The Regions of France

See the map opposite.

1. PARIS *pp116-157*
2. NORTHERN FRANCE *pp158–207*
3. NORMANDY *pp208-241*
4. BRITTANY *pp242-279*
5. CHÂTEAUX OF THE LOIRE *pp280-311*
6. ALSACE LORRAINE CHAMPAGNE *pp312-363*
7. BURGUNDY JURA *pp364-395*
8. FRENCH ALPS *pp396–425*
9. AUVERGNE RHÔNE VALLEY *pp426-481*
10. DORDOGNE BERRY LIMOUSIN *pp482–509*
11. ATLANTIC COAST *pp510–545*
12. LANGUEDOC ROUSSILLON TARN GORGES *pp546-593*
13. PROVENCE *pp594-633*
14. FRENCH RIVIERA AND CORSICA *pp634-671*

Château de Chenonceau

THE GREEN GUIDE
France

How to...

Plan Your Trip

Inspiration p22

Practical Info p42

Understand France

France Today p64

French History p70

French Art and Culture p84

Nature p112

Discover France

Paris p116

Northern France p158

Normandy p208

Brittany p242

Châteaux of the Loire p280

Alsace Lorraine Champagne p312

Burgundy Jura p364

French Alps p396

Auvergne Rhône valley p426

Dordogne Berry Limousin p482

Atlantic coast p510

Languedoc Roussillon Tarn Gorges p546

Provence p594

French Riviera and Corsica p634

Green Guides - Discover the Destination

Main sections

PLANNING YOUR TRIP
The blue-tabbed section gives you **ideas for your trip** and **practical information.**

INTRODUCTION
The orange-tabbed section explores **Nature, History, Art and Culture** and the **Region Today.**

DISCOVERING
The green-tabbed section features Principal Sights by region, **Sights, Walking Tours, Excursions,** and **Driving Tours.**

Region intros

At the start of each region in the Discovering section is a brief introduction. Accompanied by the region maps, these provide an overview of the main tourism areas and their background.

Region maps

Star ratings

Michelin has given star ratings for more than 100 years. If you're pressed for time, we recommend you visit the three or two star sights first:

★★★ **Highly Recommended**
★★ **Recommended**
★ **Interesting**

Tours

We've selected driving and walking tours that show you the best of each town or region. Step by step directions are accompanied by detailed maps with marked routes. If you are short on time, you can follow the star ratings to decide where to stop. Selected addresses give you options for accommodation and dining en route.

Addresses

We've selected the best hotels, restaurants, cafés, shops, nightlife and entertainment to fit all budgets. See the Legend on the cover flap for an explanation of the price categories. See the back of the guide for an index of where to find hotels and restaurants.

Other reading

- French Regional Green Guides
- Must Sees Paris
- Michelin Road Atlas - France
- Michelin National Map 721 - France

Welcome to France

France is seductive and alluring, a place of unique culture founded on a bedrock of village markets, café culture, friendly auberges and bistros… a place where the metronome of life is set at andante… and everything stops for lunch. Whether you come in search of history, architecture, World Heritage Sites, imposing châteaux, good food, good wine or simply a relaxing holiday on golden beaches, you'll find that France satisfies all needs… with elegance, panache and a Gallic pride that is rooted in prehistory. For those with a penchant for the outdoor lifestyle, the bright blue skies and balmy breezes of summer are conducive to walking, cycling, horse-riding and the delightful vagaries of serendipity.

Those with energy in excess will find excuses to burn it off among the high mountains… climbing, skiing, rafting along the rivers, canyoning and taking to the skies attached to parapentes.

The country is large, the geography diverse, and that means ever-changing landscapes from agricultural plains to vineyards and orchards, from volcanic uplands to stark granitic peaks, from resplendent lakes to bustling rivers, and all dotted with towns and villages, inimitable, distinctive and often very beautiful.

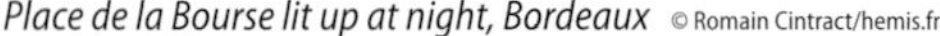

Place de la Bourse lit up at night, Bordeaux © Romain Cintract/hemis.fr

Planning Your Trip

Inspiration 22
Cities of France 23
Islands of France 26
The Great Outdoors 28
UNESCO World Heritage Sites 31
Wine Tours 32
Spas 33
Activities for Kids 33
What to Buy & Where to Shop 34
Festivals & Events 38

Practical Info 42
Before You Go 43
When to Go 43
Getting There 44
Documents 46
Customs Regulations 46
Health 47
Accessibility 47
On Arrival 47
Getting Around 47
Places to Stay 52
Places to Eat 53
Practical A–Z 54
Business Hours 54
Electricity 54
Embassies and Consulates 55
Emergencies 55
Mail/Post 55
Media and Internet 55
Money 56
Public Holidays 56
School Holidays 56
Smoking 57
Telephones 57
Time 57
Tipping 57
Tourist Offices: National 58
Tourist Offices: Regional 58
Useful Websites 59
Value Added Tax 59

Introducing France

France Today 64
French History 70
French Art and Culture 84
Nature 112

Discovering France

Paris 117
Planning Your Trip to Paris 122
A Bit of History 125
Arrondissements 1–4 132
Arrondissements 5–7 & 16 142
Arrondissements 8–10 & 17 148
Arrondissements 11–15 151
Arrondissements 18–20 152

Northern France 159
Château de Versailles 161
Disneyland Resort Paris 166
Château de Vaux-le-Vicomte 169
Fontainebleau 170
St-Germain-en-Laye 173
Parc Astérix 175
Château de Chantilly 176

Senlis	177
Compiègne	178
Laon	182
Arras	183
Amiens	185
Lille	190
Calais	196
Boulogne-sur-Mer	201
Chartres	203
Rambouillet	205
Normandy	**209**
Rouen	212
Le Havre	220
Caen	224
Normandy Landing Beaches	230
Bayeux	232
La Presqu'ile du Cotentin	235
Mont-St-Michel	238
Alençon	240
Brittany	**243**
Rennes	246
St-Malo	251
St-Brieuc	258
St-Pol-de-Léon	260
Brest	261
Quimper	263
Lorient	267
Vannes	268
Belle-Île	272
Nantes	273
Châteaux of the Loire	**281**
Angers	284
Saumur	293
Tours	298
Blois	304
Orléans	309
Alsace Lorraine Champagne	**313**
Metz	316
Verdun	321
Nancy	323
Toul	329
Strasbourg	330
Colmar	340
Riquewihr	344
Mulhouse	347
Route des Crêtes	349
Reims	350
Châlons-en-Champagne	356
Monthermé	357
Troyes	358
Provins	363
Burgundy Jura	**365**
Dijon	368
Beaune	377
Auxerre	383
Besançon	389
Lons-le-Saunier	395
French Alps	**397**
Annecy	399
Évian-les-Bains	405
Chamonix-Mont-Blanc	408
Route des Grandes Alpes	411
Courchevel	417
Grenoble	419
Briançon	422
Grand Canyon du Verdon	423

Auvergne Rhône valley **428**
Lyon 432
Vienne 452
St-Étienne 456
Le Puy-en-Velay 458
Clermont-Ferrand 464
Les Monts du Cantal 474
Vichy 476
Moulins 480

Dordogne Berry Limousin **483**
Bourges 485
Limoges 491
Périgueux 494
Sarlat-la-Canéda 496
Rocamadour 503
Cahors 506

Atlantic coast **511**
Bordeaux 513
Arcachon 522
Biarritz 523
St-Jean-de-Luz 526
Dax 528
Pau 529
Angoulême 530
Cognac 533
La Rochelle 535
Rochefort 541
Poitiers 542
Le Puy du Fou 545

Languedoc Roussillon Tarn Gorges **547**
Montpellier 550
Nîmes 558
Gorges du Tarn 562
Carcassonne 564
Narbonne 569
Perpignan 572
Toulouse 577
Albi 584
Lourdes 588

Provence **595**
Marseille 598
Aix-en-Provence 612
Arles 616
Les Baux-de-Provence 622
Avignon 624
Orange 630

French Riviera and Corsica **635**
Nice 638
Monaco 646
Menton 652
Cannes 654
St-Tropez 660
Toulon 663
Corsica 665

Index 672
Maps and Plans 698
Map Legend 699
Useful Words and Phrases 700

Regions of France

Paris (pp116-157)

Paris has been France's capital since medieval times, and ever since this lively metropolis has played a dominant role in the country's social, political and cultural life.

Northern France (pp158-207)

Besides Versailles and the delights of the Île de France, to the north lie Amiens, the cradle of Gothic architecture, and Flanders, with its distinctive Flemish architecture. Whether you prefer the urban villages of Paris or the rural hamlets of Picardy, the variety of this region is hard to beat; from the estuaries, beaches and dunes of the north and the forests and marshland of its leafy heartland, to the valleys, castles and cities of the south and west.

Abbatiale Saint-Ouen, Rouen, Normandy
© Stéphane Lemaire/hemis.fr

Normandy (pp208-241)

Famous for its ciders, cheeses and calvados, the former dukedom of Normandy boasts elegant coastal resorts, while cows, orchards and hedgerows provide rural charm. Rouen's Gothic cathedral and the ruins of the abbey at Jumièges are two of France's most impressive and important historic sights. More recent history is preserved at Caen's Memorial peace museum and the Normandy Landing Beaches.

Brittany (pp242-279)

This rugged Celtic peninsula in the northwest – with its indented coastline and islands battered by the Atlantic, narrow inlets and sandy bays – has a mysterious past that is reflected in the many prehistoric remains scattered around the region, such as the menhirs at Carnac. The separate identity and culture of the Bretons make this a fascinating part of France.

Trébeurden near St-Brieuc, Côtes-d'Armor, Brittany
© Emmanuel Berthier/hemis.fr

Hôtel-Dieu, Beaune, Burgundy
© Vidler Steve/age fotostock

Châteaux of the Loire (pp280-311)

Renowned for its magnificent Renaissance châteaux such as Chambord and Chenonceau, the Loire valley in the Centre Region is also referred to as the "Garden of France" due to the cultivation of vines, flowers and horticultural crops. The many châteaux actually sit on the banks of the River Loire's tributaries, the Indre and the Cher, and date from the 16C onwards.

Alsace Lorraine Champagne (pp312-363)

Alsace has a very Germanic character and many of its towns and villages reflect this. To the west of the Vosges mountains is Lorraine, which, despite being part of Germany for a while, is more French. Further west is Champagne, well known for its sparkling wine, and to the north, the heavily wooded Ardennes region.

Riquewihr with its vineyards, Alsace
© Walter Zerla / Tips / Photononstop

Burgundy Jura (pp364-395)

Formerly a great dukedom, Burgundy is placed on the great trade route linking the north with the Mediterranean. Coupled with the proceeds of its viticulture, this led to great wealth, which resulted in amazing buildings like the Hôtel-Dieu at Beaune. The Jura in the Franche-Comté region to the east is home to forested uplands and pasture, and such culinary delights as Vacherin and Comté cheese.

French Alps (pp396-425)

In the southeast of France, stretching from the Mediterranean to Lac Léman (Lake Geneva), the Alps are beloved by winter sports fans, but they also provide dramatic and beautiful mountain landscapes to explore when the snows are confined to the highest peaks. There are National and Regional Parks, which reflect the richness of this environment and allow access to these amazing landscapes.

Rocamadour, Dordogne valley
© Marc Dozier/hemis.fr

Auvergne Rhône valley (pp426-481)

The unique volcanic landscape of the Massif Central is at the centre of the Auvergne region and the mountains vary from classic volcanic cones to more eroded rugged shapes. To the east, the land slopes down to the Rhône valley, where the rivers Rhône and Saône converge on their journey south to meet in the great city of Lyon and flow eventually the Mediterranean Sea.

Dordogne Berry Limousin (pp482-509)

The Dordogne, or the Périgord, is well known to visitors due to its agreeable climate, its impressive castles and cave systems, not to mention the meandering Dordogne river itself. The Berry and the Limousin to the north, on the other hand, are relatively undiscovered, and provide a great deal of interest, especially at Bourges (in Berry) and Limoges (in Limousin).

Boat trip, Gorges du Tarn
© J.-P. Azam / hemis.fr

Atlantic coast (pp510-545)

In this guide, the Atlantic coast region extends from the River Loire in the north to the mighty Pyrénées in the south. It includes Bordeaux and most of Aquitaine and Poitou-Charentes – once the territory of the Dukes of Aquitaine – which, for many years, was held by the English.

Languedoc Roussillon Tarn Gorges (p546-593)

Stretching in an arc from the Rhône delta to the Pyrénées and characterised by vineyards and popular beaches, Languedoc Roussillon is steeped in history from the Roman era to the medieval. The Gorges du Tarn (Tarn Gorges) to the north are cut into the Grand Causses, from which there are amazing views from the corniche roads.

Cours Mirabeau and Fontaine du Roi René, Aix-en-Provence
© van der Meer Rene/age fotostock

Provence (pp594-633)

Centred around the impressive Rhône delta in the south, this ancient region, blessed with sunshine and occupied successively by Celts, Romans and Franks, retained its independence from the French Crown until the 15C. Fascinating cities such as Nîmes, Marseille, Aix-en-Provence and Arles, and astonishingly well-preserved Roman remains, such as those at St-Rémy-de-Provence, ensure the ongoing popularity of this region.

French Riviera and Corsica (pp634-671)

The **Côte d'Azur** – or French Riviera – runs along the Mediterranean coastline of southeast France from Menton to Cassis. What started as a popular winter health resort in the late 18C continues to draw thousands of tourists each year. Resort towns here include Cannes, Beaulieu-sur-Mer and St-Tropez. You can't beat its 300 days of sunshine per year and holiday atmosphere.
Referred to by the ancient Greeks as "Kallisté", meaning "most beautiful", and by the French as *L'Île de Beauté*, the mountainous island of **Corsica** certainly lives up to its name. Totally unspoilt, it has both Italian and French influences. From the gulfs and ruggedness of the west coast to the promontory of the Cap Corse and the cliffs of Bonifacio, this is a truly exceptional place.

Bonifacio, Corsica
© S. Sauvignier / Michelin

Plage Notre-Dame, Île de Porquerolles, Îles d'Hyères , French Riviera

Planning Your Trip

The Louvre and the Pyramid, Paris

Planning Your Trip

» **Inspiration p22**

Cities of France p23

Islands of France p26

The Great Outdoors p28

UNESCO World Heritage Sites p31

Wine Tours p32

Spas p33

Activities for Kids p33

What to Buy & Where to Shop p34

Festivals & Events p38

» **Practical Info p42**

Before You Go p43

On Arrival p47

Practical A–Z p54

Mont St-Michel, Normandy

Inspiration

WHAT'S HOT

– Located in the heart of **Lens** (p184), a former coal mining centre in Nord-Pas de Calais, the Louvre-Lens Museum, opened in 2012, exhibits masterpieces from the Paris Louvre. The museum is unique in giving a behind-the-scenes view of the museum by allowing the public to see into its stores and restoration rooms. www.louvrelens.fr.

– The construction of a pedestrian bridge, and the subsequent destruction of the ancient causeway, were the final acts in the restoration of **Mont-St-Michel** (p238) to its original marine setting.

– A major project to revitalise the **Paris docks** on the Seine (p142), has seen the creation of a new space entirely devoted to fashion and design. The unique contemporary space features restaurants, cafés, designer boutiques, event space for cultural events, a concert and club venue, and the Institut Français de la Mode. www.paris-docks-en-seine.fr.

– **Bordeaux** (p513) will open a multicultural centre in 2016 to bring new life to the world of wine, focussing on production in Bordeaux and the Aquitaine region. The centre will feature tasting rooms, restaurants, a wine bar, exhibitions, films and more. www.citedescivilisations duvin.com.

– **Toulouse** (p577) opened a new centre in 2015 (in Toulouse-Blagnac) where the public can visit the Concorde n-1 and the A300 aircraft. The centre explores the history of aeroplane design and construction. www.musee-aeroscopia.fr.

Old port and Basilique de Notre-Dame de la Garde, Marseille

Cities of France

There are 53 mainland cities in France, from large conurbations like Paris, Lyon, Marseille and Toulouse to more down-to-earth towns such as Clermont-Ferrand, Montpellier and Rennes. Yet only in Paris and Lyon is there any sense of a haphazard sprawling metropolis around which all else revolves.

ANGERS★★ See p284

Ranked among the finest of the Loire towns and cities, Angers is a vibrant and cultured city on the River Maine and formerly the centre of the Plantagenet kingdom, a realm that embraced the whole of England and half of France. In this sometime capital of Anjou, the architecture of Angers is outstanding and features the extensive use of slate and blue and white stones.

BORDEAUX★★★ See p513

Capital of Aquitaine, and a World Heritage Site, Bordeaux is a town steeped in history, a place of 18C grandeur that played an important role in the affairs of France. Victor Hugo commented: "Take Versailles, add Antwerp, and you have Bordeaux". Today, Bordeaux is one of the country's finest capitals of wine.

CLERMONT-FERRAND★★ See p464

In recent years, the urban landscape of Clermont-Ferrand, the natural capital of the Auvergne, has seen many changes, from the construction of a vast shopping complex in the Jaude district, to a new covered market at St Pierre, law courts and residential buildings. All these developments combine contemporary architecture with traditional urban development, bringing a vibrancy that is palpable and an enthusiasm that is catching.

LYON★★★ See p432

The greatness of Lyon's past is matched by today's cultural dynamism and diversity. Its location, at the meeting point of the Rhône and the Saône, was always a guarantee of distinction, and today Lyon (spelt with an 's' in English) is France's third most populous city, a place of enterprise, industry and commerce. Many would argue that for the visitor, Lyon offers so much more than Paris.

MARSEILLE★★★ See p598

Marseille is probably the oldest city in France, founded 2 600 years ago by Greeks as a trading port. Today, it is the second largest city in France. Designated the European Capital of Culture in 2013, Marseille is a city proud of its differences from the rest of France… a regional centre for culture and entertainment, with

an important opera house, history and maritime museums and five art galleries...and now with a direct rail service from London.

MONTPELLIER★★★ See p550

Capital of the Languedoc, Montpellier used to be France's twenty-fifth biggest city; now it is its eighth. Its heritage dates from 985, when the city was founded at an advantageous position at the crossroads of the Roman 'Via Domitia', the salt road a little to the south, and the 'Cami Roumieu' taken by the pilgrims bound for Compostela. Today, Montpellier is envied throughout France as a centre of intellectual excellence.

NANTES★★★ See p273

Sited at the point where the Loire becomes tidal, Nantes has long been a focus of trade and movement between Brittany and Poitou. It was selected as the European Green Capital for 2013, a distinction that rewards the city for a number of green initiatives: already, a quarter of the city's hotel rooms are eco-certified, making Nantes the leading 'green' city in France.

NICE★★★ See p638

Nice benefits both from a maritime and a mountain pedigree that has cultivated a unique personality and environment. Nice rose to fame as a fashionable place of resort among Victorians following its 'discovery' in the 19C. The adjacent coastline is well developed, creating a busy atmosphere in marked contrast to the much quieter interior, famed for its olive groves, gorges and hill villages.

PARIS★★★ See p122

The unadulterated brilliance of Paris is breathtaking; from its imposing architecture to its romantic and evocative atmosphere, its avenues, squares and gardens, its cultural wealth and its joie de vivre. A girdle of greenery surrounds the city, rippling outwards as the great forests of Fontainebleau and Rambouillet that merge with fertile landscapes and high-yielding arable lands. More than 20% of the French population lives in Paris, and its nickname – the City of Lights – is a reference to the many intellectuals, past and present, who live and lived here.

REIMS★★★ See p350

This ancient university town on the River Vesle is renowned for its magnificent cathedral, a place where French kings were traditionally crowned. Today, the city, along with nearby Epernay, is a key element in the champagne production industry. The centre offers the elegance of Art Deco façades and a relaxed atmosphere that prevails in the streets and on the café-terraces.

STRASBOURG★★★ See p330

Surrounded by two arms of the River Ill, Strasbourg's Grande Île boasts outstanding monuments: the cathedral, four ancient churches and the Palais Rohan form a district characteristic of a medieval town, and illustrate Strasbourg's evolution from the 15C–18C. This unique distinction qualifies the island as a World Heritage Site. Strasbourg is one of only a few cities in the world to accommodate pan-cultural organisations without the status of being a capital city. But the choice of Strasbourg as European capital was not a chance decision, rather it was one intended as a mark of reconciliation between the people of Europe.

TOULOUSE★★★ See p577

Within sight of the Pyrenees, Toulouse reveals the influences of Spain and, architecturally, Italy, too. The quality of life and economic dynamism attract thousands of new people each year, seduced by the region and its European metropolis capital, which enjoys an easy-going lifestyle. Any expectations of large-city pretensions are soon dispelled amid the sprawl of narrow streets and squares.

Cathédrale Notre-Dame, Reims

Islands of France

France has an extensive coastline along which are dotted idyllic islands, some as small as a field and others very large – Corsica is three times the size of a small country such as Luxembourg. The islands are perfect destinations for a change of scenery and pace; their isolation, as well as an air of mystery and charm, adds to the fascination of a way of life shaped by the sea.

ÎLES DU PONANT

(English Channel–Atlantic Ocean)

Îles Chausey★ See p256
The largest archipelago in Europe, with superb natural history. Grand Île is the only inhabited island of the group, with a population of around 30.

Île de Bréhat★ See p258
Lying off the coast north of Paimpol, Ile Bréhat is one of Brittany's loveliest islands consisting of several islets around two small islands… walk, cycle and enjoy the micro-climate brought by the Gulf Stream.

Île de Batz See p278
The main attractions of Île de Batz are its exotic garden, lovely beaches, gentle walking and superb views from the top of the lighthouse.

Île d'Ouessant★★ See p262
The island is a delight for those who enjoy long walks overlooking the sea. Discover authentic Breton houses, the smallest sheep in the world and feast on Breton pancakes.

Île de Molène
Near **Le Conquet** (see p262), this is the largest of an archipelago of 20 islands, but still very small. A local delicacy is Molène sausage, which is smoked with seaweed.

Île de Sein See p266
This is Brittany's most unusual island, being entirely flat, its highest point just 6m above sea level. Explore the museums, walk the coast to the lighthouse and the historic Free French Monument.

Îles de Glénan
Located south of Finistère (see p263), and comprising seven major islands; ideal for a day trip.

Île de Groix★ See p267
Groix is home to a wide variety of sea birds that favour the high cliffs, sandy beaches and secluded coves along its north coast.

Îles du Golfe de Morbihan★★
See p270
There are around 42 islands in the bay, many owned by celebrities. The largest, Île aux Moines and Île d'Arz, are favourite tourist destinations. Île aux Moines offers scenic walks, while Arz has lovely creeks and coves.

Belle-Île★★★ See p272
This is the largest of the French Atlantic islands, and it enjoys a wild and varied landscape of forests, valleys, beaches, small bays and dunes.

Île d'Houat
The island is located, along with two other islands, in the entrance to the **Baie de Quiberon** (see p270); its "twin sister" island is Hoëdic. The landscape is mainly granite cliffs, except for a long beach with dunes on the eastern coast.

Île d'Hoedic
A small island off the coast of the Île d'Houat (see above), characterised by sandy coves and rocky points around the edge of an undulating plateau.

Île d'Yeu★★
Ride a bike, swim, run, sunbathe, stay close to Mother Nature. A destination of choice off the coast of the **Sables d'Olonne** (see p538).

Île d'Aix★
Lying in the Bay of Biscay near **Rochefort** (see p541) and the mouth of the Charente river, Île d'Aix (pronounced "eel dex"), is a romantic place – frequented by abdicating emperors (Napoléon stayed here for 3 days in 1815) and wild birds. Come for the peace; it's palpable.

Île de Noirmoutier★
Off the coastline near **Nantes** (see p273), two-thirds of this island is below sea level. It is linked to the mainland by a bridge and the ancient Passage du Goit, a tidal causeway. A splendid place of tiny villages, and a relaxing way of life.

Île de Ré★ and Île d'Oléron★
See p538
At the top and bottom of the Charente Maritime coastline, and linked by bridges to the mainland, both islands offer delightful, relaxing breaks, superb coastlines and villages.

ÎLES DU LEVANT
(Mediterranean Sea)

Îles du Frioul See p606
The Frioul archipelago is a group of four islands off the Mediterranean coast about 4km/2.5mi from Marseille… white cliffs, crystal-clear water, breathtaking rocky inlets and sandy beaches… Paradise.

Îles des Calanques
'Calanques' are rocky coves, or inlets along the Marseille coast, facing out to a group of small islands, the largest of which is **Riou** (see p607), a wild and wonderful place, ideal for walking.

Île de Bendor★
Not far from Toulon (see p663), this small island is home to a Wine and Spirits Museum. Walk around the cliffs to discover a sculpture garden.

Vieux Château, Île d'Yeu

Îles d'Hyères★★★ See p664
A group of 4 islands off Hyères in SE France – Porquerolles (nature conservation, sea cliffs and coves), Port-Cros (national park and bird refuge), Île du Baguad, Île du Levant (some military use, and long-established nudist colony).

Îles de Lérins★★ See p658
Amazing castle; great walking; beautiful nature – away from the crowds.

Îles Sanguinaires★★
This archipelago of 4 islands, off the coast of Ajaccio (see p666) are a Nature 2000 site, which protects them as a reserve for marine birdlife… more than 150 species can be found.

Îles Lavezzia
The uninhabited Lavezzi Islands are a small archipelago of granite islands and reefs in the Strait of Bonifacio sited between Corsica (see p665) from Sardinia, and form the southernmost point of metropolitan France.

The Great Outdoors

France offers a splendid range of leisure activities from spa treatments and wine tours to outdoor sports and cruises. Below are a few suggestions of ways to enhance your stay.

OUT & ABOUT

Information and brochures for all sporting, special interest and outdoor facilities may be obtained from **RendezvousenFrance** (the **French Tourist Office**), Lincoln House, 300 High Holborn, London WC1V 7JH (*℘0207 061 66 00; http://uk.rendezvousenfrance.com*) or from the local tourist information centres shown within the *Discovering France* section of this guide.

CANOEING

A guide is published annually indicating schools and places where canoeing may be practised. Apply to **Fédération Française de Canoe-Kayak** (87 quai de la Marne, 94344 Joinville-le-Pont. ℘01 45 11 08 50; www.ffck.org).

CYCLING HOLIDAYS

A number of UK tour operators organise cycle touring holidays in France, for example **Susi Madron's Cycling for Softies** (*www.cycling-for-softies.co.uk*) and **Headwater** (*www.headwater.com*).

In France, the cyclists' touring association, **Fédération Française de Cyclotourisme**, organises cycle tours, and provides itineraries detailing distances, difficulty of the routes, and sights to visit. 12 r. Louis Bertrand 94207 Ivry-sur-Seine Cedex. ℘01 56 20 88 88; www.ffct.org.

You can also apply to the **Fédération Française de Cyclisme,** 5 rue de Rome, 93561 Rosny-sous-Bois. ℘01 49 35 69 00; www.ffc.fr. This organisation publishes a guide listing marked mountain-bike tracks. Lists of local cycle hire shops are available from Tourist Offices. Some SNCF railway stations hire out cycles, which can be returned at a different station.

FISHING

The abundance of rivers, streams and lakes provides anglers with many opportunities to catch salmon, trout, perch, tench or carp. Whatever the site, however, it is necessary to be affiliated to a fishing association and to abide by fishing regulations. Daily fishing permits are available in certain areas. Contact the local tourist office or apply to the local fishing federations or fishing tackle stores.

A folding map *Fishing in France* (*Pêche en France*) is published and distributed by the Conseil Supérieur de la Pêche (134 av. de Malakoff, 75016 Paris. ℘01 45 02 20 20), and is also available from departmental fishing organisations.

For information about regulations contact the Tourist Offices or the offices of the Water and Forest Authority (Eaux et Forêts).

GOLF

For location, addresses and telephone numbers of golf courses in France, consult the map *Golfs, les Parcours français,* published by Edition Plein Sud based on **Michelin maps**. You can also contact the **Fédération Française de Golf** (68 r. Anatole France, 92 300 Levallois-Perret. ℘01 41 49 77 00; www.ffgolf.org).

MOTOR BOATING

Enquire at local Tourist Information Centres or at resort waterfronts. Anyone who intends to drive a powered boat (6–50hp) within 5 nautical miles of a French harbour must qualify for a sea certificate (*Carte mer*). Beyond the 5 nautical mile limit an additional sea permit (*Permis mer*) is required. Yachts and boats with engines of less than 6hp are exempt.

RIDING & PONY TREKKING

Apply to the **Comité Nationale du Tourisme Équestre, Parc équestre** (41 600 Lamotte. ✆02 54 94 46 00; www.ffe.com), which publishes an annual handbook covering the whole of France.

For information about riding holidays, contact the **Comité national de tourisme équestre** (9 boulevard Macdonald 75019 Paris. ✆01 53 26 15 50), which publishes the annual handbook *Cheval Nature, l'Officiel du tourisme équestre en France,* giving details of selected riding stables and equestrian establishments throughout France.

RIVER & CANAL CRUISING

The extensive network of navigable waterways in France can be explored at leisure. Many tour operators offer touring vacations with motor cruisers. Information on boat hire companies is available from the **Féderation des Industries Nautiques** (✆01 44 37 04 00; www.france-nautic.com). Charges usually include boat hire, insurance and technical assistance. Some charter companies also offer bicycles to enable visitors to go shopping and for rides or excursions along the towpath or to neighbouring villages. Visitors usually operate the locks on small canals by themselves; otherwise, it is customary to give a hand to the lock-keeper. Two publishers produce collections of guides to cruising on French canals. Both series include numerous maps and useful information and are provided with English translations.

The publishers are: Grafocarte (125 r. J.-J. Rousseau BP 40, 92132, Issy-les-Moulineaux; ✆01 41 09 19 00) and Guides Vagnon, Les Éditions du Plaisancier (100 av. du Général-Leclerc, 69641 Caluire Cedex; ✆04 78 23 31 14).

ROCK CLIMBING

Excursions with qualified instructors are organised by sections of the **Club Alpin Français** and by local guides. Apply to the Tourist Information Centres, or to the **Fédération Française de la Montagne et de l'Escalade** (8–10, quai de la Marne, 75019 Paris; ✆01 40 18 75 50; www.ffme.fr).

SAILING

Many resorts have sailing clubs offering courses. In season it is possible to hire boats with or without crew. Apply to the **Fédération**

Rock climbing in the Forêt de Fontainebleau

Super Besse ski resort, Parc Naturel Régional des Volcans d'Auvergne

© Christian Guy/imageBROKER/age fotostock

Française de Voile: 17 r. Henri Bocquillon, 75015 Paris. ✆01 40 60 37 00; www.ffvoile.net.

WALKING

Exploring the regions of France on foot is a delightful way of discovering the landscape, and the life and culture of the countryside. Short-, medium- and long-distance footpaths network the whole country. For the nationwide system of long-distance paths, Topo-Guides are published by the **Fédération Française de la Randonnée pédestre**. Some of the guides have been translated into English. They give detailed maps of the paths and offer valuable information to the walker, and are on sale at the Information Centre (64 r. du Dessous des Berges, 75013 Paris. ✆01 44 89 93 90; www.ffrandonnee.fr) and many bookshops throughout France. A good selection of **English-language guidebooks for walkers** covering many areas of France is available from specialist UK publisher Cicerone Press, 2 Police Square, Milnthorpe, Cumbria LA7 7PY. www.cicerone.co.uk; ✆01539 562069.

SCUBA DIVING

Apply to the **Fédération Française d'Études et de Sports Sous-Marins** (24 quai de Rive Neuve, 13284 Marseille Cedex 07. ✆04 91 33 99 31; www.ffessm.fr).

SKIING & WINTERSPORTS

The French Alps are one of the world's major ski and winter sports areas, stretching from Lake Geneva in the north, to the Mediterranean, a distance of 370km/230mi. There is also excellent skiing in the Pyrenees and the Auvergne.

For all enquiries contact the **Club Alpin Français**, a national federation of 174 local mountain sports associations, based at 24 av. de Laumière, 75019 Paris. ✆01 53 72 87 00; www.ffcam.fr. Or, for general information, contact **Ski France**, an association of winter sports resorts, for their annual publications *Guide Pratique Hiver/Été* and *Guide des Tarifs* (both free), 61 boulevard Haussmann, 75008 Paris. ✆01 47 42 23 32.

UNESCO World Heritage Sites

There are no fewer than 39 sites inscribed on the World Heritage List in France: 35 of these are listed for cultural reasons, 3 for their 'natural' qualities and 1 (Mont Perdu in the Pyrenees) for a combination of reasons. A further 39 sites currently await on the Tentative List.

World Heritage sites are natural and cultural sites identified by UNESCO following the adoption, during the 1972 General Conference, of the "Convention Concerning the Protection of the World Cultural and Natural Heritage". There are 1 007 sites (779 cultural, 197 natural and 31 mixed) currently inscribed on the World Heritage List. To be included on the World Heritage List, sites must be of outstanding universal value and meet at least one out of ten selection criteria, divided into six cultural criteria and four natural criteria.

Almost 40 sites in France are of such importance internationally that they have been inscribed as World Heritage Sites. This protected cultural heritage includes monuments (buildings, sculptures, archaeological structures, etc) that have unique historical, artistic or scientific features; groups of buildings (such as religious communities, ancient cities); or sites (human settlements, examples of exceptional landscapes, cultural landscapes) which are the combined works of man and nature, and of exceptional beauty.

Some of the sites in France are multiple in nature, for example the numerous Vauban fortifications that appear across much of the country, and the various pilgrimage routes of Santiago de Compostela. Others are more esoteric – the banks of the Seine in Paris, part of the Loire valley between Sully-sur-Loire and Chalonnes and the Grande Île in Strasbourg. But most focus on one redeeming feature such as the Roman aqueduct at Pont du Gard, Amiens Cathedral and Provins, the town of medieval fairs.

A recent addition to the list for France is the stunningly beautiful episcopal city of Albi in the department of Tarn. And such is the heritage of France that another 39 properties are currently under consideration for inclusion on the World Heritage List, including the Camargue, the Fontainebleau forest, the massif of Mont Blanc, the Carnac stones, the Cévennes and the Grands Causses.

The World Heritage Convention is not only "words on paper", but a vital instrument for firm action in preserving threatened sites and endangered species. By recognising outstanding universal value of sites, governments across the world commit to their preservation and strive to find solutions for their protection.

Albi by the Tarn, Midi-Pyrénées

Wine Tours

In most wine-making regions, wine tours or wine trails, taking in the main vineyards and wineries, or caves, are signposted, leaving visitors to discover the route for themselves. Joining a wine tour is the safest way of learning about the folklore of wine and its production, leaving you to quaff amiably without worrying about the consequences. *See Introduction p69.*

ALSACE

Often overlooked, Alsace produces some excellent wines, and the Route des Vins (www.alsace-route-des-vins.com) can be driven or cycled. Almost all wines from this region are white, except for those made from the Pinot Noir grape. Gewürztraminer, Sylvaner and Reisling, the principal wines, are sold under those names, but also bear the AOC label for Alsace.

BORDEAUX

Renowned for its magnificent First Growth wines, the region offers a number of opportunities to get to know the wines of the Médoc and Saint-Émilion, which are among the finest in the world. Many tours combine visits to châteaux, cookery classes (cooking with wine, of course) and exclusive gourmet meals.

BURGUNDY JURA

The great wine centre of Burgundy is Beaune; a place riddled with tunnels and cellars. Chablis is one of the region's strengths, made in the north from 100 per cent chardonnay grapes. Farther south, superb classic red wines are produced, like Gevrey-Chambertin and Clos Vougeot, while the Côte de Beaune includes the outstanding wines of Puligny-Montrachet, Chassagne Montrachet and Meursault. Frequently, but undeservedly under-rated, the Jura, between Burgundy and Alsace, produces good-value wines that won't break the bank.

CHAMPAGNE-ARDENNE

All the major champagne producers host tours around their cellars, especially those in Reims and Épernay, but don't overlook the Côte des Bars.

LANGUEDOC-ROUSSILLON

Many of the wines of this region are labelled according to VDQS regulations, the second highest qualification for French wines. Much of the wine for daily consumption, like Corbières, comes from this area. But keep an eye out for vineyards producing the lovely Picpoul de Pinet, which has been produced near the Thau Lagoon for centuries; appropriately, given its proximity to the oyster farms of the area, Picpoul is the perfect accompaniment to seafood and shellfish.

LOIRE VALLEY

Reaching from Sancerre to Touraine, the vineyards of the Loire valley produce exceptional wines that play an important part in French gastronomy, with no fewer than 24 AOCs being listed here. Try the Sancerre Rouge; most people go for the white, but the red is light and delicate and perfect in summer.

PROVENCE & THE RHÔNE

It doesn't all have to be Châteauneuf-du-Pape in the Rhône valley; try visiting the smaller vineyards around Gigondas, Vacqueyras and on the slopes of Mont Ventoux for a completely different view of things. A little farther afield in the Côtes de Provence, the reds are full of flavour, while rosés are light and refreshing.

SOUTHERN FRANCE

Many smaller areas in the south of France produce outstanding wines: Montbazillac from south of Bordeaux is a prime example; likewise Jurançon from the Pyrenees, Gaillac from Tarn, and Crémant de Limoux.

Spas

The hectic pace of modern life has resulted in an increasing number of people visiting the country's spa resorts for a few days in which to relax, recharge their batteries and help ease certain illnesses and ailments through treatments that are based on the medicinal qualities of the resorts' mineral-rich waters.

WELL-BEING

Spas have long been part of French life. They are gradually becoming less concerned with medical treatment, and rather more with relaxation, reinvigoration and a modicum of self-indulgent pampering. There are dozens of spas in France, ranging from up-market spa resort hotels to charming small spa villages that have relaxed visitors since the days of the Ancient Romans.

TAKING A SPA BREAK

France has numerous spas ranging from indulgent, exclusive resorts to an increasing number of small spa villages, from luxury spas in the heart of Parisian chic to urban and rural oases. Facilities vary, the most luxurious – and also the most expensive – provide everything you could possibly need. Others have fewer facilities, but nonetheless are a welcome and enjoyable break, and can be found in the most unexpected places.

There are many spa break deals on offer; the concept of 'Wellness' – long ingrained in the minds of the French as synonymous with three weeks away from work among the mountains of the Alps and the Pyrenees at the expense of the government – is today a developing and successful business enterprise.

Activities for Kids

All attractions offer discounted fees for children. The following are just a few examples of places that will guarantee a fun day out for both children and their parents. In this guide, sights of particular interest to children are indicated with a KIDS symbol (👤👤).

IN THIS GUIDE

Children are welcome everywhere in France; the French are very much family-oriented. It is quite commonplace to see well-behaved children dining in restaurants in the early evening. Moreover, France is a wonderful destination to bring babies, toddlers, in fact, children of all ages. Most attractions, parks, museums and buildings offer reduced rates for children, with very young children often going free.

Some attractions may offer discount fees for children.

USEFUL WEBSITES

A useful source of ideas is **www.france4families.com**, which contains a lot of general information and tips. There are also other useful websites, like **www.takethefamily.com**, which has tips and destination guides, **www.totstotravel.co.uk** which specialises in crafting family holidays in France, and **www.babygoes2.com**, which contains pages of information to help parents travelling with small children.

What to Buy & Where to Shop

Browse one-off shops in search of gifts, kitchenware, home accessories, paintings, bric-à-brac and antiques. Buy food and wine in street markets and specialist shops, where knowledgeable staff can recommend new tastes.

SHOPPING IN FRANCE

Shopping in France is a particular delight. When travelling around the country make sure you take in the colourful local markets (see www.jours-de-marche.fr), an important domestic institution, or the various agricultural fairs that are held regularly throughout the year. These compelling and – be honest – seductive weekly markets offer everything from pot pourri to live fish, but are there primarily for local people, which is great if you're staying in a self-catering property and need groceries. Don't be afraid of doing what everyone else does, and sample what's on offer before buying... taste the cheese, sip the wine, sample the roast wild boar. All the main cities and large towns are host to a wide selection of chain stores and supermarkets, among which Printemps, Galeries Lafayette and FNAC are prominent. But many towns and large villages tend to have smaller, more regional stores and shops catering, often, more for the local population than for visitors... you can get quality goods and produce here at much less cost than in the cities.
Nor should you overlook the huge opportunities for discount and bargain shopping such as can be found in factory outlet centres and shopping malls that are dotted about France – Troyes (110+ shops) and Roubaix (many up-market labels), are just two examples. The key thing about these outlet centres is that they have excellent facilities: car parking (invariably free), children's play areas, ATM machines, restaurants and cafés, and information centres.
Many city stores in France are allowed to run special promotions, so keep an eye open for shop window posters that announce 'Promotion' or '*Soldes exceptionnels*'.

Marché aux Puces de Saint-Ouen, Paris © Jean-Daniel Sudres/hemis.fr

SHOPPING IN PARIS

Paris is one of the finest cities in the world for shopping, with major stores stocking a range of designer brand names and luxury fashions. It's worth knowing about designer/consignment stores that are generally owned and managed by people who know their stuff when it comes to fashion, and offer designer and couture clothes at excellent discounts.

Boulevard Saint Germain is a street you may not want to miss. Starting at the Seine in the 7th arrondissement, this appealing street is lined with plane trees and magnificent buildings, a great place for home décor shops, fashion boutiques and gourmet food. For an extravagant Paris shopping experience, follow Boulevard Saint Germain into the neighbouring 6th arrondissement to enjoy high-end shopping around St-Germain des Prés. But where Paris is concerned there is so much to choose from: the Triangle d'Or, across the Seine from the Eiffel Tower, is the beating heart of Paris Haute Couture and the finest fashion houses in Europe. Yet everything in Paris isn't necessarily high end: just off Boulevard Haussmann, Monoprix is a department store offering excellent deals on fashions and a wide range of other products. For more details on the best shopping places in Paris, visit www.parisperfect.com.

At the lower end of the Parisian scale, but no less (and probably more) enjoyable are the remarkable fleamarkets (Les Puces) of Saint-Ouen. This is a perfect place to find a bargain, or something a little unusual to remind you of your stay. There is much hustle and bustle here, so be wary of pickpockets, and keep your valuables out of sight, tucked away.

ANTIQUES

All the main towns and cities have their established antique dealers, and here the costs are much on a par with other countries. But, if you know what you're looking for, and can spot a real bargain, then there are hundreds of *brocante* markets all around France. You'll need to know your stuff because you can be sure that the full-time dealers were up at dawn to snaffle anything of interest, but they don't see everything, and you can still pick up the odd bargain.

At the 'serious' end of the scale there are three particularly worthwhile antique centres: Les Puces de Saint-

Ouen in Paris, mentioned above; the first weekend of each month sees the biggest *braderie* (discount sales) in Europe in Lille, while in Provence, L'Isle-sur-la-Sorgue is renowned for its antique shops, markets and fairs, especially at Easter and again in August, each with more than 200 dealers in attendance. Another great event is the Puces du Canal in Lyon-Villeurbanne, the second-biggest market in France after Paris.

If the joy of finding a bargain – or just something unusual that you like – appeals to you, keep an eye open virtually anywhere for hand-made signs announcing a 'Vide-Grenier'. It means, literally, emptying the attic, the French equivalent of the British car boot sale. These are unpredictable and can crop up anytime, anywhere, and are a mix of professional dealers (*brocanteurs*) and locals just having a clear out (http://vide-greniers.org).

CHEESE

In 1962, ex-president Charles de Gaulle famously quipped: "*Comment voulez-vous gouverner un pays qui a deux cent quarante-six variétés de fromage?*" ("How can you govern a country which has two hundred and forty-six varieties of cheese?").

There are more than 246 cheeses these days, but, perhaps surprisingly, not so many as in Britain. Virtually every village in France has someone who makes cheese and sells it locally, from tangy, aromatic goat's cheeses to the great classic of French cuisine. Visit any supermarket and you will find it overflowing with cheese, and the local markets are much the same, although they do tend to offer regional cheeses rather than those from across greater France.

COGNAC

While many visitors love to trawl the wine producing vineyards, anyone passing through Poitou-Charentes should take in one (or all) of the great cognac producing distilleries that dot the landscape around the small town of Cognac. They are accustomed to receiving visitors (and make a charge for admission): Courvoisier (in Jarnac); Martell; Camus; Otard; Rémy Martin (in Merpins and Cognac); Hennessy. A little farther afield is Château de Beaulon in Saint-Dizant-du-Gua, producing, many would say, the finest cognac of them all… but it's a matter of taste, of course. If you do succumb, be sure you know your Customs allowances (*see p46*).

CUTLERY

It may be an apocryphal tale, but it is said that one French housewife, on hearing that her husband had bought a Laguiole knife, said 'Good, now I can buy a cheaper cut of meat!' Laguiole cutlery is renowned, and available, throughout France and online, but there is no substitute for a visit to the factory (www.forge-de-laguiole.com) in the eponymous town in Aveyron, where you can see the craftsmen at work. If you arrive at the right time, you can see a demonstration of how a Laguiole knife is assembled.

But Laguiole doesn't have things all its own way: Thiers, in Puy-de-Dôme, is also famous for its cutlery industry, and, unlike Laguiole, has a town museum portraying the history of knife-making.

FAIENCE

Faience is tin glazed earthenware. It is a mixture of local clays to which oxide of tin is added, so that it becomes opaque and takes on a white colour. Faience production came to France in the 16C, and today is found in large centres such as Lyon, Marseille, Rouen, Montpellier, Nevers and Quimper, but increasingly in many small towns and villages, particularly in the south of France, beyond Toulouse. Be sure it is well protected for the journey home.

PORCELAIN

The history of French porcelain extends from the 17–18C, when it was produced in Rouen, Nevers, Saint-Cloud and Chantilly. Today, the

Thiers cutlery

place to go for exquisite porcelain is Limoges, which is the premier manufacturing city of porcelain in France. However, beware the unscrupulous use of the name, should you find anyone offering Limoges porcelain at knock-down prices; the likelihood is that it is not the genuine article.

POTTERY

Always popular as a 'take-home' souvenir of France are ceramics, an expression of a way of life, as well as something beautiful. You can buy ceramic products almost anywhere in France, but none rivals the evocative colours of Provence. Here the '*terroir*' is ideal: clay-rich soil, wood for firing and a generous amount of sunshine for baking. It is the bright colours that betray Provençal ceramics in particular, and, even on the gloomiest day back home, they will bring back memories of the heady, herby aromas of the *garrigue* and Mediterranean sunshine. Pottery markets are held throughout Provence from April to September, organised by Terres de Provence (www.terresdeprovence.org)… and, while in Provence, look for *santons*. These are small, hand-painted terracotta figures representing characters from Provençal village life, such as farmers, fishwives, fruit sellers and scissor grinders. Today, the creation of santons is a family skill, handed down from parents to children. You can find them throughout Provence, in tiny villages like Séguret, but each December there is a gathering of *santonniers* in Marseille to display and sell their santons at the Foire des Santonniers (www.foire-aux-santons-de-marseille.fr. *Festivals and Events, p38*).

SILK

The Rhône-Alpes, and Lyon in particular, are worth visiting if you are in search of silk goods: headscarves, stoles for women, ties and scarves for men, all made in the region's silk mills. The silk business for a long time was historically exclusive to Lyon, a city perfectly located for handling the silk cocoons bred in the Ardèche and throughout the southern part of the region.

SALES TAX (VAT)

In France a sales tax (*TVA* or VAT) is added to all purchases. For non-EU residents on holiday this tax can be refunded. *See VALUE ADDED TAX, p59.*

Festivals & Events

Almost every village has a festival at some time during the year. Book accommodation well in advance at festival times, even out of season.

FEBRUARY: Carnival in Limoux

JANUARY

Angoulême – International Comic Strip Festival. www.bdangouleme.com.
Clermont-Ferrand International Short-Film Festival. ✆04 73 91 65 73; www.clermont-filmfest.com.

FEBRUARY

Chalon-sur-Saône Carnival, Winter Fur and Pelt Fair. ✆03 85 48 08 39
Limoux Traditional carnival every weekend (and Shrove Tuesday). All-night *Blanquette* party follows. ✆04 68 31 11 82; www.limoux.fr.
Menton Lemon Festival. ✆04 92 41 76 76; www.fete-du-citron.com.
Nice Carnival. ✆0892 70 74 07; www.nicecarnaval.com.
Paris Paris International Agricultural Show. www.salon-agriculture.com.
Prats-de-Mollo, St-Laurent-de Cerdans, Arles-sur-Tech Traditional carnival. ✆04 68 39 70 83; www.pratsdemollolapreste.com.
Toulouse *Fête de la Violette* (violet festival). ✆05 62 16 31 31; www.toulouse-tourisme.com.
Le Touquet Motorbike race along the beach. ✆03 21 06 72 00.

MARCH

Clermont-Ferrand *Vidéoformes*: international video and multimedia art festival. ✆04 73 17 02 17; www.videoformes.com.
Clermont-Ferrand Poetry week. ✆04 73 31 72 87; www.printemps despoetes.com.
Lyon International Fair. ✆04 72 22 33 37; www.foiredelyon.com.

MID-MARCH–MID-JULY

Lille Music, art and theatre. ✆03 28 52 30 00.

LATE MARCH–LATE OCTOBER

Versailles Fountain display with musical performances *Les Grandes Eaux Musicales) – every weekend and Bank Holiday.* ✆01 30 83 78 98.

APRIL

Bourges Music Festival. ✆02 48 27 28 29.
Chartres Students' Pilgrimage. ✆02 37 21 51 91; www.chartres-tourisme.com.
Chartres Music festival. ✆02 22 06 87 87; www.chartres-tourisme.com.
Cournon-d'Auvergne Festival for young people: theatre, puppets, dance, music. ✆04 73 69 90 40.
Gérardmer Flower Festival. ✆03 29 27 27 27.
Le Mans 24-hour motorcycle race. ✆02 43 40 24 24; www.lemans.org.

APRIL–OCTOBER

Parc national des Cévennes Nature festival: themed walks, exhibitions, shows, markets ✆04 66 49 53 01; www.cevennes-parcnational.fr.

Chaumont-sur-Loire International Garden Festival. ✆02 54 20 99 22.

MAY

Aubrac *Fête de la transhumance*: seasonal shepherd's festival held on the weekend nearest to May 25 ✆05 65 44 21 15; www.traditionsenaubrac.com.
Cannes International Film Festival ✆01 53 59 61 00; www.festival-cannes.com.
Évian Classical music. ✆04 50 26 85 00.
Maguelone Festival of ancient and Baroque music (1st two weeks). ✆04 67 60 69 92.
Montauban Music festival. ✆05 63 63 66 77.
Orléans Joan of Arc Festival. ✆02 38 24 05 05; www.tourisme-orleans.fr.
Orange Music and opera. ✆02 40 14 58 60.
Rouen Joan of Arc Festival. ✆02 35 08 32 40.
Les Saintes-Maries-de-la-Mer Gypsy Pilgrimage. ✆04 90 97 82 55.
Touraine The Day of the Loire to celebrate the Loire and its countryside. ✆02 47 31 42 88.

MAY–OCTOBER

Vichy *Une Saison en Eté*: theatre, classical music, opera, variety shows at the Vichy Opera House. ✆04 70 30 50 30; www.ville-vichy.fr.

JUNE

Bellac Drama, music. ✆05 55 60 87 61.
Clermont-Ferrand Medieval Festival in Montferrand. ✆04 73 23 19 29; www.montferrandmedieval.org.
Le Mans 24-hour car race. ✆03 43 40 24 24; www.lemans.org.
Montpellier International Festival of Dance. ✆0 800 600 740; www.montpellierdanse.com.
Perpignan Saint-Jean Festa Major (with mid-summer bonfires around June 21). ✆04 68 66 30 30; www.perpignantourisme.com.
La Rochelle International Regatta. ✆05 46 41 14 68.
Toulouse Rio Loco Festival. ✆05 61 32 77 28; www.rio-loco.org.
Tours *Florilège Vocal*: Choral Festival. ✆02 47 21 65 26; www.florilegevocal.com.
Vic-le-Comte Celtrad: Celtic music festival. ✆04 73 69 02 12.
Villefranche-sur-Saône Midsummer Night: bonfires, singers, illuminations. ✆04 74 65 04 48.

MID-JUNE–MID-JULY

Pau Theatre, music and dance. ✆05 59 27 27 08.

MID-JUNE–MID-OCTOBER

Anjou Anjou Festival in the historical sites of Maine-et-Loire. ✆02 41 88 14 14; www.festivaldanjou.com.
Chaumont-sur-Loire International Garden Festival. ✆02 54 20 99 22; www.domaine-chaumont.fr.
Orléans Jazz Festival. ✆02 38 24 05 05; www.tourisme-orleans.fr.

JUNE–LATE AUGUST

Amboise "At The Court of King François". ✆02 47 57 14 47.
Toulouse Classical, jazz and rock music. ✆05 62 27 60 60.

JULY

Aix-en-Provence International Music Festival. ✆0820 922 923.
Albi Classical music. ✆05 63 49 48 80.
Ambert Festival de Folklore. ✆04 73 82 66 34; www.livradoue-dansaire.com.
Auvergne *Thermathlon du Sancy*: Fun trek along the Route des Villes d'Eaux of the Massif Central (mountain biking, walking, canoeing, archery). ✆04 73 31 20 32.
Avignon Theatre Festival. ✆04 90 27 66 50.
Béziers Classical music. ✆04 67 36 82 30.

Cap d'Agde *Fête de la Mer* (sea festival; last weekend). ✆04 67 01 04 04; www.capdagde.com.
Carcassonne Festival of the City: Medieval Cité is "set alight" by an evening firework display; classical music concerts, theatre, opera, dance, jazz (July 14). ✆04 68 11 59 15; www.festivaldecarcassonne.com.
Carpentras Music and dance ✆04 90 60 46 00.
Cordes-sur-Ciel *Fête médiévale du Grand Fauconnnier* (historical pageant and entertainments (mid-July) ✆05 63 56 34 63; www.grandfauconnier.com.
Forez Concerts of classical music in churches and castles of the region. ✆04 73 51 55 67.
Frontignan *Festival du Muscat* (mid-month). ✆04 67 18 31 60; www.tourisme-frontignan.com.
Gannat International folk music. ✆04 70 90 12 67.
Juan-les-Pins World Jazz Festival. ✆04 97 23 11 10.
Lorient Celtic festival ✆02 97 21 24 29.
Luz-St-Sauveur *Jazz à Luz* (early July). ✆05 62 92 38 30; www.jazzaluz.com.
Montpellier *Festival de Radio-France et de Montpellier Languedoc-Roussillon*: opera, symphonies, chamber music, jazz (2nd fortnight). ✆04 67 61 66 81; www.festivalradiofrance montpellier.com.
Nantes International Flower Show. ✆02 40 47 04 51.
Orcines *Open Golf des Volcans*: international golf championship (last week of the month). ✆04 73 62 15 51; www.golfdesvolcans.com.
Perpignan *Estivales* (Theatre festival). ✆04 68 62 62 00; www.theatredelarchipel.org.
Quimper Cornouaille Festival. ✆02 98 55 53 53.
Rennes Theatre, music, dance and poetry. ✆02 99 67 11 11.
St-Guilhem-le-Désert Musical season at the abbey. ✆04 67 96 86 19; www.st-guilhem-le-desert.com.
Vollore *Festival des Concerts de Vollore*: Classical music, jazz and *musique tzigane*. ✆04 73 51 55 67; www.concertsdevollore.fr.

JULY AND AUGUST

Sète Festival of St Louis: jousting, fireworks. ✆04 67 74 48 44; www.fiestasete.com.
St-Bertrand-de-Comminges, St-Just-de-Valcabrère, St-Gaudens, Martres-Tolosane. *Festival du Comminges*, classical music, chamber music. ✆05 61 88 32 00; www.festival-du-comminges.com.
Vaison-la-Romaine Theatre and dance. ✆04 90 36 02 11.

MID-JULY–MID-SEPTEMBER

Arles International Photo Festival. ✆04 90 96 76 06.
St-Rémy-de-Provence Organ music. ✆04 90 92 05 22.
Sceaux Classical music. ✆01 46 60 07 79.

AUGUST

Aurillac International Street Theatre Festival. ✆04 71 45 47 45; www.aurillac.net.
Allanche Secondhand market: the most important in the Auvergne. ✆04 71 20 48 43.
Bayonne Corrida and Street Festival. ✆0820 42 64 64.
Colmar Alsatian Wine Festival. ✆03 89 20 68 92.
Béziers Bullfighting Festival. ✆04 67 76 13 45; www.languedoc-france.info.
Chamonix Mountain Guides Festival. ✆04 50 53 00 88.
Entrecasteaux Chamber music. ✆04 94 72 91 62.
Pomarez Running of the Cows. ✆05 58 89 30 28.
Pont de Salers and other villages International Folklore Festival. ✆05 65 46 80 67; www.festival-rouergue.com.
Prades Festival Pablo Casals: chamber music. ✆04 68 96 33 07.

Monteux Fireworks Festival. ✆04 90 66 97 52.
Montesquieu-Volvestre British Film Festival. ✆05 61 90 65 74.
St-Pourçain-sur-Sioule Wine and Food Festival. ✆04 70 45 32 73; www.ville-saint-pourcain-sur-sioule.com.
St-Donat-sur-l'Herbasse Bach Festival. ✆04 75 45 10 29.
Sablé-sur-Sarthe Festival of Baroque music. ✆02 43 62 22 22; www.sablesursarthe.fr.
Salon-de-Provence Music Festival. ✆04 90 56 27 60.

SEPTEMBER

Besançon Classical music: Young Conductors Competition. ✆03 81 25 05 85
Deauville American Film Festival. ✆02 31 14 14 14; www.festival-deauville.com.
Dinan Ramparts Festival (biennial – next in 2016). ✆02 96 39 75 40.
Divonne Chamber music. ✆04 50 90 17 70.
Lyon Even years: dance; Odd years: music and modern art. ✆04 72 77 69 69.
Le Puy-en-Velay *Les Fêtes du Roi de l'Oiseau* (Festival of the King of the Birds): all the splendour of a city in the period of François I; 6 000 people in costume. ✆04 71 09 38 41; www.roideloiseau.com.

SEPTEMBER–DECEMBER

Beaujolais, Coteaux du Rhône and du Forez Grape Harvest and Wine Festivals in the wine-growing regions.
Puy-de-Dôme Les Automnales: theatre and music throughout the Auvergne ✆04 73 42 23 29; www.puydedome.com.

OCTOBER

Lannion Organ and choral music ✆02 96 35 14 14.
Montpellier International fair. ✆04 67 17 67 17; www.foire-montpellier.com.
Mourjou Chestnut Festival. ✆04 71 49 69 34; www.foirechataignemourjou.fr.
Perpignan Jazz Festival ✆04 68 86 08 51; www.jazzebre.com.
St-Malo Comics Festival. ✆02 99 40 39 63; www.quaidesbulles.com.
Sauveterre-de-Rouergue Chestnut and cider festival. ✆05 65 72 02 52.

NOVEMBER

Beaune Auction sale of the wines of the Hospices de Beaune. ✆03 80 24 47 00.
Belfort Cinema. ✆03 84 22 94 44.
Le Puy-en-Velay International Hot-Air Balloon Rally. ✆04 71 09 38 41; www.ot-lepuyenvelay.fr.

DECEMBER

Marseille Santons Fair. ✆04 91 54 91 11; www.foire-aux-santons-de-marseille.fr.
Mont-Ste-Odile Pilgrimage (the most important in Alsace). ✆03 88 95 80 53.
Strasbourg Christmas Market. (Chriskindelsmarik). ✆03 88 52 28 28; www.noel.strasbourg.eu.

DECEMBER 25

Azay-le-Rideau The Imaginary World of the Château d'Azay-le-Rideau. ✆02 47 45 44 40.
Blois The Story of Blois. ✆02 54 78 72 76.
Les-Baux-de-Provence Shepherds' Midnight Mass and Son et Lumière in the Loire valley. ✆04 90 97 34 39.
Chenonceau The Ladies of Chenonceau. ✆02 47 23 94 45.
Cheverny The River Loire down the ages. ✆02 54 42 69 03.
Loches The Strange Story of Bélisane. ✆02 47 59 07 98.
Le Lude Spectacular Historical Events. ✆02 43 94 62 20.
Valençay Esclarmonde. ✆02 54 00 04 42.

Practical Info

TOP TIPS

Best time to go: May–June and September; avoid school holidays.
Best way around: By car or rail, but certainly on foot in the towns.
Best for sightseeing: Avoid Mondays, when many sites are closed
Most authentic accommodation: Chambres d'Hôte/Table d'Hôte.
Need to know: A few words of French will get you a long way; it's just a question of making the effort (see p700).
Need to taste: Local and regional dishes in situ.

TEMPERATURE CHART

Degrees C. Maximum temperatures in red; minimum in black
The following temperatures are guidelines only

Month	Jan	Feb	Mar	Apr	May	Jun	Jul	Aug	Sep	Oct	Nov	Dec
Alsace , Lorraine, Champagne	5	6	11	13	17	21	24	25	20	15	9	6
	–1	–1	2	3	7	10	13	13	10	7	3	0
Atlantic Coast	9	11	14	16	20	24	26	26	24	19	14	11
	3	4	5	6	10	12	14	14	9	10	6	4
Auvergne Rhône valley	6	8	11	14	18	21	25	26	22	16	11	7
	–1	–1	2	3	7	10	12	12	10	7	4	0
Burgundy Jura	5	6	12	15	20	22	26	26	22	16	11	6
	0	0	3	4	9	11	14	15	11	7	4	1
Brittany	10	11	15	16	21	24	26	27	25	20	15	12
	2	3	4	6	10	12	15	15	12	9	6	4
French Riviera and Corsica	13	14	16	17	21	25	27	28	26	22	18	15
	3	4	5	7	10	14	16	16	15	11	7	4
Dordogne Berry Limousin	7	9	12	14	18	21	23	26	24	20	16	9
	1	1	2	4	7	10	13	14	12	9	7	3
Languedoc-Roussillon Tarn Gorges	11	13	15	17	21	25	29	29	26	22	16	12
	4	5	6	8	11	15	18	18	15	12	7	5
Normandy	6	7	11	13	17	20	23	25	20	15	10	7
	2	0	4	4	7	10	12	12	10	7	4	3
Northern France	8	8	10	12	16	19	22	24	19	15	11	8
	3	3	5	6	9	11	14	15	12	9	7	4
PARIS: Ile de France	10	11	15	16	21	24	26	27	25	21	15	11
	2	3	5	6	10	12	15	15	12	10	6	4
Pays de la Loire	8	10	13	15	18	22	25	26	23	17	12	10
	2	2	5	5	9	11	14	14	11	9	5	4
Provence	12	13	16	17	23	26	30	31	27	22	17	13
	3	4	5	7	11	14	16	16	14	11	7	3

Before You Go

WHEN TO GO

SEASONS

Depending on the reason for your visit, **spring**, **summer** and **autumn** are the best seasons to visit France, each having its own appeal, and there is a region to suit every season. For **winter** sports, the season runs from December to April.

For relaxing out of doors, high summer can be beautiful, but resorts and the principal sightseeing areas are much more crowded.

A better time to travel is May, June or September when French children are at school. Many visitors may prefer the moderate warmth of these early and late summer months to the higher temperatures of July and August, especially in the south of the country.

CLIMATE

In general the French climate is a moderate one; extremes of either heat or cold are rare for the most part, so that outdoor activity of some kind is almost always possible.

Inland the winters are chilly and darkness comes early, especially in the northern latitudes. As spring turns to summer, the days become long and warm and by June the sun lingers well into the evening. Spring and autumn provide opportunities to explore the outdoors and enjoy the lovely countryside and coastal areas of France. In winter, snowfall throughout much of the interior of the country, as well as in the mountainous regions, permits winter sports, including downhill skiing and snowboarding.

Weather Forecast

For **Météo-France** (national weather bureau, www.meteo.fr) reports in French, 3250, then select from the recorded choices (€0.34/min). Information about the weather can be downloaded to mobile phones and tablets from http://mobile.meteofrance.com, and from other sources. See Temperature Chart p42.

For **departmental forecasts** dial 08 92 68 02... followed by the number of the *département* you want, e.g. Ain 01; Aisne 02; Allier 03; Ardèche 04, etc.

Mountain weather forecast: 3250 (select 4); For information about snow cover and avalanche risk, 08 92 68 10 20.

GETTING THERE

BY PLANE

The main arrival point into France is Paris, which has two airports: Charles-de-Gaulle to the north and Orly to the south. Once in France, the numerous regional airports are well-connected both to the Paris airports and to each other.

Airport transfer services

Visitors arriving in **Paris** who wish to reach the city centre or a train station may use public transportation or reserve space on the airport shuttle **RoissyBus** (for Roissy-Charles-de-Gaulle 01 45 38 55 72, for Orly 01 43 21 06 78; www.ratp.fr). You can also use the **Leader Shuttle** (www.leadershuttle.net), or go by **taxi**, which is the most convenient method, but also the most expensive.

Introduced in 2015, and running up to 80 times per day, **easyBus** operates between Charles de Gaulle (Terminal 2) and central Paris, with the first bus of the day leaving Le Palais Royal/Louvre at 05:45 and the last leaving Charles de Gaulle at 01:00. Online bookings can be made at www.easyBus.co.uk.

Many airlines, especially on shorter-haul journeys, also operate services to **Nice**, **Lyon** and **Marseille**, as well as other provincial cities, including **Bordeaux**, **Clermont-Ferrand**, **Mulhouse**, **Nantes**, **Toulouse**, **Montpellier**, **Perpignan** and **Nîmes**.

BY SHIP

There are numerous **cross-Channel services** (passenger and car ferries) from the United Kingdom and Ireland, as well as the rail shuttle through the Channel Tunnel

To choose the most suitable route between your port of arrival and your destination use the Michelin Tourist and Motoring Atlas France, Michelin map 726 (which gives travel times and mileages) or Michelin maps from the 1:200 000 series (with the orange cover). For details apply to travel agencies or:

- **Brittany Ferries** ☏0871 244 0744 (UK); 0825 828 828 (France); www.brittanyferries.com. Services from Portsmouth, Poole and Plymouth.
- **Condor Ferries** ☏01202 207216 and ☏0845 609 1024 (reservations); www.condorferries.co.uk. Services from Weymouth, Poole and Portsmouth.
- **DFDS Seaways** operate routes between Dover and Calais, Dover-Dunkerque and Newhaven-Dieppe. ☏(UK) 0871 574 7235 and 0800 917 1201; www.dfdsseaways.co.uk.
- **P&O Ferries** ☏0800 130 0030 (UK), or 0825 120 156 (France); www.poferries.com. Service between Dover and Calais.

BY COACH/BUS

www.eurolines.com has information about travelling by coach in Europe. From the UK call ☏0871 81 81 81; within France ☏0892 89 9091. The main UK terminus is Victoria Coach Station, in central London.

BY CAR

France has an excellent network of major and minor roads covering long distances, including ***autoroutes*** –motorways or major highways, often with a toll to pay. Note that when entering the country at a land border, you may already be driving on an ***autoroute.*** After a short free section, a toll may be payable; increasingly this can be done using a credit card.

Eurotunnel

This is the fastest way across (under) the English Channel: drive straight onto a rail shuttle that travels through the Channel Tunnel between the M20 near Folkestone (junction 11A) and the A16 near Calais (junction 42).

Le Shuttle-Eurotunnel ☏08443 35 35 35 or ☏0810 63 03 04 (from France); www.eurotunnel.com.

BY TRAIN

The only way to France from the UK by rail is on Eurostar. **Eurostar** (www.eurostar.com) runs from London (St Pancras) to Paris (Gare du Nord) in 2hr 15 (up to 20 times daily), reducing in 2016 to just 2hr. In Lille and Paris it links to the high-speed rail network (TGV) which covers most of France. Introduced in 2015 is a direct link from London to Marseille, calling at Lyon and Avignon.

Citizens of non-European Economic Area countries will need to complete a landing card before arriving at Eurostar check-in. These can be found at dedicated desks in front of the check-in area and from Eurostar staff. Once you have filled in the card please hand it to UK immigration staff.

France Rail Pass and **Eurail Pass** are travel passes that may be purchased by residents of countries outside the European Union. Contact: www.voyages-sncf.com. At the SNCF (French railways) site (www.sncf.fr), you can book ahead, pay with a credit card, and receive your ticket in the mail at home. There are numerous discounts available when you purchase your tickets in France, from 25–50% below the regular rate. These include **discounts** for using senior cards and youth cards (which must be purchased, showing your name and a photograph), and lower rates for 2–9 people travelling together (advance purchase necessary). The best discounts are available during off-peak periods.

Gare du Nord, Paris

© Y. Kanazawa/MICHELIN

All rail services throughout France (including Eurostar) can be arranged through **Voyages-SNCF** in the UK. Personal callers are welcome to drop into Voyages-SNCF Travel Centre, 193 Piccadilly, LONDON W1J 9EU. ☎0844 848 5848; www.voyages-sncf.com.

DOCUMENTS

Passport – Nationals of countries within the EU entering France need only a national identity card (although most airlines require passports). Nationals of other countries must be in possession of a valid national **passport**.

Visa – No **entry visa** is required for Canadian, US or Australian citizens travelling as tourists and staying less than 90 days, except for students planning to study in France. Visas can be obtained from your local French Consulate.

General passport information is available by phone toll-free from the Federal Information Center ☎800-688-9889. US passport application forms can be downloaded from http://travel.state.gov.

Lift at Lyon-St-Exupéry airport station

© Brice Robert/Lyon Tourism and Conventions

CUSTOMS REGULATIONS

The UK Customs website (www.hmrc.gov.uk) contains information on allowances, travel safety tips, and to consult and download documents and guides.

There are no limits on the amount of duty and/or tax paid **alcohol and tobacco** that you can bring back into the UK as long as they are for your own use or gifts and are transported by you. If you are bringing in alcohol or tobacco goods and UK Customs have reason to suspect they may be for a commercial purpose, an officer may ask you questions and make checks. There are no customs formalities when bringing caravans, pleasure-boats and outboard motors into France for a stay of less than six months, but a boat's registration certificate should be kept on board.

HEALTH

It is advisable to take out comprehensive travel insurance cover, as tourists receiving medical treatment in French hospitals or clinics have to pay for it themselves.

Nationals of non-EU countries should check with their insurance companies about policy limitations. Keep all receipts.

British and Irish citizens, if they are not already in possession of an **EHIC** (European Health Insurance Card), should apply for one before travelling. The card entitles UK residents to reduced-cost medical treatment. Apply online at www.ehic.org.uk. The card is not an alternative to travel insurance. It will not cover any private medical healthcare or costs, such as mountain rescue in ski resorts, being flown back to the UK, or lost or stolen property. Details of the healthcare available in France and how to claim reimbursement are published in the leaflet ***Health Advice for Travellers***, available from post offices. All prescription drugs taken into France should be clearly labelled; it is recommended to carry a copy of prescriptions.

♿ ACCESSIBILITY

Sights with good accessibility are indicated in this guide with a ♿. On French TGV and Corail trains there are wheelchair spaces in 1st-class carriages available to holders of 2nd-class tickets. On Eurostar and Thalys, special rates are available for accompanying adults.

All airports offer good accessibility.

Disabled drivers may use their EU blue card for parking entitlements.

Information about accessibility is available from **Association des Paralysés de France** (17 bd Auguste Blanqui, 75013 Paris. ☎01 40 78 69 00; www.apf.asso.fr), which also has a nationwide network of branches.

On Arrival

GETTING AROUND

Once in France, the most versatile option for getting around is the car; the most relaxing is rail, and while air travel is perfect for getting to France, within the country the check-in and security times and the distance of airports from the centre of cities, make this the least appealing of the ways of getting around.

BY TRAIN

Rail travel is a pleasure in France: trains are comfortable, speedy, punctual and good value. A comprehensive rail network, provided by the state's rail operator **SNCF,** covers almost the entire country, enabling region-to-region transfers without the need to retreat to Paris before setting off again, although the closer you are to Paris the greater the likelihood that a return to the centre is needed.

Sleek, fast TGV trains operate between main towns, with door-to-door journey times that easily rival air travel, especially Paris–Lyon (2 hours) and Paris–Marseille (3.5 hours). TGVs must always be booked in advance, and all seats are reserved. However, it is often possible to reserve a **TGV** seat up to just a few minutes before the train departs.

Apart from TGVs, the main city-to-city lines are also served by other comfortable modern trains, which do not require advance booking. Away from these major lines, SNCF operates a reliable stopping service within each region, including a variety of smaller trains that reach into rural areas, sometimes supplemented by SNCF's bus services.

Before booking rail tickets, be sure to enquire at the station whether you are entitled to obtain one of the many rail **discount passes**. For example, groups of friends travelling together, or families with a young child, may be eligible.

When first starting any journey by train, remember that rail tickets **must be validated** (*composter*) by using the orange automatic date-stamping machines at the platform entrance.

BY CAR

Driving in France should not present much difficulty. For British drivers unaccustomed to driving on the right, extra care will be needed at first, but the rules of the road are otherwise similar to those in other Western countries. Road signs generally use easy-to-understand international visual symbols instead of words.

For up-to-date information on driving in France, consult www.drive-france.com.

Route planning

The road network is excellent and includes many motorways. The roads are very busy during the holiday period (particularly weekends in July and August), and to avoid traffic congestion it is advisable to follow the recommended secondary routes (signposted as ***itinéraires bis***).

The motorway network includes simple rest areas (***aires***) every 10–15km/6–10mi and service areas (***aires de service***), with fuel, restaurant and shopping, about every 40km/25mi. The rest areas are only basically provisioned, often having no more than just toilets. The main service areas are more fully equipped, but vary in

Gare des Bénédictins clock tower at night, Limoges

size and complexity from perfectly adequate "pit stop" facilities with mini-supermarkets, coffee machines and newspaper kiosks, to extensive complexes often with restaurants and overnight accommodation, too.
For **general information** on traffic and ***itinéraires bis***, contact Bison Futé. ☎0800 100 200; www.bison-fute.equipement.gouv.fr.

Documents

Driving licence – Travellers from other European Union countries and North America can drive in France with a valid national driving licence. An international driving licence is useful but not obligatory.
Registration papers – For the vehicle, it is necessary to have the registration papers (logbook).
In addition to carrying the correct documentation, the driver of a vehicle registered outside France is expected to display a nationality plate of approved size close to the registration plate on the back of the vehicle, unless this already forms part of the registration plate.

Insurance

Insurance cover is compulsory, and although an International Motor Insurance Certificate (known in the UK as a Green Card) is no longer a legal requirement for vehicles registered in the UK, it is still the most effective proof of insurance cover and is internationally recognised by the police and other authorities. If you have comprehensive insurance, you may want to check that your insurance cover is unaffected by driving abroad. Some insurers wish to be informed if you intend to take your vehicle abroad. Most British insurance policies give only the minimum third-party cover required while in France – but this amounts to less than it would in the UK. Therefore check with your insurance company before leaving to ensure you are fully covered in the event of an accident.

Enforcement

Police have wide powers to check documents at any time and to impose heavy on-the-spot fines for almost all driving offences. In the case of more serious offences, especially if alcohol is involved, they may at their own discretion confiscate the vehicle. If paying an on-the-spot fine, you should be given a copy of the officer's report form, a receipt for any money paid, and information on how to proceed if you wish to plead not guilty.

Alcohol

The regulations on **drinking and driving** are strictly enforced. The maximum permissible blood alcohol content is currently 0.50g/l, which is lower than in the UK.
From 2012, drivers and motorcyclists are obliged to carry a **breath test kit** in their vehicles. Foreign visitors and tourists also come under this law.

Highway code

In France the minimum driving age is 18. Traffic drives on the right. All passengers must wear **seat belts. Children** under the age of 10 must ride in the back seat.
In the absence of stop signs at intersections, cars must **give way to the right** (See *Priorité à droite below*). Traffic on main roads outside built-up areas (priority indicated by a yellow diamond sign) and on roundabouts has right of way. Vehicles must stop when the lights turn red at road junctions and may filter to the right, with caution, only when indicated by an amber arrow.

Priorité à Droite

On all two-way roads, traffic drives on the right. The rule of ***priorité à droite*** also means that priority must be given – in other words, you must give way – to **all vehicles coming from the right, even from minor roads (but not private property), unless signs indicate otherwise.** The principal sign indicating that you have priority over all other roads, even those on the right, is a yellow diamond. In practice, the yellow diamond normally gives priority to traffic on all main roads outside built-up areas. Traffic within a roundabout (traffic circle) has priority over vehicles entering the roundabout, unless signs indicate otherwise.

Pedestrian priority

Under legislation introduced in 2010, **pedestrians** now always **have priority over cars** when crossing a road. Until recently, they had priority only at specially designated crossings. They need to "show a clear intention to cross" a road – described as "an ostensible step forward or a hand gesture" – and vehicles are required to stop for them. The only exception is where a designated pedestrian crossing is less than 50m away. Drivers who ignore the rules face a fine.

Lights

Full or dipped headlights must be switched on in rain, poor visibility and at night; use sidelights only when the vehicle is stationary. Headlight beams should be adjusted for driving on the right. It is illegal to drive with faulty lights in France, so it is advisable to take a spare set of bulbs with you.

Speed limits

- Toll motorways (péage) 130kph/80mph (110kph/68mph when raining)
- Dual carriage roads and motorways without tolls 110kph/68mph (100kph/62mph when raining)
- Other roads 90kph/56mph (80kph/50mph when raining) and in towns 50kph/31mph
- Left lane on motorways during daylight, on level ground and with good visibility: min speed limit of 80kph/50mph.

Parking regulations

In built-up areas there are zones where parking is either restricted or subject to a charge; tickets should be obtained from nearby ticket machines (***horodateurs*** – small change necessary) and displayed inside the windscreen on the driver's side; failure to display may result in a fine, or towing away and impoundment. Other parking areas in town may require you to take a ticket when passing through a barrier. To exit, you must pay the parking fee and insert the paid-up card in another machine which will lift the exit gate.

Tolls

In France, most motorway sections are subject to a toll ***(péage)***. You can pay in cash or, increasingly, with a Visa or Mastercard.

Petrol/Gasoline

French service stations dispense ***sans plomb 98*** (super unleaded 98), ***sans plomb 95*** (super unleaded 95), ***diesel/gazole*** (diesel) and GPL (LPG), but it is cheaper to fill up at the large hypermarkets on the outskirts of towns.

Breakdown

In the case of a **breakdown**, a red warning triangle and hazard warning lights are obligatory. In the event of an emergency, all persons in a vehicle are obliged to wear **yellow fluorescent jackets**.

Millau Viaduct, Tarn Gorges

The jackets must be carried inside the car and readily accessible. Drivers not carrying the obligatory jacket may receive an instant fine (€11), and could receive a further fine of €135 for not wearing a yellow jacket at the roadside in the event of a breakdown.

Ensure you have adequate **breakdown cover** before arriving in France. UK motoring organisations, for example the **AA** and the **RAC**, offer accident insurance and breakdown service programmes, either on a yearly basis or for temporary periods, for both members and non-members. These offer an emergency phone number in the UK, and a reliable standard of service and workmanship provided locally. However, because French autoroutes are privately owned, European Breakdown Cover service does not extend to breakdowns on the autoroute or its service areas – you must use the emergency telephones, or drive off the autoroute before calling your breakdown service.

Car rental

There are car rental agencies at airports, railway stations and in all large towns throughout France. European cars have manual transmission; automatic cars are available only if an advance reservation is made. Drivers must be over 21; between ages 21 and 25, drivers are required to pay an extra daily fee; some companies allow drivers under 23 only if the reservation has been made through a travel agent. It is relatively expensive to hire a car in France.

Car hire and holders of UK driving licences

In 2015, changes to the UK Driving License came into force which mean that details of fines, penalty points and restrictions are now only held electronically.

This change will affect you if you turn up at French airport, for example, to pick up a hire car, because you are going to have to make arrangements for the hire company to be able to access your online driving record by means of a DVLA-issued pass code.

The pass code number, however, can be used only once; so if this isn't set up before you get to the hire company desk you may face delays. Moreover, the code is only valid for 21 days and then lapses so you will need internet access if trying to hire a car while already in France. The new system allows you to download a summary of your licence record, which can be printed or shared. To log into the system you will need to know your National Insurance number and postcode, so take them with you in case you need to log in to the DVLA website while abroad. To access your online driver record you need the last eight digits of your driving licence, plus the special pass code. You can view your licence at www.gov.uk/view-driving-licence. You will also be able to call the DVLA and give permission for your driving record to be checked verbally.

PLACES TO STAY

Hotel and Restaurant listings fall within the description of each principal sight. These have been recommended for their location, comfort, value for money and, in some cases, for their charm. We have also made a conscious effort to cover all budgets. The Legend on the cover flap explains the symbols and abbreviations used.
The **Addresses** in this guide describe a number of lodgings arranged by price category. They appear in many of the cities and towns described in the guide.
For an even greater selection, use the **Michelin Guide France**, with its famously reliable star-rating system and hundreds of establishments throughout France. The **Michelin Charming Places to Stay** guide contains a selection of 1 000 hotels and guesthouses at reasonable prices.
Be sure to book ahead to ensure that you get the accommodation you want, not only in the tourist season but year-round, as many towns fill up during trade fairs, arts festivals etc. Some places require an advance deposit or a reconfirmation. Reconfirming is especially important if you plan to arrive after 6pm.

The handbook of a respected federation of good-value, family-run hotels (most with restaurants), **Logis et Auberges de France**, is available from the French Tourist Office, as are lists of other kinds of accommodation such as hotel-châteaux, bed-and-breakfasts, etc. Another resource, which publishes a catalogue for each French ***département***, for vacation villas, apartments or chalets, is the **Fédération Nationale des Locations de France CléVacances** (✆05 61 13 55 66; www.clevacances.com).
Relais et Châteaux provides information on booking in luxury hotels with character. For central reservations (UK): ✆00 800 0825 1020; www.relaischateaux.com.

Hotel booking websites

There is a growing number of hotel booking agencies and user-review companies operating online these days, all of them offering hotel rooms at discounted and competitive prices from high-end hotels to budget and economy establishments. It is always worth checking websites such as these to find good value discounts.
However, the general ease of booking hotel rooms online sometimes makes it worthwhile dealing with the hotels direct, since these can often offer the best rates available at the time of booking. If your command of French is adequate, it is also worth calling the hotel to see if you can negotiate a lower rate (un bon prix) over the telephone.

Gîtes, cottages, bed and breakfast

The **Maison des Gîtes de France** is an information service on self-catering accommodation in France. Gîtes usually take the form of a cottage or apartment decorated in the local style where visitors can make themselves at home, or bed and breakfast accommodation (Chambres d'hôtes) which consists of a room and breakfast at a reasonable price.

For general information, contact the **Gîtes de France** office in Paris (40 Avenue de Flandre, 75019 Paris. ☎01 49 70 75 75; www.gites-de-france.com), which has a good English version. From the site, you can choose and book a gîte, or order catalogues for different regions illustrated with photographs of the properties, as well as specialised catalogues (bed and breakfasts, farm stays, etc.).

If you want to improve your French, then consider the category Chambres d'hôte/Table d'hôte. These are essentially B&B properties, but, being (usually) a little more remote from town centres offer an evening meal. But it's one where you have to join in with the whole family, few of whom would be able to speak English.

Regional and nationwide holiday websites are also worth looking at because they contain information about self-catering cottages, for example LaGrange Holidays (www.lagrange-holidays.co.uk) and Loire Valley Holidays (www.loire-valley-holidays.com), on which you can view and book cottages.

Equally you can contact local tourist offices direct; many of them have lists of holiday properties and local bed and breakfast establishments.

Hostels, camping

The international youth hostels movement, International Youth Hostel Federation or Hostelling International, has dozens of hostels in France.

There is an online booking service on www.hihostels.com, which you may use to reserve rooms as far as six months in advance. To stay in hostels, you may need a membership card.

To obtain an IYHF or HI card (there is no age requirement) contact the IYHF or HI in your own country for information and membership applications (in the UK ☎01707 324170. In the US, there are many HI centres; check the website to find your nearest).

There are two main youth hostel associations *(auberges de jeunesse)* in France, the **Ligue Française pour les Auberges de la Jeunesse** (67 r. Vergniaud, 75013 Paris. ☎01 44 16 78 78; www.auberges-de-jeunesse.com) and the **Fédération Unie des Auberges de Jeunesse** (27 r. Pajol, 75018 Paris. ☎01 44 89 87 27).

There are thousands of officially graded **campsites** with varying standards of facilities throughout the country.

The **Michelin Camping France** guide lists a selection of campsites. It is wise to reserve in advance.

PLACES TO EAT

French cuisine is as varied as it is delicious. We have also highlighted an array of eating places primarily for their atmosphere, location and regional delicacies.

Turn to the Addresses within the *Discovering France* section for descriptions and prices of selected places to eat in the different locations covered in this guide. The Legend on the cover flap explains the symbols and abbreviations used in these Addresses.

Use the red-cover **Michelin Guide France**, with its respected star-rating system and hundreds of establishments all over France, for an even greater choice.

Restaurants usually serve lunch from noon–2pm and dinner from 7.30–10pm. It is not always easy to find something to eat at other

Terrace of a brasserie, Île Saint-Louis, Paris

times, except for a simple baguette sandwich in a café, or an ordinary hot dish in a brasserie.
In French restaurants and cafés, the service charge and all taxes are included in the price, so tipping is not necessary. However, it is usual to leave any small change from the bill on the table when leaving.

For a glossary of gastronomic terms and for information on local specialities, see the section entitled Food and Drink in the Introduction.

Practical A-Z

BUSINESS HOURS

Offices and other businesses are open Mon–Fri, 9am–noon, 2–6pm. Many also open Sat mornings. Town and village shops are open Tue–Fri; there are local variations. Midday breaks may be much longer in the South. However, in cities, tourist centres or resorts, businesses may keep longer hours or stay open all day, seven days a week, especially if they primarily serve the tourist market.
Ordinary shop hours in towns and villages are typically open Tue–Sat 9am–noon or 12.30pm, 3–7pm. The lunch break is often longer in the South. Food shops may open earlier in the morning, but later in the afternoon, and some, especially bakeries (**pâtisseries**) and grocery stores, open on Sunday morning. In resorts, shops may keep longer hours and stay open all day, all week. Department stores are open Mon–Sat 9am–6.30pm (often with one or more later evenings per week). Hypermarkets are usually open Mon–Sat 9am–10pm.

ELECTRICITY

The electric current is 220 volts/ 50 Hz. Circular two-pin plugs are the rule. Adaptors should be bought before you leave home; they are on sale in most airports.

EMBASSIES AND CONSULATES

- **Australia Embassy**
4 r. Jean-Rey, 75015 Paris.
℘01 40 59 33 00;
www.france.embassy.gov.au.
- **Canada Embassy**
35 av. Montaigne, 75008 Paris.
℘01 44 43 29 00;
www.amb-canada.fr.
- **Ireland Embassy**
4 r. Rude, 75116 Paris.
℘01 44 17 67 00;
www.embassyofireland.fr.
- **New Zealand Embassy**
103, rue de Grenelle,
75007 Paris. ℘01 45 01 43 43;
www.nzembassy.com.
- **UK Embassy**
35 r. du Faubourg-St-Honoré,
75383 Paris Cedex 08.
℘01 44 51 31 00;
www.ukinfrance.fco.gov.uk/en.
- **UK Consulate**
18bis r. d'Anjou, 75008 Paris.
℘01 44 51 31 00

There are also UK Consulates in Bordeaux, Lille, Lyon and Marseille.

- **USA Embassy**
2 av. Gabriel, 75008 Paris.
℘01 43 12 22 22;
http://france.usembassy.gov.
- **USA Consulate**
2 r. St-Florentin, 75001 Paris.
℘01 43 12 22 22

EMERGENCIES

Europe-wide emergency number: ℘112
Police (Gendarme): ℘17
Fire (Pompiers): ℘18
Ambulance (SAMU): ℘15

Note, however, that the Europe-wide emergency number if used close to the border with another country, may connect with that country rather than France.

First aid, medical advice and chemists' night-service rotas are available from chemists/drugstores (***pharmacie,*** identified by a green cross sign).

MAIL/POST

Look for the bright yellow ***La Poste*** signs. Main post offices are generally open Mon–Fri 9am–7pm, Sat 9am–noon. Smaller branches generally open 9am–noon, 2–4pm weekdays. There are often automatic tellers (***guichets automatiques***) inside, which allow you to weigh packages and buy postage and avoid a queue.
You may also find that you can change money, make copies, send faxes and make phone calls in a post office.
To post a letter from the street look for the bright yellow postboxes. Stamps are also sold in newsagents and cafés that sell cigarettes (***tabac***). Stamp collectors should ask for ***timbres de collection*** in any post office (there is often a ***philatélie*** counter).
France uses a five-digit postal code that precedes the name of the city or town on the last line of the address. The first two digits indicate the ***département*** and the last three digits identify the ***commune*** or local neighbourhood. www.laposte.fr.

MEDIA AND INTERNET

Newspapers, both national and local, and magazines are readily available at the many ***Maisons de la presse*** (newsagents) found in all towns. English-language newspapers are usually only available in larger centres, but are often a day old by the time they arrive on the newsstand.
The internet is now widely available in hotels, fast-food outlets, internet cafés and even

the local bar. Most use WiFi connections, some for a charge, some free.

MONEY

CURRENCY

Coins and notes – The unit of currency in France is the **euro** (€). One euro is divided into 100 cents or ***centimes d'euro.*** There are no restrictions on the amount of currency visitors can take into France. Visitors wishing to export currency in foreign banknotes in excess of the given allocation from France should complete a currency declaration form on arrival.

BANKS AND CURRENCY EXCHANGE

Banks are generally open Mon–Fri 9am–5.30pm. Some branches are open for limited transactions on Saturday.

A passport or other ID may be necessary when cashing cheques in banks. Commission charges vary and hotels usually charge considerably more than banks for cashing cheques, especially for non-residents.

By far the most convenient way of obtaining French currency is the **24hr cash dispenser** or **ATM** (***distributeur automatique de billets*** in French), found outside many banks and post offices and easily recognisable by the CB (***Carte Bleue***) logo. Most accept international credit cards (don't forget your PIN) and almost all also give instructions in English. Note that many ATMs will dispense only up to a certain limit, which may be lower than the daily limit set by your bank. Do not attempt to top up funds the same day (although you can continue to use the card to pay bills in restaurants, for example); this may work with some banks, but at others your card may be declined or, worse, retained. Foreign currency can also be exchanged in major banks, post offices, hotels or private exchange offices found in main cities and near popular tourist attractions.

CREDIT CARDS

Major credit cards (Visa, Mastercard, Eurocard) are widely accepted in shops, hotels, restaurants and petrol stations. If your card is lost or stolen call the issuing bank, but also report any loss or theft to the local police who will issue you with a certificate (give this to your credit card company).

PUBLIC HOLIDAYS

France has several public holidays when attractions may be closed. There are also a number of other religious and national festivals, local saints' days, etc..

1 January	New Year's Day *(Jour de l'An)*
8 April	Easter Monday *(Pâques)*
1 May	Labour Day
8 May	VE Day
17 May	Ascension Day *(Ascension catholique)*
4 June	Whit Monday
14 July	*Fête* National France's National Day (or Bastille Day)
15 August	Assumption *(Assomption)*
1 November	All Saints' Day *(Toussaint)*
11 November	Armistice Day
25 December	Christmas Day *(Noël)*

SCHOOL HOLIDAYS

French schools close for holidays five times a year; the exact dates differ across the three zones used for this purpose. In these periods, all tourist sites and attractions, hotels, restaurants, and roads are busier than usual. These school holidays are one week at the end of October, two weeks at Christmas, two weeks in February, two weeks in spring, and the whole of July and August.

SMOKING

Smoking is forbidden in all public places in France, notably bars, restaurants, railway stations and airports. Ironically, this has created a problem for non-smokers who want to sit outside on a terrace to enjoy the open air, where smoking is not prohibited.

In 2015, the city of Paris started issuing fines of €68 to anyone responsible for dropping cigarette butts on the streets of the city. Others cities may follow suit.

TELEPHONES

The telephone system in France is still operated largely by the former state monopoly France Télécom. They offer an English-language enquiries service on 0800 364 775 (within France) or 00 33 1 55 78 60 56 (outside France).

The French **ringing tone** is a series of long tones; the engaged (busy) tone is a series of short beeps.

National Calls

French telephone numbers have 10 digits. Numbers begin with 01 in Paris and the Paris region; 02 in northwest France; 03 in northeast France; 04 in southeast France and Corsica; 05 in southwest France. However, all 10 numbers must be dialled even locally.

International calls

To call France from abroad, dial the country code 33, omit the initial zero of the French number, and dial the remaining 9-digit number. When calling abroad from France dial 00, followed by the country code (*see above*), followed by the local area code (usually without any initial zero) and the number of your correspondent.

Mobile/Cell phones

Dual- or tri-band mobile phones will work almost anywhere In France, but at international roaming rates. If you are staying for an extended period you might consider renting a mobile phone locally, including Blackberries and iPhones – www.cellhire.fr. A number of service providers now offer the facility to use home-country units rather than paying roaming charges, but make a daily charge for this. If you plan to make regular use of a mobile phone while abroad, this is worth considering. You can buy pre-paid French Euro-SIM cards to use in your own phone, and save on local and international rates (www.lefrenchmobile.com).

TIME

France is one hour ahead of GMT. In France the 24-hour clock is widely applied.

WHEN IT IS NOON IN FRANCE**, IT IS**	
3am	in Los Angeles
6am	in New York
11am	in Dublin
11am	in London
7pm	in Perth
9pm	in Sydney
11pm	in Auckland
In France "am" and "pm" are not used but the 24-hour clock is widely applied.	

TIPPING

Since a **service charge** is automatically included in the price of meals and accommodation in France, any additional tipping is up to the visitor, generally small change, and generally not more than 5 percent.

Hairdressers are usually tipped 10–15 percent.

Restaurants usually charge for meals in two ways: a ***forfait*** or ***menu***, that is a fixed price menu with two to three courses, sometimes a small pitcher of wine, all for a set price, or ***à la carte***, the more expensive way, with each course ordered separately. **Cafés** have very different prices, depending on where they are located. The price of a drink or a coffee is cheaper if you stand at the counter (***comptoir***) than if you sit down (***salle***) and sometimes it is even more expensive if you sit outdoors ***(terrace)***.

Taxi drivers do not have to be tipped, but again it is usual to give a small amount, up to 10 percent. Attendants at public toilets should be given a few cents. Hairdressers are usually tipped 10–15 percent. **Tour guides and tour drivers** should be tipped accordingly: from €2–€5 would not be unusual.

TOURIST OFFICES: NATIONAL

Australia
French Tourist Bureau, 25 Bligh Street, Sydney, NSW 2000, Australia.
✆(0)292 31 62 77;
http://au.rendezvousenfrance.com

Canada
Maison de la France, 1800 av. McGill College, Bureau 1010, Montreal, Quebec H3A 3J6, Canada.
✆(514) 288 20 26;
http://ca.rendezvousenfrance.com

France
79/81 rue de Clichy,
75009 Paris, France.
✆01 42 96 70 00;
http://rendezvousenfrance.com

South Africa
Block C, Morningside Close
222 Rivonia Road.
MORNINGSIDE 2196 –
JOHANNESBURG
✆00 27 (0)10 205 0201

UK and Ireland
Lincoln House, 300 High Holborn, London WC1V 7JH.
✆0207 061 66 00;
http://uk.rendezvousenfrance.com

USA
825 Third Avenue, New York, NY 10022 , USA. ✆(212) 838 78 00;
http://us.rendezvousenfrance.com

TOURIST OFFICES: REGIONAL

Alsace Lorraine Champagne
www.tourisme-alsace.com
www.tourisme-lorraine.fr
www.tourisme-champagne-ardenne.com

Atlantic Coast
www.tourisme-aquitaine.fr
www.poitou-charentes-vacances.com

Auvergne – Rhône valley
www.auvergne-tourisme.info
www.rhonealpes-tourisme.com

Brittany
www.brittanytourism.com

Burgundy Jura
www.bourgogne-tourisme.com
www.franche-comte.org

Châteaux of the Loire
www.visaloire.com
www.enpaysdelaloire.com

Corsica
www.visit-corsica.com

Dordogne Berry Limousin
www.tourismelimousin.com

French Alps
www.rhonealpes-tourisme.com
www.visit-southern-france.com

French Riviera
www.frenchriviera-tourism.com

Languedoc Roussillon Midi-Pyrénées
www.destinationsuddefrance.com
www.tourism-midi-pyrenees.co.uk

Normandy
www.normandie-tourisme.fr

Northern France and the Paris Region
www.crt-nordpasdecalais.fr
http://en.parisinfo.com
www.picardietourisme.com

USEFUL WEBSITES

www.uk.rendezvousenfrance.com
The French Government Tourist Office site is packed with practical information, advice and tips for those travelling to France, including choosing package tours and even buying a property. The homepage has a number of links to more specific guidance, for American or Canadian travellers for example, or to the FGTO's London pages.

www.holidayfrance.org.uk
The Association of British Travel Organisers in France has created this tidy site, which covers just about everything.

www.francediscovered.com
A practical and developing France-wide website for the traveller, written by a Francophile travel writer. Includes essential information, as well as a wide range of regional and local content to help plan and inspire a stay in France.

www.ViaMichelin.com
This site has maps, tourist information, travel features, suggestions on hotels and restaurants, and a route planner for numerous locations in Europe. In addition, you can look up weather forecasts, traffic reports and service station location, particularly useful if you will be driving in France.

www.F-T-S.co.uk
The French Travel Service specialises in organising holidays in France using the rail network. Let FTS organise your travel and hotels anywhere in France.

www.fngi.fr (Tour Guides)
Looking for a professional tour guide? This FNGIC represents and unites licensed tourist guides, while promoting and defending their profession. It is a professional non-profit organisation. It has about 700 members, all of whom passed an examination and received professional accreditation from both the Ministry of Tourism and the Ministry of Culture and Communication. FNGIC, 43, rue Beaubourg, 75003 PARIS. ☏01 44 59 29 15.

www.ambafrance-uk.org and www.ambafrance-us.org
The French Embassies in the UK and the USA have a website providing basic information (geography, demographics, history), a news digest and business-related information. It offers special pages for children and pages devoted to culture, language study and travel, as well as links to other selected French sites (regions, cities, ministries).

VALUE ADDED TAX

In France a sales tax (*TVA* or VAT) is added to all purchases. For non-EU residents on holiday this tax can be refunded as long as you have bought more than €175 worth of goods at the same time and in the same shop, and have completed the appropriate *Bordereau* form at the shop. Ask for your receipts and the form when at the sales desk, and take these and your purchases to the local customs office at the airport before you check in for your flight.
The amount permitted may vary, so it is advisable to check first with the VAT-refund counter (*Service de détaxe*). Customs Information Centre: ☏08 20 02 44 44 or www.douane.gouv.fr.

Introducing France

Cité de Carcassonne

Features

» **France Today p64**
A Way of Life p65
French Cuisine p67
French Wine p69

» **French History p70**
Key Events p71

» **French Art and Culture p84**
Prehistory to the Middle Ages p85
Romanesque (11–12C) p86
Gothic (12–15C) p89
Military Architecture p94
The Renaissance (16–17C) p96
Henri IV & Pre-Classicism (16–17C) p98
French Classicism in the Early 17C p99
Versailles Classicism (17–18C) p100
French Rocaille (18C) p101
Neoclassical Reaction (18–19C) p103
Art and Architecture in the 19C p105
Art and Architecture in the 20C p108
French Literature p110
French Films p111

» **Nature p112**
France's Landscapes p113

Maison Carrée, Nîmes

France Today

France is a wealthy country of over 66 million people, with the highest birthrate in Europe. A major economic power and an important tourist destination, the France of today is very different from the France of 100, or even just 50 years ago. However, many symbolic similarities remain: the Fifth Republic presidency has monarchic characteristics, and regional power bases compete with Paris; themes that have persisted in France for centuries. Although actively involved on the international stage, France looks after French interests first and retains a strongly nationalistic quality, with over 72 per cent of newborn children (2010) having two French parents. Life expectancy in France is high, founded on an excellent social care system, and a deeply engrained joie de vivre.

» A Way of Life p65
» French Cuisine p67
» French Wine p69

Vineyards of Hautes-Côtes de Beaune, Pernand-Vergelesses, Burgundy

A Way of Life

France embraces notions of romance, culture, liberty and intellectualism in combinations that are a pot-pourri of ideas and concepts, at once familiar and foreign, and a complicated blend of 21st century ideology and tradition.

STREET LIFE

For most French people the qualities associated with this ancestral land are encapsulated in the traditional **village** – the village where one was born, where one has chosen to live or where one spends one's holidays. Leaving aside the differences attributed to climatic conditions and building materials, all villages feature common characteristics: the **main street** lined with small shops, the **market place**, where local cattle fairs used to be held, and, of course, the **church**, whose bells continue to herald the fortunes and misfortunes of the community.

Although they see a surge of activity during municipal and trade fairs, French villages are quiet, and peaceful most of the year. Only the traditional **café** and the **boules ground** echo the conversations of the locals idly debating the meaning of life. This strong regionalism has led to frequent conflict with, and hostility to, the central government in Paris. To resolve this long-standing problem, a series of decentralisation reforms was implemented in 1982, creating regional governments with considerable autonomy.

Regional capitals were established to strike a balance between the capital and the countryside. Despite their long history and local tradition, these regional urban centres tend to be resolutely turned towards the future and illustrate the thriving character of the French regions. However, **Paris** remains the administrative core of the country and a focal point for the whole nation. The seat of political power, and an important centre for world trade, "the City of Lights" is also an exceptional destination for visitors.

This brief description would not be complete without mentioning the **French** themselves. Frequently misunderstood by foreign visitors, often condemned as brusque and unhelpful, they are nonetheless always ready to protect and safeguard their age-old traditions and support a cause in defence of the interests of France and the French way of life. To those who make the effort of going towards them, and who cherish their way of life as they do, the French will always extend a warm, genuine welcome.

PEOPLE

The total population of metropolitan France (2015) was 66 317 994, a slight increase on previous years, and growing at a rate of 0.55%. The population is projected to exceed 69 000 000 by 2020. The average age at marriage is just over 30 for men and just under 30 for women, although the rate of marriage is falling with many preferring to cohabit. In 2006, the French government introduced a law raising the age at which a woman can get married from 15 to 18. France continues to have the longest-living citizens in Europe – for men life expectancy is 78 years while for women it is 85.

Some elements of French behaviour are as deeply rooted as France itself, revealing itself in factions of cultural individuality such as in Brittany and the Basque country.

But it is a fundamental part of the French psyche to sustain regionalism, to denigrate foreigners (and each other), and, paradoxically, to oppose authority while simultaneously upholding it as necessary.

THE FAMILY

For many the concept of the French lifestyle conjures up images of good living with strong emphasis on family values and traditions. And while this remains true for many, there has been a tendency in recent years for busy families to spend less time together and eat less well. This has led some social commentators to the view that all is not well with French society. That may be the case, but an attempt in 2010 to have the traditional French lunch listed by UNESCO as worthy of cultural World Heritage status shows that the French have not lost their sense of humour.

RELIGION

Freedom of religion is guaranteed by the Constitution, but there is a strict separation of Church and state. The French government does not maintain any records of the statistics of the religion of the inhabitants of France. But since the 1970s, France has become a very secular country with a growing number admitting to being lapsed Christians, agnostic or atheist.

SPORT

Sport has always played an important role in French society, with the most watched sport being football. Both rugby codes (Union and League) are popular, as are athletics, alpine skiing, tennis and, of course, cycling. At lower energy levels, *pétanque* and *boules* are played anywhere there is a small patch of level ground, and are taken very seriously indeed. There is a difference between the two, but only the French would dare to try to explain it!

ECONOMY

France has long enjoyed a strong rural tradition, but today there are far fewer people (only 4%) employed in agriculture. Alongside this, France has a very advanced industrial economy (25% of the population), but employs the greatest proportion of the population (71.8%, 2010) in the services sector.

Economically, France has followed its own path, favouring extensive employee rights, state monopolies, state intervention, heavy subsidies and protectionism.

In 2014, France was ranked the sixth-largest economy in the world behind the US, China, Japan and Germany and the UK, with the third largest economy in Europe.

Gross Domestic Product (GDP) – $2.469 trillion – grew 0.9% in the early part of 2015, and the forecast was for 1.1% expansion during the rest of the year. The overall impression of economists, however, is that France's competitiveness has not significantly improved, and that consumer confidence remains low. A record number of people are looking for work, with unemployment at 10.3% (January 2015), the highest since 1999. Whatever the statistics show, France has the highest number of millionaires in Europe: 2.6 million of them, followed by the UK and Germany; this accounts for 3.9% of the total French population.

GOVERNMENT

The government of France is a semi-Presidential system functioning under a written constitution, and with a parliament of *Deputés* elected every five years and a President also elected every five years. The **President** has extensive personal powers.

At the same time, France is divided into large regions with a high degree of autonomy. Within each region is a multitude of communes, which enjoy a good deal of local self-determination under powerful mayors. There are 27 administrative **regions** in France (22 within metropolitan France, and five overseas), governed by elected councils. The regions are composed of **départements** (100 in all of France), each of which is divided into communes, governed by municipal councils and mayors. **Cantons** exist only to elect members to the departmental council. Proposals are afoot, however, to reduce the 22 metropolitan regions to just 13; these will take effect on 1 January 2016.

French Cuisine

France is the land of good food and fine dining, and it has a host of regional specialities. The Michelin Red Guide: France lists hundreds of hotels and restaurants throughout the country.

SOUPS

In restaurants, large and small, at least one soup of the day will always be available. The best-known, probably because they are the easiest to make, are cream of asparagus (*velouté d'asperges*), leek and potato (*soupe de poireaux-pommes de terre*), onion (*soupe à l'oignon*), *garbure* (a thick soup with cabbage popular in southwestern France) and *cotriade* (Breton fish soup). In rural village bar-restaurants you may be served a dish of raw vegetables (*crudités*) to begin your meal.

ENTRÉES & MAIN COURSES

In France, the *entrée* is commonly the first dish of a meal (and strictly speaking includes soup). Quite often the first course will be a savoury tart or salad, something light, like *salade niçoise* (tomatoes, anchovies, onions, olives) or *salade lyonnaise (endive, bacon, croutons, poached eggs)*, that leads in to the main course. If dining out in a restaurant, especially at lunchtime, do not feel pressured to go for three courses; if all you want is a main dish, just ask for that. France, of course, is renowned for its imaginative and inventive cuisine, and there are many regional dishes that are worth trying, like *aligot* (a dish traditionally made in the Aubrac (Aveyron, Cantal, Lozère) region in the Massif Central), which is a blend of melted Tomme cheese (although others are often substituted, to good effect) and mashed potatoes, often flavoured with garlic; *cassoulet* (a rich, rib-sticking white haricot bean stew containing meat, usually pork sausages, pork and duck confit. It is slow-cooked and best enjoyed at a leisurely pace with plenty of crusty bread); *tartiflette* (a dish from Savoie, made with potatoes, Reblochon cheese, cream and lardons. It often includes onions); and *ratatouille* (a stewed vegetable dish from Provence, often served as a side dish, but also as a main course). *See www.lovefrenchfood.com for French dishes to cook at home.*

CHEESE

The cheese course in French dining comes before the dessert, not after. It is intended to cleanse the palate after the main course, so to better appreciate the flavours of the final course.

Almost every village in France produces its own cheeses, and there is seldom any doubt about origin. Cheese is such a quintessential element of French cuisine that no fewer than 45 of them have been given AOC status (*Appellation d'Origine Contrôlée*), which effectively controls the production and origin of cheese: 29 cow's milk cheeses; 13 goat's milk; 2 made from sheep's milk and just 1 that is made from mixed milk. That's not it, of course; those are just the AOC cheeses, where method of production and place of origin are guaranteed. Some are also protected under the less stringent Label Régional (LR), and some have Protected Geographic Indication designation (PGI).

FRUIT AND DESSERTS

There are innumerable **desserts** to round off a meal. Apart from the baskets of fruit, strawberries and cream, strawberries in red wine, and fruit salads that make use of all the orchard fruits, there are apple, pear and peach compotes, and all manner of cake dishes, such as *tarte Tatin* (a caramelised tart cooked with the filling underneath), walnut cake (*gâteau aux noix*), *far* (a baked custard dessert from Brittany), gingerbread (*pain d'épices*) in the Gâtinais region, *clafoutis* (a blend of milk and eggs mixed with fruit and baked in the oven), and *kougelhopf* from Alsace baked in the form of a ring and served as a dessert or as an afternoon snack. For those with an especially sweet tooth there is crème caramel, baked cream desserts, and soft meringues with custard sauce (*îles flottantes*) that are found in nearly every region of France.

FOOD GLOSSARY

ail - garlic
aïoli - garlic mayonnaise
aligot - potatoes and Tomme cheese
andouillette - chitterling sausage
anis - aniseed confectionery
asperges - asparagus
bar - sea bass
bergamots - hard-boiled sweets
berlingots - more hard-boiled sweets
bêtises - hard mints
beurre blanc - butter sauce
bouillabaisse - seafood stew
bourride - fish soup
brandade - creamed salt cod
calmar - squid
canard au sang - pressed duck
cassoulet - stew with haricot beans, sausages and pork
cèpes - cèpe mushrooms
charcuterie - smoked, cured or dried meats
choucroute - Sauerkraut
confiseries - confectionery
confits - duck or goose preserved in fat
crêpes - pancakes
crêpes dentelles - thin pancakes
cuisse de grenouilles - frog's legs
daurade, dorade - sea bream
dragées - sugared almonds
encornet - squid
escargots - snails
esturgeons - sturgeon
far - Breton flan
ficelles Picardes - ham pancakes with mushroom sauce
foie gras - goose liver
fouace - dough cakes
fraises - strawberries
fruits confits - crystallised fruit
galettes - savoury pancakes
gâteau d'amandes - almond cake
garbure - meat and vegetable stew
gratins - dishes with a crusty topping
jambon - ham
jambon cru - cured ham
lait - milk
lardons - thickly sliced bacon pieces
légumes - vegetables
lotte - monkfish
loup - bass
macarons - macaroons
madeleines - small sponge cakes
magret de canard - breast of duck
marrons glacés - crystallised chestnuts
merlu - hake
miel - honey
morue - salt cod
mouclade - mussel stew
moules - mussels
moutarde - mustard
noix - nuts
nougat - sugar, honey and nut sweetmeat
nougatine - caramel syrup and almond sweetmeat
oursins - sea urchins
pain d'épice - spiced honey cake
pieds de cochon - pigs' trotters
piperade - sweet pepper and tomato omelette
poireau - leeks
poisson - fish
poulardes - fatted chickens
poulet - chicken
pralines - caramelised almond confectionery
pruneaux - prunes
quenelles - poached meat or fish dumplings
quenelles de brochet - pike dumplings
quiche (Lorraine) - egg, cream and bacon flan
rillettes - potted pork
rognons - kidneys
saucisson - sausage
seiche - cuttlefish
tripes - tripe
truffes - truffles
truite - trout
viande - meat
volailles - poultry

French Wine

There are just two key elements to wine production – apart from the fact that someone has to grow the grapes, harvest them and contrive to turn them into wine: the vague notion of 'terroir' (*see below*), and Appellation d'Origine Controllée (AOC), which sets down strict rules for wine production.

VARIETIES

The wines of France encompass every variety of taste from sweet whites to the driest, from rich, full-bodied reds to light easy-drinking rosés, from unpretentious, drinkable table wines to the greatest names in the world, including, of course, the very symbol of celebration and delight, champagne.

Understanding the labels can be critical to the health of your wallet. Not all wines are AOC, although this is a guarantee of place and method of production. But lack of AOC status doesn't mean that the wine is unfit for drinking, and many of the Vins de Pays and Vins de Table are excellent.

But knowing what the labels mean is equally important.

- **Grand cru**, applies to the very best estates of Médoc, no fewer than 61 in number.
- **Cru bourgeois** are wines from Médoc and Haut Médoc… excellent but invariably cheaper than Grand cru.
- **VDQS** (Vin Délimité de Qualité Supérieure) wines are from geographically limited areas, such as Provence and the Loire valley.
- **Vin de pays** wines do not have AOC or VDQS labels, but are excellent wines for everyday drinking.
- **Vin de table**, also known as 'Vin ordinaire' is ordinary, everyday wine; cheap but not unpleasant.

TERROIR

The French love to speak of 'terroir' and not only in the context of wine. Yet it defies adequate translation, and is meant to embrace all the natural components that go into production, including the nature and quality of the soil, the climate, the vagaries of landscape, and a healthy dose of '*Je ne sais quoi*'.

VITICULTURE

Wine is produced in 12 regions of France, their boundaries invisible but nonetheless critical and important demarcations: Alsace, Bordeaux, Burgundy, Champagne, Corsica, Jura, Languedoc-Roussillon, Loire, Provence, Rhône, Savoie and South-west France.

WINE TASTING

The opportunities to taste wine in France range from roadside bars and market stalls to the large emporiums of wine producers, and quite a range of dégustations in between. But remember: it's not the done thing to slurp, spit/swallow and wander off without buying something.

MICHELIN

For wine-lovers, the **Michelin Guide: The Wine Regions of France** offers a comprehensive introduction to French wine-making and features driving itineraries for the 14 main wine regions of the country: Alsace, Beaujolais, Bordelais (Bordeaux wines), Burgundy, Champagne, Cognac, Corse (Corsican wines), Jura, Languedoc-Roussillon, Loire valley, Provence, Rhône valley, Savoie-Bugey and the Southwest. Descriptions of over 500 restaurants, hotels and guesthouses are included in this guide to enhance your journey through these regions.

French History

For centuries, France was the giant of Europe, dominating its neighbouring countries. Few nations have influenced the modern world so dynamically. The country was fertile, prosperous and the keystone of the balance of continental power. With the Age of Discovery, France had an impact across the world from India to Canada, and from the Far East to the Caribbean, so much so that by the end of the 19C, the French Empire was second only to that of Britain. Yet conflict, in one guise or another, has been a hallmark of the history of France, making this a country born of effort and sacrifice, rather than a natural synergy of its parts.

» Key Events p71

King François I knighted after the Battle of Marignano in 1515

Key Events

The great sweep of prehistory has left abundant traces in France, and it is to Frenchmen that much of our knowledge of prehistoric times is due.
See Les EYZIES-DE-TAYAC, p498.

ORIGINS

The presence of **Neolithic** remains in the Dordogne valley are clear evidence of thriving communities more than 25 000 years ago in what was to become France. Prehistoric life flourished along the river valleys, and rudimentary villages were first settled in the Paris Basin, along the Rhône valley and in the Aude in Languedoc, more than 6 500 years ago. These settlements later gave way to **Celtic**, **Germanic** and **Roman** culture.

5000 BCE	**Megalithic** culture flourishes in Brittany (Carnac), then in Corsica, lasting for over 2 500 years.
8C	**Celtic** tribes from central Europe arrive in Gaul where they build the fortified settlements known as oppidums.
600	**Greek** traders found a number of cities, including Marseille, Glanum (*see ST-RÉMY-DE-PROVENCE p623*), and Aléria in Corsica.
2C	Celtic culture, which had spread as far as Brittany, gives way to both Germanic and Roman influences. The port of Fréjus, on the Mediterranean coast, is founded in 154 by the **Romans** as a link on the sea route to their possessions in Spain. By the year 122 they have established themselves at Aix, and four years later at Narbonne.
58–52	Julius Caesar's Gallic Wars. He defeats the Veneti in 56 BCE (*see VANNES p268*), then himself suffers defeat at the hands of Vercingetorix (*see CLERMONT-FERRAND p464*) in 52 BCE, though the latter's surrender comes only a few months later.
1C	During the reign of Augustus, Roman rule in Gaul is consolidated and expanded (*see NÎMES p558*). Fréjus is converted into a naval base and fortified.
5C	The monasteries set up by St Martin at Ligugé and by St Honorat at Lérins reinforce Christian beliefs and mark the beginning of a wave of such foundations (by St Victor at Marseille, by St Loup at Troyes, by St Maxime at Riez).

THE MEROVINGIANS (418–751)

The Frankish king, **Clovis** (482–511) was the first of the Merovingian Dynasty, a powerbase that over the next century came to control most of Gaul and left a legacy of murders and atrocities to rival Byzantium. Not until the reign of **Dagobert I**

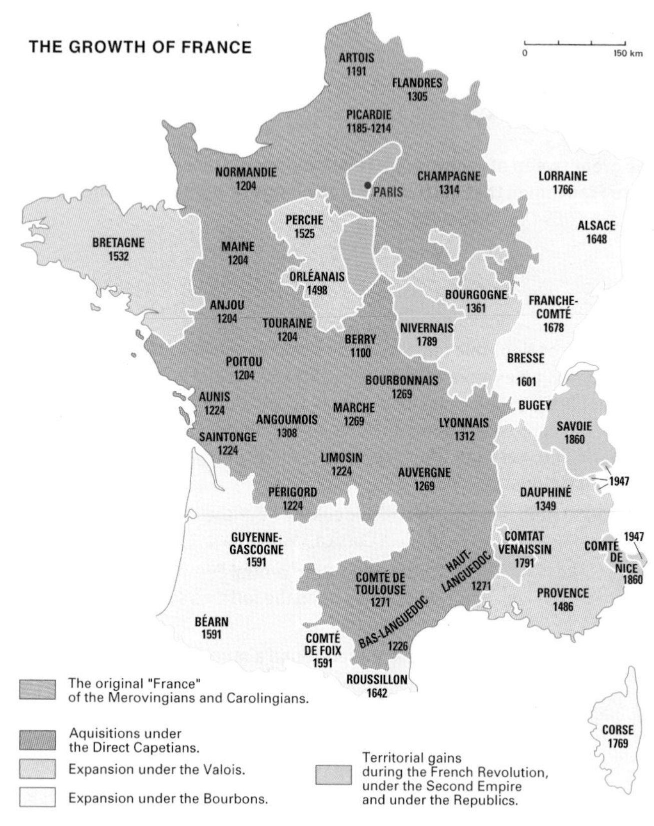

(628–637) was any attempt made to restore the Frankish kingdom, but on his death the Merovingian Dynasty descended into the hands of idle kings given to debauchery, gluttony and internecine plotting.

451	**Merovius**, king of the **Salian Franks** (from the Tournai area in present-day Belgium), defeats Attila the Hun (*see CHÂLONS-EN-CHAMPAGNE p356*). It is to him that the dynasty owes its name.
476	Fall of the Roman Empire in the West; Gaul occupied by barbarian tribes.
496	Clovis, grandson of Merovius and King of the Franks, is baptised in Reims.
507	Defeat of the **Visigoths** under Alaric II at Vouillé (*see POITIERS p542*) by Clovis.
6C	Accompanied by Christian missionaries, settlers from Britain arrive in the Breton peninsulas, displacing the original Celtic inhabitants. But they too are overcome, first by the Franks (in the 9C), then by the Angevins (11C).
732	The Arab armies invading France are defeated at Moussais-la-Bataille (*see POITIERS p542*) by **Charles Martel**.

THE CAROLINGIANS (751–986)

The coronation of **Pepin I** was essentially the product of his own aspirations and those of the church, which resented royal interference in clerical matters, but needed secular power for its security. The crowning by Pope Leo III of **Charlemagne** as Emperor in 800 was seen as an extension of the Roman Empire, and is today referred to as the Carolingian Empire.

751	Pepin the Short has himself elected king by an assembly of magnates and bishops at Soissons, sending the powerless Childeric, last of the Merovingians, to a monastery.
800	Charlemagne is crowned Emperor of the West in Rome.
842	The Strasbourg Oaths.
843	By the **Treaty of Verdun**, the Carolingian Empire is divided between the sons of Louis I, Charles the Bald receiving the territories to the west, roughly corresponding to modern France.
850	**Nominoé** (*see VANNES p268*) wrests eastern Brittany and the Rais country south of the Loire from its Frankish rulers.
910	Foundation of the great abbey at Cluny.
911	By the **Treaty of St-Clair-sur-Epte**, **Charles the Simple** and the Viking chief **Rollo** create the **Duchy of Normandy**.

THE CAPETIANS (987–1789)

Capetian France was hallmarked by a form of aristocratic anarchy involving princes, nobles and knights, who, in the absence of a defined feudal hierarchy, held the real power, especially the farther they reigned from the Île de France. As a result, political power was fragmented until a measure of consolidation began in the 13C.

987	A descendant of Robert the Strong, **Hugh Capet**, Duke of "France", ousts Charles of Lorraine and has himself elected. By having his son crowned during his own lifetime, he consolidates his family's rule, which nevertheless does not become truly hereditary until the accession of **Philippe Auguste** in 1180.
1066	**William Duke of Normandy** (*see BAYEUX p513 and CAEN p222*) sets out for the English coast from Dives. His victory over Harold at the Battle of Hastings leads to his coronation as King of England, though technically speaking he is still a vassal of the French king.
1095	The **First Crusade** is preached at Clermont-Ferrand.
1137	**Louis VII** weds **Eleanor of Aquitaine** (*see BORDEAUX, p513*); the annulment of their marriage 15 years later is a disaster for the dynasty.
1204	Gaillard Castle falls to Philippe Auguste, who goes on to conquer Normandy, Maine, Touraine and Anjou.
1209	Start of the **Albigensian Crusade**.

1214	Victory at the **Battle of Bouvines** (*see LILLE p190*); for the first time, a genuinely French patriotism appears.
1244	**Cathars** burnt on a funeral pyre at Montségur.
1270	**St Louis** (**Louis IX**) dies aboard ship off Tunis on his way to the Eighth Crusade.

THE HOUSE OF VALOIS (1328–1589)

The rejection of **Edward III** of England's claim to the throne of France (as a direct male descendant of **Philip IV** of France), on the grounds that Salic Law prohibited succession through the female line (although it didn't), was the catalyst that fuelled Edward III's attempts to claim the throne with force. This led to what became the Hundred Years' War between England and France.

THE HUNDRED YEARS' WAR (1337–1475)

Extending over six reigns, the war was both a political and dynastic struggle between **Plantagenets** and **Capetians** over who should rule in France. Accompanied by plague (including the Black Death of 1348) and religious confusion, it was a time of tribulation for the people of France, harassed as they were by bands of outlaws as well as by the English soldiery.

In **1337, Philippe VI of Valois** resisted the claims to his throne made by Edward III of England, who was the grandson, on his mother's side, of Philippe le Bel (the Fair). This marked the beginning of the war. Three years after the French defeat at Crécy, Philippe VI purchased the **Dauphiné**, up to then a territory of the Empire, from its ruler, **Humbert II**, thereby extending French rule far to the east of the Rhône.

In **1356**, **King John the Good** was defeated by the **Black Prince**, the eldest son of King Edward III of England, at the **Battle of Poitiers** (*see POITIERS, p542*).

Under **Charles V**, **Du Guesclin** succeeded in restoring internal order. But at this point in their conflict, both adversaries were beset by problems of their own caused in England by the minority of **Richard II**. In France, **Charles VI**, too, was under-age and later affected by madness. The War between the Armagnacs and Burgundians began and the Church was torn by the **Great Schism** (*see AVIGNON, p624*). Following the English victory at **Agincourt** (*see ST-OMER, p197*) and the assassination of **John the Fearless** of Burgundy at Montereau (*see DIJON, p368*), the **Treaty of Troyes**, promising the French Crown to the English king, seemed to extinguish any hope of the future Charles VII succeeding.

In **1429**, however, after having picked out the king from among the courtiers assembled at Chinon, **Joan of Arc** recaptured Orléans thereby preventing **Salisbury**'s army from crossing the Loire and meeting up with the English troops who had been stationed in central and southwestern France following the **Treaty of Brétigny** in 1360. On 17 July **Charles VII** was crowned in Reims cathedral; in **1436** Paris was freed, followed by Normandy and Guyenne.

In **1453**, the French victory at Castillon-la-Bataille was the last important clash of arms in the war, which was formally brought to an end by the Treaty of Picquigny.

FRANÇOIS I, HENRI II, FRANÇOIS II (1515–60)

1515	Accession of François I; **Battle of Marignano** and the signing of peace in perpetuity with Switzerland.
1520	Meeting of François I and **Henry VIII of England** at the **Field of the Cloth of Gold** at Guînes.

1539	The **Ordinance of Villers-Cotterêts**, one of the bases of French law, is promulgated by François I. Among its 192 articles are ones decreeing the keeping of parish registers of births and deaths, as well as law reform outlawing the founding of guilds and instituting secret criminal investigation and the compulsory use of French instead of Latin in legal matters.
1541	**Calvin**'s "Institutes of the Christian Religion" is published. In it, this native Frenchman, born at Noyon, attempts to stem the fissiparous tendencies of the Reformation and to proclaim its universality. Style, structure and significance combine in this work to make it the first classic of French literature.
1560	The **Amboise Conspiracy**, harbinger of the looming political and religious crisis.

THE WARS OF RELIGION (1562–98)

This is the name given to the 36-year-long crisis marked by complex political as well as religious conflict. During the latter half of the 16C, the French monarchy was in poor shape under **Charles IX** (ruled 1560–74) and later **Henri III** (ruled 1574–1589) to withstand the looming hegemony of Spain, with political life in chaos and debt reaching incredible dimensions. The firm stand taken on religion by Spain and Italy on the one hand and by the Protestant countries on the other was missing in the France of **Catherine de' Medici**'s regency, where both parties jostled for favour and a policy of appeasement applied. The nobility took advantage of the situation, seeking to bolster their power base in the provinces and, under cover of religion, to grasp the reins of government. The **Catholic League** was formed by the **Guise** and **Montmorency** families, supported by Spain and opposed by the **Bourbon**, **Condé** and **Coligny** factions, **Huguenots** all, with English backing. Though historians distinguish eight wars separated by periods of peace or relative tranquillity, the troubles were continuous: in the country, endless assassinations, persecutions and general lawlessness; at court, intrigues, volte-faces and pursuit of particular interests. Actual warfare, threatened ever since the Amboise Conspiracy, began at Wassy in 1560, following a massacre of Protestants. The names of Dreux, Nîmes, Chartres, Longjumeau, Jarnac, Montcontour, St-Lô, Valognes, Coutras, Arques and Ivry follow in bloody succession. The Peace of St-Germain in 1570 demonstrated a general desire for reconciliation, but only two years later came the **St Bartholomew's Day Massacre** in which some 20 000 Huguenots died. The States General were convened at Blois at the request of the supporters of the League who were opposed to the centralisation of power into royal hands. Fearful of the power enjoyed by **Duke Henri of Guise**, head of the Catholic League and the kingdom's best military commander, King Henri III had him assassinated in the château at Blois one cold morning in December 1588, only to be cut down himself by a fanatical monk the following year. This left the succession open for the Huguenot **Henri of Navarre**, the future **Henri IV**. By formally adopting the Catholic faith in 1593 and by promulgating the **Edict of Nantes** in 1598, this able ruler succeeded in rallying all loyal Frenchmen to his standard, putting at least a temporary end to the long-drawn-out crisis.

THE BOURBONS (1589–1789)

Bourbon monarchs ruled France from the time of Henri IV until the overthrow of the monarchy in 1792 during the French Revolution. The House of Bourbon was briefly restored in 1814, and then with more permanence in 1815 after the fall of the First French Empire, the empire of Napoléon I. They were finally overthrown in the July Revolution of 1830.

HENRI IV (1589–1610)

Though his political manoeuvring and his personal conduct did not endear him to everybody, Henri IV put France's affairs on a firm footing once more, attaching the provinces of Bresse and Bugey to the kingdom and setting great architects like Du Cerceau and Métezeau to work on projects in Paris such as the Place des Vosges and the Louvre Gallery, and in La Rochelle and Charleville in the provinces. Important economic reforms were undertaken, and the king's old Huguenot friend, **Maximilien de Béthune**, **Duke of Sully**, set the nation's finances in order, dug canals and laid out new roads and port facilities.
In 1600, the landowner **Olivier de Serres** published his great work on progressive farming technique "The Theatre of Agriculture and Field Husbandry", supporting Sully in his contention that "tilling and stock-keeping are the two breasts from which France feeds". The king's concern with his people's well-being found expression in his famous statement "a chicken in the pot every Sunday".

LOUIS XIII (1610–43)

1610 Louis XIII becomes king. The country's trade flourishes with the development of inland ports and there are fine planned expansions to a number of towns (Orléans, La Rochelle, Montargis, Langres). The reign is marked by an aristocratic rebellion, as well as by the pioneering work of St Vincent de Paul in social welfare (hospitals, Sisters of Mercy). In the field of ideas, **Descartes** publishes his "Discourse on Method" (1637), with its reasoning based on systematic questioning ("Cogito, ergo sum"), a starting point for the intellectual revolution which, among other achievements, led to the invention of analytical geometry.

1624 The king's first minister, **Richelieu** (1585–1642), is successful in his attempts to reduce the power of a Protestantism over-inclined to seek foreign aid (La Rochelle) or to resist the unification of the kingdom (Montauban, Privas). A few exemplary executions serve to humble the nobility (Montmorency, Cinq-Mars), a process carried further by the demolition of castles. He strengthens France's role in Europe (Thirty Years' War) and, in 1635, founds the Academy (**Académie française**).

LOUIS XIV (1643–1715)

The 72 years of the **Sun King**'s reign marked both France and Europe with the force of his personality (*see PARIS p116 and VERSAILLES p161*). At the time of his accession, the king was only five years old and **Anne of Austria** confirmed **Mazarin** in his role as first minister. Five days later, the French victory at **Rocroi** (1643) signalled the end of Spanish dominance of Europe's affairs. In 1648, the

Peace of Westphalia ended the Thirty Years' War, confirmed France's claim to Alsace (apart from Strasbourg and Mulhouse) and established French as the language of diplomacy.

In 1657, while the king looked on, the two-month siege of Montmédy was brought to a triumphant conclusion by La Ferté and **Vauban**, thereby putting an end to Spanish rule in the Low Countries. In 1662, the king's first year of personal rule was crowned by the purchase of the port of Dunkerque, a result of the statesman Lionne's diplomacy; the place became a base for smugglers and for privateers like Jean Bart operating in the service of the king.

Anglo-French rivalry for control of the seas (*see BELLE-ÎLE, p272*) now became the main theme of international politics. In 1678, the **Treaty of Nijmegen** marked the end of the war with Holland, the giving-up of the Franche-Comté and of 12 strongholds in Flanders by Spain, and the reconquest of Alsace. This was a high point in Louis' reign and in French expansion, insured by Vauban's work in fortifying the country's new frontiers. The politics of religion were not always straightforward; for 20 years, the king was in conflict with the pope in what was known as the **Affair of the Régale**; in 1685 came the **Revocation of the Edict of Nantes** with all its dire consequences, and in 1702 the suppression of the **Camisard** revolt. The monarch's later years were clouded by the country's economic exhaustion, though the **Battle of Denain** in 1712 saved France from invasion by the Austro-Dutch armies and led to the end of the **War of the Spanish Succession**.

ORIENTAL VENTURES

In 1664, a century after the voyages of **Jean Ango** and Jacques Cartier, the **French East India Company** was revived by **Colbert**, Louis XIV's great minister of finance. Two years later he authorised it to set up bases both at **Port-Louis** and on waste ground on the far side of the confluence of the Scorff and Blavet rivers. In 1671 the first great merchantman was fitted out for her journey to the East, and the new port was given the name of L'Orient (**Lorient** in 1830).

Anglo-French naval rivalry now began in earnest. Over a period of 47 years the Company put a total of 76 ships into use, which, in the course of their long and often dangerous voyages, would bring back cargoes of spices and porcelain (France alone importing over 12 million items of the latter). The initially fabulous profits eventually declined when the Company became a kind of state enterprise under the control of the bank run by the Scots financier Law. In the end, Lorient moved from a commercial role to a naval one.

The spirit of scientific enquiry leads to rapid technological progress, the growth of industry (textiles, porcelain, steam power) and to endeavours such as **Lalande**'s astronomical experiments and the **Montgolfier brothers**' balloon flights at Annonay in 1783.

LOUIS XV (1715–74)

1715	Louis XV succeeds to the crown at the age of five; the **Duke of Orléans** is Regent. The reign is marked by indecision, frivolity and corruption; many of France's colonies (Senegal, Québec, the Antilles, possessions in India) are lost. Internally, however, the country prospers, benefiting from a wise economic policy; the standard of living improves and a long period of stability favours agricultural development (introduction of the potato, artificial extension of grazing lands). **Lorraine** is absorbed into France in 1766, as is **Corsica** in 1769.

1774 Louis XVI becomes king. **Lafayette** takes part in the **American War of Independence**, brought to an end by the **Treaty of Versailles** in 1783.

THE FRENCH REVOLUTION (1789–99)

The Revolution, opening up the continent of Europe to democracy, was the outcome of the long crisis affecting the **Ancien Régime**. Hastened along by the teachings of the thinkers of the **Enlightenment**, as much as by the inability of a still essentially feudal system to adapt itself to new social realities, the Revolution broke out following disastrous financial mismanagement and the emptying of the coffers of the state. The main events unfolded in Paris but their repercussions were felt in the provincial cities such as Lyon and Nantes as well as in the countryside.
The year 1789 heralded a number of major historic events for France. The Estates General were renamed the **National Assembly**, the **Bastille** was stormed, privileges were abolished (night of 4 July) and the **Rights of Man** were proclaimed. Two years later, in 1791, the king, fleeing with his family, was arrested in Varennes (22 June) and brought back to Paris, where he was suspended from office on 30 September. The following year the **Convention** (1792–95) was signed, while in Valmy (20 September) Kellermann and Dumouriez saved France from invasion by forcing the Prussians to retreat. On 22 September, France was proclaimed a one and indivisible **Republic**. The major landmarks of 1793 were the execution of Louis XVI (21 January), the Vendée revolt, the crushing of the Lyon uprising and the siege of Toulon (July–December). In 1795 France adopted the metric system.
In 1799, **Napoléon** overthrew the **Directory** (*9 November*) and declared himself First Consul of the Republic. Finally, in 1801, the **Code Napoléon** was promulgated throughout the country.

1789 French Revolution begins in Paris.

1799 Napoléon overthrows Revolutionary government, puts new constitution in place.

FIRST EMPIRE (1804–15)

Napoléon's rise to power ended the period of the French Consulate (the government of France between the fall of the Directory in the coup of Brumaire in 1799), and led to a series of wars known collectively as the **Napoléonic Wars**, which served to extend French influence over much of western Europe. At its height, in 1812, the French Empire ruled over 44 million subjects. Undermining forces, however, began to criticise Napoléon's achievements, leading to his defeat and ultimate exile.

1804 On 2 December, Napoléon is crowned **Emperor of the French** in Notre-Dame by **Pope Pius VII**. The territorial acquisitions made in the course of the French Revolution now have to be defended against a whole series of coalitions formed by the country's numerous enemies.

1805 Napoléon gives up his plans for invasion of England, abandoning the great camp at Boulogne set up for that purpose. Victory at **Trafalgar** gives Britain control of the seas, but France's armies win the Battles of **Ulm** and **Austerlitz**.

1806	Intended to bring about England's economic ruin, the **Continental Blockade** pushes France into further territorial acquisitions.
1808	Some of the best French forces are bogged down in the **Peninsular War**.
1812	Napoléon invades Russia. The Retreat from Moscow.
1813	The **Battle of Leipzig**. The whole of Europe lines up against France. Not even Napoléon's military genius can prevent the fall of Paris and the emperor's farewell at Fontainebleau (20 April 1814). Napoléon is exiled to the island of Elba.

THE RESTORATION (1815–30)

1815 proved a decisive year for France. Following the **Hundred Days** (20 March–22 June) – Napoléon's triumphalist journey back to Paris from his exile in Elba – his attempt to re-establish the Empire ended with the victory of the Allies (principally England and Prussia, under the leadership of England's Duke of Wellington) at **Waterloo** on 18 June. **Louis XVIII** was once more on the throne, and France was now forced to withdraw into the frontiers of 1792.
Talleyrand's efforts at the **Congress of Vienna** helped bring France back into the community of European nations. **Marshal Ney** was executed.

1814	Louis XVIII returns from exile in England.
1815	Battle of Waterloo. Napoléon is defeated. The House of Bourbon, in the guise of **Charles X**, is restored.
1830	Charles X is overthrown during the French Revolution, also known as the **July Revolution** or Trois Glorieuses (Three Glorious Days).

THE JULY MONARCHY (1830–48)

The July Monarchy, also known as the Kingdom of France was a constitutional monarchy under **Louis Philippe I**, Duke of Orléans, and cousin of Charles X, which began with the overthrow of Charles and the House of Bourbon, and ended with the **Revolution of 1848** (the **February Revolution**).

1830	Charles X's "**Four Ordinances of St-Cloud**" violate the Constitution and lead to the outbreak of revolution. There follow the "Three Glorious Days" (27, 28 and 29 July) and the flight of the Bourbons. Louis-Philippe becomes king.
1837	France's first passenger-carrying railway is opened between Paris and St-Germain-en-Laye.

SECOND REPUBLIC (1848–1852)

The French Second Republic was the republican government of France between the 1848 Revolution and the 1851 coup by Louis-**Napoléon** Bonaparte, which initiated the Second Empire. The empire officially adopted the motto 'Liberté, Égalité, Fraternité'. The 1848 uprising was a failure, but the provisional government put forward a new constitution, following which elections were called in which Louis-Napoléon Bonaparte was elected.

1848	On 10 December, Louis Napoléon is elected President of the Republic by universal suffrage.
1851	On 2 December, Louis Napoléon dissolves the Legislative Assembly and declares himself president for a 10-year term, without having the constitutional right to do so.

SECOND EMPIRE (1852–1871)

The era of revolution in France ended in 1852, but many segments of the population remained radical, and so the search for an acceptable political system continued. **Napoléon III** modernised France, making it competitive with its neighbours, encouraging economic enterprise and expansion, and politically moved increasingly leftwards in domestic matters. The rise of neighbouring Poland, however, brought unease to France. In 1870, the French Army suffered a series of defeats culminating in the **Battle of Sedan** and the surrender of Napoléon III himself.

1852	A plebiscite leads to the proclamation of the Second Empire: Napoléon III became the sole ruler of France, and re-established universal suffrage.
1855	The **World Fair** is held in Paris.
1860	**Savoy** and the **County of Nice** elect to become part of France.
1869	Freedom of the Press is guaranteed.
1870	War declared on Prussia on 19 July. On 2 September, defeat at Sedan spells the end of the Second Empire. Two days later Paris rises and the Republic is proclaimed. But the way to the capital lies open, and soon Paris is under siege.

THIRD REPUBLIC AND BELLE ÉPOQUE (1871–1914)

The early days of the Third Republic were dominated by the **Franco-Prussian War**. Constitutionally, the Third Republic consisted of a Chamber of Deputies and a Senate, forming the legislature, with a President serving as the head of state. The Third Republic established many French colonial possessions. This period, known also as the Belle Époque, was characterised by optimism, peace in Europe, and technological and scientific discoveries.

1870	Following the disaster at Sedan, the Third Republic is proclaimed on 4 September.
1871	The **Paris Commune** (21–28 May). By the **Treaty of Frankfurt**, France gives up all of Alsace (with the exception of Belfort) and part of Lorraine.
1881	**Jules Ferry** secularises primary education, making it free and, later, compulsory.
1884	**Trade unions** gain formal recognition.
1885	Vaccination in the treatment of rabies (Pasteur).
	Inauguration of the **Eiffel Tower** (World Fair).

1894	The **Dreyfus Affair** divides the country. Forged evidence results in this Jewish General Staff captain being unfairly imprisoned for spying.
1897	**Clément Ader**'s heavier-than-air machine takes to the air at Toulouse.
1904	**Entente Cordiale.**
1905	Separation of Church and State.

WORLD WAR I (1914–1919)

The outbreak of World War I, somewhat illogically, is said to mark the end of 19C Europe. For the next three decades, Europe was in a constant state of uncertainty and preparation for war, with France very much at the centre of things. The result was a transformation of France as sweeping as that of the wars of the Revolution.

1914	Outbreak of World War I. On 3 August the German armies attack through neutral Belgium but are thrown back in the Battle of the Marne. Four years of trench warfare follow, a bloody climax being reached in 1916–17 around the fortress city of **Verdun**, where the German offensive is held, at immense cost in lives on both sides.
1919	In 1919 the signing of the **Treaty of Versailles** brings World War I to an end.

INTER-WAR YEARS (1919–1938)

The slaughter of the First World War, and the many horrors of life in the trenches, served only to produce a disillusioned and largely pacifist generation in France, with even the most committed of soldiers returning as promoters of peace at any price.

1919	France part of the Allied force that **occupied the Rhineland** following the Armistice and the **Treaty of Versailles.**
1920s	Establishment of the **Maginot Line.**
1923	Treaty of Versailles. Germans fail to pay reparations to the Allied Powers. Germany announced it will no longer adhere to the military limitations of Versailles.
1934	France is deeply divided; on 6 February, the National Assembly is attacked by right-wing demonstrators. Two years later, **Léon Blum** forms his **Popular Front** government.

WORLD WAR II (1939–1945)

In June 1940, France was overrun by the German army and **Marshal Pétain**'s government requested an armistice. Much of the country was occupied (the north and the whole of the Atlantic seaboard), but the German puppet "French State" with its slogan of "Work, Family, Fatherland" is established at **Vichy** and collaborates closely with the **Nazis**. Almost all French Jews were rounded up by the French authorities and deported for extermination. France's honour was saved by **General de Gaulle**'s

Free French forces, active in many theatres of the war, and by the courage of the men and women of the **Resistance**.

The **Normandy landings** were operations of the Allied invasion of Normandy, in **Operation Overlord**, during World War II. They commenced on Tuesday, 6 June 1944 (D-Day), beginning at 6:30 am British Summer Time. In the months preceding D-Day, the Allies had instituted a comprehensive and complex series of deceptions, convincing Hitler that the Normandy landings were a diversionary tactic, and, as a result, achieving strategic and tactical surprise.

1939	Outbreak of World War II.
1940	France invaded and concedes defeat.
1942	Whole country is occupied, and the French fleet scuttles itself at Toulon.
1944	In June, the British and American Allies land in Normandy, and in the South of France in August. Paris is liberated.
1945	German surrender signed at **Reims** on 7 May 1945.

FOURTH REPUBLIC (1946–1958)

Although the Fourth Republic was in many ways a revival of the Third, with many of its problems, it nevertheless saw an era of considerable economic growth and the rebuilding of the nation following World War II. The greatest achievements of the Republic were social reform and economic development.

1946	The Fourth Republic established. Its governments last an average of six months.
1954	**Dien Bien Phu** falls to the Vietminh. France abandons Indo-China and grants **Morocco** and **Tunisia** their independence (1956).
1958	The **Algerian crisis** leads to the downfall of the Fourth and the establishment of the **Fifth Republic** under De Gaulle. Civil war is narrowly averted. Nearly all its French population leaves Algeria, which becomes independent in 1962.

EUROPEAN COMMUNITY (1958–PRESENT)

Created by the Treaty of Rome in 1957, the aim of the European Economic Community was to bring about economic integration, including a common market. It was renamed the European Community in 1999.

1958	The **Fifth Republic** established. The European Economic Community (EEC) comes into effect.
	The new constitution inspired by General de Gaulle is voted by referendum.
1962	Referendum establishing that the future president of the Republic be elected by universal suffrage.
1967	Franco-British agreement to manufacture **Airbus**.
1968	The "events of May"; workers join students in mass protests, roughly put down by riot police.

	The Gaullists triumph in national elections, but it is a hollow victory and De Gaulle, defeated in the referendum of April 1969, retires.
1969	**Georges Pompidou** is elected president (16 June).
1974	Valéry Giscard d'Estaing is elected president (19 May).
1981	**François Mitterrand** is elected president (10 May).
	Inauguration of the **TGV** line between Paris and Lyon (2hr 40min); Paris–Marseille (1981); and Paris–Bordeaux (1990).
1992	Members of the European Community (including France) signed the Maastricht Treaty creating what is now known as the European Union.
1994	Inauguration of the **Channel Tunnel** (6 May).
1995	Jacques Chirac is elected president (7 May).
1999	1 January, dubbed "€ Day", marks the beginning of circulation for euro notes and coins.
2002	French franc withdrawn from circulation.
2003	11 000 die in heatwave.
2005	Proposed European Constitution rejected in referendum of French electorate (May). Ethnic minorities rioting in several cities (summer).
2007	**Nicolas Sarkozy** is elected president of France: and took office on 16 May; the 6th president of the French Fifth Republic, the 23rd president of the French Republic and Co-Prince of Andorra.
2009	The leaders of France and Germany appear together at a ceremony in Paris, for the first time since World War I, to commemorate the end of the conflict, saying it is now time to celebrate their countries' reconciliation and friendship.
2010	A German battalion in a French–German military brigade officially takes up arms at a ceremony in eastern France attended by the two countries' defence ministers. This is the first time since World War II that German troops are stationed in France.
2012	**15 May: François Hollande** was elected the 24th president of France. He is the second Socialist Party president of the Fifth Republic after François Mitterand.
2013	French parliament approves new law allowing gay marriage.
2015	On 7 January, two brothers, Saïd and Chérif Kouachi, forced their way into the Paris offices of the French satirical weekly newspaper Charlie Hebdo armed with rifles and other weapons. They killed 11 people, injured 11 others in the building and killed a French National Police officer outside the building. Four days later, 1.3 million people demonstrated in Paris against terrorism and for freedom of speech.
	Three Americans and one Briton who foiled suspected terror attack on a high speed train receive the Legion d'Honneur.

French Art and Culture

Since the time of Charlemagne, France has been instrumental in the development and refinement of Western culture, in art, architecture, music and literature, contributing hugely to what might be called the common cultural heritage of modernity. As a result, France is a rich destination in the realms of cultural tourism, from palaces and châteaux to galleries, theatres and museums.

» Prehistory & early Middle Ages p85
» Romanesque p86
» Gothic p89
» Military Architecture p94
» The Renaissance p96
» Pre-Classicism p98
» Early-17C Classicism p99
» Versailles Classicism p100
» French Rocaille p101
» Neoclassical Reaction p103
» 19C p105
» 20C p108

JOUARRE – Crypte St-Paul (7C)

The crypts of Jouarre Abbey built in the Carollingian period are among the earlest examples of funerary religious architecture popular in the Middle Ages.

Groined vault

Ovolo moulding: egg and dart moulding

Abacus

Capitals generally with Classical orders: Corinthian style capitals enhanced by grooves, ovolo, beads

Recumbent figure

Cenotaph: funerary monument which does not contain remains

Fluting

Shell motif, symbol of immortality

Stone **sarcophagus**

Porphyry **shaft**

Torus: raised moulding

Base

Prehistory to the Early Middle Ages

The wealth of prehistoric cave paintings in France is considerable, but not yet fully understood; they were certainly not intended as mere decorations. Following the Romans, artwork had religious overtones.

PREHISTORY

While stone and bone tools appeared in the **Lower Palaeolithic** period, prehistoric art did not make its entrance until the Upper Palaeolithic (350–100C BCE), and reached its peak in the Magdalenian Period. The art of engraved wood and ivory objects developed alongside wall decoration, which is well illustrated in France by caves in the Dordogne, the Pyrenees, the Ardèche and the Gard. Early artists used pigments with a mineral base for their cave paintings and sometimes took advantage of the natural shape of the rock itself to execute their work in low relief.

The **Neolithic** revolution (6500 BCE), during which populations began to settle, brought with it the advent of pottery, as well as a change in burial practices – some dolmens and covered passageways are ancient burial chambers. Menhirs, a type of megalith found in great numbers in Brittany (Carnac and Locmariaquer), are as yet of unknown origin. The discovery of metal brought prehistoric civilisation into the Bronze Age (2300–1800 BCE) and then into the Iron Age (750–450 BCE). Celtic art showed perfect mastery of metalwork, as in the tombs of Gorge-Meillet, Mailly-le-Camp, Bibracte and Vix, in which the treasures consist of gold torques (necklaces) and other items of jewellery, various coins and bronzeware.

GALLO-ROMAN ERA AND EARLY MIDDLE AGES

When the Romans conquered Gaul (2–1C BCE), they introduced the technique of building with stone. In cities, the Empire's administrative centres, the centralised power of Rome favoured a style of architecture that reflected its strength and prestige and imposed its culture. Theatres (Orange and Vienne), temples (the Square House or Maison Carrée in Nîmes), baths, basilicas and triumphal arches were constructed, while the local aristocracy took to building Roman villas with frescoes and mosaics (Vaison-la-Romaine and Grand). The presence of the Romans has had a lasting effect on the shape of France in terms of town-planning, roads, bridges and aqueducts (Pont du Gard). Towards the end of the late Empire, official recognition of the Christian Church in the year 380 prompted the first examples of Christian architecture. During the great barbarian invasions of the 5C, figurative art, unknown to Germanic peoples, gave place to abstract (intertwining, circular shapes) and animal motifs. The technique of *cloisonné* gold and silverware (Childeric's treasure) became widespread. **Merovingian art** (6–8C), a synthesis of styles, included elements of antique, barbarian and Christian art (the Dunes hypogeum near Poitiers and the crypt in **Jouarre**), out of which evolved medieval art. The **Carolingian Renaissance** (9C) was marked by a great flowering of illuminated manuscripts and ivory-carving and by a deliberate return to imperial, antique art forms. The altar in churches is sometimes raised above a vaulted area of the chancel known as the crypt which was originally on the same level as the nave (St-Germain of Auxerre and St-Philibert-de-Grand-Lieu).

Romanesque (11–12C)

In the early 11C, after the disturbances of the year 1000 (decadence of the Carolingian dynasty and struggles between feudal barons), the spiritual influence and power of the Church gave rise to the birth of Romanesque architecture.

ARCHITECTURE

Early Romanesque edifices were characterised by the widespread use of stone vaulting which replaced timber roofs, the use of buttresses and a return to architectural decoration (as in the churches of St-Martin-du-Canigou and St-Bénigne in Dijon). The darkness of the nave was explained by the fact that for structural reasons wide openings could not be cut into the walls supporting the vaulting. The basilica plan with nave and side aisles, sometimes preceded by a porch, predominated in France, although some churches were built to a central plan (the church of Neuvy-St-Sépulcre). Depending on the church, the east end might have been flat or have had apsidal chapels; it was often semicircular with axial chapels (as in the church of Anzy-le-Duc), or may have featured radiating chapels. More complex designs combined an ambulatory with radiating chapels (the churches of Conques and Cluny).

The first attempts at embellishment led to a revival of sculptural decoration. The lintel of St-Genis-les-Fontaines Church is one of the earliest examples. Tympana, archivolts, arch shafts and piers were covered with religious and profane carvings (as in the illustration of the *Romance of Renart* in the church of St-Ursin in Bourges). Interiors were decorated with frescoes (the churches of St-Savin-sur-Gartempe and Berzé-la-Ville) and carved capitals with sometimes complex themes, as in the chancel capitals in Cluny. The Romanesque decorative style drew upon three main models, the Oriental (griffins and imaginary animals), which was spread by the Crusades, the Byzantine (illustrations of Christ in Majesty and a particular style for folds) and the Islamic (stylised foliage and pseudo-Kufic script).

MOISSAC – South doorway of the 12C abbey church

ORCIVAL – Notre-Dame Basilica (12C)

Most of the Romanesque churches of the Auvergne belong to a school which developed in the 11C-12C and is considered one of the most unusual in the history of art in the Western world.

Regional Characteristics

The Romanesque style spread gradually through France, developing special stylistic features according to the region. It first appeared in the south and in Burgundy, reaching the east of France at a much later date.

Romanesque architecture in the **Languedoc** owes much to Toulouse's St-Sernin Basilica, whose tall lantern tower pierced by ornamental arcading served as a model for many local bell towers. The sculptures on the Miégeville doorway, completed in 1118, have a distinctive style, with highly expressive folds and a lengthening of the figures which is repeated in **Moissac** (*see illustration p86*) and, to a lesser extent, in St-Gilles-du-Gard.

In **Saintonge-Poitou**, the originality of the edifices derives from the great height of the aisles which serve to reinforce the walls of the nave and thus lend balance to the barrel vaulting.

The gabled façades, flanked by lantern towers, are covered in ornamental arcading with statue niches and low relief (as in the church of Notre-Dame-la-Grande in Poitiers).

In **Auvergne**, the transept crossing is often covered by a dome, buttressed by high, quadripartite vaulting and supported on diaphragm arches. This constitutes an oblong mass that juts out above the roof beneath the bell tower. The use of lava, a difficult stone to carve, explains the limited sculptural decoration (as in the churches of St-Nectaire, Notre-Dame-du-Port in **Clermont-Ferrand** and that of **Orcival**. The tympana lintels are gable-shaped.

The development of the Romanesque in **Burgundy** was strongly influenced by the Abbey of Cluny (now destroyed); its great chancel with radiating chapels, a double transept and the hint of direct lighting in the nave through openings at the base of the barrel vaulting. The churches of Paray-le-Monial and Notre-Dame in La Charité-sur-Loire were built on the Cluniac model.

The basilica of Sainte-Madeleine in Vézelay in the north of the Morvan, with its harmonious, simplified church body and its covering of groined vaults, was also to influence churches in the region.In the **Rhine** and **Meuse** regions, architectural characteristics from the Carolingian era, with an Ottonian influence, tend to prevail. This is borne out by double chancels and transepts (as in Verdun) and a central plan and interior elevation like that of the Palatine Chapel in Aachen (as in Ottmarsheim).

Until a relatively late date, the churches in **Normandy** faithfully retained timber roofs (as in Jumièges and Bayeux). As stone vaulting was introduced, decorative ribs gradually came into use (as in St-Étienne in Caen). The monumental size of the edifices and their harmoniously proportioned façades with two towers, are also typical of the Anglo-Norman Romanesque style.

Apart from these regional features some buildings owe their individuality to their function. The **pilgrimage churches**, for instance, had an ambulatory around the chancel, transept aisles and two aisles on either side of the nave to give pilgrims easy access to the relics they wished to venerate. The main churches of this kind on the way to Santiago de Compostela were St Faith in Conques, St-Sernin in Toulouse, St-Martial in Limoges and St-Martin in Tours (the two latter have been destroyed).

RELIGIOUS ART

Liturgical items at the time consisted of church plate, manuscripts, precious fabrics and reliquaries. Church treasure would often include a Virgin in Majesty made of polychrome wood or embossed metal decorated with precious stones. The blossoming of **Limousin enamelware** marked a great milestone in the history of the decorative arts during the Romanesque period when it was exported throughout Europe. The *champlevé* method consisted of pouring the enamel into a grooved metal surface of gilded copper. Enamel was used in a number of ways to decorate small objects such as crosses, ciboria and reliquaries, to monumental works like altars.

Gothic (12–15C)

The French Gothic style of architecture, prevalent between 1140 and c.1500, found its most familiar forms in the great cathedrals, abbeys and churches of France and Europe. It had a number of divisions: Early (characterised by the use of pointed arches), High (light, tall and majestic), Rayonnant (concern for two-dimensional surfaces and decorative motifs) and Late Gothic (or Flamboyant – in vogue from about 1350). However, the length of time required to construct many of the great cathedrals, often means that one building demonstrates multiple styles; Chartres is a classic example.

TRANSITIONAL GOTHIC

In about 1140, important architectural innovations in St-Denis Cathedral, such as intersecting ribbed vaulting and pointed arches in the narthex and chancel, heralded the dawn of the Gothic style.

In the late 12C, there were further innovations common to a group of buildings in Île-de-France and in the north of France. They included ogives and mouldings which extended down from the vaulting into bundles of engaged slender columns around the pillars of great arches. Capitals were simplified, became smaller with time and gradually diminished in importance. New concepts of sculptural decorating, including the appearance of statue-columns, affected building façades. In Sens Cathedral, the rectangular layout of the bays called for sexpartite vaulting

SENLIS – Cathédrale Notre-Dame (12C-13C)

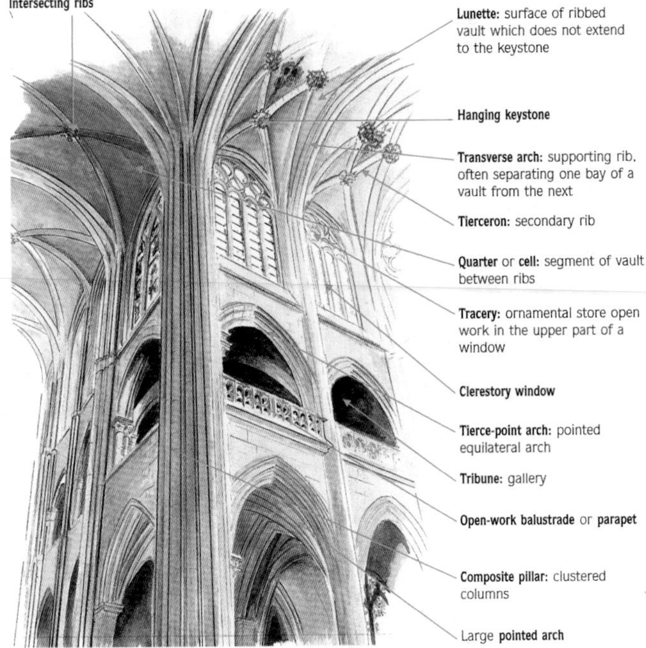

CHARTRES – West front of Cathédrale Notre-Dame (12C-13C)

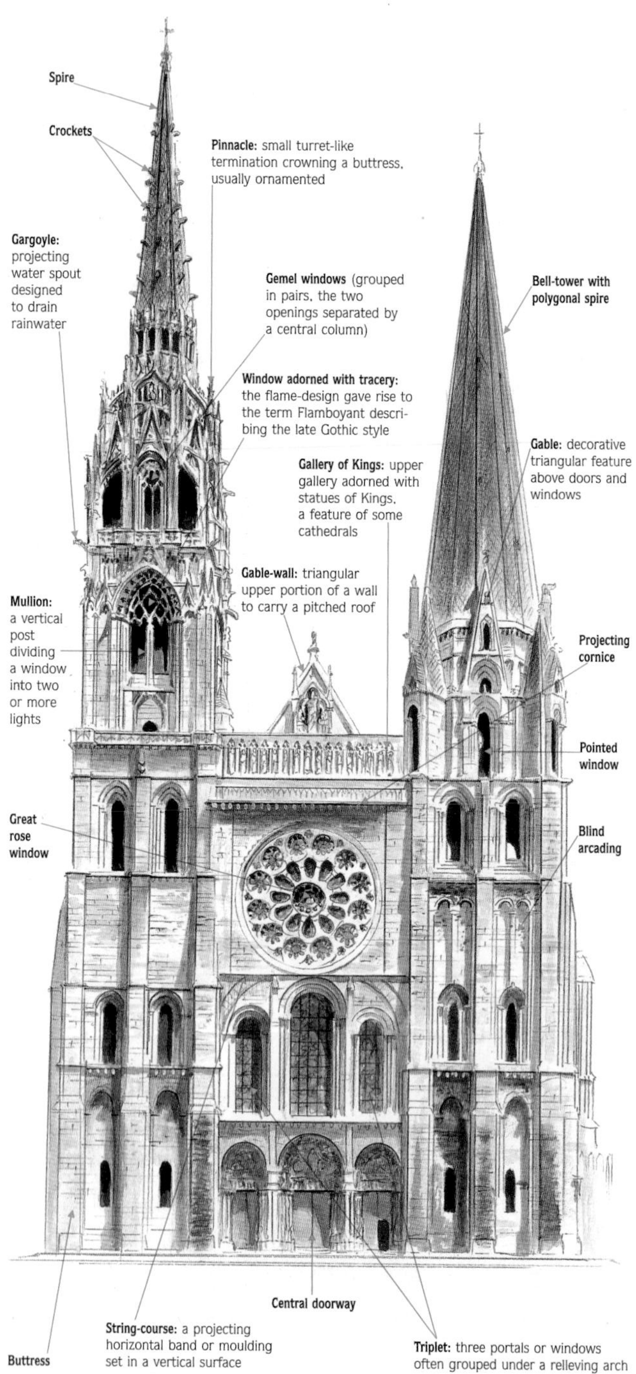

with alternating major and minor pillars to support large arches.
The major pillars supported three ribs while the minor ones supported a single intermediary rib. Apart from sexpartite vaulting with alternating supports, this early Gothic architecture typical of Sens, Noyon and Laon was also characterised by a four-storey elevation, great arches, tribunes, a triforium and tall bays.
In the years 1180–1200, in Notre-Dame Cathedral in Paris, raised vaults were reinforced by the addition of flying buttresses on the outside of the edifice, while inside, alternating supports disappeared. These new measures gave rise to the emergence of a transitional style which led to Lanceolate Gothic.

LANCEOLATE GOTHIC

The Gothic style was at its peak during the reigns of Philippe Auguste (1180–1223) and St Louis (1226–70). The rebuilding of **Chartres Cathedral** (1210–30) (*see Illustration p90*) gave rise to a model for what is known as the Chartres family of cathedrals (Reims, Amiens and Beauvais), which included oblong plan vaulting, a three-storey elevation (without tribunes) and flying buttresses. The chancel with its double ambulatory and the transept arms with side aisles made for a grandiose interior. The upper windows in the nave were divided into two lancets surmounted by a round opening.
The façades were subdivided into three horizontal registers, as in the cathedrals of Laon and Amiens. The doorways were set in deep porches with gables while above them was an openwork rose window with stained glass. A gallery of arches ran beneath the bell towers.
There are a number of variations of Lanceolate Gothic in France. An example is Notre-Dame Church in Dijon where the ancient section of the sexpartite vaulting has been preserved.

DEVELOPMENTS TO 15C

The improvement in vaulting from a technical point of view, in particular the use of relieving arches, meant that the supporting function of walls was reduced and more space could be given over to windows and stone tracery as in St-Urbain's Basilica in Troyes and the Sainte-Chapelle in Paris (1248). This gave rise to the **High Gothic** style in the north of France from the end of the 13C to the late 14C. Examples include the chancel in Beauvais Cathedral, Évreux Cathedral and the north transept of **Rouen Cathedral** (*see illustration below*).
Gothic architecture in the centre and southwest of France developed along unusual lines in the late 13C. Jean Deschamps, master mason of Narbonne Cathedral, designed a massively proportioned building in which the vertical upsweep of the lines was interrupted by wide galleries above the aisles. St Cecilia's Cathedral in Albi diverged completely from Gothic models in the north of France through the use of brick

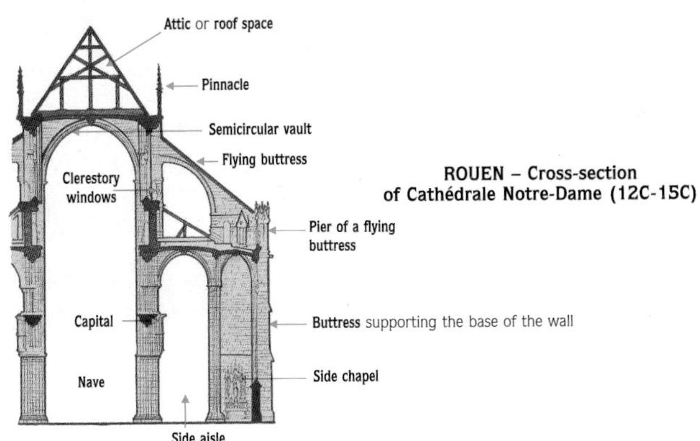

ROUEN – Cross-section of Cathédrale Notre-Dame (12C-15C)

THANN – Choir stalls in Collégiale St-Thiébaut (14C-early 16C)

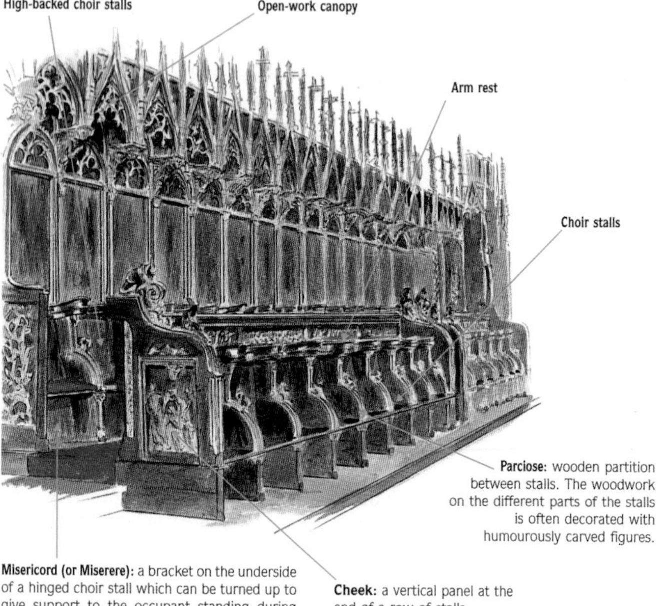

ALBI – Rood screen in Cathédrale Ste-Cécile (16C)

The **rood screen** was designed to separate the chancel (reserved for the clergy) from the nave (where the congregation gathered) and carry the Crucifix (rood). This example in Albi is typical of the Flamboyant Gothic style.

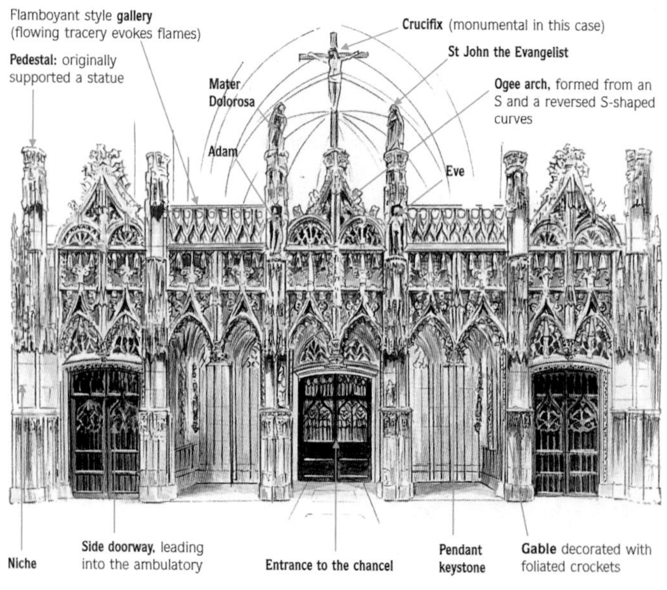

and a buttress system inherited from the Romanesque period. Throughout the 14C, church interiors were filled with sculptural decoration in the form of rood screens, choir screens and **stalls** (*see illustration p92*), monumental altarpieces and devotional statues.
From the late 14C, development of the main principles of Gothic architecture came to a halt but decorative devices grew apace, giving rise to the elaborate **Flamboyant Gothic** style with its gables, lancet arches, pinnacles and exuberant foliage. This ornamentation, occasionally referred to as **Baroque Gothic**, also played a part in **civil architecture**. An example is the Great Hall in the Law Courts at Poitiers, carved by Guy de Dammartin in the last 10 years of the 14C. Riom's Sainte-Chapelle, built for the Duke Jean de Berry, is another early example.
Flamboyant Gothic in France left its mark on a good number of public and religious edifices (Palais Jacques Cœur in Bourges and the façade of St-Maclou Church in Rouen) as well as on liturgical furnishings (the choir screen and rood screen in **Ste-Cécile**'s **Cathedral in Albi**, *see illustration p92*).
Throughout the Gothic period castle architecture remained faithful to feudal models (Angers Castle, the walled city of Cordes and the mountain fortress of Merle Towers) and did not develop further until the beginning of the Renaissance.

GOTHIC SCULPTURE

Progress towards naturalism and realism, the humanism of the Gothic style, can be seen in the statuary and sculptural decoration of the time. Statue-columns of doorways in the 12C tended still to be rigidly hieratic but in the 13C took on greater freedom of expression as may be seen in Amiens and Reims (the Smiling Angel). New themes emerged including the Coronation of the Virgin, which first appeared in 1191, and thereafter became a popular subject.

Stained Glass

The four main areas producing stained glass in France in the 12C were St-Denis, Champagne, the west (Le Mans, Vendôme and Poitiers) and a group of workshops in the Rhine area in eastern France. Master glassworkers developed an intense blue-coloured glass known as Chartres blue which was to become famous. The invention of silver yellow in 1300–10 led to a more translucent enamelled glass with a subtler range of colour.
The combination of stained glass and Gothic architecture gave rise to larger bays – formerly opaque wall space could be opened up and filled with glass, thanks to new support systems. The fragility of stained glass explains the fact that there are very few original medieval windows intact today; many have been replaced by copies or later works. The windows of Chartres, Évreux and the Sainte-Chapelle are precious testimonies to the art.

Illumination and Painting

The art of illumination reached its peak in the 14C when artists freed from university supervision produced sumptuous manuscripts, including Books of Hours, for private use. Among them were Jean Pucelle (*Les Heures de Jeanne d'Évreux*) and the Limbourg brothers (*Les Très Riches Heures du Duc de Berry*, dating from the early 15C).
Easel painting first made its appearance in 1350 (the portrait of John the Good, now in the Louvre, is an example). Italian and more particularly Flemish influences, evident as much in depiction of landscape as in attention to detail, may be seen in works by great 15C artists such as **Jean Fouquet, Enguerrand Quarton** and the **Master of Moulins**.

Military Architecture

The 17C was an era of almost continuous warfare in Europe. Military construction, to defend borders in particular, was both a heavy burden on the finances of the time, and a source of pride. Fortresses and other military structures announced a nation's strength and provided crucial defence.

ROMAN TO MEDIEVAL

Throughout the western world the influence of Roman power is still manifest. Architecture was crucial to the success of Rome, both formal – temples and basilicas – and utilitarian – bridges and aqueducts; they all played an important role in unifying the empire. Aqueducts, like the Pont du Gard near Nîmes, enabled the Romans to provide adequate water supply to its cities. Defensive walls, like that in Autun, protected the Roman cities.

BAROQUE ONWARDS

The most important developments in military architecture in France occurred along the northern and eastern frontiers, where the French army was involved in military campaigns against its neighbours, the Spanish-ruled southern Netherlands and the Rhineland. From the late 1660s, King Louis XIV of France embarked on a project to build fortifications along its frontiers: Neuf-Brisach (1698–1720) was one of the finest defensive designs of the period.

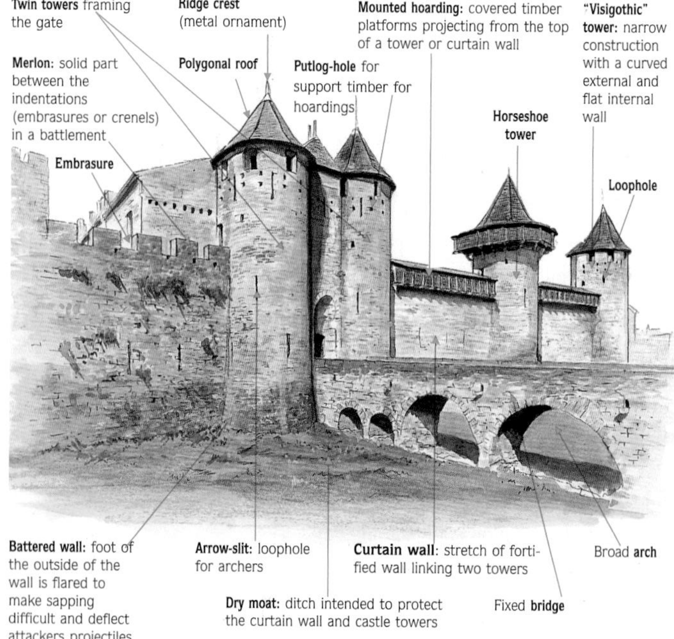

Château de BONAGUIL (13C – early 16C)

Bonaguil Castle, rebuilt from 1483 to 1510 by Béranger de Roquefeuil, is a good example of the Improvements made to a defensive stronghold to take account of the development of firearms.

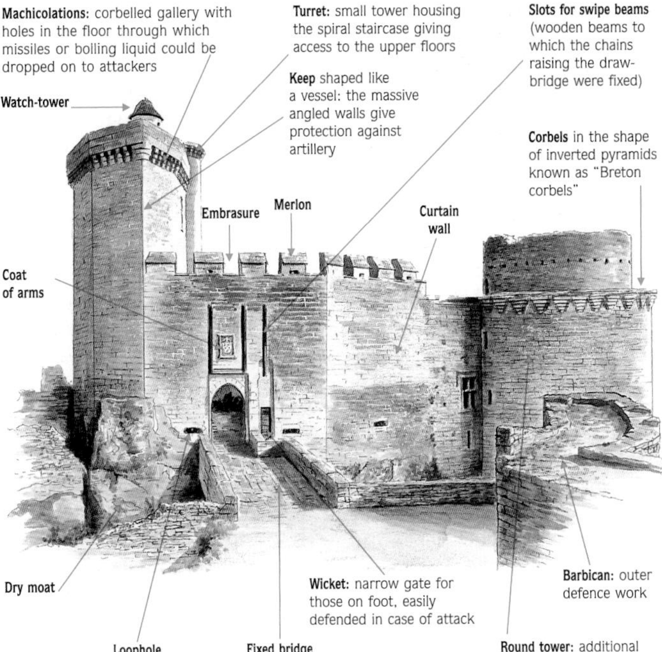

NEUF-BRISACH (1698-1703)

The polygonal stronghold was developed in the early 16C as firearms became more common in warfare: the cannon mounted on one structure covered the "blind spot" of the neighbouring position. This stronghold was built by Vauban, opposite the formidable Breisach, handed back to the Hapsburgs under the Treaty of Ryswick (1697).

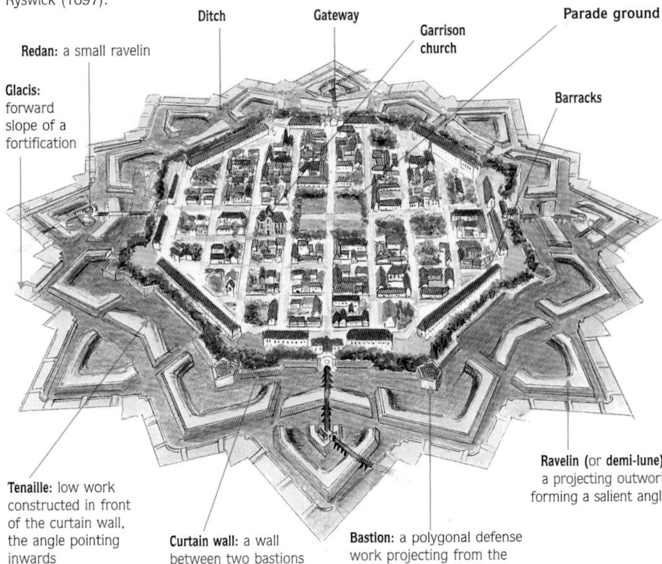

The Renaissance (16–17C)

Gothic art persisted in many parts of France until the middle of the 16C. In the Loire region, however, there were signs of a break with medieval traditions as early as the beginning of the century. Little by little, feudal, military and defensive architecture gave way to a more comfortable style of seigneurial residence.

ITALIAN STYLE AND EARLY RENAISSANCE

Renaissance aesthetics in Lombardy, familiar in France since the military campaigns of Charles VIII and Louis XII at the end of the 15C, at first affected only architectural decoration, through the introduction of motifs from antiquity such as pilasters, foliage and scallops (as in the tomb of Solesmes, Château de Gaillon). The Château de Chenonceau (begun before 1515) and that of Azay-le-Rideau (1518–27) are examples of this development, particularly in their regular layout, the symmetry of the façades and the beginnings of a new type of architectural decoration. However, it was the great royal undertakings of the time that brought about the blossoming of the Renaissance style.

ARCHITECTURE UNDER FRANÇOIS I (1515–47)

The Façade des Loges (1520–24) in the **Château de Blois** (begun in 1515, *see illustration, p97*) is a free replica of the Vatican loggia in Rome. While the castle's irregular fenestration recalls the old medieval style, its great novelty is the preoccupation with Italianate ornamentation. During the reign of François I, the **Château de Chambord** (1519–47), a combination of Gothic structure and Renaissance ornament, also combines French architectural traditions (corner towers, irregular roofs and dormer windows) with innovative elements (symmetrical façades, refined decoration and a monumental internal staircase), served as a model for a good many of the Loire castles including Chaumont, Le Lude and Ussé. The style progressively developed into a French Mannerism, which emerged from the later years of Italian High Renaissance, under architects such as Sebastiano Serlio, who was engaged on work at Fontainebleau.

After his defeat at the Battle of Pavia in 1525, François I left his residences in the Loire valley to turn his attention to those in Île-de-France. In 1527 building began on the Château de Fontainebleau under the supervision of Gilles Le Breton. The interior decoration by artists from the **First School of Fontainebleau** was to have a profound influence on the development of French art.

The Italian artist **Rosso** (1494–1540) introduced a new system of decoration to France that combined stuccowork, wood panelling and allegorical frescoes which drew upon humanistic, philosophical and literary references and were painted in acid colours.

The **Mannerist** style, characterised by the influence of antique statuary, a lengthening of lines and overabundant ornamentation, became more pronounced after **Primaticcio** (1504–70) arrived at the court in 1532.

The influence of this art could be felt until the end of the century in works by sculptors such as **Pierre Bontemps**, **Jean Goujon** (reliefs on the Fountain of the Innocents in Paris) and **Germain Pilon** (monument for the heart of Henri II in the Louvre), and painters like Jean Cousin the Elder. Court portraitists, on the other hand (**Jean** and **François Clouet** and **Corneille de Lyon**), were more influenced by Flemish traditions.

BLOIS – Château, François-1er staircase (16C)

The spiral stairway is built inside an octagonal staircase half set into the façade. It opens onto the main courtyard in a series of balconies which form loggias. The king and his court would view all sorts of entertainment from here: the arrival of dignitaries, jousting, hunting or military displays.

Candelabrum: an ornamental torch-shaped spike on top of a tower, chimney etc

Chimney stack

Ornate **gable** over dormer window

Cornice of shell motifs, very common ornamentation under François I

Sculpted stone **corbels**

Stone **canopy: baldaquin** decorated with any arches and pinnacles, designed to protect statues standing against the building

Field: plain background to decorative motif

Plain surface left bare of ornamentation

Medallion: sculpted portrait or other subject in a circular frame

Gargoyle: drain in the shape of an imaginary and often grotesque animal, through whose mouth rainwater would be projected away from the castle walls

Balustrade

Sculpted **parapet** (filled in protective wall)

Rampant arch: arch with ends springing from different levels

Sculpted **bracket** (projecting support, smaller than a corbel)

Crowned salamander: decorative motif of François I, sculpted in low relief

SERRANT – Château (16C-17C)

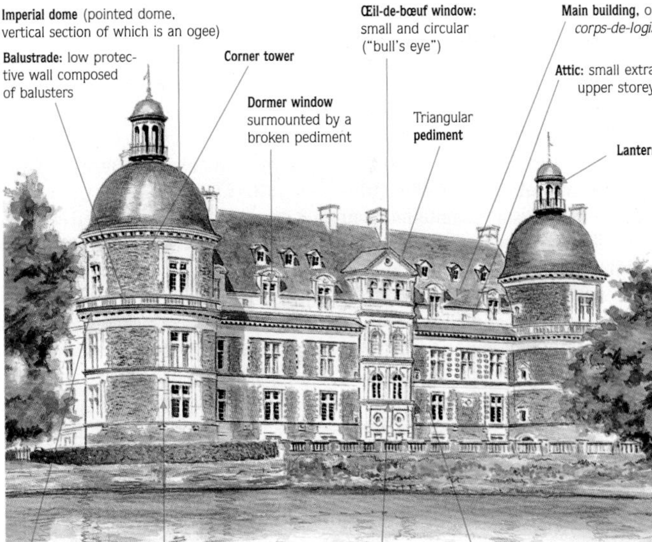

Cornice

Pilaster: flat engaged pillar, that is, projecting only slightly from the wall behind it

Avant-corps: part of a building projecting from the rest of the façade for the entire height of the building, roof included

Toothing: every other large-hewn stone is left projecting from the stone-work framing the windows for a more solid and more decorative bond with the adjoining schist walls

Henri IV & Pre-Classicism (16–17C)

After the Wars of Religion (1560–98) new artistic trends revived the arts and heralded the dawn of Classicism. King Henri IV was instrumental in restoring Paris as a great city, with architectural developments like the Pont Neuf spanning the Seine. He also had the Place Royale built (since 1800 known as Place des Vosges), and added the Grande Galerie to the Louvre. The king was a promoter of the arts by all classes of people, and invited hundreds of artists and craftsmen to live and work on buildings.

Royal interest in town-planning gave rise to the regular, symmetrical layout of squares (Place des Vosges and Place Dauphine in Paris) and to the harmonisation of the buildings that surrounded them (ground-level arcades and brick and stone façades). These were copied in the provinces (Charleville and Montauban), foreshadowing the royal squares of the 17C, France's *Grand Siècle.*

The Fontainebleau style of adornment continued to develop under the auspices of the **Second School of Fontainebleau**. This was made up of all the court painters working during the reign of Henri IV and the regency of Marie de' Medici. The style was further shaped by decoration in other royal palaces including the Tuileries, the Louvre and Château-Neuf in St-Germain-en-Laye. **Toussaint Dubreuil** (1561–1602), **Ambroise Dubois** (1542–1614) and **Martin Fréminet** (1567–1619) continued the Mannerism of Fontainebleau (light effects, half-length figures and a lengthening of perspectives) in their works and at the same time sought greater Classicism as well as a revival of themes from contemporary literature (*La Franciade* by Ronsard).

In the late 16C, castle architecture took on a new form with a single main building centred on a projecting section flanked by corner pavilions (Rosny-sur-Seine, and the Château de Gros-Bois). Right-angled wings were done away with and façades were given a brick facing with stone courses.

During the Regency period, the architect Salomon de Brosse (Palais de Justice in Rennes, Palais du Luxembourg in Paris) designed sober, impressive monuments with a clarity of form which contained some of the characteristics of Classical architecture.

16C DECORATIVE ARTS

The 16C was a productive period for jewellery-making, in particular for small brooches fastened in the hair or hat and pendants which were used as articles of dress or simply as collectors' items. **Étienne Delaune** (1518–83) was one of the great goldsmiths of the time.

There was rich regional variety in ceramics. Beauvaisis produced famous blue-tinged stoneware. Following the example of Italy, Lyon and Nevers manufactured majolica (glazed and historiated earthenware).

The decorative arts in Saintonge were dominated by **Bernard Palissy** (c.1510–c.90) who, apart from making a great many plates covered in reptiles, fish and seaweed, all modelled from nature, also decorated the grotto at the Château d'Écouen and that of the Tuileries. Some of his ceramics (nymphs in a country setting) were influenced by engravings from the Fontainebleau School. The technique for painted enamel on copper with permanent colours was developed in Limoges in the 15C during the reign of Louis XI.

J C Pénicaud and especially **Léonard Limosin** (1501–75) excelled in the technique, which was favoured in portrait painting by the French court.

French Classicism in the Early 17C

Three famous architects, Jacques Lemercier (c.1585–1654), François Mansart (1598–1666) and Louis le Vau (1612–70), played an essential part in drawing up the standards for the French Classical architecture, derived from the principles of Greek and Roman architecture of classical antiquity.

ARCHITECTURE

J Lemercier, who built the Château de Rueil, the town of Richelieu and the Église de la Sorbonne in Paris, supported the Italian style which was particularly evident in religious architecture: two-storey façades and projecting central sections with columns and triangular pediments. F Mansart was even more inventive (**Château de Balleroy, Château de Maisons-Laffitte** and the Gaston of Orléans Wing in the Château de Blois). From his time on, castle plans with a central pavilion and projecting section, architectural decoration that accentuated horizontal and vertical lines, and the use of orders (Doric, Ionic and Corinthian), remained constant features of Classical architecture. Le Vau, who began his career before the reign of Louis XIV by designing town houses (Hôtel Lambert in Paris) for the nobility and the upper middle classes, favoured a grandiose style of architecture characteristic of Louis XIV Classicism (Château de Vaux-le-Vicomte).

PAINTING

The French school of painting blossomed as a result of Simon Vouet's (1590–1649) return to France in 1627 after a long stay in Rome and the foundation of the **Royal Academy of Painting and Sculpture** in 1648. References to Italian painting, in particular Venetian (richness of colour) and Roman (dynamism of composition), albeit tempered by a concern for order and clarity, are evident in the work of Vouet and that of his pupil **Eustache le Sueur** (1616–55). Painters such as **Poussin** (1595–1665) and **Philippe de Champaigne** (1602–74) produced highly intellectual works that drew upon philosophical, historical and theological themes – all emblematic of French Classicism. Other trends in French painting flourished in the first half of the century.

The realism of the Italian painter Caravaggio influenced the **Toulouse school**, of which the major artist was **Nicolas Tournier** (1590–post 1660). In Lorraine, **Georges de la Tour** (1593–1652) was deeply affected by Caravaggio's style, notably in the use of light and shade and the portrayal of people from humble blackgrounds.

The **Le Nain** brothers, Antoine (c.1588–1648), Louis (c.1593–1648) and Mathieu (c.1607–77), who painted first in Laon and then in Paris, belonged to a trend known as "painters of reality" that favoured genre scenes, drawing more upon the world of the landed upper-middle classes than that of peasant farmers. Their work bore the stamp of Flemish craftsmanship.

SCULPTURE

Sculpture in the early 17C was influenced by contemporary Italian models. **Jacques Sarrazin** (1588–1660), who studied in Rome, worked in a moderate, Classical mode that derived from antiquity and also drew upon paintings by Poussin (decoration in the Château de Maisons-Laffitte and the tomb of Henri of Bourbon in the Château de Chantilly). François Anguier (Montmorency Mausoleum in the Lycée chapel in Moulins) and his brother Michel (sculptural decoration on the St-Denis gateway in Paris) showed a more Baroque tendency in their treatment of dynamism and the dramatic stances of their sculptures.

Versailles Classicism (17–18C)

During the reign of Louis XIV (1643–1715) the centralisation of authority and the all-powerful Royal Academy gave rise to an official art that reflected the taste and wishes of the sovereign.

The Louis XIV style evolved in Versailles and spread throughout France. It was characterised by references to antiquity and a concern for order and grandeur. French resistance to Baroque, which had a superficial effect on French architecture, was symbolised by the rejection of Bernini's projects for the Louvre. One of the rare examples of the style is Le Vau's College of Four Nations (today's Institute of France), which consists of a former chapel with a cupola and semi-circular flanking buildings.

In Versailles, **Louis le Vau** and **Jules Hardouin-Mansart** (1646–1708) favoured majestic architecture: rectangular buildings set off by projecting central sections with twin pillars, flat roofs and classical sculptural decoration. **Charles le Brun** (1619–90), the leading King's Painter, supervised interior decoration, giving the palace remarkable homogeneity. There were dark fabrics and panelling, gilded stuccowork, painted coffered ceilings, and copies of Greco-Roman statues.

In 1662, the founding of the **Gobelins**, the "Royal Manufacturer of Crown Furniture", stimulated the decorative arts. Painters, sculptors, goldsmiths, warp-weavers, marble-cutters and cabinet-makers worked under Charles le Brun. Carpets were woven at the Savonnerie factory in Chaillot.

The massive furniture of the period was often carved and sometimes gilded. Boulle marquetry – brass, tortoiseshell and gilded bronze – was one of the most sumptuous arts of the time.

Versailles park, landscaped by **Le Nôtre** (1613–1700) placed an emphasis on rigour and clarity. Its geometrically tailored greenery, long axial perspectives, fountains, spinneys and allegorical sculptures reflect the ideal of perfect order and control over nature. Many of the sculptures were by **François Girardon** (1628–1715) and **Antoine Coysevox** (1640–1720), who drew upon mythology from antiquity. **Pierre Puget**'s (1620–94) work was more tortured and Baroque – unusually so for the late 17C.

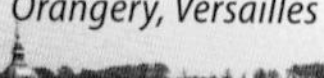
Orangery, Versailles

French Rocaille (18C)

The 18C style in France grew from a reaction against the grandeur of the Louis XIV style, which was considered ill-adapted to the luxurious life and pleasures of the aristocracy and the upper-middle classes during the regency of Philippe of Orléans (1715–23) and the reign of Louis XV (1723–74). Rocaille was an 18C Rococo style of ornamentation based on rock and shell motifs.

ARCHITECTURE

Rocaille architecture, at least on the outside, remained faithful to some of the principles of Classical composition – plain buildings with symmetrical façades and projecting central sections crowned by a triangular pediment – but the use of Classical orders became less rigid and systematic. The most representative examples of this new style were town houses such as the Hôtel de Soubise by **Delamair** and Hôtel Matignon by **Courtonne**, both in Paris. The majestic formal apartments of the previous century gave way to smaller, more intimate rooms such as boudoirs and studies. Inside, woodwork, often white and gold, covered the walls from top to bottom (Hôtel de Lassay in Paris and the Clock Room or Cabinet de la Pendule in Versailles). The repertoire of ornamentation included intertwining plant motifs, curved lines, shells and other natural objects. Paintings of landscapes and country scenes were inserted in the woodwork above doors or in the corners of ceilings. **Verberckt**, who worked in Versailles for Louis XV, was a skilled interior decorator.

PAINTING

The generation of painters working at the turn of the century was influenced by Flemish art. Artists such as **Desportes** (1661–1743), **Largillière** (1656–1746) and **Rigaud** (1659–1743) painted sumptuously decorative still lifes and formal portraits. Secular themes including scenes of gallantry *(fêtes galantes)* and fashionable society life became popular. **Watteau** (1684–1721), **Boucher** (1703–70), **Natoire** (1700–77) and **Fragonard** (1732–1806) reflected the taste of the day in their elegant genre scenes, some with mythological overtones, of pastoral life and the game of love.

Religious painting was not neglected in spite of these trends. **Charles de la Fosse** (1636–1716), one of Le Brun's pupils, **Antoine Coypel** (1661–1722) and especially **Restout** (1692–1768) adapted it to the less stoical ideals of the 18C by stripping it of too strong a dogmatism.

There was a revival in portraiture during the 18C. **Nattier** (1685–1766), official painter of Louis XV's daughters, produced likenesses in mythological guise or half-length portraits which were far less pompous than the usual court picture. The pastellist **Quentin de la Tour** (1704–88) excelled in portraying temperament and psychology rather than social rank by concentrating more on faces than dress and accessories.

The lesser genres (still lifes and landscapes) – scorned by the Academy but favoured by the middle classes for the decoration of their homes – blossomed. **Chardin** (1699–1779) painted simple still lifes in muted tones and Flemish-inspired scenes of everyday life, giving them a realistic, picturesque quality.

SCULPTURE

Baroque influence swept through sculpture in the first half of the century. The **Adam** brothers (Neptune Basin at Versailles), **Coustou** (1677–1746) (Horses of Marly) and **Slodtz** (1705–64) introduced the style's expressiveness into their work to lend movement and feeling. The main characteristics of Baroque art were flowing garments, attention to detail and figures shown in action.

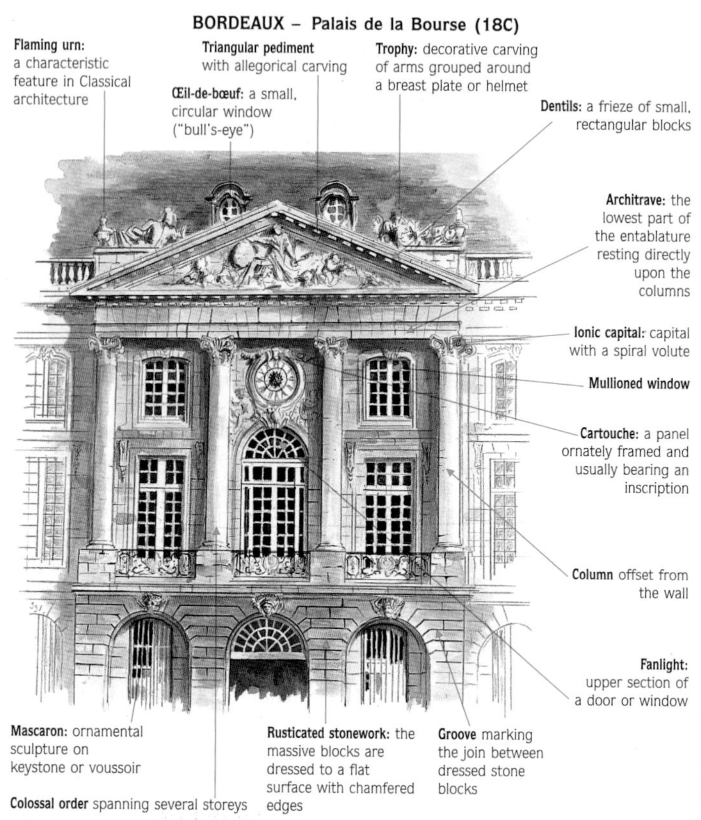

In contrast, the contemporary work of **Bouchardon** (1698–1762), who trained in Rome and was therefore influenced by antique sculpture, tended to be more Classical (Fountain in the Rue de Grenelle in Paris).

Decorative Arts

The rise of fashionable society brought with it a great need for luxury furniture that matched the style of woodwork inside elegant homes. New types of furniture were created: after commodes (chests of drawers) came writing desks – upright or inclined, escritoires, chiffoniers and countless small tables. For the comforts of conversation there were wing-chairs and deep easy chairs. There were also *voyeuses* or conversation chairs (special seats in gaming houses placed behind players to allow spectators to watch) and all manner of sofas and seats on which to recline (couches, lounging-chairs, divans and settees). Curved lines were favoured, as were rare and precious materials like exotic woods and lacquered panelling often set off by floral marquetry and finely chased gilded bronze. Among the great rocaille cabinet-makers were **Cressent**, **Joubert** and **Migeon**, while the principal seat carpenters of the time were **Foliot**, **Sené** and **Cresson**.

The **Vincennes Porcelain Factory** moved to **Sèvres** in 1756 and produced luxury items of which some were decorated in deep blue known as Sèvres blue. Gilt ornamentation was theoretically used only for royal services. Rocaille gold and silver plate was adorned with reed motifs, crested waves, scroll-work and shells often arranged in asymmetrical patterns. **Thomas Germain** (1673–1748), one of the most prestigious names in the trade, supplied the princely tables of the time.

Neoclassical Reaction (18–19C)

The middle of the 18C brought a reaction against rocaille on moral and aesthetic grounds. The style was considered to be too florid and frivolous, the result of decadence in both morals and the arts. Classical models from antiquity and the 17C were then deemed the only recourse to revive proper artistic creation.

ARCHITECTURE

The new style of architecture that emerged was austere and tended towards the monumental. Sculptural decoration on façades grew more restrained and the Doric order became widespread. Some buildings, like the Église Ste-Geneviève (the present-day **Panthéon**) in Paris by **G Soufflot** (1713–80), were direct copies of antique models. Louis XVI commissioned men like **Victor Louis** (1731–1802) who designed the Bordeaux theatre, **A T Brongniart** (1739–1813) and **J F Bélanger** (1744–1818) for most of the great architectural undertakings of the time. The philosophical influence of the Enlightenment led to a keen interest in the architecture of functional, public buildings such as the Royal Salt-works in Arc-et-Senans by **Claude-Nicolas Ledoux** (1736–1806).

SCULPTURE

Sculptors distanced themselves from rocaille extravagance by striving towards a natural portrayal of anatomy. **E M Falconet** (1716–91), **P Julien** (1731–1804) and **G C Allegrain** (1710–95) drew upon Greco-Roman models for their greatly admired sculptures of female bathers. **J A Houdon** (1741–1828), one of the greatest sculptors of the late 18C, made busts of his French and foreign contemporaries (Voltaire, Buffon and Madame Adélaïde for the first, and Benjamin Franklin and George Washington for the second) which constituted a veritable portrait gallery. The busts, executed in an extremely realistic manner, many without wigs or articles of dress to detract from the faces, were the culmination of modelled portraiture in France. Houdon also sculpted tombs

Panthéon, Paris

Oath of the Horatii (18C) by Jacques-Louis David, Musée du Louvre

and mythological statues. **J B Pigalle** (1714–85) maintained the style of sculpture predominant at the beginning of the century that the Neoclassical reaction had not managed to stifle entirely (mausoleum of the Marshal de Saxe in the Église St-Thomas in Strasbourg).

PAINTING

In the 1760s, attempts by the Royal Academy to restore a style of painting known as the grand manner encouraged the emergence of new themes such as antique history, civic heroism and 17C tragedies. These were adopted by painters like **J L David** (1748–1825), **J B M Pierre** (1714–89) and **J F P Peyron** (1744–1814). The style drew upon low-reliefs and statuary from antiquity and followed the principles of composition used by painters like Poussin and other 17C masters. Works by **J M Vien** (1716–1809) and **J B Greuze** (1725–1805) showed a less austere approach to painting, with more room for sensibility and emotion, which heralded the romanticism that was to blossom after the Revolution.

DECORATIVE ARTS

Louis XVI furniture kept some of the characteristics inherited from the beginning of the century such as the use of precious materials and chased gilt bronze ornamentation, but curves and sinuous shapes gave way to straight lines. As far as decoration was concerned, while the floral motifs and ribbons of the past were maintained, ovoli friezes, Greek fretwork and fasces were willingly introduced. **René Dubois** (1738–99) and **Louis Delanois** (1731–92) initiated the Greek style derived from antique furniture seen in friezes at Herculaneum and Pompeii. Prestigious artists of the genre included Oeben and Riesener, while Carlin, followed by Beneman and Levasseur, specialised in furniture adorned with plaques of painted porcelain. At the end of the century new decorative motifs, including lyres, ears of corn, wickerwork baskets and hot-air balloons, were imported from England.

The technique of hard-paste porcelain that was introduced into France at the beginning of the 1770s took the lead over soft-paste porcelain in the factory at Sèvres. Figurines of **biscuit** porcelain (white, fired, unglazed pottery) shaped on models by Fragonard, Boucher and other artists, became very popular.

The iconoclasm that prevailed during the **Revolution** marked a break in the history of French art. The Louvre opened in 1793, paving the way for many more museums in France.

Art and Architecture in the 19C

Some of the world's most famous art was created in the 19C, spurred on by industrialisation and the new horizons and individualism carved out by the emergence of train travel and modern technology. Art and ideas travelled faster, and exchanges of information journeyed farther. The century also witnessed dramatic societal changes: for artists, the birth of new viewpoints, new painting techniques; for architects and builders, new construction methods. France was at the forefront of these innovations.

FIRST EMPIRE

After his investiture in 1804, Napoléon favoured the emergence of an official style of art by commissioning palace decoration (Tuileries, destroyed in 1870, and Fontainebleau) and paintings that related the great events of the Empire. The artists to benefit from the Emperor's patronage were men like J L David and his pupils **A J Gros** (1771–1835) and **A L Girodet-Trioson** (1767-1824).

Paintings of the time took on new themes derived from the romanticism in contemporary literature, orientalism and an interest in the medieval. National historic anecdotes were painted by artists who, like the troubadours, praised heroic deeds and fine sentiment.

Architecture was less innovative. Napoléon commissioned large edifices commemorating the glory of the *Grande Armée* including the Carrousel Arch, the column in Place Vendôme and the Temple de la Madeleine (now a church). The official architects **Percier** (1764–1838) and **Fontaine** (1762–1853) were responsible for the overall supervision of the undertakings, setting models not only for buildings but also for decoration at official ceremonies and guidelines for the decorative arts.

Ambitious town-planning projects like the reconstruction of Lyon were also completed under the Empire.

Former royal palaces were refurnished. The style of First Empire furniture derived from the Neoclassical with massive, quadrangular, commodes and jewel-cases made of mahogany with gilt bronze plating and antique deco-

19C column set in 18C Place Vendôme, Paris

rative motifs. **Desmalter** (1770–1841) was the main cabinet-maker of the imperial court. The sculptors **Chaudet** (1763–1810) and **Cartellier** (1757–1831) supplied models for furniture ornamentation in the Neoclassical style which also inspired their statues. After the Egyptian Campaign, motifs such as sphinxes and lotuses began to appear in the decorative arts.

RESTORATION AND THE JULY MONARCHY

Two major trends affected French art between 1815 and 1848. The first was the gradual disappearance of the Neoclassical style which, however, still influenced church building (Notre-Dame-de-Lorette and St-Vincent-de-Paul in Paris); and the second was the birth of historicism, a style that fostered regard for the architecture of the past, particularly of the medieval period (Église Notre-Dame in Boulogne-sur-Mer and Marseille Cathedral by Léon Vaudoyer). The trend was furthered by the *Monuments Historiques* (a body set up for the classification and preservation of the national heritage) in 1830 and the enthusiasm of **Viollet-le-Duc** (1814–79).

THE SECOND EMPIRE

On the accession of Napoléon III the arts in general were affected by a spirit of **eclecticism**. The Louvre, completed by Percier's disciple Visconti (1791–1853) and **H Lefuel** (1810–80), and the Paris Opera by **Garnier** (1825–98) were among the greatest undertakings of the century. References to architectural styles of the past (16C, 17C and 18C) were present everywhere. Nevertheless, the introduction of new materials such as glass and cast iron (the Gare du Nord by **Hittorff** and the Église St-Augustin by **V Baltard**) showed the influence of technological progress and a new rational approach to building.

Baron Haussmann (1809–91), Prefect of the *département* of the Seine, laid down the principles for a public works programme that was to modernise the capital. Prefect C M Vaïsse carried out a similar plan in Lyon.

Academicism reigned over the **painting** of the time. **Cabanel** (1823–83), **Bouguereau** (1825–1905) and the portraitist **Winterhalter** (1805–73) drew their inspiration just as easily from antique statuary as from works by 16C Venetian masters or Rococo ornamentation.

However, **Courbet** (1819–77), **Daumier** (1808–79) and **Millet** (1814–75) formed an avant-garde group that fostered realism in painting with subjects from town and country life.

Ingres (1780–1867) who represented the Classical trend, and **Delacroix** (1798–1863), the great romantic painter of the century, were both at the height of their powers. Great architectural projects stimulated the production of **sculpture. Carpeaux** (1827–75), responsible for the high-relief of Dance on the façade of the Paris Opera, transcended the eclecticism of his time by developing a very personal style that was reminiscent of, and not simply a copy of, Flemish, Renaissance and 18C art. **Dubois** (1829–1905), **Frémiet** (1824–1910) and **Guillaume** (1822–1905) were more academic in their approach.

A taste for pastiche prevailed in the decorative arts.

The shapes and ornamental motifs of the Renaissance, the 16C and 18C were reproduced on furniture and *objets d'art*. The advent of **industrialisation** affected certain fields. The goldsmith Christofle (1805–63) and the bronze-founder Barbedienne (1810–92) made luxury items for the imperial court as well as mass-produced articles for new clients among the rich upper-middle classes.

LATE-19C TRENDS

Architecture during the Third Republic was mainly marked by edifices built for Universal Exhibitions held in Paris (the former Palais du Trocadéro, the Eiffel Tower, the Grand-Palais and the Pont Alexandre-III). The pompous style of the buildings with their exotic ornamentation derived from the trend for eclecticism.

La Gare Saint-Lazare (1877) by Claude Monet, Musée d'Orsay

In the 1890s, **Art Nouveau** architects, influenced by trends in England and Belgium, distanced themselves from the official style of the day. They harmonised external and internal decoration and designed their creations as a whole – stained glass, tiles, furniture and wallpaper. Decoration included plant motifs, stylised flowers, Japanese influences and asymmetrical patterns. **Guimard** (1867–1942) was the main proponent of the style in France (Castel Béranger in Paris and entrances to the capital's metro stations).

The decorative arts followed the Art Nouveau movement with works by the cabinet-maker **Majorelle** (1859–1929) and the glass and ceramics artist **Gallé** (1846–1904) in Nancy.

In the field of painting, the **Impressionists** began exhibiting their work outside official salons in 1874. **Monet** (1840–1926), **Renoir** (1841–1919) and **Pissarro** (1830–1903) breathed new life into the technique and themes of landscape painting by working out of doors, studying the play of light in nature and introducing new subjects drawn from contemporary life. **Manet** (1832–83) and **Degas** (1834–1917) joined the group temporarily.

Between 1885 and 1890, Neo-Impressionists like **G Seurat** (1859–91) and **Signac** (1863–1935) brought the Pointillist (painting with small dots) technique known as divisionism to a climax. The Dutch painter **Van Gogh** (1853–90) settled in France in 1886. His technique of using pure and expressionist colours with broad, swirling brushstrokes coupled with his belief that expression of emotional experience should override impressions of the external world were to have a great influence on early 20C painters. **Cézanne** (1839–1906) and **Gauguin** (1848–1903), who were influenced by primitive and Japanese art, partly dispensed with Impressionism to give more importance to volume. In 1886, seeking new inspiration, Gauguin moved to Pont-Aven, a small town east of Concarneau in Brittany that had often been visited by the painter **Corot** in the 1860s. Fellow artists **Émile Bernard** and **Paul Sérusier** formed the **Pont-Aven School** that favoured synthesist theories and symbolic subjects which paved the way for the **Nabis**.

Among the Nabis were artists like **Denis** (1870–1943), **Bonnard** (1867–1947) and **Vuillard** (1868–1940) who advocated the importance of colour over shape and meaning. Sculpture at the end of the century was dominated by **Rodin** (1840–1917). His expressionistic, tormented, symbolic work stood free from formal academic conventions and was not always understood in his time.

Art and Architecture in the 20C

The early years of the 20C were largely dominated by the experiments in colour and content that hallmarked the styles known as Impressionism and Post-Impressionism. The dynamic evolution of art was little hindered by war, fuelled by the continuing advances of humanity. The late 1950s and 1960s saw even greater experimentation into the realms of Pop Art.

THE AVANT-GARDE

At the beginning of the 20C, proponents of the avant-garde reacted against the many trends of the 19C including the restrictions laid down by official art, academicism in painting and Art Nouveau in architecture.

The **De Stijl** movement created simple, geometric buildings adorned with sober low-reliefs. One of its most magnificent examples was the Théâtre des Champs-Élysées by the **Perret brothers** with sculptural decoration by **Bourdelle** (1861–1929). In the field of sculpture, the artists **Maillol** (1861–1944), **Bartholomé** (1848–1928) and **J Bernard** (1866–1931) opposed Rodin's aesthetic concepts and produced a very different type of art by simplifying their figures, in some cases to the point of schematic representation.

Fauvism was the great novelty at the Autumn Salon of painting in 1905.

A Derain (1880–1964), **A Marquet** (1875–1947) and **M de Vlaminck** (1876–1958) broke up their subject matter through the vivid and arbitrary use of colour, a technique which was to pave the way for non-figurative painting. After an early period with the Fauvist movement, **Matisse** (1869–1904) went his own way, developing a personal style based on the exploration of colour. A further major avant-garde movement in painting followed on from **Cézanne**'s structural analysis in which he broke up his subject matter into specific shapes. The trend was taken up by artists like **Braque** (1882–1963) and **Picasso** (1881–1973), whose exploration led to **Cubism**, a new perception of reality based not on what the eye saw but on an analytical

Statue by Aristide Maillol in Jardin des Tuileries, Paris

© Bruce Bi / age fotostock

approach to objects, depicting them as a series of planes, usually in a restricted colour range. The style dominated their work from 1907 to 1914.

Members of the *Section d'Or* (golden section) Cubist group like **A Gleizes**, **J Metzinger** and **F Léger** (his early works) were less revolutionary and more figurative. The main French Cubist sculptures came from **Henri Laurens**, who was influenced by Braque. **Surrealism** breathed new life into the art world in the 1920s and 1930s. It was a subversive art form that created an irrational, dreamlike, fantasy universe. For the first time chance and prompting from the subconscious were integrated into the creative process. **Duchamp** (1887–1968), **Masson** (1896–1997), **Picabia** (1879–1953) and **Magritte** (1898–1967) all formed part of the movement.

1945 ONWARDS

Abstract art began to affect the field of painting after World War II. **Herbin** defined it as the triumph of mind over matter. In 1949 he published Non-figurative, Non-objective Art (L'Art non figuratif non objectif) and greatly influenced young artists of the **geometric abstract** art movement. All his works from the 1950s onwards have been one-dimensional patterns of letters and simple geometric shapes painted in pure colours.

The **lyrical abstract** artists focused on the study of colour and texture. **Riopelle** applied his paint with a knife while **Mathieu** applied it directly from the tube. **Soulages**, who was influenced by art from the Far East, produced meditative, expressive work in shades of black. **Nicolas de Stael**'s art constituted a link between abstract and figurative in that his abstract compositions were the result of observations of real objects which could sometimes be distinguished in the final work.

In the 1960s, **New Realism** (*Nouveau Réalisme*), a form of pop art, with **Pierre Restany** as its leading theoretician, attempted to express the reality of daily life. Industrial items, the symbols of modern society, were broken up (by the artist **Arman**) and assembled (by **César**) or trapped in glass.

Yves Klein (1928–62) took his adherence to New Realism a step further in his Monochromes by trying to capture the universal essence of objects. He rejected formal and traditional values, as did **Dubuffet** (1901–85) who, in 1968, wrote a pamphlet entitled Asphyxiating Culture (Asphyxiante culture), which made a stand for permanent revolution. Dubuffet's later art consisted of puzzles of coloured or black and white units.

Since the 1960s, the problems posed by town-planning have led to a re-evaluation of the relationship between architecture and sculpture and an attempt to reconcile the two arts.

The **Support-Surface** movement (**Claude Viallet**, **Pagès** and **Daniel Dezeuze**) of the 1970s reduced painting to its pure material state by focusing on the way the paint was applied. Paintings were removed from their stretchers and cut up, suspended and folded. The 1980s saw the return of Figuration in manifold ways. References to tradition are evident in the work of artists like **Gérard Garouste, Remi Blanchard, François Boisrond, Robert Combas** and **Jean-Charles Blais.** The great vitality of contemporary art can be seen in the extremely wide variety of styles and trends favoured by artists today. Many modern artists still focus on the horrors of war, notably **Boltanski**, and his wife, **Annette Messager**, who portrays issues of identity and feminism.

The photographer, installation and conceptual artist **Sophie Calle**'s work is distinguished by its use of arbitrary sets of constraints, and evokes the French literary movement of the 1960s.

The death of sculptor **Louise Bourgeois** in May 2010 marked the end of an extraordinarily long career, in which she produced work (first in France, then New York) during most of the 20C avant-garde artistic movements. Exploring themes of femininity, sexuality and isolation, her most famous pieces include the monumental spider bronzes *Maman*.

French Literature

This selection of further reading will help you to delve deeper into modern France and its culture.

1000 Years of Annoying the French – Stephen Clarke (*Bantam Press, 2010*). An idiosyncratic, and occasionally tongue-in-cheek, look at the long-lasting relationship with the French.

Paris Revealed: The Secret Life of a City – Stephen Clarke (*Bantam Press, 2011*). The latest in Stephen Clarke's gentle take on the curiosities of France.

More, More France Please – Helena Frith Powell (*Gibson Square, 2007*). Real-life stories from France.

France in the New Century: Portrait of a Changing Society – John Ardagh (Penguin, 2001). An acclaimed overview of the political landscape, by one of the most respected commentators on French life.

François Théodore Thistlethwaite's Frenglish Thoughts – Barry A. Whittingham (Self-published, 2012). Idiosyncrasy at its best. Some things are better for coming at you from the direction you least expect. So, it is with this essay in biological and familial conflict; you never quite know what's going to happen next. A worthy addition to the writings on France for anyone in love with the country and its people.

The French – T Zeldin (*Kodansha Globe, 1996).* A perceptive and entertaining look at the nation's character.

The Man who married a Mountain – Rosemary Bailey (*Bantam Books, 2005*) A tale in search of a man, Count Henry Russell, 19C explorer and mountaineer who lived in a cave high in the Pyrenees.

Searching for the New France – J Hollifield and G Ross (Routledge, 1998). Why France is so anxious about its identity, its role and its future.

Betrayal: France, the Arabs and the Jews – David Pryce-Jones *(Encounter Books, 2008).* How France's relations with the Arab world have led it into trouble.

Horrible Histories: France – Terry Deary (Scholastic Hippo, 2002). A comical cartoon summary of French history.

Speak the Culture – France (*Thorogood Publishing, 2008*). A general guidebook that shows you where to go in France and what to say when you get there, reasoning that through exploring the people and their lifestyles you will achieve an intimate understanding of France and its people.

Something to Declare – Julian Barnes (Picador, 2002). A collection of essays written over 20 years that attest to Barnes' appreciation of the Land Without Brussels Sprouts.

Exploring Rural France – Andrew Sanger (*Passport Books, 1994*). Itineraries for off-the-beaten-track tourists.

The Wines and Winelands of France – Geological Journeys – C Pomerol (McCarta Publishing, 1990). What lies behind the extraordinary diversity of the French wine list.

Green Guide to the Wine Regions of France. All you need to visit and taste your way around the country.

Paris to the Past: Traveling through French history by train – Ina Caro (W W Norton and Company, 2011). A rare breed of travel book; one that blends scholarship, story-telling and public transport.

Only in Paris: A Guide to Unique Locations, Hidden Corners and Unusual Objects – Duncan J D Smith (Brandstatter, 2013). This delightful compendium of all things unexpected to be encountered in Paris is so much more than you will get from a conventional travel guide… discover a counterfeit museum, concealed courtyards and secret squares.

French Films

France has inspired and served as a location for innumerable films. The ones featured here provide some insight into regional Gallic sensibilities.

Jean de Florette and Manon des Sources (1986)
Two peasants in rural Provence outwit the new owner of the neighbouring property. In the second movie, his death is avenged by his daughter Manon.

French Kiss (1995)
Comic romance about a Canadian out to save her marriage plans and the petty crook using her, who travel to Cannes together.

La Haine (1995)
Violence and racism as three youths, one black, one a Jew, one an Arab, get involved in riots in the Paris suburbs.

Le Fabuleux destin d'Amélie Poulain (2001)
Touching and lighthearted adventures of the naive Amélie as she looks for love in Paris.

Être et Avoir (To Be and to Have) (2001)
There are still single-classroom schools that bring together, under the same schoolteacher, all the children from the same village, from nursery age to 11. This documentary follows one such rural class over the course of a year.

7 years (2005)
Maïté is married to Vincent who has just been sentenced to seven years in prison. The only intimacy left to them lies in the prison's visiting rooms. Twice a week, she picks up his laundry, washes it, irons it, and brings it back.

La Vie en Rose (2007)
Released in France as La Môme, La Vie en Rose is a French and Canadian biographical musical film about Edith Piaf.

Bienvenue Chez les Ch'tis (Welcome to the Sticks) (2008)
Although living a comfortable life in Salon-de-Provence, Julie has been feeling depressed for a while. To please her, Philippe Abrams, her post office administrator husband, tries to obtain a transfer to a seaside town, on the French Riviera, at any cost…

Partir (Leaving) (2009)
Suzanne is a well-to-do wife and mother in the south of France. Her idle bourgeois lifestyle gets her down and she decides to go back to work as a physiotherapist.

L'Arnacœur (Heartbreaker) (2010)
Alex (Romain Duris) and his sister Mélanie (Julie Ferrier) run a business designed to break up relationships. Taking on a job on the French Riviera, will icy Juliette (Vanessa Paradis) be the client who scuppers the mission?

The Artist (2011)
A silent movie star meets a young dancer, but the advent of the 'talkies' takes their careers in different directions. Filmed in the style of a black-and-white silent film, this French romantic comedy drama is set in Hollywood in the late 1920s and early 1930s. Winner of multiple BAFTAs, Golden Globes and Oscars.

Blue Is the Warmest Colour (la vie d'Adèle, 2013)
An intimate portrayal of the relationship between Adèle (Adèle Exarchopoulos) and art school rebel Emma (Léa Seydoux). Winner of the Palme d'Or at the 2013 Cannes Film Festival.

Nature

Amid all the wonders of art, architecture, history and culture bestowed on France, the country is also richly endowed in a natural history of prime importance from an international perspective. Specifically, France corrals almost 15 per cent of its territory (7 000 000 hectares/17 000 000 acres) into 49 Regional Natural Parks (Parc natural régional).

Each park serves a common purpose: to manage human habitation, to sustain economic development, to protect the natural environment, foster ecological research and public education in the natural sciences. Collectively, these parks embrace over 4 200 communes, with a population in excess of 3 000 000.

» Landscapes p113

Parc Naturel Régional des Pyrénées near Angoustrine in the Cerdagne

France's Landscapes

France has a fortunate location in the European continent – not detached from it like the British Isles, nor projecting away like Iberia or Greece, nor set deep in its interior like the countries of Central Europe, yet in touch with the resources and the life of the whole of Western Europe and the seas around it, Atlantic, Channel, Mediterranean and North Sea.

TOPOGRAPHY

There are four main river systems in France: in the east is the valley of the Rhône, which together with its tributary the Saône links the Paris basin with the Mediterranean; in the north, the Seine drains into the English Channel; in the west, the longest of all, the Loire, rises in central France and flows into the Atlantic, as does its southern cousin the Garonne, which rises in the Pyrénées and drains into the Gironde estuary. Within this unified and robust framework there flourishes a geographical identity which is unmistakably French yet of an unrivalled local richness and variety.

GEOLOGICAL HISTORY

The whole of Earth's history – the building of the planet – can be traced within the confines of France. The complex geological history starts 600 million years ago, when the Hercynian folding raised the great mountain ancestors of today's Massif Central, Armorican Peninsula, Vosges and Ardennes. Beginning 200 million years ago, the Paris region, Aquitaine, the Rhône and Loire valleys and the southern part of the Massif Central all lay under a sea that gradually filled them with sediments. New mountain ranges reared up 60 million years ago: the Alps, Pyrénées, the Jura and Corsica. The Quaternary Era (2 million years ago) saw an alternation of warm and cold periods; glaciers advanced and retreated and rivers swelled and shrank, sculpting much of the land surface into its present forms.

CLIMATE AND RELIEF

In climatic terms too, France experiences Atlantic, Continental and Mediterranean influences (in northern and western France, central and eastern parts of the country, and the south, respectively), all contributing decisively to the formation of soils and their mantle of vegetation as well as to the processes which have shaped the geological foundation into the patterns of today's relief.

Climate change is impacting on France as elsewhere, affecting winter sports (50 percent decrease in snow in the French Prealps, for example), inducing an upward migration of alpine plants, a higher incidence of heat waves, forest fires and droughts, such as that of 2003, and an advance of fruit tree flowering. In Alsace, the number of days with a mean daily temperature above 10°C has increased from 170 to 210 since 1970.

The north of the country is largely composed of great sedimentary basins, scarp (*côtes*) and vale country, drained by slow-flowing rivers like the Seine and the Loire. At the extremities of these lowlands are rugged areas formed of Primary rocks, the much-eroded granites of Brittany and the gneisses and schists of the Ardennes, and the higher massifs of the Vosges and the centre. Beyond lie the fertile plains of Aquitaine and Languedoc while the corridor carved by the Rhône and Saône links the north and south of the country. Finally come the "young" mountains of the Jura, Alps and Pyrénées; their high peaks and ranges, while forming fine natural frontiers, are by no means impermeable to political, commercial and cultural currents.

Discovering France

Tournette trail near Lac d'Annecy, Haute-Savoie

Paris

» Region map p118–119
Planning Your Trip to Paris p122
A Bit of History p125
Arrondissements 1–4 p132
Arrondissements 5–7 & 16 p142
Arrondissements 8–10 & 17 p148
Arrondissements 11–15 p151
Arrondissements 18–20 p152

Introduction

The brilliance and greatness of Paris – its evocative spirit, the imposing dignity of its avenues and squares, its vast cultural wealth and unique flair and style – are known the world over. The dominance of Paris in France's intellectual, artistic, scientific and political life can be traced back to the 12C when the Capetian kings made it their capital.

Paris is France's most populated city, its national capital, and the regional capital of Île-de-France. Lying on the banks of a loop formed by the Seine river, the ordinary Gallo-Roman village of Lutetia became an important urban centre during the 10C thanks to its location at a crossroads of trade routes, in the heart of a rich agricultural region.

Two hundred years later, Paris' cultural influence was felt all over Europe. With the kings of France choosing it as their capital city (and the basilica of the neighbouring town of St-Denis as their necropolis), Paris' political weight continued to grow until it became a major focal point of the Christian world at the beginning of the 14C. As a centre of all powers in France, the only real challenge to Paris came from Versailles, where the monarchy settled from the late 17C until the French Revolution of 1789. A world capital of arts and leisure in the 19C and early 20C, Paris' unrivalled heritage and culture have given it the honour of becoming the world's most popular tourist destination.

Highlights

1. Visit one of the world's finest collections of Impressionist paintings at **Musée d'Orsay** (p143)
2. Take a stroll down the **Champs-Élysées** from the Arc de Triomphe, and then walk back up on the opposite side (p147)
3. If you enjoyed the award-winning film Amélie, follow in the character's footsteps in **Montmartre** (p150)
4. Strange as it may seem, visit the **Père-Lachaise Cemetery** in the 20th arrondissement (p151)
5. Make the most of a little Parisian **café culture** (p153)

Today, Paris is breathtaking at every turn, from its outstanding architecture to its romantic atmosphere, its profound cultural wealth and its unassailable ***joie de vivre***.

Musée d'Orsay © Jean-Luc Bohin / age fotostock

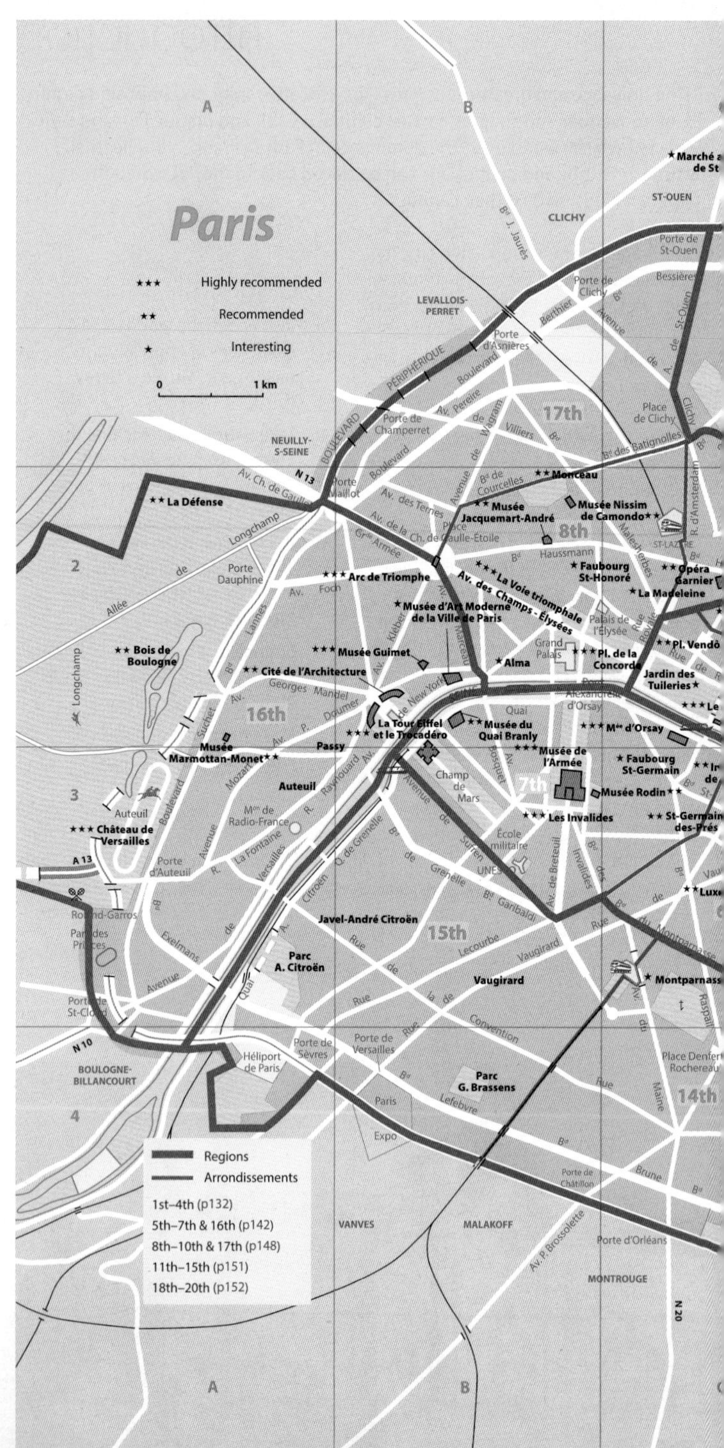

Paris
★★★ Highly recommended
★★ Recommended
★ Interesting
0 1 km
Regions
Arrondissements
1st–4th (p132)
5th–7th & 16th (p142)
8th–10th & 17th (p148)
11th–15th (p151)
18th–20th (p152)
★★ La Défense
★★ Bois de Boulogne
★★★ Arc de Triomphe
★★★ La Voie triomphale
Av. des Champs-Élysées
★ Musée d'Art Moderne de la Ville de Paris
★★★ Musée Guimet
★★ Cité de l'Architecture
★★★ La Tour Eiffel et le Trocadéro
★★ Musée du Quai Branly
★★★ Musée de l'Armée
★★★ Les Invalides
★★ Musée Rodin
★★ Musée Jacquemart-André
★★ Monceau
Musée Nissim de Camondo ★★
★ Faubourg St-Honoré
★★ Opéra Garnier
★ La Madeleine
★★ Pl. Vendô
★★★ Pl. de la Concorde
Jardin des Tuileries ★
★ Alma
★★★ M^{ée} d'Orsay
★ Faubourg St-Germain
★★ St-Germain-des-Prés
★★ Luxe
★ Montparnass
★ Marché a de St
Musée Marmottan-Monet ★★
★★★ Château de Versailles
Passy
Auteuil
Javel-André Citroën
Vaugirard
Parc A. Citroën
Parc G. Brassens
17th
8th
16th
7th
15th
14th
CLICHY
ST-OUEN
LEVALLOIS-PERRET
NEUILLY-S-SEINE
BOULOGNE-BILLANCOURT
VANVES
MALAKOFF
MONTROUGE
Porte d'Asnières
Porte de Champerret
Porte Maillot
Porte Dauphine
Porte d'Auteuil
Porte de St-Cloud
Porte de Sèvres
Porte de Versailles
Porte de Châtillon
Porte d'Orléans
Porte de Clichy
Porte de St-Ouen
Héliport de Paris
Paris Expo
Champ de Mars
École militaire
Grand Palais
Palais de l'Élysée
Roland-Garros
Parc des Princes
M^{on} de Radio-France
Place de Clichy
Place Denfert Rochereau
Av. Foch
Bd Haussmann
Av. des Ternes
Boulevard Périphérique
A 13
N 13
N 10
N 20
A
B
2
3
4

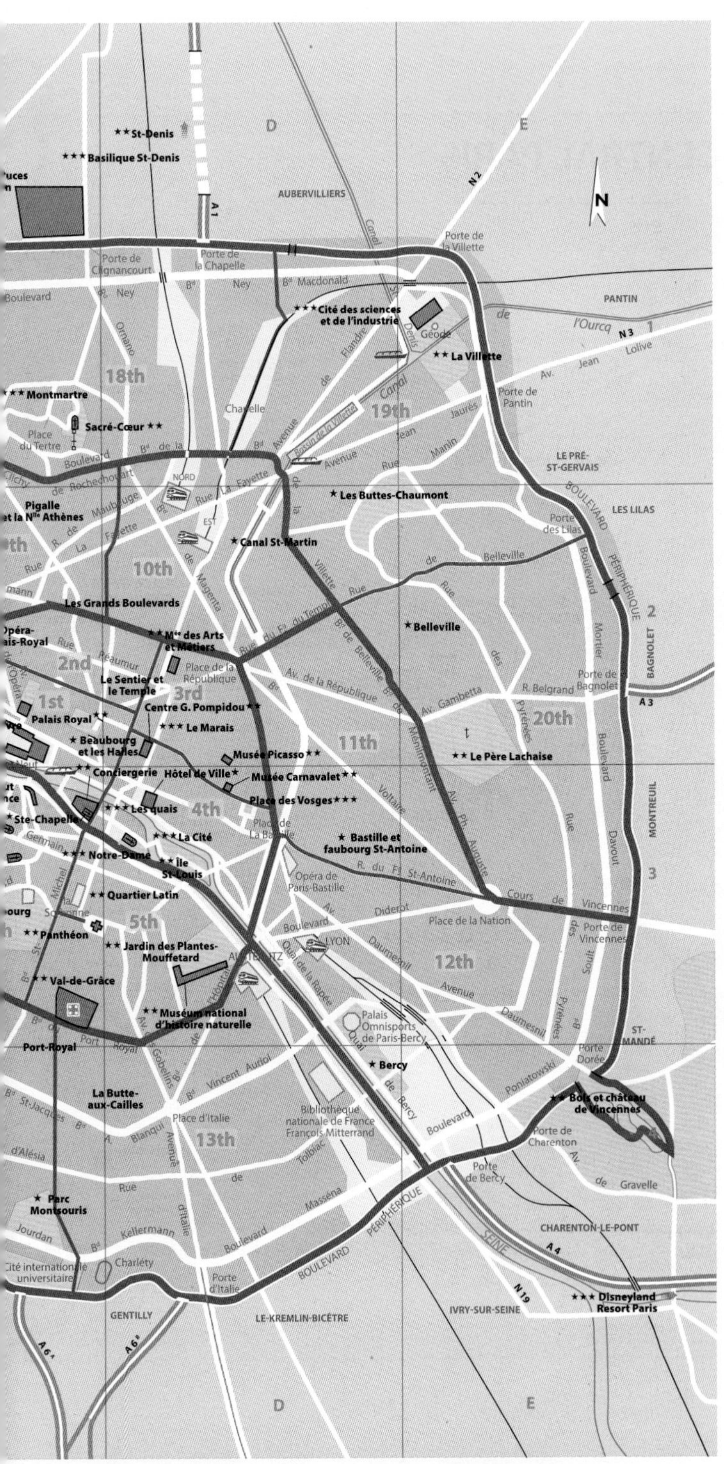
★★St-Denis
★★★Basilique St-Denis
AUBERVILLIERS
N2
N
Porte de la Villette
Porte de Clignancourt
Porte de la Chapelle
PANTIN
★★★Cité des sciences et de l'industrie
Géode
★★La Villette
18th
19th
★★★Montmartre
Sacré-Cœur★★
Place du Tertre
Porte de Pantin
LE PRÉ-ST-GERVAIS
★Les Buttes-Chaumont
LES LILAS
Pigalle et la Nlle Athènes
★Canal St-Martin
Porte des Lilas
BOULEVARD PÉRIPHÉRIQUE
10th
Les Grands Boulevards
★★Mts des Arts et Métiers
★Belleville
Place de la République
2nd
Le Sentier et le Temple
3rd
Centre G. Pompidou★★
Porte de Bagnolet
BAGNOLET
20th
1st
Palais Royal★★
★★★Le Marais
11th
★Beaubourg et les Halles
Musée Picasso★★
★★Le Père Lachaise
★★Conciergerie
Hôtel de Ville★
Musée Carnavalet★★
Place des Vosges★★★
★★★Les quais
4th
MONTREUIL
★Ste-Chapelle
★★★La Cité
★Bastille et faubourg St-Antoine
★★★Notre-Dame
★★Île St-Louis
Opéra de Paris-Bastille
★★Quartier Latin
Place de la Nation
Porte de Vincennes
5th
★★Panthéon
★★Jardin des Plantes-Mouffetard
12th
★★Val-de-Grâce
★★Muséum national d'histoire naturelle
Palais Omnisports de Paris-Bercy
ST-MANDÉ
Port-Royal
Porte Dorée
★Bercy
La Butte-aux-Cailles
★★Bois et château de Vincennes
Place d'Italie
Bibliothèque nationale de France François Mitterrand
13th
Porte de Charenton
Porte de Bercy
★Parc Montsouris
CHARENTON-LE-PONT
SEINE
A4
Cité internationale universitaire
Charléty
Porte d'Italie
N19
★★★Disneyland Resort Paris
GENTILLY
LE-KREMLIN-BICÊTRE
IVRY-SUR-SEINE
A6A
A6B
D
E

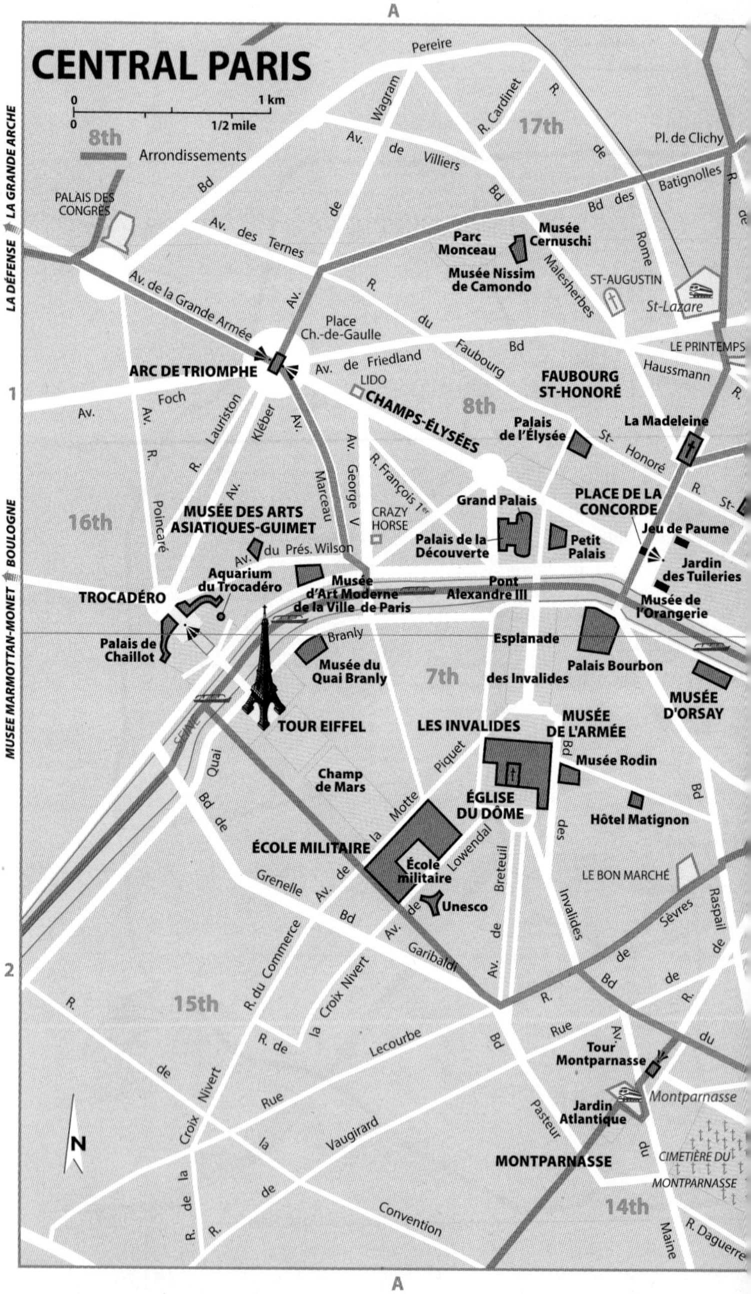

CENTRAL PARIS

0 1 km
0 1/2 mile
8th Arrondissements

A

LA DÉFENSE / LA GRANDE ARCHE
BOULOGNE
MUSÉE MARMOTTAN-MONET

Pereire
Av. de Wagram
R. Cardinet
R. de
17th
Pl. de Clichy
Av. de Villiers
Bd
Bd des Batignolles
R. de
PALAIS DES CONGRÈS
Av. des Ternes
Parc Monceau
Musée Cernuschi
Musée Nissim de Camondo
Malesherbes
Rome
ST-AUGUSTIN
St-Lazare
Av. de la Grande Armée
R. du Faubourg
Place Ch.-de-Gaulle
Bd
LE PRINTEMPS
Haussmann
ARC DE TRIOMPHE
Av. de Friedland
LIDO
FAUBOURG ST-HONORÉ
Av. Foch
CHAMPS-ÉLYSÉES
8th
R.
Av. Kléber
Av. Marceau
Av. George V
R. Lauriston
Av. R. Poincaré
R. François 1er
Palais de l'Élysée
St-Honoré
La Madeleine
Grand Palais
PLACE DE LA CONCORDE
R. St-
16th
MUSÉE DES ARTS ASIATIQUES-GUIMET
CRAZY HORSE
Av. du Prés. Wilson
Palais de la Découverte
Petit Palais
Jeu de Paume
Jardin des Tuileries
Aquarium du Trocadéro
Musée d'Art Moderne de la Ville de Paris
Pont Alexandre III
TROCADÉRO
Musée de l'Orangerie
Branly
Esplanade des Invalides
Palais de Chaillot
Palais Bourbon
Musée du Quai Branly
7th
MUSÉE D'ORSAY
SEINE
TOUR EIFFEL
LES INVALIDES
MUSÉE DE L'ARMÉE
Quai
Piquet
Bd
Musée Rodin
Champ de Mars
Bd de Grenelle
Av. de la Motte
ÉGLISE DU DÔME
Hôtel Matignon
Bd
ÉCOLE MILITAIRE
École militaire
Lowendal
Av. de Breteuil
Bd des Invalides
LE BON MARCHÉ
Av. de
Unesco
Bd de Sèvres
Raspail
Garibaldi
2
R. du Commerce
R. de la Croix Nivert
Bd de
R.
Rue de
15th
Lecourbe
Tour Montparnasse
Av. du
R. de
Bd Pasteur
Montparnasse
Jardin Atlantique
N
R. de la Croix Nivert
Rue de Vaugirard
MONTPARNASSE
Av. du Maine
CIMETIÈRE DU MONTPARNASSE
R. de la Convention
14th
R. Daguerre
R. de
R.

A

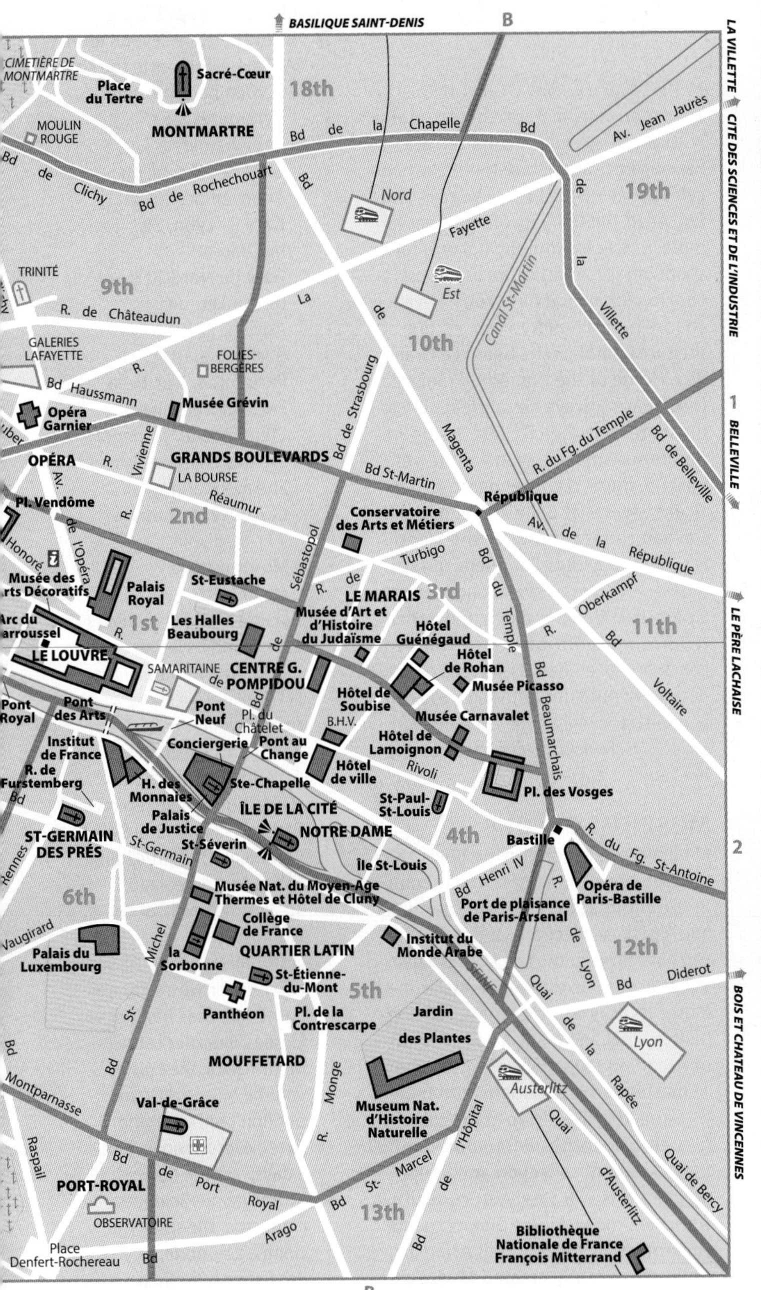

BASILIQUE SAINT-DENIS
B
LA VILLETTE
CITE DES SCIENCES ET DE L'INDUSTRIE
BELLEVILLE
LE PÈRE LACHAISE
BOIS ET CHATEAU DE VINCENNES
1
2
CIMETIÈRE DE MONTMARTRE
Place du Tertre
Sacré-Cœur
MONTMARTRE
MOULIN ROUGE
18th
19th
9th
10th
2nd
3rd
1st
11th
4th
12th
6th
5th
13th
Bd de la Chapelle
Av. Jean Jaurès
Bd de Clichy
Bd de Rochechouart
Nord
Est
La Fayette
Bd de la Villette
Canal St-Martin
TRINITÉ
R. de Châteaudun
GALERIES LAFAYETTE
FOLIES-BERGÈRES
Bd Haussmann
Musée Grévin
Opéra Garnier
OPÉRA
GRANDS BOULEVARDS
Bd de Strasbourg
Bd de Magenta
R. Vivienne
LA BOURSE
Réaumur
Bd St-Martin
R. du Fg. du Temple
Bd de Belleville
République
Pl. Vendôme
Av. de l'Opéra
Conservatoire des Arts et Métiers
Av. de la République
Sébastopol
Turbigo
Honoré
Musée des Arts Décoratifs
Palais Royal
St-Eustache
LE MARAIS
Musée d'Art et d'Histoire du Judaïsme
Bd du Temple
R. Oberkampf
Arc du Carroussel
Les Halles Beaubourg
Hôtel Guénégaud
Bd Voltaire
LE LOUVRE
SAMARITAINE
CENTRE G. POMPIDOU
Hôtel de Rohan
Musée Picasso
Bd Beaumarchais
Pont Royal
Pont des Arts
Pont Neuf
Pl. du Châtelet
Hôtel de Soubise
B.H.V.
Musée Carnavalet
Institut de France
Conciergerie
Pont au Change
Hôtel de Lamoignon
R. de Furstemberg
H. des Monnaies
Hôtel de ville
Rivoli
Ste-Chapelle
Pl. des Vosges
Palais de Justice
ÎLE DE LA CITÉ
St-Paul-St-Louis
ST-GERMAIN DES PRÉS
NOTRE DAME
Bastille
R. du Fg. St-Antoine
Bd St-Germain
St-Séverin
Île St-Louis
Bd Henri IV
Opéra de Paris-Bastille
Rennes
Musée Nat. du Moyen-Age Thermes et Hôtel de Cluny
Port de plaisance de Paris-Arsenal
Vaugirard
Collège de France
R. de Lyon
Palais du Luxembourg
la Sorbonne
QUARTIER LATIN
Institut du Monde Arabe
Bd Diderot
SEINE
St-Étienne-du-Mont
Quai de la Rapée
Panthéon
Pl. de la Contrescarpe
Jardin des Plantes
Lyon
Bd St-Michel
MOUFFETARD
Austerlitz
Bd Montparnasse
R. Monge
Val-de-Grâce
Museum Nat. d'Histoire Naturelle
Bd de l'Hôpital
Quai d'Austerlitz
Quai de Bercy
Raspail
Bd de Port Royal
Bd St-Marcel
PORT-ROYAL
OBSERVATOIRE
Bd Arago
Place Denfert-Rochereau
Bibliothèque Nationale de France François Mitterrand

Planning Your Trip to Paris

A PARISIAN WAY OF LIFE

Your mornings in Paris should begin with a *café-croissant* on a terrace, a Parisian institution since the 18C, when cafés attracted the likes of Voltaire and Rousseau. But the "City of Light" has far more in store for you, and not only for a shopping spree at the *Grands Magasins*. Looking for a good film? You'll have to choose from a hundred venues, one of the most emblematic being Le Grand Rex. Home of the Comédie-Française (17C), Paris always has a great classic on stage, but the city also harbours numerous smaller, avant-garde venues. The music scene ranges from classical concerts at Salle Pleyel or Salle Gaveau to jazz shows at the trendy New Morning Club. For opera and ballet, the 19C Opéra-Garnier and modern Opéra-Bastille offer a rich and varied repertoire. Night owls may want to check out the Champs-Élysées or the Bastille-République, although you can happen upon nightclubs, cabarets, variety shows, reviews, cafés-theatres and bars almost anywhere.

MUSEUMS GALORE

Magnificently restored in the 1990s, the Louvre is one of the largest art museums in the world. Don't miss the Egyptian and Assyrian collections, and make sure you have time for the French and Italian sculpture. Just across the Seine river, the Musée d'Orsay, a former railway station built in steel and glass, awaits with its outstanding collections of impressionist masterpieces. If modern art is more your speed, make a stop at the colourful Centre Georges Pompidou: both the permanent collection and temporary exhibits will sate your curiosity. The lesser-known Musée Guimet boasts an impressive collection of Asian art, while the recently created Musée du Quai Branly is a vibrant tribute to indigenous arts from around the globe. Heading outside Paris, exploring the Palace

---

Population: 2 243 833.

Michelin Map: 312 D 2

Info: There are several tourist Welcome Centres in the city: http://en.parisinfo.com.

- **Pyramides,** 25 r. des Pyramides;
- **Gare de l'Est,** pl. du 11 novembre 1918;
- **Gare de Lyon,** 20 bd Diderot;
- **Gare du Nord** 18 r. de Dunkerque;
- **Anvers,** 72 bd Rochechouart;
- **Paris Expo,** 1 pl. de la Porte de Versailles;
- **Clémenceau,** corner of ave des Champs-Élysées and ave Marigny;
- **Carrousel du Louvre** 99 r. de Rivoli;
- **Montmartre** 21 pl. du Tertre.

Location: Paris is France's capital and its largest city. It lies in the middle of the Île-de-France region, which sits between the Centre, Bougogne, Champagne-Ardennes, Picardie and Haute Normandie regions. Paris is 85.6km/53mi SW of Compiègne; 69km/42.8mi NW of Fontainebleau; 104km/64.6mi SE of Les Andelys.

Don't Miss: Arc de Triomphe, Eiffel Tower, Notre-Dame Cathedral, the Champs-Élysées, Quartier Latin, Montmartre, the Louvre and the Musée d'Orsay, but don't fall for trying to see everything in 1 or 2 days… come back.

Kids: Cité des Sciences et l'Industrie, the spherical cinema La Géode, Cité des Enfants, Jardin de Luxembourg, Palais de Découverte.

GETTING THERE

BY AIR – Paris is served by two major international **airports**: Roissy-Charles de Gaulle 23km/14.3mi to the north of Paris on the A1, and Orly 11km/6.8mi to the south along the A6. Domestic flights are handled by Orly.

Public services giving access to and from the city include Air France coaches, public transport (RATP) buses, private minibuses, easyBus, RER trains and taxis.

BY TRAIN – Eurostar runs via the Channel Tunnel between **London** (St Pancras) and **Paris** (Gare du Nord) in 2hr 15min (www.eurostar.com).

All rail services throughout France (including Eurostar) can be arranged through **Voyages-SNCF** in the UK. Personal callers are welcome to drop into Voyages-SNCF Travel Centre, 193 Piccadilly, LONDON W1J 9EU. ✆0844 848 5 848; www.voyages-sncf.com.

GETTING AROUND

The **Seine river** flows east–west across the city. Places north of the river are on the ***rive droite***, while those to the south are on the ***rive gauche***. Paris is divided into 20 **arrondissements** (districts or neighbourhoods), each one with its own local government and characteristics. Each *arrondissement* is further divided into a number of neighbourhoods determined by history and the people who live there.

BY RAIL – **The métro** and **RER** are the easiest and most economical way of moving around the city. **Line 1**, which crosses **Paris east–west**, services many of the most famous attractions: the Louvre, the Champs-Élysées and the Arc de Triomphe. **Line 4** is useful for travelling across the **city from north–south**. The metro also services the immediate suburbs of Paris, but for those a bit farther out, use the **RER suburban** trains.

BY BUS – Like all forms of public transport, Parisian buses – depending to some extent on the line – can be slightly unpredictable in terms of punctuality and comfort: they can get extremely crowded, so it is best to avoid rush hours if possible. Nonetheless, the bus remains a great way to see Paris. All bus trips in Paris and the immediate suburbs require one ticket (no transfers). These are the same as the tickets used in the metro, and you can save money by buying a pass or a book of ten tickets ahead of time. On board the bus, you can buy tickets individually from the driver, at a higher price.

BY TAXI – There are over 18 000 taxis in Paris, cruising the streets day and night and parked in over 700 ranks close to road junctions and other frequented points beneath signs labelled 'Taxis'.

Taxis may also be hailed in the street when the white taxi sign is fully lit. However, you cannot hail a taxi if it is less than 50m from a taxi rank, it is in a bus lane, or if it is already reserved. The rate (between €1 and €1.55 per km) varies according to the zone and time of day (higher rates between 5pm and 10am, and in the suburbs and beyond). The white, orange and blue lights correspond to the three different rates A, B and C and these appear on the meter inside the cab. A supplementary charge is made for baggage over 5kg, or unwieldy items such as skis, baby stroller, as well as for a fourth or fifth person (www.taxi-paris.net).

Since 2007 in Paris, a unique number to call (01 45 30 30 30) has been in place allowing you to call taxis equipped with a terminal. ♿See also the Porte-à-Porte taxi service between stations for a fixed price starting at €9.90 – www.pap.sncf.com/starcab.

BY BICYCLE – **Vélib'** – There is a popular self-hire bike service in Paris, available 24hr a day, seven days a week. Simply go to the self-service machines and follow the instructions to choose from a range of bikes, using your credit card (www.velib.paris.fr).

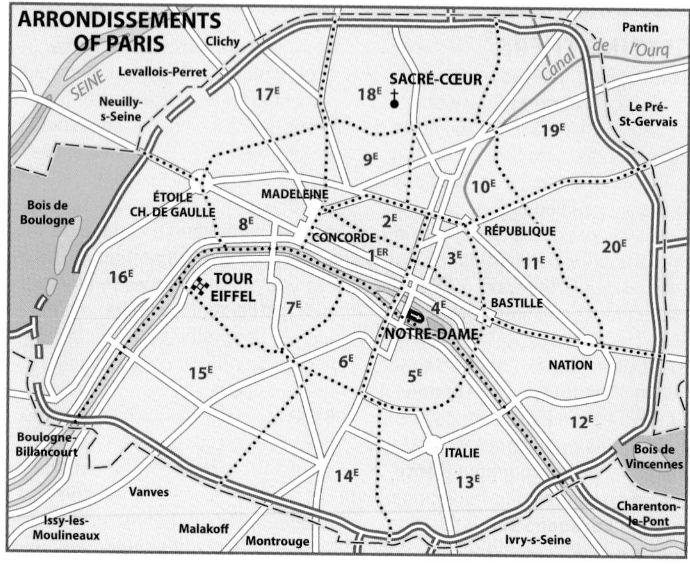

Paris Pass

The Paris Pass is valid for 2, 4 or 6 consecutive days (€122, €182 and €219 respectively) and provides unlimited access to more than 60 museums and monuments; to the best attractions; free unlimited travel on the Metro; free hop-on hop-off bus tours of Paris… and much more, including a 120-page guidebook to Paris. www.parispass.com.

of Versailles (UNESCO World Heritage site) is a must. The National Museum of Archeology in St-Germain hosts unique sculptures from prehistoric France. Why not pay a visit to the workshops of the National Manufacture of Porcelain in Sèvres? You might also explore Rodin's house in Meudon, where the sculptor produced some of his legendary works.

URBAN LANDSCAPE

Can you imagine picnicking in the Gallo-Roman-era Arènes de Lutèce? Or relaxing on a lounge chair overlooking the Seine? Each summer, several kilometres of a usually busy road are converted into Paris-Plage, a sunny beach complete with palm trees and sand. Civil architecture in and around Paris ranges from the bizarre – witness the colourful pipes of Centre Georges Pompidou, built by Renzo Piano in the 1970s – to the pure classicism of Versailles and the Louvre. The fashionable Marais abounds in quaint 17C mansions, but the city's dominant style is 19C Haussmanian cut- stone buildings. But Paris isn't merely a city dwelling in its glorious past. The skyscrapers and imposing cubic Arche at La Défense and newborn Bibliothèque Nationale district remind us that Paris is a dynamic urban community.

PARKS AND GARDENS

Paris' oldest public garden, the Jardin des Plantes, dates to the early 17C. But most green spaces in the Paris region were created in the 19C; outstanding examples include the Buttes-Chaumont, Bois de Vincennes and Bois de Boulogne. The royal park at Versailles is a remarkable composition of gardens, musical fountains and canals. Quiet Parc de Sceaux and Parc de St-Cloud also merit a visit. Finally, don't miss the views of the capital from the gardens of the castle at St-Germain-en-Laye.

A Bit of History

ORIGINS

At the time of the fall of the Roman Empire towards the end of the 5C, Paris was a modest township founded seven centuries previously by Gallic fishermen. Following its occupation by the **Romans**, the settlement was extended south of the river to where the remains of the Cluny Baths and a 2C amphitheatre now stand: the **Quartier Latin**. In the 3C, St Denis, Paris' first bishop, had met his martyrdom and the Barbarians had razed the place to the ground. This destruction, together with the threat posed by Attila's hordes (but supposedly averted by the intervention of St Geneviève, patron saint of the city), had prompted inhabitants to withdraw to the security of the Île de la Cité.

Clovis, King of **the Franks**, settled in Paris in 506. Two years later, he founded an abbey south of the Seine in honour of St Geneviève, just as 35 years previously a basilica had been erected over the tomb of St Denis. In 885, for the fifth time in 40 years, the Norsemen sailed up the river and attacked Paris; **Odo**, son of Robert the Strong, bravely led the local resistance, and was elected king of "France" in 888. From then on, Paris was the seat of royal power, albeit with some interruptions.

THE CAPETIAN DYNASTY (987–1328)

In 1136, **Abbot Suger** rebuilt the abbey church of St-Denis in the revolutionary Gothic style, an example soon followed by Maurice de Sully at Notre-Dame. Between 1180 and 1210, **Philippe Auguste** surrounded the growing city with a continuous ring of fortifications anchored on the Louvre fortress. In 1215 France's first university was founded on the St-Geneviève hill.

THE HOUSE OF VALOIS (1328–1589)

On 22 February 1358, **Étienne Marcel**, the merchants' provost, succeeded in rousing the townsfolk to break into the Law Courts (Palais de Justice); entering the Dauphin's apartments, he slew two of the future Charles V's counsellors before the former's eyes. On becoming king, **Charles V** quit this place of ill memory. In 1370, he built himself a stronghold in the eastern part of the city, the **Bastille**, which became the centrepiece of a new ring of fortifications. Paris was taken by the English in 1418. **Joan of Arc** was wounded in front of Porte St-Honoré trying to retake the city in 1429. Paris was won back for France eight years later by Charles VII.

In 1492, the discovery of America marked the first beginnings of a new outlook and the modern age. The Neapolitan artists brought back by **Charles VIII** from his campaigns in Italy were introducing new trends in taste and thought; the influence of the Renaissance became apparent in many new buildings. In the 1560s, the brothers **Du Cerceau** drew up the plans for the Flore Pavilion abutting the Louvre to the west, then set about the construction of the Pont Neuf (New Bridge), which today is the city's oldest surviving bridge. On 24 August 1572, bells rang out at St-Germain-l'Auxerrois to signal the start of the **St Bartholomew's Day Massacre** (of Protestants); Henri of Navarre, the future **Henri IV**, just married to Marguerite of Valois, barely escaped with his life. In 1589, **Henri III** was assassinated at St-Cloud in 1589 by the monk **Jacques Clément**, ending the Valois line.

THE BOURBONS (1589–1789)

In 1594 Paris opened its gates to **Henri IV**, the new king who had renounced his Protestant faith and succeeded in pacifying the country. But on 14 May 1610 in the Rue de la Ferronnerie, this monarch too fell victim to an assassin. Under **Louis XIII** (1610–43), **Métezeau** designed an imposing Classical west facade for St-Gervais Church, the first of its kind in Paris; **Salomon de Brosse** built the Luxembourg Palace for Marie de' Medici; Jean Androuet Du Cerceau laid out the courtyards and gardens of the Hôtel de Béthune-Sully. As well as erecting a church for the Sorbonne with Classical columns on its courtyard side, **Lemercier** built the Palais-Royal for **Richelieu**. On the king's death in 1643, **Anne of Austria** became Regent, acting in concert with Mazarin and continuing the policies of Richelieu. Paris fell prey to the series of disturbances caused by unrest among the nobility and known as the **Fronde**; the young king concluded that it might be advantageous to separate Court from city.

The 23-year-old **Louis XIV** began his long and highly personal reign in 1661. Even more than the splendour of court life, it was the extraordinary advancement of the arts and literature at this time that gave Paris and France such prestige in Europe. Under the protection of a king keen to encourage artistic endeavour and promote creative confidence, writers, painters, sculptors and landscapers flourished as never before. In the space of 20 years, the great **Le Nôtre** redesigned the parterres of the Tuileries; Claude Perrault provided the Louvre with its fine colonnade and built the Observatory; Le Vau completed the greater part of both the Institut de France and the Louvre. France's "Century of Greatness" came to an end with Louis XIV's death in 1715.

The country now found itself, for the second time, under the rule of a five-year-old. The running of the country was therefore put into the hands of a regent, **Philippe d'Orléans**; the first action of the court was to pack its bags and quit the boredom of Versailles for the gaiety of the capital. A long period of peace accompanied the years of corruption; for 77 years France experienced no foreign incursions. Literary salons flourished, notably those of the Marquise de Lambert, Mme Du Deffand and Mme Geoffrin, all helping the spread of new ideas in what became known as the **Age of Enlightenment**. The Palais Bourbon (1722–28), which now houses the National Assembly, was erected at this time.

The personal rule exercised by **Louis XV** was discredited by his favourites, but Paris nevertheless witnessed a number of great personalities and important advances; such as **Charles de la Condamine**, a surveyor and naturalist responsible for the discovery of rubber (1751); **Jussieu**, incumbent of the Chair in Botany at the Botanical Gardens, responsible for a systematic classification of plants (1759) and for many advances in pharmacology; **Diderot**, author, together with **d'Alambert**, of the great *Encyclopaedia*, a splendid summary of the technology of the age; **Chardin**, who had lodgings in the Louvre, devoted himself to working in pastel; **Robert Pothier**, who wrote the *Treatise of Obligations*, or **Ange-Jacques** Gabriel, the last and most famous of a line of architects linked to **Mansart** and **Robert de Cotte**, who between them gave France a hundred years of architectural unity. It was **Gabriel** who designed the magnificent façades fronting the Place de la Concorde, the west front of St-Roch Church and the École Militaire (Military Academy). Finally there was **Soufflot**, creator of the dome which crowns the Panthéon.

Distinguished furniture-makers were at work too: **Lardin** with his cabinets and commodes with rosewood inlay, and **Boudin** with his virtuoso marquetry and secret compartments; they anticipated the masters who were to emerge in the following reign.

REVOLUTION AND EMPIRE (1789–1814)

In 1788, King **Louis XVI (1774–92)** decided to convene the States-General. The delegates assembled at Versailles on 5 May 1789. As a result, on 17 June, the States-General transformed itself into a **National Assembly** which styled itself the Constituent Assembly on 9 July; the monarchy would eventually become a constitutional one.

On **14 July 1789**, in the space of less than an hour, the people of Paris took over the **Bastille** in the hope of finding arms there; the outline of the demolished fortress can still be traced in the paving on the west side of the Place de la Bastille (14 July became a day of national celebration in 1879). On 17 July, in the City Hall (Hôtel de Ville), Louis XVI kissed the recently adopted tricolour cockade. The feudal system was abolished on 4 August, and the Declaration of the **Rights of Man** adopted on 26 August; on 5 October, the Assembly moved into the riding-school of the Tuileries, and the royal family was brought from Versailles and installed in the Tuileries Palace.

On 12 July 1790 the Church became subject to the Civil Constitution for the Clergy. Two days later, a great crowd gathered on the Champ-de-Mars to celebrate the anniversary of the fall of the Bastille; **Talleyrand**, Bishop of Autun as well as statesman and diplomat, celebrated mass on the altar of the nation and the king reaffirmed his oath of loyalty to the country.

After his attempt to join **Bouillé**'s army at Metz had been foiled, Louis was brought back to Paris on 25 June 1791; on 30 September, he was forced to accept the constitution adopted by the Assembly which then dissolved itself.

The Legislative Assembly – The new deputies met the following day in the Tuileries Riding School. On 20 June 1792, encouraged by the moderate revolutionary faction known as the Girondins, rioters invaded the Tuileries and made Louis put on the red bonnet of liberty. On 11 July, the Assembly declared France to be in danger, and during the night of 9 August the mob (*sans-culottes*) instituted a "revolutionary **commune**" with the status of an organ of government. The next day, the Tuileries were sacked and 600 of the Swiss Guards massacred. The Assembly responded by depriving the king of his few remaining responsibilities and confining him with his family in the tower of the Templar Prison (Tour du Temple). Soon after, the "**September Massacres**" began; 1 200 prisoners, some "politicals", but most of them common offenders, were hauled from the city's jails and arbitrarily executed on the Buci crossroads in a frenzy of fear and panic precipitated by fear of invasion. This grisly event marked the beginning of a particularly violent period known as the Terror. On 21 September, the day after the French defeat at the Battle of Valmy, the Legislative Assembly gave way to the Convention.

The Convention – At its very first meeting, the new assembly, now in the hands of the Girondins, formally abolished the monarchy and proclaimed the **Republic**. This day, 21 September 1792, became Day 1 of Year One in the new revolutionary calendar (which remained in force until 31 December 1805). At the end of May, beset by difficulties at home and abroad and bereft of popular support, the Girondins fell, to be replaced by the "Mountain" (the extreme Jacobin faction, so-called because they occupied the upper tiers of seating in the Assembly).

In one of the faction's first acts, Louis XVI was guillotined on 21 January 1793 on the Place de la Concorde. On 17 September, the Law of Suspects was passed, legalising **the Terror**. The first to be executed by the revolutionary tribunals were the Girondins, in October 1793. On 8 June 1794, **Robespierre** the "Incorruptible" presided over the **Festival of the Supreme Being**. The event was orchestrated by the painter **David**, beginning in the Tuileries Gardens and proceeding to the Champ-de-Mars.

On 10 June (9 Prairial), the Great Terror began. Over a period of two months, the "national razor", as the guillotine was known, was to slice off 2 561 heads. Among those executed was Lavoisier, former Farmer-General and eminent chemist, responsible for the formulation of the theory of the conservation of mass on which much of modern chemistry rests, and **André Chénier**, the lyric poet who had condemned the excesses of the regime in his verse. The end of the Terror came with the fall and execution of Robespierre himself, on 27 July.

The **Thermidorian Convention** now attempted to put the sickening spectacle of the scaffold behind it with a policy calculated to promote stability. Among its most important achievements were measures designed to advance science and learning, including the founding of the École Polytechnique (School of

Engineering); the creation of the Conservatoire des Arts et Métiers (National Technical Institution), and the setting up of the École Normale (the prestigious college). In 1795, the metric system was adopted and the Office of Longitudes founded. Just before the Assembly's dissolution on 25 October, **public education** was instituted and the Institut de France founded, embracing the nation's learned academies, including the **Académie Française**.

The Directory and the Consulate – The period of the Directory was marked, in 1798, by the very first Universal Exhibition, but was brought to an end with the *coup d'état* of 9 November (18 Brumaire) 1799, when the Council of Elders persuaded the legislature to move to St-Cloud as a precautionary measure against Jacobin plots. On the following day, **Napoléon Bonaparte** entered the chamber to address the delegates, but was booed; he was saved by the presence of mind of his brother Lucien, who used the guard to disperse the members. By the same evening, power was in the hands of three consuls; this marked the end of the Revolution. In less than five years, the Consulate allowed Napoléon to centralise power, opening the way to the realisation of his Imperial ambitions.

The Empire – Proclaimed Emperor of France by the Senate on 18 May 1804, Napoléon I was anointed on 2 December by Pope Pius VII at Notre-Dame, though it was he himself who actually put the crown on his head in a ceremony immortalised by David. His reign was marked by the promulgation in 1804 of the **Civil Code**, which he had helped draft himself when he was still First Consul, and which, as the *Code Napoléon*, has since formed the legal basis of many other countries. In order to make Paris into a truly imperial capital, Napoléon ordered the erection of a great column in the Place Vendôme; cast from the melted-down metal of guns taken at the Battle of Austerlitz (Slavkov), it commemorated the victories of his *Grande Armée*. **Vignon** was commissioned to design a temple, which nearly became a railway station before ending up as the Madeleine Church; **Chalgrin** was put to work drawing up plans for a great triumphal arch (Arc de Triomphe); **Brongniart** built the Stock Exchange (Bourse); **Percier** and **Fontaine**, the promoters of the Empire style, constructed the north wing of the Louvre and the Carrousel Arch (Arc du Carrousel); **Gros** painted the battles and **Géricault** the cavalry of the *Grande Armée*.

On 31 March 1814, despite strong resistance offered by **Daumesnil** at Vincennes, the Allies occupied Paris. On 11 April, the Emperor, "the sole obstacle to peace in Europe", put his signature to the document of abdication at Fontainebleau.

THE RESTORATION (MAY 1814–FEBRUARY 1848)

The reign of Louis XVIII – 1814–24 The period of rule by Louis XVI's brother was interrupted by the Hundred Days of Napoléon's attempt to re-establish himself between his sojourn on Elba and his final exile to St Helena. During the years of Louis XVIII's reign, **Laënnec** invented the stethoscope, wrote his *Treatise on Mediate Auscultation* and founded the anatomo-clinical school together with **Bayle** and **Dupuytren**; **Pinel** studied mental illness at the Salpêtrière Hospital; **Cuvier** put biology on a sounder footing, formulated the principles of subordination of organs to their function and established a zoological classification; **Bertholet** studied the composition of acids, **Sadi Carnot** thermodynamics and temperature equilibrium, and **Arago** electromagnetism and the polarisation of light; **Daguerre** laid the foundations of his fame with his dioramas, and Lamartine conquered literary society with his *Méditations Poétiques* – its elegaic rhythms soothed Talleyrand's sleepless nights.

The reign of Charles X – 1824–30 Painting flourished with the brilliant sweep of **Delacroix**' great canvases and **Corot**'s landscapes. At the same time, Laplace was establishing the fundamental laws of mathematical analysis and providing a firm basis for astronomical mechanics, and **Berlioz** was composing his *Fantastic Symphony*, the key work of the Romantic Movement in music.

On 21 February 1830, **Victor Hugo**'s drama *Hernani* provoked a literary battle between "moderns" and "classicals" in which the latter were temporarily routed. In the summer, Charles' press ordinances provoked a crisis which led to his abdication; he was succeeded by **Louis Philippe**, a member of the cadet branch of the Bourbons.

Reign of Louis-Philippe – 1830–48

During the 1830s, the mathematician **Evariste Galois** put forward the theory of sets; Victor Hugo wrote *Notre-Dame de Paris* and **Alfred de Musset** *Caprices*. Chopin, the darling of Parisian society, composed scherzos, waltzes and his celebrated Polonaises. In 1838, while on holiday in Paris, **Stendhal** wrote *The Charterhouse of Parma*, a masterpiece of psychological observation which can be read on a number of levels. The first news agency was founded by **Charles Havas**. In 1839, a railway line was opened between Paris and St-Germain. The 1840s saw the publication of the *Mysteries of Paris* by **Eugène Sue**, the *Count of Monte Cristo* and the *Three Musketeers* by **Dumas** and many of the works of **Balzac**'s prodigious Human Comedy as well as the *Treatise on Parasitology* by **Raspail**. The abuses of the July monarchy, meanwhile, were satirised in the drawings of **Daumier**.

At the age of 79, Chateaubriand brought his finely chiselled *Memories from beyond the Tomb* to a triumphant conclusion. On 23 February 1848, the barricades went up on the Boulevard des Capucines and the monarchy fell; the next day, at the City Hall, amid scenes of wild enthusiasm, **Lamartine** saluted the tricolour: "the flag which has spread the name of France, freedom and glory around the wide world".

SECOND REPUBLIC

The abolition of the National Workshops in June 1848 led to rioting in the St-Antoine district, in which the archbishop of Paris was killed. In 1849, **Léon Foucault** proved the rotation and spherical nature of the earth by means of a pendulum (the experiment was repeated in 1855 from the dome of the Panthéon). On 2 December 1851 the short life of the Second Republic was ended by a *coup d'état*.

SECOND EMPIRE – 1852–70

Two great exhibitions (in 1855 and 1867) proclaimed the prosperity France enjoyed under the rule of Bonaparte's nephew, **Napoléon III. Baron Haussmann**, Prefect of the *Département* of the Seine, was responsible for an ambitious programme of public works which transformed the capital, giving it many of the features which now seem quintessentially Parisian. Among them were the laying out of the Bois de Boulogne and the Bois de Vincennes, and the building of railway stations and the North Wing of the Louvre. But the Baron is remembered above all for the ruthless surgery he performed on the capital's ancient urban tissue, opening up new focal points (Place de l'Opéra) and linking them with great axial roadways (Grands Boulevards), splendid exercises in traffic engineering and crowd control. In 1852, **Alexandre Dumas** wrote *The Lady of the Camellias* at the same time Rudé was working on the memorial to Marshal Ney, which was to be placed on the spot where the great soldier had been executed in 1815; in Rodin's opinion, it was Paris' finest statue. In 1857 Baudelaire, the first poet of the teeming modern metropolis, published *Les Fleurs du Mal (The Flowers of Evil)*. In 1859, Gounod presented *Faust* at the Opéra Lyrique. In 1860, Étienne Lenoir registered his first patent for the internal combustion engine.

The year 1863 was marked by the scandals caused by **Manet**'s *Déjeuner sur l'herbe* and *Olympia*; Baltard masked the masterly iron structure of the St-Augustin Church with the stone cladding still obligatory in a religious building. In 1896 Pierre de Coubertin created the **International Olympic Committee**.

REPUBLICAN CONTINUITY (1870 – PRESENT DAY)

On 4 September 1870, the mob which had invaded the National Assembly was led by Gambetta to City Hall, declaring the Republic. The new government prepared to defend Paris against the advancing Prussians; the St-Cloud Château was set on fire and a fierce battle took place at Le Bourget.

The ensuing siege subjected Parisians to terrible hardships; food ran out and the winter was exceptionally severe. The city surrendered on 28 January 1871. The revolutionary **Commune** was ruthlessly suppressed by military force, but not before the Communards had burnt down the City Hall, the Tuileries and the Audit Office (Cours des Comptes – on the site of what is now the Orsay Museum), pulled down the column in the Place Vendôme and shot their prisoners at the Hostages' Wall in the Rue Haxo. They made their last stand in the Père-Lachaise Cemetery, where those Communards who had survived the bitter fighting were summarily executed at the Federalists' Wall (**Mur des Fédérés**).

Political institutions were re-established and the nation revived; the Republic was consolidated as France's political regime, notwithstanding **Marshal Pétain**'s 'État Français', Nazi occupation and the provisional government following the end of World War II.

Third Republic – **Carpeaux** sculpted the Four Corners of the World for the Observatory Fountain, and **Émile Littré** published his *Dictionary of the French Language*. **Bizet** wrote *L'Arlésienne (The Woman of Arles)* for the Odéon theatre and followed it with *Carmen*, based on a story by **Mérimée**.

In 1874, **Degas** painted *The Dancing Class* and **Monet** *Impression: Rising Sun*, which inspired the initially derisive term "Impressionism". Later, **Renoir** worked at the Moulin de la Galette, and **Puvis de Chavannes** decorated the walls of the Panthéon. Rodin sculpted the *Thinker*, followed by figures of Balzac and Victor Hugo.

In 1879, **Seulecq** presented the principle of sequential transmission on which television is based and **Pasteur** completed his vast body of work. **Seurat**'s Grande Jatte heralded the establishment of the Pointillist school of painting. The engineer **Gustave Eiffel** completed his great tower, centrepiece of the Universal Exhibition of 1889. In the century's final decade, **Toulouse-Lautrec** painted cabaret scenes and **Pissarro** Parisian townscapes, and **Forain** gained fame as a marvellous caricaturist. At the Catholic Institute, Édouard **Branly** discovered radio conductors.

In 1891, René **Panhard** built the first petrol-engine motor car, which drove across Paris. In 1898, the young Louis

Sacré-Cœur Basilica, Montmartre

Famous artists

On 19 December 1915, Édith Giovanna Gassion was born to abject poverty at the Tenon Hospital (but popular legend had her come into the world under a lamppost on the steps of No. 72 r. de Belleville). She later sang in the streets, before becoming a radio, gramophone and music-hall success in 1935 under the name of **Édith Piaf**. Beloved for the instinctive but deeply moving tones of her voice, she came to embody the spirit of France *(La vie en rose, Les cloches).*

Another famous figure was **Maurice Chevalier** (1888–1972), film star, entertainer and cabaret singer; he paired with Jeanne Mistinguett at the Folies Bergère (1911) and sang at the Casino de Paris between the World Wars. Before attaining fame on Broadway in blacktie and boater, he was known at home for songs that are rooted in Belleville: *Ma Pomme, Prosper and un gars du Ménilmontant.*

Renault built his first car, then founded his Billancourt factory; in 1902 he patented a turbocharger. The factory turned out cars, lorries, planes and, in 1917, light tanks that contributed to the German defeat in 1918. In 1898 Pierre and **Marie Curie** isolated radium and established the atomic character of radioactivity; their laboratory has since disappeared, but its outline is shown in the courtyard of the school at 10 rue Vauquelin. **Girault** used steel, stone and glass to construct the Grand Palais and Petit Palais exhibition halls for the 1900 Exhibition. This occasion also saw the bridging of the Seine by the great flattened arch of the Pont Alexandre III. In 1906, **Santos-Dumont** took off in a aircraft, staying aloft for 21 seconds and travelling 220m.

At Montparnasse, artists **Soutine**, **Zadkine**, **Chagall**, **Modigliani** and **Léger** took up studios; **Brancusi**'s work was evolving towards abstraction (*The Sleeping Muse*). In 1913, the Théâtre des Champs-Élysées theatre opened with a controversial performance of **Stravinsky**'s *Rite of Spring*. In 1914 construction of the Sacré-Cœur Basilica was completed. On 31 July, the eve of the outbreak of World War I, **Jean Jaurès** was assassinated.

THE WORLD WARS

World War I (1914–18) put civilians and soldiers to the severest of tests. After three years of conflict, **Clemenceau** assumed leadership of France, earning the title "Father of Victory". In 1920, the interment of an unknown soldier at the Arc de Triomphe marked France's recognition of the sacrifices made by ordinary soldiers.

In the 1920s, **Le Corbusier** built the La Roche Villa, **Bourdelle** sculpted *"France"* at the Palais de Tokyo; **Georges Rouault** completed *Miserere*, **Maurice Ravel** composed *Boléro* for the dancer Ida Rubinstein and **Cocteau** wrote *Les Enfants Terribles*. In 1934, André Citroën introduced the front-wheel drive car.

Paris was bombed in 1940 during **World War II**, then **occupied**. In July 1942, police rounded up over 13 000 French Jews at the **Vélodrome d'Hiver** prior to deporting them to Nazi death camps; 4 500 members of the Resistance also perished in the clearing on Mount Valérien, where the National Memorial of Fighting France now stands. On 19 August 1944, Paris was **liberated.**

Fourth and Fifth Republics – Post-WWII thinkers like Jean-Paul Sartre, Simone de Beauvoir and Albert Camus brought new ideas in art and philosophy, including Existentialism, to the fore.

In May 1968, a student-led revolt at the Sorbonne ushered in a major social and cultural revolution, propelled by others around the world.

MODERN ERA

The Opera house at la Bastille, the Ministry of Finance buildings at Bercy, the Grande Arche at la Défense and the Bibliothèque nationale de France François-Mitterand at Tolbiac are distinctive modern landmarks.

Arrondissements 1–4

Harbouring the historic Île de la Cité, the awe-inspiring Notre-Dame Cathedral and Sainte-Chapelle, the Louvre, Tuileries, Palais Royal, and the Marais district with its heady mixture of Renaissance charm and hip urban culture, arrondissements 1–4 make up the heart of classical Right-Bank Paris.

- **Michelin Map:** 312 D 2. See p118–119.
- **Info:** 08 92 68 30 00 or http://en.parisinfo.com.
- **Location:** Stretching from the city centre, through the Sentier, Temple and Marais districts, the Île de la Cité and Île St-Louis.
- **Don't MIss:** Notre-Dame Cathedral, Louvre, Marais.
- **Kids:** Ice cream from Berthillon on the Île St Louis.

NOTRE-DAME CATHÉDRAL ★★★

r. du cloître Notre-Dame.
Cathedral open daily 8am–6.45pm (Sat-Sun 8am–7.15pm). No charge. Guided tours in English Wed and Thu 2pm, Sat 2.30pm. **Towers** open Apr–Sep 10am–6.30pm; Oct–Mar 10am–5.30pm; €8.50. 01 53 10 07 00; www.notredamedeparis.fr.

A bronze star embedded in the pavement outside Notre-Dame is the point from which distances to Paris are measured.

Maurice de Sully began work on the cathedral in 1163, but people have worshipped at the site for 2 000 years and the present building has witnessed the great events of French history.

Notre-Dame is the last great galleried church building and one of the first with flying buttresses. In 1245 the bulk of the work was complete and St Louis held a ceremony for the knighting of his son, also placing the Crown of Thorns in the cathedral until the nearby Sainte-Chapelle was ready to receive it. In 1250 the twin towers were finished.

In 1430, the cathedral hosted the coronation of the young Henry VI of England as King of France; in 1455, the late Joan of Arc was rehabilitated here in a ceremony; in 1558, Mary Stuart was crowned here on becoming Queen of France by her marriage to François II; in 1572, the Huguenot Henri IV married Marguerite of Valois; in 1594 the king converted to the Catholic faith.

East end of Notre-Dame

Notre Dame has endured mutilations of various kinds throughout its history: in 1699 the choir screen was demolished, and later some of the original stained glass was removed to let in more light; the central portal was also demolished (18C) to facilitate processions. During the 1789 Revolution, statues were destroyed and the cathedral declared a Temple of Reason. It was in a much-dilapidated building that Napoléon Bonaparte crowned himself Emperor and the King of Rome was baptised. In 1831, Hugo's novel *Notre-Dame de Paris* sensitised public opinion to the poor state of the building, and in 1841 Louis-Philippe charged Viollet-le-Duc with its restoration. In the space of 24 years, he completed his work in accordance with his own, idealised vision of the Gothic style. Though often criticised, it should be seen in the context of the wholesale demolition of the medieval Île-de-la-Cité and its replacement with administrative buildings.

The magnificent Cloister Portal (Portail du Cloître–north transept) is 30 years older than the west front portals; with its richly carved gables and smiling figure of the Virgin – the only original large sculpture to have survived – it demonstrates how far the art of sculpture had advanced over the period. At the beginning of the 14C, the bold array of flying buttresses was sent soaring over the ambulatory and galleries to hold the high vaults of the east end in place.

Above the Kings' Gallery is the great rose window, which conserves its medieval glass. An enterprise of considerable daring – it was the largest such window of its time – it shows no sign of distortion after 700 years and has often been imitated. Inside, the rose window has particularly fine stained glass of a deep bluish-mauve.

SAINTE-CHAPELLE★★★

4 bd. du Palais. ♿ Open Mar–Oct 9.30am–6pm (until 9pm on Wed from mid-May–mid-Sept); Nov–Feb 9am–5pm. Closed 1 Jan, 1 May, 1 and 25 Dec. €8.50. ✆ 01 53 40 60 80; http://sainte-chapelle.monuments-nationaux.fr.

Only 80 years separate this definitive masterpiece of the High Gothic from the Transitional Gothic of Notre-Dame, but the difference is striking; in the lightness and clarity of its structure, the Sainte-Chapelle pushes Gothic ideas to the limit. The chapel was built on the orders of St Louis to house the recently acquired relics of the Passion within the precincts of the royal palace; it was completed in a record time of 33 months.

The upper chapel resembles a shrine, with walls made almost entirely of remarkable stained glass covering a total area of 618sq m; 1 134 different scenes are depicted, of which 720 are made of original glass. The windows rise to a height of 15m. By 1240, the stained glass at Chartres had been completed, and the king was able to summon the master craftsmen who had worked on them to Paris. This explains the similarity between the glass of the cathedral and of the chapel, in terms of the scenes shown and the luminous colour which eclipses the simplicity of the design.

The original rose window is shown in a scene from the Très Riches Heures du Duc de Berry; the present rose window is a product of the Flamboyant Gothic, ordered by Charles VII, and depicts the Apocalypse of St John. It is characteristic of its age in the design of its tracery and in the subtle variations of colour which had replaced the earlier method of juxtaposing numerous small coloured panes.

PALAIS DE JUSTICE AND CONCIERGERIE★★

2 bd. du Palais. **Palais** open Mon–Sat 8.30am–6pm. Closed public holidays. Visitors are normally allowed to attend a civil or criminal hearing. ✆ 01 44 32 52 52. **Conciergerie** open daily Mar–Oct 9.30am–6pm; Nov–Feb 9am–5pm. Closed 1 Jan, 1 May, 25 Dec. €7.50. ✆ 01 53 40 60 80.

Known as the Palace (Palais), this is the principal seat of civil and judicial authority. Before becoming the royal palace of the rulers of medieval France, it served as the residence of Roman governors, Merovingian kings and the children of Clovis.

The Capetian kings built a chapel and fortified the palace with a keep. Philippe le Bel (the Fair) entrusted Enguerrand de Marigny with construction of the Conciergerie as well as with the extension and embellishment of the palace; its Gothic halls of 1313 were widely admired. Later, Charles V built the Clock Tower (Tour de l'Horloge), the city's first public clock; he also installed Parliament here, the country's supreme court. Survivals from this period include the Great Hall (Salle des gens d'Armes) with its fine capitals, the Guard Room (Salle des Gardes) with its magnificent pillars, and kitchens with monumental corner fireplaces.

The great hall on the first floor was restored by Salomon de Brosse after the fire of 1618; it was refurbished again in 1840 and once more after the fire of 1871.

The First Civil Court is in the former Grand'chambre du parlement: this is where kings dispensed justice, where the 16-year-old Louis XIV dictated his orders to Parliament, where that body in its turn demanded the convocation of the States-General in 1788, and where the Revolutionary Tribunal was set up under public prosecutor Fouquier-Tinville. The entrance to the royal palace was once guarded by the twin towers gracing the north front of the great complex; this is the oldest part of the building, albeit now hiding behind a 19C neo-Gothic façade.

The **Conciergerie** served as antechamber to the guillotine during the Terror, housing up to 1 200 detainees at a time. The Galerie des Prisonniers, Marie-Antoinette's cell and the Chapelle des Girondins are most moving.

HÔTEL DE VILLE★

pl. de l'Hôtel de Ville.

Hôtel de Ville is home to the Parisian government. Municipal government was introduced in the 13C, under the direction of leading members of the powerful watermen's guild appointed by Louis IX.

The vast plaza outside City Hall has long been the epicentre of uprising and revolt (and the scene of gory executions during the Medieval period). Throughout the French Revolution it was in the hands of the Commune, and in 1848 it became the seat of the Provisional Government. The Republic was proclaimed from here in 1870, and, on 24 March 1871, the Communards burnt it down. It was rebuilt from 1874.

ARC DE TRIOMPHE DU CARROUSEL★

This delightful pastiche, inspired by the Roman triumphal arch of Septimus Severus, was built between 1806 and 1808. Six bas-relief sculptures commemorate the Napoléonic victories of 1805. On the platform, where Napoléon placed the four horses removed from the basilica of San Marco in Venice (until these were returned in 1815), **Bosio** sculpted an allegorical goddess, representing the Restoration of the Bourbons, accompanied by Victories and driving a quadriga.

The square takes its name from the lavish equestrian and theatrical tournament held there in honour of the birth of the Dauphin (Prince) in 1662.

Standing beneath the arch affords a magnificent **view★★★** along the axis that runs from the Louvre through the Tuileries, place de la Concorde, the Champs-Élysées and the Arc de Triomphe, to the Grande Arche at La Défense.

▶ Descend one of the flights of stairs near the Carrousel, or go through the Pyramid and the main entrance.

LA GALERIE CARROUSEL DU LOUVRE

The inverted crystalline pyramid provides a well of light in the central area of the arcade; concrete masonry, rows of windows and subdued lighting combine to give the main arcade the appearance of a large entrance hall.

Hôtel de Ville

PALAIS DU LOUVRE★★★ (MUSÉE DU LOUVRE)

For eight centuries the Louvre was the seat of kings and emperors. Today it is famous for one of the richest collections of art and antiquities in the world.

Philippe Auguste (1180–1223) lived in the Palais de la Cité. In 1190 he had the Louvre fortress built on the north bank of the Seine, at the weakest point in his capital's defences against its English neighbours. This fortress was located on the southwest quarter of the present Cour Carrée. **Philip the Fair** (1285–1314) installed his arsenal and royal treasury in the Louvre, where they would remain for the next four centuries.

Charles V (1364–80) transformed the old fortress into a comfortable residence. Here he installed his famous **library** of 973 books, the largest in the kingdom. A miniature in the *Very Rich Hours* of the Duke of Berry depicts this attractive Louvre, surrounded by new ramparts, which put an end to its military career. After Charles V, the Louvre was not inhabited by royalty for the next 150 years.

François I (1515–47) lived mainly in the Loire Valley or the Marais. In 1528, in desperate need of money, he planned to tax the Parisian population. To soften them up, he announced his intention to take up residence in the Louvre. Rebuilding began: the keep, a bulky form, which cast a shadow over the courtyard, was razed, and the advance defences were demolished; however, orders for a new palace were not given to **Pierre Lescot** until 1546. Lescot's Renaissance-style plans, popular on the banks of the Loire, were new to Paris. By 1547, at the king's death, construction was barely visible above ground level.

Henri II (1547–59) took up residence in the Louvre and retained Lescot as chief architect. The old great hall was transformed into the **Salle des Caryatides**; on the first floor, the Salle des Cent-Suisses, reserved for the Palace Guard, preceded the royal suite in the south wing.

Catherine de' Medici (1519–89) withdrew after the death of her husband Henri II. Once declared regent, she decided to take up residence in the Louvre, on the floor since known as the Logis des Reines (Queens' Lodging), but was not content to reside in the middle of Lescot's building site. In 1564, she ordered **Philibert Delorme** to build her a residence on the site known as Les Tuileries, in which she would have greater freedom of movement. The Queen Mother planned to have a covered passage built between the two palaces to enable people to walk the 500m unnoticed and shelter from inclement weather. The connecting galleries were duly begun, but work was brought to a halt by the Wars of Religion. The old Louvre was to keep its two Gothic and two Renaissance wings until the reign of Louis XIV.

Henri IV (1589–1610) continued work on his arrival in Paris in 1594. **Louis**

Brief History of the Collections at the Louvre

François I was the first eminent patron of Italian artists of his day. Twelve paintings from his original collection, including the *Mona Lisa* by Leonardo da Vinci, *La Belle Jardinière* by Raphael and *A Portrait of François I* by Titian, are among the most important works presently in State hands. By the time Louis XIV died, over 2 500 paintings hung in the palaces of the Louvre and Versailles.

The idea of making the collection accessible to the public, as envisaged by Marigny under Louis XVI, was finally realised by the Convention on 10 August 1793, when the doors of the Grande Galerie were opened to visitors. Napoléon subsequently made the museum's collection the richest in the world by exacting a tribute in works of art from every country he conquered; many of these were reclaimed by the Allies in 1815.

In turn, Louis XVIII, Charles X and Louis-Philippe all further endowed the collections: scarcely had the *Venus de Milo* been rediscovered when she was brought to France by Dumont d'Urville. Departments for Egyptian and Assyrian art were opened. Gifts, legacies and acquisitions continue to enrich the collections of the Louvre, with over 350 000 works now catalogued.

Métezeau added an upper floor to the Galerie du Bord de l'Eau; **Jacques II Androuet Du Cerceau** completed the Petite Galerie and built the **Pavillon de Flore**, with another gallery leading off to link it with the Tuileries Palace.

Louis XIII (1610–43) undertook to enlarge the Louvre fourfold. Lemercier built the **pavillon de l'Horloge** in 1640 and the northwest corner of the courtyard, a Classical statement in response to Lescot's design.

After the death of Louis XIII, Anne of Austria moved to the Palais-Royal with the young **Louis XIV** (1643–1715). Nine years later, they moved to the Louvre, intimidated by the *Fronde* uprisings. **Le Vau** resumed work on the extension; building the **Galerie d'Apollon** and in 1662 ordered a grand new façade to close off the Cour Carrée (**Colonnade★★**). In 1682, the king moved to Versailles and construction halted.

18C–19C – The Louvre was by now so dilapidated that there was talk of tearing it down. After the brief interval of the Regency (1715–22), Louis XV lived at Versailles, whence Louis XVI was brought to Paris on 6 October 1789, briefly occupying the Tuileries until his incarceration at the Temple prison.

The Convention used the theatre and the Committee of Public Safety installed itself in the Tuileries royal apartments.

Napoléon I (1799–1814), while living in the Tuileries, took great interest in the Louvre. The emperor commissioned architects **Percier** and **Fontaine** to complete the Cour Carrée, enlarge the place du Carrousel and build the Arc de Triomphe du Carrousel. Napoléon's fall in 1814 interrupted works.

Napoléon III (1852–70), also resident of the Tuileries, oversaw completion of the Louvre. He entrusted first **Visconti**, then **Lefuel** with closing off the Grande Cour to the north. The latter compensated for the difference in levels of the two arms of the Louvre by rebuilding the **Pavillon de Flore★** in a grandiose style (high relief by **Carpeaux, The Triumph of Flora★**) and modifying a section of the Galerie du Bord de l'Eau.

The Republic – The bloody uprising of the Paris Commune resulted in the Tuileries Palace's destruction in 1871, but collections were saved. In 1875, **Lefuel** began restoration of the Louvre, proposing to rebuild the Tuileries. In 1882 the Assembly removed the ruins, obliterating associations with the past. **François Mitterrand** initiated the **Grand Louvre** project from 1981. Most work was finished by 1993, with the opening of the Richelieu wing and a fashion museum.

Colonnade

THE LOUVRE: **PRACTICAL INFORMATION**

General information: *Open daily except Tue 9am–6pm (9.45pm on Wed and Fri). 01 40 20 53 17; www.louvre.fr.* Some galleries are closed on certain days (or for restoration); check the schedule of open rooms online or call in advance. Video screens in the hall provide information about daily events at the museum. There is also a general activity programme (six languages) available at the main information desk, which comes out every three months.

Audioguides can be hired at 4 counters: under the Pyramid, at the Denon, Sully and Richelieu entrances. €5.

Location: The main entrance to the museum is at the **Pyramid**. There is also an entrance through the shopping mall of the **Carrousel du Louvre** (*metro stop Palais-Royal-Musée-du-Louvre (lines 1 and 7)*), on either side of the Arc du Carrousel, or at the Porte des Lions. You will find yourself in the well-lit **Napoléon Hall**, which leads you towards the three wings of the museum: **Denon, Richelieu** and **Sully**. There is a bookshop, restaurant and auditorium.

Parking: The closest underground car park (80 coaches, 620 cars) is **Parking Carrousel-Louvre**, on avenue du Général Lemonnier. Open daily 7am–11pm. After parking, enter the museum via the shopping mall of the Carrousel by the fortifications of Charles V.

Don't Miss: Of all the artworks inside the museum, probably the most famous are Leonardo's masterpiece, the *Mona Lisa* (La Joconde), and, among the classical works, the *Victoire de Samothrace* and the *Vénus de Milo*. All three are in the Denon section.

Timing: The Louvre cannot be enjoyed in its entirety even in several visits, let alone one. Decide what you would like to see and head for your selections. Cost notwithstanding, it is worth just concentrating on one or two sections per visit, and then keep coming back if time allows.

The information desks offer a variety of aids and amenities to enhance your visit. If not using an audioguide, choose one of the thematic trails (provided on leaflets) designed for all ages that allow you to discover both masterpieces and less well-known works while exploring a particular theme, such as the Da Vinci Code.

Kids: Children aged 4 and up can take part in one of the many workshops for young people or follow a Children's Route through the museum. See website for details.

WALKING TOUR

LOUVRE EXTERIOR

The exhibition on the History of the Louvre and the underground excavations provide insight into the palace. *For this you need an entrance ticket.*

Start from the church of St-Germain l'Auxerrois, near Metro Louvre-Rivoli. From rue de Rivoli, head for the Seine. Opposite is the immense colonnade of the Louvre Palace.

COLONNADE★★

The height and Classical harmony of the structure are fully apparent now that moats have been cleared to a depth of 7m around the rusticated base.

Head towards the river and turn right. At Pont des Arts, cross the Jardin de l'Infante to the Cour Carrée.

COUR CARRÉE★★★

The Renaissance façade is the work of **Pierre Lescot**. The expressive sculpture of the avant-corps (projecting bay) and upper storey are by **Jean Goujon**, depicting allegorical scenes, and animated figures. A nocturnal lighting system highlights the most impressive remnants of the old Louvre.

Pass under the Clock Pavilion.

Pavillon de l'Horloge (p136)

Enter Cour Napoléon.

PYRAMID★★

The Pyramid, 21m high and 33m wide at the base, was designed by architect **Ieoh Ming Pei**; it is built of sheet glass supported on a framework of stainless-steel tubes. An **equestrian statue of Louis XIV** stands on the axis leading to the Champs-Élysées.

Cross the road that traverses place du Carrousel, in the direction of the Jardins des Tuileries.

Guided tours

English-language guided tours are available Mon, Thu, Sat–Sun 9am–5.15pm, Wed and Fri 9am–8.15pm. Visitors should buy their tickets at the window marked "Accueil des groupes" under the Pyramid, 01 40 20 52 63; €12 (does not include entry to the museum). In many rooms, there are explanatory texts in several languages, placed in racks near the door.

CENTRE GEORGES-POMPIDOU★★★

pl. Georges-Pompidou. Wed–Sun 11am–10pm. Atelier Brancusi daily except Tue and 1 May, 2–6pm. €14. 01 44 78 12 33; www.centrepompidou.fr.

The "inside-out" building known to locals as "Beaubourg" is easily spotted on the Parisian skyline with its bright red, blue and white pipes and beams. Built in 1977 on the grounds that once served as parking for the marketplace at Les Halles, it's home to a modern art museum, public library, music research centre, café, several shops, an arthouse cinema and rooftop restaurant. A splendid panoramic **view★★** extends over Paris' rooftops (free with museum ticket). The architects **Richard Rogers** (British) and **Renzo Piano** (Italian) achieved a totally futuristic building. The façade appears a tangle of pipes and tubes latticed along its glass skin, earning the establishment the nickname of "the inside-out museum".

The **Musée national d'Art moderne** (National Museum of Modern Art) occupies the 4th and 5th levels. The **Bibliothèque publique d'information**, the public library known as the BPI, is on the 1st, 2nd and 3rd levels. The **IRCAM** (Institute for Acoustic and Musical Research) lies beneath place Stravinski. The centre also houses several **temporary exhibition halls** on the 1st (mezzanine) and 6th levels.

In addition, the centre provides live entertainment (dance, music, theatre), cinema performances and spoken reviews. The library is especially popular with Parisians, thanks to its late hours, open access and up-to-date collection of printed and other resources. There's an arts bookshop on level 0, a design shop and mezzanine café (with view over the main entrance) on level one, and a good restaurant, Georges (*reservations required.* ✆*01 44 78 47 99*) on level 6.

Musée national d'Art moderne★★★

pl. Georges-Pompidou. Daily except Tue and 1 May 11am–9pm (Thu 11pm). Museum and exhibitions: €14.

Ranking high among the most significant collections dedicated to modern art in the world (50 000 works and objects), this museum traces the evolution of art from Fauvism and Cubism to contemporary movements. The modern collection (1905–60) is housed on the fifth floor, whereas contemporary exhibitions from the 1960s onwards are on the fourth floor.

Outside the museum on the vast, sloping square, the Parisian sculpture workshop of **Constantin Brancusi** (1876–1957) has been entirely reconstituted in a small building, featuring the artist's tools, major works and personal art collection.

Modern collection

Fifth floor.

Forty galleries present around 900 works. Throughout the exhibition, the juxtaposition of painting and sculpture with the design and architecture of the same decade enables the visitor to obtain an overview of 20C artistic creation.

Galleries dedicated to a single artist (Matisse, Léger, Picasso, Rouault, Delaunay) alternate with thematic rooms. All the main movements of the first half of the 20C are represented here, including **Fauvism** (1905–10; Derain, Marquet, Dufy and Matisse); **Cubism** (**Braque** and **Picasso** in 1907), **Dada** (from 1913; **Marcel Duchamp**), the **Paris School** (1910–30; **Soutine, Chagall, Modigliani**, Larionov, Gontcharova), the Abstract School (from 1910; **Kandinsky, Kupka, Mondrian, Klee**), and the **Bauhaus School**.

Surrealism is represented by De Chirico, **Salvador Dalí**, Max Ernst, **Magritte**, Brauner, André Masson, Tanguy, Giacometti, Picasso and **Miró**.

The **Cobra** movement (1948–51) advocated spontaneous expression through the free use of bold colour and energetic brushstrokes (Alechinsky, Appel, Jorn). American art from the 1940s to the 1960s is represented by **Pollock, Rothko** and **Newman**.

Centre Georges-Pompidou

Contemporary collection

Fourth floor.

This collection is regularly changed and updated to reflect contemporary artistic trends and highlight the work of major personalities from around the world. The result is a dynamic, colourful world of form and movement linking art with everyday life.

Major works include *Requiem for a Dead Leaf* (Tinguely) and *Red Rhinoceros* (Veilhan). **Pop Art** is represented by **Warhol** and Rauschenberg, **New Realism** by **Klein**, **Arman**, **César**, **Niki de Saint-Phalle**, **Op** and **Kinetic Art** by **Agam** (Antechamber of the Élysée Palace private apartments) and Vasarely. There are also installations by **Dubuffet** (*The Winter Garden*), **Beuys** (*Plight*) and **Raynaud** (*Container Zero*).

Three rooms offer examples of design and architecture from the 1960s to the present (Starck, Nouvel, Perrault, Toto Ito). Space is also devoted to film, multimedia installations and Happening (**Gutaï** and **Fluxus**).

ÉGLISE ST-EUSTACHE★★

2 Impasse Saint-Eustache. Open Mon–Fri 9.30am–7pm, Sat 10am–7pm, Sun 9am–7pm. Audioguides available. No charge, but suggested donation €3. 01 42 36 31 05; http://saint-eustache.org.

Église St-Eustache interior columns

©H. Chajmowicz/Michelin

This was once the richest church in Paris, centre of the parish which included the areas around the Palais-Royal and the Halles market. It was modelled after Notre-Dame when construction began in 1532. But St-Eustache took over a hundred years to complete; tastes changed, and the building's Gothic skeleton is fleshed out with Renaissance finishes and detail.

The Flamboyant style is evident in the three-storeyed interior elevation, the vaulting of the choir, crossing and nave, lofty side aisles and flying buttresses. The Renaissance is exemplified in the Corinthian columns and in the return to the use of semicircular arches, and Classicism in P. de Champaigne's choir windows and in Colbert's tomb, designed by Le Brun in collaboration with Coysevox and Tuby. The Chapelle St-Joseph houses English sculptor Raymond Mason's commemoration of the fruit and vegetable market's move out of Paris in 1969.

MUSÉE DES ARTS ET MÉTIERS★★

60 r. Réaumur. Open daily except Mon 10am–6pm (Thu 9.30pm). Closed public holidays. €6.50. 01 53 01 82 00; www.arts-et-metiers.net.

This museum illustrates technical progress in industry and science. The visit begins with instruments used to explore the "**infinitesimal** and **infinitely remote**".

Next come **machines** and models showing **building techniques**. **Communication** is illustrated through printing, television, photography, etc. **Energy** is represented by a model of the Marly machine (1678–85), turbines, boilers and engines, while **locomotion** explores means of transport: cycles, cars, aircraft and 19C railways. The chapel displays the first steam buses and models of the Statue of Liberty, the engine of the European rocket Ariane and of Foucault's pendulum (the latter proved the Earth's rotation).

LE MARAIS★★★

Charles V's 14C move to the Hôtel St-Paul in the Marais district marked the incorporation of a suburban area into Paris. Charles VI, Henri IV and Louis XIII also resided here, making the former swamplands increasingly fashionable. The characteristic French town house, (*hôtel*) assumed its definitive form here; it became the setting for literary or philosophical *salons*.

The **Hôtel Lamoignon★** (*24 r. Pavée*) of 1584 is a typical example of a Henri III-style mansion. Jean-Baptiste Androuet Du Cerceau applied the Giant Order style with flattened pilasters, Corinthian capitals and sculpted string-course for the first time in Paris.

The Henri IV style emerges in the **Place des Vosges★★★** designed by Louis Métezeau, completed in 1612. The 36 houses retain their original symmetrical appearance with arcades, two storeys of alternating brick and stone facades and steeply pitched slate roofs pierced with dormer windows. The King's Pavilion (Pavillon du Roi) lies at the southern end, balanced by the Queen's Pavilion (Pavillon de la Reine) at the sunnier northern end.

Louis XIII's reign heralds the Classical style. In 1624, Jean Androuet Du Cerceau built the **Hôtel de Sully★** (*62 r. Saint-Antoine*) with a gateway framed between massive pavilions, and a main courtyard (**cour d'honneur★★★**) with triangular and curved pediments complemented by scrolled dormer windows.

The early Louis XIV style is seen in Mansart's 1648 **Hôtel Guénégaud★★** (*60 r. des Archives*), where a majestic staircase and small formal garden make it one of the finest Marais houses. Other examples include Le Pautre's **Hôtel de Beauvais★** (*68 r. François Miron*) with its curved balcony on brackets and its ingenious internal layout; the **Hôtel Carnavalet★** (*23 r. de Sévigné*), a Renaissance house rebuilt by Mansart in 1655, and Cottard's **Hôtel Amelot-de-Bisseuil★** (*47 r. Vieille-du-Temple*) of somewhat theatrical design with its cornice and curved pediment decorated with allegorical figures.

The later Louis XIV style features in two adjoining *hôtels* built by Delamair: the **Hôtel de Rohan★★** (*87 r. Vieille-du-Temple*) with its wonderful sculpture of the *Horses of Apollo (Chevaux frémissants d'Apollon à l'abreuvoir)* by Robert Le Lorrain; and the **Hôtel de Soubise★★** (*60 r. des Francs-Bourgeois*) with its horseshoe-shaped courtyard and double colonnade. They are characterised by raised ground floors, massive windows, roof balustrades and the sculpture of their projecting central sections.

Arrondissements 5–7 & 16

Moving across the Seine to the Left Bank, arrondissements 5–7 harbour many of Paris' legendary places, from the quaint streets of the Quartier Latin or St-Germain-des-Prés and their dizzying intellectual heritage, to the Musée d'Orsay and Eiffel Tower, symbols of a city ushering itself into modernity.

- **Michelin Map:** 312 D 2. See p118–119.
- **Info:** ℘08 92 68 30 00 or http://en.parisinfo.com.
- **Location:** Beginning near St-Michel and heading west to St-Germain-des-Prés, then toward the Quai d'Orsay and the Eiffel Tower.
- **Don't MIss:** Quartier Latin, Musée d'Orsay, Eiffel Tower.
- **Kids:** The Jardin des Plantes and its quaint zoo.

QUARTIER LATIN★★★

Lying on the left bank of the Seine and the slopes of the mount "**Montagne" Ste-Geneviève**, the Quartier Latin concentrates many of the capital's most venerable institutions, notably the Sorbonne, one of Europe's oldest universities, founded 1253. Though anchored in the past, the area is marked by the ebb and flow of students and young people who make up the population of the "Latin" Quarter (Latin was the language of tuition up to the French Revolution). The area also abounds in publishing houses, bookshops, and terrace cafés, including the legendary Procope (*13 r. de l'Ancienne Comédie*), one of Paris' oldest cafés and former haunt of philosophers such as Voltaire. Head to **Quai Austerlitz** to see its latest expression of youth in the **Paris docks**.

ÉGLISE ST-SÉVERIN★★

3 r. Prêtres St Séverin.
www.saint-severin.com.

This much-loved Latin Quarter church features a number of architectural styles. The lower part of the portal and the first three bays of the nave are High Gothic; while much of the rest of the building was remodelled in Flamboyant style. In the 18C, the pillars in the chancel were clad in wood and marble.

LUXEMBOURG PALACE★★

15 r. de Vaugirard.

The historic gardens of Luxembourg Palace (*see Parks in Paris box, p153*), seat of the French Senate, are a magnificent oasis of greenery in the heart of the Latin Quarter, making it a popular place where you can sit and absorb the atmosphere of Paris. In 1257 a community of Carthusians, with the help of St Louis, laid claim to the area and built a vast monastery with extensive grounds.

After the death of Henri IV, Queen Marie de' Medici, who wished to have a place of her own that would remind her of the Pitti Palace in Florence. Construction started in 1615, with a commission in 1621 for **Rubens** to paint 24 large allegorical pictures representing the queen's life (these are now in the Louvre).

In 1790 when the monastery was suppressed, the palace gardens were extended to the avenue de l'Observatoire.

Today the palace is the seat of the **Sénat** (the French Upper House), composed of 319 members.

The **Petit Luxembourg**, now the residence of the President of the Senate, comprises the original Hôtel de Luxembourg given to Richelieu by Marie de' Medici, but also the cloister and chapel of a convent founded by the queen. The **Musée du Luxembourg** houses temporary exhibitions in the former orangerie. (Enter at 19 r. de Vaugirard; open daily except 1 May, 10am–7pm (Mon 10pm). €12. ℘01 40 13 62 00; www.museedu-luxembourg.fr.)

Jardin du Luxembourg

PANTHÉON★★

pl. du Panthéon. Open daily 10am–6pm. Closed public holidays. €7. ☎01 44 32 18 00; www.pantheonparis.com.

The Panthéon's distinctive silhouette on the hilltop and its role as the necropolis of France's greatest citizens make it a popular national monument.

Louis XV vowed, when desperately ill in 1744, that should he recover he would replace the semi-ruined church of the abbey of Ste-Geneviève. The project was given to the architect Jacques **Soufflot**. A lack of funds and cracks in the structure caused by ground movements delayed completion until after Soufflot's death (1780), in 1789.

In April 1791 the structure's function as a church was suspended by the Constituent Assembly in order to "receive the bodies of great men who died in the period of French liberty" – it thus became a Pantheon. Voltaire and Rousseau are buried here, and Mirabeau and Marat were for a short while.

The Panthéon subsequently served as a church under the empire, a necropolis in the reign of Louis-Philippe, a church under Napoléon III, the headquarters of the Commune and finally as a lay temple to receive the ashes of Victor Hugo in 1885.

The **dome★★**, strengthened with an iron framework, can be best surveyed from a distance. Eleven steps rise to the peristyle, composed of fluted columns supporting a triangular pediment – the first of its kind in Paris.

The great edifice is built in the shape of a Greek Cross. The upper section has a fresco by Baron Antoine Jean Gros (1771–1835) depicting St Geneviève's Apotheosis. Stairs lead up to the dome from a place affording a fine **view★★** over Paris.

Although strangely eerie and empty, the crypt contains the tombs of great thinkers throughout France's history: La Tour d'Auvergne, Voltaire, Rousseau, Victor Hugo, Émile Zola, Marcelin Berthelot, Louis Braille, Jean Jaurès, the explorer Bougainville. More recent figures honoured here are Nobel Prize winners Pierre and Marie Curie, and French Resistance leader Jean Moulin.

Foucault's Pendulum – In 1851 Léon Foucault took advantage of the dome's height to repeat publicly his experiment that proved the rotation of the earth, which deviated from its axis during oscillation in a circular movement.

The pendulum can now be seen at the **Musée des Arts et Métiers** (*see p140*).

MUSÉE DE CLUNY ★★ (Musée National du Moyen Âge)

6 pl. Paul Painlevé. Open Wed–Mon 9.15am–5.45pm. Closed 1 Jan, 1 May, 25 Dec. €8; no charge 1st Sun of the month. ℘01 53 73 78 00; www.musee-moyenage.fr.

This museum encompasses the residence of the abbots of Cluny, the ruins of Roman thermal baths and a collection of medieval arts.

Together with the Hôtel de Sens, Hôtel de Cluny is one of only two remaining 15C private houses in Paris. Despite much restoration, original medieval details survive in features such as wall crenellations and turrets.

The left wing is articulated with arches; the central building has mullioned windows; a frieze and Flamboyant balustrade, from which gargoyles spurt, line the base of the roof. A pentagonal tower juts out from the central building.

QUARTIER DE ST-GERMAIN-DES-PRÉS★★

Antique dealers, literary cafés and chic nighlife on side streets combine to maintain the reputation of this former centre of international Bohemian life. Notable landmarks include Café de Flore (*172 bd. St Germain*) and Les Deux Magots (*6 pl. St Germain des Prés*).

ÉGLISE DE ST-GERMAIN-DES-PRÉS★★

pl. Saint-Germain des Prés.

This venerable church offers more than aesthetic delights to those who know something of the history of its ancient stones. With the exception of Clovis, the Merovingian kings were buried here. The church was subsequently destroyed by the Normans, but was restored during the 10C and 11C. Not surprising, then, that the tower rising above the west front has a fortress-like character. Around 1160, the nave was enlarged and the chancel rebuilt in the new Gothic style.

"Improvements" followed in the 17C, and in 1822 a somewhat over-zealous restoration took place.

The church's years of glory were 1631–1789, when the austere Congregation of St Maur made it a centre of learning and spirituality: monks studied ancient inscriptions (epigraphy) and writing (paleography); the Church Fathers (Patristics), archaeology and cartography. Their library was confiscated during the French Revolution.

ÉGLISE DE SAINT-SULPICE★★

33 r. Saint-Sulpice.
Open daily from 7.30am–7.30pm.

The church, dedicated to the 6C Archbishop of Bourges, St Sulpicius, was founded by the abbey of St-Germain des-Prés as a parish church for peasants living in its domain.

Rebuilding began in 1646 with the chancel. Six architects took charge over a period of 134 years. The **interior** is impressive for its size.

Of the 20 artists who worked on the interior paintings, Delacroix's genius dominates. His **murals★**, painted between 1849 and 1861, illustrate *St Michael Killing the Demon* (ceiling), *Heliodorus Being Driven from the Temple, and Jacob Wrestling with the Angel* (left wall).

INSTITUT DE FRANCE★★

quai Conti. ℘01 44 41 44 41; www.institut-de-france.fr.

Founded by Mazarin for scholars for provinces incorporated into France during his ministry, the building (1662) was first called the College of Four Nations. Designed by Le Vau, it stands on the far side of the river from the Louvre. The Institute comprises five academies, including the highly exclusive Académie Française, founded 1635 and honouring France's great intellectual achievers.

FAUBOURG SAINT-GERMAIN★★

The Faubourg St-Germain was originally the aristocratic suburb (faubourg) of the abbey of St-Germain-des-Prés.

The Revolution closed its sumptuous town houses and today the district is known primarily for its government ministries. Curious travellers wandering outside the well-known St-Germain and St-Sulpice districts will find the elegant, residential Sèvres-Babylone district dotted with shops and lively cafes.

PALAIS BOURBON★

126 r. de l'Université.

This palace of 1722 has been the seat of the Lower House of France's parliament, the Assemblée Nationale, for more than 150 years.

MUSÉE D'ORSAY★★★

62 r. de Lille. ♿ Open daily except Mon 9.30am–6pm (Thu 9.45pm). Closed 1 May, 25 Dec. €11 for permanent and temporary collections; €8.50 from 4.30pm, except Thu (from 6pm); no charge 1st Sun in the month. ✆ 01 40 49 48 14; www.musee-orsay.fr.

The focus of this museum is the period 1848 to 1914. The upper floor is dedicated to the Impressionists, with one of the world's finest collections. There is also a considerable collection of pre- and post-Impressionist works, as well as sections consecrated to decorative arts and photography.

Major artists include the sculptors Degas and Rosso and the painters Degas, Sisley, Cézanne, Manet, Berthe Morisot, Pissarro, Gustave Caillebotte, Pierre-Auguste Renoir, and Claude Monet. Among the best-known works from this group of artists are

Les Deux Magots and Église de St-Germain-des-Prés

Planing the floor (1875) by Caillebotte (gallery 30), Renoir's Le Moulin de la Galette (1876), and the bronze Little 14-Year-Old Dancer (1881) by Degas.

LES INVALIDES★★★

129 r. de Grenelle.

The plans for the vast edifice were drawn up by Libéral Bruant between 1671–76 and implemented under by Louvois. The main façade, nearly 200m long, is dominated by an attic storey decorated with masks and dormer windows in the form of trophies. Napoléon once paraded his troops in the main courtyard (Cour d'honneur); here the South Pavilion (Pavillon du Midi) forms the façade of the Église St-Louis, the resting-place of some of France's great

Hôtel des Invalides and Pont Alexandre III

Eiffel Tower

© Mark Soskolne / iStockphoto.com

Gustave Eiffel (1832–1923)

Engineer and entrepreneur in equal measure, Eiffel was to enjoy both success and failure during his long life. Mostly remembered today for his Tower, he was also responsible for several other massively impressive structures both in France and further afield. The Garabit viaduct, the Pest railway station and the internal structure of the Statue of Liberty are just three examples of his fine work still in use. Unfortunately, Eiffel became embroiled in the scandal caused by the French Panama Canal Company. Although not involved in the finances of the enterprise, Eiffel was found guilty of fraud, a decision which was later reversed. He spent the rest of his life as a scientist, using his Tower for wind resistance experiments, as an aerial mast and a weather station.

soldiers, and the interior is hung with flags taken from the enemy. Berlioz' Requiem was performed for the first time in 1837 here.

MUSÉE DE L'ARMÉE★★★

♿Open daily: Nov–Mar 10am–5pm; Apr–Oct 10am–6pm. Closed 1st Mon of the month in Oct–Jun, 1 Jan, 1 May, 1 Nov, 25 Dec. €9.50. Guided tours available: ✆01 44 42 38 77 or 08 10 11 33 99; www.musee-armee.fr.

Containing over 500 000 military artefacts, this museum lies on either side of the main courtyard at the Invalides. Arms and armour (*west side*) illustrate the evolution of methods of defence and attack, with weapons and armour from prehistoric times to the 16C. The Ancien Régime and 19C (*east side*) section features weapons and uniforms from the 17C through to the Second Empire, including many of Napoléon's. Banners and artillery grace the courtyard, including 200 cannons in the **Salle Gribeauval** (*west side*).

The World War I and **II** (*west side*) sections feature displays showing the development of World War I, and three floors are devoted to World War II, following a chronological order.

ÉGLISE DU DÔME★★★

Open 10am–6pm Wed–Mon Apr–Jun and Sep, 9pm Tue. Jul–Aug 10am–7pm. Oct–Mar 10am–5pm.

The church of Les Invalides, designed by, **Jules-Hardouin Mansart**, was begun in 1677. With its beautiful gilded dome, it is one of the great works of the Louis XIV style, bringing to perfection the Classicism introduced in the churches of the Sorbonne and the Val-de-Grâce. In 1735, Robert de Cotte completed the building by replacing the planned south colonnade and portico with the splendid vista offered by the Avenue de Breteuil. On the far side he laid out the Esplanade, and set up the guns captured at Vienna in 1805 by Napoléon to defend the gardens and fire ceremonial salvoes on great national occasions. The church became a military necropolis after Napoléon had Marshal Turenne (d. 1675) buried here.

Note the memorial to Vauban, the great military architect, and the tomb of Marshal Foch. In Visconti's crypt of green granite from the Vosges stands the "cloak of glory", the unmarked **Tombeau de Napoléon,** completed in 1861 to receive the Emperor's remains.

EIFFEL TOWER★★★

7 r. de Belloy. Open daily.
Lift: mid–Jun–early Sept 9am–midnight; rest of year 9.30am–11pm. €9, child €7 (elevator to 2nd floor); €15.50, child €13.50 (elevator to top floor).
Stairs (1st and 2nd floors only): €5, child €4. 08 92 70 12 39; www.tour-eiffel.fr.

The Eiffel Tower is Paris' most famous symbol. The first proposal for a tower was made in 1884; construction was completed in 26 months and the tower opened in March 1889 for the Universal Exhibition of that year.

The structure highlights Eiffel's imagination and daring; in spite of the tower's weight of 7 000 tonnes and a height of 320.75m and the use of 2.5 million rivets, it is a masterpiece of lightness. It is difficult to believe that the tower actually weighs less than the volume of air surrounding it and that the pressure it exerts on the ground is that of a man sitting on a chair.

The best light for viewing is usually 1hr before sunset. At night the illuminated tower has a jewel-like quality, sparkling for the first 5 minutes of every hour. At level 3, Eiffel's sitting room can be seen through a window. The second floor houses a restaurant, brasseries and boutiques. On the first floor is a museum, a gift shop, a post office and another restaurant.

PALAIS DE CHAILLOT★★

pl. du Trocadéro.

This remarkable example of inter-war architecture was built for the 1937 Universal Exhibition. Its twin pavilions are linked by a portico and extended by wings which frame the wide terrace with its statues in gilded bronze.

From here there is a wonderful **view★★★** of Paris; in the foreground are the Trocadero Gardens with their spectacular fountains, and beyond the curving river the Eiffel Tower, the Champ-de-Mars, and the École Militaire. The Palais houses the **Théâtre de Chaillot** (01 53 65 30 00; www.theatre-chaillot.fr); **Musée de l'Homme★★** (closed for renovations until Oct 2015; www.museedelhomme.fr); **Musée National de la Marine★★** (01 53 65 69 53; www.musee-marine.fr); **Musée de l'Architecture et du Patrimoine★★** (01 58 51 52 00; www.citechaillot.fr); **Musée du Cinéma Henri-Langlois★** (01 45 53 21 86; www.cinematheque.fr)

ÉCOLE MILITAIRE★★

1 pl.Joffre.

Though the original design could not be fully implemented because of lack of financial resources, the Military Academy by Jacques-Ange Gabriel is one of the outstanding examples of French 18C architecture. It was begun in 1752, financed in part by Mme de Pompadour, and completed in 1773. Under the Second Empire, cavalry and artillery buildings of nondescript design were added, together with the low-lying wings which frame the main building. True to its original function, it now houses the French Army's Staff College. The superb main courtyard **(cour d'honneur★)**, lined on either side by beautiful porticoes with paired columns, is approached via an exercise yard; the imposing central section and the projecting wings form a harmonious composition.

MUSÉE DU QUAI BRANLY★★

37 quai Branly. Open Tue–Wed and Sun 11am–7pm (9pm on Thu, Fri, Sat). €9 (€11 combined for the permanent and temporary exhibitions). Audioguides available in several languages, €5. 01 56 61 70 00; www.quaibranly.fr.

Designed by eminent architect Jean Nouvel, this recent museum dedicated to indigenous arts from around the world opened in summer 2006.

The setting is remarkable: undulating leather-clad low walls lead visitors through the glass and metal structure to sections dedicated to the arts and civilizations of Africa, Asia, Oceania and the Americas. Video and multimedia installations are interspersed throughout. Surrounding gardens add to a sense of luxurious distance from the bustle of the city.

Arrondissements 8–10 & 17

Pomp and grandeur: this might best describe the atmosphere of prestige and royalty dominating in these arrondissements. But notwithstanding the bustling, gilded settings of the Champs-Élysées, Madeleine and Grands Boulevards, this area also harbours quiet, off-the-beaten-track spots such as the Canal St-Martin and the little-known Batignolles district, where artists like Edouard Manet drew inspiration.

- **Michelin Map:** 312 D 2. See p118–119.
- **Info:** ℘08 92 68 30 00 or http://en.parisinfo.com.
- **Location:** Beginning near Madeleine and Champs Élysées; northeast to Opéra Garnier and Gare du Nord, Place de Clichy.
- **Don't MIss:** Voie Triomphale, Champs Élysées
- **Kids:** Grevin wax museum.

LA VOIE TRIOMPHALE★★★

The most famous thoroughfare in Paris is at once an avenue with a spectacular view, a place of entertainment and a street full of smart luxury shops. The vista extending down the Champs-Élysées, with the Arc de Triomphe silhouetted against the sky, is world-renowned, and Parisians call it the *Voie Triomphale* or Triumphal Way. The avenue continues to be the rallying point for protests.

JARDIN DU CARROUSEL

Burned down by the rioters of the Paris Commune in 1871, the ruins of the Tuileries were razed in 1883 and replaced by the Carrousel Garden, named after an equestrian parade, or *carrousel*, that took place here in the 18C. Two flowerbeds frame yew hedges radiating out from the Arc du Carrousel. 18 statues of female nudes by the sculptor Maillol are placed among the hedges, which are framed by the two wings of the Louvre Museum.

JARDIN DES TUILERIES★

Catherine de' Medici envisaged an Italian-style park, complete with fountains, maze, and grotto, populated with terracotta figures by Bernard Palissy, and a menagerie for her palace next to the Louvre. Henri IV later added an orangery and a silkworm farm. In 1664 Le Nôtre raised two lengthwise terraces of unequal height to level the sloping ground, creating the magnificent central axis; he created the pools and designed formal flower beds, quincunxes and slopes. Colbert was so delighted that he intended the gardens to be kept for the royal family, but was subsequently persuaded by Charles Perrault to allow access to the public.

MUSÉE DE L'ORANGERIE★★

♿Open daily except Tue 9am–6pm. Closed 1 May, 25 Dec. €9. ℘01 44 50 43 00; www.musee-orangerie.fr.

Two pavilions, the Orangerie and the Jeu de Paume, were built during the Second Empire and have served as art galleries since the beginning of the 20C. The two oval rooms on the ground floor are hung with panels from Claude Monet's water-lily series of his garden at Giverny, in Normandy, known as the Nymphéas. The lower-level galleries accommodate the Walter-Guillaume Collection (Impressionists to 1930), including the work of artists like Picasso, Cézanne, Renoir and Rousseau.

PLACE DE LA CONCORDE★★★

Everything about this square – site, size, general elegance – is impressive, particularly the obelisk, which dominates the scene. Place de la Concorde is one of the most beautiful squares in Paris, but also one of the busiest. The point of the obelisk indicates international time – it is the largest sundial in the world.

It was designed by Ange-Jacues Gabriel in 1755 and completed over a period of 20 years. On Sunday 21 January 1793, a guillotine was erected in the northwest corner (near where the Brest statue now stands) for the execution of **Louis XVI**.

The colossal **mansions ★★**on either side of the opening to rue Royale are among the finest examples of the early Louis XVI style. The right pavilion, the **Hôtel de la Marine**, was until 1792 the royal store; it then became the Admiralty Office. Today it houses the Navy headquarters. The **Hôtel de Crillon**, across the street, was at first occupied by four noblemen.

In the centre of the square stands an **obelisk★** from the ruins of the temple at Luxor, given to France in 1831 by Mohammed Ali, Viceroy of Egypt. The pink granite monument is 3 300 years old and covered in hieroglyphics.

The obelisk provides the best **views★★★** of the Champs-Élysées, framed by the **Marly Horses** looking up the avenue. Coysevox's Winged Horses frame the view across the Tuileries. Replicas have replaced the two marble groups of horses, which are in the Louvre.

GRAND PALAIS★

This great exhibition hall is formally fronted by an Ionic colonnade running the length of the building, before a mosaic frieze. Enormous quadrigae punctuate the corners; the Belle-Epoque building is elsewhere dotted with turn-of-the-19C decorative elements. Inside, a single glazed space is covered by a flattened dome. With an exhibition area of 5 000sq m, the **Galeries du Grand Palais** have become a cultural centre for major temporary exhibitions of artefacts and art from around the world (3 ave. du Général Eisenhower. Opening hours and charges vary according to exhibition; check website for details – www.rmn.fr).

PALAIS DE LA DÉCOUVERTE★★

Inside the Grand Palais; entrance on avenue Franklin D Roosevelt. Open daily except Mon 9.30am–6pm (Sun and public holidays 10am–7pm). Closed 1 Jan, 1 May, 14 Jul, 25 Dec. €9 (children €7; Planetarium €3 supplement. ☏01 56 43 20 20; www.palais-decouverte.fr.

This museum is a centre for scientific study and popular discovery. Many interactive attractions are intended for kids; some for visitors who are relatively knowledgeable in the field.

The domed **planetarium★** (*level 2*) is a fascinating introduction to the heavens.

AVENUE DES CHAMPS-ÉLYSÉES★★★

Today, the iconic Champs-Élysées is lined with restaurants and cafés, showrooms and banks, cinemas and nightclubs. Most of the shops are international chains, with the majority of the fashion boutiques found along the side streets like avenues George V and Montaigne. The Second Empire private houses and amusement halls that once lined the Avenue have since vanished; the only exception is no. **25**, a mansion built by La Païva, a Polish adventuress, whose house was famous for dinners attended by philosophers, painters and writers. **Le Colisée**, an amphithea-

Canal Saint-Martin

Napoléon ordered the construction of the canal in 1802 to provide much-needed fresh water from the Canal de l'Ourq. It was not completed until 1825. Subsequently allowed to deteriorate, the area received a boost in 1938 when the area was refurbished for the Marcel Carné film *Hôtel du Nord*, starring the Parisian actress Arletty. However, during the 1960s the canal began to fall into disuse. New boutiques and trendy cafés opened in the past ten years have renewed popularity for the canal among strolling tourists, locals with their picnics, and "bourgeois bohemian" professionals who snap up the canalside apartments.

tre built in 1770 to hold an audience of 40 000, has left its name to a street, café and cinema.

ARC DE TRIOMPHE★★★

pl. Charles-de-Gaulle. Open daily Apr–Sep 10am–11pm; Oct–Mar 10am–10.30pm. Closed public holidays. €9.50. ✆01 55 37 73 77; www.arcdetriompheparis.com.

Twelve avenues radiate from the arch and **place Charles de Gaulle★★★ (place de l'Étoile)**, like the points of a star. The arch commemorates Napoléon's victories and the fate of the Unknown Soldier, laid to rest in the tomb in 1921. **Napoléon** commissioned **Chalgrin** to construct a giant arch in 1806. It wasn't finished until 1836, under **Louis-Philippe**. In 1840 the carriage bearing the emperor's body passed beneath the arch. **Haussmann** redesigned the square in 1854, while Hittorff planned its façades.

On 14 July 1919, Allied armies, led by the marshals, marched in victory here. The **arch platform** has an excellent **view★★★** of the capital: here you are halfway between the Louvre and La Défense.

PALAIS DE L'ÉLYSÉE

55 r. du Faubourg St-Honoré. The gardens of the palace are open to the public on the last Sun of each month, Oct–Mar noon-5pm; Apr–Sept 1–7pm (entrance from ave Gabriel).

Staircase, Opéra Garnier

The mansion was constructed in 1718 for the Count of Évreux. During the Revolution it became a dance hall. It was home to Caroline Murat, Napoléon's sister, then Empress Josephine. Napoléon signed his second abdication here after his Waterloo defeat, on 22 June 1815, and the future **Napoléon III** planned his successful coup d'état of 1851 here. Since 1873 the Élysée Palace has housed the French president.

PALAIS-ROYAL★★

pl. du Palais-Royal.

In 1632, Richelieu ordered Lemercier to build what was first dubbed the Palais Cardinal (**Cardinal's Palace**), an edifice remarkable for its impressive central façade, surmounted by allegorical statues and a curved pediment.

Richelieu bequeathed it to Louis XIII, whereupon its name was changed to the Palais-Royal. In 1783, Victor Louis laid out the charming formal gardens and arcades. In 1986, **Daniel Buren** designed the 260 striped columns of varying heights which occupy the outer courtyard.

PALAIS GARNIER – OPÉRA NATIONAL DE PARIS★★

pl. de l'Opéra, entrance on r. Scribe. Open daily except during matinée or special event 10am–5pm (mid-Jul–Aug 10am–6pm. €10. ✆08 92 89 90 90; www.operadeparis.fr.

This stunning building housed the Paris Opera from 1875 to 1989, and is now home to the city's ballet company. The architect **Charles Garnier** built it in 1861. The theatre accommodates up to 450 performers. Considered a monument of the Second Empire, the main façade overlooking the place de l'Opéra features a series of sculpted figures.

Garnier used multicoloured marbles quarried in France for the **interior★★★**. The **Great Staircase** and **Grand Foyer** are used as sumptuous venues.

Arrondissements 11–15

In many ways the heart of a dynamic, contemporary Paris, arrondissements 11–15 offer an exciting nightlife scene (Bastille, Oberkampf, Montparnasse), a glimpse into new ideas in architecture and urban planning (Bercy, Bibliothèque Nationale), as well as quiet, village-like areas little-trodden by tourists.

Michelin Map: 312 D 2. See p118–119.
Info: 08 92 68 30 00 or http://en.parisinfo.com
Location: Beginning near Bastille, then crossing the Seine to Bercy, Gare de Lyon, and Montparnasse.
Don't Miss: Bastille nightlife, the view from Montparnasse.
Kids: The Cirque d'hiver (11th arrond)

BASTILLE

Scene of the historic revolutions of 1789, 1830 and 1848, the **place de la Bastille** remains a symbolic rallying point for demonstration and public celebrations, dominated by the commemorative **July Column** (52m high) and the **Opéra Bastille★**. It also has a lively bar and club scene.

BERCY

The modern district boasts a Palais Omnisports by architects Andrault, Parat and Gavan; the **Cinémathèque Française** (*51 r. de Bercy; www.cinematheque.fr*), holding the world's largest film archive, and the imposing **Finance Ministry**, designed by Chemetow and Huidobro.

The **Bibliothèque nationale de France★** (*Quai François-Mauriac; www.bnf.fr*) by Dominique Perrault – four tower blocks resembling open books – was the last of the "great projects" carried out by the eponymous president.

ÉGLISE NOTRE-DAME-DU-VAL-DE-GRÂCE★★

1 pl. Laveran. Open Mon–Sat 2–6pm, Sun 9am–noon, 2–6pm. 01 43 29 12 31.

Anne of Austria commissioned this church to commemorate the birth of Louis XIV in 1638. The church recalls Roman Renaissance architecture; the dome, with its double triangular pediment, is particularly ornate. The **cupola★★** was decorated by Mignard and features a fresco with 200 figures.

LES CATACOMBES★

1 avenue du Colonel Henri Rol-Tanguy (place Denfert-Rochereau). Open Tue–Sun 10am–8pm. Closed public holidays. €10. Audioguide €5. 01 44 59 58 58. www.carnavalet.paris.fr.

Long stairways, no restrooms. visitor numbers restricted.

These Gallo-Roman quarries were deposited with millions of skeletons from overcrowded Parisian cemeteries between 1785 and 1810. After descending 130 steps, visitors encounter uncountable femurs, skulls and tibias, artfully arranged along the walls with plaques naming cemeteries of origin.

MONTPARNASSE★★

Although this neighbourhood has changed since artists and philosophers resided here in the early 20C, Montparnasse is still a great place to spend an evening.

TOUR MONTPARNASSE★

Open Apr–Sep 9.30am–11.30pm; Oct–Mar, Sun–Thu 9.30am–10.30pm, Fri–Sat 9.30am–11pm. €15. 01 45 38 52 56; www.tourmontparnasse56.com.

Completed in 1973, this 209m tower dominates Montparnasse. It takes 40 seconds to reach the 56th floor, offering a magnificent **panorama★★★** of Paris and surrounds. There is also a bar and panoramic restaurant.

Arrondissements 18–20

Seat of arty, romantic Montmartre with its winding cobblestone streets and precipitous views, but also of edgy, urban Belleville and quiet nooks like the Père-Lachaise Cemetery and Buttes-Chaumont park, arrondissements 18–20 harbour some of Paris' most untouched spots. It's also the traditional working-class bastion of Paris.

- **Michelin Map:** 312 D 2. See p118–119.
- **Info:** 08 92 68 30 00 or http://en.parisinfo.com.
- **Location:** Stretching from the Montmartre hill to the Buttes-Chaumont Park, bustling Belleville neighborhood and Père-Lachaise.
- **Don't Miss:** Montmartre, Père-Lachaise Cemetery.
- **Kids:** The carrousel in Montmartre is great for kids.

MONTMARTRE★★★

The "Martyrs' Hill" was an independent village before becoming the haunt of artists in the late 19C. It retains the picturesque quality of a village in its steep, narrow lanes and precipitous stairways. The "Butte", or mound, rises from the city's sea of roofs; at its centre is the **Place du Tertre★★** with the former town hall at no. 3. The area still enjoys some semblance of local life, at least in the morning; by the afternoon, the "art market" is flooded with tourists. Nearby rises the dramatic outline of the **Basilique du Sacré-Cœur★★**, a place of perpetual pilgrimage. The dome gallery offers an incomparable **panorama★★★** over Paris (r. du Chevalier-de-la-Barre. 01 53 41 89 09; www.sacre-coeur-montmartre.com).

LA VILLETTE★★

The city's largest park stretches between the Porte de la Villette and the Porte de Pantin, a vast green space boasting two museum complexes, concert venues, cinemas, and play areas.

CITÉ DES SCIENCES ET DE L'INDUSTRIE★★★

30 ave. Corentin-Cariou. Open Tue–Sat 10am–6pm, Sun 10am–7pm. Closed 1 Jan, 1 May and 25 Dec. €10. 01 40 05 70 00; www.cite-sciences.fr.

Built in an effort to educate young and old alike about scientific and industrial advances, this museum encourages visitors to investigate, learn and have fun through entertaining scenarios, and an updated programme of exhibits. **Cité des Enfants★** – (*See above for opening times*). The ground floor of the Cité is designed to encourage young scientific discovery through experimentation, and is divided into two sections: ages 2–7 and ages 5–12.

LA GÉODE★★★

In the park just outside the museum. Open Tue–Sun 10.30am–8.30pm (hourly sessions). €12, child €9. 01 44 84 44 84; www.lageode.fr.

This spherical cinema and circular screen (diameter: 36m), which rests on a sheet of water, is a technical achievement from engineer Chamayou.

MARCHÉ AUX PUCES DE SAINT-OUEN★

Espace Accueil et Information du Marché aux Puces, 7 Impasse Simon, St-Ouen. 01 58 61 22 90. The flea market is situated just outside Paris in the suburb of St-Ouen (five-min walk from metro Clignancourt – go north under bd. Périphérique to reach the markets). 01 40 11 77 36; www.st-ouen-tourisme.com.

The most famous flea market in Paris; there are up to 3 000 stalls on display. If you are willing to search and bargain you may find something to treasure among the bric-a-brac – a collector's paradise.

PARKS IN PARIS

Parc Montsouris

© J-C.&D. Pratt/Photononstop

The city boasts some 450 parks, public gardens and green spaces. Some are prestigious and historic, and adorned with fine sculpture.

Highlights include:

Bois de Vincennes, 4 458 acre/995ha including the Parc Floral.

Bois de Boulogne, 2 090 acre/846ha with the Bagatelle, iris and rose gardens.

Jardin des Plantes, historic Botanical Gardens of Paris (opened to the public in 1640).

Jardin des Tuileries, with its ancient and modern statuary.

Jardin du Luxembourg, a pleasant Latin Quarter park with a pond alongside a palace, popular with students and young children.

Parc Montsouris and Square des Batignolles, examples of "Jardins Anglais", albeit with a less formal layout.

Parc Paysager des Buttes-Chaumont, possibly the city's most picturesque, boasting dramatic bluffs and man-made grottos.

Jardin du Palais-Royal, a haven of elegance in the very heart of Paris.

Jardin japonais de l'UNESCO, a Japanese-style garden at the UNESCO headquarters, also known as "Garden of Peace".

Jardin du Musée Rodin, ideal spot to prolong your museum visit and discover magnificent city views.

Parc Monceau, offering memorable statues of Musset, Maupassant, Chopin and other noteworthy French figures.

Parc André-Citroën, sophisticated and contemporary, with several themed gardens.

Parc de La Villette, the largest in Paris.

Parc de Belleville, offering panoramic views of the whole city.

Parc de Bercy, recalling the wine-dealing past of this modernised district.

PÈRE-LACHAISE CEMETERY★

bd. de Ménilmontant; main entrances: Porte de Repos (Metro Philippe Auguste), Porte d'Amandiers (Metro Père-Lachaise) Open Mid-Mar–Nov, 8am–6pm, Sat 8.30am–6pm, Sun and holidays 9am–6pm; Nov–mid-Mar, 8am–5.30pm, Sat 8.30am–5.30pm, Sun and public holidays 9am–5.30pm. Guided tours (2hr) possible: 01 55 25 82 10. Maps at Repos and Gambetta entrances.

Père-Lachaise Cemetery is the city's oldest and largest, sprawling across 44 hectares (109 acres) and housing the tombs of greats from Balzac to Molière, Edith Piaf to Oscar Wilde. Addressing a problem of painfully overcrowded graveyards, Emperor Napoléon I ordered the creation of Père-Lachaise (along with several others) in the early 19C. The lush site – boasting thousands of trees, plants and flowers – was designed to resemble an English garden.

Père-Lachaise houses two important war memorials. The **Mur des Fédérés** is a wall commemorating the 147 insurgents of the Paris Commune who were executed at the site in 1871.

In the cemetery's southeast corner are monuments dedicated to World War II deportees and victims of extermination.

ADDRESSES

STAY

Aberotel – 24 r. Blomet, 75015 Volontaires. 01 40 61 70 50; www.aberotel.com. 28 rooms. A popular hotel with stylish rooms and an inner courtyard for summer breakfasts. It has a pleasant lounge adorned with paintings of playing cards.

Delambre – 35 r. Delambre, 75014. Edgar Quinet. 01 43 20 66 31. 30 rooms. French poet André Breton stayed in this hotel located in a quiet street close to Montparnasse railway station.

Nord et Est – 49 r. Malte, 75011. Oberkampf. 01 47 00 71 70; www.hotel-nord-est.com. 45 rooms. The warm family atmosphere and reasonable prices draw regulars to this hotel near Place de la République.

7 Eiffel – 17 bis r. Amélie, 75007. La Tour Maubourg. 01 45 55 10 01; www.hotel-7eiffel-paris.com. 32 rooms. and junior suites. Sleek contemporary design reigns in this elegant Left-Bank hotel. A rooftop summer terrace complete with bee hives affords great city views.

Hôtel des Archives – 87 r. des Archives, 75003. Temple. 01 44 78 08 00; www.hoteldesarchives.com. 19 rooms. Charming hotel near the National Archives, with small yet prettily decorated, comfortable rooms.

Beaubourg – 11 r. S. Le Franc, 75004. Rambuteau. 01 42 74 34 24. www.beaubourg-paris-hotel.com. 28 rooms. Located in a tiny street behind the Georges-Pompidou Centre.

Eiffel Park Hôtel – 17 bis, r. Amélie, 75007. La Tour Maubourg. 01 45 55 10 01. 36 rooms. From the Indian and Chinese artefacts to the ethnic fabrics, exoticism reigns through this elegant hotel.

Élysées Mermoz – 30 r. J. Mermoz, 75008. Franklin D. Roosevelt. 01 42 25 75 30; www.hotel-elysees mermoz.com. 22 rooms and 5 suites. This cosy hotel has rooms in sunny colours or shades of grey. Varnished wood panelling and blue stone in the bathrooms as well as a cane-furnished lounge.

Etats-Unis Opéra – 16 r. d'Antin, 75002. Opéra. 01 42 65 05 05; www.hotel-etats-unis-opera.com. 45 rooms. In a quiet street, this hotel in a 1930s building offers modern, comfortable rooms.

Familia – 11 r. des Ecoles, 75005. Cardinal Lemoine. 01 43 54 55 27; www.familiahotel.com. 30 rooms. Notre-Dame and the Collège des Bernardins provide the backdrop for rustic rooms adorned with sepia frescoes.

Le Hameau de Passy – 48 r. Passy, 75016. La Muette. 01 42 88 47 55; www.hameaudepassy.com. 30 rooms. A private lane leads to this hamlet with a charming inner courtyard overrun with greenery.

Louvre Ste-Anne – 32 r. Ste-Anne, 75001. Pyramides. 01 40 20 02 35; www.paris-hotel-louvre.com. 20 rooms. In a street lined with Japanese restaurants, this hotel has small but well-equipped rooms decorated in pastel shades.

Hôtel de Nesle – 7 r. de Nesle. 75006. Odéon or St-Michel. 01 43 54 62 41; www.hoteldenesleparis.com. 18 rooms. An almost magical address, where rooms are each decorated in their own theme (colonial, Oriental, country, Molière…). The garden is planted with Tunisian palm trees, a quiet haven in the centre of the Latin Quarter!

Hôtel de la Place des Vosges –12 r. de Birague. 75004. Bastille or St-Paul. 01 42 72 60 46; www.hotel placedesvosges.com. 16 rooms. This hotel within the 17C walls has real character. The rooms, of adequate size, either have a sober minimalist style, or have been prettily renovated. The lobby combines ancient stone walls, exposed wooden beams and old tapestries. A charming stay near one of the most beautiful squares in Paris.

Hôtel Favart – 5 r. de Marivaux. 75002. Richelieu Drouot. 01 42 97 59 83; www.hotel-favart.com. 37 rooms. Goya stayed at this charming hotel, where a timeless atmosphere prevails. The rooms of the main façade, overlooking the Opéra-Comique, are the most attractive.

Hôtel Libertel Gare de l'Est Français –13 r. du 8 Mai 1945. 75010. Gare de l'Est. 01 40 35 94 14; www.hotelfrancais.com. 70 rooms. This hotel located across from the Gare de l'Est train station is in a lively neighbourhood. Rooms are soundproofed, air conditioned, well equipped and renovated with style. The 1900 reception salon beneath a large stained-glass atrium is open for the breakfast buffet 6am–11am.

Grand Hôtel St-Michel – 19 r. Cujas. 75005. Luxembourg. 01 46 33 33 02; www.hotel-saintmichel-paris.com. 47 rooms. This Haussmannian building has plush rooms with painted furniture in a Napoléon III style. Breakfast served in the vaulted cellar

Hôtel Signature – 5 r. Chomel. 75007. Sèvres-Babylone or St-Sulpice. 01 45 48 35 53; www.signature-saintgermain.com. 26 rooms. One of the craftsmen who helped build Lindbergh's famous plane *Spirit of St-Louis* stayed at this hotel near the Bon Marché in the 19C. All of the rooms were redecorated in the 1930s–1940s style. Very friendly welcome.

Hôtel Malar – 29 r. Malar. 75007. École Militaire, La Tour Maubourg or Invalides. 01 45 51 38 46; www.hotelmalar.com. 22 rooms. These two buildings constructed under Louis-Philippe's reign (19C) have been renovated many times. Rooms have period furnishings and pretty two-toned bathrooms. In summer breakfast is served in the tiny private courtyard.

Hôtel du Palais-Bourbon – 49 r. de Bourgogne. 75007. Varenne. 01 44 11 30 70; www.hotel-palais-bourbon.com. 29 rooms. Built in 1730, this hotel between the Rodin Museum and the Invalides is a pleasant surprise. Well-decorated rooms with air conditioning and wooden furnishings. Singles are quite small, but well priced. Breakfast included in the rates.

Hôtel Pavillon de la Reine – 8 pl. des Vosges. 75003. Bastille. 01 40 29 19 19; www.pavillon-de-la-reine.com. 54 rooms. Behind one of the 36 brick pavillions of the place des Vosges, two buildings, including one from the 17th-century, house this hotel with its refined rooms overlooking a private garden.

Hôtel St-Thomas-d'Aquin – 3 r. du Pré-aux-Clercs. 75007. Rue du Bac or St-Germain-des-Prés. 01 42 61 01 22; www.hotel-saint-thomas-aquin-paris.com. 21 rooms. Chic boutiques, antique shops, art galleries and literary cafés: Paris' celebrated Left Bank is right outside this hotel. Rooms have modern comforts and boat-cabin- style bathrooms.

Hôtel de la Tulipe – 33 r. Malar. 75007. Invalides or La Tour Maubourg. 01 45 51 67 21; www.paris-hotel-tulipe.com. 21 rooms. This yellow house dating back to the 17C is now a Provençal-style hotel with a pretty paved garden courtyard. The small rooms are nicely furnished, with a nice mix of wicker, exposed stone and wooden beams.

Hôtel Verneuil – 8 r. de Verneuil. 75007. Rue du Bac. 01 42 60 82 14; www.hotel-verneuil-saint-germain.com. 26 rooms. This old building has been arranged like a private mansion, with beautiful 18C engravings in the cosy bedrooms. Nearby is the house where legendary French singer Serge Gainsbourg lived.

EAT

Atelier Maître Albert – 1 r. Maître Albert, 75005. Maubert Mutualité. 01 56 81 30 01; www.ateliermaitrealbert.com. A huge medieval fireplace and spits for roast meat take pride of place in this handsome interior. Guy Savoy is responsible for the mouth-watering menu.

Bofinger – 5 r. Bastille, 75004. Bastille. 01 42 72 87 82; www.bofingerparis.com. The famous clients and remarkable décor have bestowed enduring renown on this brasserie created in 1864.

Le Carré des Vosges – 15 r. St-Gilles, 75003. Chemin Vert. 01 42 71 22 21. Friendly bistro a stone's throw from the Rue des Francs-Bourgeois and its trendy boutiques.

Chardenoux – 1 r. Jules Vallès, 75011. Charonne. 01 43 71 49 52. Reopened under the chef Cyril Lignac on its 100th anniversary, this bistro specialises in traditional cuisine.

Florimond – 19 av. La Motte-Picquet, 75007. Ecole Militaire. 01 45 55 40 38. Pocket-sized restaurant named after Monet's gardener in Giverny.

La Maison de l'Aubrac – 37 r. Marbeuf, 75008. Franklin D. Roosevelt. 01 43 59 05 14; www.maison-aubrac.com. Aveyron farmhouse-style décor, generous portions of rustic cuisine (with emphasis on Aubrac beef) and an excellent wine list. Close to Champs-Élysées.

Pharamond – 24 r. de la Grande-Truanderie, 75001. Châtelet-Les-Halles. 0173 20 21 03; www.pharamond.fr. An institution dating back to the heyday of Les Halles. The Pharamond still serves traditional dishes.

Vaudeville – 29, r. Vivienne, 75002. Bourse. 01 45 26 41 43. This large brasserie with its sparkling Art Deco details in pure Parisian style is especially lively after theatre performances.

Bistro les Deux Théâtres – 10 chaussée de la Muette, 75016. Mo La Muette. 01 45 03 14 84; www.lesdeuxtheatres.com. The very attractive, all-inclusive formula of this elegant bistro explains part of its appeal in the neighbourhood.

La Coupole – 102 bd Montparnasse, 75014. Vavin. 01 43 20 14 20. The spirit of Montparnasse lives on in this huge Art Deco brasserie opened in 1927. The 24 pillars were decorated by artists of the period, while the cupola sports a contemporary fresco.

Ma Salle à Manger – 26 pl. Dauphine. Pont Neuf or Cité. 01 43 29 52 34. 11am–10.30pm. This restaurant wears its name well: you're in "My Dining Room" of the owner, Florence. The atmosphere is warm and friendly, with inventive cuisine by chef Gaétan. Don't miss the belote competition every Sunday evening in the square.

Le Troquet – 21 r. François Bonvin, 75015. Cambronne. 01 45 66 89 00. An authentic Parisian bar: single set menu shown on the blackboard, retro-style dining room, and tasty market-based cuisine.

Benoit – 20 r. St-Martin. Châtelet-Les Halles. 01 42 72 25 76; www.esprit-bistrot.com. Closed 25 Feb–2 Mar and 26 Jul–25 Aug. Alain Ducasse surpervises this chic and lively bistro, one of the oldest in Paris. Classic French cuisine that respects the historic spirit of this authentic establishment.

ENTERTAINMENT

Consult L'Officiel des Spectacles, Une Semaine à Paris and Pariscope, and the daily press for details of time and place of exhibitions. The monthly booklet Paris Selection, edited by the Paris Tourist Office, lists exhibitions, shows and other events in the capital.

Paris may be said to be one huge "living stage", as it boasts a total of 100 **theatres** and other venues devoted to the performing arts, representing a seating capacity of 56 000. Most of these are located near the Opéra and the Madeleine, but from Montmartre to Montparnasse, from the Bastille to the **Latin Quarter★★★** and from Boulevard Haussmann to the Porte Maillot, state-funded theatres (**Opéra-Garnier★★**, Opéra-Bastille, Comédie Française, Odéon, Chaillot, La Colline) are to be found side by side with local and private theatres, singing cabarets and café-théâtres.

Cinemas, more than 400 in number, are to be found in every part of the city, with particular concentrations in the same areas as the theatres and on the Champs-Élysées. There are also two open-air cinema festivals in the city in the summer: one at **Parc de la Villette★**; the other, **Cinéma au Clair de Lune**, is held in parks and squares across Paris.

Music-hall, **variety shows** and **reviews** can be enjoyed at such places as the Alcazar de Paris, the Crazy Horse, the Lido, the Paradis Latin, the Casino de Paris, the Folies Bergère and the Moulin Rouge.

As well as the **Opéra-Garnier★★**, the Opéra-Bastille and the Comic Opera (Opéra-Comique), there are a number of concert halls with resident orchestras like the Orchestre de Paris at the Salle Pleyel, the Ensemble Orchestral de Paris at the Salle Gaveau, and the orchestras of the French Radio at the Maison de Radio-France. In addition there are many other halls in which full-scale performances are put on.

There are also nightclubs, cabarets, dens where chansonniers can be heard, café-théâtres, television shows open to the public, concerts and recitals in churches, circuses, and other entertainment.

SHOPPING

SHOPPING DISTRICTS

Most major stores are concentrated in a few districts, whose names alone are suggestive of Parisian opulence.

Champs-Élysées

All along this celebrated avenue and in the surrounding streets (avenue Montaigne, avenue Marceau), visitors can admire dazzling window displays and covered shopping malls (Galerie Élysée Rond-Point, Galerie Point-Show, Galerie Élysée 26, Galerie du Claridge, Arcades du Lido) devoted to fashion, cosmetics and luxury cars.

Rue du Faubourg-St-Honoré

Here haute couture and ready-to-wear clothing are displayed alongside perfume, fine leather goods and furs.

Place Vendôme

Some of the most prestigious jewellery shops (Cartier, Van Cleef & Arpels, Boucheron, Chaumet) stand facing the Ritz Hotel and the Ministry of Justice.

Place de la Madeleine and r. Tronchet

An impressive showcase for shoes, ready-to-wear clothing, luggage, leather goods and fine tableware.

DEPARTMENT STORES

For locals and visitors alike, the city's great department stores are the ideal way to find a vast choice of high-quality fashions and other goods under one roof. Most leading names are represented. Some have free fashion shows.

Department stores are usually open Monday–Saturday 9.30am–7pm.

Bazar de l'Hôtel de Ville (52 r. de Rivoli)

Galeries Lafayette (40 bd Haussmann)

Printemps (64 bd Haussmann)

Le Bon Marché (r. de Sèvres).

ANTIQUE SHOPS AND DEALERS

Le Louvre des Antiquaires (1 pl. du Palais Royal), **Le Village Suisse** (r. du Général de Larminat), the **Richelieu-Drouot** auction room and the **rues Bonaparte** and **La Boétie** specialise in antiques. Good bargains can also be found at the flea market at the **Porte de Montreuil** and **Porte de St-Ouen** (Sat–Mon).

FAIRS AND EXHIBITIONS

Paris hosts a great number of trade fairs and exhibitions all year round. The following events are among the most important.

Paris – Expo, pl. de la Porte de Versailles. www.viparis.com. Over 200 exhibitions, conventions and events per year including the Paris Nautical Trade Show.

Parc International d'Expositions, Paris-Nord Villepinte. www.viparis.com. Trade Show for Crafts (SMAC) in March, the Maison & Objet home style expo, the International food industry exhibition (SIAL) and Japan Expo.

Parc des Expositions, Le Bourget aerodrome. www.siae.fr. Paris Air Show (odd years: next is in 2017).

SPORT

Among the most popular sporting events held in and around Paris are the International Roland Garros Tennis Championships, the Paris Marathon, the legendary **Tour de France** with its triumphant arrival along the Champs-Élysées, and several prestigious horse races (Prix du Président de la République in Auteuil, Prix d'Amérique in Vincennes, Prix de l'Arc de Triomphe in Longchamp).

The **Parc des Princes stadium** (24 r. Claude Farrère; www.leparcdesprinces.fr) is host to the great football and rugby finals, attended by an enthusiastic crowd, and the **Palais Omnisport de Paris-Bercy** (8 bd Bercy; www.bercy.fr) organises the most unusual indoor competitions: indoor surfing, North American rodeos, ice figure-skating, tennis championships (Open de Paris), moto-cross races, martial arts, Six-day Paris Cycling Event, and also pop concerts by international stars.

Northern France

» Region map p160

Château de Versailles p161

Disneyland Resort Paris p166

Château de Vaux-le-Vicomte p169

Fontainebleau p170

St-Germain-en-Laye p173

Parc Astérix p175

Château de Chantilly p176

Senlis p175

Compiègne p178

Laon p182

Arras p183

Amiens p185

Lille p190

Calais p196

Boulogne-sur-Mer p201

Chartres p203

Introduction

The Île-de-France, defined by the rivers Seine, Aisne, Oise and Marne, is the wealthiest of the regions of France, and from which the French state has grown. Where its limestone plateaux have been cut into by the rivers, lush valleys have been formed, contrasting with the vast arable tracts of the Beauce, Vexin and Brie. A girdle of greenery surrounds the capital, made up of great forests such as those of Fontainebleau and Rambouillet, into which merge the landscapes of leisure and pleasure. Further north, landscapes are open and high-yielding arable land is broken by a number of valleys, such as that of the Somme.

Geography – Northeast is Flanders, consisting largely of low-lying reclaimed land. Inland is the ***pays noir***, stretching from Béthune to Valenciennes. The coal industry has now disappeared and, in its place, textile, processed food and car part industries provide employment.

History – Away from Paris, the Île-de-France, together with Amiens, was the cradle of Gothic architecture, while to the north, Flanders has long been a battleground and completely devastated during both world wars.

Today – the whole region is part of a highly successful modern economy, which, while heavily industrialised, retains much woodland and huge tracts of agricultural land to the north, particularly in Picardy.

Culturally speaking, Picardy has more in common with Nord-Pas-de-Calais than with Île-de-France. But its geography closely links it with the Parisian Basin. The culture of Nord-Pas-de-Calais has unique features of its own, such as the widespread use of Flemish. Its rich privateer past has given birth to some of the wildest festive Carnival celebrations.

Overall, this is a complex and vibrant region making up an interesting array of similarities and differences.

Highlights

1. French Classicism at its best: **Château de Versailles** (p161)
2. Europe's only Disney resort: **Disneyland Resort Paris** (p166)
3. Railway carriage at Compiègne: **Clairière de l'Armistice** (p179)
4. **Grand'Place, Place des Héros** at Arras: **Les Places** (p184)
5. Rodin's bronze figures: **Monument des Bourgeois de Calais** (p197)

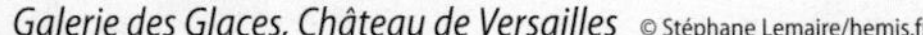

Galerie des Glaces, Château de Versailles © Stéphane Lemaire/hemis.fr

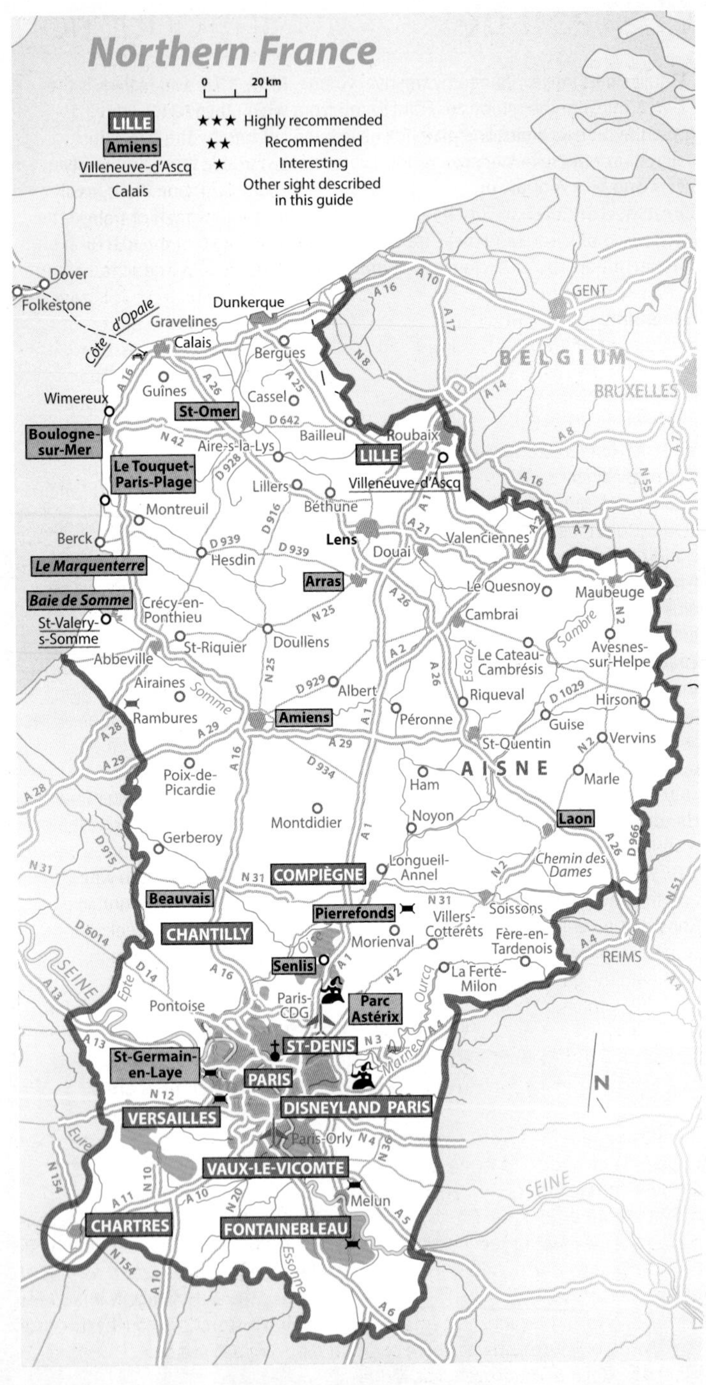

Northern France
0
20 km
LILLE ★★★ Highly recommended
Amiens ★★ Recommended
Villeneuve-d'Ascq ★ Interesting
Calais Other sight described in this guide
Dover
Folkestone
Côte d'Opale
Dunkerque
Gravelines
Calais
Bergues
Guînes
Wimereux
Cassel
St-Omer
Boulogne-sur-Mer
Bailleul
Roubaix
Aire-s-la-Lys
LILLE
Le Touquet-Paris-Plage
Villeneuve-d'Ascq
Lillers
Béthune
Montreuil
Berck
Lens
Valenciennes
Douai
Hesdin
Le Marquenterre
Arras
Le Quesnoy
Maubeuge
Baie de Somme
Crécy-en-Ponthieu
Cambrai
St-Valery-s-Somme
St-Riquier
Doullens
Le Cateau-Cambrésis
Avesnes-sur-Helpe
Abbeville
Sambre
Escaut
Airaines
Albert
Riqueval
Hirson
Somme
Rambures
Amiens
Péronne
Guise
St-Quentin
Vervins
Poix-de-Picardie
AISNE
Ham
Marle
Montdidier
Noyon
Laon
Gerberoy
Longueil-Annel
Chemin des Dames
COMPIÈGNE
Beauvais
Pierrefonds
Soissons
Villers-Cotterêts
CHANTILLY
Morienval
Fère-en-Tardenois
Senlis
La Ferté-Milon
REIMS
SEINE
Epte
Oise
Ourcq
Pontoise
Paris-CDG
Parc Astérix
ST-DENIS
Marne
St-Germain-en-Laye
PARIS
N
DISNEYLAND PARIS
VERSAILLES
Eure
Paris-Orly
VAUX-LE-VICOMTE
SEINE
Melun
CHARTRES
FONTAINEBLEAU
Essonne
GENT
BELGIUM
BRUXELLES
A 10
A 16
A 17
N 8
A 14
A 26
A 25
D 642
N 42
D 928
A 8
A 1
A 16
N 55
D 916
A 21
A 2
A 7
D 939
N 25
A 26
N 2
A 2
D 929
A 1
D 1029
A 28
A 29
A 29
A 29
D 934
A 28
A 16
N 2
A 1
A 26
D 966
D 915
N 31
N 31
N 2
N 31
N 51
D 6014
D 14
A 16
A 1
N 2
A 4
A 13
A 13
N 3
A 4
N 12
N 4
N 36
N 154
N 10
A 11
A 10
N 20
A 5
N 154
A 10
A 6

Château de Versailles★★★

Versailles is the creation of the French monarchy at the moment of its greatest splendour. Consisting of the château, the gardens, and the Trianon★★, it is a wonderfully harmonious composition of building and landscape, the definitive monument of French Classicism.

- **Michelin Map:** 311 I 3
- **Info:** 2 bis, ave de Paris. ℘01 39 24 88 88. www.versailles-tourisme.com.
- **Location:** Versailles is only 18km/11mi from Paris, easily reached by road or train (take line C of the RER to Versailles-Rive gauche, or SNCF rail link from St-Lazare to Versailles-Rive droite or from Montparnasse to Versailles-Chantiers). The château and park form one side of the town of Versailles. Place du Marché is the town's focal point, offering a variety of delightful restaurants, shops, cafés, brasseries and weekly markets.
- **Don't Miss:** The Grand Canal – rent a rowing boat and enjoy an impressive view of the palace and its gardens.
- **Timing:** A number of guided tours for the interior of the palace are offered, from 1–2hr. Allow 3hr for the gardens, and even more time if you wish to visit the Grand and Petit Trianons. The park is best seen when the Grands Eaux (fountains) are in operation (weekends and holidays in summer).
- **Kids:** Beyond the Petit Trianon is the Queen's Hamlet (Le Hameau de la Reine), where farm animals roam about, serving as a great attraction for children.

A BIT OF HISTORY

The birth of the Sun King's palace – The original château was a small hunting lodge around the present Marble Court, built in 1624 for Louis XIII, who had Philibert le Roy reconstruct it in brick and stone in 1631.

The young **Louis XIV** saw Versailles as the perfect place to build his own château far from the mobs of Paris, a magnificent palace of immense proportions and opulence never seen before. He wanted to demonstrate the glory of the French arts as well as establish the absolute power of the Sun King. He commissioned a renowned team to realise his dream: the architect Louis Le Vau, the landscape architect Le Nôtre and the decorator Le Brun.

Construction began – and continued to some extent for almost a century – in 1661 with the gardens, embellished for Louis XIV's splendid festivals.

In 1668 Le Vau constructed stone façades around the original château, creating an "envelope" which concealed the old façades.

Revolution and Restoration – Under Louis XV changes to the interior included the creation of the Petits Cabinets. He added the Petit Trianon and gardens in the château park next to the Grand Trianon, which was eventually given to Louis XVI's queen Marie-Antoinette, who would expand and embellish it with a private theatre and hamlet. When the Revolution drove Louis XVI from Versailles, a century of royal occupation came to a close. The artworks were placed in the Louvre and the furnishings auctioned off. Today, the palace is listed as one of UNESCO's World Heritage Monuments following restoration work by the state and private patronage.

CHÂTEAU★★★

The enjoyment of even the shortest of visits will be greatly enhanced if the **Michelin Green Guide Northern France and the Paris Region** *is used.*

A complete tour of the palace, gardens, park and Marie-Antoinette's Estate takes two days. If you have only one day begin with the interior of the château, where the most magnificent apartments are to be found.

The park and gardens are best enjoyed at leisure.

This "pink marble and porphyry palace with delightful gardens", as Mansart described it, is widely regarded as the most refined set of buildings within the Versailles compound.

HIGHLIGHTS

Full appreciation of Versailles demands a knowledge of Classical mythology and its symbols, the château and its gardens being in effect a temple dedicated to worship of the Sun God.

Grands Appartements★★★

Open Tue–Sun: Apr–Oct 9am–6.30pm; Nov–Mar 9am–5.30pm. Closed 1 Jan, 1 May, 25 Dec. €15 (Palace only), Passport €18 (1 day), €25 (2 days). 01 30 83 76 20; http://.en.chateauversailles.fr.

These comprise the King's Suite on the north and the Queen's Suite to the south, facing the sun.

The six-room suite with decoration by Le Brun was the king's apartment from 1673 to 1682. Then Louis XIV took up residence definitively at Versailles and had a new apartment designed around the Marble Court.

Three times a week on Mondays, Wednesdays and Thursdays from 6pm to 10pm the king held court in the Grands Appartements.

Cour de Marbre★★

This is the heart of Louis XIII's château. Built in brick with stone dressings and reserved for the King's private use, it has fine raised paving in black and white marble, façades graced by 40 busts (some of them by Coysevox), mansard roofs decorated with urns, and a colonnaded portico supporting the wrought-iron balcony of the King's Bedchamber.

Galerie des Glaces★★★

Jules Hardouin-Mansart completed this splendid reception room begun by Le Brun, and built over Le Vau's terrace. It lies between the War Salon and the Peace Salon; its mirrors catch the rays of the setting sun. Its decoration was completed in 1687.

Appartement de la Reine★★

Entrance to the Queen's Suite is through the **Salon de la Paix★**, decorated with a canvas by Lemoyne of Louis XV presenting peace to Europe. The suite was constructed for Louis XIV's wife Queen Marie-Thérèse, who died here in 1683.

Chambre de la Reine

Le Brun's original decoration for Marie-Thérèse was redone for Queen Maria Leczczynska between 1729 and 1735. The white and gold woodwork, the greyish tones of the ceiling by Boucher, and the doors decorated by Natoire and De Troy demonstrate the inclination towards the Rococo under Louis XV. Marie-Antoinette had other renovations made in 1770; the two-headed eagle and the portraits of the house of Austria recall the queen's origins.

The floral wall hangings were rewoven to the original pattern in Lyon, matching exactly the original hanging of the queen's summer furnishings of 1786.

In France, royal births were public events: in this room 19 children of France were born, among them Louis XV and Philip V of Spain.

The Gardens (Jardins)★★★

Open daily: Apr–Oct 8am–8.30pm; Nov–Mar 8am–6pm.

Laid out by Le Nôtre, the gardens are a masterpiece of French landscape style, going beyond the evocation of the idea of majesty (as at Vaux-le-Vicomte) to celebrate the supreme authority of the monarch by the systematic use of Classical symbolism. Among the 200 statues of this open-air sculpture museum are Keller's bronzes in the

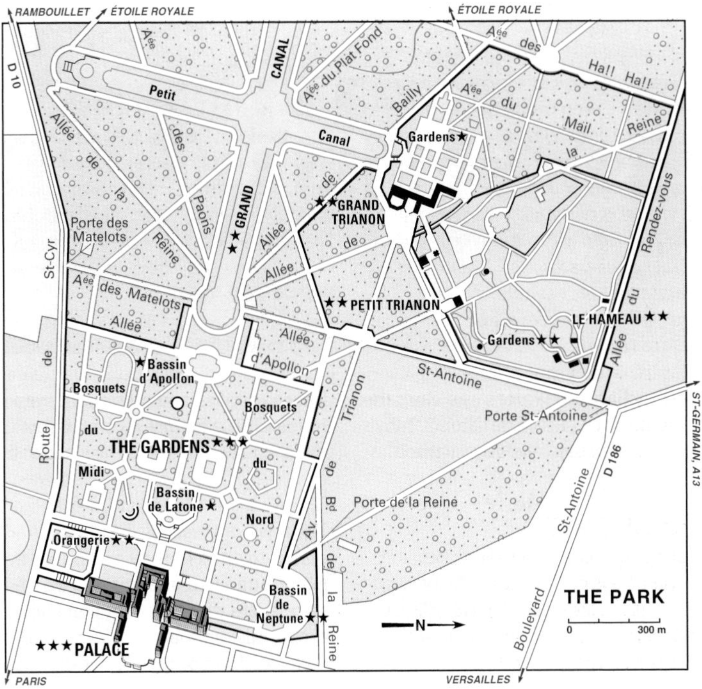

RAMBOUILLET ÉTOILE ROYALE ÉTOILE ROYALE
D 10
Petit Canal
★★ GRAND CANAL
Allée de la Reine
Allée des Paons
Aée du Plat Fond
Bailly
Aée des Ha!! Ha!!
Aée du Mail
Allée de la Reine
Gardens★
★★GRAND TRIANON
Allée de
Allée de Rendez-vous
Porte des Matelots
Aée des Matelots
Allée
★★ PETIT TRIANON
LE HAMEAU ★★
Gardens★★
Allée du
★Bassin d'Apollon
Allée d'Apollon
St-Antoine
Bosquets
Bosquets
Trianon
Porte St-Antoine
ST-GERMAIN, A13
Route de St-Cyr
du
THE GARDENS★★★
du
Midi
Bassin de Latone★
Nord
Bd. de la Reine
Av. de
Porte de la Reine
D 186
St-Antoine
Orangerie★★
Bassin de Neptune★★
★★★PALACE
Boulevard
THE PARK
N
0 300 m
PARIS
VERSAILLES

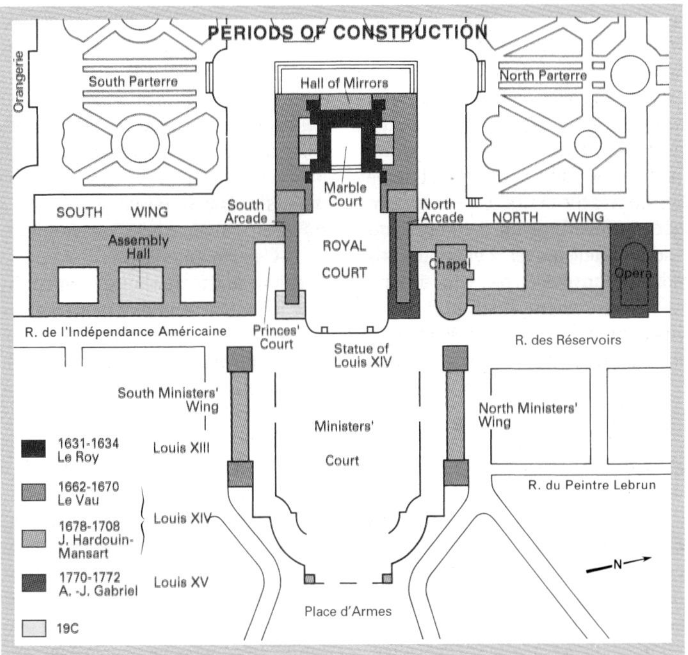

Hameau de la Reine

© S. Sauvignier / Michelin

Water Gardens (Parterres d'eau), the Latona Basin (Bassin de Latone), Tuby's Apollo, and bas-reliefs by Girardon.

Domaine de Marie-Antoinette★★

Open daily except Mon: Apr–Oct, noon–6.30pm (8.30pm for the gardens); Nov–Mar, noon–5.30pm. €10. ℘01 30 83 76 20; www.chateauversailles.fr.

No trip to Versailles would be complete without visiting Marie-Antoinette's Estate located on the northern edge of the Grand Park.

Formed by the **Petit Trianon** and its **gardens** and **hamlet**, the area has been returned to its former arrangement. This is where Louis XVI's wife would retire, away from the Court's rigorous etiquette expected from a woman of her rank. It started with the **Grand Trianon★★**, built as a personal retreat for Louis XIV in 1687, with its own gardens overlooking the Petit Canal and romantic groves. Next door is the **Petit Trianon★★** (1768), where Marie-Antoinette spent much of her time with her children. She had a private theatre, an English-style garden with lakes and follies, and a replica village, le **Hameau de la Reine★★**, complete with thatched-roof houses, animals and mill.

Guided Tours

Take one of the tours offered by the tourist office to get better acquainted with both the château and its gardens, and with the town itself. There is also a choice of guided tours at the château, each starting at a different entrance.

VILLE DE VERSAILLES★★

The town of Versailles was built as an annex to the château to house the numerous titled and untitled people who served the court. It has retained a certain austere charm. It was originally conceived in the symbol of the sun, with the château at the centre and the three main avenues radiating away like rays of light. There are few 17C houses left in Versailles; most of the old town dates from the 18C. The pedestrianised r. Satory, in the heart of old town, has become as lively as Quartier Notre-Dame, where antique dealers and outdoor cafés abound.

EXCURSIONS

HARAS DE JARDY

2km/1.2mi NE on N 182. Leave by ave de St-Cloud towards Paris.

This huge stud farm, a horse-lover's paradise, forms part of an important complex of leisure activities (tennis, golf, riding, show jumping). The vast park offers fine walks and is the site of numerous show-jumping competitions.

CHÂTEAU DE BRETEUIL★★

24km/15mi SSW of Versailles.

Breteuil is one of the most charming châteaux in the Île-de-France region, owned by the Le Tonnelier de Breteuil family since 1712. The estate boasts many charms: its architecture, fine furniture, souvenirs of a family of famous diplomats, a pleasant park and, a special treat for children, an exhibit dedicated to well-known fairytale characters.

CHÂTEAU DE DAMPIERRE★★

19km/12mi SW of Versailles.

Dampierre is closely associated with two distinguished families, the Luynes and the Chevreuse, who still own it today. From 1675 to 1683 Jules Hardouin-Mansart rebuilt the Château de Dampierre for Colbert's son-in-law the Duke of Chevreuse, a former student at Port-Royal and the mentor of the Duke of Burgundy. The castle and its park, laid out by Le Nôtre, form one of the rare well-preserved estates close to Paris.

ADDRESSES

STAY

Ibis – 4 ave Gén. de Gaulle. ℘01 39 53 03 30; www.ibis.com. 85 rooms. Near the château and town hall, offering the chain's latest standards of comfort. Poppy red rooms, which are functional and attractive.

Mercure – 19 r. Ph. de Dangeau. ℘01 39 50 44 10; www.mercure.com. 60 rooms. Practical rooms in a quiet area. Well-furnished lobby giving on to a pleasant breakfast room.

Novotel Château de Versailles – 4 bd St-Antoine, 78152 Le Chesnay. ℘01 39 54 96 96; www.novotel.com. 105 rooms. Restaurant. Hotel at the entrance to the town, on the place de la Loi. Functional rooms lead off an atrium made into a lounge. Modern bistro-style restaurant.

Hôtel Le Versailles – 7 r. Ste-Anne. ℘01 39 50 64 65; www.hotel-le-versailles.fr. 45 rooms. In a quiet side street not far from the château. Spacios, Art Deco-style rooms. Cosy bar-lounge and breakfast terrace.

Résidence du Berry – 14 r. d'Anjou. ℘01 39 49 07 07; www.hotel-berry.com. 38 rooms. Located in the Saint-Louis quarter, this 18C edifice has been entirely restored by Les Bâtiments de France. Comfort and top-quality materials await you in rooms with time-worn beams overhead.

EAT

La Brasserie du Théâtre – 15 r. des Réservoirs. ℘01 39 50 03 21; www.brasserietheatre.com. Closed 25 Dec, 1 May. Reservations advisable evenings. The walls of this 1895 brasserie situated next to the theatre are covered with photos of artists who have frequented it over the years. 1930s-style décor, covered terrace and traditional cuisine.

Le Bœuf à la Mode – 4 r. au Pain. ℘01 39 50 31 99. A typical 1930s bistro with a convivial, relaxed atmosphere. The décor – red wall-seats, knick-knacks, posters, mirrors – is a hit and the regional specialities are delicious. Very busy on market days.

Le Potager du Roy – 1 Mar.-Joffre. ℘01 39 50 35 34. Closed Sun–Mon. Delightfully retro setting. Meat and fish dishes with plenty of vegetables.

Au Chapeau Gris – 7 r. Hoche. ℘01 39 50 10 81; www.auchapeaugris.com. Closed Tue eve and Wed. Reservations required. This restaurant, said to date back to the 18C, is a veritable institution hereabouts. Quintessential Versailles ambience and décor are the setting for appetising, traditional cuisine. Reliable, very much sought-after establishment.

Valmont – 20 r. au Pain. ℘01 39 51 39 00; www.levalmont.com. Closed Sun eve and Mon. This old house on the Place des Halles is bound to catch your eye. First-rate reception, charming decoration, elegant tables and succulent cookery.

SHOPPING

Shops – The principal shopping areas are: Rue de la Paroisse, Rue Royale, Rue du Général-Leclerc, Place du Marché and Les Manèges, opposite the Rive-Gauche station. You'll find many antique dealers in the Passage de la Geôle, near La Place du Marché.

Major stores – From the FNAC (books, CDs, cameras, etc.) to Printemps or BHV (department stores), the shopping complex Le Centre Commercial de Parly II, on your way out of Versailles towards St-Germain, has it all.

Disneyland Resort Paris★★★

Opened in 1992 under the name EuroDisney, Disneyland Paris is an enormous holiday resort outside Paris with hotels, a 27-hole golf course, Disney Village entertainment and shopping complex, and campsite. The Disney Studios opened in 2002, and other new developments are planned through to 2017.

- www.disneylandparis.com.
- **Location:** The resort is located 30km/18.6mi east of Paris in Chessy.
- **Parking:** Parking on-site, €15/car, €10/motorcycle, €20/camping-cars.
- **Don't Miss:** The Disney Parade of characters down Main Street daily at 4pm.
- **Timing:** Allow two days to visit the entire resort.
- **Kids:** "Meet & Greet" Disney characters at specific restaurants.

A BIT OF HISTORY

Born in Chicago in 1901, Walt Disney showed great ability in drawing. After WWI, in which he served as an ambulance driver in France, he returned to the United States where he met a young Dutchman called Ub Iwerks, who was also passionate about drawing.

In Hollywood in 1923 the pair produced a series of short films called **Alice Comedies** and in 1928 Mickey Mouse was created, ushering in an era of Oscar-winning animated feature films: **Three Little Pigs** (1933), **Snow White and the Seven Dwarfs** (1937), **Dumbo** (1941). Disney productions also developed to include films starring real people, such as **Treasure Island** (1950), and some mixing of the two, for instance **Mary Poppins** (1964), which won six Oscars.

DISNEYLAND PARK★★★

This theme park, like those in the United States and Japan, is a realisation of Walt Disney's dream of creating a small, enchanted park where children and adults can enjoy themselves together. The large Disneyland Paris site (over 55ha/136 acres) is surrounded by trees and comprises five themed lands.

Every day the **Disney Parade★★** procession of floats carries Disney characters down Main Street USA. On some evenings and in the summer the **Main Street Electrical Parade★★** adds extra illuminations to the fairy-tale setting.

Main Street USA

Enter the park onto the main street of an American town at the turn of the 20C, bordered by shops with Victorian-style fronts. Horse-drawn street cars, double-decker buses, fire engines and Black Marias transport visitors from Town Square to Central Plaza while colourful musicians play favourite ragtime, jazz and Dixieland tunes. From Main Street station a small steam train, the **Euro Disneyland Railroad★**, travels across the park and through the **Grand Canyon Diorama**.

Frontierland

The conquest of the West, the gold trail and the Far West with its legends and folklore are brought together in Thunder Mesa, a typical western town. The waters here are plied by two handsome **steamboats★**, the *Mark Twain* and the *Molly Brown*.

In the bowels of **Big Thunder Mountain★★★** lies an old gold mine which is visited via the mine train: this turns out to be a runaway train which hurtles out of control to provide a thrilling ride. A tour of the dilapidated **Phantom Manor★★★** overlooking the rivers of the Far West is a spine-chilling house of hundreds of mischievous ghosts. The horseshoe-shaped **Lucky Nugget Saloon★** – every western town had

GETTING THERE

RER: (line A) Marne-la-Vallée–Chessy; by TGV from Lille, Lyon, Avignon, Marseille, Bordeaux, Nantes and Toulouse; by shuttle from Orly and Roissy-Charles de Gaulle Airports; by car via *autoroute* A 4 direction Metz; exit at junction 14 and follow signs .

GENERAL INFORMATION

Entry – Hours vary daily; check the website for current details.
For information on offers, quotes or booking, contact the Reservations Office (☎0844 8008 898: Open: Mon–Fri 9am–8pm; Sat 9am–6pm; Sun 10am–5.30pm).
Visiting – The charges for visiting Disneyland are complex and vary depending on your intentions. Check the website to build a profile of your planned visit, which can include everything from parking to hotel accommodation and restaurant reservations.
Disney Studios – High season and weekends 10am–9pm; low season 10am–6pm. For **guided tours**, contact the City Hall (Disneyland Park) on Town Square in Main Street, USA.
Hotel reservations – ☎01 60 30 60 30.
Internet – www.disneylandparis.com.
Booking a show – Entertainment programmes and booking facilities are available from City Hall, located in Town Square, inside Disneyland Park.
Currency exchange – Facilities are available at the parks' main entrance.
Disabled guests – A guide detailing special services available can be obtained from City Hall (Disneyland Park) or from the information desk inside Walt Disney Studios Park.
Lockers and storage – At the entrance and Main Street Station.
Rental – Guests can rent cameras from Town Square Photography, pushchairs and wheelchairs in Town Square Terrace (Disneyland Park) and in Front Lot (Walt Disney Studios Park).
Animals – They are not allowed in the theme parks, in Disney Village or in the hotels. The Animal Care Centre is located near the visitors' car park.
Baby Care Centre, Meeting Place for Lost Children, First Aid – Near the Plaza Gardens Restaurant (Disneyland Park) or in Front Lot (Walt Disney Studios Park).

MAKING THE MOST OF IT

Tips – To avoid long queues at popular attractions, it is best to visit these attractions during the parade, at the end of the day, or get a **Fast Pass** issued by distributors outside the most popular attractions in both parks; this ticket bears a time slot of 1hr during which there is access to the attraction without waiting in line.
Disneyland Park – Indiana Jones (Adventureland); Space Mountain (Discoveryland); Buzz Lightyear Laser Blast (Discoveryland); Peter Pan's Flight (Fantasyland); Big Thunder Mountain (Frontierland); Star Tours (Discoveryland).
Walt Disney Studios Park – Rock'n Roller Coaster (Backlot); Flying Carpets (Animation Courtyard); The Twilight Zone Tower of Terror (Production Courtyard).
Where to eat – Park maps include a list of eating places, with symbols indicating those offering table service and vegetarian meals. For quick meals go to **Bella Notte**, **Colonel Hathi's** or **Plaza Gardens** in Disneyland Park, or to the **Backlot Express Restaurant** in Disney Studios.
Take time and go to one of the following table service restaurants to enjoy a fine meal enhanced by an original décor (booking recommended. ☎01 64 74 28 82 or call at City Hall): **Silver Spur Steakhouse**, **Blue Lagoon Restaurant**, **Walt's American Restaurant** and **Auberge de Cendrillon** in Disneyland Park or **Café des Cascadeurs** in Walt Disney Studios Park.

its saloon – presents the dinner show **Lilly's Follies.**

Adventureland

Access this land of exotic adventure from Central Plaza, through Adventureland Bazaar. In the tropical Caribbean seas, marauding pirates attack and loot a coastal fort and village in the famous action-packed encounter, **Pirates of the Caribbean★★★**.

Courageous archaeologists brave the ruined temple deep in the jungle in **Indiana Jones et le Temple du Péril... à l'envers★★★**, while the giant tree, **La Cabane des Robinson★★** (27m high), offers panoramic views from the ingeniously furnished home of the shipwrecked Swiss family Robinson.

Fantasyland

Based around Walt Disney's familiar trademark, Sleeping Beauty's castle, this land recalls favourite fairy tales by authors such as Charles Perrault, Lewis Carroll and the Brothers Grimm. **Le Château de la Belle au bois dormant★★**, with its blue and gold turrets crowned with pennants, is at the very heart of Disneyland. **It's a Small World★★** is a delightful musical cruise in celebration of the innocence and joy of children throughout the world, while **Alice's Curious Labyrinth★** is a maze leading to the Queen of Hearts' castle. Fly in a boat through the skies above London and in Never-Never Land on **Peter Pan's Flight★★**, or visit the lovable puppet Pinocchio and his friends on **Les Voyages de Pinocchio★**. Enjoyable tours lead through the mysterious forest in mining cars from the dwarfs' mine with **Blanche-Neige et les Sept Nains★**.

Discoveryland

This is the world of past discoveries and future dreams of great visionaries such as Leonardo da Vinci, Jules Verne and HG Wells and their wonderful inventions. **Space Mountain★★★ – Mission 2** is a fantastic journey through space, while **Star Tours★★★** presents a breathtaking inter-planetary experience full of special effects inspired by the film *Star Wars*. Zap alien invaders in **Buzz Lightyear's Laser Blast**, or zoom around **Autopia**.

WALT DISNEY STUDIOS PARK

This park is dedicated to the wonders of the cinema, taking visitors backstage to discover the secrets of filming, animation techniques and television. The park entrance is overlooked by a watertower, a traditional landmark in film studios. In the centre of the Spanish-style courtyard, planted with palm trees, is a fountain dedicated to Mickey. Highlights include **Animagique★★★**, **Art of Disney Animation★★**, **Flying Carpets★★** and **Cinémagique★★★**.

DISNEY VILLAGE★

Across from the theme parks is Disney Village. In the main street of this American town it's always party time. On summer evenings there is plenty going on in the shops, restaurants and bars. Nightbirds can end the evening in the Sports Bar or Country Western Saloon.

The famous adventures of pioneer William Frederick Cody (1846–1917), alias Buffalo Bill, are the inspiration for **La Légende de Buffalo Bill★★**, a cabaret dinner which evokes the story of the Wild West, complete with horses, bison, cowboys and Indians.

EXCURSION

PROVINS★★

➲ 60km/37mi SE of Disneyland.

Whether approaching Provins from the Brie plateau to the west or from Champagne and the Voulzie valley, this medieval town presents the eye-catching and distinctive outlines of the Tour César and of the dome of St-Quiriace Church. Splendid remparts contribute to the town's medieval atmosphere, and the rose gardens add to its visual appeal. The lower town, a lively shopping centre, sits at the foot of the promontory and extends along the River Voulzie and the River Durteint. The town, which boasts 58 historic monuments, is now a UNESCO World Heritage Site.

Château de Vaux-le-Vicomte★★★

This splendid château, one of the masterpieces of the 17C, lies at the heart of French Brie, a countryside of vast fields broken with occasional copses.

- **Michelin Map:** 312 F 4
- **Info:** Vaux-le-Vicomte. 01 64 14 41 90; www.vaux-le-vicomte.com.
- **Location:** Vaux-le-Vicomte is 50km/31mi SE of Paris.
- **Don't Miss:** A walk through the gardens.
- **Timing:** Plan to enjoy a candlelit tour of the château (May–early Oct Sat 8pm–midnight). €19.50 (children 6–16, €15).
- **Kids:** There are Easter egg hunts, quizzes and costume rental all year.

Château de Vaux-le-Vicomte

© Vaux-le-Vicomte

A BIT OF HISTORY

Nicolas Fouquet had been Superintendent of Finances since the days of Mazarin and built a vast personal fortune. In 1656, he decided to construct at Vaux a palace to symbolise his success. As architect, he chose Louis Le Vau, as interior decorator Charles Le Brun, as landscaper André Le Nôtre.

By 1661, Vaux looked as it does today. A connoisseur, a man of lavish tastes, but sadly lacking in political judgement, Fouquet had counted on being appointed in Mazarin's place right up to the moment when Louis XIV decided to take power into his own hands.

Furthermore, he had alienated Colbert, and, even worse, had made advances to one of the king's favourites, Mlle de La Vallière.

By May, the decision to place him under arrest had already been taken. On 17 August, the unwitting Fouquet threw the most sumptuous of festivities among the Baroque splendours of Vaux. Hoping to impress the young Louis, he succeeded only in offending his monarch more deeply by the unparalleled extravagance of the proceedings. Dinner was presented on a solid gold service, at a time when the royal silverware had been melted down to repay the expenses of the Thirty Years' War! On 5 September, Fouquet was arrested at Nantes, his property confiscated, and his brilliant team of designers put to work on Versailles.

VISIT

Open mid-Mar–mid-Nov 10am–6pm. Day pass: €16.50 (children 6–16, €10). Audioguide €3. Gardens: €8.50.

Le Vau's château is the definitive masterpiece of the early Louis XIV style. It is majestic in its impact.

It is to be understood as the central feature of a grandiose designed landscape, an archetype of immense influence over the whole of Europe in the course of the following century and a half.

Le Brun's talent is here made manifest in all its richness and diversity.

His King's Bedroom anticipates the splendour of the Royal Apartments at Versailles.

In the **gardens** ★★★, Le Nôtre showed himself to be a master of perspective.

Fontainebleau★★★

As early as the 12C, the Capetian kings had built a hunting lodge here, drawn by the abundant game which thrived in the vast forest. It was to become an extraordinarily majestic palace and park listed as a World Heritage site.

- **Population:** 15 945
- **Michelin Map:** 312 F 5
- **Info:** 4 r. Royale. ✆01 60 74 99 99; www.fontainebleau-tourisme.com.
- **Location:** Fontainebleau and its château are in the midst of a large forest, 64km/39.7mi S of Paris.
- **Don't Miss:** The Grand Apartments and famous horseshoe staircase.
- **Timing:** The exterior of the Palace will take about an hour, the interior more than an hour.

A BIT OF HISTORY

The woodland covers 25 000ha/62 000 acres, much of it high forest of sessile oak, Norway pine and beech. It grows on the low east–west sandstone ridges, among the crags and boulders of stony wastelands, and in the sandy depressions between the ridges.

The forest is traversed by a network of well-signposted footpaths. Since the days of Colbert's Forestry Ordinance of 1669, "a masterpiece of forestry administration" (J L Reed), it has been carefully managed to ensure its long-term survival. In spite of the forest's fame and popularity, it is the palace begun by François I which has made the reputation of Fontainebleau. A taste for natural surroundings together with its role as a military base (notably for cavalry) led to the growth of the town of Fontainebleau in the 19C. Between 1947 and 1967 it was home to the headquarters of NATO.

CHÂTEAU★★★

77300 Fontainebleau. **Château** open Wed–Mon: Oct–Mar 9.30am–5pm; Apr–Sep 9.30am–6pm. Closed 1 Jan, 1 May, 25 Dec. €11. ✆01 60 71 50 70; www.musee-chateau-fontainebleau.fr.

From the days of the Capetian kings to the time of Napoléon III, the Palace of Fontainebleau has been lived in, added to and altered by the sovereigns of France. Napoléon Bonaparte liked it; here, in contrast to Versailles, he was free of the overwhelming presence of Louis XIV, a formidable predecessor in the quest for glory. He called Fontainebleau "the house of Eternity", furnished it in Empire style and set about altering it for himself, Josephine and Pope Pius VII.

In 1528, François I commissioned Gilles Le Breton to replace the existing medieval buildings with two structures linked by a gallery. Like his predecessor Charles VIII, while campaigning in Italy, François had acquired a taste for agreeable surroundings adorned with works of art. He brought in gifted and prolific artists who are known as the **First School of Fontainebleau**. They included Rosso (of Florence), Primaticcio (from Perugia), Niccolo dell'Abbate (from Parma), as well as architects, thinkers, cabinet-makers, goldsmiths and decorators.

He also acquired works of art including Leonardo's Mona Lisa and paintings by Raphael. France was thus permeated by Renaissance taste, by Renaissance mathematics and by an appreciation of the rules of proportion derived from the architecture of Greece and Rome. The pleasures of life were savoured anew, and painters and sculptors abandoned religious subjects in favour of older divinities. This era endowed the palace with many of its most splendid features: on the outside, the left wing and façade of the Court of the White Horse or Farewell Court (**Cour du Cheval-Blanc ou des Adieux★★**), the concave section of the Oval Court (**Cour Ovale★**), the

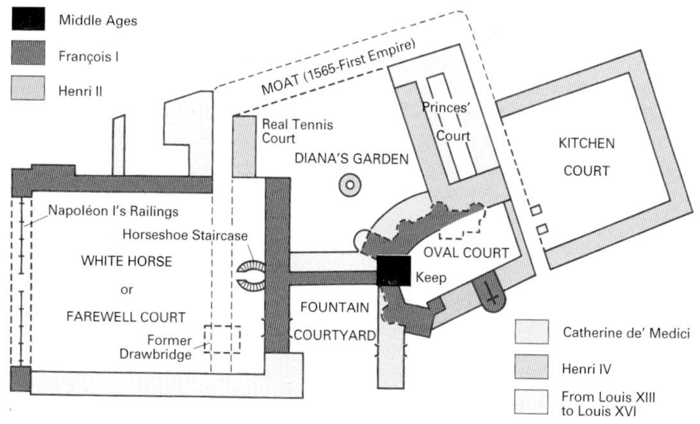

Golden Gate (**Porte Dorée★**) with its loggia painted by Primaticcio; and on the inside, the François I Gallery (**Galerie François I★★★**) by Rosso, the first important French interior to mix frescoes and stucco work, and the Ballroom (**Salle de Bal★★★**) painted by Primaticcio and dell'Abbate and completed by Philibert Delorme in the reign of Henri II.

Henri II, Catherine de' Medici and Charles IX carried on the work initiated during this most creative and productive period. Henri IV enlarged the palace further by building the real tennis court (Jeu de Paume), and the Diana Gallery (Galerie de Diane). He also completed the enclosure of the Oval Court. There was a change of style; the Second School of Fontainebleau looked to Flanders for its inspiration and found its artists in the Île-de-France; oil was now the preferred medium for painting. Louis XIII completed the Farewell Court. It was here, from the famous horseshoe staircase built by Du Cerceau, that Napoléon bade his men farewell on 20 April 1814, following his abdication.

Musée Napoléon I★

The **museum** is dedicated to the Emperor and his family; it occupies 15 rooms on the ground and first floors of the Louis XV wing and is only accessible by guided tour. Exhibits include portraits, silverware, arms, medals, ceramics (Imperial service), clothing (coronation robes, uniforms) and personal memorabilia. The rooms on the first floor evoke the Coronation (paintings by François Gérard), the Emperor's various military campaigns, his daily life (remarkable folding desk by Jacob Desmalter), the Empress Marie-Louise in formal attire or painting the Emperor's portrait (picture by Alexandre Menjaud) and the birth of Napoléon's son, the future King of Rome (cradles).

Château de Fontainebleau

Gardens★

Open daily Nov–Feb 9am–5pm; Mar–Apr and Oct 9am–6pm; May–Sep 9am–7pm. Closed 25 Dec, 1 Jan. **Park**: open 24/7. 01 60 71 50 70; www.musee-chateau-fontainebleau.fr.

Grotte du Jardin des Pins★

This rare ornamental composition carved in sandstone reveals the popular taste, copied from the Italians, for ponds, man-made features and bucolic landscapes in vogue toward the end of François I's reign. The rusticated arches are supported by giant telamones. The frescoes have disappeared.

The **Jardin anglais★** was created in 1812 on the site of former gardens (featuring a pine grove) redesigned under Louis XIV and abandoned during the Revolution. The Bliaut or Blaut fountain, which gave its name to the palace, plays in a small octagonal basin in the middle of the garden. The **park** was created by Henri IV, who filled the canal (in 1609) and had the grounds planted with elms, pines and fruit trees. Sixty years before the installation of the Grand Canal at Versailles, this dazzling sight was a great novelty for the *Ancien Régime*, as were the aquatic displays.

EXCURSION

CHÂTEAU DE COURANCES★★

19km/12mi W of Fontainebleau.

The still-inhabited château de Courances is a dramatic example of the Louis XIII style. It's famous for its park and numerous bodies of water. A superb "water garden" with bold geometric lines, the park is at once contemporary and a rare vestige of a little-known 16C landscaping style.

ADDRESSES

STAY

Hôtel Belle Fontainebleau – 1 r. de la Chancellerie. 01 64 22 21 70; http://hotel-belle-fontainebleau.com. 25 rooms. This small hotel in the heart of the city is located in the former buildings of the chancellery. The small rooms are bright and practical.

Hôtel Victoria – 112–122 r. de France. 01 60 74 90 00; www.hotelvictoria.com. 37 rooms. This 19C building is a pleasant, relaxing place to stay only five minutes on foot from the Château and the centre of town. Most of the rooms on its three floors have been redecorated in shades of yellow and blue; five of them have a marble fireplace.

EAT

Croquembouche – 43 r. de France. 01 64 22 01 57. Closed Sat & Mon for lunch, Sun. A plain and simple restaurant in the city centre frequented by regulars who appreciate the warm reception, the inviting dining room decorated in soothing colours, and the traditional food prepared from fresh produce.

L'Île aux Truites – 6 chemin Basse-Varenne, Vulaines-sur-Seine. 7km/4.3mi E of Fontainebleau dir. Samoreau. 01 64 23 71 87. Closed Thu lunch and Wed. Reservations required. A pretty thatched-roof country house on the banks of the Seine. Diners can savour trout and salmon from the restaurant's fish tank while enjoying an incomparable view of the river and forest.

NIGHTLIFE

Le Franklin-Roosevelt – 20 r. Grande. 01 64 22 28 73. Wine bar with mahogany furniture and red leatherette wall seats, a library dedicated to the period between 1890 and 1920, intimate ambience with jazz in the background, and some fine vintages on offer.

SPORT & LEISURE

Jeu de Paume de Fontainebleau – Château de Fontainebleau. 01 60 71 50 70; www.musee-chateau-fontainebleau.fr. The jeu de paume, a sport whose descendants include tennis and squash, has been played since 1601 in this indoor court of the Château de Fontainebleau. Visitors can watch a match or try a game themselves.

St-Germain-en-Laye★★

A residential suburb of Paris, and also a popular weekend resort, St-Germain's attractions are a château with delightful terraces and gardens, and a forest with pleasant walks.

- **Population:** 40 481.
- **Michelin Map:** 311 I 2
- **Info:** Maison Claude Debussy, 38 r. au Pain. ℘01 30 87 20 63. www.saintgermainenlaye-tourisme.fr.
- **Location:** The town is 19km/11.8mi W of Paris and easily reached from the city on the RER (line A1).
- **Don't miss:** The main area of interest is the château.
- **Timing:** Allow an hour or so to visit the château.

A BIT OF HISTORY

Now a residential town forming part of the Paris suburbs, St-Germain's significance in the course of French history goes back hundreds, if not thousands, of years. A strategic site 60m above a bend in the Seine persuaded Louis VI le Gros (the Fat) to build a stronghold here. Later, when the **Hundred Years' War** was at its height, the castle was restored by Charles V. Three French kings were born here (Charles IX, Henri II, Louis XIV), as well as several princes, writers, historians and composers. **Louis XIII** died here. It was here that in 1641 Richelieu promulgated the edict limiting the rights of the French parliament. On 28 February 1837, the first passenger railway in France was inaugurated, running to Paris.

CHÂTEAU★

Pl. Charles de Gaulle. ℘01 39 10 13 00.

Its appearance is still much as it was when François I had it rebuilt by Pierre de Chambiges in the taste of the 16C. Louis XIV brought in Mansart to replace the corner turrets with pavilions, and Le Nôtre, who designed the park, laid out the very long **terrasse★★** and replanted the forest.

The château houses the **Musée des Antiquités nationales★★** (www.musee-antiquitesnationales.fr); its priceless collection of archaeological exhibits traces French history from the Paleolithic to the Middle Ages.

EXCURSION

AUVERS-SUR-OISE★★

32km/20mi NW of Paris, along the A 115.

Tourist office, 38 Rue du Général de Gaulle, 95430 Auvers-sur-Oise. ℘01 30 36 71 81; www.auvers-sur-oise.com.

In the early 19C, this pleasant river village just outside Paris became the favoured stomping ground for a new generation of painters known as the "Impressionists" (*see Introduction, p107*), who came here to stay and paint, including Monet. Later, Van Gogh visited and subsequently committed some of the village sights to canvas, such as the church and town hall. An old walking trail, now a series of narrow streets, still carries the memory of the artists who brought it fame.

In Van Gogh's Footsteps

During his stay in Auvers, Vincent Van Gogh was extremely active. The restful countryside, where he hoped to find peace after his internment in Provence, encouraged his quest for freedom and his frantic need to work. He completed over 70 paintings in a very short time.

Auberge Ravoux★

Open Mar–Oct Wed–Sun 10am–6pm. €6. ℘01 30 36 60 60; www.maisondevangogh.fr.

Known as the **Maison de Van Gogh**, this is the inn where Van Gogh stayed for two months before his tragic death. Feeling guilt towards his brother Theo, upon whom he was entirely dependent, Van Gogh shot himself in the chest while he was out in a field; he died two days later in his room. He was 37 years old. The inn has been carefully restored and has retained its interior decoration and restaurant. Outside are panels describing the artist's eventful life. The small garret he occupied has remained unchanged and, despite the absence of furniture, gives an insight into the ascetic conditions in which he lived.

Follow rue des Colombières past the museum and studio of Charles-François Daubigny.

A path to the right leads to a cemetery set among the corn fields that Van Gogh loved to paint.

Vincent and Theo Van Gogh's graves

The famous Dutch painter's tomb stands against the left-hand wall. His brother Theo, who supported him and who died soon after him, rests by his side.

Musée de l'Absinthe

44 rue Callé. Open Mar–Oct, Sat–Sun and public holidays 1.30–6pm (Jul–Aug Wed–Sun 1.30–6pm). €5. 01 30 36 83 26; www.musee-absinthe.com.

The famous green liqueur reached the peak of its popularity in the cafés of the 19C. It was often described as the **green fairy** and was closely linked to the life of the artists of the day who spent a great deal of time in cafés. The documents, posters and objects displayed in the museum bring back to life the history of a drink which had a profound social influence until it was banned in 1915.

Musée Daubigny

Open daily except Mon–Tue: Apr–Oct 2–5.30pm (Sat–Sun and public holidays 10.30am–12.30pm, 2–6pm); Nov–Mar 2–5pm (Sat–Sun and public holidays 2–5.30pm). €4. 01 30 36 80 20; www.museedaubigny.com.

Housed in the Manoir des Colombières, this museum displays a collection of 19C paintings, watercolours, drawings and engravings illustrating the birth of Impressionism.

Maison-Atelier de Daubigny★

Open late Apr–Sep (except mid-Jul–mid-Aug) Thu–Sun 2–6.30pm. €6. 01 30 36 60 60; www.atelier-daubigny.com.

Charles-François Daubigny (1817–78), a landscape painter, settled in Auvers on the advice of his friend, Camille Corot. He had a studio-house built in 1861 and asked his family and friends to take part in the interior decoration. Charles, his son Karl and his daughter Cécile, as well as Corot and Daumier, left their marks of artistic inspiration on the walls and doors.

Château d'Auvers

Open Apr–Sep Tue–Sun and public holidays 10.30am–6pm; Oct–Mar 10.30am–4.30pm. €14.25 (children, 6–18, €10.15). 01 34 48 48 48; www.chateau-auvers.fr.

This restored 17C château, laid out with extensive use of audiovisual presentations, offers visitors a chance to enjoy a **Journey Back to the Days of the Impressionists★** and gain some insight into the wonderful adventure that was art in the 19C. Using reconstructions of interiors and the projection of some 600 works, it brings to life the Paris of the time, a city undergoing immense change thanks to the work of Baron Haussmann, and a city where the wealthy middle classes led a bustling, frivolous life with little appreciation of the new style of painting.

CHÂTEAU DE THOIRY★★

50km/31mi W of Paris.

Thoiry is a vast estate comprising a large Renaissance château and 250ha/ 625 acres of gardens and park. The family who has owned it for the past 400 years or more has undertaken a considerable amount of work to turn it into a magical spot where history and nature merge.

ADDRESSES

EAT

Auberge Ravoux – 01 30 36 60 60; www.maisondevangogh.fr. Reservations required. This old artists' café was Van Gogh's last home.

Parc Astérix★★

Astérix the Gaul, comical hero of the famous cartoon strip by Goscinny and Uderzo known throughout the world and translated into several languages, provides the theme for this 50ha/123-acre fun park which opened in 1989. It is a fantasy world for all ages that offers a madcap journey into the past.

Michelin Local Map: 312: G-6 or map 106 fold 9. 30km/18.6mi north of Paris.

Location: By car: 30min from central Paris on *autoroute* A 1; by **Métro**/RER train: line B3 from Châtelet or Gare du Nord stations (alight at Roissy-Charles de Gaulle 1 station); by **coach**: from Roissy coach station with Courriers Île-de-France (CIF; www.cif-bus.com).

Kids: Camp de Petitbonum, La Ronde des Rondins, Les Petits Drakkars, La Forêt des Druides, Au Pied du Grand Huit, La Petite Tempête, Les Petits Chars Tamponneurs.

VISIT

Open from 10am Apr–Oct, but at variable hours and days, check website for current details. €46 (under-11, €38). Parking €10 per day. Reservations: ✆08 26 46 66 20 (€0.15/min); www.parcasterix.fr.

The park is basically divided into five "historical" sections, complete with various attractions, shows, and a choice of snacks and meals. To explore this enchanting world, start at **Via Antiqua**, a "street" lined with stalls symbolising Asterix's journeys across Europe.

Gaul

At the very heart of the park, Astérix's **Village Gaulois★** consists of huts where visitors can meet the little hero and his fellow characters. Nearby, the atmosphere is much damper at the **Grand Splatch★**. But perhaps the most popular site is a Stone Age village built on piles, where an ingenious delivery system called **Menhir Express★★** takes anybody who dares on a trip through a network of canals bristling with surprises! You will also love the ride known as the **Trace du Hourra★★★** aboard a small train.

Roman Empire

In the arena, witness a charming young Gallic spy become the heroine of acrobatic fights in a show called **La Légion recrute★★**. Join the **Espions de César★** who have devised an efficient surveillance system above ground level. If you are really serious about a spy career, go through intensive spy training and meet the four challenges of the **Défi de César**.

Greece

The **Vol d'Icare** (Icarus' flight) takes you out of Daedalus' labyrinth, but you still have to defeat the terrible **Hydre de Lerne**. Once you are safe and sound, you may want to embark on a daring journey aboard a giant roller coaster called **Tonnerre de Zeus★★**, with the angry god watching you from atop Mount Olympus! After so much action, relax and enjoy a wonderful **spectacle of dolphins ★★** at the Theatre of Poséidon or a trip down the **Elis River**.

Vikings

The hiighlights of this section of the park include **Goudurix★★**, a gigantic roller coaster; **La Galère**, a funny swing in the shape of a boat; and for your little ones, **Les Petits Drakkars** (boats slipping on water) and **Les Petites Chaises Volantes** (flying chairs).

Across Time

A long journey in time takes place along **Avenue de Paris★★**. Ten centuries of history are illustrated here, each period represented by people in costume, typical shops and the avenue's own special atmosphere.

Château de Chantilly★★★

A synonym for elegance, Chantilly is home to wonderful art collections, a great park and forest, and the cult of the horse as well as the château itself.

- **Michelin Map:** 305 F-G 6
- **Info:** Office de Tourisme, 73 rue du Connétable, Chantilly. ☎03 44 67 37 37; www.chantilly-tourisme.com.
- **Location:** Chantilly is 50km/31mi N of Paris. When you arrive, the château is well signposted from here.
- **Timing:** Allow at least 2hr for the château.
- **TGV/Train:** Chantilly Gouvieu station is just 23min from Paris Nord.

THE CHÂTEAU★★★

Open: Apr–Oct daily 10am–6pm; Nov–Mar daily except Tue 10.30am–5pm. €16. Park and gardens €7. Parking €4. ☎03 44 27 31 80; www.chateaudechantilly.com.

Anne de Montmorency, the great Constable of France who served six monarchs (from Louis XII to Charles IX), had a Renaissance castle built here in 1528. The foundations of an earlier building (1386) were re-used. In 1560 the architect Jean Bullant designed a charming little château (Petit Château) to the south of the main building. The Great Condé and his descendants later made the state rooms of the Petit Château into their living quarters; today, there is much to delight the eye, including Rococo woodwork, manuscripts, silver caskets and icons.

The greatest treasure is in the Library *(Cabinet des Livres; open daily 9.15am–5pm)*; this is the **Limbourg** brothers' sumptuously illuminated *Book of Hours for the Duke of Berry (Les Très Riches Heures du Duc de Berry)* of about 1415, completed 60 years later by Jean Colombe (on display in reproduction). Under Louis II of Bourbon, known as the Great Condé, Le Nôtre laid out the park and gardens; François Mansart redesigned the principal façade and the layout of the rooms.

During the Revolution, the château was dismantled to first-floor level, the Petit Château was ruined and the park laid waste. On the death of Louis-Joseph de Condé, the estate passed into the hands of the Duke of Aumale, who rebuilt the great edifice (1875–83) in a neo-Renaissance style.

The château houses a **museum★★** – manuscripts, furniture, paintings, sculpture – whose wealth would prove difficult to rival today. The landscaped **English-style garden★** (open same hours as the château) was laid out on the surviving relics of Le Nôtre's park in 1820.

Musée du Cheval – Grandes Écuries★★

Open same hours as the château.

These stables were built in 1721 by Jean Aubert for Louis-Henri of Bourbon, the Great Condé's great-grandson. Much admired in its time, it is the finest example of 18C building at Chantilly to have come down to us. The stables house the **Musée Vivant du Cheval et du Poney★**, which has stalls from the time of the Duke of Aumale, historic harnessing, costumes, and all kinds of objects associated with equitation. Riding displays take place in the central rotunda. More than 3 000 horses are stabled and trained in and around Chantilly; race meetings and hunts both perpetuate the tradition begun on 15 May 1834 when France's first great official race meeting was held, and maintain Chantilly's reputation as the country's thoroughbred capital. The French Derby (*Prix du Jockey Club*) is held here every April.

Senlis★★

A tributary of the Oise, the Nonette River runs through this picturesque medieval town surrounded by the rich cornfields of Valois and the wooded expanses of Ermenonville, Chantilly and Halatte forests. Strolling along the winding streets of the Old Quarter, paved with flagstones and lined with relics of its past, you may still feel the powerful presence of the Frankish rulers and cathedral builders who left behind an invaluable legacy for us to enjoy.

- **Population:** 16 170.
- **Michelin Local Map:** 305 G 5 or map 106 folds 8, 9
- **Info:** Office du tourisme de Senlis, pl. du Parvis-Notre-Dame, 60300. ✆03 44 53 06 40; www.senlis-tourisme.fr.
- **Location:** Access from Paris: by car, via the A 1 (51.5km/32mi); by train, from Gare du Nord to Chantilly, then bus link to Senlis.
- **TGV/Train:** Senlis is about 1hr via Chantilly from Paris Gare du Nord.
- **Parking:** The car park near the cathedral fills early in the day. Try those off the rue de la République.
- **Don't Miss:** Notre-Dame's magnificient spire; the view over the remains of the old ramparts from the Jardin du Roy; the Gallo-Roman and Merovingian collections of the Musée d'Art et d'Archéologie; St-Frambourg Royal Chapel and its stained-glass windows by Joan Miró.
- **Timing:** Allow a half day to explore the town and 1hr to visit the cathedral.

A BIT OF HISTORY

The election of Hugues Capet – The conquerors of Senlis built a massive stronghold over the first Gallo-Roman ramparts of the town. The kings of the first two **Frankish dynasties** would often take up residence here, lured by the game in the nearby forests. The Carolingian line died out when Louis V suffered a fatal hunting accident. In 987, the Archbishop of Reims called a meeting at Senlis Castle in which he and the local lords decided that **Hugues Capet**, then Duke of France, would be the next king. The last king of France to have stayed in Senlis was Henri IV. The city went out of fashion as a royal place of residence and was gradually replaced by Compiègne and Fontainebleau.

CATHÉDRALE NOTRE-DAME★★

The construction of Senlis cathedral started in 1153 – 16 years after St-Denis and 10 years before Notre-Dame in Paris – but progressed at a slow pace due to insufficient funds. The cathedral was not consecrated until 1191. It was only toward the mid-13C that the right tower was crowned with the magnificent **spire★★** which was to have such a strong influence over religious architecture in the Valois area. The **main doorway★★** is strongly reminiscent of the doorways at Chartres, Notre-Dame in Paris, Amiens and Reims.

South front – Constructed by **Pierre Chambiges** (1509–44) in the 16C, the **transept façade★★** contrasts sharply with the main façade. You can follow the evolution of Gothic architecture from the austere 12C to the 16C, when Late Flamboyant showed signs of Renaissance influence, introduced after the Italian wars.

North side – The cathedral's setting on this side features several patches of greenery and is extremely picturesque. Skirt the little garden that follows the east façade of what was once the bishop's palace. The building rests on the ruins of Gallo-Roman ramparts.

Compiègne★★★

- **Population:** 40 517.
- **Michelin Map:** 305 H 4
- **Info:** pl. de l'Hôtel-de-Ville. ☎03 44 40 01 00; www.compiegne-tourisme.fr.
- **Location:** Hidden in the Forest of Compiègne, the town is 60km/37mi E of Beauvais, in southern Picardy.
- **TGV/Train:** Compiêgne is 40min–1hr direct from Paris Gare du Nord.
- **Don't Miss:** The royal private apartments in the palace; the forest surrounding the town, one of the most beautiful of its type in France.
- **Timing:** The Palace will take about 2hr to visit.

The site of Compiègne had been appreciated by the Merovingians long before Charles the Bald built a château here in the 9C. A fortified town grew up around this nucleus. In 1429, Philippe le Bon (the Good), Duke of Burgundy, had designs on Picardy, which he hoped to incorporate into his realm by means of a joint operation with the English. The French line of defence along the Oise was reinforced on the orders of Joan of Arc; disgusted with the inertia prevailing at Sully-sur-Loire where the French Court had established itself, she had come to Compiègne on her own initiative. But on the evening of 23 May 1430, she was seized by the Burgundians. Wary of possible consequences, Philip the Good sold her on to the English; one year later she was burnt at the stake in Rouen.

CHÂTEAU★★★

Open Wed–Mon 10am–6pm. Closed 1 Jan, 1 May, 25 Dec. €7.50 (free for under 26, and on 1st Sun in the month). ☎03 44 38 47 02; www.musee-chateau-compiegne.fr.

Compiègne had been a royal residence since the time of the later Capetians, but Louis XV was dissatisfied with the ill-assorted and crumbling buildings inherited from his great-grandfather, and in 1738 he gave orders for the château to be reconstructed.

The architect was **Ange-Jacques Gabriel**, who succeeded in building one of the great monuments of the Louis XV style. Begun in 1751, the great edifice made use of the foundations of the previous structure, partly for reasons of economy, partly because the site was pitted with old quarries. Gabriel chose to emphasise the horizontality of his buildings, stretching them out and providing them with flattened roofs with balustrades, themes he took up again in the Place de la Concorde and École Militaire in Paris. The palace took 40 years to build; after Gabriel's retirement the work was carried on by his draughtsman, and a general movement in the direction of greater simplicity is very evident, with features like entablatures, ornamental window-brackets and attic floors tending to disappear. This evolution can be traced in the left wing of the main courtyard (1755), the principal façade facing the park, which was designed in 1775 and completed 10 years later (Napoléon's staircase of 1801 spoils the effect wished for by Gabriel), and the peristyle of 1783.

While the place was still a building site, it formed the background to the first meeting (1770) between Louis XVI and Marie-Antoinette. Later, in 1810, it was where Napoléon met Marie-Louise, Marie-Antoinette's great-niece.

Guided Tours

Compiègne offers themed discovery tours from mid-May–mid-Jul and mid-Aug–mid-Oct at weekends and on public holidays. Enquire at the tourist office.

© Yann Guichaoua / age fotostock

Château de Compiègne

During the Second Empire, Napoléon III made Compiègne his favourite residence, where he took much pleasure in the house-parties to which like-minded celebrities would be invited, some 80 at a time. Inside, the palace is decorated and furnished in 18C and Empire style (chests of drawers, applied ornament, wall-cupboards, tapestries).

Musée de la Voiture et du Tourisme★★

In addition to 18C and 19C coaches, the vehicles exhibited include: the **Mancelle** of 1898, a steam mail-coach designed by Amédée Bollée; a No 2 **Panhard**; a Type A **Renault** of 1899 with direct drive; the **Jamais Contente** ("Never Satisfied") of 1899, an electric car with tyres by Michelin, the first to reach 100kph/62mph; a Type C **Renault** of 1900, one of the first cars to have enclosed bodywork (by Labourdette); and a **Citroën** half-track of 1924.

ADDITIONAL SIGHTS

Hôtel de Ville★

Musée de la Figurine historique★
(*pl. de l'Hôtel de Ville*)

Musée Vivenel – Greek vases★★
(*2 r. d'Austerlitz*)

EXCURSIONS

CLAIRIÈRE DE L'ARMISTICE★★

8km/5mi E.

This is the place where, at 5.15am on 11 November 1918, the armistice was signed, which put an end to WWI at 11am on the same day. At the time the site was sheltered by forest trees. A restaurant-car identical to the carriage **(wagon-bureau)** (open Apr–mid-Sep daily 10am–6pm; mid-Sep–Mar daily except Tue 10am–5.30pm. €5. 03 44 85 14 18; www.musee-armistice-14-18.fr) used by Marshal Foch displays the original objects handled by the delegates in 1918. **Ferdinand Foch** (1851–1929) is generally held to have been the architect of Allied victory in the Great War of 1914–18. He was born in Tarbes in the Pyrénées in an 18C middle-class home (now a museum). He taught strategy at the Military Academy (École de Guerre), then became its commandant. In 1914 he distinguished himself both in the Battle of the Frontiers in Lorraine and in the "Miracle of the Marne".

After the German breakthrough in the Ludendorff offensive of early 1918, Foch was appointed supreme commander of the French and British armies. Promoted to marshal, it was he who launched the final Allied offensive on 8 August.

After the Battle of France in 1940, it was the turn of a French delegation to present itself here to the dignitaries of the Nazi regime in order to hear the victors' terms for an armistice. It was signed on the evening of 22 June. The clearing and its historic monuments were then ransacked by the occupation forces; only the statue of Marshal Foch was spared.

Château de Pierrefonds

© Arenysam / Fotolia.com

CHÂTEAU DE PIERREFONDS★★

14km/8.7mi SE.

Open May–early Sept daily 9.30am–6pm; Sept–Apr daily except Mon 10am–1pm, 2–5.30pm. €7.50.

The stronghold seems to embody everything that a medieval castle should be as it looms over the village crouching at its feet. For the most part, however, it is a creation of the 19C. Pierrefonds was part of the Duchy of Valois, and its castle, whose origins go back as far as Carolingian times, was rebuilt in the middle of the Hundred Years' War by Louis d'Orléans, the brother of Charles VI, as part of a chain of defences between the rivers Oise and Ourcq. It was dismantled during the reign of Louis XIII.

The castle ruins were bought by Napoléon I. In 1857 Louis Napoléon, inspired by romantic ideals, commissioned **Viollet-le-Duc** (1814–79) to restore the keep; four years later he was entrusted with a complete rebuilding of the castle as an Imperial residence and a picturesque place for receptions given to entertain the emperor's guests at Compiègne. From the ramparts the view extends over the Vallée de Pierrefonds. Little of Louis d'Orléans' building is left save the base of the walls and the towers.

Viollet-le-Duc's contributions, in the neo-Gothic style, are not without merit, but are notable more for originality than for strict historical accuracy, in terms of both architecture and decoration (arcading and gallery of the main façade in the courtyard, tribune in the chapel, roof of the Salle des Preuses). Nevertheless, it gives an excellent idea of a castle's defensive system prior to the age of cannon (north rampart walk).

CHÂTEAU DE BLÉRANCOURT

31km/19mi NE.

During WWI the château was taken over by Ann Morgan, who set up a temporary hospital here. Blérancourt subsequently became the headquarters for the organisation of relief for the civilian population.

When the war was over, Miss Morgan's efforts were directed towards the establishment of a museum of Franco-American history. In 1929, she presented the place to the French state, whereupon its name was changed to the **Musée National de la Coopération Franco-Américaine** (open daily except Tue 2–6pm. 03 23 39 60 16; www.museefrancoamericain.fr). About a dozen rooms in the left wing (at present closed for reconstruction) are devoted to the American War of Independence.

The exhibits on show in the right wing (Pavillon Florence Gould) illustrate aspects of the long and close relationship between the two countries; there are displays on the 1801 Treaty of Friendship, the Louisiana Purchase, emigration to the United States, the Gold Rush, etc. Other rooms evoke the two world wars, notably by means of relics of the **La Fayette** Squadron and of the American Field Service.

CATHÉDRALE DE BEAUVAIS (ST-PIERRE)★★★

Beauvais lies on the A 16 in southern Picardy. Open daily: Jun–Oct 10am–6.15pm; Nov–May 10am–12.15pm, 2–5.15pm. 03 44 48 11 60; www.cathedrale-beauvais.fr.

An extraordinary Gothic cathedral stands at the centre of this fortified city. The strange spireless building is the result of a long effort, technical and financial, which eventually ended in failure. In 1225 the Bishop of Beauvais decided to build the biggest and highest cathedral of the age in honour of St Peter. Its vaults were to top 48m. But in 1272, ten years after completion, the vault collapsed; it was rebuilt but fell again in 1284. Work had to start immediately on strengthening the walls, increasing the number of flying buttresses at the east end and using external struts at the base of the roof, 40m above ground, concealing the sheer daring of the original enterprise. The interior was treated similarly. In the southern bays, additional pillars underpinned the structure above. The windows were given more lancets to subdivide and strengthen them, and glazing was added to the elevation, lightening it considerably.

After the Hundred Years' War, Martin Chambiges began the construction of the transepts and crossing. He designed the great gable and rose window of the south transept, then, instead of the nave, he built the crossing tower. It was completed in 1539, a century later, 11m higher than the tower of Strasbourg cathedral. With no nave to buttress it, the great structure collapsed in 1573.

The dizzying height of the vaults is still most impressive and there is much decorative work to admire, from the Renaissance doors of the south portal, to the **stained-glass windows (vitraux)**★★ created by the Beauvais workshops founded by Ingrand Leprince. There's also the remarkable **astronomical clock** (horloge astronomique)★.

ADDRESSES

STAY

Auberge de la Vieille Ferme – 58 r. de la République, Meux. 03 44 41 58 54. 14 rooms. Restaurant. This old farmhouse built of Oise valley brick offers rooms that are simple but well-kept and practical. The restaurant sports exposed beams, rustic furniture, a tile floor and gleaming copperware. Traditional and regional cuisine.

Hôtel des Beaux Arts – 33 cours Guynemer. 03 44 92 26 26; www.bestwestern.com. 50 rooms. Located along the Oise waterfront, here's a contemporary hotel whose modern, well-soundproofed rooms have been furnished in teak or laminated wood. Some are larger and have a kitchenette.

EAT

Le Bistrot des Arts – 33 cours Guynemer. 03 44 20 10 10. Closed Sat lunch and Sun. Located on the ground floor of the Hôtel des Beaux-Arts, an appealing, authentic bistro decorated with various objects and etchings. In the kitchen, the chef concocts appetising dishes using market-fresh produce.

Brasserie du Nord – pl. de la Gare. 03 44 83 58 84. Closed Sun & public holidays. This has become quite an institution locally for its seafood dishes. The dining room is modern and bright.

Auberge du Buissonnet – 825 r. Vineux, Choisy-au-Bac. 5km/3mi NE of Compiègne via N 31 and D 66. 03 44 40 17 41. Closed Sun eve, Tue eve and Mon. Reservations recommended. Ask for a table near the bay windows of the dining room or on the terrace, weather permitting, and watch ducks and swans glide peacefully over the pond, then shake themselves off and waddle proudly toward the garden.

Le Palais Gourmand – 8 r. du Dahomey. 03 44 40 13 13. Closed Sun eve and Mon . This spruce-timbered house (1890) has a string of rooms and an attractive verandah where heaters, Moorish pictures and mosaics create an agreeable atmosphere. Traditional cuisine.

Laon★★

This ancient town dominates the surrounding countryside from its magnificent hilltop site★★, a 100m-high limestone outlier rising abruptly from the plain. Its defensive potential was noted by the Carolingian kings who made it their capital for 150 years, from the reign of Charles le Chauve (the Bald) (840) to Louis V (987). It was only in the reign of Hugh Capet that the capital was moved to the Île-de-France.

- **Population:** 25 986.
- **Michelin Map:** 306 D 5
- **Info:** pl. du Parvis Gautier de Mortagne. ℘03 23 20 28 62; www.tourisme-paysdelaon.com.
- **Location:** Laon lies 138km/86mi NE of Paris, mid-way between Reims and Saint-Quentin.
- **TGV/Train:** Laon is 1½–2hrs direct from Paris Gare du Nord.
- **Parking:** Driving and parking are difficult in the Upper Town. Parking is available at the foot of the cathedral and along Promenade de la Couloire.
- **Timing:** Allow at least half a day to explore the town. The quickest and most enjoyable way to reach the Upper Town is on the cable railway, called Poma (Mon–Sat 7am–8pm. ℘03 23 23 52 01; www.tul-laon.net).
- **Kids:** There is a wide range of activites for children, from treasure hunts to following in the footsteps of Knights Templar.

Lantern tower of the cathedral

SIGHT

CATHÉDRALE NOTRE-DAME★★

The present cathedral was begun in 1160 and completed towards 1230. It is in the early Gothic style, still caught up in the Romanesque idiom (as in its Norman-style lantern-tower).

The west front is a masterpiece, with its deep porches and stepped towers flanked by openwork turrets. The immensely long **nave★★★** shows the persistence of Carolingian traditions, but "nowhere else did the development of 12C Gothic achieve such breadth and unity" (Henri Focillon). The elevation is four-storeyed, with great arches carried on circular columns, a gallery with bold double arches, a blind triforium and a clerestory. In the nave, transept and chancel the bays are marked – in a less emphatic way than at either Sens (1140) or Senlis (1153) – by a pattern of major and minor clustered columns.

ADDITIONAL SIGHTS

Quartier de la Cathédrale★★ (Cathedral area)
Rempart du Midi★ (southern Ramparts) – **views★**
Musée Archéologique Municipal★ (*32 r. George-Ermant*). **Chapelle des Templiers★** (*r. Paul Doumer*). **Église St-Martin★** (*r. Eglise St Martin*).
Porte de Soissons★

Arras★★

The Abbey of St-Vaast formed the nucleus around which the capital of Artois grew in the Middle Ages. Between the 12C and 14C it gained privileges from the Counts of Artois encouraging an economy based on corn, banking and, especially, fabrics. The city prospered; poetic and literary societies thrived in which Arras' notables could enjoy hearing themselves lampooned by minstrels and entertainers. In the 15C, Artois passed into the hands of the Dukes of Burgundy, ensuring steady orders for its fine tapestries, which were notable for dealing realistically with secular themes.

- **Population:** 41 611.
- **Michelin Map:** 301 J 5-6
- **Info:** pl. des Héros. ☏03 21 51 26 95; www.ot-arras.fr.
- **Location:** 62.5km/39mi NE of Amiens.
- **TGV/Train:** Arras is 50min direct from Paris Gare du Nord.
- **Timing:** Half a day for a leisurely explore.
- **Don't Miss:** The outstanding architectural details of the Grand Place and the Place des Héros.

A BIT OF HISTORY

The notorious **Maximilien Robespierre** was born in Arras in 1758 to a well-to-do legal family. He was called to the Bar before becoming a Deputy in 1789, a Republican in 1792, and a prominent member of the feared Committee of Public Safety in 1793. Determined and indifferent to favours, "Robespierre the Incorruptible" embodied the spirit of the Revolution. Backed by Saint-Just and Couthon, he harried plotters and crushed deviationists, going so far as to take part in the condemnation of his allies, the Girondins. Discredited in the end by the consequences of his extremist ideology, on 27 July 1794 he himself fell victim to the guillotine to which he had condemned so many others.

SIGHTS

ANCIENNE ABBAYE ST-VAAST★★

In 667, a small chapel found itself the site of the building of a new abbey intended for Benedictine monks.
The chapel had been erected by St Vaast (453–540), whose remains were moved from Arras cathedral into the new abbey. It was St Auburt who began the abbey's development, which was completed by his successor and richly endowed by King Theodoric. Independent until 1778, the abbey enjoyed huge importance in the surrounding area.
After the Revolution the monastery was used as a hospital and later a barracks. In 1838, part of it was turned into a museum; the bishop held residence in the other part. In 1833, the abbey church was rebuilt and now serves as

Grand'Place

Arras cathedral, replacing the former Gothic building destroyed during the Revolution. The abbey houses the **Musée des Beaux-Arts★** which displays a variety of medieval and archaeological artworks, paintings and ceramics.

Les Places★★★ (Squares)

Dating from the 11C, the **Grand'Place, Place des Héros** and the **Rue de la Taillerie** linking them celebrate the city's status as an important regional market centre. Their present splendidly harmonious appearance is the fruit of the city fathers' purposeful civic design initiatives in the 17C and 18C.

The existing Spanish Plateresque buildings of the 16C and 17C (Arras was effectively under Spanish rule from 1492–1640) were given Flemish Baroque façades from 1635 onward. To the north of the Grand'Place a brick building with a stone-built ground floor is topped by a stepped gable, the only one of its kind. Arras' civic pride was symbolised by the construction of its Town Hall, **Hôtel de Ville★** (pl. des Héros) in 1572; its bell tower (beffroi) (open when the tourist office is open; closed 1 Jan, 25 Dec. ✆03 21 51 26 95) blends Flemish Gothic with Henri II-style ornamentation. It was destroyed in WW I but rebuilt in 1919.

Circuit des souterrains (The Boves)

Guided tours 40min from tourist office. Closed 1 and 7–25 Jan, 18–22 Mar, 3–4 Jul and 25 Dec. €5.50.

The 10C galleries, or boves, cut into the limestone bank on which the town stands, served as a refuge in wartime (during WWI the British set up a field hospital here for 24 000 troops) and above all as an enormous wine cellar; the caves (boves) are at the ideal temperature for storing wine.

Wellington Quarry memorial

Rue Arthur Delétoille. Open daily 10am–12.30pm, 1.30–6pm. Guided and audioguided tours only. €7. ✆03 21 51 26 95; www.explorearras.com.

A fascinating visit to underground quarries that played an unsuspected and vital role during World War I. A very moving experience.

Cité Nature

Open Tue–Fri 9am–5pm, Sat–Sun 2–6pm. €7. www.citenature.com.

An old warehouse renovated by Jean Nouvel in 2004 houses an interactive exposition on nature, ecology, and agriculture, with a green labyrinth in the gardens.

EXCURSIONS

Vimy Canadian Memorial★

10km/6.2mi N.

A gripping sight that brings home some of the realities of WWI. The summit of this chalky ridge was taken by the Canadian Expeditionary Force, part of the British Third Army, in April 1917.

It is crowned by the Canadian Memorial. There are extensive views over a farmed landscape dotted with the conical tips of coal mines.

To the west are the cemetery and basilica of Notre-Dame-de-Lorette, and nearby, entrenchments and pitted landforms left by trench warfare, which can be visited.

Musée Louvre-Lens★★

18.7km/11.6mi N. Maison du projet. R. Georges-Bernanos. www.louvrelens.fr. Open Wed–Sun 11am–6pm. No charge.

A satellite of the Louvre in Paris, this 20ha/50acre museum and park is located on the site of a former pithead.

ADDRESSES

STAY

Le Clos Grincourt – 18 r. du Château, 62161 Duisans. 9km/5.4mi W of Arras via N 39 then D 56. ✆03 21 48 68 33; www.leclosgrincourt.com. 3 rooms. A tree-lined lane leads to a lovely B&B.

EAT

Astoria – 12 pl. Foch, Arras. ✆03 21 71 08 14. Brasserie-style restaurant. Traditional breakfast dishes and regional specialities.

Amiens★★

The largest Gothic cathedral in France, one of the finest in the world, is the majestic centrepiece of the historic capital of Picardy.

- **Population:** 133 448.
- **Michelin Map:** 301 G 8
- **Info:** 40 pl. Notre-Dame. ✆03 22 71 60 50; www.amiens-tourisme.com.
- **Location:** 125km/78mi S and E of Boulogne-sur-Mer. Walk across the River Somme to explore the narrow streets of Quartier St-Leu, which contain craft and antique shops, cafés and restaurants.
- **Parking:** Leave the car in place St Michel, next to the cathedral, or in Saint-Leu underground car park.
- **Don't miss:** The Hortillonnages; the Son et Lumière at the cathedral; the Saint-Leu district.
- **Timing:** Amiens requires a full day as a minimum; longer would be better.

A BIT OF HISTORY

Amiens' great legend is that of the Roman soldier who, passing near Amiens, sliced his cloak in two and gave half to a wretched beggar. Later becoming Bishop of Tours, the former soldier was eventually canonised as St Martin, patron saint of France. In 1477, on the death of Charles le Téméraire (the Bold), this ancient capital of Picardy became subject to the French Crown.

In the 17C its textile industry prospered (Amiens velvet). The city suffered in both world wars, in 1918 during the Ludendorff Offensive, in 1940 during the Battle of France. Later attractively restored and now a university town, it is again a major centre for the arts and the economy.

SIGHTS

Cathédrale Notre-Dame★★★

Open daily Apr–Sep 8.30am–6.30pm; Oct–Mar 8.30am–5.30pm. Guided tours available. ✆03 22 71 60 50.

A UNESCO World Heritage Site, this harmonious building was begun in 1220 and completed just 68 years later. The architect, Robert de Luzarches, had all the stonework cut to its finished dimensions before it left the quarry, then simply assembled it on site. The cathedral is in Gothic Lanceolate style, with three-storey elevations including a blind triforium in nave and transept. The wonderfully elegant nave is the highest in France (42.5m).

At an early date problems arose through water from the Somme penetrating the foundations; movement occurred along the length of the building, evidence of which can be seen in cracks in the nave near the transept. The weight of the vaults aggravated the effect; to remedy it, in the 16C a brace of Toledo steel was inserted into the triforium, heated red-hot, and allowed to cool.

For four centuries it has served its purpose admirably. The building was further strengthened by increasing the number of buttresses at the east end and by adding side chapels in the form of double aisles to the nave in order to spread the downward forces as widely as possible.

The famous slender steeple rising above the crossing was built by the master carpenter Cardon in two years (1528–29). Much of the cathedral's decoration is of very high quality indeed: the sculpture of the west front (including the noble figure of Christ known as the "Beau Dieu"), and the rose windows of the main façade, including the 16C Sea Window (rose de la Mer), of the north transept; the 14C Window of the Winds (rose des Vents); and of the south transept, the 15C Window of Heaven (rose du Ciel). Inside, the wrought-iron choir screen dates from the 18C and the oak choir stalls from the beginning of the 16C. The third chapel of the north aisle

© S. Sauvignier / Michelin

Detail of the central doorway, Cathédrale Notre-Dame

houses a remarkable Romanesque Crucifixion probably influenced by oriental art. Christ's feet are nailed to the Cross separately; clad in a long robe, He wears His royal crown in glory. The figure was carved before the arrival in Paris of the relics of the Passion (including the Crown of Thorns) purchased by St Louis.

Chés Cabotans Puppet Theatre

Puppet shows mid-Oct–Mar 2–6pm; Apr–Aug 10am–noon, 2–6pm. Tariffs vary for each performance; check website for details. 03 22 22 30 90; www.ches-cabotans-damiens.com.

Visiting this theatre you will get to learn a bit about famous local characters such as Lafleur and his wife Sandrine (*see Puppets panel, page 186*). While you may not understand everything that's said why not watch one of the shows given in this miniature theatre where the characters express themselves in a mixture of Picardy dialect and French?

Hortillonnages★

€6 (children, €4.50–€5.50). Boat trip daily Apr–Oct 1.30pm onwards. 03 22 92 12 18; www.hortillonnages-amiens.fr.

The small allotments known as **aires**, which stretch over an area of 300ha/7 491 acres amid a network of canals (**rieux**) fed by the many arms of the Somme, have been worked since the Middle Ages by market gardeners or *hortillons*. At present, fruit trees and flowers are tending to replace vegetables and the gardeners' sheds are becoming weekend holiday homes. Kids will enjoy the Île-aux-Fagots, where there is an **aquarium** and an **insectarium**.

ADDITIONAL SIGHT

Musée de Picardie★★

Open: Tue, Fri–Sat 10am–noon, 2–6pm, Wed 10am–6pm, Thu 10am–noon, 2–9pm, Sun 2–7pm. Closed 1 Jan, 1 and 8 May, 14 Jul, 1 and 11 Nov, 25 Dec and Mon. €5 (no charge 1st Sun in the month). 03 22 97 14 00.

Puppets

Amiens' puppet shows date back to about 1785. Known in Picardy dialect as **cabotans**, the puppets are carved out of wood and are about 50cm tall. The main character **Lafleur** is the King of St-Leu (the medieval quarter) and undoubtedly embodies all the spirit and character of the Picardy people. Since at least the 19C, this truculent, irreverent, bold character with his fiery temper has expressed plain common sense and acclaimed the proud nobility of the province in the language of his ancestors. Even from a distance, he is recognisable by his impressive stature, characteristic gait, and 18C valet's livery of fine red Amiens velvet. He is often accompanied by his wife **Sandrine** and his best friend Tchot Blaise. His motto is "Drink, walk and do nothing".

In the 19C, each of the 20 quarters in the city had its own puppet theatre. With the arrival of the cinema and sporting events at the turn of the 20C, however, the theatres gradually closed down.

The Henson horse breed

This small, robust horse is a cross between a French saddle horse and a Norwegian Fjord pony. Its coat varies from light yellow to brown, and its mane is a mixture of black and gold. This breed was developed in 1978 in a small village of the Baie de Somme area, thanks to the determination of **Doctor Berquin**. Hensons show remarkable endurance; they can remain out in the fields all year round and cover great distances without getting tired. Their docile and affectionate behaviour makes them ideal companions for children and long-distance riders. They also fare very well in team competitions and horse shows generally.

The museum's significant collections of archaeology, medieval art and fine arts are housed in a Napoléon III building constructed between 1855 and 1867 for the Picardy Society of Antiquaries. Upon entering the central hall, visitors will not miss the rotunda and its colourful mural (1992) created by American artist Sol LeWitt (1928–2007).

EXCURSION

PARC DU MARQUENTERRE★★

The Park is accessible from Abbeville via the D 940, direction Crotoy. Open: mid-Jan–mid Feb Sat–Sun 10am–5pm; and daily mid-Feb–Mar and Oct–mid-Nov 10am–6pm; Apr–Sept 10am–7pm; Christmas period 10am–5pm. €10.50. 03 22 25 68 99; www.parcdumarquenterre.com.

It is advisable to visit on a rising tide when the birds leave the stretches of the Baie de Somme, or during the spring and autumn migration periods. There are three different paths around the park that will take you from 45min for the shortest one to 2hrs for a more in-depth tour. The red discovery trail is tailored just for kids! No dogs, but free kennel available.

The Marquenterre area is an alluvial plain reclaimed from the sea, which lies between the Authie and Somme estuaries. Its name derives from ***mer qui entre en terre*** (sea which enters the land). The stretches of land are made up of briny marshes, salt-pastures and sand dunes secured to the land by vegetation.

Today this reserve is home to 344 species of birds, 265 species of plants, and 27 species of mammals living both on land and in the water, including a large colony of seals; the most inquisitive of them are sometimes spotted at high tide near the quayside at St Valéry-en-Somme and Le Crotoy.

Reclaimed from the sea – The process of reclaiming the land was started in the 12C by monks from **St-Riquier** and **Valloires** who erected the first dikes and attempted to canalise the rivers. Many drainage canals were built.

Perched on a hill, **Rue**, the future capital of the Marquenterre area, ceased to be an island in the 18C. During the 19C, dikes and beaches were strengthened, which allowed the development of vegetable and cereal growing.

In 1923, the industrialist **Henri Jeanson** bought an area of marshland along the coast, which his successors drained and diked using Dutch methods, so that it was eventually possible to grow bulbs. At the same time, trees were planted. But the plans failed, and this gave rise to the idea of a bird sanctuary.

The birth of the bird sanctuary – The Marquenterre lands have always been an important habitat for migratory and non-migratory birds. Alas, it was also a paradise for hunters who brought many species close to extinction.

As a result, in 1968 the Hunting Commission created a reserve on the maritime land, to ensure the protection of the birds along 5km/3mi of coastline.

The owners of the Marquenterre estate next to the reserve decided to set up a bird sanctuary within it to allow the public to watch bird life in a natural habitat. Thirteen years later, the site

MAKING THE MOST OF THE PARK

When to Go

Each season is interesting and enables visitors to watch different species. **Spring** is the nesting season for many species such as stork, small waders (avocet, oystercatcher, plover), greylag geese, shelduck. The herons' nesting place is particularly spectacular since five species of large waders, including spoonbill, nest at the top of pine trees. **Summer** is the migrating season for black stork; it is also the time when small waders gather at high tide and when large gatherings of spoonbill, cormorant and egret can be seen. **Autumn** sees the mass arrival of many species of ducks coming to spend the winter in the park (up to 6 000 birds, some of them arriving from Russia and Finland, can be observed). The park is the most important wader ringing centre in France, and studies on migration are carried out in cooperation with the National Natural History Museum in Paris.

What to take with you

Solid walking shoes, a wind- water-proof coat, and a pair of binoculars (*also available for rent at the park*).

Riding tours

Espaces Equestres Henson – *34 chemin des Garennes, 80120 St-Quentin-en-Tourmont. 03 22 25 03 06; www.henson.fr.* The Henson horse-riding centre organises guided riding tours for all levels of ability, including beginners and children.

became the property of the Office of Coastal Preservation. In 1994, it was granted the status of "protected nature reserve."

Discovering the Bird Sanctuary

The Bird Sanctuary covers 250ha/618 acres on the edge of the reserve and houses numerous species of birds, including shelduck, geese, tern, avocet, gull, heron, sandpiper and spoonbill. Three marked **trails** and trained guides will help you discover the riches of the park at your own pace:

Red discovery trail – *1.5km/0.9mi.* This introductory tour of the park will offer you a close-up view of the birds that live here permanently: ducks, seagulls, geese and herons. Their calls attract wild birds of the same species. A few familiar mammals can be seen on the way – Henson horses, weasels and hares – as well as amphibians such as toads and insects such as dragonflies.

Blue observation trail – *4km/2.5mi.* This walk follows a path through the dunes to various observation hides.

Green extended observation trail – *5km/3.1mi.* An additional path shows the reserve from a completely different angle, allowing an in-depth discovery of its fauna and flora.

ADDRESSES

STAY

Hôtel Alsace-Lorraine – 18 r. de la Morlière. 03 22 91 35 71. 14 rooms. This comfortable, likeable little hotel hides behind an imposing carriage entrance a five-minute walk from the town centre and train station. Bedrooms, brightened with colourful fabrics, give onto the inner courtyard.

Hôtel Carlton – 42 r. de Noyon. 03 22 97 72 22; www.lecarlton.fr. 24 rooms. Behind the attractive 19C façade discover a modern, plush interior. Every room features waxed furniture and murals. Their simple restaurant, Le Bistrot, serves grilled meats.

Chambre d'hôte Le Petit Château – 2 r. Grimaux, Dury. 6km/3.6mi S of Amiens via N 1 dir. Beauvais. 03 22 95 29 52. 4 rooms. In the countryside, 10min from central Amiens, a massive 19C residence whose comfortable guest rooms are housed in an outbuilding.

EAT

Le Petit Poucet – 52 r. des Trois-Cailloux. ℘03 22 91 42 32. Closed Mon. This attractive establishment is very popular with the people of Amiens who come for a slice of quiche, a ficelle picarde (baked crepes, stuffed and rolled), or a mixed salad for lunch, a delectable chocolate for tea, or a box of divine pastries to enjoy at home.

Le Bouchon – 10 r. Alexandre Fatton. ℘03 22 92 14 32; www.lebouchon.fr. Closed Sun eve. A Parisian-style bistro near the railway station specialising in typically Lyonnais dishes and traditional cuisine of the region.

Les Marissons – Pont de la Dodane, Quartier St.-Leu. ℘03 22 92 96 66; www.les-marissons.fr. Closed Wed and Sat for lunch, and Sun. The place to be in the Saint-Leu quarter is this old marine workshop transformed into a restaurant. The flowery mini-garden becomes a terrace in summer, while in winter diners sit under the sloping wooden frame which has a pleasant décor of handsome beams and round tables.

GUIDED TOURS

Contact the tourist office for guided tours of the town in French, several times daily.

Barge Tours – Explore the **canals of St-Leu** in traditional style. Depart from chemin du port Cappy. ℘03 22 76 12 12.

NIGHTLIFE

After dark, the Quai Belu canalside area in the St Leu quarter is the place for pubs, discos and nightlife.

Texas Café – 13 r. des Francs-Mûriers, Quartier St.-Leu. ℘03 22 72 19 79. This enormous Confederate-themed "saloon" of brick and wood is always crowded and popular. Before midnight, drink (beer and cocktails), dance and sing (karaoke). After midnight, it's a disco and dance venue.

ENTERTAINMENT

"The cathedral in living colour" – ℘03 22 22 58 90. The artist Skertzò uses lighting to highlight the colourful entrance on the cathedral's west side. The presentation is held mid-Jun–Sep at dusk, and during December at 7pm. Commentary in French and then English.

Comédie de Picardie – 62 r. des Jacobins. ℘03 22 22 20 20; www.comdepic.com. This venerable old manor, entirely restored, houses a very pretty 400-seat theatre. The region's creative and dramatic hub, producing 15 different shows for a total of 250 performances per season.

Maison de la Culture d'Amiens – pl. Léon-Gontier. ℘03 22 97 79 79; www.maisondelaculture-amiens.com. Two halls (1 070 and 300 seats), a movie theatre devoted to art and experimental films, and two exhibition rooms. This complex offers an unusually interesting and eclectic selection of events.

Théâtre de Marionnettes – Chés Cabotans d'Amiens, 31 r. Édouard-David, quartier St-Leu. ℘03 22 22 30 90; www.ches-cabotans-damiens.com. This fascinating family-orientated show, established in 1933, takes place in a veritable miniature theatre with a beautifully designed set. The puppets all have their own history and language (French or Picard).

SHOPPING

Atelier de Jean-Pierre Facquier – 67 r. du Don. ℘03 22 92 49 52. Transforming them into traditional and invented wooden Picardy puppets, Monsieur Facquier carves life into pieces of wood before your eyes. Madame Facquier sews their clothes using fabric chosen with care.

Jean Trogneux – 1 r. Delambre, & 2nd branch at Parvis de la Cathédrale. ℘03 22 71 17 17; www.trogneux.fr. The city's speciality since the 16C, the Amiens macaroon, a blend of almonds and honey, is ever popular.

Marché des Hortillons – The local market gardeners, who grow their produce in the hortillonnages, come to market Saturday mornings at **Place Parmentier**. On the third Sunday in June, a market is held as in years gone by: the gardeners, wearing traditional attire, come in flat-bottomed punts and unload their produce onto the docks.

Lille★★★

Lively, convivial capital of French Flanders and close to the Belgian border, the city successfully combines vibrant forward-looking appeal with its splendid Baroque heritage.

- **Population:** 227 560.
- **Michelin Map:** 302 G 4
- **Info:** pl. Rihour. ℘0891 56 20 04; www.lilletourism.com. English-language walking tours of Lille (2hr, €9.50) are on Thu at 10.15am. Book at the Lille tourist office, by phone, or you can reserve online not less than 48hr in advance. ℘03 59 57 94 00.
- **Location:** Lille is a large city close to the Belgian border, 220km/138mi N of Paris, and 110km/69mi from Calais. It is easily reached by high-speed TGV and Eurostar trains which arrive in the centre, or by road on A 1 from Paris and A 25 from the English Channel.
- **TGV/Eurostar:** Lille Europe is about 1hr from Paris Gare du Nord, and on a direct service from London via Eurostar. Certain train connections allow a few hours in Lille. There is a Left Luggage facility at the station.
- **Transport:** Lille has 2 Metro lines covering 60 stations and 45km/28mi; 2 tram lines cover more than 35 stations, linking Lille with Roubaix and Tourcoing.
- **Parking:** Street-level car parks offer 20 000 parking spaces as well as several metro car parks in the city centre, plus on-street pay-and-display parking.
- **Don't Miss:** The picturesque lanes and shops of the old quarter Le Vieux Lille; Centre Euralille, a huge indoor mall with more than 130 shops.
- **Timing:** Old Lille will take half a day.

A BIT OF HISTORY

A medieval trading city, Lille moved into manufacturing, wool and cloth predominating from the 14C. In the 15C Lille belonged to Burgundy, which held the whole of Flanders; in 1454 Duke Philippe le Bon (the Good) of Burgundy was responsible for the fine brick-built Palais Rihour.

The marriage of Marie de Bourgogne to Charles V brought first Austrian, then Spanish, rule. In 1667, after a nine-day siege, Lille fell to Louis XIV, subsequently becoming the capitalof France's northern provinces.

In October 1914 Lille, which was poorly defended, surrendered to the Germans. Some 900 buildings were destroyed. During WWII, the French troops capitulated on 1 June 1940.

From the 1960s to 1990s, a plan to restore the old district successfully preserved its artistic heritage, while modernisation has proceeded apace with new buildings.

OLD LILLE★★★

Beautiful façades of 17–18C buildings line the bustling old streets where there are numerous good little shops and brasseries. The distinctive Lille style combines brick and carved stonework.

Vieille Bourse★★

The Old Exchange designed and built in 1652–3 by the architect Julien Destrée is an example of the persistence of the Louis XIII style adapted to Flemish tastes (doors with broken pediments, caryatids supporting the entablatures, columns, pilasters and window-surrounds in sandstone, fruit and floral decoration and a little bell tower). The whole building proclaims the importance of textile manufacturing in the life of the city as well as paying tribute to great men and their contributions to progress with the statues lining the arcades.

Musée des Beaux-Arts★★★

♿ Open daily except Tue: Mon 2–6pm, Wed–Sun 10am–6pm. Closed public holidays. €7 (free 1st Sun in the month). ✆ 03 20 06 78 00; www.palaisdesbeauxarts.fr.

The collection includes many masterpieces of French painting, among them the *Mystical Fountain* by Jean Bellegambe (early 16C) with its symbolic treatment of renewal and redemption, a serenely Classical *Nativity* by Philippe de Champaigne (1643), a beautifully modelled *Portrait of Madame Pélerin* by Maurice Quentin de la Tour, and another portrait, *Jean-Baptiste Forest* (1704), by Nicolas de Largillière.

Rue de la Monnaie★

The Mint once stood in this street where the restored houses now attract antique dealers and interior decorators. On the left there is a row of 18C houses (note the apothecary's shop sign of a mortar and distilling equipment at No 3). The houses at Nos 5 and 9 are decorated with dolphins, wheat-sheaves, palms etc. At No 10 a statue of Notre-Dame-de-la-Treille adorns the front and at Nos 12 and 14 the crow-stepped gable has been rebuilt. Neighbouring houses date from the first third of the 17C and flank the rusticated door (1649) of the Hospice Comtesse.

Place Louise-de-Bettignies

The square bears the name of a WWI heroine. The **Demeure de Gilles de la Boé★**, at No 29 on a corner, was built

City Pass

This inclusive ticket (1, 2 or 3 days: €25, €35 and €45 respectively) gives you access to **metropolitan Lille's public transport** network (Transpole) plus 26 interesting sights, museums and tourist attractions in Lille, Roubaix, Tourcoing, Villeneuve-d'Ascq and Wattrelos, but not to museum guided visits. Information and sales available at the tourist office.

Vieille Bourse

© Gérard Labriet/Photononstop

in about 1636 and is a superb example of Flemish Baroque. The abundant ornamentation includes cornices and prominent pediments. In the past this building stood on the edge of the Basse-Deûle port, in the days when there was a great deal of river traffic.

QUARTIER ST-SAUVEUR

Now a smart business district, this former working-class slum inspired the author of the lullaby Le P'tit Quinquin, Emile Desrousseaux.

Porte de Paris★

This gate, built from 1685 to 1692 by Simon Vollant in honour of Louis XIV, is the only example of a town gate which also served as a triumphal arch; it was formerly part of the ramparts. On the outward side, it appears as an arch decorated with the arms of Lille (a lily) and of France (three lilies). Victory stands at the top, honoured by Fames, about to crown Louis XIV represented in a medallion. From the inner side the gate has the appearance of a lodge.

LA CITADELLE★

The Citadel is a military base. Guided tours only. May–Aug Sun 3pm. Contact tourist office for details and reservation.

Within four months of Louis XIV's troops entering the town, Vauban began to reconstruct the citadel. The great complex is set in a marshy site that could

Vauban, a Military Genius

Sébastien Le Prestre (1633–1707) was born at St-Léger (*25km/15.5mi SE of Avallon in the Morvan*). Better known as the Marquis de **Vauban**, he was one of the truly great figures of the age of Louis XIV, a soldier who personally conducted 53 sieges, an engineer who created the French army's corps of engineers and who studied the science of gunnery, and not least an architect and town planner who redesigned ports, dug canals, spanned the Eure at Maintenon with a fine aqueduct, and built from scratch 33 new fortresses as well as improving no fewer than 300 others (many have of course disappeared).

Appointed Commissioner of Fortifications in 1678, he took his inspiration first of all from his predecessors, bringing their work to a new peak of perfection; in the case of Belfort he added a second external line of defences as well as strengthening the existing bastions by means of demilunes and a deep moat, while at Neuf-Brisach his innovations included supplementing the internal walls with bastions and placing demilunes in front of the redoubts. But above all he was able to assimilate new inventions and changes in tactics, and to adapt his designs to the particular characteristics of the site. His main concern was to defend France's new, expanded frontiers. His work thus took him to Flanders, the Ardennes and Alsace, to the Franche-Comté, to the Pyrénées, the Alps and to many places along the country's coastline. Some of his fortresses proved their worth to the retreating French and British forces in 1940.

be flooded when necessary. With its masterly handling of brick and sandstone, its economical design, its logical plan and its response to the geometry of artillery, it was a great masterpiece, the "Queen of citadels".

EAST OF THE CENTRE

MUSÉE D'ART MODERNE★★

Open Tue–Sun 10am–6pm. €7. ✆03 20 19 68 68; www.musee-lam.fr.

Lying by a lawn above Lac du Héron, the huge building (1983) by architect Rolland Simounet suggests a set of brick and glass cubes. The sculpture park displays contemporary works by **Alexander Calder** and **Picasso**. The foyer leads to the permanent and temporary exhibitions, and to the reception and other services: library, cafeteria, classrooms used for courses in the plastic arts.

The collection – Roger Dutilleul's collection, which contains over 230 works mainly from the first half of the 20C, recognised the talent of artists who were not then understood: one of the first paintings he bought was Braque's *Houses and Tree* which had just been refused entry at the Salon d'Automne.

The collection contains many Fauvist, Cubist, primitive and abstract works. The Fauvists include Rouault, Derain and Van Dongen. Cubism is represented in paintings by **Braque** and **Picasso**.

Several works by **Fernand Léger** follow his development from a 1914 landscape to his sketch for a mural (1938). One room is devoted to **Modigliani** paintings, drawings and the unique, white marble *Head of a Woman* (1913).

Works of abstract art featured are by Kandinsky, Klee and **De Staël**. De Staël knew Roger Dutilleul through the painter **Lanskoy**, who was the collector's protégé, and many examples of the latter's work are also on show. Other artists from the Paris School include **Charchoune**, **Buffet**, **Chapoval** and **Utrillo**.

EURALILLE

Covering an area of almost 70ha/173 acres beyond Lille city centre is a whole new urban district designed by Dutch town planner Rem Koolhaas. Since May 1993, Lille's railway station, which was renamed **Lille-Flandres**, has catered to most of the high-speed trains from Paris. Linked by a viaduct with four arches, the new station, **Lille-Europe**, easily recognisable by its huge glass frontage, was built as part of the Paris–London and London–Brussels routes using the Channel Tunnel and for the high-speed train services between Lille and Lyon, Bordeaux, Nice, Montpellier etc. Two towers span the new stations, the **Tour Lille-Europe WTC** designed by architect Claude Vasconi and the L-shaped **Tour du Crédit Lyonnais★** designed by Christian de Portzampac. The **Centre Euralille** was designed by the acclaimed French architect Jean Nouvel. Its spacious walkways and two floors contain more than 130 shops, a hypermarket, restaurants and a cultural centre called the Espace Croisé. It also has a theatre, private apartments, and a business school.

HOSPICE COMTESSE★

Open daily except Tue: Mon 2–6pm, Wed–Sun 10am–6pm. ✆03 28 36 84 00.

The hospital was built in 1237 by Jeanne de Constantinople, Countess of Flanders, to ask for divine intervention on behalf of her husband Ferrand de Portugal, taken prisoner at Bouvines. It was destroyed by fire in 1468 but was rebuilt and enlarged in the 17C and 18C. It became a hospice during the Revolution, then an orphanage. It changed again in 1939 and is today a museum of history and ethnography which also holds concerts and exhibitions.

Hospital ward – A long, sober building, rebuilt after 1470 on the old 13C foundations, flanks the main courtyard. Inside, the immense proportions of the interior and its panelled timber **vault★★** in the shape of an upturned boat are striking. The ward contains two beautiful tapestries, woven in Lille in 1704. One represents Baudouin of Flanders with his wife and two daughters; the other portrays Jeanne, the hospital's founder, flanked by her first and second husbands. The vault is decorated with the heraldic arms of the hospital's benefactors. The former dormitory on the first floor has carved ceiling beams. It contains 17C Flemish and Dutch paintings and a superb 16C wooden Crucifixion from Picardy. Two rooms flanking the dormitory are filled with exhibits relating to regional history.

EXCURSION

DOUAI★

The town is in French Flanders, close to the Belgian border.

70 pl. d'Armes. ✆03 27 88 26 79; www.douaitourisme.fr.

The town preserves the 18C layout and grand buildings that gave it the aristocratic look that Balzac evoked.

In the 11C and 12C, Douai provided winter quarters for merchants and merchandise using the great trading routes of Northern Europe. The painter **Jean Bellegambe** (1470–1534) was born here. Around 1605, a number of Benedictine monks from England and Wales came to Douai and established the monastery of St Gregory the Great. It was here that the "Douai Bible", an English version of the Old Testament, was published in 1609. The monastery buildings were destroyed at the time of the Revolution and the community recrossed the Channel, eventually settling at Stratton-on-the-Fosse in Somerset, where they founded Downside abbey.

One of the best **belfries★** of its kind is atop Douai's town hall (Enquire at the

Les fêtes des Gayants

On the Sunday after 5 July, five giant figures of the Gayant family, dressed in medieval costume, are paraded though Douai accompanied by folk groups: Gayant, the father (7.5m tall, weighing 370kg, his wife Marie Cagenon (6.5m) and their children Jacquot, Fillion and Binbin. The giants appear in town on the next two days. Gayant, the oldest giant in northern France (1530), is also the most popular. The inhabitants of Douai refer to themselves in jest as "Gayant's children". *www.nordmag.fr/nord_pas_de_calais/douai/gayant.htm.*

tourist office or the Mairie for visiting information).

Both Victor Hugo and Corot were much taken by the Gothic tower of 1390 with its elaborate crown. The Flemish Renaissance courtyard front was rebuilt in 1860.

ADDRESSES

STAY

As Hôtel – 98 r. Louis-Braille. 59790 Ronchin. 3km/2mi SE Lille via autoroute heading towards Paris, exit1 Ronchin. 03 20 53 05 05; www.ashotel.com. 62 rooms. This contemporary hotel offers functional, comfortable rooms and a pleasant dining room. A convenient stopover just off the A1 autoroute.

B & B (B&B) – 78 r. Caumartin. 03 61 50 16 42 or 06 85 70 06 64. Closed mid-Jul–mid-Aug. 3 rooms. "B & B" as in Béatrice and Bernard, the owners of this Napoléon III house. Minimum 2-night stay.

Chez Julie – 8 r. de Radinghem, 59134 Beaucamps-Ligny. 12km/7mi to the W of Lille via A 25, exit 7 and D 62 rte du Radinghem. 03 20 50 33 82; www.chezjulie.fr. 3 rooms. This homely red-brick smallholding on the edge of a village near Lille boasts well-maintained bedrooms.

Hotel Kanaï – 10 r. de Béthune. 03 20 57 14 78; www.hotelkanai.com. Ideally located 2 min from Palais Rihour. Trendy decor, contemporary furniture and free WiFi access. Warm welcome. No lift.

Nord Hôtel – 48 r. du Fg-d'Arras. 0320 53 53 40; www.nord-hotel.com. 80 rooms. Conveniently located near the Porte d'Arras metro station and easily accessible from the road. Modern, spacious rooms.

Hôtel Flandre Angleterre – 13pl. de la Gare. 03 20 06 04 12; www.hotel-flandreangleterre-lille.com. 44 rooms. Situated opposite the train station and near the pedestrian streets, this family-run hotel presents modern rooms that are comfortable and cosy.

Hôtel Novotel Centre Grand Place – 116 r. de L'Hôpital-Militaire. 03 28 38 53 53. www.novotel.com. WiFi. 104 rooms. This chain hotel boasts spacious, contemporary rooms with modern bathrooms.

Hôtel Brueghel – Parvis St-Maurice. 03 20 06 06 69; www.hotel-brueghel.com. WiFi. 65 rooms. This Flemish-style house near the train station marries bygone charm with modern facilities.

EAT

Aux Moules – 34 r. de Béthune. 03 20 57 12 46. Closed 1 Jan, 24–25, 31 Dec. Steamed mussels and other Flemish specialities await customers in this 1930s style brasserie set in a lively pedestrian street.

Restaurant La Cave aux Fioles – 39 r. de Gand. 03 20 55 18 43; www.lacaveauxfioles.com. Closed Sat lunch, Sun, Mon and public holidays. A warm, pleasant bistro housed in two 17C and 18C residences.

Omnia – 9 r. Esquermoise 03 20 57 55 66; www.omnia-restaurant.com. Closed 24, 25 Dec. Successively a cabaret, brothel, movie theatre and microbrewery, this Baroque-Rococo bar and restaurant serves traditional fare.

Brasserie de la Paix – 25 pl. Rihour. 03 20 54 70 41. Closed Sun. This friendly brasserie kitted out with banquettes and Desvres earthenware serves bistro cuisine.

Les 3 Brasseurs – 22 pl. de la Gare. 03 20 06 46 25; www.les3brasseurs.com. closed 24 Dec (eve) and 25 Dec. The pungent scent of hops greets visitors to this brasserie. Sample one or four kinds of beer from the tuns.

La Petite Cour – 7r. du Curé-Saint-Étienne. 03 20 51 52 81. A covered courtyard and chic terrace with a vintage vibe. Generous, hearty portions.

Tous les Jours Dimanche – 13r. Bartholomé-Masurel. 03 28 36 05 92. Noon–6.30pm. Closed Sun and Mon (Oct–Apr) eve. Bohemian chic. Lunch menus prepared using fresh produce; a wide selection of teas.

⊜ **La Bottega** – 8 r. Péterinck. ℘03 20 21 16 85; www.la-bottega.com. Until 10pm. Closed Sun eve and Mon. Italian restaurant serving up perfect pizzas and white pasta (piles of mozzarella, no tomato sauce). Italian deli opposite.

⊜ **Chez Max** – 164 r. de Solferino. ℘03 20 77 59 86. Closed Sun and Mon. Spare a thought for Max as he shuttles up and down the stairs in this new eatery serving traditional cuisine.

⊜ **La Vieille France** – 51 r. de Gand. ℘03 20 31 00 57. Closed Tue & Wed lunch. Old school regional dishes chalked up on a blackboard and served on chequered tablecloths.

⊜ **Chez la Vieille** – 60 r. de Gand. ℘03 28 36 40 06. Closed Aug, 24 Dec– 2 Jan, Sun and Mon. Step back in time in this friendly Flemish estaminet favoured by locals for its authentic local cuisine.

⊜⊜ **Le Bistrot de Pierrot** – 6 pl.de Béthune. ℘03 20 57 14 09; www.bistrot depierrot.com. Closed Jan, 10–16 Aug, Sun and Mon. Authentic, friendly bistro serving a wide range of hearty dishes with lighter choices.

⊜⊜ **L'Assiette du Marché** – 61 r. de la Monnaie, 59000 Lille. ℘03 20 06 83 61; www.assiettedumarche.com. Closed 2–24 Aug, Sun (contact for details). ♿. Contemporary decor and a large skylight over the inner courtyard complements the 18C architecture of this former treasury mint.

⊜⊜ **La Tête de l'Art** – 10 r. de l'Arc. ℘03 20 54 68 89. Closed Mon, Tue & Sun eves. Behind the pink façade of this 1890 house hides a cosy dining room serving traditional cuisine.

⊜⊜ **Le Passe-Porc** – 155 r. de Solferino. ℘03 20 42 83 93. Closed 3 weeks in Aug, Sun and eve (ex. Fri). ♿. The enamelled wall plaques act as the backdrop for a vast collection of pigs. Plentiful fare.

⊜⊜ **Le Why Not** – 9 r.Maracci. ℘03 20 74 14 14; www.lewhynot-restaurant.fr. Closed 1–6 Jan, 28 Jul–Aug,Sat lunch, Sun and Mon. The trendy vibe of this relaxed eatery in Old Lille matches the cutting-edge cuisine prepared by its globe-trotting chef.

⊜⊜ **L'Ecume des Mers** – 10 r. du Pas. ℘03 20 54 95 40; www.ecume-des-mers.com. Not far from the Grand' Place, this elegant restaurant specialises in seafood and seasonal game.

⊜⊜ **Clément Marot** – 16 r. de Pas. ℘03 20 57 01 10; www.clement-marot.com. Closed Sun eve. A traditional menu served in a friendly restaurant run by the descendants of poet Clément Marot.

⊜⊜ **Au Vieux de la Vieille** – 2–4 r. des Vieux-Murs. ℘03 20 13 8164. Closed Mon and Tue. A candle-lit estaminet serving hearty northern fare. Very popular.

ENTERTAINMENT

Le Grand Bleu – 36 ave Max-Dormoy. ℘03 20 09 88 44; www.legrandbleu.com. Closed Aug. €13 (6–25, €11). This performance hall caters to a young audience. Dance, circus, theatre, story-telling, hip-hop and other nice surprises.

Orchestre National de Lille – pl. Mendès -France. ℘03 20 12 82 40; www.onlille.com. Closed Aug. Since 1976, The Orchestre National de Lille has given an average of 120 concerts per season. Performances are held in the Lille area, the Nord-Pas-de-Calais region and abroad (30 countries altogether).

Théâtre de Marionnettes du Jardin Vauban – 1 ave Léon-Jouhaux, Chalet des Chèvres in the Jardin Vauban, Armentières. ℘03 20 42 09 95. Closed Oct–Mar, Sat, Mon. An outdoors puppet show of the Guignol tradition starring characters of local repute, such as Jacques de Lille and Jean-Jean La Plume.

SHOPPING

Marché de Wazemmes – 59000 Armentières. Tue, Thu and especially Sun mornings, the Wazemmes market takes over the Place de la Nouvelle-Aventure.

Rue de Gand – Paved, animated and highly colourful, La Rue de Gand is well worth a visit. Butcher's shops, taverns, bars and especially restaurants serving various types of cuisine line the pavements.

Calais

Calais is the leading passenger port in France and the second in the world with traffic totalling 20 million passengers a year. The town gave its name to the Pas-de-Calais, the strait known on the north side of the Channel as the Straits of Dover. The history of the town has been considerably influenced by its proximity to the English coast, only 38km/23.5mi away. The white cliffs of Dover are often clearly visible from the promenade and the vast sandy beach west of the entrance to Calais harbour. Calais is the ideal starting point for excursions along the Opal Coast to Le Touquet.

- **Population:** 73 636.
- **Michelin Map:** 301 E 2
- **Info:** 12 bd Georges Clemenceau. 03 21 96 62 40; www.calais-cotedopale.com.
- **Location:** Calais is on the channel coast 34km/21mi NE of Boulogne-sur-Mer and 54km/34mi SW of the border with Belgium.
- **TGV:** Calais Frethun is 1h40 direct from Paris Gare du Nord; Calais Ville is 3h10 via Lille.
- **Parking:** There is plenty of metered street parking in Calais-Sud. Place d'Armes in Calais-Nord is a useful parking area.
- **Don't Miss:** Rodin's remarkable *Burghers of Calais*, near the town hall.
- **Timing:** As well as the sights, allow plenty of time to browse Calais' excellent shops.

A BIT OF HISTORY

The Channel Tunnel

The "Chunnel" is the realisation of more than two centuries of dreams and unfinished projects. Over the past 250 years there have been 27 proposals, the oldest of which was made in 1750 by M Desmarets, who wanted to rejoin Britain to the mainland by a bridge, tunnel or causeway. From 1834 onwards, Aimé Thomé de Gamond, known as the "Father of the Tunnel", put forward several propositions, all technically viable. In 1880, 1 840m/over 1mi of galleries were dug out on the site called the "Puits des Anciens"; 2 000m/1.25mi were tunnelled out on the English side before the work was stopped. A fresh approach was tried in 1922. The technical progress of the 1960s gave the project a boost but a 400m gallery was abandoned once again.

During a Franco-British summit in September 1981, the idea of building a fixed link was again mooted by British Prime Minister Margaret Thatcher and French President François Mitterrand. In October 1985, after an international competition, four projects were shortlisted and the Eurotunnel was finally selected on 20 January 1986. A Franco-British treaty was signed on 12 February 1986 in Canterbury cathedral with a view to the tunnel's construction. The first link between France and England was established on 1 December 1990. The official opening of the tunnel and Shuttle service took place on 6 May 1994. Most of the tunnel lies 40m below the seabed in a layer of blue chalk. The **trans-Channel link** consists of two railway tunnels 7.60m in diameter, connected every 375m to a central service gallery 4.80m in diameter, built for ventilation, security, and system maintenance. Each tunnel contains a single track along which run trains in one direction only, taking passengers and freight. The tunnels have a total length of 50km/31mi, of which 40km/24mi are beneath the Channel.

The Burghers of Calais

After his success at Crécy, **Edward III** of England needed to create a power-base in France. He began the siege of

Calais on 3 September 1346, but eight months later had still not been able to breach the valiant defence led by the town governor, Jean de Vienne; in fact, it was famine that forced the inhabitants to capitulate in the end.

Six burghers, led by **Eustache de Saint-Pierre**, prepared to sacrifice themselves in order that the other citizens of Calais would be spared the sword. In thin robes, "barefoot, bareheaded, halters about their necks and the keys to the town in their hands", they presented themselves before the king to be delivered to the executioner. They were saved by the intercession of Edward's wife, Queen Philippa of Hainault.

Calais was in the hands of the English for over two centuries and liberated only in 1558, by the Duke of Guise.

This was a mortal blow to **Mary Tudor**, Queen of England, who said: "If my heart were laid open, the word 'Calais' would be engraved on it."

Calais Lace

Together with Caudry-en-Cambrésis, Calais is the main centre of machine-made lace, employing about 2 000 workers using over 350 looms. Englishmen from Nottingham introduced the industry at the beginning of the 19C; quality was improved around 1830 when the first Jacquard looms were introduced. Three-quarters of the lace made in Calais is exported. Traditional lace made with the Leavers machine is entitled to a quality label created in 1991, representing a peacock.

SIGHTS

Monument des Bourgeois de Calais★★

This famous work by **Rodin**, *The Burghers of Calais,* is located between the Hôtel de Ville and Parc St-Pierre. It dates from 1895 and exemplifies the sculptor's brilliance. The six life-size figures' veins and muscles are exaggerated, their forms tense and haughty.

Hôtel de ville

The beautiful and graceful town hall is built of brick and stone in the 15C Flemish style yet dates only from the turn of the last century. The **belfry** (75m) can be seen for many kilometres in all directions. Inside, a **stained-glass window** recalling the departure of the English diffuses the sunlight over the grand staircase.

Place d'Armes

Before the devastation of the war, this was the heart of medieval Calais. Only the 13C **watchtower** has survived. The belfry and the town hall beside it are popular subjects for artists. To the left is the Bassin Ouest; to the right is the Bassin du Paradis.

The Lighthouse (Le phare)

Guided visits (30min) Tue–Sun 10am–noon, 2–5.30pm. €4.50 (children, €2). ☎03 21 34 33 34; www.pharedecalais.com.

The lighthouse (53m tall; 271 steps) was built in 1848 to replace the watch-tower beacon. From the top there is a surprisingly wide and splendid panoramic **view★★** over Calais, the harbour, the basins, the town's stadium, place d'Armes and the unexpectedly large Church of Our Lady.

Musée des Beaux-Arts et de la Dentelle★★

♿Open daily except Mon 10am–noon, 2–6pm (Sun 2–6pm); Nov–Mar 10am–noon, 2–5pm (Sun 2–5pm). Closed public holidays. €4. ☎03 21 46 48 40; www.calais.fr.

The fine arts and lace museum gives an insight into changes in sculpture over the 19C and 20C and styles of painting between the 17C and 20C.

19C and 20C sculpture features works by Rodin and the studies he made for *The Burghers of Calais*. Also works by Rodin's predecessors, including Carrière-Belleuse, Carpeaux, Barye, and his students, Bourdelle and Maillol.

Paintings from the 17C to the 20C by the Flemish and North European schools. There are also works by modern and contemporary artists such as Jean Dubuffet, Félix Del Marle, Picasso, Fautrier, Lipchitz and Arp.

The **lace section**, in a former tulle-making factory, deals with machine-made and hand-made lace (the museum owns more than 400 000 samples of machine-made lace).

EXCURSIONS

DUNKERQUE

Dunkerque is 50km/31mi E of Calais; 78.8km/49mi NW of Boulogne-sur-Mer. Beffroi, r. de l'Amiral-Ronarc'h. 03 28 66 79 21; www.ot-dunkerque.fr.

Although it was almost entirely destroyed in WW II, the rebuilt town has an attractive centre with a pleasant atmosphere, appealing bars and good shops and museums. Dunkerque (Church of the Dunes in Flemish) was originally a fishing village, whose transformation into the principal port of Flanders began as early as the 14C. It was taken by Turenne after his victory in the Battle of the Dunes in 1658, and given to England in recognition of her help in the struggle against Spain. The town was repurchased by France in 1662. It was now that Dunkerque became the abode of smugglers and of pirates pressed into the service of the king. In the course of Louis XIV's reign, a total of 3 000 foreign ships were captured or destroyed and the trade of the Netherlands completely wrecked. The most intrepid of these privateers was **Jean Bart** (1651–1702). Despite his vocation, the town is proud of him: his statue of 1848 by David d'Angers stands in the square named after him.

Demolition of the fortifications in 1713 (one of the conditions of the Treaty of Utrecht) brought about a decline in Dunkerque's fortunes, notwithstanding improvements in the port facilities. The German breakthrough at Sedan in mid-May 1940 and subsequent dash to the coast near Abbeville had led to the Allied forces in the north being trapped with their backs to the sea. Despite a magnificent rearguard action by French troops endeavouring to protect them, defeat and retreat were inevitable. The subsequent evacuation codenamed "Operation Dynamo" was turned into the "Miracle of Dunkerque", the name given to the successful evacuation from 26 May–4 June of more than 338 000 troops from the beaches of Dunkerque and its resorts of Malo, Zuydcoote and Bray-Dunes, an operation carried out in the face of intense bombardment on land and from the air. A fleet of over 900 small vessels, dubbed the "Little Ships of Dunkerque", helped to transport the troops safely back to the UK.

Le Port★★

Dunkerque is the third-largest port in France and the major French port of the North Sea. A vast industrial zone has emerged, based on shipbuilding, steelworks, refineries and petrochemicals. It is the first port in France for ore, coal copper and container fruit imports, and the second port in France for traffic with the UK. A vehicle ferry service operates between Dover and Dunkerque (Gravelines), providing an alternative to the traditional Dover–Calais route.

Belfry

Mon–Sat 10am–12.30pm, 2–6.30pm; (Jul–Aug Mon–Sat 10am–6.30pm), Sun and public holidays 10am–noon, 2–4pm. €3.50 (children, 7–12, €2.50). 03 28 66 79 21; www.dunkerque-tourisme.fr.

Built in the 13C and heightened in 1440, this served as the bell tower to **Église St-Éloi** which burnt down in 1558. This high tower contains a peal of 48 bells which play "Jean Bart's tune" on the hours and other popular tunes on the quarter-hours. The tourist office is housed on the ground floor. A war memorial has been erected under the arch opposite Église St-Éloi.

Musée Portuaire★

Open Jul–Aug 10am–12.30pm, 1.30–6pm. Rest of year Wed–Mon 10am–12.30pm, 1.30–6pm. 03 28 63 33 39; www.museeportuaire.fr.

Laid out in a former tobacco warehouse dating from the 19C, this attractive museum gives an insight into the history and operating of the port of

Dunkerque, Northern France's huge maritime gateway, through dioramas, model ships, maps, paintings, engravings and the tools once used by dockers. In the 17C, Dunkerque became the main privateering harbour, with Jean Bart to defend it. *The Battle of Texel* (a copy of a painting by Isabey kept in the Musée de la Marine in Paris), engravings, and models of privateers' boats illustrate Bart's exploits.

Musée des Beaux-Arts★ (Fine Arts Museum)

Open daily except Mon and public holidays: Apr–Oct 10am–noon, 2–6pm (Sun 2–6pm); Nov–Mar 10am–noon, 2–5pm (Sun 2–5pm). €4. ✆03 21 46 48 40.

This museum (rebuilt in 1973) houses beautiful collections of 16–20C paintings and documents tracing Dunkerque's history. One room is dedicated to the privateer Jean Bart. Note the strange 17C money box in the shape of a chained captive from the Église St-Eloi. The money placed in it was used to buy back slaves.

Lieu d'Art et Action Contemporaine (LAAC)★

Open Tue–Sun 10am–12.15pm, 2–6pm. ✆03 28 29 56 00.

The museum is devoted to contemporary earthenware and glassware from 1950–80, including CoBrA, César, Soulages, Warhol and Télémaque.

Working with the theme **"Dialogues in ceramics"**, the museum aims to increase public awareness of this art form.

The Museum of Contemporary Art stands in the middle of a **sculpture park★** designed by Gilbert Samel.

The paths climb outcrops and run down slopes, leading past great stone pieces by the sculptor Dodeigne, metal structures by Féraud and compositions by Viseux, Arman and Zvenijorovsky, all against the backdrop of the North Sea.

ST-OMER★★

This northern town is 49km/30mi SE of Calais. ✆03 21 98 08 51; www.tourisme-saintomer.com.

A market centre of some importance, St-Omer has kept many fine town houses dating from the Classical period.

The town lies at the junction of Inland Flanders, with its watery landscapes of poplars, elms and willows, and Coastal Flanders, won from the sea in medieval times and now dominated by industry and arable farming.

A border town, St-Omer was in turn part of the Holy Roman Empire, Flanders, Burgundy and then Spain, finally passing into French hands in 1677. The town's industry, predominantly metalworking, chemicals and glass-making, is concentrated in the Arques district. 38km/23.6mi to the south lies the site of the Battle of **Agincourt**, where, on 25 October 1415, France suffered its worst defeat of the Hundred Years' War at the hands of Henry V of England.

Cathédrale Notre-Dame★★

Open daily Nov–Mar 8am–5pm; Apr–Oct 8am–6pm. www.cathedrale-saint-omer.org.

Completed at the end of the Hundred Years' War, the building shows signs of the influence of the English Perpendicular style. There are numerous high-quality **works of art★★**, including 18C woodwork, and 13C floor tiles.

Hôtel Sandelin and museum★

Open Wed–Sun 10am–noon, 2–6pm. €5.50. ✆03 21 38 00 94; www.musenor.com.

The house was built in 1777 for the Viscountess of Fruges. It is set between a courtyard and a garden, with a huge portal and an elegant Louis XV gate.

Ground Floor – The drawing rooms overlooking the gardens form a charming suite of rooms with finely carved wainscoting, 18C fireplaces and Louis XV furnishings. The woodcarving room (religious sculptures and medieval tapestries) and the Salle Henri Dupuis, containing ebony cabinets made in Antwerp, lead to the **Salle du Trésor** where exhibits include the famous gilt and enamelled **base of the St Bertin Cross★** (12C), a masterpiece of Mosan art. The upper floors house a collection of local ceramics, and **Delftware**.

Jardin public★

A vast park is located on part of the old 17C ramparts, with gardens and views of the bastion, rooftops and the cathedral tower.

CÔTE D'OPALE★

The road linking Calais and Boulogne takes the visitor along the most spectacular part of this coastline with its high chalk cliffs, heathlands and vast sandy beaches backed by dunes.

BLÉRIOT-PLAGE

3km/1.8mi W of Calais.

The little resort has a fine beach stretching as far as Cap Blanc-Nez. On a clifftop knoll is the obelisk commemorating the **Dover Patrol**, mounted continuously between 1914 and 1918 to protect the vital supply routes across the English Channel. At Les Baraques just to the west of the resort is a monument marking **Louis Blériot's** flight across the Channel in 1909.

CAP BLANC-NEZ★★

11km/6.8mi W of Calais, along D 940.

From the top of the white cliffs the **view★** extends from Calais to Cap Gris-Nez and right across the Channel to the English coast.

WISSANT

19km/12mi W of Calais, along D 940.

With its superb beach of fine hard sand, one of France's main centres for land yachting, Wissant enjoys its privileged position in the middle of the National Conservation Area which includes both Cap Gris-Nez and Cap Blanc-Nez.

CAP GRIS-NEZ★★

31km/19.2mi SW of Calais.

This lofty limestone headland makes a contrast with the chalk cliffs to the south. It gives a **view★** of the white cliffs of the English coast.

WIMEREUX

27km/16.7mi SW of Calais.

This sizeable family resort is pleasantly situated between Cap d'Alprech to the south and the cliffs running up to Cap Gris-Nez in the north.

From the raised seafront promenade there are fine views over the Channel and along the coast from the monument **(Colonne de la Grande Armée)** to Boulogne.

BOULOGNE-SUR-MER★

See BOULOGNE-SUR-MER, p201.

Cap Blanc-Nez

Boulogne-sur-Mer★★

Considered the most attractive and interesting of the "short crossing" Channel ports, Boulogne has a historic walled upper town built on the site of the Roman fortress with 13C ramparts, interesting shops and a traditional market in the lower town, and a busy quayside where fishermen's wives sell their husbands' fresh catch at traditional tiled stalls.

- **Population:** 43 070.
- **Michelin Map:** 301 C 3
- **Info:** Parvis de Nausicaä. 03 21 10 88 10; www.tourisme-boulognesurmer.com.
- **Location:** 34km/21mi SW of Calais.
- **TGV/Train:** Boulogne Ville is 2hrs–2hrs 45 mins direct from Paris Gare du Nord.
- **Parking:** There are car parks by the seafront – it's much easier than trying to park in town.
- **Don't Miss:** The quiet streets of Ville Haute within its ring of sturdy ramparts.
- **Kids:** Nausicaä is a family destination and kids will love it.

A BIT OF HISTORY

Boulogne's location along the chalk cliffs facing the English coast made it a cross-Channel port at an early date. It was from here that Emperor Claudius set sail to conquer Britain; he even established regular boat services to Dover and built a 12-storey landmark tower 200 Roman feet high (1 Roman ft = 2.96cm), which stood until the 16C. Fishing has long been the town's principal activity, the ship-owners' guild being regulated as early as 1203.

NAUSICAÄ★★★

Open daily 9.30am–6.30pm (Jul–Aug 9.30am–7.30pm). Closed first 3 weeks in Jan, 25 Dec, 1 Jan (until 2pm). €19 (child, 3–12, €12.50). 03 21 30 98 98; www.nausicaa.fr.

Designated as the national sea life centre, Nausicaä is an extraordinary complex, at once educational and entertaining. There are many serious elements which have an overall theme of conservation, but there are also amusements such as highly trained sea lions. Within the centre, there is a cinema, a shop, some restaurants and bar.

SIGHTS

Ville haute★★

The upper town, Boulogne's historic district built on the site of the Roman fortress, is still surrounded by its 13C ramparts, which have a walkway on top.

Basilique Notre-Dame

Open Apr–Aug daily 9am–noon, 2–6pm; Sep–Mar daily except Mon 10am–noon, 2–5pm. 03 21 99 75 98.

The basilica was built from 1827 to 1866 on the site of the old cathedral (destroyed after the Revolution) and has preserved the Romanesque crypt. The superb, soaring **dome**★ with its circle of large statues rises behind the chancel; in the central chapel stands the wooden statuette of Our Lady of Boulogne (Notre-Dame de Boulogne), crowned with precious stones.

Under the basilica, a labyrinth of underground passages links 14 chambers.

Château-musée★

Open Mon–Sat 10am–12.30pm, 2–5.30pm, Sun 10am–12.30pm, 2.30–6pm. €5 (free first Sun of month). 03 21 10 02 20.

Formerly the residence of the counts of Boulogne, this polygonal building was the first in western Europe to abandon the traditional keep. Flanked by round towers, it protected the most vulnerable part of the ramparts facing the plateau.

Château-musée

The archaeology of the Mediterranean is represented by an Egyptian section (sarcophagi and numerous funerary objects, the gift of Mariette the Egyptologist) and also by a beautiful group of **Greek vases★★** dating from 5–6C BCE, among them a black-figure jug portraying the suicide of Ajax.

Among the ethnographic collections, the **Eskimo and Aleutian masks★★** brought back from a voyage to North America by the anthropologist Pinart, and the objects from the South Sea Islands including a Maori battle canoe from New Zealand, are particularly interesting.

EXCURSIONS

COLONNE DE LA GRANDE ARMÉE★★

3km/2mi north by N 1 and turn left on a small road. Open mid-Jun–Sept Wed–Sun 10am–12.30pm, 2.30–6.30pm; Oct–mid-Nov and mid-Dec–mid-Jun Fri–Sun 10am–noon, 2–4pm. Closed 1 Jan, 1 May, 1 Nov, 25 Dec. €3. ✆03 21 80 43 69; www.wimille.monuments-nationaux.fr.

Designed by the architect **Eloi Labarre** (1764–1833) to commemorate the Boulogne Camp, the column was started in 1804 but only finished under Louis-Philippe. On its base, a bronze low-relief sculpture portrays Field Marshal Soult offering the plans of the column to the Emperor.

A staircase (*263 steps*) leads to the square platform from where the **panorama★★** extends over the lush countryside of the Boulogne region and, on a clear day, across the Channel as far as the white cliffs of Dover.

LE TOUQUET★★★

The town is on the Channel coast S of Boulogne. Palais de l'Europe, pl. de l'Hermitage. ✆03 21 06 72 00; www.letouquet.com.

With its casinos, grand villas, immense beach, designer stores, gourmet restaurants and luxury hotels, the "Pearl of the Opal Coast" enjoys an international reputation.

Occupied by the Germans during WWI, Le Touquet like many French towns suffered badly, especially towards the end of the war when most of the resort's hotels were destroyed. It also had the distinction of being the most mined town in France, with over 100 000 devices to deal with at the end of the hostilities.

Seaside

Along the seafront, the **promenade** is edged by gardens and car parks. The south end leads to a yachting club and a thalassotherapy centre. The fine sand beach stretches as far as the mouth of the River Authie. The **coast road** follows the line of the dunes and leads to the marina and the water-sports club, well sheltered by Pointe du Touquet.

Chartres★★★

Chartres' magnificent cathedral, the "Acropolis of France" (Rodin), still beckons to the pilgrim far off across the endless cornfields of the Beauce. The area was occupied by the Carnutes, and Druids once worshipped here; there is also evidence of the pagan cult of a holy spring, and possibly also of a mother-goddess, whom the first missionaries may have Christianised as a forerunner of the Virgin Mary.

- **Population:** 38 931.
- **Michelin Map:** 311 E 5
- **Info:** 8, rue de la Poissonnerie. ℘02 37 18 26 26. www.chartres-tourisme.com.
- **TGV/Train:** Chartres is about 1hr direct from Paris Gare du Nord.
- **Timing:** Allow 1hr for the cathedral, plus a good half day for the rest of the town.

A BIT OF HISTORY

The picturesque old town **(le Vieux Chartres★)** lies at the point where the Eure cuts into the plain of the Beauce. Today, the old mill-races and laundry-houses have been restored, and a number of 17C houses have kept their embossed doorways topped by a bull's-eye. The most attractive townscape is to be found in the St-André quarter, by the riverbanks, and in Rue des Écuyers and Rue du Cygne. Loëns Granary (Grenier de Loëns) is a fine 12C building which once housed the tithes of grain and wine.

Chartres attracted pilgrims at an early date, first of all to Our Lady of the Underground Chapel (*Notre-Dame-de-Sous-Terre*), then to the cathedral which Bishop Fulbert built in the 11C but which was burnt down in 1194.

CATHÉDRALE NOTRE-DAME★★★

Open daily 8.30am–7.30pm (Jun–Aug Sun, Tue and Thu until 10pm. Guided tours available €6.50. ℘02 37 21 75 02; www.cathedrale-chartres.org.

See Introduction: Art – Architecture, p90.

Reconstruction began immediately and was completed in the short space of 25 years. The north and south porches were added only 20 years later and the building consequently has a unity of style possessed by few other Gothic churches. Pilgrims have been coming here for eight centuries.

The new cathedral raised the Transitional Gothic style to new levels. The bays of the nave, previously square in plan, are now oblong and have sexpartite vaults; the arches of arcades

Cathédrale Notre-Dame

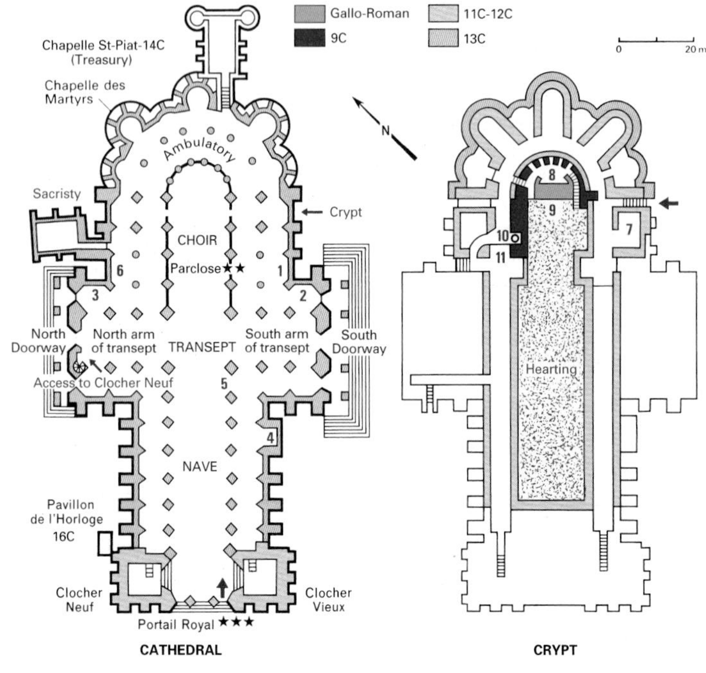

1	Notre-Dame-de-la-Belle-Verrière	5	Organ	10	Puits des Saints-Forts
2	St Fulbert's window	6	Vierge du Pilier	11	Chapelle Notre-Dame-de-Sous-Terre
3	Window of Peace	7	Chapelle St-Martin		
4	Chapelle Vendôme	8	Crypte St-Lubin		
		9	Gallo-Roman wall		

and windows are more pointed; a round opening is inserted in the space above the highest windows; the structural functions of galleries are taken over by flying buttresses.

Gothic verticality reigns outside, too, but the architect wisely kept two Romanesque masterworks, the Old Bell Tower (Clocher vieux) of 1145 and the Royal Doorway, **Portail Royal★★★**, of the west front, with its long-bodied but intensely expressive sculpted figures.

The cathedral's interior is subtly lit by its superb stained glass (**vitraux★★★**) which covers a total area of 2 700sq m and depicts 5 000 figures.

Most of the windows date from the 12C and 13C and are the greatest achievement of this art form. "Chartres blue" is famous for the clarity and depth which can be seen in the wonderful Notre-Dame-de-la-Belle-Verrière Window (*first window on the south side of the ambulatory*). In 1964, the American Society of Architects gave a window and in 1971 the German Friends of the Cathedral did likewise (*north transept*).

ADDITIONAL SIGHTS

Musée des Beaux-Arts★
(29 cloître Notre Dame)

Église St-Pierre★ – stained glass★
(5 pl. St-Pierre)

ADDRESSES

SHOPPING

Marché aux légumes et volailles – pl. Billard. Each Saturday morning, the covered Vegetable and Poultry Market displays colourful stands featuring authentic Beauce produce. This carrousel of sights, tastes and fragrances is one of the most popular markets in the area.

Rambouillet★

The combination of an attractive château, park and forest makes Rambouillet one of the main sights in the Île-de-France. Since 1883 it has been the official summer residence of the President of the French Republic. Distinguished guests include Nelson Mandela (South Africa, July 1996), Boris Yeltsin (Russia, October 1995), George Bush (United States, July 1991) and Mikhail Gorbachev (USSR, October 1990).

- **Population:** 26 159.
- **Michelin Map:** 106 fold 28.
- **Info:** Hôtel de Ville, pl. de la Libération, 78120 Rambouillet. 01 34 83 21 21; www.rambouillet-tourisme.fr.
- **Location:** 53km/33mi SW of Paris, via the A 13 and A 12.
- **Train:** Rambouillet is about 1hr direct from Paris Montparnasse (SNCF).
- **Parking:** Near the château or on the place Jeanne d'Arc.
- **Don't Miss:** Visit the deer observation points in the Forêt des Cerfs.
- **Kids:** Espace Rambouillet, shows. The toy train collection (Musée Rambolitrain).
- **Timing:** The château itself will not take more than an hour.

CHÂTEAU

Guided tours daily except Tue: Apr–Sep 10am, 11am, 2pm, 3pm, 4pm, 5pm; Oct–Mar 10am, 11am, 2pm, 3pm, 4pm. Closed 1 Jan, 1 May, 1 and 11 Nov, 25 Dec. €8.50. 01 34 83 00 25; http://chateau-rambouillet.monuments-nationaux.fr.

Leave from place de la Libération, the site of the town hall. The château presents a triangular shape after Napoléon dismantled the left wing. The large round tower, where François I is believed to have died, belonged to the 14C fortress. It is difficult to distinguish because of the numerous additions made by the Comte de Toulouse. The façades are essentially 19C.

Mezzanine – The reception rooms commissioned by the Comte de Toulouse

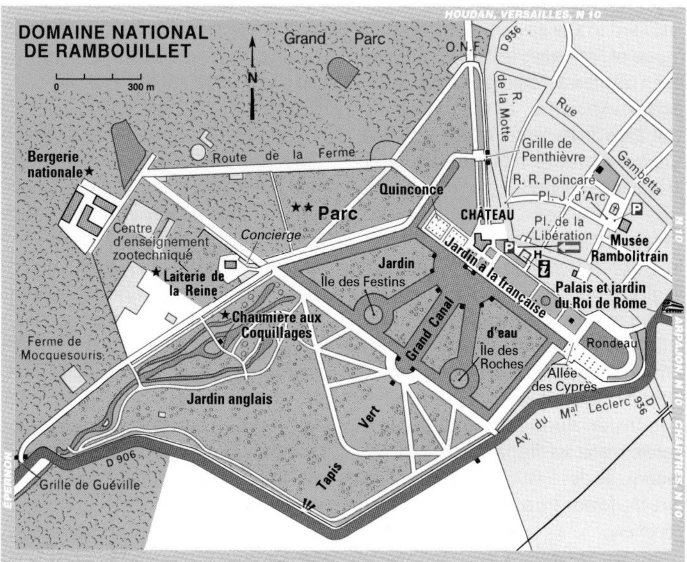

are embellished with superb Rococo **wainscoting★**. Note the charming boudoir designed for the Comte's wife.
The corridor adjoining the François I tower leads through to the Imperial bathroom suite, adorned with Pompeian frescoes. This opens onto the Emperor's Bedchamber, where he spent the night of 29 June 1815. It was in the dining room – the former ballroom – that Charles X signed the abdication document. Stunning view.

PARK★★

♿Open daily May–Sep 8am–7pm (Jun–Aug 7.30pm); Feb–Apr 8am–6pm; Nov–Jan 8am–5pm. ✆01 34 94 28 79.
The château is set in a pleasant park, renowned for the variety of its gardens remodelled throughout the 17C and 18C, which reflect the evolution of taste during that period, from the formal parterres to the winding alleyways lined with exotic trees.

Jardin à la française

Walking back towards the château, one goes through the "petit bosquet" (small copse), the "miroir" (mirror) and the "grand bosquet" (large copse) forming a French-style garden.

Quinconce

Situated to the east of the château, a group of lime trees from Holland have been planted according to a geometric pattern known as a "quinconce", or quincunx. In its centre stands *La Barque* solaire, a bronze sculpture by Karel, inaugurated in 1993.

Jardin à l'anglaise

In 1779, Hubert Robert designed an English-style garden beyond the green carpet of lawn. It is essentially planted with exotic species. The **Grotte des Amants** (Lovers' grotto) was named after a couple of lovers who took refuge inside during a thunderstorm. Canals crisscross the park, forming small islands: Île des Festins, Îles des Roches etc. 18C follies are scattered among the greenery.

Chaumière des Coquillages★

Open same hours as château.
Guided tours only (45min). €3.
✆01 34 94 28 79.
The **landscape garden** in the park features a cottage built for the Princesse de Lamballe. The walls of the rooms are encrusted with a variety of seashells, chips of marble and mother-of-pearl. A boudoir with painted panelling adjoins the main room.

Laiterie de la Reine★

Open same hours as château. Guided tours only (45min). €3. ✆01 34 94 28 79.
Louis XVI had the Dairy built in 1785 to amuse his wife Marie-Antoinette. The small sandstone pavilion resembling a Neoclassical temple consists of two rooms. The first – which houses the actual dairy – features marble paving and a marble table from the First Empire. The room at the back was designed as an artificial grotto adorned with luxuriant vegetation. It includes a marble composition by Pierre Julien depicting a nymph and the she-goat Amalthea (1787).

FORÊT DE RAMBOUILLET★

This vast forest has some delightful footpaths for those who enjoy walking, as well as 60km/37mi of cycle tracks, 20 or more lakes with picturesque banks, and a number of villages with old houses. The forest is home to a thriving game population.
Rambouillet is part of the ancient Yveline forest, which in Gallo-Roman times stretched as far as the outskirts of Nogent-le-Roi, Houdan, Cernay-la-Ville and Etampes. A large part of it is now included in the Parc Naturel Régional de la Haute Vallée de Chevreuse.
In the Middle Ages, wide-scale deforestation took place and the vast clearances now divide it into three main areas of woodland: St-Léger and Rambouillet itself, the most popular areas with tourists situated north of Rambouillet, and Yvelines to the south, which is rather more divided up into private estates.
The forest around Rambouillet is damper and has more rivers, lakes and

ponds than Fontainebleau. From time immemorial it has been particularly well stocked with game such as roe deer and wild boar – and it remains so today.

ESPACE RAMBOUILLET

Open Feb–Mar and Nov daily except Mon 10am–5pm; Apr and Jul–Oct daily 10am–6pm (Sat–Sun and public holidays 6.30pm); May–Jun daily 9.30am–6pm (Sat–Sun and public holidays 6.30pm). €9–€14 (children, 3–12, €6–€11), according to season. 01 34 83 05 00; www.onf.fr/espaceramb.

This 250ha/625-acre wildlife park has been divided into various areas (binoculars are recommended), including the **Forêt des Cerfs** (deer and wild oxen), **Forêt Sauvage** (a free-roaming-wilderness), **Forêt des Aigles** (more than 100 birds of prey) and **Coin des Fourmis** where young children can discover industrious ants. Free flight shows.

WALKS AND TOURS

The **GR 1** trail runs through the forest north/south from Montfort-l'Amaury to Rambouillet. The **GR 22** trail runs in a northwest/southwest direction from Gambaiseuil to St-Léger-en-Yvelines.

Rochers d'Angennes

8.5km/5.3mi from Rambouillet via D 936 then D 107. Leave from the "Zone de Silence des Rabières". Walk 100m through the village up the steeper slope of the valley to find the right path leading to the summit.

Go past an arena-shaped shelf circled by boulders to reach the crest: **view** of the Guesle valley and Angennes Lake, bordered by aquatic plants.

Balcon du Haut Planet★

12km/7.4mi from Rambouillet along D 936 to Carrefour du Haut-Planet, then turn right onto the unsurfaced road which crosses rough, hilly ground and leave your vehicle in the car park at La Croix Pater.

After passing the Blue Fountain spring on the right, the lane reaches a shaded terrace on the plateau edge, un-folding the most spectacular panorama of the whole massif: to the north, the **view** extends across the Vesgre valley and the Château du Planet.

Étangs de Hollande

8km/5mi from Rambouillet along N 10 then D 191 to St-Hubert; leave the car near the Étang de St-Hubert.

4hr there and back.

The ponds were part of one of Vauban's projects to create water reservoirs for Versailles. Six ponds separated by paths were laid out near the **Étangs de Hollande.** Only the two end basins are filled with water. In summer, the ponds offer swimming and fishing. Head west out of St-Hubert, follow the Corbet forest track, cross the Villarceau alleyway, and walk to the Petites-Yvelines crossroads then the Malmaison crossroads. Turn left towards the Bourgneuf crossroads and, to the southeast, the Route des Étangs which skirts the north shore of the **Bourgneuf** pond. Follow D 60 to the south shore of the **Corbet** pond.

Walk past the sluice-gate which separates it from the **Pourras** pond and skirt the Pourras woods to Croix Vaudin. A path on the left runs through the woods to the Pont Napoléon; on the right lies the **St-Hubert** pond. This leads back to the Corbet forest track.

Carrefour du Grand Baliveau

8km/5mi from Montfort-l'Amaury via D 138. At the crossroads, follow the path to the right of the panel marked "Route forestière du Parc-d'en-Haut". 30min there and back.

A charming walk through a lovely green glade. Good **view★** of a secluded valley.

Étang de la Porte Baudet

4km/2.5mi from Montfort by D 112 and D 13: go past the turning to Gambais (right) and turn left onto rue du Vert-Galant. Follow the plateau along the winding road. Starting point: parking des Brûlins; 45min there and back.

This is one of the finest sites in the forest; farther on, Route Belsédène then Route Goron lead (1km/0.6mi) to Chêne Baudet, a splendid 550-year-old oak tree.

Normandy

» **Region map p210–211**
Rouen p212
Le Havre p220
Caen p224
Normandy Landing Beaches p230
Bayeux p232
La Presqu'ile du Cotentin p235
Mont-St-Michel p238
Alençon p240

Introduction

Taking its name from the Norsemen or Normans, this old dukedom extends from the edge of the Paris Basin towards the Breton peninsula. To many it is reminiscent of southern England with its shared heritage of glorious Norman architecture and lush, pastoral countryside. There is great diversity in the buildings here; Norman masons fashioned the fine Caen limestone into great churches while humbler structures were built from cob, chalk, pebbles in mortar, brick, timber, shingles and thatch.

Highlights

1. Gothic architecture at **Rouen**'s Cathédrale Notre-Dame (p212)
2. Castle above the Seine: **Château Gaillard** (p217)
3. The old town and picturesque port: Vieux **Honfleur** (p221)
4. 11C masterpiece of tapestry: The **Bayeux Tapestry** (p232)
5. The Romanesque Benedictine **Mont-St-Michel** abbey (p238)

Lower Normandy (Basse-Normandie) is built of the old rocks from the Primary Era. In the north, the Cotentin peninsula projects into the English Channel dividing the Bay of the Seine from the Gulf of St-Malo. To the southeast lies the ***bocage*** (pasture) – its hedgebanks offered excellent cover to the Germans in 1944. On either side of the Seine valley extends Upper Normandy (Haute-Normandie), centred on the historic city of Rouen. To the south is the Pays d'Auge, quintessential ***bocage*** country, famous for its ciders, cheeses and calvados, while to the north stretches the vast chalk plain of the Pays de Caux, bordered by the Channel coast with its white cliffs and hanging valleys.

History – Originally occupied by Celts, by the 1C BCE the Romans were establishing towns here. The collapse of the Roman Empire led to occupation by the Franks, but raiding Vikings took over c. 911. Normandy remained independent until 1204 before becoming a French dukedom subject to English control for long periods, until 1469 when it became a province of France. The 15–17C saw the discovery of new territories by Norman sailors, such as Quebec. More recently, on 6 June 1944, Normandy beaches were the scene of what became known as the "D-Day Landings".

Today – The major economies are dairy farming, agriculture and, in Upper Normandy, industry; products include calvados and cider. Tourism is also a major contributor to the economy.

Rouen with the Cathédrale Notre-Dame and the Seine

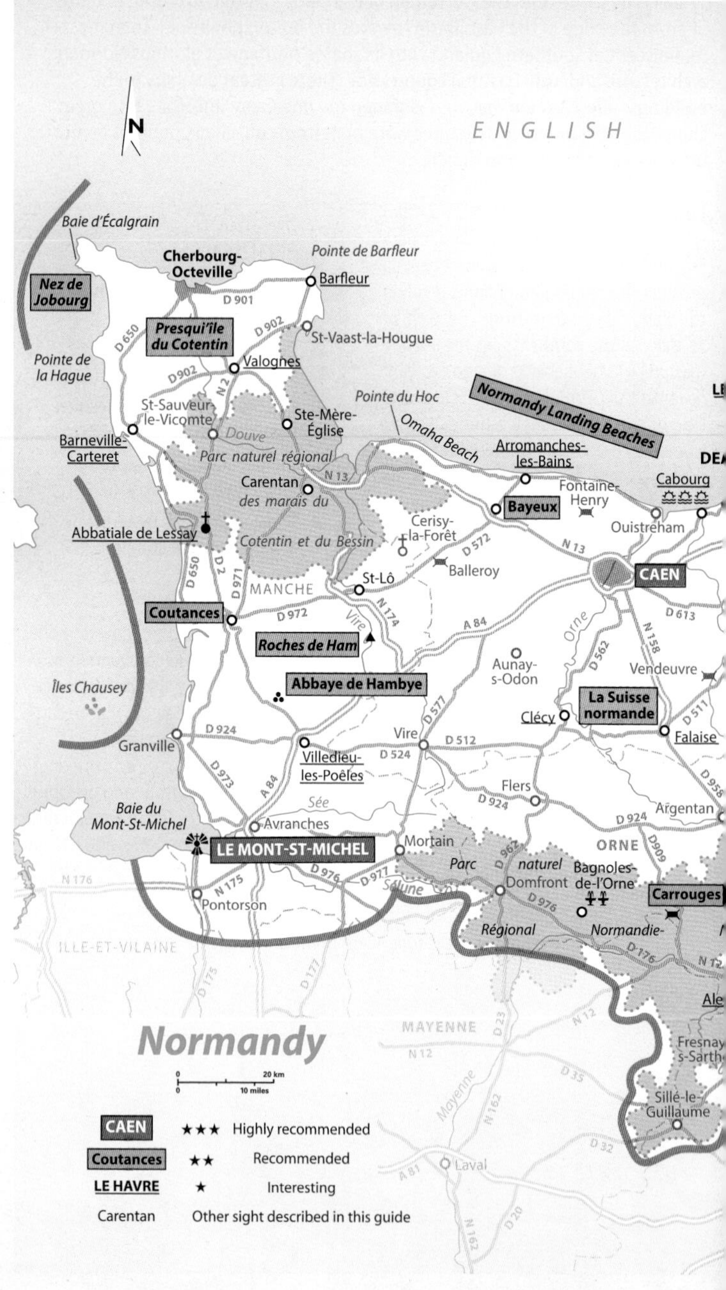

N
ENGLISH
Baie d'Écalgrain
Nez de Jobourg
Cherbourg-Octeville
Pointe de Barfleur
Barfleur
D 901
Presqu'île du Cotentin
D 902
St-Vaast-la-Hougue
D 650
Pointe de la Hague
Valognes
D902
N 2
Pointe du Hoc
Normandy Landing Beaches
St-Sauveur-le-Vicomte
Ste-Mère-Église
Omaha Beach
Barneville-Carteret
Douve
Parc naturel régional
Arromanches-les-Bains
Carentan
N 13
des marais du
Fontaine-Henry
Cabourg
Bayeux
Cerisy-la-Forêt
Ouistreham
Abbatiale de Lessay
Cotentin et du Bessin
D 572
N 13
Balleroy
D 650
D 2
D 971
MANCHE
St-Lô
CAEN
Coutances
D 972
N 174
Vire
D 613
A 84
Roches de Ham
Orne
N 158
Aunay-s-Odon
D 562
Vendeuvre
Îles Chausey
Abbaye de Hambye
D 577
La Suisse normande
D 511
Clécy
Falaise
D 924
Vire
D 512
Granville
Villedieu-les-Poêles
D 524
D 973
A 84
Flers
D 958
D 924
Sée
Argentan
Baie du Mont-St-Michel
Avranches
D 924
Mortain
ORNE
LE MONT-ST-MICHEL
D 962
D909
Parc
naturel
Bagnoles-de-l'Orne
N 176
D 976
D 977
Domfront
Sélune
Carrouges
N 175
D 976
Pontorson
Régional
Normandie-
ILLE-ET-VILAINE
D 176
D 175
D 177
N 12
Normandy
MAYENNE
D 23
N 12
Fresnay-s-Sarthe
0
20 km
0
10 miles
D 35
Mayenne
N 162
Sillé-le-Guillaume
CAEN ★★★ Highly recommended
Coutances ★★ Recommended
LE HAVRE ★ Interesting
Carentan Other sight described in this guide
D 32
A 81
Laval
D 20
N 162

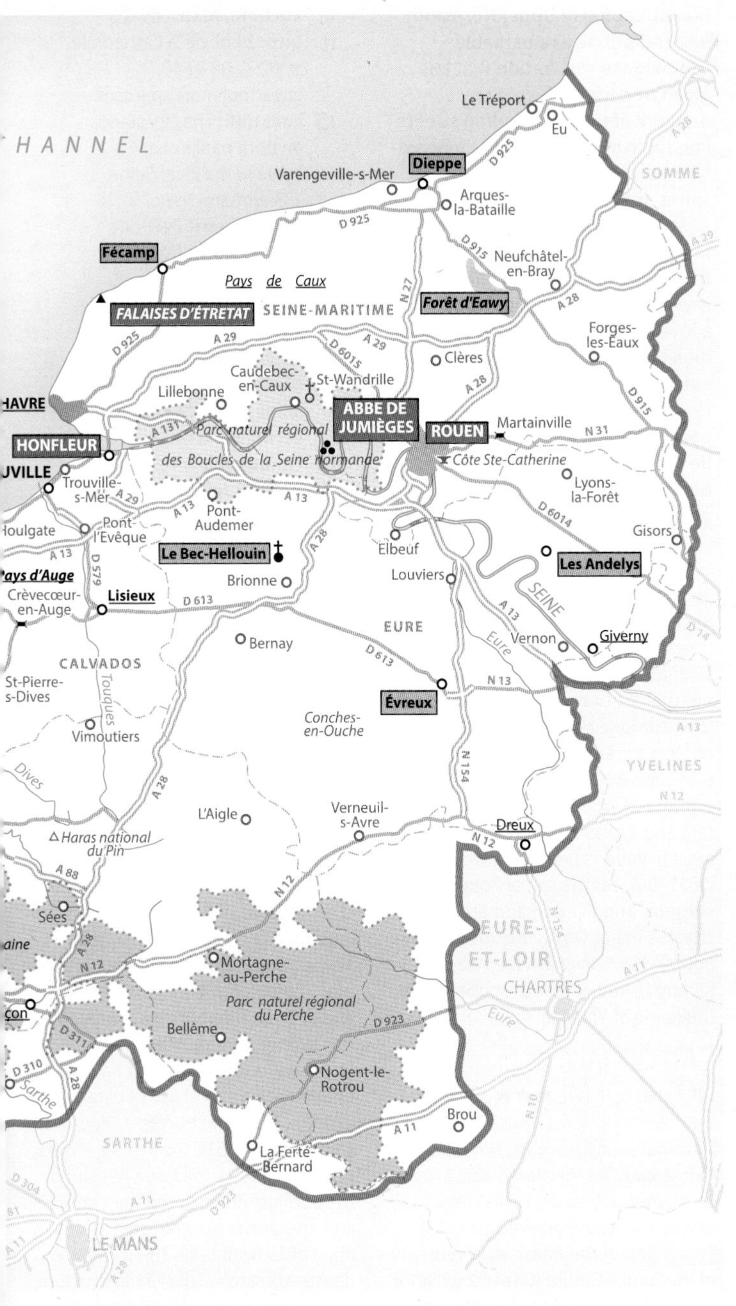
CHANNEL
Le Tréport
Eu
Dieppe
Varengeville-s-Mer
Arques-la-Bataille
SOMME
D 925
D 915
Neufchâtel-en-Bray
Fécamp
Pays de Caux
SEINE-MARITIME
N 27
Forêt d'Eawy
A 28
A 29
FALAISES D'ÉTRETAT
D 6015
Forges-les-Eaux
Clères
Caudebec-en-Caux
St-Wandrille
Lillebonne
HAVRE
ABBE DE JUMIÈGES
ROUEN
Martainville
N 31
HONFLEUR
A 131
Parc naturel régional des Boucles de la Seine normande
Côte Ste-Catherine
Lyons-la-Forêt
UVILLE
Trouville-s-Mer
A 13
Pont-Audemer
D 6014
Gisors
Houlgate
Pont-l'Evêque
Elbeuf
Le Bec-Hellouin
Les Andelys
Pays d'Auge
D 579
Brionne
Louviers
Crèvecœur-en-Auge
Lisieux
D 613
SEINE
EURE
Bernay
Vernon
Giverny
CALVADOS
St-Pierre-s-Dives
Touques
Évreux
N 13
Vimoutiers
Conches-en-Ouche
YVELINES
Dives
N 154
N 12
L'Aigle
Verneuil-s-Avre
Dreux
Haras national du Pin
A 88
Sées
EURE-ET-LOIR
Mortagne-au-Perche
CHARTRES
Parc naturel régional du Perche
Eure
Bellême
D 923
D 311
D 310
Sarthe
Nogent-le-Rotrou
A 11
Brou
SARTHE
La Ferté-Bernard
D 304
LE MANS

Rouen★★★

Rouen, capital of Upper Normandy, has undergone a remarkable campaign of restoration that has given new life to the old city's network of narrow, winding streets lined with magnificent half-timbered houses. With its skyline of towers, spires and fine buildings, it offers a wealth of artistic delights and is a city of first-rate museums – the Musée de Beaux-Arts alone is worth the trip. Rouen sits in a lovely valley surrounded by high hills, from which there are extensive views over the city and the Seine. Established at the lowest point on the Seine which could be successfully bridged, Rouen developed into a hugely successful port and industrial centre.

- **Population:** 110 933.
- **Michelin Map:** 304 G 5
- **Info:** 25 pl. de la Cathédrale. ✆02 32 08 32 40. www.rouentourisme.com.
- **Location:** The city stands on both banks of a curve in the River Seine, 133km/83mi NW of Paris.
- **TGV:** Rouen Rive Droite is 1hr40 direct from Paris St Lazare.
- **Flights:** The Aéroport de Rouen Vallée de Seine (✆02 35 79 41 00; www.rouen.aeroport.fr) is linked to the city by the TCAR bus network and by taxis.
- **Timing:** Allow 1–2 hours for a walk through Old Rouen with its beautiful 15–18C half-timbered houses. The quays on the north bank and the surrounding streets are the city centre.
- **Don't miss:** The Musée des Beaux-Arts is, in such a busy city, a relaxing place to be – the collection is excellent, too.

A BIT OF HISTORY

Rouen has been important since Roman times owing to its position as the lowest bridging point on the Seine; the alignment of its two main streets (Rue du Gros-Horloge and Rue des Carmes) still reflects the layout of the early city.
Although Rouen is the birthplace of a number of scientists, it is men of letters and artists who have contributed most to Rouen's fame. Gustave Flaubert (1821–80) was the son of Rouen's chief surgeon and lived in and around the city. His major works include *Madame Bovary* (1857), in which the village of Ry (20km/12.4mi east) is described under the name of Yonville.

CATHÉDRALE NOTRE-DAME★★★

Open Apr–Oct Mon 2–7pm, Tue–Sat 9am–7pm, Sun 8am–6pm; Nov–Mar Mon 2–6pm, Tue–Sat 9am–noon, 2–6pm, Sun 8am–6pm. Closed 1 Jan, 1 May, 11 Nov. www.cathedrale-rouen.net.

This is one of the finest achievements of the French Gothic; it was rebuilt after a fire in 1200. Thanks to the generosity of John Lackland, Duke of Normandy, as well as the king of England, reconstruction was swift; the transepts were extended and the choir enlarged.
The spaciousness of the interior is striking. The choir, with 14 soaring pillars and delicate triforium, is a masterpiece of harmonious proportion.
The great edifice seems to have been under repair for most of its existence for varied reasons: the Hundred Years' War, another fire in 1514, the Religious Wars, the hurricane of 1683, the Revolution, the burning-down of the spire in 1822, and the aerial bombardment of the night of 19 April 1944. This most recent disaster threatened the whole structure; restoration work is still under way.

WALKING TOUR

OLD ROUEN★★★

Rouen map, p214. Allow about 30min.

- **Place de la Cathédrale** – Opposite the cathedral on the corner of rue du Petit-Salut stands the former Bureau des Finances, an elegant Renaissance building (1510).
- **Rue Saint-Romain★★** – One of Rouen's most fascinating streets with its beautiful 15–18C half-timbered houses.
- **Archevêché** – Closed for tours. Next to the Booksellers' Court stands the 15C Archbishop's Palace (altered in the 18C). A gable pierced by the remains of a window is all that is left of the chapel where the trial of Joan of Arc ended on 29 May 1431, and where her rehabilitation was proclaimed in 1456.
- **Église St-Maclou★★** – Beautiful church of Gothic-Flamboyant style, built between 1437 and 1517.
- **Rue Martainville★** – The street has preserved some marvellous 15–18C half-timbered houses.
- **Aître St-Maclou★★** – This 16C ensemble is one of the last examples of a medieval plague cemetery.
- **Rue Damiette★** – The street is lined with half-timbered houses.
- **Rue Eau-de-Robec** – In this street, lined with old houses boasting recently restored timber framing, flows a little stream, spanned by a series of footbridges. Several of these tall buildings have workshop-attics, where drapers would leave their skeins of cotton and sheets of fabric out to dry.
- **Musée national de l'Éducation★** – The National Museum of Education is housed in a handsome 15C residence known as the Maison des Quatre Fils Aymona. It was once a notorious trysting spot referred to as the House of Marriages on account of the many casual encounters that took place there.
- **Abbatiale Saint-Ouen★★** – This former abbey church is one of the jewels of High Gothic architecture.
- **Église Saint-Godard★** – This late-15C church contains wonderful stained-glass **windows★**.
- **Musée Le Secq des Tournelles★★** – The Wrought Ironwork Museum is housed in old Église St-Laurent, a fine Flamboyant building, and is exceptionally rich (3–20C).
- **Musée de la Céramique★★** – The 17C Hôtel d'Hocqueville houses the Ceramics Museum, which presents an outstanding collection of 16C to 18C Rouen faïence.
- **Musée des Beaux-Arts★★★** – Open Wed–Mon 10am–6pm (last entry 1hr before closing). €5. ℘02 35 71 28 40. www.rouen-musees.com. The museum has a magnificent collection of 15–20C painting, especially in the earlier period, as well as fine sculpture, and other pieces including furniture and gold-work. See Gérard David's *Virgin and Saints*, an oil painting on wood, one of the masterpieces of Flemish Primitive art, as well as several choice pieces from the French School: *Diana Bathing* by François Clouet, The *Concert of Angels* by Philippe de Champaigne, and *Venus Arming Aeneas* by Nicolas Poussin. Other outstanding works from European countries are *The Adoration of the Shepherds* by Rubens, *St Barnabé Healing the Sick* by Veronese, and especially *Democritus* by Velasquez.
- **Palais de Justice★★** – This splendid 15C and early 16C Renaissance building was built to house the Exchequer of Normandy (law courts).
- **Place du Vieux-Marché★** – In the Middle Ages the square was the scene of public mockery and executions. On the north, the foundations of the pillories have been excavated, and on the South, an outline marks the tribune from where the judges of Joan of Arc watched her execution. A cross has been erected at the spot where she was burned at the stake on 30 May 1431.

ROUEN

0 100 m
0 100 yds

WHERE TO STAY

Andersen (Hôtel) ... 1
Auberge de jeunesse ... 3
Bertelière (Hôtel La) ... 5
Camp du Drap d'or (Hôtel du) ... 7
Cardinal (Hôtel le) ... 4
Carmes (Hôtel des) ... 6
Cathédrale (Hôtel de la) ... 8
Dandy (Hôtel) ... 10
Dieppe (Hôtel de) ... 12
Muette (Chambre d'hôte La) ... 16
Vieux Carré (Hôtel le) ... 18
Versan (le) ... 2

WHERE TO EAT

Bistrot de Panurge (Le) ... 4
Bistrot du Siècle (Le) ... 6
Couronne (La) ... 10
Écaille (L') ... 12
Gill ... 14
Maraîchers (Les) ... 16
Marmite (La) ... 20
Pascaline ... 22
P'tits Parapluies (Les) ... 23
Réverbère (Le) ... 25
Toque d'Or (La) ... 27
37 (Le) ... 29

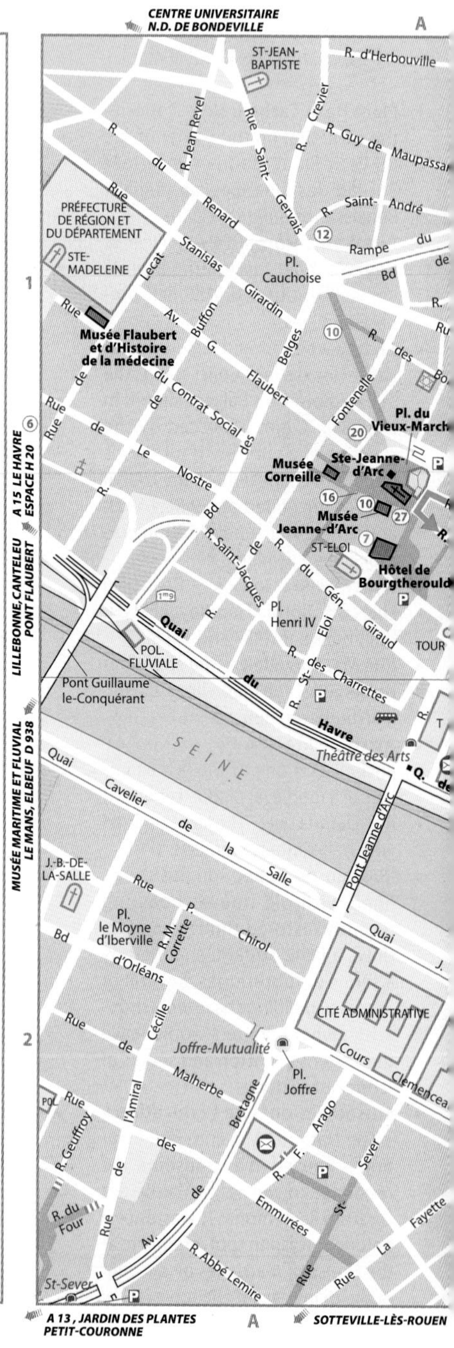

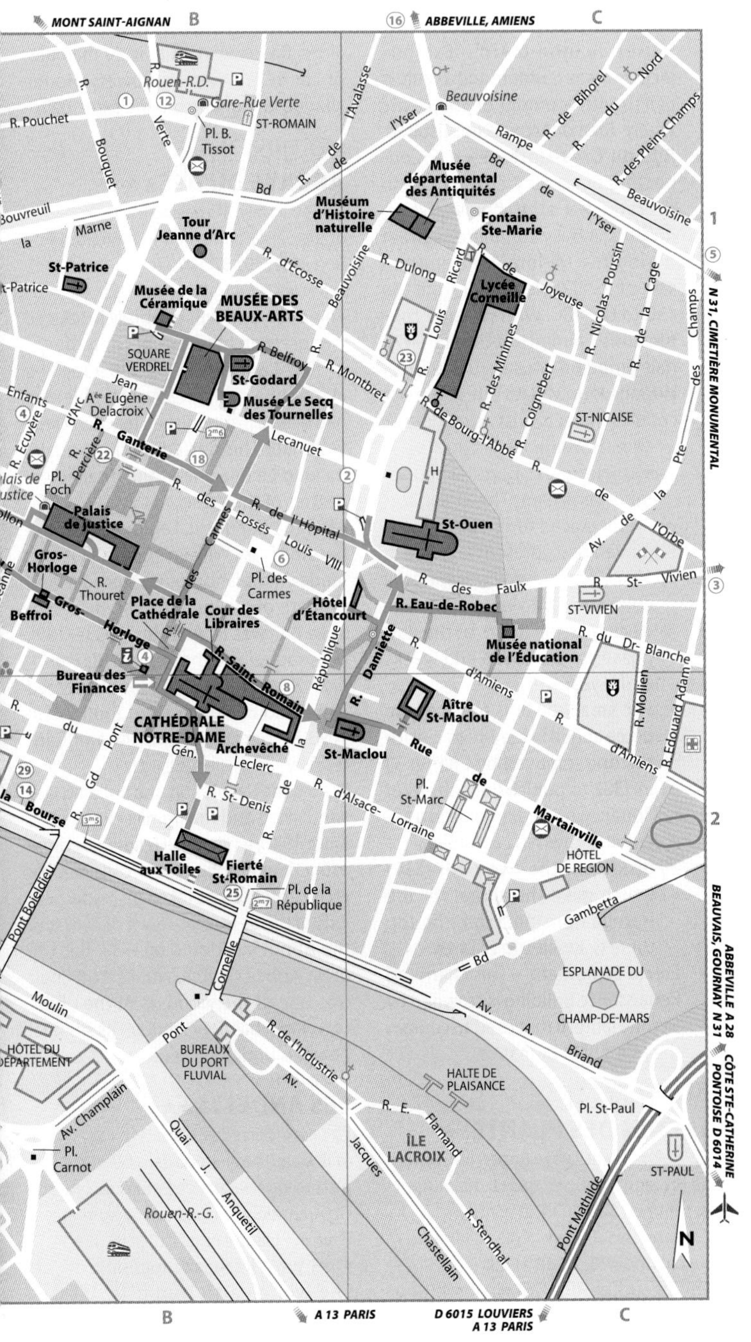
MONT SAINT-AIGNAN
ABBEVILLE, AMIENS
MUSÉE DES BEAUX-ARTS
Musée de la Céramique
Tour Jeanne d'Arc
St-Patrice
Muséum d'Histoire naturelle
Musée départemental des Antiquités
Fontaine Ste-Marie
Lycée Corneille
St-Godard
Musée Le Secq des Tournelles
SQUARE VERDREL
Palais de Justice
Gros-Horloge
Beffroi
Place de la Cathédrale
Cour des Libraires
Bureau des Finances
CATHÉDRALE NOTRE-DAME
Archevêché
St-Maclou
Aître St-Maclou
Hôtel d'Étancourt
St-Ouen
Musée national de l'Éducation
ST-NICAISE
ST-VIVIEN
ST-ROMAIN
Gare-Rue Verte
Beauvoisine
Halle aux Toiles
Fierté St-Romain
Pl. de la République
HÔTEL DE REGION
ESPLANADE DU CHAMP-DE-MARS
HÔTEL DU DÉPARTEMENT
BUREAUX DU PORT FLUVIAL
HALTE DE PLAISANCE
ÎLE LACROIX
Pl. St-Paul
ST-PAUL
Pl. Carnot
Rouen-R.-G.
Rouen-R.D.
N 31, CIMETIÈRE MONUMENTAL
ABBEVILLE A 28 BEAUVAIS, GOURNAY N 31
CÔTE STE-CATHERINE PONTOISE D 6014
A 13 PARIS
D 6015 LOUVIERS A 13 PARIS

- **Église Ste-Jeanne-d'Arc** – This 1970s church is shaped like an upturned ship.
- **Musée Jeanne-d'Arc** – Exhibits include a wax museum and a vaulted cellar with a model of the castle where Joan of Arc was imprisoned.
- **Rue du Gros-Horloge★★** – Connecting place du Vieux-Marché to the cathedral is the abbreviated rue du Gros, a busy commercial street during the Middle Ages and the seat of local government from the 13C to the 18C. With its large cobblestones and attractive 15C–17C half-timbered houses, rue du Gros-Horloge is nowadays one of the city centre's major tourist attractions.

  Gros-Horloge – Tue–Sun 2–6pm; €6. The most popular monument in Rouen. The clock, formerly placed in the belfry, was moved to its present location in 1527 when the arch was specially constructed to receive it. The clock tells the hours of the day, phases of the moon and weeks of the year.

  The small tower is topped by a dome added in the 18C to replace the one removed by Charles VI in 1382 to punish the citizens of Rouen, who had organised a tax revolt, known as La Harelle.

  Inside are the two bells (13C) which gave the signal for the Harelle uprising. From the top there is a majestic vista★★.
- **Fierté St-Romain** – This charming Renaissance building is crowned by a stone lantern that used to contain the relics of St Romanus.

ADDITIONAL SIGHTS

JARDIN DES PLANTES★

▶ 2.5km/1.5mi. Leave Rouen by avenue de Bretagne. ♿Open daily 8.30am-8pm in summer; 8am–dark in winter. Greenhouses 9–11am, 1.30–4.30pm. No charge. ☎02 32 18 21 30.

This beautiful 10ha/25-acre park, originally designed in the 17C, contains around 3 000 plant species inside the conservatories and **tropical hothouses** and a further 5 000 out in the open air. A star attraction is the **Victoria Regia**, a giant water lily from the Amazon, whose large, flat leaves can reach a diameter of 1m in summer. Its flowers bloom, change colour and die the same day.

EXCURSIONS

ABBAYE DU BEC★★

▶ The abbey sits beside the Risle, S of the Seine, about 40km/25mi from Rouen. ℹ☎02 32 43 72 60. www.abbayedubec.com.

This once-prestigious abbey produced two great archbishops of Canterbury. In 1042 **Lanfranc** (1005–89) appeared at the abbey. This great yet humble man had been a distinguished teacher. Three years later, he started teaching again, making Le Bec one of the intellectual centres of the West.

After the Conquest, Lanfranc, who had become Duke William's Counsellor, was made Archbishop of Canterbury and Primate of all England. His successor at Le Bec was **St Anselm** (1033–1109), philosopher and theologian. His *Proslogion*, written here in 1078, is considered a great source of Western thought. In 1093 he became Archbishop of Canterbury.

During the Revolution, the building was vandalised and the monks expelled.

Since 1948, when Bec-Hellouin became a functioning abbey again, considerable reconstruction has taken place, particularly of the St-Nicolas Tower of 1467 and the Abbot's Lodging of 1735. But the great Abbey Church, whose 42m choir was one of the wonders of the Christian world, has gone, though its spiritual power is undiminished.

LES ANDELYS★★

▶ Les Andelys lies 39km/24mi SE of Rouen. The château rises beside picturesque waterside Petit Andelys. Grand Andelys extends away from the river. ir. Philippe Auguste. ☎02 32 54 41 93. www.lesandelys-tourisme.fr.

The white castle rising beside Les Andelys commanded the Seine valley on the border of Normandy. Its strategic position was valued by Richard the Lionheart, Duke of Normandy as well as King of England. In 1196, he decided to break his agreement with the king of France, and construct a mighty fortress of his own. Within the year, so legend has it, the work was complete.

Château Gaillard★★

Accessible by car from Grand Andelys or on foot (30min climb) from Petit Andelys. Open Apr–early Nov, daily except Tue 10am–1pm, 2–6pm. Closed 1 May. €3.20. Guided tours 4.30pm daily, and 11.30am on Sun. €4.50.

Despite its 17 towers, thick walls, three rings of defences and a moat, King Philippe Auguste succeeded in taking the castle in 1274 after a siege of only eight months. This victory enabled him to incorporate Normandy, Maine, Anjou and Touraine into the French kingdom. In 1419 Henry V of England took it back. La Hire, companion to Joan of Arc, won it again for France ten years later, only to lose it to Henry once more.

ABBAYE DE JUMIÈGES★★★

Jumièges is on a big loop of the River Seine just W of Rouen.

The great abbey in its splendid setting on the Lower Seine forms one of the most evocative groups of ruins in France. The abbey was founded in the 7C and within 50 years housed 700 monks and 1 500 lay-brothers. Its great wealth was based on the generosity of the Merovingian rulers and on tithes drawn from a vast area. Destroyed by the Vikings, the abbey was raised again in the early 11C, but suffered in the Wars of Religion. The monks were scattered at the outbreak of the Revolution.

In 1793 it was auctioned and a purchaser started dismantling it to re-use the stone, blowing up the chancel and lantern-tower in the process. In 1852 a new owner saved it from complete destruction, but by then the great edifice was already a ruin.

ÉVREUX★

The town is 56km/35mi S of Rouen. 02 32 24 04 43. www.grandevreuxtourisme.fr.

The history of Évreux could read like a series of unmitigated disasters, from the burnings and sackings perpetrated by Vandals, Vikings and Plantagenets, to the devastation wreaked from the air by Luftwaffe (in 1940) and Allied air forces (in 1944). But after each disaster, the townspeople have re-created prosperity from ruin.

Evidence of this spirit can be seen in the promenade laid out on the old Roman rampart on the banks of the river Iton, and in the treatment of the Clock Tower (Tour de l'Horloge) which was built by Henry V in 1417, two years after his victory over the French at Agincourt.

Cathédrale Notre-Dame★

19 r. Charles Corbeau. Open 8.30am–7pm. 02 32 24 04 43.

The cathedral, begun in the 12C, is essentially a harmonious Gothic building of the 13C. Much restoration had to take place after John the Good's siege in 1356 and during the reign of Louis XI (1461–83). In the 16C the aisles of the nave were rebuilt in Flamboyant style, and after WW II much of the upper part of the cathedral was replaced. It has many beautiful 13–14C stained-glass windows★.

Abbaye de Jumièges

DREUX★

Dreux is 85km/52.8mi W of Paris via N 12, and 48km/29.8mi E of l'Aigle.

02 37 46 01 73. www.ot-dreux.fr.

Dreux is set on the boundary between Normandy and Île-de-France; it is a lively regional market town earning its living from diverse industrial activities. The town is the final resting place of members of the Orléans family, one of France's royal lines; they can be viewed in the crypt of the Royal Chapel of St-Louis where their tombs comprise an impressive collection of 19C sculpture. Nearby, the Eure valley contains lovely surprises, notably the château of Anet. Dreux rose to importance when the Normans settled west of the River Avre and Dreux Castle had to defend the French frontier against a very belligerent neighbour.

The castle, which stood on the hill now occupied by St Louis' Chapel, was besieged many times. It was dismantled on the orders of Henri IV, who razed the town in 1593.

ADDRESSES

STAY

€ **Hôtel Andersen** – 4 r. Pouchet. 02 35 71 88 51. www.hotelandersen.com. 14 rooms. Pleasantly quiet and refined. A little street noise on weekends.

€ **Youth Hostel** – Le Robec, 3 r. du Tour, route de Darnétal. 02 35 08 18 50. www.fuaj.org. 7am–12pm, 5–10pm, weekends and holidays 6pm–10pm – reservation 48 hours prior. 108 beds. In old Auvray dyers installations, typically 18C architecture. Simple, functional rooms.

€€ **Chambre d'hôte La Muette** – 1057 r. des Bosquets, 76230 Isneauville, 10km/6mi NE. 02 35 60 57 69. www.charmance-lamuette.com. Closed mid-Dec–mid-Mar. 5 rooms. Spacious, themed rooms in stunning 18C Norman building.

€€ **Hôtel des Carmes** – 33 pl. des Carmes. 02 35 71 92 31. www.hoteldescarmes.com. 12 rooms. Not far from the cathedral. Delightful, artistic reception; clutter-free bedrooms.

€€ **Hôtel Le Cardinal** – 1 pl. de la Cathédrale. 02 35 70 24 42. www.cardinal-hotel.fr. Closed 18 Dec–14 Jan. 15 rooms. Near Notre Dame Cathedral, family hotel with distinctive red façade; moderate-sized rooms, modern furnishings.

€€ **Hôtel Le Vieux Carré** – 34 r. Ganterie. 02 35 71 67 70. www.hotel-vieux-carre.com. 13 rooms. Charming, half-timbered property (1715), modern rooms.

€€ **Le Versan** – 3 r. Jean-Lecanuet. 02 35 07 77 07. 4 rooms. Practical, on boulevard near hôtel de ville. Functional rooms, efficient soundproofing.

€€–€€€ **Hôtel de la Cathédrale** – 12 r. St-Romain. 02 35 71 57 95. www.hotel-de-la-cathedrale.fr. 26 rooms. Beautiful 17C building in a pretty, pedestrian street near cathedral. Rooms comfy, atmosphere delightful.

€€€ **Hôtel La Bertelière** – 1641 av. Mesnil-Grémichon, 76160 Saint-Martin-du-Vivier. 02 35 60 44 00. www.laberteliere.com. Open all year. 44 rooms. Restaurant €€–€€€. Comfy rooms on Rouen heights, wide salons open on gardens. 10 min from central Rouen. Rooms with access for disabled.

€€€ **Hôtel Dandy** – 93 bis. r. Cauchoise. 02 35 07 32 00. www.hotels-rouen.net. Closed 26 Dec–2 Jan. 18 rooms. Near Place du Vieux-Marché; tearoom, charming bar. Rooms refined, pretty breakfast room.

€€€ **Hôtel de Dieppe** – pl. Bernard Tissot (opposite train station). 02 35 71 96 00. www.hotel-dieppe.fr. 41 rooms. Run by the same family since 1880. Neat rooms each with own décor.

€€€€ **Hôtel du Camp du Drap d'or – Hôtel de Bourgtheroulde** – 5 pl. de la Pucelle. 02 35 14 50 50. www.hotelsparouen.com. 78 rooms. Pleasant, contemporary rooms. Spacious, light. Marble bathrooms, steam bath, sauna, brasserie, upscale restaurant l'Aumale.

EAT

€ **Le Bistrot de Panurge** – 91 r. Ecuyères. 02 35 15 97 02. Closed Sat noon and Sun €€. Roast lamb with flageolet beans is house speciality.

Bistrot d'Adrian – 37 pl. du Vieux-Marché. ☎02 35 71 57 73. www.les-maraichers.fr. Parisian style in half-timbered house. Norman-style second dining room on ground floor.

Pascaline – 5 r. de la Poterne. ☎02 35 89 67 44. www.pascaline.fr. Reservations advised. Restaurant with bistro façade. Brasserie décor, handsome wood counters, long seats, yellow walls. Fixed-price menus.

La Marmite – 3 r.de Florence. ☎02 35 71 75 55. http://lamarmiterouen.unblog.fr. Near place du Vieux-Marché. Delicately flavoured cuisine, fresh products, attentively prepared.

La Toque d'Or – 11 pl. du Vieux-Marché. ☎02 35 71 46 29. Well-placed, pretty half-timbered house with two restaurants. Ground floor: elegant, with refined fare; upstairs, more casual and served faster.

Le Bistrot du Siècle – 75 r. Jules Ferry, 76480 Duclair, 20km/12.4mi NW. ☎02 35 37 62 36. Closed 25 Dec–1 Jan, Sun and Mon. Little bistro with fine reputation. Flame-grilled meats, a few dishes from Reunion Island.

Le 37 – 37 r. St-Étienne-des-Tonneliers. ☎02 35 70 56 65. Closed Sun, Mon, 11–19 Apr and 1–25 Aug. Trendy bistro, casual. Daily specials.

Les P'tits Parapluies – pl. Rougemare. ☎02 35 88 55 26. Closed 3–19 Aug, 2–8 Jan, Sat lunch, Sun eve, Mon. 16C former umbrella factory. Pleasant, modern, yet with period beams.

Reverbère – 5 pl. de la République. ☎02 35 07 03 14. Closed 28 Apr–4 May, 28 Jul–17 Aug, Sun, public holidays. A discreet glass front on small square, near river. Modern dining room, low-key lounge, wooden staircase to a rustic lounge.

L'écaille – 26 rampe Cauchoise. ☎02 35 70 95 52. Seafaring restaurant with blue-green décor, modern paintings, up-to-date fish dishes.

La Couronne – 31 pl. du Vieux-Marché. ☎02 35 71 40 90. www.lacouronne.com.fr. Superbly preserved, 1345 home is France's most beautiful inn. Rustic setting, flower-decked terrace in summer.

Gill – 9 quai de la Bourse. ☎02 35 71 16 14. www.gill.fr. Closed 4–20 Apr, 1–25 Aug, Sun. On the Seine, elegant, comfortable, simple dining room. Inventive cuisine, Norman ingredients.

NIGHTLIFE

Bar de la Crosse – 53 r. de l'Hôpital. ☎02 35 70 16 68. Closed Sun, Mon, fortnight in Aug and public holidays. When spending time in Rouen, pay a visit to this small, unpretentious bar. It owes its fine reputation to its singular atmosphere; between concerts and exhibits, laughter abounds, and it isn't unusual to see tourists and regulars chatting here like old friends.

La Taverne St-Amand – 11 r. St-Amand. ☎02 35 88 51 34. Closed 3 weeks in Aug & Sun. Transformed into a bar 30 years ago, this 17C house attracts painters, writers and actors.

SHOWTIME

Théâtre de l'Écharde – 16 r. Flahaut. ☎02 35 89 42 13. Theatre with 100 seats where the troupe's creations and shows for young theatregoers are performed.

Théâtre des Deux Rives – 48 r. Louis Ricard. ☎02 35 70 22 82. www.cdn-hautenormandie.fr. Ticket office open Tue–Sat 2–7pm. Closed Jul–Aug. Classical and modern theatre.

SHOPPING

Markets – pl. Saint-Marc (*Tue, Fri and Sat all day*); Place des Emmurés (*Tue and Sat all day*); Place du Vieux-Marché (*daily except Mon, mornings*).

Faïencerie Augy-Carpentier – 26 r. St-Romain. ☎02 35 88 77 47. The last handmade and hand-decorated earthenware workshop in Rouen. They offer copies of many traditional motifs on white and pink backgrounds, from blue monochrome to multicoloured, and from lambrequin to cornucopia.

Maison Hardy –22 pl. du Vieux-Marché. ☎02 35 71 81 55. In this alluring delicatessen, the Hardys offer Rouen specialities such as terrine de canard, duck being a highly prized fowl in this city (also known for its mutton). Mr Hardy's andouilles de Vire and his Caen tripe cooked in calvados and cider, specialities from Normandy, have clinched his reputation.

Le Havre★★

Destroyed in WWII and rebuilt in a striking modern style, this is one of Europe's most important ports and a Unesco World Heritage site.

- **Population:** 175 497.
- **Michelin Map:** 304 A 5
- **Info:** 186 bd Clemenceau. 02 32 74 04 04. www.lehavretourisme.com.
- **Location:** Le Havre is 42.6km/26.4mi SW of Fécamp and 88km/55mi W of Rouen.
- **TGV:** Just over 2hrs direct from Paris St Lazare; 2hr 45min via Rouen.
- **Parking:** Between the Bassin du Commerce and the Espace Niemeyer (pl. du Gén.-de-Gaulle).
- **Timing:** Spend 2hr walking around the modern town starting from the place du Géneral-de-Gaulle.
- **Don't miss:** The Musée des Beaux-Arts André-Malraux is worth seeking out.

A BIT OF HISTORY

By 1517, the harbour at Harfleur to the east had silted up. To remedy this François I ordered the building of a new port, which was to be called "Havre-de-Grâce" (Harbour of Grace). The marshy site selected by Admiral Bonnivet seemed unpromising, but his choice was a happy one since the tide remained at the flood two hours longer here than elsewhere. The port area subsequently spread some 20km/12.4mi upstream with a parallel industrial development of chemical, engineering and motor industries, shipyards and refineries.

The town and its region have an important Impressionist history and feature in several Impressionist works, notably Claude Monet's *Terrace at Ste-Adresse* (in the Metropolitan Museum in New York), a key work. The old town and resort of **Ste-Adresse★★** is still a pleasant place; from the clifftop at La Hève there are fine views out over the estuary and the English Channel.

Le Havre today comprises a large port and industrial area, the residential district of Ste-Adresse and the old port of Harfleur. The newer part of town centres around the Espace Niemeyer, which provides a modern architectural face-lift to Place Gambetta.

SIGHTS

Quartier Moderne (Modern Town)★

During the bombing that preceded Le Havre's liberation on 13 September 1944, the old centre was obliterated and more than 4 000 people were killed; the besieged Germans completed the destruction by dynamiting the port. The architect Auguste Perret (1874–1954), already famous for his innovative work with reinforced concrete, was given the task of rebuilding the devastated town from scratch. His initial concept involved a vast deck covering all the new city's services (energy, pipelines, gas, traffic). This bold scheme was rejected, so Perret laid out the town largely using the old street pattern, but in an uncompromisingly modern idiom which remains striking.

Among the highlights of Perret's remarkable work are **Place de l'Hôtel de Ville★**, one of the largest squares in Europe; **Avenue Foch★**, with a vista down to the sea, and **Église St-Joseph★**, whose interior walls are a lattice of stained glass.

Musée d'art moderne André-Malraux★★

2, bvd Clémenceau. Open Wed–Fri and Mon 11am–6pm, Sat–Sun 11am–7pm. Closed 1 Jan, 1 May, 14 Jul, 11 Nov, 25 Dec. €5 (no charge 1st Sat of month). 02 35 19 62 62. www.ville-lehavre.fr.

The glass and metal building looks out to the sea through a monumental concrete sculpture known locally as Le

Signal. The roof, designed to provide the best possible light to the galleries inside, consists of six sheets of glass covered by an aluminium sun blind.

The museum presents a fine **collection★** of works by **Raoul Dufy** (1877–1953), who was born in Le Havre, and **Eugène Boudin** (1824–98), a native of Honfleur.

ACROSS THE NORMANDY BRIDGE★★★

HONFLEUR★★★

Honfleur is reached via the **Pont de Normandie★★**, a soaring cable-stayed bridge crossing the Seine with a record-setting main span of 856m between 214m-high towers. The town is on the seafront at the mouth of the Seine.

quai Lepaulmier. ✆02 31 89 23 30. www.ot-honfleur.fr.

Honfleur lies at the foot of the **Côte de Grâce★★** hill, overlooking the wide waters of the Seine estuary. With its old harbour, its church, its characterful old houses and lanes combining in a singular harmony, it is truly the most picturesque of ports.

Many maritime ventures began on the quayside at Honfleur. Paulmier de Gouneville sailed from here to Brazil in 1503, and in 1506 Jean Denis explored the mouth of the St Lawrence River.

In 1608 Samuel de Champlain set out to found Quebec City, and in 1681 La Salle started the voyage which was to make him the first European to descend the Mississippi all the way to the sea, thereby opening up those vast territories to which he gave the name Louisiana in honour of his king, Louis XIV.

Great artists have appreciated the soft light and breadth of sky over the Seine estuary as seen from Honfleur.

The town appealed to English watercolourist Richard Parkes Bonington, locally born Eugène Boudin and later to Claude Monet and the other Impressionists. Erik Satie composed some of his music in Honfleur, and several distinguished writers have lived and worked here.

Le Vieux Honfleur (Old Honfleur)★★ – The streets and quaysides of the ancient port are full of character. The **old harbour★★** shelters a fishing fleet as well as yachts and pleasure craft. A richly varied townscape is formed by the fine stone residences along the Quai St-Etienne, the narrow, slate-faced houses on the Quai Ste-Catherine, the church (Église St-Etienne), and the Governor's House (Lieutenance), all seen against the foreground of masts and rigging.

Nearby is the **Église Ste-Catherine★** with its detached **bell tower★**(r. des Logettes. Open mid-Mar–mid-Nov Wed–Mon 10am–noon, 2–6pm; closed May, 14 Jul. €2.50. ✆02 31 89 11 83). The church was rebuilt after the Hundred Years' War by the ships' carpenters. All around are houses built in like fashion: a fine group of timber buildings, unusual in Western Europe.

Rue Haute, a former pathway outside the fortifications, has kept many fine houses of brick, stone and timber once lived in by shipbuilders.

Musée Eugène Boudin

Open May–Sept daily except Tue 10am–noon, 2–6pm. Closed 14 Jul, 25 Dec. €7. ✆02 31 89 54 00. www.musees-honfleur.fr.

This museum houses temporary exhibitions of Impressionist works from Normandy. There is also a room devoted to the works of the French Impressionist painter, Eugène Boudin (1824–98).

LISIEUX★

The town is a short distance inland from Honfleur.

11 r. d'Alençon. ✆02 31 48 18 10. www.lisieux-tourisme.com.

Lisieux, on the east bank of the Touques, is the market centre of the prosperous **Auge★★** region. It is also a well-known pilgrimage centre. The town is famous in France for Ste Thérèse de Lisieux (1873–97), canonised in 1925.

Manor Houses of the Pays d'Auge

With its closely packed hedgerows, thatched cottages and old manors, the **Pays d'Auge★★** is a countryside of great charm. The farmhouses and manors of this tranquil landscape are set within an enclosure planted with apple trees and defined by a hedge. All the buildings are timber-framed, from the house itself to the cider-press, apple-store, stables and dairy grouped around it. Among the finest are the moated site at Coupesarte (*16km/10mi SW*) and Château Crèvecœur★ (*18km/11mi W*) with its museum devoted to the story of petroleum research (Musée de la recherche pétrolière).

DEAUVILLE★★

See p227.

NORTH OF LE HAVRE

ÉTRETAT★★

pl. Maurice Guillard. 02 35 27 05 21. www.etretat.net.

Sited where a dry valley in the chalk country of the **Pays de Caux★** meets the sea, Étretat was a humble fishing village well into the 19C. It was then favoured by writers such as Maupassant and painters like Courbet and Eugène Isabey.

Falaise d'Aval★★★

1hr round-trip on foot from the end of the promenade. Take the steps and then the path to the clifftop known as Porte d'Aval.

There are fine views of the Manneport Arch, the solitary 70m Needle (Aiguille), the long shingle beach and the Amont Cliff on the far side of the bay.

Falaise d'Amont★★

1hr round-trip on foot from the end of the promenade.

At the end of the promenade, the memorial was put up to mark where two aviators, Nungesser and Coli, were last seen as they set out in their "White Bird" (*Oiseau Blanc*) to attempt a non-stop westward crossing of the Atlantic (8 May 1927).

FÉCAMP★★

The town is on the N Normandy coast, 43km/27mi from Le Havre.

quai Sadi Carnot. 02 35 28 51 01. www.fecamptourisme.com.

Today the fishing industry dominates Fécamp, but as early as the 11C the town had seen considerable monastic activity. Guy de Maupassant (1850–93) used the town as the setting for many of his short stories.

Abbatiale de la Sainte-Trinité★★

The ancient abbey church marks an important stage in the evolution of Gothic architecture in Normandy.

Built mostly between 1168 and 1219, it was influenced by the developments in the Île-de-France (use of tribunes as in the churches derived from St-Denis outside Paris, the combination of flying buttresses and triforium pioneered at Chartres, which made the tribunes redundant and which here is seen in the south wall of the chancel).

Falaise d'Aval

Norman regionalism reasserts itself however in a number of ways: in the slender lantern-tower high above the crossing, and in the inspection gallery at the base of the triforium windows.

Palais Bénédictine★★

The building, designed by Camille Albert in the late 19C, is a mixture of neo-Gothic and neo-Renaissance styles. The **museum** displays a large collection of objets d'art: silver and gold work, ivories, Nottingham alabasters (late-15C), wrought-iron work, statues and many manuscripts.

The Gothic Room is covered by a fine pitched roof made of oak and chestnut, shaped as the upturned hull of a ship; it houses the library: 15C Books of Hours with fine **illuminations**, numerous **ivories**, a collection of **oil lamps** dating from the early days of Christianity and a Dormition of the Virgin, a painted low-relief wooden carving of the German School.

Musée des Terre-Neuvas et de la Pêche★

♿Open daily except Tue, 10am–noon, 2–5.30pm (Jul–Aug 10am–7pm). Closed 1 Jan, 1 May, 25 Dec. ✆02 35 28 31 99.

The Newfoundland and Fishing Museum evokes memories of the Fécamp fishing industry. The lower gallery explores the great adventure of the cod fishermen on the Newfoundland banks in the days of the sailing ship and the dory, a flat-bottomed craft rising at bow and stern.

One room is devoted to shipbuilding, featuring a model of the *Belle Poule*, the naval training ship built in Fécamp in 1931. Exhibits trace the development of fishing methods and types of craft.

DIEPPE★★

Pont Jehan Ango. ✆02 32 14 40 60. www.dieppe.fr.

The nearest seaside resort to Paris, Dieppe is sometimes referred to as Plage de Paris. Its famous sea-front lawns were laid out in 1863 by Empress Eugénie and Napoléon III.

Dieppe's history as a major port goes back to the 11C, the English wool trade, and the import of spices from the Orient. As early as the 14C, Dieppe sailors were landing on the coast of the Gulf of Guinea and Jean Cousin was exploring the South Atlantic. In 1402 Jean de Béthencourt founded the first European colony on the Canary Islands. Jean Ango (1480–1551), whose privateers once captured a fleet of 300 Portuguese vessels, equipped many a voyage of discovery to remote shores.

ESTRAN Cité de la Mer★

Open daily 10am–noon, 2–6pm. €7 (children, €3.50). ✆02 35 06 93 20. http://estrancitedelamer.free.fr.

This museum is dedicated to the maritime history of Dieppe as a port. It also includes an aquarium containing fish species that live in the Channel and the North Sea.

Château-Musée de Dieppe (Dieppe Castle Museum)

Open Oct–May Wed–Mon 10am–noon, 2–5pm; Jun–Sep until 6pm. Closed 1 Jan, 1 May, 1 Nov, 25 Dec. €4. ✆02 35 06 61 99. www.musees-haute-normandie.fr.

Housed in a 15C fortress, this museum's collection includes fine art, archaeology, ethnology, history, music and ceramics. About a thousand ivory items created by Dieppe craftsmen are also on display.

CÔTE D'ALBÂTRE (ALABASTER COAST)★ From Dieppe to Étretat

104km/64.6mi

Sheer white cliffs cut into by dry valleys (*valleuses*) drop to sandy beaches.

Little resorts – **Pourville-sur-Mer, Ste-Marguerite-sur-Mer** and **Veules-les-Roses** – are sited at the seaward end of a series of lush valleys.

In **Varangeville-sur-Mer**, the graveyard of the 11–15C church overlooks the sea and shelters the tomb of the Cubist painter, **Georges Braque**. The stained glass of Chapelle St-Dominique (on the outskirts) by the artist are of interest.

Caen★★★

Tough and enduring, the city of Caen rebuilt itself after being almost destroyed by bombing during WWII. Today the city proudly preserves an impressive historical legacy, while being committed to peace and the future.

- **Population:** 108 954.
- **Michelin Map:** 303 E-J 3-4
- **Info:** pl. St-Pierre. ✆02 31 27 14 14. www.caen-tourisme.fr.
- **Location:** 15km/9mi inland from the coast and ferry terminal at Ouistreham, and 94km/59mi from Le Havre.
- **TGV:** Caen is just over 2hrs direct from Paris St Lazare.
- **Don't Miss:** The Mémorial de la Paix and the Abbaye-aux-Hommes.
- **Timing:** Allow 2hr for the château and the nearby museums, 2hr for the abbeys, and 2hr for the Peace Memorial.

A BIT OF HISTORY

The City of the Normans – After the invasions of the Norsemen in the 9C and 10C, and the establishment of the duchy of Normandy, Benedictines built the first major religious buildings in Normandy. Caen's architectural heritage reveals the affection felt for the city by William, Duke of Normandy, and his wife Mathilda, who chose this as their residence. They married in 1053, against papal opposition, which arose because they were cousins. This led to their excommunication until they made amends when William founded the Abbey for Men and Mathilda, the Abbey for Women.

Caen Stone – The light limestone quarried locally was used not only here but in great buildings of the Normans in England (Canterbury Cathedral, the White Tower at the Tower of London and Westminster Abbey).

WALKING TOUR

Caen map, p224.

- **Hôtel d'Escoville★** – This mansion, which now houses the tourist office and the Artothèque, was built between 1533 and 1538 by Nicolas Le Valois d'Escoville, a wealthy merchant.
- **Église St-Pierre★** – Although only a parish church, St Peter's is richly decorated. The impressive tower (78m), which dated from 1308, was destroyed during the Battle of Caen in 1944. "The king of Norman belfries" has, however, been rebuilt, as well as the nave into which it once fell.
- **Rue St-Pierre** – Lively shopping.
- **Musée de la Poste et des Techniques de Communication** – Illustrates the history of the postal service.
- **Cour des Imprimeurs** – These early 16C houses used to be home to major printing presses that were in operation until the early 20C.
- **Rue Froide** – In the shadow of St-Saviour's church, this very discreet little street still has interesting houses from the 15C to 19C.
- **Église St-Sauveur** – St Saviour's church has twin chevets facing rue St-Pierre: Gothic (15C) on the left and Renaissance (1546) on the right. Rue Froide contains interesting old houses, dating from the 15C to the 19C.
- **Place de la République** – The pedestrian precinct, between place St-Pierre and place de la République, is lively both day and night. Place de la République, which is laid out as a public garden, is bordered by beautiful Louis XIII houses (Hôtel Daumesnil at Nos 23–25) and the modern offices of the Préfecture.
- **Place Malherbe** – This square is named after a beautiful restored

house where the poet Malherbe is said to have been born in 1555.

- **Place St-Sauveur** – A fine collection of 18C houses borders the square, where the pillory stood until the 19C. At the centre is a statue of Louis XIV. The north-east side of the square is the site of the old St Saviour's, which was destroyed in 1944.
- **Place St-Martin** – Note the statue of Constable Bertrand du Guesclin. There is an interesting view of the two towers of St-Étienne.
- **Rue du Vaugueux** – Rue Montoir-Poissonnerie leads to this lovely pedestrian street, which has kept its quaint charm: cobblestones, stone and timber houses, old-fashioned street lights.

Abbaye-aux-Hommes★★

Guided tours (1hr30min) daily 9.30am, 11am, 2.30pm and 4pm. €3. ✆02 31 30 42 81.

The church of the Abbey for Men was founded by William the Conqueror; it was begun in 1066 and took 12 years to build. The west front with its soaring towers (the octagonal spires were added in the 13C) dates from this time. The nave is vast; it is a fine example of Romanesque construction with great square bays divided in two by minor piers and with high galleries over the aisles. The great lantern-tower over the crossing is probably the work of Lanfranc and William themselves; in its simple perfection it is a masterpiece of Romanesque art. The choir, which was extended and altered in the 13C, is a very early example of Norman Gothic which set the standard for buildings all over the duchy.

Château Ducal★

Guided tours Fri during Jul–Aug. No charge. ✆02 31 27 14 14.

This great fortress, perched on a bluff overlooking the city, was built by William in 1060, and subsequently strengthened and extended.

From its ramparts there are extensive views over Caen.

Musée des Beaux-Arts★★

♿Open Wed–Mon 9.30am–6pm. Closed 1 Jan, Easter Sun, 1 May, 1 Nov and 25 Dec. €3.50. ✆02 31 30 47 70. www.mba.caen.fr.

Situated within the precinct of William the Conqueror's castle, the Fine Arts Museum offers its collections from a chronological, thematic and geographical point of view. Large religious paintings and imposing historical and allegorical scenes hang in vast halls, bathed in light, whereas works of religious fervour and smaller paintings are essentially displayed in the small cabinets.

Musée de Normandie★★

Open daily 9.30am–6pm. Closed Tue Nov–May, 1 Jan, Easter Sun, 1 May, 1 Nov and 25 Dec. No charge. ✆02 31 30 47 60. www.musee-de-normandie.caen.fr.

This great museum displays the history of the Normandy region, its culture and people.

Abbaye-aux-Dames★★

Open daily 2–5.30pm. Guided tours (1hr) daily 2.30pm and 4pm. No charge. ✆02 31 06 98 98.

The Norman building, with its nave of nine bays, round-headed arches, and blind arcades in the triforium, was founded by Mathilda in 1062 as the church of the Abbey for Women. As at St Stephen's, the upper storey was altered when the timber roof was replaced by sexpartite vaulting.

Le Mémorial★★★

♿Open mid-Feb–Oct daily 9am –7pm; Nov–Dec daily except Mon (except last 2 Mon in Dec) 9.30am–6pm. Closed Jan and 25 Dec. €19. ✆02 31 06 06 44. www.memorial-caen.fr.

The memorial erected by the city, which in 1944 was at the centre of the Battle of Normandy, takes the form of a Museum for Peace; it is primarily a place of commemoration and of permanent meditation on the links between human rights and the maintenance of peace.

The façade of the sober building of Caen stone, facing Esplanade Dwight-

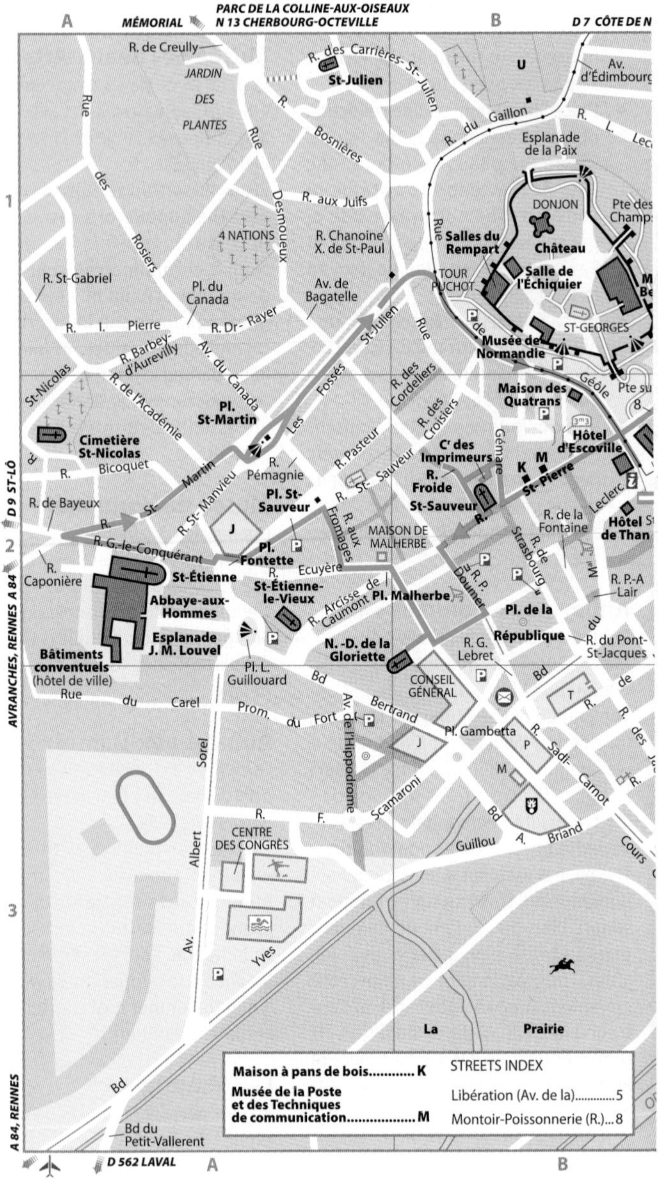

Maison à pans de bois........... K

Musée de la Poste et des Techniques de communication.................. M

STREETS INDEX

Libération (Av. de la)............. 5

Montoir-Poissonnerie (R.)... 8

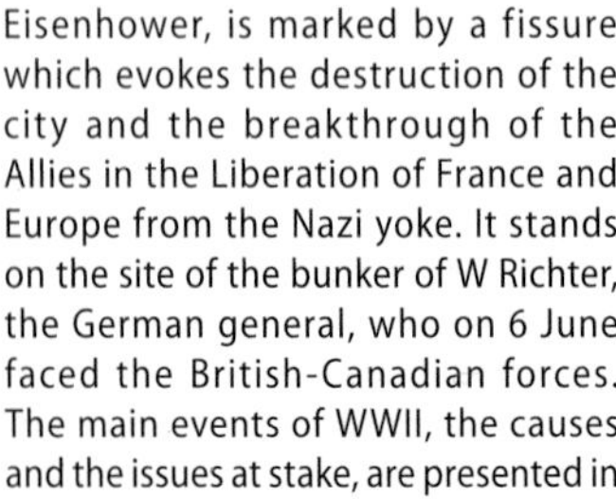

Eisenhower, is marked by a fissure which evokes the destruction of the city and the breakthrough of the Allies in the Liberation of France and Europe from the Nazi yoke. It stands on the site of the bunker of W Richter, the German general, who on 6 June faced the British-Canadian forces. The main events of WWII, the causes and the issues at stake, are presented in the light of the latest historical analysis. The collection includes a particularly imaginative display, centred on a spiral ramp on such themes as the inter-war years and the advance of Fascism; the use of extensive archive material, including a gripping panoramic projection of D-Day seen simultaneously from the Allied and the German standpoints; as well as moving testimonies

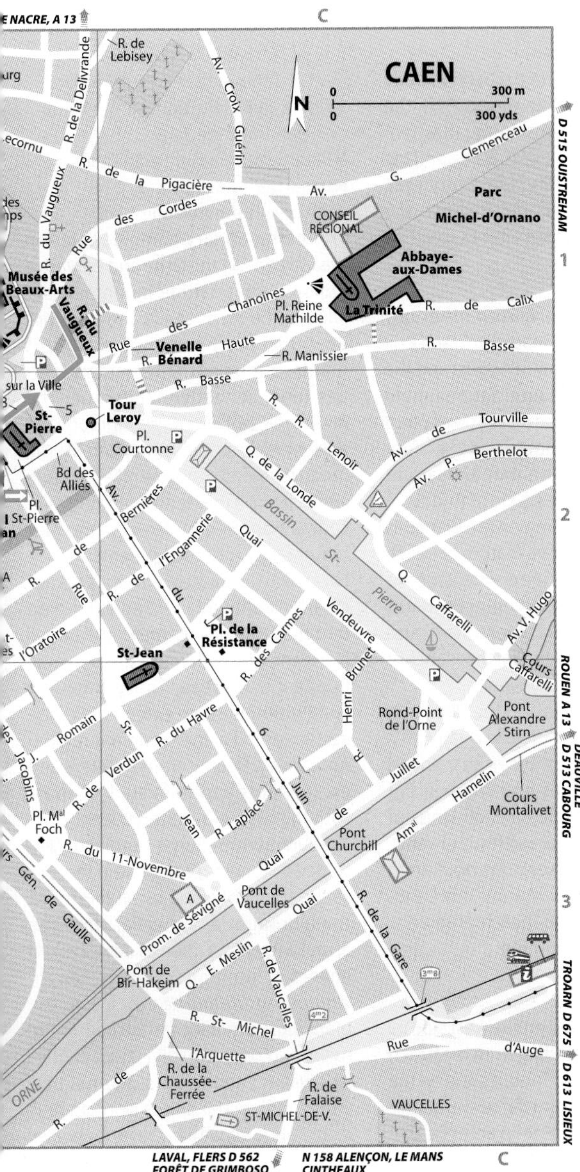

by witnesses of and participants in the drama. Lived experience is given priority so that the impact of WWII can be appreciated on a human level.

The **Mur de la Liberté** (Wall of Freedom) pays tribute to the hundreds of thousands of American soldiers who fought for freedom in Europe.

EXCURSIONS

DEAUVILLE★★

Located 94km/59mi from Rouen and 43km/27mi from Le Havre, Deauville lies on the Côte Fleurie.

112 rue Victor Hugo. 02 31 14 40 00. www.deauville.org.

Deauville, a popular resort since the mid-19C, is known for the luxury and refinement of its various establishments and the elegance of its entertainments. Events of the summer season include racing (including the Grand Prix), the polo world championship, regattas, tennis and golf tournaments, galas, and the international yearling fair. Every year, in early September, the city hosts the prestigious **American Film Festival**.

The Resort

The season in Deauville opens in July and ends with the Deauville Grand Prix on the fourth Sunday in August and the Golden Cup of the international polo championship. Horse racing takes place alternately at La Touques and Clairefontaine and the international yearling sales are held in Deauville in August.

The coming and going on the **Planches** is the most distinctive feature of beach life in Deauville. Lined with elegant buildings such as the Pompeian Baths and the Soleil Bar, where stars and celebrities like to be seen, the Planches draws fashionable strollers.

Between the casino and the Planches, the Centre International de Deauville is a remarkable ensemble of suspended gardens, fountains and transparent façades which welcomes all kinds of professional, cultural and festive events. A walk along the seafront boulevard Eugène-Cornuché will prove that Deauville is not called the "beach of flowers" (*plage fleurie*) for nothing.

Deauville Port

The port is enclosed on the west side by a breakwater extending from the beach to the mouth of the Touques and on the east by a jetty marking the port entrance to the channel. The deep access channel means that the port is accessible 80 percent of the time. It consists of three docks, entered through a double lock, which provide deep water moorings and ample capacity: 800 berths along 4 000m of quays. At the centre are the slate-roofed marinas, the Deauville harbour master's office, an annexe of the Marina Deauville Club (quai des Marchands, near the lock) and space for shops and hotel services.

LA SUISSE NORMANDE★★

The Suisse Normande takes in the Orne valley as well as the Noireau, the Vère, the Rouvre and the Baize.

ℹ Place Saint Sauveur, 14220 Thury Harcourt. ✆02 31 79 70 45. www.ot-suisse-normande.com.

This extraordinary name denotes an area straddling the **Orne** and **Calvados** regions. It has neither mountains nor lakes in the Swiss sense and does not even include Normandy's highest points, but nevertheless draws tourists to its attractive landscape. The River Orne, as it cuts its way through the ancient rocks of the Armorican Massif, produces a kind of hollow relief through which flows a pleasantly winding river course bordered by steep banks surmounted by rock escarpments.

Located in the midst of Calvados *bocage* country south of Caen and extending into the Orne *département*, the Suisse Normande lies between the towns of **Condé-sur-Noireau, Thury-Harcourt** and **Putanges**; some extend the range eastwards to **Falaise**★ and the rugged Ante valley. Deeply eroded valleys and escarpments appear in stark contrast with the flat plain around Caen.

The curious name Suisse Normande was coined by tourism promoters in the 19C, as the train, followed by an improved road, brought city-dwellers into the area. Switzerland, then as now, evoked images of inspiring scenery, clean air, vigorous sports and healthy living. The branding was not too far-fetched, as the rivers and canyons still attract canoeists, walkers and anglers. Tourists notwithstanding, the Suisse Normande is resolutely rural, with pastures for horses and cattle, fields of rapeseed, winding roads between ancient hedgerows, swathes of forest and little villages.

Thury-Harcourt

The town, rebuilt, stands on the banks of the Orne and is now a tourist centre for the Suisse Normande to the south. Thury adopted the name Harcourt from the Harcourt family, who came from the town of Harcourt in the county of Évreux; in 1700 Thury became the

Harcourt ancestral seat. Near the ruins of the Harcourt family château, burnt by the Germans in 1944, the **park★** has walkways bordered with trees, shrubs and flower beds.

Clécy★

This township, the tourist centre of the Suisse Normande, is close to some of the most picturesque beauty spots in the Orne valley.

ADDRESSES

STAY

Hôtel Bernières – 50 r. de Bernières. 02 31 86 01 26. www.hotelbernieres.com. 17 rooms. Friendly hotel, charming breakfast room, lounge.

Hôtel St-Étienne – 2 r. de l'Académie. 02 31 86 35 82. www.hotel-saint-etienne.com. 11 rooms. Dating from 1789, this house is near Abbaye-aux-Hommes.

Hôtel des Quatrans – 17 r. Gémare. 02 31 86 25 57. www.hotel-des-quatrans.com. 47 rooms. Central family hotel with colourful, functional rooms. Rear rooms quieter.

Hôtel du Château – 5 av. du 6-Juin. 02 31 86 15 37. www.hotel-chateau-caen.com. 24 rooms. In the town centre, between marina and château. Rooms small but pleasant.

Hôtel du Havre – 11 r. du Havre. 02 31 86 19 80. www.hotelduhavre.com. 19 rooms. Near La Prairie and racecourse; post-war hotel with modern, quiet rooms.

Hôtel la Glycine – 11 pl. du Commando no. 4, 14970 Bénouville. 02 31 44 61 94. www.la-glycine.com. P. 35 rooms. Restaurant. Near Pegasus Bridge; pleasant lodgings.

Hôtel Moderne – 116 bld Mar.-Leclerc. 02 31 86 04 23. http://en.bestwestern-moderne-caen.com. 40 rooms. Discreet post-war building.

EAT

Le Bouchon du Vaugueux – 12 r. Graindorge. 02 31 44 26 26. Closed 3 weeks in Aug, Sun and Mon. Reservations required. Popular tavern near château and old Caen.

Maître Corbeau – 8 r. Buquet. 02 31 93 93 00. www.maitre-corbeau.com. Closed 3 weeks in Aug, 1 Jan and 25 Dec, Sat noon, Mon noon and Sun. Entirely devoted to cheese: boxes, adverts, implements, etc.

Stiffler – 72 r. St-Jean. 02 31 86 08 94. www.stifflertraiteur.com. Closed Mon–Tue 9am–1pm, 2.30–7.30pm, Sun 8am–6pm and school holidays. Closed 27 Jul–18 Aug. Magnificent pastry shop.

Café Mancel – At the Château. 02 31 86 63 64. www.cafemancel.com. Closed Sun evening and Mon. This café and shop has high-quality local produce and also goods from Italy, Flanders, Holland and England.

Le Carlotta – 16 quai Vendeuvre. 02 31 86 68 99. Closed Sun. Art Deco-inspired brasserie.

L'Embroche – 17 r. Porte-au-Berger. 02 31 93 71 31. Closed Sat noon, Mon noon and Sun. Reservations advised. 3 specialities: Camembert with Calvados, steak with a caramelised balsamic sauce, and tripes Père Michel.

L'Insolite – 16 r. du Vaugueux at foot of château. 02 31 43 83 87. www.restaurantlinsolite.com. Closed Sun–Mon except May–Sep. Reservations advised. Half-timbered 16C house with unconventional interior, rustic and retro.

Pain et Beurre – 46 r. Guillaume-le-Conquérant. 02 31 86 04 57. Closed Sun noon, Sun evening and Mon. Near Abbaye-aux-Hommes. Fine cuisine: authentic and exotic.

Saint-Andrew's – 9 quai de Juillet. 02 31 86 26 80. http://restaurant.st.andrew.free.fr. Reservations advised. Good place to eat after a stroll along the Orne. Recalls an English pub.

Auberge de l'Île Enchantée – 1 r. St-André, 14123 Fleury-sur-Orne. 02 31 52 15 52. www.aubergelileenchantee.com. Closed first 2 wks Aug, 24 Feb–8 Mar, 13–28 Jul, Sun eve, Wed eve and Mon. Riverside; warm welcome, gourmet French cuisine.

LEISURE ACTIVITIES

Festyland – bd Péripherique 50 N, exit for Carpiquet, 14650 Carpiquet. 02 31 75 04 04. www.festyland.com. Closed Oct–Mar. €19 (children under 12, €16). Family leisure with some 30 attractions.

Normandy Landing Beaches★★

The choice of Normandy as the landing point for the invasion of Europe was not an obvious one. Defended by the Atlantic Wall, the coast had choppy water and tricky tides. Italy seemed a more likely option, but the invasion, begun in July 1943, proved slow and costly; to the east, the Germans still besieged Leningrad. At the Teheran Conference in late 1943, Churchill, Roosevelt and Stalin agreed on a French front. Men and arms were massed in Britain and intense bombing raids over Germany and France were intended to soften defences. The tour described in this section includes that part of the Calvados coast between the mouths of the Orne and the Vire, also known as the Côte de Nacre, where the D-Day landings took place on 6 June 1944. The marked itineraries, known as Overlord – L'Assaut (Overlord – The Onslaught) and D-Day – Le Choc (D-Day – The Impact), are two of several such itineraries in the Historical Area of the Battle of Normandy.

- **Michelin Map:** F3-K4.
- **Info:** Port-en-Bessin: ✆02 31 22 45 80. Longues-sur-Mer: ✆02 31 21 46 87.
- **Location:** This section covers the Calvados coast between the mouths of the Orne and the Vire, also known as the Côte de Nacre (Mother-of-Pearl coast) where the Normandy landings took place on D-Day, 6 June 1944.
- **Timing:** Each of the circuits described below takes half a day.

D-DAY LANDINGS

Operation Overlord – The Normandy Landings, or D-Day, for which the code name during preparations for this massive Allied invasion was Operation Overlord, were commanded by US General Dwight D Eisenhower, with British General (later Field Marshal) Bernard Montgomery in charge of land forces. Transport involved an armada of 7 000 ships and landing craft, and 12 500 aircraft. Some 156 000 troops landed, supported by 195 000 sailors. Preparations were epic: finally, all depended on the tides, to bring landing craft to shore.

D-Day Landings: A Turning Point – Field Marshal Erwin Rommel, inspecting the Atlantic Wall, pointed out that if the Allies succeeded in breaching it, the Third Reich would fall. Germany fell on 8 May 1945, after a long struggle, but the end had begun 11 months earlier.

Dawn of D-Day – The formidable armada, which consisted of 4 266 barges and landing craft together with hundreds of warships and naval escorts, set sail from the south coast of England on the night of 5 June 1944; it was preceded by flotillas of minesweepers to clear a passage through the mine fields in the English Channel. As the crossing proceeded, airborne troops were flown out and landed in two detachments at either end of the invasion front. The British 6th Division quickly took possession of the Bénouville-Ranville bridge, since named Pegasus Bridge after the airborne insignia, and harried the enemy positions between the River Orne and the River Dives to prevent reinforcements arriving. West of the River Vire the American 101st and 82nd Divisions mounted an attack on key positions such as **Ste-Mère-Église** or opened up the exits from Utah Beach.

BRITISH SECTOR

Although preliminary bombing and shelling had not destroyed Hitler's Atlantic Wall, the British forces succeeded in disorganising German defences. Land forces were able to

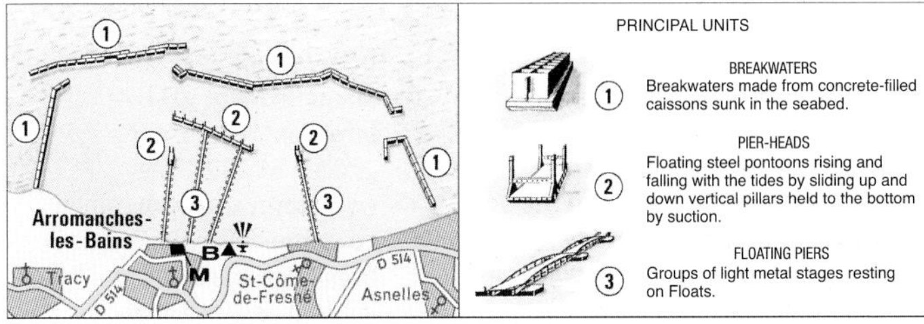

reach their objectives, divided into three beachheads:

Sword Beach

14.5km/9mi NE of Caen.

The Franco-British commandos landed at Colleville-Plage, Lion-sur-Mer and St-Aubin. They captured Riva-Bella and the strongpoints at Lion and Langrune and then linked up with the airborne troops at Pegasus Bridge. The main strength of the British 3rd Division then landed. This area, exposed to the Germans' long-range guns in Le Havre, became the crucial point in the battle.

Juno Beach

20km/12.5mi N of Caen.

The Canadian 3rd Division landed at Bernières and Courseulles, reaching Creully by 5pm. They were the first troops to enter Caen on 9 July 1944.

Gold Beach

35km/21mi NW of Caen.

The British 50th Division landed at Ver-sur-Mer and Asnelles; by the afternoon they were sufficiently established so the artificial Mulberry harbour could be brought into position. The 47th Commandos advanced and captured Port-en-Bessin during the night of 7 June. On 9 June the British sector joined up with the Americans from **Omaha Beach**. On 12 June, after the capture of **Carentan** had enabled the troops from Omaha and Utah beaches to join forces, a single beachhead was established.

AMERICAN SECTOR

A mighty Allied armada of over 4 000 specially made craft, together with hundreds of warships and naval escorts, sailed from the south coast of England on the night of 5 June 1944. The following morning they arrived: it was D-Day. The liberation of France, and of Europe, had begun.

Omaha Beach★

20km/12mi northwest of Bayeux.

Here the US 1st Division made its first contact with French soil and here the bloodiest engagement of D-Day was fought. Omaha Beach, which until 6 June 1944 existed only as an operational code name, has continued to designate the beaches of St-Laurent-sur-Mer, Colleville-sur-Mer and Vierville-sur-Mer, in memory of the American soldiers of the 1st (5th Corps of the 1st Army) Division.

Utah Beach

10km/6.25mi S of Cherbourg.

This beach, northeast of **Carentan**, entered history following the landing of American forces on 6 June 1944. Despite murderous fire from the Germans, the American 4th Division managed on 12 June to link up with the forces who had landed at Omaha Beach.

The Normandy invasion, and its significance in European and world history, is marked all along this coastline by cemeteries, monuments and museums.

ARROMANCHES-LES-BAINS★

On the coast, 10km/6.2mi NE of Bayeux via D 516, 38km/23.6mi NE of Caen via D 516 and N 13.

A modest seaside resort that owes its fame to the gigantic landing operation of June 1944. In the little port are the remains of a Mulberry harbour (*see illustration, above*), the most extraordinary maritime achievement of the war.

Bayeux★★

The Bayeux Tapestry still presents its unique record of the events of 1066 and the Battle of Hastings. Its home, the former capital of the Bessin, was the first French town to be liberated (7 June 1944) in WWII. The town escaped damage during the war, leaving a cathedral and old houses – many tastefully restored – as well as a pedestrian precinct, for explorers in the 21C.

- **Population:** 13 222.
- **Michelin Map:** 303 H 4
- **Info:** Pont St-Jean. 02 31 51 28 28. www.bayeux-tourism.com.
- **Location:** 30km/18.6mi from Caen, the town is just inland from the Omaha and Arromanches landing beaches.
- **TGV:** Bayeux is about 2hrs 15mins direct from Paris St Lazare, and just under 3hr via Caen.
- **Kids:** Special child-friendly audioguides are available to help youngsters enjoy the Bayeux Tapestry.

A BIT OF HISTORY

First a Roman town, then an early episcopal city until the 9C when it became a Norse-speaking Viking city, Bayeux was the "cradle of the Dukes of Normandy" and home of William, who invaded and conquered England.

Almost 900 years later the invasion came the other way when on 6 June 1944 the Allies landed on the Normandy beaches. On 7 June Bayeux became the first French town to be liberated and here on D-Day + 7, General de Gaulle made his first speech on French soil.

SIGHTS

Bayeux Tapestry (Tapisserie de la Reine Mathilde)★★★

Open early Jan, Feb and Nov–Dec 9.30am–12.30pm, 2–6pm; Mar–Oct 9am–6.30pm (7pm May–Aug). Closed: last 3 weeks of Jan, 25 Dec. €9 (children, €4). 02 31 51 25 50. www.tapisserie-bayeux.fr.

Beautifully displayed in specially designed premises, it is most likely that this extraordinary masterpiece of embroidery was made by talented nuns – in fact noble Saxon women who had chosen the convent – in England, soon after the Conquest in 1066.

Using a style similar to today's strip cartoon, its 72 scenes, or pictures, recount the epic of the Norman invasion with striking truthfulness; in addition, it is an irreplaceable source of information on the ships, weapons, clothes and way of life of the mid-11C.

Cathédrale Notre-Dame★★

Guided tours of Cathedral 10.30am, 11.45am, 2.30pm, 3.45pm, 5pm. €4. 02 31 51 28 28.

Numerous changes contributed to this impressive edifice. The Romanesque vaulted crypt and lower nave date from the 11C. The 12C added intricate stonework including profusely decorated walls and cornerstones as well as rib-vaulting in the aisles. In the 13C (the High Gothic period) further elegant additions were made, including the superb chancel with radiating chapels, transepts with three-pointed arches, and a gallery with a fretwork design.

Hôtel du Doyen

A huge 17C porch leads into the 18C mansion, which houses the collection of the **Baron-Gèrard Museum**, which is closed for repairs.

Musée d'Art et d'Histoire Baron-Gérard

Open Mar–Apr and Oct–Dec 10am–12.30pm, 2–6pm; May–Sept 9.30am–6.30pm. €7. 02 31 51 25 50. www.bayeuxmuseum.com.

Bayeux was once an important manufacturing centre for porcelain. Founded in 1812 by J Langlois, the workshop's

Detail of the Bayeux Tapestry - Harold's Oath to Duke William of Normandy

famous glazing (red, gold and blue) made the reputation of the town. Production ended in 1951. The museum displays several of these decorated porcelain pieces

The upstairs rooms contain furniture and painting, mainly 15C and 16C Italian and Flemish Primitive works, and 17–19C French works.

Musée-Mémorial de la Bataille de Normandie★

♿Open mid-Feb–Apr and Oct–Dec 10am–12.30pm, 2–6pm; May–Sep 9.30am–6.30pm. Closed mid-Jan–mid-Feb. €5.50 (children, from €4). ☏02 31 51 25 50. www.bayeuxmuseum.com.

Situated on the line that separated the British and American sectors in 1944, the Memorial Museum recalls the dramatic events of summer 1944. Two large galleries, named Overlord and Eisenhower, explain the chronology of the Battle of Normandy and give a detailed account of the equipment and uniforms of the various nations involved in the conflict.

The closing of the **Falaise Pocket** is illustrated by a diorama re-creating the village of Chambois where, on 19 August, part of the 90th US Infantry Division joined forces with the 1st Polish Armoured Division.

A great variety of heavy equipment is exhibited.

The Norman Conquest

Edward the Confessor (c.1003–66) died without a clearly designated heir to the English throne. **Harold Godwinson** (c.1022–66) claimed that Edward had left England in Harold's "protection" on his deathbed. **William the Bastard, Duke of Normandy** (Edward's distant cousin, c.1028–87), claimed that Harold had sworn on sacred relics at Bayeux to support his own claim to the throne and had therefore perjured himself of this oath. Having secured the support of Pope Alexander II and his barons by the promise of English lands and titles, and with the resources of the cities of Caen and Rouen at his disposal, William organised a punitive expedition in just seven months.

The Norman fleet was assembled at **Dives**; its 600 ships carried 8 000 soldiers and cavalry who were landed on the coast at Pevensey Bay on 28 September 1066. Harold's army was already depleted and tired when it arrived at the Norman battlefield, having just arrived from fighting off a Viking invasion at the Battle of Stamford Bridge on 25th September. On 14 October, William won the **Battle of Hastings**, the Saxon army was routed and Harold was dead. William was crowned King at a ceremony in Westminster Abbey on 25 December. The situation was ambiguous: William was both King of England and Duke of Normandy; the latter making him a vassal to the King of France. Difficulties arose, worsening in 1152 after the divorce of Louis VII and **Eleanor of Aquitaine**, only to be resolved at the end of the Hundred Years' War.

ADDRESSES

STAY

La Ferme des Châtaigniers – Vienne-en-Bessin, 7.5km/4.6mi E of Bayeux via D 126. 02 31 92 54 70. 3 rooms. Set apart from the farmhouse, this converted farm building contains simple, yet pleasant, comfortable rooms. Guests have the use of a fitted kitchen. Peace and quiet is guaranteed in this house set in the fields.

La Ferme de Fumichon – Vaux-sur-Aure, 3km/1.8mi N of Bayeux via D 104. 02 31 21 78 51. www.fermedefumichon.com. 4 rooms. Once part of Longues-sur-Mer Abbey, this fortified 17C farm is today a dairy and cider-making farm.

Hôtel Reine Mathilde – 23 r. Larcher. 02 31 92 08 13. www.hotel-reinemathilde.com. Closed 15 Nov–15 Feb. 16 rooms. If you wish to stay in the old town, this small family hotel is conveniently situated a stone's throw from the cathedral and the famous tapestry.

Chambre d'hôte Le Moulin de Hard – Area called "Le Moulin de Hard", 14400 Subles, 6km/3.7mi SW of Bayeux. 02 31 21 37 17. 3 rooms. Large rooms in a restored 18C watermill near a small river with a beautiful garden.

Chambre d'hôte Manoir de Crépon – Anne-Marie Poisson, Crépon, 14km/8.7mi NE of Bayeux via D 12. 02 31 22 21 27. www.manoirdecrepon.com. Closed 10 Jan–10 Feb. 4 rooms. This 17C and 18C house is typical of the area, with its oxblood-coloured roughcast.

Hotel Le Bayeux – 9 r. Tardif. 02 31 92 70 08. www.lebayeux.com. 31 rooms. WiFi. Functional and well-kept in a modern style, hidden in a quiet side street.

EAT

Hostellerie St-Martin – 6 pl. Edmond Paillaud, Creully. 02 31 80 10 11. Closed 1–14 Jan. Today it's a restaurant, but in the past the large vaulted rooms dating from the 16C housed the village market. Exposed stone, a fireplace, sculptures and a view of the wine cellar make up the curious décor. Classic cuisine. A few bedrooms.

Le Petit Bistrot – 2 r. du Bienvenu. 02 31 51 85 40. Closed Sun, Wed, Mon (low season). An inventive cuisine prepared by a keen chef is the main attraction of this small establishment facing the cathedral. Original dishes inspired by Mediterranean cuisine are served in a Provençal-style décor with an ochre colour scheme, watercolours and drawings.

Le Pommier – 38–40 r. des Cuisiniers. 02 31 21 52 10. www.restaurantlepommier.com. Closed 14 Dec–18 Jan, Sun (Nov–Mar). No place could be more centrally located, near the cathedral, its inviting apple-green façade announcing its rich Norman cuisine: smoked ham, tripes à la mode de Caen, cream sauces and, of course, apples. There are also vegetarian dishes.

La Rapière – 53 r. St-Jean. 02 31 21 05 45. Closed mid-Dec–mid-Jan, Wed & Thu. A 15C house situated in old Bayeux. A lovely, rustic interior and tasty food using local produce.

SHOPPING

Markets – r. St-Jean. Open Wed 7.30am – 2.30pm; and pl. St-Patrice Sat 6.30am–2.30pm. Bayeux's two markets are quite different, each with its own charm. St-Jean pedestrian street **Wednesday** market features greengrocers, butchers, fishmongers, cheesemakers and honey-sellers. On the Pl. St-Patrice, every **Saturday**, some 120 merchants offer their wares, about half of them foodstuffs.

Naphtaline – 14, 16 parvis de la Cathédrale. 02 31 21 50 03. Closed Jan–Feb and Sun. Three boutiques housed in a fine 18C building offer antique and modern lace, Bayeux porcelain and reproductions of traditional tapestries woven on Jacquard looms.

NIGHTLIFE

Café Inn – 67 r. St-Martin. 02 31 21 11 37. www.cafeinn-bayeux.com. Coffee beans are roasted on the spot and 75 sorts of tea are served in a bustling ambience. Salads, omelettes and quiches are offered as prelude to the delicious *Tarte Tatin.*

La Presqu'ile du Cotentin★★

The pronounced thrust of the Cotentin peninsula, or La Presqu'Ile du Cotentin, into the Atlantic corresponds with an equally uncharacteristic landscape: the austere surroundings of La Hague are more like Brittany than Normandy. Geographically speaking, the area can be divided into three parts: the Cotentin Pass is the lower plain, the Val de Saire includes the river valley and the whole northeast part of the peninsula, the Cap de la Hague is the granite spine jutting out into the sea. The wooded hinterland was the cradle of Norman adventurers who once controlled the central Mediterranean area.

- **Michelin Map:** 303 H 4
- **Info:** The area is served by a number of different tourist offices – see www.encotentin.com.
- **Location:** The Cotentin Peninsula is in the extreme NW of France.
- **TGV:** Cherbourg is about 3hrs 15mins direct from Paris St Lazare, and 4–5hrs via Caen.

SIGHTS

ST-LÔ

74km/46mi WSW of Caen.

In 1944 St-Lô acquired the sad title of Capital of Ruins. On 19 July, the day the town was liberated, only the battered towers of the collegiate church and a few suburban houses remained standing. Since then St-Lô has been rebuilt and is now the site of one of the largest **stud farms** in France. Outside of town in the **Vallée de la Vire** is the **Roches de Ham★★**(Alt 80m); from the magnificent escarpment there is a view of a beautiful bend in the river Vire.

COUTANCES★★

29km/18mi WSW of St-Lô.

Coutances is perched on a hillock crowned by a magnificent cathedral, miraculously saved from the bombardments that destroyed two-thirds of the town in June 1944. The name of this religious and judicial centre of the Cotentin peninsula recalls the Roman Emperor Constantins-Chlorus (293–306). In the 14C Coutances acquired an aqueduct of which only three arches remain to the northwest of the town on the Coutainville road.

Cathédrale Notre-Dame de Coutances★★★

The present building (1220–75) made use of some of the remains of Geoffroy de Montbray's Norman cathedral, as well as drawing on the experience gained in the then recently completed abbey at Fécamp. The west front is framed by two towers, whose soaring lines are emphasised by the tall, narrow corner turrets. The great octagonal lantern rises imposingly over the crossing; it, too, is flanked by turrets, and has strikingly delicate ribbing and slender openings. Within, the nave has clustered piers and highly moulded arches, a triforium with double openings and tall windows behind the typically Norman balustraded inspection gallery. The transept is in a more advanced style. Built in 1274, it is a masterpiece of ingenious construction.

Jardin des Plantes★

Open 9am–5pm. No charge.

The garden's entrance is flanked by an old cider press on one side and the **Quesnel-Morinière Museum** on the other. The terraced promenade traverses the sloping gardens with its many flower beds and pine trees. The obelisk in the centre commemorates a former mayor.

LESSAY★★

38km/24mi NW of St-Lô.

Lessay grew up round a Benedictine abbey founded in 1056 by a Norman lord. The first monks came from Le Bec-Hellouin. The town is particularly lively in September during the Holy Cross Fair, which originated in the 13C, today attended by about 400 000 people.

Abbey Church★★

The magnificent Romanesque abbey church, damaged during the war, was reconstructed between 1945 and 1957, using original building materials wherever possible; the result is one of the most perfect examples of Romanesque architecture in Normandy.

CHÂTEAU DE PIROU★

10km/6mi SW of Lessay.

The 12C fortress, which once stood on the coast beside an anchorage, since silted up, is one of the oldest Norman castles and served as an outpost for the defence of Coutances under the lords of Pirou who owned it from the 11–14C.

BARNEVILLE-CARTERET★

37km/23mi SSW of Cherbourg.

This popular seaside resort, the closest port to the Channel Islands, is lively, the dunes windswept, and the long beach is of fine sand.

CAP DE LA HAGUE★★

32km/20mi NW of Cherbourg.

Some of the highest cliffs in Europe, interspersed with small sandy beaches and charming ports, all linked by the Customs Path, which is well known to walkers. This "end of the world" place with its dramatic cliffs is renowned for its spectacular scenery as well as the beauty of its gardens, which have a tropical feel. Although often associated with the nuclear power industry the name of La Hague is associated with the generosity of nature.

CHERBOURG★

123km/77mi NW of Caen.

Cherbourg is a seafaring town with the largest artificial harbour in the world. Here, on the northern shore of the Cotentin peninsula, this city has beautiful monuments and is known for its remarkable breakwater.

Cité de la Mer★★

The Art Deco former hall of the transatlantic passenger station has information kiosks, but the core of the museum lies in adjacent wings with basins and tanks that present marine fauna and flora. Le Redoutable, the first French nuclear submarine, is here.

NEZ DE JOBOURG★★

28km/17.5mi W of Cherbourg.

The long, rocky and barren promontory is now a bird sanctuary (seagulls). Walk along the Nez de Voidries. From the Auberge des Grottes there is a view north of **Écalgrain Bay**, the lighthouse off **Cap de la Hague** and the Channel Islands: Alderney, the nearest, Sark, Guernsey and Jersey. Farther south the **Nez de Jobourg** itself comes into view, separated from the Nez de Voidries by Senneval Bay.

BARFLEUR★

28km/17.5mi E of Cherbourg.

This charming fishing port, with its granite houses and quays, is one of the Most Beautiful Villages of France. Tradition has it that the boat that carried William, Duke of Normandy, to England was built here. A bronze plaque placed in 1966 at the foot of the jetty marks his departure (1066).

VALOGNES★

21km/13mi SE of Cherbourg.

Valognes is an important road junction at the heart of the Cotentin Peninsula and is the market town for the surrounding agricultural area. The aristocratic town described by Barbey d'Aurevilly was partially destroyed in June 1944; it has been rebuilt in the modern style and expanded. Several traces of the past have survived including Gallo-Roman ruins, 11C–18C churches, and private mansions built in the 18C when local high society made Valognes the Versailles of Normandy.

ADDRESSES

STAY

ST-LÔ

€€ Chambre d'hôte Château de Dampierre – 14350 Dampierre, 9km/5.6mi from Torigny-sur-Vire via D 13, then right on D 53. ☎02 31 67 31 81. 15 rooms. A magnificent tree-lined approach leads to this 16C manor. Well-kept rooms overlooking the moat, the gatehouse and a superb dovecot, in the midst of the *bocage* countryside.

BARNEVILLE-CARTERET

€€€ Chambre d'hôte Le Logis de la Mare du Parc – Village de La Mare-du-Parc, 50270 Surtainville, 11km/6.9mi north of Carteret by the D 650, then the D 66 to the left. ☎02 42 10 55 49. www.logisdelamareduparc.com. 5 rooms. In this extensive lovely 18C house are five well-equipped comfortable en-suite rooms. Four on the first floor for 2 or 3 people and one on the ground floor accessible for people of reduced mobility, with an adapted bathroom.

CHERBOURG-OCTEVILLE

€€€ Hôtel Renaissance – 4 r. de l'Église. ☎02 33 43 23 90. www.hotel-renaissance-cherbourg.com. 12 rooms. This hotel has bright, soundproofed rooms.

ST-VAAST-LA-HOUGUE

€€ Hôtel de France et Fuchsias – 20 r. du Mar.-Foch. ☎02 33 54 40 41. www.france-fuchsias.com. Closed 2 Jan 2–12 Feb and Mon Sep–May, Tue Nov–Mar. 35 rooms. Restaurant€€. When the fuchsias are in bloom they cover the walls of this 100-year-old hotel set back from the harbour. Some rooms overlook the garden. Meals in the dining room, on the veranda or the terrace.

VALOGNES

€€ Grand Hôtel du Louvre – 28 r. des Réligieuses. ☎02 33 40 00 07. www.grandhoteldulouvre.com. Closed 28 Dec 6, 23 Dec–15 Jan and 4–12 Mar. 18 rooms. P. Restaurant€€. Near the centre of town, this hotel has character: Barbey d'Aurevilly, a 19C Gothic novelist, stayed in room No 4. Rooms, reached by a spiral staircase, have been renovated but retain their 19C character.

EAT

ST-LÔ

€€ Le Péché Mignon – 84 r. du Maréchal-Juin. ☎02 33 72 23 77. www.peche-mignon-saint-lo.fr. Closed Sun eve and Mon, except for group bookings. Near the Haras national, the owner/chef prepares regional dishes adapted to today's tastes.

COUTANCES

€€ Le Tourne-Bride – 85 r. d'Argouges, 50200 Gratot. ☎02 33 45 11 00. Closed 1–15 Jul, Feb holidays, Sun eve and Mon. The proprietors of this former post-coach relay, Martine and Denis Poisson, offer a warm and attentive welcome. In the two rustic-style dining rooms, the menu focuses on traditional Norman cuisine.

BARNEVILLE-CARTERET

€€ Pom'Cannelle – 10 r. du Gén.-Leclerc (à côté de la Poste), 50250 La Haye-du-Puits. ☎02 33 46 45 57. www.restaurantpomcannelle.fr. Closed Mon and Wed eve 15 Sep–15 Jun). Crêpes and country cooking, fish and seafood, duck foie-gras, duck cutlet with camembert cream.

CHERBOURG-OCTEVILLE

€€€ Le Faitout – 25 r. Tour-Carrée. ☎02 33 04 25 04. www.restaurant-le-faitout.com. Closed last 2 weeks Dec. Reservations required. An attractive retro façade, and a handsome wood-panelled décor, like that of a ship, inside. Normandy specialities.

ST-VAAST-LA-HOUGUE

€€ Le Chasse Marée – 8 pl. du Gén. de Gaulle. ☎02 33 23 14 08. Closed mid-Dec–Jan, Mon lunch in Jul–Aug, Sun eve and Mon–Tue from Sep–Jun. Locally caught seafood.

VALOGNES

€ L'Agriculture –18 r. Léopold-Delisle. ☎02 33 95 02 02. www.hotel-agriculture.com. In the centre of Valognes, this vine-covered building sits on a quiet little square. The interior is charming and rustic. Delicious house specialities. Guest rooms are modern and comfortable.

Mont-St-Michel★★★

Le Mont-St-Michel has been called "the Wonder of the Western World"; its extraordinary site, its rich and influential history and its glorious architecture combine to make it the most splendid of all the abbeys of France.

- **Population:** 43.
- **Michelin Map:** Local map 59 303 C8 - Manche (50).
- **Info:** Tourist office: Le-Mont-St-Michel. ✆02 33 60 14 30. www.ot-montsaintmichel.com. Car park (cars €9) and visitor centre 2.5km/1.5mi from the Mont. Access the Mont from here on foot, free shuttle, or horse-drawn carriage.
- **Location:** The Mount is at the extreme north end of the D 976.
- **TGV/Train: From Paris Montparnasse TGV to Rennes** (2hr). Connection by train TER from Rennes to Pontorson and then bus to Le Mont Saint-Michel, or bus from Rennes to Mont Saint-Michel
  - **From Paris Montparnasse TGV to Dol de Bretagne** (2hrs 40mins) and direct connections from de Dol de Bretagne by bus to Mont Saint-Michel.
  - **From Paris Saint-Lazare local train** to Caen and local train from Caen to Pontorson and bus from Pontorson to Mont Saint-Michel.
- **Timing:** Get information on the tide times from the tourist office website.

A BIT OF HISTORY

At the beginning of the 8C St Michael appeared to Aubert, the bishop of Avranches. Aubert founded an oratory on an island then known as Mont Tombe. This oratory was soon replaced by an abbey, which adopted the Benedictine Rule in the 10C, thereby assuring its importance. Two centuries later the Romanesque abbey reached its peak of development. In the 13C, following a fire, a great rebuilding in Gothic style took place, known as *la Merveille* – the Marvel. Even though the English besieged it during the Hundred Years' War, the Mount did not fall.

SIGHTS

L'Abbaye (Abbey)★★★

Open 9.30am–6pm. Closed 1 Jan, 1 May, 25 Dec. €9. ✆02 33 89 80 00.

The architecture of the Abbey was determined by the constraints imposed by the rock on which it stands. Crowned as it is by the Abbey church and the buildings of the Merveille (c.1225), the result bears little resemblance to the conventional Benedictine monastery.

Église★★

There is a striking contrast between the stern character of the Romanesque nave and the well-lit Flamboyant choir. The axis of the sanctuary is aligned on the rising sun on 8 May, the spring Feast of St Michael under the Eastern calendar.

La Merveille★★★

The name, which means the Marvel, applies to the superb Gothic buildings on the north face of the mount. The eastern block, the first to be built between 1211 and 1218, comprises, from top to bottom, the refectory, the Guests' Hall and the Almonry; the western block, built between 1218 and 1228, consists of the cloisters, the Knights' Hall and the cellar.

From the outside the buildings look like a fortress, although their religious connections are indicated by the simple nobility of the design. The interior is a perfect example of the evolution

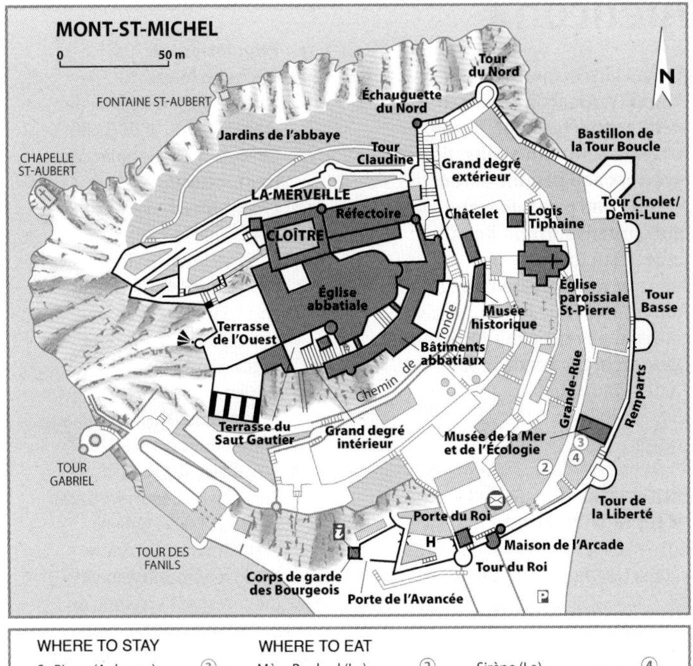

WHERE TO STAY	WHERE TO EAT	
St-Pierre (Auberge)..............③	Mère Poulard (La)................②	Sirène (La)..............................④

of the Gothic style, from an almost Romanesque simplicity in the lower halls, through the elegance of the Guests' Hall, the majesty of the Knights' Hall and the mysterious luminosity of the Refectory, to the cloisters, which are a masterpiece of delicacy and line.

Cloisters★★★ – The cloisters seem to be suspended between the sea and the sky. The gallery arcades display heavily undercut sculpture of foliage ornamented with the occasional animal, human figure, or religious symbol. The different colours of the various materials add to the overall charm. The *lavatorium* (washroom) on the right of the entrance recalls the ceremonial washing of the feet every Thursday.

Refectory★★ – The effect is mysterious; the chamber is full of light, although it appears to have only two windows in the end wall. To admit so much light without weakening the solid side walls, the architect introduced a very narrow aperture high up in each recess. The vaulted ceiling is panelled with wood and the acoustics are excellent.

Jardins de l'Abbaye★

From the gardens there is a view of the north face of the mount, the "most beautiful wall in all the world", according to Victor Hugo.

ADDRESSES

STAY

Auberge St-Pierre – Grande-Rue. ✆02 33 60 14 03. www.auberge-saint-pierre.fr. 21 rooms. Restaurant. This half-timbered inn has a restaurant and small, well-kept bedrooms.

EAT

La Sirène – 16 Grande-Rue. ✆02 33 60 08 60. Take the spiral staircase to enter the crêperie in this 14C house.

La Mère Poulard – Grande-Rue, BP 18 50170, Mont-St-Michel. ✆02 33 89 68 68. www.merepoulard.com. This hotel-restaurant is famous for Mother Poulard's omelette.

Alençon★

A royal lace manufactory under Louis XIV, Alençon has a rich architectural heritage, a Fine Arts Museum with a collection of lacework and paintings from the 15–19C, and pleasant waterways and gardens surrounding the pedestrian town centre.
Alençon was liberated on 12 August 1944 due to the decisive role of the French 2nd Armoured Division in the Battle of the Falaise-Mortain Pocket.

- **Population:** 26 704.
- **Michelin Map:** 310 J-4
- **Info:** Maison d'Ozé, pl. de la Madeleine. ✆02 33 80 66 33. www.paysdalencontourisme.com.
- **Location:** From Alençon, roads lead to Paris (195km/122mi E via N 12), and to Brittany, Belgium and Spain. The A 28 leads to Le Mans (58km/36mi to the S) and to Rouen (160km/100mi to the N).
- **Don't Miss:** The little villages of the Alpes Mancelles, especially St-Léonard-des-Bois and St-Céneri-le-Gérei.
- **Timing:** Take a half-day in the town, then enjoy the lovely countryside in the forest of Perseigne or in the Alpes Mancelles.
- **Kids:** At St-Léonard-des-Bois, the domaine of Gasseau offers nature walks under the trees.

SIGHTS

Musée des Beaux-Arts et de la Dentelle★

♿Open daily except Mon: 10am–noon, 2–6pm (Jul–Aug, every day). Closed 1 Jan, 1 May, 25 Dec. €4.50. ✆02 33 32 40 07.

The Museum of Fine Arts and Lace houses paintings from the 15C to the 19C as well as collections of lace.

The presentation of the **lace collection★** offers a broad review of the principal lacemaking centres in Italy and France. Its display of Alençon lace, which uses a needlepoint technique unique in France, includes the elegant creations of the Alençon lacemakers from the 17C to the present day.

There is also a collection of Cambodian objects brought back by **Adhémar Leclère** (1853–1917), a native of Alençon and 19C governor of Cambodia.

Église Notre-Dame★

The beautiful 14–15C Flamboyant Gothic Church of Our Lady was begun during the Hundred Years' War. The tower, transept and chancel were rebuilt in the 18C. The elegant three-sided **porch★**, built by Jean Lemoine from 1490 to 1506, is an example of the purest Flamboyant style. All the decoration is concentrated on the upper parts of the church. Inside, the sweeping lines of the nave rise to the lierne and tierceron **vaulting** which is highly decorated. The lines of the triforium merge with those of the clerestory to form a unified whole.

Note the admirable **stained glass★** by the master-glaziers of Alençon and the Maine region. The glass in the clerestory windows dates from 1530.

In place de la Madeleine, to the left of the church, is the attractive 15C **Maison d'Ozé**, now the Tourist Information Centre, where the future King Henri IV is said to have stayed in 1576.

EXCURSIONS

LAVAL★

Laval is 32km/20mi S of Mayenne by D 162. Le Mans is 86km/53.4mi to the E on N 157.

1 allée du Vieux-St-Louis. ✆02 43 49 46 46. www.laval-tourisme.com.

The River Mayenne defines Laval, flowing gently through the centre of town, as it has since the city was founded in the year 1000. The town has a picturesque château and old half-timbered houses, and has produced many distinguished citizens.

BAGNOLES-DE-L'ORNE★

Bagnoles is 2km/1mi N of the N 176, which links Alençon (47km/29mi SW) to Mont-St-Michel (90km/56mi W).
The town comprises two distinct parts: to the W Bagnoles-Château, and E, Bagnoles-Lac.
02 33 37 85 66. www.bagnolesdelorne.com. Parking near the château, the museum, the casino and the place du Marché.

In addition to its healing waters, Bagnoles-de-l'Orne has a lovely **lakeside setting★** that invites calm.
The lake is formed by the Vée, a tributary of the Mayenne, before it enters a deep gorge cut through the massif of the Andaines Forest. The site can be seen best by walking from Tessé-la-Madeleine to the Roc au Chien.
The spot known as Capuchin's Leap received its name when a Capuchin monk, cured of his ills by a magical spring, fulfilled a vow by making a gigantic leap (4m) between the rock spikes high above the water.

Parc de l'établissement thermal★

The park surrounding the spa building is planted with pines, oaks and chestnut trees. The Allée du Dante on the east bank of the Vée, which is often crowded with bathers, leads from the lake to the spa building. Other alleys in the park wind towards Capuchin's Leap and to the site known as the Abri Janolin. Shops line the lake-front rue des Casions.

Le Roc au Chien★

45min round-trip on foot.

Start from the church and walk up the avenue du Château; the main gateway opens on to the avenue and the public park of Tessé. The château, built in the 19C in the neo-medieval style, now houses the town hall.
Take the avenue on the right which overlooks the Bagnoles gorge and leads to the rocky promontory, the Roc au Chien, where there is a lovely **view★** of Bagnoles beside the lake and the spa building and its park.

CHÂTEAU DE CARROUGES★★

Carrouges is 26km/16mi E of Bagnoles-de-l'Orne and 30km/18.5mi NE of Alençon. Open daily Apr–mid-Jun, and Sep 10am–noon, 2–6pm; mid-Jun–Aug 9.30am–noon, 2–6.30pm; Oct–Mar 10am–noon, 2–5pm. Closed 1 Jan, 1 May, 1 and 11 Nov, 25 Dec. €7.50. 02 33 27 20 32.

For almost five centuries this immense château and park belonged to a famous Norman family, Le Veneur de Tillières; in 1936 it was bought by the nation.
The château itself is austere but imposing. Surrounded by a moat, the buildings are arranged around an inner courtyard. The stables and domestic quarters occupy the ground floor; the apartments and state rooms are on the first floor.
From the **park** with its fine trees and elegant flower beds there are good views of the château.
The Conservatoire botanique des pommiers de Bretagne et de Normandie, at the entrance to the property, includes 152 varieties of apple trees.
The 16C **gatehouse★** is an elegant brick building with decorative geometric patterns. It was almost certainly built by Jean Le Veneur, Bishop of Lisieux and Abbot of Bec, who helped fund Jacques Cartier's 1534 expedition to Canada.

The Village

The village of Carrouges stands within the boundary of the **Parc naturel régional Normandie-Maine**.
The **Maison du Parc** (02 33 81 75 75; www.parc-naturel-normandie-maine.fr) occupies the restored buildings of a 15C chapter of canons, an outbuilding of the château.

Brittany

» Region map p244–245

Rennes p246

St-Malo p251

St-Brieuc p258

St-Pol-de-Léon p260

Brest p261

Quimper p263

Lorient p267

Vannes p268

Belle-Île p272

Nantes p273

Introduction

Populated by Celts since its birth, Brittany retains many affinities with the other Celtic lands fringing the Atlantic. Its identity, quite distinct from that of the rest of France, is expressed in its language (Breton, akin to Welsh), traditions and landscape. The province's long and mysterious past makes itself felt in the abundance of prehistoric remains, menhirs, dolmens and megaliths. Granite distinguishes Breton building whether in church or castle, harbour wall or humble house, and is used to great effect.

Geography – Brittany has an extraordinarily indented coastline, called "Armor" (country near the sea) by the Gauls. Its cliffs, rocky headlands and offshore islands are battered by Atlantic breakers, while its narrow drowned valleys, ***abers***, and sandy bays are washed by tides of exceptional range. Inland is the "Argoat" (country of the wood), once thickly forested, now a mixture of bocage, heath and moor.

History – The Channel coast is punctuated by historic towns, elegant resorts, dramatic corniches and headlands. The original Celts were subjugated by the Romans in the 1C AD, but fresh waves of Celtic settlers arrived here from Cornwall following the collapse of the Roman Empire, and the country remained anarchic until 799, when Charlemagne took control. The Duchy of Brittany was soon established and independence achieved in AD 845. Although later Dukes paid homage to the French monarch, this autonomy was retained till the late 15C following the marriage of Anne of Brittany to the King. The Bretons were enthusiastic supporters of the Revolution and helped put down those who revolted against the new state.

Economy – Much of France's fishing fleet operates from Brittany. Other industries include food processing and car manufacturing. Tourism is vitally important and many summer visitors are attracted to the resorts on the Atlantic and Channel coasts.

Highlights

1 Village set in aspic: **Locronan** (p264)
2 Spectacular coastal landscape: **Pointe du Raz** (p266)
3 Small inland sea near Vannes: **Golfe de Morbihan** (p268)
4 Megaliths at **Carnac** (p270)
5 The stunning beauty of **Belle-Île** (p272)

The standing stone alignments, Carnac, Morbihan © Hiroshi Higuchi/age fotostock

ENGLISH
ATLANTIC
OCEAN
N
Côte de Granit rose
Trégastel-Pla
Ploumanach
Perros-Guir
Trébeurden
Roscoff
Baie de Morlaix
Kerd
Tréguier
Phare de l'Île Vierge
Meneham
St-Pol-de-Léon
Locquirec
Lannion
L'Aber-Wrac'h
D 10
Carantec
St-Michel-en-Grève
D 786
ROCHERS, CÔTE SAUVAGE
St-Thégonnec
Les Abers et l'Iroise
Morlaix
N 12
Pnte de Pern
ÎLE D'OUESSANT
Élorn
Plougonven
Guimiliau
D 787
Le Conquet
D 789
BREST
Parc Natural Régional d'Armorique
Monts d'Arrée
Plourac'h
Callac
Pnte de St-Mathieu
Pnte des Espagnols
Huelgoat
PNTE DE PENHIR
Crozon
Landévennec
D 887
MÉNEZ HOM
Pnte de Dinan
Aulne
N 164
Montagnes Noires
PRESQU'ÎLE DE CROZON
Locronan
La Trinité-Langonnet
Pnte du Van
Douarnenez
Mgne de Locronan
Île de Sein
D 765
Odet
D 15
D 769
Ellé
Foré Quéné
PNTE DU RAZ
Cornouaille
Quimper
Kernascléden
FINISTÈRE
Scorff
D 2
D 785
Bénodet
Poul Fetan
Pont-l'Abbé
Quimperlé
Phare d'Eckmühl
Penmarch
Concarneau
Pont-Aven
N 165
Pont-Scorff
Port-Manech
Hennebc
Laïta
Le Pouldu
Lorient
Merleve
Îles de Glénan
Larmor-Plage
Port-Louis
Île de Groix
Port-Lay
Carnac
Presqu'île de Quiberon
La Trin s-M
Quiberon
Pnte Des Poulains
Stêr-Vrazet Stêr-Ouen
Sauzon
Port-Donnant
CÔTE SAUVAGE
BELLE-I
Aiguilles de Port-Coton
Port-Goulph
Brittany
0 30 km
0 15 miles
ST-MALO ★★★ Highly recommended
Rennes ★★ Recommended
Quiberon ★ Interesting
Lorient Other sight described in this guide

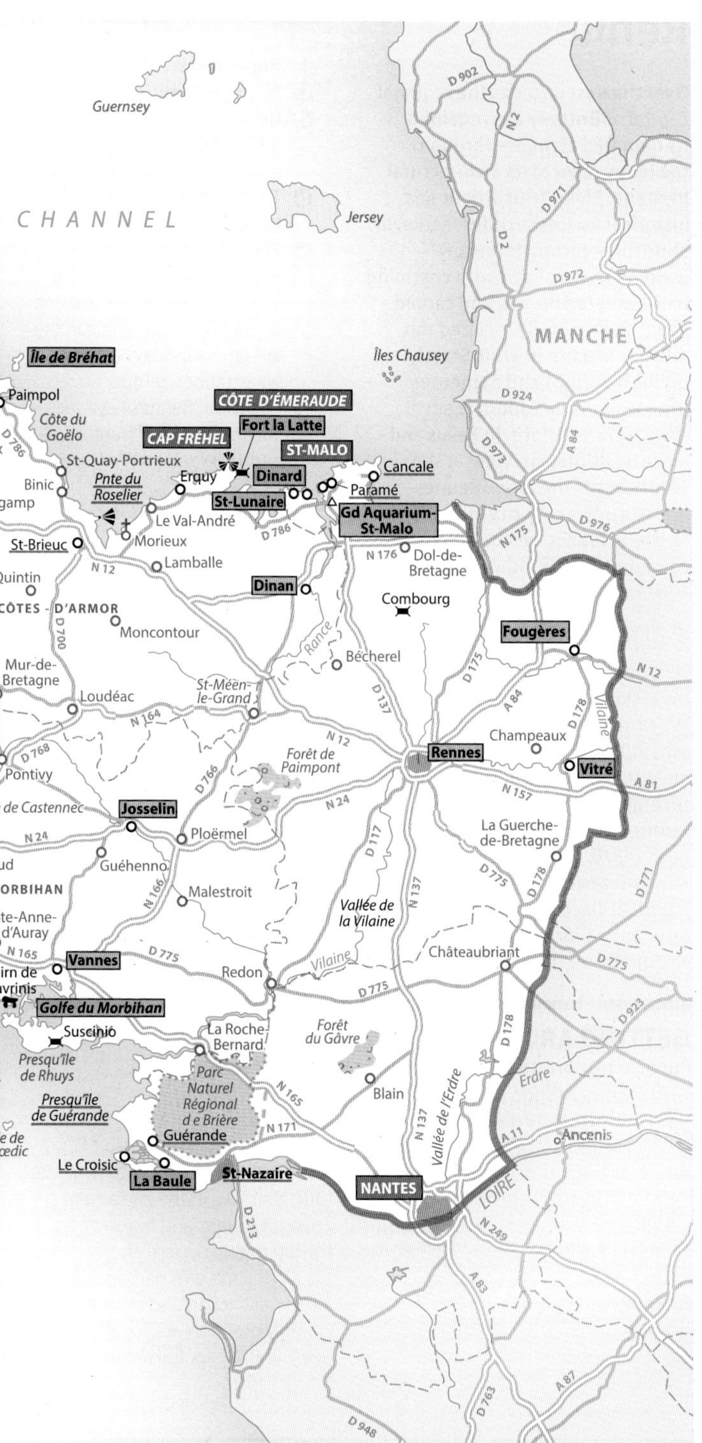

Guernsey
CHANNEL
Jersey
MANCHE
Îles Chausey
Île de Bréhat
Paimpol
Côte du Goëlo
CÔTE D'ÉMERAUDE
Fort la Latte
CAP FRÉHEL
ST-MALO
St-Quay-Portrieux
Erquy
Dinard
Cancale
Binic
Pnte du Roselier
St-Lunaire
Paramé
Gd Aquarium-St-Malo
Le Val-André
Morieux
St-Brieuc
Lamballe
Dol-de-Bretagne
Quintin
Dinan
Combourg
CÔTES-D'ARMOR
Moncontour
Fougères
Rance
Bécherel
Mur-de-Bretagne
Loudéac
St-Méen-le-Grand
Champeaux
Vilaine
Forêt de Paimpont
Rennes
Vitré
Pontivy
Josselin
Ploërmel
La Guerche-de-Bretagne
Guéhenno
MORBIHAN
Malestroit
Vallée de la Vilaine
Ste-Anne-d'Auray
Vannes
Châteaubriant
Redon
Golfe du Morbihan
Suscinio
La Roche-Bernard
Forêt du Gâvre
Presqu'île de Rhuys
Parc Naturel Régional de Brière
Blain
Presqu'île de Guérande
Erdre
Île de Hœdic
Guérande
Vallée de l'Erdre
Ancenis
Le Croisic
La Baule
St-Nazaire
NANTES
LOIRE
D 902
N 2
D 971
D 2
D 972
D 924
A 84
D 973
N 175
D 976
N 176
D 786
N 12
D 700
N 164
D 766
D 175
D 137
D 178
A 81
N 157
N 24
D 117
N 137
D 775
N 165
N 166
D 768
D 771
D 923
N 171
A 11
D 213
N 249
A 83
A 87
D 763
D 948

Rennes★★

Over the past decades the regional capital of Brittany has regained its dignified elegance through the restoration of its architectural heritage. This city of artistic and historical interest exudes medieval atmosphere from its narrow, winding streets lined with charming half-timbered houses and carved sills that thankfully escaped the ravages of a fire in 1720. Stately public buildings and numerous private mansions adorn the two royal squares (place du Palais and place de l'Hôtel-de-Ville) at the very heart of the town. Rennes is also a university city at the centre of France's electronics and communications industries.

- **Population:** 207 178.
- **Michelin Map:** 309 L-M 6
- **Info:** 11 r. St Yves. ℘02 99 67 11 11. www.tourisme-rennes.com.
- **TGV:** Paris Montparnasse to Rennes (2h 15min).
- **Flights:** Rennes Brittany Airport is 7km/4mi from the centre of Rennes; information on transfers is available in the arrivals hall, 7 days a week. www.rennes.aeroport.fr.
- **Location:** Rennes lies 105km/66mi N of Nantes, and 152km/95mi W of Le Mans.
- **Timing:** Rennes is not a city to rush around; allow a full day or more to get the most from your visit.

A BIT OF HISTORY

Du Guesclin's Beginnings (14C) – Bertrand Du Guesclin (*see p74*) was born in a castle southwest of Dinan. The eldest of 10 children, he entered a tournament at Rennes at age 17 and unseated several opponents. In the service of France, he freed Périgord from English rule in 1370, and Normandy in 1378.

The great fire of 1720 – In the evening of 22 December 1720, a drunken carpenter set fire to a heap of shavings with his lamp. The house burned like a torch and immediately others around it caught fire. Ravaged areas were rebuilt to the plans of **Jacques Gabriel**, the descendant of a long line of architects and father of Gabriel who built the place de la Concorde in Paris. A large part of the town owes its rectangular street pattern and granite houses to this event. Apartments were sold separately, the beginning of co-ownership.

GETTING AROUND

Public transport – Rennes has a bus network and a metro (VAL), which goes northwest (J-F Kennedy) to southeast (La Poterie). Tickets cost €1.50 for one journey and €13.70 for a book (carnet) of 10 tickets. Information and sales from Infostar, 12 rue du Pré Botté. ℘09 70 821 800. www.star.fr.

On foot – strolling around this remarkable city is by far the best way of ensuring that you make the most of your time here. Or, for something a bit less energetic, you can try a **gyropod**, silent, clean and environmentally friendly.

TOURS

Rennes is a "Town of Art and History" and offers guided and audio-guided tours that take in the Parliament, Thabor Gardens and highlights of the old town, modern architecture, the city's parks and gardens. There are general tours, and tours of full- or half-day duration. €7.50. ℘02 99 67 11 66. Enquire for full details at the tourist office.

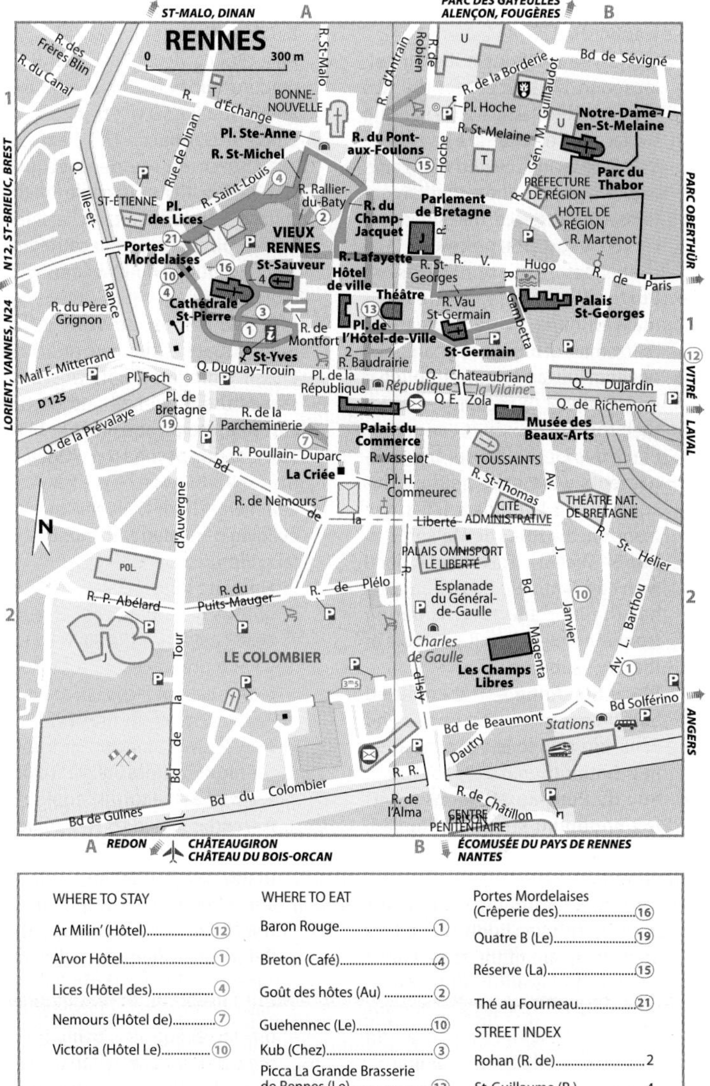

WALKING TOUR

OLD TOWN★★

This is the part of the old town that escaped the 1720 fire. It contains a maze of 15C and 16C houses with overhanging storeys and lordly mansions with sculpted façades. Begin at the Basilique St-Saveur.

- **Basilique St-Sauveur** – Inside this 17C and 18C basilica are a fine gilded wooden **canopy** and an **organ loft** (17C). To the right is a chapel consecrated to Our Lady of Miracles who is belived to have saved Rennes from the English during the siege of 1357.
- **Cathédrale St-Pierre** – Carrefour de la Cathédrale. Open 9am–noon, 3–6pm. ✆02 99 78 48 80. The third built on the site since the 6C, this cathedral

was finished in 1844 after 57 years' work. The previous building collapsed in 1762 except for the two towers in the Classical style flanking the façade. The **interior★** is very rich, its stucco facing covered with paintings and gilding. The cathedral contains a masterpiece: the gilded and carved wood **altarpiece★★** in the chapel before the south transept.

- **Portes Mordelaises** – The city's main entrance, these gates are all that remain of the 15C ramparts. The dukes of Brittany passed through it on their way to the cathedral for their coronation.
- **Place des Lices** – Jousts and tournaments were once held on this square. At 34 stands a 17C stone mansion, the Hôtel de Molant
- **Rue St-Michel** – This street is lined with half-timbered houses and still has the inns and taverns dating from the time when it was part of the city's suburbs.
- **Place Ste-Anne** – The coloured half-timbered houses, Gothic and Renaissance in style, surround a 19C neo-Gothic church.
- **Rue du Pont-aux-Foulons** – This is a shopping street leading off the square with 18C half-timbered houses.
- **Rue du Champ-Jacquet** – This street leads to an oddly shaped triangular square of the same name. It is lined to the north with tall half-timbered 17C houses and is overlooked by the stone and wood façade of Hôtel de Tizé (number 5).
- **Palais du Parlement de Bretagne★★** – pl. du Parlement de Bretagne. Guided tours only (1hr30); reservations at the tourist office. Closed 1 May. €7.50. ✆02 99 67 11 66. Brittany's Parliament initially had its seat in Rennes for part of the year and Nantes for the other, before finally the decision was taken in 1561 to establish a single seat in Rennes.
- **Rue St-Georges** – This animated street, lined with cafés and restaurants, has many old houses.
- **Palais St-Georges** – Preceded by a beautiful garden, this former Benedictine abbey (1670) now houses administrative services.
- **Église St-Germain** – This Flamboyant church on rue de Coëtquen (15C–16C) with its 17C gable (on the south side) retains certain characteristics typical of a Breton cathedral: wood vaulting and its beams with sculpted ends.
- **Place de l'Hôtel-de-Ville** – This regal square is the centre of the Classical district. On its west side stands the town hall and on the east side, the theatre, built in 1832. To the south, beyond rue d'Orléans, the view is blocked by the Palais du Commerce (Trade Hall), an imposing building decorated with monumental sculpture.

  Hôtel de Ville – Open Mon–Sat, guided tours only. Closed public holidays. ♿ ✆02 99 67 11 08. www.tourisme-rennes.com. Built to the plans of Jacques Gabriel in 1734–43, after the fire of 1720. A central tower, standing back from the façade, carries the great clock – *le gros*, as the townspeople call it – and is joined by two curved buildings to two large annexes. Inside are the former chapel and a lovely 17C Brussels tapestry. The right wing contains the Pantheon of Rennes, a hall dedicated to the memory of men who have died for France. Provided no official reception is being held, the public is admitted to the left wing of the building and can see the monumental staircase, the 18C Brussels tapestries and the hall where wedding ceremonies are performed.

ADDITIONAL SIGHTS

Les Champs Libres★

10 cours Alliés. Open Tue–Fri noon–7pm (Tue until 9pm), Sat-Sun 2–7pm. ♿ €7 (day pass). ✆02 23 40 66 00. www.leschampslibres.fr.

This cultural centre brings together three institutions: the Musée de Bretagne, the Espace des Sciences and the library. The ultra-modern building is the work of architect Christian de Portzamparc.

Musée des Beaux-Arts★

20 quai Émile Zola. Open Tue 10am–6pm, Wed–Sun 10am–noon, 2–6pm. Closed Mon and public holidays. ♿. €5. ✆02 23 62 17 45. www.mbar.org.

The permanent collection rooms at the Museum of Fine Arts have recently been restyled, extended and enriched with new works that have never been shown. It now contains fine examples of painting, sculpture, drawing, prints and objects from the 14C to the present.

EXCURSIONS

FOUGÈRES★★

Distance from Rennes 51km/32mi.
2 r. Nationale. ✆02 99 94 12 20. www.ot-fougeres.fr.

In the 19C Fougères was the most industrialised town in Brittany, having abandoned cloth-making in favour of shoe production. The area formed part of the frontier region taken from the Franks in AD 850 by **Nominoé** (*see p73, 268*).

Château de Fougères★★ – pl. Pierre Symon. Open daily except Mon other than public holidays: May–Sept 10am–1pm, 2–7pm (Jul–Aug daily 10am–7pm); Oct–Apr 10am–12.30pm, 2–5.30pm. Closed Jan and 25 Dec. €7.50. ✆02 99 99 79 59. www.chateau-fougeres.com. The first fortifications date from the 10C. In the 13C the castle's mighty towers protected Brittany from Capetian France. After its 14C role in the **War of the Breton Succession**, Richelieu partly demolished the castle.

VITRÉ★★

Distance from Rennes 40km/25mi.
pl. Gen.-de-Gaulle, 35500 Vitré. ✆02 99 75 04 46. www.ot-vitre.fr.

This is the best-preserved "old world" town in Brittany; its fortified castle, its ramparts and its streets have remained just as they were 4–500 years ago, giving the town a picturesque appeal. The old town is built on a spur, commanding the deep **Vallé de la Vilaine** on one side and a railway cutting on the other; the castle stands proudly on the extreme point. Vitré was one of the more prosperous Breton cities from the 15–17C. It made hemp, woollen cloth and cotton stockings that were sold not only in France, but also in England, Germany, Spain and even America and the Indies. Gathered together to form the powerful brotherhood known as "Marchands d'Outre-Mer", the Vitré tradesmen commissioned highly distinctive houses with half-timbering, many of which survive today.

Château★★ – Open Apr–Sep daily 10.30am–12.15pm, 2–6.30 pm; Oct–Mar daily except Tue and Sun am, 10.30am–12.15pm, 2–5.30pm. Guided tours available. Closed 1 Jan, Easter Sun, 1 Nov and 25 Dec. €4. ✆02 99 75 04 46. www.ot-vitre.fr. The 11C château was rebuilt from the 13–15C. The entrance is guarded by a drawbridge and entrance fort (Châtelet) flanked by two towers. The St-Laurent Tower houses the **Musée St-Nicolas**, which contains 15C and 16C sculpture from the houses of Vitré, the 15C tomb of Gui X (a local lord) as well as 16C Flemish and 17C Aubusson tapestries.

Old Town – Rue de la Baudrairie★★ is a curious street, taking its name from the baudroyeurs (leather craftsmen).

COMBOURG★

38km/24mi.
pl. Albert-Parent, 35270 Combourg. ✆02 99 73 13 93.

This picturesque old town stands at the edge of Lac Tranquille and is dominated by an imposing castle. Those who want to take only a quick look at the castle from the outside should walk along the local road that branches off the Rennes road and runs beside the lake.

The **château★** (€8. ✆02 99 73 13 93. www.chateau-combourg.com) has a fortress-like appearance.

ADDRESSES

STAY

Hôtel Arvor – 31 av. Louis-Barthou. 02 99 30 36 47. www.arvorhotel.com. 16 rooms. Near station, this hotel has simple, functional rooms.

Hôtel des Lices – 7 pl. des Lices. 02 99 79 14 81. www.hotel-des-lices.com. 48 rooms. In the centre of Old Rennes, these comfortable rooms with soundproofing are vividly decorated, with contemporary furniture. WiFi.

Hôtel de Nemours – 5 rue de Nemours. 02 99 78 26 26. www.hotelnemours.com. 29 rooms. Well located in a busy street near the République metro, this hotel's rooms are soundproofed and reached by a small lift. Attractive breakfast room.

Le Victoria – 35 av. Jean Janvier. 02 99 31 69 11. www.hotel-levictoria.com. 37 rooms. Restaurant. This hotel near the station has been rejuvenated. Its clean rooms make for a convenient stay. A brasserie atmosphere prevails in the restaurant and frescoes depict a trip made by Queen Victoria.

Ar Milin' – 24km/15mi E of Rennes by N 136 then N 157 at 30 r. de Paris, 35220 Châteaubourg. 02 99 00 30 91. www.armilin.com. Closed 20 Dec–5 Jan and Sun eve. Nov–Feb. 32 rooms. Restaurant closed Tue–Sat lunch and Mon Jul–Aug. Ar Milin', "the windmill" in Breton, has been converted into an attractive hotel. Choose between the intimate rooms with period furniture in the main building or the more contemporary park hotel. Restaurant.

EAT

Le Baron Rouge – 15–17 rue du Chapitre. 02 99 79 08 09. www.lebaronrouge.fr. Closed Sun and Mon. Original cuisine and a wild atmosphere where Bacchus himself is celebrated makes for rustic and surprisingly charming.

Chez Kub – 20 r. du Chapitre 02 99 31 19 31. www.chezkub.fr. Closed Sun lunch and Mon. Grilled specialities prepared on a wood stove in convivial surroundings close to the chimney. In good weather the terrace opens out onto the medieval street.

Crêperie des Portes Mordelaises – 6 rue des Portes Mordelaises. 02 99 30 57 40. www.portesmordelaises.fr. Closed Tue, Wed eve and Sun. Crêpes and galettes opposite one of the old town gates and the house of Anne of Brittany.

Le Picca La Grande Brasserie de Rennes – pl. de la Mairie. 02 99 78 17 17. www.lepicca.com. Open daily 8am–midnight. This Rennes institution founded in 1832 welcomes clients from midday to midnight in its attractive dining room. Pleasant terrace backs onto the theatre.

Le Quatre B – 4 pl. Bretagne. 02 99 30 42 01. www.quatreb.fr. Closed Mon & Sat lunch and Sun. Refined dining room with banquettes, modern chairs and large, floral-themed canvasses. Pleasant terrace. The modern style successfully extends to the cuisine.

Au Goût des Hôtes – 8 pl. Rallier-du-Baty. 02 99 79 20 36 . Closed 2 Jan. Away from the hubbub of the Quartier de la Soif, this restaurant boasts an inventive menu sustained by quality ingredients and an excellent wine cellar.

Thé au Fourneau – 11 rue des Portes Mordelaises. 02 99 78 25 36. Closed third week of Aug and Sun. Under the low ceiling of this welcoming 17C tea house, you will taste wonderful homemade pies, prodigious salads and, of course, an excellent choice of teas.

Le Café Breton – 14 rue Nantaise. 02 99 30 74 95. www.cafe-breton.fr. Closed Mon evenings, Sun, 3 weeks in Aug. The haphazard décor of this restaurant has created both a popular and an energetic dining atmosphere.

Le Guehennec – 33 r. Nantaise. 02 99 65 51 30. Closed 2 weeks in Aug, Sat lunch, Mon eve and Sun. Light coloured panelling and dark brown contemporary furnishings contribute to a warm welcome in this small restaurant. The gourmet menu is inspired by market produce.

La Réserve – 36 r. de la Visitation. 02 99 84 02 02. www.lareserve-rennes.fr. Closed Sun & Mon. Quality traditional cuisine. Don't miss the foie gras, the mango and pineapple chutney or the crème brûlée with vanilla and bourbon!

St-Malo★★★

The site★★★ of the walled town of St-Malo on the east bank of the Rance is unique in France, making the ancient port one of the country's great tourist attractions.

- **Population:** 46 342.
- **Michelin Map:** 309 J 3
- **Info:** espl. St-Vincent. ℘0825 135 200. www.saint-malo-tourisme.com.
- **Location:** St Malo is on Brittany's northern coast 70km/44mi NNW of Rennes.
- **Parking:** Park near the port by the Esplanade St-Vincent.
- **Timing:** Walk right around the town on top of the ramparts in about 30min. Spend another 2hr seeing the château and cathedral.
- **Kids:** Le Grand Aquarium.

A BIT OF HISTORY

The town's prosperity began in the 16C. In 1534, **Jacques Cartier** had set out from here on the voyage which led to the discovery and naming of Canada; very soon a thriving commerce had begun, based on furs and fish. Local ship-owners began to build themselves fine manor houses in the surrounding countryside, as well as tall timber-built residences in the town itself.

By the 1660s their boats were trading in the Pacific, and their ever-increasing wealth enabled them to build in granite. Parisian architectural fashions began to prevail over local traditions. Anticipating the coming naval rivalry between England and France, Colbert became aware of the vulnerability of his country's western coasts; in 1689, Vauban was commissioned to strengthen the defences of St-Malo.

In the 19C, the invention of floating docks ended the advantage which the great tidal range of the port had long given its ship-builders and -repairers.

WALKING TOUR

1 WALLED CITY★

St-Malo map II, p254.

- **Château★★** – You can enter the courtyard and see the façades of the former 17C–18C barracks (now the town hall), the well, the keep and the gatehouse.

  Musée d'Histoire de la Ville et d'Ethnographie du Pays Malouin★ – The museum, which is installed in the great keep and gatehouse, records the development of the city of St-Malo and its celebrities.

  Tour Quic-en-Groigne★ – This tower (65 steps), which is located in the left wing of the castle, bears the name Quic-en-Groigne from an inscription Queen Anne had carved on it in defiance of the bishops of St-Malo: "*Qui-qu'en-groigne, ainsi sera, car tel est mon bon plaisir*" ("Thus it shall be, whoever may complain, for that is my wish").
- **Place Chateaubriand** – As a child, Chateaubriand lived at number 2 (hôtel White).
- **Cour La Houssaye** – The 15C tower in this small courtyard is part of a house said to belong to Duchess Anne.
- **Cathedral St-Vincent** – The nave vault of 1160 is one of the oldest in Brittany, albeit rebuilt after the last war. Note the stained-glass windowsa by Jean Le Moal.
- **Maison de Corsaire –Hôtel d'Asfeld** – Saved in 1944, this 18C dwelling belonged to François Auguste Magon de La Lande, the King's Corsair, Director of The India Company and a very influential *malouin* (native of St-Malo).

  The little keep was built as part of the ramparts in 1395. From the great keep's watchtower (1424) there is a **panorama★★**.

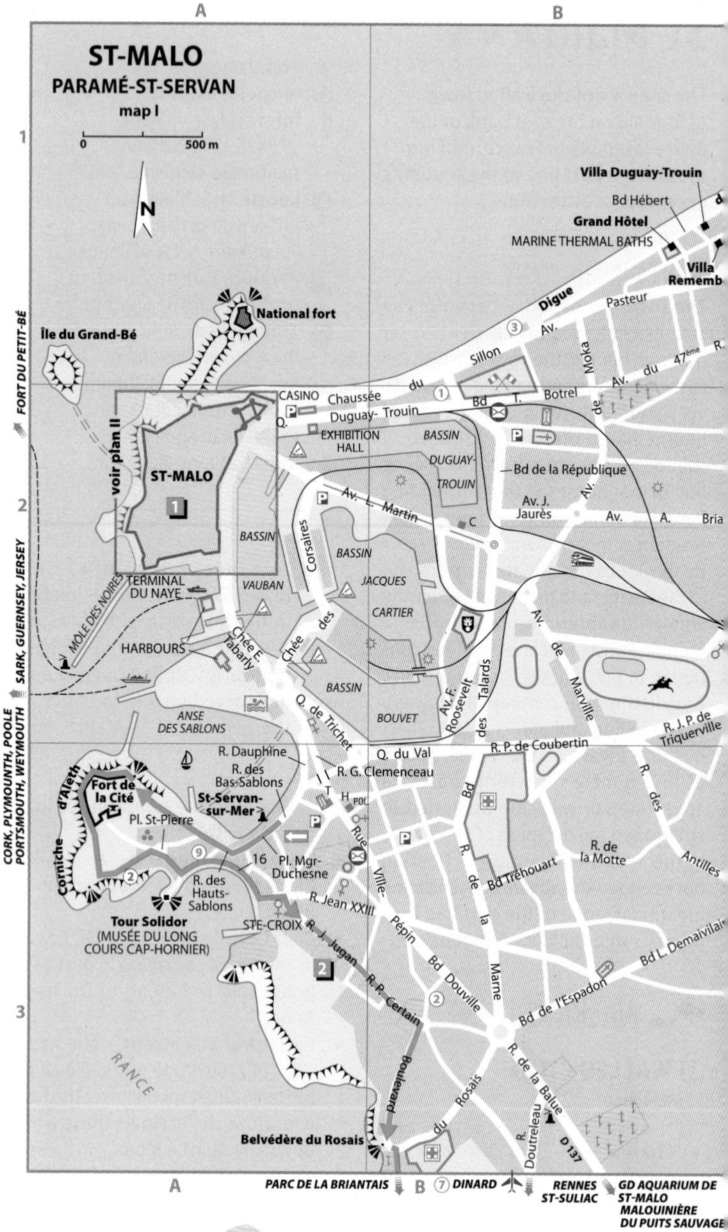

ST-MALO
PARAMÉ-ST-SERVAN
map I

2 RAMPARTS★★★

St-Malo map I, above.

St-Malo and the surrounding area were turned into an entrenched camp by the Germans and became the prize for which a merciless battle raged from 1–14 August 1944. The town was left in ruins. With a great sense of history, its restorers were determined to bring the old city back to life. They have been completely successful in their quest.

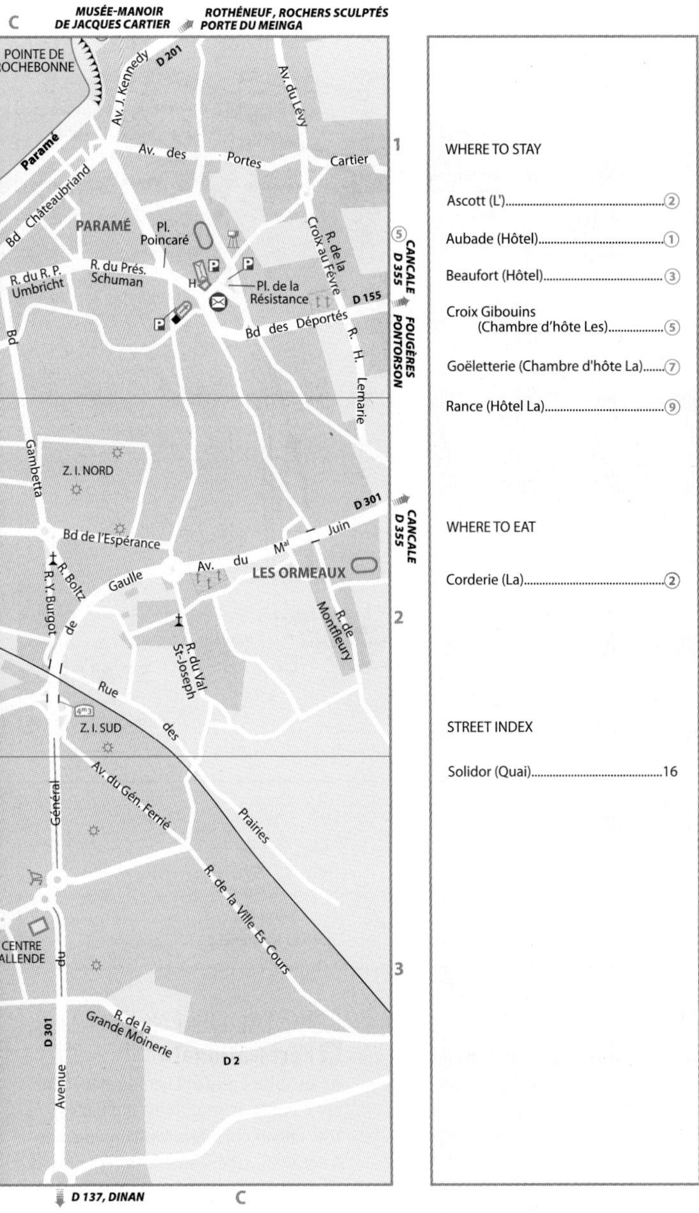

The statue near the esplanade, at the entrance to the Casino garden, portrays Chateaubriand by Armel Beaufils. It was erected in 1948 on the centenary of his death.

The ramparts, started in the 12C, were enlarged and altered up to the 18C and survived the wartime destruction. The rampart walk commands magnificent views, especially at high tide, of the coast and islands.

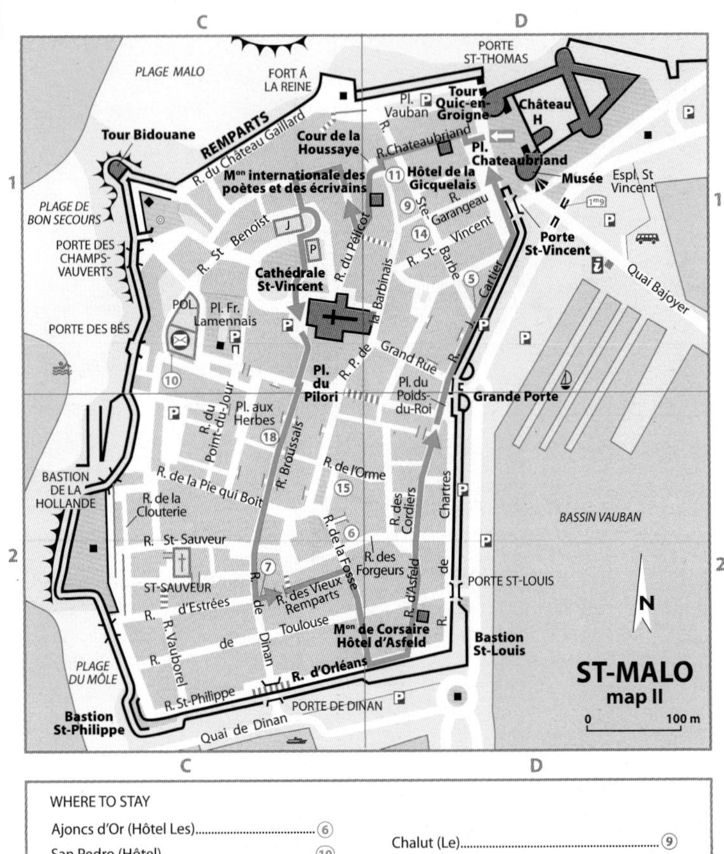

WHERE TO STAY

Ajoncs d'Or (Hôtel Les)........ 6
San Pedro (Hôtel)........ 10

WHERE TO EAT

Au Pied d'Cheval........ 5
Brigantine (La)........ 7
Chalut (Le)........ 9
Coquille d'Œuf (La)........ 11
Margaux (Crêperie)........ 15
Petit Crêpier (Le)........ 14
Ti Nevez (Crêperie)........ 18

ADDITIONAL SIGHT

Le Grand Aquarium★★

ave du Général Patton. Open daily, times vary. Closed mornings of 25 Dec and 1 Jan, 2 weeks in Jan, 2 weeks Nov. €16 (children, 3–12, €12). ☎02 99 21 19 07. www.aquarium-st-malo.com.

The aquarium presents collections of great scientific interest, as visitors trace the history of great sailors from St-Malo. Attractions of special interest include the ring **(Anneau)**, a remarkable round aquarium containing 600 000 litres in which shoals of pelagic species of fish swim endlessly; and a life-size reconstruction of a sunken wreck **(Vaisseau englouti)** with sharks.

COASTAL DEFENCE

Fort National★

Access by Plage de l'Éventail at low tide only. 15min on foot there and back. Tours (45min) Easter, Whitsun, Jun–Sep daily at low tide (variable times). Closed high tide. €5 (children, 6–16, €3). ☎02 72 46 66 26. www.fortnational.com.

Historical monument built in 1689 by the great military architect Vauban to protect the port of St-Malo.

EXCURSIONS

DINAN★★

Dinan is at the top of the Rance estuary, about 30km/18.6mi S of St-Malo.

9 rue du Château, 22105 DINAN.

GETTING AROUND

BY BUS – Map of the bus network at the **Infobus** kiosk, espl. St-Vincent, terminal du Naye. ✆02 99 56 06 06.
BY TOURIST TRAIN – Departs porte St-Vincent every 30min. ✆02 99 40 49 49. www.lepetittrain-saintmalo.com. Adults €6 (children €4).
BY BIKE – Les Vélos Bleus – 19 rue Alphonse Thébault. ✆02 99 40 31 63. www.velos-bleus.fr. Closed Nov–Mar. From €13 for 1 day, up to €53 for 7 days.

TOURS

Guided tours of Intra-Muros – from early Jun–late Sep leaving from the Tourist Office. 1hr 30. €6.
Audio-guide – Voyage Corsaire – Maison de Corsaire, 5 rue d'Asfeld. ✆02 99 56 09 40. www.saint-malo-tourisme.com. Rental of audio-guides: €12 for two hours for two people. Discover the old town at your own pace via an audio tour narrated by actors in a lively style.

✆02 96 87 69 76.
www.dinan-tourisme.com.
Dinan is a gem of a town, surrounded by ramparts and guarded by a castle. The great hero of the town is **Bertrand du Guesclin** (c.1315–80), a redoubtable warrior. Jean le Bon (John the Good) had been taken prisoner by the English at the Battle of Poitiers in 1356. During the four years of captivity he spent in England he became aware of the extent to which feudal rights imposed limitations on royal power, and conceived the idea of a body of knights attached to the monarch. In pursuit of this aim, he took Du Guesclin into his service shortly after his release and return to France.
This middle-aged knight had until then experienced little but rebuffs and difficulties due to his modest ancestry, lack of means and exceptionally ugly appearance. John's successor, Charles V, kept him on, doubtless in view of his great popularity and reckless bravery and his hatred of the English.
In 1366, after ridding France of the Free Companies, he was made High Constable of France. He freed Périgord from the English in 1370 and Normandy in 1378. In 1379 he handed his sword to the king rather than use it against fellow Bretons.

La Vieille Ville

The houses of the old town cluster behind the long circuit of walls, built by the Dukes of Brittany in the 14C to defend their domain against the Normans, the English, and the French.

Château★

pl. du Guesclin. Open Jun–Sep daily 10am–6.30pm; Oct–Dec and Feb–May daily 1.30–5.30pm. €4.
✆02 96 87 58 72.
Begun by Duke John IV about the middle of the 14C. Its 15C towers project outwards in order to facilitate enfilading fire. The exceptionally fine machicolations of Duchess Anne's Keep (Donjon de la Duchesse Anne) are of interest.

Basilique St-Sauveur

pl. St-Sauveur.
The west front is much influenced by the Poitiers version of the Romanesque. In the north aisle is the Evangelists' Window, a fine example of late 15C Breton glass, famous for its yellows. In the north transept is the cenotaph containing the heart of Du Guesclin.

Vieilles maisons

Duke John was happy to let Dinan run its own affairs, and the town's prosperity is reflected in the rebuilding of timber houses in stone. A picturesque townscape emerges of buildings with overhanging storeys, half-timbering, arcades and granite side-walls.
The most interesting houses are on Rue de l'Apport (the 15C Mère Pourcel House), **Place des Merciers★** (triangular gables and porches), **Rue du Jerzual★** which links the main part of the town with the port (15C and 16C shops where craftsmen have worked for six centuries) and on Place du Guesclin (17C and 18C town houses).

DINARD★★

This smart resort is on the left bank of the Rance across from St-Malo.
2 bd Féart. 0821 235 500. www.ot-dinard.com.

On the magnificent estuary of the River Rance opposite St-Malo, Dinard, once a small fishing village, is an elegant resort with sheltered sandy beaches and luxuriant Mediterranean vegetation flourishing in the mild climate.

The resort came into being when a wealthy American called Coppinger built a château here in 1850. He was followed two years later by a British family, who in turn attracted many of their fellow-countrymen. By the end of the 19C its reputation rivalled that of Brighton; sumptuous villas and luxurious hotels abounded, frequented by an international smart set.

Promenades lead from **Plage de l'Écluse★** – a fine beach bordered by hotels, the casino and convention centre – to the **Plage du Prieuré. Pointe du Moulinet★★** enjoys good views. In summer, the **Promenade du Clair de Lune★** forms a setting for evening concerts.

Fort La Latte★★

Open Apr–Sep 10.30am–6pm (Jul–Aug 10.30am–7pm); Oct–Mar 1.30–5.30pm. €5.50 (children €3.50). 02 96 41 57 11. www.castlelalatte.com.

This stronghold, built by the Goyon-Matignons in the 14C, remodelled in the 17C and restored in the early 20C, has kept its feudal appearance. It stands on a spectacular **site★★**, separated from the mainland by two gullies, which are crossed by drawbridges.

Follow the lane to the fort; you will pass a menhir known as **Gargantua's Finger**. Cross the thick walls and go to the **Tour de l'Échaugette** and the cannon-ball foundry. From the parapet walk, there is a **panorama★★**.

CÔTE D'ÉMERAUDE★★★

The name Emerald Coast has been given to Brittany's picturesque northern shore from **Cancale★ (headland – Pointe du Grouin★★)** to **Le Val André★★** and includes some famous beaches: Dinard, **St-Lunaire★★, Paramé★** etc. and the city of privateers, St-Malo.

The Emerald Coast scenic road runs through the major resorts (Dinard, St-Malo) and offers detours to the tips of the numerous headlands, including **Fort de Latte★★, Cap Fréhel★★★** and **Cap d'Erquy★** from which the views of the jagged coastline are in places quite spectacular.

Cap Fréhel★★★

Between St-Brieuc and Dinard, on the Emerald Coast.
pl. de Chambly, 22240 Fréhel. 02 96 41 57 23. www.paysdefrehel.com.

The **site** of this cape is one of the grandest on the Breton coast. Its red, grey and black cliffs rise vertically to a height of 70m and are fringed with reefs on which the swell breaks heavily. Overlooking the English Channel, legend has it that in ancient times you could walk to the UK from here! Of course, scientists have since proven otherwise. This wild, protected site covers 400ha/988.4 acres of heathland and includes an ornithology park.

Panorama – The coastal panorama is vast in clear weather: from the Pointe du Grouin, on the right, with the Cotentin in the background, to the Île de Bréhat, on the left. The famous outline of Fort la Latte is visible on the right.

Tour du Cap – 30min walk. At the extremity of the headland stands the **lighthouse**, built in 1950 and lit automatically; the light can be seen 120km/75mi away on a clear night. From the gallery there is an immense view: you may see Bréhat to the west, Jersey to the north, Granville, a part of the Cotentin Peninsula and the **Îles Chausey** to the northeast. After passing the furthest point where a siren stands, you can look down on the **Fauconnière rocks**, crowded with seagulls and cormorants; the contrast between the mauvish-red of the rocks and the blue or green of the sea is striking. Near the Restaurant de la Fauconnière, take a steep path on the right; halfway down it reaches a platform with a fine view.

ADDRESSES

STAY

Hôtel San Pedro – 1 rue Ste-Anne. ℘02 99 40 88 57. www.sanpedro-hotel.com. 12 rooms. Closed mid Nov–late Feb. Budget hotel a short hop from Bon Secours beach.

Hôtel Les Ajoncs d'Or – 10 rue Forgeurs. ℘02 99 40 85 03. www.st-malo-hotel-ajoncs-dor.com. 22 rooms. Closed Dec & Jan. Well-kept rooms in a peaceful street in the old town.

OUTSIDE WALLED TOWN

Hôtel La Rance – 15 quai Sébastopol. ℘02 99 81 78 63. www.larancehotel.com. 11 rooms. Lovely, small hotel, located in the shadow of the Solidor tower.

L'Ascott – 35 rue Chapitre. ℘02 99 81 89 93. www.ascotthotel.com. 10 rooms. Contemporary and classic details in a quiet residential neighbourhood.

Hôtel Aubade – 8 place Duguesclin. ℘02 99 40 47 11. www.aubade-hotel.com. 20 rooms. Closed 31 Jan–9 Feb. Homely place where each floor has its own colour scheme.

Hôtel Beaufort – 25 chausée du Sillon. ℘02 99 40 99 99. www.hotel-beaufort.com. 22 rooms. Colonial-style rooms. Avoid the noisier rooms overlooking rue du Sillon.

NEARBY

Chambre d'Hôte Les Croix Gibouins – 6km/3.7mi E of St-Malo on the D 301 rte de Cancale and D 155 rte de St-Méloir-des-Ondes. ℘02 99 81 12 41. www.les-croix-gibouins.com. 3 rooms. Don't worry about the road that passes near this 16C gentleman's residence as its thick walls guarantee calm inside. Restored rooms overlooking a meadow.

Chambre d'Hôte La Goëletterie – 20 rue Goëletterie, quartier Quelmer. 5km/3mi from St-Malo towards Dinard then Quelmer. ℘02 99 81 92 64. www.la-goeletterie.fr. Closed 15 Dec–15 Feb. 4 rooms. This pretty farm overlooking the Rance offers tranquillity aplenty. Rooms have been recently renovated. Friendly welcome.

EAT

La Brigantine – 13 rue de Dinan. ℘02 99 56 82 82. http://la-brigantine.fr. Closed Tue and Wed off season except school holidays. Galettes and crêpes made from organic products are the order of the day in this bright dining room.

Ti Nevez – 12 rue Broussais. ℘02 99 40 82 50. Closed Jan and Tue–Wed except school holidays. Traditional *crêperie* with a rustic setting, well-known for its flat cake, egg-cheese-andouille and its crêpe Québécoise with maple syrup.

Crêperie Margaux – 3 place du Marché aux légumes. ℘02 99 20 26 02. www.creperie-margaux.com. Closed Tue & Wed, except for school holidays. Enjoy freshly-made *crêpes* on a lovely terrace in fine weather. Tea room.

Le Petit Crêpier – 6 rue Ste. Barbe. ℘02 99 40 93 19. Closed Jan, 15 days in Nov, Tue & Wed, except for school holidays. Traditional *crêpes* and some fillings too in a maritime-themed atmosphere.

Au Pied d'Cheval – 6 rue Jacques Cartier. ℘02 99 40 98 18. Closed 15 Nov–30 Mar. The Le Moal family raise their own shellfish in nearby Cancale, which they serve in their restaurant.

La Coquille d'Oeuf – 20 rue de la Corne-de-Cerf. ℘02 99 40 92 62. Closed Mon. The contemporary style of this restaurant in the town centre is lovely. Add to the mix great service and delicious food and you'll understand why it makes a good pit stop.

Le Chalut – 8 rue de la Corne de Cerf. ℘02 99 56 71 58. Closed Mon and Tue. Reservations obligatory. Well-known address for its fish, seafood and lobsters, this cosy setting fittingly evokes the sea and its ships. Excellent value for money.

OUTSIDE WALLED TOWN

La Corderie – Cité d'Aleth, 9 chemin de la Corderie, St-Servan-sur-Mer. ℘02 99 81 62 38. www.lacorderie-restaurant.com. Closed Mon except public holidays. Perched above the Solidor tower, this villa offers fine views over the Rance and its dam. Famous for its fish specialities, there's a terrace for fine days and two dining rooms with panoramic windows.

St-Brieuc★

to Côte de Granit Rose★★

The town is built 3km/1.8mi from the sea on a plateau deeply cleft by two water courses: the Gouëdic and the Gouet. Bold viaducts span their valleys. The Gouet is canalised and leads to the commercial and fishing port of Légué. St-Brieuc is the administrative, commercial and industrial centre of the *département* (Côtes-d'Armor). The markets and fairs of the town are much frequented, especially the Fair of St-Michael (Foire St-Michel) on 29 September. On Saturdays, a market is held in front of the cathedral. The peaceful provincial city has retained some fine timber-framed houses.

- **Population:** 46 209.
- **Michelin Map:** Local map 309 F3 – Côtes-d'Armor (22).
- **Info:** 7 r. St-Gouéno, 22000 St-Brieuc. ✆02 96 33 32 50. www.baiedesaintbrieuc.com.
- **Location:** St-Brieuc is crossed by the N 12, which comes from Dinan (60km/37mi E) and goes to Brest (145km/90mi W). The D 786 follows the coast, serving the resorts of the Côte d'Émeraude.
- **Kids:** A walk through the Galerie des Oiseaux at the Maison de la Baie.
- **Timing:** Allow a day to visit the town and beaches.
- **Don't Miss:** The views from **pointe du Roselier**.

A BIT OF GEOGRAPHY

La Côte de Granit Rose★★ – The Pink Granite Coast boasts a remarkable stretch of pink-coloured rocky coastline between **Trégastel★★** and **Trébeurden★**. While there are many places in the world that have pink or red rock, there are only two other places that have the same type of pink granite found at the northern Brittany coast: the Bavella range of mountains in southeast Corsica, and in southeast China. Due to the fragility of this spectacular environment, the Pink Granite Coast has been designated a conservation area.

SIGHTS

Cathédrale St-Étienne★ – This great 13–14C cathedral has been reconstructed several times and restored in the 19C; its mass bears striking witness to its original role of church fortress.

Old Houses – The area to the north of the cathedral still retains many 15–16C half-timbered and corbelled houses.

Fontaine de St-Brieuc is sheltered by a lovely 15C porch, and stands against the east end of the Chapelle of Notre-Dame-de-la-Fontaine. Brieuc, the Welsh monk who came to the region in the 5C, is believed to have settled here.

Tertre Aubé★ – The hill commands a fine **view★** of the **vallée du Gouët**, crossed by the viaduct which carries the road to **Paimpol**; also of the partly hidden port of **Légué**, below, and, to the right, of St-Brieuc bay and the ruined tower of Cesson.

EXCURSIONS

ST-QUAY-PORTRIEUX★

19km/12mi N of St-Brieuc.

St-Quay-Portrieux, a popular seaside resort, owes its name to an Irish monk, **St Ké**, who, legend has it, landed on this coast c. 472.

Its beautiful beaches – **Casino, Châtelet** and **Comtesse** – are sheltered by a rocky fringe known as the **Roches de St-Quay**.

ÎLE DE BRÉHAT★★

53km/33mi NNW of St-Brieuc.

Bréhat is a much-frequented holiday resort. Its pink rocks stand out against the sea. Cars are not allowed; tractors are used for transportation.

TRÉGUIER★★

72km/45mi NW of St-Brieuc.
1 pl. Général Leclerc. 02 96 92 30 19. www.ville-treguier.fr.

Tréguier is a little medieval city, overlooking the estuary of the Jaudy and Guindy rivers, one of the drowned valleys characteristic of the Breton coast. The town and its surroundings were no strangers to misfortune. In 1345–47. the area was devastated by the English allies of Jean de Montfort in retribution for having supported Jeanne de Penthièvre in the **War of the Breton Succession**. In 1592 it was pillaged by the Catholic Leaguers for having taken the side of Henri IV, then punished again in 1789 for its opposition to taxes and reforms introduced at the French Revolution.

Cathédrale St-Tugdual★★ – Begun in 1339, this is one of the finest buildings of its kind in Brittany, Anglo-Norman in style in spite of the use of the local granite. The **cloisters (cloître)★** of 1458 are among the few to survive in Brittany. Timber-roofed and with a carved frieze, it has 48 elegant arches giving onto a hydrangea-planted courtyard.

Jardins de Kerdalo★★ – To the east of Tréguier, in the village of Trédarzec. Created by Peter Wolkonsky in 1965, these botanic gardens can be found in a romantic setting of 18ha/44.5acres. The paths wind through the majestic trees, woods and perfumed areas. Lovely **view★** over the port of Tréguier.

LANNION★

67km/42mi NW of St-Brieuc.

Lannion, spread out on both banks of the River Léguer, has retained its typical old Breton character. From the bridge, there is a good view of the port and of the vast Monastère Ste-Anne. The Centre de Recherches de Lannion and the Centre National d'Études des Télécommunications, where research is undertaken in telecommunications and electronics, have been built north of Lannion at the crossroads of the road to Perros-Guirec and that of **Trégastel-Plage**. Lannion's annual organ festival takes place in Église St-Jean-du-Baly (16–17C).

Old Houses★ – Note the beautiful façades of the 15C and 16C houses, half-timbered, with slate roofs.

Église de Brélévenez★ – Built on a hill by the Templars in the 12C and remodelled in the Gothic period.

PERROS-GUIREC★★

77km/48mi NW of St-Brieuc.

This much-frequented seaside resort (with casino and seawater therapy centre), built in the form of an amphitheatre on the Pink Granite Coast, overlooks the fishing and pleasure boat harbour and the two gently sloping fine sand and sheltered beaches of Trestraou and Trestignel.

Le Sentier des Douaniers★★ – 3hr on foot there and back. The best time to go is in the morning, and if possible, at high tide. Follow the edge of the cliff as far as Pors-Rolland to reach the lighthouse via the Pointe de Squéouel, the Ploumanac'h lighthouse and the Maison du Littoral information centre. Bring your camera.

Ploumanach★★ – 6.5km/4mi NW of Perros-Guirec. This little fishing port on the Pink Granite Coast, belonging to the municipality of Perros-Guirec and well situated at the mouths of the two picturesque Traouiéros valleys, has become a well-known seaside resort, famous for its **rock formations★★**.

Les Sept-Îles – Access to the islands: Apr–Sep, 8.30am–6.30pm. 02 96 91 10 00. www.armor-decouverte.fr. This archipelago has been an ornithological centre since 1912. You can observe more sea birds in the morning and in the evening.

ADDRESSES

STAY

ST-BRIEUC

€€€ Hôtel Le Duguesclin – 2 Pl. Duguesclin. 02 96 33 11 58. www.hotel-duguesclin.com. 17 rooms. Pub cuisine and seafood dominate the terrace and a comfortable upstairs dining room in this friendly brasserie.

St-Pol-de-Léon★

St-Pol is one of the main market-gardening centres of the rich band of fertile soils running all round the Breton coast from St-Malo to St-Nazaire. Where the wind can be kept out, the otherwise mild climate allows excellent crops of vegetables to be grown, artichokes, onions, early potatoes, cauliflowers, salad vegetables... eagerly bought in the markets of Paris and on the far side of the English Channel. Mechanisation means that much of the characteristic pattern of tiny fields bounded by stone walls is doomed to disappear.

- **Population:** 6 904.
- **Michelin Map:** 308 H
- **Info:** pl. de l'Evêché. 02 98 15 05 69. www.saintpoldeleon.fr.
- **Location:** 5km/3mi S of Roscoff.

The town centre is an agreeable place to explore, and is often overlooked by visitors. Here, not far from the harbour, is the church of **Notre-Dame-de-Kroaz-Batz★** with its remarkable lantern-turret belfry (*clocher★*) of Renaissance date. Inside, four alabaster **statues★** grace an altarpiece in the south aisle.

SIGHTS

Chapelle du Kreisker★

2 r. Verderel.

The chapel was rebuilt around 1375; in the 15C, when the coastal towns were prospering from their sea-borne trade, it housed the meetings of the town council. In about 1430, Duke John V of Brittany tried to introduce the Gothic style into Brittany in order to boost his prestige. But the response of the Breton architects was to adapt Flamboyant Gothic to local ways, as in evidence here.

Ancienne Cathédrale★

r. de Morlaix.

The old cathedral was erected on 12C foundations in the 13–14C. This fine building with its characteristically Breton balustraded belfry was restored by the dukes of Brittany 1431 onwards.

EXCURSIONS

ROSCOFF★

5km/3mi N.

The harbour town with its fishing fleet and important export trade (vegetables) to Britain also has ferry services linking Brittany to Plymouth and Cork. It is a flourishing resort and a medical centre using sea-water treatment.

ENCLOS PAROISSIAL DE ST-THÉGONNEC★★

The village lies 12km/7.4mi SW of the town of Morlaix, in northern Brittany.

The parish close at St-Thégonnec is among the most famous of these typically Breton monumental groupings of church, cemetery, calvary and ossuary. The magnificent 17C parish close at St-Thégonnec was to be the last of the great parish closes of Brittany. By good fortune, the village has managed to preserve it in fine condition.

Although of older origin, parish closes began to develop in this form during the second half of the 16C. They formed a useful tool for the Catholic Church, trying to promote a veneration of apostles and saints in opposition to Brittany's heritage of local cults.

ENCLOS PAROISSIAL DE GUIMILIAU★★

8km/5mi SW.

This example of a parish close pre-dates the one at St-Thégonnec by some 30 years. The **calvary★★** (*calvaire*, 1581) has an attractively naïve quality; its 200 figures are full of a sense of vigorous movement and are carved in a robust way which recalls the sculpture of the Romanesque period.

Brest★

An ancient port built on a magnificent natural lagoon that, being nowhere less than 10m deep, is almost an inland sea, Brest remains wedded to its maritime tradition.

- **Population:** 141 303.
- **Michelin Map:** 308 A 4, E 4-5
- **Info:** pl. de la Liberté. 02 98 44 24 96. www.brest-metropole-tourisme.fr.
- **TGV:** Just under 5h from Paris Montparnasse.
- **Flights:** Aéroport Brest Bretagne is 9km/5.5mi from the centre of Brest (www.brest.aeroport.fr); a shuttle service operates to Porte de Guipavas (10min).
- **Location:** The town is 71km/42mi N of Quimper.
- **Kids:** Océanopolis centre.

A BIT OF HISTORY

Although used as a port by Gauls and then Romans, the importance of Brest was firmly established from the 13C onwards. A French garrison moved in and has been there ever since.

At the beginning of the 17C, Richelieu's wish was to have French naval forces which could be permanently ready for action. He founded the naval dockyard and its first warship was launched in 1634. The Rue de Siam, running in a straight line between the arsenal and Place de la Liberté, formed the main axis of the ancient town and its fame was spread worldwide by the sailors who frequented it. The town had to be completely rebuilt after World War II, in which it suffered four years of air attack and a 43-day siege.

SIGHTS

Océanopolis★★★ – Port de Plaisance du Moulin Blanc. Days and hours vary for each exhibition; check website for current details. €20 (children, 3–13, €13). 02 98 34 40 40. www.oceanopolis.com. In this ultra-modern building, shaped like a giant crab, visitors discover the marine life of Brittany's coastal waters in the saltwater aquariums, and the many sea birds of the coast in their nesting places on the cliff face (entrance level).

Cours Dajot★ – This fine promenade was laid out in 1769 on the old ramparts. It gives splendid **views★★** of the port and of the great roadstead of 150sq km/58sq mi.

Musée des Beaux-Arts★ – 24 r. Traverse. Open Tue–Sat 10am–noon, 2–6pm, Sun 2–6pm. Closed public holidays (except 14 Jul and 15 Aug, 2–6pm). €4. 02 98 00 87 96. www.musee-brest.com. The collections illustrate the advances made by the painters of the Pont-Aven School, for example *Yellow Sea (Mer jaune)* by Lacombe, as well as a curious study of the town of Ys (*see QUIMPER p263*), Manet's *Parrots*, and *Bouquet of Roses* by Suzanne Valadon.

EXCURSIONS

CALVAIRE DE PLOUGASTEL-DAOULAS★★

11km/6.8mi E, S of the church.

The calvary was built from 1602 to 1604 by the Priget brothers to mark an outbreak of plague four years earlier. Its 180 figures are sculpted in the round; a certain stiffness of posture is set off by the size of the heads and the vigorous expressions.

LES ABERS★★

The coastline from the **Pointe St-Mathieu★★** to **Brignogan-Plages** is wild and rugged, and is broken up by estuaries called "abers" (Aber-Wrac'h, Aber-Benoît, Aber-Ildut).

The term *aber* is of Celtic origin and is found in Scottish and Welsh place names. In Brittany *abers* are picturesque, fairly shallow estuaries on the low, rocky northwest coast of **Finistère**.

The entrance to the **aber Wrac'h** is guarded by the resort of the same name near which there are fine views of the **lighthouse on Vierge Island**, the tallest in France (82.5m). A **scenic road★** runs along the rugged coastline through a number of charming resorts.

ÎLE D'OUESSANT★★★

The island is open to pedestrians and cyclists only, and reached from the coast of Brittany by a 15min flight from Brest or by ferry from Brest (2hr15min), **Le Conquet★** (30min–1hr) or Camaret (1hr15min). Almost all ferry crossings are early in the morning. Bourg de Lampaul. 02 98 48 85 83. www.ot-ouessant.fr.

Most of the island's residents are professional seamen, many in the navy; a few fishermen trap lobsters. The population lives in scattered hamlets or in the little capital, **Lampaul**, with its tiny harbour and the mausoleum where the Proella crosses representing those lost at sea are assembled.

The island is a fragment of the **Léon plateau** on the mainland. Two outcrops of granite running northeast–southwest enclose a sunken area of mica-schist much eroded by the sea to form the **Baie de Lampaul** and the **Baie du Stiff**. Where there is shelter from the wind, camellias, aloes and agaves can grow, but the characteristic vegetation of the island is heather and dwarf gorse.

For ferry information, contact Compagnie Maritime Penn Ar Bed (02 98 80 80 80. www.pennarbed.fr). For flights, contact Finistair (02 98 84 64 87. www.finistair.fr).

Côte Sauvage★★★

4hr round-trip on foot from Lampaul.

The headlands and inlets of Ushant's rocky northwestern coastline have a rugged and dramatic beauty. The most spectacular locations include Keller Island (**Île de Keller**), **Penn-ar-Ru-Meur** and the Cadoran islet (**Îlot de Cadoran**). The 300 or so vessels which pass each day are guided by five great light-houses. The one at **Creac'h**, which houses the **Centre d'Interpretation des Phares et Balises** (open daily Apr–Sep 10.30am–6.30pm; Nov–Dec 1.30–5pm, Jan–Mar and Oct 1.30–5.30pm, excl. holidays; closed winter holidays, Easter and 1 Nov; 02 98 48 80 70), a historical museum on lighthouses and beacons, is the most powerful in the world; together with its counterpart at Land's End in Cornwall it marks the western limit of the English Channel. The light at **Stiff** gives a splendid **view★★** over the rolling sea. The lighthouses play a vital role: over the last hundred years over 50 wrecks have been recorded.

CROZON PENINSULA★★★

Crozon Peninsula (Presqu'île de Crozon) lies between Brest to the N and Douarnenez Bay to the S.

The peninsula is a place of craggy cliffs and golden sand beaches, windswept moorland and tiny coves, not least at **Morgat** a little to the south of the main town Crozon.

The **beach★** here is a gentle arc, backed by a scattering of brightly painted shops and bars that provide everything you need for a short break or an uncomplicated, encore le pastis, life style. The nearby **Lagrange holiday village** is perfectly placed (www.lagrange-holidays.co.uk).

Pointe de Penhir★★★ – Penhir Point is the most impressive of the four headlands of the Crozon peninsula, which has some of the finest coastal landscapes in the whole of Brittany.

Camaret-sur-Mer★ – At the end of the peninsula, Camaret-sur-Mer is a dizzy little place favoured by artists, and with brightly coloured shop and restaurant fronts that would do Scotland's Tobermory proud. Nearby are the **Alignements Mégalithiques de Lagatjar★**.

Cap de la Chèvre★★ – From the former German observation point there is a fine view over the Atlantic.

Pointe des Espagnols★★ – From here there is a remarkable **panorama**.

Pointe de Dinan★★ – A fine **panorama** can be seen from the edge of the cliff. Skirting the cliff to the right is the enormous rocky mass of **Dinan castle**, joined to the mainland by a natural arch.

Quimper★★

Quimper is in Brittany's far west and is the capital of Finistère. It lies in a pretty valley at the junction (*kemper* in Breton) of two rivers.

- **Population:** 63 550.
- **Michelin Map:** 308 G 6-7
- **Info:** pl. de la Résistance. ✆02 98 53 04 05. www.quimper-tourisme.com.
- **Location:** 72km/45mi SE of Brest, and 69km/43mi NW of Lorient.
- **Don't Miss:** The Old Town.

A BIT OF HISTORY

The town was first of all a Gaulish foundation, sited on the north bank of the Odet estuary. Towards the end of the 5C BCE, Celts sailed over from Britain (hence the area's name of Cornouaille, i.e. Cornwall) and drove out the original inhabitants. This was the era of the legendary King Gradlon and of the fabulous city of Ys, which is supposed to have sunk beneath the waves of Douarnenez Bay. The town has a long tradition of making faïence (fine earthenware), and is a centre of Breton folk art.

The statue of **René-Théophile-Hyacinthe Laënnec** (1781–1826) commemorates Quimper's most illustrious son – the man who invented the stethoscope.

CATHÉDRALE ST-CORENTIN★★

The cathedral is dedicated to one of the figures responsible for founding Brittany. Much of the cathedral is Gothic, although the twin spires were added only in the 19C. Much of the interior decoration was stripped away during the Revolution and the Reign of Terror (1793), and while the lime-washed interior that remains may not suit some tastes, it does leave the cathedral with a bright and appealing atmosphere.

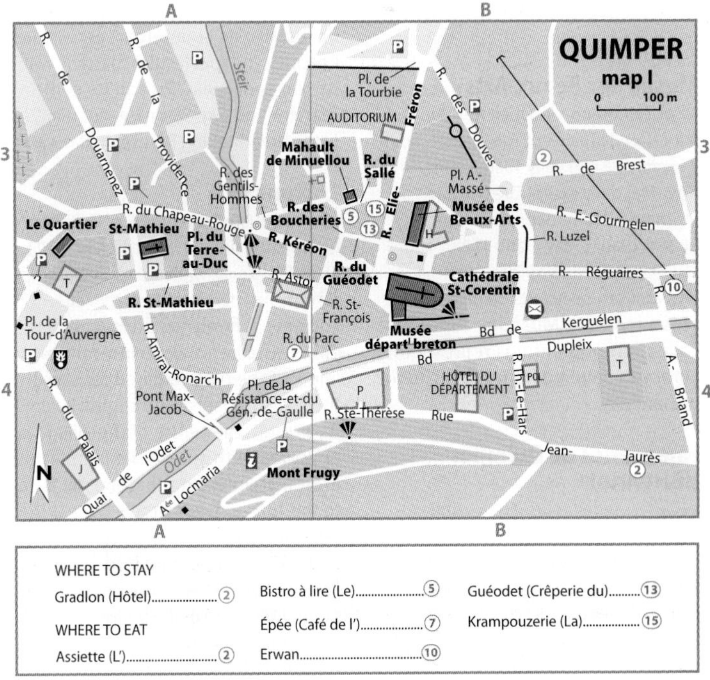

OLD QUIMPER★

The medieval town lies between the cathedral and the River Odet and its tributary, the Steyr. There are fine old houses with granite ground floors and timber-framed projecting upper storeys.

- **Rue Élie-Fréon** – North of place St-Corentin. Walk up the no. 22 to admire a 17C corbelled house with a slate roof, and a Renaissance porch at number 20. From here go to charming place au Beurre.
- **Rue du Sallé** – It was in the Middle Ages that the street of sausage and meat sellers got its name. Note the beautiful old house of the Mahault de Minuellou family at number 10.
- **Rue Kéréon★** – A busy shopping street and the most attractive in the town. It was once where the shoemakers were to be found (kereon in Breton – hence its name).
- **Place Terre-au-Duc** – A picturesque square lined with old half-timbered houses. This was the lay town opposite the episcopal city and included the Law Courts, prison and the Duc de Bretagne market.

ADDITIONAL SIGHTS

Musée des Beaux-Arts★★

40 pl. St-Corentin. ♿Open Apr–Jun and Sept–Oct daily except Tue 9.30am–noon, 2–6pm; Jul–Aug daily 10am–7pm; Nov–Mar daily except Tue and Sun morning 9.30am–noon, 2–5.30pm. Closed 1 Jan, 1 May, 1 and 11 Nov and 25 Dec. ✆02 98 95 45 20. www.musee-beauxarts.quimper.fr.

This Fine Arts Museum contains a collection of paintings representing European painting from the 14C to the present day.

Faïenceries de Quimper HBHenriot

r. Haute. Guided tours (French and English) Mon-Fri. ♿ ✆02 98 90 09 36. www.hb-henriot.com.

The 300-year-old faïence workshops were bought in 1984 by Paul Janssens, an American citizen of Dutch origin. Earthenware is still entirely decorated by hand with traditional motifs such as Breton peasants in traditional dress, birds, roosters and plants. A tour of the workshops enables visitors to discover in turn the various manufacturing stages, from the lump of clay to the firing process.

Musée Départemental Breton★

1 r. du Roi Gradion; open daily except Mon and public holidays: 9am–12.30pm, 1.30–5pm (Sun 2–5pm); mid-Jun–late Sept daily 9am–6pm. ✆02 98 95 21 60. www.museedepartementalbreton.fr.

The museum, housed in the former palace of the Bishops of Cornwall, is the most remarkable monument after the cathedral of Quimper, and presents a synthesis of the archaeology, folk and decorative arts of Finistère.

EXCURSIONS

LA CORNOUAILLE★★

Although the area today is limited to the coast and immediate hinterland west of its capital Quimper, Cornouaille was once the Duchy of medieval Brittany, stretching as far north as **Morlaix**. Brittany's "Cornwall" juts out into the Atlantic just like its counterpart across the Channel. The spectacular coastline with its two peninsulas, **Presqu'île de Penmarch★** and **Cap Sizun★★**, culminates in the breathtaking **Pointe du Raz★★★**.

Locronan★★

E of Douarnenez and NE of Quimper. pl. de la Mairie, 29180 Locronan. ✆02 98 51 80 80. www.villedelocronan.fr. You must park outside the village.

Locronan is firmly rooted in times past. This used to be a major centre for woven linen, of the type required for sails by the French, Spanish and English navies. As a result, the centre of the village is endowed with splendid examples of Breton architecture that mostly date to the 18C, and was largely built at the behest of wealthy sail merchants.

In the 19C, competition from Vitré and Rennes, coupled with the general economic downturn of the period, brought ruin and stagnation for Locronan. Just how wealthy a place this must have

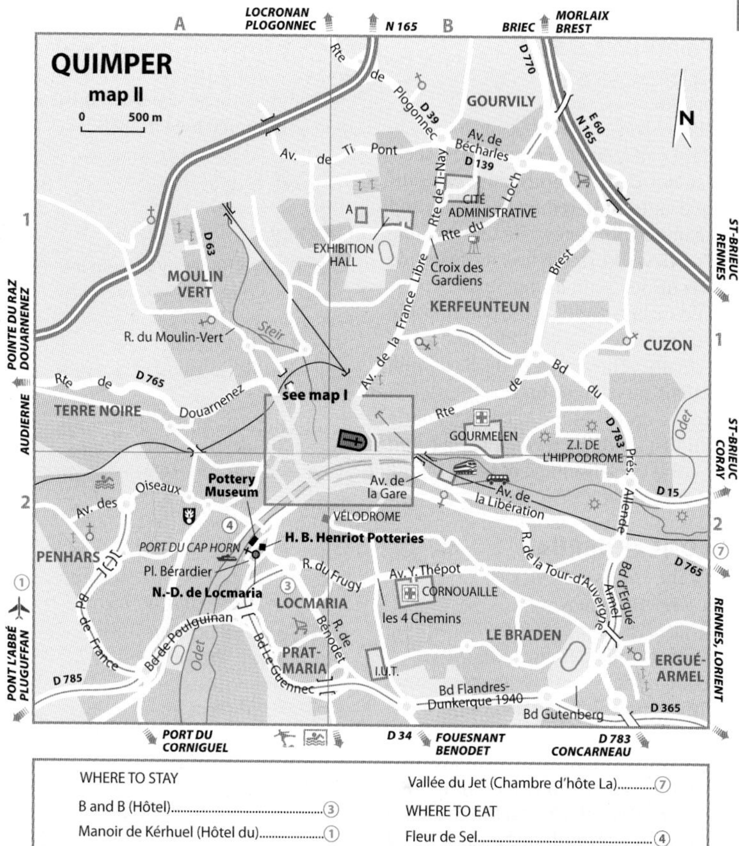

been is self-evident if you study the quality of the opulent architecture, especially in the place de l'Église.

It takes a while to register, but there is something not quite right about Locronan. And then you notice that there are no spaghetti tangles of telephone cables festooned from building to building, no television aerials or satellite dishes, no road markings, no permanent road signs; in fact, nothing that visually places the setting in the 21C.

Montagne de Locronan★

2km/1.2mi E of Locronan. Open only during the Troménies held every year on the 2nd Sun in July, and the Grandes Troménies held every six years from the 1st–2nd Sun in July. 02 98 91 70 14.

From the top (289m), crowned by a **chapel** (note the stained-glass windows by Bazaine), you will see a fine **panorama★** of Douarnenez bay. On the left are Douarnenez and the Pointe du Leydé; on the right Cap de la Chèvre, the Presqu'île de Crozon, Ménez-Hom and the **Monts d'Arrée★★**.

Ste-Anne-la-Palud

8km/5mi NW of Locronan. Leave Locronan by D 63 to Crozon. After Plonévez-Porzay, turn left. Open Easter–1 Nov daily 9am–8pm; rest of the year Sun only. 02 98 92 50 17.

The 19C **chapel** contains a much-venerated painted granite statue of St Anne dating from 1548. The *pardon* on the last Sunday in August, one of the finest and most picturesque in Brittany, attracts thousands.

Pointe du Raz★★★

The point is at the farthest tip of Brittany's Cornouaille peninsula, about 51km/32mi W of Quimper.

Raz Point is one of France's most spectacular coastal landscapes. Its jagged cliffs, battered by the waves and seamed with caves, rise to over 70m. The **view★★** extends over the fearsome Raz de Sein with its multitude of reefs and rocky islands (on the outermost of which is sited the lighthouse, Phare de la Vieille). The outline of the **Île de Sein** can be seen on the horizon.

To the north lies the headland, **Pointe du Van**, perhaps less impressive, but having the advantage of being off the tourist track.

CONCARNEAU★

The town is S of Quimper, in western Brittany.

quai d'Aiguillon. 02 98 97 0144. www.tourismeconcarneau.fr.

Concarneau owes its success to its fishing port. Trawlers and cargo-boats moor in the inner harbour up the estuary of the Moros, while the outer harbour is lively with pleasure craft. There are many vegetable and fish canneries and plenty of bustle as the catch is sold at the morning "criée" (fish market).

Walled Town★★ – On its islet in the bay, this was one of the strongholds of the ancient county of Cornouaille; as at Dinan and Guérande, its walls proclaim the determination of the citizens to maintain their independence, particularly in times of trouble (as during the **War of the Breton Succession** in 1341). The English nevertheless seized the place in 1342, and were thrown out only by Du Guesclin in 1373.

PONT-AVEN★

33.5km/21mi SE of Quimper.

The town lies in a very pleasant setting at the point where the River Aven opens out into a tidal estuary. The Aven used to drive numerous mills, hence the saying: "Pont-Aven, a famous town; 14 mills, 15 houses".

Today, only one mill remains in operation. Pont-Aven is also famous for Galettes de Pont-Aven (butter cookies) and as a favourite resort of painters; the Pont-Aven School, headed by Gauguin, was formed here in 1888.

ADDRESSES

STAY

Chambre d'hôte La Vallée du Jet – Kervren, 29140 St-Yvi. 14km/8.7mi SE of Quimper on the D 765 rte de Rosporden. 02 98 94 70 34. Closed Feb. 5 rooms. 2 gîtes. This 19C longhouse overlooks the Jet valley.

Hôtel du Manoir de Kérhuel – 29720 Plonéour-Lanvern. 12km/7.4mi S of Quimper on the D 785 rte de Pont l'Abbé then D 156 rte de Plonéour-Lanvern. 02 98 82 60 57. http://manoirdekerhuel.fr. Closed Jan–Mar 20, 11 Nov–27 Dec. Restaurant. 20 rooms. A long tree-lined drive leads to this 15C manor.

Hôtel Gradlon – 30 rue de Brest, Quimper. 02 98 95 04 39. www.hotel-gradlon.fr. Closed 12 Dec–11 Jan. 20 rooms. One of the nicest hotels in town.

EAT

Le Bistro à Lire – 18 rue des Boucheries. 02 98 95 30 86. Closed Sun and Mon off season. Since 2001, this bookshop-restaurant in the heart of the pedestrian area marries a love of books with the delights of eating.

La Krampouzerie – 9 rue du Sallé (Place au Beurre). 02 98 95 13 08. Closed Sun and Mon off season. Savour unexpected specialities such as crêpes with algae or with onion jam from Roscoff, paired with caramel and ginger.

Café de l'Épée – 14 rue du Parc. 02 98 95 28 97. www.quimper-lepee.com. Artists of stage and screen, writers and politicians have frequented this brasserie and local institution.

Erwan – 1 r. Aristide-Briand. 02 98 90 14 14. Breton cuisine of simple small dishes taken from grandmothers' recipe books.

Fleur de Sel – 1 quai Neuf. 02 98 55 04 71. Closed 24 Dec-2 Jan, Sat lunch and Sun. Situated in a picturesque quarter of Quimper on the Quai neuf, serving traditional dishes.

Lorient

The modern city of Lorient boasts proudly of being the site of five ports: the fishing port of Keroman; a military port, with dockyard and submarine base (capacity for 30 submarines); a passenger port, with ships sailing to the Île de Groix★; the Kergroise commercial port, which specialises in the importing of animal foodstuffs; and the Kernevel pleasure boat harbour, with a wet dock located in the centre of the city: it is the starting point for transatlantic competition. An annual Interceltic Festival (Festival Interceltique, see Festivals and Events, p38**) is held in Lorient.**

- **Population:** 57 204.
- **Michelin Map:** Local map 308 KB - Morbihan (56).
- **Info:** 6 quai de Rohan, 56100 Lorient. ℘02 97 84 78 00. www.lorient-tourisme.fr.
- **Location:** 69km/43mi SW of Brest, and 56km/35mi W of Vannes.
- **Kids:** La Thalassa; out of town, the **Pont-Scorff Zoo★**.
- **Timing:** Use the Batobus: very practical and pleasant "boat-buses".

VISIT

Ancien Arsenal – Until 2000, the naval dockyard was located in the former India Company's area; four docks were used for the repair of warships. The area is now being modernised.

Enclos du Port de Lorient – A tour of the dockyards recalls the heyday of the India Company.

La Thalassa – This ship, launched in 1960 by Ifremer, is enjoying retirement in Lorient.

Port de Pêche de Keroman – Partly reclaimed from the sea, the port of Keroman is the only French harbour designed and equipped for commercial fishing.

Base de Sous-marins Keroman★ – At the end of WWII, the French Navy took over the base for their Atlantic submarine operations, but have discontinued operations. The last active submarine left the base for Toulon in 1997.

EXCURSIONS

LARMOR-PLAGE

6km/3.7mi S of Lorient by the D 29.

Looking out over the ocean, across from Port-Louis, Larmor-Plage has lovely, fine, sandy beaches much appreciated by the people of Lorient.

PORT-LOUIS★

17km/10.5mi S of Lorient by road.

Port-Louis is a small fishing port and seaside resort popular with the inhabitants of Lorient. It still has its 16C citadel, 17C ramparts, as well as several interesting old houses.

The town also has two fishing harbours: Locmalo in Gâvres cove and, opposite Lorient, La Pointe, a marina equipped with 200 moorings for yachts.

HENNEBONT

17km/10.5mi NE of Lorient. Route passes through Lanester.

Hennebont is a former fortified town on the steep banks of the River Blavet. The 16C basilica, **Basilique Notre-Dame-de-Paradis**, has a big **bell tower★** and is surmounted by a steeple 65m high. At the base of the tower is a fine Flamboyant porch ornamented with niches leading into the nave, which is lit up by a stained-glass window by Max Ingrand.

KERNASCLÉDEN★★

The village is about 34km/21mi N of the coastal town of Lorient.

Built in granite 1430–1455, the **church★★** typifies the Breton version of Flamboyant Gothic. It has two **porches** on the south side (one with statues of the **Apostles★**). Inside there is a fine window at the east end. The **frescoes★★** are striking: the choir vault depicts 24 scenes from the Life of the Virgin.

Vannes★★

& the Golfe du Morbihan

Vannes is a pleasant city in the shape of an amphitheatre at the highest point to which tides flow at the head of the Morbihan Gulf. The picturesque old town, enclosed in its ramparts and grouped around the Cathedral, is a pedestrian zone where elegant shops have been established in old half-timbered town houses.

- **Population:** 52 515.
- **Michelin Map:** 308 O 9
- **Info:** quai Tabarly. ✆02 97 47 24 34. www.tourisme-vannes.com.
- **Location:** Vannes is a lively, popular resort on the SE coast of Brittany. The historic centre is by the cathedral and Pl. Henri IV.
- **Don't Miss:** A boat trip on the Gulf.
- **Kids:** Adults and kids will love the Aquarium du Golf.

A BIT OF HISTORY

In pre-Roman times, it was the capital of the **Veneti** tribe. One of Gaul's most powerful peoples, they were intrepid sailors, crossing the seas to trade with the inhabitants of the British Isles. They nevertheless suffered a terrible defeat at sea in 56 BCE at the hands of the Romans, losing 200 ships in a single day. As a result, Brittany's fate was to remain a backwater for a very long time. In the 9C, Vannes was where Breton unity was achieved under **Nominoé**, who made Vannes his capital.

WALKING TOUR

OLD TOWN★★

Vannes map, p269.

Surrounded by **ramparts★**, the area around the cathedral, the successor to a much more ancient place of worship, still has the air of a medieval town.

- **Place Gambetta** – This semicircular square, built in the 19C, frames Porte Saint-Vincent (St Vincent Gateway), which leads into the old town along a road of the same name, lined with beautiful 17C mansions.
- **Ramparts** – After crossing from the Promenade de la Garenne you will get a **view★★** of the most picturesque corner of Vannes.
- **La Cohue★** – This term (literally, a bustling crowd) is commonly used in Brittany to designate the market place.

  La Cohue Musée des Beaux-Arts – The beautifully restored building is now a museum, and offers visitors a permanent collection of 19C and contemporary paintings as well as religious sculpture.
- **Cathédrale St-Pierre★** – A robust granite construction. Note in particular the stained-glass windows and Renaissance **chapel★**.
- **Place Henri-IV★** – Walk along rue des Halles then rue St-Salomon with its old town houses to this picturesque square, lined with 16C gabled houses.
- **Musée d'Histoire et Archéologique de Morbihan★** – This museum occupies three floors of Château Gaillard (15C), which once contained Brittany's Parliament.
- **Maison de Saint Vincent-Ferrier** – In this house, remodelled in the 16C, Vincent Ferrier died in 1419. A fine example of a timber-framed house.
- **Maison de Vannes** – An old dwelling adorned with two carved wood busts of jovial peasants known as "Vannes and his wife."
- **Place des Lices** – This square used to be the tilt-yard, where tilts and tournaments were held in 1532, the year France and Brittany were united under one crown.

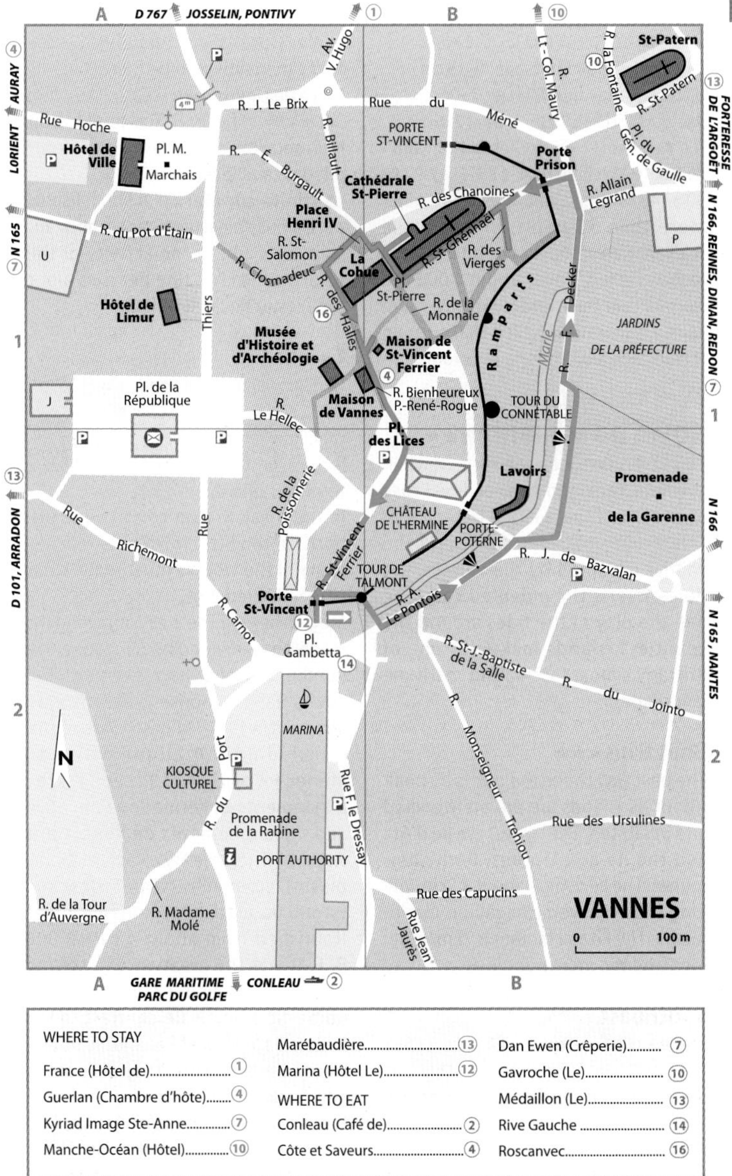

ADDITIONAL SIGHTS

Hôtel de Ville

pl. Maurice-Marchais. ✆02 97 01 60 00. www.mairie-vannes.fr.

This building in the Renaissance style, erected at the end of the 19C, stands in **place Maurice-Marchais**, which is adorned with a **statue** of the Constable de Richemont, one of the great figures of the 15C. It was he who created and commanded the French army which defeated the English at the end of the Hundred Years' War. He became Duke of Brittany in 1457, but died in 1458.

Aquarium du Golfe★

Parc du Golfe du Morbihan. Open daily: Jan–Mar and Oct–Dec 2–6pm; Apr–Jun and Sep 10am–noon, 2–6pm; Jul–Aug 9am–7.30pm. Closed 1 Jan and 25 Dec. €13 (children, 4–11, €9). 02 97 40 67 40. www.aquarium-du-golfe.com.

More than 50 pools, in which the relevant natural environment has been reconstructed, house about 1 000 fish from all over the world (cold seas, warm seas, freshwater), which make up an incredible kaleidoscope of colour.

EXCURSIONS

GOLFE DU MORBIHAN★★

This little inland sea was formed when the land sank and the sea level rose as a result of the melting of the great Quaternary glaciers, drowning the valleys occupied by the Vannes and Auray rivers. The indented coastline and the play of the tides around the countless **islands** make this one of Brittany's most fascinating maritime landscapes.

Boat trips★★★

The best way to see the gulf is by boat. About 40 islands are privately owned and inhabited. The largest are **Île d'Arz** and the **Île aux Moines**, both communes. The Île d'Arz is about 3.5km/2mi long and has several megalithic monuments. The Île aux Moines is 7km/4.3mi long and the most populous.

Southeast

Château de Suscinio★ – 30km/18.5mi S of Vannes by D 780. Sarzeau. This was once the summer residence of the Dukes of Brittany.

Port-Navalo★ – 40km/25mi SW Vannes by D 780. The little port and seaside resort guards the entrance to the Gulf. There are fine views.

West

Auray Port St Goustan★★ – 18.5km/11.4mi W of Vannes. **Ensemble Mégalithique de Locmariaquer★★** – 32km/20mi SW Vannes by N 165, D 28 and D 781. This group of megaliths is an important part of a programme of conservation and restoration of megalithic sites. Three megaliths can be found here.

Cairn de Gavrinis★★ – 16.5km/10mi SW of Vannes by D 101. This tumulus, 6m high and 50m round, is made of stones piled on a hillock.

La Trinité-sur-Mer★ – A small fishing port, a busy pleasure boat harbour and shipyards add to the activity of this resort, which has fine beaches along the Presqu'île de Kerbihan.

Carnac★

33km/20mi SW of Vannes by N 165, D 768 and D 119 at the base of the Quiberon Peninsula.

74 ave desDruides. 02 97 52 13 52. www.ot-carnac.fr.

In the bleak Breton countryside just north of the little town of Carnac are some of the world's most remarkable megalithic remains.

Megaliths★★ – The area containing the megaliths is divided up by roads and a number of stones have been lost, but altogether it comprises 2 792 menhirs, arranged in 10 or 11 lines – *alignements* – including the **alignements du Ménec★★** with 1 150 menhirs, the **alignements de Kermario★** with 1 029 and the **alignements de Kerlescan★** with 594. There are also dolmens (burial places), cromlechs (semicircles) and tumuli (mounds). Megalithic culture flourished from about 4 670–2 000 BCE. It was the creation of a settled population growing crops and with domestic animals (in contrast to the hunter-gatherers of Paleolithic times), who produced polished objects, pottery and basket-work and who traded in flints. The inhabitants of Carnac had commercial relations with people from Belgium and from Grand-Pressigny in the north of Poitou.

PRESQU'ÎLE DE QUIBERON★

45km/28mi SW of Vannes by N 165 and D 768.

Quiberon used to be an **island**, but over the years sand has accumulated north of Penthièvre Fort to form an isthmus linking it to the mainland. The peninsula's rocky and windswept western shore is known as the **Côte Sauvage** (Wild Coast), but to the east there are sheltered sandy beaches. The ferries for **Belle-Île★★** (see p272) leave from Quiberon harbour.

CHÂTEAU DE JOSSELIN★★

45km/28mi N of Vannes by D 778. The château is in the heart of the inland village of Josselin, W of Rennes, Place de la Congregation. Open Apr–Oct. €9 (children 7–14, €5.50). 02 97 22 36 45. www.chateaujosselin.fr.

This famous stronghold of the Rohan family, who have owned the castle for more than 500 years and still live here in the private apartments, has stood guard over the crossing of the Oust for 900 years and seen many battles.

ADDRESSES

STAY

Hôtel Le Marina – 4 Place Gambetta. 02 97 47 22 81. 14 rooms. Most of the rooms in this town-centre hotel have harbour views.

Chambre d'Hôte Guerlan – 56400 Plougoumelen. 12km/7.5mi W of Vannes on the N 165, exit Ploeren towards Mériadec then first right after 3.5km/2.2mi 02 97 57 65 50. Closed 10 Nov–10 Mar. 5 rooms. Imposing 18C building ideally placed to explore the Gulf of Morbihan.

Hôtel de France – 57 av. Victor Hugo. 02 97 47 27 57. www.hotelfrance-vannes.com. 30 rooms. Closed 21 Dec–5 Jan. Comfortable rooms near the town centre.

Hôtel Manche Océan – 31 rue du Lt.-Col.-Mauray. 02 97 47 26 46. www.manche-ocean.com. Closed 22 Dec–6 Jan. 42 rooms. Rooms in the heart of the town in this 1950s building.

Kyriad Vannes Centre – 8 pl. de la Libération. 0207 519 50 45. www.kyriad-vannes-centre.fr. 45 rooms. This central hotel offers comfortable rooms with air conditioning and sound insulation. The Breton-style restaurant provides a warm welcome and a traditional menu.

Marébaudière – 4 r. A.-Briand. 02 97 47 34 29. www.marebaudiere.com. 14 rooms. Five minutes on foot from the ramparts, this typical regional-style house has rooms decorated in blue, yellow and russet.

EAT

Crêperie Dan Ewen – 3 pl. du Gen.-de-Gaulle. 02 97 42 44 34. Closed one week in Feb and two weeks in Oct. Breton culture is cultivated with passion in this restaurant near the préfecture – old-style crêpes, antique furniture, Celtic music.

Café de Conleau – 10 allée des Frères-Cadoret. 02 97 63 47 47. www.le-roof.com. An annexe of the hotel serving a brasserie menu. Low prices in a pleasant setting.

Le Gavroche – 17 rue de laFontaine. 02 97 54 03 54. Closed Sun. Reservations advised. In a street filled with restaurants serving cuisine from around the world, here's one that stands out. Delicious traditional cuisine.

Côte et Saveurs – 8 r. Bienheureux-Pierre-René-Rogues. 02 97 47 21 94. Closed Wed Sep–Mar. The restaurant's name is well chosen as you can travel the world with the menu's exotic specialities such as ostrich steak with green pepper and red fruits.

Rive Gauche – 5 pl. Gambetta. 02 97 47 02 40. Ground floor restaurant with small wooden tables and fabric tablecloths in a charming bourgeoise house located on the port. Menus and winelist on blackboard.

Le Médaillon – 10 rue Bouruet-Aubertot, 56610 Arradon. 02 97 44 77 28. http://lemedaillon.chez-alice.fr. Closed 21–27 Dec, Sun eve, Tue eve and Wed except 14 Jul–31 Aug. Don't be put off by the plain exterior of this restaurant; inside is a rustic dining room with beams and stonework and a terrace.

Roscanvec – 17 rue des Halles. 02 97 47 15 96. www.roscanvec.com. Closed Sun eve and Mon (exc school hols). Reservations advised. In a half-timbered house in the old town, the wonderful cuisine here is no-nonsense, with a menu that ranges from oysters with jelly of pork feet to caviar.

Belle-Île★★★

The name alone is enticing, but the island's beauty surpasses expectations. This, the largest of the Breton islands, is a schist plateau measuring about 84sq km/32sq mi; 17km/10.5mi long and 5–10km/3–6mi wide. Valleys cut deep into the high rocks, forming beaches and harbours. Farmland alternates with wild heath, and whitewashed houses stand in lush fields.

- **Population:** 4 489
- **Michelin Map:** 308 L-M 10-11
- **Info:** quai Bonnelle, Le Palais. ✆02 40 08 97 97. www.belle-ile.com.
- **Location:** Regular car ferries linking Quibéron (Brittany) and Le Palais in 45min are operated by SMN (✆08 20 05 60 00. www.navix.fr). Passenger-only speedboats operate in summer between Le Palais and Lorient (Brittany) in 60min. Access from La Trinité in summer. Perfect for a day trip, but hire a car locally if you intend to stay longer.

SIGHTS

Le Palais

This is the island's capital, known to locals simply as "Palais". Most of the island's amenities are to be found here. The natural harbour is dominated by the imposing citadel and fortifications, known as **Citadelle Vauban★**. The proximity of Belle-Île to the ports of the south coast of Brittany and the mouth of the Loire gave it great importance in the fight for the control of the high seas conducted by England and France. In 1658 the island came into the hands of chancellor Fouquet. He consolidated the defences and installed 200 new batteries.

From 1682, the great military engineer **Vauban** adapted the citadel following improvements in the technology of war, converting an old chapel into a powder-magazine with a projecting roof to fend off broadsides, rebuilding the old arsenal as well as laying out an officers' walk with a gallery giving fine seaviews.

Côte Sauvage★★★

The Côte Sauvage, literally "wild coast", runs from the Pointe des Poulains to the Pointe de Talud. Battered by the Atlantic waves, the schists of which the island's plateau is composed have been formed into spectacular coastal scenes. **Port-Donnant★★** has a splendid sandy beach between high cliffs, but is known for its great rollers and perilous currents. The **Aiguilles de Port-Coton★★** are pyramids hollowed out into caverns and grottoes. The different colours of the rock have been exposed by the action of the sea. **Sauzon★** is a small port with a busy marina lying in a pretty **setting★** on the east bank of the River Sauzon's estuary. At **Pointe des Poulains★★** a sandy isthmus connects the island with the Pointe des Poulains on which stands a lighthouse and which is completely cut off at spring tide. **Port-Goulphar★** is a long, narrow channel at the foot of picturesque cliffs.

ADDRESSES

STAY

€€ Hôtel- Restaurant de Bretagne – Quai Macé, Le Palais 56 360. ✆02 97 31 80 14. www.hotel-de-bretagne.fr. Open all year. 32 rooms. This impressive hotel with its splendid mansard roof stands proudly on the quayside overlooking the pier.

EAT

Le Palais has plenty of restaurants.

€€€ Roz Avel – 56360 Sauzon. ✆02 97 31 61 48. Closed 1 Jan–15 Mar, 11 Nov–15 Dec and Wed. Reservations obligatory. Behind the church, this traditional old house filled with Breton furniture is well loved by locals who like to catch rays on the terrace or enjoy seafood in the dining room.

Nantes★★★

Nantes is Brittany's largest city, sited at the point at which the Loire becomes tidal. The presence of islets (inhabited from the 17C on) in the river had long facilitated the building of bridges, making Nantes the focus of trade and movement between Lower Brittany and Poitou.

- **Population:** 284 970.
- **Michelin Map:** 316 G 4
- **Info:** 3 cours Olivier de Clisson. ℘08 92 46 40 44. www.nantes-tourisme.com.
- **TGV:** Just over 2hrs from Paris Montparnasse.
- **Flights:** Nantes Atlantiques airport (www.nantes.aeroport.fr), operates an airport shuttle that takes you to the heart of the city in just 20 minutes (€8).
- **Location:** Three tramway lines and over 60 bus routes make for easy movement throughout the city.
- **Timing:** You'll need at least 3hr to visit the château and the surrounding sights.
- **Parking:** It is not easy to move around Nantes by car. Find parking in one of several lots surrounding the central area and move around the city by tramway, bus or foot.
- **Don't Miss:** Find a bar or restaurant in the Ste-Croix neighbourhood for an authentic Nantes evening.
- **Kids:** Planète Sauvage at Port-St-Père.

A BIT OF HISTORY

In the 9C the city was disputed between the first Duke of Brittany, and the Franks to the east. In 939 it was chosen as his capital by King Alain Barbe-Torte (Crookbeard). By the 14C, Nantes had become a trading port, with a fleet of 1 300 ships, but it was only in the 15C, under Duke François II, that the city reached its full importance.

It was in its cathedral, on 13 April 1598, that Henri IV signed the **Edict of Nantes**, establishing equality between Catholics and Protestants. Louis XIV revoked the Edict in 1685, provoking the Huguenot exodus to England, Holland and Germany and depriving France of some of its most valuable craftsmen.

In the early 18C Nantes grew rich on trade, including slavery. Nantes became France's premier port until the loss of French territories abroad and the abolition of slavery.

Château des Ducs de Bretagne

WHERE TO STAY

- Coin chez soi (Un)........ 12
- Graslin (Hôtel)........ 4
- Ibis Styles Place Centre Royale........ 7
- Ibis Styles Centre Place Graslin........ 2
- Petit-Port (Camping Le)........ 9
- Pommeraye (Hôtel)........ 10

WHERE TO EAT

- Amour de Pomme de Terre........ 1
- Atlantide (L')........ 4
- Café Cult' (Le)........ 7
- Chez l'Huître........ 11
- Cigale (La)........ 13
- Embellie (L')........ 17
- Enfants Terribles (Le Bistrot des)........ 19
- Heb-Ken (Crêperie)........ 21
- Montesquieu (Le)........ 22
- Paludier (Le)........ 3
- Tim Fish........ 2

STREET INDEX

- Bouffay (Pl. du)........ 1
- Flesselles (Allées)........ 3
- Fosse (R. de la)........ 5
- Kervégan (R.)........ 7
- Paix (R. de la)........ 9
- Petite-Hollande (Pl. de la)........ 11
- Pré-Nian (R.)........ 13
- St-Léonard (R.)........ 15
- St-Vincent (Pl.)........ 17
- Ste-Croix (Pl.)........ 19

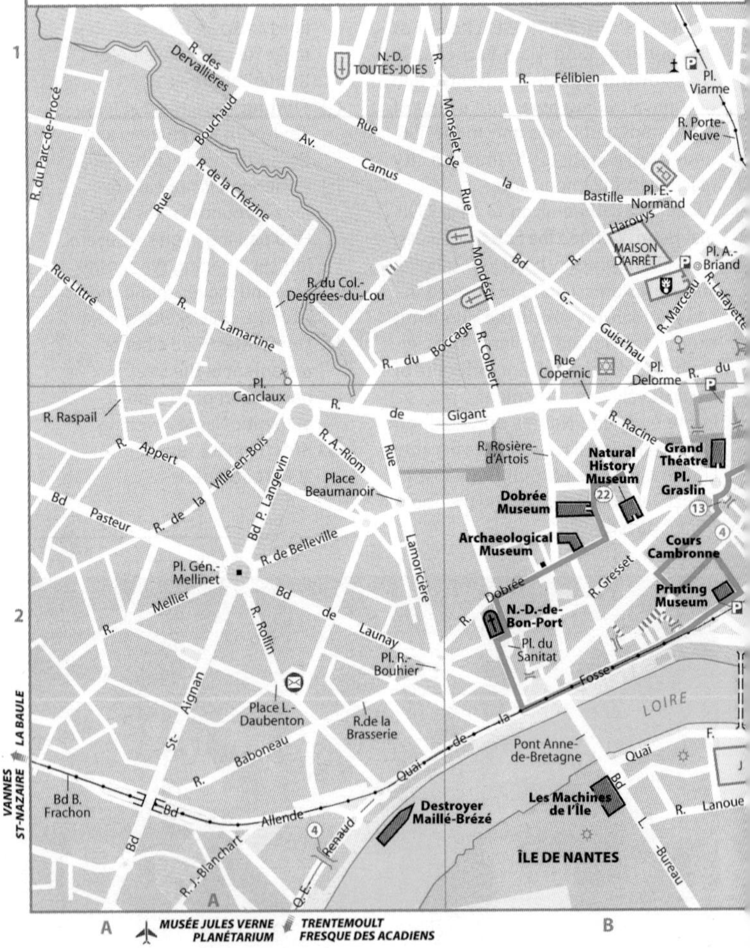

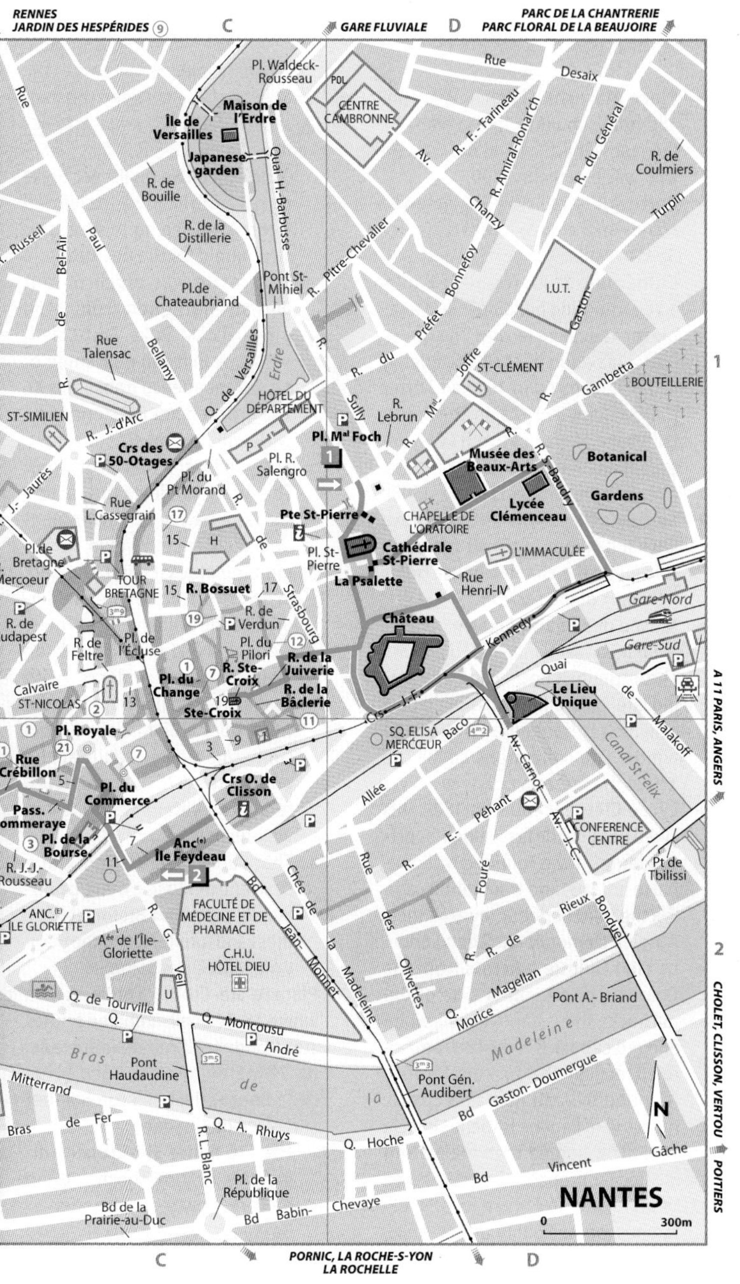
RENNES
JARDIN DES HESPÉRIDES
GARE FLUVIALE
PARC DE LA CHANTRERIE
PARC FLORAL DE LA BEAUJOIRE
Maison de l'Erdre
Île de Versailles
Japanese garden
CENTRE CAMBRONNE
Musée des Beaux-Arts
Botanical Gardens
Lycée Clémenceau
Cathédrale St-Pierre
La Psalette
Château
Le Lieu Unique
Pl. Mal Foch
Pte St-Pierre
Crs des 50-Otages
R. Bossuet
Pl. du Change
Ste-Croix
R. Ste-Croix
R. de la Juiverie
R. de la Bâclerie
Pl. Royale
Rue Crébillon
Pl. du Commerce
Pass. Pommeraye
Pl. de la Bourse
Crs O. de Clisson
Anc. Île Feydeau
FACULTÉ DE MÉDECINE ET DE PHARMACIE
C.H.U. HÔTEL DIEU
CONFERENCE CENTRE
Gare-Nord
Gare-Sud
Canal St Félix
A 11 PARIS, ANGERS
CHOLET, CLISSON, VERTOU
POITIERS
PORNIC, LA ROCHE-S-YON
LA ROCHELLE
NANTES
0
300m

WALKING TOUR

1 AROUND THE CASTLE★★

Nantes map, p274–275. Allow 3hrs.

- **Place Maréchal-Foch** – Two fine 18C hotels, built from the plans by Ceineray, flank the Louis XVI Column that was erected in 1790.
- **Porte St-Pierre** – This 15C gateway stands on the remains of a 3C Gallo-Roman wall.
- **Cathédrale St-Pierre-et-St-Paul★** – This imposing building is remarkable for its austere façade. The cathedral was begun in 1434, completed in 1893, restored in 1930 and after fire damage in 1972. In the south transept of the cathedral is the exceptionally fine tomb of François II (**tombeau de François II★★** – 1502).
- **La Psalette** – This 15C building with a polygonal turret formerly contained the chapter-house but is now part of the sacristy.
- **Musée des Beaux Arts★★** – Open Wed–Mon 10am–6pm, Thu until 8pm. The museum is housed in an imposing late-19C building, the main part of which is flanked by projecting wings. The collections cover the 13C to the present.
- **Lycée Clemenceau** – In 1886 this Lycée became the first French "sports academy". It was founded by Bonaparte in 1803, and then rebuilt during the third Republic, by architects Antoine Demoget and Léon Lenoir.
- **Le Lieu Unique** – Across from the Château, on the other side of the rail tracks, there stands a blue, white and red cupola. It is the last remaining trace of the biscuit factory founded by Jean Romain Lefèvre, husband of Pauline Isabelle Utile, in 1885. They joined their initials and created Lu, probably the best known of all bicuits in France, especially famous for the Petit Beurre. In 1986, the machinery moved to premises south of town. In 1999 the former factory was redesigned by architect Patrick Bouchain and renamed Lieu Unique.
- **Château des Ducs de Bretagne** – 4 pl. Marc-Elder. Open (museum): daily except Mon 10am–6pm (Jul–Aug 9am–7pm). Closed 1 Jan, 1 May, 1 Nov and 25 Dec. €5 (access to the courtyard, moat and ramparts is free). ♿ ✆02 51 17 49 48. www.chateau-nantes.fr.

  "God's teeth! No small beer, these dukes of Brittany!" exclaimed Henri IV on seeing this massive stronghold for the first time.

  The castle was much rebuilt and strengthened from 1466 onwards by Duke François II who saw in it the guarantee of his independence from Louis XI. The great edifice is defended by wide moats, and six stout towers with Breton machicolations. The interior reflects the castle's role as a palace of government and residence, known for its high life of feasts and jousting. Many of its features are of interest, like the Golden Crown Tower (Tour de la Couronne d'oraa), the main building (Grand Logis) with its massive dormer windows, the Governor's Major Palace (Grand Gouvernement) rebuilt at the end of the 17C, and the well (puits★★) with its wrought-iron well-head.

  There are two museums in the castle: the Musée d'Art populaire★ featuring Breton coiffes, dress and furniture, and the maritime Musée des Salorges.
- **Plateau Ste-Croix** – This is an area where 15–16C half-timbered houses still stand: no. 7 rue de la Juiverie, no. 7 rue Ste-Croix, nos. 8 and 10 rue de la Boucherie, no. 5 rue Bossuet and place du Change.

  The 17C **Église Ste-Croix** is surmounted by the former town **belfry★** crowned with angels.

  Bars and restaurants liven up the district in the evening and pavement cafés welcome visitors.

WALKING TOUR

2 OLD NANTES

Nantes map, p274–275. Allow 3hrs.

- **Ancienne Île Feydeau★** – Between 1926 and 1938 the islet was linked to the mainland and a second island, the Île Gloriette, by filling in several arms of the Loire. The islet has retained its 18C appearance, especially between place de la Petite Hollande and cours Olivier-de-Clisson (number 4 was the birthplace of Jules Verne).

  It was here that rich shipowners used to build their vast mansions, which stretch from the central street, rue Kervégan, right back to one of the outer avenues, allées Turenne or Duguay-Trouin.
- **Quartier Graslin★** – It was the financier Graslin, Receiver General for farmlands at Nantes, who was responsible for the creation of this area in the late 18C.

  The Stock Exchange, built in 1811–13, stands on place du Commerce.

  Opening onto rue Santeuil is a curious stepped shopping arcade on three levels, **Passage Pommeraye★**, built in 1843.

  Place Graslin – Narrow and busy, Rue Crébillon is very lively. It is the hub for taking a stroll in the town. It leads to a fine esplanade which houses the Corinthian theatre dating from 1783. La Cigale brasserie is classed as a national monument and has a fine 19C interior with mosaics. Just further on is Cambronne Square, created by Mathurin Crucy. Fine Napoléon I houses flank the square.
- **Musée de l'Imprimerie** – The history of printing.
- **Quai de la Fosse** – Several 18C mansions line this quay (numbers 17, 54, 70), including number 86, Hôtel Durbé, whose outbuildings served as a warehouse for the India Company.

Un bon vin blanc

This expression, well known for being part of a phonetics exercise for Anglo-Saxon learners of French – literally "a fine white wine" – adequately describes the local **Muscadet**, dry but not too sharp, perfect with seafood. The vineyards are located to the south and east of Nantes, alongside or near the Sèvre and towards **Ancenis** on the banks of the Loire.

- Opposite quai de la Fosse, the **île Beaulieu**, renamed île de Nantes, is subject to a vast programme of urbanisation. The architect Jean Nouvel is responsible for the new glass and concrete law courts (palais de justice).
- **Église Notre-Dame-de-Bon-Port** – Also known as Église St-Louis, this unusual building overlooks Place Sanitat. The great cubic mass (1846–58) is adorned by frescoes and a triangular pediment supported by massive hexagonal pillars and topped by a majestic dome decorated with panels of stained glass and frescoes.
- **Musée Archéologique★** – Archaeological museum featuring prehistoric, Greek, Etruscan, Egyptian, Gallo-Roman and Norse artefacts.
- **Musée Dobrée★** – This Romanesque-style mansion was built in the 19C by the Nantes shipowner and collector Thomas Dobrée (1810–95). Romanesque, Gothic and Chinese collections
- **Muséum d'Histoire Naturelle ★★** – 12 rue Voltaire. Open Wed–Mon 10am–6pm. Closed public holidays. €3.50 (under 18, no charge), no charge on 1st Sun of every month (Sept–Jun). 02 40 41 55 00. www.museum.nantes.fr. Originally set up in the Cabinet Dubuisson in 1799, this Natural History Museum was moved to the former Mint (Hôtel de la Monnaie).

EXCURSIONS

PLANÈTE SAUVAGE★★

20km/12.4mi SW, on D 758.
www.planetesauvage.com.

This safari park at the heart of the Pays de Retz has over 1 500 animals roaming free in its 140ha/350-acre enclosure. The visit includes two circuits: one to be toured on foot, the other by car.

ST-NAZAIRE★

62km/39mi W of Nantes.

A visit to St-Nazaire, which is above all a great ship-building centre, is well worthwhile. Originally a small fishing port in the 15C, the town developed rapidly in 1856, when large ships, finding it difficult to sail up to Nantes, stopped at its deep-water port. Rebuilt in 1945 in the plainest fashion, St-Nazaire is nevertheless worth seeing for its port where everything is spectacular: the former submarine base, Escal'Atlantic, the museum show devoted to transatlantic sea journeys of bygone days and the docks where the world's largest liners are built.

LA BAULE★★

The resort stands on the N bank of the wide Loire estuary. It is reached on autoroute A11 and then by expressway from Nantes. 8 pl. de la Victoire. 02 40 24 34 44. www.labaule.fr.

Perhaps the ultimate in modern seafront development on the French Atlantic, the resort of La Baule is today one of Europe's major resorts and considered to have one of its most beautiful beaches. It was only in 1879 that construction of the town began, after 400ha/1 000 acres of maritime pines had been planted to halt the steady encroachment of sand dunes.

The older houses retain much of their original charm and stand mostly hidden behind the more recent constructions along the shaded and well laid-out avenues. Water-sports, tennis, a casino and golf make this one of the most popular seaside resorts on the Atlantic coast.

Many kilometres of beautiful sandy beaches are protected by the headlands, **Pointes de Penchâteau** and **Chémoulin** to the northwest and southeast respectively. The elegant promenade lined with modern buildings stretches for 7km/4.3mi.

Numerous hotels and apartment complexes, some comfortable, others luxurious, in the proximity of delightful resorts such as **Le Croisica**, **Le Pouliguen★** and **Pornichet★**, with their pleasure-boat harbours, make La Baule, together with its neighbour **La Baule-les-Pins★★**, the ideal spot for discovering the splendour of the **"Côte d'Amour"** and the **Guérande Peninsula**.

La Côte Sauvage

This Wild Coast is on the mainland (the other is on Belle-Île, *see BELLE-ÎLE, p272*) and stretches from Pointe du Croisic in the west to Pointe de Penchâteau in the east. Skirted by a road and footpaths, the coastline alternates rocky parts with great sandy bays and numerous caves accessible only at low tide such as the cave of the Korrigans, the little elves of Breton legends.

PRESQU'ÎLE DE GUÉRANDE★

88km/55mi W of Nantes.

In the Roman era, a gulf stretched between the island, **Île de Batz**, and the Guérande ridge. Just a channel remains open opposite **Le Croisic★** through which the sea flows at high tide.

Guérande★

The town lies behind the beach resort of La Baule. 1 pl. du Marché au Bois. 08 20 15 00 44. www.ot-guerande.fr.

Standing on a plateau overlooking the salt marshes and secure behind its circle of ramparts, Guérande has kept its appearance as a medieval town.

Ramparts★ – Begun in 1343, the ramparts were completed in 1476 and remain unbreached. They were flanked by six towers and pierced by four fortified gateways.

Collégiale St-Aubin★ – Built between the 12C and the 16C, the church has a striking west front in granite. Embedded in a buttress is an **outdoor pulpit**. Inside, the **capitals** are decorated with grotesque figures and foliage.

ADDRESSES

NANTES

STAY

Camping Le Petit Port – 21 bd du Petit-Port, Bord du Cens. ☎02 40 74 47 94. www.nge-nantes.fr/camping. Reservation advised. 200 pitches. The campsite has 200 pitches for tents, caravans and campervans just minutes from the town. Free access to the swimming pool in Petit Port for campers.

Hotel Ibis Styles Place Centre Royale – 3 r. Couëdic. ☎02 40 35 74 50. www.accorhotels.com. 65 rooms. Near the place Royale, this hotel has modern rooms (flat screen TV, internet), with a view of neighbouring rooftops from upper floors.

Hôtel Pommeraye – 2 r. Boileau. ☎02 40 48 78 79. www.hotel-pommeraye.com. 50 rooms. Close to the well known Passage Pommeraye and rue Crébillon's shops, lovers of contemporary design will delight in this hotel which is classified as a Clef Verte venue.

Hôtel Graslin – 1 r. Piron. ☎02 40 69 72 91. 47 rooms. This hotel offers two types of accommodation. Choose either the Art Deco style rooms or the traditional pine furnished ones.

Un coin chez soi – 1 r. de Briord. ☎06 14 57 22 41. www.uncoinchezsoi.net. This hotel offers an alternative to a traditional hotel as it consists of private apartments situated in the town centre which can accommodate 2–4 persons. Immaculate decoration.

Hotel Ibis Styles Centre Place Graslin – 5 rue du Chapeau Rouge. ☎02 40 48 79 76. 40 rooms. The breakfast room at this contemporary hotel serves as an exhibition space for local artists.

EAT

Crêperie Heb-Ken – 5 r. de Guérande. ☎02 40 48 79 03. www.heb-ken.fr. Closed 20 Jul–19 Aug, Sun and public hols. Reasonable prices for crêpes.

Tim Fish – 4 r. de l'Arche Sèche. ☎02 40 47 11 46. http://timfish.unblog.fr. Closed Mon–Wed eve and Sun. This small restaurant has developed a new way of tasting seafood. The assortment of fresh seasonal fish is served in a buckwheat cornet with vegetables.

Amour de Pomme de Terre – 4 rue des Halles. ☎02 40 47 66 37. www.amourdepommedeterre.fr. The potato reigns here in all its forms: as an accompaniment to grills or raclettes…

Le Café Cult' – 2 pl. du Change. ☎02 40 47 18 49. http://cafe-cult.com. Closed two weeks in Aug and Sun. Take a trip back in time as you admire the façade of this 15C Nantes house, then open the door to discover its medieval interior where history inspires the food.

La Cigale – 4 pl. Graslin. ☎02 51 84 94 94. www.lacigale.com. With its listed tiles dating from 1900, which have appeared in several films, this atmospheric, animated brasserie is a favourite of the locals. A great place to come for market-fresh plats du jour and weekend brunches.

Le Bistrot des Enfants Terribles – 4 rue Fénelon. ☎02 40 47 00 38. Closed Sat lunch, Sun and Mon. Reservations advised. Cosy restaurant where the dining room has fireplaces dating from the 16C and 17C, mirrors and benches. The caramelised pigs' cheeks, house terrines and St-Jacques (scallops) with mushroom sauce are delicious.

Chez l'Huître – 5 rue des Petites-Écuries. ☎02 51 82 02 02. Closed 23 Dec–15 Jan and Sun except from 15 Jun–15 Sep. Lovers of seafood are going to like this place, which has several varieties of oyster on offer.

Le Montesquieu – 1 r. Montesquieu. ☎02 40 73 06 69. www.lemontesquieu.fr. Mon–Fri noon–2pm and Wed–Sat 7pm–10.30pm. Authentic cuisine near to the Musée Dobrée.

Le Paludier – 2 r. de Santeuil. ☎02 40 69 44 06. Closed Mon and Sat lunch, Sun and three weks August. Restaurant dedicated to seafood.

L'Atlantide – Quai Ernest-Renaud. ☎02 40 73 23 23. www.restaurant-atlantide.net. Closed 20–23 May, 31 Jul–30 Aug, Sat lunch, Sun and holidays. A contemporary dining room with Japanese influences on the fourth floor of this modern building. Views over the Loire and city.

L'Embellie – 14 r. Armand Brossard. ☎02 40 48 20 02. www.restaurantlembellie.com. Closed Aug, Sun and Mon. Close to the Anne de Bretagne tower. Dishes prepared with care.

Châteaux of the Loire

» Region map p282–283
Angers p284
Saumur p293
Tours p298
Blois p304
Orléans p309

Introduction

Rising far to the southeast in the Massif Central, France's longest river, the Loire, was once a busy waterway. Many of the towns along its banks bear traces of this former activity: from Orléans, once the Loire's foremost port, Blois, Tours, Langeais and Saumur. As with other great rivers, navigation was never easy and, once the railways came, the Loire was left to its caprices. Nowadays the region is famous for its magnificent Renaissance châteaux, which adorn the banks of the Loire's tributaries, the Indre and the Cher.

Geography – This "garden of France", as the Loire valley has been called, has also been described as "a home-spun cloak with golden fringes", a reference to the contrast between the fertile valleys of the Loire and the low plâteaux that separate them.
History – Following the withdrawal of the Romans the Franks occupied the region. Viking incursions affected Tours and Angers during the 9C, but until the 12C most of the area was held by powerful barons. After 1202 King Philippe-Auguste was able to take charge following the seizure of the territory from King John of England. In the late medieval period the region was involved in the Hundred Years' War with much of the Loire falling into English hands again. During the 16C, however, the great château-building period began as new ways of thinking about art and architecture were ushered in by the Renaissance at Chenonceau, Azay, Blois and Chambord. Their elegance and architectural exuberance contrasted with the sterner fortresses of an earlier age, like the great castle at Angers. Other buildings have white tufa walls and slate roofs; around Amboise and Tours are troglodytic dwellings.
Economy – The Loire valley is a major agricultural region. Manufacturing is important, with the production of car parts and tyres made possible partly by excellent communications. Tourism, also vitally important, is based on the châteaux and the great cathedrals of Orléans and Tours.

Highlights

1. Exceptional tapestry of Angers' **Tenture de l'Apocalypse** (p284)
2. Château partly built on a bridge: **Chenonceau** (p300)
3. French Gothic style: **d'Azay le Rideau** (p302)
4. Formal gardens (Jardins) at **Villandry** (p302)
5. First of France's Classical palaces: **Chambord** (p306)

Gardens and Château de Villandry © J Moreno Arco / age fotostock

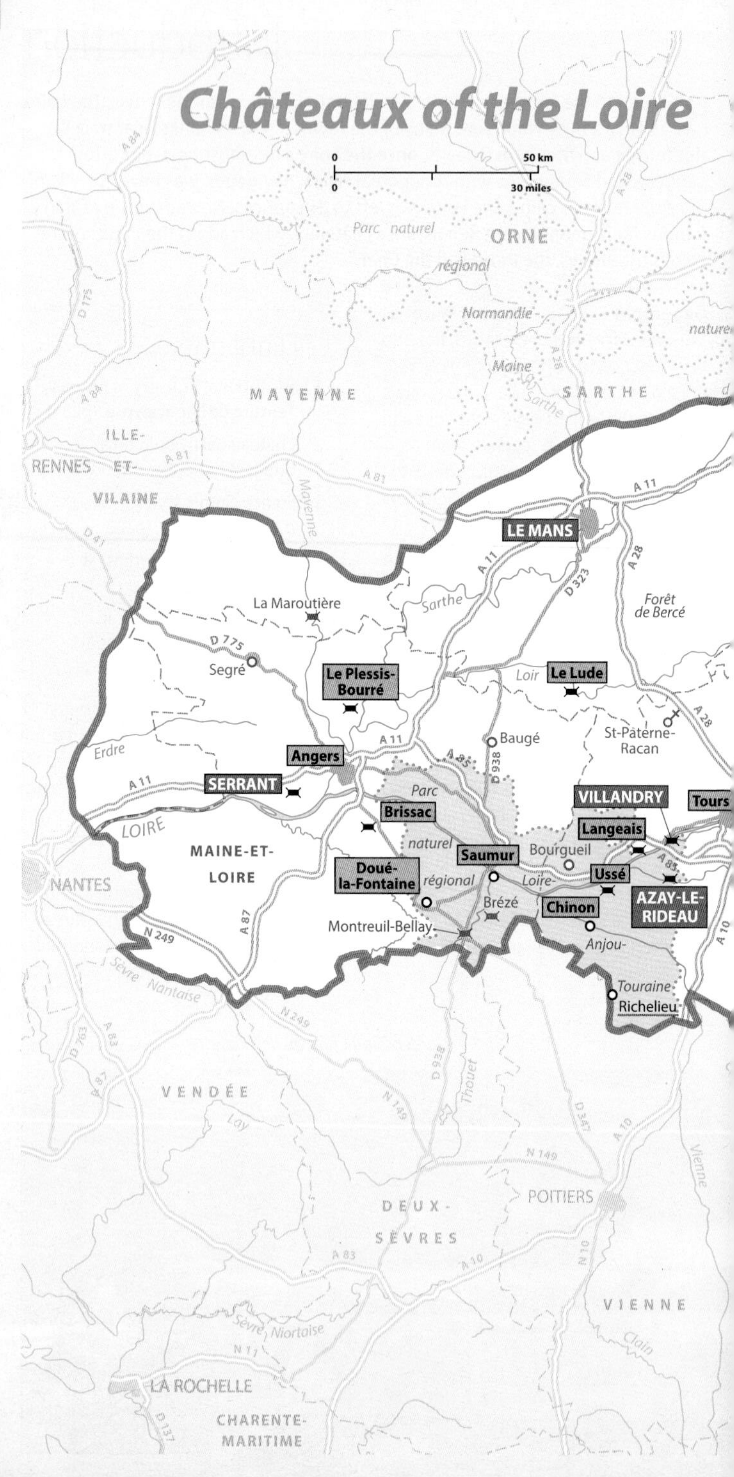
Châteaux of the Loire
0
50 km
0
30 miles
Parc naturel
régional
Normandie-
Maine
ORNE
MAYENNE
SARTHE
ILLE-
RENNES
ET-
VILAINE
LE MANS
Forêt
de Bercé
La Maroutière
Segré
Le Plessis-
Bourré
Le Lude
Baugé
St-Paterne-
Racan
Angers
SERRANT
Brissac
Parc
naturel
régional
VILLANDRY
Tours
Langeais
Bourgueil
Saumur
Ussé
AZAY-LE-
RIDEAU
Chinon
Doué-
la-Fontaine
Brézé
Montreuil-Bellay
Anjou-
Touraine
Richelieu
MAINE-ET-
LOIRE
NANTES
VENDÉE
DEUX-
SÈVRES
POITIERS
VIENNE
LA ROCHELLE
CHARENTE-
MARITIME

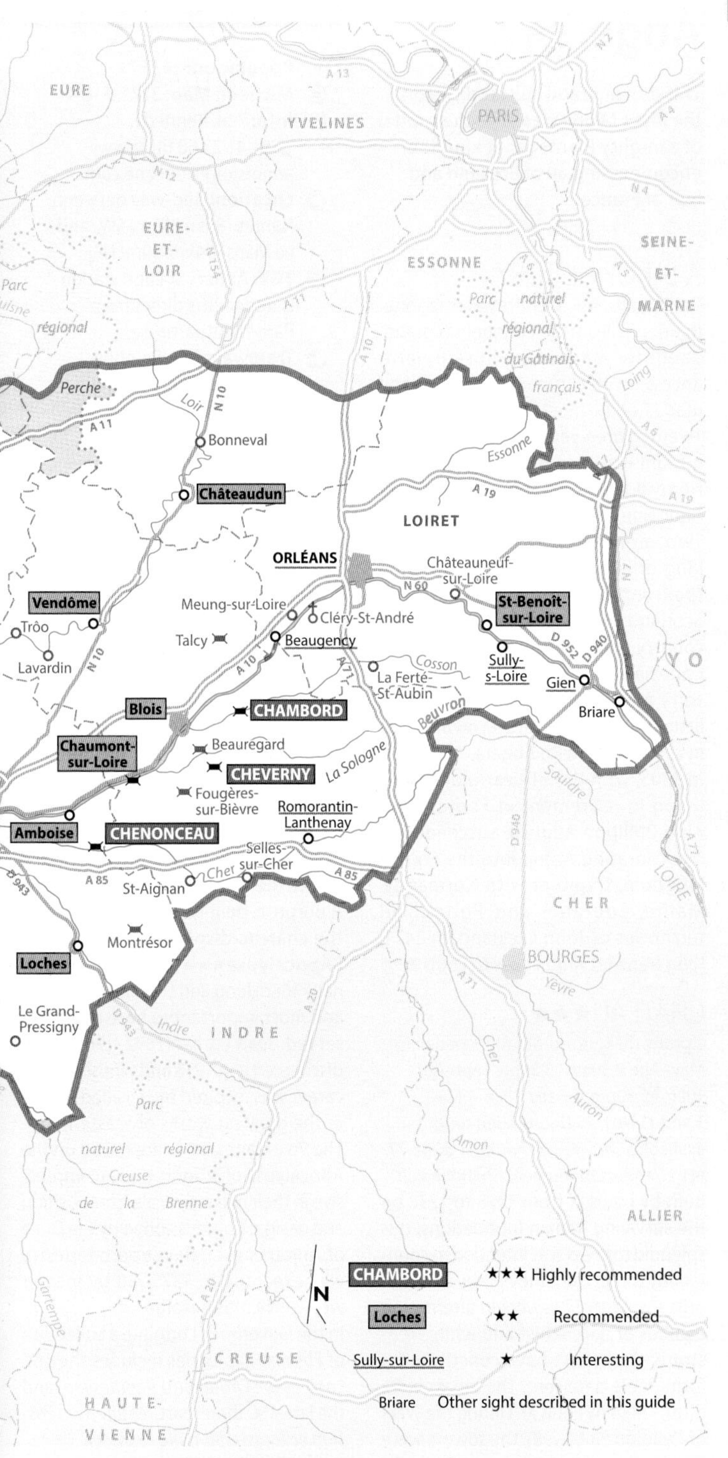
EURE
YVELINES
PARIS
EURE-ET-LOIR
ESSONNE
SEINE-ET-MARNE
Parc naturel régional du Gâtinais français
Perche
Bonneval
Châteaudun
LOIRET
ORLÉANS
Châteauneuf-sur-Loire
St-Benoît-sur-Loire
Meung-sur-Loire
Cléry-St-André
Vendôme
Trôo
Lavardin
Talcy
Beaugency
Sully-s-Loire
Gien
Briare
La Ferté-St-Aubin
Blois
CHAMBORD
Chaumont-sur-Loire
Beauregard
CHEVERNY
La Sologne
Fougères-sur-Bièvre
Romorantin-Lanthenay
Amboise
CHENONCEAU
Selles-sur-Cher
St-Aignan
Montrésor
Loches
Le Grand-Pressigny
INDRE
CHER
BOURGES
ALLIER
CREUSE
HAUTE-VIENNE
Parc naturel régional de la Brenne
N
CHAMBORD ★★★ Highly recommended
Loches ★★ Recommended
Sully-sur-Loire ★ Interesting
Briare Other sight described in this guide

Angers★★

This dynamic and cultured city on the River Maine was once the capital of a mighty Plantagenet kingdom encompassing all of England and half of France.

- **Population:** 147 571.
- **Michelin Map:** 317 E-F-G 4
- **Info:** 7 pl. Kennedy. ℘02 41 23 50 00. www.angersloiretourisme.com.
- **Location:** mid-way between Nantes (88km/55mi SW) and Le Mans (94km/59mi NE).
- **TGV:** Angers St Laud station is under 2hrs direct from Paris Montparnasse.
- **Tramway:** The 'Rainbow' tram system links many tourist sites across the greater Angers region.
- **Parking:** Parking is available by the château on Esplanade du Port-Ligny.
- **Don't Miss:** The 14C Tenture de l'Apocalypse.
- **Timing:** After visiting the château (2hr), allow at least half a day for the Old Town. A fun way to discover the city is a tour on the Petit Train. There are also taxi tours, and city tours on foot.

A BIT OF HISTORY

On 9 June 1129, Geoffrey Plantagenet married William the Conqueror's granddaughter Mathilda, whose inheritance of both Normandy and England made her the most desirable of brides. Twenty-three years later another significant marriage took place, between Henry II, Geoffrey's son, and Eleanor of Aquitaine, the divorced wife of Louis VII. Two months later Henry became king of England, thereby extending the frontiers of the Angevin state to Scotland in the north and the Basque country in the south. By contrast, the Capetian kingdom to the east cut a sorry figure; its capital, Paris, seemed little more than an overgrown village in comparison with Angers.

In 1203, with the 81-year-old Eleanor living in retirement at Fontevraud, King Philippe Auguste succeeded in incorporating Anjou into the French kingdom, together with Normandy, Maine, Touraine and Poitou, all territories of John Lackland. In 1471, King **René** let Anjou pass to Louis XI.

CHÂTEAU★★★

2 prom. du Bout-du-Monde. Open daily: May–Aug 9.30am–6.30pn; Sept–Apr 10am–5.30pm. Closed 1 Jan, 1 May, 1 and 11 Nov, 25 Dec. Guided tours available (2hr). €8.50. ℘02 41 86 48 77. http://angers.monuments-nationaux.fr.

Built by Louis IX from 1228 to 1238 on the surviving Roman foundations, this splendid fortress was intended to counter any threat from the nearby Dukes of Brittany. With 17 towers in alternating courses of dark schist and white freestone, they must have constituted a formidable deterrent. The moats were dug in 1485 by Louis XI. During the Wars of Religion (1562–98), the towers were reduced in height and terraces added to give the defenders a clear field of fire.

A purpose-built gallery at the heart of the château displays the **Tenture de l'Apocalypse★★★**, a tapestry, originally 168m long and 5m high, the oldest and most important to have been preserved. Jean Lurçat (1892–1966), who discovered it in 1938 and whose artistic career was inspired by it, called it "one of the greatest works of Western art". The 76 extant scenes are based on the Apocalypse of St John, and are impressive in their masterly scale, composition and design. Commissioned by the Duke of Anjou Louis I, this superb tapestry was executed in 1375–80 by master weaver **Nicolas Bataille**.

In the Governor's Lodging, a collection of Flemish tapestries includes the 16C *Lady at the Organ* and *Penthesilea*, and the late-15C three-part *Tenture de la Passion et Tapisseries mille-fleurs*★★.

Château d'Angers

© Liane Matrisch/Dreamstime.com

WALKING TOUR

OLD TOWN★

Angers map, p286. Allow a half day.

Walking through the streets of the old town is like visiting an open-air museum. If the weather is nice, you can enjoy a pleasant break for a picnic lunch in the Jardin des Plantes.

- **Hôtel du Croissant** – This 15C mansion, with mullion windows and ogee arches, housed the registrar of the Order of the Crescent (Ordre du Croissant), a military and religious chivalrous order founded by King René.
- **Cathédrale St-Maurice★** – The cathedral is a fine 12–13C building. The Calvary standing to the left of the façade is the work of David d'Angers. Inside, the cathedral is majestically furnished. Note the chancel's 13C stained **glass★★**, which has vivid blues and reds.
- **Maison d'Adam★** – This 16C half-timbered house has posts decorated with numerous carved figures. It owes its name to the apple tree which appears to hold up the corner turret and which was flanked by statues of Adam and Eve until the Revolution.
- **Galerie David-d'Angers★** – The gallery in this restored 13C abbey church houses the vast majority of plaster casts donated by the sculptor David d'Angers (1788–1856) to his native town.
- **Musée des Beaux-Arts★★** – This beautiful late-15C residence housing a Fine Arts Museum was built by Olivier Barrault, the King's Secretary, Treasurer to the Brittany States and Mayor of Angers. In the 17C it was taken over by the seminary, whose pupils included Talleyrand, the future Bishop of Autun. On the first floor are archaeological collections evoking the history of Anjou from the 12C to the 14C, including the 16C terracotta Virgin of Tremblay. The second floor is devoted to paintings.
- **Tour St-Aubin** – This is the belfry (12C) of the former St-Aubin monastery, a wealthy Benedictine abbey founded in the 6C.
- **Monastery buildings★** – The abbey buildings, extensively restored in the 17C and 18C, presently house local government offices.
- **Collégiale St-Martin** – The first church was built on this site in the 5C, outside the city walls. The nave is one of the few remaining examples in France of Carolingian architecture on a large scale. Forty religious artefacts illustrate terracotta techniques of the Angevine and Le Mans schools (17C).
- **Place du Ralliement** – This lively square is the centre of town.
- **Hôtel Pincé★** – This elegant Renaissance mansion, built for a mayor of

ANGERS

WHERE TO STAY

- Chambre d'hôte du Domaine des Chesnaies .... ①
- Chambre d'hôte La Béchalière .... ④
- Chambre d'hôte La Rousselière .... ⑦
- Chambre d'hôte Le Grand Talon .... ⑩
- Château de Noirieux .... ⑪
- Gîte de charme La Pointerolle .... ⑫
- Grand Hôtel de la Gare .... ⑬
- Hôtel d'Anjou Best Western .... ⑭
- Hôtel de France .... ⑮
- Hôtel Cavier .... ⑯
- Hôtel de Champagne .... ⑰
- Hôtel Le Continental .... ⑲
- Hôtel Le Progrès .... ㉒
- Hôtel Mail .... ㉕

WHERE TO EAT

- Chez Rémi .... ①
- Le Crèmet d'Anjou .... ②
- L'Hoirie .... ④
- Le Favre d'Anne .... ⑤
- La Ferme .... ⑦
- Le Grand Jardin .... ⑧
- Le Napoli .... ⑨
- Le Petit Comptoir .... ⑩
- Le Relais .... ⑬
- Le Théâtre .... ⑯
- La Villa Toussaint .... ⑱
- Ma Campagne .... ⑳
- Provence Caffé .... ㉒
- Une Île .... ㉔

Angers and bequeathed to the town in 1861, houses the **musée Turpin de Crissé** (1772–1859) and its exotic collection.

- **St-Laud district** – The small rue St-Laud is the axis of a pleasant pedestrian and shopping district, where a number of very old façades can be admired.
- **Muséum des Sciences Naturelles** – Two charming historic buildings in the town centre house this treasure trove of a museum which includes stuffed animals, fossils, shells and birds.
- **Église St-Serge★** – Until 1802 this was the church of the Benedictine abbey of the same name founded in the 7C. The 13C **chancel★★** is remarkably wide, elegant and well lit, a perfect example of the Angevin style

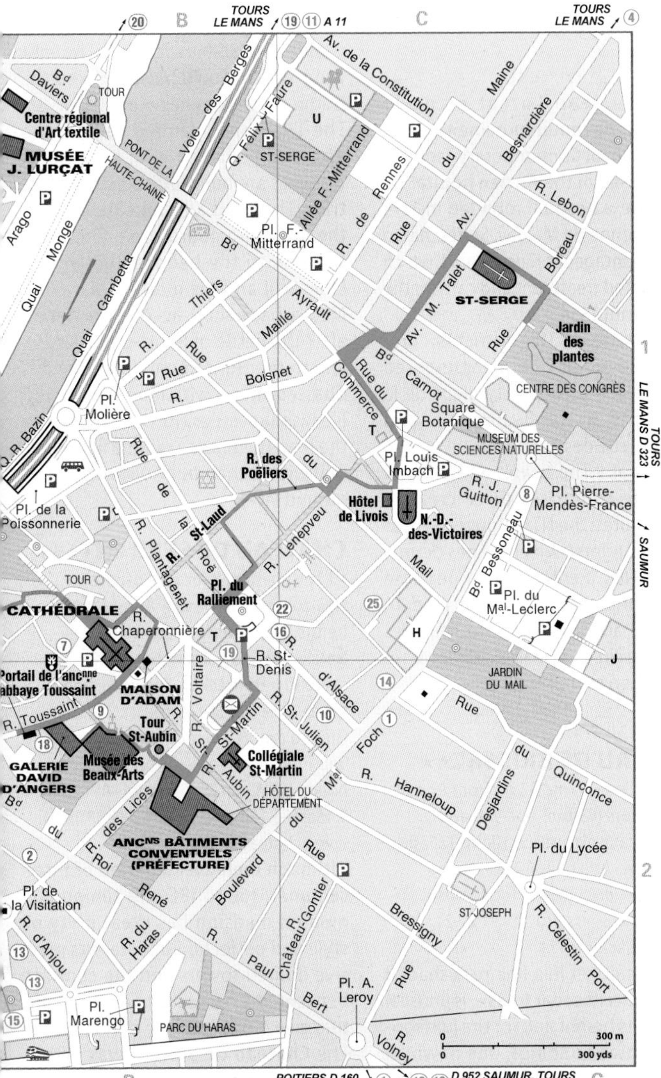

GARDENS★

- **Jardin des Plantes** – Located behind the Centre des Congrès and opposite the old conventual buildings (18C) of St-Serge abbey church, this botanical garden is home to some beautiful, rare species of tree.
- **Jardin du Mail** – A Neoclassical garden.
- **Parc de l'Arboretum, le jardin des collections★** – Southwest of the town centre, this innovative garden is sheltered by the great trees of the Gaston-Allard arboretum.
- **Parc de Balzac★** – The floodplains are typical of the marshes between here and the Atlantic coast with hedgerows, poplar trees, donkeys and cattle herds.
- **Parc St-Nicolas** – Four parks form a necklace of greenery along the St-Nicolas pond.
- **Parc de la Maine** – 200ha/490 acres of woods and lawns surround the Lac de Maine.

NORTH BANK OF THE RIVER MAINE

- **Musée Jean-Lurçat et de la Tapisserie contemporaine★★** – This Museum of Contemporary Tapestry is housed in the **Ancien hôpital St-Jean★**, a hospital founded in 1174 by Étienne de Marçay, Seneschal to the Plantagenet King Henry I, which provided treatment and care for the sick until 1854.
- **La Doutre★** – This district has preserved some fine half-timbered houses: on the pretty place de la Laiterie, in rue Beaurepaire and along rue des Tonneliers.
- **Le Quai** – The town's new cultural centre comprises three creative structures: the NTA (Nouveau Théâtre d'Angers), which stages drama, the CNDC (Centre national de danse contemporaine), a school of modern dance, and Open-Arts which focuses on the circus, visual and street art in addition to music.

EXCURSIONS

CHÂTEAU DE BRISSAC★★

Brissac lies 18km/11.2mi from Angers.
Guided tours (45min) Apr–Jun and Sep–Oct daily except Tue 10am–12.15pm, 2–6pm; Jul–Aug daily 10am–6pm; Nov–Mar check website for details, which vary. €10. 02 41 91 22 21. www.brissac.net.

The château, set in a fine park shaded by magnificent **cedar trees★**, is unusual both for its height and for the juxtaposition of two buildings, one of which was intended to replace the other rather than stand next to it. Be sure to see the tapestries inside the château.

As the original building had been damaged during the Wars of Religion, Duke Charles de Cossé commissioned a new residence designed by Jacques Corbineau, the architect responsible for the citadel at Port-Louis in Lorient. Work ceased on his death in 1621 and the château was left as we see it today. There is an unfinished main façade flanked by medieval towers. The central pavilion and the left wing are abundantly ornamented with rusticated pilasters and statues in niches. The right wing, which would have replaced the Gothic tower, was never built.

The 17C French painted **ceilings** are often embellished with sculptures; the walls are hung with superb **tapestries**. The Louis XIII staircase leads to the imposing guard room (Salle des Gardes), to the bedchamber where Louis XIII and his mother, Marie de' Medici, had a short-lived reconciliation after the Battle of Ponts-de Cé (1620), and to the Hunt Room (Chambre des Chasses), hung with magnificent 16C Flemish tapestries.North of Brissac, on the road to Angers, stands a fine windmill with a chamber hollowed out at ground level.

CHÂTEAU DE SERRANT★★★

The château is located off the N23 20km/10mi west of Angers, just before Saint-Georges-sur-Loire.
Take the 1hr guided tour of the château before taking the excursion to the abbey at St-George.
Guided tours (1hr) mid-Mar–Jun and Sep–mid-Nov Wed–Sun and public holidays 9.45am–5.15pm; Jul–Aug daily 9.45am–5.15pm. €10. 02 41 39 13 01. www.chateau-serrant.net.

Although built over a period of three centuries, 16C to 18C, this sumptuous moated mansion has great unity of style and perfection of detail. Its massive domed towers and the contrast between the dark schist and the white tufa give it considerable character.

The **Château de Serrant** was begun in 1546 by Charles de Brie supposedly after drawings by Philibert Delorme, the architect responsible for the construction of Fontainebleau.

The castle was bought by Hercule de Rohan, Duke of Montbazon, in 1596, and sold in 1636 to Guillaume Bautru whose granddaughter married the Marquis of Vaubrun, Lieutenant-General of the king's army. On the death of her husband, the Marchioness continued construction work until 1705. She commissioned Jules Hardouin-Mansart to build the beautiful chapel in memory of her husband, and Coysevox to design the mausoleum. During the 18C, the property was acquired by Antoine Walsh, a member of the Irish nobility who followed James II into exile in France and became a shipowner in Nantes.

Interior

In addition to the superb Renaissance staircase surmounted by coffered vaulting, the whole interior is very attractive. The **apartments★★★** are magnificently furnished and this exceptional collection of furniture was added to the list of Historic Monuments. Sumptuous Flemish and Brussels tapestries hang in the reception rooms which contain rare pieces of furniture such as the unique ebony cabinet by Pierre Gole (17C) adorning the Grand Salon. Note also 17C, 18C and early 19C furniture by prestigious cabinet-makers (Saunier, JE de Saint-Georges) and Empire-style furniture by Jacob, upholstered with Beauvais tapestry, commissioned for Napoléon and Josephine's visit.

There are fine paintings representing the French and Italian schools, a bust of the Empress Marie-Louise by Canova (Empire-style bedroom on the first floor), and two terracotta nymphs by Coysevox in the sumptuous **Grand Salon★★**.

The **library★★★** houses 12 000 volumes. Some of the books are marked with the Trémoille seal showing four T's symbolising the main estates owned by the family: Trémoille, Thouars, Talmont and Tarente. Opening onto the main courtyard, the chapel built by Jules Hardouin-Mansart contains the magnificent white-marble funeral monument of the Marquis de Vaubrun killed at the battle of Altenheim (1673).

ST-GEORGES-SUR-LOIRE

2km/1mi by N 23.

St-Georges, on the north bank of the Loire, is situated not far from the famous vineyards, the **Coulée de Serrant** and the **Roche aux Moines**, where some of Anjou's finest white wines are produced. The **abbey** (open Jul–Aug Tue–Sun 11am–12.30pm, 2.30–6.30pm; rest of the year by request, enquire at town hall; 02 41 72 14 80) was founded in 1158 by the Augustinian Order. The building dates from 1684 and contains a grand staircase with a wrought-iron banister and the chapterhouse with original wainscoting.

LE MANS★★

95km/59mi NW of Angers.

TGV: Le Mans is about 1hr direct from Paris Montparnasse. The city centre is the old quarter on the left bank of the Sarthe. 02 43 28 17 22. www.lemans-tourisme.com.

P There is usually plenty of parking space in Place des Jacobins.

Le Mans, a large, modern provincial capital, hosts several fairs and events every

Library, Château de Serrant

© Nicolas Thibaut / Photononstop

The Birthplace of the French Motor-Car Industry

In the second half of the 19C **Amédée Bollée** (1844–1917), a local bell-founder, began to take an interest in the incipient motor-car industry. His first car *(L'Obéissante)* was completed in 1873. Later he built the *Mancelle*, the first car to have the engine placed in front under a bonnet and to have a transmission shaft. The Austrian emperor, Franz-Josef, went for a ride in the *Mancelle*.

Bollée's son Amédée (1867–1926) devoted himself mainly to racing cars; they were fitted with **Michelin** tyres and reached 100kph/62mph. After WWI he began to produce an early form of piston rings, which became the main line of manufacture in his factory.

On 27 June 1906, the first prize on the Sarthe circuit was won by Szisz driving a Renault fitted with Michelin detachable rims.

In 1908 his brother, Léon Bollée, invited **Wilbur Wright** to attempt one of his first flights in an aeroplane at Les Hunaudières. When asked how the aircraft had performed, Wright replied, "Like a bird". In 1936 Louis Renault set up his first decentralised factory south of Le Mans in the Arnage plain.

year, most famously the 24hr Grand Prix, the *"24 Heures de Mans"*.

An old town, enclosed by ramparts in the 4C, Le Mans was part of the Plantagenet estates. It has long been the site of trade fairs and festivals, which today include a Spring Fair (late Mar–early Apr), a great Four-Day Fair (mid-Sep) and an Onion Fair (first Fri in Sep). As a result, Le Mans has a long gastronomic tradition; local specialities include potted pork (*rillettes*), plump pullets (*poulardes*), capons (*chapons*) accompanied by cider, as well as the delicious reinette apple.

Vieux Mans★★

The historic centre of Le Mans stands on the site of a Celtic settlement, overlooking the lowlands on either side of the Sarthe. This part of the city is still enclosed within its 4C Gallo-Roman ramparts, some of the few extant in western France.

Cathédrale St-Julien★★

This magnificent building makes a fine spectacle from Place des Jacobins. Its Gothic **chevet★★★**, supported on intricate Y-shaped two-tier buttresses, is a spectacular demonstration of the boldness and ambition of its architect. The transition from nave to choir is one of the clearest demonstrations anywhere – even for the architecturally uninitiated – of the great technical and stylistic changes which took place over a period of some 160 years. The arches of the south porch are pleasingly decorated, and the **doorway★★** has splendid statue-columns. The Gothic choir was completed in 1254. The whole is lit on three levels by 13C **stained-glass windows★★**; in the chapels opening out onto the outer ambulatory, in the inner ambulatory and in the clerestory. Note how in the south transept (1385–92) the junction has been effected between the Gothic choir and the older, Romanesque, transept.

Churches

Several of Le Mans' churches are worth a visit, including: **Église de la Couture★** (*22 r. Berthelot*); **Église Ste-Jeanne d'Arc★** (*pl. George-Washington*) and **Notre-Dame de L'Épau★** (*r. de l'Esterel*).

Museums

Le Mans has its fair share of museums: discover old Le Mans with historical maps and pictures at **Musée de la Reine Bérengère★** (r. de la Reine-Bérengère au Mans; ℘02 43 47 38 51); visit the half-timbered 16C house **Maison du Pilier Rouge** (*Grand Rue*); admire the paintings at **Musée de Tessé★** (2 av. de Paderborn-au-Mans; ℘02 43 47 38 51).

Motor-Racing Circuits

To the S of Le Mans between N 138 and D 139.

Le Mans 24-hour Race – In 1923 Gustave Singher and Georges Durand launched the first Le Mans endurance test which was to become a sporting event of universal interest and an ideal testing ground for car manufacturers.

The difficulties of the circuit and the duration of the race are a severe test of the quality of the machine and of the endurance of the drivers.

The track has been greatly improved since the tragic accident in 1955 when 83 spectators died and 100 were injured. Whether seen from the stands or from the fields or pine woods that surround the track, the race is an unforgettable experience: the roaring of the engines, the whining of the vehicles hurtling up the Hunaudières section at more than 350kph/200mph, the smell of petrol mingled with the resin of the pine trees, the glare of the headlights at night, the emotion and excitement of the motor car enthusiasts. Every year there is also a Le Mans 24-hour motorcycle race and a Le Mans 24-hour truck race. A Grand Prix de France motorcycle race is held here regularly.

Circuit des 24 Heures – The 24-hour circuit (13.6km/8.5mi long) begins at the Tertre Rouge bend *(virage)* on N 138. The racetrack, which is about 10m wide, is marked in kilometres. The double bend on the private road and the Mulsanne and Arnage hairpin bends are the most exciting hazards on the 24-hour course. In 1972 the course was laid out to give a better view.

Circuit Permanent Bugatti – From the main entrance to the track on D 139 a tunnel leads to the Bugatti circuit and the museum. Guided, individual and group tours – see website. 02 43 40 24 30. www.lemans.org. Apart from being used by its school for racing drivers, the track is also a permanent testing ground for teams of racing-car drivers and motorcyclists who use it for private trials.

Musée des 24 Heures du Mans –Circuit de la Sarthe★★

9 pl. Luigi Chinetti. Open: Apr–Sept 10am–7pm; Oct–Dec and Feb–Mar daily except Tue 11am–6pm; Jan Fri–Sun 11am–6pm. Closed 25 Dec, 1 Jan. €8.50 (10–18 years: €6). 02 43 72 72 24. www.lemusee24h.com.

Rebuilt in 1991, the Motor Museum displays 110 vehicles in an extremely modern and instructive setting.

The section on racing cars, in particular those that won the Le Mans 24-hour race, presents a superb collection of outstanding automobiles, including a 1924 Bentley, a 1949 Ferrari, a 1974 Matra, a 1983 Rondeau, a 1988 Jaguar, a 1991 Mazda and a 1992 Peugeot.

ADDRESSES

STAY

Chambre d'hôte la Béchalière – 49480 St Sylvain-d'Anjou. 5km/3mi NE. 02 41 76 72 22. 5 rooms. A convivial B&B amid verdant loveliness.

Chambre d'hôte du Domaine des Chesnaies – La Noue, 49190 Denée. 02 41 78 79 80. www.domainedeschesnaies.com. 4 rooms. Spacious and opening onto a 19C-style garden.

Chambre d'hôte Le Grand Talon – 3 rte. des Chapelles. 49800 Andard. 11km/6.8mi E. 02 41 80 42 85. 3 rooms. This elegant 18C house, decked out with leafy vines, is a haven of peace.

Grand Hotel de la Gare – 26 r. Denis-Papin. 02 41 88 40 69. www.hotel-angers.fr. 52 rooms. A traditional, welcoming hotel overlooking the jet d'eau.

Hôtel Cavier – La Croix-Cadeau, 49240 Avrillé. 8km/5mi NW of Angers on N 162. 02 41 42 30 45. www.lacroixcadeau.com. 43 rooms. Modern bedrooms in the recent wing of an 18C windmill, which houses the restaurant.

Hôtel de Champagne – 34 av. Denis-Papin, 49100 Angers. 02 41 25 78 78. www.hoteldechampagne.com. 29 rooms. Renovated rooms are tastefully decorated. Near the city centre.

Gîte La Pointerolle – chemin des Landes, 49800 Trélazé. 06 47 03 38 20. http://gitelapointerolle.monsite.orange.fr. P. Near the Château de Pignerolle, this charming gîte sleeps 2 people in a haven of vegetation. Attractive pond in the garden. Bikes available.

Hotel le Continental – 14 r. Louis-de-Romain. 02 41 86 94 94. www.hotellecontinental.com. 25 rooms. A central location, with traditional furnishings.

Hotel de France – 8 pl. de la Gare. 02 41 88 49 42. 55 rooms. A popular hotel, with a fine restuarant and good selection of wines. Cosy rooms.

Hôtel du Mail – 8 r. des Ursules. 02 41 25 05 25. www.hotel-du-mail.com. P. 28 rooms. The thick walls of this former convent keep out the noise from the nearby town centre.

Hotel le Progrès – 26 r. Denis-Papin. 02 41 88 10 14. www.hotelleprogres.com. Closed 7–15 Aug, 24 Dec–1 Jan. 41 rooms. Near the train station, this is a friendly place with modern rooms. Enjoy coffee in the breakfast room, with its décor inspired by the bright colours of Provence.

Chambre d'hôte la Rousselière – 49170 La Possonnière. 18km/11mi SE. 02 41 39 13 21. 5 rooms. Closed 20 Nov–15 Dec. Refined rooms with antique furnishings, set in a large park with a swimming pool.

Best Western – 1 bd. Maréchal-Foch. 02 41 21 12 11. www.hoteldanjou.fr. 53 rooms. 3-star hotel with plenty of character set in the heart of the city in a historic townhouse.

Château de Noirieux – Relais et châteaux. 26 rte. du Moulin 49125 Briollay. 17km/10.5mi NE of Angers. 02 41 42 50 05. www.chateaudenoirieux.com. Closed 14 Feb–25 Mar, 14 Nov–1 Dec and Sun–Mon Oct–May. Elegant château overlooking the Loir, set in grounds that are ideal for a stroll. Superbly decorated rooms and sophisticated cuisine.

EAT

Le Théâtre – 2 pl. du Ralliement. 02 41 24 15 15. Easy to find opposite the theatre; excellent and fresh cuisine.

Le Napoli – 5 r. Toussaint. 02 41 87 68 09. Closed Sun and Mon. Considered the best pizza restaurant in Angers. Reserve.

Chez Rémi – 7 bis bd. Foch. 02 41 24 95 44. Closed Sat lunch, Sun and Mon lunch. Inventive cuisine using fresh local market produce. Good value; reservations recommended.

Ma Campagne – 14 prom. de Reculée. 02 41 48 38 06. Closed Sun eve, Mon, and Tue eve. Rustic décor and views of the river Maine at this good value place.

La Villa Toussaint – 43 r. Toussaint. 02 41 88 15 64. Closed Sun. World cuisine in a trendy, zen atmosphere.

La Ferme – 2 pl. Freppel. 02 41 87 09 90. Closed 20 Jul–12 Aug, Sun eve, Wed. Reservations required. Traditional local cooking in a simple setting.

L'Hoirie – r. Henri-Faris, 49070 Beaucouzé. 02 41 72 06 09. Closed Sun eve, Mon. Serves appetising, modern cuisine in a quiet room.

Le Grand Jardin – 1 pl. Mendès-France. 02 41 60 34 81. The restaurant of the Hôtel Mercure opens onto the Jardin des plantes.

Provence Caffé – 9 pl. du Ralliement. 02 41 87 44 15. Closed 3 Jan, 1–24 Aug, 19 Dec, Sun–Mon. Reservations required. Carefully prepared cuisine at moderate prices.

Le Relais – 9 r. de la Gare. 02 41 88 42 51. Closed 22 Aug–13 Sep, 24 Dec–4 Jan, Sun–Mon and public holidays. The woodwork and the murals in this tavern recall the vineyard and grape harvest.

Le Favre d'Anne – 18 quai des Carmes. 02 41 36 12 12. Closed 29 Jul-13 Aug, Sun–Mon. Creative and modern cuisine, plus a view of the Château.

Le Petit Comptoir – 40 r. David d'Angers. 02 41 88 81 57. 16–25 Jan, 30 Jul-21 Aug, Sun–Mon. Relaxed atmosphere; inventive cuisine.

Une Île – 9 r. Max-Richard. 02 41 19 14 48. Closed weekends. Refined cuisine and an emphasis on regional wines.

Saumur★★

Lying on the banks of the Loire, beneath its imposing fortress, Saumur is famous for its Cavalry School, its wines (especially sparkling wines), its medal makers and its mushrooms (production of which is 42 percent of the national figure).

- **Population:** 27 283.
- **Michelin Map:** 317: I-5
- **Info:** pl. de la Bilange, BP 241, 49418 Saumur. ℘02 41 40 20 60. www.ot-saumur.fr.
- **Location:** Saumur lies 65km/40mi SE of Angers, 32km/20mi NE of Chinon.
- **Don't Miss:** Every year a tattoo using horses and motor transport is given by the **Cadre Noir** on the vast place du Chardonnet (*see Planning Your Trip, Festivals and Events, p38*). Repeat performances are given in the Riding School of the National Equitation Centre in Terrefort.
- **Timing:** You can easily fill a day in Saumur.

A BIT OF HISTORY

Charles the Bald built a fortified monastery in the 9C to house the relics of St Florent, but it was not long before it was destroyed by the Vikings. In the 11C Saumur was the subject of numerous conflicts between the Count of Blois and the Count of Anjou. In 1203, **Philippe Auguste** captured the town. In the late 16C and early 17C the town enjoyed its true heyday. It was one of the great centres of Protestantism. Henri III gave it as a stronghold to the king of Navarre, the future **Henri IV**, who appointed as governor **Duplessis-Mornay**, a great soldier, scholar and fervent Reformer, who was known by the Roman Catholics as the Huguenot Pope. In 1611 a general assembly of the Protestant churches was held there to consolidate their organisation following the death of Henri IV and the departure of Sully. Louis XIII grew alarmed at the Protestant danger and ordered the town walls to be demolished in 1623. The **Revocation of the Edict of Nantes** in 1685 dealt Saumur a fatal blow; many of the inhabitants emigrated and the Protestant church was demolished.

École d'application de l'arme blindée et de la cavalerie (EAABC) – It is interesting to note the mementoes of officers who served in the cavalry of the African Army between 1830 and 1962: Bugeaud, Gallifet, Charles de Foucault, who was an officer before he became a recluse, Lyautey, Henry de Bournazel and Leclerc de Hauteclocque.

SIGHTS

- **Château★★** – Open: Apr–mid-Jun and mid-Sep–Oct Tue–Sun 10am–1pm, 2–5.30pm; mid-Jun–mid-Sep daily, 10am–6.30pm. €7 (Jul–Aug); €6 (rest of year). ℘02 41 40 24 40. The château is compact and solid, and despite being a fortress is decorated in the style of a country house with machicolations and balustrades at the windows overlooking the courtyard.

  A succession of fortresses has been erected on the promontory. The present building, which succeeded Louis IX's castle, was rebuilt at the end of the 14C. The interior was altered in the 15C by René d'Anjou and external fortifications were added in the late 16C by Duplessis-Mornay.

  Under Louis XIV and Louis XV it was the residence of the governor of Saumur; it subsequently became a prison and then barracks, and it now houses two museums.
- **Old Town★** – The narrow twisting streets between the castle and the bridge still follow their original course; in some areas the old houses have been preserved whereas in

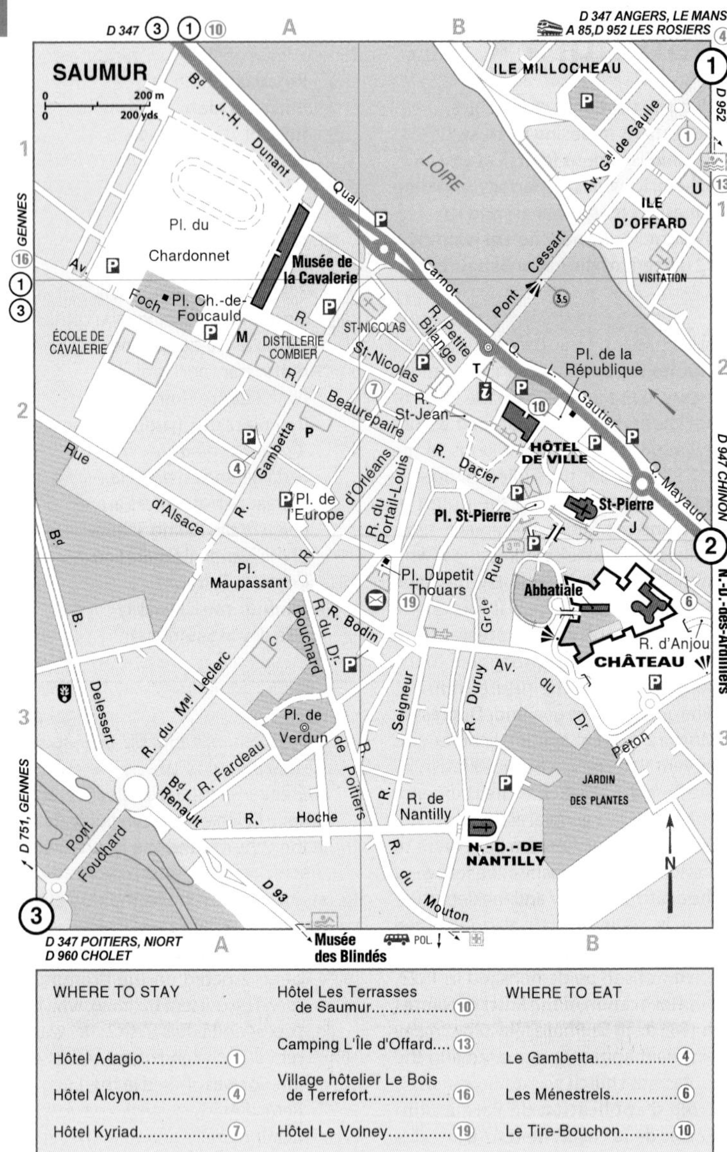

others new constructions have been built in the medieval style or are resolutely modern but full of surprises *(south of St Peter's Church)*.

Along the main shopping street, rue St-Jean, and in the square, **place St-Pierre**, half-timbered houses and 18C mansions with wrought-iron balconies stand side by side.

- **Église St-Pierre** – The church is Plantagenet Gothic except for the west front which collapsed in the 17C and was rebuilt. The Romanesque door in the south transept leads into the interior which is hung with two series of 16C **tapestries★**.
- **Hôtel de Ville★** – Only the left-hand section of the town hall is old (16C). Originally the Loire flowed past the

foundations and the building was a bridgehead and part of the town walls, hence its military appearance.

The façade facing the courtyard is in the Gothic Renaissance transitional style with some fine sculpture.

- **Église Notre-Dame-de-Nantilly★** – This is a fine Romanesque church. Louis XI added the right aisle. A pillar on the left in the same aisle bears an epitaph composed by King René d'Anjou.

  The 12C painted wooden statue of Our Lady of Nantilly was placed in the apse on the right of the chancel. The organ case dates from 1690. There are fine **tapestries★★** dating from the 15C and 16C except for eight in the nave which were made at Aubusson in the 17C.

MUSEUMS

Musée de la Cavalerie

Open mid-Feb–Jun and Sept–mid-Nov Sat–Mon 2–6pm, Wed–Fri 10am–noon, 2–6pm; Jul–Aug daily 10am–noon, 2–6pm. €5. 02 41 83 69 23.

In 1763 the Carabiniers Regiment, a crack corps recruited from the best horsemen in the army, was sent to Saumur. The present central building was constructed between 1767 and 1770 as their barracks. This museum's rich display of souvenirs, created in 1936 from Barbet de Vaux collections, traces the heroic deeds of the French Cavalry and the Armoured Corps since the 18C.

Musée des Blindés

Via boulevard Louis-Renault; follow the signposts. Open daily: Jan–mid-Apr and Nov–Dec Mon–Fri 10am–5pm, Sat–Sun and public holidays 11am–6pm; mid-Apr–Jun and Sep daily 10am–6pm; Jul–Aug 9.30am–6.30pm. €8. 02 41 83 69 95. www.museedesblindes.fr.

This museum and information centre on tanks houses over 100 vehicles (tanks, armoured vehicles, artillery equipment), many of which are still in working order, coming from a dozen or more countries. The most prestigious or rare exhibits are the **St-Chamond** and the **Schneider** (the first French tanks), the Renault FT 17 (French tank used in the very last stages of the WWI), the Somua S 35, the B1bis (issued to the 2nd Armoured Division under General de Gaulle in 1940) and German tanks dating from the French Campaign until the fall of Berlin (Panzers III and IV, Panther, Tiger), the Comet A 34 (the British tank used in the Normandy landing), the Churchill A 22, the Sherman M 4 and AMX 13 and 30.

EXCURSIONS

FONTEVRAUD L'ABBAYE★★★

The abbey occupies the heart of the village of the same name, which is 15km/9.3mi SE of Saumur, close to the Loire and Vienne rivers. 02 41 51 73 52. www.abbayedefontevraud.com.

Fontevraud abbey, close to the hearts of the Plantagenets, stands on the borders of Anjou, Tourraine and Poitou. Despite the ravages of history, it remains the largest group of monastic buildings in France, having retained some interesting features typical of Anjou architecture, in particular the lofty vaulting of the abbey church and the impressive kitchen. There is a good view of the Abbey from the Loudun road on the south side of the village.

The Order of Fontevraud was founded in 1099 following the failure in France of Pope Gregory's reform, which had been designed to enhance both the competence and the respectability of the clergy. The success of the new Order was immediate and it quickly took on an aristocratic character accommodating both sexes. It was presided over by an abbess at a time when the growing cult of the Virgin Mary was influencing the status of womanhood, and the abbesses, who were members of noble families, procured rich gifts and powerful protection for the abbey.

The Plantagenets chose the abbey as their last resting place and Eleanor of Aquitaine, her husband Henry II and her son Richard the Lionheart were buried here. Later, the hearts of John Lackland

(King John) and his son Henry III, who built Westminster abbey, were transferred to the crypt.

Église Abbatiale★★

The abbey church has a vast nave with delicately carved capitals and is roofed by a series of domes, characteristic of churches found in the southwest of France. Built several decades earlier than the nave, the transept and chancel are reminiscent of the Benedictine plan: an ambulatory and radiating chapels where the luminosity and repetition of vertical lines signify the aspiration to reach up to heaven.

In the transept crossing are a number of **Plantagenet tombs★**, good examples of Gothic funerary sculpture. The figures of Henry Plantagenet, Richard the Lionheart and Eleanor of Aquitaine are in painted tufa, while the figure of Isabel of Angoulême, John Lackland's wife, is of polychrome wood.

The **kitchen★★** is a highly individual structure (27m high), dating from around 1160 and restored in 1902. It is a rare example of a Romanesque kitchen, with a tiled roof characteristic of the Poitiers area.

CHINON★★

Chinon is 32km/20mi SE of Saumur.
02 47 93 17 85.
www.chinon-valdeloire.com.

Chinon occupies a sunny site on the Vienne, surrounded by the fertile Veron countryside, and known for the mildness of its climate.

Le Vieux Chinon★★

The old town has kept its medieval and Renaissance appearance. The old gabled houses with corner turrets and the 16C and 17C mansions, most of them in white tufa, make up a most evocative townscape. Many fine old buildings stand in its main street Rue Voltaire, including the Gothic dwelling where Richard the Lionheart is supposed to have died in 1199.

At the crossroads **(Grand Carroi★★)** the oldest houses of all press closely together. On her arrival from Vaucouleurs on Sunday 6 March 1429, **Joan of Arc** is thought to have used the coping of the well-head here to dismount from her horse. The following day she picked out the Dauphin (the heir apparent) hiding among his courtiers, and declared, "You are the heir of France and true son of the king, Lieutenant of the King of Heaven who is King of France".

Château★★

Open daily: Jan–Feb and Nov–Dec 9.30am–5pm; Mar–Apr and Sep–Oct 9.30am–6pm; May–Aug 9.30am–7pm. €8.50. 02 47 93 13 45. www.forteressechinon.fr.

The spur overlooking the town was the site of a Gallic oppidum, then of a fortress, long before Henry II of England (born at Le Mans in 1133) built the present castle to protect Anjou from Capetian designs. The castle was taken by Philippe Auguste in 1205 from John Lackland; it subsequently became a royal residence, was strengthened by Charles VII, but then abandoned by the court at the end of the 15C and gradually dismantled. The remains of the castle include, to the east, St George's Fort (Fort St-Georges), watching over the most vulnerable approach, the Middle Castle (Château du Milieu) which has a 14C clock tower, the royal apartments and gardens, and finally the Coudray Fort (Fort de Coudray) at the far end of the spur.

CHÂTEAU DE LANGEAIS★★

The town and château are on the right bank of the Loire between Tours and Saumur, approached by taking the left bank road and crossing the river into the town.

Open daily: Feb–Mar 9.30am–5.30pm; Apr–Jun and Sept–mid-Nov 9.30am–6.30pm; Jul–Aug 9am–7pm; mid-Nov–Jan 10am–5pm (25 Dec 2–5pm). €9. 02 47 96 72 60. www.chateau-de-langeais.com.

The castle is built on a promontory, beneath the high walls of which are nestled the town's white houses.

The great Angevin ruler Foulques Nerra built a sturdy keep to command the Loire valley. Completed in 994, now in ruins in the park of the château, it is considered to be the oldest such building in the whole of France.

The château itself was built to protect France from Brittany. In 1491, the marriage of Charles VIII of France and Anne of Brittany ended the threat. Seen from outside, the château still looks like a medieval fortress, with drawbridge, towers, battlemented sentry-walk and almost windowless walls. But the façade facing the courtyard has the features of a Renaissance country house, including pointed dormers, turrets, sculptures and mullioned windows.

Inside, the **apartments★★★** have kept their medieval layout, one room commanding the next through narrow doors and laid out along diagonal lines. The last owner, Jacques Siegfried (a mill- and ship-owner and banker from Le Havre), refurnished the interior very expertly, and Langeais gives a good impression of aristocratic life in the early Renaissance period. The rooms contain fine tapestries. In the Charles VIII Room is a 17C clock with a single hand.

ADDRESSES

STAY

Camping l'Ile d'Offard – 02 41 40 30 00. www.cvtloisirs.com. Open Mar–Nov. Occupying a great part of the island, with 260 places.

Hotel Alcyon – 2 bis r. de Rouen. 02 41 67 51 25. www.alcyon-saumur.com. P. 16 rooms. Close to the centre, newly renovated. Hotel shuttle.

Hotel Volney – 1 r. Volney. 02 41 51 25 41. www.levolney.com. Closed 15 Dec–2 Jan. 14 rooms. A central location, modest but stylish rooms, a nice reception and regular room service: here is a small, pleasant hotel perfect for discovering "the pearl of Anjou" without breaking the bank.

Chambre d'hôte La Butte de l'Épine – 37340 Continvoir. 2km/1mi E of Gizeux on D 15. 02 47 96 62 25. Closed 24 Dec–5 Jan. 3 rooms. This 16C–17C property has been charmingly restored. The main room has old furniture and a huge fireplace, the bedrooms are really exquisite and romantic, and the park is full of flowers.

Hotel Kyriad – 23 r. Daillé. 02 07 519 50 45. www.central-kyriad.com. 29 rooms. A central location, but in an area of calm; agreeable on all levels.

Hotel les Terrasses de Saumur – chemin de l'Alat, 49400 St-Hilaire-St-Florent. 02 41 67 28 48. Closed 21 Dec–19 Jan. 22 rooms. P. Overlooks the château, and offers tasteful rooms, and a swimming pool.

Village hôtelier Le Bois de Terrefort – av. de l'Éducation-Nationale-d'Équitation, 49400 St-Hilaire-St-Florent. 2km/1.5mi W of Saumar on D 751. 02 44 27 67 56. www.villagehotelier.com. P. 14 rooms. A hotel-village near the national riding school, not far from Saumur. The peaceful country setting and reasonable prices make it an ideal place to stay for those on a tight budget.

Hotel Adagio – 94 av. du Gén-e-Gaulle. 02 41 67 45 30. www.hoteladagio.com. Closed 23 Dec–2 Jan. P. 36 rooms. A fine hotel located on the Ile de la Loire, facing the château. Rooms have been renovated.

EAT

Le Tire-Bouchon – 10 pl. de la République. 02 41 67 35 05. Closed Sun eve in Jan–Feb, Tue. Reservation recommended. Delicious food in generous portions, a relaxed atmosphere with pleasant décor explains the success of this small restaurant ideally situated on the wharf.

Le Gambetta – 12 r. Gambetta. 02 41 67 66 66. www.restaurantlegambetta.com. Closed Sun and Mon, Feb holidays. Simple, delicious food.

Mercure bord de Loire – r. du Vieux Pont . 02 41 67 22 42. Located on the Ile d'Offard and with a great view of the river.

Les Ménestrels – 11 r. Raspail. 02 41 67 71 10. Closed 21-28 Dec, Mon (except Apr–Oct), and Sun. Delicious modern cuisine and excellent range of wines. Moroccan influences.

Tours★★

With a civilised air, under dazzling Loire valley skies, built in bright white tufa and roofed in black slate, the ancient city of Tours makes a perfect base for excursions into the château country.

- **Population:** 134 817.
- **Michelin Map:** 317 N 4
- **Info:** 78–82 r. Bernard-Palissy. ☏02 47 70 37 37. www.tours-tourisme.fr.
- **Location:** 80km/50mi NE of Saumur, Tours spans the Loire and fills the isthmus between the Loire and its tributary the Cher.
- **TGV:** Tours is about 2hrs 15mins via Orléans from Paris Austerlitz, but just 1hr 15mins via St Pierre des Corps from Paris Montparnasse.
- **Timing:** Allow half a day to visit the Old Town along the left bank of the Loire.

A BIT OF HISTORY

The place originated in Gallic times, becoming an important centre of trade and administration under the Romans in the 1C AD. Throughout the Middle Ages it was an important religious centre and was the capital of Touraine; indeed, Tours became the capital of France during the reign of Louis XI.

SIGHTS

Old Town★★★

The vast restoration work begun about 1970 around place Plumereau, and the building of the Faculté des Lettres beside the Loire, have brought the old quarter to life; its narrow streets, often pedestrian precincts, have attracted shops and craftsmen, and the whole quarter near the university has become one of the liveliest parts of town.

Château★

Not comparable in grandeur to the more typical Loire châteaux, this is a heterogeneous collection of buildings from the 4–19C. The lower parts of the wall on the west side go back to Roman times and here too is the 11C residence of the Counts of Anjou; the Guise Tower (Tour de Guise) with its machicolations and pepper-pot roof is of the 13–15C, while the dormer-windowed Governor's Lodging (Logis du Gouverneur) is 15C and other additions were made as recently as the 17–19C.

Cathédrale St-Gatien★★

Following a fire, the cathedral was rebuilt from 1235 onwards. The work

Place Plumereau

© Nicolas Thibaut / Photononstop

lasted all of 250 years. As a result it demonstrates the complete evolution of the Gothic style, from a chevet in the early phase, to a Flamboyant west front, and even a lantern crowning the twin towers that is characteristic of the Early Renaissance. The stained glass ranges in date from the 13C (high windows in the chancel) via the 14C (transept rose windows) to the 15C (rose window of the west front).

Cloître de la Psalette★

Open: Apr daily (except Sun am), 10am–12.30pm, 2–5.30pm; May–Aug daily (except Sun am), 9.30am–12.30pm, 2–6pm; Sept–Mar daily (except Mon, Tue and Sun am) 9.30am–12.30pm, 2–5pm. €3. ✆02 47 47 05 19. http://la-psalette.monuments-nationaux.fr.

This is the name given to the cathedral cloisters where canons and choir-master used to meet. The tiny Archive Room (Salle des Archives) of 1520 and the vaulted Library (Librairie) are reached by means of a spiral staircase, Gothic in structure but Renaissance in detail.

Place Plumereau★

This busy and picturesque square is located at the old "meeting of the ways" (carroi); it is bordered by fine 15C residences built of stone and timber. On the corner with the Rue du Change and the Rue de la Monnaie is a corner post with a depiction of the Circumcision.

Musée des Beaux-Arts★★

Open Wed–Mon. €4. ✆02 47 05 68 73.

In the former Bishops' Palace (17–18C), its rooms are beautifully decorated with Louis XVI panelling and silk hangings made locally. It houses works of art from the châteaux at **Richelieu★** and **Chanteloup** (now the site of the Parc de la Pagode, *see AMBOISE, p300*) as well as from the great abbeys of Touraine. The collection of paintings consists mostly of French works of the 19–20C, but there are also two outstanding Mantegnas, a Resurrection and Christ in the Garden of Olives (late 15C).

Musée du Compagnonnage★★

Open daily. €5. ✆02 47 21 62 20.

The city long prided itself on its craftsmen, and even at the end of the 19C there were still three guilds jealously guarding their traditions. The museum contains many fine examples of the work of master craftsmen, such as roofers and slaters, blacksmiths and locksmiths, saddlers and carpenters.

ADDITIONAL SIGHTS

- **Rue Briçonnet★** – This street is bordered by houses showing a rich variety of local styles, from the Romanesque façade to the 18C mansion.
- **Place Grégoire-de-Tours★** – This square gives a view of the east end of the cathedral and the Gothic flying buttresses; to the left is the medieval gable of the **Archbishop's Palace** (the Musée des Beaux-Arts).
- **Hôtel Gouin★** (*26 r. du Commerce*) – This mansion, a fine example of living accommodation during the Renaissance, is one of the most interesting of its kind in Tours.
- **Musée de la Société archéologique de Touraine★** (*26 r. du Commerce*)
- **L'Historial de Touraine★(in the castle)** (*25 quai d'Orléans*)
- **Jardin de Beaune-Semblançay★** – The **Hôtel de Beaune-Semblançay** belonged to the unfortunate Minister of Finance who was hanged during the reign of François I.
- **Musée des Équipages militaires et du Train★** (r. du Plat d'Etain, Quartier Beaumont) Open Mon–Fri Sep–Jul 2–5.30pm. No charge. ✆02 47 77 33 07. In 1807 Napoléon created the service corps to remedy the problem of insufficient transport means: up to then, the army administration had resorted to using the services of civilian companies, whose efficiency left something to be desired.

  The museum has been set up in the **Pavillon de Condé** (the only vestiges of the abbey of Ste-Marie in Beaumont). Ten carefully laid out rooms retrace the history of the service corps.

EXCURSIONS

AMBOISE★★

The busy town centre rises from the S bank of the Loire.
quai du Gén.-de-Gaulle. 02 47 57 09 28. www.amboise-valdeloire.com.
On the edge of town, kids will love the Parc des Mini-Châteaux (La Menaudière; 0 2 47 23 44 57) and the Parc de la Pagode de Chanteloup (Route de Blere. 02 47 57 20 97. www.pagode-chanteloup.com).

Amboise is a bridge-town, built at the foot of an escarpment already fortified in Gallo-Roman times, on which stand the proud remains of its great **château**.

Château★★

Open daily from 9am (closing times vary). €11. 08 20 20 50 50. www.chateau-amboise.com.

The 15C saw the Golden Age of Amboise. Charles VIII was born here in 1470; from his 22nd year onwards he carried on the work begun by his father, Louis XI. By the time he left on his Italian campaign, work was well in hand on a number of projects: the round towers, the great Gothic roof of the wing overlooking the Loire, and the Flamboyant St-Hubert Chapel, which served as an oratory for Anne of Brittany and has particularly fine Flemish door panels. In 1496 Charles returned from Italy, bringing with him not only works of art but a whole retinue of artists, architects, sculptors, cabinet-makers and gardeners.

With these Italians came a taste for antiquity and a decorative sense unknown at the time in France (doorways resembling triumphal arches, inlaid ceilings, superimposed arches, etc.). Charles' liking for luxury enhanced the prestige of the monarchy; his promotion of the artistic ideas of the Renaissance was continued by Louis XII and even more by François I, under whom château life became a whirl of princely gaiety with festivals, entertainments and hunting parties. However, this first French château of the Renaissance was destined to disappear; partly demolished by the troops of Louis XIII, it was further dismantled on the orders of Napoléon's Senate. Now it is known only from an engraving by Du Cerceau.

Tour – From the **terrace**, there is a fine view of the Loire Valley and the slate-blue roofs of the town. Inside, the **Royal Apartments** are the only part of the château that escaped demolition from 1806–10.

Laid out in informal English style, the pleasant **gardens** are worth seeing.

Clos-Lucé★

Very near the château.
Open daily: Jan 10am–6pm; Feb–Jun and Sept–Oct 9am–7pm; Jul–Aug 9am–8pm; Nov–Dec 9am–6pm. €14 (winter €12). 02 47 57 00 73. www.vinci-closluce.com.

To this manor house of red brick with stone dressings François I invited **Leonardo da Vinci** in 1516. The great Florentine was then aged 64. At Amboise he neither painted nor taught, devoting himself instead to organising royal festivities, designing a château at **Romorantin★**, planning the drainage of the Sologne and amusing himself designing mechanical inventions, some of which have now been constructed and are in a display of "fabuleuses machines".

CHÂTEAU DE CHENONCEAU★★★

14km/8.7mi S of Amboise, the château straddles the River Cher.
Open daily (times vary). €12.50. 08 20 20 90 90. www.chenonceau.com.

Chenonceau is a jewel of Renaissance architecture, built 1513–21 on the site of a fortified mill on the River Cher by Thomas Bohier, François I's treasurer. Over the years the place has been in the charge of six women, of whom three marked it strongly with their personality: Catherine Briçonnet, Diane de Poitiers and Catherine de' Medici.

CHÂTEAU DE CHAUMONT-SUR-LOIRE★★

43km/27mi NNE of Tours.
Open daily: 11am–6pm. 02 54 20 99 22. www.domaine-chaumont.fr.

The Château de Chaumont is as well sited as Amboise on the south bank

Château de Chaumont-sur-Loire

of the Loire, overlooking the town and the river. The feudal austerity of the structure is softened by its Renaissance influence, its elegant stair tower and its sumptuous Council Room.

The International Garden Festival★★★ (✆02 54 20 91 73; www.domaine-chaumont.fr) – Every year, 30 landscape gardeners create individual plant displays in 30 separate plots, many influenced by Pop Art. Visitors enter a curious and fascinating plant kingdom, which is neither a landscape garden nor a botanical park, but rather a unique site that pays tribute to the beauty of nature, where the creative genius of gardeners can be given free rein. This annual festival aims to introduce new creations and unusual combinations of plants and flowers.

CHÂTEAU D'USSÉ★★

➤ 45km/28mi SW of Tours.

The château stands with its back to a cliff on the edge of Chinon forest, its terraced gardens overlooking the Indre. Its impressive bulk and fortified towers contrast sharply with the white stone and myriad roofs, turrets, dormers and chimneys rising against a green background. Tradition has it that when Charles Perrault, the famous French writer of fairy tales, was looking for a setting for Sleeping Beauty, he chose Ussé as his model.

LOCHES★★

➤ Loches lies on the River Indre, 49km/30.4mi SE of Tours.
✆02 47 91 82 82. www.loches-tourainecotesud.com.

Modern Loches lies mostly on the left bank of the Indre, at the foot of the fortified bluff that dominates the valley and that set natural limits to the growth of the medieval town.

Cité médiévale★★

The medieval town is contained within a continuous wall some 1 000m long in which there are only two gates.

To the south, the great square **keep ★★** was built by the Counts of Anjou in the 11C on even earlier foundations.

In the 13C, it was strengthened by wide ditches hewn into the solid rock, by buttress towers and the Martelet Tower with its impressive dungeons, then given additional accommodation including service buildings.

In the centre of the old town is a church, **Église St-Ours★**, with its Angevin porch built around a Romanesque portal, and pyramid vaults in its nave.

To the north is the **Château★★** (open daily. €8.50. ✆02 47 59 01 32), begun at the end of the 14C as an extension of the 13C watchtower known as **Tour Agnès Sorel**. Part of the royal apartments are medieval (Vieux logis), part Renaissance (Nouveau logis). It was in the great hall of the Vieux Logis on 3 and 5 June 1429 that Joan of Arc persuaded the Dauphin

Château d'Azay-le-Rideau

© Philippe Body/hemis.fr

to undertake his coronation journey to Reims. There is a tiny Flamboyant oratory, dedicated to Anne of Brittany and decorated with the ermine of Brittany and the girdle of St Francis, and, in the Charles VIII Room, a recumbent figure (**gisant d'Agnès Sorel★**) of Charles VII's "Lady of Beauty".

CHÂTEAU D'AZAY-LE-RIDEAU★★★

25km/15.5mi from Tours in the direction of Chinon.

Open daily (times may vary). €8.50. 02 47 45 42 04. http://azay-le-rideau.monuments-nationaux.fr.

Sitting in a verdant setting where the waters of the Indre act as reflecting pools, this castle was built for financier Gilles Berthelot from 1518–29.

The château d'Azay-le-Rideau was built in French Gothic style. Its defences (machicolated cornice, pepperpot towers and turrets) are purely decorative. By contrast, the interior shows Italianate influences. The decoration includes Florentine shells in the gable of the great dormer window, pilasters, moulded entablatures, and, above all, the grand staircase with straight flights and rectangular landings. The interior is also notable for the French-style ceiling in the dining room and the chimney piece in the François I Room.

JARDINS ET CHÂTEAU DE VILLANDRY★★★

Coming from Langeais, take D 16, which has scenic views. Coming from Tours, take D 288, which crosses the Loire at Savonnières. Gardens and château open daily. Château closes early Jan–mid-Feb and mid-Nov–mid-Dec. €10 (château and gardens); mid-Nov–Mar €8. 02 47 50 02 09. www.chateauvillandry.com.

In 1536, Jean Le Breton, who had been France's ambassador in Italy, rebuilt the château here on the foundations of an earlier one. The new building had a number of features which made it unusual in Touraine: ditches and canals, an esplanade and a terrace, rectangular pavilions in place of round towers, and, above all, its gardens.

Château★★

The interior is distinguished by Louis XV panelling in the Great Salon and Dining Room, by the fine ramped staircase in wrought iron, and by a surprising 13C Mudejar ceiling from Spain, brought here by Joachim de Carvallo (1869–1936).

Gardens★★★

In 1906, Dr Carvallo, founder of the French Historic Houses Association (Demeure Historique), bought the Villandry estate and began to restore the gardens. The plan of the gardens shows both the influence of the agricultural writer **Olivier de Serres** and the synthesis of the monastery garden with the Italian garden proposed by Jacques II Androuet du Cerceau.

Covering a total area of 7ha/17.3 acres, the gardens have many fascinating features. There are three terraces, one above the other, separated by shady avenues of limes and vines; the high-

est is the water garden with its mirror-like stretch of water, then comes an ornamental garden with box clipped into patterns symbolising the varieties of love: tragic (sword and dagger blades), fickle (butterflies and fans), tender (masks and hearts) and passionate (broken hearts).
Finally there is a kitchen garden with 85 000 plants contained in clipped-box beds. The use of the humblest of vegetables, chosen for their culinary value, symbolism, therapeutic value or colour, is here raised to an art form.

ADDRESSES

STAY

⊖⊖ **Chambre d'hôte Le Moulin Hodoux** – 37230 Luynes, 14km/8.7mi W of Tours on N 152 and minor road. ℘02 47 55 76 27. 5 rooms. In a peaceful country setting not far from Tours, near the castle at Luynes, this 18–19C watermill provides comfortable, well-equipped rooms. In the garden there are tables, chairs, a barbecue, and swimming pool.

⊖⊖ **Hôtel Le Cygne** – 6 r. du Cygne. ℘02 47 66 66 41. Closed Christmas. 16 rooms. One of Tours' oldest hotels (18C). Rooms have been renovated, but their character has been preserved. In winter, a fine 16C fireplace warms the lounge.

⊖⊖ **Hôtel du Relais St-Éloi** – 8 r. Giraudeau. ℘02 47 38 18 19. 56 rooms. Recent building with small, practical rooms. Some, with a mezzanine, are particularly suitable for families. No-frills décor and regular maintenance. Modern dining room, but traditional culinary repertoire.

⊖⊖⊖⊖ **Central Hôtel** – 21 r. Berthelot. ℘02 47 05 46 44. 37 rooms. A quiet, comfortable hotel in the old part of Tours, near the busy pedestrian-only districts. The staff are reserved but pleasant. There is a small, peaceful garden behind the hotel and you can eat breakfast on the terrace.

EAT

⊖ **Bistrot de la Tranchée** – 103 ave Tranchée. ℘02 47 41 09 08. Closed Sun and Mon. Dark wood panelling, bottles of wine, comfortable wall sofas and old-fashioned pizza ovens make up the décor of this pleasant bistro. Enjoy a good selection of small dishes typical to this type of restaurant.

⊖⊖ **Cap Sud** – 88 r. Colbert. ℘02 47 05 24 81. Closed weekends and Mon. This little restaurant has a Mediterranean atmosphere, both in its warm décor and up-to-date cuisine.

⊖⊖ **Léonard de Vinci** – 19 r. de la Monnaie. ℘02 47 61 07 88. Closed Sun eve and Mon. Reservations required in eve. A taste of Tuscany in the heart of the Touraine. This Italian restaurant's claim to fame is that it doesn't serve pizzas! A chance to discover different Italian dishes, with a décor that highlights models of Leonardo da Vinci's inventions.

⊖⊖⊖⊖ **La Roche Le Roy** – 55 rte de St-Avertin. ℘02 47 27 22 00. www.rocheleroy.com. Closed Sun and Mon. The restaurant in this Touraine manor house will be much appreciated by gourmets. Sample the cooking in the intimate dining room or the enclosed courtyard.

CAFÉS

Le Vieux Mûrier – 11 pl. Plumereau – ℘02 47 61 04 77. Closed Sun, Mon. This is one of the oldest cafés in place Plumereau and it has that extra hint of character that is so often missing from modern establishments.

SHOPPING

Markets – **Second-hand goods:** 1st and 3rd Fri of the month, r. de Bordeaux; 4th Sun in the month, bd Bérange; Wed and Sat mornings, pl. de la Victoire.

Au Vieux Four – halles centrale, Place G.Paihoux. ℘02 47 38 63 55. Closed Sun and Mon. This boulangerie reveals the secrets of traditional bread-making.

La Chocolatière – 6 r. de la Scellerie. ℘02 47 05 66 75. www.la-chocolatiere.com. Closed Mon. "Le pavé de Tours" is one of the great specialities of this exceptional maker of pâtisseries, confectionery and top-of-the-range chocolates.

Blois★★

Blois looks northwards to the Beauce and south to the Sologne, and is situated at that point on the Loire at which the limestone landscapes around Orléans give way almost imperceptibly to the chalk country of Touraine downstream. Originally defended by a medieval castle, the town was transformed from 1503 onwards when the kings moved there from Amboise, bringing in their train all the trades devoted to satisfying the royal taste for luxury.

- **Population:** 46 492.
- **Michelin Map:** 318 C-D-E-F 5-6-7
- **Info:** 23 pl. du Château. ✆02 54 90 41 41. www.bloischambord.com.
- **TGV:** Blois is about 2hrs via Orléans from Paris Austerlitz.
- **Location:** Blois is roughly mid-way between Tours (66km/41mi SW) and Orléans (61km/38mi NE).
- **Don't Miss:** Be sure to stroll in the old quarter, which rises behind the town centre.
- **Kids:** The Maison de la Mogie will entertain young ones. Or ask at the tourist office about taking a boat trip on the Loire.

CHÂTEAU★★★

Open daily: Jan–Mar and Nov–Dec 9am–12.30pm, 1.30–5.30pm; Apr–Jun and Sept 9am–6.30pm; Jul–Aug 9am–7pm; Oct–Nov 9am–6pm. Closed 1 Jan and 25 Dec. €10 (children, 6–17, €5). ✆02 54 90 33 33. www.chateaudeblois.fr.

The whole development of secular French architecture from feudalism to the Classicism of Louis XIII's reign can be traced at Blois. The medieval remains include the round towers, spiral stairways and steep-pitched roofs of the Foix Tower and the Chamber of the States-General of 1205; with its panelled ceiling, this is where the States-General held its Assemblies in 1576 and 1588.

The transition from the Gothic to the Renaissance is evident in the Charles of Orléans Gallery and particularly in the Louis XII Wing of 1498–1501. Louis had been born at Blois in 1462 and, together with Anne of Brittany, carried out a number of improvements including the construction of a new wing. This was right up to date with its triumphal arch doorways, Italianate arabesque decoration applied to the three Gothic pillars on the courtyard side, and the use of galleries to link rooms rather than having them run directly into one another.

Built only 15 years later, possibly by Claude de France, the François I wing exemplifies the preoccupation with ornamentation that swept in with the first phase of the French Renaissance. The work remained incomplete but the new taste for sumptuous decoration is very apparent, not only in the Façade des Loges (built in front of the old rampart) with its still-irregular fenestration, but also in Pierre Trinquart's François I staircase; though somewhat over-restored in the view of some archaeologists, this is a richly decorated masterpiece with openings between its buttresses forming a series of balconies. The much-modified interior includes, on the first floor, Catherine de Medici's study with its secret cupboards, and on the second floor, Henri III's apartments, scene of the murder of Henri de Guise.

The King's brother employed François Mansart, who, however, failed to deploy the full range of his talents, his work here being stiff rather than dignified. Building stopped when the birth of Louis XIV put paid to his uncle's hopes of succeeding to the throne.

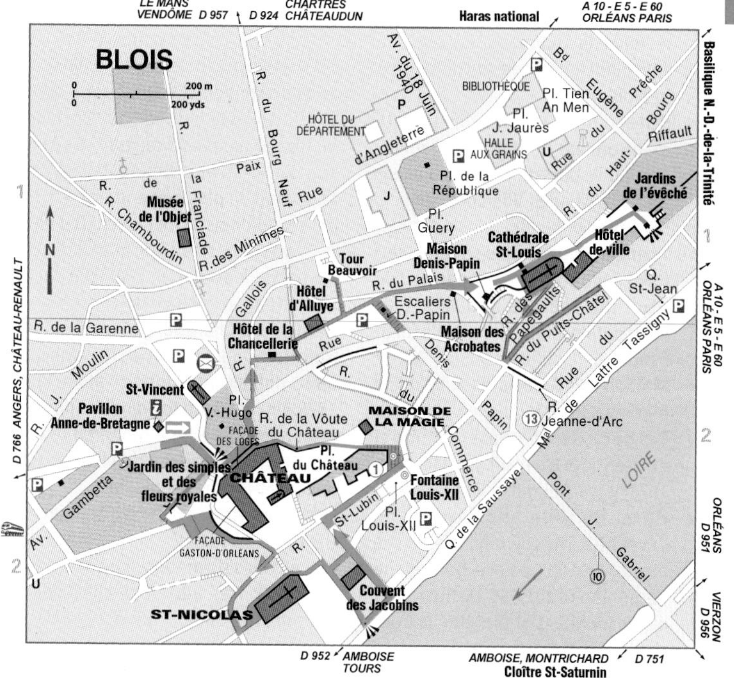

WALKING TOUR

OLD TOWN★

Blois map, above. Allow at least 2hrs.

Every street corner of this fascinating town has something to offer the dedicated visitor prepared to stroll through the old districts.

- **Pavillon Anne-de-Bretagne★** – This graceful little building of stone and brick, crowned by a high slate roof, once the belvedere of the Royal Gardens, is now the tourist centre.
- **Jardin des Simples et des Fleurs Royales** – This small terraced garden is all that remains of the vast château gardens. Standing near the balustrade one has an excellent **view★**.
- **Façade des Loges** – The interior part of François I's initial construction backed on to the medieval rampart wall and had no outside view. This troubled the King and so he decided to add a second building with as many openings as possible against the outside of the ramparts.
- **Église St-Nicolas★** – This fine 12–13C church formed part of the Benedictine abbey of St-Laumer whose monastic buildings stretch down to the river bank.
- **Couvent des Jacobins** – As early back as the 15C–16C, these convent buildings already housed the **Musée d'Art religieux**, devoted to religious art collections on the first floor and, on the second floor, beneath a fine timber roof shaped as an inverted hull, the **Muséum d'Histoire naturelle**.
- **Fontaine Louis XII** – This Flamboyant Gothic fountain is a copy of the monument erected during the reign of Louis XII. The weather-worn original is kept in the Château.
- **Maison de la Magie Robert-Houdin★** – Set up in a 19C hôtel particulier facing the château, the Maison de la Magie enlightens visitors on the history of magic and serves as a national centre for the art of illusionism.

- **Hôtel de la Chancellerie** – This late 16C mansion is one of the largest in Blois.
- **Hôtel d'Alluye** – This fine private mansion was built in 1508 for Florimond Robertet, treasurer successively to Charles VIII, Louis XII and François I.
- **Tour Beauvoir** – This square keep (11C) belonged to a separate fief from the château and was later incorporated into the town's fortifications.
- **Maison des Acrobates** – A typical medieval house.
- **Cathédrale St-Louis** – Almost entirely destroyed by a storm in 1678, it was rebuilt in Gothic style.
- **Hôtel de Ville and Jardins de l'Évêché** – The town hall lies in the former bishop's palace, built at the beginning of the 18C by the father of the architect of place de la Concorde in Paris.

EXCURSIONS

BOAT TRIPS

Sailing along the Loire in a traditional boat will offer you the opportunity of observing at leisure the local fauna and flora. For information, apply to the tourist office.

CHÂTEAU DE CHAMBORD★★★

The château is S of the Loire, between **Beaugency★** and **Blois★★**, at the end of a long avenue through woodland. Open daily: Jan–Mar and Oct–Dec 9am–5pm; Apr–Sep 9am–6pm. Closed 1 Jan, 1st Thu of Feb, 25 Dec. €11. 02 54 50 40 00. www.chambord.org.

The first of France's great Classical palaces, Chambord stands in a vast park enclosed by a wall. Beyond stretches the forest of Sologne, teeming with the game that the rulers of France have long loved to hunt.

At the age of 21, François I had just returned in triumph from his victory over the Swiss at Marignano which had given him possession of the Duchy of Milan. Dissatisfied with the old royal residence at Blois in spite of the improvements he had made, he had a vision of a dream castle to be built four leagues away on the forest edge. Leonardo da Vinci may have helped with the plans for this fabulous edifice; its feudal keep and corner towers belied its purpose as a palace of pleasure and status symbol for a Renaissance prince. The château was begun in 1519; later Philibert Delorme, Jean Bullant and the great Mansart all worked on it.

Hardly had Chambord started to rise from its foundations when the king suffered defeat and captivity at Pavia in 1525. On his return to France he judged it more suitable for a monarch to live close to his capital, at either Fontainebleau or St-Germain-en-Laye.

From the entrance there is a fine view of the keep linked to the corner towers by two arcades surmounted by galleries.

A gallery was added to the façade towards the end of the reign of François I at the same time as the two spiral staircases in the north corners of the courtyard.

The château's famous double staircase, undoubtedly conceived by Leonardo da Vinci, is justly famous for its interlocking spirals opening onto internal loggias and for its vaults adorned with salamanders, François' crest. The extraordinary roof terrace was where the king and his entourage spent much of their time watching tournaments and festivals or the start and return of the hunt; its nooks and crannies lent themselves to the confidences, intrigues and assignations of courtly life, played out against this fantastic background of pepper-pot turrets, chimney stacks, dormers peeping from the roofs, false windows embellished with shells, all decorated with inset slatework and dominated by the splendid lantern.

The state rooms contain rich furnishings: wood panelling, tapestries, furniture, portraits and hunting collections.

CHÂTEAU DE CHEVERNY★★★

17km/10.5mi S of Blois, the château can be seen from afar. Open daily including Sun and public holidays:

Jan–Mar and Oct–Dec 10am–5pm; Apr–Sept 9am–6.30pm. (château and park) €10 (children, €7). ☏02 54 79 96 29. www.chateau-cheverny.com.

Cheverny was built between 1604 and 1634 with that simplicity and distinction characteristic of the Classical architecture of the reigns of Henri IV and Louis XIII.

The elevation is strictly symmetrical, extending to either side of the well containing the staircase, and terminated by massive corner pavilions with square domes. The prominent slate roofs are in Louis XIII style, pierced with mansards and bull's-eye windows.

The first-floor windows are crowned with scrolls; between them are medallions of Roman emperors (Julius Caesar in the central pediment).

The elegant doorway is adorned with two concentric collars. The state rooms, served by a majestic Louis XIII ramped staircase with massive balustrades and rich sculptural decoration, contain a fine collection of furniture from the 17–19C.

VENDÔME★★

▶ The River Loir flows parallel to the Loire, to its N. The town's setting is complicated and unusual, the islands fitting together like a jigsaw puzzle. Rue Poterie runs north–south across the town centre. ☏02 54 77 05 07. www.chateaux-valdeloire.com/Vendome.html.

At the foot of a steep bluff, which is crowned by a **château**, the Loir divides into several channels. Vendôme stands on a group of islands crowded with bell towers, gables and steep slate roofs.

Ancienne Abbaye de la Trinité★

Founded in 1040 by Geoffroy Martel, Count of Anjou, the Benedictine abbey expanded considerably and became one of the most powerful in France. Pilgrims flocked here to venerate the supposed Holy Tear Christ shed at Lazarus' tomb and which Martel brought back from a Crusade. The Flamboyant Gothic **abbey church**★★ has a remarkable west front, which contrasts with the plain Romanesque tower. The transept, all that is left of the 11C building, leads to the chancel and ambulatory with its five radiating chapels. In the 14C chancel are fine late 15C **stalls**★ decorated with naïve scenes. The axial chapel contains a window dating from 1140 depicting the Virgin and Child (Majesté Notre-Dame).

CHÂTEAU DE VALENÇAY★★★

Open daily: Apr 10.30am–6pm; May and Sept 10am–6pm; Jun 9.30am–6.30pm; Jul–Aug 9.30am–7pm; Oct–mid-Nov and mid-end Dec 10.30am–5pm. €12.50. ☏02 54 00 15 69. www.chateau-valencay.fr.

Château de Cheverny

Many events are held here, notably the re-enactments of 19C life in period costume in the afternoons, and evening Son et Lumière shows.

Vast and superbly proportioned, richly furnished, and standing in an exquisite park, this is a place dedicated to the good life. The original medieval castle was rebuilt in the 16C and the defensive features were retained as decoration. In 1803, the estate was acquired by **Charles-Maurice de Talleyrand-Périgord** (1754–1838), paid for mostly by Napoléon, at the time still First Consul.

For almost a quarter of a century, the château served as a glittering background to international diplomacy conducted by its owner, who held high offices of state from the time of Louis XVI to the Restoration.

Inside are opulent furnishings of the Régence and Empire periods, including 18C Savonnerie carpets and the round table from the Congress of Vienna.

ADDRESSES

STAY

Hôtel Anne de Bretagne – 31 ave J.-Laigret. 02 54 78 05 38. Closed 9 Jan–6 Feb . 28 rooms. This small family hotel is near the castle and the terraced Jardin du Roi. The rooms are decorated in attractive colours and well soundproofed; those on the third floor are under the sloping roof.

Chambre d'hôte La Villa Médicis – 1 r. St-Denis, Macé, 41000 St-Denis-sur-Loire. 4km/2.5mi NE of Blois on N 152 towards Orléans. 02 54 74 46 38. Reservations required in winter. 6 rooms. Marie de Medici came to take the waters at the springs in the park in which this 19C villa was built, as a hotel for spa patrons at the time.

EAT

Au Bouchon Lyonnais – 25 r. des Violettes. 02 54 74 12 87. Closed Sun, except public holidays. Reservations recommended. Located just at the bottom of the hill crowned by the château, this restaurant is a favourite with residents of Blois, who enjoy the rustic décor with exposed beams and stone walls. The menu features regional fare.

Au Rendez-vous des Pêcheurs – 27 r. Foix. 02 54 74 67 48. Closed Mon lunchtime and Sun. Reservations recommended. A provincial-style bistro in the old part of Blois. Stained-glass windows filter the light in the quiet dining room. Fish features prominently among the fresh market produce on the menu.

Le Bistrot du Cuisinier – 20 quai Villebois-Mareuil. 02 54 78 06 70. You'll find a real bistro atmosphere here, simple and relaxed, and from the front dining room there is a splendid view of Blois and the Loire.

SHOPPING

Rue du Commerce and the adjacent streets in the pleasant pedestrian-only town centre (r. du Rebrousse-Pénil, r. St-Martin) offer all kinds of shops.

SON ET LUMIÈRE

Shows are put on nightly at the château from Easter–Sep from 10pm. The Wed show is in English.

02 54 90 33 32. www.blois.fr.

Alain Decaux of the Académie Française wrote the texts that retrace the history of Blois – "a thousand years' history spanning ten centuries of splendour" – and they are read by famous French actors including Michael Lonsdale, Fabrice Luchini, Robert Hossein, Pierre Arditi and Henri Virlojeux. Enormous projectors, combining photographs with special lighting effects, and the very latest in sound transmission systems make for a lively, entertaining and visually stimulating show, despite there being no live actors participating in the show.

Orléans★

Orléans grew up on the great bend in the Loire between the rich cornfields of the Beauce to the north and the heaths and forests of the Sologne to the south. For a time the city was the capital of France. Place du Martroi, with its statue of Joan of Arc, is the centre of the historic town.

- **Population:** 114 167.
- **Michelin Map:** 318 I 4
- **Info:** 2 pl. de l'Etape. ☎02 38 24 05 05. www.tourisme-orleans.com.
- **TGV/Train:** Orléans is 1–1hrs 30mins direct from Paris Austerlitz.
- **Tram:** The Tao network operates 2 tram lines, daily until 11.30pm.
- **Location:** The city lies 131km/82mi SW of Paris and 62km/39mi NE of Blois, at the closest point of the Loire to the capital.

A BIT OF HISTORY

The **Siege of 1428–29** was one of the great episodes in the history of France, marking the country's rebirth after a period of despair. It began on 12 October 1428, as the Earl of Salisbury attempted to take the bridge over the Loire and thus link up with the other English forces in central and southern France. Lasting almost seven months, the siege was the scene of one of the first-ever (albeit inconclusive) artillery duels.

On 29 April 1429, **Joan of Arc** arrived from Chinon; she skirted Orléans to the south and entered the city by the Burgundy Gate (Porte de Bourgogne), several days ahead of the army advancing along the north bank of the river. By 7 May, victory seemed assured, and on 8 May the English capitulated.

In Orléans, Joan enjoyed the hospitality of Jacques Boucher, whose fine half-timbered dwelling with its **museum** is known as **Maison de Jeanne d'Arc★** (3 pl. de Gaulle; ☎02 38 68 32 63; www.jeannedarc.com.fr/maison/maison.htm).

SIGHTS

Cathédrale Ste-Croix★★

Construction of the cathedral lasted from the 13C to the 16C. The nave was torn down by the Huguenots in 1568, but rebuilt in composite Gothic style by **Henri IV**, mindful of the city's loyalty to him.

The woodwork (**boiseries★★**) of the choir stalls (1706) includes splendidly carved medallions and panels adorning the high backs.

Half-timbered houses (colombages), Orléans

Musée des Beaux-Arts★★

♿Open Tue–Sun 10am–6pm. €3 (no charge 1st Sun in the month). ✆02 38 79 21 55. www.orleans.fr.

This museum houses some of the richest collections in France, especially of French painting from the 16–20C, including Courbet, Boudin and Gauguin.

Musée historique et archéologique★

Opening times vary (call for details). ✆02 38 79 21 55. www.musees.regioncentre.fr.

The Museum of History and Archaeology is housed in an elegant little mansion, **Hôtel Cabu** (1550), next to another Renaissance façade.

On the ground floor is the **Gallo-Roman treasure★** from Neuvy-en-Sullias which consists of a series of expressive statues, a horse and a wild boar in bronze.

The first floor is devoted to the Middle Ages and the Classical period, as well as typical local ceramic ware. The second floor is occupied by local folklore, pewter ware, gold and silverware, and clocks. Another room presents the history of the port of Orléans, describing the various industries associated with river traffic in the 18–19C.

Maison de Jeanne d'Arc★

3 pl. de Gaulle. Open daily except Mon: Oct–Mar 2–6pm; Apr–Sep 10am–6pm. €4. ✆02 38 68 32 63. www.jeannedarc.com.fr.

The tall timber-framed façade contrasts with the modernity of the square, place du Général-de-Gaulle, which was heavily bombed in 1940. The building is a reconstruction of the house of Jacques Boucher, Treasurer to the Duke of Orléans, where Joan stayed in 1429. An audiovisual show on the first floor recounts the raising of the siege of Orléans by Joan of Arc on 8 May 1429.

The centre's resources include a book library, a film library, and microfilm and photographic archives.

The old **museum** houses displays of a scientific and cultural nature. The four upper floors of the museum are devoted to the marine world, aquatic ecosystems (aquarium), reptiles and amphibians, higher vertebrates, mineralogy, geology, palaeontology and botany (greenhouses of temperate and tropical plants on the top floor).

EXCURSIONS

PARC FLORAL DE LA SOURCE★★

▶ In Olivet take D 14 E to the Source Floral Park. Open daily. €6 (children, 6–16 years, €4). ✆02 38 49 30 00. www.parcfloraldelasource.com.

This park was laid out in the wooded grounds of a 17C château to host the 1967 Floralies Internationales horticultural exhibition. As the seasons change, so does the display: in spring, the flower beds are in bloom with tulips, daffodils, then **irises★**, rhododendrons and azal-

Châteaudun

eas; mid-June to mid-July is when the rose bushes are at their best; in September the late-flowering rose bushes come into bloom with the dahlias. The **butterfly house** is a great attraction. The **Loiret spring★** can be seen bubbling up from the ground. The spring is the resurgence of the part of the river which disappears underground near St-Benoît-sur-Loire. Throughout the year, flocks of cranes and emus and herds of deer roam the park, while flamingoes stalk by the banks of the Loiret.

ABBAYE DE ST-BENOÎT-SUR-LOIRE★★

The abbey is at the village of St-Benoît, beside the Loire between Gien and Orléans. A pretty way to approach it is along the riverside road, D 60.

Enthralling by its majestic size, exquisite harmony and utter simplicity, Fleury abbey at St-Benoît-sur-Loire is justly one of the most famous Romanesque buildings in France.

The original abbey was founded here on a river terrace well above flood level. In around AD 675, it was presented with the remains of St Benedict and of his sister, St Scholastica, brought from Monte Cassino in Italy. Hitherto known as Fleury Abbey, the monastery rededicated itself to the founder of Western monasticism.

Basilica★★

Open daily. Closed during services. ✆02 38 35 72 43. www.abbaye-fleury.com.

Built between 1067 and 1108, the Romanesque basilica has a fine **crypt★** with a double ambulatory and a massive central pillar containing the relics of St Benedict. The **choir★★** is remarkable for its paving (a Roman mosaic brought here from Italy) and for the elegant arcading.Outside, the **belfry porch★★** is one of the finest examples of Romanesque art in France.

GERMIGNY-DES-PRÉS★

5.5km/3.4mi NW.

The much-restored church is the **oratory** that Abbot Theodulf built for himself. It is a typical example of Carolingian architecture of the 9C, with an unusual plan, alabaster window-panes filtering the light, and a remarkable **mosaic★★**.

CHÂTEAUDUN★★

130km/80mi southwest of Paris, between Chartres (45km/28mi) to the N and Vendôme (40km/25mi) to the SW.

On the south bank of the Loir at the point where the **Perche** region joins the Beauce, Châteaudun and its castle stand on a bluff, indented by narrow valleys called *cavées*.

Château★★

Open daily. €7.50. ✆02 37 94 02 90.

Châteaudun is the first of the Loire châteaux to come into sight on the road from Paris. It stands on a bluff rising steeply above the Loir. Crude and fortress-like from the outside, the buildings resemble a stately mansion when seen from the courtyard. The keep, which is 31m high without the roof, dates from the 12C; it is one of the earliest circular keeps, and one of the most impressive and best preserved.

The **south oratory** collection of 15 **statues★★** is an excellent example of the work produced in Loire valley workshops in the late 15C.

The **Aile de Dunois** was begun towards 1460 and is built in the true Gothic tradition, although the interior furnishings suggest a desire for comfort following the Hundred Years' War. The huge living rooms have massive overhead beams and are hung with tapestries, including, on the first floor, a superb series from Brussels depicting the Life of Moses.

CHÂTEAU DE SULLY-SUR-LOIRE★

48km/30mi SE from Orléans.

The Château de Sully commanded one of the Loire crossings. Its history is dominated by four great names: Maurice de Sully, Bishop of Paris who commissioned the building of Notre-Dame; Joan of Arc; statesman duc de Sully and Voltaire. Today an agreeable charm pervades the mellow stones of the fortress reflecting in the still waters of the moat.

Alsace Lorraine Champagne

» Region map p314–315
Metz p316
Verdun p321
Nancy p323
Toul p329
Strasbourg p330
Colmar p340
Riquewihr p344
Mulhouse p347
Route des Crêtes p349
Reims p350
Châlons-en-Champagne p356
Monthermé p357
Troyes p358
Provins p363

Introduction

Alsace is France's window onto Central Europe. Its capital, Strasbourg, was part of the Holy Roman Empire. Together with the towns and villages along the left bank of the Rhine, it has a decidedly Germanic character. **Lorraine** owes its name to ancient Lotharingia, central of the three kingdoms into which Charlemagne's inheritance was divided. The **Champagne** region to the west is renowned for its sparkling wine, and the **Ardennes** to the north is one of Europe's most extensive areas of forest.

Geography – The Rhine forms a frontier between Alsace and Germany, flowing through a broad rift valley defined by the Black Forest and the Vosges uplands. Further west in Lorraine, a series of limestone escarpments is pierced by major rivers flowing northwest. Around Reims, steep slopes carry vineyards, and beyond stretch productive agricultural regions. To the north, the Ardennes merges with Belgium and the German Eifel.

History – Alsace and Lorraine have long been fought over by France and Germany, and the territory has changed hands four times since 1871. At some point over the years, both France and Germany have claimed the people of Alsace as their own, and that has influenced everything from the food to the music to their livelihoods. In 1900, 86.8 per cent of those living in Alsace-Lorraine spoke German. Today, most residents speak German, French and Alsatian. Alsace has become a symbol of the trans-national European economy. Strasbourg, seat of the Council of Europe, was one of the first "Eurocities" on the continent.

Highlights

1. UNESCO World Heritage Site Place Stanislas, **Nancy** (p323)
2. La Petite France, **Strasbourg** (p334)
3. Grünewald's masterpiece, The Issenheim Altarpiece, **Colmar** (p340)
4. Gothic Cathédrale Notre-Dame, **Reims** (p351)
5. Old timber-framed houses, Vieux Troyes at **Troyes** (p358)

Economy – Alsace produces many varieties of wine. Lorraine depends heavily on timber production and dairy produce, while retaining an important metal sector. Farms in Lorraine are France's leading producers of rape seed, used for making oil. Champagne's economy is mainly agriculture, while the Ardennes depends heavily on timber, tourism and its agricultural industries.

Place Stanislas, Nancy

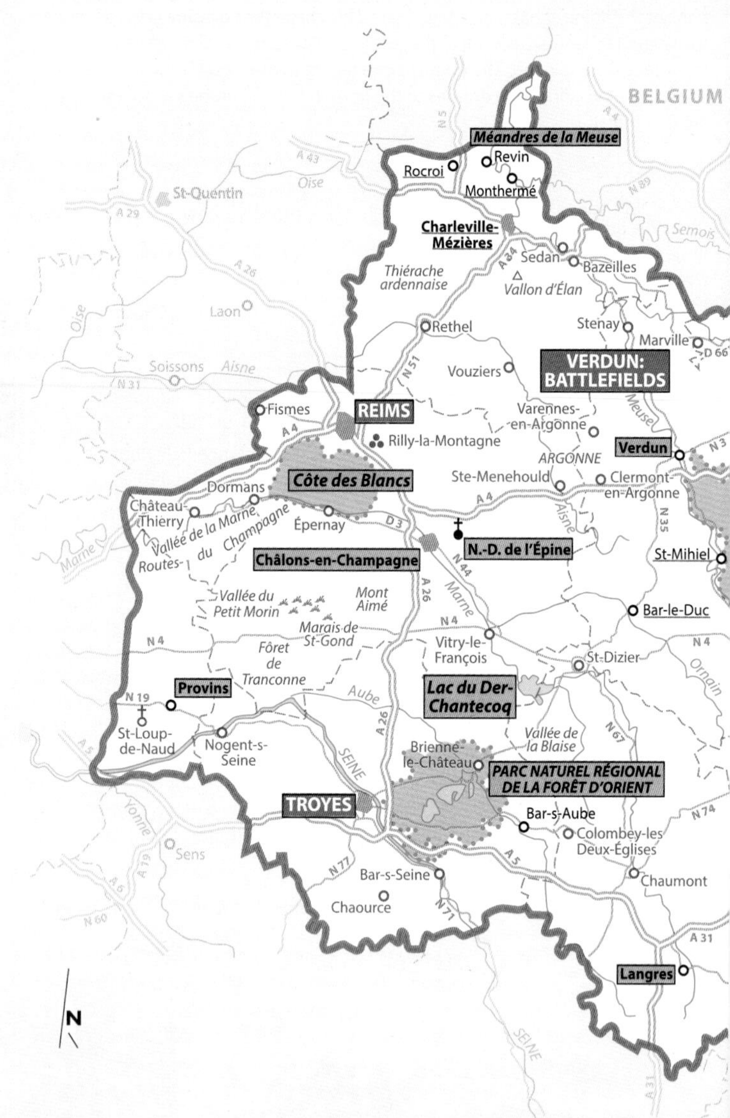

BELGIUM
Méandres de la Meuse
Rocroi
Revin
Monthermé
St-Quentin
Oise
Charleville-Mézières
Sedan
Bazeilles
Semois
Thiérache ardennaise
Vallon d'Élan
Laon
Stenay
Marville
Rethel
Vouziers
VERDUN: BATTLEFIELDS
Soissons
Aisne
Fismes
REIMS
Varennes-en-Argonne
Meuse
Rilly-la-Montagne
Verdun
ARGONNE
Côte des Blancs
Dormans
Ste-Menehould
Clermont-en-Argonne
Château-Thierry
Épernay
Vallée de la Marne
Routes du Champagne
N.-D. de l'Épine
St-Mihiel
Châlons-en-Champagne
Marne
Vallée du Petit Morin
Mont Aimé
Bar-le-Duc
Marais de St-Gond
Vitry-le-François
St-Dizier
Fôret de Tranconne
Provins
Lac du Der-Chantecoq
Ornain
Aube
St-Loup-de-Naud
Nogent-s-Seine
Vallée de la Blaise
Brienne-le-Château
PARC NATUREL RÉGIONAL DE LA FORÊT D'ORIENT
SEINE
Yonne
TROYES
Bar-s-Aube
Colombey-les-Deux-Églises
Sens
Bar-s-Seine
Chaumont
Chaource
Langres
N

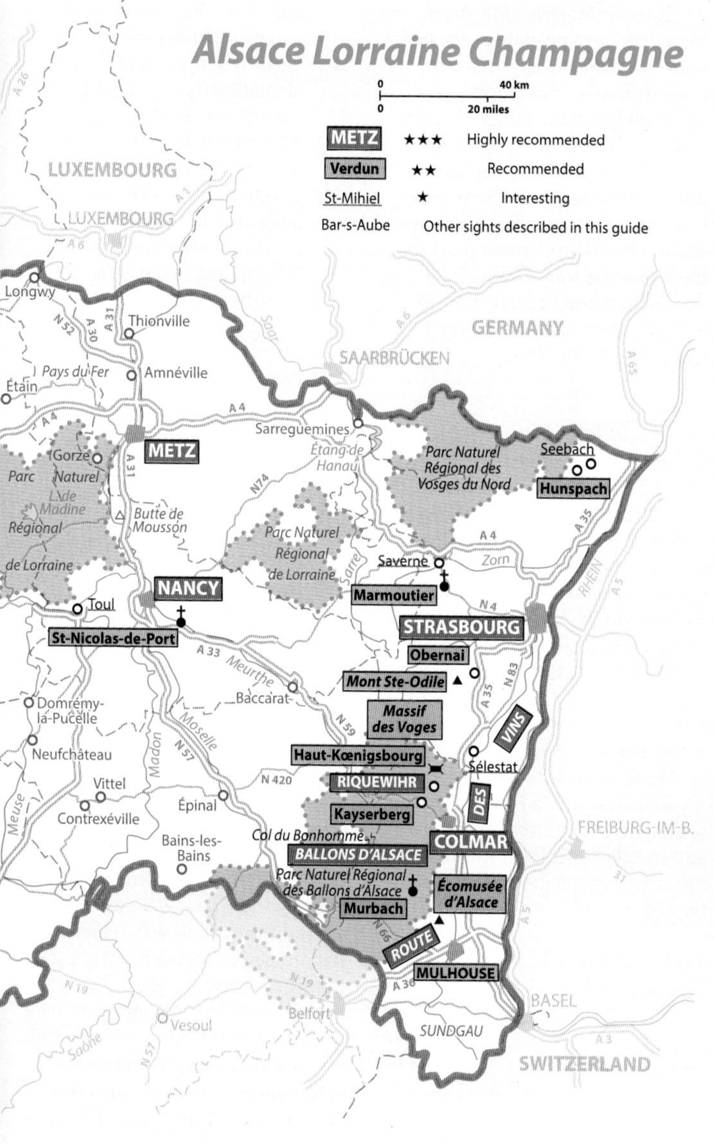
Alsace Lorraine Champagne
0 40 km
0 20 miles
METZ ★★★ Highly recommended
Verdun ★★ Recommended
St-Mihiel ★ Interesting
Bar-s-Aube Other sights described in this guide
LUXEMBOURG
LUXEMBOURG
GERMANY
SAARBRÜCKEN
Longwy
Thionville
Pays du Fer
Amnéville
Étain
Sarreguemines
Étang de Hanau
METZ
Gorze
Parc Naturel Régional de Lorraine
L. de Madine
Butte de Mousson
Parc Naturel Régional de Lorraine
Parc Naturel Régional des Vosges du Nord
Seebach
Hunspach
Saverne
Zorn
Marmoutier
NANCY
Toul
St-Nicolas-de-Port
STRASBOURG
Obernai
Mont Ste-Odile
Meurthe
Baccarat
Domrémy-la-Pucelle
Massif des Voges
Neufchâteau
Moselle
Madon
Haut-Kœnigsbourg
Sélestat
RIQUEWIHR
Vittel
Contrexéville
Épinal
Kayserberg
Meuse
Col du Bonhomme
FREIBURG-IM-B.
Bains-les-Bains
BALLONS D'ALSACE
COLMAR
Parc Naturel Régional des Ballons d'Alsace
Murbach
Écomusée d'Alsace
ROUTE DES VINS
MULHOUSE
Belfort
Vesoul
Saône
SUNDGAU
BASEL
SWITZERLAND
RHEIN
Sarre
Saar

Metz★★★

Lorraine

From the limestone escarpment of the Côtes de Moselle high above Metz, the Lorraine plateau can be seen stretching away eastwards towards the German frontier. The city itself lies at the meeting point of the Moselle with the Seille, a strategic site whose importance was appreciated by the Romans; it was here that their great highways leading from the Channel coast to the Rhine and from Trier to Italy were linked, their course marked today by Metz' busy shopping street, Rue Serpenoise.

- **Population:** 120 738.
- **Michelin Map:** 307 I 4
- **Info:** 2 Place d'Armes. ℘03 87 39 00 00. www.tourisme-metz.com. Discover Metz on foot with a tour guide (French only), by mini-train, boat, or at total liberty at your own pace with an audio-guide.
- **TGV:** Metz Ville is 1hr 30mins direct from Paris Est.
- **Location:** Metz is a major junction at the heart of Lorraine, and lies due S of Luxembourg, 50km/31mi from the German border and 160km/100mi NW of Strasbourg.
- **Parking:** Numerous car parks with over 7 000 parking spaces, most underground. Much of the centre is traffic free.
- **Timing:** Metz is a large city, and exploring it will take time. Allow at least a full day to visit the historic heart of the city.

A BIT OF HISTORY

In the 4C, as a response to the threat posed by the Germanic tribes to the east, fortifications were built. In the early part of the Middle Ages, the city was the residence of the Merovingian rulers of Eastern Gaul (Austrasia); it then became the capital of the kingdom of Lotharingia (Lorraine), before being attached to the Holy Roman Empire. In the 12C, Metz declared itself the capital of a republican city-state, with an elected High Magistrate as ruler. But in 1552, together with Verdun and Toul, it was annexed by a French kingdom seeking to push its frontier eastwards, and its role henceforth was that of a fortress-town standing guard over the border.

1871–1918–1944

On 6 August 1870, the Prussian armies conquered the city, which became part of the newly declared German Empire. The city lost a quarter of its population, people who chose to resettle in France; artists left and so did many businessmen, at the very moment when industry was expanding rapidly. Metz's loss was Nancy's gain.

The town began to take on a Germanic character. In 1898 the cathedral was given a neo-Gothic portal, complete with a statue of the Prophet Daniel looking uncommonly like Kaiser Wilhelm II (though his moustache was subsequently clipped). With its surrounding forts, Metz became the centre of the greatest fortified camp in the world. From 1902–08 the area around the station was rebuilt; the station itself was constructed in a style which mixed Rhenish neo-Romanesque and Second Reich symbolism (the emperor himself designed the bell tower); an imposing central post office rose nearby, together with hotels providing accommodation for the officers of the garrison. Metz was in fact the linchpin of the Schlieffen Plan, the strategy to be followed in the event of a future war with France; this plan envisaged the adoption of a defensive posture to the south of the city coupled

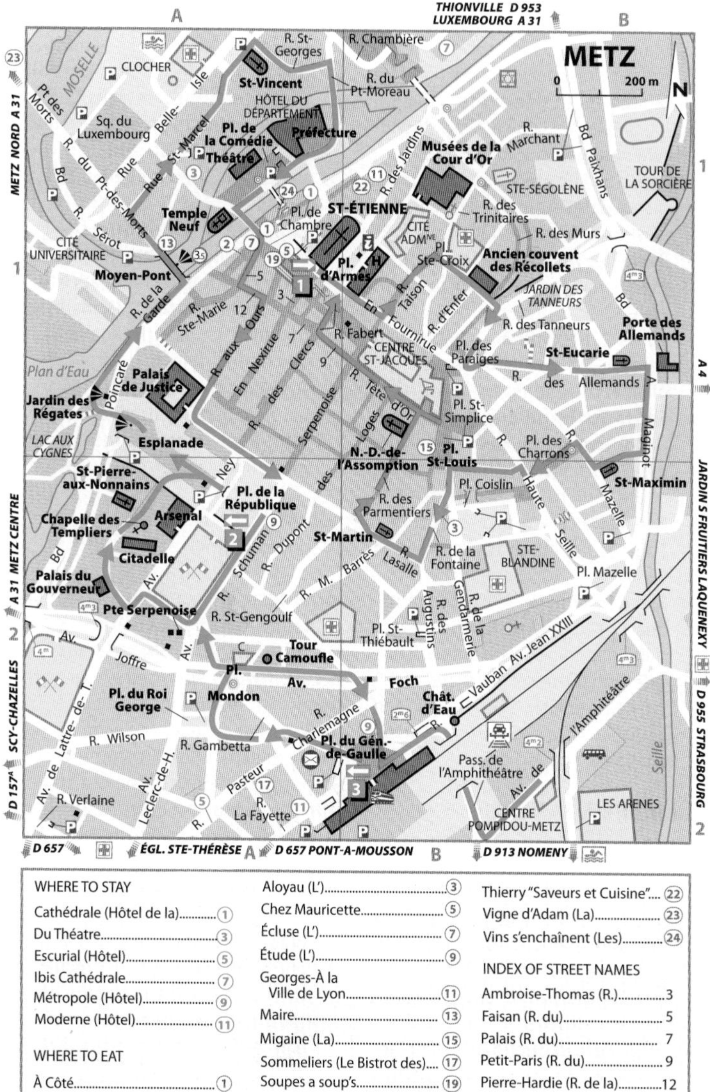

WHERE TO STAY

Cathédrale (Hôtel de la)............ 1
Du Théatre.................................. 3
Escurial (Hôtel)........................... 5
Ibis Cathédrale............................ 7
Métropole (Hôtel)......................... 9
Moderne (Hôtel)........................... 11

WHERE TO EAT

À Côté.. 1
Aloyau (L')................................... 3
Chez Mauricette............................ 5
Écluse (L')................................... 7
Étude (L')..................................... 9
Georges-À la Ville de Lyon.............. 11
Maire.. 13
Migaine (La).................................. 15
Sommeliers (Le Bistrot des).... 17
Soupes a soup's............................ 19
Thierry "Saveurs et Cuisine".... 22
Vigne d'Adam (La)........................ 23
Vins s'enchaînent (Les)............. 24

INDEX OF STREET NAMES

Ambroise-Thomas (R.)............... 3
Faisan (R. du)............................ 5
Palais (R. du)............................ 7
Petit-Paris (R. du)..................... 9
Pierre-Hardie (R. de la)............. 12

with a vast turning movement to the northwest, which would sweep through Belgium and then descend on Paris. In 1914 this plan all but succeeded; the German armies marched steadily forward for six weeks, coming within 50km/30mi of Paris, only to be thrown back by Marshal Joffre at the Miracle of the Marne.

In the inter-war period, the ring of forts around Metz was incorporated into the Maginot Line. Their defensive strength was such that the Allied armies took two and a half months to eject their German occupants in the autumn of 1944.

WALKING TOUR

1 OLD TOWN

Metz map, above.

- **Place d'Armes** – The square was designed in the 18C by Jacques

François Blondel on the site of the former cloisters. The town hall, facing the south side of the cathedral has an elegant Louis XVI façade with two pediments.

- **Église St-Eucaire** – The fine square belfry dates from the 12C and the west front from the 13C.
- **Porte des Allemands★** – This massive fortress formed part of the town walls.
- **Église St-Maximin★** – A fine carved head of Christ decorates the central pillar at the entrance.
- **Église St-Martin-aux-Champs** – A Gallo-Roman wall, once part of the town's fortifications, forms the base of the church
- **Notre-Dame-de-l'Assomption** – This Jesuit church was erected in 1665
- **Place St-Louis★** – Situated in the heart of the old town, the rectangular place St-Louis is lined on one side with buttressed arcaded buildings dating from the 14C, 15C and 16C that once housed the money-changers' shops.

2 ESPLANADE★

Metz map, p317.

This is a splendid walk laid out at the beginning of the 19C on the site of one of the citadel's moats: from the terrace, there is a fine view of Mount St-Quentin crowned by a fort and of one of the arms of the River Moselle.

- **Place de la République** – This place has long been the location of military parades.
- **Jardin des Régates** – This pretty turn-of-the-20C landscaped garden is at the foot of the citadel.
- **Moyen Pont★** – Pleasant **view★**.
- **Palais de Justice** – Built in the 18C, during the reign of Louis XVI, this edifice was intended to be the military governor's palace but the Revolution changed all that.
- **Église St-Pierre-aux-Nonnains★** – Around 390, during the reign of Emperor Constantine, a palæstra or gymnasium was built on this site. When Attila plundered the town in 451, the edifice was partially destroyed, but the walls built of rubble stones reinforced at regular intervals by ties of red bricks were spared and used in the building of a chapel c 615.
- **Chapelle des Templiers** – This chapel, built at the beginning of the 13C by the Knight Templars established in Metz since 1133, marks the transition between the Romanesque and Gothic styles.
- **Arsenal** – The walls of the 19C arsenal were partially used to build this ultra-modern centre dedicated to music and dance.

3 MODERN TOWN

Metz map, p317.

After 1870, William II wanted to turn Metz into a prestigious German city. He entrusted his plan to Kröger, an architect from Berlin, who used pink and grey sandstone, granite and even basalt. The new district includes the wide Avenue Foch, the chamber of commerce, the imposing building of the old station (1878), and the post office designed by Kröger in neo-Romanesque style and constructed between 1908 and 1911.

- **Place du Général-de-Gaulle★** – The station (1908) a huge, profusely decorated, neo-Romanesque edifice, is one of several buildings erected by the Germans at the beginning of the 20C to assert the power of the empire.

ADDITIONAL SIGHTS

Cathédrale St-Étienne★★★

The cathedral grew out of the joining together around 1240 of two churches which up to then had been separated by an alleyway. The 13C and 14C interior recalls the Gothic style of Champagne; its relative narrowness combines with the modest height of the aisles to exaggerate the loftiness of the nave which does in fact reach 41.77m.

The late Gothic chancel, crossing and transepts were completed at the beginning of the 16C.

The cathedral is known as "God's Lantern" (Lanterne du Bon Dieu) due to its stained-glass windows (**verrières★★★**). The rose window of the west front is 14C work, the lower part of the north transept window 15C, and the upper part of this window together with the glass of the south transept and the chancel, 16C. Contemporary glass can be seen beneath the towers and above all in the north ambulatory and on the southwest side of the north transept (the *Earthly Paradise* by Chagall).

Musées de la Cour d'Or ★★

The museums are housed in the buildings of a former Carmelite convent (17C), a 15C tithe barn (Grenier de Chèvrement) and several link rooms and extensions. In the basements are the remains of ancient baths. The complex uses the latest display techniques to present a fascinating survey of times past.

Centre Pompidou-Metz★★★

This is the first so-called "decentralised" branch of Paris's famous Centre Pompidou to open outside Paris. It exhibits artworks of the 20C and 21C to further its mission of promoting art in Europe. The building, with exhibits spread across three galleries, has a 77m-high spire. The exhibitions, most taken from the Musée National d'Art Moderne in Paris, are all temporary to allow for the continuing evolution of artistic styles that prove ripe for presentation.

14C rose window, Cathédrale St-Étienne

ADDRESSES

STAY

Hotel Ibis Metz Centre Cathédrale – 47 rue Chambière Quartier Pontiffroy. ✆03 87 31 01 73. 79 rooms. Ideal for exploring the city centre. Air conditioned rooms, WiFi and a restaurant overlooking the Moselle make for a convenient and pleasant stay.

Métropole – 5, pl. Gén.de Gaulle. ✆03 87 66 26 22. www.hotelmetropole-metz.com. 72 rooms. This hotel is housed in a nice freestone building opposite the station, providing rooms with warm tones, modern furnishings and a welcoming atmosphere.

Hôtel Moderne – 1, r. Lafayette. ✆03 87 66 57 33. www.hotel-moderne-metz.com. In the centre of town offering comfort and good taste. The rooms are equipped with functional furniture but are nevertheless pleasant and those overlooking the street are soundproofed.

Hôtel de la Cathédrale – 25 pl. de Chambre. ✆03 87 75 00 02. www.hotelcathedrale-metz.fr. Closed 1–15 Aug. 20 rooms. A charming hotel situated in a lovely 17C house that was completely restored in 1997. The attractive rooms have cast iron or cane beds, old parquet flooring and furniture, some of which is oriental. Most rooms face the cathedral, just opposite.

Du Théâtre – 3 r. du Pont-St-Marcel. ✆03 87 31 10 10. www.hoteldutheatre-metz.com. 65 rooms. Restaurant. An ideally located hotel in the historic town centre, providing freshly renovated rooms, more peaceful on the Moselle side. Fine regional furnishings in the reception area and regional wall paintings in the restaurant.

Escurial – 18 r. Pasteur. ✆03 87 66 40 96. www.escurial-hotel.com. Closed Dec 29–Jan 1. 36 rooms. This hotel in the Imperial district has recently had a facelift. Providing modern and practical rooms, a breakfast area and large lounge with a warm and colourful atmosphere.

EAT

Chez Mauricette – Marché couvert, Place de la Cathédrale. 03 87 36 37 69. www.chezmauricette.com. Closed Sun and Mon. This enticing market stall run by Mauricette and his team offers delicious food to go – French, Corsican, Swiss, German, Italian and Spanish – for those in a hurry to see the sites!

La Migaine – 1–3 pl. St-Louis. 03 87 75 56 67. Closed Aug 1–15 and Sun. You can eat at any time here, from morning to late afternoon. The tearoom in a pretty square surrounded by arcades serves copious breakfasts, meat pies, quiche Lorraine, cakes and tea – the choice is yours. Terrace in summer.

Soupes a soup's – Marché Couvert, pl de la Cathédrale. 06 08 31 11 04. Situated in a splendid covered market constructed in 1785 the soup bar owned by M.Grumberg, a self-taught passionate cook, is a real success. Delicious soups of vegetables or fruit, hot or cold, traditional breads, kebabs and more can be sampled here.

Les Vins s'enchainement – 8 r. Piques. 03 87 36 19 01. Closed Sat, Sun eve and Wed. In a small 18C pedestrianised street you can find this wine bar with its contemporary decor done by the clients. The owner, an informed sommelier, can suggest more than 30 cru served by the glass to accompany meats, cheeses, tartes, traditional cuisine and the famous house terrine.

L'Aloyau – 3 pl. de-la-Fontaine. 03 87 37 33 72. Closed Jul 19–Aug 9, Sun and Mon. Grandson and son of a butcher and one himself for 15 years before opening a restaurant. Well known for his beef, lamb and suckling pig dishes accompanied by delicious sauces, not to mention the sea food.

L'Étude – 11, Avenue Robert Schuman. 03 87 36 35 32. Closed Sun. Very popular with the locals, this quintessentially French establishment marries books with food by lining the walls of the restaurant with well stocked bookshelves. Live music on Friday and Saturday.

Georges – À La Ville de Lyon – 9 r. Piques. 03 87 36 07 01. www.alavilledelyon.com. Closed Jan 1–10, Mon (except lunch on public hols) and Sun eve. The restaurant rooms are split between outbuildings of the Cathedral – one room is set in a 14C Chapel – and the walls of a coaching house.

Thierry "Saveurs et Cuisine" – 5 r. des Piques, "Maison de la fleur de Lys". 03 87 74 01 23. www.restaurant-thierry.fr. Inventive cuisine enhanced by herbs and spices, an attractive brick and wood setting and a summer terrace all contribute to this stylish bistro's popularity.

À Côte – 43 pl du Chambre. 03 87 66 38 84. Closed Sun and Mon. Next door to L'Ecluse, the chef Eric Maire offers accessible modern cuisine which can be sampled at the bar first unlike the neighbouring restaurant.

L'Écluse – 45 pl. de la Chambre. 03 87 75 42 38. Closed Aug 5–20, Sun and Mon. A taste of Brittany, near the cathedral. The chef's enthusiasm for the region is evident in the decor, inspired by the Breton coast, with blue chairs and a menu that includes seafood served in an attractive, bright dining room.

Le Bistrot des Sommeliers – 10 r. Pasteur. 03 87 63 40 20. Closed Dec 24–Jan 4, Sat lunch, Sun and Hols. Colourful facade and decor on a wine theme in this bistro near the station. A good selection of wines by the glass and dishes based on market produce on a blackboard.

La Vigne Adam – 50 r. Gén. de Gaulle F, 57050 Plappeville. 03 87 30 36 68. Closed Sun. In the heart of the village, this old winegrower's house is now a trendy, modern wine bar/restaurant. Modern cuisine and a fine selection of wines.

Maire – 1 r. du Pont-des-Morts. 03 87 32 43 12. Closed Wed lunchtimes and Tue. There is a superb view of the Moselle from this town-centre restaurant. You will enjoy the young chef's carefully prepared dishes, whether in the salmon-pink dining room with its pale wood furniture or on the attractive terrace.

Verdun★★

This ancient stronghold occupies a strategic position on the Meuse. The Upper Town with its cathedral and citadel is poised on an outcrop overlooking the river.

- **Population:** 18 513.
- **Michelin Map:** 307 D 4
- **Info:** Place de la Nation. ℘03 29 86 14 18. www.verdun-tourisme.com.
- **TGV:** Verdun is about 1h 40 from Paris Est via Meuse (change).
- **Location:** Roughly mid-way between Metz (80km/50mi E) and Reims (120km/75mi W).

A BIT OF HISTORY

The Gauls were the first to build a fortress here on the left bank of the Meuse. They were followed by the Romans, but Verdun entered the mainstream of history with the signing of the **Treaty of Verdun** in 843. By its terms, Charlemagne's realm was divided up among his grandsons. The repercussions have been felt throughout the centuries.

The town was besieged in 1870 at the start of the Franco-Prussian War, then occupied for three years. In World War I, Verdun was the scene of some of the bloodiest fighting of the Western Front, in a battle that lasted 18 months.

WALKING TOUR

VILLE HAUTE★

Verdun map, p322.

The seat of a bishop, the fortified upper town rises in stages from the banks of the river. The city's historic buildings include **Cathédrale Notre-Dame★**, laid out like the great Romanesque basilicas of the Rhineland, and the Bishop's Palace **(Palais épiscopal★)**, constructed by Robert de Cotte in the 18C.

ADDITIONAL SIGHT

Citadelle Souterraine (Underground Citadel) – self-guided vehicle travels 7km/4.3mi of tunnels equipped to fulfil the needs of the army.

BATTLEFIELDS★★★

10km/6.2mi NE of Verdun.

The name of Verdun is forever linked to the decisive struggle on which turned the outcome of the First World War (1914–18). The gaze of the world was fixed for a year-and-a-half on the violence endured by both sides, in a battle which inspired the utmost steadfastness and courage.

At the outbreak of war in August 1914, Verdun lay 40km/25mi from the frontier. The 21 February 1916 dawned bright but cold. A devastating bombardment preceded the Germans' frontal assault on the French lines. Within four days Douaumont Fort had fallen.

This was the moment at which General Pétain took effective charge of the battle; by the time of his replacement in April 1917, it was clear that the German attempt to break the French army had failed. Verdun, the hinge of the Western Front, could not be taken.

A series of battles raged throughout March and April in the Argonne, around Les Éparges; and, closer to Verdun, on Hill 304 and the other eminence known chillingly as the Mort-Homme (Dead Man's Hill). On 11 July, the final German offensive ground to a halt in front of the Souville fort, a mere 5km/3mi from the city. The French counter-offensive began in October 1916. By 20 August 1917, the Hell of Verdun, which had cost the lives of over 700 000 men, was over.

ADDRESSES

STAY

Camping Les Breuils – 8 allée des Breuils. ℘03 29 86 15 31. www.camping-lesbreuils.com. Apr–Sep. Reservation advised. 162 places. Pleasant, quiet, well equipped campsite.

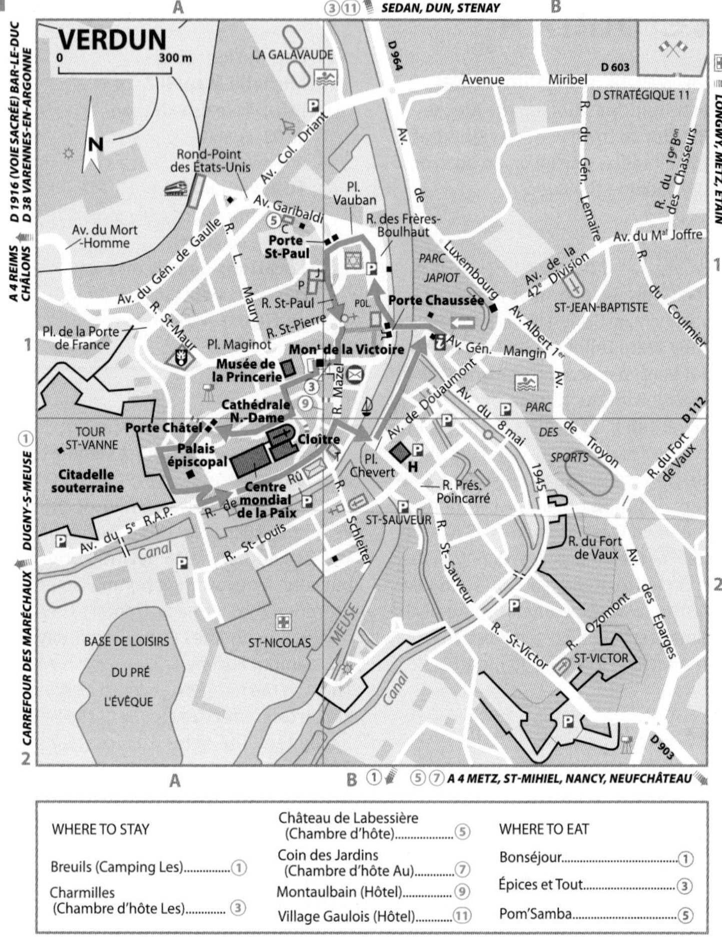

Montaulbain – 4 r. Vieille-Prison. ☎03 29 86 00 47. 10 rooms. Cramped rooms, but well-kept.

Chambre d'hôte Charmilles – 12 Rue de la Gare. ☎03 29 86 93 49. 3 rooms. Pretty rooms.

Chambre d'hôte Coin des Jardins – 13 bis, Grande rue, 55160 Pareid. ☎03 29 83 97 76. www.aucoindesjardins.com. 5 rooms. A restored Lorraine farm.

Village Gaulois – 11 rue du Parge Marre, 55100, 12km/7.5m north of Verdun on the D964. ☎03 29 85 03 45. www.villagegaulois.com. 11 rooms. Rustic ambience.

Chambre d'hôte Château de Labessière – 55320 Ancemont. 15km/9.3mi S of Verdun on D 34 (St-Mihiel road). ☎03 29 85 70 21. www.labessiere.com. Closed Dec 25, Jan 1. 4 rooms. Dinner. 18C château.

EAT

Pom Samba – 7 ave Garibaldi. ☎03 29 83 49 34. Closed Sun. An imaginative restaurant.

Bonsejour – 33 route de Metz. ☎03 29 84 66 63. www.lebonsejour.fr. Pizzas and Flammeküche.

Epices et Tout – 33 rue Gros Dégres. ☎03 29 86 46 88. Closed Sun and Wed eve. Modern, inventive cuisine.

Nancy★★★

Capital of the industrial area of Lorraine, Nancy is sited on the low-lying land between the River Meurthe and the Moselle Heights (Côtes de Moselle).

- **Population:** 105 421.
- **Michelin Map:** 307 I 6
- **Info:** 14 pl. Stanislas. ℘03 83 35 22 41. www.ot-nancy.fr.
- **TGV:** Nancy Ville is 1hr 40mins direct from Paris Est.
- **Tram:** Runs from Vandoeuvre-les-Nancy to Essey-les-Nancy (www.reseau-stan.com).
- **Location:** Nancy lies 56km/35mi due S of Metz.
- **Don't Miss:** Place Stanislas.
- **Timing:** Discover Nancy using *Les Taxis de Nancy* with multi-language commentary (www.taxis-nancy.com; ℘03 83 37 65 37).

A BIT OF HISTORY

The city was founded in the 11C, but its history begins in the 15C when the Dukes of Lorraine asserted their independence. In the 17C, the new town (*Ville neuve*) was planned on a regular pattern by the artist **Claude Lorrain** (1600–82). Louis XIV 's architect Mansart designed the town hall **(Palais du Governement★)** in 1699. Ever since the Treaty of Munster in 1648, the Duchy of Lorraine had been in a precarious situation; an independent enclave in French territory, it still formed part of the Holy Roman Empire. Though French in language and culture, its people were proud of their independence.

In 1738, following the War of the Polish Succession, Duke François I, son of Leopold and husband of Maria-Theresa of Austria, found himself having to cede Lorraine in exchange for Tuscany. In his place, Louis XV appointed, as ruler for life, his own father-in-law Stanislas Leszczynski, and by 1766 the Duchy had been painlessly incorporated into the French kingdom, a notable success for Cardinal Fleury's foreign policy. Stanislas was a man of peace, fond of his daughter the Queen of France, a lover of good living and of the opposite sex, and a passionate builder.

He set out to join together the old quarter of Nancy with the "New Town" by means of a set-piece of civic design in honour of his son-in-law. The great project was completed between 1752 and 1755.

WALKING TOURS

1 LORRAINE'S CAPITAL

Nancy map II, p325.

- **Place Stanislas★★★** – The collaboration between architect Emmanuel Héré and craftsman Jean Lamour resulted in a superb architectural ensemble (1751–60) characterised

PRACTICAL INFORMATION

Guided tours – Nancy, City of Art, organises 1hr30 guided tours (French only). Audioguides are also available. Enquire at tourist office or buy online for all tours and passes.

Tourist train (le Train touristique) – Apr–mid-Nov: 40min tour of the historic town by miniature train. Departs from place de la Carrière, daily 9am–6pm. €7 (children 6–14 years, €5). ℘03 89 73 74 24. www.petit-train-nancy.fr.

City pass – This pass gives entry to six museums, also serves as a 24-hr public transport ticket, and gives discounts on a range of products: €16. There is also a separate **Museum Pass**, giving access to 2–6 museums only, and valid for 10 days: €10.

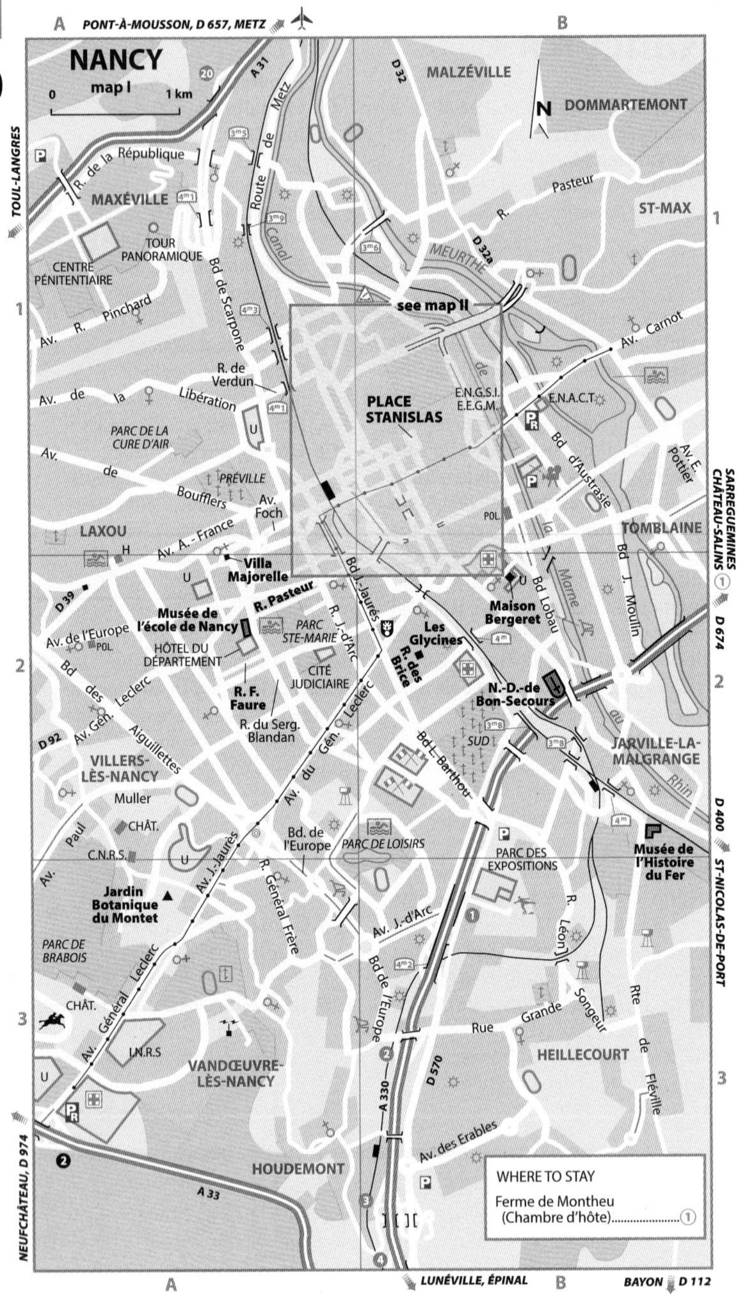

by the perfect harmony of its proportions, layout and detail. The square is surrounded by pavilions, emphasising the impression of space and harmony.

- **Hôtel de ville** – The town hall was erected between 1752 and 1755. The interior rooms offer a splendid vista of the surrounding squares.

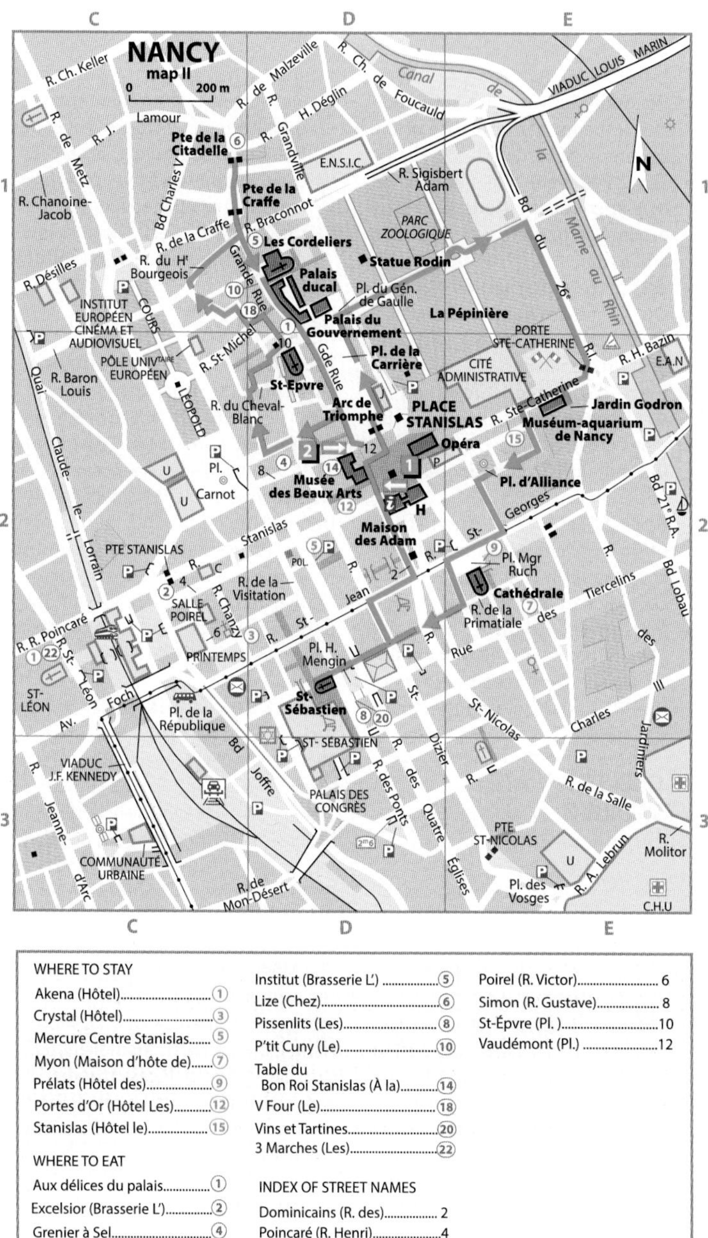

- **Arc de Triomphe★** – This deep triumphal arch, built between 1754 and 1756 to honour Louis XV, is modelled on Septimus Severus' arch in Rome.
- **Place de la Carrière★** – This elongated square dates from the time of the dukes of Lorraine; originally used for cavalry drills, it was remod-

elled by Héré and is now lined with beautiful 18C mansions.

- **Palais du Gouverneur★** – This edifice is the former residence of the governors of Lorraine.
- **La Pépinière** – This fine 23ha/57 acre open space includes a terrace, an English garden, a rose garden and a zoo.
- **Musée-aquarium de Nancy** – On the ground floor is the tropical **aquarium★**, upstairs is a collection of stuffed animals.
- **Place d'Alliance** – Designed by Héré, the square is lined with 18C mansions.
- **Cathédrale** – An imposing 18C construction.
- **Église St-Sébastien** – This masterpiece by architect Jenesson was consecrated in 1732; it has a striking concave Baroque **façade★**.
- **Maison des Adam** – This is the elegant home of the Adam family, who were renowned sculptors in the 18C and decorated the house themselves.

2 OLD TOWN AND NEW TOWN

Nancy map II, p325.

The Old Town is the historic heart of the city, centred on place St-Epvre. When it extended outside its original gates, the New Town was born. There are a number of attractive hôtels to see.

- **Basilique St-Epvre** – Built in the 19C, in neo-Gothic style, this imposing church is dedicated to a 6C bishop of Toul. Its elegant west front is preceded by a monumental staircase (a gift from the emperor of Austria). The roof was blown off during the severe storm in December 1999.
- **Porte de la Craffe★** – This gate, which formed part of the 14C fortifications, is decorated with the thistle of Nancy and the cross of Lorraine (19C). The gate was used as a prison until the Revolution. To the north stands the Porte de la Citadelle which used to secure the old town.
- **Palais ducal★★** – Dating from the second half of the 13C, the palace was in ruins when René II had it rebuilt after his victory over Charles the Bold of Burgundy. In the 16C, Duke Antoine had the **Porterie★★** (gateway) completed together with the Galerie des Cerfs (Deer Gallery). In 1850 the palace was skilfully restored.

ADDITIONAL SIGHTS

Musée de l'École de Nancy★★

36–38 rue du Sergent Blandan. Open Wed–Sun 10am–6pm. €6. Closed 1 Jan, 1 May, 14 Jul, 1 Nov, 25 Dec. 03 83 40 14 86. www.ecole-de-nancy.com.

Housed in an opulent residence dating from the turn of the 20C, this museum offers a remarkable insight into the renewal movement in the field of decorative arts that took place in Nancy between 1885 and 1914 and became known as the **École de Nancy**.

Musée des Beaux-Arts★★

3, pl. Stanislas. Open daily except Tue 10am–6pm. Closed 1 Jan, 1 May, 14 Jul, 1 Nov, 25 Dec. €6. 03 83 85 30 72.

The impressively refurbished Museum of Fine Arts, housed in one of the pavilions on place Stanislas, contains rich collections of European art from the 14C to the present day which are not arranged chronologically – to great advantage. The Modern Art collection, housed in the contemporary extension, is essentially represented by Manet, Monet, Henri Edmond Cross, Modigliani, Juan Gris, Georg Grosz, Picasso, and a few early 20C artists from Lorraine. Sculptures include works by Rodin, Duchamp-Villon, Lipchitz, and César.

Musée Lorrain★★★

64 Grande-Rue in the Palais ducal. Open daily except Tue 10am–12.30pm, 2–6pm. Closed 1 Jan, 1 May, 14 Jul, 1 Nov, 25 Dec. €4. 03 83 32 18 74.

The museum contains a wealth of exceptional documents illustrating the history of Lorraine, its artistic production and its folklore, displayed on three floors. The pavilion at the bottom of the garden houses an **archaeological gallery** concerned with prehistory, the Celtic period, and Gallo-Roman and Frankish times.

Église des Cordeliers★

Open daily except Mon 10am– 12.30pm, 2–6pm. Closed 1 Jan, 1 May, 14 Jul, 1 Nov, 25 Dec. €4. ✆03 83 32 18 74.

The now-restored 15C Franciscan convent and adjacent church were erected on the initiative of Duke René II.

The **church★** has only one nave, as is usual for the church of a mendicant order. A chapel on the left-hand side contains the **recumbent figure of Philippa of Gelderland★★**, René II's second wife, carved in fine limestone, one of the finest works of Ligier Richier. Against the south wall (near the high altar), note the funeral recess of **René II's funeral monument★**, carved by Mansuy Gauvain in 1509. The effigy of Cardinal de Vaudémont (d 1587) is the work of Florent Drouin. The latter is also the author of a remarkable Last Supper, a low-relief sculpture after the famous painting by Leonardo da Vinci.

Built from 1607 onwards, the **Chapelle ducale★** was modelled on the Medici Chapel in Florence. The cloisters and some rooms of the former monastery are restored and now house a rich **Musée d'Arts et Traditions populaires**.

Jardin botanique du Montet★

100 r. du Jardin Botanique. Opening times vary. €4 greenhouses (gardens: no charge). ✆03 83 41 47 47. www.cjbn.uhp-nancy.fr.

The botanical gardens contain some 15 thematic collections (Alpine, ornamental, medicinal plants, an arboretum etc), and 6 500 species grow in the hot houses: orchids, and insect-eating and succulent plants.

Église Notre-Dame-de-Bon-Secours★

Avenue de Strasbourg.

Built in 1738 for Stanislas by Emmanuel Héré, on the site of René II's chapel commemorating his victory over Charles the Bold (1476), this church is a well-known place of pilgrimage.

The richly decorated interior includes carved confessionals in Louis XV style, railings by Jean Lamour and a splendid Rocaille pulpit.

The chancel contains **Stanislas' tomb★** and the monument carved by Vassé for the heart of Marie Leszczynska, Louis XV's wife, on the right-hand side and, on the left, the **mausoleum of Catherine Opalinsk★★**, Stanislas' wife.

ADDRESSES

STAY

Weekends in Nancy – At some hotels stays of two nights and more are rewarded by a welcome gift and reductions on visits to the town. Ask at the tourist office for the list of hotels and conditions.

⊖ **Hôtel Stanislas** – 22 rue Ste Catherine. ✆03 83 37 23 88. www.hotel-lestanislas.fr. 16 rooms. In the centre of Nancy adjacent to Place Stanislas and only 100m from the splendid Parc de la Pépinière, this small is ideally placed for exploring the old town.

⊖ **Chambre d'hôte Ferme de Montheu** – 54770 Dommartin-sous-Amance. 10km/6.25mi NE of Nancy, Sarreguemines and Agincourt direction. ✆03 83 31 17 37. 5 rooms. Evening meal ⊖. This working farm in the middle of the country has lovely uninterrupted views, apart from a nearby high-tension power line. But that's soon forgotten in the peace of the simple rooms with their old furniture. Evening meal by arrangement.

⊖⊖ **Hôtel Revotel –** 41–43 avenue Raymond Poincarré. ✆03 83 28 02 13. 58 rooms. Part of a chain located in the town centre near to the station, metro, bus and shops/restaurants. Pleasant receptionists and comfortable rooms in 2 categories; prestige or standard.

⊖⊖ **Portes d'Or** – 21 r. Stanislas. ✆03 83 35 42 34. www.hotel-lesportesdor.com. 20 rooms. The main advantage of this hotel is its proximity to the Place Stanislas. The pastel-coloured rooms are not very large, but are reasonably well equipped.

Hôtel Crystal – 5 r. Chanzy. 03 83 17 54 00. Closed Dec 24–Jan 2. 58 rooms. This entirely renovated Best Western hotel near the station is a good place to stay in Nancy. Its modern, spacious rooms have been nicely arranged and decorated and feel welcoming. Cosy bar-lounge.

Mercure Centre Stanislas – 5 r. Carmes. 03 83 30 92 60. www.mercure.com. 80 rooms. Ideally situated in the town centre shopping area, this hotel has complete, well-kept facilities. Rooms have furniture in the Art Nouveau style.

Maison d'hôte Myon – 7, rue Mably. 03 83 46 56 56. www.maisondemyon.com. 5 rooms. An entirely restored 18C hotel transformed into a maison d'hôte in the heart of Nancy near the Place Stanislas. The individual rooms are tastefully decorated and equipped with stylish furniture.

Des Prélats – 56 pl Mgr Ruch. 03 83 30 20 20. www.hoteldesprelats.com. 42 rooms. This 17C building attached to the Cathedral has been wonderfully restored with spacious, individually styled rooms and a pleasant veranda opening onto an inner courtyard.

EAT

Aux délices du Palais – 69 Grande Rue. 03 83 30 44 19. Closed Aug and Dec 24–31. Small restaurant cheerfully decorated. Excellent cuisine and menus regularly updated. Specialities include lasagne with salmon and spinach.

Les Pissenlits – 25 bis r. des Ponts. 03 83 37 43 97. www.les-pissenlits.com. Closed Aug 1–15, Sun and Mon. There's always a crowd in this bistro near the market, and with good reason: the atmosphere is relaxed, the cuisine innovative and diverse.

Le V Four – 10 r. St-Michel. 03 83 32 49 48. Closed Feb 1–10, Sep 14–24, Sun evening and Mon. It may be small, but this restaurant in the heart of the old city is popular among the locals, who enjoy its simple modern decor and its trendy cuisine. Terrace.

Excelsior Brasserie – 50, rue Henri-Poincaré. 03 83 35 24 57. www.brasserie-excelsior.com. A belle époque brasserie complete with beautiful école de Nancy windows and fittings and fixtures by all the leading artisans of the period. Typical brasserie cuisine.

Brasserie de l'Institut – 2, rue Braconnot. 03 83 32 24 14. One of Nancy's oldest cafés dating from 1903 designed by the architect Charbonnier and situated in the old town.

Chez Lize – 52 rue Henri Déglin. 03 83 30 36 26. Closed Jul 12–Aug 9, Dec 28–Jan 4, Sat lunch, Sun eve, and Mon. Restaurant fitted out in a former bar. The dining room offers the appropriate rustic setting for serving Alsatian as well as Lorraine specialities.

Le P'tit Cuny – 95 Grande Rue. 03 83 32 85 94. Closed Dec 25 and Jan 1. Authentic Lorraine cuisine such as ***choucroute, tête de veau*** and veal pie are served in this rather cramped but welcoming small restaurant.

A La Table du Bon Roi Stanislas – 7 r. Gustave-Simon. 03 83 35 36 52. http://tablestan.free.fr. Closed Sun eve and Mon. Reservation advised. Dedicated to King Stanislas who became Duke of Lorraine in the 18C and was said to be a good amateur cook. This historic restaurant has original recipes and sobre period decor not to be missed.

Vins et Tartines – 25bis rue des ponts. 03 83 35 17 25. www.vins-et-tartines.com. Closed Aug 1–15. As the name suggests, the concept of this restaurant is light meals with wine and bread.

Les 3 Marchés – 8 r st Léon. 03 83 41 33 00. Reservation advised. Small restaurant with excellent traditional cuisine. Decorated with large mirrors and corner library.

Grenier à Sel – 28 r. Gustave-Simon. 03 83 32 31 98. Closed Jul 23–Aug 13, Sun and Mon. This restaurant is on the first floor of one of the oldest houses in town. In the large country-style dining room you can enjoy food with a modern flair.

Toul★

On the banks of the river Moselle, the handsome fortified town occupies a strategic position at the intersection of highways and waterways.

- **Population:** 15 693.
- **Michelin Map:** 307 G 6
- **Info:** Parvis de la Cathédrale. ℘03 83 64 90 60. www.toul.fr.
- **TGV:** Toul is 2h 15 from Paris Est via Nancy Ville.
- **Location:** Toul lies on a wide loop in the Moselle river, 22km/14mi W of Nancy, and 75km/47mi to the E of Saint-Dizier.

A BIT OF HISTORY

Together with Metz and Verdun, the city was one of the three Imperial Bishoprics which were annexed by Henri II in 1552 and were finally recognised as belonging to the French Crown by the Peace of Westphalia in 1648.

Vauban built new ramparts round the city in 1700 (the Porte de Metz is all that remains today), which were subsequently improved at intervals so that on the eve of World War I Toul was acknowledged as one of the best-defended strongholds in Europe.

SIGHTS

Cathédrale St-Étienne★★

Built from 1221 to 1496, cathedral has a very simple elevation. The highly pointed arches of the first five bays of the nave are in the High Gothic style of the 14C. The west front (**façade★★**), almost overloaded with architectural ornament, lost its statuary at the time of the French Revolution. The **cloisters★**, adorned with fine gargoyles, are among the most extensive in France.

Musée d'Art et d'Histoire★

25 rue Gouvion Saint Cyr. Open daily (except Tue): Apr–Oct 10am–noon, 2–6pm; Nov–Mar 2–6pm. Closed 1 Jan, Easter, 1 May, 25 Dec. ℘03 83 64 13 38. www.toul.fr/Musee-70.

Housed in the Hôtel-Dieu, there are numerous collections tracing the history of Toul. The themed rooms cover everything from the prehistoric period to recent history.

Église St-Gengoult★

This former Collegiate church, erected in the 13C and 15C, is a fine example of Champagne Gothic architecture. The West front has an elegant doorway dating from the 15C. The Cloister★★ dates from the 16C and the outside decoration of the galleries is Renaissance.

ADDRESSES

STAY

⊖⊜ **La Villa Lorraine** – 15 r. Gambetta. ℘03 83 43 08 95. 21 rooms. Closed Nov school hols. This small hotel in the heart of the city has well soundproofed bedrooms with rustic furnishings and pleasant breakfast room.

⊖⊜ **Hôtel l'Europe** – 373 ave. Victor Hugo. ℘03 83 43 00 10. www.hotel-europe54.com. 21 rooms. A convenient hôtel when travelling by train. The ground floor still has a 1930s atmosphere. The well-kept rooms have all been renovated. Family hospitality.

EAT

⊖⊜ **Auberge du Pressoir** – 7 pl. des Pachenottes. ℘03 83 63 81 91. Closed Sun & Wed eve, Mon and last 2 weeks in Aug. The old village station has become a restaurant with a simple renovated decor. Regional country ornaments decorate the walls. Sunny terrace.

⊖⊜ **Aux Bouchons Lyonnais** – 10 r. de la République. ℘03 83 43 00 41. Closed Sun eve. In the centre of Toul discover a restaurant specialising in traditional cuisine and Lyonaise dishes. The warm decor with ceramic panels helps to give an authentic feeling of times past.

Strasbourg★★★

This important modern city, with a busy river port and renowned university, is not just the lively capital of Alsace. It is also where the Council of Europe and European Parliament are located. At the same time, the Grande Île, the historic centre around the cathedral, has been listed as a UNESCO World Heritage Site since 1988.

- **Population:** 271 782.
- **Michelin Map:** 315 K 5
- **Info:** 17 pl. de la Cathédrale. www.otstrasbourg.fr. There are satellite offices at the TGV station and in the Parc de l'Etoile.
- **TGV:** Strasbourg is 2hrs 15mins direct from Paris Gare de l'Est.
- **Flights:** Strasbourg-Entzheim International Airport (www.strasbourg.aeroport.fr) is 10km/6.25mi from Strasbourg centre via autoroute. The airport is linked to Strasbourg railway station by a train shuttle (4 times per hour, journey time of 9 minutes). ☎0800 77 98 67 (freephone within France). www.ter-sncf.com/alsace.
- **Location:** On the banks of the river Ill, Strasbourg is less than 8km/5mi W of the Rhine, and 150km/95mi E of Nancy.
- **Don't Miss:** Notre-Dame Cathedral and the Musée de l'Œuvre Notre-Dame. For a relaxing time and to see chimney nesting storks visit the parc de l'Orangerie.
- **Timing:** Allow at least a full day to explore the Grande Île and Petite France, preferably more, much more.
- **Parking:** Parking areas around the outskirts of Strasbourg allow you to leave your car and travel into the town centre by tram. City-centre parking is not easy for visitors.

A BIT OF HISTORY

Strasbourg's name comes from the German meaning "City of the roads", and the place is indeed a meeting point for the highways, railways and waterways linking the Mediterranean with the Rhineland, Central Europe, the North Sea and the Baltic via the Belfort Gap and the Swabian Basin.

On 14 February 842, the **Strasbourg Oaths** were sworn by two of the sons of Louis the Pious (son of Charlemagne). Brothers Charles and Louis undertook to be loyal to one another in their attempt to frustrate the ambitions of their elder brother Lothair. Protocol demanded that each declare the oath in a language comprehensible to his brother's entourage; thus it was that the text read out by Louis the German is considered to be the oldest such document in a Romance language, the first written example of the language which has evolved into modern French.

Strasbourg remained a **free city** within the Holy Roman Empire even after the virtual incorporation of the rest of Alsace into France by the Peace of Westphalia in 1648, but eventually submitted to annexation by Louis XIV in 1681.

On 24 April 1792, **Frédéric de Dietrich**, Strasbourg's first constitutional mayor, threw a farewell celebration for the volunteers of the Army of the Rhine. The conversation turned to the need for a marching song to match the troops' enthusiasm. Rouget de Lisle was asked to compose "something worth singing"; by morning he had finished, and sang his "marching song for the Army of the Rhine". Not long after, it was adopted by the Federates of Marseille, and ever since has been known as the **Marseillaise**.

PRACTICAL INFORMATION

PARK & RIDE – Car parks on the outskirts of the city make it possible to park your vehicle close to a tram station and to travel to the centre in just a few minutes. After paying your parking fee for the day, all occupants of the vehicle receive a ticket entitling them to a return journey by tram. The Park & Ride car parks are open from Mon–Sat, 7am–8pm. Outside the opening hours the car park is free, but payment is required to use the tram.The car parks are indicated by a square panel with the letters P+R on a violet background.

TRAMWAYS – CTS. ℘03 88 77 70 70. www.cts-strasbourg.fr. 5 tram lines link tourist sights in and around Strasbourg (Lines A, B and C operate Mon–Sun 4.30am–0.30am; line D operates Mon–Sat 7am–7pm except during the summer school holidays).

BUSES – CTS. ℘03 88 77 70 70. 29 bus routes crisscross the conurbation; in addition, intercity buses link the city with many Alsatian villages.

TICKETS: A **Unipass** (€1.60) is a single-journey ticket valid for an hour on the bus and tram network; A **Tourpass** (€4.50) is valid for 24 hours for an unlimited number of journeys. A **24H Trio Pass** (€6.50) is valid for 24 hours for an unlimited number of journeys, for 2 to 3 persons travelling together (minimum: 1 adult and 1 child).

Strasbourg Pass – Issued by the tourist office, this pass allows free or half-price admission to 10 sights and monuments. Valid for 3 days, it is on sale in the tourist office information centres (place de la Cathédrale, place de la Gare and Pont de l'Europe) and hotels. €19.

Guided tours – The town organises guided tours (1hr 30min) by approved guides. Enquire at the tourist office.

Audio-guided tours – The city has created a 15-stage trail that highlights the way in which Europe has shaped the city over the centuries.

Mini-train – Apr to Oct. Departure place du Château, next to the cathedral, every half-hour or every hour depending on time of year. €5. ℘03 88 77 70 03. Guided tour of the old town (50min, in French) with a stop at Barrage Vauban.

Boat trips on the Ill – ♿ A choice of two multi-lingual trips along the River Ill: (1) **20 Centuries of History**, (1hr 10min, all year, 8–38 sailings daily depending on season: €12.50, children 4–12, €7.50), and (2) **Grande Île**, a tour of the central part of the city (45min, Apr–Dec, except Jul–Aug, just one sailing daily: €9.50, children 4–12, €6). ℘03 88 84 13 13. www.batorama.fr.

In 1870, Strasbourg was seized by Germany after a long siege. It continued to grow, under the influence of Prussian culture. It became French at the 1918 Armistice, but was again taken by Germany from 1940 to 1944.

Two parts of the old city evoke the delightful spectacle of a bygone Alsace of timber-framed houses with the whole array of traditional features, wooden galleries, loggias on brackets, windows with tiny panes of coloured glass, as well as the overhanging upper storeys, which continued to be built here after 1681 even though they had been banned in France proper.

CATHÉDRALE NOTRE-DAME★★★

1 r. Rohan. Open daily 7–11.20am, 12.40–7pm; no visits during services. ℘03 88 21 43 34. www.cathedrale-strasbourg.fr.

In 1176, the cathedral was rebuilt in red Vosges sandstone on a site above flood-level but nevertheless using bundles of oak piles as a foundation (these were recently reinforced with concrete). Externally, this is still a Romanesque building as far as choir, transept and lantern-tower are concerned. The famous Gothic **spire★★★** (€5, and 332 steps) is an architectural master-

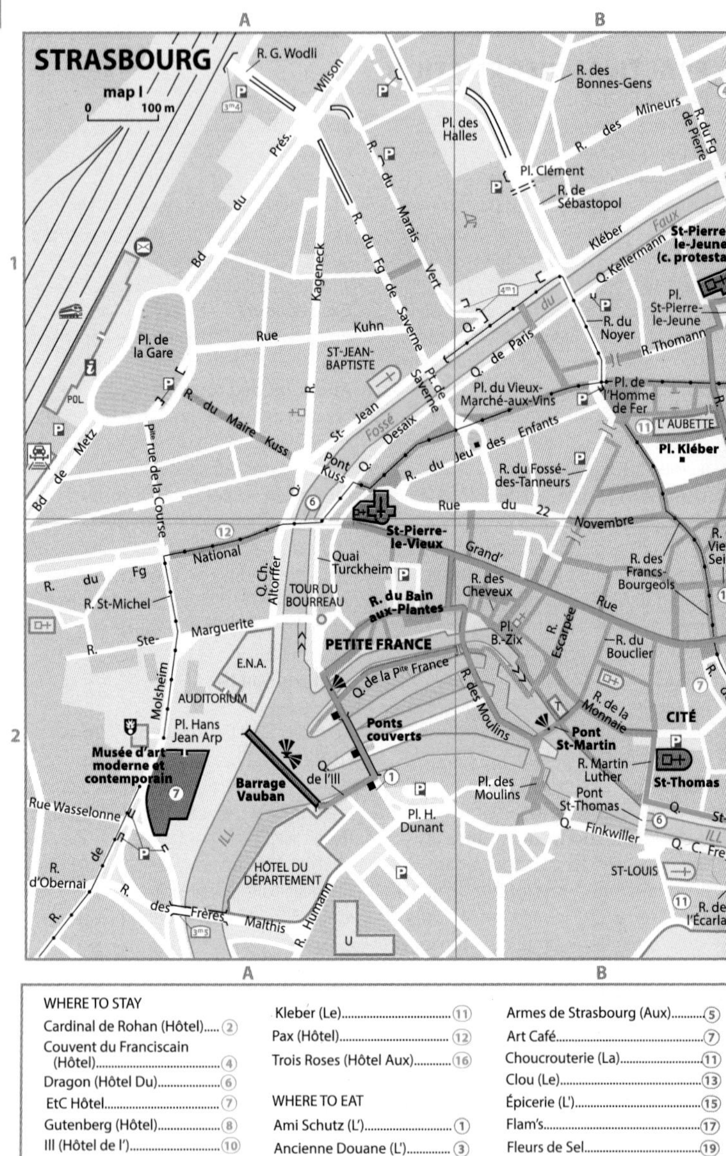

piece, its verticality emphasised by its forward position immediately over the west front. An unmistakable landmark, visible over much of the Alsace plain, it rises to a height of 142m. The openwork octagon supporting it was erected between 1399 and 1419 by a Swabian architect and given an extra 7m in height during the course of construction for reasons of prestige. Its final stage was designed and built between 1420 and 1439 by a Cologne architect, using techniques from the previous century; it is particularly notable for the projecting structures carrying the external staircases.

The High Gothic west front (**façade★★★**) was the work of Erwin von Steinbach.

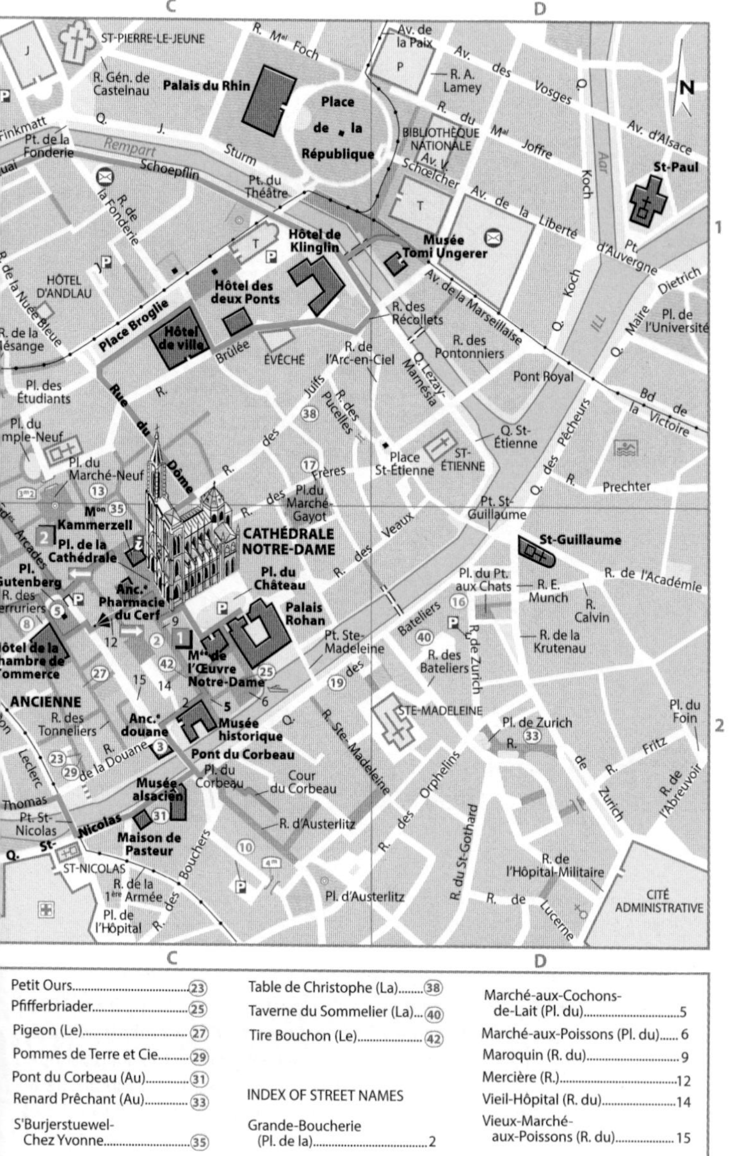

Petit Ours.......... 23
Pfifferbriader.......... 25
Pigeon (Le).......... 27
Pommes de Terre et Cie.......... 29
Pont du Corbeau (Au).......... 31
Renard Prêchant (Au).......... 33
S'Burjerstuewel-Chez Yvonne.......... 35
Table de Christophe (La).......... 38
Taverne du Sommelier (La).......... 40
Tire Bouchon (Le).......... 42

INDEX OF STREET NAMES

Grande-Boucherie (Pl. de la).......... 2
Marché-aux-Cochons-de-Lait (Pl. du).......... 5
Marché-aux-Poissons (Pl. du).......... 6
Maroquin (R. du).......... 9
Mercière (R.).......... 12
Vieil-Hôpital (R. du).......... 14
Vieux-Marché-aux-Poissons (R. du).......... 15

It is decorated with a wealth of sculpture (statues and low-reliefs of many different periods), especially in the central portal **(portail central)** with its double gable and delicate lancets masking part of the rose window. The three lower levels of the tympanum have particularly fine 13C work, including depictions of the Entry into Jerusalem, scenes of the Passion and Resurrection, and the Death of Judas; in the arching can be seen the Creation, the story of Abraham, the Apostles, the Evangelists and the Martyrs.

In the south doorway **(portail Sud)** is a famous portrayal of the Seducer about to succeed in tempting the most daring of the Foolish Virgins (she is undoing

WHERE TO STAY

Maison du Charron (Chambre d'hôte La)..... ①

Princes (Hôtel des)..... ③

WHERE TO EAT

Buerehiesel..... ①

Vignette (La)..... ③

her dress). The statues of the Church and Synagogue (copies) on the south side of the cathedral are equally celebrated.

Inside, the nave elevation is a straightforward example of the High Gothic style of the 14C, with an openwork triforium and wide aisles lit by elegant window-openings.

In the south transept is the 13C Angel pillar (**pilier des Anges★★**) or Last Judgement (**du Jugement dernier**); its delicate statuary, on three levels, raises Gothic art to a peak of perfection. **Stained-glass windows★★★** from the 12C, 13C and 14C are remarkable. The **astronomical clock★** *(clock chimes at 12.30pm)* nearby, dating from 1838, continues to draw crowds with its automata ringing out the quarter-hours (the figure of Death has the privilege of sounding the hours) and the crowd of figures brought out to mark midday (12.30pm).

WALKING TOURS

1 OLD TOWN★★★

Allow one day. Strasbourg map I, p332.

The old town nestles round the cathedral, on the island formed by the two branches of the River Ill.

- **Place de la Cathédrale★** – The Pharmacie du Cerf on the corner of rue Mercière, which dates from 1268, was the oldest chemist's in France until it closed in 2000. On the north side of the cathedral, the Maison Kammerzella (1589), restored 1954 and now a restaurant, has splendid carved wood.
- **Place du Château** – Here are the **Musée de l'Œuvre Notre-Dame★★** (*see MUSEUMS, p336*) and the **Palais Rohan★**.
- **Place du Marché-aux-Cochons-de-Lait★** – A charming square lined with old houses including a 16C house with wooden galleries.
- **Pont du Corbeau** – This is the former "execution" bridge from which those condemned for infanticides and parricides, tied up in sacks, were plunged into the water.
- **Cour du Corbeau★** – Once a fashionable inn, which welcomed illustrious guests, such as Turenne, King Johann-Casimir of Poland, Frederick the Great and Emperor Joseph II, the picturesque courtyard dates from the 14C.
- **Quai St-Nicolas** – The embankment is lined with some fine old houses; three are now the **Musée Alsacien ★★** (*see MUSEUMS, p336*).
- **Église St-Thomas** – This five-naved church, rebuilt at the end of the 12C, became a Lutheran cathedral in 1529. It contains the 18C **mausoleum★★** of the Maréchal de Saxe.
- **La Petite France★★** – Once the fishermen's, tanners' and millers' district, this is today one of the most interesting and best-preserved areas of the old town. Quai de la Petite France runs alongside the canal, offering a romantic **view★** particularly at dusk of the old houses reflected in the water.
- **Ponts Couverts★** – This is the name given to three successive bridges spanning the River Ill; each guarded by a massive square tower, remaining from the 14C fortifications. The bridges once had wooden roofs.
- **Barrage Vauban** – There's a striking **view★★** of the Ponts Couverts, la Petite France and the cathedral from the terrace of the casemate bridge (part of Vauban's fortifications).
- **Rue du Bain-aux-Plantes★★** – The street is lined with timber-framed corbelled houses dating from the Alsatian Renaissance (16–17C).
- **Église St-Pierre-le-Vieux** – This church consists of two adjacent churches: one Catholic and the other Protestant.

2 OLD TOWN VIA PLACE BROGLIE

Strasbourg map I, p332.

- **Place Gutenberg** – Here stand the Renaissance Hôtel de la Chambre de Commerce and Gutenberg's statue by David d'Angers. No 52 rue du Vieux-Marché-aux-Poissons is the birthplace of Jean Arp (1887–1966), a sculptor, painter and poet.
- **Place Kléber** – On the north side is an 18C building called "l'Aubette" because the garrison came here at dawn (aube) to get their orders. In the centre is a statue of Strasbourg native Jean-Baptiste Kléber (1753–1800), a brilliant general of the Revolutionary period.
- **Église St-Pierre-le-Jeune** – Three successive churches have stood on this site. All that remains of the first church is a tomb believed to date from the end of the Roman occupation (4C AD); the lovely restored cloisters belonged to the church built in 1031. The present Protestant church (13C, restored 1900) contains a fine Gothic rood screen decorated with paintings from 1620.
- **Place Broglie** – This square was laid out in the 18C. On the south side is the **town hall★** built by Massol, former residence of the counts of Hanau-Lichtenberg.
- **Rue du Dôme and adjacent streets** – The old aristocratic district adjoining place Broglie has preserved several 18C mansions.

PALAIS DE ROHAN★ AND ITS MUSEUMS

The beautiful classical bishop's palace was built in 1704 for Cardinal Armand de Rohan-Soubise by royal architect Robert de Cotte.

Musée des Arts Décoratifs★★ – Includes the State Apartments (**Grands Appartements**) and tells the story of the city's crafts and craftsmen. It has one of the finest **ceramic collections★★** in France, particularly rich in Strasbourg and Niderwiller faience and porcelain.

Musée des Beaux-Arts★ – for its Italian paintings (Primitives and Renaissance), its Spanish works (Zurbaran, Murillo and Goya) and 15–17C Netherlandish Old Masters. Don't miss Nicolas de Largillière's 1703 portrait of *La Belle Strasbourgeoise*, the elegant, black-robed beauty.

Musée Archéologique★★ – Covers the period between the Quaternary era and the end of the first millennium AD. There are displays on prehistory, extinct animals, ceramics, and on Roman and Merovingian times.

MORE MUSEUMS

Musée Alsacien★★

23–25 quai St-Nicolas. Open daily except Tue 10am–6pm. Closed 1 Jan, Good Friday, 1 May, 1 and 11 Nov, 25 Dec. €6.50. ✆03 88 52 50 01. www.musees-strasbourg.eu.

This museum of popular art, in a maze of quaint rooms in three 16–17C houses, gives a good insight into the history, customs and traditions of Alsace.

Musée de l'Œuvre Notre-Dame★★

3 pl. du Château. Open daily except Mon 10am–6pm. Closed 1 Jan, Good Fri, 1 May, 1 and 11 Nov, 25 Dec. €6.50 (no charge 1st Sun of the month). ✆03 88 52 50 00. www.musees-strasbourg.eu.

Housed in a number of old dwellings just to the south, this museum greatly enhances the visitor's appreciation of the cathedral. Its great treasure is the famous **Tête de Christ★★** from Wissembourg in northern Alsace.

In addition, there is the oldest stained glass in existence and, above all, many of the cathedral's original statues, including the Church and the Synagogue, the Wise and Foolish Virgins. The architect's drawings of the west front and the spire are here too.

Musée d'Art Moderne et Contemporain★★

1 place Hans-Jean-Arp. ♿ Open daily except Mon 10am–6pm. Closed 1 Jan, Good Friday, 1 May, 1 and 11 Nov, 25 Dec. €6.50. ✆03 88 23 31 31. www.musees-strasbourg.eu.

Standing on the bank of the River Ill, this modern building was designed by Adrien Fainsilber, architect of the Cité des Sciences et de l'Industrie at La Villette in Paris. The display covers the diverse artistic strands that left their stamp on the history of modern art. Several rooms are devoted to **Jean Arp** and his wife Sophie Taeuber-Arp, who, in collaboration with Theo Van Doesburg, made a series of stained-glass panels re-creating the constructivist interiors (1926–28) of l'Aubette on place Kléber. As a reaction against World War I, the Dadaists signed derisory, even absurd, works (Janco, Schwitters). Following in their footsteps, the Surrealists Brauner, Ernst and Arp tried to introduce the world of dreams into their works.

19C GERMAN QUARTER

After 1870, the Germans erected a great number of monumental public buildings in neo-Gothic Renaissance style. They intended to transfer the town centre to the north-east, and include the orangery and the university. This district with its broad avenues is a rare example of Prussian architecture.

Place de la République – This vast square has a shady circular garden in the centre, with a war memorial by Drivier (1936). On the left is the Palais du Rhin, the former imperial palace (1883–88); on the right are the National Theatre, housed in the former Landtag Palace, and the National Library.

Parc des Contades – This park situated north of place de la République is named after the military governor of Alsace who had it laid out. On the edge of the park, the Synagogue de la Paix was built in 1955 to replace the synagogue destroyed in 1940.

Maison de la Télévision FR3-Alsace – This was built in 1961; a monumental (30x6m) ceramic by Lurçat, symbolising the Creation, decorates the concave façade of the auditorium.

CAPITAL OF EUROPE

Palais de l'Europe★

Allée Spach, av de l'Europe. ♿ Guided tour (1hr) by reservation. Service des visites, Conseil de l'Europe, 67075 Strasbourg Cedex. ✆03 88 41 20 29.

The palace houses the **European Council**, including the council of ministers, the parliamentary assembly and the international secretariat. The buildings, inaugurated in 1977 were designed by the French architect Henri Bernard. The palace contains 1 350 offices, meeting rooms, a library and the largest parliamentary amphitheatre in Europe. Opposite, the **Parc de l'Orangerie★** was laid out by Le Nôtre in 1692 and remodelled in 1804 for Empress Josephine's stay. It includes a lake, a waterfall, a zoo and two excellent restaurants; storks are seen everywhere.

Palais des Droits de l'Homme

Nearby, on the banks of the river Ill, stands the futuristic new Palais des Droits de l'Homme, designed by Richard Rogers, which houses the European Court of Human Rights.

PORT AUTONOME & RHINE

Strasbourg is one of the most important ports along the River Rhine. Its impact on eastern France's economy equals that of a major maritime port because of the good navigable conditions and the network of waterways, railway lines and roads linking the region with Western and Central Europe.

EXCURSIONS

WINE VILLAGES

Some of the most picturesque villages in Alsace are a short drive from the city.

Saverne★ – The town at the entrance to the **Vosges** uplands has **old houses★** and a splendid red sandstone **château★** with a monumental Louis XVI **façade★★** giving onto the park.

Église de Marmoutier★★ – This 12C former abbey church has a fine **west front ★★** in the red sandstone of the region, in Romanesque style incorporating Carolingian and Rhineland influences.

Hunspach★★

Hunspach is in the extreme NE of France, close to the Rhine and the German border. Carefully preserved and free from incongruous modern additions, it is one of Alsace's most charming villages. Flowers fill the streets of timber-framed houses with projecting roofs and bull's-eye windows (a Baroque feature). Many of the buildings are old farmhouses, with yards opening off the street; orchards, vines and long-handled pumps complete the picturesque scene.

Nearby **Seebach★** (*5km/3mi NE by D 249*) is a wonderful example of the flower-decked Alsatian village with its half-timbered houses adorned with awnings and gardens.

Obernai★★

Obernai is north of Colmar on the main highway to Strasbourg. Sited where the lower, vine-covered slopes of Mont Ste-Odile meet the plain, its ruined walls eloquent of its ancient independence and its narrow, winding streets lined with high-gabled houses, the little town of Obernai seems to represent the very essence of Alsace. With its cheerfully coloured timber-framed buildings, the picturesque **Place du Marché★★** is Obernai's centrepiece, graced by a fountain with a statue of St Odile. Its Town Hall (**Hôtel de Ville★**, 15–16C) has a fine oriel window, a 16C Corn Hall (**Ancienne Halle aux blés★**) with a stork's nest above its doorway, and the Chapel Tower (**Tour de la Chapelle★**), a 13C bell tower.

There are many **old houses★** in the streets around place du Marché. In rue des Pèlerins, note the three-storey stone house dating from the 13C.

ADDRESSES

STAY

Couvent du Franciscain – 18 r. du Fg-de-Pierre. 03 88 32 93 93. www.hotel-franciscain.com. Closed last week Jul, 1st week Aug. 43 rooms. At the end of a cul-de-sac you will find these two joined buildings. We recommend the rooms in the new wing. Walking distance of the old city.

Hôtel Pax – 24 r. du Fg-National 03 88 32 14 54. www.paxhotel.com. Closed 23 Dec–4 Jan. 90 rooms. Restaurant. A family hotel in a busy street on the edge of the city's old district. Its plain rooms are well kept, and its restaurant serves regional dishes.

EtC Hôtel – 7 r. de la Chaine. 03 88 32 66 60. www.etc-hotel.com. 35 rooms. Situated in a peaceful area beside the cathedral and la Petite France in the heart of the old city.

Aux Trois Roses – 7 r. Zürich. 03 88 36 56 95. www.hotel3roses-strasbourg.com. 32 rooms. Cosy duvets and pine furniture add to the welcoming feel of the quiet guest rooms in this elegant building on the banks of the Ill. Fitness area with sauna and jacuzzi.

Hôtel de l'Ill – 8 r. des Bateliers. 03 88 36 20 01. www.hotel-ill.fr. 27 rooms. Renovated hotel with family atmosphere. The rooms of differing sizes are impeccably clean, while the old-fashioned breakfast room has a cuckoo clock.

Le Kléber – 29 pl. Kléber. 03 88 32 09 53. http://hotel-kleber.com. 30 rooms. "Meringue", "Strawberry" and "Cinnamon" are just a few of the names of the rooms in this comfortable hotel. Contemporary, colourful décor with a sweet-and-savoury theme.

Des Princes – 33 r. Geiler. 03 88 61 55 19. www.hotel-princes.com. Closed 25 Jul–25 Aug, Jan 2–10. 43 rooms. A welcoming hotel in a quiet residential neighbourhood. Guest rooms with classic furnishings and large bathrooms.

Hôtel Cardinal de Rohan – 17 r. du Maroquin. 03 88 32 85 11. www.hotel-rohan.com. 36 rooms. Named after the nearby palais de Rohan, this little hotel is on a pedestrian street near the cathedral. Its quiet, pleasant rooms are furnished in Louis XV, Louis XVI or rustic style.

Gutenberg – 31 r. des Serruriers. 03 88 32 17 15. www.hotel-gutenberg.com. 42 rooms. This building dating back to 1745 is now a hotel with an eclectic mix of spacious guest rooms.

EAT

Pommes de Terre et Cie – 4 r. de l'Écurie. 03 88 22 36 82. www.pommes-de-terre-cie.com. Booking advisable. If you want a change from ***choucroute***, this friendly restaurant specialises in jacket potatoes accompanied by meat, fish or cheese. Local produce.

Flam's – 29 r. des Frères. 03 88 36 36 90. www.flams.fr. Booking advisable at weekends. This half-timbered house very close to the cathedral houses a restaurant specialising in *flammekueches*. 15C painted ceiling.

Pfifferbriader – 6 pl. du Marché-aux-Cochons-de-Lait. 03 88 32 15 43. Closed Sun. Feel at home in this low-beamed dining room, with windows decorated with wine-making scenes. Tasty regional dishes including *käseknefples, choucroute* and *bäeckehoffe* are served along with classic French cuisine. Good choice of regional wines.

Le Pigeon – 23 r. des Tonneliers. 03 88 23 31 30. This typical *winstub* owes its name to two pigeons sculpted on the façade of one of the oldest houses in Strasbourg.

La Taverne du Sommelier – Ruelle de la Bruche (Krutenau distict). 03 88 24 14 10. Booking essential. The type of little restaurant it's always a pleasure to discover. The décor is perfect to set off the intimate atmosphere. The menu follows the seasons, while the wine list features wines from the Languedoc and the Rhône valley.

Petit Ours – 3 r. de l'Écurie (quartier des Tonneliers). 03 88 32 13 21. Booking advisable. Great little restaurant decorated with Tuscany-inspired colours. Light floods through the bay windows of one room, and the cellar is also very pleasant. Each dish (mostly fish) is characterised by a herb or spice.

Au Renard Prêchant – 34 r. de Zürich. ☎03 88 35 62 87. Closed lunchtime on Sat, Sun and public holidays. A 16C chapel in a pedestrianised street, which takes its name from the murals decorating its walls telling the story of the preaching fox. Rustic dining room, pretty terrace in summer, and reasonable fixed-price lunches.

L'Ami Schutz – 1 Ponts Couverts. ☎03 88 32 76 98. www.ami-schutz.com. Closed Christmas Holidays. Between the Meanders of the Ill, typical cosy *winstub* with wood panelling (the smaller dining room has greater charm). Terrace beneath the lime trees.

Au Pont du Corbeau – 21 quai St-Nicolas. ☎03 88 35 60 68. Closed Sun lunch and Sat except Dec. A renowned restaurant on the banks of the Ill, next to the Alsatian Folk Art Museum. Regionally inspired menu that focuses on local specialities.

La Vignette – 29 rue Mélanie at La Robertsau. ☎03 88 31 38 10. An earthenware stove and old photos of the neighbourhood adorn the dining room of this café-restaurant. Appetising, market-inspired cuisine.

Ancienne Douane – 6 r. de la Douane. ☎03 88 15 78 78. www.anciennedouane.fr. This building, on the banks of the River Ill, dating from 1358 has had a variety of uses, but is now a charming restaurant in the centre of the old city.

Le Tire Bouchon – 5, rue des Tailleurs de Pierre. ☎03 88 22 16 32. www.letirebouchon.fr. Charming restaurant located near the cathedral in a typical narrow Alsatian street, with an extensive wine cellar and offering traditional cuisine.

Aux Armes de Strasbourg – 9 pl. Gutenberg. ☎03 88 32 85 62. An oasis of peace in the famous place Gutenberg.

L'Épicerie – 6 r. de Vieux Seigle. ☎03 88 32 52 41. www.lepicerie-strasbourgcom. Closed 22 Dec–7 Jan, holidays. Nostalgic atmosphere with a 1960s ambience.

S'Burjerstuewel – Chez Yvonne – 10 r. Sanglier. ☎03 88 32 84 15. www.chez-yvonne.net. Closed Christmas holidays. This *winstub* is one of the city's institutions, evidenced by the photos and dedications of its famous guests.

© Jacques Loic/Photononstop

Le Clou – 3 r. du Chaudron. ☎03 88 32 11 67. www.le-clou.com. Closed Wed lunchtime, Sun and holidays. This small wine bar in a little street near the cathedral is eternally popular, with its typical décor, friendly atmosphere and good Alsace cooking.

Fleur de Sel – 22 quai des Batelliers. ☎03 88 36 01 54. Opened in 2005 on the south bank of the Ill across the Pont Ste Madeleine. Traditional Alsatian and French cuisine.

Le Buerehiesel – 4 Parc de l'Orangerie. ☎03 88 45 56 65. www.buerehiesel.fr. Closed 2 Aug–24 Aug, 30 Dec–21 Jan, Sun and Mon. Famous chef Antine Westermann has handed over to his son Eric in the kitchens, but this outstanding Michelin restaurant, set amid the greenery of the parc de l'Orangerie, remains one of Alsace's gastronomic temples.

ON THE TOWN

Au Brasseur – 22 r. des Veaux. ☎03 88 36 12 13. Daily 11.30am–1am. This micro-brasserie proposes a wide variety of beers brewed on the premises. Locals also come here to dine and for jazz, rock and blues concerts at weekends.

Bar à Champagne – 5 r. des Moulins. ☎03 88 76 43 43. www.regent-hotels.com. 5pm–2am. This is the hotel bar of the luxurious Regent Petite France, which was a mill for 800 years. No effort has been spared to ensure that you spend a relaxing evening here: the fine contemporary décor, the riverside terrace, discreet background jazz, a good choice of cocktails and the best champagnes.

Colmar★★★

The capital of Upper Alsace is situated at the point where the Munster valley widens out into the broad plain of the Rhine. Since the 13C the town has prospered on the proceeds of the wine trade and boasts fine monuments. More recently, industries have spread along the Logelbach Canal.

- **Population:** 67 615.
- **Michelin Map:** 315 I 8
- **Info:** 4 r. Hunterlinden. ℘03 89 20 68 92. www.ot-colmar.fr.
- **TGV:** Colmar is around 3–3hrs 45mins from Paris Est via Strasbourg or Mulhouse .
- **Location:** Colmar is located 71km/44mi SSW of Strasbourg, 40km/25mi N of Mulhouse.
- **Don't Miss:** The Old Town; Retable d'Issenheim, on display at the Musée Unterlinden; Colmar by Night – The town's most beautiful buildings are lit up at night; a Boat Trip.
- **Kids:** Musée Animé du Jouet et des Petits Trains.
- **Timing:** Allow half a day to explore the Old Town and as much again to explore Little Venice.

A BIT OF HISTORY

In 1834 **Frédéric Bartholdi** was born here, the patriotic sculptor responsible for many striking works, including New York's Statue of Liberty.

Between 1871 and 1918 Alsace and Lorraine were part of Germany. A particular irritant to authority was the Colmar writer and caricaturist Jean-Jacques Waltz (1872–1951), known as "Hansi", who was imprisoned at the outbreak of war in 1914, but escaped to enlist in the French army. In early February 1945, the French army under General de Lattre de Tassigny launched an attack on Colmar to eliminate German resistance. On 1 February the German lines north of Colmar were overrun by American troops, who stood aside to let the French 5th armoured division enter Colmar.

MUSÉE UNTERLINDEN★★★

1 r. d'Unterlinden. Open May–Oct daily 9am–6pm; Nov–Apr Wed–Mon 9am–noon, 2–5pm. Closed 1 Jan, 1 May, 1 Nov, 25 Dec. €8. ℘03 89 20 15 50. www.musee-unterlinden.com.

The museum, situated on place d'Unterlinden through which flows the Logelbach canal, is housed in a former 13C monastery. The ground floor is devoted to religious art and presents rich collections of paintings and sculpture dating from the late Middle Ages and the Renaissance.

Retable d'Issenheim★★★

In 1512 **Matthias Grünewald** was called to Issenheim 22km/14mi south of Colmar to paint the **Issenheim altarpiece** for the chapel of the Antonite convent. This extraordinary work should be seen, not as a collection of separate masterpieces, but as an integrated whole, conceived and executed as a programme whose logic, while still puzzling to the specialist of today, probably lies in the convent superior's particular vision of the meaning of suffering. Everything contributes to the overall effect, not only the choice of themes and their relationship to one another, but also the pose and expression of the figures, the symbolic meaning of the various themes, animals and monsters.

WALKING TOURS

1 OLD TOWN★★

Colmar map II, p343.

The heart of the old town comprises the Place de l'Ancienne Douane, Rue des Marchands and Rue Mercière (Haberdasher Street). There are many picturesque old houses, with corner turrets, oriel windows and half-timbering, and balconies adorned with flowers. Particularly striking are the **Maison Pfister★★**, with frescoes and medallions and a pyramidal roof, and the Old Customs House, **Ancienne Douane★**, of 1480, with a timber gallery and canted staircase tower.

- **Temple protestant St-Matthieu** – This former Franciscan church, now Protestant, is decorated with fine 14C and 15C stained-glass windows.
- **Place de l'Ancienne-Douane** – This picturesque square features timber-framed houses such as the Maison au Fer Rouge.
- **Ancienne Douane★ or "Koifhus"** – This former customs house is the most important civilian edifice in Colmar.
- **Maison Pfister★★** – A hatter from Besançon had this lovely house built in 1537 and decorated with frescoes and medallions.
- **Place de la Cathédrale** – On the square stand the oldest house in Colmar, Maison Adolphe (1350), and the **Ancien Corps de garde★** (1575).
- **Collégiale St-Martin★** – This imposing edifice decorated with glazed tiles and red-sandstone projections was built in the 13C and 14C on the site of a Romanesque church.
- **Église des Dominicains** – Work began on the chancel in 1283, but the main part of the edifice was only completed in the 14C and 15C. Inside, altars and stalls date from the 18C.

2 PETITE VENISE★ (LITTLE VENICE)

- **Quartiers des tanneurs** – Timber-framed houses were narrow but high, creating lofts to dry skins.
- **Krutenau district★** – Once a fortified area; this district's market gardeners once used flat-bottomed boats, similar to Venetian gondolas.
- **Explore** – The quays and Pont St-Pierre provide a pleasant end to the stroll.

ADDITIONAL SIGHTS

Musée Animé du Jouet et des Petits Trains

Housed in a former cinema, collections include numerous railway engines, trains, and dolls in different materials.

EXCURSIONS

KAYSERSBERG★★

12km/7.4mi NW of Colmar.

Kaysersberg is a typically pretty Alsace village; its flower-bedecked streets have many old houses, several dating from the 16C, and behind the pretty little town rise the serried ranks of vines on the slopes of the Vosges hills.

Kaysersberg was a Roman town known as *Caesaris Mons*, due to its strategic position along one of the most important routes linking ancient Gaul and the Rhine valley.

The great doctor, theologian and pioneer of Third World aid, Albert Schweitzer (1875–1965), was born at 126 Rue du Général de Gaulle.

CHÂTEAU DU HAUT-KŒNIGSBOURG★★

The castle is roughly 21km/13mi N of Colmar. It is reached via a steep, winding road between Sélestat and Ribeauvillé.

This vast, mock-medieval edifice in pink sandstone overlooks the Alsace plain from its lofty rock rising through the treetops of the Vosges forest. The castle, which was first mentioned in 1147, was built by the Hohenstaufens on a promontory overlooking the Alsace plain, at an altitude of 700m.

In 1479 it passed to the Habsburgs who had it rebuilt with a modern system of defence. Sadly this did not prevent the Swedes taking and sacking the castle 150 years later.

For the next 200 years it was an imposing ruin, until in 1899 it was offered for sale by the town of **Sélestat★**.

The present building is the outcome of an almost complete reconstruction in neo-feudal style carried out on the orders of Emperor William II between 1900 and 1908 during the period when Alsace and Lorraine had been reincorporated into Germany.

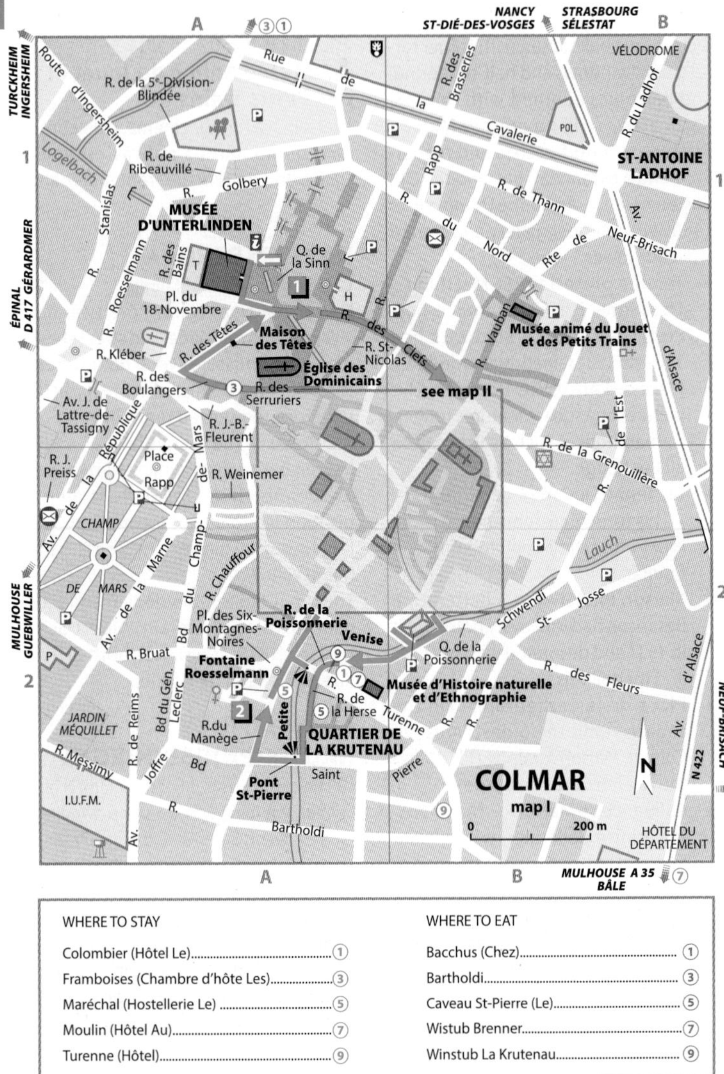

ADDRESSES

STAY

Chambre d'hôte Les Framboises – 128 r. des Trois-Épis, 68230 Katzenthal. 5km/3mi NW of Colmar, Kaysersberg direction then D 10. 03 89 27 48 85. Closed Jan. 4 rooms. Accommodation in wood-panelled attic rooms.

Hôtel Au Moulin – Rte d'Herrlisheim, 68127 Ste-Croix-en-Plaine. 10km/6.2mi S of Colmar on A 35 and D 1. 03 89 49 31 20. Closed Dec 20–Apr 1. 17 rooms. This old mill deep in the country is perfect for those seeking peace and quiet.

Hôtel Turenne – 10 rte de Bâle. 03 89 21 58 58. www.turenne.com. 83 rooms. On the edge of the old town, this hotel occupies a large, pleasing building with a pink and yellow façade. Renovated rooms.

Hôtel Le Colombier – 7 r. de Turenne. 6km/3.5miles south of Colmar

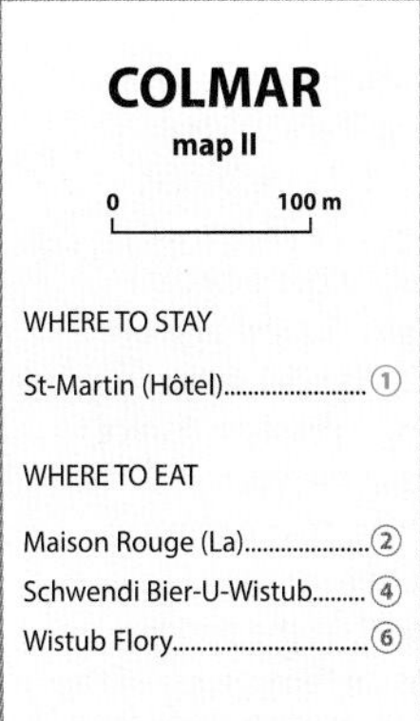

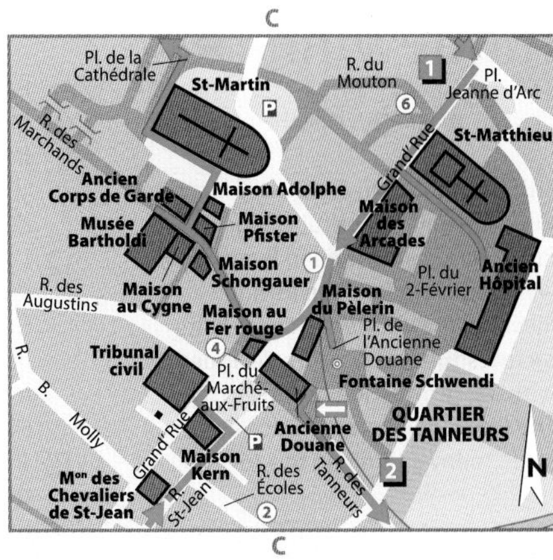

on D 14, then D 45. ✆03 89 23 96 00. www.hotel-le-colombier.fr. Closed Dec 24 –Jan. 24 rooms. This lovely 15C house in old Colmar retains elements from its past, such as the superb Renaissance staircase.

⊜⊜⊜ **Hôtel Le Maréchal** – 4/6 pl. Six Montagnes Noires. ✆03 89 41 60 32. www.hotel-le-marechal.com. 30 rooms. The rooms of these delightful Alsatian houses in Little Venice, most of which have a chocolate box charm, are furnished with brocades and antiques.

⊜⊜⊜ **Hôtel St Martin** – 38 Grand'Rue. ✆03 89 24 11 51. www.hotel-saint-martin.com. Closed Dec 23–26, Jan 1–8. 40 rooms. Three 14C and 17C houses in the old quarter, set around an inner courtyard with a turret and a Renaissance staircase.

EAT

⊜ **Winstub La Krutenau** – 1 r. de la Poissonnerie. ✆03 89 41 18 80. Closed Christmas to end Jan, Sun eve and Mon out of season. At this winstub beside the River Lauch you can go boating in Little Venice and eat beside the canal.

⊜ **Schwendi Bier-U-Wistub** – 23–25 Grand'Rue. ✆03 89 23 66 26. Closed evenings on Christmas and New Year's Day. A charming winstub with an ideal location in the heart of old Colmar. The wooden decor and the cooking are a tribute to Alsace.

⊜⊜ **Le Caveau St-Pierre** – 24 r. de la Herse (Little Venice). ✆03 89 41 99 33. www.lecaveausaintpierre-colmar.com. Closed Jan. Booking advisable. A pretty wooden footbridge across the Lauch leads to this 16C house, which offers a little slice of paradise with its rustic, local-style decor, cuisine, and a terrace.

⊜⊜ **Chez Bacchus** – 2 Grand'Rue, 68230 Katzenthal. 5km/3mi NW of Colmar, Kaysersberg direction, then D 10. ✆03 89 27 32 25. Closed Jan 7–31, 1 week in Jul and in Nov. Open Thu–Sat evening from Oct 1–Jul 14, Sun and Jul 15–Sep 30 every evening except Tue. Booking advisable at weekends. There's a friendly atmosphere in this 18C wine bar. Massive exposed beams and helpings of Alsatian cuisine guaranteed to satisfy the healthiest of appetites.

⊜⊜ **Wistub Flory** – 1 rue Mangold. ✆03 89 41 78 80. Wide selection of regional dishes (ample portions), which can be enjoyed on the terrace when the weather is suitable.

⊜⊜⊜ **Bartholdi** – 2 rue Boulangers. ✆03 89 41 07 74. Closed Jun 30–Jul 7, Feb hols, Sun eve and Mon. Lovers of Alsatian wines cannot fail but be delighted by the vast choice of local vintages offered by this spacious restaurant with the appearance of a Winstub.

⊜⊜⊜ **Wistub Brener** – 1 r. de Turenne ✆03 89 41 42 33. Closed Feb 22–Mar 12, Jun 15–20, Nov 16–25, Dec 24–Jan 2, Tue and Wed. The terrace by the Lauch in Little Venice is very popular on fine days. The whole of Colmar meets here.

⊜⊜⊜ **La Maison Rouge** – 9 rue des Écoles. ✆03 89 23 53 22. http://maison-rouge.net. Closed Sun and Mon. The somewhat ordinary façade hides a delightful rustic interior.

Riquewihr★★★

and the Route des Vins

Situated along the Route des Vins, the tiny, beautiful village of Riquewihr is surrounded by medieval walls. It prides itself on its fine Riesling; the vintners' houses in its picturesque streets were designed with the production of wine in mind. The town looks pretty much the same today as it did in the 16C.

- **Population:** 1 203.
- **Michelin Map:** 315 H 8
- **Info:** 2 r. de la 1re Armée. ℘03 89 73 23 23. www.ribeauville-riquewihr.com.
- **Location:** Riquewihr is on the Rhine border with Germany, in eastern France, nuzzled in the Vosges mountains, 16km/10mi NW of Colmar.
- **Parking:** Use the parking facilities on the outside of the town: place des Charpentiers; rue de la Piscine; rocade Nord.
- **Timing:** Allow 2hr and time to try a glass of the region's famous Riesling.

WALKING TOUR

Riquewihr map, p345.

- **Château des Ducs de Wurtemberg** – Completed in 1540, the castle has kept its mullioned windows, its gable and its turret. It houses a museum.
- **Maison Liebrich★** – A well dating from 1603 and a huge winepress from 1817 stand in the picturesque courtyard of this 16C house.
- **Maison Brauer** – This house, at the end of the street, has a fine doorway dating from 1618.
- **Place des Trois-Églises** – The square is framed by two former churches, St-Érard and Notre-Dame.
- **Maison Preiss-Zimmer★** – The house that belonged to the wine-growers' guild stands in the last but one of a succession of picturesque courtyards.
- **Rue et cour des Juifs** – Narrow rue des Juifs leads to the Cour des Juifs, the old ghetto, from which a narrow passageway and wooden stairs lead to the ramparts and Musée de la Tour des Voleurs.
- **Dolder★** – Built in 1291, this gate was reinforced 15–16C.
- **Obertor** (upper gate) – Note the portcullis and the place where the former drawbridge was fixed. **Maison Kiener★** – This 1574 house has a pediment with an inscription and a bas-relief.
- **Rue Latérale** – Lovely houses on this street include the Maison du march- and Tobie Berger at no 6, which has a 16C oriel and a Renaissance doorway in the courtyard.
- **Maison du Bouton d'Or** – The house goes back to 1566. An alleyway, just

Driving the Route des Vins

The 180km/112mi itinerary, known as the Route des Vins (Wine Road), winds its way along the foothills of the Vosges from Marlenheim to Thann, the northern and southern gateways to Alsace where there are information centres about Alsatian vineyards and wines. The first driving tour from Marlenheim to Châtenois *(68km/42mi)* takes in the pretty villages of Wangen and Itterswiller. From Châtenois to Colmar *(54km/34mi)*, the road passes the WWII cemetery near Bergheim and Hunawihr, famous for Alsacian storks. A final stretch between Colmar and Thann (59km/37mi) will take you to the birthplace of Alsacian vine-growing, Wettolsheim, and Pfaffenheim, which has a 13C church.

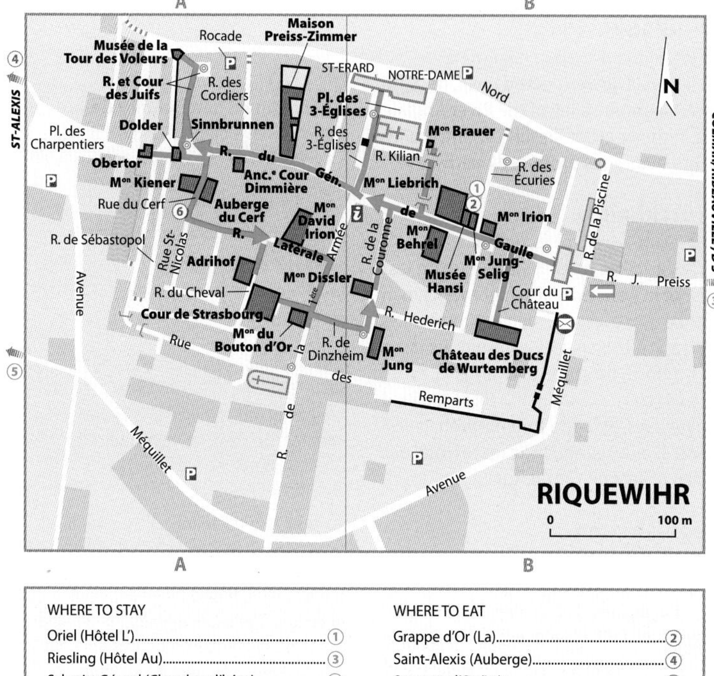

WHERE TO STAY		WHERE TO EAT	
Oriel (Hôtel L')	1	Grappe d'Or (La)	2
Riesling (Hôtel Au)	3	Saint-Alexis (Auberge)	4
Schmitt Gérard (Chambre d'hôte)	5	Sarment d'Or (Le)	6

round the corner, leads to another tithe court known as the Cour de Strasbourg dating from 1597.

- **Maison Dissler★** – This stone house (1610) is an interesting example of Renaissance style.

ADDITIONAL SIGHTS

Musée du Dolder

Access by staircase to left of the Porte du Dolder. Open early Jul–Aug daily, 2–6.30pm. Apr–early Jul and Sep–Oct Sat–Sun and holidays 2–6.30pm. Closed 1 Nov to Easter. €4. ✆03 89 58 44 08. www.musee-riquewihr.fr.

The museum houses mementoes, prints, weapons, tools and furniture, associated with local history.

Musée de la Tour des Voleurs

Open Easter–Oct daily 10.30am–1pm, 2–6pm. Closed Nov to Easter. €4.

The tour includes the torture chamber, the dungeon, guardroom and the caretaker's lodgings of this former prison.

EXCURSION

ROUTE DES VINS

180km/112mi.

The numerous flower-decked villages along the route, nestling round their church and town hall, are one of the most charming aspects of the Alsace region, no doubt enhanced by convivial wine-tasting opportunities.

Obernai★★

45km/28mi NNE of Riquewihr.

In the heart of wine-growing country, Obernai is a pleasant holiday resort. The picturesque old town, with its narrow streets, gabled houses, old shop signs and its well, is still partly surrounded by 12C ramparts.

Mont Saint Odile★

50km/31mi NNE of Riquewihr.

Mont Ste-Odile (alt. 764m) is one of the most popular sights in Alsace, drawing both pilgrims and tourists for the spectacular setting and views, with its pink cliffs rising out of the forest.

Andlau★

42km/26mi NNE of Riquewihr.

This small flower-decked town, nestling in the green valley of the River Andlau, is in the heart of Riesling country, with three vintages produced nearby.

Turckheim★

12km/7.5mi S of Riquewihr.

This ancient fortified town is the last place in Alsace where a night watchman (May–Oct every evening at 10pm) walks through the streets carrying his lamp and horn; he stops and sings at every street corner. Admire the three fortified gateways, Place de Turenne with its 16C and 17 houses and the ornate Hôtel des Deux-Clefs on Grand'Rue.

Eguisheim★

17.5km/11mi S of Riquewihr.

This ancient village developed round an octagonal 13C castle. Surrounded by 300ha/741 acres of vines and lying at the foot of three ruined towers, used as sundials by workers in the plain below, the village has hardly changed since the 16C. Two famous wines are produced locally. The wine-growers festival takes place during the fourth weekend in August. Visitors can follow the wine trail (1hr on foot; guided tours of cellars with wine-tasting included).

Rouffach★

27km/17mi S of Riquewihr.

Nestling at the foot of vine-covered hills, Rouffach is a prosperous agricultural centre, which has preserved many traces of its medieval past.

Guebwiller★

38km/24mi S of Riquewihr.

This small yet lively town, situated along the Route des Vins, has retained a wealth of architectural features.

ADDRESSES

STAY

Chambre d'hôte Schmitt Gérard – 3 chemin des Vignes. 03 89 47 89 72. Closed Jan–Mar. 2 rooms. A house with a garden at the top of the village, on the edge of a vineyard. Impeccably clean panelled rooms under the roof.

Hôtel Au Riesling – 5 rte des Vins, 68340 Zellenberg. 03 89 47 85 85. www.au-riesling.com. Closed Jan–Feb. 36 rooms. In the heart of the vineyards this hotel proudly carries the name of the famous wine. The rooms of this long building are partly modernised and rather sedate. The rustic style restaurant offers a pretty view of the vines. Traditional menu.

Hôtel L'Oriel – 3 r. des Écuries-Seigneuriales. 03 89 49 03 13. www.hotel-oriel.com. 22 rooms. This 16C hotel is easily recognised by its wrought-iron sign. The sloping walls, maze of staircases, exposed beams and bedrooms with Alsatian furniture create a romantic atmosphere.

EAT

Auberge St-Alexis – 68240 St-Alexis 6km W of Riquewihr on minor road and forest track. 03 89 73 90 38. www.saintalexis.fr. Closed Fri. It's definitely worth venturing into the forest to this old 17C hermitage. You will be rewarded with simple authentic dishes made from local farm produce.

Le Sarment d'Or – 4 r. du Cerf. 03 89 86 02 86. Closed Jan 5 – Feb 11, Jun 28 – Jul 6, Sun evening, Tue lunch and Mon. Pale wood panelling, a pretty fireplace and huge beams create a lovely warm atmosphere in this restaurant in one of Riquewihr's fine 17C houses. The cooking is traditional with some modern touches.

Le Grappe d'Or – 1 r. Ecuries Seigneuriales. 03 89 47 89 52. Closed Jun 25–Jul 10, Jan, Wed Feb–Mar and Thu. This welcoming house from 1554 has two dining rooms with well-worn walls, one adorned with rustic tools and the other with a pretty earthernware stove. Locally sourced menu.

Mulhouse★★

Mulhouse became a free imperial city in the 13C, and was part of the Decapolis (Décapole), an alliance formed in 1354 by ten Imperial cities of the Holy Roman Empire in the Alsace region.

A BIT OF HISTORY

A historic manufacturing and trading centre, the city's independent spirit led it into an association with the cantons of Switzerland. In 1524, the Republic's government adopted the principles of the Reformation and a little later on adhered to Calvinism. Theatrical performances were banned and inns had to close by 10pm. However, the spirit of the new religion spurred on industrial development and prompted social and cultural initiatives. It joined France voluntarily in 1798. Mulhouse was already long established as a textile centre, when, in 1746, three of its citizens, J-J Schmaltzer, the painter J-H Dollfus and the merchant S Koechlin together founded the first mill producing calico cotton fabrics. Production advanced by leaps and bounds. In 1812 the Dollfus and Mieg mill was the first to install steam power.

OLD TOWN

Hôtel de Ville★★

Since 1558, the City Hall has symbolised Mulhouse's civic and political liberties. It is a unique example in France of a building of the Rhineland Renaissance by a Basle architect; the exterior is decorated solely by artists from Konstanz. It was remodelled in 1698. It is this later decoration which has been restored to its former glory. The coats of arms of the Swiss cantons painted on the main façade on either side of the covered double flight of steps recall the historical link with Switzerland. The streets surrounding the hôtel de ville include the neo-Gothic **Temple St-Étienne**, the oldest pharmacy in Mulhouse (on rue des Boulangers), and the mansion built by the Feer family on rue des Franciscains.

- **Population:** 109 588.
- **Michelin Map:** 315 i 10
- **Info:** 1 avenue Robert Schuman. ℘03 89 35 48 48. www.mulhouse.fr.
- **TGV:** Mulhouse Ville is less than 3hr direct from Paris Gare de Lyon.
- **Tram:** Mulhouse has several modes of transport to help you get around: trams, trains, buses. Much of the centre is pedestrianised.
- **Location:** 40km/25mi S of Colmar, this large city lies at the meeting point of France, Germany and Switzerland.
- **Don't Miss:** Find time for the fascinating textile museum, where beautiful fabrics with historic designs are on sale.
- **Timing:** At least a full day is needed here.
- **Kids:** Those who love cars – old and new – will enjoy the Musée de l'Automobile.

INDUSTRIAL MUSEUMS

Musée de l'Automobile – Collection Schlumpf★★★

Open daily: mid-Apr–Oct 10am–6pm; Nov –mid-Apr 10am–5pm. Closed 25 Dec and 1 Jan. €11.50 (children 7–12, €9); combined ticket with Cite du Train €19. ℘03 89 33 23 23. http://citedelautomobile.com.

The splendid, definitive collection of 500 vehicles was lovingly built up by the mill-owning Schlumpf brothers. The collection vividly evokes the history of the motor car from the steam-powered Jacquot (1878) to the latest models.

Cité du Train: Musée français du Chemin de fer★★★

Situated near Lutterbach. Open daily: mid-Apr–Oct 10am–6pm; Nov–mid-Apr 10am–5pm. €11.50 (children 7–12, €9); combined ticket with Cite de l'Automobile €19. Closed 25 Dec and 1 Jan. €03 89 42 83 33. www.citedutrain.com.

The French Railways (SNCF) collection, splendidly displayed, illustrates the evolution of railways from their origins until today. The main hall includes footbridges offering a view inside carriages, pits making it possible to walk beneath engines, and drivers' cabins.

The panorama of steam engines includes famous engines such as the Saint-Pierre, which ran between Paris and Rouen from 1844 onwards, the Crampton (1852), which reached speeds of around 120kph/75mph, and the 232 U1 (1949), the last operating steam engine.

The museum also boasts the drawing-room carriage of Napoléon III's aides-de-camp (1856) decorated by Viollet-le-Duc, and the French president's carriage (1925) decorated by Lalique and fitted with a solid-silver washbasin. In striking contrast, the bottom of the range includes one of the fourth-class carriages of the Alsace-Lorraine line.

Musée de l'Impression sur étoffes★

14, rue Jean-Jacques Henner. ♿ Open daily except Mon, 10am– noon, 2–6pm. Closed 1 Jan, 1 May, 25 Dec. €9. ✆03 89 46 83 00. www.musee-impression.com.

The Museum of Printed Fabric is housed in a former industrial building, which once belonged to the Société Industrielle de Mulhouse. The Museum of Printed Fabric (created in 1857) illustrates the birth and development of the industry from 1746 onwards: engraving and printing techniques are explained, and impressive machines used throughout the ages are employed for regular demonstrations. There are displays of original 18C shawls with oriental motifs. This museum and its lovely shop are a must for anyone interested in fashion, interior design and the decorative arts.

ADDITIONAL SIGHTS

Parc zoologique et botanique★

S of the town centre, on the edge of the Rebberg district. Opening times and charges vary. €14.50 (out of season – Nov –late Mar) – and children €8.50). ✆03 89 31 85 10. www.zoo-mulhouse.com.

This zoological and botanical garden, covering an area of 25ha/62 acres and sheltering more than 1 000 animals, aims at preserving, breeding and studying rare and endangered species by collaborating with other zoos and various agencies. Interesting animals include gibbons, lemurs, deer, wolves, panthers, sea lions and penguins.

EXCURSION

ECOMUSÉE D'ALSACE★★

68190 Ungersheim, about 16km/10mi NW of Mulhouse. Check website for opening times. €14 (children 4–14, €10) ✆03 89 62 43 00. www.ecomusee-alsace.fr.

An open-air museum founded in 1984 to preserve local heritage comprises some 60 old buildings dotted over an area of 25ha/50 acres. The buildings dating from the 15–19C, which were saved from demolition and carefully dismantled and re-erected to create a village setting, are fine examples of rural habitats from the regions of Alsace. The museum also includes industrial structures; next to the museum are the restored buildings of a potassium mine that was worked from 1911–1930. Walk around the half-timbered buildings grouped by region (Sundgau, Reid, Kochersberg, Bas-Rhin) and complete with courtyards and gardens, to appreciate the development of building techniques and the varied architecture of farm buildings according to the regions and periods.

Specific buildings such as a fortified structure, a chapel, a school and a wash-house evoke community life in a traditional Alsatian village. Old plant varieties are grown in a typical field that also serves for farming demonstrations. An area devoted to funfairs includes a rare merry-go-round (1909). Many local people act as volunteers and help with various entertainments that bring the trades of yesteryear to life. Visitors will discover the age-old crafts of carpenters, blacksmiths, clog makers, potters, coopers, coalmen and masons as well as the evolution of living conditions, including reconstructed interiors complete with kitchens, alcoves and "stube", the living area with its terracotta stove.

Route des Crêtes★★★

This strategic road was built during WWI at the request of the French High Command, in order to ensure adequate north-south communications between the various valleys along the front line of the Vosges. The magnificent (80km/49.7mi) itinerary enables motorists to admire the most characteristic landscapes of the Vosges mountains, its passes, its ballons (rounded summits), its lakes, its chaumes (high pastures where cattle graze in summer) and offers wide panoramas and extended views. Between the Hohneck and the Grand Ballon, the road is lined with fermes-auberges where snacks and regional dishes are served from June to October. In winter the snowfields offer miles of cross-country tracks.

- **Michelin Map:** 315 G 8, F 8, F 9 and G 9
- **Location:** The route starts 30km/18.6mi W of Colmar and heads S to Thann.
- **Don't Miss:** The panoramas between Le Hohneck and the Grand Ballon.

EXCURSION
COL DU BONHOMME TO THANN

83km/52mi. Allow half a day.

Col du Bonhomme

Alt 949m. The pass links the two regions of Alsace and Lorraine.

Beyond the pass, the road offers fine vistas of the Béhine valley to the left, with the Tête des Faux and Brézouard towering above. Farther on, the Col du Louchbach affords a beautiful view of the valley of the River Meurthe.

Col de la Schlucht

1 139m.

This is the steepest but also one of the busiest of the routes through the Vosges. The eastern slopes are subject to intense erosion because of the gradient of the torrential rivers; at a distance of only 9km/5.6mi from the pass, the town of **Munster★** lies 877m below, while Colmar is 1 065m lower.

Hohneck★★★

1 362m.

Rising near the central point of the range, this is one of the most visited of the Vosges summits. From the top there are superb **views★★★**; to the east, the **Munster valley★★** plunges steeply towards the broad expanses of the Alsace plain, while to the west is the Lorraine plateau.

Grand Ballon★★★

1 424m.

The Grand Ballon forms the highest point of the Vosges. From the top (*30min round-trip*) the **panorama★★★** extends over the southern part of the range. The eastern and western slopes are quite dissimilar; the drop to the Alsace plain is abrupt, while to the west the land falls gently to the Lorraine plateau. Glacial action in the Quaternary era is responsible for features like the massive rounded humps of the summits *(ballons)*, and the morainic lakes in the blocked valleys. Above the tree line, the forest clothing the hillsides gives way to the short grass of the wide upland known as the Hautes-Chaumes.

Vieil-Armand★★

The war memorial marks one of the most bitterly contested battlefields of World War I.

Thann★

This small town is renowned for having the most richly decorated Gothic church in the Alsace. The steep, south-facing vineyards and volcanic soils of the Rangen mountain produce a reputed Alsatian appellation.

Reims★★★

The ancient university town on the banks of the River Vesle is famous for its magnificent and important cathedral, where French kings were traditionally crowned.
It has a wealth of other architectural masterpieces. Reims is also (along with Epernay) the capital of Champagne's wine industry. Most of the great champagne houses are open to the public.

- **Population:** 179 992.
- **Michelin Map:** 306 G 7
- **Info:** 2 r. Guillaume de Machault. ✆03 26 77 45 00. www.reims-tourisme.com.
- **TGV:** Reims is less than 1hr direct from Paris Gare de l'Est.
- **Tram:** 11km/7mi urban tramway, running N to S.
- **Location:** Reims is 143km/89mi NE of Paris on the A 4 *autoroute*, and 275km/171mi from Calais on the A 26, which skirts the town.
- **Timing:** Reims can easily consume two full days.

A BIT OF HISTORY

Under the Romans, Reims was the capital of the province that was to become Belgium. It was at Reims, in 496, that Clovis, King of the Franks, was baptised by St Remigius (St Rémi). This was a political event of some significance, since it made the ambitious 35-year-old warrior the only Christian ruler in the chaotic times following the collapse of the Roman Empire. It was he who halted the advance of the Visigoths at Poitiers, subsequently pushing them back, first to Toulouse, then all the way into Spain. With him, the source of political authority in Gaul passed from Provence to the north.

At the time of the Carolingians, a feeling for beauty became evident at Reims; ancient texts were carefully copied, manuscripts illuminated, ivory carved and masterpieces of the goldsmith's art created. The period produced Charlemagne's Talisman (now in the Bishops' Palace) as well as the Épernay Gospel. In 816, Louis I the Pious had himself crowned here, as Charlemagne had done at Rome 16 years before. It was from this point that the dynasty acquired a sort of religious character, though it was not until the crowning of Louis VIII, 400 years later, that the city became the recognised place for coronations, with a ceremonial ever more

Champagne

Though covering only 2 percent of the total area planted with vines in France, this northernmost of the country's wine-growing regions is perhaps its most prestigious. The product was known in Roman times, when it was a still wine. It was Dom Pérignon (1638–1715), cellar-master of Hautvillers abbey (abbaye de Hautevilliers), who had the idea of making it sparkle by means of double fermentation, a process carried out today by the use of cane sugar and yeasts. The vines are spread over an area totalling 30 000ha/74 000 acres, on the lower slopes of the chalk escarpment of the Côte de l'Île-de-France for preference. The most renowned vineyards are the Montagne de Reims (robust, full-bodied wines), the valley of the Marne (fruity wines with plenty of bouquet) and the Côte des Blancs (fresh and elegant wines). Champagne is a blended, branded wine, the prestige of the great labels dependent on the expertise of the master-blenders. Some 215 million bottles are produced in an average year, with over 75 million of them for export.

elaborate and charged with symbolism. By the time of Charles X, 25 kings had been crowned here. The most moving coronation was that of Charles VII on 17 July 1429, which took place in the middle of the Hundred Years' War in the presence of Joan of Arc; the Maid of Orléans had given Frenchmen the first inklings of national identity, and had persuaded the king to make his way to Reims, even though this involved him in crossing the hostile Burgundian territory of Philippe le Bon (the Good).

On 7 May 1945, in a modern technical college near the station, the document was signed which marked the surrender of Germany. Confirmed the day after in Berlin, this brought to an end World War II in Europe.

CATHÉDRALE NOTRE-DAME★★★

Place Cardinal Luçon. Open daily 7.30am–7.30pm; no visits during services.

The present building was begun in 1211. It is one of the great cathedrals of France, built in the Lanceolate Gothic style pioneered at Chartres, but with more sophisticated ornamentation, especialy in its window tracery. The west front has wonderfully soaring lines and superb 13C sculpture, whose masterpiece is the world-famous Smiling Angel (in a splay of the north portal). Inside is one of the greatest achievements of the Gothic, the west end of the nave, best seen towards the end of the afternoon when the sun lights up the two rose windows.

Reims was occupied by the German army from 3–12 September 1914, and for four years remained in the battle zone. By the end of the war, out of a total of 14 130 houses, only 60 remained habitable. The cathedral, one of the country's most precious buildings in terms of both artistic and historic value, was in ruins. The artillery bombardments of 19 September 1914 and April 1917 had been particularly destructive. The skilful restoration has largely been financed by the Rockefeller Foundation.

WALKING TOUR

TOWN CENTRE

Reims map, p352. Allow 2hr.

- **Église St-Jacques** – The 13–14C church has a Gothic and Renaissance interior.
- **Place Drouet-d'Erlon** – Named after one of Napoléon's generals, this lively pedestrian-friendly space lined with cafés, restaurants, hotels and cinemas is the heart of the city.
- **Hôtel Saint-Jean-Baptiste de la Salle★** – This Renaissance house, built in 1545–56, is the birthplace of Jean-Baptiste de la Salle.
- **Hôtel de ville** – The imposing 17C façade survived the fire that destroyed the building in 1917.
- **Basses et Hautes Promenades** – These vast, shady squares were laid out in the 18C to replace the moat and glacis of the old fortifications.
- **Porte Mars★** – This triumphal arch of the Corinthian order was erected in honour of the Roman Emperor Augustus after the 3C AD. During the Middle Ages, it was incorporated into the ramparts and used as a town gate.
- **Rue de Mars** – The façade of no 6 is decorated with mosaic panels illustrating the Champagne-making process.
- **Hôtel des Comtes de Champagne** – This Gothic mansion belongs to the Taittinger Champagne house.
- **Cryptoportique gallo-romain** – This large half-buried Gallo-Roman monument, dating from the 3C AD, stands on the site of the ancient city's forum.
- **Place Royale★** – This arcaded square with balustraded roofs, designed by Legendre in 1760, is characteristic of the Louis XVI style.
- **Porte du Chapitre** – This 16C gate, flanked by two corbelled turrets, formed the main entrance to the chapter house.

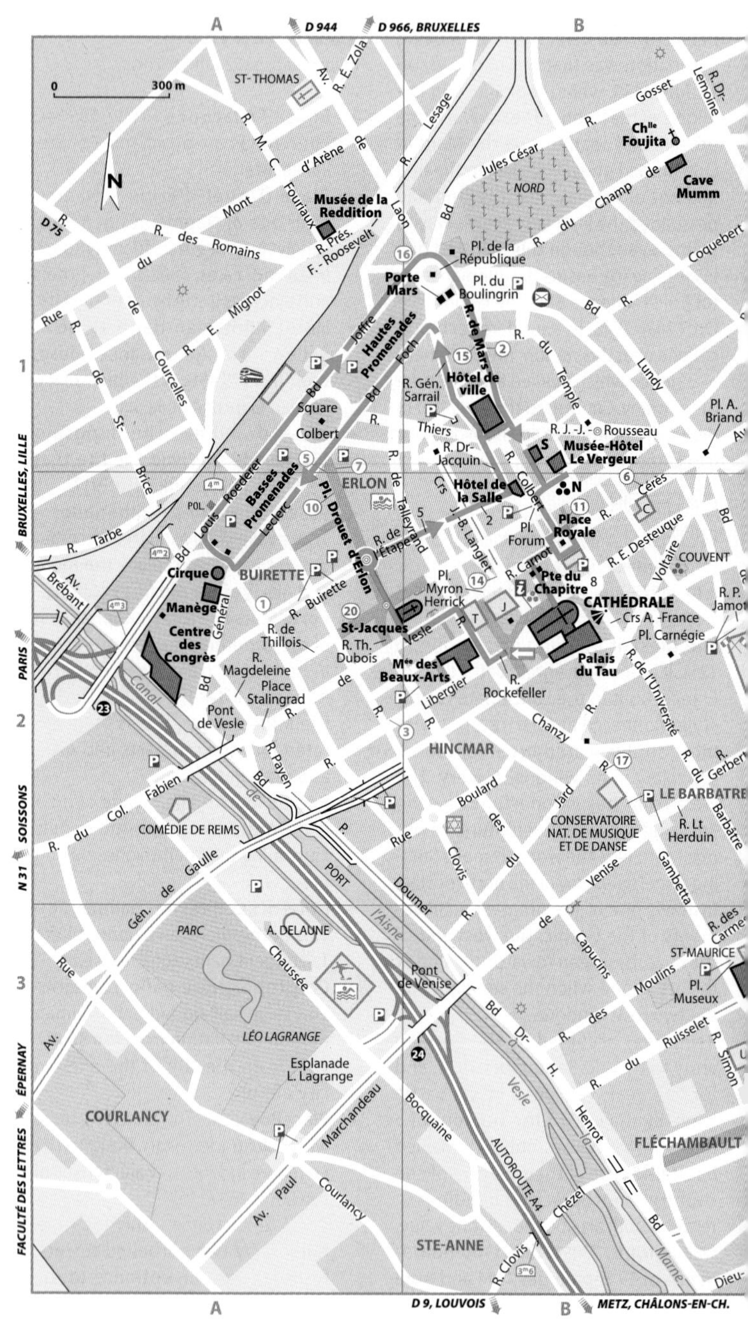
A
B
D 944
D 966, BRUXELLES
BRUXELLES, LILLE
PARIS
N 31 SOISSONS
ÉPERNAY
FACULTÉ DES LETTRES
D 9, LOUVOIS
METZ, CHÂLONS-EN-CH.
1
2
3
0
300 m
N
ST-THOMAS
Musée de la Reddition
Cave Mumm
Chlle Foujita
NORD
Pl. de la République
Porte Mars
Pl. du Boulingrin
Hautes Promenades
Basses Promenades
Square Colbert
Hôtel de ville
R. de Mars
Musée-Hôtel Le Vergeur
Hôtel de la Salle
Place Royale
Pl. Forum
Pte du Chapitre
CATHÉDRALE
Palais du Tau
Pl. Carnégie
Crs A.-France
ERLON
Pl. Drouet d'Erlon
BUIRETTE
Cirque
Manège
Centre des Congrès
St-Jacques
Mée des Beaux-Arts
Pl. Myron Herrick
R. Rockefeller
Place Stalingrad
Pont de Vesle
HINCMAR
LE BARBATRE
CONSERVATOIRE NAT. DE MUSIQUE ET DE DANSE
COMÉDIE DE REIMS
PARC
A. DELAUNE
LÉO LAGRANGE
Esplanade L. Lagrange
Pont de Venise
COURLANCY
STE-ANNE
FLÉCHAMBAULT
ST-MAURICE
Pl. Museux
COUVENT
Pl. A. Briand
AUTOROUTE A4
PORT
Canal
Vesle
l'Aisne
Marne

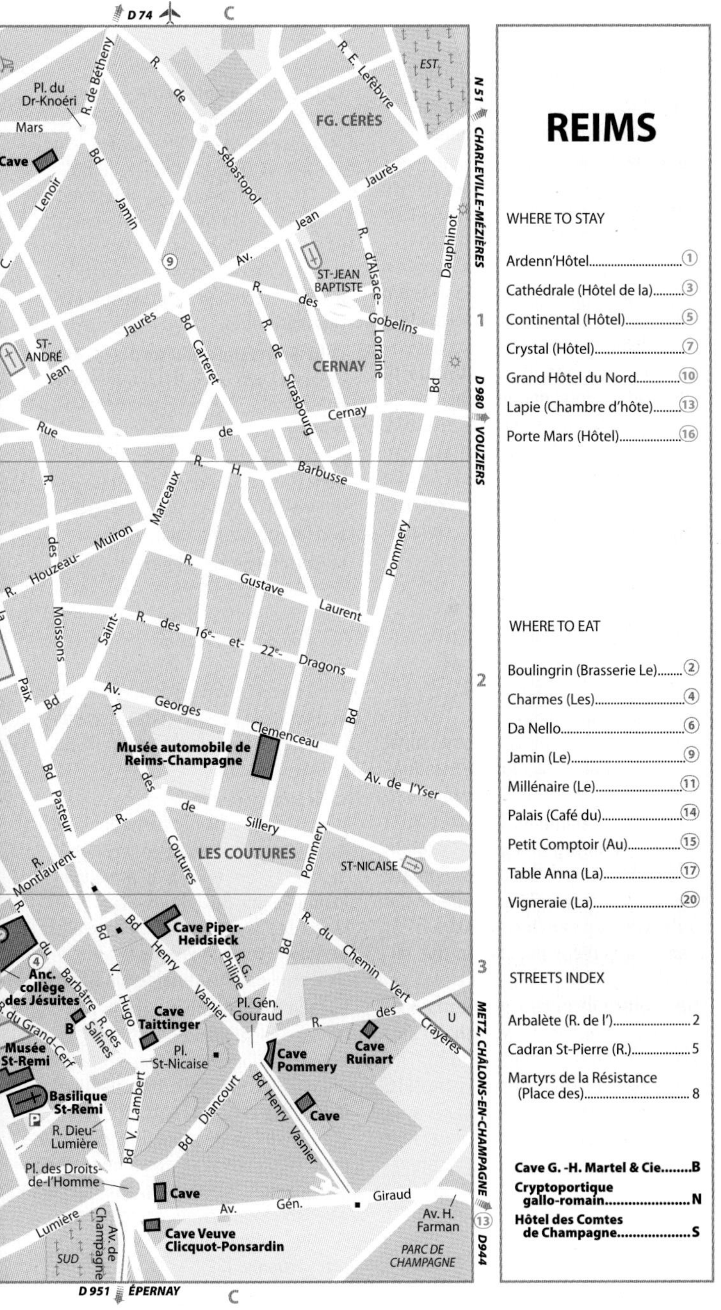
REIMS
WHERE TO STAY
Ardenn'Hôtel 1
Cathédrale (Hôtel de la) 3
Continental (Hôtel) 5
Crystal (Hôtel) 7
Grand Hôtel du Nord 10
Lapie (Chambre d'hôte) 13
Porte Mars (Hôtel) 16
WHERE TO EAT
Boulingrin (Brasserie Le) 2
Charmes (Les) 4
Da Nello 6
Jamin (Le) 9
Millénaire (Le) 11
Palais (Café du) 14
Petit Comptoir (Au) 15
Table Anna (La) 17
Vigneraie (La) 20
STREETS INDEX
Arbalète (R. de l') 2
Cadran St-Pierre (R.) 5
Martyrs de la Résistance (Place des) 8
Cave G. -H. Martel & Cie B
Cryptoportique gallo-romain N
Hôtel des Comtes de Champagne S
D 74
C
N 51 CHARLEVILLE-MÉZIÈRES
D 980 VOUZIERS
METZ, CHÂLONS-EN-CHAMPAGNE D944
D 951 ÉPERNAY
1
2
3
Pl. du Dr-Knoéri
R. de Béthény
Mars
Cave
Lenoir
Bd Jamin
R. de Sébastopol
R. E. Lefèbvre
EST
FG. CÉRÈS
Av. Jean Jaurès
ST-JEAN BAPTISTE
R. des Gobelins
R. d'Alsace-Lorraine
Bd Dauphinot
ST-ANDRÉ
Jaurès
Jean
Bd Carteret
R. de Strasbourg
CERNAY
Rue de Cernay
R. H. Barbusse
Bd Pommery
R. des Moissons
R. Houzeau-Muiron
Marceaux
R. Gustave Laurent
R. des 16e- et- 22e- Dragons
Saint-
Paix
Av. Georges Clemenceau
Musée automobile de Reims-Champagne
Av. de l'Yser
Bd Pasteur
R. des Coutures
R. de Sillery
LES COUTURES
Pommery
ST-NICAISE
R. Montlaurent
Bd Henry Vasnier
Cave Piper-Heidsieck
R. du Chemin Vert
R. du Barbâtre
Anc. collège des Jésuites
Bd V. Hugo
R. G. Philipe
R. des Salines
R. du Grand-Cerf
B
Cave Taittinger
Pl. Gén. Gouraud
R. des Crayères
U
Musée St-Remi
Pl. St-Nicaise
Cave Pommery
Cave Ruinart
Basilique St-Remi
Bd Diancourt
Bd Henry Vasnier
Cave
R. Dieu-Lumière
Bd V. Lambert
Pl. des Droits-de-l'Homme
Cave
Av. Gén. Giraud
Av. H. Farman
Lumière
Av. de Champagne
SUD
Cave Veuve Clicquot-Ponsardin
PARC DE CHAMPAGNE

PALAIS DU TAU★★

2 place du Cardinal-Luçon. Open early May–early Sept daily 9.30am–6.30pm. Rest of the year 9.30am–12.30pm, 2–5.30pm. Closed 1 Jan, 1 May, 1 and 11 Nov, 25 Dec. €8. 03 26 47 81 79. http://palais-tau.monuments-nationaux.fr.

Dating from 1690, the former palace of the bishops of Reims was built by Mansart and Robert de Cotte. In it is housed some of the cathedral's original statuary and tapestries, among them two huge 15C Arras tapestries depicting scenes from the life of Clovis.

The treasury has many objects of outstanding interest, such as the 9C Talisman of Charlemagne, the 11C cut-glass Holy Thorn reliquary, the 12C coronation chalice, the St Ursula reliquary with its cornelian casket, the Holy Ampulla reliquary, and a collar of the Order of the Holy Ghost.

BASILIQUE ST-RÉMI★★

Place Chanoine Ladame. Open daily 8am–7pm. Son-et-Lumière shows Jul–Sep Sat 9.30pm. No charge. Guided tours on request.

Dating from 1007, this is the city's most venerable church, though restorations have left little that is Romanesque and less that is Carolingian. The west front was rebuilt during a major restoration in 1170; it is remarkable for its Romanesque south tower. The façade of the south transept with its statue of St Michael was reconstructed in the 14C and 15C.

The sombre interior **(intérieur★★★)** is remarkable for its length (122m) in proportion to its width (26m). The oldest part of the church is the 11C transept. In the 12C, the choir was rebuilt in the Early Gothic manner and the whole nave given Gothic vaulting.

ADDRESSES

STAY

Ardenn'Hôtel – 6 r. Caqué. 03 26 47 42 38. 14 rooms. This hotel with an attractive brick façade has many points in its favour. You will certainly be won over by its location in a quiet little town-centre street, the unfailing cleanliness of the tastefully decorated rooms and the smiling service.

Chambre d'hôte Lapie – 1 r. Jeanne-d'Arc, 51360 Val-de-Vesle. 21km/12.5mi SE of Reims on N 44 and left on D 326. 03 26 03 92 88. Closed 15 Dec–15 Jan. 5 rooms. Five lovely pastel-toned rooms are available on this farm in the heart of a village. The attractive decor mixes old and modern styles and there's an immaculate downstairs breakfast room.

Grand Hôtel du Nord – 75 pl. Drouet-d'Erlon. 03 26 47 39 03. www.hotel-nord-reims.com. Closed Christmas holidays. 50 rooms. Mostly refurbished rooms in a 1920s building set on Reims' pedestrian main square. The rooms at the rear are quieter. Many restaurants and lots going on nearby.

Hôtel de la Cathédrale – 20 r. Libergier. 03 26 47 28 46. www.hotel-cathedrale-reims.fr. 17 rooms. This smart but welcoming hotel stands in one of the streets that lead to the cathedral. The small rooms have comfortable beds and are bright and cheerful, while the breakfast room is decorated with old engravings.

Hôtel Crystal – 86 pl. Drouet-d'Erlon. 03 26 88 44 44. 69 rooms. An astonishing haven of greenery right in the centre of town is an attractive feature of this 1920s house. The renovated bedrooms all have excellent bedding. Breakfast is served in a delightful courtyard-garden in summer.

Hôtel Continental – 93 pl. Drouet-d'Erlon. 03 26 40 39 35. www.grandhotelcontinental.com. Closed 21 Dec–7 Jan. 61 rooms. The attractive façade of this central hotel adorns the city's liveliest square. The rooms, renovated in varying styles, are reached by a splendid staircase (if you're for calm avoid the rooms overlooking bd du Général-Leclerc). Elegant Belle Epoque sitting rooms.

Hôtel Porte Mars – 2 pl. de la République. 03 26 40 28 35. www.hotelportemars.com. 24 rooms. It's a pleasure to drink tea near the fire in the cosy sitting room, or enjoy a drink in the sophisticated bar. A delicious breakfast is also served in the attractive glass-roofed dining room decorated with photographs and old mirrors. Each of the well-sound-proofed rooms have a personal touch.

EAT

Brasserie Le Boulingrin – 48 r. de Mars. 03 26 40 96 22. Closed Sun. This Art Deco restaurant dating from 1925 is an institution in Reims. The owner is much in evidence, overseeing operations and ensuring a convivial mood. The menu is inventive and the prices reasonable.

La Table Anna – 6 r. Gambetta. 03 26 89 12 12. www.annas-latable amoureuse.com. Closed Mon. Champagne takes pride of place in the window of this establishment next door to the music conservatory. Some of the paintings adorning the walls are the work of the owner, an artist at heart.

La Vigneraie – 14 r. de Thillois. 03 26 88 67 27. www.vigneraie.com. La Vigneraie, situated just off pl. Drouet-d'Erlon, boasts a fantastic collection of carafes. Tasty classical menu and fine wine list. Excellent value-for-money.

Le Jamin – 18 bd. Jamin. 03 26 07 37 30. www.lejamin.com. Closed Mon, Sun dinner, end Jan, end Aug. In this little local bistro, perfectly mastered traditional cooking is served in a rustic dining room. Look for the good-value daily specials on the blackboard.

Café du Palais – 14 pl. Myron-Herrick. 03 26 47 52 54. Closed Sun and public holidays. This lively café near the cathedral was founded in 1930, and still has its original glass roof. Popular with locals for its generous salads, daily dishes and home-made patisseries.

Les Charmes – 11 r. Brûlart. 03 26 85 37 63. Closed spring hols, 23 Jul–23 Aug, Sat lunch, Mon evening and Sun. Close to the famous champagne cellars and St-Remi basilica, this convivial family restaurant is decorated with paintings on wood. Good selection of whiskies.

Au Petit Comptoir – 17 r. de Mars. 03 26 40 58 58. Closed Sat lunch, Mon lunch and Sun and 24–31 Dec–2 Jan. This trendy restaurant behind the town hall has a striking modern interior to match the dishes of Patrice Maillot.

Da Nello – 39 r. Cérès. 03 26 47 33 25. Closed Aug. A Mediterranean welcome awaits you at this Italian restaurant where the tables all have a view of the kitchen and the pizza oven is right in the centre of the room. Fresh pasta, grills and daily specials according to what the market has to offer.

Le Millénaire – 4 r. Bertin. 03 26 08 26 62. www.lemillenaire.com. A spacious dining room near place Royale is hung with modern paintings.

NIGHTLIFE

Place Drouet-d'Erlon – This square is the starting point for anyone wanting to go out on the town, whether you are looking for a bar, pub, restaurant, tearoom or brasserie.

CALENDAR

Fêtes Johanniques – 2nd weekend in June. 2 000 walk-ons in period costume accompany Joan of Arc and Charles VII during a massive street festival.

Flâneries musicales d'été – Jun–Jul. Over 150 street concerts throughout the town, including shows by major international stars in some of the town's most prestigious and unlikely venues.

CHAMPAGNE HOUSES

Several of the world's most renowned champagne-makers have their cellars in Reims, and offer guided tours, tastings and discount purchases.

Mumm 34 r. du Champ-de-Mars. www.mumm.com.

Piper-Heidsieck 51 bd Henry-Vasnier. www.piper-heidsieck.com.

Pommery 5 pl. du Gén.-Gouraud. www.pommery.com.

Ruinart 4 r. des Crayères. www.ruinart.com.

Taittinger 9 pl. St-Nicaise. www.taittinger.fr.

Veuve Clicquot-Ponsardin 1 pl. des Droits-de-l'Homme. www.veuve-clicquot.fr.

Châlons-en-Champagne★★

Its centre traversed by the River Marne and two canals, the Mau and the Nau, Châlons, formerly known as Châlons-sur-Marne, is a dignified and attractive commercial town with some fine buildings.

- **Population:** 45 299.
- **Michelin Map:** 306 I 9
- **Info:** 3 quai des Arts. 03 26 65 17 89. www.chalons-tourisme.com.
- **TGV:** Chalons is 1hr 30mins from Paris Gare de l'Est.
- **Location:** 46km/29mi SE of Reims, and 32km/20mi E of Épernay.

A BIT OF HISTORY

The valley of the Aube to the southwest of the town was the setting in 451 for the series of battles known as the Catalaunian Fields **(Champs catalauniques)**. Having given up his intention of sacking Paris, then known as Lutetia, because of the intervention of St Genevieve, Attila the Hun was engaged here by the Roman army under Aetius; after fierce fighting, he quit the battlefield and fled eastwards.

During the Wars of Religion, the town remained loyal to the King who declared it to be the "main town of the Champagne region" and in 1589 it became the seat of an annexe of the Paris Parliament. Châlons was the birthplace in 1749 of Nicolas Appert, a pioneer of the food industry and the inventor of a system of preserving food by sterilisation.

SIGHTS

Cathédrale St-Étienne★★

Open Feb–Dec, call for opening hours. Admission charge. 05 61 03 03 03.

The present building was begun around 1235 in the Lanceolate Gothic style invented 40 years previously at Chartres, though there is little evidence of stylistic development having taken place.

The cathedral is famous for its stained glass (**vitraux**), Renaissance as well as medieval. The 13C glass includes the tall windows in the choir, the north transept (with the wonderful hues of green characteristic of the region), and the first bay on the north side (the Tanners' window – note the hanging skins). The finest windows, however, are those of Renaissance date, in the side chapels of the south aisle, showing scenes from the Creation, the earthly Paradise, the Passion, the Life of Christ and the Lives of the Saints.

Église Notre-Dame-en-Vaux★

Open daily 10am–noon, 2–6pm, Sun 2.30–6pm. 03 26 65 63 17.

This typical early Gothic church with a characteristic four-tier elevation has a particularly noteworthy ambulatory, inspired by the one at St-Rémi in Reims, together with the stained glass in the windows of the north aisle, again showing superb skill in the use of green.

To the left of the church, the **Musée du Cloître de Notre-Dame-en-Vaux★★** houses **sculptures★★** from the old Romanesque cloisters, a rare example of the most accomplished medieval architecture.

EXCURSION

Bar-le-Duc★

Bar-le-Duc sits halfway between Strasbourg and Paris.

7 r. Jeanne-d'Arc. 03 29 79 11 13. www.barleduc.fr.

This old capital of the Duchy of Bar is divided into two sections. The historic Ville Haute rests on a plateau, while the industrial Ville Basse is laid out along the River Ornain and the Rhine-Marne canal. The upper town is a beautiful ensemble of grand and aristocratic 16–18C houses, especially notable in the triangular Place St-Pierre.

Monthermé★

Monthermé has a spectacular site★ just downstream from the meeting point of the Semoy with the Meuse, and makes a good starting point for walks or cycle rides into the Ardennes.

- **Population:** 2 459.
- **Michelin Map:** 306 K 3
- **Info:** pl. J.-B. Clément. ☏03 24 54 46 73. www.montherme.fr.
- **Location:** The little town is close to Charleville-Mézières, 104km/65mi to the NE of Reims, not far from the Belgian border.

EXCURSION

La Meuse Ardennaise★★ (The Meuse Gorge through the Ardennes)

72km/45mi.

One of Europe's great rivers, 950km/590mi in length, the Meuse rises on the Langres uplands. It flows between the escarpment of the Côte des Bars and the dip-slope of the Côte de la Meuse, before penetrating the high plateau of the Ardennes in a deep gorge. Its meanders here mark the course it traced out in Tertiary times; since then, the plateau has been uplifted, but the river has succeeded in entrenching itself in the landscape. From **Charleville-Mézières★** to Givet there is a succession of single meanders (Monthermé, Fumay, Chooz), double (Revin) and even triple ones (Charleville). The valley has long formed a corridor of human activity, with its water, rail and road communications, and with a skilled workforce producing engineering products and domestic appliances.

Downstream from Monthermé the most interesting sites are: the **Roches de Laifour★** and the **Dames de Meuse★** opposite one another; **Revin**, where the old town and the industrial area each occupy their own peninsula; **Fumay**, with its old quarter, once famous for its quarries producing violet slate, and **Givet**, sited at the exit from a side valley originally fortified by Charles V and strengthened by Vauban.

EXCURSION

Rocroi★

Rocroi stands close to the Belgian border.

Place d'Armes. ☏03 24 54 20 06. www.otrocroi.com.

First laid out in the 16C in a clearing in the Ardennes forest, Rocroi is a typical Renaissance fortified town. After the principality of Sedan had been incorporated into France in 1642, the death of Richelieu and the ill health of Louis XIII made a long period of uncertain rule by a regent seem likely. The prospect whetted the expansionist appetites of Philip IV of Spain, for whom the capture of Rocroi would open the way to Paris via the valleys of the Aisne and the Marne.

On 19 May 1643, three days after the death of Louis XIII, a bold manoeuvre by the Duke d'Enghien, the future Grand Condé, routed the redoubtable Spanish infantry. This, the first French victory over the Spaniards for more than a century, reverberated around Europe. Mazarin was now able to implement Richelieu's foreign policy. After his involvement in the disturbances known as the Fronde, Condé went over to the Spaniards, and, in 1658, was responsible for capturing Rocroi for them. But in the following year, the Treaty of the Pyrenees gave the fortress town back to France and Condé to his king.

Ramparts

The ramparts of Rocroi were improved by Vauban. With their glacis, bastions, demi-lunes and deep defensive ditches they are a fine example of the great engineer's mastery of his art.

Troyes★★★

The lively centre of this distinguished old trading town is a charming collection of picturesque half-timbered houses, many beautifully restored.

- **Population:** 60 280.
- **Michelin Map:** 313 E 4
- **Info:** 16 bd Carnot (by the station) ℘03 25 82 62 70, and r. Mignard (pedestrian zone, opposite Saint Jean church). ℘03 25 73 36 88. http://en.tourisme-troyes.com.
- **Location:** 125km/78mi S of Reims by *autoroute*, and 176km/110mi SE of Paris in the cradle formed by the A 5 and A 26 *autoroutes*.
- **Parking:** If you are visiting the old town, park the car behind the town hall (place Alexandre-Israël) or along boulevard Gambetta.
- **Don't Miss:** For shopping bargains, visit the big factory outlet malls on the edge of town.
- **Timing:** Allow a day to enjoy Vieux Troyes.

A BIT OF HISTORY

Today Troyes shares with Reims the distinction of being one of the capitals of the province of Champagne, though historically the city looks southeast towards Burgundy rather than northwards to the Ardennes. The town developed in the Seine valley on the great trade route between Italy and the cities of Flanders. It had a considerable Jewish population, among them the influential scholar Rashi (1050–1105).

In the Middle Ages the town hosted two huge annual fairs, each lasting three months, and attracting merchants and craftsmen from all over Europe. But by the end of the 14C, the pattern of commercial exchanges had changed, and these gatherings fell into decline.

Troyes has long been France's most important centre of hosiery manufacture, an industry introduced at the beginning of the 16C. The city's wealth enabled it to overcome the great fire of 1524; houses and churches were rebuilt in a style showing both the Italianate influence of artists who came from Fontainebleau around 1540, as well as the persistence of medieval traditions.

Guided Tours

Guided tours, including audio-tours, can be booked all year round at the tourist office, who also sell the useful **Pass'Troyes** (€12). *Ask at the tourist office.*

WALKING TOUR

HISTORIC CENTRE★★

Troyes map, p360-361. Allow 4hr.

Medieval Troyes consisted of two separate districts: the Cité, the aristocratic and ecclesiastical centre surrounding the cathedral, and the Bourg of the commercial burghers where the Champagne fairs took place. In 1524, a fire swept through the town. The prosperous inhabitants took this opportunity to build the more opulent houses that are still visible today. The timber-framed houses had pointed gables, cob walls and corbelled upper floors. More opulent houses had walls of limestone rubble and brick in the traditional Champagne style. The most elegant mansions were built of stone, an expensive material in the region due to the absence of hard-stone quarries.

SIGHTS

Maison de l'Outil et de la Pensée ouvrière★★

7 r. de la Trinité. Open daily 10am–6pm (Oct–Mar daily except Tue). Closed 1 Jan and 25 Dec. €7. ℘03 25 73 28 26. www.maison-de-l-outil.com.

Housed in the Hôtel du Mauroy, it is a fine architectural setting for the fascinating range of objects displayed. The dignity of labour is celebrated here in the subtle diversity of forms as much as in the individual character and highly specialised function of each object.

Église Ste-Madeleine

This church is Troyes' oldest place of worship. Much rebuilt in the 16C, it is famous for the rood screen (**jubé★★**); this has scalloped arches with no intermediate supports, fine glass (**verrières★**), as well as a statue of **Sainte Marthe★** of striking gravity.

Musée de Vauluisant★

4 r. Vauluisant. Open Wed–Sun: 10am–1pm, 2–6pm (Nov–Mar 5pm). €3. ✆03 25 73 05 85.

The fine 16C Renaissance **Hôtel de Vauluisant★** contains a museum of **local art** and a **museum of hosiery** with exhibits depicting the industry's evolution, including historic looms and other machinery.

Cathédrale St-Pierre et St-Paul★★

The cathedral was begun in 1208 and continued until the 17C, enabling the regional Gothic style to be traced over the whole period of its evolution. The building has remarkable proportions, exceptionally rich decoration and a beautiful nave. The stained-glass windows (**vitraux★★**) of the cathedral cover a total area of 1 500sq m. One of the supreme achievements of this art form, they transform the building into a cage of glass.

Musée d'Art Moderne★★

14 Place Saint-Pierre. ♿ Open Tue–Sun: 10am–1pm, 2–6pm (Nov–Mar 5pm). €5. ✆03 25 76 26 80.

This is the collection built up since 1939 by Pierre and Denise Lévy, noted hosiery manufacturers. It comprises thousands of items dating from 1850–1950, many of them donated to the State and now on display in the former Bishops' Palace. Particularly well represented here are the **Fauves**, who, together with Braque, Dufy, Matisse and Van Dongen, "made colour roar". Derain too, one of the first to appreciate the art of Africa, is very much present, as is Maurice Marinot, a local artist and glass-maker.

ADDITIONAL SIGHTS

Basilique St-Urbain★ – 13C Gothic architecture.

Église St-Pantaléon★ – Collection of religious statuary.

Musée St-Loup *(1 r. Chrestien de Troyes)*– Fine art and **archaeology★**.

Apothicairerie de l'Hôtel-Dieu-le-Comte *(Quai des Comtes de Champagne Troyes)* – Rich collection of 18C earthenware.

ADDRESSES

STAY

⊖ **Les Comtes de Champagne** – 54–56 r. de la Monnaie. ✆03 25 73 11 70. www.comtesdechampagne.com. 29 rooms. It is said that the counts of Champagne used to mint coins in the four 12C houses which make up this hotel.

⊖⊜ **Hôtel de Troyes** – 168 av. du Gén. Leclerc. ✆03 25 71 23 45. www.hoteldetroyes.com. 23 rooms. Rooms are spread over two buildings either side of a bright plant-filled veranda.

⊖⊜ **Citôtel La Bonne Fermière** – Pl. de l'Église, 10450 Bréviandes – 5km S of Troyes, on the road to Dijon. ✆03 25 82 45 65. 13 rooms. This small, peaceful hotel offers comfortable refurbished rooms brightened up by lovely colours.

⊖⊜ **Hôtel Ibis** – R. Camille-Claudel. ✆03 25 75 99 99. 77 rooms. New establishment benefiting from the latest Ibis standards: air-conditioned rooms, new-look bathrooms, pleasant breakfast room.

⊖⊜ **Chambre d'hôte Moulin d'Eguebaude** – 10190 Estissac. ✆03 25 40 42. Closed 1 Jan and 25 Dec. ⊭. 8 rooms. Located on a vast fish-farming estate, this typical wheat mill from the Champagne region (1789) offers fresh, simple rooms.

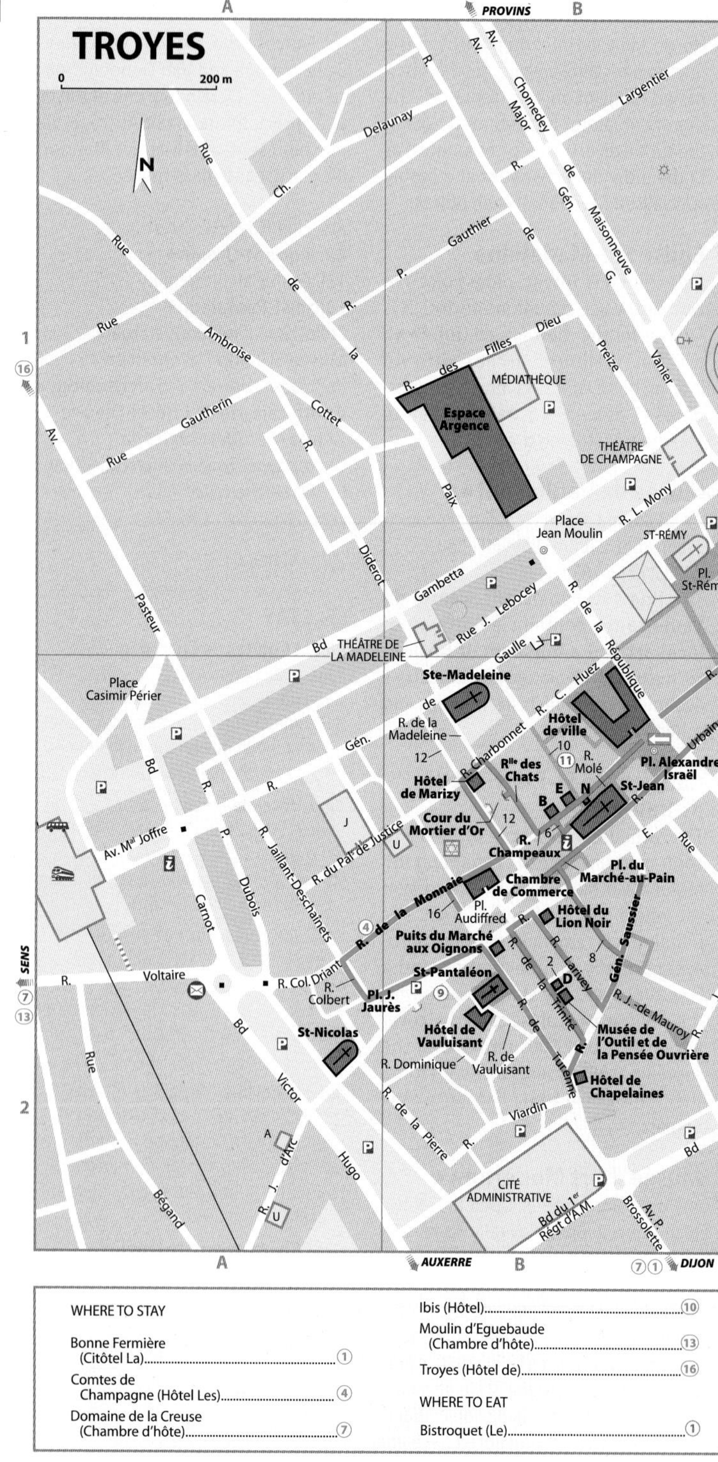

WHERE TO STAY

Bonne Fermière (Citôtel La) .... ①
Comtes de Champagne (Hôtel Les) .... ④
Domaine de la Creuse (Chambre d'hôte) .... ⑦
Ibis (Hôtel) .... ⑩
Moulin d'Eguebaude (Chambre d'hôte) .... ⑬
Troyes (Hôtel de) .... ⑯

WHERE TO EAT

Bistroquet (Le) .... ①

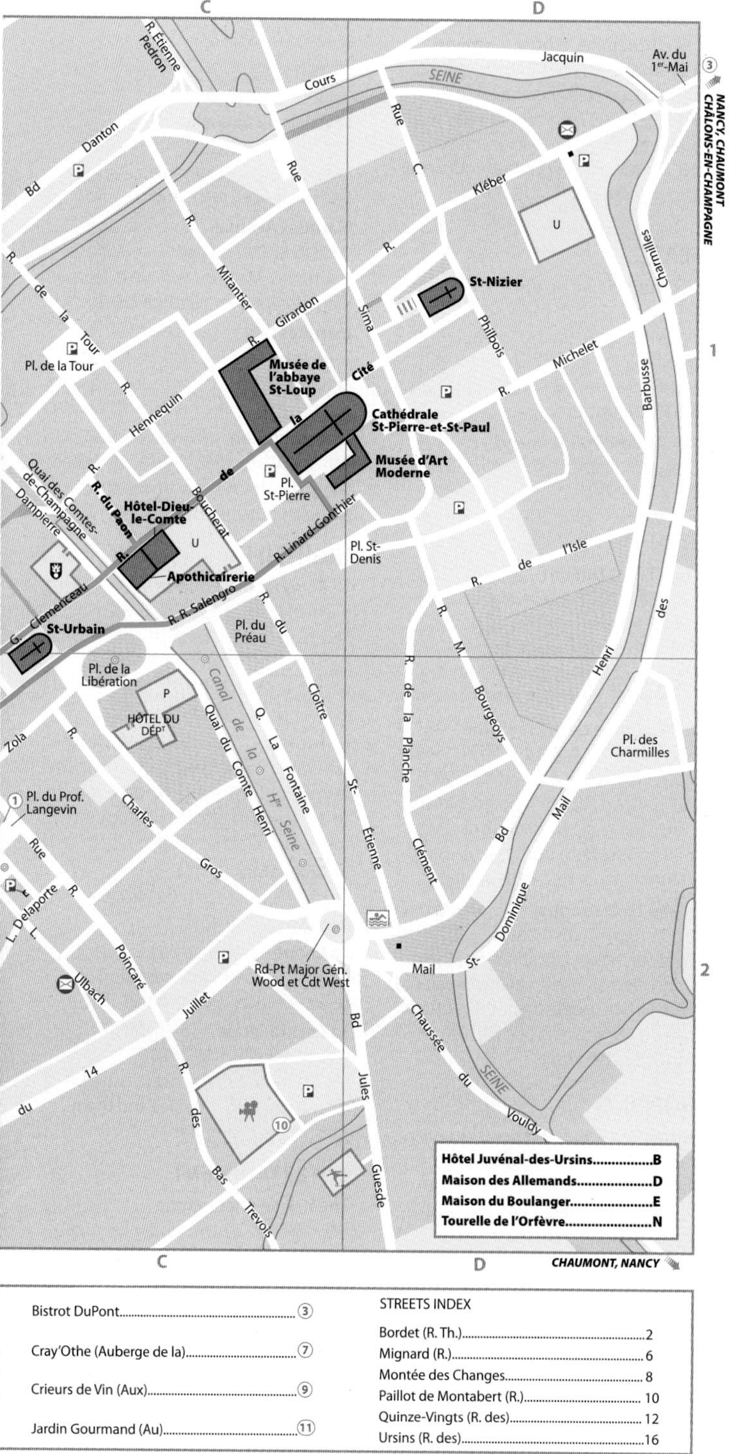

Bistrot DuPont.......................................③
Cray'Othe (Auberge de la)......................⑦
Crieurs de Vin (Aux)................................⑨
Jardin Gourmand (Au)..............................⑪

STREETS INDEX

Bordet (R. Th.)...2
Mignard (R.)...6
Montée des Changes.....................................8
Paillot de Montabert (R.)..............................10
Quinze-Vingts (R. des)..................................12
Ursins (R. des)..16

Chambre d'hôte Domaine de la Creuse – 10800 Moussey. 03 25 41 74 01. www.domainedelacreuse.com. Closed 22 Dec–3 Jan. 3 rooms. This traditional 18C Champagne house is built around a lovely central courtyard laid out as a garden.

EAT

Aux Crieurs de Vin – 4–6 pl. Jean-Jaurès. 03 25 40 01 01. Closed Sun and Mon. Wine connoisseurs will appreciate this establishment, which is part wine and spirits shop, part atmospheric pre-1940s style bistro.

Au Jardin Gourmand – 31 r. Paillot de Montabert. 03 25 73 36 13. Closed 2 weeks Mar, 2 weeks Sep, Mon lunch and Sun. Andouillette reigns at this restaurant in old Troyes.

Bistrot DuPont – 5 pl. Charles-de-Gaulle, 10150 Pont-Ste-Marie, 3km/1.8mi NE of Troyes on N 77. 03 25 80 90 99. Closed Sun evening and Mon. In a simple but carefully planned setting, the cheerful dishes suit the bistro's style.

Auberge de la Cray'Othe – 31 Grande-Rue, 10190 Messon. 12km/7.5mi W of Troyes on N 60 and left on D 83. 03 25 70 31 12. Open Thu–Sun. Closed 2 weeks in Jan, 2 weeks in Sep. Booking necessary. This beautiful farm houses a pleasant restaurant decorated with paintings.

Le Bistroquet – Pl. Langevin 03 25 73 65 65. www.bistroquet-troyes.fr. Closed Sun except lunchtimes from Sep –June. This restaurant occupying an old cinema in the pedestrianised centre of Troyes, is reminiscent of a Parisian belle époque brasserie.

SHOPPING

Specialities – *Andouillettes* (chitterling sausages): grilled, unaccompanied or drizzled with olive oil flavoured with fines herbes and garlic. Other specialities include Chaource cheese, cider or champagne *choucroute*.

Market – Daily market in the Place St-Remy halls. The main market is held on Saturdays. There is another in the Chartreux area on Wed and on Sun morning. Country market every 3rd Wed on Boulevard Jules-Guesde.

Jean-Pierre-Ozérée – Halles de l'Hôtel-de-Ville. 03 25 73 72 25. Maturing of cheeses, including Chaource.

Le Palais du Chocolat – 2 r. de la Monnaie. 03 25 73 35 73. www.pascal-caffet.com. Closed Sun afternoon. Chocolate, ice cream and pastries.

Marques Avenue – 114 bd de Dijon, 03 25 82 00 72. Closed Sun. With 120 boutiques, Marques Avenue is Europe's biggest centre for discount fashion.

Marques City – Pont-Ste-Marie. Closed Sun. Stores offering almost 200 labels at discount prices, from sportswear to formal wear. Three restaurants on site.

McArthur Glen – Voie des Bois, 10150 Pont-Ste-Marie. 03 25 70 47 10. Closed Sun and 1 May. 84 end-of-line shops along an outside covered gallery.

NIGHTLIFE

Le Bougnat des Pouilles – 29 r. Paillot-de-Montabert. 03 25 73 59 85. The high-quality vintages in this wine bar are sought out by the young proprietor himself, from among the smaller producers in the region.

Le Tricasse – 16 r. Paillot-de-Montabert. 03 25 73 14 80. Closed Sun. This most famous of Troyes' nightspots is in a smart area and offers a glorious mix of music, from jazz to salsa to house.

Le Chihuahua – 8 r. Charbonnet. 03 25 73 33 53. This fashionable cellar bar also has dancing.

La Chope – 64 ave du Gén.-de-Gaulle. 03 25 73 11 99. Wide selection of beers, whiskies and cocktails.

La Cocktaileraie – 56 r. Jaillant-Deschainets, BP 4102. 03 25 73 77 04. A hundred or so cocktails are on offer, around 45 whiskies and many prestigious champagnes.

ENTERTAINMENT

Théâtre de Champagne – r. Louis-Mary. 03 25 76 27 60 / 61. Closed Jul–Aug. Opera, comedy, art-house theatre, variety shows.

Provins★★

- **Population:** 12 301.
- **Michelin Map:** 312 I 4
- **Info:** Chemin de Villecran. ☎0 64 60 26 26. www.provins.net.
- **Location:** 70km/44mi NW of Troyes, and 93km/58mi SE of Paris, Provins is easily reached by road or rail from the capital.
- **Don't Miss:** A relaxing stroll around the upper town.

The ancient fortified city of Provins sits atop a ridge overlooking the Seine valley and the Champagne chalklands, roughly equidistant from both Paris and Troyes.
The town has a famous outline (once painted by Turner), dominated by a tower (Tour de César) and the dome of Église St-Quiriace. Provins' role as an important centre of commerce was confirmed in the 12C when it became one of the two capitals of the County of Champagne.
Its annual fairs were renowned, part of a round of such events which also took place at Lagny, Bar-sur-Aube and Troyes. For a number of years in the 13C, Edmund of Lancaster was Lord of Provins, at a time when the place was known for its roses, in those days a rare flower.
He incorporated a red rose into his emblem; a century-and-a-half later it was this flower which triumphed over the white rose of York in the Wars of the Roses.

A BIT OF HISTORY

The lower town developed from the 11C on around a Benedictine priory built on the spot where the relics of St Ayoul (or Aygulf) had been miraculously found. Under the leadership of Henri I (1152–81), Count of Champagne, known as the Liberal, Provins became a prosperous trading town and one of the two capital cities of the Champagne region.

Roses – According to tradition it was Thibaud IV the Troubadour who brought roses back from Syria and grew them successfully in Provins. Edmund Lancaster (1245–96), brother of the King of England, married Blanche of Artois and was for a while suzerain of Provins, at which time he introduced the red rose into his coat of arms.

VILLE HAUTE★★

Still protected to north and west by its 12C and 13C **walls★★**, its most splendid feature is the **Tour de César★★**, a massive 12C keep with an additional rampart built by the English in the Hundred Years' War as an artillery emplacement. There is also a 13C tithe barn (*Grange aux Dîmes*), which belonged to the canons of St-Quiriace.

Also of note is the group of **statues★★** at the Église St-Ayoul.

EXCURSION

Église de St-Loup-de-Naud★

11km/6.8mi SW.

The church belonged to a Benedictine priory of the Archbishopric of Sens, and was one of the first in the area to be vaulted in stone. Erected in the 11C and 12C, it demonstrates the gradual evolution of the Romanesque into early Gothic. The choir dates from the 11C, as does the early Romanesque cradle-vault next to it. The dome over the crossing, the barely projecting transepts and the first two bays of the nave were built at the beginning of the 12C.

Finally, around 1160, the last two bays of the nave were completed; they are square in plan and have alternating pillars and twin columns on the model of Sens Cathedral. The well-preserved **doorway★★**, under the main porch, shows similarities with the Royal Doorway (*Portail royal*) of Chartres Cathedral; Christ in Majesty surrounded by symbols of the Evangelists on the tympanum, apostles in arched niches on the lintel, statue-columns in the splays, and figures in between the arch mouldings.

Burgundy Jura

» Region map p366–367
Dijon p368
Beaune p377
Auxerre p383
Besançon p389
Lons-le-Saunier p395

Introduction

Burgundy's unity is based more on history than on geography. Fortunately located on the trade route linking northern Europe to the Mediterranean, the territory was consolidated by its great Dukes in the 15C. It comprises a number of *pays* of varying character, though its heartland lies in the limestone plateaux stretching eastwards from the Auxerre area and terminating in escarpments, which drop down to the Saône valley. To the east the Jura's limestone uplands run in a great arc for some 240km/150mi from Rhine to Rhône, corresponding roughly to the old province of Franche-Comté.

Geography – Of the Burgundian escarpments La Côte is the most renowned, with its slopes producing some of the world's finest wines. To the north is the Morvan, a granite massif of poor soils, with scattered hamlets and extensive forests. Further north and west the Nivernais stretches to the Loire and to the south the lower reaches of the Saône are bordered by the broad Bresse plain. The limestone uplands of the Jura were folded into long parallel ridges and valleys by the pressure exerted on them in the Alpine-building period. This is a verdant landscape with extensive forests and vast upland pastures.

History – Burgundy was independent of France in the Middle Ages, but by the 15C the powerful Dukes had extended their rule to include the Jura. In the late 15C and early 16C, Burgundy provided a power base for the rise of the Habsburgs, after Maximilian of Austria had married into the ducal family. In 1477, at the battle of Nancy during the Burgundian Wars, the last duke, Charles the Bold, was killed in battle and Burgundy itself taken back by France.

Economy – The name Burgundy has been synonymous with fine wines since the 14C. The region also produces cheese, cereals and poultry, although tourism is increasingly important. In the Jura region, world-famous cheeses are produced, along with the yellow wine of Arbois.

Highlights

1. 17C Ducal Palace at **Dijon** (p369)
2. 6C BCE grave goods at **Trésor de Vix** (p373)
3. The 1C **abbaye de Fontenay** (p373)
4. Flemish-Burgundian Hospital, Hôtel Dieu, at **Beaune** (p377)
5. The Benedictine **abbaye de Cluny** (p381)

Ducal Palace, Dijon © Christophe Lehenaff / Photononstop

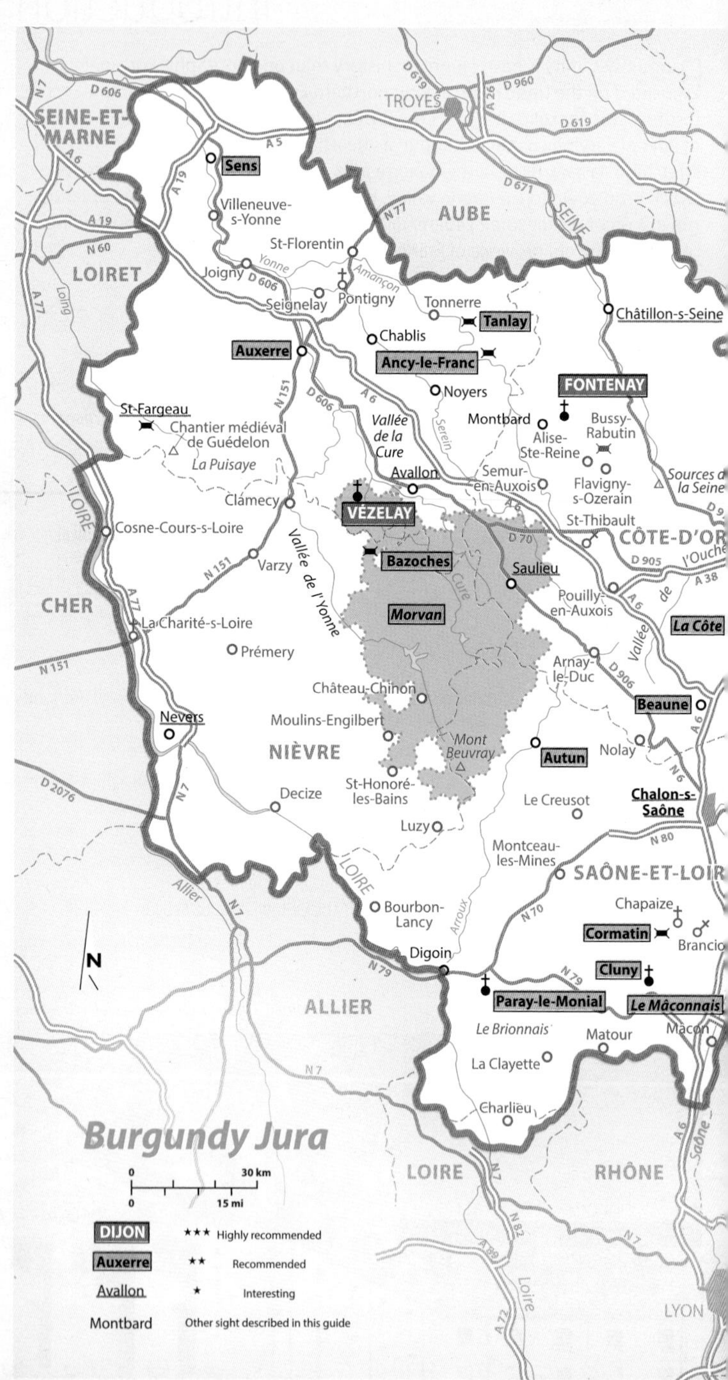

Burgundy Jura
Sens
Villeneuve-s-Yonne
St-Florentin
Joigny
Pontigny
Seignelay
Tonnerre
Tanlay
Chablis
Auxerre
Ancy-le-Franc
Noyers
Châtillon-s-Seine
FONTENAY
Montbard
Bussy-Rabutin
Alise-Ste-Reine
St-Fargeau
Chantier médiéval de Guédelon
La Puisaye
Vallée de la Cure
Avallon
Semur-en-Auxois
Flavigny-s-Ozerain
Sources de la Seine
Clamecy
VÉZELAY
St-Thibault
CÔTE-D'OR
Cosne-Cours-s-Loire
Varzy
Bazoches
Saulieu
Pouilly-en-Auxois
Vallée de l'Yonne
Morvan
La Côte
CHER
La Charité-s-Loire
Prémery
Arnay-le-Duc
Château-Chinon
Beaune
Nevers
Moulins-Engilbert
Mont Beuvray
Autun
Nolay
NIÈVRE
Decize
St-Honoré-les-Bains
Le Creusot
Chalon-s-Saône
Luzy
Montceau-les-Mines
SAÔNE-ET-LOIRE
Bourbon-Lancy
Chapaize
Cormatin
Digoin
Cluny
Paray-le-Monial
Le Mâconnais
ALLIER
Le Brionnais
Matour
Mâcon
La Clayette
Charlieu
LOIRE
RHÔNE
LYON
SEINE-ET-MARNE
TROYES
AUBE
LOIRET
N
0 30 km
0 15 mi
DIJON ★★★ Highly recommended
Auxerre ★★ Recommended
Avallon ★ Interesting
Montbard Other sight described in this guide

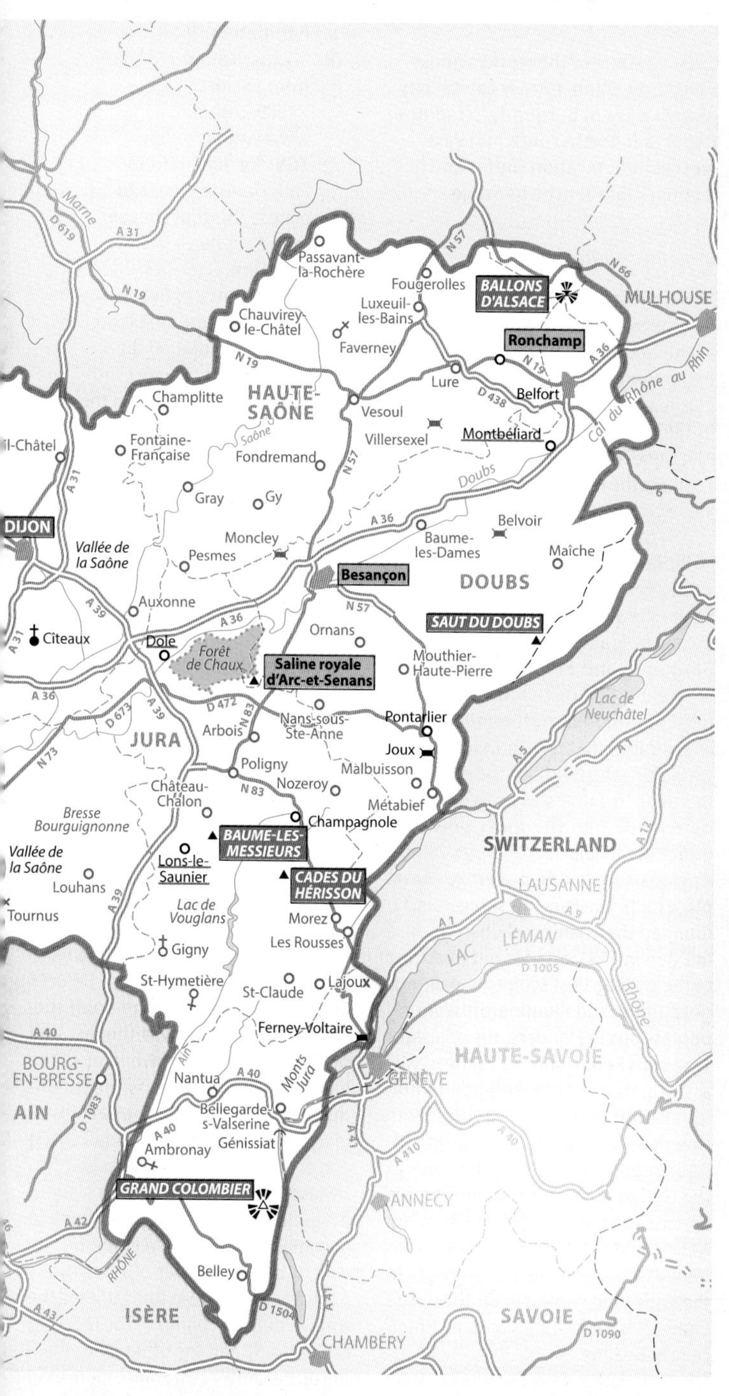

Marne
D 619
A 31
N 19
Passavant-la-Rochère
N 57
Fougerolles
BALLONS D'ALSACE
N 66
MULHOUSE
Chauvirey-le-Châtel
Luxeuil-les-Bains
Faverney
Ronchamp
N 19
A 36
Lure
Belfort
Canal du Rhône au Rhin
Champlitte
HAUTE-SAÔNE
Vesoul
D 438
Villersexel
Montbéliard
Saône
Fontaine-Française
Fondremand
N 57
Doubs
Gray
Gy
A 31
DIJON
A 36
Belvoir
Moncley
Baume-les-Dames
Maîche
Vallée de la Saône
Pesmes
Besançon
DOUBS
Auxonne
N 57
A 39
SAUT DU DOUBS
Cîteaux
A 36
Ornans
Dole
Forêt de Chaux
Saline royale d'Arc-et-Senans
Mouthier-Haute-Pierre
A 36
D 673
A 39
D 472
N 83
Lac de Neuchâtel
Nans-sous-Ste-Anne
Pontarlier
JURA
Arbois
A 5
N 73
Joux
Poligny
Malbuisson
Nozeroy
N 83
Château-Chalon
Métabief
Bresse Bourguignonne
Champagnole
BAUME-LES-MESSIEURS
SWITZERLAND
Vallée de la Saône
Lons-le-Saunier
Louhans
CADES DU HÉRISSON
LAUSANNE
A 39
Lac de Vouglans
Tournus
Morez
A 1
A 9
Les Rousses
LAC LÉMAN
Gigny
D 1005
St-Hymetière
St-Claude
Lajoux
Rhône
A 40
Ferney-Voltaire
Ain
BOURG-EN-BRESSE
HAUTE-SAVOIE
Nantua
A 40
Monts Jura
GENÈVE
AIN
D 1083
Bellegarde-s-Valserine
A 40
A 41
A 410
A 40
Génissiat
Ambronay
GRAND COLOMBIER
ANNECY
A 42
RHÔNE
Belley
A 43
ISÈRE
D 1504
A 41
SAVOIE
D 1090
CHAMBÉRY

Dijon★★★

Close to some of the world's finest vineyards, Dijon, former capital city of the Dukes of Burgundy, straddles important north–south and east–west communication routes and has a remarkable artistic heritage.

- **Population:** 151 212.
- **Michelin Map:** 320 K 5-6
- **Info:** 11 r. des Forges. ℘0892 700 558. www.visitdijon.com.
- **TGV:** 1hr 30mins from Paris Gare de Lyon, and almost 3hrs (but cheaper) from Paris Bercy (SNCF).
- **Location:** Dijon lies 46km/29mi N of Beaune.
- **Parking:** There are plenty of car parks around the perimeter of the city centre, and metered parking in the city; consider making use of the free shuttle buses, the *Diviaciti,* that run in the city centre from 7am–8pm.
- **Timing:** At least one full day to explore the centre.

A BIT OF HISTORY

Dijon had been the capital of Burgundy ever since the rule of Robert the Pious at the beginning of the 11C. In 1361, Philippe de Rouvres died without an heir, leaving the duchy without a ruler. In 1363, the French King Jean II le Bon (the Good) handed the duchy to his son Philippe, the first of an illustrious line of Valois Dukes who made the Dijon court one of the most brilliant of Europe.

Philippe became duke in 1364, at the same time as his brother Charles V le Sage (the Wise) was acceding to the throne of France. Thus from this time Burgundy and France were closely entwined. Philippe stood out as the most able of four royal brothers; cool, analytical on the one hand, well-named "le Hardi" (the Bold) on the other. His marriage in 1369 to Margaret of Flanders made him the most powerful prince of Christian Europe.

Anxious to provide a worthy burial place for himself and his successors, he founded the Champmol Charterhouse in Dijon in 1383, and set out to attract to the city the best sculptors, painters, goldsmiths and illuminators from his possessions in Flanders. His successor **Jean sans Peur** (John the Fearless) was assassinated in 1419. **Philippe le Bon** (the Good) inherited the title. From this time on, Burgundy saw its cultural importance waning in favour of the Netherlands and Flanders, where Renaissance ideas were blossoming. Nevertheless, artistic production continued throughout his 48-year reign. At the same time, Nicolas Rolin, the duke's Chancellor, was establishing the Hôtel-Dieu at Beaune.

The boundaries of the Burgundian state had never been more extensive nor the life of its court more exuberant; on his wedding day in 1429, Philippe founded the Order of the Golden Fleece; never had the French king and his court, lurking in relative obscurity at Bourges, been more pitiful. But Burgundy's alliance with England had become unpopular just as Joan of Arc was awakening national sentiment. Philippe decided it was prudent to submit himself to the authority of the French king, marking the beginning of the end of the Hundred Years' War.

Charles le Téméraire (the Bold) succeeded in 1467; he was the last and perhaps the most renowned of all the Valois Dukes of Burgundy. He squandered its resources in the search for glory. Charles' death in 1477 marked the end of the great days of the Burgundian dynasty, but in the same year Mary of Burgundy, Charles' daughter, married Maximilian, Holy Roman Emperor. She was to be the mother of **Philippe le Beau** (the Fair), who in turn fathered the future Emperor Charles V. The recovery of Burgundy and the other lands making up her dowry cost France more than two and a half centuries of struggle.

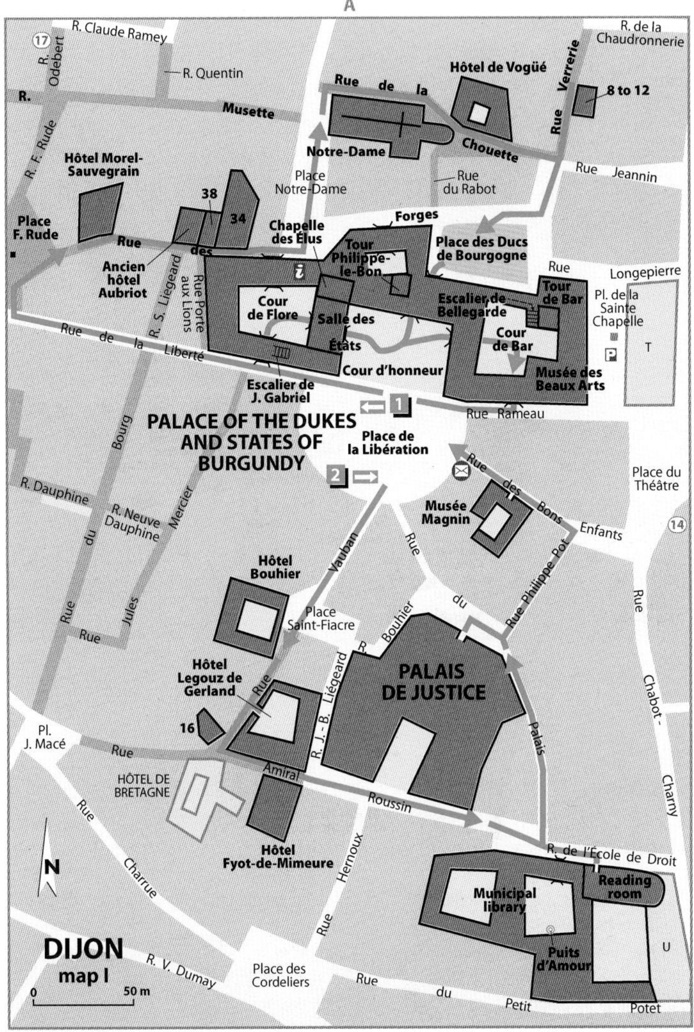

WHERE TO EAT

DZ'Envies (Le).. 14

Comédie (La).. 17

PALACE OF THE DUKES AND STATES OF BURGUNDY★★

pl. des Ducs-de-Bourgogne. Open Mon–Fri 8.45am–12.15am, Sat 9.30am–12.30pm. No charge. ℘03 80 74 52 71.

The ducal palace had been neglected since the death of Charles the Bold. In the 17C, it was restored and adapted and given a setting of dignified Classical buildings. At the time the city was keen to emphasise its parliamentary role and needed a suitable building in which the States-General of Burgundy could meet in session. The exterior of the Great Hall of the States-General (Salle des États) recalls the Marble Court (Cour de Marbre) at Versailles. By contrast, the east wing with its peristyle anticipates the architectural style of the 18C.

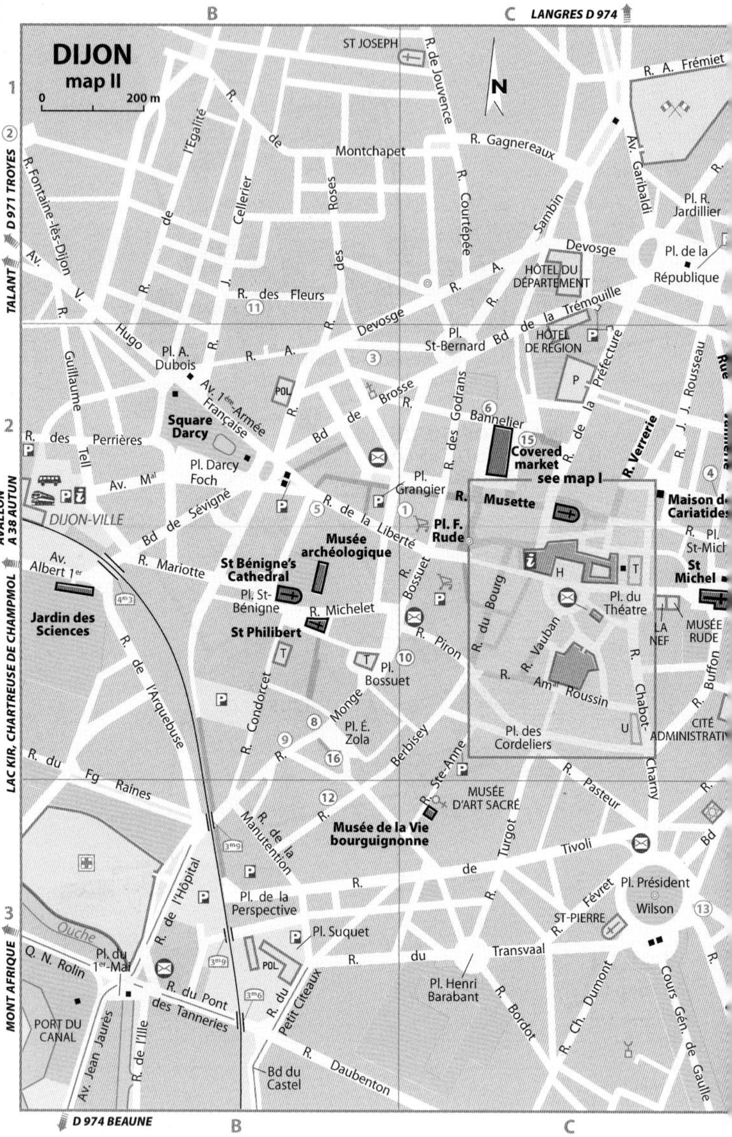

Musée des Beaux-Arts★★

Cour de Bar entrance, Palais des Etats de Bourgogne. ♿Open daily except Tue: Nov–Apr 10am–5pm; May–Oct 9.30am–6pm. No charge (audioguide, €4). ✆03 80 74 52 09. http://mba.dijon.fr.

The huge fine arts museum created in 1799 is in the former ducal palace.

WALKING TOUR

1 PALAIS DES DUCS★★

Dijon map I, p369. Allow 3hrs.

The old district around the palace of the dukes of Burgundy is charming. Much of the area is pedestrianised; you will come across beautiful old stone mansions and half-timbered 15–16C houses.

WHERE TO STAY

B & B Hôtels ... (1)
Montigny (Hôtel) ... (3)
Nord (Hôtel du) ... (5)
Relais de la Sans-Fond (Hôtel Le) ... (7)
Sauvage (Hostellerie Le) ... (9)
Victor Hugo (Hôtel) ... (11)
Wilson (Hôtel) ... (13)

WHERE TO EAT

Auberge de la Charme (L') ... (2)
Bento (Le) ... (4)
Bistrot des Halles (Le) ... (6)
Chabrot (Le) ... (8)
Dame d'Aquitaine (La) ... (10)
Dôme (Le) ... (15)
Émile Brochette (L') ... (16)
Mère Folle (La) ... (12)

- **Place de la Libération** – This is the former place Royale. In the 17C, when the town was at the height of its parliamentary power, the ducal palace was transformed and its approaches rearranged.
- **Place François-Rude** – In the pedestrian zone is this irregularly shaped, lively square, with one or two half-timbered houses.
- **Rue des Forges★** – This is one of the most characteristic old streets of the town. At no. 40, the Ancien Hôtel Aubriot was the birthplace of Hugues Aubriot, provost of Paris under Charles V. He was responsible for building the Bastille, several of the bridges over the Seine (e.g. St-Michel Bridge), and the first vaulted sewers.
- **Église Notre-Dame★** – 13C Burgundian Gothic architecture. The chapel to the right of the choir houses the statue of Notre-Dame-de-Bon-Espoir (Our Lady of Good Hope). This 11C Virgin has been the object of particular veneration since the Swiss raised the siege of the town on 11 September 1513.
- **Quartier Notre-Dame** – Rue Musette gives a good view over the façade of the church and leads to the market. Local merchants have congregated in this quarter since the Middle Ages.

- **Hôtel de Vogüé** – This early-17C mansion with its colourful tiled roof was one of the early meeting places of the representatives of the province.
- **Rue Verrerie** – Attractive half-timbered houses, buildings with decorated facades, a Renaissance house and a watchtower.
- **Place des Ducs-de-Bourgogne** – From this little square, one can imagine what the palace must have looked like at the time of the dukes. The handsome Gothic façade is that of the Salle des Gardes, dominated by Philip the Good's tower.

WALKING TOUR

2 PALAIS DE JUSTICE

Dijon map I, p369.

The great feature of this walk is the splendid architecture, which includes fine examples of Renaissance work and half-timbered houses.

- **Rue Vauban** – Various Classical, Renaissance and half-timbered houses.
- **Hôtel Fyot-de-Mimeure** – The façade in the inner courtyard of no. 23 rue Amiral-Roussin is in the style of Hugues Sambin (16C).
- **Municipal Library** – The 17C chapel of the former college of Les Godrans, founded in the 16C by a rich Dijon family, has been transformed into a reading room. Among its 300 000 or more items, the are precious illuminated manuscripts.
- **Palais de Justice** (Law Courts) – The gabled façade of the former Burgundian Parliament is in the Renaissance style and has a covered porch supported by columns.
- **Musée Magnin★** – The museum is in an elegant 17C mansion, the home of art lovers Maurice Magnin (a magistrate) and his sister Jeanne, herself a painter and art critic. Their collection of more than 1 500 paintings covers lesser-known painters, but as well as great masters.

AROUND SAINT-BÉNIGNE

Dijon map II, p370.

- **St-Bénigne's Cathedral** – The ancient abbey church is on the site of an earlier Romanesque building, and is pure Burgundian-Gothic in style.
- **Musée Archéologique★** – The museum is in the eastern wing of what used to be the cloisters of St-Bénigne. Works include Gallo-Roman sculpture; medieval sculpture, displayed within the 13C Gothic monks' dormitory; and on the top floor a collection of prehistoric artefacts.
- **Église Saint-Philibert** – Built in the 14C and reworked in the 15C, the church is currently disused.
- **Square Darcy** – Named after the engineer who brought drinking water to Dijon in 1839 and helped set up the PLM (Paris-Lyon- Mediterranean) railway line.
- **Jardin des Sciences★** – Explores the flora and fauna of the Dijon area, and the world.

  Muséum de la ville de Dijon★ – Founded in 1836 by Léonard Nodot, a Dijonnais with a passion for nature, the museum is housed in the old crossbowmen's barracks built in 1608. Displays cover geology and biology of the last 300 million years.

  Jardin de l'Arquebuse★ – This park owes its name to the company of harquebusiers, who occupied the site in the 16C. Botanical gardens, arboretum, tropical glasshouses and a vivarium.

ADDITIONAL SIGHTS

- **Église St-Michel★** – This Flamboyant Gothic church was consecrated in December 1529, although its façade was eventually completed in the full Renaissance style.
- **Chartreuse de Champmol★** – This former monastery was largely destroyed in the Revolution; a psychiatric hospital now occupies the site.

Cloisters, Abbaye de Fontenay

© John Frumm / hemis.fr

- **Musée de la Vie bourguignonne★** – This museum of local history uses furnishings, household items, clothing and other souvenirs of times past to bring to life the daily habits, ceremonies and traditions of Burgundy at the end of the 19C.
- **Musée Amora** – This museum, created by the Amora mustard company, recounts the history of the condiment, its origins, and every aspect of its production.

EXCURSIONS

CHÂTILLON-SUR-SEINE★

83km/51.5mi N of Dijon.
9–11 r. de la Libération. 03 80 81 57 57. www.chatillonnais.fr.

Châtillon occupied a strategic location on the ancient north–south trade route. It was here that the Seine ceased to be navigable; as a result, the place developed all the facilities that transshipment needed, and grew prosperous on the merchandise being exchanged between Cornwall and Etruria – amber, tin, coral, ceramics.

Two major events in Chatillon's history are separated by exactly 100 years. In 1814 a Congress was held here between France and her enemies.

Napoléon rejected the terms, fighting resumed and the downfall of the Empire soon followed. In 1914 General Joffre set up his Headquarters here and issued the famous order which led to the halting of the German advance by French troops.

Le Trésor de Vix★★ – Found in the tomb of a young Celtic queen, 6C BCE grave goods (the treasure of Vix) can be found on display in the **Abbaye Notre-Dame de Châtillon** (r. de l'Abbaye; for information and opening times, contact tourist office).

ABBAYE DE FONTENAY★★★

72km/45mi NW of Dijon, next to **Montbard.** Open daily mid-Nov–Mar 10am–noon, 2–5pm; Apr–mid-Nov 10am–6pm. 03 80 92 15 00. www.abbayedefontenay.com.

Tucked away in its lonely valley near the River Brenne, Fontenay is very evocative of the self-sufficient life of a Cistercian abbey of the 12C. **St Bernard** (1091–1153), unhappy with the wealth and power of Cluny, found greater asceticism and spirituality at the abbey of **Cîteaux**, 23km/14mi south of Dijon. He was made responsible for establishing the abbey at **Clairvaux** on the River Aube; then, in 1118, at the age of 27, he founded **Fontenay**, his "second daughter".

The abbey church **(église abbatiale)** was built between 1139 and 1147. It is the first example of the "monastic simplicity" characteristic of the architecture promoted by St Bernard, and is laid out in a straightforward way, with a square chancel and chapels of square plan.

DRIVING TOUR

CÔTE DE NUITS★★

Leave Dijon on D 122, known as the Route des Grands Crus.

The Côte de Nuits road follows foothills covered with vines and passes through villages with world-famous names. In 2015, the Burgundy vineyards (Climats du vignoble de Bourgogne) became the 4th UNESCO World Heritage Site in Burgundy.

Chenôve

The Clos du Roi and Cls du Chapitre recall the former owners of these vineyards, the dukes of Burgundy and the canons of Autun. The dukes' wine cellar, **Cuverie des ducs de Bourgogne** (♿ open Jul–Sep 2–7pm; rest of the year by appointment. ☎03 80 51 55 00) contains two magnificent 13C presses.

Marsannay-la-Côte

Part of the Côte de Nuits, Marsannay produces popular rosé wines, obtained from the black Pinot grapes.

Fixin

This village produces wines that some consider among the best of the Côte de Nuits appellation. The small **Musée Noisot** (open mid-Apr to mid-Oct Sat–Sun 2–6pm. €4.50. ☎03 80 52 45 62) houses mementoes of Napoléon's campaigns. The 10C church in nearby **Fixey** is thought to be the oldest in the area.

Brochon

Brochon, which is on the edge of the Côte de Nuits, produces excellent wines. The **château** was built in 1900 by the poet Stephen Liégeard who coined the phrase Côte d'Azur for the Provençal coast. The name has stuck long after the poet has faded into obscurity, together with his poem which was honoured by the French Academy.

Gevrey-Chambertin

This village is typical of the wine-growing community immortalised by the Burgundian writer **Gaston Roupnel** (1872–1946). It is situated at the open end of the gorge, Combe de Lavaux, and surrounded by vineyards. The older part lies grouped around the church and château whereas the Baraques district crossed by N 74 is altogether busier.

The famous Côte de Nuits, renowned for its great red wines, starts to the north. In the upper village is this square-towered fortress **château** (open Jun–Sep; guided tours (1hr) 10am–noon, 2–6pm. €6. ☎03 80 34 36 77), lacking its portcullis; it was built in the 10C by the lords of Vergy.

Chambolle-Musigny

The road from Chambolle-Musigny to Curley passes through a gorge, Combe Ambin, to a charming beauty spot: a small chapel stands at the foot of a rocky promontory overlooking the junction of two wooded ravines.

Vougeot

Vougeot red wines are highly valued. The walled vineyard of Clos-Vougeot, owned by the abbey of Cîteaux from the 12C up to the French Revolution, is one of the most famous of La Côte. Since 1944 the **Château du Clos de Vougeot★** (♿ open daily: Apr–Oct 9am–6.30pm; Nov–Mar 10am–5pm; closed 1 Jan, and 24–25 and 31 Dec. €7. ☎03 80 34 36 77. www.closdevougeot.fr) has been owned by the **Confrérie des Chevaliers du Tastevin** (Brotherhood of the Knights of the Tastevin). The château was built in the Renaissance and restored in the 19C. The rooms visited include the Grand Cellier (12C cellar) where the *disnées* (banquets) and the ceremonies of the Order are held, the 12C cellar containing four huge winepresses, the 16C kitchen with its huge chimney, and the monks' dormitory with a spectacular 14C roof.

Vosne-Romanée

These vineyards produce only red wines of the highest quality. Among the various sections (*climats*) of this vineyard, Romanée-Conti and De Richebourg have a worldwide reputation.

Nuits-St-Georges

This attractive little town is surrounded by the vineyards to which it has given its name. The fame of the wines of Nuits goes back to Louis XIV.

When the royal doctor advised him to take some glasses of Nuits and Romanée with each meal as a tonic, the whole court wanted to taste it. The **museum** (open May–Oct daily except Tue 10am–noon, 2–6pm. €2.30. ☎03 80 62 01 37), in the cellars of an old wine business, shows items found in the Gallo-Roman settlement excavated at Les Bolards near Nuits-St-Georges.

ADDRESSES

STAY

B & B Hôtels – 5 r. du Château. 0892 707 506. www.hotel-bb.com. 55 rooms. Chain hotel, keenly priced. All rooms come with functional contemporary style and air-con.

Hostellerie le Sauvage – 64 r. Monge. 03 80 41 31 21. www.hotellesauvage.com. P. 22 rooms. This 15C coaching inn has a prime spot, just a ten minute walk from the Ducal Palace and smack in the middle of a lively quarter with a great café and restaurant scene. Cobbled courtyard.

Hôtel Montigny – 8 r. Montigny. 03 80 30 96 86. www.hotelmontigny.com. Closed 18 Dec–2 Jan. WiFi. 28 rooms. Efficiently run hotel near the town centre with secure parking. Rooms, although rather functional, are spotlessly kept and well soundproofed.

Hôtel Victor Hugo – 23 r. des Fleurs. 03 80 43 63 45. www.hotelvictorhugo-dijon.com. WiFi. 25 rooms. A friendly place with bright, smartly decorated and well-kept rooms. Bag one over the courtyard for more space.

Hôtel Wilson – 1 r. de Longvic. 03 80 66 82 50. www.wilson-hotel.com. WiFi. 27 rooms. This former post house has retained its traditional charm and charisma. You immediately feel at home in its bright rooms, which come prettily decorated with light wood furniture and exposed beams.

Hôtel Du Nord – Pl. Darcy. 03 80 50 80 50. www.hotel-nord.fr. Closed 17 Dec–2 Jan. 27 rooms. Right on the bustle of Dijon's central shopping square, this hotel has serviceable, well-soundproofed rooms.

NEAR DIJON

Hôtel Le Relais de la Sans-Fond – 33 rte de Dijon, 21600 Chevigny, 16km/10mi south. 03 80 36 61 35. www.lerelais-delasansfond.com. Closed 15 Dec–5 Jan. P. WiFi. 17 rooms. A simple and well-kept family inn with airy, uncluttered rooms. Traditional cuisine served in contemporary dining rooms or on the garden terrace.

EAT

Le Chabrot – 36 r. Monge. 03 80 30 69 61. If you're after traditional tastes and a laid-back ambience, this bistro is right up your street. Choose your wine from the racks along the walls to go with classic Burgundian dishes.

La Comédie – 3 pl. du Théâtre. 03 80 67 11 62. www.la-comedie.com. This bistro appeal to those seeking traditional flavours and atmosphere.

Le Dôme – 16 bis r. Quentin. 03 80 30 58 92. This modern restaurant is near the market hall. The mouth-watering menu deals in traditional and contemporary cooking, with a good showing of Burgundian specialities.

L'Émile Brochettes – 16 pl. Émile-Zola. 03 80 49 81 04. Closed 25 Dec–1 Jan. This quirky cavern-style restaurant looking onto lovely place Émile Zola celebrates the kebab in all of its savoury and sweet forms.

La Mère Folle –102 r. Berbisey. 03 80 50 19 76. Closed Mar. This small, town-centre restaurant offers regional specialities such as snails, eggs *en meurette* (poached eggs with red wine sauce) and *sandre* (pike-perch) *au Chablis*. 1930s-style décor.

Le Bistrot des Halles – 10 r. Bannelier. 03 80 49 94 15. Closed 25 Dec–2Jan, Sun and Mon. A typical bistro, a stone's throw from the covered market. Choose one of the dishes of the day, chalked up on a slate.

Le Bento – 29 r. de la Chaudron-nerie. 03 80 67 11 50. Lunch set menu. Sun brunch noon–6pm. The chef invents new sushi, sashimi and maki dishes daily.

La Dame d'Aquitaine – 23 pl. Bossuet. 03 80 30 45 65. www.ladamedaquitaine.fr. Closed for lunch 20 Jul–20 Aug, Mon lunch and Sun. In the town centre, a paved courtyard and a long flight of steps descend to a superb 13C vaulted dining hall. The décor is medieval, with tapestries and stained glass.

Le DZ'Envies – 12 r. Odebert. 03 80 50 09 26. www.dzenvies.com. This recently opened contemporary gastronomic bistro on the market square reworks French cuisine with Japanese and North African touches.

BURGUNDY'S LEGENDARY VINEYARDS

The lie of the land

The Côte runs along the east-facing slopes of the "mountain", dominating the plains of the Saône at an altitude varying from 200–300m, and slashed by cross-cut combes in a similar layout to the blind valleys of the Jura vineyards. Only the east- and south-facing slopes of the combes are planted with vines – around 8 000 hectares of first-quality grapes; the north-facing slopes are often densely wooded. While the hilltops are crowned with scrubland or thickets, the vineyards carpet the limestone slopes, basking in the morning sunlight and well protected from cold winds. This exposure to sunlight is what determines the production of sugar in the grapes and the final alcohol content of the wine. The slopes also ensure that rain runs off, keeping the soil well drained and nicely dry – just how the vines like it – to produce top-class wines.

Burgundy's fine wines – the "Grands crus"

For much of its length, the D 974 marks the dividing line between the "noble" grape varieties and the rest, with the grands crus generally planted mid-way up the slopes. Pinot Noir is the king of Burgundy grapes: it is used to make red wines, whereas the great white wines are made from the Chardonnay grape. After the devastation of the phylloxera blight in the 19C, the vineyards were entirely replanted with resistant vines grafted from North American stock. But it's an ill wind that blows no good. Paradoxically, the pesky parasites brought beneficial changes in their wake: small producers were able to buy back land from the big boys, and a reduction in the quantity of wine produced led to much-improved quality. The Côte d'Or divides into two main areas: the superstars are the Côte de Nuits and the Côte de Beaune. The wines of the Côte de Nuits are prized for their robustness, while those of the Côte de Beaune are admired for their delicacy.

The Côte de Nuits

The Côte de Nuits extends from Fixin to Corgoloin. Its vineyards cover around 3 740 hectares and produce 104 950 hectolitres annually – that's 14 million bottles, give or take. The vineyards are planted on limestone slopes rich in calcium from fossils. This is red wine country whose most famous *crus*, running from north to south, are Chambertin, Musigny, Clos-Vougeot et Romanée-Conti. Rich and beefy, these wines need eight to ten years to develop the incomparable body and character of the best Burgundy. To the south, the Hautes-Côtes de Nuits vineyards produce uncomplicated wines on the west-facing slopes of the Côte.

The Côte de Beaune

The Côte de Beaune stretches over 5 950 hectares from north of Aloxe-Corton to Santenay, producing not only top-notch white wines, but also superb reds. On the upper slopes, the vineyards grow in limestone-rich soil, which changes its character to brown marly earth mingling with pebbles and clay as it washes down towards the lower reaches. The bottom line is an annual production of some 214 335 hectolitres, equating to 28 million bottles. Its most prestigious *crus* are, in the red corner, Corton, Volnay, Pommard and Beaune; in the white camp are Meursault and Montrachet. The reds are muscular and fruity – rather like the whites, which deliver a fabulously rich intensity on the nose and palate.

Beaune★★

Right at the heart of the Burgundian vineyards lies Beaune, a name synonymous with good wine; a visit to this ancient city, which boasts a splendid architectural heritage and some fine museums, is not complete without a tour of the vineyards of La Côte.

- **Population:** 22 394.
- **Michelin Map:** 320: I-7
- **Info:** 6 bd Perpreuil, 21200 Beaune. ☎03 80 26 21 30. www.beaune-tourisme.fr.
- **TGV:** Paris Gare de Lyon to Beaune, 2hrs 15mins–3hrs.
- **Location:** 46km/29mi S of Dijon.
- **Parking:** Parking can be difficult in the very centre of Beaune on busy days.
- **Timing:** Beaune is a glorious place to explore; allow a full day, or stay overnight.

A BIT OF HISTORY

Birth of a town – First a Gaulish centre and then an outpost of Rome, Beaune was the seat of the Dukes of Burgundy to the 14C. After the death of Charles the Bold, last Duke of Burgundy, in 1477, the town refused Louis XI's efforts to annex it and gave in only after a five-week siege.

Wine auction at the Hospices de Beaune – This is the main event of the year and draws a large crowd. The Hospices de Beaune (this name includes the Hôtel-Dieu, the Hospice de la Charité and the hospital) acquired a very fine vineyard between Aloxe-Corton and Meursault through Chancellor Rolin. The wines from this vineyard have won international acclaim. The proceeds of the auction sales, **Les Trois Glorieuses**, known as the "greatest charity sale in the world", go to the modernisation of the medical facilities and maintenance of the Hôtel-Dieu.

HÔTEL-DIEU★★★

Open daily: 9am–6.30pm. €7. ♿. ☎03 80 24 45 00. www.hospices-de-beaune.com.

The Hôtel-Dieu is a marvel of Burgundian-Flemish art, founded as a hospital by Chancellor Nicolas Rolin in 1443. The building with its medieval décor has survived intact and was used as a general hospital until 1971.

Exterior – The main decorative elements of the external façade with its tall and steeply pitched slate roof are the dormer windows, the weather vanes, the delicate pinnacles and lacework cresting of lead. The roof line is broken by the bell turret surmounted by a slim Gothic spire. The delicate roof above the porch is composed of three slate gables terminating in worked pinnacles.

Each weather vane bears a different coat of arms. On the panelled door, note the ironwork grille and the door knocker, a magnificent piece of sculpted wrought-iron work.

Courtyard – The wings to the left and rear have magnificent roofs of coloured glazed tiles (recently restored) in geometric patterns. These roofs are punctuated by turrets and a double row of dormer windows, surmounted by weather vanes adorned with heraldic bearings and small spires of worked lead.

Interior – The highlight of the interior is the **Grand'Salle or Chambre des Pauvres** ★★★. This immense hall, used as the poor ward, has a magnificent timber roof in the shape of an upturned keel which is painted throughout; the ends of the tie-beams disappear into the gaping mouths of monsters' heads.

WALKING TOURS

1 TOWN CENTRE

Among the many old houses, those at nos. 18, 20, 22 and 24 **rue de Lorraine** form a fine 16C ensemble. The town hall (**Hôtel de ville**) is in a 17C former Ursuline convent. The right wing houses

two museums. At no. 10 **rue Rousseau-Deslandes** there is a house with its first floor decorated with trefoiled arcades.

- **Hôtel de la Rochepot★** – This 16C building has an admirable Gothic façade. In place Monge is a 14C belfry and a statue of **Gaspard Monge** (1746–1818), a local shopkeeper's son who became a famous mathematician. no. 4 **place Carnot** is a 16C house with attractive sculptures.
- **Place de la Halle** – The Hôtel-Dieu with its fine slate roof overlooks the square. Avenue de la République and rue d'Enfer lead to the former mansion of the dukes of Burgundy, dating from the 15C and 16C, now the museum of Burgundy wine.

  No 13 **place Fleury** is the **Hôtel de Saulx**, a mansion with a quaint tower and an interior courtyard. The Maison des Vins is on rue Rolin, beyond the Hôtel-Dieu.
- **Musée du Vin de Bourgogne★** – The museum is in the former mansion of the dukes of Burgundy, dating mainly from the 15C and 16C. The history of Burgundian vineyards and vine cultivation is explained in a comprehensive exhibit on the ground floor. The large first-floor room decorated with two huge Aubusson tapestries is the headquarters of the Ambassade des Vins de France.
- **Collégiale Notre-Dame★** – The daughter house of Cluny, begun about 1120, was considerably influenced by the church of St-Lazare in Autun; it is a fine example of Burgundian Romanesque art despite successive additions.

  Tapestries★★ – In the choir behind the high altar are some magnificent tapestries which mark the transition from medieval to Renaissance art. Five richly coloured panels, worked in wool and silk, trace the whole life of the Virgin Mary in a series of charming scenes. They were commissioned in 1474 and offered to the church in 1500 by Canon Hugues le Coq.

2 THE RAMPARTS★

The relatively well-preserved ramparts form an almost continuous walk (2km/1mi). They were built between the end of the 15C and the middle of the 16C, and are adorned with a few surviving towers and eight rustic bastions of various shapes – the double one, originally a castle, is known as the **Bastion St-Jean**. The moat is now occupied by gardens, tennis courts etc.

- The north tower of the Bastion St-Jean has gargoyles and a niche occupied by a Virgin and Child. Pass the Blondeau Tower to get to the **Bastion Notre-Dame**, with a charming turret covering the spur. The line of the ramparts is broken by the 18C Porte St-Nicolas at the end of rue Lorraine.
- Next come the **Bastion des Filles**, spoilt by the addition of an ugly new roof, and the now filled-in Bastion St-Martin forming a triangular terrace **(square des Lions)** overlooking a shaded garden.
- The route now takes you past the Bastion des Dames, the **Rempart des Dames** and the now-abandoned Bastion de l'Hôtel-Dieu.
- The 15C Grosse Tour on the **Rempart Madeleine** is followed by the Bastion Ste-Anne with a turret overlooking the moat. The tour ends in front of the **south tower**.

EXCURSIONS

CHÂTEAU DE SAVIGNY-LÈS-BEAUNE★

5km/3mi NW.

Open daily: mid-Apr–mid-Oct 9am–6.30pm; mid-Oct–mid-Apr 9am–noon, 2–5.30pm. Call for charges. 03 80 21 55 03. www.chateau-savigny.com.

This village, known for its quality wines, has a 14C castle with some interesting collections on display. The smaller 17C château is now home to a wine-tasting and sales room and an exhibit of **Arbath endurance cars**. Visitors to the park

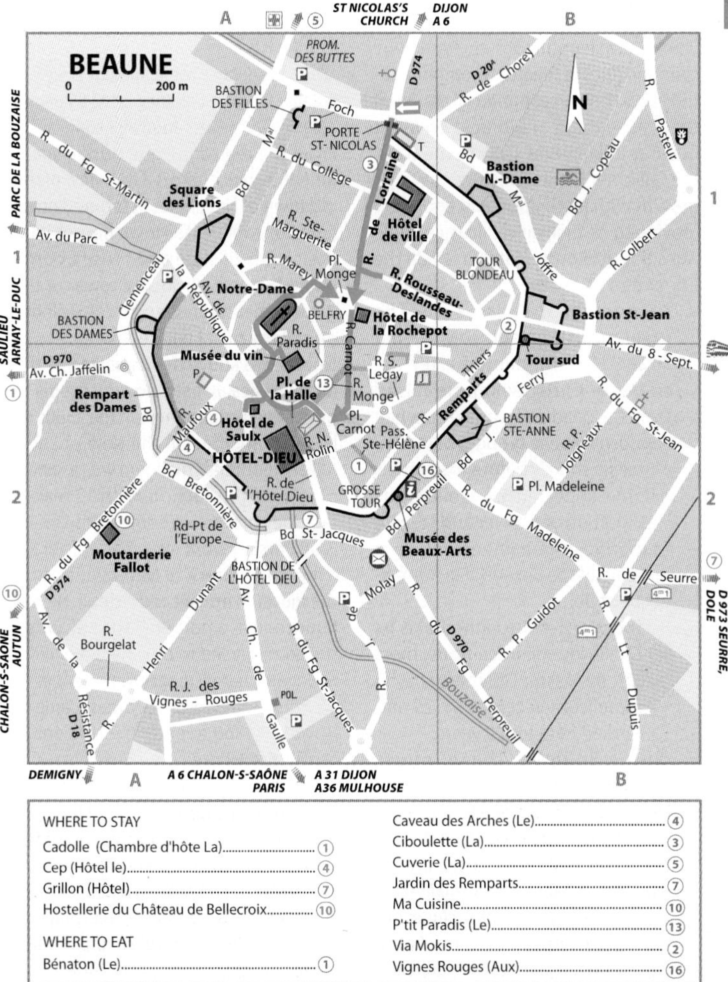

will see 60 **jet fighter planes**, including Mirages (I to V), MIG 21 US (1962), Sikorsky helicopters and more.

The château was built by Jean de Frolois, Maréchal de Bourgogne, and restored by the Bouhier family in the 17C. An upper floor has been set aside for the **motorcycle collection★**, including over 500 models.

MONTAGNE DE BEAUNE

5km/3mi NW along D 970.

Seen from the orientation table near the war monument south of the statue of Notre Dame-de-la-Libération, a lovely view extends over the brown-tiled roofs of the town to the vineyards beyond, and the **Mâconnais★★** hills to the south. The light is at its best in the afternoon.

AUTUN★★

48km/30mi W from Beaune on D 973.

13 r. Général Demetz. 03 85 86 80 38. www.autun-tourisme.com.

Flanked by wooded hills, this dignified country town in northern Burgundy has a cathedral, museums and Roman remains that bear witness to its past. Autun was founded by the Emperor Augustus, half a century after Caesar's conquest of Gaul. Rome itself was taken as the model for the new town; its walls

(6km/4mi in length) soon sheltered fine civic buildings (a theatre, an amphitheatre) and a thriving commercial life. From their stronghold at Bibracte on Mont Beuvray 29km/18mi away to the west, the Gallic Aedui tribe watched the city's growth with fascination and ended up moving there themselves. In the Middle Ages the city consolidated itself on the upper part of its site.

- **Cathédrale St-Lazare★★** – The great sandstone edifice was built from 1120–46, named after the friend of Christ whom He raised from the dead and whose relics had supposedly been brought here from Marseille shortly before. Though its external appearance was altered by the addition of a tower and steeple in the 15C, it remains essentially a building of the Burgundian Romanesque style.

  The glory of the cathedral is its 12C Burgundian sculpture, most of it by Master Gislebertus, who came from Vézelay in 1125 and worked here for 20 years.
- **Musée Rolin★** – The 20 rooms contain many noteworthy exhibits. Here you will find masterpieces of Roman **statuary★★**, mostly by the two great sculptors of the Burgundian School, Gislebertus and Martin, a monk. Other exhibits include 14C and 15C sculptures from the Autun workshops and works by French and Flemish Primitive painters.
- **Gallo-Roman Town** – The ruins of the **Roman Theatre** were once the largest theatre in Gaul (capacity 12 000). **Porte St-André★** is where the roads from Langres and Besançon meet. It is the sole survivor of four original gates in the Gallo-Roman fortifications, which were reinforced with 54 semicircular towers. **Porte d'Arroux** was the Roman Porta Senonica, leading towards Sens and the Via Agrippa, which ran from Lyon to Boulogne. The upper arcading dates from the time of Emperor Constantine.

NEVERS★

152km/95mi W of Beaune by D 978.
Palais Ducal, r. Sabatier. 03 86 68 46 00. www.nevers-tourisme.com.

From the red sandstone bridge spanning the Loire, there is a fine view of the old town of Nevers set in terraces on its limestone hill. Its tall town houses with their roofs of slate and tile are dominated by the high square tower of the great cathedral and the graceful silhouette of the ducal palace.

Nevers was known for its pottery in the Middle Ages. Artistic pottery seems to have been brought here in the 1560s by Italian craftsmen. In the time of Louis XIII and Louis XIV the town was a centre of faïence production, with 12 manufactories producing some of the finest Blue Persian work ever made. There is a fine **collection★** of Nevers pottery in the museum **(musée municipal)**. Nevers flourished as a port until the 19C when the Loire ceased to be navigable.

Following her visionary experiences at Lourdes, Bernadette Soubirous came to Nevers in 1866 to enter the convent of **St-Gildard★** here.

- **Palais Ducal★** – r. Sabatier. The former residence of the Dukes of Nevers is a fine example of French Renaissance architecture.
- **Cathédrale Saint-Cyr-et-Ste-Julitte★★** –This vast basilica displays all the architectural styles from the 10C to the 16C.
- **Église St-Étienne★** – This splendid Romanesque church has a magnificently tiered east end and a beautiful overall pattern of windows in the style of the great abbey church of Cluny. The height of the interior is particularly impressive for a building of its date (1063–97).

CHALON-SUR-SAÔNE★

30km/19mi S of Beaune by A 6.
2–4 pl. du Port Villiers. 03 85 48 37 97. www.achalon.com.

Chalon is Burgundy's second town, a prosperous place in the heart of an area of arable farming, stock raising and vineyards; the best wines are worthy of their great neighbours in the Côte d'Or.

Chalon is the urban centre for the fertile lowlands bordering the Saône river as it makes its way between the Jura and the Massif Central. Its most famous son is the father of photography, Joseph Nicéphore Niépce (1765–1833).

The Central Canal (completed 1790), is one of Europe's great commercial waterways, flowing south to join the Rhône at Lyon. Long before the present age, however, the Saône had been an important commercial route.

- **Musée Nicéphore Niépce★★** – The museum is housed in the 18C Hôtel des Messageries on the banks of the Saône. The rich collection comprises photographs and early photographic equipment, including the earliest cameras ever made, which were used by Joseph Nicéphore Niépce, as well as his first heliographs. There are also works by well-known contemporaries of Niepce in the world of photography.

CLUNY★★

A climb to the top of the Tour des Fromage gives the best view of the town and its historic structures.

6 r. Merciere. 03 85 59 05 34. www.cluny-tourisme.com. P Plenty of parking available at pl. de l'Abbaye and pl. du Marche.

The conditions for the future renown and prosperity of the great **abbaye de Cluny★★** existed at the very moment of its foundation. The abbey, founded in 910, deep in forest and far removed from the centres of power in either France or Germany, was subject to no authority other than that of the pope himself. It answered – like its daughter houses and other dependencies – to no one but its elected abbot. It thus became a powerful papal instrument.

Cluny's development was rapid, its prestige immense and its influence pre-eminent. In under a century, the abbey had amassed considerable power as well as much property and already had 1 184 daughter- and dependent houses. One hundred and fifty years later their numbers had risen to 3 000, scattered all over Europe. For two and a half centuries this capital of monasticism found leaders of exceptional calibre, some of whom ruled for up to 60 years. The decline of the order began in the 13C, but its prosperity lasted until the 18C.

- **Abbaye Bénédictine de Cluny** – Palais Jean de Bourbon. Open daily: Apr–Jun and Sept 9.30am–6pm; Jul–Aug 9.30am–7pm; Oct–Mar 9.30am–5pm. Closed 1 Jan, 1 May, 1 and 11 Nov, 25 Dec. €9.50. 03 85 59 15 93. http://cluny.monuments-nationaux.fr. The abbey church, started 1088, was completed in 1130 and later destroyed during the Revolution. All that remains are the lower parts of two towers; the bell tower known as "the Holy Water" **(Eau bénite★★)**, an octagon, and another known as the Clock Tower (Tour de l'Horloge); of the great transept, the south arm with its two chapels and an octagonal vault (32m high); of the minor transept, the chapel (Chapelle de Bourbon) with sculpted heads of the Prophets. Reduced in height, the flour store (*Farinier*) has a fine 13C timber roof, and eight capitals from the abbey. The abbey buildings were rebuilt in the 18C.

CHÂTEAU DE CORMATIN★★

13km /8mi N of Cluny.

Guided tours (45min) daily Apr–mid-Nov, 10am–noon, 2–5.30/6.30pm (mid-Jul–mid-Aug 10am–6.30pm). €10 (children 8–17, €5). 03 85 50 16 55. www.chateaudecormatin.com.

The château, probably built by Jacques II Androuet du Cerceau, is a good example of the Henri IV style (late 16–early 17C): the monumental gates framed by antique orders, the basement built of stone and the windows decorated with mouldings. The mannerist style which evolved in the literary salons under Louis XIII (1610–43) reached its peak with the gilding and the lapis-lazuli decoration of the St Cecilia Room **(Cabinet Ste-Cécile★★★)**.

ADDRESSES

STAY

Chambre d'hôte La Cadolle – Grande-Rue, 21200 Bouze-les-Beaune. 6km/3.7mi northwest of Beaune on D970. 03 80 26 08 99. Closed Dec and Jan. P. 3 rooms. This delightfully renovated stone house offers three rooms with original wood parquet flooring. Those on the first floor open onto their own little balconies, while the third is more cosy.

Hôtel Grillon – 21 rte Seurre. 03 80 22 44 25. www.hotel-grillon.fr. Closed 1–7 Dec and all Feb. WiFi. 20 rooms. A spruce little bolthole tucked away in a walled garden, with attractive personal touches in the bedrooms.

Hôtel Le Parc – 13 r. du Golf, 21200 Levernois. 6km/3.7mi southeast of Beaune on D970. 03 80 24 63 00. www.hotelleparc.fr. Closed 31 Jan–13 Mar. P. WiFi. 17 rooms. Charming hotel clad with Virginia creeper and bursting with flowers in summer.

Hostellerie du Château de Bellecroix – 20 chemin de Bellecroix, 71150 Chagny. 18km/11mi southeast of Beaune on D974 then N6. 03 85 87 13 86. www.chateau-bellecroix.com. Closed 15 Dec–13 Feb and Wed (except Jun–Sep). 19 rooms. The two towers of this 18C château stand amid wooded parkland. Nearby lie the turrets of a former 12C Knights Templar building of the Order of Malta.

Hôtel Le Cep – 27 r. Maufoux. 03 80 22 35 48. www.hotel-cep-beaune.com. WiFi. 61 rooms. Ravishing 16C house in the old quarter. Cosily old-fashioned bedrooms are named after famous vintages from the Côte-d'Or. Breakfast is served in the vaulted cellar or in the courtyard with pretty Renaissance arcades.

EAT

Aux Vignes Rouges – 4 bd Jules-Ferry. 03 80 24 71 28. www.auxvignesrouges.com. Closed Mar and Wed. Two dining rooms in a stone vaulted cellar done out with a natural look are the setting for regional cuisine built on fresh local produce.

Le Bénaton – 25 r. fg Bretonnière. 03 80 22 00 26. www.lebenaton.com. Closed 1–7 Jul, 5–15 Dec, Feb holidays, Sat lunch Apr–Nov, Thu lunch Apr–Nov and Wed. Small, tranquil restaurant with a covered terrace for warm days. Delicious meals made with seasonal produce are great value for money.

Caveau des Arches – 10 bd Perpreuil. 03 80 22 10 37. www.caveau-des-arches.com. Closed 18 Jul–19 Aug, 20 Dec–19 Jan, Sun and Mon. Savour fine classic Burgundy cooking in the cosy dining rooms on the ramparts.

La Ciboulette – 69 r. de Lorraine. 03 80 24 70 72. Closed 2–20 Aug, 1–25 Feb, Mon and Tue. Two cheerful dining rooms furnished with green rattan and wood panelling. Traditional dishes with a Bourguignon spin.

La Cuverie – 5 r. Chanoine-Donin, 21420 Savigny-lès-Beaune. 03 80 21 50 03. Closed 20 Dec–20 Jan, Tue and Wed. This 18C stone wine cellar with bourguignon furniture and a snazzy collection of cafetières is just the job for traditional dining and local produce.

Le Jardin des Remparts – 10 r. Hôtel-Dieu. 03 80 24 79 41. www.le-jardin-des-remparts.com. Closed Dec, Sun and Mon except public holidays. P. Comfy dining rooms and a delightful garden terrace in this 1930s house up against the ramparts.

Ma Cuisine – passage Ste-Hélène. 03 80 22 30 22. Closed Aug, Wed, Sat and Sun. Located along a tiny street, this small dining room is decorated in the colours of Provence.

Via Mokis – 1 r. Eugène Spüller. 03 80 26 80 80. www.viamokis.com. Closed 23 Dec–2 Jan. 5 rooms. Masterfully creative cooking in a trendy bistro setting. Good choice of wines by the glass. Spacious, individual, modern rooms and there's a basement spa.

Le P'tit Paradis – 25 r. Paradis. 03 80 24 91 00. Closed 2 weeks in Aug, 2 weeks in Dec, 2 weeks in Apr, Sun and Mon. Dining room and terrace by a flower garden. Modern cuisine with regional flair and wines from boutique producers.

Auxerre★★

A port on the River Yonne, surrounded by rustic, wooded farm country and hillsides planted with vines and orchards, the city was once an important staging post on the great Roman highway which led from Lyon to Boulogne via Autun and Lutetia (Paris).

- **Population:** 36 200.
- **Michelin Map:** 319 E-F-G 5
- **Info:** quai de la République. ℘03 86 52 06 19. www.ot-auxerre.fr.
- **TGV:** About 2hrs from Paris Gare de Lyon or Paris Bercy.
- **Location:** Auxerre lies 149km/93mi NW of Beaune, and 78km/49mi SW of Troyes.
- **Timing:** A day trip or overnight stay from Paris will be well spent.

A BIT OF HISTORY

The Romans built Autessiodurum on the road from Lyon to Boulogne, near a simple Gaulish village, and from the 1C it thrived. By the Middle Ages, Auxerre was a spiritual centre, and was declared a Holy City by the Pope in the 12C. Two great figures have visited Auxerre. In 1429 **Joan of Arc** passed through twice; and on 17 March 1815, **Napoléon** arrived on his return from Elba.

WALKING TOUR

TOWN CENTRE

Auxerre map, p384.

- **Quartier de la Marine** – This part of town with its narrow streets was once home to the boatmen. Take rue de la Marine to see the remains of the north-east tower of the Gallo-Roman fortified wall. Walk across pretty place St-Nicolas, overlooking quai de la Marine. The square is named after the patron saint of boatmen. Rue du Mont-Brenn leads to the place du Coche-d'Eau. At no. 3, a 16C house hosts temporary exhibitions as part of the Musée du Coche-d'Eau.
- **Ancienne Abbaye St-Germain★★** – This Benedictine abbey was built in the 6C by Queen Clotilda, wife of Clovis, on the site of an oratory where St Germanus, the 5C Bishop of Auxerre, was buried. In the time of Charles the Bald the abbey had a famous school; St Patrick, who converted the Irish, was a student.

  Abbey church – The upper part of the church is Gothic in style (13–15C); it replaced a Carolingian Romanesque church.

  Crypt★★ – The crypt forms a semi-underground church consisting of a nave and two aisles.

  Musée St-Germain – This museum is in the old conventual buildings of the abbey, including the abbot's residence rebuilt at the beginning of the 18C (entrance to abbey and museum), 14C cellars, 12C chapter-house (the latter's façade was found behind the cloisters – restoration work in progress) and sacristy. There is an archaeological collection in the monks' dormitory.
- **Cathédrale Saint-Étienne★★** – The fine Gothic cathedral was built between the 13C and 16C to replace the existing Romanesque one. The building was practically finished by 1525.

  West front – Set within a Flamboyant façade, the sculptures (13C–14C) were mutilated in the 16C during the Wars of Religion, and the stone has weathered badly. Among the scenes are the Last Judgement (lintel) and Christ between the Virgin Mary and St John (tympanum).

  Romanesque crypt★ – The crypt, the only remaining part of the 11C Romanesque cathedral, has 11–13C frescoes.

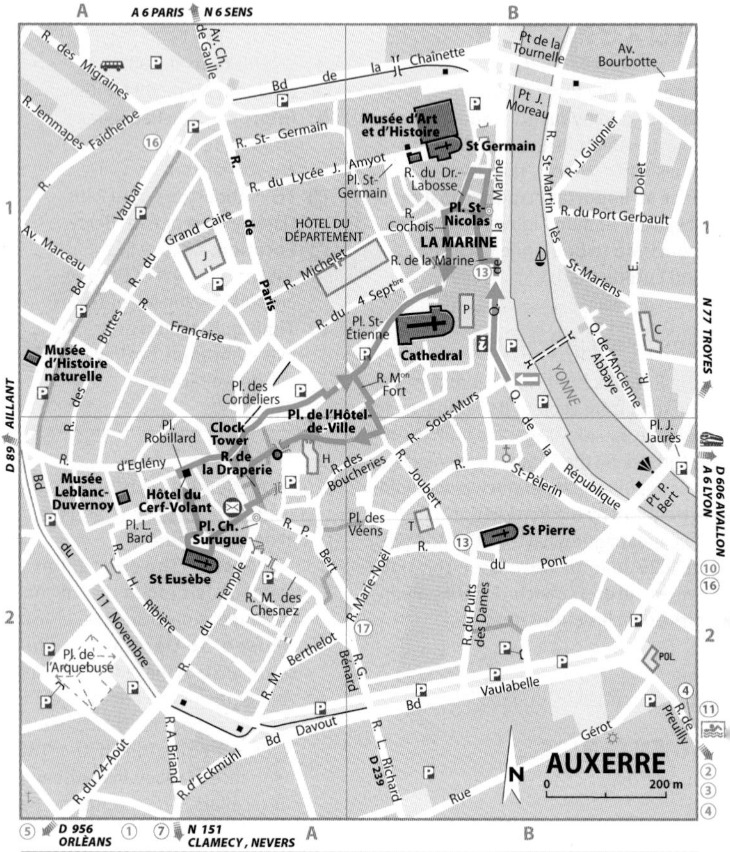

AUXERRE

WHERE TO STAY

- Abbaye de Reigny (Chambre d'hôte) 2
- Château de Ribourdin (Chambre d'hôte) 1
- Clos du Merry (Chambre d'hôte Le) 4
- Mas des Lilas (Hôtel) 10
- Maxime (Hôtel Le) 13
- Maison des Randonneurs (La) 17
- Moulinot (Chambre d'hôte Le) 3
- Normandie (Hôtel) 16
- Petit Manoir des Bruyères (Le) 5

WHERE TO EAT

- Bourgogne (Le) 4
- Chamaille (La) 7
- P'tite Beursaude (La) 13
- Tilleuls (Auberge Les) 16
- Voutenay (Auberge Le) 11

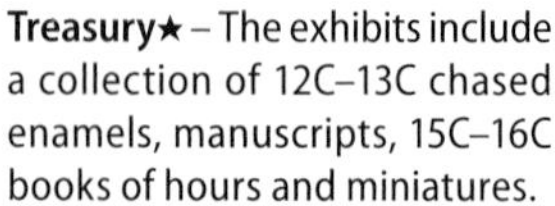

Treasury★ – The exhibits include a collection of 12C–13C chased enamels, manuscripts, 15C–16C books of hours and miniatures.

- **Town centre** – There are many interesting old houses here, mostly 16C with half-timbering. Rue Fécauderie intersecting with rue Joubert has two half-timbered houses with a sculpted corner post; it leads to place de l'Hôtel-de-Ville; note nos. 4, 6, 16, 17 and 18.
- **Tour de l'Horloge** (Clock Tower) – This tower, also called the Tour Gaillarde, was built in the 15C. The astrological clock (17C) has faces showing the movement of the sun and moon.
- **Streets** – The remainder of the tour passes through a series of streets, starting with a vaulted passageway beside the clock tower leading to place du Maréchal-Leclerc. The walk takes in the church of St-Eusèbe,

White Wines of Chablis

Chablis has been made in Burgundy since the 12C, when the vineyards stretched as far as the eye could see. Tending them was the population's sole occupation, and the source of an enviable prosperity. Today, the land is used more selectively, and the soil is the determining factor in the appellation on the bottle, which is a reference to the silica, limestone and clay content of the soil (as in Champagne), rather than to domaines, or specific vineyards (as in Bordeaux, for example). The best vintages are the Grands Crus, mostly grown on the steep hillsides of the east bank: Vaudésir, Valmur, Grenouilles, Les Clos, Les Preuses, Bougros and Blanchots. Rich in aroma yet dry and delicately flavoured, distinguished by their golden hue, these generally bloom after three years in the bottle, but are rarely kept more than eight. Premier Cru wines are grown on both banks of the river; lighter in colour and less full-bodied, they are best aged three years, never more than six. More than half of the production, bearing the Appellation Chablis Contrôlée label, is very dry and pale, to be aged one to three years before reaching its best.

Often described as crisp or fresh, a good Chablis made exclusively from Chardonnay grapes is delightful with oysters, freshwater fish, ham or chicken dishes with creamy sauce. Lesser vintages, including hearty Bourgogne Aligoté or fruity Petit Chablis, are best enjoyed young with local country fare (grilled sausage, crayfish) or regional cheese (Chaource, St-Florentin) and fresh bread.

which is all that remains of an old priory, and the town's oldest house at no. 5 place Robillard, known as the Kite House (14C and 15C). Its lovely weather vane recalls the days when it was a musical instrument shop.

ADDITIONAL SIGHT

Musée Leblanc-Duvernoy

This museum is mainly devoted to faience ware, with many exhibits from French or local ceramists, It also houses 18C Beauvais tapestries depicting scenes from the life of the Emperor of China.

EXCURSIONS

BRIARE

The Briare canal is reached 70km/44mi SW of Auxerre.

pl. Charles de Gaulle. 02 38 31 20 08. www.briare-le-canal.com.

Briare is a busy town on the banks of the Loire, known for its ceramic floor mosaics and its stoneware.

- **Pont-Canal★** – The Loire was used by river traffic from the 14–19C, but the navigation companies found it difficult to cope with the river's irregular flow on the one hand, and shallowness on the other.

  To rectify this, and as part of his policy of economic unification, Henri IV began building the Briare Canal in 1604; completed in 1642, it linked the basins of the Loire and the Seine via its junction with the River Loing at Montargis. It was the first connecting canal in Europe.

  The Loire Lateral Canal (1822–38) extends it south to **Digoin**. It crosses the Loire at Briare on an aqueduct built 1890–94 (58 years after those at Le Guétin and Digoin). The channel is the longest in the world and rests on 15 granite piers designed by Gustave Eiffel.

SENS★★

80km/50mi NW of Auxerre.

pl. Jean-Jaurès. 03 86 65 19 49. www.office-de-tourisme-sens.com.

The once-important old town is girded by boulevards that replaced the ancient ramparts. In the city centre stands the first of France's great Gothic cathedrals. The tribe of the Senones, who gave the town its name, was one of the most powerful in Gaul. In 390 BCE, they even invaded Italy and seized Rome. Its central position in relation to Burgundy, Champagne and the Île-de-France gave Sens considerable importance for centuries; for a long time it was the Bishop of Sens who crowned French kings.

- **Cathédrale St-Étienne★★** – In its general conception this is the very first of France's great Gothic cathedrals, its foundations laid in the years 1128–30, though most building took place between 1140 and 1168.

  The influence of the Romanesque can be discerned in a number of features, like the slightly pointed "Burgundian" arches of the nave, but it is the Gothic which is decisive in its visual makeup. Inside, the eye is drawn to the 12C **stained glass★★**.

- **Museum, Treasury and Palais Synodal★** – The Musées de Sens are housed in the Old Archbishop's Palace (16–18C) and the Synodal Palace which stand on the south side of the cathedral.

  François I and Henri II wings – These 16C galleries are devoted to the history of Sens its district.

  Cathedral treasury (Trésor)★★ (access via the museum) – One of France's richest treasure houses, containing a magnificent collection of materials and liturgical vestments: the shroud of St Victor, a 13C white silk mitre embroidered with gold thread, St Thomas à Becket's alb; handsome 15C high warp tapestries *(Adoration of the Magi and Coronation of the Virgin)*; ivories (5C and 6C pyx, the 7C liturgical comb of St Lupus, an 11C Byzantine coffret and a 12C Islamic one) as well as gold plate (late 12C ciborium).

  Synodal Palace – A beautiful 13C palace restored by Viollet-le-Duc. The great vaulted chamber on the ground floor was the seat of the ecclesiastical tribunal (*officialité*). In the 13C two bays served as a prison and there are still traces of graffiti on the walls.

CHABLIS

21km/13mi E of Auxerre.
1 rue du Maréchal de Lattre de Tassigny. 03 86 42 80 80. www.tourisme-chablis.fr.

This small town, with the feel of a big village, is tucked away in the valley of the River Serein, between Auxerre and Tonnerre. Chablis is the capital of the prestigious wine-growing region of lower Burgundy. Thanks to its many old buildings, harking back to its heyday in the 16C, it still has a medieval feel.

The annual wine fair and the village fairs of November and late January, held in honour of St Vincent, patron of wine-growers (*see Festivals and Events, p38*), recall the town's lively commercial past.

- **Church** – The **Église St-Martin** dates from the late 12C. It was founded by monks from St-Martin-des-Tours, who carried their saint's relics with them as they fled the Normans.

CHÂTEAU D'ANCY-LE-FRANC★★

The château stands in N Burgundy countryside, SE of Tonnerre.
18 pl. Clermont-Tonnerre. Open 10.30am–12.30pm, 2–5pm (Apr–Jun and Sept 6pm; Jul–Aug 10.30am–6pm). €9 (guided visits €10). 03 86 75 14 63. www.chateau-ancy.com.

This dignified château marks the end of the early, Italian-influenced French Renaissance in all its brilliance. Designed by Sebastian Serlio, Italian architect invited to France in 1541 by François I, the château was begun in 1546 and completed 50 years later.

The exterior gives an impression of great order, combining symmetry with a masterly handling of spaces and surfaces according to the rules of the Golden Section. The courtyard is particularly subtle, with deeply sunken twin pilasters topped by Corinthian capitals and separating scalloped niches.

The interior is equally fine. There are ancient bindings in the library, secret cabinets from Italy, dell'Abbate's *Battle of Pharsalus* and oval medallions by Primaticcio representing the Liberal Arts.

VÉZELAY★★★

Vézelay is W of Avallon.
r. St-Étienne. 03 86 33 23 69. www.vezelaytourisme.com.

The quiet and picturesque little village of Vézelay climbs a steep slope among the northern foothills of the Morvan countryside, overlooking the **vallée de la Cure**. Its fame is due to the majestic basilica which numbers among the greatest treasures of France.

The Celts were the first to settle this hilltop site. In 878 an abbey was founded here, and in 1050 it was dedicated to Mary Magdalene, whose remains were supposedly here, and the place soon became one of France's great pilgrimage destinations. It was here that St Bernard preached the Second Crusade in 1146. In 1279, however, the monks of St-Maximin in Provence claimed to have discovered the bones of Mary Magdalene in a cave; the certification of the relics as authentic led to the decline of Vézelay as a place of pilgrimage; it was pillaged by the Huguenots, razed at the time of the French Revolution and given its *coup de grâce* by lightning.

- **Basilique Ste-Marie-Madeleine★★★** – First built between 1096 and 1104 and restored following the fire of 1120. The principal external features are the fine Romanesque body of the church, **Tour St-Antoine**, and a particularly harmonious chevet with radiating chapels. From the terrace, there is a fine **view★** over the valley of the river Cure.

  In the dimly lit narthex (1140–60) is the marvellous **tympanum★★★** of the central doorway. The greatest contribution to the basilica's decoration is made by the many **capitals★★★** adorning the pillars; these were sculpted in the 12C.

ADDRESSES

STAY

A few kilometres from Seignelay, take exit 19 off the motorway to a cluster of hotels and restaurants. They may be well-known and unexciting chain establishments, but they offer perfectly good services at good prices.

La Maison des Randonneurs – 5 r. Germain-Bénard. 03 86 41 43 22. www.maison-rando.fr. 8 rooms. The rather spartan rooms of this hostel have 4 to 8 bunks, but you can't fault the location, smack in the town centre next to a wooded park.

Gîte de séjour municipal – 1 r. Hérisson, 58500 Surgy. 38km/24mi S on N 151 and D 144. 03 86 27 97 89. www.domaine-de-surgy.com. Closed Nov–Mar. 7 rooms. Set in huge grounds, this handsome 18C building has been recently restored.

Chambre d'hôte Le Clos du Merry – 4 r. Crété, 89440 Joux-la-Ville. 9km/6mi NE of Voutenay-sur-Cure on D 32. 03 86 33 65 54. Closed Oct–Easter (except weekends by reservation). 5 rooms. This working grain-growing farm has strictly non-smoking rooms (some well-suited to families) spread around the vast breakfast room. Large garden with children's games.

Chambre d'hôte Le Moulinot – D 606, 89270 Vermenton. 24km/15mi SE on D 965 and N 6. 03 86 81 60 42. www.moulinot.com. Closed 25 Dec–2 Jan. 6 rooms. You cross a skinny bridge over the River Cure to reach this 18C mill bracketed by the river and a pond. The dreamily idyllic setting oozes charm and relaxation. A wooden staircase leads to lovely spacious bedrooms. The lounge-dining room looks over the water, and there's a swimming pool too.

Chambre d'hôte Les Vieilles Fontaines – 89270 Sacy. 6km/4mi E of Vermenton on D 11. 03 86 81 51 62. http://lesvieillesfontaines.free.fr. Closed Nov–Mar. 3 rooms. Three simple but very comfy rooms in a stone house that was once home to a wine producer.

Chambre d'hôte Place Voltaire – 15 pl. Voltaire, 89270 Vermenton. 24km/15mi SE on D 965 and N 6. 03 86 81 59 63. www.15placevoltaire.com. Closed Nov–Mar. 4 rooms. This stone-built village house has four rooms decorated with old furniture. The King's Room is named after Louis-Philippe, who legend has it, stayed here for the inauguration of the canal.

Hôtel Mas des Lilas – Hameau de la Cour Barrée, 89290 Champs-sur-Yonne. 9.5km/6mi SE on D 965 and D 606. 03 86 53 60 55. www.lemasdeslilas.com. Closed 23 Oct–4 Nov. P. WiFi. 16 rooms. These villas nestling in a lovely flower-filled gardens offer well-kept little ground-floor rooms with terraces opening onto the greenery.

Hôtel Normandie – 41 bd Vauban. 03 86 52 57 80. www.hotelnormandie.fr. Closed 18 Dec–2 Jan. WiFi. 47 rooms. A tranquil courtyard terrace, comfy rooms (go for those in the main house), an Art Deco bar-lounge, billiard room and gym.

Hôtel Le Maxime – 2 quai de la Marine. 03 86 52 14 19. www.lemaxime.com. WiFi. 25 rooms, 1 suite. This former salt warehouse on the banks of the River Yonne has views over the river or the courtyard.

Château de Ribourdin – 89240 Chevannes. 7km/4.5mi SW on N 151 then D 1. 03 86 41 23 16. www.chateauderibourdin.com. P. 5 rooms. This magnificent 16C château and dovecote rise proudly from the wheat fields beneath the village. The bedrooms are in a converted barn.

Chambre d'hôte Le Puits d'Athie – 1 r. de l'Abreuvoir, 89380 Appoigny. 11km/7mi NW on N 6. 03 86 53 10 59. www.puitsdathie.com. Closed Jan–Feb. 5 rooms. Individually-decorated rooms: Porte d'Orient with its authentic Rajasthani door, stands out. Regional and Mediterranean dishes.

Chambre d'hôte abbaye de Reigny – 89270 Vermenton. 24km/15mi SE on D 965 and N 6. 03 86 81 59 30. www.abbayedereigny.com. P. 5 rooms. Peace and quiet guaranteed in the verdant fringes of the abbey, shaded by linden trees. Old-fashioned style.

Le Petit Manoir des Bruyères – Les Bruyères, 89240 Villefargeau. 7km/4.3mi W on D 965. 03 86 41 32 82. www.petit-manoir-bruyeres.com. 5 rooms. This manor house with a glazed tile roof is a peaceful hideaway on the edge of a forest. Classy 18C rooms and a truly royal Montespan suite. **Table d'hôte** Burgundian dishes.

EAT

La P'tite Beursaude – 55 r. Joubert. 03 86 51 10 21. Closed 28 Jun–6 Jul, 28 Dec–11 Jan, Tue and Wed. The essence of the Burgundian countryside. Dining room with exposed beams, heavy stone walls and an open kitchen.

Auberge Les Tilleuls – 12 quai de l'Yonne, 89290 Vincelottes. 16km/10mi S on D 606 and D 38. 03 86 42 22 13. www.auberge-les-tilleuls.com. Closed 20 Dec–24 Feb, Tue and Wed. This small village inn will delight you with its setting, its summer terrace along the banks of the Yonne and succulent cuisine.

Auberge Le Voutenay – N 6, 89270 Voutenay-sur-Cure. 03 86 33 51 92. www.aubergelevoutenay.com. Closed 16–24 Jun, 1–21 Jan, Sun eve, Mon and Tue. P. 7 rooms. Roadside 18C residence in pleasant grounds. Smart rustic dining room, a bistro area, and a little shop selling local produce.

La Chamaille – 4 rte Boiloup, 89240 Chevannes. 8km/5mi SW on N 151 then D 1. 03 86 41 24 80. Closed 25 Oct–3 Nov, 21 Feb–8 Mar, Sun eve and Mon. P 3 rooms. Chamaille is surrounded by a delightful garden with a small stream meandering through fields stretching as far as the eye can see. The tastefully restored farmhouse has a pretty veranda.

Le Bourgogne – 15 r. Preuilly. 03 86 51 57 50. www.lebourgogne.fr. Closed 25 Apr–3 May, 8–23 Aug, 19 Dec–3 Jan, Thu eve, Sun and Mon P. Agreeably rustic setting, nice summery terrace, and a market menu that reads as appetisingly on the chalkboard menus as it looks on the plate.

Besançon★★

The capital of the Franche-Comté occupies a superb site★★★ on a meander of the River Doubs, overlooked by a rocky outcrop on which Vauban built a fortress which has resulted in the town being an outstanding example of 17C military architecture. The birthplace of the writer Victor Hugo, Besançon is also known for its many museums and fine architecture.

- **Population:** 116 914.
- **Michelin Map:** 321 G 3
- **Info:** 2 pl. de la 1ére-Armée-Française. ℘03 81 80 92 55. www.besancon-tourisme.com.
- **TGV:** About 2hrs 15min from Paris Gare de Lyon.
- **Location:** 109km/68mi NE of Beaune.
- **Timing:** The historic centre of town lies within the circle of the Doubs river. Shops and restaurants can be found on Grande-Rue, near the bridges. The modern town is on lower ground across the river. Allow a day or more to appreciate everything.

A BIT OF HISTORY

A 2C triumphal arch called the Black Gate (Porte Noire) survives from a Gallo-Roman settlement (Vesontio) first mentioned by Julius Caesar as the home of the Gaulish *Sequani* tribe: the modern Grande-Rue still follows the course of its main street in the heart of old Besançon. Later the town became an important archbishopric.

The city is closely connected with the Holy Roman Empire and was given the title of Imperial Free City in 1184. Through inheritance and marriages, in the 15C and 16C the town – like the rest of Franche-Comté – became part of the Austro-Spanish empire. It marked a high point in the province's commercial life, illustrated by the rise of the Granvelle family. Although born into the humblest of peasant families, the son Perrenot was given an education, rose rapidly, becoming chancellor to Charles V, and built himself the Palais Granvelle. In 1674 Louis XIV conquered the Franche-Comté, made Besançon its capital and had Vauban construct the citadel.

CITADELLE★★

99 r. des Fusillés-de-la-Résistance. Open daily except Tue: Nov–Mar 10am–5pm; Apr–Oct 9am–6pm (Jul–Aug daily until 7pm). Closed 25 Dec, 1 and 14 Jan. €10.60 (children, 4–17, €8.50). ℘03 81 87 83 33. www.citadelle.com.

From 1675–1711 Vauban constructed this mighty fortress. Its great mass is best appreciated from the sentry-walk along the encircling ramparts. The building houses a zoo, the Musée d'Histoire naturelle (aquarium, insectarium, climatorium, noctarium), and the **Musée de la Résistance et de la Déportation★**.

WALKING TOUR

1 OLD TOWN★★

Besançon map II, p392.

Bound by the meander of the River Doubs, this part of town was once walled. Before going down the Grande-Rue, take a few steps back along the bridge to get a better view of the 17C residences with beautiful grey-blue stone **façades★** that line the banks of the Doubs.

- **Place de la Révolution** – This lively square, better known as place du Marché, is at a junction with the Musée des Beaux-Arts et d'Archéologie on one side and old buildings along rue des Boucheries.
- **Musée des Beaux-Arts et d'Archéologie★★** – The Museum of Fine Arts and Archaeology is in

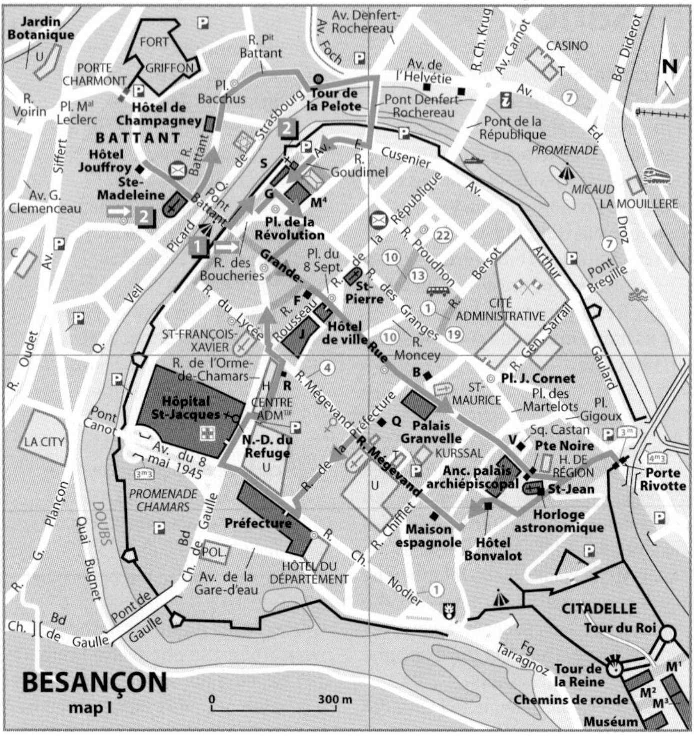

BESANÇON
map I

WHERE TO STAY		WHERE TO EAT			
Citotel Granvelle (Hôtel)	1	Barthod	1	Femme du Boulanger (La)	10
Mercure Parc Micaud (Hôtel)	7	Cavalier Rouge (Le)	4	Miam	13
Nord (Hôtel du)	10	Chaland (Le)	7	Petit Polonais (Au)	19
				Poker d'As (Le)	22

Ancien hôpital du St-Esprit	**G**	**Musée de la Résistance et de la Déportation**	**M³**	**Promenade Granvelle**	**S**
Bibliothèque municipale	**B**	**Musée des Beaux-Arts et d'Archéololgie**	**M⁴**	**Promenade Vauban**	**Q**
Espace Vauban	**M¹**	**Palais de Justice**	**J**	**Statue de Victor Hugo**	**R**
Hôtel d'Emskerque	**F**			**Vestiges romains (Square archéologique A.-Castan)**	**V**
Musée Comtois	**M²**				

the old grain hall, which dates from 1835. It was extended in 1971 by a follower of Le Corbusier, Louis Miquel, who built an original construction of concrete in the courtyard consisting of a succession of gently sloping ramps with landings in between them.

The museum contains some rich collections of works of art, some of which come from the Granvelle family, more particularly from Nicolas de Granvelle.

Expect Egyptian antiquities; statues and objects from the Middle Ages and the Renaissance; **paintings★** includes a wide variety of works by non-French schools,

- **Grande-Rue** – This street is an old Roman highway and is still the main road through the city. There are a number of houses and mansions of interest, some with pretty courtyards.

  Hôtel de Ville – The town hall dates from the 16C.

Palais de Justice – The law courts have a pretty Renaissance **façade★** by Hugues Sambin. The Franche-Comté's Parliament sat in session inside, on the first floor.

- **Palais Granvelle★** – The mansion was built from 1534 to 1542 for Chancellor Nicolas Perrenot de Granvelle.
- **Musée du Temps** – The clockmaking industry, established in Besançon in 1793, remained the town's main activity until the 1920s. This museum, in the restored Palais Granvelle, celebrates that history.
- **Vestiges Romains** (Roman ruins) – Sights include a pretty park with Roman columns, the channels of an aqueduct, and the Porte Noire, a triumphal arch built in the 2C.
- **Cathédrale Saint-Jean★** – Most of this cathedral was built in the 12C. The astronomical clock, **Horloge Astronomique★** is a marvel of mechanics comprising 30 000 parts. It was designed and made between 1857 and 1860 by A-L Vérité from Beauvais, and reset in 1900 by F Goudey from Besançon. It is connected to the clock faces on the bell tower. The 62 dials indicate among other things the days and seasons, the time in 16 different places all over the world, the tides in 8 ports, the length of daylight and darkness, the times at which the sun and the moon rise and set and, below the clock, the movement of the planets around the sun.
- **Porte Rivotte** – This gate is the remains of 16C fortifications. The cliffs of the citadel tower above the gate. These cliffs once plunged straight into the river; the narrow strip of land along which the road passes was blasted out of the rock face. A 375m-long canal cuts through the cliffs in a tunnel, providing a shortcut past the Doubs meander.
- **Hôtel Bonvalot** – Built between 1538 and 1544, this rather austere mansion is brightened up by its ogee-arched stained-glass windows.
- **Maison espagnole** – Although built after the region was united to the kingdom of France, this house has clear Spanish features.
- **Rue Mégevand** – There is a lovely 18C fountain representing the River Doubs, while a little further on to the right, place du Théâtre offers a very appropriate setting to the Classical-style theatre.
- **Préfecture★** – The erstwhile Palais des Intendants was built in the 18C after designs by the architect Louis.
- **Hôpital Saint-Jacques** – This hospital dates from the 17C. It has a splendid **wrought-iron gate★** and a pretty 18C pharmacy.
- **Chapelle Notre-Dame-du-Refuge** – This chapel owes its name to an establishment founded in 1690 by the Marquis de Broissia to shelter young girls in danger of falling into vice.

WALKING TOUR

2 OLD TOWN★★

Besançon map I, p390.

This lively district on the north-west bank of the Doubs, once the vine-growers' area, is one of the oldest in the city.

- **Collégiale Sainte-Madeleine** – This church was built in the 18C; the towers were added in 1830. The interior is vast, with elegant vaulting supported on fluted columns.
- **Hôtel de Champagney** – This mansion was built in the 16C.
- **Tour de la Pelote** – The rather curious late-15C tower was integrated into Vauban's defence system.

EXCURSIONS

SAUT DU DOUBS★★★

On the border 10km/6mi E of Morteau. r. Berçot, 25130 Villers-le-Lac. 03 81 68 00 98. www.villers-le-lac-info.org. The waterfall is at its best viewed in autumn after heavy rain. Allow 1hr.

Bursting out of the Chaillexon lake, the waters of the Doubs plunge down in a

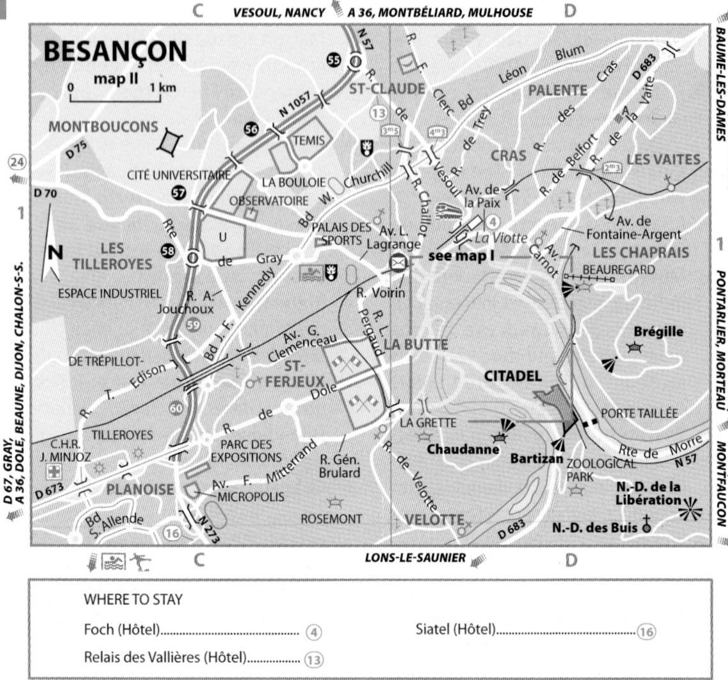

magnificent drop, known as "le Saut du Doubs", one of the most famous natural phenomena you can admire in the Franche-Comté. From the raised level of the lake, the Doubs tumbles to its natural level in a noisy and turbulent cascade of spume. There is a **boat service** (Apr–Oct; during Mar and Nov call for information. €14.50, children 4–12, €10. 03 81 68 13 25; www.sautdudoubs.fr) from Villers-le-Lac. The boats follow the river's meanders as they open into the Chaillexon Lake; then they continue through a gorge, the most picturesque part of the trip. From the landing-stage, take the path (30min round-trip on foot) to the two viewpoints.

Villers-le-Lac★

This small town in the Doubs valley, where the river spreads to form the **Lac de Chaillexon★**, is the starting point of boat excursions to the **Saut du Doubs★★★** waterfall.

Two slopes on either side of the River Doubs crumbled in and blocked a part of the valley, creating a natural dam which in turn formed the lake.

In the town, the interesting **Musée de la Montre★** (open school holidays daily except Tue 10am–noon, 2–6pm; €5.50;. 03 81 68 44 53) celebrates the history of traditional watchmaking in Jura.

ARC-ET-SENANS★★

The royal saltworks of Arc-et-Senans are located in Jura, not far from the River Loue. They are situated SW of Besançon and N of Arbois.

Institut Claude-Nicolas Ledoux. 03 81 54 45 45. www.salineroyale.com.

Erected 1775–80, the Classical buildings of the former royal saltworks are an extraordinary essay in utopian town planning of the early Industrial Age and are on UNESCO's World Heritage List. In 1773, the King's Counsel decreed that the royal saltworks should be built at Arc-et-Senans. Only the cross-axis and half the first ring of buildings envisaged by the visionary French architect **Claude-Nicolas Ledoux** (1736–1806), inspector general of other saltworks, were actually completed; what we see today is however enough to evoke the idea of an ideal 18C city.

His plan was ambitious; a whole town laid out in concentric circles with the Director's Residence at the centre, flanked by storehouses (*Bâtiments des sels*), offices and workshops, and extending out to include a church, a market, public baths and recreational facilities. Ledoux's vision makes him one of the forerunners of modern architecture and urban design and while the enterprise was never really viable, being closed down in 1895, the amazing buildings of the *Saline Royale* remain.

Saline Royale (Royal Saltworks)★★

The complex today consists of the gatehouse, Director's Residence, courtyard, coopers' building and salt storehouses. Badly damaged by fire in 1918 and a subsequent dynamite attack, the **Director's Residence** has been the object of much-needed restoration. In the **coopers' building** architectural models, photographs and prints depict Ledoux' ideas about an ideal society. The old **salt storehouses** have been converted into venues for concerts and other events.

PONTARLIER

The town lies near the Swiss border at the foot of the Jura mountains.
14 bis r. de la Gare. 03 81 46 48 33. www.pontarlier.org.

Between the 13C and17C this proud upland town (pop 19 227), was the capital of the area known as the Baroichage. This statelet, consisting of Pontarlier and the 18 surrounding villages, enjoyed an independent regime of republican character which was only extinguished by Louis XIV's conquest of the Franche-Comté.

Cluse de Pontarlier★★

5km/3mi S. of Pontarlier.

The Jura has many such *cluses* – lateral clefts through the high ridges separating two valleys that facilitate communication between valley communities. This example, with the road and railway tightly squeezed together in the narrow defile, is strategically located on the route to Switzerland and overlooked by the Larmont and **Joux**★ forts high above (the Cluse de Joux is one of the Jura's most beautiful *cluses*).

Lac de St-Point★

8km/5mi S of Pontarlier.

Nearly 7km/4.3mi long, it is the largest lake in the Jura, fed by the waters of the River Doubs and sited among mountain pastures and pine forests.

Source de la Loue★★★

16km/10mi W. of Pontarlier

The River Loue rises in one of the blind valleys that penetrate deeply into the high plateau of the Jura. In its setting of high cliffs and luxuriant vegetation, it is one of the region's finest natural sites.

Grand Taureau★★

11km/7mi E. Leave Pontarlier S along N 57 and turn left onto a minor road climbing to the ski resort of Montagne du Larmont.

This is the highest point (1 323m) of the Larmont mountains, less than 1km/0.5mi from the Franco-Swiss border. The **view**★ from here stretches over Pontarlier and the Jura plateaux to the west.

Chapelle de Ronchamp★★

Ronchamp is a small former mining town bordering Alsace.
Open daily: Apr–Sep 9am–7pm; Oct–Mar 10am–5pm. €8.
Rue de la Chapelle, Ronchamp. 03 84 20 65 13. www.collinenotredameduhaut.com.

Built by **Le Corbusier** (1887–1965), the Chapelle Notre-Dame-du-Haut on its hilltop site is one of few great works of religious architecture produced by the early 20C Modern Movement. The 'Hill Notre-Dame du Haut' project has been designed with several environmental ideas in mind – nature playing a fundamental role.

ADDRESSES

STAY

Hôtel Siatel Chateaufarine Hôtel du Nord – 8 r. Moncey. 03 81 81 34 56. www.hotel-du-nord-besancon.com. 44 rooms. Situated in the historic quarter, this hotel dating from the 19C is a perfect base for venturing out into the old town. The rooms are practical and sound-proofed.

Hôtel Foch – 7 bis av. Foch. 03 81 80 30 41. www.hotel-foch-besancon.com. 27 rooms. The rather severe façade of this large building on the corner reveals a well-run hotel. The entrance hall with a reception area and lounge lead through to the buffet breakfast room. Above, the rooms are equipped with all comforts offering good value for money.

Best Western Citadelle – 13 r. Général-Lecourbe. 03 81 81 33 92. www.bestwesterncitadelle.com. 28 rooms. This stone building has an ideal location just a few steps from the historic town centre. Most of the comfortable rooms lead onto a paved interior courtyard.

Hôtel Siatel Chateaufarine – 6 Rue Louis Aragon. 03 81 41 12 22. www.hotelsiatel.com. 120 rooms. A functional hotel close to a busy main road, but the rooms are well sound-proofed. The dining rooms offers buffets, traditional meals and grills. WiFi.

Mercure Parc Micaud – 3 av. Ed.-Droz. 03 81 40 34 34. www.mercure.com. 91 rooms. Opposite the Doubs river, close to the old town where Victor Hugo was born in 1802. Rooms suit the demands of a business clientele; there is a decent bar and the modern-styled restaurant has a view to the gardens of the casino.

EAT

Le Cavalier Rouge – 3 r. Mégevand. 03 81 83 41 02. Closed Sun. A trendy urban atmosphere and speedy service attracts plenty of local regulars, who talk shop over the specialities of the day.

Au Petit Polonais – 81 r. des Granges. 03 81 81 23 67. Open lunch Tue–Sun; evenings Thu–Sat. Closed Mon, 3 weeks end-Jul–mid-Aug and 2 weeks around Christmas. A simple, unpretentious setting for traditional local cuisine.

La Femme du Boulanger – 8 r. Morand. 03 81 82 09 56. Closed Sun. This friendly tea room and baker's café offers sandwiches made with Poilâne bread, salads and a dish of the day served both lunchtimes and evenings. The bright colour scheme, old tiles and wooden tables give a relaxed atmosphere.

Miam – 8 r. Morand. 03 81 82 09 56. Closed Sunday. A very chic, designer restaurant which will whisk your palate far away from the banks of the Doubs river. International specialities include lamb tagine and fresh pasta dishes prepared the Italian way.

Maison Barthod – 22 r. Bersot. 03 81 82 27 14. www.barthod.fr. Closed Sun and Mon. Sit down on the terrace among the shrubs and potted plants and admire the view of the nearby waterfall. The owner is a wine buff who offers carefully planned menus (prices include wine) washed down by an interesting selection of wines.

Le Poker d'As – 14 sq. St-Amour. 03 81 81 42 49. Closed 12 Jul–11 Aug, Christmas holidays, Sun eve and Mon. A 100 percent family affair: the young chef cooks up traditional and contemporary dishes in a rustic dining room decorated with wooden sculptures made by his grandfather.

Le Chaland – Promenade Micaud near the Bregille bridge. 03 81 80 61 61. Closed Sat lunch and Sun eve. This charming old barge built in 1904 was converted into a restaurant in the 1960s. Moored along the Doubs, offering views of the old town and the Promenade Micaud. In fair weather, the meals are served on the upper deck, from where you can watch the boats negotiating the river.

La Source – 4 r. des Sources, 25170 Champvans-les-Moulins. 8km/5mi NW of Besançon. 03 81 59 90 57. www.lasource-besancon.com. Closed 31 Aug–9 Sep, 28 Dec–18 Jan, Wed eve except Jun–Aug, Sun eve and Mon. Big bay windows bathe the main room on the mezzanine with light, while the locals add a pleasant, lively atmosphere. Regional and traditional food is served.

Lons-le-Saunier★

The capital of the Jura is a spa town with an interesting heritage, and makes a good base for excursions to the vineyards or the Jura plateau. The local *Vin Jaune* or yellow wine is similar in taste to dry sherry.

- **Population:** 17 681.
- **Michelin Map:** 321 D 6
- **Info:** pl. du 11-novembre. 03 84 24 65 01. www.ville-lons-le-saunier.fr.
- **Location:** Near the Swiss border. 85km/53mi SW of Besançon.

RUE DU COMMERCE★

The town was ravaged by fire between 25 June and 4 July 1636 when it was attacked by Condé on Richelieu's orders. Seven years later, the population was amnestied by Mazarin and allowed to return. The Rue du Commerce was rebuilt in accordance with a detailed plan in the second half of the 17C; it is elegantly laid out on a slight curve and is famous for its great variety of shops with their attractive displays.

EXCURSIONS

DOLE★

The brown-tiled roofs of Dole's old houses cluster around the church and its imposing bell tower. The citizens of Dole are proud of their city; it was the capital of the free province of Burgundy (the Franche-Comté) for many centuries. The present city is adorned with monuments to its illustrious past.

Old Town★★ – The old town is clustered around the church of Notre-Dame. Its narrow, winding streets are closely packed with houses dating from the 15C to the 18C, many of which have interesting details: coats of arms above doorways, turrets, arcaded inner courtyards and so on. Start at place Nationale.

Collégiale Notre-Dame★ – The size of the 16C church's interior is striking. Its sober lines are a resolute departure from the excessive ornamentation of the Late Gothic style. It contains some of the first Renaissance works of art to manifest themselves in Dole, such as the works in polychrome **marble★**.

Walking Tours

Follow the marked **Sentier des Cascades** footpath which starts 8km/5mi E of Doucier as far as the Ilay crossroads (3hr round-trip).

CIRQUE DE BAUME★★★

19km/11.8mi E.

This is one of the most spectacular of the blind valleys characteristic of the western rim of the Jura.

The action of water has been particularly significant here in undermining the upper beds of limestone, which have caved in, thus forming the impressive gorge we see today. The viewpoint at Roches de Baume (*near the D 471*) gives splendid prospects over this great natural amphitheatre marking the boundary between the high plateau of the western Jura and the Bresse plain.

CASCADE DU HÉRISSON★★★

E of Lons-les-Saunier, and approached from the villages of Bonlieu, Doucier or Ilay, and then reached on foot.

6 Grande-rue, Clairvaux-les-Lacs. 03 84 25 27 47. www.juralacs.com.

High up at the foot of the cirque of Chaux-de-Dombief is little Lake Bonlieu, drained by the River Hérisson (hedgehog). The river crosses the narrow Frasnois plateau, then drops via a series of rapids and falls through its famous wooded gorge to the **Champagnole** plain below.

The path climbs over a series of limestone outcrops laid down during Jurassic times; it is they that form the succession of splendid falls, the **Éventail★★★** (Fan Falls), the **Grand Saut★★** (Great Leap), Château Garnier, the **Saut de la Forge★** and Saut Girard.

French Alps

» **Region map p398**
Annecy p399
Évian-les-Bains p405
Chamonix-Mont-Blanc p408
Route des Grandes Alpes p411
Courchevel p417
Grenoble p419
Briançon p422
Grand Canyon du Verdon p423

Introduction

Stretching from the Mediterranean to Lac Léman (Lake Geneva), the French Alps display all the varieties of mountain scenery, from the tranquility of bare rock and eternal snow to the animation of densely settled valleys. Nowhere, more than among these incomparable mountains, does human habitat show such close adaptation to natural conditions. Centuries of endurance and ingenuity have overcome formidable obstacles and brought all possible resources into play, settling valley floors, pushing grazing and cultivation to its highest limits and developing widely varied local traditions of living and building.

Geography – The north of the French Alps is marked by the great sweep of Lac Léman. To the south rise the Alps of Savoy, first the Chablais and Faucigny country and beyond that the famous peaks and glaciers around Mont Blanc. Westward lie other graceful stretches of water, Lake Annecy and Le Bourget Lake. Geologists divide the French Alps into four main areas: the **Préalpes**, or Alpine foothills; the **Alpine trench**, a depression cut through marl; the **central massifs** – Mont Blanc, Belledonne, Grandes Rousses, Écrins and Mercantour; and the **intra-Alpine zone**, forming the axis of the Alps, and consisting of sedimentary rocks.

History – The Alps have been inhabited since the Stone Age, but it was the Romans who first made an impact on the region. After the Romans, the area eventually became the County of Savoy which, during the 15C, was integrated with Piedmont and became the Duchy of Savoy.

Economy – Traditionally the Alps were an area of cattle rearing, and observed the traditional practice of transhumance, when man and beast would head into the high mountain pastures, returning just before winter. Now year-round tourism is of major importance, with many activities available in summer as well as traditional winter sports.

Highlights

1. Sea of ice above Chamonix: **Mer de Glace** (p409)
2. High road through the Alps: **Route des Grandes Alpes** (p411)
3. Spectacular view of Grenoble from **Fort de la Bastille** (p419)
4. Natural fortress: **Massif du Vercors** (p421)
5. Europe's most spectacular gorge: **Grand Canyon du Verdon** (p423)

Grenoble with the Alps behind

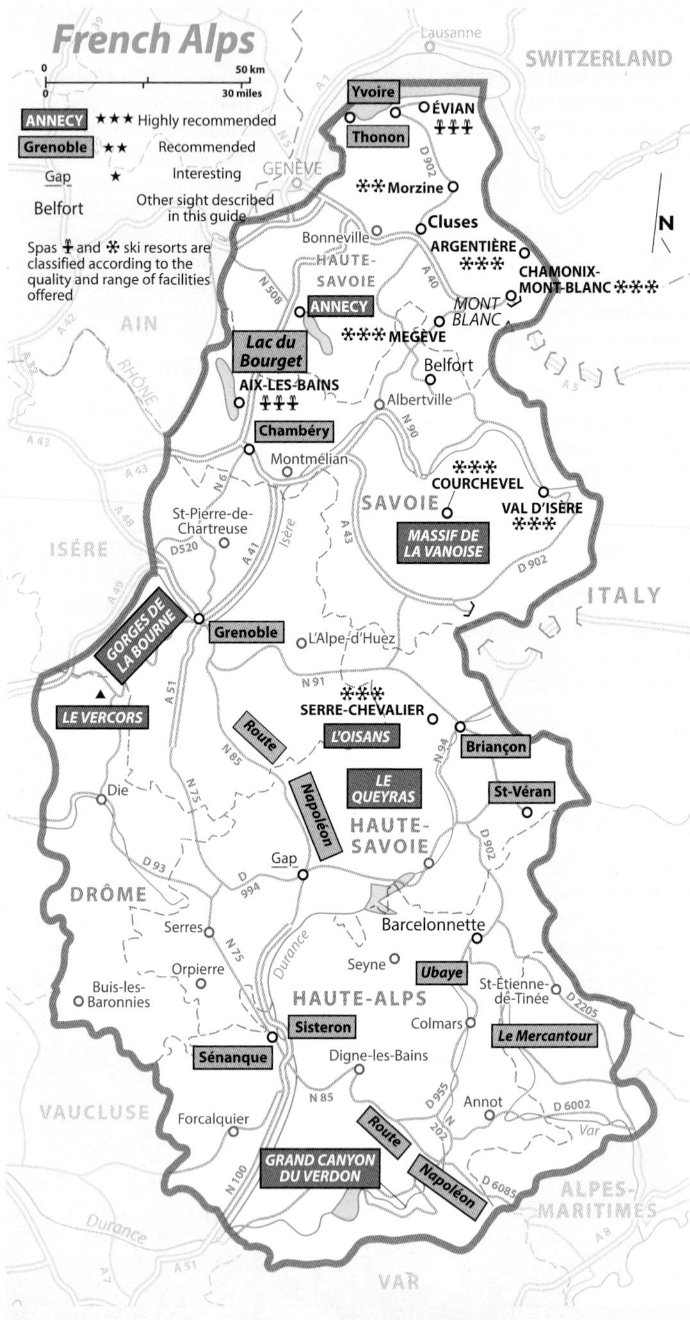
French Alps
0 50 km
0 30 miles
ANNECY ★★★ Highly recommended
Grenoble ★★ Recommended
Gap ★ Interesting
Belfort Other sight described in this guide
Spas and ski resorts are classified according to the quality and range of facilities offered
N
Lausanne
SWITZERLAND
Yvoire
Thonon
ÉVIAN
GENÈVE
Morzine
Cluses
Bonneville
ARGENTIÈRE
CHAMONIX-MONT-BLANC
HAUTE-SAVOIE
ANNECY
MONT BLANC
MEGÈVE
AIN
Lac du Bourget
AIX-LES-BAINS
Belfort
Albertville
Chambéry
Montmélian
COURCHEVEL
VAL D'ISÈRE
SAVOIE
MASSIF DE LA VANOISE
St-Pierre-de-Chartreuse
ISÈRE
ITALY
GORGES DE LA BOURNE
Grenoble
L'Alpe-d'Huez
LE VERCORS
SERRE-CHEVALIER
Briançon
Route
L'OISANS
Napoléon
LE QUEYRAS
St-Véran
Die
HAUTE-SAVOIE
Gap
DRÔME
Barcelonnette
Serres
Seyne
Ubaye
Orpierre
Buis-les-Baronnies
St-Étienne-de-Tinée
HAUTE-ALPS
Colmars
Sisteron
Le Mercantour
Sénanque
Digne-les-Bains
VAUCLUSE
Annot
Forcalquier
Var
Route
GRAND CANYON DU VERDON
Napoléon
ALPES-MARITIMES
Durance
VAR

Annecy★★★

Lakeside Annecy enjoys an exquisitely beautiful setting of water and mountains, and has a picturesque old centre clustered around the River Thiou.

- **Population:** 50 379.
- **Michelin Map:** 328 J-K 5
- **Info:** Centre Bonlieu,1 r. J.-Jaurès, 74000 Annecy. ✆04 50 45 00 33. www.lac-annecy.com.
- **Location:** The town is 39.4km/24.5mi NE of Lac du Bourget.
- **TGV:** Annecy is just under 4hrs direct from Paris Gare de Lyon.
- **Flights:** Aéroport d'Annecy Haute-Savoie Mont-Blanc (✆02 50 322 322; www. annecy.aeroport.fr). The airport is just 13min from the centre of Annecy, best reached by taxi.
- **Parking:** You won't need the car; leave it at the central Bonlieu car park, or park at the train station.
- **Don't Miss:** A boat trip on the lake is a must.
- **Timing:** The pedestrianised Old Annecy is the heart of the city, and will take a few hours to explore fully. On market days (Tue, Wed, Sun), visit Old Annecy in the morning, when it is in fuil swing. See the *Michelin Green Guide French Alps* for suggestions on where to stay and eat.

A BIT OF HISTORY

Ancient lake settlement, then a hillside Gallo-Roman town, Annecy moved back downhill in the Middle Ages to its present site by the Thiou, whose rapid waters powered its many mills.

In the 16C Annecy became the regional capital, displacing Geneva, and in the 17C was the home of the influential **St Francis of Sales**, bitter opponent of Calvinism, which had spread throughout the region.

WALKING TOUR

LES BORDS DU LAC★★

Annecy map, II p401. Allow 2hrs.

- **Avenue d'Albigny** – This royal avenue, lined with ancient plane trees, crosses the Champ de Mars where the locals used to watch military manoeuvres. On the left, the enormous Préfecture building, constructed after the Savoie region was annexed to France (1860), is in Louis XIII Revival style.
- **Parc de l'Impérial** – Shaded by beautiful trees, this pleasant park at the east end of avenue d'Albigny takes its name from a luxury hotel, built in Belle Époque style, which today incorporates a conference centre and a casino. The park includes the main lakeside beach.
- **Pont des Amours** – The bridge spans the Canal du Vassé, offering lovely views of the canal one way, with its small wooden boats, and of the wooded Île des Cygnes the other.
- **Jardins de l'Europe★** – At the time of the annexation of Savoie to France, these gardens were laid out as an arboretum with species from Europe, America and Asia.

OLD ANNECY★★

Annecy map, II p401. Allow 1hr 30 min.

The waterways of the Thiou and the Vassé wind through the colourful old part of town, which is now largely pedestrianised. The sizeable churches of St-Maurice and St-François-de-Sales mark the transition between the Sardinian architecture of the 19C old town and the commercial town of the first part of the 20C.

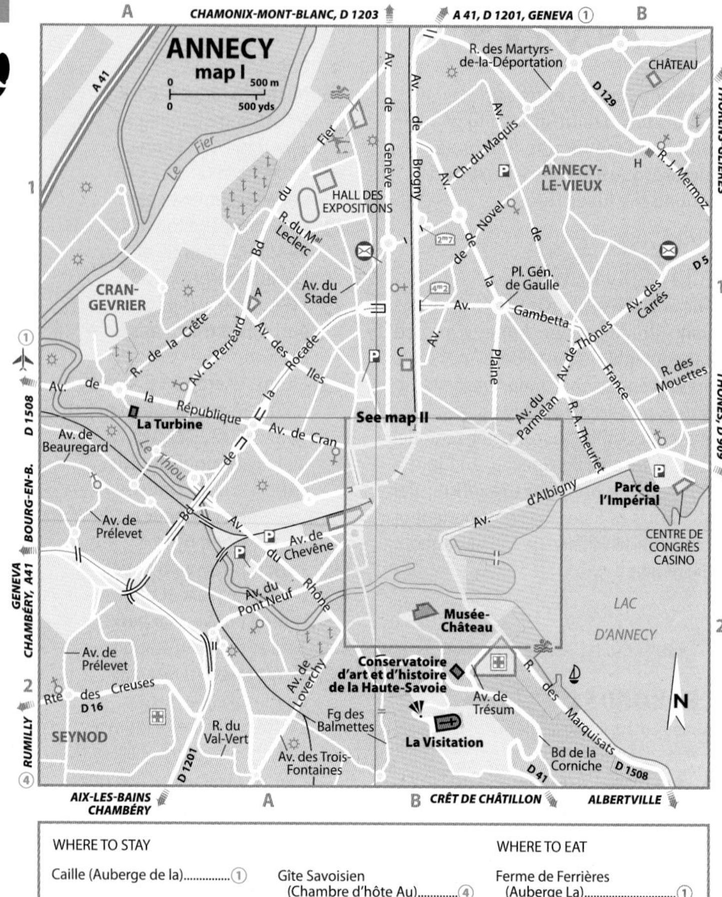

- **Église St-Maurice** – The church was built in the 15C with a large overhanging roof in typical regional style.
- **Église St-François-de-Sales** – St François de Sales and St Jeanne de Chantal were originally buried in this Baroque-fronted 17C church, which once belonged to the order they founded.
- **Pont sur le Thiou** – The oddly shaped **Palais de l'Île★★** in the middle of the river offers the most famous **view★★** of Old Annecy.
- **Palais de l'Île★★** – This monument is so photographed, it has become a local symbol. Built on an island in the 12C, when Annecy was little more than a small fisherman's town, the palace was used in turn as the Count of Geneva's residence, the mint, the law courts and a fearsome prison, which it remained until 1870, resuming that grim role for a time during World War II.

  It now houses a centre for urban and local patrimony, with displays of the town at different periods.
- **Musée-Château d'Annecy★** – This handsomely restored former residence of the lords of Geneva, from a junior branch of the House of Savoie, dates from the 12C to the 16C. The castle was damaged by fire several times, abandoned in the 17C, then used as a garrison before being restored with the help of public funds.

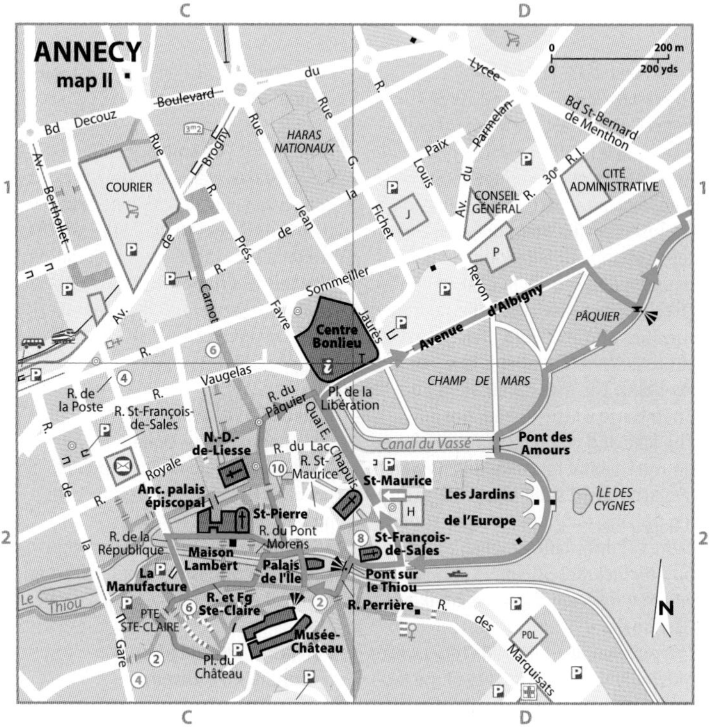

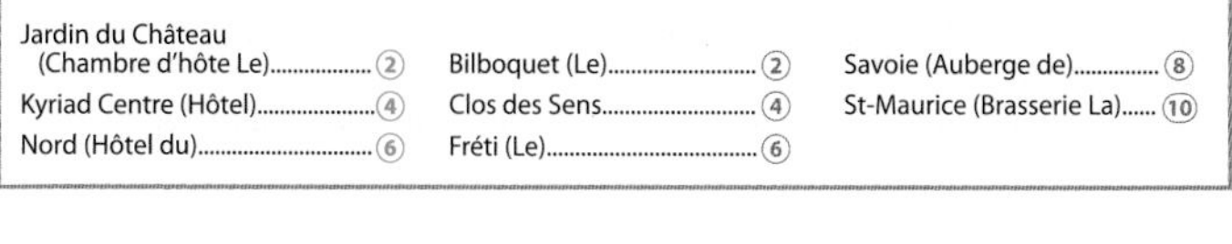

WHERE TO STAY	WHERE TO EAT	
Jardin du Château (Chambre d'hôte Le) ②	Bilboquet (Le) ②	Savoie (Auberge de) ⑧
Kyriad Centre (Hôtel) ④	Clos des Sens ④	St-Maurice (Brasserie La) ⑩
Nord (Hôtel du) ⑥	Fréti (Le) ⑥	

- **Rue Ste-Claire★** – The high street of Old Annecy is lined with arcaded houses. The 16C mansion at no. 18 has a particular link to the bishopric of St François de Sales. Thirty years before Richelieu's Académie Française was inaugurated, de Sales became the co-founder of the Académie Florimontane, a literary institution intended to promote the public good, influence opinion and spread the cult of beauty.
- **Ancien Palais Épiscopal** – The old episcopal palace was built in 1784, at which time the house belonging to Madame de Warens was demolished. In memory of their special encounter, in the courtyard a bust of Jean-Jacques Rousseau was placed, surrounded by his famous "gold balustrade".
- **Cathédrale St-Pierre** – Built in the 16C with a Renaissance façade and a Gothic interior, it became the episcopal seat of Bishop François de Sales when he was evicted from Geneva by the Calvinists; however, it was elevated officially to a cathedral only in 1822. Jean-Jacques Rousseau sang in the choir and played the flute in the cathedral.
- **Place Notre-Dame** – Enlarged in 1793 at the expense of the 14C church chevet, on one side of the square is the old hôtel de ville with its elegant 18C façade.
- **Église Notre-Dame-de-Liesse** – Dedicated to the Mother of God since the 12C, in 1338 anti-pope Clément VII of Avignon founded a seven-year jubilee here known as the grand Annecy pardon.

EXCURSIONS

LAC DU BOURGET★★

The lake is 39km/24.5mi SW of Annecy. The ideal base for a tour of the lake is Aix-les-Bains, a famous resort with lively streets, opulent hotels near the spa baths, and an attractive lakeshore.

Enclosed within an impressive mountain setting, this is France's largest, deepest and most celebrated natural lake, lying in a glaciated valley between the Jura and the Alps. On its eastern shore is the elegant spa town of Aix-les-Bains. The lake is best seen from La Chambotte a little further north.

The lake and its banks form a rich and unusual habitat for wildlife. In its waters live around 50 species of fish, including pollans, migratory members of the salmon family, and crayfish. Its varied birdlife includes 300 or so cormorants which winter on the west bank at La Grande Cale.

The poet Lamartine (1790–1867) wrote movingly about the beauty of the lake, and of Mme Lulie Charles Julie whom he met here in October 1816. The popular spa Aix-les-Bains is one of the best-equipped resorts in the Alps, and has been known for its health-giving waters for over 2 000 years. Queen Victoria visited here three times.

Abbaye royale de Hautecombe★★

On the west bank of the lake. Open Wed–Mon 10am–1.15am, 2–5pm. ✆04 79 54 58 80.

Jutting into the lake, the abbey (founded 1125) houses the tombs of 42 princely members of the House of Savoy. The abbey's little harbour has an unusual 12C building **(grange batelière)** with covered moorings, allowing goods to be unloaded and stored under the same roof.

CHAMBÉRY★★

10km/6.2mi S of Lac du Bourget.

24 bd de la Colonne. ✆04 79 33 42 47. www.chambery-tourisme.com.

Don't miss the many fascinating trompe-l'œil decorations around the town.

The well-restored old centre recaptures something of Chambéry's past splendour as the capital of Savoy.

Château de Chambéry

This fortress was occupied by the counts of Savoy in 1285, who expanded it during the 14C to serve as their residence and seat of administration. The **Sainte-Chapelle★**, adjoined to the château, displays Flamboyant Gothic architecture (guided tours (1hr) daily; €4. ✆04 79 70 15 94).

Musée Savoisien★

sq. Lannoy de Bissy. Open Wed–Mon 10am–noon, 2–6pm. Closed public holidays. €4 (no charge 1st Sun of the month). ✆04 79 33 44 48.

The museum houses interesting exhibits of prehistory, religious art and regional ethnography.

Fontaine des Éléphants (Elephants' Fountain)

r. de Boigne.

This famous – and originally disliked – landmark was erected in 1838. The shape of the Savoyan cross is achieved by the truncation in a column of the forelimbs of four elephants.

AIX-LES-BAINS ★★

Aix-les-Bains lies at the foot of Mont Revard, on the eastern shore of Lac du Bourget. Follow A 41 and A 43, 10km/6.25mi from Chambéry.

pl. Maurice-Mollard, 73100 Aix-les-Bains. ✆04 79 88 68 00. www.aixlesbains.com. P. The town-hall car park is located at the heart of the town, near spas, gardens and pedestrian malls.

After touring the town, stop by the Faure museum for the bronze sculptures by Rodin.

This well-known spa, which specialises in the treatment of rheumatism and respiratory ailments, is also one of the best-appointed tourist centres in the Alps, with lively streets, splendid palace hotels near the baths and attractive lake shores.

Taking the waters: a fashionable pastime – Aix's health-giving waters have been famous for almost 2 000 years. The Romans excelled in the art of hydropathy and the baths were at once a social club, a casino and a fitness club. The name of the town comes from *Aquae Gratianae*, "the waters of Emperor Gratianus".

During the Middle Ages, the baths were severely neglected. Taking the waters became fashionable again in the 16C, but the first real establishment dating from the 18C was only equipped with showers.

The treatment offered became more sophisticated in the 19C with the introduction of the steam bath and shower-massage, a technique brought back from Egypt by Napoléon's doctors.

The splendour of Aix-les-Bains at the turn of the century – The expansion of the spa town, which began in 1860, reached its peak during the Belle Époque. Luxury hotels were built in order to attract the aristocracy and the crowned heads of Europe: the "Victoria", for instance, welcomed Queen Victoria on three occasions, whereas the Splendide and the Excelsior counted among their guests a maharajah from India, the Emperor of Brazil and Empress Elizabeth ("Sissi") of Austria-Hungary. Most of the buildings in the spa town were designed by an architect from Lyon, Jules Pin the Elder (1850–1934), whose masterpiece was undoubtedly the Château de la Roche du Roi. After WWII, most of these magnificent hotels closed down for economic reasons.

THE SPA TOWN

The life of the spa town is concentrated round the baths, the municipal park with its vast open-air theatre, the Palais de Savoie and the new casino, as well as along the lake with its beach and marinas. Rue de Genève, rue du Casino and adjacent streets form the shopping centre of the town.

THE ROMAN TOWN★

Arc de Campanus

Erected by a member of the "Pompeia" family, this arch stood 9m high in the centre of the Roman town. The remains of the **Roman baths** can only give a rough idea of their former splendour (24 different kinds of marble were used to decorate them).

Temple de Diane

This remarkable rectangular Roman monument has its stones set in place without mortar. Note the classic Italianate façade on the former **Grand Hôtel** (1853) on the corner.

Musée Faure★

♿Open daily 10am–noon, 1.30–6pm. Closed Tue, public holidays and 22 Dec–3 Jan. €4. ✆04 79 61 06 57.

In 1942, Dr Faure bequeathed to the town a rare collection of paintings and sculptures including a large number of works by the Impressionists and their predecessors.

Thermes nationaux and caves

Open May–Oct. Guided tours (1hr) daily at 3pm, except Sun and Mon. Closed public holidays. €4. ✆04 79 35 38 50.

Inaugurated in 1783, renovated and enlarged during the 19C, the baths were completed by the Nouveaux Thermes in 1934, and modernised in 1972; these are open to visitors.

ADDRESSES

STAY

⊖ Chambre d'hôte Au Gite Savoisien – 98 rte de Corbier, 74650 Chavanod. 6km/3.7mi SW of Annecy by D 16, towards Rumilly, in the village of Corbier. ✆04 50 69 02 95. www.gite-savoisien.com. P. 4 rooms. This old farm on the slopes above Annecy in the heart of a small village offers simple and comfortable rooms, three of them air-conditioned. In summer, guests can relax in the garden with a view of the mountains, or play a game of pétanque. A gîte is also offered. Evening meal available on request on Monday, Wednesday and Friday.

⊜⊜ **Auberge de la Caille** – 18 chemin de la Caille, 74330 La Balme-de-Sillingy. 12km/7.4mi NW of Annecy by D 1508 and D 3. ℘04 50 68 85 21. Closed 25 Dec–1 Jan, Sun eve and Sep–Jun Wed. 🅿. 7 rooms, restaurant⊜⊜⊜. The auberge is set in a 4ha/10-acre park with lawns, a pool and tennis courts. There is a choice of accommodation between 7 comfortable rooms, 10 brand new chalets with kitchens, 2 gîtes and a small campsite. Tasty regional cooking is served in a wood-panelled dining room or on the terrace.

⊜⊜ **Chambre d'hôte Le Jardin du Château** – 1 pl. du Château. Exit Annecy Sud, follow Albertville, then Château. ℘04 50 45 72 28. http://annecy-chambre-dhote.monsite-orange.fr. Open all year for rental of studios (non-serviced), weekly only in Jul–Aug, breakfast provided May–Jun and Sep. ⊭. 5 rooms. This friendly accommodation is well located in the heart of the old town. All rooms have a kitchenette and several have balconies. Terrace with a view of Annecy, pretty garden and small snackbar.

⊜⊜ **Hôtel du Nord** – 24 r. Sommeiller. ℘04 50 45 08 78. www.annecy-hotel-du-nord.com. WiFi. 30 rooms. An unpretentious little hotel in the centre of town, ideally situated for a short visit. The rooms are functional and you should receive a friendly welcome.

⊜⊜ **Hôtel Kyriad Centre** – 1 fg Balmettes. ℘0207 519 50 45. www.kyriad-annecy-centre.fr. WiFi. 24 rooms. This modern hotel at the entrance to the pedestrian district occupies a 16C building. The rooms, decorated in blue and yellow, are pleasant. Good service.

ϒ/EAT

⊜ **Auberge La Ferme de Ferrières** – 800 rte des Burnets, 74370 Ferrières. 7km/4.3mi NW of Annecy by D 1201 and D 172, towards Les Burnets. ℘04 50 22 04 00. Closed Feb–Mar and Wed. Reservations essential Sun–Tue eve. The family farm provides pigeons, chickens, ducks, rabbits, fruit and vegetables for your meal. The kitchen can also offer several cheese-based Savoyard specialities. Rustic dining room, terrace with view. There are also eight bed-and-breakfast rooms.

⊜⊜ **Auberge de Savoie** – 1 pl. St-François. ℘04 50 45 03 05. www.aubergedesavoie.fr. Closed 3–13 Jan, 24 Oct–10 Nov, Wed and Sep–Jun Tue. Right next to the St-François church, this contemporary and warm restaurant is most professionally run. The terrace on a little square looks towards the Thiou and the castle.

⊜⊜ **Clos des Sens** – 13 rue Jean Mermoz. ℘04 50 23 07 90. www.closdessens.com. Closed 28 Dec–10 Jan and Sun–Mon. Be prepared to eat at this popular restaurant side by side with the "whole of Annecy". In the style of a modern bistro, the menu is adventurous and tasty. Terrace on the pavement.

⊜⊜ **La Brasserie St-Maurice** – 7 r. Collège-Chapuisien. ℘04 50 51 24 49. www.stmau.com. Closed Sun–Mon. This building dates from 1675. The attractively decorated dining room includes original wooden columns. Traditional cuisine is offered, and there is a terrace for summer.

⊜⊜ **Le Bilboquet** – 14 fg Ste-Claire. ℘04 50 45 21 68. www.restaurant-lebilboquet.fr. Closed 15 Feb–10 Mar, Mon and Sep–Jun Sun except eves. Adjoining the Ste-Claire gateway, the thick old walls of this restaurant keep it delightfully cool. Traditional cooking according to seasonal availability.

⊜⊜ **Le Fréti** – 12 r. Ste-Claire. ℘04 50 51 29 52. www.lefreti.com. Closed Mon–Sat lunch and public holidays. Reservations recommended. This establishment at the heart of the old town is above the arcades and the family-run cheese-making business, from which issue mouth-watering specialities and the scent of raclettes, fondues and tartiflettes to tempt food lovers. Simple décor. Summer terrace.

Évian-les-Bains★★

Poetically known as the "pearl of Lake Geneva", Évian is remarkably well situated between the lake and the foothills of the Préalpes du Chablais. The resort town, renowned for its old palaces and thermal spas, climbs up from the flat lake area like an amphitheatre, with steep little roads parting in every direction. You can enjoy splendid architecture, walks, lazy evenings by the lake, and the town makes a fine base for exploring the Chablais.

- **Population:** 8 142.
- **Michelin Map:** 328 M2
- **Info:** pl. de la Porte d'Allinges, 74501 Évian-les-Bains. ☎04 50 75 04 26. www.evian-tourisme.com.
- **Location:** Évian-les-Bains is about 45min from exit 15 of A 40, or 10km/6.25mi from Thonon-les-Bains.
- **TGV/Train:** Evian is 4 – 5hrs 30mins from Paris Gare de Lyon via either Lyon or Bellegarde.
- **Don't Miss:** A boat ride on Lake Geneva. The amazing panorama from the Pic de Mémise.
- **Kids:** The Pré-Curieux is both fun and educational.
- **Timing:** You can spend quite a few hours just strolling along the waterfront.

WALKING TOUR

THE LAKESIDE★

Évian-les-Bains map, p406. Depart from the tourist office.

Simply the most enjoyable walk in Évian. Firstly, because of the rare trees that border the lake, along with lawns and pretty flowerbeds. Next, because it is here that you will find the important buildings of the **Palais Lumière**, the **Villa Lumière**, today's town hall, and the **casino.**

All along the promenade up to the pleasure port Les Mouettes, the water in **musical fountains** plays in time to the music. Behind you, appearing through the chestnut groves of Neuvecelles, are the grand hotels, stacked up on the lower slopes of the Gavot.

Église Notre-Dame-de-l'Assomption – Pl. des Anciens-Combattants. Typical of early Gothic art in Savoie (end of 13C), the church has been rebuilt and restored frequently. To the right of the chancel in the Rosaire Chapel is a Burgundian painted wooden bas-relief of the Virgin Mary. The stalls are a masterpiece of Flamboyant Gothic art from the mid-15C, partly rebuilt in the 19C.

Villa Lumière (hôtel de ville) – Open Mon–Fri 9–11.30am, 1.30–5pm. ☎04 50 83 10 00. Once owned by Antoine Lumière, father of the cinema pioneer, this grand 1896 villa now houses the town hall; the ground-floor rooms and the **grand staircase★** are especially elegant, while the next-door **theatre** is a splendid relic of 19C excess.

Also on the lakeside, on the same site as the Château de Blonay, willed to the town in 1877, are the **casino**, built in 1911 by the same architect as for the **Buvette Cachat**, and the **Palais Lumière**, a thermal spa until 1984 when it was converted to a cultural centre.

Buvette and Source Cachat – Open mid-Jun–mid-Sep daily 10.30am–12.30pm, 3–7pm; mid-May–mid-Jun and end Sep Mon–Sat 2.30–6.30pm. Free. ♿☎04 50 84 80 80. The centre is housed in the former pump room (1905) of the **Cachat spring**, an Art Nouveau building surmounted by a cupola. The spring is named after its owner, who improved the installations in 1824.

Parc thermal – The new baths are situated here. The pump room, designed by Maurice Novarina, was erected in 1956 and the Espace Thermal in 1983. This is

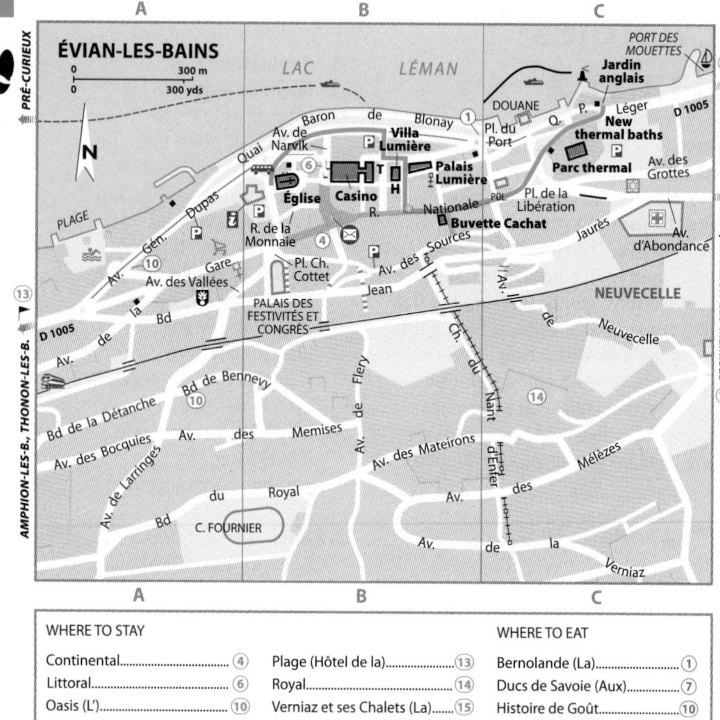

partly built below ground in order to preserve the appearance of the park.

Jardin anglais – Beyond the harbour where yachts find a mooring and where the lake's pleasure boats come alongside, the Jardin anglais offers a view of the Swiss shore.

Le Pré Curieux Water Gardens★

Guided tour (2hrs, by reservation 4 days ahead; leaves from pontoon opposite the casino) May–Sept daily departures at 10am, 1.45pm and 3.30pm. €10 (children P7). ♿ ✆04 50 75 04 26.

This pretty garden demonstrates the rich variety of marshland ecosystems. You reach the elegant, Colonial-style villa on a solar-powered boat.

EXCURSIONS

The nearby town of **Amphion-les-Bains** (4km/2.5mi to the west) was the first spa resort of the Chablais region, which became fashionable as early as the 17C, when the Dukes of Savoie regularly took the waters. The medicinal properties of Évian water were discovered in 1789, when a gentleman from Auvergne realised it was dissolving his kidney stones. The water, filtered by sand of glacial origin, is cold (11.6°C) and low in minerals. As well as for drinking, it is prized for its beneficial effects on kidney disorders and rheumatism.

You can visit the very modern **bottling factory** (guided tour (1hr30) by appointment at the Évian information centre. ✆04 50 84 86 54), which produces an average of 5 million litres of water per day, the highest output of any producer.

YVOIRE★★

26km/16mi W along the shore from Évian-les-Bains.

Place de la Mairie. ✆04 50 72 80 21.

This picturesque village, bedecked with flowers, has retained its medieval character. It enjoys a magnificent site on the shores of Lake Geneva (Lac Léman), at the tip of a headland separating the Petit Lac and the Grand Lac.

Village Médieval (Old Town)★

Pedestrian access only.

Rebuilt in the 14C on the site of a former fortress, Yvoire has kept part of its original ramparts, including two gates protected by towers and its castle (closed to the public) with a massive square keep framed by turrets. The bustling streets lined with old houses and craft shops lead to delightful squares decked with flowers which afford fine views of the lake.

Jardin des Cinq-Sens★

Le Labyrinthe. Open mid-Apr–mid-Oct, daily 10am–6.30pm. €12 (children 6–18, €7). 04 50 72 88 80. www.jardin5sens.net.

The former kitchen garden of the castle has been turned into a reconstruction of a medieval enclosed garden, situated in the centre of Yvoire's Old Town.

ADDRESSES

STAY

Continental – 65 r. Nationale. 04 50 75 37 54. www.hotel-continental-evian.com. WiFi. 32 rooms. Family-owned hotel. Attractive old furniture collected by the proprietor. Pedestrian street.

Hôtel de la Plage – 431 r. de la plage, 74500 Amphion-les-Bains. On D 1005. 04 50 70 00 06. www.hotelplage74.com. Closed Nov–Apr. P. 39 rooms, restaurant. You could not stay closer to the lake. Bright, quiet rooms have all been renovated. Eating in the restaurant on stilts is adorable.

Le Littoral – 5 quai Besson. 04 50 75 64 00. http://en.hotel-littoral-evian.fr. Closed 29 Oct–14 Nov. WiFi. 30 rooms. A 1990s hotel built next to the casino. Rooms in regional style, with lake views (most have balconies).

L'Oasis – 11 bd Bennevy. 04 50 75 13 38. www.oasis-hotel.com. Closed Oct–Mar. WiFi. 17 rooms. On the heights of Évian, a charming hotel with pretty rooms. Some face the lake; others are in small houses nestled in the pretty shaded garden.

La Verniaz et ses Chalets – Rte d'Abondance. 04 50 75 04 90. www.verniaz.com. Closed 12 Nov–11 Feb. P. 32 rooms, restaurant. This lovely hotel has several buildings set in a beautiful garden. Large bedrooms have a view over the lake.

Hotel Royal – 04 50 26 85 00. www.evianroyalresort.com. WiFi. 140 rooms. Built in Art Nouveau style in 1907, this luxurious hotel, renovated in 2015, is set in a park. Well-equipped wellness centre and spacious, stylish rooms. Variety of dining options, including special diet dishes at the Jardin des Lys.

EAT

La Bernolande – 1 pl. du Port. 04 50 70 72 60. Closed Jan, Wed and Sep–Apr Thu. On a fine day, the terrace of this little restaurant is the perfect spot to sit back and enjoy homestyle cooking whilst watching ferry boats on the lake.

Aux Ducs de Savoie – R. 23 juillet 44, 74500 St-Gingolph. 04 50 76 73 09. www.ducsdesavoie.net. Closed 4–26 Jan, Mon and Sep–Jun Tue. Pleasant chalet in the middle of the village. Tasty, classic recipes are served in a bourgeois setting inside or on the shady terrace with lake view.

Histoire de Goût – 1 av. Gén. Dupas. 04 50 70 09 98. www.histoires-de-gout.fr. Closed 3–18 Jan and Mon. Choose between a room with a wooden/zinc bar and décor of wine boxes, or another vaulted room with ironwork décor.

ACTIVITIES

Good to know – The **sailing centre** offers courses and races for all levels. The **Évian-Plage** swimming centre has two heated pools. At Cité de l'Eau in Amphion-les-Bains you will find an indoor pool, wave pool, diving pool sauna and jacuzzi.

Rencontres musicales d'Évian – La Grange au lac. 04 50 71 39 47. www.evianroyalresort.com. 2nd and 3rd weeks of May. Évian hosts a renowned festival of classical music. Check the website for details of each year's programme.

Chamonix-Mont-Blanc★★★

Chamonix lies at the foot of the famous 3 000m Chamonix Needles (Aiguilles de Chamonix) at a point where the glacial valley of the Arve widens out. All around are the high mountains of the Mont Blanc massif. This is the most renowned of the massifs of the French Alps because of its dramatic relief, crystalline rocks and glacial morphology. The upper slopes of the great White Mountain is just visible from the town.

- **Population:** 8 972.
- **Michelin Map:** 328 M-O 5
- **Info:** 85 pl. du Triangle de l'Amitié. ☎04 50 53 00 24. www.chamonix.com.
- **Location:** Chamonix is 101km/63mi E of Annecy.
- **TGV/Train:** Chamonix is 10–11hrs 30 mins via St Gervais les Bains from Paris Austerlitz.
- **Don't miss:** A cable-car ride up the Aiguille du Midi, or to Montenvers on the train, but be sure to check the weather in advance. See the *Michelin Green Guide French Alps* for suggestions on where to stay and eat.
- **Timing:** You can wander aimlessly for hours, although there are really only two main streets.

RESORT

Already the mountaineering capital thanks to its Compagnie des Guides, Chamonix has also become one of the best-equipped ski resorts in the Alps. The development of the town as a skiing destination began when the first Winter Olympic Games were held here in 1924. Today, the Chamonix valley offers a mixture of architectural styles and incessant traffic throughout the high season. Hardly beautiful in itself, its main attraction lies in its magnificent landscapes, lively atmosphere and numerous opportunities to practise sports and enjoy cultural events.

Rue du Dr-Paccard, extended by rue Joseph-Vallot, is the town's main artery. The short rue de l'Église, perpendicular to it, leads to the church at the heart of the old town and to the **Maison de la Montagne**, which houses the offices of the Compagnie des Guides.

In the opposite direction, avenue Michel-Croz leads past the **statue** of Docteur Michel Gabriel Paccard to the station and the newer districts of Chamonix lying on the left bank of the Arve. A **bronze sculpture** by Salmson, depicting the naturalist Horace Bénédict de Saussure (1740–99) and the mountain guide Jacques Balmat (1762–1834) admiring Mont Blanc, decorates the widened Pont de Cour.

Musée Alpin

89 avenue Michel-Croz. ♿ Open daily except Tue 2–6pm (every day in Jul–Aug). Closed mid – to end May. €5.50 (Entrance to the Alpine Museum allows free access to Espace Tairraz). ☎04 50 53 25 93.

This museum illustrates the history of the Chamonix valley, daily life in the 19C, the conquest of Alpine summits, scientific experiments and early skiing in the valley.

Tairraz Centre (Crystal Museum)

Rocade du Dr. Payot. Open Jan–Jun 2–7pm. €5.50 (entrance to Musée Alpin gives free admission to Espace Tairraz). ☎04 50 55 53 93.

The space is shared between the **Musée des Cristaux**, with remarkable examples of crystal from Mont Blanc and around the world, and temporary exhibits about the regional heritage.

Mer de Glace and the Montenvers Railway

SIGHT

The tongue of the Glacier des Bossons hangs 500m above the valley on the approach to Chamonix. The Geneva naturalist **Horace Benedict de Saussure** based himself here in the course of his scientific studies in Savoy. In 1760, he offered a reward for the first ascent of Mont Blanc. On 8 August 1786, Dr Michel Paccard and Jacques Balmat reached the summit, thereby inaugurating the age of mountaineering, as well as the development of the town as an Alpine resort.

EXCURSIONS

AIGUILLE DU MIDI★★★

Cable car: Runs daily subject to weather conditions. www.compagniedumontblanc.fr. Trip in two stages: Chamonix–Plan de l'Aiguille and Plan de l'Aiguille–Aiguille du Midi. €57 round-trip (children 4–15, €48.50).

The **panorama★★★**, especially from the central peak (3 842m), is staggering, taking in Mont Blanc, Mont Maudit, the Grandes Jorasses, and the dome of the Goûter whose buttresses are buried in 30m of ice.

The **Vallée Blanche**, also known as the Glacier du Géant, can be reached by taking the cable-car *(téléphérique)* to Pointe Helbronner. From here can be seen the glacial cirques with their flanks worn down by the incessant attacks of the ice.

MER DE GLACE★★★

Montenvers train: Runs daily subject to weather conditions. €30.50 (children 4–15, €26) includes train, cable car and visit to the ice grotto.

The view from the upper station of the railway built in 1908 takes in the whole of this "sea of ice". The glacier is 7km/4.3mi long, in places 200m thick, and moves 90m a year.

The rocky material it carries with it scores and scratches the mountain walls on either side as well as giving the glacier its characteristic rather grimy appearance. At the foot of the glacier this material is deposited, forming a terminal moraine.

Beyond, the eye is led from one peak to another; this **panorama★★★** is one of the most beautiful in the region.

ARGENTIÈRE★

8km/5mi northeast of Chamonix.

24 Route du Village, 74400 Argentière.

04 50 54 02 14. www.chamonix.com.

At 1 252m, Argentière is the highest resort in the Chamonix valley; with its annexes of Montroc-le-Planet and Le Tour, it forms an excellent holiday and mountaineering centre offering a wide choice of expeditions to the Massif du Mont Blanc and Massif des Aiguilles Rouges. The slopes of the upper Arve valley provide pleasant walks through a fringe of larch woods.

A legend in the French Alps, **Armand Charlet** (1900–75), a native of Argentière, was held to be the king of mountain guides until the early 1960s. He set a record, which has never been equalled, by climbing the Aiguille Verte more than 100 times.

AIGUILLE DES GRANDS-MONTETS★★

Access by the Lognan and Grands-Montets cable cars. ℘04 50 54 00 71. www.compagniedumontblanc.fr. About 2hr30min return.

The **panorama★★★** is breathtaking. The view extends to the Argentière glacier over which tower the Aiguille du Chardonnet and Aiguille d'Argentière to the north, Mont Dolent to the east, Aiguille Verte and Les Drus to the south, with the Aiguille du Midi, Mont Blanc and Dôme du Goûter further away.

COL DE BALME★★

Access all year round by the Col de **Balme gondola**. ℘04 50 54 00 58. www.compagniedumontblanc.fr. Allow 10min to walk from the lift to the pass.

The **view★★** extends northeast to the Swiss Alps and southwest to the Aiguille Verte, Mont Blanc and the Aiguilles Rouges massif.

CHAMONIX VIEWPOINTS BY CABLE CAR

Aiguille du Midi★★★

Minimum 2hr return.

The Aiguille du Midi cable car, suspended part of the time 500m above ground, and the gondola form the most thrilling attraction in the French Alps.

Plan de l'Aiguille★★

This midway stop, situated at the foot of the jagged Aiguilles de Chamonix, is the starting point for walks. Good view of the upper Mont Blanc massif.

Le Brévent★★★

Minimum 1hr30 min return by gondola (to Planpraz, 20 min) then by cable car (Planpraz–Brévent 20 min).

Planpraz★★ relay station offers a splendid view of the Aiguilles de Chamonix and an excellent lunch. From Le Brévent, the **panorama** extends over the French side of the Mont Blanc massif.

La Flégère★

Cable car Les Praz–La Flegère (15min) plus l'Index chair lift (20min).

From Les Praz, there is an impressive **view** of the Aiguille Verte and the Grandes Jorasses summits closing off the Mer de Glace depression.

Les Houches

Les Houches is 6km/3.75mi S of Chamonix. BP 9, 74310, Les Houches. ℘04 50 55 50 62. www.leshouches.com.

The view of the massif from this resort at the foot of Mont Blanc is spectacular. Les Houches has extended across the widest and sunniest part of the Chamonix valley, while still keeping its village character. Even if the setting is not on a par with Chamonix, Les Houches is a pleasant family resort; well equipped and ideal for skiers who prefer not to take on the steeper, high-altitude slopes.

Ski area

The resort offers skiers a wide range of difficulties in the Lachat, Bellevue and Prarion areas, and 110 snow cannon are on standby to make good any lack of snow. The famous "green run" (black in fact!) requires a high level of skill. There are, in addition, some 30km/18.6mi of cross-country skiing trails.

Bellevue★★

1hr there and back.

It is possible to continue up to the Nid d'Aigle (*Glacier de Bionnassay*) and go back down via St-Gervais on board the Tramway du Mont Blanc.

The Nid d'Aigle★★ (Glacier de Bionnassay)

Allow 3hr there and back by the Tramway du Mont Blanc.

This journey provides a good introduction to high-altitude mountain landscapes by opening up the wild setting of the Bionnassay Glacier stretched out at the foot of the Aiguilles de Bionnassay (*spectacular avalanches*) and of the Aiguille du Goûter.

Route des Grandes Alpes★★★

Among the many routes inviting visitors to explore the French Alps, this high-altitude road is the most famous. Rarely far from the frontier, the Great Alpine Road links Lake Geneva with the Riviera, crossing mountain passes as it leaps from valley to valley. The route is open from end to end during the summer months only.

Michelin Map: 332, 334, 340 and 341.

Info: Association Grande Traversée des Alpes, 14 r. de la République, Grenoble. ℘04 76 42 08 31. www.grande-traversee-alpes.com.

Location: From Thonon-le-Bains to Menton, across 25 mountain passes.

DRIVING TOUR

734km/458mi.

Thonon-les-Bains★★

From the Place du Château the view extends over the great sweep of **Lake Geneva (Lac Léman★★★)**.

On the Swiss shore to the north rise the terraces of the great Lavaux vineyard, and beyond are the mountains of the Vaudois Alps (to the east) and the Jura. Saint Francis of Sales once preached in St Hippolytus' Church (Église St-Hippolyte); its vault (**voûte★**) has retained its original stucco and 18 painted medallions, together with the stucco decoration of its false pillars (visible from the adjoining basilica), all done by the Italian craftsmen who restored the interior in Rococo style in the 18C.

© Pierre Jacques/hemis.fr

Thonon-Les-Bains by Lake Geneva

The road rises in a series of steps through the damp beech woodland of the gorges cut by the River Dranse de Morzine. This marks the transition between the gently rolling hill country fringing the great lake and the **Chablais★★** massif, a complex of high ridges and peaks, with rich pastures grazed by Abondance cattle.

The most spectacular part of the route is known as the **Gorges du Pont du Diable★★**, marked by a number of rock-falls, one of which has formed the bridge attributed to the Evil One.

Morzine★★

33km/20.5mi SE of Thonon

The valleys around the resort are dotted with hamlets; the chalets have patterned balconies. All around grow sombre forests of spruce.

After the pass at Les Gets, the small industrial town of Tanninges marks the beginning of the **Faucigny★★** country. Drained by the Giffre, this is a landscape of pastures and sprucewoods, fashioned by the action of glacial moraines on calcareous rocks deposited here far from their point of origin.

Cluses

29km/18mi SW of Morzine.

The town commands the most important lateral valley (*cluse*) in the French Alps. The River Arve has cut down

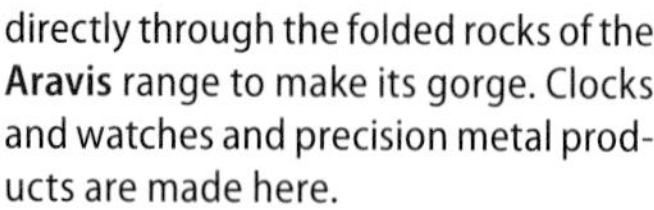

directly through the folded rocks of the **Aravis** range to make its gorge. Clocks and watches and precision metal products are made here.

The upland Sallanches basin is bounded to the north by the dramatic peaks of a number of ranges, but dominating all is the great mass of Mont Blanc itself, the "Giant of the Alps".

La Clusaz★★

44km/27.3mi SW of Cluses.

The most important ski resort in the **Massif des Aravis** owes its name to the deep gorge, or cluse, downstream of it, through which the Nom torrent gushes. The village, situated in the middle of pine forests and mountain pasture, is tightly huddled around the big church characterised by its onion-dome tower. The jagged outlines of the Aravis mountains can be seen in the distance.

Two-Day Programme

By driving hard it is possible to get from Thonon to Menton in two days, but to do so would be to deprive yourself of a number of sights that in themselves would make the trip worthwhile. They include Chamonix, with the Aiguille du Midi and the Vallée Blanche, La Grave and the splendid viewpoint at Le Chazelet, St-Véran.

Five-Days

Thonon–Beaufort
144km/89.4mi –allow 5hr30min including sightseeing.
Beaufort–Val d'Isère
71km/44mi – allow 3hr including sightseeing.
Val d'Isère–Briançon
180km/111.8mi – allow 7hr30min including sightseeing.
Briançon–Barcelonnette
133km/82.6mi – allow 6hr30min including sightseeing.
Barcelonnette–Menton
206km/128mi – allow 6hr including sightseeing.

In the summer, La Clusaz offers excellent walking, and in winter plenty of thrills for ski enthusiasts.

At the top of the climb out of the valley, Val d'Arly, the Notre-Dame de Bellecombe road gives good views, first of the whole Aravis massif, then of the wooded gorges cut by the Arly.

Col des Saisies

18km/11mi SE of La Clusaz.

At this point the route leaves the Sub-Alpine Furrow (*Sillon alpin*); from here as far as St-Martin-d'Entraunes to the south of the Cayolle Pass (*Col de Cayolle*), its course lies entirely within the High Alps (*Grandes Alpes*).

The broad depression of the **Saisies Pass**, 1 633m high, is one of the most characteristic Alpine grazing grounds to be seen along the route; it is browsed by sturdy little reddish-brown cattle as well as by the dark-brown Tarines breed and the white-spotted Abondances. The landscape is studded with innumerable chalets.

Beaufort

18km/11mi SE of Col des Saisies.

This little crossroads town (its church has fine woodcarvings and interesting sculptures) has given its name to the **Beaufortain★★** country, an area of folded limestone beds on a base of ancient crystalline rocks. Virtually continuous forest cover forms a background to sweeping alpine past-ures. Above the 1 450m contour, the pastoral economy is marked by the seasonal movement of the herds up and down the slopes. The village of **Boudin★** (*7km/4.3mi S*) is particularly picturesque.

Cormet de Roselend★

20km/12.4mi SE of Beaufort.

This long valley, 1 900m high, links the Roselend and Chapieux valleys. It is a vast, treeless, lonely place, dotted with rocks and shepherds' huts.

A rushing mountain stream descends the steep valley, **vallée des Chapieux★**, in a series of abrupt steps towards **Bourg-St-Maurice**. This strategically sited town commands the routes coming down from the Beaufortain country and the Little St Bernard (Petit-St-Bernard) and Iseran passes. Around it is the **Tarentaise★★** country of the upper Isère valley where transhumance is still practised. By the time the route reaches Ste-Foy in the upper Tarentaise, the landscape has become more mountainous in character. The Tignes Valley (Val de Tignes) is characterised by gorges and glacial bars; the avalanche protection works are impressive, as is the **Tignes Dam★★**, a major engineering feat of the 1950s.

Val d'Isère★★★

50km/31mi SE of Cormet de Roselend

In its high valley, 1 000m above Bourg-St-Maurice, this is the most important town in the upper Tarentaise. With an excellent sunshine record, the resort is surrounded by splendid mountain landscapes; to the south and west are the glaciers and peaks (several rising to more than 3 500m) of the Vanoise National Park, much favoured by walkers. As the road climbs amid the crystalline massifs, it gives views of the imposing peaks of the Gran Paradiso in Italy to the left and of the Vanoise massif (Grande Motte peak) to the right.

Col d'Iseran★

16km/10mi SE of Val d'Isère. 2 770m.

The road across this high pass is the only link between the Tarentaise and the **Maurienne** country to the south which centres on the long valley of the River Arc. Industry is more important here than agriculture. The location of settlements has been determined by the sharp breaks in slope marked by glacial bars.

Modane

55.5km/34.5mi SW of Col d'Iseran.

This is a border town at the French end of rail and road tunnels into Italy. At Valloire, the route once more enters the ancient Hercynian mountains and begins to climb to the Galibier Pass.

Col du Galibier★★★

52km/32.3mi SW of Modane. 2 642m.

From the viewing table there is a superb panorama which takes in the Maurienne country (to the north), and the Pelvoux region (to the south), which is separated from the Briançonnais country by the high ridge of the Massif des Écrins. The pass marks the dividing line between the northern and southern part of the French Alps.

At the pass, **Col du Lautaret★★**, with its fine views of the Meije mountains, turn right in the direction of La Grave in the Romanche Valley, then turn left at the entrance to the second tunnel.

Oratoire du Chazelet★★★

23km/14.3mi W of Col du Galibier.

From the viewing table, the view extends over the high peaks of the Écrins National Park from the Col des Ruillans on the right to the broken ridges of the Meije (including le Doigt

Val-d'Isère

de Dieu). The upper course of the glacier, fed by frequent snowfall, is of a staggering whiteness.

La Grave★

5km/3mi E of Oratoire du Chazelet.

The village has a particularly fine **site★★** in the Romanche valley at the foot of the Meije. A two-stage cable-car ride takes the visitor to the col on the western flank of Mont du Râteau, from where there are unforgettable views over the Meije and the Écrins glaciers.

Back at the Col du Lauteret, the route now enters the southern part of the French Alps. At Monêtier in the Guisanne valley, it re-enters the sedimentary zone of the High Alps; oak, beech and ash reappear, the valleys open out and the whole landscape takes on a lighter air.

Briançon★★

38km/23.6mi SE of La Grave.

See BRIANÇON, p422.

Col d'Izoard★★

14km/8.7mi SE of Briançon. 2 361m.

The pass is in a desolate setting fringed by dramatic peaks. From the viewing tables magnificent views extend over the Briançonnais to the north and the Queyras country to the south.

The road descends in a series of hairpin bends through a strange landscape of screes and jagged rocks known as the **Casse Déserte★★**. At this high altitude, the processes of erosion are greatly accelerated by the extremes of temperature to which the rocks are exposed.

The high **Queyras★★** country is centred on the valley of the River Guil.

Closed off downstream from the outside world by a series of narrow gorges, and cut off from main communication routes, it has fine examples of Alpine houses. Above Château-Queyras, the valley sides are sharply differentiated; the gentler south-facing slopes are covered with well-watered meadows, while the north-facing slopes grow only larches and Arolla pines.

Saint-Véran★★

34km/21mi SE of Col d'Izoard.

Lying between the 1 990m contour and the 2 040m contour, this is the highest village in France and the third highest in Europe. Its chalets, timber-built on a basement of schist, are a unique example of adaptation to the rigours of a high-altitude mountain life which combines arable cultivation and grazing, forestry, and the exercise of craft skills during the long winters. The south-facing dwellings are sited in groups, most with hay-barns and balconies on which cereals are ripened.

The little town of **Guillestre**, with its church characterised by a beautiful **porch★**, is situated at the end of the **Combe du Queyras★★**, a canyon carved out by the clear waters of the Guil.

Saint-Véran

Embrun★

51km/31.6mi SE of Saint-Véran.

High up on its terrace overlooking the River Durance as it emerges from the mountains, the little town was once the seat of an archbishop. From the Place de l'Archevêché there are fine views over the valley slopes with their well-cultivated terraced fields. The torrents entering the main valley have spread their debris over its floor in alluvial fans. The upper slopes are gouged by deep ravines, while dominating the scene are sombre high mountain crests.

The former **Notre-Dame Cathedral**, the finest church in the whole of the Dauphiné Alps, dates from the 12C. It has fine black-and-white marble stonework, and the **north porch★** is supported on pretty pink columns.

Col de Vars

38.5km/24mi E. 2 111m.

This pass forms the gateway to the Ubaye valley. The valley floor, littered with boulders and studded with ponds, is grazed by sheep.

Beyond the pass, the south-facing slopes with their scattered hamlets are given over to stock-farming. In its upper reaches, the River Ubaye has cut deeply into the dark schists. Near La Condamine, the 19C **Fort Tournoux** seems part of the high rock on which it is built. After Jausiers, the route enters the Barcelonnette basin; the valley pastures are interspersed with woodland and the scene becomes more cheerful.

Barcelonnette★

31km/19mi SW of Col de Vars.

The little capital of the Ubaye district was laid out as a bastide on a regular plan in 1231 by Raimond Béranger, Count of Barcelona. It belonged to the House of Savoy until passing to France under the provisions of the Treaty of Utrecht in 1713.

On the edge of town are the houses of the "Barcelonnettes" or "Mexicans", locals who made their fortunes in the textile trade in Mexico before returning home. A museum, **Musée de la Vallée**, traces the history of the migrations. The road climbs around the flank of Mont Pelat, the highest (3 035m) peak in the Provence Alps.

Col de la Cayolle★★

30km/18.6mi SE of Barcelonnette.

2 327m.

This pass links the Ubaye country and the Upper Verdon to the upper reaches of the Var. From the top there are views over the deep valley of the Var towards the Grasse Pre-Alps in the far distance.

THE UPPER VALLEY OF THE RIVER VAR★★

See region maps for French Alps, p398 and French Riviera p637.

The source of the Var is on the left as the road drops away from the pass to follow the river through the sombre mountains.

At **St-Martin-d'Entraunes** the route passes from the High Alps into the sedimentary zone, the Pre-Alps of **Provence**. Downstream from **Villeneuve d'Entraunes** water coursing through drainage channels draws attention to the changes that take place in the landscape of the countryside around **Guillaumes**.

Gorges de Daluis★★

3.5km/2mi S of Guillaumes.

These deep gorges have been cut by the river into thick beds of red porphyry and Urgonian limestone, giving striking colour effects. The road from **Guillaumes** to **Beuil** leads to the **Gorges du Cians** in the upper stretch of the River Var.

The road climbs steadily to the **Col de Valberg**, offering views of the different sides of the valley: woody to the north, compared to the southern one covered with vineyards and fruit trees. The descent towards **Roubion** from **Col de Couilloie** (1 678m) reveals the valleys of **La Vionèse** and **La Tinée**.

After the impressive **site★★** of **Roubion** (the village is perched 1 300m up on a ridge), the road travels through a red schistose landscape, enlivened by several waterfalls.

Roure★

12.4km/7.7mi E of Roubion.

This village is characterised by its architectural unity: houses with red schist walls and limestone tile roofs *(lauze)*. The route then follows the River Vionèse until it flows into the River Tinée at **St-Sauveur-sur-Tinée**. Outside the village, on the left, a small road leads to the striking **site★** of **Ramplas** village.

La Bolline

22km/13.7mi SE of Roure.

This pleasant summer resort is situated in the middle of a chestnut grove.

La Colmiane

8km/5mi E of La Bolline.

The chalets and hotels of this winter sports resort are set amidst a wonderful larch forest. From the **Col de St-Martin**, there is a possibility of taking a chairlift up to the **Pic de Colmiane★★** (beautiful **panorama★★** from the top).

St-Martin-Vésubie★

8.4km/5.2mi E of La Colmiane.

A Baroque church and channelled stream flowing down the Rue du Docteur-Cagnoli characterise this famous mountaineering centre from which visitors can go rambling in the **vallon du Boréon★★** or the **vallon de la Madone de Fenestre★**.

La Bollène-Vésubie

16km/10mi SE of St-Martin-Vésubie.

The concentric streets of this peaceful village, in the middle of a beautiful chestnut grove, converge on the church, which crowns the hill. The forest, **Fôret de Turini★★**, which spreads across the valleys of the Vésubie and the Bévéra, demarcates the southern border of the Parc national du Mercantour.

Le Massif de l'Authion★★

32.5km/20.2mi SE of La Bollène.

North of the **Col de Turini**, this massif constitutes a wonderful natural fortress which seems to stand guard over the roads between the Vésubie and Roya valleys. This strategic value has caused it to be, throughout the centuries, the stage for several conflicts. In April 1945, it was the last sector of France to be liberated. A stele commemorates the fierceness of the combat.

After crossing the forest of Turini, the river Bévéra winds its way towards the **Gorges du Piaon★★** where the corniche road overlooks the river. Before reaching the gorges, the road goes through **Moulinet**, a charming village set in a verdant valley before passing the **Chapelle de Notre-Dame-La-Menour** with its Renaissance façade on the left.

Sospel★

28.6km/17.7mi SE of Le Massif.

This Alpine resort was a bishopric during the Great Schism and a stop on the Salt Road linking Turin with the coast. Old houses line both banks of the Bévéra which is traversed by an ancient fortified bridge.

On the Nice road, 1km/0.6mi from the centre of the village stands the **Fort St-Roch**, one of the last elements of the "Alpine Maginot line" built in the 1930s. The road follows the old railway line which used to link Sospel to Menton, along the course of the Merlanson, a tributary of the Bévéra. On the opposite side of the valley, the road to Nice via the **Col de Braus** winds its way, amidst olive groves, towards the capital of the French Riviera.

Menton★★

21km/13mi SE of Sospel. See p652.

ADDRESSES

STAY

Good to know – It may not be as fashionable as Courchevel, but it remains hard to find inexpensive lodgings in **Val d'Isère**. The central reservation office gives details of self-catering options, while the tourist office caters for B&Bs and campsites.

Hôtel Le Kern – La Grange. 04 79 06 06 06. http://le-kern.valdisere.com. Closed May–Nov. 18 rooms. Comfort of an old beamed house, with polished wood and antiques.

Courchevel★★

Courchevel is undoubtedly one of the major and most prestigious winter sports resorts in the world. Founded in 1946 by the Conseil général de la Savoie (regional council), it played a leading role in the development of the Trois Vallées❄❄❄ complex. Émile Allais, who was the downhill world champion in 1937, was the first to introduce to French resorts the idea of grooming ski runs. Après-ski activities are just as exciting: art exhibitions, classical and jazz concerts, an impressive number of luxury shops, sports centres, fitness clubs and famous nightclubs. However, Courchevel also owes its reputation to the quality of its hotels and gastronomic restaurants, unrivalled in mountain areas. Even in summer, when Courchevel changes radically and becomes a peaceful resort, this diversity sets it apart.

- **Population:** 1 967.
- **Michelin Map:** 333 M5
- **Info:** Le Coeur de Courchevel. BP 37, 73122 Courchevel. ℘04 79 08 00 29. www.courchevel.com.
- **Location:** The drive is 50km/31.25mi from Albertville to Courchevel, partly on D 91 with its spectacular panoramic views.
- **Don't Miss:** The cable-car trip up the Saulire is a high point of any visit; a guided tour in the mountains: ℘04 79 01 03 66.
- **Timing:** The "Forfait de Loisir" gives access to many activities. See the *Michelin Green Guide French Alps* for suggestions on where to stay and eat.

THE RESORTS

The Trois Vallées, comprising Courchevel, Méribel, Les Menuires, Val Thorens and several smaller resorts, is the largest linked ski resort in the world, having 200 lifts on a single pass and 600km/375mi of ski runs.

At Courchevel, snow cover is guaranteed from early December to May, owing to the north-facing aspect of the slopes and an impressive array of more than 500 snow cannons. There are excellent runs for beginners along the lower sections of the Courchevel 1850 ski lifts (Verdon, Jardin Alpin). Advanced skiers prefer the great Saulire corridor and the Courchevel 1350 area. Cross-country skiers can explore the network of 130km/81.25mi of trails linked across the Trois Vallées area.

The Courchevel area includes four resorts on the slopes of the Vallée de St-Bon, among pastures and wooded areas, in a vast open landscape framed by impressive mountains.

Le Praz 1300

Ski jumps used during the 1992 Olympic Games are close to the old village.

A picturesque 7km/4.3mi-long forest road leads to the resort of **La Tania**.

Courchevel 1550

Family resort situated on a promontory near woodlands.

Moriond-Courchevel 1650

Sunny resort where urban architecture contrasts with traditional chalets.

Courchevel 1850

Courchevel 1850 is the main resort of the complex as well as the liveliest and most popular. There is an impressive **panorama★** of Mont Jovet, the Sommet de Bellecôte and the Grand Bec peaks.

EXCURSIONS

LA SAULIRE★★★

Access from Courchevel 1850 by the Verdon gondola and the Saulire cable car. The well-equipped summit links the Courchevel and Méribel valleys and is the starting point of a dozen famous runs. Non-skiers can take a gondola to Méribel or Mottaret and a cable car to Courchevel.

From the top platform, the view embraces the Aiguille du Fruit in the foreground, the Vanoise Massif and glaciers further away, the Péclet-Polset Massif to the south, the Sommet de Bellecôte and Mont Pourri to the north with Mont Blanc on the horizon.

Sommet de la Saulire

Alt 2 738m. *1hr return on foot.*

This excursion is recommended in summer to tourists at ease in mountain conditions. The summit can be reached from the cable-car station, along a wide path and a steep lane on the right.

MASSIF DE LA VANOISE★★★

Numerous Neolithic monuments, cairns and stone roads high on the mountains show that this magnificent landscape has been a centre of human activity for many tens of thousands of years.

This famous massif lies between the valleys of the Arc and the Isère. It was proclaimed a national park in 1963.

La Vanoise Massif, which is dotted with charming villages and lovely forests, remains nonetheless a high mountain area with over 100 summits in excess of 3 000m.

The massif is noted for its diverse fauna (marmot, ibex, chamois) and flora (around 2 000 species).

MORE EXCURSIONS

Val-d'Isère★★★ – a prestigious winter sports resort with impressive views.

Rocher de Bellevarde★★★ – Access by cable railway. Views of the Tarentaise and Mont Blanc.

Refuge de Prariond★★ – 2hr round-trip on foot. A pleasant walk with varied landscapes (gorges, rock faces).

Réserve naturelle de la Grande Sassière★★ – A backdrop of lakes and glaciers frames Tignes Dam. The park boasts a wealth of animal and plant species which may be easily observed. From the Saut car park, walks to **Lac de la Sassière★★** (1hr on foot) and the **Glacier de Rhême-Golette★★** *(2hr30min)*, at an altitude of 3 000m.

Tignes★★★ – Alt. 2 100m. Resort around a lake in a **site★★** dominated by the breath-taking view of the Grande Motte Glacier (3 656m). Seasoned ramblers may want to tackle **Col du Palet★★**, **Pointe du Chardonnet★★★** (very steep slope) or the **Col de la Croix des Frêtes★★**, the **Lac du Grattaleu★**, **Col de Tourne★**.

Peisey-Nancroix★ – This village, nestling in the lush **Vallée de Ponturin★**, opens onto the park and is linked to the skiing area of Les Arcs.

Lac de la Plagne★★ – 4hr round-trip on foot. A route in a delightful, flowery setting, at the foot of the Bellecôte summit, 3 417m) and Mont Pourri (3 779m).

Pralognan★ – Alt. 1 410m. One of the main stopping places for ramblers in La Vanoise Massif.

Col de la Vanoise★★ – 4hr round-trip. Alt. 2 517m. Views of the Grande Casse (3 855m).

Col d'Aussois★★★ – Alt. 2 916m. Ascent 5hr. Sweeping panorama. These two passes may also be reached from Termignon and Aussois en Maurienne.

Réserve naturelle de Tuéda★ – Beautiful pine forest by Tuéda Lake.

Cime de Caron★★★ – round-trip by cable car and cable railway. Alt. 3 198m. Panorama of the Écrins, Tarentaise and Mont Blanc.

ADDRESSES

STAY

Good to know – In this ultra-fashionable resort, the tourist office can help you find lodgings that provide a compromise between value and comfort.

Les Peupliers – 73120 Le Praz. 04 79 08 41 47. www.lespeupliers.com. Closed May–Jun and Sep–Oct Sat–Sun. WiFi. 35 rooms. This family hotel close to a little lake gives a warm welcome with wood-panelled rooms.

Grenoble★★

Capital of the French Alps, Grenoble is a flourishing modern city of broad boulevards at the confluence of the Drac and Isère rivers.

- **Population:** 155 637.
- **Michelin Map:** 336 H 6 -7
- **Info:** 14 r. de la République. ✆04 76 42 41 41. www.grenoble-tourisme.com.
- **Location:** Grenoble lies 104km/65mi SE of Lyon.
- **TGV:** From Paris Gare de Lyon, 3hr direct, or 3hrs 45mins via Lyon.
- **Flights:** Grenoble Isère airport (www.grenoble-airport.com): Grenoble Altitude operates coach transfers to the city centre.
- **Don't Miss:** A walk along the heights of the Bastille is a highlight of any trip.
- **Kids:** The beach at La Bifurk.
- **Timing:** This is not a place to rush around; allow at least one full day, preferably more.

A BIT OF HISTORY

The vast quantities of material brought down by the restless River Drac ("that most brutal, most violent of Alpine tributaries": R Blanchard) formed an alluvial fan on which by the late 3C a fortified Roman town was sited.

Development of the town was held back by the precarious nature of its communication links; though Grenoble was well sited on the roads leading from the Rhône valley to Turin and Cannes, frequent floods and challenging gradients made travelling an uncertain business.

In the reign of Henri IV the city was captured by Lesdiguières, commander of the armies of Piedmont and Savoy, who re-fortified it. Later fortifications doubled the area of the city to the south.

SIGHTS

Fort de la Bastille

Access by cable car. Allow 1hr.

The fort was built in the 16C to protect the approaches to the city, and strengthened in the 19C. It has the best **view★★★** over the town in its magnificent setting.

Vieille Ville (Old Town)★

The Roman town lay close to the present-day Place Granette (celebrated by Stendhal) and on either side of the Grande-Rue, itself a Roman road.

By the 13C the town had spread northeastwards as far as the Isère, where today a number of courtyards and porches dating from the 16C can be found (No 8 Rue Brocherie, Nos 8 and 10 Rue Chenoise).

Musée de Grenoble★★★

Open Wed–Mon 10am–6.30pm. Closed public holidays. €8 (no charge 1st Sun of the month). ✆04 76 63 44 44. www.museedegrenoble.fr.

On the bank of the Isère in the heart of the old town, this Fine Arts museum has a remarkably plain and sober appearance. Huge windows look out on massive sculptures which enhance the parvis and the Parc Michallon, outside the north building.

This is one of France's most important provincial museums, with painting from the 16C to the 20C, including an exceptionally rich collection of modern art. The collections include fine modern works like Matisse's *Interior with Aubergines* and Picasso's *Woman Reading* as well as Old Masters like de Champaigne's *John the Baptist*, Rubens' *Pope Gregory surrounded by Saints* or de La Tour's *St Jerome*. Most art movements after 1945 are represented: Abstraction lyrique, New Realism, "Supports-surfaces", Pop Art and Minimalism.

ADDITIONAL SIGHTS

Musée archéologique, église St-Laurent★★

Open: daily except Tue, 10am–6pm. No charge. ✆04 76 44 78 68.

Rare in Europe, this archaeological museum is housed in a disused church ranked among the top historic monuments of France. The Merovingian **crypt** is unique and splendid testimony to the art and architecture of the Middle Ages.

Musée de la Résistance et de la Déportation★

14 r. Hébert. Open daily: 9am–6pm (Tue, 1.30–6pm; Sat–Sun, 10am–6pm). No charge. ✆04 76 42 38 53. www.resistance-en-isere.fr.

The Museum of the Resistance and Deportation is intended as a museum of history. The Grenoble Resistance movement and the story of deportation are covered, from aspects of the local history to the men who were involved and the events that took place.

Note the three doors on the first floor that are the remains of the Gestapo dungeons, covered with Resistance graffiti. A large relief map illustrates the activities of the Resistance forces and the events that hallmarked this troublesome time.

Musée dauphinois★

30 r. Maurice Gignoux. ♿Open daily except Tue: Sep–May 10am–6pm; Jun–Aug 10am–7pm. Closed 1 Jan, 1 May, 25 Dec. No charge. ✆04 57 58 89 01. www.musee-dauphinois.fr.

This interesting regional museum is located in a 17C **convent of the Visitation of Ste-Marie-d'En-Haut** clinging to the side of a hill in a superb setting. The main galleries are devoted to the Dauphinois heritage, and display a fine collection of domestic furniture and traditional tools, symbolic of rural life in the Alps.

The history of skiing is also illustrated in a comprehensive account of the impact of this winter sport on daily life in the mountains. The wealth and quality of the themed exhibitions make this museum of particular importance in the history of the region. A visit to the museum also enables you to discover a part of the original convent, the **chapel★★**, a real gem of Baroque art completed in 1662 for the beatification of St Francis de Sales.

EXCURSIONS

L'OISANS★★★

The region is largely within the Parc National des Écrins, between the rivers Romanche and Drac.

L'Oisans is the second-highest massif in France, after Mont Blanc. Its population is grouped in villages sited on high terraces reached by spectacular narrow roads.

LES ÉCRINS

These bare mountains between the valleys of the Romanche, Drac and Durance look down on more than 100sq km/38.6sq mi of glaciers.

The Route des Grandes Alpes (*see ROUTE DES GRANDES ALPES, p411*) gives fine views of the north and east faces of the massif (from the Col du Galibier, the Oratoire du Chazelet, and from La Grave), cut by isolated valleys with their typical way of life and served by long cul-de-sac roads; the best known is the valley of the Vénéon leading to La Bérarde.

BASSIN DU BOURG D'OISANS★

Until the 13C the fertile basin was a glacial lake, now filled in by material brought down by the Romanche and its tributary, the Vénéon. This is the economic centre of the region.

VALLÉE DU VÉNÉON★★★

31km/19mi from Bourg-d'Oisans to La Bérarde.

The road up to **La Bérarde** is a lesson in glacial geomorphology made more dramatic by the scale of the great U-shaped valley and the ruggedness of its high granite walls, moraines, waterfalls in hanging valleys, and compact little villages, before reaching La Bérarde, now a climbing centre.

MASSIF DU VERCORS★★★

The area is to the W and SW of Grenoble.

La-Chapelle-en-Vercors. 04 75 48 22 54. www.vercors-drome.com.

Rising above Grenoble like a fortress, the massive limestone plateau of the Vercors forms the largest regional park in the northern Alps.

The Vercors is the most extensive of the Pre-Alpine massifs. Protected by sheer cliffs, it is a natural citadel, inside which grow fine forests of beech and conifers interspersed with lush pasturelands. In places, the immensely thick limestone has been cut into by the rivers to form deep and spectacular gorges.

In 1944, the Resistance in these mountains numbered several thousand.

In June of that year, the Wehrmacht stepped up its assault on the Resistance, and brought in parachute troops on 21 July. With many of their number lost, the surviving members of the Resistance were given the order to disperse on 23 July. 700 of the inhabitants and defenders of the Vercors had died; several of its villages lay in ruins.

North of the rebuilt village of **Vassieux-en-Vercors** is a National Cemetery with the graves of some of those who died during that terrible summer, and at the Col de Lachan stands a monument to the fallen (Mémorial du Vercors).

The **Vercors Regional Natural Park★★★** (04 76 94 38 26. www.parc-du-vercors.fr) is France's largest natural reserve; there are no roads, no villages, only shepherds and forestry workers, along with 65 species of mammals, 135 species of birds and 17 species of reptiles. The flora is extremly diverse with 1 800 species, of which 80 are protected. There are 60 species of orchids alone.

GORGES DE LA BOURNE★★★

18.7km/11.6mi N of Vassieux-en-Vercors.

The unusually regular walls of the gorge open out downstream. Its entrance is marked by the old cloth town of **Pont-en-Royans** with its houses clinging picturesquely to the rock face.

COMBE LAVAL★★★

24.6km/15.3mi SW of Gorges de la Bourne.

One of the finest sights in the Vercors. The road clings dizzily to a vast limestone wall rising 600m above the upper valley of the Cholet.

GRANDS GOULETS★★★

17.7km/11mi SE of Combe Laval.

An epic piece of construction dating from 1851, the narrow road was hewn directly from the rock. From its upper section it is possible to see the river beginning the process of eroding an as yet intact geological formation. The village of **Les Barraques-en-Vercors** was destroyed by enemy action in 1944.

COL DE ROUSSET★★

22.6km/14mi S of Grands Goulets.

Go to the southern entrance to the disused tunnel.

The pass marks the climatic as well as the morphological boundary between the northern and southern Alps.

There are spectacular views, not only of the road twisting its way downwards, but also of the great limestone walls protecting the Vercors, of the Die valley 960m below, and of a succession of bare ridges extending into the far distance.

ADDRESSES

STAY

Hôtel Acacia – 13 r. de Belgrade. 04 76 87 29 90. P. 20 rooms. This hotel is located close to the cable car of la Bastille. The guest rooms are modern; the reception area and breakfast room are decorated in Provençal colours.

Chambre d'hôte Le Manoir du Berlioz – 636 chemin du Berlioz, 38190 Villard-Bonnot. 5km/3mi from Grenoble towards Villard-Bonnot. 04 76 71 40 00. http://domaineduberlioz.pagesperso-orange.fr. Closed Nov–Feb. P. WiFi. 3 rooms. Today this 12C residence is an equestrian centre and includes two spacious rooms and one suite, with fine furniture. They look out to the vegetable garden or the horses.

Briançon★★

The highest town in Europe (1 321m), Briançon is best viewed from the terraces of the UNESCO site, La Fort de Salettes, where stands the 9m-high statue of France★ sculpted by Antoine Bourdelle.

- **Population:** 11 627.
- **Michelin Map:** 334 H 3
- **Info:** 1 pl. du Temple. ☎04 92 21 08 50. www.ot-briancon.fr.
- **Location:** Briançon lies 118km/73.3mi SE of Grenoble. After arriving at the town, follow signs to "Briançon Vauban" to find the Old Town.

A BIT OF HISTORY

Since ancient times, two great routes into Italy have met here, one coming from the Romanche valley via the Col de Lautaret, the other following the Durance up from Embrun.

The strategic value of the site was appreciated by the Gauls. It seems likely that the survivors of the Germanic tribes routed by the Roman general Marius outside Aix-en-Provence found their way here, and Briançon may have provided a refuge too for some of the persecuted members of the Vaudois, a 15C sect. The town played an important commercial and military role, the latter enhanced by the presence of great rock bars lending themselves naturally to fortification.

SIGHT

Ville Haute (Upper Town) ★★

In January 1692, the War of the League of Augsburg had been raging for six years; mercenaries in the pay of Vittorio-Amadeo II, Duke of Savoy, invaded the Dauphiné and torched Briançon – only two houses out of 258 escaped the fire. Vauban was working in Burgundy, but was immediately dispatched by Louis XIV to Briançon with a brief to rebuild the town and make it impregnable.

A week sufficed for the great engineer to draw up his plans, but age and ill health made it impossible for him to supervise their execution.

With its gate (Porte Pignerol) and its fortified church, Briançon-Vauban, in contrast to the lower town Briançon-Ste-Catherine, still has the look of a frontier town of Louis XIV's reign, while its narrow, steeply sloping streets, especially the **Grande Gargouille★** (also known as the Grande Rue), express the drama of its precipitous site. East of town, the **Pont d'Asfeld★** (bridge) was built in 1734 and is also part of the town's collection of UNESCO sites.

Collégiale Notre-Dame, Briançon

Grand Canyon du Verdon★★★

The modest-looking River Verdon has cut Europe's most spectacular canyon through a remote, wild landscape.

- **Michelin Map:** 334 E-F 10.
- **Info:** Maison des Gorges du Verdon, La Palusur-Verdon. 04 92 77 32 02. www.lapaludsurverdon.com.
- **Location:** The gorge is best reached from Castellane on the east side or Moustiers-Ste-Marie on the west. On the north side, the canyon can be followed on D 952 and D 23, while the spectacular D 71 (the Corniche Sublime) runs along the south side.
- **Timing:** The road on either side is slow and tiring, so allow a full day.

GEOGRAPHY

The canyon extends 26km/16mi from the meeting point of the Verdon with the Jabron in the east to where it flows into Ste-Croix Lake in the west at the Galetas bridge. The height of the canyon's walls emphasise the sheer scale of the Jurassic sedimentation.

VISIT

La Corniche Sublime★★★

South bank scenic route.

The steep and twisting (20km/12.4mi) road was engineered so as to open up the most spectacular views. They include: the **Balcons de la Mescla★★★** overlooking the swirling waters where the Verdon is joined by the Artuby; the bridge, Pont de l'Artubya, linking sheer walls of rock; the Fayet tunnels above the Étroit des Cavaliers (Knights' Narrows), and the **Falaise des Cavaliers★** (Knights' Cliff) 300m high.

La Route des Crêtes★★★

North bank scenic route.

The road (23km/14.3mi long) links a series of viewpoints overlooking the most spectacular section of the canyon. Further eastwards, the viewpoint known as the **Point Sublime★★★** dominates the canyon and the impressive narrows, the **Couloir de Samson★★★**.

Castellane★

This rustic village (04 92 83 61 14; www.castellane.org) is the gateway to the Verdon Gorge, a magnificently set village hemmed in by sheer cliffs.

Moustiers-Ste-Marie★★

The small town is the centre for the Valensole plateau. It has an extraordinary **site★★** at the foot of a cleft in the limestone cliff, across which a knight returning from the Crusades stretched the chain which can still be seen today. The church has a **tower★** with arcading in Lombard style. Faïence was introduced here in 1679; the most sought-after pieces were fired at high temperatures (*see LIMOGES, p491*) and are decorated with charming hunting scenes in blue.

WALKING IN THE GRAND CANYON★★★

1 SENTIER MARTEL★★★

Between the Chalet de la Maline and the Point Sublime, GR 4, known as the Sentier Martel, offers those who do not mind a tiring day's walking in unforgettably close contact with the Grand Canyon.

Chalet de la Maline to the Point Sublime

5hr walk, along a difficult itinerary – headtorch essential. GR 4 is marked in white and red.

From the steps going down to the river, there are fine views of the Pas de l'Estellié.

Ignore the path branching off to the right towards the Estellié Footbridge;

Grand Canyon du Verdon from the Corniche Sublime

it leads to the Restaurant des Cavaliers and the Corniche Sublime.

At the Pré d'Issane (*after 1hr 30min walking*), the path runs close to the river and follows it through the **Étroit des Cavaliers** with sheer cliffs towering 300m above. The gorge widens and the path reaches the **Talus de Guègues**, a scree framed by steep slopes.

Continue upstream past the vast Baumes-aux-Bœufs Cave and take the second path to the right leading to the **Mescla★★★** (*30min return*), where the flow of the Verdon mixes with that of the Artuby. There is a splendid view upstream of the Défilé des Baumes-Frères.

Retrace your steps to the intersection and turn right.

The path winds its way up to the Brèche Imbert *(steps)*: superb view of the Baumes-Frères and the Barre de l'Escalès. The canyon, overlooked by very high cliffs, becomes wider and the walk (*1hr30min*) is a bit monotonous, until the cliffs narrow. The **Chaos de Trescaïre**, on the right, is an extraordinary jumble of fallen rocks. The hilltop village of Rougon can be seen in the distance. Next come two tunnels; inside the second, metal steps lead to the **Baume-aux-Pigeons★**, a vast cave, 30m/98ft high, situated at the foot of a high cliff. From the bottom of the stairs, you can see, on the opposite bank, the huge blocks which fell when the roof caved in. This cave and the collapsed roof indicate that in the past the Verdon flowed partly underground. From the last opening, there is a view of the **Couloir Samson★★**, a very narrow corridor with smooth vertical sides. Beyond the tunnel, the path goes over the footbridge across the Baou and climbs to the parking area. The walk ends at the **Belvédère du Point Sublime★★★**.

Walk to the inn where you can call a taxi. You can join D 952 from the Auberge du Point Sublime by taking short cuts.

If you wish to go to La Palud-sur-Verdon without going past the Point Sublime, take the path on the left just before the footbridge over the Baou; it goes up along the south bank of the stream and joins D 952 4km/2.5mi from La Palud-sur-Verdon.

2 SENTIER DE DÉCOUVERTE DES LÉZARDS

From Point Sublime★★★

This well-marked nature trail starts from the Plateau des Lauves. A small explanatory booklet is available at the Auberge du Point Sublime or at the tourist office in La Palud-sur-Verdon. Another itinerary leads to the Pont de Tusset along GR 49.

3 BELVÉDÈRE DE RANCOUMAS★★

East bank starting from Point Sublime★★★

3hr 30min return. It is possible to start from the Point Sublime car park and to walk south, following GR 49 markings, or to drive towards the Couloir Samson (D 23B) and park the car on the last bend before the straight stretch ending in the car park.

2km/1.2mi before reaching the car park, take GR 49 on the left, marked in white and red; it leads through an oak forest down to the **Pont de Tusset★**, a bridge dating from the early 17C.

The path starts rising through a forest of pines, maples and beeches, then joins a wide track.

Leave the marked path and follow the track on the right; it crosses a stream before reaching the ruins of Encastel. Go up to the edge of the cliff.

The natural Belvédère de Rancoumas offers a striking **panorama★★** of the whole Falaise de l'Escalès with the Sentier Martel running below. The **Mourre de Chanier**, the highest summit of the Verdon region, soars in the distance to the northwest.

Return along the same route.

EXCURSION

SISTERON★★

Sisteron is located on the Route Napoléon between Gap and Digne.

Hôtel de Ville. ℘04 92 61 36 50. www.sisteron.com.

The lofty citadel of Sisteron, sternly guarding a narrow ravine and looking down on the clustered lanes of the 14C town, still makes an impressive spectacle despite the battering it took from Allied bombing raids during 1944.

Sisteron lies on the Route Napoléon and the River Durance and is the main mountain gateway to Provence.

The town is situated between the Laragne valley to the north and the valley of the middle Durance to the south. As well as marking the historic boundary between Dauphiné and Provence, this is also the northern limit of the cultivation of the olive.

Citadel★

Open daily: Apr and Oct 9am–6pm; May 6.30pm; Jun and Sep 7pm; Jul–Aug 7.30pm. €6.50 (children 6–14, €2.80). ℘04 92 61 27 57. www.citadelledesisteron.fr.

There is nothing left of the 11C castle. The keep and the watch-path are late 12C and the mighty walls set around the rock are the work of **Jean Errard**, Henri IV's chief military engineer. New defences, designed by **Vauban**, Louis XIV's military engineer, in 1692, were added to the powerful 16C fortifications. Part of the citadel, including the chapel, was damaged by bombing in 1944 but later tastefully restored.

A marked tour leads up a succession of steps and terraces, offering views of the town and the Durance valley, and on to the watch-path. Walk on below the keep, where Jan Kazimierz, Prince of Poland, was imprisoned in 1639, to reach the terrace and enjoy the bird's-eye **view★** of the lower part of town, the reservoir and the mountains dominating the horizon to the north.

Walk to the north side of the citadel, to the **"Guérite du Diable"** offering an impressive **view★** of the Rocher de la Baume. The steps leading downwards were once part of an underground staircase, built to link the citadel to the Porte de Dauphiné, destroyed in 1944.

Musée Terre et Temps★

6 pl. Gén-de-Gaulle. Open Tue–Sat: Mar–Sep, 9am–noon, 2–6pm; late Sep–Nov 9–10m, 3–6pm. No charge. ℘04 92 61 61 30.

In the Visitandine chapel, this museum, set up by the Réserve Géologique de Haute-Provence, explores the development of the idea of time, from geological time to modern timepieces. A Foucault's pendulum shows the rotation of the Earth.

Auvergne Rhône Valley

» Region map p430–431
Lyon p432
Vienne p452
St-Étienne p456
Le Puy-en-Velay p458
Clermont-Ferrand p464
Les Monts du Cantal p474
Vichy p476
Moulins p480

St-Jean Cathedral and the Lyon skyline

Introduction

The Auvergne forms the core of the Massif Central. It is a volcanic landscape unique in France, with mountains, lakes and rivers in deep gorges where the great variety of relief makes for fine upland walking country, while the towns and villages of sombre granite have their own allure heightened by the presence of some of France's finest Romanesque churches. To the east an escarpment leads down to the sun-drenched Rhône valley with its mighty river charging down to the Mediterranean, which could not be in greater contrast to the verdant, rugged uplands of the Auvergne.

Highlights

1. The view from La Colline de Fourvière **in Lyon** (p438)
2. The huge Statue of the Virgin Mary at **Puy-en-Velay** (p458)
3. Walk up **Puy Mary** (p475)
4. **Viaduc de Garabit** at St-Flour (p475)
5. Le Quartier Thermal at **Vichy** (p476)

Geography

The volcanoes of the Auvergne vary from the classic cones of the Monts Dômes to the rugged shapes of the much-eroded Monts Dore. Mainly agricultural, the grazing grounds of the higher land complement the rich alluvial soils of the lower ground. The volcanic activity has created an array of lakes and other water bodies; at Aydat a lava flow has blocked a valley trapping its waters, while the same effect has been produced at Chambon by a volcano erupting into the valley itself.

Elsewhere the hollows produced by a series of volcanic explosions have filled with water while elsewhere lakes have formed inside a crater. Further east the valley of the Rhône, and its tributary the Saône, seem to divide the ancient uplands to the west from the younger, folded rocks of the Alps to the east. This natural ruggedness has impeded accessibility from the rest of France, and bred generations of people who are proud and austere, whose way of life rests on a vibrant agrarian economy.

Passerelle Saint Vincent over the Saône and Vieux Lyon

History

The Auvergne, was originally the feudal domain of the Counts of Auvergne, was named after the Arveni, a Gallic tribe renowned for its fierce resistance, whose King, Vincingetorix, had the distinction of defeating Julius Caesar. The victory was short-lived, however, and the region was in turn ruled by Romans, Visigoths and Franks before becoming a Duchy and, later, a Province. That historic province is today embraced within the region of Auvergne, with its capital at Clermont-Ferrand.

The Rhône valley, long and wide, has served as a communications corridor of great importance for centuries, linking northwestern Europe to the Mediterranean. For this reason the Romans founded Lyon, and the châteaux perched on spurs high above the river provide further evidence of its importance.

Today, is it very much a crucible of differing cultures, and an area at the leading edge of industrial progress.

Economy – In Auvergne, the economy is based mainly on tourism, *charcuterie* (celebrated in many "La Mangona" village festivals), cheese (Saint Nectaire, Bleu d'Auvergne, Cantal, Salers, Fourme d'Ambert), mineral water, including Volvic, and the Michelin tyre plants around Clermont-Ferrand.

In the Rhône valley the area around the great city of Lyon is marked by centuries of industrial activity. Industry came to the area in the 16C with the introduction of silk production around Lyon. Coalfields later enabled the expansion of industry, but once the seams ran out, energy supply was derived from hydroelectric installations upstream and downstream of Lyon, and, since the 1970s, by nuclear power plants along the Rhône valley.

The taming of the Rhône means 2 000t barges can reach the city. However, the improved waterway carries only a fraction of the total traffic using its corridor; it is supplemented by the A 6 motorway, two national highways, a main-line railway on each bank, and gas and oil pipelines. A series of canals provides a total of 330km/205mi of navigable waterway between Lyon and the sea. Increasingly, the area's economy today is bolstered by tourism, both urban and rural.

The region is dominated and influenced by Lyon, the second-largest city in France, with a lively cultural life, fine architecture and heritage, and with a long-held reputation for good food.

Puy Pariou, the Puy de Dôme in the background

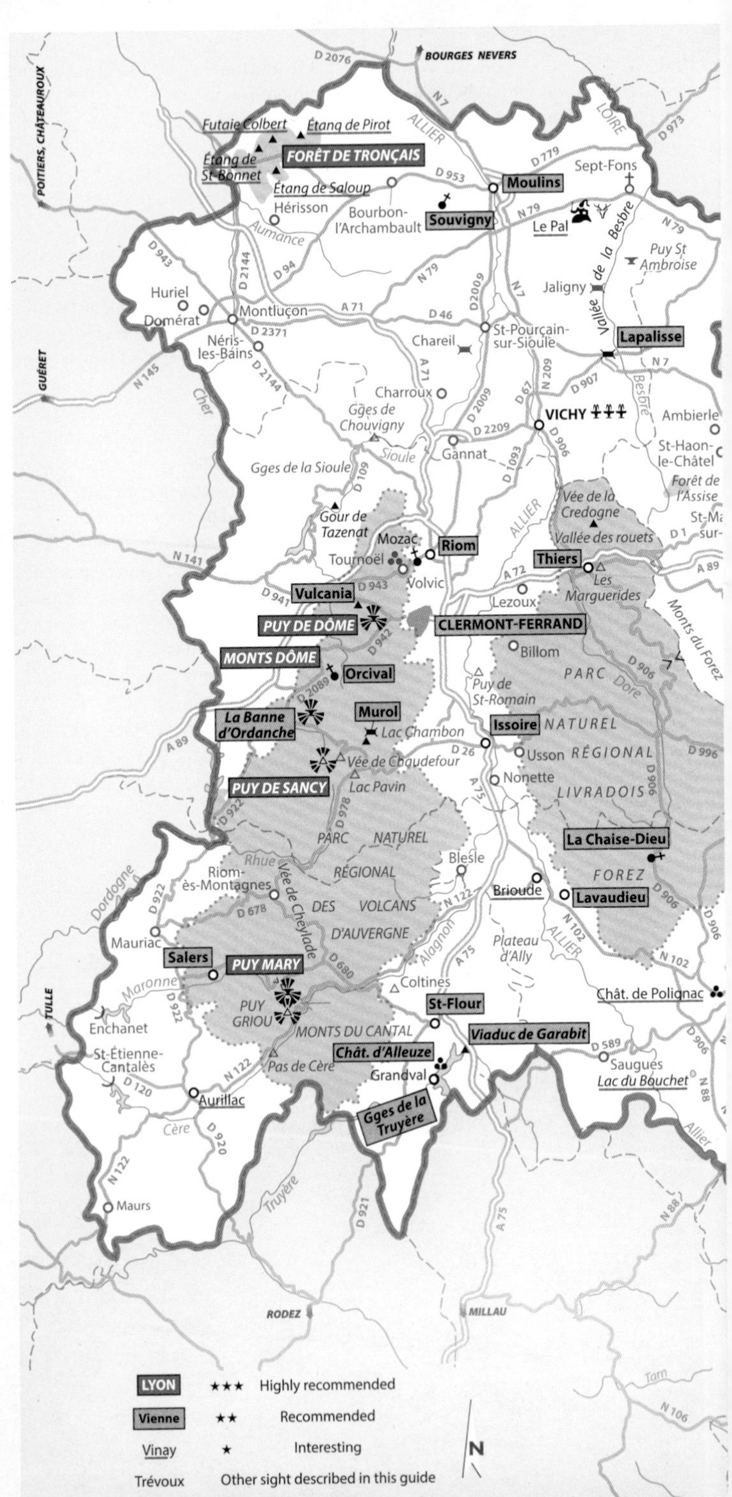
BOURGES NEVERS
POITIERS, CHÂTEAUROUX
Futaie Colbert
Étang de Pirot
Étang de St-Bonnet
FORÊT DE TRONÇAIS
Étang de Saloup
Hérisson
Bourbon-l'Archambault
Moulins
Souvigny
Sept-Fons
Le Pal
Puy St Ambroise
Vallée de la Besbre
Jaligny
Huriel
Domérat
Montluçon
Néris-les-Bains
Chareil
St-Pourçain-sur-Sioule
Lapalisse
GUÉRET
Charroux
Gges de Chouvigny
VICHY
Ambierle
St-Haon-le-Châtel
Forêt de l'Assise
Gannat
Gges de la Sioule
Gour de Tazenat
Mozac
Riom
Tournoël
Volvic
Vée de la Credogne
Vallée des rouets
Thiers
Les Margueride
Lezoux
Vulcania
PUY DE DÔME
CLERMONT-FERRAND
MONTS DÔME
Orcival
Billom
Monts du Forez
Puy de St-Romain
PARC NATUREL RÉGIONAL LIVRADOIS FOREZ
La Banne d'Ordanche
Murol
Lac Chambon
Issoire
Usson
Vée de Chaudefour
Nonette
PUY DE SANCY
Lac Pavin
La Chaise-Dieu
PARC NATUREL RÉGIONAL DES VOLCANS D'AUVERGNE
Blesle
Riom-ès-Montagnes
Vée de Cheylade
Brioude
Lavaudieu
Mauriac
Plateau d'Ally
Salers
PUY MARY
Coltines
Chât. de Polignac
TULLE
PUY GRIOU
St-Flour
Enchanet
MONTS DU CANTAL
Viaduc de Garabit
St-Étienne-Cantalès
Chât. d'Alleuze
Saugues
Pas de Cère
Grandval
Lac du Bouchet
Aurillac
Gges de la Truyère
Maurs
RODEZ
MILLAU
LYON ★★★ Highly recommended
Vienne ★★ Recommended
Vinay ★ Interesting
Trévoux Other sight described in this guide
N

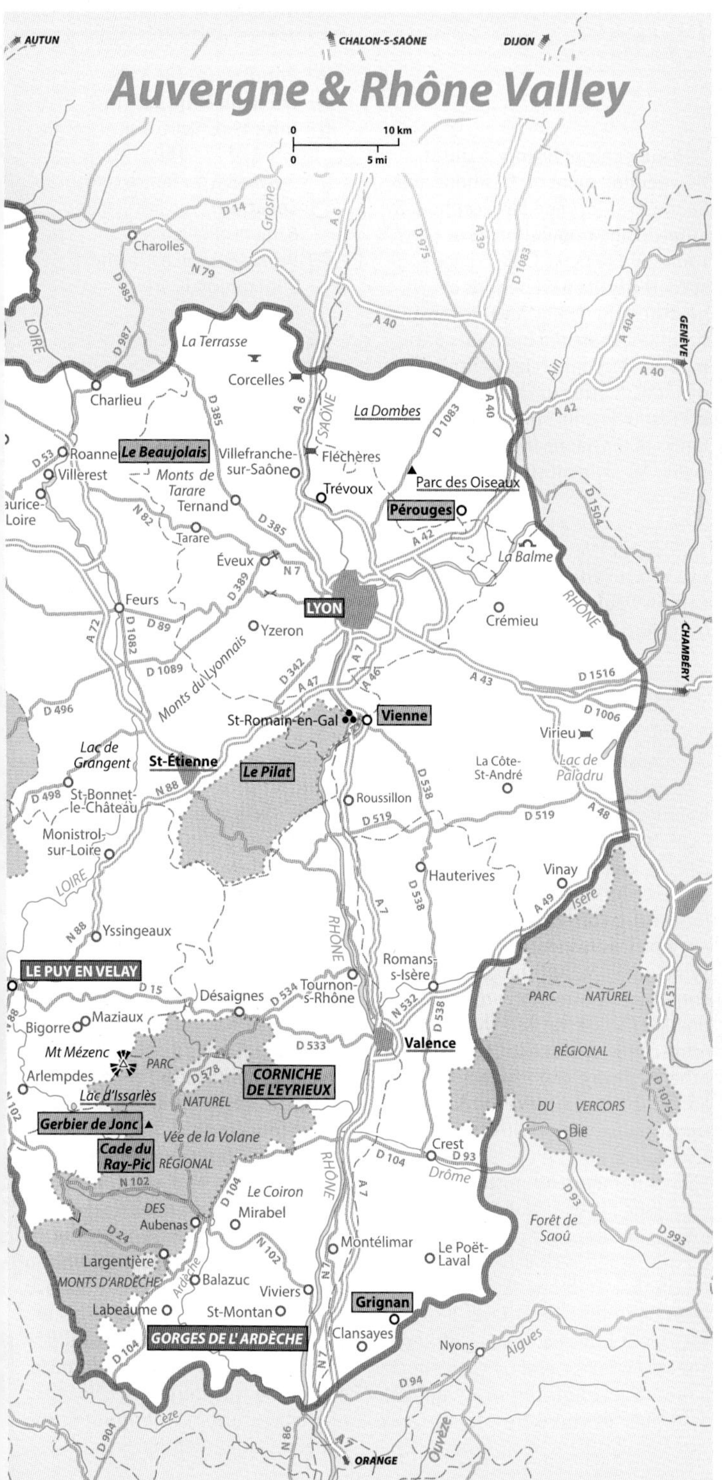
Auvergne & Rhône Valley
AUTUN
CHALON-S-SAÔNE
DIJON
GENÈVE
CHAMBÉRY
ORANGE
Charolles
Charlieu
Roanne
Villerest
Le Beaujolais
Monts de Tarare
Ternand
Tarare
Éveux
Feurs
Yzeron
Monts du Lyonnais
La Terrasse
Corcelles
Villefranche-sur-Saône
Flèchères
Trévoux
La Dombes
Parc des Oiseaux
Pérouges
La Balme
LYON
Crémieu
Vienne
St-Romain-en-Gal
Virieu
La Côte-St-André
Lac de Paladru
Lac de Grangent
St-Étienne
Le Pilat
St-Bonnet-le-Château
Monistrol-sur-Loire
Roussillon
Hauterives
Vinay
Yssingeaux
LE PUY EN VELAY
Romans-s-Isère
Tournon-s-Rhône
Désaignes
Maziaux
Bigorre
Valence
Mt Mézenc
Arlempdes
Lac d'Issarlès
CORNICHE DE L'EYRIEUX
Gerbier de Jonc
Cade du Ray-Pic
Vée de la Volane
PARC NATUREL RÉGIONAL DES MONTS D'ARDÈCHE
PARC NATUREL RÉGIONAL DU VERCORS
Die
Crest
Drôme
Le Coiron
Mirabel
Aubenas
Largentière
Balazuc
Labeaume
St-Montan
Viviers
Montélimar
Le Poët-Laval
Forêt de Saoû
Grignan
Clansayes
Nyons
GORGES DE L'ARDÈCHE
LOIRE
SAÔNE
RHÔNE
Isère
Ain
Ardèche
Cèze
Aigues
Ouvèze
Grosne
A 6
A 7
A 40
A 42
A 43
A 46
A 47
A 48
A 49
A 51
A 72
A 39
N 7
N 79
N 82
N 88
N 86
N 102
N 532
D 14
D 15
D 24
D 53
D 89
D 93
D 94
D 104
D 342
D 385
D 389
D 496
D 498
D 519
D 533
D 534
D 538
D 578
D 904
D 975
D 985
D 987
D 993
D 1006
D 1075
D 1082
D 1083
D 1089
D 1504
D 1516
0 10 km
0 5 mi

Lyon★★★

Rhône

Two millennia of history, a site at the meeting point of the Rhône and Saône corridors and an exceptionally enterprising population have combined to make Lyon France's second city. Its past periods of greatness, in Roman and Renaissance times, are matched by its present industrial, commercial and cultural dynamism. Truly the heart of the city, la Presqu'île offers great views of the quays of the Saône River and Vieux Lyon. Department stores, boutiques, cinemas and bars line rue de la République, well known for its 19C architecture. Stretching from north to south, rue du Président-Herriot and rue Paul-Chenavard are also good for shopping.

- **Population:** 484 344.
- **Michelin Map:** 327 H-I 5
- **Info:** 19 pl. Bellecour. 04 72 77 69 69. www.en.lyon-france.com.
- **Location:** Lyon lies 100km/62mi W of Chambéry.
- **Parking:** Lyon has many underground parking garages.
- **Don't Miss:** The Renaissance old quarter, Vieux Lyon, on the right bank of the Saône.
- **Timing:** You should aim to spend a few days here.

A BIT OF HISTORY

A Celtic, then Gallic, settlement, Lyon was chosen as a base camp by Julius Caesar for his conquest of Gaul. Under Augustus it became the capital of the Roman Empire's "Three Gauls" (Aquitaine, Belgium and the province around Lyon), complementing the older province centred on Narbonne.

Agrippa was responsible for choosing Lyon as the hub of the road system, constructed originally in pursuit of political ends. It was here that the great route coming north from Arles met the other highways from Saintes, Orléans and Rouen, from Geneva and Aosta, and from Chalon with its links to Amiens, Trier and Basle.

The manufacture of pottery became established here as early as the 1C AD, only to move later to La Graufesenque on the Tarn (*see MILLAU, p561*). The Amphitheatre of the Three Gauls on the hill, Colline de la Croix-Rousse, was joined by the Temple of Rome and of Augustus and by the Federal Sanctuary where the noisy annual assembly of the 60 tribes of Gaul was held under Roman supervision.

Christianity reached Lyon via Vienne by the middle of the 2C, brought by soldiers, traders and Greek missionaries. In 177, there were riots on the occasion of the annual assembly, and Saints Pothinus and Blandina, along with 48 others, became the city's first Christian martyrs. Twenty years later, Saint Irenaeus, head of the Church in Lyon, was to meet the same fate. According to St Gregory of Tours, the Gospel was reintroduced to Lyon around 250 by Roman missionaries, and, under Constantine, Christianity is supposed to have flourished here as in the other cities of the Empire.

The era of invention – Lyon played a leading role in science and technology at this time. Among its eminent citizens should be noted the following: **Marie-Joseph Jaquard** who built a power-loom in 1804; **André Ampère,** inventor of the galvanometer, electromagnetism and electrodynamics; **Barthélemy Thimonnier**, who invented the sewing machine in 1829; **Jean-Baptiste Guimet**, who, in 1834, succeeded in making the dye ultramarine; the **Lumière brothers** (Auguste and Louis), the creators of cinematography; **Hector Guimard**, one of the founders of Art Nouveau in architecture, the designer of the entrances to the metro stations of Paris.

GETTING AROUND

Maps – In addition to the maps included in this guide, Michelin town plans 30 and 31 and Michelin map 110 (the surroundings of Lyon) will be useful.

Access – By road via motorways A 6, A 7, A 42 and A 43. The city also boasts a regular 2hr link with Paris by TGV. Perrache and La Part-Dieu stations are close to the town centre by métro. There are flights to and from most major cities via Lyon-St-Exupéry airport, linked to the town centre by a shuttle service.

Parking – There are several underground car parks strategically placed for easy access to the town centre. Some of these are architectural gems, the most spectacular being the Parc Célestins by Buren, whose columns adorn the Jardins du Palais-Royal in central Paris.

Public transport – The underground train/subway (métro) is the most convenient mode of public transport, and is especially well adapted to the needs of tourists. The best-value ticket to buy is the **1-day Ticket-liberté**, for unlimited travel on the Lyon urban transport network (métro, bus, funicular railway, trolley-bus). Details from TCL (Transports en Commun Lyonnais) kiosks and www.tcl.fr.

Cultural Pass: You can buy a 1-, 2- or 3-day **Lyon City Card** which will gain you admission to museums, sights and transport, as well as reductions in theatres, on shopping, etc. Adult prices range between 1 day (€22), 2 days (€32) and 3 days (€42). (discount for online purchase at www.lyoncitycard.com).

TOURING THE TOWN

Planning your visit – If you have only **one day** to spend in Lyon, then you must devote the morning to Old Lyon (on foot), to the Fourvière terrace and the Roman theatres (use the funicular), but you will not have time to visit the museums; the afternoon should be spent touring Presqu'île with its Fabric Museum, and either visiting the Fine Arts Museum or taking an enjoyable walk around the Gros Caillou, on the slopes of the Croix-Rousse.

Two days will enable you to get better acquainted with Fourvière and the various museums and to stroll along the River Saône on the first day. The second day should be devoted to touring Presqu'île and to visiting its museums; you should even have time to take a stroll in the Croix-Rousse district.

Organised tours – **Lyon**, which is listed as a "Town of Art and History" by the French government, offers discovery tours conducted by guide-lecturers approved by the Ministry of Culture and Communication. Information at the tourist office or on www.vpah.culture.fr. The Lyon tourist office offers tours of the city on foot, or by bus, boat, taxi or even helicopter.

Lecture tours are available around Old Lyon, Croix-Rousse and the Tony Garnier district.

Bateaux-mouches river trips – 13 bis quai Rambaud. ✆04 78 42 96 81. www.lyoncityboat.com. These unique boats enable visitors to discover a different face of Lyon, seen from its four river banks: one trip explores the confluence of the Saône and Rhône; the other follows the Saône up to and round the Île-Barbe.

SHOPPING

Markets – The **Marché de la Création, quai Romain-Rolland**, and the **Marché de l'Artisanat, quai Fulchiron**, are held on Sunday mornings. These are no run-of-the-mill craft markets, as the workmanship is outstanding. There are regional products and small taverns at the Halles de Lyon, 102 cours Lafayette. For food, head for the quai Saint-Antoine, where food markets with producers from all over the region set up stall and sell their produce. There is also a Farmers' Market twice a week in the place Carnot, in front of the Gare Perrache.

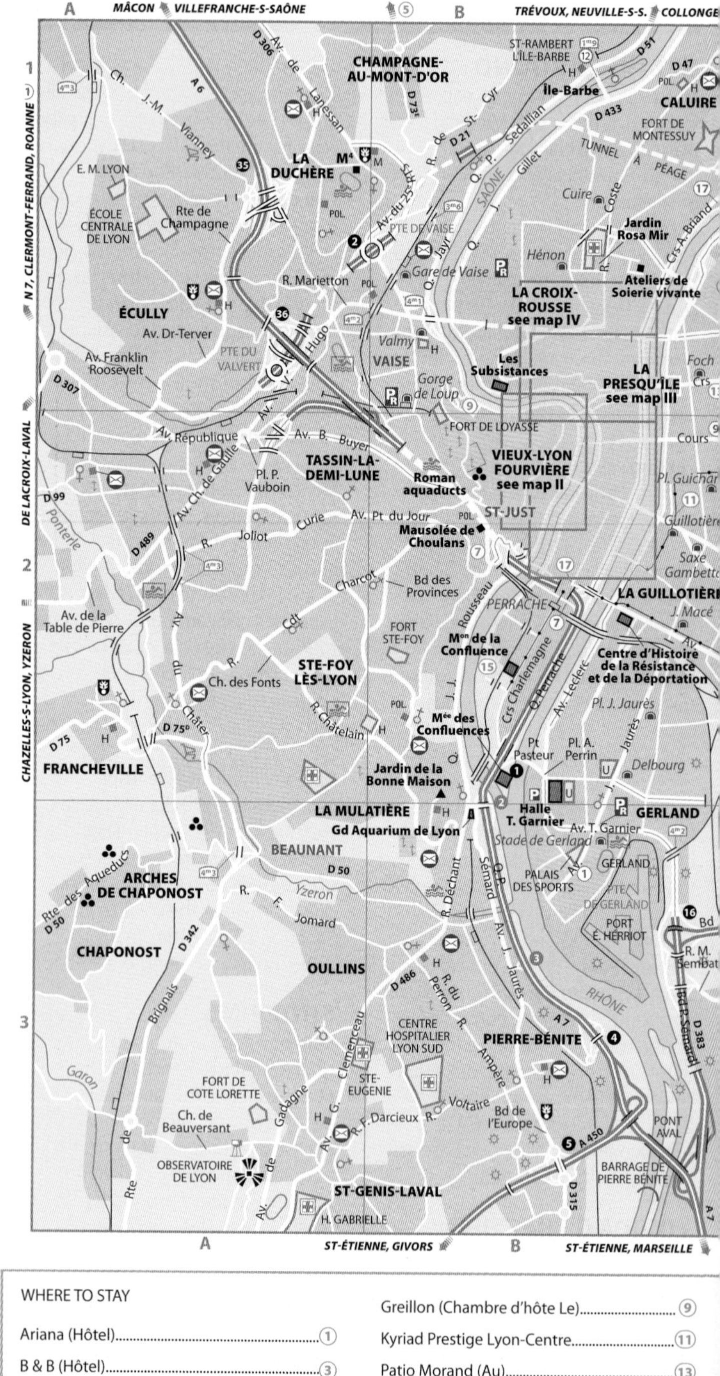

WHERE TO STAY

Ariana (Hôtel)............ ①
B & B (Hôtel)............ ③
Chaumière (Hôtel la)............ ⑤
Grange de Fourvière (Chambre d'hôte La)... ⑦
Greillon (Chambre d'hôte Le)............ ⑨
Kyriad Prestige Lyon-Centre............ ⑪
Patio Morand (Au)............ ⑬
Péniche El Kantara (Chambre d'hôte)............ ⑮
Savoies............ ⑰

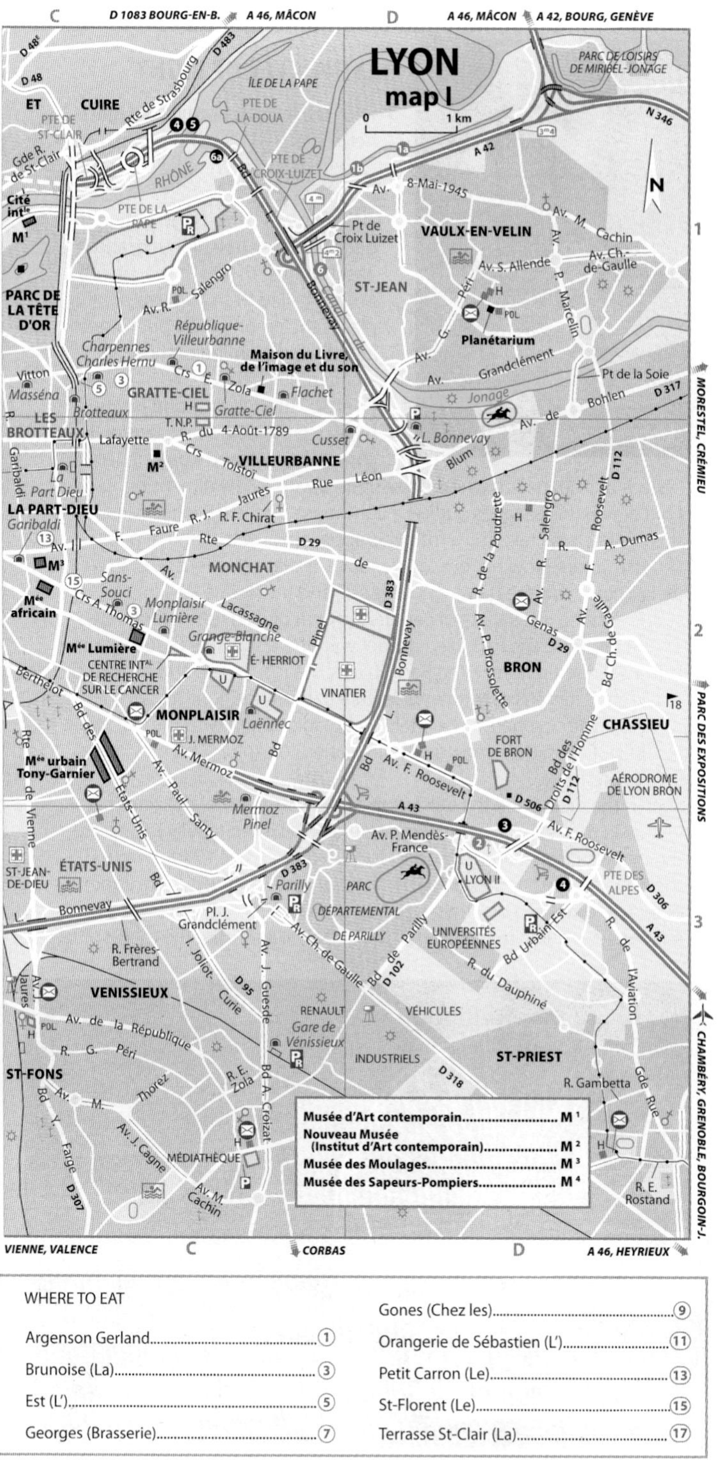

WHERE TO EAT

Argenson Gerland.......... 1
Brunoise (La).......... 3
Est (L').......... 5
Georges (Brasserie).......... 7
Gones (Chez les).......... 9
Orangerie de Sébastien (L').......... 11
Petit Carron (Le).......... 13
St-Florent (Le).......... 15
Terrasse St-Clair (La).......... 17

Jardin Botanique

© Jakezc / Fotolia.com

LYON, CITY OF LIGHT

With the famous **Festival of Lights** held here on 8 December, when the city twinkles with the light of thousands of candles, Lyon was already predisposed to investing generously in street lighting, and it has done just that in the shape of a project called "Plan Lumière", which places the emphasis on public safety and the highlighting of the city's architectural heritage.

Over 100 monuments and locations have been selected for inclusion in a comprehensive and homogeneous system of illumination which gives them a whole new dimension. Fourvière Basilica stands out like a lighthouse on the top of its hill; the opera house takes on a futuristic appearance with its huge glass superstructure glowing red; squares such as place des Terreaux or place de la Bourse and the banks of the Saône and the Rhône are lit up by subtle lighting in a variety of colours in warm or cold tones depending on the location. The Part-Dieu district with the distinctive Crédit Lyonnais tower soaring up from it, the Port St-Jean, the Hôtel-Dieu and many more of the city's famous monuments feature in this huge light show which weaves an atmosphere of fairy tale and magic. Along with the various events put on in the evenings, this invitation to explore "Lyon by night" proves irresistible.

Such is the drama and the skill of the artists, that many of the sites that feature in the Fêtes des Lumières need to be revisited to fully appreciate the magic of it all. During the four days, visitors are free to stroll around the "City of Light", appreciating a life-size art show at the cutting edge of technology. It is a breathtaking experience, and rightly praised and renowned. A guide to the "Plan Lumière" is available from the tourist office.

Place Bellecour

© Jakezc / Fotolia.com

VIEUX LYON★★★

The medieval and Renaissance quarter of Lyon, the precursor of today's city, extends along the west bank of the Saône at the foot of the **Colline** (hill) **de Fourvière**. Of interest in the old town are the many passages or alleyways known as "traboules" – from the Latin trans ambulare meaning "walking through". The passageways run perpendicular to the streets and link the buildings by means of corridors with vaulted or coffered ceilings leading to inner courtyards.

QUARTIER ST-JEAN★★★

Lyon was incorporated into the French kingdom at the beginning of the 14C. In the Middle Ages it was a border town facing the Dauphiné, Savoy, and the Holy Roman Empire.

Charles VII made it a trading centre of European importance when he founded the twice-yearly fair in 1419. Louis XI introduced the weaving of raw silk imported from the Levant and from Italy, but local opposition led the only silk-mill to transfer its operations to Tours. Forty-four years later, Louis doubled the number of fairs; long-distance trade was encouraged and patterns of commercial activity developed which were far in advance of the time; accommodation at inns and hostels was improved, and clearing houses were set up, forerunners of the great bank founded in the 16C.

Trade flourished, and with it came a period of great prosperity for the city, its merchants, bankers and high officials. Lyon seethed with activity and ideas; its streets were lined with elegant Flamboyant Gothic façades with asymmetrical window patterns; behind them, down narrow alleys, lay courtyards like the ones at 11 and 58 rue St-Jean. More numerous are houses of Renaissance date, decorated with Italianate motifs such as (polygonal turrets, superimposed galleries, baskethandle arches and corner signs like the figure of the ox at the junction of rue du Bœuf – Hôtel Paterin (4 r. de la Juiverie), sculpted in the 16C by John of Bologna.

The **Hôtel de Gadagne★** houses the **Musée historique de Lyon★** (*1 pl. du Petit Collège; www.museegadagne.com*) and the **Musée international de la Marionnette★** (*as for the Musée historique de Lyon*), the latter created by Laurent Mourget (1769–1844), whose **Guignol** is the very embodiment of the spirit of the Lyon populace.

With the development of the characteristic forms of the French Renaissance come superimposed orders, as in the Hôtel Bullioud (*8 r. de la Juiverie*) with its gallery and corner pavilions by the local architect **Philibert Delorme**.

Printing had been invented in Korea in 1403, then again at Mainz in 1447, and made its first appearance on the banks of the Saône in 1485. The world of the transcriber or of the illuminator would never be the same again. The spread of books transformed Europe with its diffusion of learning, in literature, science and technology and accounts of voyages. The Reformation, born from widespread reading of the Bible, came about some 50 years after the invention of the printing press.

This was also the age of Louise Labé, known as la "Belle Cordière" (Ropemaker's wife), whose salon became a centre for literature and the arts; among those writing was the Lyon poet Maurice Scève.

By 1548 there were almost 400 printers working in the city, including Sébastien Gryphe, Guillaume Rouille and Étienne Dolet, the publisher of Marot and of Rabelais; the latter served as a doctor at the Pont-du-Rhône hospital for three years, carrying on a correspondence with Erasmus and Du Bellay. It was Du Bellay who published **Rabelais**' *Pantagruel* in 1532 and Gargantua in 1534 to coincide with the Lyon fairs.

Walking Tour 1

Vieux Lyon / Fourvière map, p439.

- **Place St-Jean.**
- **Manécanterie.**
- **Primatiale St-Jean★** – Dating originally from the 12C, St-Jean Cathedral is a Gothic building erected to

complete a Romanesque apse. On the exterior the most notable features are the four towers, two on the west front and two over the arms of the transept. They are only slightly higher than the nave. In 1245 and 1274 the cathedral was the setting for the two Councils of Lyon. In the following century it was chosen for the consecration of Pope John XXII. In 1600, Henri IV married Marie de' Medici here.

- **Jardin Archéologique.**
- **Rue St-Jean★★** – This was the main street in the old town of Lyon and, as such, royal corteges and religious processions passed along it.
- **Rue des Trois-Maries.**
- **Place du Gouvernement.**
- **Place du Change.**
- **Rue Lainerie.**
- **Rue Juiverie★** – The Jews were expelled from this street in the late 14C and the Italian bankers who replaced them had luxurious mansions built.
- **Musée Gadagne★** – This mansion stretches from no. 10 to no. 14 rue de Gadagne and is the largest Renaissance building in the old town.
- **Musée Historique de Lyon★** – In the Local History Museum the rooms on the ground floor have been laid out with religious sculpture.
- **Musée International de la Marionnette★** – The exhibits of this museum include not only Guignol and a number of glove puppets, but also an outstanding collection of string and rod puppets and shadow figures.
- **Rue du Bœuf.**
- **Place Neuve-St-Jean.**

ST-GEORGES DISTRICT

The St-Georges district of Lyon is the area where, from the 16C, silk weavers settled before moving to Croix-Rousse in the 19C. It was here that the first traboules were built in the Middle Ages.

Walking Tour 2

Vieux Lyon / Fourvière map, p439.

- **Place de la Trinité.**
- **Montée du Gourguillon.**
- **Rue St-Georges.**

COLLINE DE FOURVIÈRE★

The name of the hill is derived from the old forum (*Forum vetus*) which was still here in the reign of King Louis I in the 9C. Its site is now occupied by the pilgrimage chapel (with its Black Virgin) next to the basilica of 1870. Roman Lyon had numerous public buildings, including the imperial palace (the Capitol) giving onto the forum, a theatre and an odeon (both rebuilt) on the slope of the hill, baths, a circus building and several temples, as well as the amphitheatre on the east bank of the river.

The terrace to the north of the basilica forms a splendid **viewpoint★** overlooking the confluence of the Rhône and Saône and encompassing the hills and Dauphiné plain over which the great city has spread.

THE MONTÉES

The *montées,* or rises, consist of winding flights of steps or steeply sloping streets that climb the Fourvière hill, providing superb views down over the old town. Each of them has its own charm.

Walking Tour 3

Vieux Lyon / Fourvière map, p439.

- **Montée des Chazeaux.**
- **Jardin du Rosaire★** – The great rose gardens are laid out between the lake and quai Achille-Lignon, and boast 70 000 plants representing 350 varieties, which are a stunning sight between June and October.
- **Basilique Notre-Dame★** – Built on the site of the Roman forum, the massive basilica standing today at the top of Fourvière hill is an integral part of the Lyon landscape.
- **Ancienne Chapelle de la Vierge.**
- **Musée de Fourvière.**

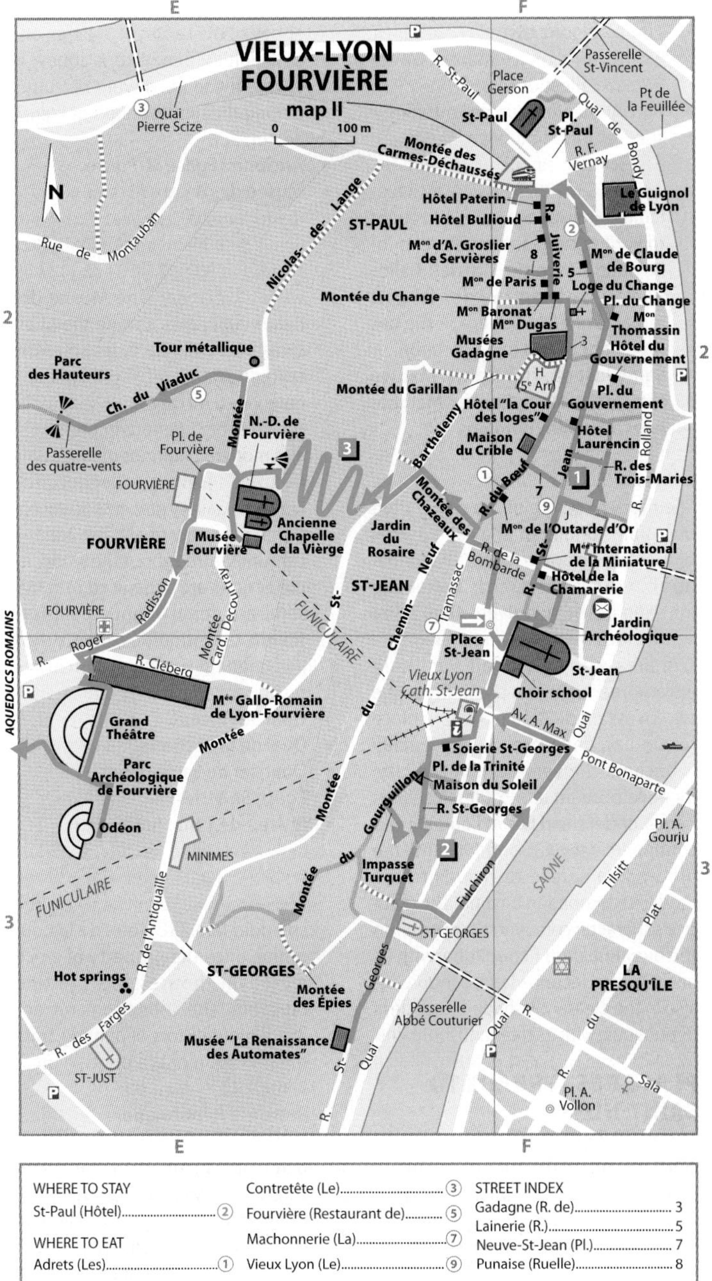

- **Montée Nicolas-de-Lange.**
- **Parc des Hauteurs.**
- **Musée de Gallo-Romains de Lyon-Fourvière★★** – Open daily Tue-Sun 10am-6pm. Closed 1 Jan, 1 May, 1 Nov, 25 Dec. ♿. €7, free Thu. ✆04 72 38 49 30. www.musees-gallo-romains.com. Fourvière, at the heart of the district that was once the plateau of the ancient town of Lugdunum.

The museum displays thematic exhibitions of its mainly Gallo-Roman collections.

- **Parc Archéologique de Fourvière★** – Same opening times as the Musée de Gallo-Romains de Lyon-Fourvière. ℘04 72 38 49 30. Fourvière archaeological site, opened in 1933, brought to light ancient and medieval public buildings in the district: Gallo-Roman baths in rue des Farges, remains of early basilica in rue des Macchabées and quai Fulchiron.
- **Saint-Just quarter sights: Mausolées de Choulans, Rue des Macchabées, Thermes Romains.**

LA PRESQU'ÎLE★★

The modern centre of the city is sited on a long tongue of alluvial material brought down by the Rhône. The formation of the "Peninsula" has shifted the junction of the two rivers 4km/2.5mi southwards since Roman times.

The area was first of all a military encampment, then its proximity to the two rivers made it a favourable place for trading and warehousing. Finally it became the very core of the city; its development along Classical lines begun under Henri IV and Louis XIII was continued in the 18C and 19C, until the urban area spread outwards to the modern suburbs and beyond. The great city's character comes across not only in the busy Rue de la République, with its fine 19C façades and elegant shops, but also in the pleasantly shaded Place de la République, with its trees and fountains.

PLACE DES TERRAUX TO SAINT-NIZIER

The place des Terraux is a square in central Lyon, at the foot of the hill of La Croix-Rousse; it is part of the area classified as a World Heritage Site, and is itself listed as a Monument Historique.

Walking Tour 1

Lyon la Presqu'île map, p441.

- **Place des Terreaux.**
- **Palais St-Pierre★** – This 17C and 18C building was formerly the abbey of the Ladies of St Peter, one of the oldest Benedictine abbeys in Lyon, whose nuns were recruited among the highest ranks of French aristocracy.
- **Ancienne Église St-Pierre.**
- **Musée des Beaux-Arts★★★** – 20 pl. des Terreaux. ♿Open Wed–Sun 10am–6pm (Fri 10.30am–6pm). Closed public holidays. €7–12. ℘04 72 10 17 40. www.mba-lyon.fr. The Musée des Beaux-Arts ranks among the finest museums in France. Its splendid collections, carefully displayed, have been further enriched by the donation of 35 famous Impressionist and modern paintings of Jacqueline Delubac's private collection. The Fine Arts Gallery presents an exceptional overview of art through the centuries, throughout the world. Its collections are organised into five separate departments: painting, sculpture, antiquities, objets d'art and medals. Excellent lunchtime restaurant.
- **Quai St-Vincent.**
- **Quai de la Pêcherie.**
- **Quartier de Saint-Nizier: Église St-Nizier.**
- **Musée de l'Imprimerie★★** – 13 r. de la Poulaillerie. ♿Open Wed–Sun 9.30am–noon, 2–6pm. €5. ℘04 78 37 65 98. www.imprimerie.lyon.fr. The splendid late-15C Hôtel de la Couronne, once the property of a rich merchant, houses this printing museum. The collections retrace the glorious history of printing, from the invention of the printing press in the 15C.
- **Rue de la République.**
- **Rues de Bouchons.**
- **Opéra de Lyon** – On the south side of the square, opposite the Hôtel de Ville, stands the new Lyon opera house, the result of a successful modernisation scheme. The façade of the old building has been preserved and the eight muses of the pediment appear to hold up the immense and splendid glass semi-cylindrical roof, the design of the architect Jean Nouvel. With a

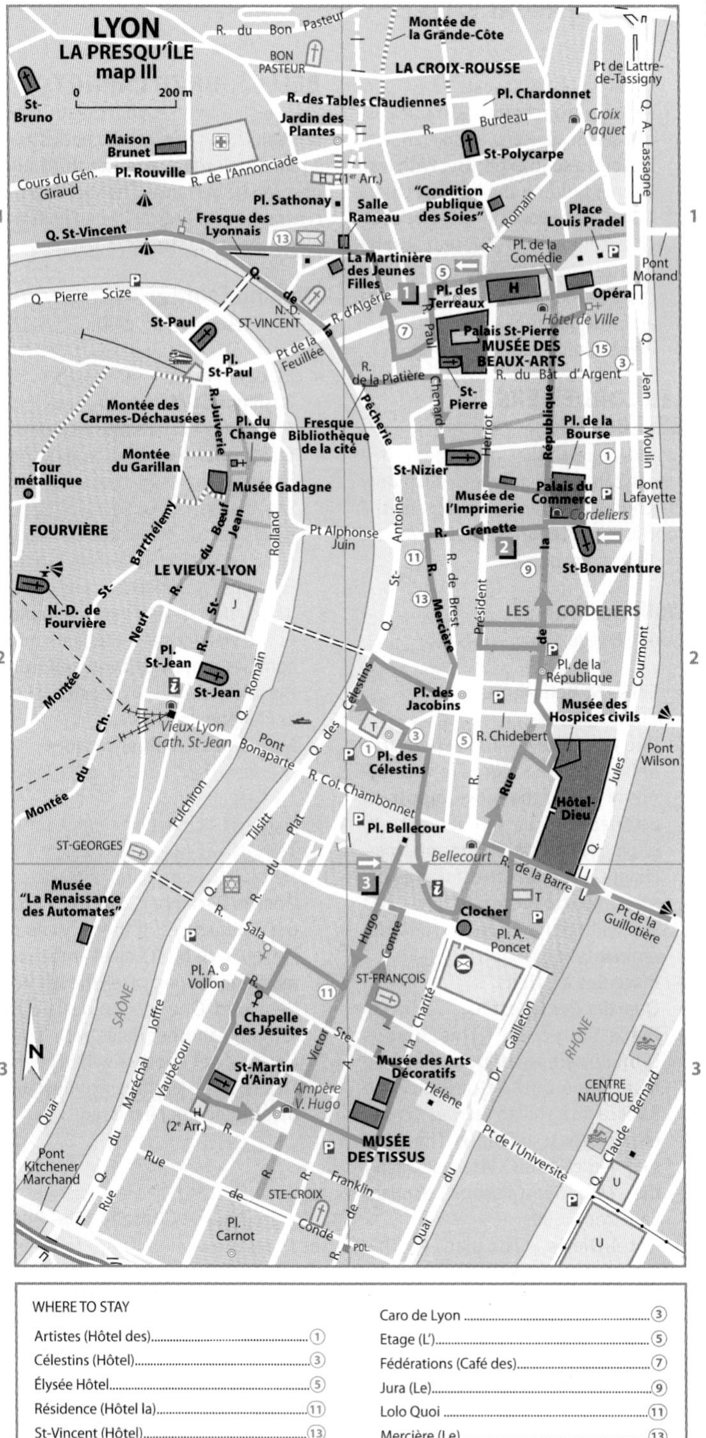

WHERE TO STAY

Artistes (Hôtel des)............ (1)
Célestins (Hôtel)............ (3)
Élysée Hôtel............ (5)
Résidence (Hôtel la)............ (11)
St-Vincent (Hôtel)............ (13)

WHERE TO EAT

Brunet............ (1)
Caro de Lyon............ (3)
Etage (L')............ (5)
Fédérations (Café des)............ (7)
Jura (Le)............ (9)
Lolo Quoi............ (11)
Mercière (Le)............ (13)
203 (Café le)............ (15)

capacity of 1 300 seats, The Opéra includes an orchestra (60 musicians), a ballet (30 dancers), a choir (26 singers) and a solid expertise. With Ivan Fischer holding the baton, l'Opéra National de Lyon is an international-class company. A 200-seat amphitheatre is the stage for a more varied programme, including classical, jazz and world music.

- **Place Louis-Pradel.**

LES CORDELIERS TO BELLECOUR

Les Cordeliers takes its name from a Franciscan monastery, of which only the church now remains following the confiscation of church property during the French Revolution.

Walking Tour 2

Lyon La Presqu'île map, p441.

- **Église St-Bonaventure.**
- **Rue Grenette.**
- **Rue Mercière★** – Today pedestrianised, the rue Mercière was formerly one of the most important arteries of Lyon; the name itself, originally "Mercatoria", means "merchants". Today the street stands as a monument to those past times, and you will see many arches, and the remnants of old shops.
- **Place des Jacobins.**
- **Quartier des Célestins.**
- **Place Bellecour** – This famous Lyon square, overlooked by the distinctive outline of Fourvière Basilica on its hill to the west, is one of the largest in France. The huge symmetrical Louis XVI façades lining the west and east sides of the square date from 1800.
- **Hôtel-Dieu★** – The plans for this were drawn up by Soufflot in 1740. It marks a significant stage in the evolution of French architecture with its long façade facing the Rhône, its projecting central section with Ionic columns and its dome rising from a square base and crowned with a square lantern.

BELLECOUR TO CARNOT

Place Bellecour takes your breath away; it is said to be the largest pedestrian square in Europe, and the third biggest square in France. The square is the central focus of Presqu'Ile and links the major shopping streets.

Walking Tour 3

Lyon La Presqu'île map, p441.

- **Place Bellecour** – See left.
- **Basilique St-Martin-d'Ainay.**
- **Musée des Tissus & Musée des Arts Décoratifs★★★** – 34 r. de la Charité. Open Tue–Sun 10am–5.30pm. Closed public holidays. €10 (combined ticket with the Musée des Arts Décoratifs). 04 78 38 42 00. www.musee-des-tissus.com. Apart from its exhibits devoted to very early examples of the weaver's art, the collection consists mostly of Lyon silk from the 17C onwards, by masters such as Philippe de Lasalle.
- **Musée des Confluences★★★** – 86 Quai Perrache. Open Tue–Wed and Fri 11am–7pm; Thu 11am–10pm; Sat–Sun and public holidays 10am–7pm. Closed 1 Jan, 1 May, 1 Nov, 25 Dec. €9. 04 28 38 11 90. www.museedesconfluences.fr. Open in December 2014, the Musée des Confluences, at the very end of Presqu'île, is Lyon's most ambitious museum, seeking to tell the story of the world. One section deals with 'Origins', another deals with 'Species' and yet another with 'Death'. This is an all-embracing museum that should not be missed.

LA CROIX-ROUSSE

La Croix-Rousse (literally "The Russet Cross") owes its name to a coloured stone cross that stood at one of the district's crossroads in the days before the French Revolution. The district still has all the character and flavour of a small village community and today remains the last bastion of true Lyon traditionalism. The most fiercely proud inhabitants of

La Croix-Rousse are deeply attached to the "Plateau" and look down from a distance on the hustle and bustle below. They might even spend months on end without going down the hill.

HISTORIC TEXTILE WORKERS DISTRICT

The invention of new looms by Joseph-Marie Jacquard (1752–1834) led the "canuts" or silk-workers to abandon the low cottages in the St-Jean district and move to larger austere buildings with wide windows that let in the light. The traboules in La Croix-Rousse were used to move bolts of silk about the district without any risk of damage from inclement weather.

In 1831, and again in 1834, they were the scene of bloody uprisings when the silk-workers waved black flags symbolising poverty and bearing the famous motto: "Life through work or death through conflict."

Walking Tour 1

Lyon La Croix-Rousse map, p444.

- **Condition Publique des Soies.**
- **Place Chardonnet.**
- **Rue des Tables-Claudiennes.**
- **Cour des Voraces.**
- **Grande-Côte★** – The Grande-Côte "montée" is well named; fortunately, you go down it. To compensate for the destruction of many old houses in its upper part, the Grande-Côte has benefited from much redevelopment.
- **Amphithéâtre des Trois Gaules.**
- **Jardin des Plantes.**
- **Place Rouville.**
- **Place Sathonay.**

LE PLATEAU★

The plateau is part of La Crois-Rousse hill, an area hallmarked by the industry of silk makers, who moved here from Vieux Lyon in the 18C, but who experienced very poor working conditions, which in turn led to a number of worker uprisings.

Walking Tour 4

Lyon La Croix-Rousse map, p444.

- **Place des Tapis.**
- **Quartier des Canuts★** – At the junction of boulevard des Canuts, rue Denfert-Rochereau and rue Pelletier stands a tall **wall★** adorned with a trompe-l'œil mural covering an area of 1 200sqm/12 840sq ft. Painted in December 1987 and updated in 1997, it serves as a picturesque reminder of life in one of the districts in La Croix-Rousse. Note, in the windows, the puppet-theatre characters of Guignol, his wife Madelon and the Bailiff.
- **Maison des Canuts.**

LEFT BANK

The Left Bank of the Rhône has allowed the original 18C town to expand. From the Parc de la Tête d'Or to the very modern Gerland, passing buildings of glass and brick of the International City, the extension has brought together the most diverse areas and offers an ideal ecological lifestyle, combining water and green spaces.

Banks of the Rhône

Lyon map I, p434.

- **Cité Internationale** – This vast complex, comprising an imposing Conference Centre (Palais des Congrès), cinemas (14 screens), hotels and a Museum of Contemporary Art, was installed between the Tête d'Or Park and the Rhône.
  Musée d'Art Contemporain★ – Cité Internationale – 81 Quai Charles-de-Gaulle. Open daily except Mon, Tue noon–7pm. ♿€6. Closed 1 May, 25 Dec. ☎04 72 69 17 17. www.mac-lyon.com. This new cultural focus is built around the atrium of the old market hall. Its modern structure allows for great flexibility of display and for works of art to be exhibited to their best advantage. The museum collection is very varied.

LYON
LA CROIX-ROUSSE
map IV

0 — 200 m

WHERE TO STAY

Lyon Guest House.......................... ②

WHERE TO EAT

Comptoir du Mail.......................... ②
Deux Places (Restaurant des).......................... ④
Maison Villemanzy.......................... ⑥
Table d'Hippolyte (La).......................... ⑧

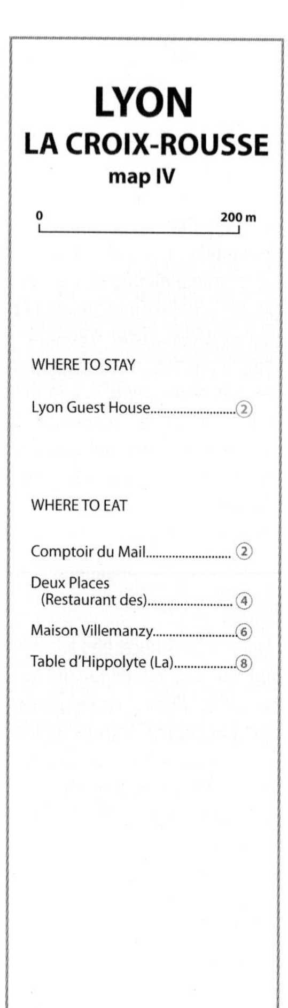

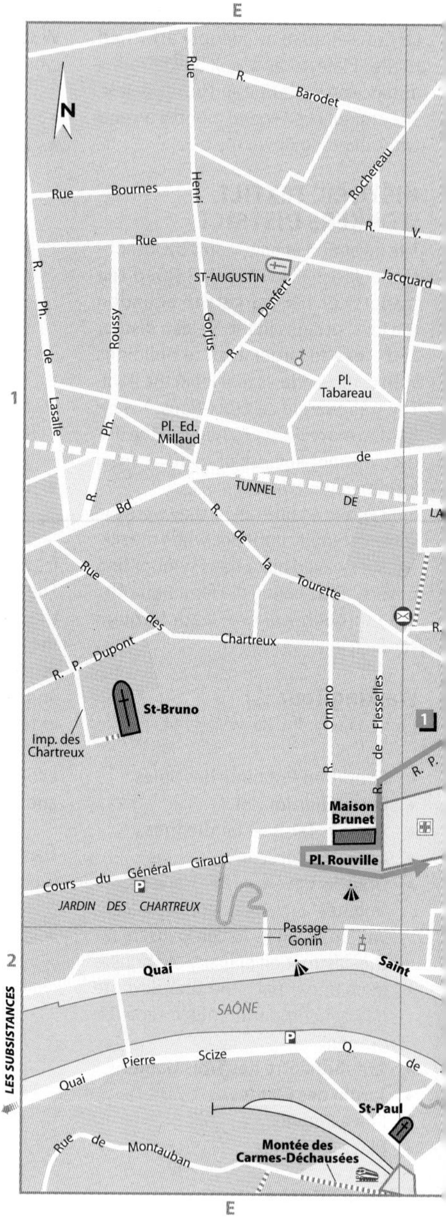

- **Parc de la Tête d'Or★** – The name of the English-style gardens surrounding the Conference Centre derives from local folklore, which claims that a golden head of Christ is buried here. The entrance is marked by huge wrought-iron gates. The park is an ideal place to go walking and cycling and there is also a narrow-gauge railway. **Serres★ and Jardin Botanique** – The botanical gardens are laid out to the south-east end of the park and consist of acres of outdoor plants,

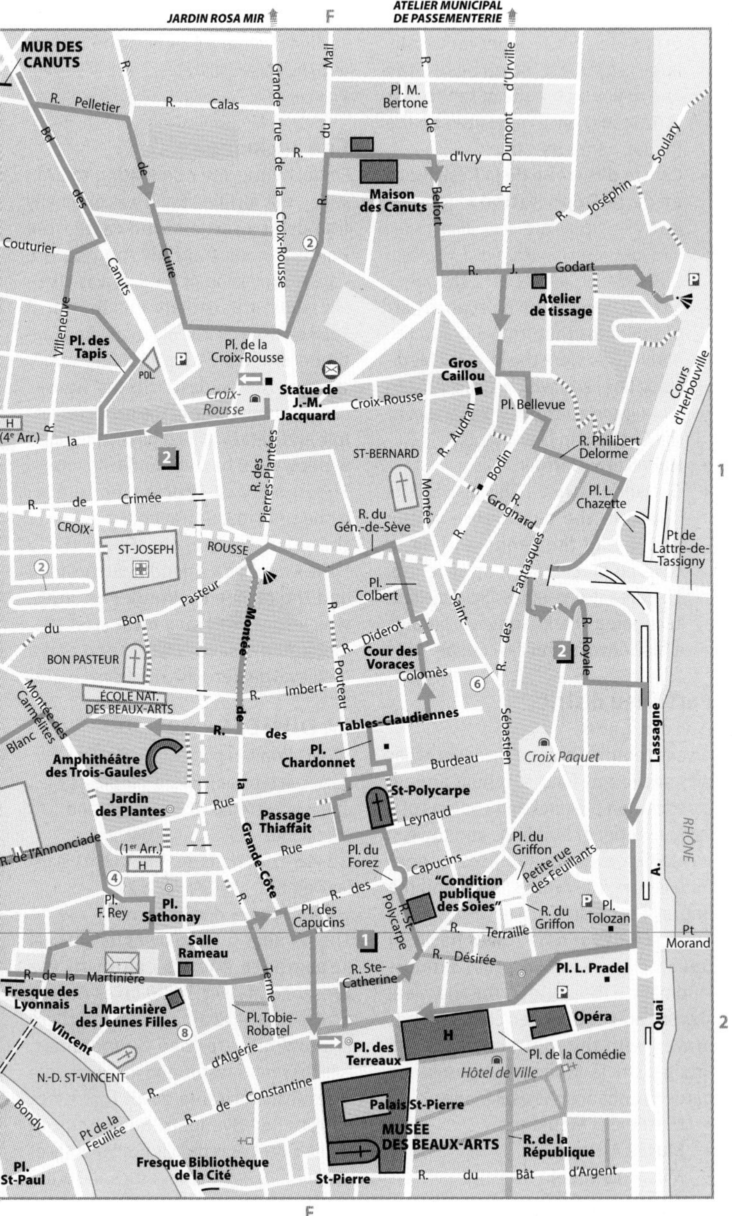

great glasshouses containing tropical vegetation including numerous palm trees, and an Alpine garden. **Jardin Zoologique.**

- **Quaysides** – Quai Augagneur, by the Hôtel-Dieu, is lined with imposing bourgeois houses built in the late 19C. This wonderful esplanade beneath the plane trees is enhanced by the lively atmosphere of an open-air market (except Mondays), and is particularly attractive in misty weather, when the river is turbulent and fast-flowing. The district of Les

Brotteaux, with its geometrically laid-out streets, stretches to the east; it lies on the site of sandbanks (brotteaux) once deposited by the Rhône, hence its name.

- **Centre d'Histoire de la Résistance et de la Déportation★** – 14 av. Berthelot. Open Wed–Sun, 10am–6pm. Closed Christmas public holidays except 8 May. €4. ✆04 78 72 23 11. www.chrd.lyon.fr. The museum is set up in part of buildings that from 1882 to the early 1970s were the Military Medical School and which, from 1942 to 1944, housed the headquarters of the Gestapo in this region.
- **Halle Tony-Garnier.**
- **Gerland District** – This district sits opposite the confluence of the Rhône and the Saône and has a covered meat market at its centre. The area is one large "Science and Technology Park" and incorporates a high-level technical college.

Part-Dieu district

Lyon map I, p434.

A vast complex spread out over what was once Army land, it is built around a pedestrian precinct and consists of a large number of buildings and towers, including government offices, a shopping centre, the radio studios and the impressive library.

The **Crédit Lyonnais Tower** has now become the second most famous landmark in the city after the Fourvière Towers, and its brick-red colour blends in well with the rooftops of the old urban districts. Modern sculptures and gardens enhance the esplanades.

- **Musée des Moulages.**
- **Musée Africain.**
- **Musée Lumière.**
- **Aquarium.**

EXCURSIONS

PÉROUGES★★

25km/15.5mi NE of Lyon.

Entrance of the Cité. ✆04 74 46 70 84.

Tightly contained within the ramparts, the tortuous streets and ancient houses of the old town have formed the perfect setting for many a period film including *The Three Musketeers* and *Monsieur Vincent*.

Cité ancienne★★

On its hilltop site dominating the Ain valley, this fortified town was originally founded by settlers who came from Perugia in central Italy long before Caesar's invasion of Gaul. It was virtually rebuilt in its entirety after the war of 1468 with Savoy. The older buildings are timber-framed with projecting upper storeys. The modest artisans' houses contrast with those of the richer townsfolk and gentry, which have mullioned windows and basket-handle arches.

The Upper Gate (**Porte d'en Haut★**) is the principal entrance to the town; the main square, the **Place de la Halle★★★**, has a splendid old hostelry and the **Musée du Vieux-Pérouges**, which contains many local artefacts, a restored weaver's workshop and a medieval garden with medicinal herbs.

LA DOMBES★

The Dombes plateau is situated between Lyon and Bourg-en-Bresse and is bordered by the River Ain and the Saône.

3 Place de l'Hôtel de Ville, 01330 Villars les Dombes. ✆04 74 98 06 29. www.villars-les-dombes.com.

The Dombes plateau owes its unusual appearance and its charm to the presence of over 1 000 lakes dotted across its entire area. Here and there are low hills, formed by moraines, which were transformed in the Middle Ages into veritable earth fortresses surrounded by moats. Rural housing in the Dombes region is built mainly of cob (*pisé*), whereas the castles and outer walls are built of rough red bricks known as *carrons* (terracotta).

The region's history, too, is somewhat out of the ordinary. Dombes was raised to the rank of a principality by François I following the confiscation of the property belonging to the Constable of Bourbon in 1523. A sovereign Parliament sat in **Trévoux**, its main town, until the mid-18C.

A Bit of Geography

The impermeable soil encouraged local people very early on in their history to turn their fields into lakes enclosed by mud dikes. The Grand Étang de Birieux, one of the most extensive of the lakes, but now subdivided, dates from the 14C. In the 16C, Dombes boasted almost 2 000 lakes, many filled with stagnant water, which led to an unhealthy climate. Most of the lakes are intermittent, one being emptied to fill another: they are filled with water and stocked with fish for a period of six or seven years, then drained and for one year turned over to agriculture.

Sight

The **Parc des Oiseaux★** bird sanctuary (1km/0.6mi south of Villars-les-Dombes on N 83; open daily Mar–mid Apr, Oct–Nov 10am–5.30pm, late Apr–Aug 9.30am–7pm (6.30pm Mon–Fri in May and Jun), Sep 9.30am–6.30pm; closed Dec–Feb; from €16 (children 3–12, years, €12); 04 74 98 05 54; www.parcdesoiseaux.com) close to the Dombes Nature Reserve, lies along one of the main migration routes in Europe. Over 2 000 birds from five continents live in the park. At the entrance, the "Birds' House" provides a warm, humid atmosphere for a wonderful selection of brightly coloured exotic birds.

Enjoy a walk round the park along the footpaths running round the lakes, which are the breeding ground for large birds such as common and night heron as well as rarer species in giant aviaries. Besides the spectacular Vallée des Rapaces, the Volière du Pantanal and the Cité des Perroquets are also fascinating. The park is engaged in several conservation programmes aimed at endangered species. These are explained to children through various activities in the Maison des Enfants.

BOURG-EN-BRESSE

62km/39mi NE of Lyon, via the D 1083. Allow half a day to explore at a leisurely pace.

Bourg is the capital of the Bresse area, famous in France for its high-quality poultry, which bears its own label of authentication. It is situated to the west of the Jura Mountains on the River Reyssouze, a tributary of the Saône.

Old houses

A couple of half-timbered houses, dating from the 15C, are worth visiting: the **Maison Hugon**, on the corner of the rue Gambetta and the rue V-Basch, and the **Maison Gorrevod**, in the rue du Palais. Equally noteworthy is the beautiful 17C stone façade of the **Hotel de Bohan**, and, in rue Teynière, the **Hotel de Marron de Meillonnas**, which dates from the 18C and has impressive wrought-iron balconies.

Monastère royal de Brou★★

63 bd de Brou. Open daily: Apr–Jun 9am–12.30pm, 2–6pm; Jul-mid-Sept 9am–6pm; Jul–mid-Sept 9am–12.30pm, 2–6pm; Oct–Mar 9am–12.30pm, 2–5pm. Closed 1 Jan, 1 May, 1 and 11 Nov, 25 Dec. €7.50. 04 74 22 83 83. www.brou.monuments-nationaux.fr.

The church – now deconsecrated – was built from 1513 to 1532 in exuberant Flaboyant Gothic style. The work was undertaken by a Flemish master builder and a team of artists and craftsmen, mostly from Flanders, where Margaret was now living. The interior decoration was already much influenced by the Renaissance. In the elegant nave, built of pale stone from the Jura, a finely sculptured balustrade was substituted for the more usual triforium.

The stone **rood screen★★** has three basket-handle arches and is profusely decorated with leaves, cable-moulding and scrolls. The 74 **choir stalls★★** were built by local carpenters. An array of statuettes represents biblical figures. In the **Margaret of Austria chapel★★★** an altarpiece is a masterwork of amazing craftsmanship. There are also superb **stained-glass windows★★**.

The three **tombs★★★** give the church its truly regal character. On the right is that of Margaret of Bourbon, in a Gothic niche with Flamboyant decoration. Philibert the Fair's elaborate tomb is completely Renaissance in character.

Monastère Royal de Brou

Margaret of Austria's tomb forms part of the parclose screen; she is first shown lying in state on a black marble slab, then, underneath, in her shroud. Its richly carved canopy incorporates her motto.

The **museum★** is housed in the monastic buildings which are ranged around two-storey **cloisters★**, unique in France. On the ground floor of the small cloisters the sacristy and the chapterhouse, now one room, are used for temporary exhibitions. The great cloisters lead to the second chapterhouse, now the museum reception. A staircase leads up to the dormer where the old monks' cells now house collections of paintings and decorative art. The cells on the south side are devoted to 16–18C art, including a fine portrait of Margaret of Austria★ painted by B Van Orley c.1518.

GRAND COLOMBIER★★★

125km/77mi E of Lyon. r. de la Mairie, Culoz. 04 79 87 00 30. http://culoz.interarb.com/colom.

At 1 571m, the Grand Colombier forms the highest point in the Bugey area. The viewpoint at the summit is one of the finest in the whole of the Jura.

It's possible to drive almost to the top. Leave the car in the car park and continue to the summit on foot. It's a tough climb.

From Virieu-le-Petit to Culoz

The road rises steeply, passing first through splendid pine forests. At the summit, with its cross and triangulation point, there is the widest of panoramas, taking in the Jura, the Dombes plateau, the valley of the Rhône, the Massif Central and the Alps.

In the distance the Grand Fenestrez, crowned by an observatory **(Observatoire★★)**, rears up from the Culoz plain, which can be reached by car via a boldly designed hairpin road.

ADDRESSES

STAY

VIEUX-LYON

Hôtel St-Paul – 6 r. Lainerie. 04 78 28 13 29. 20 rooms. A small Renaissance hotel at the centre of the quarter.

FOURVIÈRE

Chambre d'Hôte la Grange de Fourvière – 86 r. des Macchabées. 04 72 33 74 45. www.grangedefourviere.fr. 5 rooms. A former 19C barn and stable completely renovated are the basis of this charming B&B.

Chambre d'Hôte le Greillon – 12 montée du Greillont. 06 08 22 26 33. www.legreillon.com. 4 rooms. Away from the noise of the city, this 18C house has a terraced garden, unique for hotels in the centre of the city.

PRESQU'ÎLE

Chambre d'Hôte Péniche "El Kantara" – Quai Rambaud. ℘04 78 42 02 75. 2 rooms. What could be more romantic or unusual than this magnificently restored barge moored on the river?

Hôtel St-Vincent – 9 r. Pareille. ℘04 78 27 22 56. www.hotel-saintvincent.com. 30 rooms. Located in a narrow street close to the Saône, this hotel, formerly cloisters, is very comfortable, with large rooms.

Élysée Hôtel – 92 r. du Prés.-Edouard-Herriot. ℘04 78 42 03 15. 29 rooms. A small family-run hotel where you can enjoy the vitality of the Presqu'île at affordable prices.

Kyriad Prestige Lyon-Centre – 4–6 r. du Mortier. ℘0892 23 48 13. www.kyriadprestige.com. 126 rooms. Just a five minute walk from place Bellecour, this modern hotel with a glass front is rather agreeable; all the rooms are identical; functional and well-equipped.

Hôtel La Résidence – 18 r. Victor-Hugo. ℘04 78 42 63 28. www.hotel-la-residence.com. 67 rooms. Managed by the same family since 1954, this hotel borders on a pedestrian street quite near the place Bellecour.

Hotel des Savoies – 80 r. de la Charité. ℘04 78 37 66 94. www.hotel-des-savoies.fr. 46 rooms. Look for a façade decorated with the Savoie coat of arms in the Perrache train station quarter. The cleanliness of the standard rooms, with their simple furniture and pastel carpets, the convenient garage and reasonable prices make this a popular address.

Hotel Célestins – 4 r. des Archers. ℘04 72 56 08 98. www.hotelcelestins.com. 25 rooms. Charming hotel in the heart of the city between place Bellecour and place des Jacobins, and perfect for exploring the city on foot.

Hotel des Artistes – 8 r. G-André. ℘04 78 42 04 88. www.hotel-des-artistes.fr. 45 rooms. Giving onto the adorable place des Célestins and the theatre, this hotel has lovely rooms and a theatrical ambiance.

RIVE GAUCHE

Hôtel B&B – 93 cours Gambetta. ℘08 92 707 534. www.hotel-bb.com. 114 rooms. A chain hotel offering a central location near the railway station, and with spacious and comfortable rooms with king-size beds.

Au Patio Morand – 99 r. de Créqui. ℘04 78 52 62 62. www.hotel-morand.fr. 31 rooms. This hotel has a patio where you can breakfast. The elegant rooms have large bed and plasma screen TV.

Hotel Mercure Saxe-Lafayette – 29 rue de Bonnel. ℘04 72 61 90 90. www.mercure.com. 156 rooms. In the centre of Lyon, the 4-star Mercure Lyon Centre Saxe Lafayette hotel is a 10-minute walk from Vieux Lyon, slightly off-centre and cheaper for it. If arriving by rail, take a taxi. Excellent restaurant as part of hotel complex.

THE OUTSKIRTS OF LYON

Hôtel la Chaumière – 11 av. du Gén-de-Gaulle, 69410 Champagne-au-Mont-d'Or. ℘04 78 35 10 60. This contemporary building has bright, very well maintained rooms. A delightful alternative to chain hotels.

Hôtel Ariana – 163 cours Émile-Zola, 69100 Villeurbanne. ℘04 78 85 32 33. www.ariana-hotel.fr. 102 rooms. This is a practical address for those who wish to stay amid the 1930s high-rises of Villeurbanne. The hotel is modern; it has air-conditioned, soundproofed rooms with a sober interior.

EAT

VIEUX-LYON

Le Vieux Lyon – 44 r. St-Jean. ℘04 78 42 48 89. Closed Sun evening. Local epicureans are all familiar with this tavern, in operation since 1947, where good humour and hospitality reign. Home-made Lyonnais cooking.

Un, Deux, Trois – 1 place Neuve Saint-Jean. ℘04 26 00 94 13. Traditional, small bouchon serving generous portions of Lyonnais cuisine. Very popular, so either make a reservation or turn up at 12 noon. 60s' and 70s' music often in the background.

La Machonnerie – 36 r. Tramassac. ℘04 78 42 24 62. Closed Sun and lunchtimes except Sat. This restaurant perpetuates the traditions of attentiveness and authentic recipes. Lovely room dedicated to jazz.

⊖⊖ **Les Adrets** – 30 r. du Boeuf. ☎04 78 38 24 30. Closed Sat and Sun. Exposed beams and tiled floor. Traditional dishes.

FOURVIÈRE

⊖⊖ **Le Contretête** – 55 quai Pierre-Scize. ☎04 78 29 41 29. Closed Sat lunch and Sun. This bistro cultivates authenticity and offers "grandmother's" slow-cooked recipes of yesteryear.

⊖⊖ **Restaurant de Fourvière** – 9 pl. de Fourvière. ☎04 78 25 21 15. Perfectly situated, this restaurant enjoys a superb panorama and serves traditional cuisine.

PRESQU'ÎLE

⊖ **Le Café 203** – 9 r. du Garet. ☎04 78 28 66 65. Customers come here for the fresh fare, slate menu and bistro setting.

⊖⊖ **Lolo Quoi** – 42 r. Mercière. ☎04 72 77 60 90. In this pedestrian street, those in the know go to Lolo. Minimalist furnishings, thoughtful lighting and modern Italian cuisine.

⊖⊖ **La Brasserie Georges** – 30 cours de Verdun. ☎04 72 56 54 54. www.brasseriegeorges.com. Open since 1836, this brasserie near the Perrache train station is still a favourite Lyon haunt.

⊖⊖ **Le Jura** – 25 r. Tupin. ☎04 78 42 20 57. Closed Mon from Sep–Apr, Sat from May–Sep, and Sun. Reservations requested. Not far from the Rue de la République, this eatery with its 1920s decor and aproned matron overseeing the stoves, it's as genuine as they come.

⊖⊖ **Brunet** – 23 r. Claudia. ☎04 78 37 44 31. Closed Sun-Mon and Tue lunch. Reservations recommended. An authentic Lyon bouchon, Brunet has elbow-to-elbow tables, Guignol-marked tableware and tasty little dishes enhanced by an enticing selection of wines by the carafe.

⊖⊖ **Café des Fédérations** – 8 r. Major-Martin. ☎04 78 28 26 00. www.lesfedeslyon.com. Closed Sun. Unrivalled guardian of the Lyonnais culinary traditions, served in a perfect setting and relaxing atmosphere.

⊖⊖ **Le Mercière** – 56 r. Mercière. ☎04 78 37 67 35. www.le-merciere.fr. Reservations recommended. Located in a passageway giving onto one of the most sought-after restaurant streets in town, this old house serves traditional fare in a classic Lyonnais setting.

⊖⊖ **Le Caro de Lyon** – 25 r. du Bât-d'Argent. ☎04 78 39 58 58. Closed Sun. This restaurant behind the Opera House, designed to resemble a library, welcomes diners into an intimate atmosphere comprised of Murano chandeliers and antique knick-knacks.

⊖⊖ **L'Étage** – 4 pl. des Terreaux. ☎04 78 28 19 59. Closed Sun and Mon. The locals never tire of climbing the stairs leading to the humble silk workshop on the second floor. Charming setting and seductive and creative menus.

LA CROIX-ROUSSE

⊖⊖ **Restaurant des Deux Places** – 5 pl. Fernand-Rey. ☎04 78 28 95 10. Closed Sat-Mon. A few steps from the Place Sathonay, this traditional little restaurant boasts a convivial atmosphere, a décor full of rural knick-knacks and time-honoured cuisine.

⊖⊖ **La Table d'Hippolyte** – 22 r. Hippolyte-Flandrin. ☎04 78 27 75 59. Closed Sat lunch, Sun-Mon. Located in a small street near the Halles de la Martinière; curios, old mirrors and hefty objects co-exist peacefully. The ideal setting for a candlelit supper.

⊖⊖ **Comptoir du Mail** – 14 r. du Mail, (Croix-Rousse). ☎04 78 27 71 40. The local population wasted no time in adopting this restaurant serving dishes straight from the marketplace.

⊖⊖ **Maison Villemanzy** – 25 montée St-Sébastien. ☎04 72 98 21 21. www.maison-villemanzy.com. Closed Sun, and Mon lunch. Perched on the slopes of Croix-Rousse, this restaurant offers a superb terrace view over the city. Family recipes and inventive cuisine.

RIVE GAUCHE

⊖ **Chez les Gones** – 102 cours Lafayette. ☎04 78 60 91 61. Closed Sun and Mon. This tavern set in the bosom of the marketplace boasts typical Lyon dishes.

⊖ **Le Petit Carron** – 48 av. Félix-Faure. ☎04 78 60 00 57. Closed 3 wks in Aug, Sat lunch and Sun. Reservations recommended. The little puppet who inhabits the window of this tavern beckons you into a muted dining room featuring a slate menu du jour.

⊖⊜ **L'Est** – 14 pl. J-Ferry. ✆04 37 24 25 26. www.bocuse.fr. The last of Paul Bocuse's bastions in Lyon. The décor is that of a big, old-fashioned brasserie where electric trains circumnavigate the dining room.

⊖⊜ **Le St-Florent** – 106 cours Gambetta. ✆04 78 72 32 68. Closed Sat and Mon lunches, Sun and public holidays. The place to appreciate Bresse chicken. From floor to ceiling, from entrée to dessert this restaurant honours the chicken in all its forms.

THE OUTSKIRTS OF LYON

⊖⊜ **La Brunoise** – 4 r. A-Boutin, 69100 Villeurbanne. ✆04 78 52 07 77. www.labrunoise.fr. Closed Sun and Mon evenings, Tue and Wed. The varied specialities are displayed outside and invite you into this bright restaurant.

⊖⊜ **La Terrasse St-Clair** – 2 Grande Rue St-Clair, 69300 Caluire-et-Cuire. ✆04 72 27 37 37. www.terrasse-saint-clair.com. Closed Sun and Mon. This tavern-like restaurant has a terrace sheltered by plane trees where you can dine on traditional cuisine.

⊖⊜ **L'Orangerie de Sébastien** – Domaine de Lacroix-Laval, 69280 Marcy-l'Étoile. ✆04 78 87 45 95. www.orangeriedesebastien.fr. Closed Sun evening, Mon and Tue. The orangery is part of a 17C château, and serves dishes of the day on a beautiful terrace.

ON THE TOWN

Rue Ste-Catherine – A very lively street featuring many establishments open until the early hours of the morning. *The Albion Public House* is the most British pub in town, *The Shamrock* the most Celtic. Rum fans convene at *La Taverne du Perroquet Bourré* (The Tavern of the Plastered Parrot), while *L'Abreuvoir* is highly recommended for those who fancy good French music.

THEATRE AND ENTERTAINMENT

Le Guignol de Lyon – Compagnie des Zonzons, 2 r. Louis-Carrand. ✆04 78 28 92 57. www.guignol-lyon.com. Wed and Sat: 3pm and 4.30pm, Sun 3pm; daily during school holidays. La Compagnie des Zonzons stages children's performances that marry burlesque and fantasy. The

Vieux Lyon

shows for adults, inspired by aspects and events of life in Lyon, are more malicious.

Auditorium-Orchestre national de Lyon – 149 r. Garibaldi. ✆04 78 95 95 95. www.auditoriumlyon.com. Tickets: Mon–Fri 11am–6pm, concert Saturdays 2pm–6pm. Closed most of Aug. The Auditorium Maurice Ravel regularly hosts l'Orchestre National de Lyon.

Maison de la Danse – 8 av. Jean-Mermoz. ✆04 72 78 18 00. www.maisondeladanse.com. Tickets: Mon–Fri 11.45am –6.45pm. Closed mid-Jul–mid-Aug. From flamenco and tap dancing to ballet and the traditional dances of East and West, welcome to this, the citadel of the art.

Opéra National de Lyon – 1 pl. de la Comédie. ✆04 72 00 45 00 or 04 69 85 54 54 (ticket office). www.opera-lyon.com. Tickets: Mon–Sat 11am–7pm. Closed late Jul–end Aug. *See p440.*

Halle Tony-Garnier – 20 pl. Antonin-Perrin. ✆04 72 76 85 85. www.halle-tony-garnier.com. Visits following schedule; phone ahead. Since its restoration in 2000, this huge metallic structure presents a remarkable diversity of events from the Moscow State Circus to Lionel Richie and Johnny Hallyday.

Vienne★★

Vienne is favoured with a sunny site★ on the east bank of the Rhône. The town overlooks the bend formed by the river as it makes its way through the crystalline rocks marking the last outcrops of the Massif Central.

- **Population:** 29 328.
- **Michelin Map:** 333 C 4
- **Info:** 14 Cours Brillier. 04 74 53 80 30. www.vienne-tourisme.com.
- **Location:** Vienne lies 38km/24mi S of Lyon.
- **Timing:** Half a day will suffice, but stay longer to better appreciate the place.

A BIT OF HISTORY

Vienne came under Roman rule 60 years before Caesar's conquest of Gaul. In the 3C and 4C, the city was the centre of the vast province known as the Viennoise stretching from Lake Geneva to the mouth of the Rhône. Great public buildings were erected at the foot of Mount Pipet, opposite **St-Romain-en-Gal**, the Gallo-Roman city **(cité gallo-romaine★)** with its houses and shops. In the 5C, Vienne became the capital of the Burgundians, who ruled over the east bank of the Rhône before being chased away by the Franks in 532. Ruled subsequently by its archbishops, the city became the object of the rivalry between the Kingdom of France and the Holy Roman Empire, until its final incorporation into France at the same time as the Dauphiné, in 1349.

WALKING TOUR

Vienne map, p454.

- **Cathédrale St-Maurice★★** – pl. Saint Maurice. Open daily 10am–6pm. No charge. 04 74 53 80 30. www.cathedraledevienne.com. Built from the 12–16C, the cathedral combines Romanesque and Gothic elements. Only 35 years after its completion, the cathedral suffered mutilation during the Wars of Religion. It underwent extensive restoration in the 19C, but much remains to be admired, including the fine Renaissance window in the south aisle, the 13C low-relief between the sixth and seventh chapels in the north aisle depicting Herod and the Magi, and the rare 11C Bishop's Throne (*in the apse behind the high altar*).
- **Temple d'Auguste et de Livie★★** – pl. Charles de Gaulle. This Classical temple was first built in the reign of Emperor Augustus shortly before the beginning of the Christian era; it seems likely that it was then reconstructed about 50 years later. At the time it would have dominated the Forum to the east. It has been well preserved through successive re-use as a public building of various kinds (church, Jacobin club, tribunal, museum, library), and subsequently through its restoration by Prosper Mérimée in 1850. The 16 Corinthian columns rise from a podium rather than directly from the ground in the Greek manner. In the pediment are traces of a bronze inscription to the glory of Augustus and Livia.
- **Église St-André-le-Bas★** – This church is mainly 12C.
- **Cloître St-André-le-Bas★** – These small, trapezoidal cloisters date from the 12C. They have a series of blind arcades, resting alternately on twinned colonnettes and the piers marking the bays.
- **Église St-André-le-Haut.**
- **Théâtre Romain★** – The Roman theatre had been abandoned since the time of Emperor Constantine, in the early 4C, and was one of the largest theatres in Roman Gaul.
- **Jardin Archéologique.**
- **Musée des Beaux-Arts et d'Archéologie.**

Temple d'Auguste et de Livie

© Sime/Photononstop

ADDITIONAL SIGHTS

- **Ancienne Église St-Pierre★** – The church of St-Pierre is the oldest building of Christian Vienne, dating to the 5C.

ADDRESSES

STAY

Camping Bontemps – 38150 Vernioz. 19km/12mi S of Vienne via N 7, D 131 and D 37. ℘04 74 57 83 52. Open Apr–Sep. Reservations recommended. 100 sites. Food service. Tourism and sports are on this campground's programme. Set off walking or sightseeing to discover the region – unless you'd rather stay put and take advantage of the on-site sports facilities to go horseback riding, mountain biking or swimming.

Hôtel Central – 7 r. de l'Archevêché. ℘04 74 85 18 38. 25 rooms. In the heart of the city, as its name implies, this simple hotel's best feature is its central location.

Chambre d'Hôte Le Pré Neuf – 9 r. des Guillemottes. ℘04 74 31 70 11. 3 rooms. On the edge of town, this 19C house has a nice garden; the rooms are furnished with homely items.

La Gabetière – 269 Le Logis-Neuf, 38780 Estrablin. ℘04 74 58 01 31. www.la-gabetiere.com. 12 rooms. A beautiful 16C mansion surrounded by a park. Swimming pool.

EAT

La Chamade – 24 r. Juiverie. ℘04 74 85 30 34. Closed mid Aug. The decor of white walls, yellow tablecloths and indirect lighting is simple, the service efficient and the prices quite affordable.

L'Estancot – 4 r. de la Table-Ronde. ℘04 74 85 12 09. Closed 1–15 Sep, Christmas to mid-Jan, Sun-Mon and public holidays. Interested in trying some criques, the delicious Ardéchois potato-pancake dish? Then take a seat in this restaurant. Featured for dinner daily, they can be ordered with vegetables, foie gras or prawns.

La Medina – 71 r. de Bourgogne. ℘04 74 53 51 35. Here the emphasis is on Morocco; cuisine, decor and furnishings. The perfect place to try a tagine and couscous.

ON THE TOWN

Canicule – 5 r. Cornemuse. ℘04 74 85 40 22. Tue-Thu, Sun 8pm-1am, (Fri-Sat, 3am). "La canicule" means "the dog days" - will this new cocktail bar succeed in turning up the heat in the rather complacent city of Vienne? In a pretty, exotic setting, you can order sizeable cocktails spiked with varying quantities of alcohol.

Bar du Temple – 5 pl. du Gén.-de-Gaulle. ℘04 74 31 94 19. Summer: 7am–midnight; rest of the year: Mon-Sat. Closed public holidays. This is THE café that everyone who's anyone in Vienne knows about.

VIENNE

WHERE TO STAY

Bontemps (Camping)........................③
Central (Hôtel)....................................⑤
Gabetière (La)....................................⑦
Pré Neuf (Chambre d'hôte Le)......⑨

WHERE TO EAT

Chamade (La)......................................②
Estancot (L')..④
Medina (La)..⑥

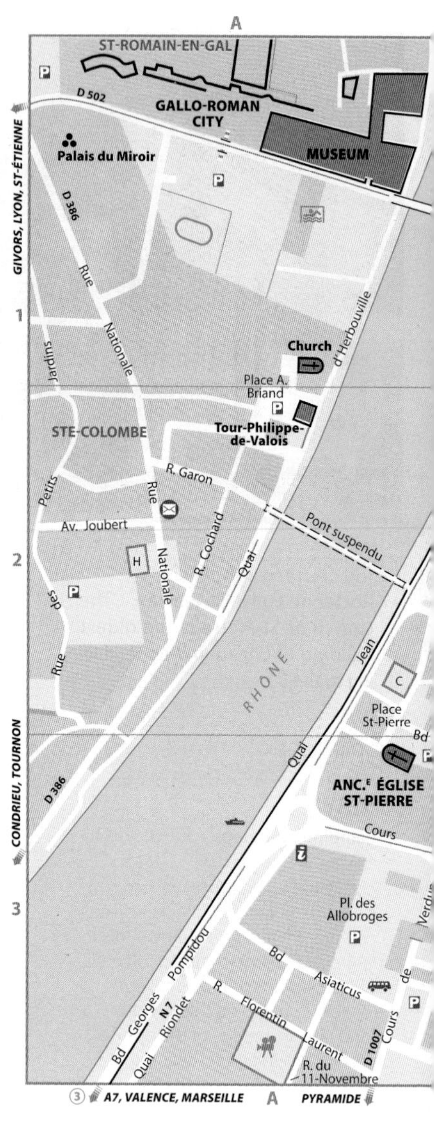

Its best feature is the superb terrace at the foot of the Temple d'Auguste and de Livie.

O'Donoghue's Pub – 45 r. Francisque-Bonnier. ✆04 74 53 67 08. 4pm–3am. All year round, this Little Brittany in Vienne holds Celtic music concerts attended by a cluster of Breton "ex-pats". If you've never tasted a Coreff, typical Breton beer, this is your chance.

SHOPPING

Markets – On Saturday mornings, the streets of the city centre, from the banks of the Rhône to the Jardin de Cybèle, overflow with market stalls. This is the perfect time to shop for a few bottles of Côte-Rôtie, a delicious Côtes-du-Rhône wine made in the region.

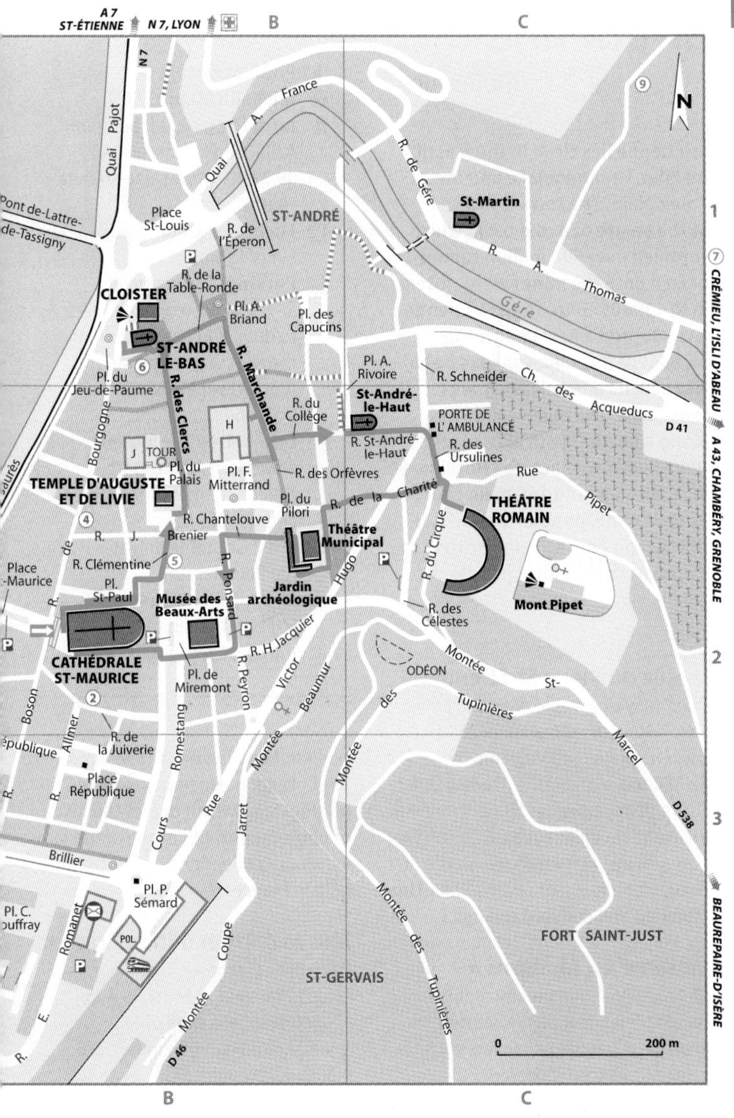

Ets Patissier Jean-Guy – 16 pl. de Miremont. ℘04 74 85 08 77. Tue-Sun 8am–7.30pm. Founded in the 1970s and remodelled in 2000, this pastry shop/tearoom's fine reputation has spread throughout the province. Its chocolate, (made with the finest cocoa beans), pastries (made with grade AA butter), ice cream and cakes are delicious.

THEATRE

Théâtre de Vienne – 4 r. Chantelouve. ℘04 74 85 00 05. Mid Sep–Jul Mon-Fri 10am-noon, 2–6.30pm, Sat 3–6pm performance days. Built in the early 18C, when Marivaux, Goldoni and Beaumarchais prevailed, this theatre exudes history and charm. Events of all genres are staged here, including drama, classical and pop music, dance, opera and children's shows.

St-Étienne★

Rhône-Alpes

St-Étienne lies close to the Massif du Pilat, Grangent lake and the Forez plain. The town is located at the centre of a coal basin which supplied over 500 million tonnes of coal until the mines were closed in the 1980s. Since then St-Étienne has adopted a new image: the façades of its buildings have been cleaned, its gardens and parks renovated. The busiest area lies along a north–south axis: place Jean-Jaurès to place de l'Hôtel-de-Ville. The 15C and 16C main church of St-Étienne, popularly known as the "Grand'Église", remains dear to the hearts of the local people.

- **Population:** 171 260.
- **Michelin Map:** 327 F 7
- **Info:** 16 av. de la Libération. 42000 St-Étienne. ℘04 77 49 39 00. www.saint-etienne tourisme.com.
- **Location:** 62km/39mi SW of Lyon.
- **Parking:** The centre of St-Étienne is a difficult place to drive and park. The tram is the best way to get around. A one-day pass is available from the tourist office.
- **Don't Miss:** The Museum of Modern Art's superb collection of photographs and the Old Town.
- **Kids:** Go stargazing at the Planetarium.
- **Timing:** There is more to St-Étienne than meets the eye; allow a full day.

VISITS

Musée du Vieux St-Étienne★

Open daily except Sun, Mon and public hols, 2.30–6pm. €3. ℘04 77 25 74 32. www.vieux-saint-etienne.com.

An 18C toll-marker from the old Outre-Furan district signals the entrance to the Hôtel de Villeneuve (18C). The City Museum inside is arranged on the first floor, in a series of rooms with fine moulded and coffered ceilings.

Musée d'Art Moderne★★

4.5km/3mi from the city centre. Leave St-Étienne N via rue Bergson towards La Terrasse and follow signs to the Musée d'Art Moderne.

Open daily except Tue 10am–6pm. Closed 1 Jan, 1 May, 14 Jul, 15 Aug, 1 Nov, 25 Dec. ♿ €5.50. ℘04 77 79 52 52. www.mam-st-etienne.fr.

The Museum of Modern Art of St-Étienne Métropole houses one of the largest collections of art from the 20C and 21C in France. The building was designed by the architect Didier Guichard in 1987 and offers a wide and luminous exhibition space.

The Collection includes works from many different movements such as Cubism, Surrealism, Neo-expressionism, Pop Art, New Realism and Minimal Art. The Collection also contains about 2 300 photographs which depict the history of photography and is one of the largest single collections of photographs held in France.

Musée d'Art et d'Industrie★★

Open daily except Tue 10am–6pm. Closed 1 Jan, 1 May, 14 Jul, 15 Aug, 1 Nov and 25 Dec. ♿ €7.50. ℘04 77 49 73 00. www.musee-art-industrie.saint-etienne.fr.

This Art and Industry Museum, located in the former Palais des Arts, is a real repository of local and regional know-how relating to tool-making and the evolution of equipment and machinery from the 16C up to the present day.

Planetarium★

Espace Fauriel, 28 rue P.-et-D.-Ponchardier. Open: call or check website for times of shows and visits. Closed Sep, 1 Jan, 1 May, 25 Dec. ♿ €7.50–€10.30 (children €6). ℘04 77 33 43 01. www.planetarium-st-etienne.fr.

Crowned by a hemispherical dome, this planetarium is fitted with highly sophisticated equipment which enhances its shows about the universe.

ADDRESSES

STAY

Hôtel Carnot – 11 bd Jules-Janin. 04 77 74 27 16. Closed 2–24 Aug. 24 rooms. This hotel near the Carnot train station has a steady flow of regular customers who appreciate the warm reception and reasonable prices.

Chambre d'Hôte du Domaine de Bonnefond – 42660 St-Romain-les-Atheux. 04 77 39 04 06. 3 rooms. This former farmhouse is situated in beautiful countryside. Indoor pool.

Chambre d'Hôte Mme Grimand - Pracoin – 42230 St-Victor-sur-Loire. 04 77 90 37 95. www.chambre-hotes-loire.com. 3 rooms. WiFi. Close to the gorges of the Loire and of the medieval village of St-Victor, this house has three harmonious and comfortable rooms.

Hôtel du Midi – 19 bd. Pasteur. 04 77 57 32 55. www.hotelmidi.fr. 33 rooms. Two buildings linked by a cosy lounge with an original fireplace. The rooms are a bit small, but practical and soundproofed.

Les Cèdres Bleus – Rte de Bas-en-Basset, 43110 Aurec-sur-Loire. 04 77 35 48 48. www.lescedresbleus.com. Closed Jan. 15 rooms. Restaurant (closed Sun evening, Mon and Tue lunches). WiFi. Between the gorges of the Loire and the Grangent lake, in a park, are three wooden chalets completely renovated.

EAT

La Presqu'Île – Rte du Port, 42230 St-Victor-sur-Loire. 04 77 53 70 08. Closed evenings. Located just outside the medieval village with a beautiful view of the gorges of the Loire and the peninsula of the Chatelet.

Corne d'Aurochs – 18 r. Michel-Servet. 04 77 32 27 27. Closed Mon lunch, Sat lunch and Sun. Just a short walk from the hôtel de ville, here's a bistro serving cuisine of the Lyon tavern genre.

Evohé – 10 pl. Villebœuf. 04 77 32 70 22. Closed Mon evening, Sat lunch, and Sun. Opposite a green square, near the Maison de la Culture; the walls are decorated with colourful paintings (some for sale), and the table arrangement preserves privacy.

La Nouvelle – 30 r. St-Jean. 04 77 32 32 60. Closed Sun and Mon. The refined setting is in perfect harmony with the inventive cuisine concocted by the owner-chef.

THEATRE AND ENTERTAINMENT

Comédie de St-Étienne, Centre Dramatique National – 7 av. du Prés.-Émile-Loubet. 04 77 25 01 24. www.lacomedie.fr. Tickets: Mon-Fri 2–7pm. Closed Aug and public holidays. This centre was founded in 1947 in order to initiate and promote drama outside of the capital. Today it orchestrates a permanent troupe of actors, a stage set workshop and a costumes atelier.

L'Esplanade – Opéra Théâtre de St-Étienne – Allée Shakespeare, Jardin des Plantes, BP 237. 04 77 47 83 40. www.opera.saint-etienne.fr. Tickets: Mon-Fri 2–7pm. Closed mid Jul–Aug. The focal point of cultural animation in St-Etienne offering theatre, ballet and operetta.

Le Triomphe – 4 sq. Violette. 04 77 32 22 16. Tickets: Tue-Sat, 2–8pm. Closed Jul–Aug. This café-theatre in a converted cinema cultivates in its shows the spirit, the culture, the accents and the language of the region.

Le Tamora – 15 r. Dormoy. 04 77 32 36 97. Wed, 10pm-3am, Thu 7pm-3am, Fri-Sat 7pm-4am. Known in St-Étienne for its karaoke evenings, this club has hosted the popular French songsters Gilbert Montagné, Zouk Machine, and Larusso.

Nouvel Espace Culturel – 9 r. Claudius-Cottier, 42270 St-Priest-en-Jarez. 04 77 74 41 81. Tickets: Mon-Fri, 8.30am-4.30pm. Closed Aug and weekends. The Nouvel Espace Culturel was created in 1991 in a suburb close to Saint-Étienne. Many professional and amateur theatre troupes from all over France appear here performing new works or repertory pieces.

Le Puy-en-Velay★★★

Haute-Loire

The town occupies one of the most amazing sites in France, its most striking landmark being the huge statue of the Virgin Mary atop a tall column of volcanic rock. Le Puy has been famous for pilgrimages since Bishop Gotescalk made one of the first pilgrimages to Santiago de Compostela from here in 962.

- **Population:** 18 521.
- **Michelin Map:** 331 F 3
- **Info:** 2 place du Clauzel. ✆04 71 09 38 41. www.ot-lepuyenvelay.fr.
- **Location:** Le Puy-en-Velay lies 75km/46.5mi SW of St-Étienne, and 126km/79mi SE of Clermont-Ferrand.
- **Don't Miss:** The fantastic views from the upper rim of the basin, especially during sunset, or the lively Saturday market at Place du Breuil.

THE TREASURE TRAIL★★★

The city's growth dates from the 11C, when it took over the urban functions of nearby St-Paulien and when it formed an important destination on the pilgrimage road to Santiago de Compostela in Spain. The cathedral's fortifications are evidence of the bishops' quarrels with the local lords over sovereignty and taxes raised from the pilgrims.

In the centre of the old town, the area around the cathedral has a sombre air, with its buildings of granite and lava, narrow arcaded entranceways, mullioned windows, heavy iron grilles and paving stones.

Walking Tour 1

Le Puy-en-Velay map, p461.

- **Cathédrale Notre-Dame★★★** – Guided tours available; contact the tourist office. ✆04 71 09 38 41. www.cathedraledupuy.org.

The first building to occupy the site was a Roman temple, followed in 430 by a sanctuary dedicated to the Virgin, built at the same time as Santa Maria Maggiore in Rome. Rebuilding and extension took place from the 10C on, and in the 19C major restoration was carried out.

St-Michel-d'Aiguilhe, Rocher Corneille and Cathédrale Notre-Dame

The lofty west front rises from its monumental steps to dominate the Rue des Taules. The windows in the third storey mark the extension to the nave which took place at the end of the 12C and which is supported on massive arcading. The overall impression is highly ornamental, due to the pierced or blind Romanesque arches, the use of polychrome granite and basalt stonework, the mosaics in the gables and the columns with carved lava capitals.

The steps continue to rise, giving a good view of the carved doors of the Golden Doorway (Porte Dorée) with, on the left, a depiction of the Nativity, and on the right, Christ's Passion. In the 10C and 11C, the apse was rebuilt and the transepts and first two bays of the nave erected. At the beginning of the 12C the two adjacent bays were built and vaulted with splendid domes. The two last bays were added at the end of the 12C.

Dating from the 11C and 12C, the cathedral **Cloisters★★** have polychrome mosaics, an allegorical Romanesque frieze at the base of the roof, a fine 12C wrought-iron **grille★** and, in the Reliquary Chapel (Chapelle des Reliques), a celebrated Renaissance fresco depicting the Liberal Arts. It also qualifies as one of the starting points of the pilgrim route to Santiago de Compostela.

Religious Art Treasury★★ – The Treasury, displayed in the former Velay State Room above the Chapel of Relics, contains a large number of works of art, including an 11C silk cope, a 13C engraved enamel reliquary, a polychrome-stone 15C Nursing Virgin, a magnificent 16C embroidered cloak for the Black Virgin, and a piece of 15C parchment showing the Genesis of the World to the Resurrection.

Lace

Lace-making was widespread in the area around Le Puy as early as the 17C, though its high point was reached in the 19C, in part due to the efforts of Théodore Falcon (1804–56), who encouraged high standards in both design and quality. Before World War I, bobbin lace and needlepoint lace were equally popular, but after 1919, the former (also known as pillow lace) became dominant, with threads of linen, silk and wool used to form patterns of great variety and delicacy.

◆ **Rocher Corneille** – This is an outlier of the volcano of which the Rocher St-Michel was the vent. It is topped by a 16m statue of Notre-Dame of France made in 1860 from more than two hundred melted-down cannons captured at the Siege of Sebastopol during the Crimean War. Reached by a steep path, the terrace at the foot of the statue offers the best viewpoint over the extraordinary **site★★★** of Le Puy.

THE OLD QUARTER★

The tall, red-roofed houses of the old town cluster around Corneille rock, while the circular boulevards mark the start of the lower, more modern town.

Walking Tour 2

Le Puy-en-Velay map, p461.

ADDITIONAL SIGHT

St-Michel-d'Aiguilhe★★

Open daily: Feb–mid-Mar 2–5pm; mid-Mar–Apr and Oct–mid-Nov 9.30am–noon, 2–5.30pm; May–Jul 9am–6.30pm; Jul–Aug 9am–7pm; Sep 9am–6.30pm. Closed 1 Jan and 25 Dec. €3.50. ℘04 71 09 50 03. www.rochersaintmichel.fr.

268 steps lead to the chapel perched on its 82m lava pinnacle. Arabesques and polychrome mosaics of Byzantine inspiration decorate the chapel

doorway. Inside, the complex vaulting gives some indication of the difficulties the 11C architect had to overcome in transforming the original Carolingian sanctuary; one of his contributions was the addition of a gallery to the narthex. Note two capitals reused in the smaller gallery, the 10C murals in the apse depicting the heavenly kingdom, and a Romanesque Christ-reliquary carved in wood.

EXCURSIONS

Château de Polignac

5km/3mi NW.

There is a striking view of this medieval fortress from the N 102 main road. Its defences were so strong that its lords were known as the "Kings of the Mountain". From the 17C to the 19C, their descendants held prominent positions in political and diplomatic life.

Lac du Bouchet★

21km/13mi SW.

The clear waters of the lake, surrounded by coniferous woodland, occupy the almost perfectly circular crater of an ancient volcano. Around it stretch the extensive Devès uplands, formed by a series of fissure-eruptions and overlying the even older granite foundation of the landscape.

Massif Du Ézenc★★★

The area lies SE of Le Puy-en-Velay.

These dramatic volcanic uplands in the southern part of the Velay region form the watershed between Atlantic and Mediterranean. They lie at the centre of a belt of igneous rocks cutting across the axis of the Cévennes.

Brioude★

The town is mid-way along the road from Clermont-Ferrand to Le Puy-en-Velay. Le Doyenné, Pl. Lafayette. 04 71 74 97 49. www.ot-brioude.fr.

Brioude is a bustling market town overlooking the lush plain of the River Allier. Allow half a day to fully explore the St Julien Basilica and the rest of the town.

Basilique St-Julien★★ – pl. Grégoire-de-Tours. Open daily 9am–noon, 2–5pm. Guided tours available. No charge. 04 71 74 94 59. This vast Romanesque church was built at the spot where, according to tradition, Julian, a centurion of a Roman legion based at Vienne, was martyred in 304. For many years it attracted throngs of pilgrims on the road which, beyond Le Puy, passed through Langogne and Villefort, at the time the only route between the Auvergne and Languedoc. Work on the present building began with the narthex in 1060, and was completed in 1180 with the construction of the choir and east end. The nave was raised in height and given a ribvault in 1259. The east end **(chevet★★)** is one of the final examples of Romanesque architecture in the Auvergne. Its five slate-roofed radiating chapels have richly decorated cornices and capitals, above which runs a band of mosaic masonry. The warm colouring of the interior is due to the combination of sandstones and basalts of red, pink and brown hue. The nave is paved with cobblestones laid in the 16C and only recently exposed again.

Lavaudieu★

10km/6.2mi SE of Brioude

The 11C Benedictine priory, attached to the great abbey at La Chaise-Dieu, has charming cloisters **(cloître★)** with timber-built galleries and 14C **frescoes★**in the chapel and refectory.

La Chaise-Dieu★★

The village is 40km/25mi from Le Puy. 04 71 00 06 06.

Set amid lush green countryside and rolling hills between Le Puy and Thiers, the ornate abbey comes as a magnificent surprise.

Église abbatiale de St-Robert★★ – Open year-round; hours vary, so call ahead. Closed Mon in Dec and Feb (except school holidays), 25 Dec, 1 Jan. €4. Guided tours available. Over 1 000m up on the high granite plateau of Livradois, **La Chaise-Dieu abbey**, from the Latin *Casa Dei* or House of God, was already a famous monastery in the 11C. Founded in 1043 by St Robert, it had a thriving community of about 300 monks

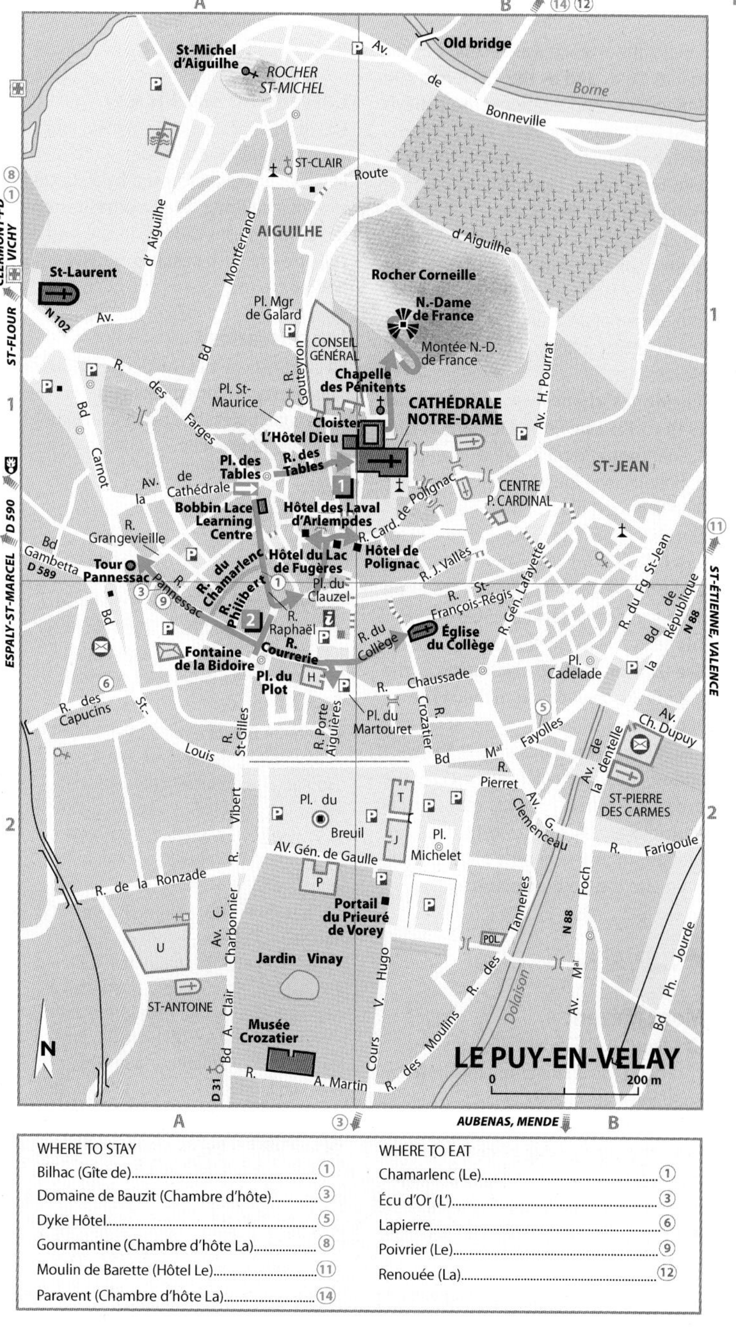

WHERE TO STAY

Bilhac (Gîte de) ... 1
Domaine de Bauzit (Chambre d'hôte) ... 3
Dyke Hôtel ... 5
Gourmantine (Chambre d'hôte La) ... 8
Moulin de Barette (Hôtel Le) ... 11
Paravent (Chambre d'hôte La) ... 14

WHERE TO EAT

Chamarlenc (Le) ... 1
Écu d'Or (L') ... 3
Lapierre ... 6
Poivrier (Le) ... 9
Renouée (La) ... 12

at the time of his death in 1067. In the 12C its importance was second only to that of Cluny and by the 13C it had 300 dependent congregations. The abbey's decline set in after 1518, when abbots were henceforth appointed by the king, with fiscal, rather than religious, considerations taking first place.

The granite west front with its twin towers (the spires have disappeared) speaks strongly of the abbey's former grandeur and austerity. Within, the structure is of a noble simplicity, a single-storeyed elevation.

The **Monks' chancel★★** was built from 1344 to 1352 by Pope Clement VI (the former monk Pierre Roger who went on to become the fourth Avignon Pontiff), who is buried here in the Choir. The 14 Flemish **tapestries★★★** (1500–18), of wool, linen and silk, came from Arras and Brussels. The tapestries are hung over the richly carved 15C **stalls★★**, 144 in number. In the **Dance macabre (Dance of Death)★** figures of the mighty are shown next to their likeness in death.

A great organ was installed at the west end in 1683 and enlarged in 1726; the organ-case **(buffet★)** is elaborately sculpted and contrasts with the spirit prevailing in the choir's architecture. Note also the Gothic **cloisters★**.

WALKS

Mont Mézenc

34km/21mi SE from Le Puy-en-Velay. 2hr-round trip on foot from the Croix de Boutières pass.

Two great lava flows extend downwards from the twin summits of the mountain, from which a vast **panorama★★★** extends over the Velay. Quite close at hand can be seen the village of Les Estables.

Gerbier de Jonc★★

43km/27mi SE from Le Puy-en-Velay. 1hr30min round-trip on foot.

Screes of bright phonolite clatter under the feet of the many who clamber to the summit of this lava pinnacle, from which there is a fine **view★★**.

Cascade du Ray-Pic★★

11km/6.8mi S of the Gerbier de Jonc. 1hr30min round-trip on foot.

In a harsh setting formed by a succession of lava flows, the Bourges torrent drops in a series of falls. In the bed of the stream, dark basalt contrasts with lighter granite.

Lac d'Issarlès★

20km/12.4mi E of the Gerbier de Jonc.

This pretty, rounded lake with its blue waters occupies the crater of an extinct volcano, 138m deep.

ADDRESSES

STAY

Dyke Hôtel – 37 bd du Mar.-Fayolle. 04 71 09 05 30. Closed Christmas week, 1 Jan. 15 rooms. The contemporary rooms are small but tidy. Breakfast is served in the bar room.

Gite de Bilhac – Bilhac, 43000 Polignac. 04 71 09 72 41. www.gite-bilhac.com. 5 rooms. This beautiful fully restored family farm has kept the rustic character of the hostel it was a few years ago. Accommodation is very simple but well maintained.

Chambre d'Hôte Domaine de Bauzit – 43750 Vals-Près-le-Puy. 04 71 03 67 01/06. http://ch.bauzit.free.fr. Closed mid Oct-mid Mar. 5 rooms. Nestled in a vast area, this former monastery exudes serenity. The decor of the room pays tribute to four different countries in Asia, while the fifth and last, "Auvergne", is simpler but equally comfortable.

Chambre d'hôte La Gourmantine – Chemin de Ridet – 43000 Polignac. 04 71 05 94 29. www.gourmantine.fr. 5 rooms. Located at the foot of the 10C castle, this farmhouse enjoys a quiet corner of the village. Cosy rooms. Home cooking.

Hôtel Le Moulin de Barette – 43700 Blavozy. 04 71 03 00 88. www.lemoulindebarette.com. Closed mid Jan-mid Feb. 42 rooms. In addition to the main ivy covered building, there are many "motel" rooms, simple and functional. Camping site adjacent; swimming pool.

⊜⊜ **Chambre d'Hôte La Paravent** – 43700 Chaspinhac, 10km/6mi NE of Le Puy via D 103 dir. Retournac, then D 71. ☎04 71 03 54 75. 5 rooms. Restaurant⊜⊜. The decor is authentic and the cosy bedrooms are very welcoming.

EAT

⊜⊜ **La Renouée** – In Cheyrac, 43800 St-Vincent. 16km/10mi N of Le Puy via D 103 and secondary road. ☎04 71 08 55 94. Closed Jan, Feb, Tue, Wed and Thu evenings from 12 Nov–31 Dec. Country-style dining room with a stone fireplace featuring tasty regional cuisine.

⊜⊜ **Le Chamarlenc** – 19 r. Raphaël. ☎04 71 02 17 72. http://lechamarlenc.free.fr. Mon-Wed lunch only; Thu-Sat lunch-dinner. Closed Sun. This small restaurant in the historic centre serves a cuisine based on local produce and organic cereals.

⊜⊜ **L'Écu d'Or** – 59–61 r. Pannessac. ☎04 71 02 19 36. www.restaurant-lecudor.fr. Closed Sun evening and Wed Oct–May. In the pedestrianised part of town, this picturesque restaurant has an arched dining room decorated with murals. Regional cuisine.

⊜⊜ **Le Poivrier** – 69 r. Pannessac. ☎04 71 02 41 30. www.lepoivrier.fr. Closed Sun (except Sun evening in Aug), Mon evening, Tue evening. Sleek restaurant; specialities include beef from Haute-Loire.

⊜⊜⊜ **Lapierre** – 6 r. des Capucins. ☎04 71 09 08 44. Closed Dec–Jan, weekends and public holidays. A little family restaurant off the beaten path serving flavourful traditional fare.

SHOPPING

Market – Pl. du Plot. Sat morning. On the public square with a water fountain, the country comes to pay its respects to the city in the form of baskets overflowing with the finest farm produce.

Marché aux Puces (Flea Market) – Pl. du Clauzel. Sat and fair days. Bargain hunters, second-hand buffs and bric-a-brac enthusiasts should visit the Place du Clauzel.

Centre d'Enseignement de la Dentelle au Fuseau (lace making centre) – 38/40 r. Raphaël. ☎04 71 02 01 68. www.ladentelledupuy.com. Apr–Oct Mon–Fri 9am–noon, 1.30–5.30pm, Sat 9.30am–4.30pm; Jan–Mar and Nov–Dec Mon–Fri 9am–noon, 1.30–5.30pm. Closed public holidays. We can thank St. François-Régis, patron saint of lace workers, for inspiring the creation of this establishment allowing us to discover lace in an original manner!

La Lentille Verte du Puy– 16 Bd Président Bertrand . ☎04 71 02 21 33. www.lalentilleverteduppuy.com. Emblem of the region, the Le Puy green lentil was the first vegetable in France to receive an AOC (Appellation d'Origine Controllée).

Distillerie de la Verveine du Velay-Pagès – Z.I. de Blavozy, approx. 6km/3.6mi E of Le Puy via N 88, exit ZI de Blavozy, dir. St-Étienne, 43700 St-Germain-Laprade. ☎04 71 03 04 11. All year: Mar–Dec: Tue-Sat 10am-noon, 1.30–6.30pm (Jul–Aug: daily); Jan–Feb: Tue-Sat, 1.30–4.30pm. Closed public holidays. The Pagès distillery takes visitors on a discovery tour of the production of Verveine du Velay liqueur.

Sabarot – Z.A. Lacombe, 43320 Chaspuzac. ☎04 71 08 09 10. www.en.sabarot.com. Mon-Thu 9am-noon, 2–5pm, Fri 9am-noon, 2–4pm. Closed Wed and Fri afternoons in summer. Founded in 1819, Sabarot was originally a flour mill. The company later branched out into the Le Puy lentil.

ON THE TOWN

Le Michelet – 5 bis pl. Michelet. ☎04 71 09 02 74. Mon-Wed 7.30am–1am, Thu 7.30am–2am, Fri–Sat 9am–4am. 1960s America and its symbols seem to attract the young people of Le Puy.

Le Bistrot – 7 pl. de la Halle. ☎04 71 02 27 08. Tue–Fri 5pm–1am; Sat 10am–12.30pm, 5pm–2am. Closed Sun–Mon and last 2 wks of Aug. The terrace is calm despite its proximity to the old town.

The King's Head English Pub – Pl. du Marché-couvert. ☎04 71 02 50 35. Mon–Fri 5pm–1am, Sat 10am–1am. Closed 1st week of Jul. The decor is rustic, the choice of beers and whiskies inspired and the atmosphere English. Light meals.

Clermont-Ferrand★★

Puy-de-Dôme

The site★★ of Clermont is unique; the old town, including the cathedral, is built on a volcano, whose black lava makes for an unusual townscape. To the north are the plateaux of Chanturgue and Les Côtes, once the site of a Gallic oppidum, and an example of the phenomenon known as relief inversion, which has protected them from erosion and left them standing out from the surrounding country. To the west are the summits of the Puys, the mountain range that gives Clermont its incomparable setting, best viewed from the Place de la Poterne with its pretty fountain (Fontaine d'Amboise★) of 1515.

- **Population:** 139 860.
- **Michelin Map:** 326 E-G 7-10
- **Info:** Pl. de la Victoire. ✆04 73 98 65 00. www.clermont-fd.com.
- **Location:** 126km/79mi NW of Le Puy-en-Velay.
- **TGV/Train:** 3hrs 30mins from Paris Bercy.
- **Flights:** 1hr flight from Paris. Airport (www.clermont-aeroport.com) is 6.7km/3.6mi east of the city. Airport bus.
- **Tram:** The tram make getting around easy.
- **Timing:** Allow at least half a day to explore the centre. Start at the place de Jaude, the focal point for anything that's going on.

A BIT OF HISTORY

Clermont was the great oppidum of the Arverni (the Celts who gave their name to the Auvergne). Here in the spring of 52 BCE, Julius Caesar and his legions were roundly defeated at the battle of Gergovie by the forces of the Gallic chieftain **Vercingétorix**, whose spirited equestrian statue by Bartholdi stands at one end of Clermont's Place de Jaude. Caesar soon returned, this time winning a decisive battle at Alésia (modern Alise Ste-Reine), and captured Vercingétorix who was taken to Rome where he was paraded in triumph and ritually strangled after being imprisoned for six years in the Tullianum in Rome.

The Capital of the Motor Tyre

© MICHELIN

Two men, Aristide Barbier and Édouard Daubrée came together around 1830 to make agricultural machinery as well as gunshot, and rubber belts and tubes. In 1889, their factory was taken over by brothers **André** and **Édouard Michelin**, the grandsons of Barbier. Building on their tradition of applying scientific method to the work of industry, the company has subsequently flourished through study of clients' needs, scrupulous observation of reality and previous experience. This process has led from the detachable bicycle tyre of 1891, the car tyre of 1895, the low-pressure "Confort" tyre of 1923, the "Metalic" of 1937, the radial tyre of 1946 (designated "X" in 1949), to the Michelin Energy tyre (1990s). This "green" tyre technology – based on reduced rolling resistance – enables fuel savings.

It was at Clermont on 28 November 1095 that Pope Urban II launched **the First Crusade**. Clermont was also the town of the remarkable writer, mathematician, thinker and inventor **Blaise Pascal** ("The heart has its reasons that reason knows not" – Blaise Pascal 1623–62). Among other things, at 19 he invented an adding machine (*on display in Musée du Ranquet*).

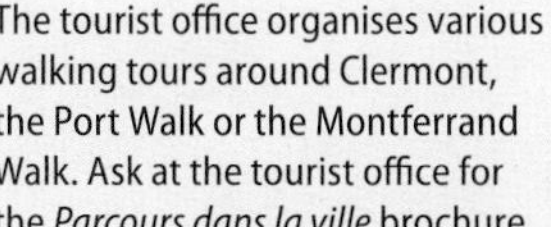

Guided Tours

The tourist office organises various walking tours around Clermont, the Port Walk or the Montferrand Walk. Ask at the tourist office for the *Parcours dans la ville* brochure.

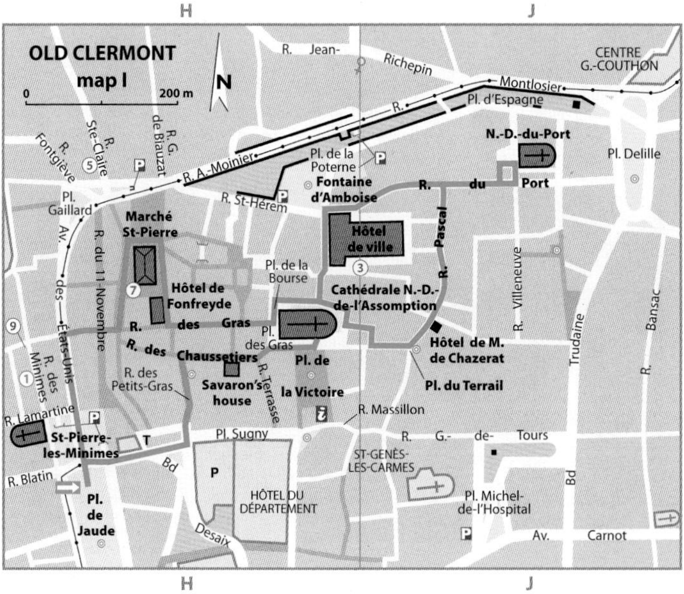

OLD CLERMONT★

A leisurely stroll in the old district will take you through the narrow alleys laid out around the cathedral and place de la Victoire, featuring quaint, old-fashioned fountains and houses with lava stone courtyards.

Walking Tour

Old Clermont map, below.

- **Place de Jaude** – Place de Jaude is the centre of life in Clermont. It is bordered by trees and surrounded by department stores, cinemas and, on the south side, by the Centre Jaude, a vast shopping complex.
- **Église St-Pierre-les-Minimes** – This vast domed church building in the Classical style has fine wood panelling in the chancel.
- **Rue des Gras** – A flight of steps used to lead from here right up to the cathedral.
- **Marché St-Pierre** – This market is situated at the heart of an old district that has been renovated, and stands on the site of a Romanesque church.
- **Fontaine d'Amboise★** – This fountain, erected in 1515 by the Bishop

OLD CLERMONT map I

WHERE TO STAY

Dav'Hôtel Jaude .... (1)

WHERE TO EAT

Chardonnay (Le) .... (3)

Comptoir des Saveurs (Le) .... (5)

Danièle Bath (Brasserie) .... (7)

Pile-Poêle .... (9)

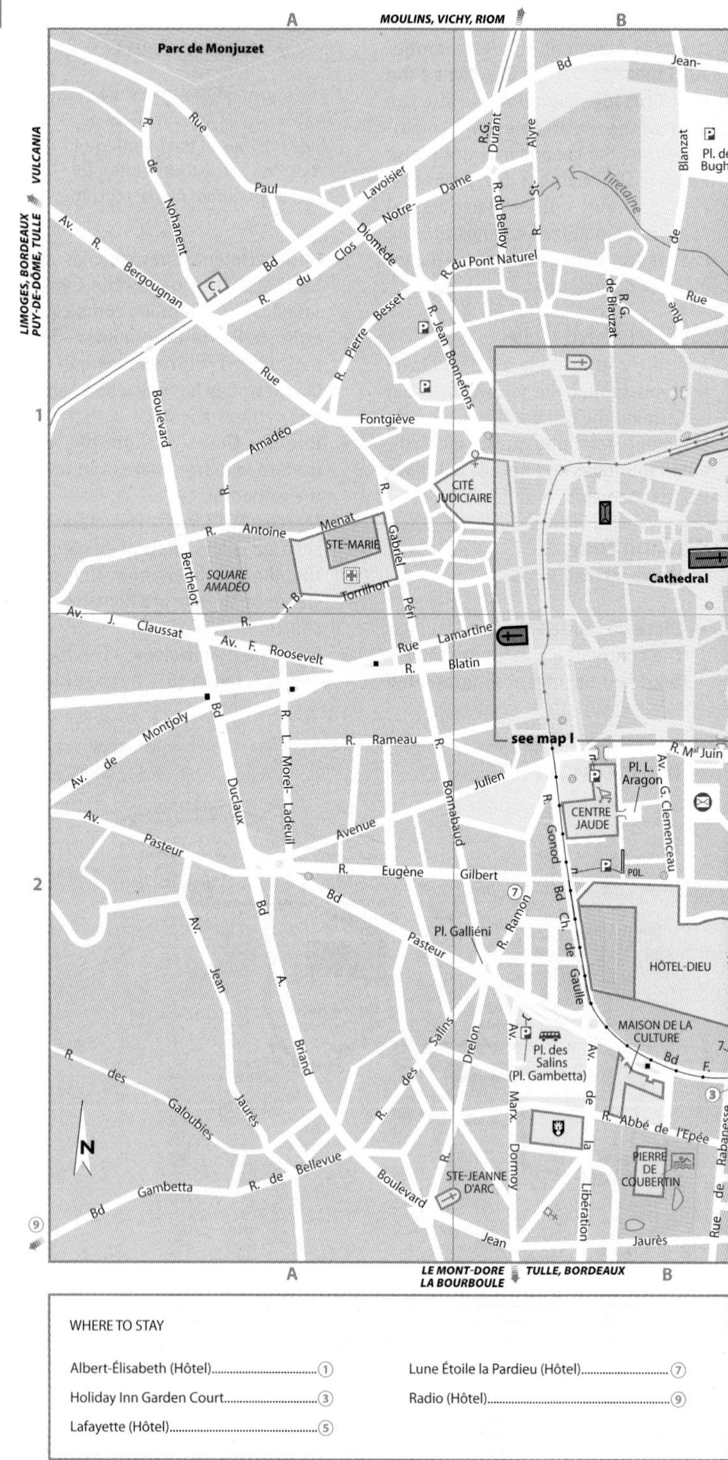

WHERE TO STAY

Albert-Élisabeth (Hôtel) 1
Holiday Inn Garden Court 3
Lafayette (Hôtel) 5
Lune Étoile la Pardieu (Hôtel) 7
Radio (Hôtel) 9

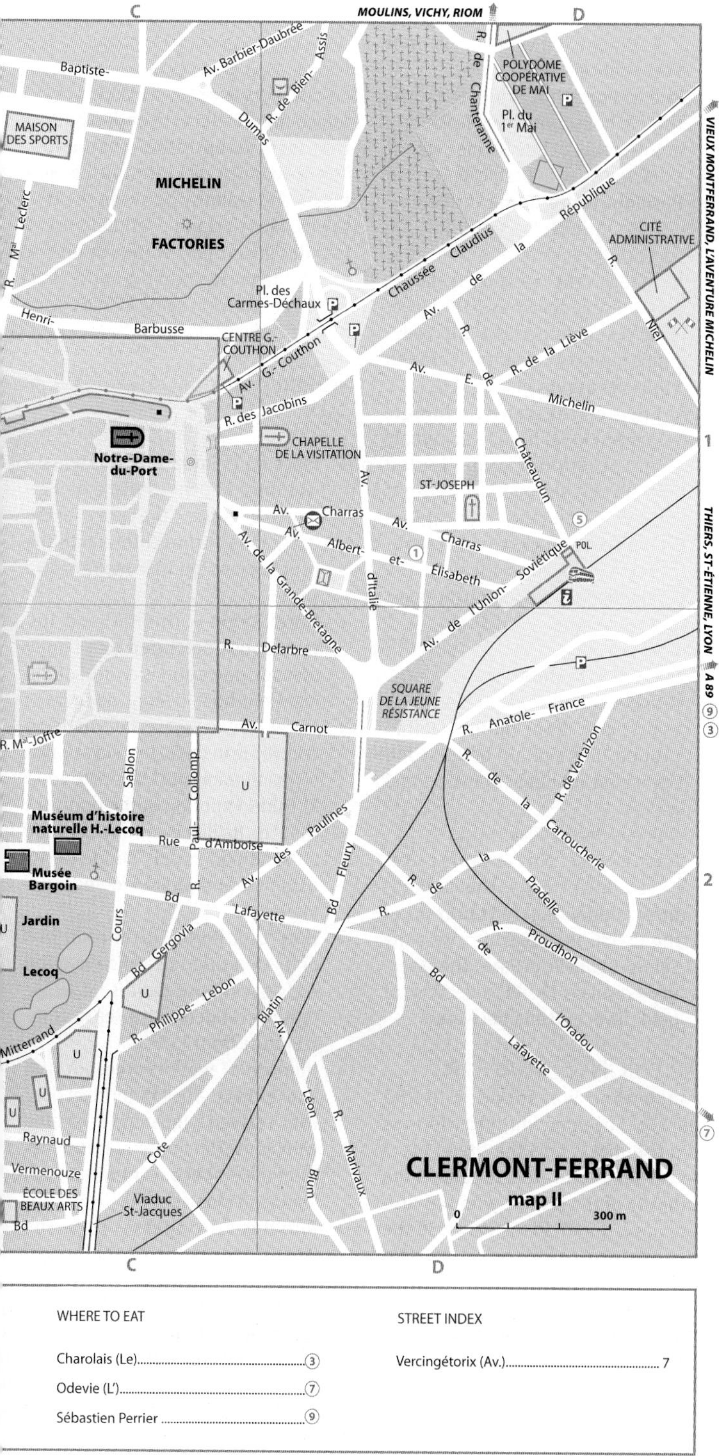

WHERE TO EAT

Charolais (Le) ③

Odevie (L') ⑦

Sébastien Perrier ⑨

STREET INDEX

Vercingétorix (Av.) 7

of Clermont, is a very fine piece of Renaissance architecture.

- **Rue du Port** – No. 21 (right) is a narrow old house with machicolations; at the corner of Rue Barnier, stands a 16C house with barbican.
- **Basilique Notre-Dame-du-Port★★** – 5 r. Saint-Laurent. ℘04 73 91 32 94. See Introduction: Art – Architecture, p86. This is the finest of the larger Romanesque churches of the Lower Auvergne, unforgettable in its beautiful simplicity. It was built around 1150 over a crypt of the 11C.

  Inside, the raised chancel (**chœur★★★**) is quite admirably proportioned and divided from the ambulatory by eight slender columns; their capitals (**chapiteaux★★**), together with those of the wall of the ambulatory, are among the finest in Auvergne.
- **Rue Pascal.**
- **Place de la Victoire.**
- **Rue des Chaussetiers** – Furniture and carpet shops fill the vaulted ground floors of old houses, and there is an abundance of doors and arches.
- **Rue des Petits-Gras.**
- **Cathédrale Notre-Dame-de-l'Assomption★★** – The stained-glass medallions (**vitraux★★**) of the 12–15C are copies of those in the Sainte-Chapelle in Paris. The **Treasury★** displays 12–19C collections of gold, silver and enamel ware.

OLD MONTFERRAND★

Montferrand was founded by the counts of Auvergne who built a fortress on a rise that is now the site of place Marcel-Sembat, in order to counter the authority of the bishop, who was also Lord of Clermont. In the early 13C the town was rebuilt on the orders of a powerful woman named Countess Brayère and was turned into a bastide, a fortified hilltop town laid out to a strictly symmetrical geometric pattern.

Montferrand was a commercial centre at the junction of several roads and, in the 15C, the wealthy middle classes began to commission townhouses. The narrow plots of land made available by Countess Brayère's town plan, however, forced the architects to design houses that were deep rather than wide. The proximity of Clermont caused rivalry and jealousy between the two towns. Montferrand eventually went into decline. In 1962 work was undertaken to renovate the old Montferrand, a project involving some 80 old townhouses and mansions.

Walking Tour

Old Montferrand map, p469.

- **Place de la Rodade** – This square was once known as place de Belregard because of the view over the Puys range. In the centre stands the Four Seasons fountain made of lava stone.
- **Hôtel Regin** – This 15C and 16C townhouse belonged to a family of magistrates and is typical of the mansions built in Montferrand.
- **Hôtel Doyac** – Late 15C mansion built for Jean de Doyac, Royal Bailiff of Montferrand and Minister to Louis XI. Huge, imposing Gothic doorway.
- **Hôtel du Bailliage** – Bailiwick House is the former Consuls' Residence. Its gargoyles and vaulted rooms are of interest.
- **Hôtel de la Porte** – In the courtyard of this mansion, also known as the Architect's House, there is a staircase turret decorated with a Renaissance sculpture from 1577.
- **Hôtel de la Faye des Forges** – A glass door protects a delightful inner door with a carved tympanum decorated with lions. The house opposite has a double timber gallery, an unusual feature in Montferrand.
- **Rue des Cordeliers** – Note the Renaissance ground floor flanked by pilasters and the delightful little inner courtyard.
- **Carrefour des Taules** – This is the central junction in the old town. Its name is a reminder that this was a butchers' market.

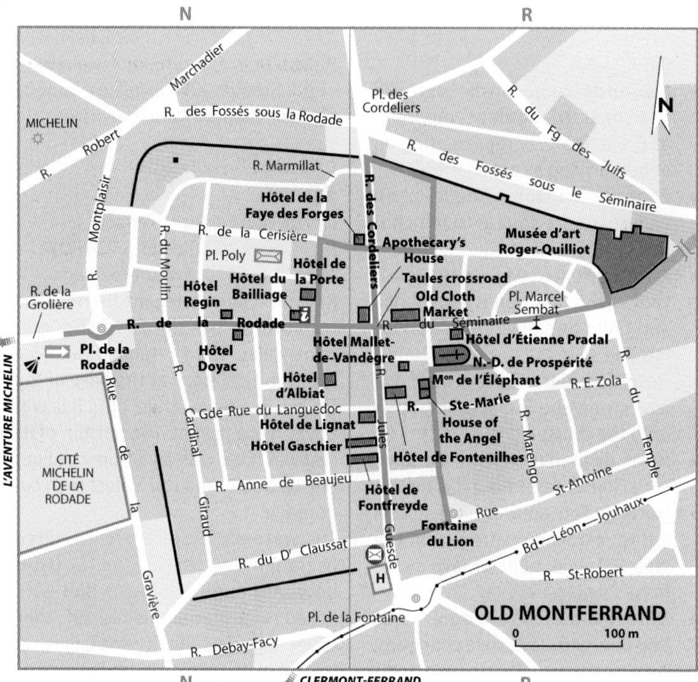

- **Maison de l'Apothicaire** – The old Apothecary's House dates from the 15C and has two timbered upper storeys.
- **Halle aux Toiles** – The old cloth market has a long balcony supporting a fine row of four basket-handled arches and corresponding side doors.
- **Hôtel d'Étienne Pradal** – The ground floor of this mansion has superb semicircular and basket-handled arches. Its "Montferrand roughcast" and cornerstones made of lava stone are typical of the town's architecture.
- **Musée d'Art Roger-Quilliot★★** – Open daily except Mon 10am–6pm. Closed 1 Jan, 1 May, 1 Nov, 25 Dec. €5, no charge 1st Sunday of the month. ℘04 73 16 11 30. The history of these premises reflects the history of Montferrand and Clermont, each in turn the seat of official bodies.

  The museum stands on the site of the Palais Vieux above the town walls. It was the seat of the royal bailiwick of the Cour des Aides of the Auvergne, the Limousin and the Marches; the monumental gateway built in the early 17C in front of the courtyard that precedes the chapel is all that remains of this building.

  When Montferrand and Clermont were combined, the Cour des Aides moved to Clermont and the Ursuline Order of nuns took over and reconstructed the buildings. The site was turned into a seminary after the Revolution, then into a military hospital from 1914 to 1918, and into barracks for riot police and gendarmerie, before being transformed into a museum.
- **Église Notre-Dame-de-Prospérité** – The west front still has its north tower which was used as a watch-tower. It is topped by a 16C lantern.
- **Maison d'Adam et d'Eve** – In the courtyard on a balustrade is a 15C **bas-relief★** of Adam and Eve.
- **Maison de l'Élephant★** – A 13C Romanesque house. The great arches on the ground floor support

the twin bay windows on the first floor.

- **Maison de l'Ange** – In the courtyard is a small, triangular tympanum above a doorway representing an angel carrying a coat of arms.
- **Fontaine du Lion** – The fountain comes from a square to which it had given its name.
- **Hôtel de Fontfreyde** – In the courtyard of this mansion is a Madonna and Child on the Gothic doorway into the staircase turret.
- **Hôtel Gaschier** – Three rows of galleries, one above the other, open onto the courtyard (15C–16C).
- **Hôtel de Lignat★** – This, the Lawyer's House, dates from the 16C.
- **Hôtel de Fontenilhes** – The house, a fine residence dating from the late 16C, was built of lava stone from Volvic.
- **Hôtel Mallet-de-Vandègre** – This building, with its austere courtyard, is said to have been the women's prison

ADDITIONAL SIGHTS

Musée Bargoin★

45 r. Ballainvilliers. Open daily except Mon 10am–noon, 1–5pm (Sun, public holidays 2–7pm). Closed 1 Jan, 1 May, 1 Nov, 25 Dec. €5, no charge 1st Sunday of the month. ✆04 73 42 69 70. www.clermont-ferrand.fr.

This museum houses a sizeable **prehistoric and Gallo-Roman archaeological collection★** on the ground and basement floors, comprising artefacts discovered locally, particularly during recent excavations in the city of Clermont itself.

L'Aventure Michelin★★

32 r. du Clos Four, Cataroux industrial site, N of the city. ♿Open daily except Mon Sep–Jun 10am-6pm; Jul–Aug 10am–7pm. €9.50 (children 7–18, €5.50). P ✆04 73 98 60 60. www.aventure-michelin.com.

An exhibition space, opened in March 2009 and spanning two floors, displays the workings of Michelin, past, present and future. Visitors learn about the history of Michelin tyres, the Michelin Man (Bibendum), and can admire a replica of the Bréguet XIV aeroplane built by Michelin during World War I.

EXCURSIONS

ROYAT

1km W of Clermont-Ferrand.
1 av. Auguste-Rouzaud, 63130 ROYAT. ✆04 73 29 74 70. www.ot-royat.com.

Royat is a large, elegant thermal spa terraced on the slopes of the Tiretaine valley. The Tiretaine flows from the granite plateau at the base of the Dômes mountain range; until it leaves Royat, it is a torrent. The bottom of its bed was filled with lava from the Petit Puy de Dôme, and the waters then cut gorges in it.

The **waters** of Royat were exploited by the Romans, who built public baths here. Although the baths met with mixed success until the mid-19C, they have enjoyed popularity and fame ever since. A hydropathic establishment was built, and the visit here by Empress Eugénie in 1862 launched Royat as a spa.

Parc Thermal – This spa garden, completed by the new English-style park through which flows the Tiretaine, contains the hydropathic establishment and the casino.

The remains of the **Gallo-Roman public baths** can be seen. One of the pools had mosaic-covered arches and marble-covered walls. Terracotta pipes brought the water into the pool in small, semi-circular cascades.

Grotte des Laveuses – The "Washerwomen's Cave" is on the banks of the Tiretaine. Several springs gush from the volcanic walls before flowing into the Tiretaine.

Église St-Léger★ – Built in the 11C, this fortified building deviates significantly from the churches of the Auvergne, for it more resembles the churches of Provence. The bell tower is 19C.

PARC EUROPÉEN DU VOLCANISME VULCANIA★★

15km/9.3mi W of Clermont-Ferrand along D 941B. Open 10am–6/8pm daily Jun–mid-Nov. Closed Mon and Tue Sep–

mid-Nov. Closed mid-Nov–mid-Mar. €24–€28 (children €17–€19.50). ✆04 73 19 70 00. www.vulcania.com. This gigantic theme park is devoted to the history of Auvergne and more specifically to its geological formation. Designed after plans by the architects Hans Hollein and Philippe Tixier, the park aims to spread knowledge about volcanoes and other Earth sciences, while contributing towards the protection of natural sites in Auvergne.

LE PUY DE DÔME★★★

16km/10mi W of Clermont-Ferrand via toll road.

At 1 465m, this mountain is the highest of the peaks in the volcanic landscape known as the Puys. The Gauls erected a sanctuary to their god Lug here, and the Romans built a temple to Mercury. In 1648, Pascal conducted an experiment here proving Torricelli's theory about atmospheric weight, taking readings of the height of a column of mercury while his brother-in-law simultaneously did the same in Clermont-Ferrand; the difference was a decisive 8.4cm.

From the summit there is a vast **panorama★★★** over the city of Clermont-Ferrand, the Grande Limagne basin and the Puys themselves. The Puys, or the Monts Dômes as they are sometimes known, extend over an area 30km/18.6mi long and 5km/3mi wide; in it, there are a total of 112 extinct volcanoes, all more than 50 000 years old.

ORCIVAL★★

26km/16mi SW of Clermont-Ferrand. Le Bourg. ✆04 73 65 89 77. www.terresdomes-sancy.com.

Many houses in this tiny Auvergne village still have their original roof coverings of tiles cut from the phonolitic lavas of the nearby Roche Tuilière, the core of an ancient volcano. Founded by the monks of La Chaise-Dieu in the 12C, Orcival had become an important parish by the middle of the 13C and has been a centre of pilgrimage since that time. More recently, it was the home town of the ex-president of France (1974–81), Valéry Giscard d'Estaing.

Basilique Notre-Dame★★ – Open year-round. Guided tours available; ask at the tourist office. Illustration – see Introduction, p87. Completed around 1130, this basilica is a fine example of Auvergne Romanesque, with a many-tiered apse, powerful buttresses and massive arches. Inside, the majestic crossing is lit by 14 windows, while both chancel and crypt, the latter with a spacious ambulatory, are masterpieces of their kind.

ISSOIRE★★

37km/23mi S of Clermont-Ferrand. 9 place Saint Paul, 63500 Issoire. ✆04 73 89 15 90. www.sejours-issoire.com.

This old Auvergne town is situated at the point where the Pavin valley meets the flatter fertile country of the southern Limagne. In 1540 the town became a notable centre of Protestantism. More recently it has acquired an industrial character, with important engineering works. But there is still an agreeable, provincial ambience about the place that rewards even the shortest break.

Abbatiale St-Austremoine d'Issoire★★ – ♿Guided tours (1hr30min) available. ✆04 73 89 15 90. Built around 1135, this is the largest Romanesque church in the Auvergne. It was extensively restored in the 19C (west front, roof, bell tower, many of the capitals, the polychrome interior decoration).

The east end (**chevet★★**) is a fine example of Auvergne Romanesque, generously and harmoniously proportioned and rich in detail. Inside, an impression of strength and solidity, characteristic of these Auvergne churches, is given by the four great arches at the crossing and by the ambulatory with its ribbed vault. The influence of the Mozac School of sculpture is clearly seen in the capitals (**chapiteaux★** – c. 1140) carved from the local volcanic rock; particularly fine are those showing the Last Supper and Christ washing the feet of the disciples. In the narthex is a 15C mural of the **Last Judgement★**, a favourite subject of the time, here treated with verve and satire.

LES MONTS DORE★★

The Monts Dore consist of three major volcanoes: the Puy de Sancy (see PUY DE SANCY, below), the Puy de l'Aiguiller and the **Banne d'Ordanche★★**, which together with their secondary cones form a region characterised by rugged mountains whose steep, grassy upper slopes provide summer pasture.

Traditionally these animals produced the famous St Nectaire cheese, although nowadays beef cattle are also fattened here before they are taken to the autumn markets.

The Monts Dore are very popular with those seeking outdoor pursuits, and walking, paragliding, canoeing and sailing can all be found here. During the winter there are also plenty of skiing opportunities. The mighty River Dordogne rises on the Puy de Sancy, beginning as two separate streams, the Dore and the Dogne, and plunges down its slopes before becoming the meandering giant which flows through the verdant countryside of the Corrèze, the Lot and the Aquitaine region to the west where it finally reaches the Gironde estuary north of Bordeaux.

Le Puy de Sancy★★★

48km/30mi SW of Clermont-Ferrand. Sancy station sits 4km/2.5mi along D 983. Take the cable-car ride (3min), then 20min on foot to the summit.

The Puy de Sancy, the highest peak in central France, rises to 1 885m from the set of extinct volcanoes called the Mont Dore massif, one of the most picturesque areas in the Auvergne.

Panorama★★★ – 1hr30min to the summit and back on foot by a rough path from the top station of the cable railway. With the heights of the Mont Dore massif in the foreground, the immense views extend northeastwards over the Puys and to the Cantal massif in the south. The hedged fields of the valley bottoms give way, at 1 100–1 400m, to a forest of beech, spruce and fir, while the landscape as a whole is enhanced by the presence of volcanic lakes. On the eastern slope is the pretty mountain village of **Basse-en-Chandesse★**, made of lava, with picturesque **streets** and houses, a barbican, and a little **church★** with sturdy columns and rough capitals.

St-Nectaire★

37km/23mi SW of Clermont Ferrand.

Two villages are grouped together under this name: the thermal spa of St-Nectaire-le-Bas (Lower St-Nectaire), which spreads out over a green valley, and the old village of St-Nectaire-le-Haut (Upper St-Nectaire) dominated by its church. In the Middle Ages a Benedictine priory was established as an offshoot of La Chaise-Dieu abbey; a castle, no trace of which remains, was also built on the hill. It was inhabited by the glorious St-Nectaire family whose most famous member was Madeleine de St-Nectaire – young, beautiful and virtuous, widowed early, always followed by 60 men on horseback; she sided with the Protestants in the Wars of Religion, defeated the king's lieutenant in Upper Auvergne and ended up killing him by her own hand. The name "St-Nectaire" is also given to a well-known cheese, made with pasteurised or unpasteurised milk, which has been produced for centuries in a well-defined area within the Cantal and Puy-de-Dôme départements.

Château de Murol★★

6km/3.7mi E of St-Nectaire.

The ruined castle rises from a basalt platform formed by a lava flow from the Tartaret volcano. The site with its polygonal keep was fortified as early as the 12C because of its strategic position between Auvergne and Cantal. At the end of the 14C, it became one of the main seigneurial residences of the province; Guillaume de Murol was responsible for those features which still distinguish the stronghold today (internal courtyard, main tower, and north and east walls) and which serve to remind us both of the medieval obsession with security and of the fiercely guarded independence of the Auvergnat nobility.

A century later, the castle was brought into line with Renaissance tastes. However, the Wars of Religion led to the place being modernised in a military sense, with the building of bastions and watch towers, as well as an outer wall rising directly from the cliff, all reinforcing the site's natural defensive ability to withstand bombardment or sapping. Now no longer impregnable, the fortress was spared Richelieu's demolition programme, but fell into ruin in the 19C.

ADDRESSES

STAY

CLERMONT-FERRAND

Hôtel Lune Étoile La Pardieu – 89 bd Gustave-Flaubert. 04 73 98 68 68. www.hotel-lune-etoile.com. 45 rooms. Close to La Pardieu, and cubic in design; modern and functional.

Dav'Hôtel Jaude – 10 r. des Minimes. 04 73 93 31 49. www.davhotel.fr. 28 rooms. This modern hotel within walking distance of the cathedral is located in a tranquil side street a few steps from the old quarter.

Hôtel Albert-Élisabeth – 37 av. Albert-Élisabeth. 04 73 92 47 41. www.hotel-albertelisabeth.com. 38 rooms. A small hotel near the station.

Hôtel Radio – 43 av. P. et M. Curie. 63400 Chamalières. 04 73 30 87 83. www.hotel-radio.fr. Closed Jan and early Nov. 26 rooms. Restaurant. Drawing its inspiration from the very beginnings of the radio era, this hotel has a 1930s decoration scheme.

Hôtel Lafayette – 53 av. de l'Union-Soviétique. 04 73 91 82 27. www.hotel-le-lafayette.com. Closed 24 Dec–4 Jan. 48 rooms. This hotel next to the station has been completely refurbished.

Holiday Inn Garden Court – 59 bd F.-Mitterrand. 04 73 17 48 48. www.holidayinn.com. 94 rooms. Restaurant. Modern hotel close by the botanic garden, with easy access to the town centre.

ROYAT

Le Chalet Camille – 21 bd Barrieu. 04 73 35 80 87. 11 rooms. Restaurant. This family boarding house in a 1920s pavilion blends right in with the spirit of the nearby spa.

EAT

CLERMONT-FERRAND

Le Chardonnay – 1 pl. Philippe-Marcombes. 04 73 90 18 28. Closed Sat lunch and Sun. The generous bistro style and the easy-going ambience make for a very enjoyable meal.

Le Pile-Poêle – 9 r. St-Dominique. 04 73 36 08 88. Closed Sun. Contemporary restaurant with a vaulted basement, and a fine menu.

Le Charolais – 77 r. Pré-la-Reine. 04 73 91 65 35. Closed weekends and weekday evenings. A favourite with meat-lovers. Generous dishes.

L'Odevie – 1 r. Eugène-Gilbert. 04 73 93 90 00. www.restaurantodevie.com. Closed 3 wks in Aug. A few steps from Place de Jaude; brasserie-style cuisine.

Le Comptoir des Saveurs – 5 r. Ste-Claire. 04 73 37 10 31. www.le-comptoir-des-saveurs.fr. Closed Tue, Wed, Thu evenings, Sun and Mon. A kind of pick "n" mix approach to dining, chosing whatever takes your fancy.

Sébastien Perrier – 6 r. Caire 63800 Lempdes. 04 73 61 74 71. Closed Sun eve and Mon. Dishes inspired by the Mediterranean, served in a traditional setting.

Brasserie Danièle Bath – pl. Marché St-Pierre. 04 73 31 23 22. Closed Sun, Mon and public holidays. Opulent dining brightened by contemporary art; good selection of wines by the glass.

Les Monts du Cantal★★★

Michelin Map: 330: D-3 to E-5.

Location: These peaks are NE from the town of Aurillac.

The mountains of Cantal, formed by the largest extinct volcano in France, embrace the most magnificent scenery in the Auvergne. Several of the peaks rise to more than 1 700m. Some, like the Puy Griou, are jagged; others, such as Puy Mary, are pyramid-shaped. The highest summit, Plomb du Cantal, is rounded and soars to a height of 1 855m. From the mountain heartlands, deep, picturesque valleys fan out, providing easy access.

GEOGRAPHY

Sharp ridges divide the country up into a series of amphitheatres, in each of which the same set of activities is carefully staged. Meadows and cropland fill the valley bottoms around villages, though in areas less exposed to the sun there are birchwoods, grown for fuel. On the middle slopes are beeches, used for a range of purposes, and recently planted conifers. Higher still come the upland pastures, dotted with stone-built huts used until lately as summer dwellings by shepherds or for cheese-making. Known as burons, they are planted round with ash trees, a useful source of fodder in times of drought. The basaltic lava (unlike the trachytes of Mont Dore) yields rich herbage which is grazed by the reddish Salers cattle, which in their turn yield the milk for the famous Cantal cheese.

ACTIVITIES

The authorities are determined that any development in the area should be compatible with the concept of sustainable tourism. While a large range of sport and leisure facilities is offered to suit all tastes and interests, they are closely monitored and must fit in with the long-term plans for the site. *For further details see: www.puymary.fr.*

Mountain biking – This is ideal territory to explore on two wheels. Mountain bike rental and guided tours available.

Horse riding – If you prefer four legs then various circuits both on horseback and even by donkey are available.

Other activities – Walking, hang-gliding, canyoning, cross-country skiing, fishing, rock climbing and white-water sports.

Le Puy Mary

SIGHTS

LE PUY MARY★★★

The summit of Puy Mary is reached by a steep but paved path from Pas-de-Peyrol – 1hr round-trip on foot.

At 1 787m, Puy Mary is one of the main peaks of the once immense Cantal volcano, which had a circumference of 60km/37mi and a cone rising to 3 000m. It is also the most visited natural reserve of the Auvergne region and has to be managed very sensitively. As a consequence, the local authoriies have implemented "Operation Grand Site: Puy Mary – Volcan du Cantal".

Panorama★★★ – Glacial action has decapitated the volcano and worn it down. The view from the top takes in a landscape punctuated by the remains of volcanic vents and lava flows which seem to have only just cooled. The **Pas-de-Peyrol★★** too affords fine views.

SALERS★★

43km/26.7mi north of **Aurillac★**. pl. Tyssandier d'Escous. 04 71 40 70 68. www.pays-de-salers.com.

High up among the vast grazing-grounds of the volcanic Cantal uplands, Salers, one of the "Most Beautiful Villages of France", has long been a market centre and staging-post for travellers. The tiny town has a maze of tortuous streets leading to the main square.

The **Grande-Place★★** is something of a stage-set, overlooked by the corner-towers and turrets of the grandiose 16C lava-built **houses** of the local notables. The Renaissance **Ancien Bailliage** has typically Auvergnat window-mouldings and angle-towers, while the **Hôtel de la Ronade** has a five-storey Gothic turret. The church **(église★)** has a 12C porch and, inside, a fine 15C polychrome sculpture of the **Entombment★**.

Salers is also the name of a locally produced tasty farmhouse AOC cheese made from unpasteurised cow's milk.

ST-FLOUR★★

St-Flour is 63km/39mi SE of Riom along the A 72/E 70. 17 bis, pl. Armes. 04 71 60 22 50. www.saint-flour.com.

Occupying a spectacular **site★★**, St-Flour comprises two little towns; one perched on a huge rock; the other a modern, busy place at its foot. Although all the interest is in the Upper Town, it is more convenient to park, eat and stay in the Lower Town.

At the eastern end of the Upper Town with its old lava-built houses stands the 15C **cathedral★**. From the Terrasse des Roches nearby there are extensive **views** over the rich grasslands of the Planèze de St-Flour, an inclined plateau.

VIADUC DE GARABIT★★

12km/7.4mi S of St-Flour.

This daring steel structure carries the Clermont-Ferrand-Millau railway across the **Truyère** valley with its many hydro-electric works built in the **gorges★★** gouged in the granite plateaux. Its central arch is 116m across. The viaduct was built from 1882–84 by Gustave Eiffel.

SITE DU CHÂTEAU D'ALLEUZE★★

26km/16mi W from Garabit via the Mallet viewpoint and the Grandval Dam.

The square keep and round towers of this most romantic of ruins loom menacingly over the lake held back by the **Grandval** Dam.

ADDRESSES

STAY

Chambre d'Hôte M. et Mme Prudent – R. des Nobles. 04 71 40 75 36. 6 rooms. In the heart of Salers, this stunning 17C house has a charm all its own. The simple rooms are comfortable, the pretty garden looks out towards the volcanoes, and breakfast is served either outdoors or in a handsome room typical of the region, unless you'd rather be served in bed.

Hôtel Le Gerfaut – rte de Puy Mary – 1km/0.5mi NE via the D 680. 04 71 40 75 75. www.salers-hotel-gerfaut.com. Open Mar–Oct. 25 rooms. Above the town, a modern and functional place to sleep peacefully. Some rooms have balconies or terraces with views.

Vichy★

Allier

- **Population:** 24 774.
- **Michelin Map:** 326 H 6
- **Info:** 19 rue du Parc. ✆04 70 98 71 94. www.ville-vichy.fr.
- **Location:** 70km/43.mi NE of Clermont-Ferrand.
- **TGV/Train:** 3hrs from Paris Bercy

Pleasantly sited in the Allier valley, and well endowed with lush parks and luxurious thermal establishments, as well as high-quality entertainment, racing, a casino and good shopping, Vichy is a world-famous spa town. The virtues of the waters drew visitors here in Roman times and again from the 17C onwards.

A BIT OF HISTORY

The Roman spa town here was relatively small. In medieval times, the river crossing was commanded by a castle and later the town grew during the reign of Henri IV.

It began to flourish as a spa resort from the 17C onwards, and the renowned letter writer Madame de Sévigné came here during the latter part of the century, soon to be followed by the daughters of Louis XV. It was the visits of Napoléon III during the 1860s, however, which really placed Vichy in the top rank of spa towns.

More recently, Vichy gave its name to the Nazi collaborationist government of France led by Marshal Pétain, whose regime ruled the country from Vichy under close German supervision from 12 July 1940 until 20 August 1944. Vichy's reputation was somewhat tarnished by this episode, but its fortunes were revived by the damming of the Allier in the 1960s which created a town-centre lake for watersports.

LE QUARTIER THERMAL★

The florid spa architecture of the second half of the 19C is well represented by a number of constructions such as the Grand Casino of 1865, the Napoléon Gallery (Galerie Napoléon) of 1857, the covered galleries bordering the park (Parc des Sources), which formed part of the 1889 Paris Universal Exhibition before being re-erected here, and the Great Baths (Grand établissement thermal) of 1900.

EXCURSIONS

MOULINS★★

58km/36mi N of Vichy.

Moulins lies on the banks of the River Allier and is the quietly charming main town of the Bourbonnais area. It boasts a range of economic activities linked to

Clock tower, Riom

the rich farmland of the Moulins region, with food industries, shoe factories and machine tool production. The wide avenues and streets of the old town are ideal for a stroll.

SOUVIGNY★★

62km/38.5mi N of Vichy.

Souvigny, which lies among wooded hills in the middle of a rich farming area, retains the most beautiful sanctuary in the Bourbonnais region, a reminder of the town's past splendour. It is renowned for its 11C **church★★** wherein lie the tombs of many of the most influential dukes of Bourbon. The town has the status of "Grand Site of the Auvergne" and is keenly promoting its important architectural heritage.

RIOM★★

Riom is 63km/39mi SW of Vichy along the D 984 and D 2009.

www.riom.net.

The old town of Riom, market centre of the Limagne district, still reflects the splendour of bygone days with its black stone houses and fountains. Be sure to have a leisurely wander in the Old Town.

Quartier Ancien (Old Town) – The medieval town was the capital of the Duchy of Auvergne, then in the 16C and 17C an administrative and legal centre, giving it a heritage of fine houses. Note the 16C **Maison des Consuls★** (*5 r. de l'Hôtel de Ville*); and the Renaissance **clock tower** and 16C **Hôtel Guimoneau★** in Rue de l'Horloge. A ring of boulevards is built on the former ramparts enclosing the Old Town.

Rue du Commerce – The modern sculptures made of lava contrast with the traditional decoration of the houses using the same material (No 36 has 17C caryatids). 16C **Église Notre-Dame-du-Marthuret★** houses the splendid late 14C sculpture – **Virgin with a bird★★★**, a masterpiece of harmonious proportion with a graceful Madonna and infant Jesus holding a bird in his hand.

Ste-Chapelle★ (*r. Jean de Berry*) – remarkable 15C stained-glass windows.

Musée régional d'Auvergne★ (*10 bis r. Delille*) – folk art and local customs.

Musée Francisque Mandet★ (*14 r. de l'Hôtel de Ville*) – 17–18C French and Flemish painting and decorative arts.

Église de Mozac★

2km/1.2mi W. of Riom.

This ancient abbey was founded towards the end of the 7C by St Calminus, becoming subordinated to Cluny in 1095. Until its collapse in 1460, the abbey church was one of the finest in Auvergne.

All that remains of the 1095 building are arches and pillars and the north aisle, together with the 47 capitals (**chapiteaux★★**) which are the oldest and perhaps the most beautiful in the whole of the province. They are products of a workshop which was active from the end of the 11C until the middle of the 12C and which enjoyed considerable influence. Those depicting Jonah (first bay of the nave), the Apocalypse (on the ground in the choir) and the Centaur (third pillar on the left) are justly famous, but it is the capital showing the Resurrection which is truly outstanding (on the ground at the end of the nave). The Shrine of St Calminus (**châsse de Saint Calmin★★**) in champlevé enamel is an exquisite example of Limoges work with chased and gilded inlay figures.

Église de Marsat

3km/1.8mi SW of Riom.

The church here has one of Auvergne's great works of medieval art, a 12C **Black Virgin★★** (in the choir of the north chapel). Few will be untouched by this depiction of Mary as a simple countrywoman, holding out the Child in a maternal gesture of great dignity.

Château de Tournoël★★

8km/5mi W of Riom.

This is one of the province's most celebrated castles. It dominates the town of Volvic, famous for its lava quarry and, of course, its spring water (on sale worldwide), whose exceptional purity is due to the filtering effect of one of the lava flows from the Puy-de-la-Nugère. Picturesquely perched on a crag, the castle dates from the turn of the 13C and was first owned by Guy II the Count of Auvergne. It has two keeps, one round, one square, joined together by ancillary buildings now in ruins. Mullioned windows of Renaissance date look down onto the courtyard, some of them blocked up to avoid window tax.

Gour de Tazenat★

22km/14mi NE of Riom.

This lovely upland lake (32ha/79 acres, 60m deep) in its wooded setting marks the northern limit of the Auvergne volcanoes, one of whose craters it now fills.

CHÂTEAU DE LA PALICE★★

Town and château are 25km/15.5mi NE of Vichy.

Guided tours (1hr) Apr–Oct daily 9am–noon, 2–6pm. Reservations required. €7. 04 70 99 37 58.

The little crossroads town of Lapalisse (pop 3 285) has grown up at the foot of the château which has commanded the crossing of the **Besbre★** since the 11C. Its most famous owner was Jacques II de Chabannes (1470–1525), a Marshal of France who distinguished himself in the conquest of Milan but who was killed by a blast from a harquebus received during the Battle of Pavia.

Little remains of the medieval castle. The present building, started at the beginning of the 16C, is very much in the style of the early Renaissance, the work of Florentine craftsmen brought from Italy by Jacques.

The courtyard façade is enlivened by heraldic motifs and polychrome brickwork, by sandstone courses on the towers and around the windows, by bracketed lintels and mullioned windows, by medallions in the portal of the central tower, by foliated scrolls, pilasters and Corinthian capitals.

Inside, there is interesting Louis XIII furniture in the main reception room. The **Salon doré★★** has a coffered ceiling and 15C Flemish tapestries. The chapel, built in granite, is in Flamboyant style, and there is a fine timber ceiling in the service range **(communs)**.

ADDRESSES

STAY

Arverna Hôtel – 12 r. Desbrest. 04 70 31 31 19. www.arverna-hotels-vichy.com. Closed 17–26 Oct, 17 Dec-5 Jan and Sun Dec–Feb. 26 rooms. A family hotel in a shady street between the train station and the spas. Bedrooms are small but functional.

Hôtel Chambord – 82 r. de Paris. 04 70 30 16 30. www.hotel-chambord-vichy.com. Closed Jan. 27 rooms. Three generations of the same family welcome you to this hotel; sound-proofed rooms.

Les Nations – 13 bd Russie. 04 70 98 21 63. www.lesnations.com. Open Apr–Oct. 70 rooms. Enjoys a central location, functional rooms and traditional food.

Aletti Palace Hôtel – 3 pl. Joseph-Aletti. 04 70 30 20 20. 126 rooms. Belle Epoque architecture and ambience in this palatial former spa near the Parc d'Allier.

Sofitel Les Célestins – 111 bd des États-Unis. 04 70 30 82 00. 131 rooms. A big, modern and very chic hotel on the banks of the Lac d'Allier. Bright, sizeable rooms.

EAT

Brasserie du Casino – 4 r. du Casino. 04 70 98 23 06. Closed Tue-Wed. Experience an authentic brasserie from the 1930s!

La Colombière – 03200 Abrest, 5km/3mi SE of Vichy via D 906. 04 70 98 69 15. Closed Sun evening and Mon. This 1950s villa with a dovecote by the side of the road is rather imposing. Bountiful cuisine.

SHOWTIME

Palais des Congrès – Opéra de Vichy, 5 r. du Casino, BP 2805. 04 70 30 50 30/ 04 70 30 50 56. Tickets: Tue-Sat 1.30–6.30pm; phone reservations: Tue–Fri 10am–12.30pm. Closed Sun–Mon except performance days. A citadel of Vichy culture, this handsome Art Nouveau-style opera house has opted for an exacting programme alternating opera, theatre, dance and even pop music.

Centre Thermal des Dômes

© Franck Guiziou/hemis.fr

THE VICHY SPRINGS

Vichy's mineral and thermal springs contain mainly bicarbonate of soda and carbonic acid. The main springs belong to the State and are operated by a contracting company founded in 1853. The waters here are used to treat conditions of the liver, gall bladder and stomach, diabetes, migraines, nutritional and digestive disorders, and also rheumatological complaints. Waters from the Grande Grille, Hôpital and, in particular, Célestins springs are bottled and exported the world over.

Hot springs – These are the basis of the Vichy drinking cures. The **Grande Grille** is named after the grille which used to protect it from thirsty animals. The bubbling water (temperature 40°C) comes up from a depth of 1 000–1 200m. The **Chomel** (temperature 41°C) is named after the doctor who captured the spring in 1750 and managed the waters. A third hot spring, the **Hôpital** (temperature 33°C), rises in a rotunda-shaped pavilion behind the Casino.

Taste the natural spring water

© S. Sauvignier / Michelin

Cold springs – Part of the regimen includes drinking the water. The **Parc** (temperature 24°C) gushes forth in the Parc des Sources. The **Lucas** (temperature 24°C) is named after the doctor and inspector who bought the spring at the beginning of the 19C on behalf of the State.
The **Célestins** has a temperature of 21.5°C.

Thermal establishments – The Centre Thermal des Dômes can provide up to 2 500 people with thermal and related treatments each morning. The Callou pump room, like that of the Célestins, boasts the latest technical innovations.

Forêt de Tronçais

© Christian Guy/hemis.fr

Moulins★

Moulins, on the River Allier, is the quiet, charming capital of the Bourbonnais region dominated by the twin spires of its Flamboyant Gothic cathedral and the Église du Sacré Coeur. Le Pal★ amusement park is well worth a visit – especially if you have children in tow. Activities on offer include horse riding, kayaking and golf.

- **Population:** 19 590.
- **Michelin Map:** 326 H 3
- **Info:** 11 r. François Péron. ✆04 70 44 14 14. www.moulins-tourisme.com.
- **Location:** In the centre of France, 54km/34mi N of Vichy and 58km/36mi S of Nevers.

A BIT OF HISTORY

The city was founded by the Bourbon lords at the end of the 11C. In time, the Bourbons rose to the rank of dukes. The 15C was the duchy's golden age, with many artists commissioned to work here. The independence of the Bourbonnais became an irritant to the king and François I took advantage of the supposed treason of Charles III, the Ninth Duke, to confiscate his estates. After a series of battles against the French forces, Charles was killed (1527) and the Bourbonnais attached to the French Crown.

CATHÉDRALE NOTRE-DAME★

Pl. des Vosges. Open year-round daily 9am–6pm. Guided tours available. Closed 1 Jan, 1 May, 14 Jul, 25 Dec. No charge; donation suggested. ✆04 70 20 57 77.

From the 17C arcaded covered market there is a good view of the cathedral, which has exemplary **stained-glass windows★★** depicting famous figures from the Bourbons' court. Among the works of art displayed in the cathedral is the **Triptych by the Master of Moulins★★★**, from about 1498 – a triumph of late Gothic painting. The Master has never been conclusively identified. The poses of the figures depicted suggest the Flemish School, while their faces recall the work of Florentine masters. Note also the **Jaquemart★** (bell tower). The **Mausolée du Duc de Montmorency★** (guided tours available; ✆04 70 48 51 18) dating from 1585–1632, is not to be missed.

EXCURSION

Forêt de Tronçais★★★

The forest lies N of Montluçon, and is easily reached on autoroute A71.
Pl. du Champ-de-Foire, Cérilly. ✆04 70 67 55 89.

This splendid oak forest, regarded by many as one of the finest in France, if not Europe, lies at the southeastern end of the great plains of central France, bounded by the rivers Allier and Cher.

A Bit of History

Today's forest passed into the hands of the French Crown when François I put an end to the independence of the Bourbonnais in 1527.

A steady process of deterioration set in which was reversed by the great Colbert in 1670; anxious to maintain the supply of ship timber for the expanding French navy, he instituted measures for the conservation and renewal of the woodland. However, in 1788 an iron foundry was opened, and to satisfy its demands for charcoal, two-thirds of the area was converted from high forest to a coppice regime. In 1832 a new policy of conservation was adopted, and since 1928 six blocks of high forest totalling 650ha/1 606 acres have been managed on a long rotation of 225 years.

Visit

The forest consists largely of sessile oak. The finest stands are called the **Hauts-Massifs★★★**; here there are a number of exceptional trees with their own names, some more than 300 years old. East of the Gardien clearing are the Carré, Émile-Guillaumin and Charles-Louis-Philippe oaks, and to the west of the Buffévent clearing in the Richebout block are other venerable trees called Jacques-Chevalier, de la Sentinelle and des Jumeaux.

The Tronçais region straddles the boundary between the north and south of France. To the north is the langue d'oïl, four-wheeled carts, and slate or flat-tiled roofs; to the south, the langue d'oc, two-wheeled carts, and pantiled roofs in the Roman fashion.

ADDITIONAL SIGHTS

Séries de l'Ouest★ – Western forest stands.

Futaie Colbert★ – Colbert Stand.

Étangs de St-Bonnet★

Pirot★ and **Saloup★** – lakes.

ADDRESSES

STAY

⊖⊖ **Le Parc** – 31 av. du Gén.-Leclerc. ✆04 70 44 12 25. www.hotel-moulins.com. 28 rooms. Restaurant⊖⊖. A few steps from a verdant park and the train station. Modest, well-kept bedrooms and two dining rooms.

⊖⊖ **Chambre d'Hôte La Grande Poterie** – 9 r. de la Grande-Poterie, 03000 Coulandon. ✆04 70 44 30 39. www.lagrandepoterie.com. 4 rooms. Restaurant⊖⊖. Closed Nov-mid Mar. Ancient farm at the centre of a woodland park. Auvergne specialities.

⊖⊖⊖ **Le Chalet Montégut** – 26 rte du Chalet, 03000 Coulandon. ✆04 70 46 00 66. www.hotel-lechalet.fr. 28 rooms. In the centre of a park; quiet, delightful and provincial.

EAT

⊖ **Auberge Saint-Martin** – Le Bourg, 03000 Coulandon. ✆04 70 46 06 10. Closed Sun, Mon and Tue evenings. Traditional dishes served in a rustic but homely dining room.

⊖⊖ **Restaurant des Cours** – 36 cours Jean-Jaurès. ✆04 70 44 25 66. Closed Wed. This fetching bourgeois house in the heart of the city is embellished by a lacework of Virginia creeper. Fixed-price menus.

⊖⊖⊖ **Logis Henri IV** – 03340 Neuilly-le-Réal. ✆04 70 43 87 64. Closed Sun evening and Mon. The logis was a hunting lodge back in the 16C. You'll enter the half-timbered dining room with its pretty tiled floor via the perron.

TAKING A BREAK

Le Grand Café – 49 pl. d'Allier. ✆04 70 44 00 05. Summer: daily 8am-1am; rest of the year: closed Sun, Tue, 1 Jan and 25 Dec. Built in 1899, this café is classified as a historic monument. An imposing fresco honouring Gambrinus, the god of ale, surrounds customers.

Le Vieux Moulins – 2 r. de l'Ancien-Palais. ✆04 70 20 67 81. Summer: Mon-Sat noon-4pm, 7.30–11.30pm, Sun 7–11.30pm. Rest of the year: closed lunch, Sundays, public holidays and 2 wks in Nov. This eminently agreeable establishment has always been a crêperie.

Dordogne Berry Limousin

» **Region map p484**

Bourges p485

Limoge p491

Périgueux p494

Sarlat-la-Canéda p496

Rocamadour p503

Cahors p506

Introduction

The Dordogne, with its hills, its mature and varied agricultural landscapes, its deciduous woodlands and its mellow stone buildings, is not unlike parts of southern England, albeit with a more genial climate and a general atmosphere of good living. Little touched by industrialisation or mass tourism, the regions of Berry and Limousin seem to represent the quintessence of rural France. Berry centres on Bourges which, with its great cathedral, was once the seat of the French court. The Limousin is the name of the old province around Limoges forming the northwestern extremity of the Massif Central.

Geography – The Dordogne incorporates the Périgord region, a plateau dissected by the Dordogne where maize, tobacco, sunflowers and cereals grow. In Quercy, layers of Jurassic limestone form ***causses,*** covered by scrubby oaks and carob trees, dissected by dry valleys and spectacular canyons. The vast limestone plateau, which forms Berry's heartland, is devoted to arable farming, contrasting with the ***bocage*** of the Boischaut and the Brenne.

History – The Dordogne has been settled since the earliest times, as evidenced by prehistoric cave paintings at Lascaux and Font-de-Gaume. The Limousin and the Berry, like the Dordogne, were both part of Aquitania in Roman times and later ruled by the Franks. Contested during the Hundred Years' War, they were eventually annexed to France in the reign of Henri IV.

Economy – The climate of the Dordogne enables the successful cultivation of crops and production of foie-gras, while the Lot valley, west of Cahors, is renowned for its wine. Tourism is important and the area is much loved by northern Europeans. Berry and Limousin are largely rural; agriculture is the mainstay of both, but tourism is important as is the porcelain industry at Limoges. This section also covers towns in Quercy. Although less well known to tourists, tourism is of increasing importance here.

Highlights

1. Palace of wealthy financier, Jacques Coeur, at **Bourges** (p487)
2. Tranquil riverside village and Abbey: **Brantôme** (p495)
3. World famous prehistoric cave painting at **Grotte de Lascaux** (p499)
4. Pilgrimage site clinging to a cliff **Rocamadour** (p503)
5. Medieval bridge with towers at Cahors: **Pont Valentré** (p506)

The Dronne at Brantôme

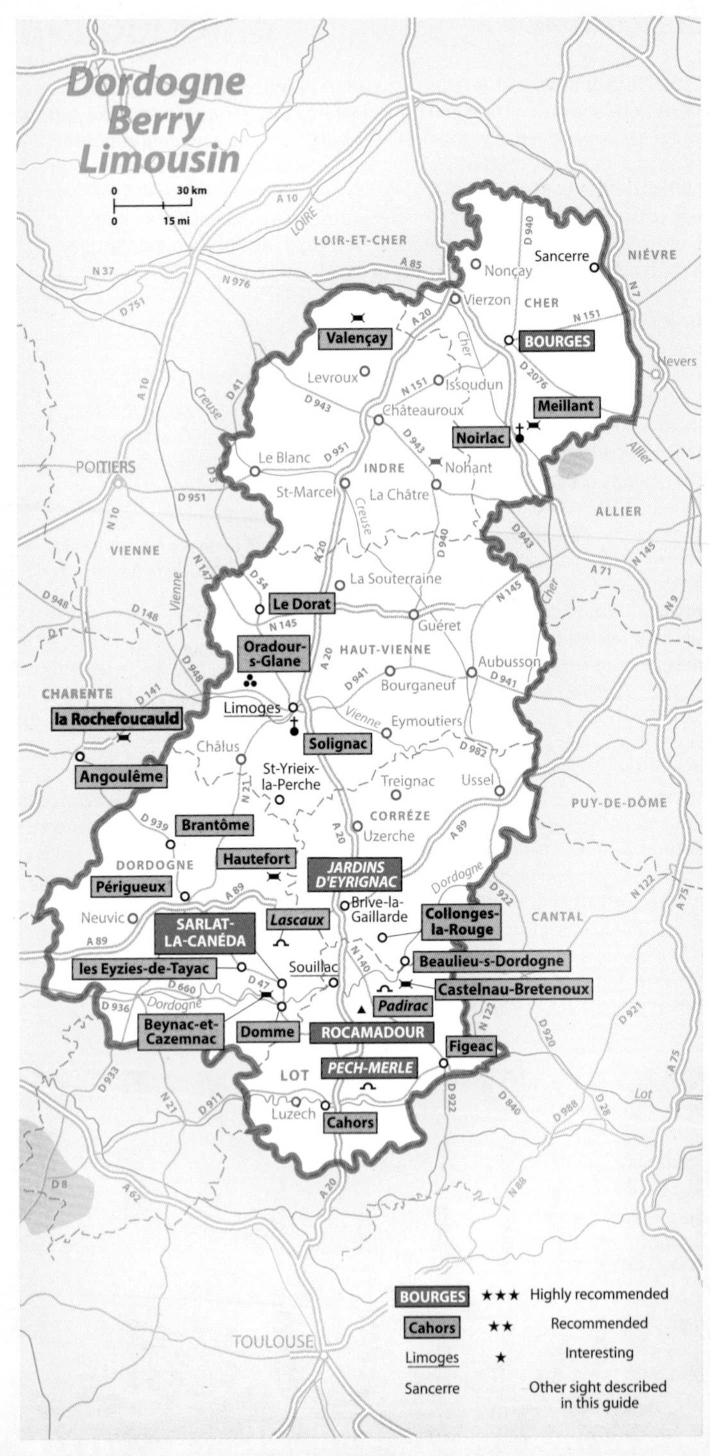
Dordogne
Berry
Limousin
0 30 km
0 15 mi
LOIR-ET-CHER
NIÈVRE
CHER
Sancerre
Nonçay
Vierzon
BOURGES
Valençay
Levroux
Issoudun
Châteauroux
Meillant
Noirlac
Nohant
Le Blanc
INDRE
St-Marcel
La Châtre
POITIERS
ALLIER
VIENNE
La Souterraine
Le Dorat
Guéret
Oradour-s-Glane
HAUT-VIENNE
Aubusson
Bourganeuf
CHARENTE
Limoges
la Rochefoucauld
Eymoutiers
Solignac
Châlus
Angoulême
St-Yrieix-la-Perche
Treignac
Ussel
PUY-DE-DÔME
Brantôme
CORRÈZE
Uzerche
DORDOGNE
Hautefort
JARDINS D'EYRIGNAC
Périgueux
Brive-la-Gaillarde
Neuvic
SARLAT-LA-CANÉDA
Lascaux
Collonges-la-Rouge
CANTAL
les Eyzies-de-Tayac
Souillac
Beaulieu-s-Dordogne
Castelnau-Bretenoux
Padirac
Beynac-et-Cazemnac
Domme
ROCAMADOUR
Figeac
LOT
PECH-MERLE
Luzech
Cahors
TOULOUSE
BOURGES ★★★ Highly recommended
Cahors ★★ Recommended
Limoges ★ Interesting
Sancerre Other sight described in this guide

Bourges★★★

The centre of Bourges is a majestic ensemble of dignified medieval buildings, dominated by the magnificent cathedral, a striking symbol of the town's rich past.

- **Population:** 66 381.
- **Michelin Map:** 323 K 4-6
- **Info:** 21 r. Victor Hugo. ☎02 48 23 02 60. www.bourges-tourisme.com.
- **Location:** 122km/76.5mi S of Orléans.
- **TGV:** Bourges is about 2hrs direct from Paris Austerlitz.
- **Timing:** A ride on the P'tit train touristique gives you a good look at the city's history and architecture (Apr–mid-Nov daily). There are also guided tours offered by the tourist office (*see p485*).

A BIT OF HISTORY

Bourges was already a place of some importance at the time of the conquest of Gaul; in 52 BCE it was sacked by Julius Caesar, who is supposed to have massacred 40 000 of its inhabitants. In the 4C, the city became the capital of the Roman province of Avaricum.

Its significance increased over the years, but only at the end of the 14C did it take on a national role, under Jean de Berry. He made Bourges a centre of the arts to rival Dijon and Avignon, commissioning works like the Très Riches Heures, perhaps the most exquisite miniatures ever painted.

CATHÉDRALE ST-ÉTIENNE★★★

Guided tours Apr–Sep 9.30am–7.30pm; Oct–Mar 8.15am–5.45pm. €8. ☎02 48 65 49 44.

In the 12C, Bourges was the seat of an archbishopric linked by tradition to the royal territories to the north, whereas the regions to the south west came under the sphere of influence of the Angevin kingdom. The great new cathedrals of the Île-de-France were taking shape, and the Archbishop, Henri de Sully, Primate of Aquitaine, dreamed of a similar great edifice for his city.

In drawing up his plans, the anonymous architect exploited all the new techniques of the Gothic in order to control and direct the thrusts exerted by and on his great structure. Other innovations of his included leaving out the transepts, retaining six sexpartite bays and incorporating the Romanesque portals of the old cathedral into the north and south doorways of the new building.

By 1200 the crypt was completed, by 1215, the choir. In 1220 the great nave with its splendid row of two-tiered flying buttresses was ready. Overenthusiastic restoration at the start of the 19C included the remodelling of the external gables and the unfortunate addition of round windows, balustrades and pinnacles. The huge west front has five doorways, anticipating the nave and four aisles adorned with the radiating motifs of the High Gothic (mid-13–14C) style; they were begun in 1230. Ten years later the two right-hand portals were in place.

By 1250, the central portal (*Last Judgement*) had been finished. But 60 years later, subsidence made it necessary to prop up the South Tower by means of a massive pillar-buttress and to strengthen the west front.

This was to no avail; on 31 December 1506, the north tower fell into ruins. Guillaume Pellevoysin, the new architect, worked for 30 years on its replacement, including many architectural

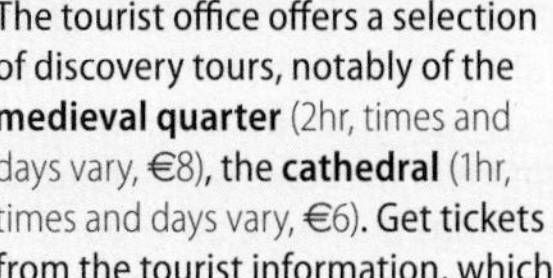

Guided Tours

The tourist office offers a selection of discovery tours, notably of the **medieval quarter** (2hr, times and days vary, €8), the **cathedral** (1hr, times and days vary, €6). Get tickets from the tourist information, which is also the starting point of tours.

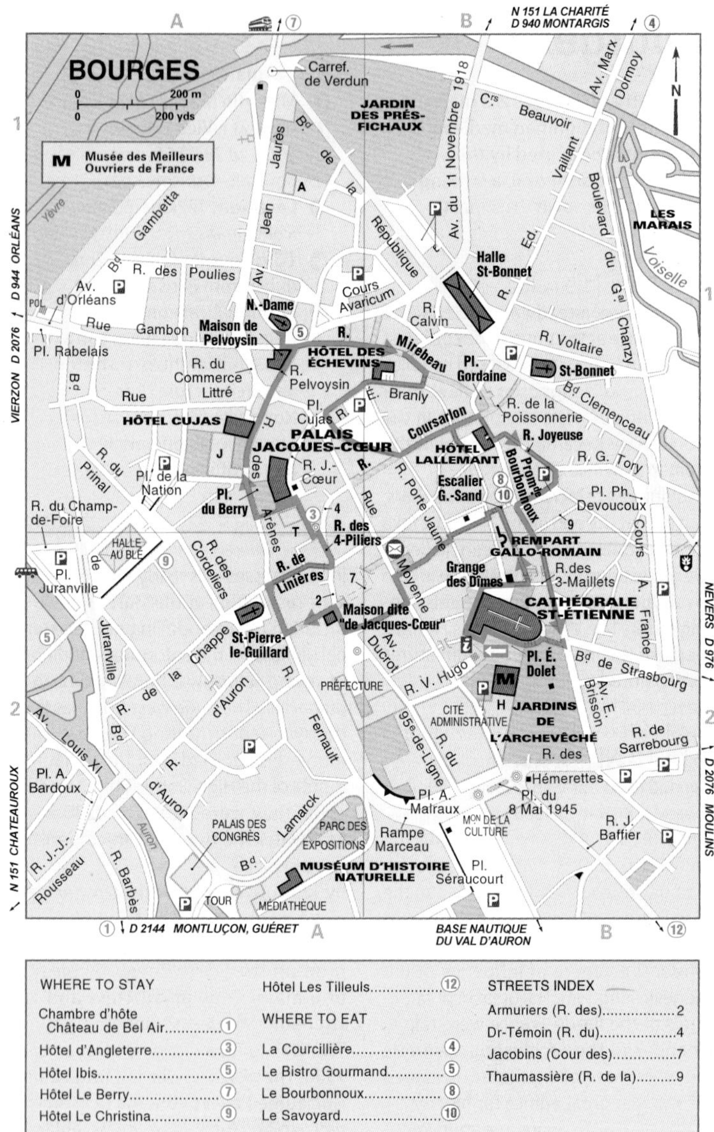

WHERE TO STAY		WHERE TO EAT		STREETS INDEX	
Chambre d'hôte Château de Bel Air	①	Hôtel Les Tilleuls	⑫	Armuriers (R. des)	2
Hôtel d'Angleterre	③	La Courcillière	④	Dr-Témoin (R. du)	4
Hôtel Ibis	⑤	Le Bistro Gourmand	⑤	Jacobins (Cour des)	7
Hôtel Le Berry	⑦	Le Bourbonnoux	⑧	Thaumassière (R. de la)	9
Hôtel Le Christina	⑨	Le Savoyard	⑩		

and decorative features of the Early Renaissance. Inside, the nave and four **aisles**, completed in 1270, make a striking impression by virtue of their great height and the light filtering through the stained glass. Beneath the choir a **crypt★★** of the same layout takes up a 6m change in level of the ground.

A fine example of a 13C crypt, it has an outer ambulatory with triangular vaulting and arcades mounted on twisted diagonal arches to allow the keystones to set.

The stained glass (**vitraux★★★**) – some of the finest in the whole of France – demonstrates the whole evolution of the art of glass-making between the 12C and 17C. The 13C windows in the choir recall the techniques of the master glass-makers of Chartres. The great nave is illuminated by light streaming in through all its windows.

PALAIS JACQUES CŒUR★★

10 bis, r. Jacques Coeur. Open daily, times vary, but generally 9.30/10am–noon, 2–5/6pm. €7.50 (combined ticket with cathedral tour, €11).
☎02 48 24 79 42. www.palais-jacques-coeur.monuments-nationaux.fr.

The son of a Bourges fur-trader, **Jacques Cœur** (1395–1456) started out as a goldsmith, first at the court of Jean de Berry, then with Charles VII. He soon became aware of the economic recovery just beginning and of the opportunities opening up in the Mediterranean. Before long he had many commercial interests and he supplied the royal court with luxury goods and became the king's Minister of Finance. At the peak of his career at the age of 50 he decided to build himself a worthy residence.

His palace, begun in 1445, was completed in the short space of 10 years. It shows how the will to build had revived after the stagnation due to war and also demonstrates the success of the Flamboyant Gothic style. It is a sumptuous building, incorporating certain pioneering comforts like a bathhouse and an arcaded courtyard.

Other innovations that it contributed to the evolution of late medieval domestic architecture included the provision of a large number of rooms with independent access, sculptures indicating the purpose of the rooms served by the various staircases, and, in the chapel, two oratories reserved for the proprietor and his wife.

WALKING TOUR

OLD TOWN

Bourges map, p486.

The whole town centre is part of a preservation and renovation scheme that aims to restore the half-timbered **houses★** to their former glory. Many date from the 15C and 16C,. The old district lying north of the cathedral offers a particularly pleasant stroll.

- **Jardins de l'Archevêché★** – 17C and 18C gardens.
- **Place Étienne-Dolet** – Note the façade of the former archbishop's residence which houses Musée des Meilleurs Ouvriers de France.
- **Grange aux Dîmes** – This massive tithe barn was used to store the dues paid to the church.
- **Promenade des Remparts★** – Ingeniously integrated into the fabric of the contemporary town, the dressed stone wall dates back to the 3C, when it was erected for protection against barbarian invasions.
- **Jacques Cœur's "Birthplace"** – In fact it was built early in the 16C on the site of a house that came to Jacques Cœur through marriage.
- **Église St-Pierre-le-Guillard** – According to legend, funds for building the church were provided by a Jewish man, Zacharie Guillard, whose mule knelt before the Holy Sacrament as it was being carried by St Antony of Padua through Bourges in 1225.
- **Rue des Linières** – A steep, attractively cobbled street.
- **Place des Quatre-Piliers** – Three splendid 17C and 18C mansions.
- **Hôtel Cujas★** – This elegant building was designed in about 1515 by Guillaume Pelvoysin for Durando Salvi, a rich Florentine merchant who had settled in Bourges.
- **Musée du Berry★** – This quiet, unpretentious museum, housed in the Hôtel Cujas, contains archaeological **collections★**.
- **Maison de Pelvoysin** – The house of Pelvoysin, the cathedral's architect.
- **Église Notre-Dame** – This church was gutted by the fire of 1487 and modified as it was rebuilt.
- **Rue Mirebeau** – This pleasant pedestrianised street is lined with timber-framed houses.
- **Hôtel des Échevins★** – This former town hall now houses the **Musée Estève★★**, home to a unique collection of 130 works by the artist Maurice Estève.

- **Rue Coursalon** – Fine view of place Gordaine along this lively pedestrianised street.
- **Place Gordaine** – Flower-decked square at the intersection of the pedestrianised streets.
- **Hôtel Lallemant★** – This mansion has retained the name of Jean Lallemant, the rich cloth merchant who had it built. It now houses the **Musée des Arts Décoratifs.**
- **Rue Joyeuse** – Peaceful street lined with private mansions.
- **Rue Bourbonnoux** – Craftsmen's workshops along this former high street among the timber-framed houses.
- **Musée des Meilleurs Ouvriers de France** – Fine objects made by gifted craftsmen.

LES MARAIS

Before you take a stroll through the town's unusual wetlands, go into Église St-Bonnet, which links the historic part of the city and the rural district known as the Marais.

- **Église St-Bonnet** – This 1510 church was remodelled in the 20C, when two bays and a neo-Flamboyant facade were added.
- **Les Marais★** – A pleasant walkway wanders through the wetlands and canals of the River Voiselle.
- **Digue de l'Yèvre** – Flat-bottomed boats are moored beneath a willow tree.
- **Jardin des Prés-Fichaux★** – A beautiful garden has been laid out on marshland between the river and the close of St-Ambroise abbey where Protestants would gather in the 16C to sing.

EXCURSIONS

CHÂTEAU DE MEILLANT★★

The castle is located 39km/24.2mi S of Bourges.

Open daily: Mar 2–6pm; Apr and Sep–mid-Nov 10am–noon, 2–6pm; May–Jun 10am–noon, 2–6.30pm; Jul–Aug 10am–6.30pm. Closed mid Nov–Feb. €8. 02 48 63 32 05. www.chateau-de-meillant.com.

This château is a fine example of how stylistic change was allied to the growing desire for domestic comfort towards the end of the 15C, to transform what had been a typical medieval castle into an agreeable country residence.

The medieval south front lapped by the waters of a moat is the only remnant of the old fortress built in the early 14C by Étienne de Sancerre; the towers retain their narrow loopholes although the wall-walk has been demolished.

The ornate east façade, which is in a different style recalling that of the châteaux of the Loire, includes two projecting stair turrets in the late Gothic style featuring a pierced balustrade at the base of the roof, dormer windows adorned with carvings, chimneys with elaborate Gothic balustrades, and in particular the splendidly decorated tower (Tour du Lion) by Giocondo, one of Michelangelo's assistants.

The interior, notably the formal dining room (Grande Salle à Manger) and the Bishop of Amboise's chamber, is furnished with period pieces, fireplaces, tapestries and carpets.

ABBAYE DE NOIRLAC★★

The abbey is just outside the town of St Amand-Montrond.

Open daily: Feb–Mar and Nov– 23 Dec 2–5pm; Apr–Oct 10am–6.30pm. €7. 02 48 62 01 01. www.abbayedenoirlac.fr.

Between the River Cher and the Meillant Forest, this 12–14C abbey is one of the best-preserved medieval monasteries in France. It occupies an exceptional setting for the Gregorian chants, concerts and cultural events that take place here. The perfect simplicity of the **abbey church** dates from 1150–60. It follows the plan of the great abbey at Clairvaux. The modern glass is the work of Jean-Pierre Raynaud, aided by craftsmen from Chartres and Bourges. The Gothic cloisters were added in the 13C.

SANCERRE★

46km/28.7mi NE of Bourges via D955. 02 48 54 08 21. www.ville-sancerre.fr.

High above the banks of the River Loire, Sancerre roosts above St-Satur and St-

Thibault. From this **vantage point★**, a wide panorama embraces the river and the Nivernais to the east, and Berry to the west. This little city, reigning over a land of trim vineyards and frisky goats, is renowned for its delicious white wine, flinty in flavour, and its little round cheeses, especially those from Chavignol. The steep streets of the town are enticing for their tempting food shops, restaurants and wine merchants.

A strategic location – Sancerre, already well known in Roman times has long stood watch over the Loire. It may have been the 9C residence of Robert le Fort, an early member of the Capetian dynasty. Later, the city played an important role in the Hundred Years' War, as the gateway to Berry, placed between the Burgundians and the English. Charles VII, the so-called king of Bourges, assembled 20 000 warriors there, personally commanding them for a time.

Sancerre became a stronghold of Protestantism, withstanding the assault of royal forces. The Treaty of St-Germain (1570) and the St Bartholomew's Day Massacre (1572) had no effect on those who held to their reformed views of religion, and refused to give in.

So, on 3 January 1573, the Maréchal de La Châtre, accompanied by 7 000 men, laid siege to Sancerre. After an intense artillery preparation, an assault took place on three fronts, but the local resistance was strong.

Capitulation came after seven long months of struggle. The population's surrender was accepted with honour, and they were allowed the freedom of their religion.

Sancerre wine – "Wine," wrote Balzac in 1844 in *La Muse du Département*, "is the main industry and the most important trading item of this land, which produces many generous vintages of rich bouquet, so similar to those of Burgundy that an untrained Parisian palate cannot taste the difference. Sancerre wines are therefore popular in Parisian cabarets where they flow steadily, which is a good thing, as they cannot be kept more than seven or eight years."

Vineyards are planted on every hill where the sun shines. The Sancerre label is only applied to white Sauvignon wines, and to red and rosé wines made from the Pinot grape.

Old Town

Visitors will enjoy strolling in the old neighbourhoods, where many of the interesting houses and vestiges are marked with informative signs. There are many architectural details to attract the eye.

Esplanade de la Porte César★★ – From this terrace, there is a great **view★★** over the vineyards, St-Satur and the viaduct, St-Thibault and the Val de Loire, and even farther afield to the Puisaye region of woods and lakes, between the Loire and the Loing, north-east of Sancerre.

Tours des Fiefs – This 14C cylindrical keep is the only vestige of the château of the counts of Sancerre, a Huguenot citadel bitterly defended during the 1573 siege. From the top, there is a wide **scenic view★** of the Loire valley and the hills of Sancerre.

ADDRESSES

STAY

⊖⊖ Hotel Ibis Bourges – R. Vladimir Jankelevitch, Quartier du Prado. ℘02 48 65 89 99. www.accorhotels.com. 86 rooms. Smart chain hotel in the centre of town.

⊖⊖ Chambre d'hôte Château de Bel Air – Lieu-dit le Grand-Chemin, Arcay. 16km/10mi S of Bourges on the D 73. ℘02 48 25 36 72. 6 rooms. Surrounded by spacious grounds, this 19C château is calm and comfortable. The dining room has a massive fireplace.

⊖⊖ Hôtel Christina – 5 r. Halle. ℘02 48 70 56 50. www.le-christina.com. 64 rooms. Chic, or small and functional rooms in this city-centre hotel.

⊖⊖ Hôtel Les Tilleuls – 7 pl. Pyrotechnie. ℘02 48 20 49 04. www.les-tilleuls.com. 39 rooms. Situated in a quiet part of town, this hotel offers guests accommodation in the main building. In the annex, the rooms are less spacious, more basic but they are air-conditioned.

Le Berry – 3 pl. du Général Leclerc. 02 48 65 99 30. www.le-berry.com. This modern hotel close to the historic centre offers attractive, colourful bedrooms and a pleasant restaurant, all of which belie its plain exterior.

Best Western Hôtel d'Angleterre – 1 pl. des Quatre-Piliers 02 48 24 68 51. www.bestwestern-angleterre-bourges.com. 30 rooms. The city's former court of justice is located close to the Palais Jacques-Cœur. All the mod cons in the bedrooms, including air-conditioning for most; their décor is sober yet modern. Buffet breakfast.

EAT

Le Bourbonnoux – 44 r. Bourbonnoux. 02 48 24 14 76. You'll find this restaurant among craft shops, along a street just a few steps away from St-Étienne Cathedral. Dining room pleasantly decorated with bright colours and exposed beams.

Le Bistro Gourmand – 5 pl. de la Barre. 02 48 70 63 37. Reservation recommended. A delightful candle-lit bistro specialising in regional and Lyonnais cuisine. The terrace looks onto the Église Notre-Dame.

Le Savoyard – 40 r. Bourbonnoux. 02 48 02 57 27. The focus here is on the cuisine of Savoy, with a menu of cheese fondues, raclettes, tartiflettes etc. Wooden skis, clogs, cowbells and other Savoyard objects adorn the cool stone vaults of this former coal cellar.

La Courcillière – R. de Babylone. 02 48 24 41 91. www.lacourcilliere.com. Located in the Marais district just a stone's throw from the city centre, this pleasant, rustic restaurant has a terrace by the water facing the gardens. Down-to-earth, reasonably priced cuisine.

Le Jardin Gourmand – 5 pl. de la Barre. 02 48 70 63 37. This pleasant bistro is just off the lively centre of town. Offers specialities from the Berry and Lyon regions with seasonal products.

Le d'Antan Sancerrois – 50 r. Bourbonnoux. 02 48 65 96 26. Enjoy the elegant setting among the old stones and modern furniture with greyish-blue hues. The chef will delight your tastebuds with original cuisine.

BARS / CAFÉS

Pub des Jacobins – Enclos des Jacobins. 02 48 24 61 78. Closed Sun. This piano-bar is wholeheartedly devoted to jazz. Top-quality concerts monthly.

Pub Jacques Cœur – 1 r. d'Auron. 02 48 70 72 88. This 16C half-timbered residence, now a pub, was built on the site where Jacques Cœur, a wealthy and influential 15C merchant and councillor to King Charles VII, was born.

ENTERTAINMENT

Maison de la Culture de Bourges – pl. André-Malraux. 02 48 67 74 70. www.mcbourges.com. This lively and popular venue hosts plays, dance performances and classical music and jazz concerts.

Les Nuits Lumières de Bourges – 02 48 23 02 60. Every eve in Jul–Aug and during the Printemps de Bourges festival. A walk through the historic city centre at night to view illuminated buildings.

LEISURE ACTIVITIES

Base de Voile du Val-d'Auron – 23 chemin Grand Mazières. 02 48 20 07 65. Closed Oct–Apr and Mon. This watersports centre at the Val d'Auron Lake offers swimming, canoeing, fishing, rowing, and more.

SHOPPING

The main shopping area is in the pedestrianised zone that includes rue Coursarlor and rue Mirebeau (near the Palais Jacques-Cœur), and rue Bourbonnoux and rue Moyenne (near the cathedral).

Markets – Every Sat morning, the listed **Halle au Blé** comes to life with 200 stallholders selling all types of food. A permanent daily market is also held at the **Halle St-Bonnet**, selling fresh seasonal produce, local cheeses and other regional specialities.

La Maison des Forestines – 3 pl. Cujas. 02 48 24 00 24. This confectionery business founded in 1825 occupies an attractive Haussmann-style building.

Épicerie du Berry – 41 r. Moyenne (Îlot Victor-Hugo). 02 48 70 02 38. This small boutique at the foot of the cathedral sells only regional products.

Limoges★

A dynamic regional capital with a long history, and a great tradition of high-quality enamel, ceramics and porcelain, Limoges is a lively university town with a notable heritage, and a place synonymous with affluence and prosperity.

- **Population:** 139 150.
- **Michelin Map:** 325 E 5-6
- **Info:** 12 bd de Fleurus. ℘05 55 34 46 87. www.limoges-tourisme.com.
- **Location:** On the north bank of the River Vienne, Limoges is 125km/78.5mi SE of Poitiers, and 171km/107mi W of Clermont-Ferrand.
- **TGV:** Limoges is about 3hrs 15mins direct from Paris Austerlitz.
- **Flights:** Limoges International Airport (www.aeroportlimoges.com) is 10km/6mi from the centre of the city, which is easily reached by taxi.
- **Don't Miss:** The Adrien-Dubouchée porcelain museum.
- **Timing:** A basic circuit of its principal sights will not consume more than half a day, but with attendant visits to its parks and ancient buildings, you need at least a whole day.

A BIT OF HISTORY

Limoges originated as a ford over the River Vienne at a meeting point of Roman highways, but remained a small provincial centre, specialising in ceramics, until the early 19C, when the manufacture of porcelain moved here from **St-Yrieix** where there were kaolin deposits but no workforce.

It became a prestigious industry, the town's name synonymous with the highest quality porcelain. The town was the birthplace of the Impressionist painter Auguste Renoir (1841–1919).

SIGHTS

Musée Municipal de l'Évêché –Musée de l'Émail★

pl. de la Cathédrale. Open Apr–Sept Wed–Mon 10am–6pm; Oct–Mar daily (except Tue and Sun am) 10am–noon, 2–5pm. No charge. ℘05 55 45 98 10.

The museum is housed in the former Bishops' Palace and features a stunning collection of some 300 *champlevé or cloisonné* enamels (*ground floor*) by Limoges masters. The palace gardens, **Jardins de l'Évêché★**, include a themed and a "wild" garden.

Musée Adrien-Dubouché★★

8 bis, pl. Winston Churchill. Open Wed–Mon, 10am–12.30pm, 2–5.45pm. €6. ℘05 55 33 08 50. www.musee-adriendubouche.fr.

This remarkable collection of international importance features items illus-

Limoges Enamel

In the 12C, Limoges became an important centre of production, partly due to the variety of minerals found in the area. The technique consists of crushing leadglass, coloured with metal oxides, applying it to a metal surface, then heating it to a temperature of up to 800°C, resulting in a crystalline effect. In the 12C Limoges specialised in champlevé enamels, in which the enamel is poured into grooves let into a copper surface, then polished level with the metal. In the 14C painted enamels made their appearance. In the reign of François I, Léonard Limosin was made Director, and enamels of great brilliance and colour were produced.

trating the evolution of pottery from ancient times to today, with many examples of the finest Limoges ware.

Ville and Cité

Early in its history, Limoges developed two rival centres, known as Cité and Ville (or Château). Overlooking the Vienne, **La Cité** is the historic core of Limoges. It spreads out around the **Cathédrale St-Étienne★**, which has a fine portal **(portail St-Jean★)** and which has kept its **rood screen★** of 1533, now located at the west end of the nave. In the chancel are a number of **tombs★**. The **Château** quarter, or Ville, serves as the modern centre of Limoges, with busy shopping streets. **St-Michel-des-Lions★** is an old hall-church that has retained its original rectangular plan.

EXCURSIONS

LE DORAT★★

Le Dorat is in a rural location 58km/36mi N of Limoges.

17 pl. de la Collégiale. 05 55 60 76 81.

Le Dorat lies in the gently rolling countryside of the old province of Marche, whose patchwork of pastureland feeds the yellowish-fawn Limousin cattle bought and sold in the great market at **St-Yrieix-la-Perche**. The little town has a collegiate church of impressive size and harmonious proportions.

Collégiale St-Pierre★★

Open daily. 05 55 60 72 20.

The great edifice was rebuilt in Romanesque style over a period of 50 years beginning in 1112. It is firmly rooted in its region by virtue of its siting, the coarse granite from which it is built, and by a number of characteristic Limousin features. These include the massive square west tower flanked by bell turrets, the portal with its scalloped archivolts, the openwork lantern (inspired by the one built 50 years earlier at St-Junien, but vastly more original), and the mouldings used in the arches and arcades through out the building.

ORADOUR-SUR-GLANE★★

The site is located 24km/15mi NW of Limoges. Access to the ruins of the martyred village is via the Centre de la Memoire. The centre offers a permanent exhibit dedicated to the rise of Nazism and the massacre of the villagers.

Open daily, Feb–mid-Dec from 9am. €8. 05 55 43 04 30. www.oradour.org.

Scene of a horrific massacre, Oradour was chosen by the Germans for its very innocence and insignificance in order to terrorise ordinary French people.

This small country town where the 642 inhabitants were massacred in a revenge attack by retreating Germans on 10 June 1944 is preserved unchanged as a fascinating and deeply moving memorial. The stark walls of the burnt-out village have been kept as a sombre reminder. Harassed by the Resistance, the troops made a characteristically brutal example of this entirely innocent place, massacring its inhabitants (men, women and children), and laying waste the village itself. The victims are buried in the village cemetery; a memorial commemorates the terrible deed. Only six escaped.

SOLIGNAC★★

Solignac is 10km/6.2mi S of Limoges. 05 55 00 42 31.

The 12C abbey church, robust and harmonious, has multiple domes. As well as being among the last of their kind to be built in Aquitaine, these are some of the finest examples to be seen in the region. There is an extraordinarily deformed dome over the choir and one of ovoid shape covering the north transept.

Eglise Abbatiale★★

Founded in 632 by St Eligius and rebuilt around 1175, the abbey church shows Limoges influence in its use of granite, but its domes are based on the ones at Souillac in Quercy. From the steps of the porch, there is a view of the interior, beautifully proportioned. Among the last of their kind, the pointed arches and pendentives are some of the finest examples in the region.

ADDRESSES

STAY

Hôtel de la Paix – 25 pl. Jourdan. 05 55 34 36 00. 31 rooms. This Napoléon III-style hotel in the heart of the city features an entertaining phonographic collection. Bright and airy bedrooms, some with wicker furnishings.

Hôtel Jeanne-d'Arc – 17 ave du Gén.-de-Gaulle. 05 55 77 67 77. Closed 21 Dec–8 Jan. 50 rooms. This pleasant, well-located hotel is close to the city's famous train station. The well-maintained bedrooms and pleasant breakfast room have managed to retain their old French charm.

EAT

Le Bœuf à la Mode – 60 r. François-Chenieux. 05 55 77 73 95. Closed Sat lunch, Sun and public holidays. If you love meat, then this is definitely the place for you! Excellent cuisine served in a friendly and traditional ambience.

Chez Alphonse – 5 pl. de la Motte. 05 55 34 34 14. Closed Mon eve, Sun and public holidays. Tucked away behind the *halles*, this bistro is a popular local haunt. Tables are decorated with chequered tablecloths and a menu is written up on the blackboard.

L'Escapade du Gourmet – 5 r. des 71ème-Mobiles. 05 55 32 40 26. Closed Sat lunch, Sun and Mon. A Belle-Époque décor of wood, frescoes, moulded ceilings and coloured glass is the backdrop to this popular traditional restaurant located between the château and the Cité Episcopale. Classical French cuisine. Good value for money.

Le Pont St-Étienne – 8 pl. de Compostelle. 05 55 30 52 54. Reservations required at weekends. Attractive bay windows with views of the old stone bridge and the river. The à la carte menu features a number of imaginatively named dishes. Summer terrace.

Les Petits Ventres – 20 r. de la Boucherie. 05 55 34 22 90. Closed Sun and Mon. Classic, high-quality French cuisine is to the fore in these two typical 15C houses, run by two enthusiastic owners. Traditional dishes based on liver, tongue, pig's trotters, tripe, etc.

BARS / CAFÉS

Brasserie Artisanale St Martial – 8 pl. Denis-Dussoubs. 05 55 79 37 98. This brewery (in the true sense of the term) perpetuates an old local tradition. Beer has been brewed in the region since the 18C; in the 19C there were no fewer than 50 brewers in the Limoges area.

Café des Anciennes Majorettes de la Baule – 27 r. Haute-Vienne. 05 55 34 34 16. Closed Mon, and mid-Jul–mid-Aug. This renowned local bar is the venue for regular concerts and plays.

L'Irlandais – 2 r. Haute-Cité. 05 55 32 46 47. This lively Irish pub is jointly run by a fisherman from Brittany who has travelled the world and established a bakery and a pub in Ireland, and by a concert violinist who has played in royal circles. Over recent years they've hosted jazz, Celtic music and other concerts.

SHOPPING

Most of the city's shops are located in the area around the castle.
The main boutiques selling porcelain are along boulevard Louis-Blanc and along the streets heading west from the city centre.

Le Pavillon de la Porcelaine – Av. du Prés.-John-Kennedy – 05 55 30 21 86. Factory outlet of Haviland, makers of prestigious porcelain sets. A wide choice of tableware on sale.

Buissières – 27 r. Jean-Jaurès. 05 55 34 10 44. At this chic confectioner's, the Art Deco décor is almost worth a visit on its own. Chocolates, pastries and desserts, including the house speciality black chocolate with chestnut cream.

Périgueux★★

Périgueux is an ancient town built in the fertile valley of the River Isle. Its long history can be traced in its urban architecture and two distinctive districts, each of which is marked by the domes of its sanctuary: the Cité district, overlooked by St Stephen's tiled roof, and the Puy St-Front district, with the Byzantine silhouette of the present cathedral bristling with pinnacles. There is a good overall view of the town from the bridge beyond Cours Fénelon to the southeast. Périgueux's gastronomic specialities, with truffle and foie gras occupying prize position, have become famous around the world and attract many visitors.

- **Population:** 29 573.
- **Michelin Map:** 329 F 4
- **Info:** 26 pl. Francheville, Tour Mataguerre. ☎05 53 53 10 63. www.tourisme-perigueux.fr.
- **Location:** Périgueux is 93km/60mi SW of Limoges.
- **TGV:** 5–6hrs via Limoges from Paris Austerlitz or via Bordeaux from Paris Montparnasse.
- **Parking:** Underground car parks at pl. Montaigne, pl. Francheville and espl. du Théâtre.

A BIT OF HISTORY

Five distinct historical periods have contributed to the formation of this ancient town. First was the Gaulish settlement which prospered in Roman times under the name of Vesunna; its site, the "Cité", is marked by the amphitheatre gardens and St Stephen's Church (St-Étienne).

In the Middle Ages, the quarter known as "Puy St-Front" became established on a rise to the north; the cathedral was built here and the area became the heart of Périgueux, eventually, in 1251, absorbing the older Cité.

In the 18C, the provincial governors, the Intendants, were responsible for a planned northward extension of the city, which linked the two districts by means of broad streets lined with public buildings. At the end of the 19C, the station area was developed, and more recently vast modern suburbs have grown up on the outskirts.

SIGHTS

St-Étienne-de-la-Cité★

Two of the domes of the original sanctuary have survived. The earlier is thought to have been built in 1117.

The second dome, built half a century later, is altogether lighter.

Cathédrale St-Front★★

Of the original early Romanesque church there remain only two small octagonal domes at the eastern end of the nave. The church was an important stopping-place for pilgrims on their way to Santiago de Compostela since it was here that the remains of St Front, the apostle of Périgord, could be seen. His tomb dates from 1077.

St-Front District★★★

The old artisans' and merchants' district has been given a face-lift. A conservation programme for safeguarding this historic area was set up, and the area has been undergoing major restoration. Its Renaissance façades, medieval houses, courtyards, staircases and shops are gradually being brought back to life; the pedestrian streets have rediscovered their role as commercial thoroughfares.

Place du Coderc and place de l'Hôtel-de-Ville are colourful and animated every morning with their fruit and vegetable market, whereas place de la Clautre is where the larger Wednesday and Saturday markets are held.

During the winter, the prestigious truffle and foie gras markets held in place St-Louis attract hordes of connoisseurs.

Vesunna – Musée Gallo-Romain de Périgueux★★★

Open daily (except Mon): Oct– Mar 9.30am–12.30pm, 1.30–5pm, Sat–Sun 10am–12.30pm, 2.30–6pm; Apr–Sept 9.30am–5.30pm, Sat–Sun 10am–12.30pm, 2.30–6pm (Jul–Aug daily 10am–7pm). Closed 2 wks in Jan, and 1 Jan, 1 and 11 Nov and 25 Dec. €6. ✆05 53 53 00 92. www.perigueux-vesunna.fr.

Designed by Jean Nouvel, this museum houses the remains of an opulent Gallo-Roman residence covering 4 000sq m. Built in the centre of a garden, it is like a large glassed-in inner courtyard reflecting the surroundings and blending perfectly with them. On one side, a mezzanine on two storeys overlooks the ancient *domus*. This section of the museum is devoted to the ancient town of Vesunna: a scale model of the town in the 2C shows how extensive it was in Roman times.

Digs have revealed the presence of a 1C building, considerably extended in the 2C. Elaborate murals can be seen on the base of the walls of the primitive house. The frieze surrounding the central pond, on the other hand, was painted when the house was extended. Along the way, the daily life of the inhabitants is illustrated: hypocaust heating system, decoration, water distribution (oak water pump) and various handicrafts.

EXCURSIONS

BRANTÔME★★

27km/17mi N of Périgueux.
✆05 53 05 70 21. www.ville-brantome.fr.

Brantôme lies in the midst of lush countryside, in the charming vallée de la Dronne, north of the town of Périgueux. Its old abbey and picturesque setting make it one of the most delightful little places in Périgord. This riverside village has old dwellings with slate roofs built like manor houses, a crooked bridge seen across the tranquil surface of the water, and great trees growing on the lawns of its lovely gardens. The 18C abbey has a fine west front and a Romanesque **bell tower★★**.

CHÂTEAU DE HAUTEFORT★★

The castle is 41km/25.4mi E of Périgueux.
Open daily Apr–Oct (times vary); Sat–Sun and public holidays Mar and early Nov. Closed mid-Nov–Feb. €9.50 (children 7–14, €5). ✆05 53 50 51 23. www.chateau-hautefort.com.

The elegant château rises up proudly on its hilltop site, overlooking its extensive and well-kept grounds. In the 16C, an ancient fortress was strengthened, and, a century later, reconstructed in Renaissance and Classical style. It has been further restored since a fire in 1968. The interior has fine Flemish tapestries saved from the flames, a 17C Felletin landscape, good pieces of furniture and unusual paved floors. The tower has magnificent **chestnut timberwork★★**.

ADDRESSES

STAY

⊖⊜ Comfort Hôtel Régina – 14 r. Denis-Papin (opposite the railway station). ✆05 53 08 40 44. 41 rooms. It is easy to spot this hotel, thanks to its yellow façade.

⊖⊜ Hôtel-Restaurant L'Écluse – at Antonne-et-Trigonant, 10km/6.2mi NE of Périgueux. ✆05 53 06 00 04. 43 rooms. The River Isle flows gently past the hotel's small waterfront. Rooms on the main façade have balconies that overlook the river.

EAT

⊖ Au Temps de Vivre – 10 r. St-Silain. ✆05 53 09 87 18. Closed eves (except summer 7–9.30pm), Sun and Mon. Reservations recommended. Tucked away in a pleasant street, this restaurant serves daily specials.

⊖⊜ Le Clos Saint-Front – 5 r. de la Vertu. ✆05 53 46 78 58. This old house, with its exposed beams, fireplace and Louis XVI furniture, is now home to an elegant restaurant resolutely devoted to Périgourdine cuisine with an inventive twist.

Sarlat-la-Canéda★★★

This attractive old Dordogne market town has narrow medieval streets lined with restored Gothic and Renaissance houses.

- **Population:** 9 739.
- **Michelin Map:** 329 I 6
- **Info:** r. Tourny. ℘05 53 31 45 45. www.sarlat-tourisme.com.
- **Location:** 64km/40m SE of Périgueux.
- **Parking:** There are plenty of car parks; spaces also in the old town, except Sat.
- **Timing:** It might be tempting to whizz around this lovely town in an hour or so. But allow at least half a day or more.
- **Don't Miss:** Saturday market, and the panoramic elevator in St Mary's church.

A BIT OF HISTORY

Sarlat is the capital of the Périgord Noir (Black Périgord) country, a fortunate and abundant region between the Dordogne and Vézère rivers.

The town grew up around the Benedictine abbey founded in the middle of the 9C. The wealth of the surrounding countryside poured into the town, enabling it to support a prosperous population of merchants, clerics and lawyers. Sarlat reached its peak during the 13C and 14C. The town long played host to fairs and markets, which still take place every Saturday, when the stalls are loaded with seasonal produce, poultry, cereals, horses, nuts, geese, foie gras, truffles and other goods.

WALKING TOUR

1 OLD TOWN★★★

Sarlat map, p497.

Sarlat's old district was cut in two in the 19C by the Traverse (rue de la République). The townhouses are quite unique: built with quality ashlar-work in a fine golden-hued limestone, with interior courtyards; the roofing, made of heavy limestone slabs (lauzes), necessitated a steeply pitched framework so that the enormous weight (500kg per m^2) could be supported on thick walls. Over the years new floors were added: a medieval ground floor, a High Gothic or Renaissance upper floor and Classical roof cresting and lantern turrets.

This architectural unit escaped modern building developments and was chosen in 1962 as one of the new experimental national restoration projects, the goal of which was to preserve the old quarters of France's towns and cities. The project, which began in 1964, has allowed the charm of this small medieval town to be recreated.

- **Cathédrale St-Sacerdos** – Built in the 12C, then rebuilt in the 16–17C.
- **Ancien Évêché** – The former bishopric. Its **façade★** has windows in the Gothic style.
- **Maison de la Boétie★** – This house, built in 1525, is the birthplace of Étienne de La Boétie.
- **Hôtel de Maleville★** – This edifice is also known as the Hôtel de Vienne after the man who built it, Jean de Vienne.
- **Rue des Consuls** – The townhouses in this street are beautiful examples of Sarlat architecture from the 14–17C.
- **Hôtel Plamon★** – A group of buildings built in different periods, illustrating the evolution of the different architectural styles used in Sarlat.
- **Fontaine Ste-Marie** – Opposite the Hôtel de Plamon, the fountain splashes in a cool grotto.
- **Place du Marché aux Oies★** – This was the traditional area of the Saturday morning market where live geese were sold.

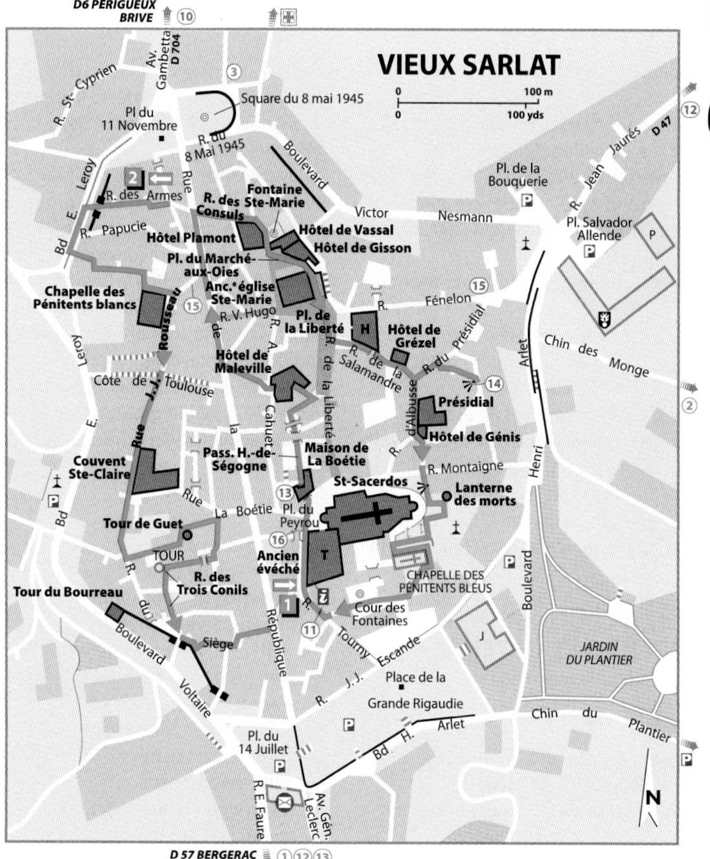

WHERE TO STAY		WHERE TO EAT	
Cordeliers (Chambre d'hôte Les)	3	Bistrot de l'Octroi (Le)	10
Etape des Peupliers (Chambre d'hôte L')	1	Chez le Gaulois	11
Maison des Peyrat (Hôtel La)	2	Jardins d'Harmonie (Les)	13
Mas de Castel (Hôtel)	12	Présidial (Le)	14
Montaigne (Hôtel)	13	Rossignol	15
Récollets (Hôtel des)	15	Rapière (La)	16

- In 2008, architect Jean Nouvel transformed the church of St Mary into a covered market. Take the **panoramic elevator** up through the steeple of the church for a unique view of Sarlat.
- **Hôtel de Vassal** – This 15C townhouse consists of two buildings at right angles flanked by twin corbelled turrets.
- **Place de la Liberté** – Many pavement cafés liven up Sarlat's main square.
- **Hôtel de Grézel** – Half-timbered façade with a tower and a lovely Flamboyant Gothic doorway.
- **Lanterne des Morts** – Built at the end of the 12C, this mysterious cylindrical tower is the tallest of its kind in Europe.

2 WEST SIDE★

Sarlat map, p497.

This part of town, on the opposite side of rue de la République (the so-called Traverse), is currently under renewal. Its steep and winding lanes are quieter, off the main tourist track, and offer another image of Sarlat.

- **Chapelle des Pénitents Blancs** – Used by the Order of Pénitents Blancs, the chapel (1626) was part of the religious establishment of the Pères Récollets.
- **Rue Jean-Jacques Rousseau** – The main street in this part of town, with many attractive old houses.
- **Tour de Guet** – Watchtower.
- **Tour du Bourreau** – Executioner's Tower, which was part of the ramparts, was built in 1580.

EXCURSIONS

BEYNAC-ET-CAZENAC★★

The castle and village are on the N bank of the Dordogne, 12km/7.4mi S of Sarlat.

Open daily. €8. 05 53 29 50 40. www.beynac-en-perigord.com.

As well as the château, the beautiful Renaissance village at the foot of the cliff is also worth visiting.

One of the great castles of Périgord, **Château de Beynac** is famous for its history, its architecture and for its panoramic setting on top of a rugged rock face. Defended on the north side by double walls, the castle looms over the river from a precipitous height of 150m. Crouching beneath its cliff is a tiny village, once the home of poet Paul Eluard. A square keep existed here as early as 1115; it was strengthened at the time of the great rivalry between the Capetians and the Plantagenets.

DOMME★★

The village is S of the River Dordogne, 12km/7.4mi from Sarlat.

Place de la Halle. 05 53 31 71 00.

One of the many medieval fortified towns (*bastides*) founded in southwest France by both French and English, Domme was laid out by Philippe le Hardi (the Bold) in 1281. The normal rectangular plan of such settlements was here distorted in order to fit it to the rocky crag overlooking the Dordogne 145m below.

A Royal Bastide – Domme was founded by Philip the Bold in 1283 in order to keep watch on the Dordogne valley and check the desire for expansion of the English established in Gascony. The king granted the town important privileges including that of minting coins and Domme played an important role during the Hundred Years' War.

In the 17C, its wine-growing and river-trading activities were thriving and its markets were renowned throughout the region.

Panorama★★★

There are splendid views over the alluvial valley of the Dordogne from the Barre belvedere or, better still, from the cliff-top walk (Promenade des Falaises) just below the public gardens. All around is an opulent landscape of castles, well-wooded slopes dotted with stone-built villages, lush meadows, walnut trees and corn.

American writer Henry Miller described the area as perhaps the nearest thing to Paradise on Earth.

LES EYZIES-DE-TAYAC★★

The village is in the heart of the Dordogne region, 20km/12.4mi from Sarlat. The best of the many fascinating sites are Grotte de Font-de-Gaume, Grotte du Grand Roc and the Musée National de la Préhistoire.

The sites are not all in the village – they are mostly spread along the Vézère valley. It is rewarding to spend a full day in the area.

The village occupies a grandiose setting of steep cliffs crowned with evergreen oak and juniper, at the confluence of two rivers. In the base of the cliffs are caves that were prehistoric habitations, where the art and crafts of our distant ancestors can still be seen.

Grotte du Grand-Roc★★ – Laugerie-basse, 24620 Les Eyzies de Tayac. Guided tours (30min) Apr–Oct 10am–6pm (Jul–

Place de la Liberté at night, Sarlat-la-Canéda

©Tibor Bognár/agefotostock

Aug 9.30am–7pm). €8. ℘05 53 06 92 70. The cave is set in a magnificent cliff overlooking the Vézère, and is renowned for its stalagmites and stalactites which display considerable variety.

Musée National de Préhistoire★ – Open daily from 9.30am. ℘05 53 06 45 65. www.musee-prehistoire-eyzies.fr. Comprehensive displays of prehistoric artefacts in an old 13C fortress with good views.

Grotte de Font-de-Gaume★ – Just outside village on road to St-Cyprien; footpath to cave entrance. Open Thu–Tue. €6. ℘05 53 06 86 00. Advance booking essential; only 200 visitors allowed per day. Since its discovery in 1901, dozens of polychrome paintings have been found in the tunnel-like Grotte de Font-de-Gaume.

Abri de Laugerie-Haute – On D 47 where it turns away from the Vézère. ♿Guided tours by appointment; call for other opening times. Information at the Grotte de Font-de-Gaume. ℘05 53 06 86 00. Representing 7 000 years of civilisation, this rock shelter was used during the Upper Palaeolithic period as a workshop for flints.

GROTTE DE LASCAUX

The cave is situated 2km/1.2mi S of the village of Montignac, and 26km/16mi S of Sarlat.

The actual Lascaux cave is closed to the public. However, a replica, known as Lascaux II, is open for visits at Montignac, just 200m away. ℘05 53 05 65 65. www.lascaux.culture.fr.

The world-famous cave paintings of Lascaux were discovered by accident on 12 September 1940 by a young man looking for his dog, which had disappeared down a hole.

The Paintings – Most of the paintings in the cave appear to date from the end of the Aurignacian period, others from the Magdalenian. They cover the walls and roofs of the cave with a bestiary of bulls, cows, horses, deer and bison, depicted with such skill as to justify Abbot Breuil's epithet "the Sistine Chapel of prehistoric times". Unfortunately, the damage caused by visitors was such that the caves were closed to the public and a full-size replica was constructed.

BERGERAC★

49km/30.5mi S of Périgueux.

97 r. Neuve-d'Argenson, 24100 Bergerac. ℘05 53 57 03 11. www.bergerac.fr.

Spread out on both banks of the Dordogne where the river tends to be calmer and the valley widens to form an alluvial plain, this distinctly southern town is surrounded by prestigious vineyards and fields of tobacco, cereals and maize. A project to restore the old quarter has seen the embellishment of a number of Bergerac's 15C and 16C houses.

Intellectual/commercial crossroads – The town's expansion began as early as the 12C. Benefiting from the town's situation as a port and bridging point, the local merchants profited from successful trade between the Auvergne and the Limousin and Bordeaux on the coast. This flourishing city and capital of the Périgord became one of the bastions of Protestantism as its printing presses published pamphlets which were widely distributed. In August 1577 the Peace of Bergerac was signed between the king of Navarre and the representatives of King Henri III; this was a preliminary to the Edict of Nantes (1598). Despite this, in 1620, Louis XIII's army took over the town and destroyed the ramparts. After the Revocation of the Edict of Nantes (1685), the Jesuits and Recollects tried to win back their Protestant disciples. A certain number of Bergerac citizens, faithful to their Calvinist beliefs, emigrated to Holland, a country where they had maintained commercial contacts.

Bergerac was the capital of Périgord until the Revolution, when the regional capital was transferred to Périgueux, which also became Préfecture of the Dordogne *département*.

In the 19C, wine-growing and shipping prospered until the onslaught of phylloxera and arrival of the railway.

Bergerac today – Essentially an agricultural centre, Bergerac is the capital of tobacco in France and, as a result, the Experimental Institute of Tobacco and the Tobacco Planters Centre of Advanced and Refresher Training are located here. In addition, the vineyards (12 000ha/29 650 acres) surrounding the town produce wine with an *appellation d'origine contrôlée* (which means it is of an officially recognised vintage) including: Bergerac, Côtes de Bergerac, Monbazillac, Montravel and Pécharmant. The Regional Wine Council, which establishes the *appellation* of the wines, is located in the Recollects' Cloisters. The main industrial enterprise of the town is the powder factory producing nitro-cellulose for use in such industries as film-making, paint, varnish and plastics.

Famous citizens – Oddly enough, the Cyrano of Edmond Rostand's play was inspired by the 17C philosopher **Cyrano de Bergerac** whose name had nothing to do with the Périgord town. Not discouraged in the slightest, the townspeople took it upon themselves to adopt this wayward son and erect a statue in his honour in place de la Myrpe.

Musée du Tabac★★

pl. du Feu. ♿ Open Jun–Sept daily 10am–1pm, 2–6pm; Oct–Mar Tue–Fri 10am–noon, 2–6pm, Sat 10am–noon; Apr–May Tue–Sat 10am–noon, 2–6pm, Sun 2.30–6.30pm. €4. ℘05 53 63 04 13.

This remarkable and beautifully presented collection, which includes satirical engravings, traces the history and evolution of tobacco through the centuries. On the **second floor** works of art depicting tobacco and smokers are displayed. *Two Smokers* from the 17C Northern French School, *Three Smokers* by Meissonier, and the charming *Interior of a smoke den* by Teniers the Younger, are among the works exhibited.

A section is devoted to the cultivation of tobacco (planting, harvesting, drying etc), with special reference to the Bergerac region.

Another room is set aside to display the techniques used to manufacture smoking accessories both in the past and throughout the world.

MUSÉE DE LA BATELLERIE★ – Musée de la Ville

5 rue des Conférences. ♿ Open Tue–Sun, times vary. €3. ℘05 53 63 04 13.

This museum is located at the end of place de la Myrpe. On the first floor, the importance of barrel-making to the Bergerac economy is explained. The section on wine shows the evolution of the Bergerac vineyards over the centuries and the type of houses the winegrowers lived in. On the second floor there are models of the various kinds of river boats, *gabares*, flat-bottomed boats sometimes with sails.

Musée Donation Costi

pl. de la Petite Mission. Open Jul–Aug Tue–Sun 2–7pm. No charge. ☏05 53 63 04 13.

This third Bergerac museum was created thanks to the gift of the sculptor Constantin Papachristopoulos, whose work it displays.

Maison des Vins – Cloître des Récollets

Open all year except Jan. Tue–Sun (times vary). No charge. ☏05 53 63 57 55.

The brick and stone cloister building was built on 12C foundations. The interior courtyard has a 16C Renaissance gallery beside an 18C gallery where exhibitions devoted to wine are staged. There is a fine view of the Monbazillac vineyards from the sumptuously decorated great hall on the first floor.

The wine-testing laboratory includes the wine-tasting room *(open to visitors)*, where all the Bergerac wines are tasted annually to determine whether they are worthy of the *appellation d'origine contrôlée* – the AOC mark on the label. The AOC system is a method of ensuring the quality of wine, and here one can learn how it works. The vineyards on the banks of the Dordogne cover 12 000 hectares/29 653 acres, producing wine for the 13 local appellations including Bergerac and Montravel.

DORDOGNE IN THE PÉRIGORD★★★

Round-trip from Sarlat – 70km/44mi.

Start at the **Site de Montfort★** and its advantageous site on the River Dordogne; it gave its name to the famous meander in the river, the **Cingle de Montfort★**. The nearby **Château de Montfort★** has a long history of sieges and battles. Carry on to **Domme★★** (*see p498*) and then **Cénac**, where the small 11C church is all that remains of a large priory. Continue to **Château de Castelnaud★★** and Château de Fayrac, tucked into the greenery on the south bank of the Dordogne. Further stops include the **Château de Milandes★**, **Beynac-et-Cazenac★★**, **Jardins de Marqueyssac** and **La Roque-Gageac**.

CHÂTEAU DE CASTELNAUD★★

19km/12mi NE from Sarlat.

The impressive ruins of the Château de Castelnaud stand on a wonderful **site★★** commanding the valleys of the Céou and the Dordogne. Just opposite stands the Château de Beynac (*see BEYNAC-ET-CAZENAC, p498*), Castelnaud's implacable medieval rival.

JARDINS DE MARQUESSAC★★

54km/34mi NNW from Sarlat.

On the tip of a rocky outcrop overlooking the Dordogne valley, the hanging gardens of Marqueyssac offer a landscape that varies according to the light, shifting as the seasons pass and taking on nuances as the hours go by. A storm that revives the scent of the box hedges, a morning mist that settles over the topiaries, the summer sun that flickers through the leaves of the green oaks… each moment has its own enchantment.

JARDIN EYRIGNAC★★

13km/8mi NE from Sarlat.

Laid out in the 18C by the Marquis de la Calprenède, these gardens were remodelled many times during the 19C and finally given their present aspect in the 1960s by Gilles Sermadiras de Pouzols de Lile. Five gardeners work full time to look after the 4ha/10-acre gardens. The result is a happy compromise between the French-style garden and Tuscan topiary art, rich in evergreens which make for year-round delight.

LA ROQUE GAGEAC★★

18km/11mi SW from Sarlat.

The village of La Roque-Gageac, huddled against a cliff which drops vertically to the River Dordogne, occupies a wonderful **site★★** – one of the finest in this part of the valley, in which Domme, Castelnaud and Beynac-et-Cazenac are all within a few miles of each other. At the top of the cliff there are clear traces to remind visitors of the tragic day in 1957 when a huge block of rock broke away from the cliff, killing three inhabitants.

ADDRESSES

STAY

Chambre d'hôte L'Étape des Peupliers – 25 ter r. de Cahors. 05 53 59 03 53. 5 rooms. Just next to the historic district of Sarlat, enjoy simple, perfectly clean rooms. These open onto the hidden back garden, where you may also enjoy a splash in the swimming pool.

Hôtel des Récollets – 4 r. Jean-Jacques-Rousseau. 05 53 31 36 00. www.hotel-recollets-sarlat.com. 18 rooms. This unique hotel is in a former convent (17C). The rooms are not large, but they are quiet and all have been renovated with contemporary furniture, original beams and stone walls. Enjoy breakfast in a vaulted room or on the patio.

Le Mas de Castel – 3km/1.8mi S of Sarlat via the D 704 and C 1. 05 53 59 02 59. www.hotel-lemasdecastel.com. 13 rooms. An attractive hotel occupying an old farm in a peaceful rural setting. Pastel tones and rustic furniture in the bedrooms, some of which are on garden level. Swimming pool.

La Maison des Peyrat – Lac de la Plane (0.6mi E of the town centre). 05 53 59 00 32. www.maisondespeyrat.com. 10 rooms. Secluded in the hills of Sarlat, this gorgeous house, full of character, surrounded by walnut trees and pastures, offers light, airy rooms, refined breakfast and dinner upon reservation. Swimming pool.

Montaigne – Pl. Pasteur, Sarlat la Canéda. 05 53 31 93 88. www.hotelmontaigne.fr. 28 rooms. 150m from the cobbled medieval centre of Sarlat and housed in a beautiful historical building, the hotel offers comfortable and well-equipped rooms with free WiFi.

Chambre d'hôte Les Cordeliers – 51 r. des Cordeliers. 05 53 31 94 66. www.hotelsarlat.com. 5 rooms. Located at the gateway to the historic centre, this pretty bourgeois house with royal blue shutters offers spacious rooms with large, sprung beds. The traditional breakfast is served in the living room which looks out onto a tree-lined square.

EAT

Chez le Gaulois – 9 r. Tourny. 05 53 59 50 64. This convivial "ham cellar"-themed restaurant offers a selection of regional products. Copious cold meat platters with cheese and salad served on chopping boards. Delicious handmade ice cream.

La Rapière – Pl. du Peyrou. 05 53 59 03 13. One of Sarlat's classic restaurants, where locals come to enjoy flavoursome regional cuisine, such as chicken breast in a verjus sauce, goose Parmentier with bolete mushrooms, and roasted preserved duck. Pleasant service.

La Petite Borie – 4 r. de Tourny. 05 53 31 23 69. This pretty little spot offers refined regional cuisine for very reasonable prices. Large platters, homemade foie gras and wine bought directly from the winemaker.

Le Bistrot de l'Octroi – 111 av. de selves (600m N of town centre). 05 53 30 83 40. www.lebistrodeloctroi.fr. Enjoy fine local and regional cuisine and a warm welcome in this 1830s building. Choose from upstairs, downstairs or the outdoor terrace.

Les Jardins d'Harmonie – Pl. André Malraux. 05 53 31 06 69. www.lesjardinsdharmonie.com. Closed Mon–Tue. Very attractive little restaurant set in the old cobbled part of town, spilling out onto the streets beneath its awnings. Try one of their speciality salads, steaks or foie gras. They also have a tearoom.

Rossignol – 15 r. Fénelon. 05 53 31 02 30. Closed Thu. A simple, central, family-run restaurant, with one rustic-style dining room. Copious and unpretentious local cuisine, including fish.

Le Présidial – 6 r. Landry. 05 53 28 92 47. Formerly the royal court of justice, this beautiful 17C building features a vast garden in the heart of historic Sarlat, making it an ideal setting for a romantic dinner. Good, classic cuisine and refined service.

Rocamadour★★★

Clinging dramatically to the sheer cliffs of the gorge cut by the little River Alzou, the tiny medieval town of Rocamadour is one of the most visited places in the Dordogne. All around stretches the Causse de Gramat★, a vast limestone plateau, known as good sheep country and for its pâté de foie gras.

- **Population:** 675.
- **Michelin Map:** 337 F 3
- **Info:** The tourist office is at L'Hospitalet. ✆05 65 33 22 00. www.rocamadour.com.
- **Location:** 53km/33mi S of Brive-la-Gaillarde. You can enter Rocamadour only on foot, so park on the plateau and walk into town (or pay and take the elevator), or take the little train (fee). To reach Place St-Amadour (and the seven sanctuaries), take the stairway at Via Sancta or the elevator.
- **Don't Miss:** The view of Rocamadour from the Hospitalet belvedere (*2km/1.2mi NE*), or from the Couzou road. The castle, rising 125m above the valley floor.

A BIT OF HISTORY

Long ago, Rocamadour was chosen by a hermit, Saint Amadour, as his place of retreat.

From the 12C onwards, and above all during the 13C, Rocamadour was one of the most popular places of pilgrimage in the whole of Christendom. Just as they do today, souvenir stalls tempted the throngs of tourists, among them Henry III of England, who is said to have experienced a miraculous cure here.

VISIT

A stairway with 216 steps leads to the Place St-Amadour (or Parvis des églises) around which are grouped seven sanctuaries, including the Chapel of Notre-Dame or Miraculous Chapel.

The stream of pilgrims eventually dried up, unsurprisingly, in view of the destruction which was caused by the great rock-fall of 1476 and completed by the Huguenots a century later.

In the 19C, the place was restored by the Bishops of Cahors in an attempt to revive the pilgrimages.

EXCURSIONS

GOUFFRE DE PADIRAC★★

The Gouffre lies about 2km/1.2mi from the village of Padirac, in the Lot département.

Padirac Chasm (Gouffre de Padirac) provides access to wonderful galleries hollowed out of the limestone mass of the Gramat plateau (Causse de Gramat) by a subterranean river. A tour of this mysterious river and the vast caves adorned with limestone concretions leaves visitors with a striking impression of this fascinating phenomenon.

The chasm served as a refuge for the people living on the *causse* during the Hundred Years' War and the Wars of Religion, but it would appear that it was towards the end of the 19C, following a violent flooding of the river, that a practicable line of communication opened between the bottom of the well and the underground galleries.

The speleologist, **Edouard A Martel**, was the first to discover the passage, in 1892. He then undertook nine expeditions and finally reached the Hall of the Great Dome.

Padirac was opened to tourists for the first time in 1898. Since then, numerous speleological expeditions have uncovered 22km/13.6mi of underground galleries. The 1947 expedition proved that the Padirac River reappears above ground 11km/6.8mi away where the Lombard rises, and at St George's spring in the Montvalent Amphitheatre near the Dordogne. During the expeditions of 1984 and

1985, a prehistoric site was discovered, with bones of mammoths, bison, bears and other animals, all found to date from between 150 000 and 200 000 years ago. Among the bones were chipped flints dating from between 30 000 and 50 000 years ago. Thanks to the efforts of **Guy de Lavaur** (1903–86), the total known length of the subterranean network at Padirac rose from 2km/1.2mi to 15km/9.3mi.

Visit

Exhibited in the entrance hall are copies of some of the bones found in the prehistoric site. The chasm is like a gigantic well of striking width and depth to the rubble cone formed by the collapse of the original roof. With its walls covered in vegetation and the overflow from stalagmites, it is one of France's most atmospheric underground domains.

The Grand Pilier, Grande Pendeloque of the Lac de la Pluie and the **Salle du Grand Dôme** are among the most striking of all natural monuments of the underground world.

The underground river flows beneath the surface of the plateau, to reappear on the surface near the natural amphitheatre at Montvalent on the Dordogne.

SOUILLAC★

Along the N 20, 29km/18mi E of Sarlat-la-Canéda and 39km/24mi S of Brive-la-Gaillarde. ✆05 65 37 81 56.

At the confluence of the Corrèze and the Dordogne, in the centre of a fertile region, Souillac is a small town bustling with trade and tourists.

After the Benedictines settled in the plain of Souillès (*souilh* meaning bog or marshland where wild boar wallow), they transformed the marsh into a rich estate. **Souillac abbey** was plundered and sacked several times by the English during the Hundred Years' War and the Wars of Religion, but rose from its ruins each time thanks to the tenacity of its abbots. During the Revolution, its buildings were used for storing tobacco.

Abbey church – Dedicated to Mary, Mother of Christ, this became a parish church to replace the church of St Martin, destroyed during the Wars of Religion. Built in the 12C, the church is related to the Romanesque cathedrals of Angoulême, Périgueux and Cahors with their Byzantine inspiration, but it is more advanced in the lightness of its columns and the height of its arcades than the others. From place de l'Abbaye one can admire the attractive east end with its five pentagonal, apsidal chapels and an unusual tower on the other side of the building. *The disfigured bell tower is all that remains of the church of St Martin.*

Musée National de l'Automate★

Open Tue–Sun, times vary. €5.50 (children 5–12, €3). ✆05 65 37 07 07.

The museum contains some 3 000 objects, including 1 000 automata donated by the **Roullet-Decamps** family, who for four generations were leaders in the field. In 1865 Jean Roullet created his first mechanical toy: a small gardener pushing a wheelbarrow. Note especially the **Jazz band** (1920), a group of electric automata with black musicians performing a concert.

BEAULIEU-SUR-DORDOGNE★★

Beaulieu is in the Limousin region, some distance upriver from the popular Dordogne resorts. ✆05 55 91 09 94. www.beaulieusurmer.fr.

Rising from the River Dordogne, picturesque Beaulieu has a fine church and former abbey.

Église St-Pierre★★ – This is the church of a former Benedictine abbey. Its **doorway★★**, dating from 1125, has as its theme the opening stages of the Last Judgement, with the dead being summoned from their graves. The Treasury in the north transept houses a remarkable 12C Romanesque **figure of the Virgin★** in a 13C shrine.

COLLONGES-LA-ROUGE★★

20km/12.4mi SE of Brive, in the Limousin region. Cars are not allowed in the village in summer. Use the car park by the old station.

Collonges-la-Rouge boasts mansions, old houses and a Romanesque church built of red sandstone; the surrounding countryside is dotted with nut orchards and vineyards. In the 13C the village was granted franchises and other privileges by the county of Turenne. In the 16C it became a holiday centre for county dignitaries who built charming mansions and residences flanked by towers and turrets.

The exclusive use of the traditional building stone and the balanced proportions of the various structures give a harmonious character to the town. Some are of special interest: the **Maison de la Sirène** with an elegant carved porch; the imposing mansion **Hôtel des Ramades de Friac**; the **Château de Benge**; and the elegant **Castel de Vassinhac★**.

CHÂTEAU DE BONAGUIL★★

54km/33.5mi W of Cahors. Open Mar–Oct daily 10am–5.30pm (Jul–Aug 7pm); Nov–Feb school holidays only, 2–5pm. Closed 1 Jan and 25 Dec. €7. 05 53 71 90 33. www.chateau-bonaguil.com.

This majestic fortress on the border of Périgord Noir (Black Périgord, so-called because of its extensive woods) and Quercy, makes a stunning sight. It exemplifies the state of military architecture of the late 15C and the 16C.

The castle was enlarged in 1445 around the existing 13C keep, and further extended between 1482 and 1520. It is unusual in that underneath its old-fashioned appearance of a traditional stronghold it is actually remarkably well adapted to the new firearms then coming into use, and thus has loopholes for both cannon and muskets.

Furthermore, it was conceived not as an offensive establishment but as a place of refuge, able to withstand any attack, with its firearms used in a purely defensive role. In 1480–1520 this was something new, and it anticipated the concept of the fort.

CHÂTEAU DE CASTELNAU-BRETENOUX★★

27km/17mi NE from Rocamadour.

The scale of this castle's defence system makes it one of the finest examples of medieval military architecture. This landmark, as Pierre Loti wrote, "...is the beacon... the thing you cannot help looking at all the time from wherever you are. It's a cock's comb of blood-red stone rising from a tangle of trees, this ruin poised like a crown on a pedestal dressed with a beautiful greenery of chestnut and oak trees."

CHÂTEAU DE MONTAL★★

26km/16mi from Rocamadour.

This harmonious group of buildings with pepperpot roofs sits on a wooded hillside above a nine-hole golf course. In 1523 Jeanne de Balsac d'Entraygues had a country mansion built on the site of a feudal stronghold for her eldest son, Robert, who was away fighting in Italy for François I. The chatelaine had the best artists and workmen brought to Quercy, and by 1534 the masterpiece begotten of a mother's loving pride was there for all to see.

Everything was ready to welcome home the proud knight. She waited day after day for her eldest son's arrival but alas, Robert's body was all that returned to the castle. The beautiful dream crumbled. Jeanne had the high window from which she had watched for her son blocked up. Beneath it, she had the despairing lament carved: Hope Is No More ("Plus d'Espoir").

Jeanne's second son, Dordé de Montal, a church dignitary, was absolved from his ecclesiastical duties by the Pope in order that he might continue the family line; he subsequently married and had nine children.

Montal was declared a national asset but suffered during the Revolution. In 1879 it fell into the hands of a certain Macaire. This impecunious adventurer made a bargain with a demolition group and divided the palace into lots. 120t of carved stone were sent to Paris. The masterpieces of Montal were then auctioned off. In 1908 a new and devoted owner set about reclaiming the lost works and refurbishing the castle, before donating it to the State in 1913.

Cahors★★

Impressively sited on a promontory almost completely surrounded by a bend in the River Lot, Cahors enjoyed fame and fortune in the Middle Ages and is a pleasant country town today. Cahors is well known for its "black" wine.

- **Population:** 20 194.
- **Michelin Map:** 337 E 5
- **Info:** pl. Mittérrand. ℘05 65 53 20 65. www.tourisme-cahors.com.
- **Location:** 112km/70mi N of Toulouse via the D 820 or A 20.
- **Parking:** Several car parks around the town centre.
- **Timing:** Allow at least half a day to explore the town, and another day to visit the nearby villages and vistas of the Lot valley. For a different perspective on the town, take a boat trip on the Lot.
- **Don't Miss:** Pont Valentré.

SIGHTS

Pont Valentré★★

The city's merchants were responsible for building this superb six-arched stone bridge; its construction lasted from 1308 to 1378. Its fortifications are a reminder of the importance attached to the defence of Cahors by Philippe le Bel (the Fair), whose relationship with the city was based on an act of pariage (equality between a feudal lord and a town).

Cathédrale St-Étienne★

pl. Chapou.

The cathedral is one of the first of the domed churches of Aquitaine. The 13C **north door★★** shows Christ beginning to rise, while the angels are stilling the fears of the disciples.

WALKING TOUR

THE CATHEDRAL AND ITS SURROUNDINGS★★★

Cahors map, p507.

The city has organised a circuit called "Les Jardins Secrets de Cahorsa". Follow the copper nails marked with acanthus leaves hammered into the pavement. You'll see signs explaining the connection between the garden theme and the landmarks.

The circuit begins at the Valentré bridge. You can request the brochure from the Tourist Office. The allées Fénélon, running perpendicular to boulevard Gambetta, have been set up and landscaped for pedestrian use.

- **Cathédrale St-Étienne★** – The clergy built this church as a fortress to provide a place of safety in troubled times, as well as to bolster prestige.
  North doorway★★ – This Romanesque door was once part of the western façade. The tympanum depicts the Ascension.
  Cloisters★ – These Renaissance cloisters were built in 1509 after those of Carennac and Cadouin, with which they share a number of stylistic similarities.
- **Chapelle St-Gausbert** – 16C Italian Renaissance-style paintings decorate the ceiling of this former chapter-house.
- **Rue Nationale** – This was the main thoroughfare of the active Badernes Quarter.
- **Rue du Docteur-Bergounioux** – At no 40, a 16C townhouse features an interesting Renaissance façade.
- **Rue Lastié** – Note the Rayonnant windows at no 35.
- **Rue St-Urcisse** – The late-12C church of St-Urcisse is entered through a 14C doorway.
- **Hotel de Roaldès** – The mansion is also known as Henri IV's Mansion because it is said that the king of Navarre stayed there during the siege of Cahors in 1580.

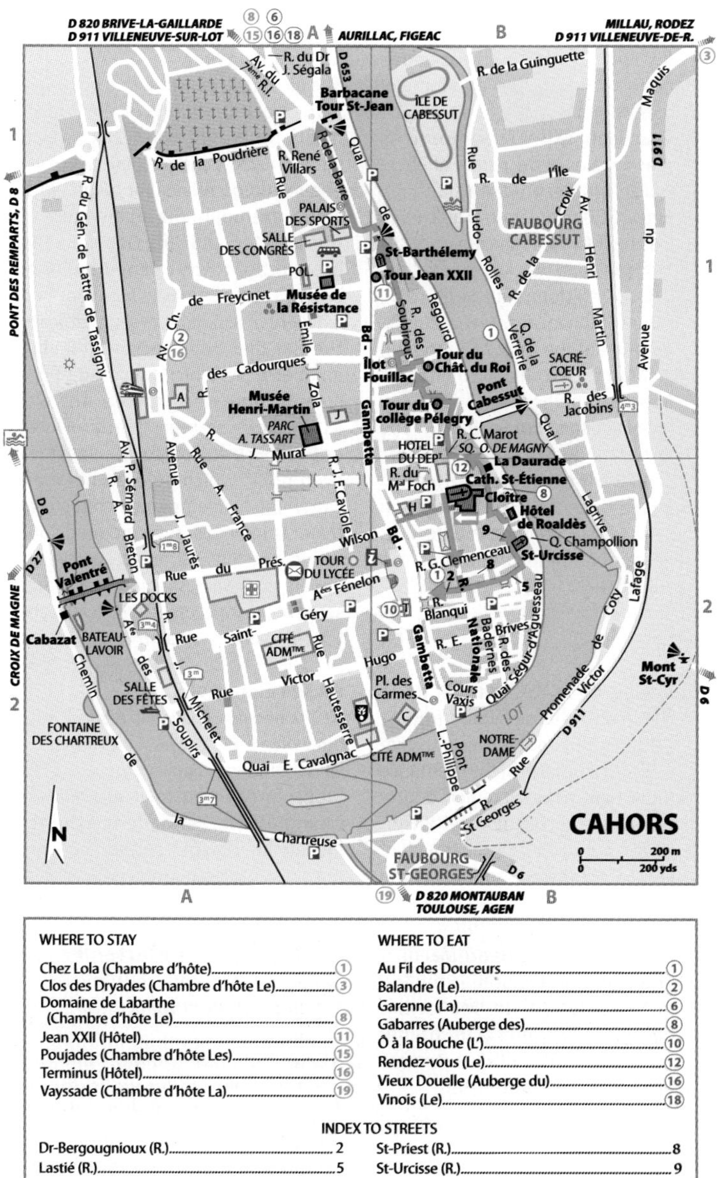

- **La Daurade** – Varied set of old residences around the Olivier-de-Magny square.
- **Pont Cabessut** – From the bridge there is a good **view★** of the upper part of the city.
- **Tour du Collège Pélegry** – The college was founded in 1368 and at first took in 13 poor university students; until the 18C, it was one of the town's most important establishments.
- **Tour du Château du Roi** – Near Pélegry College stands what is today the prison and was once the governor's residence.

- **Îlôt Fouillac** – This area has undergone an extensive programme of redevelopment.
- **Tour Jean-XXII** – This tower is all that remains of the palace of Pierre Duèze, brother of John XXII.
- **Église St-Barthélémy** – This church was built in the highest part of the old town, and was known until the 13C as St-Etienne de Soubiroux, Sancti Stephani de Superioribus (St Stephen of the Upper Quarter), in contrast to the cathedral built in the lower part of the town.
- **Barbican and Tour St-Jean★** – The ramparts, constructed in the 14C, completely cut the isthmus formed by the meander of the River Lot off from the surrounding countryside. Remains of these fortifications can still be seen.

MUSEUMS

- **Musée de la Résistance, de la Déportation et de la Libération** – Housed in six rooms, this museum illustrates the birth of the Resistance movement in the Lot region, deportations and persecutions which followed, fighting for the liberation of France and the epic journey of the Free French from Brazzaville to Berlin.
- **Musée de Cahors Henri-Martin** – This museum is housed in the former Episcopal palace. One room is devoted to the works of the painter Henri Martin (1860–1943), a member of the pointillist movement.

EXCURSIONS

FIGEAC★★

70km/43.5mi W of Cahors via D 653.
Hôtel de la Monnaie, Place Vival. ℘05 65 34 06 25. www.tourism-figeac.com.
Parking in centre.

Sprawled along the north bank of the Célé, Figeac developed at the point where the Auvergne meets Upper Quercy. A commercial town, it had a prestigious past, seen in the architecture of its tall sandstone town houses.

Le Vieux Figeac★

The old quarter, surrounded by boulevards tracing the line of the former moats, has kept its medieval town plan with its narrow and tortuous alleys.
The buildings, of elegant beige sandstone, exemplify the architecture of the 13C, 14C and 15C. Generally the ground floor was opened by large pointed arches and the first floor had a gallery of arcaded bays. Underneath the flat tiled roof was the soleilho, an open attic, which was used to dry laundry, store wood, grow plants, etc. Its openings were separated by columns or pillars in wood or stone, sometimes even brick, which held up the roof. Other noticeable period architectural features to be discovered during your tour of the old quarter are: corbelled towers, doorways, spiral staircases and some of the top storeys, which are half-timbered and of brick.

Musée Champollion★

pl. Champollion. Open Tue–Sun (times vary). €5. ℘05 65 50 31 08. www.musee-champollion.fr.
Museum devoted to Jean-François Champollion. Permanent exhibits include hieroglyphs and letters written by Champollion to his brother. Learn how and why people started writing.

Grotte du Pech-Merle★★★

The cave is located 7km/4.3mi N of St. Cirq-Lapopie and 32km/19.8mi E of Cahors.
Guided tours Apr–mid-Nov. 700 visitors per day max (reservations recommended 3 days in advance in Jul and Aug). €11 (children 5–14, €7). ℘05 65 31 27 05. www.pechmerle.com.

Sited high above the River Célé just before it flows into the Lot, the Pech-Merle cave is one of the most fascinating in terms of prehistory and speleology. On the lower level of the cave are **paintings** of a fish, two horses covered in coloured dots, and "negative hands" (made by stencilling around hands placed flat against the rock). Something like a three-dimensional effect is produced by the way in which

Pont Valentré over the Lot, Cahors

© Da Ros Luca/Sime/Photononstop

the Late Perigordian artists integrated their work with the irregularities of the rock surface. There are also representations of bisons and mammoths, as well as petrified human footprints from the Early Magdalenian. The upper level has strange, disc-like concretions, "cave pearls", and eccentrics with protuberances defying the laws of gravity.

ADDRESSES

STAY

⊖ Chambre d'hôte le Clos des Dryades – 46090 Vers. 19km/11.8mi NE of Cahors on the D 653, towards St-Cirq-Lapopie and the D 49 road to Cours. ✆05 65 31 44 50. 5rms, 3 gîtes. Nestled deep in the woods, this house with its tiled roof is the perfect place to get away from it all. The rooms are comfortable and the large swimming pool is a great place to cool off on a hot summer's day. Two self-catering cottages are also available.

⊖ Hôtel Les Chalets – 46090 Vers, 14km/9mi E of Cahors on the D 653. ✆05 65 31 40 83. 23 rooms. This small modern hotel situated in an attractive leafy setting is particularly welcoming. The bedrooms, with balconies or small gardens, overlook the river.

⊖⊖ Hôtel A l'Escargot – 5 bd Gambetta. ✆05 65 35 07 66. Closed Feb school hols, Dec and Sun out of season. 9rms. Near the Tour Jean-XXII, this hotel occupies the old palace built by the pontiff's family.

EAT

⊖⊖ Auberge du Vieux Douelle – 46140 Douelle, 8km/5mi W of Cahors on the D 8. ✆05 65 20 02 03. The dining room in the vaulted cellar of this popular inn, known locally as "Chez Malique", is decked out with bright red tablecloths.

⊖⊖ Le Dousil – 124 r. Nationale. ✆05 65 53 19 67. Closed Sun and Mon. This wine bar near the town's covered market has an extensive list of vintages.

⊖⊖ La Garenne – In Saint-Henri, 7km/4.5mi N towards Brive. ✆05 65 35 40 67. Closed Mon eve and Tue eve (except Jul–Aug) and Wed. This typically Quercy-style building once served as a stable. But the main attraction here is the delicious regional cuisine.

⊖⊖ Le Rendez-Vous – 49 r. Clément-Marot. ✆05 65 22 65 10. Closed 28 Mar–14 May, Sun and Mon. Reservations recommended. Located close to the cathedral, Le Rendez-Vous has a reputation for modern cuisine.

SHOPPING

Market – A traditional market is held on Wednesday and Saturday mornings at **Place Chapou**, with farmers' stalls selling a range of local produce.

Les Délices du Valentré – 21 bd Léon-Gambetta. ✆05 65 35 09 86. Try the Coque de Cahors, a brioche with candied citron and flavoured with orange water, and *Cabecou*, a chocolate sweet.

Atlantic Coast

» Region map p512
Bordeaux p513
Arcachon p522
Biarritz p523
St-Jean-de-Luz p526
Dax p528
Pau p529
Angoulême p530
Cognac p533
La Rochelle p535
Rochefort p541
Poitiers p542
Le Puy du Fou p545

Introduction

The Atlantic Coast region of France stretches from the estuary of the Loire in the north to the mighty natural frontier of the Pyrénées to the south. It is bounded on the west by the apparently endless Atlantic coastline and to the east by the lush countryside of the Limousin, the Périgord and Gascony. It encompasses some of the modern region of the Pays de Loire, the whole of Poitou-Charentes and the western half of the Aquitaine.

Geography – With the exception of the Pyrénées in the south, the region consists for the most part of flat coastal plain, rising gently to more undulating countryside in the east. In the north there are marshy tracts like the Marais Poitevin and dunes bordering sandy beaches. To the south is the Gironde, the name given to the broad estuary of the Garonne, and the Atlantic coast south of here runs in a straight line almost to Spain, interrupted only by the Bay of Arcachon. Behind the sandy beaches rise the highest sand dunes in Europe, while inland is the Landes, an immense area planted with pine trees.

History – In Classical times, Aquitania included all the Atlantic coast. Following the collapse of the Roman Empire, it was controlled by the Visigoths and then the Franks. During the medieval period, the region passed to the English crown, and not until the end of the Hundred Years' War did it revert to France.

Economy – The Poitou Charentes region is mainly agricultural and cereal production is very important, as are cattle rearing and dairy farming. Cognac is produced in the area around the town of the same name and exported worldwide.

The area around Bordeaux is renowned for its fine wines, and the produce of the famous châteaux are much sought after. The Landes area produces vast quantities of timber and is the largest maritime pine forest in Europe.

Highlights

1. **Aubeterre**'s monolithic church, dedicated to St John (p532)
2. Medieval towers of the **Old Port at La Rochelle** (p535)
3. 1C Roman arena at **Saintes** (p541)
4. Science-based leisure park near Poitiers: **Futuroscope** (p544)
5. History theme park based round a castle, **Le Puy de Fou** (p545)

Grande Plage, Biarritz Y. Kanazawa/MICHELIN

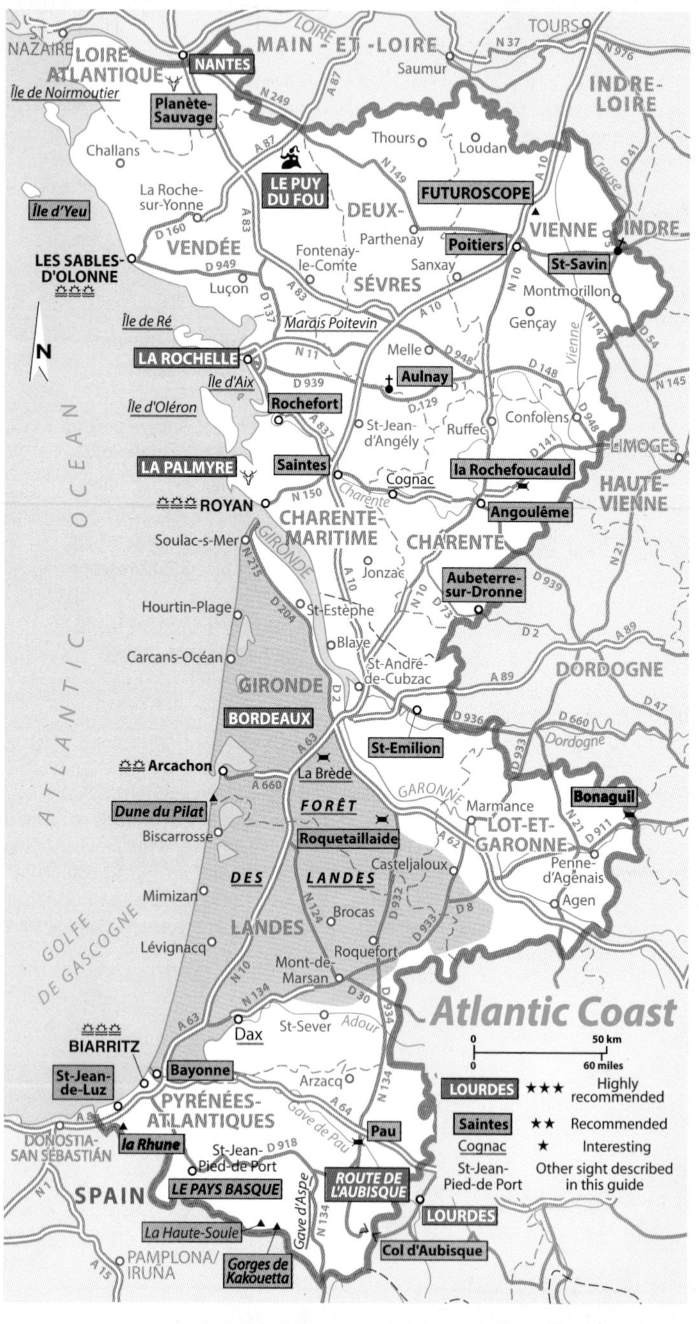
Atlantic Coast
NANTES
Planète-Sauvage
LE PUY DU FOU
FUTUROSCOPE
Poitiers
St-Savin
Île d'Yeu
LES SABLES-D'OLONNE
LA ROCHELLE
Aulnay
Rochefort
LA PALMYRE
Saintes
la Rochefoucauld
ROYAN
Angoulême
Aubeterre-sur-Dronne
BORDEAUX
St-Emilion
Arcachon
Dune du Pilat
Roquetaillaide
Bonaguil
BIARRITZ
Bayonne
St-Jean-de-Luz
la Rhune
LE PAYS BASQUE
Pau
ROUTE DE L'AUBISQUE
LOURDES
Col d'Aubisque
La Haute-Soule
Gorges de Kakouetta
LOIRE ATLANTIQUE
MAIN-ET-LOIRE
INDRE-LOIRE
VENDÉE
DEUX-SÈVRES
VIENNE
INDRE
CHARENTE-MARITIME
CHARENTE
HAUTE-VIENNE
GIRONDE
DORDOGNE
LOT-ET-GARONNE
FORÊT DES LANDES
LANDES
PYRÉNÉES-ATLANTIQUES
SPAIN
ATLANTIC OCEAN
GOLFE DE GASCOGNE
ST-NAZAIRE
Île de Noirmoutier
Saumur
TOURS
Thours
Loudan
Challans
La Roche-sur-Yonne
Parthenay
Fontenay-le-Comte
Sanxay
Luçon
Montmorillon
Gençay
Île de Ré
Marais Poitevin
Melle
Île d'Aix
Île d'Oléron
St-Jean-d'Angély
Ruffec
Confolens
LIMOGES
Cognac
Soulac-s-Mer
Jonzac
Hourtin-Plage
St-Estèphe
Blaye
Carcans-Océan
St-André-de-Cubzac
La Brède
Marmance
Biscarrosse
Casteljaloux
Penne-d'Agenais
Agen
Mimizan
Brocas
Lévignacq
Roquefort
Mont-de-Marsan
Dax
St-Sever
Arzacq
DONOSTIA-SAN SEBASTIÁN
St-Jean-Pied-de-Port
PAMPLONA/IRUÑA
Loire
Creuse
Vienne
Charente
Dordogne
Garonne
Adour
Gave de Pau
Gave d'Aspe
N
0
50 km
0
60 miles
LOURDES ★★★ Highly recommended
Saintes ★★ Recommended
Cognac ★ Interesting
St-Jean-Pied-de-Port Other sight described in this guide

Bordeaux★★★

"Take Versailles, add Antwerp, and you have Bordeaux" was Victor Hugo's description of the city, impressed as he was by its 18C grandeur and its splendid tidal river. Bordeaux had, however, played an important role in the affairs of France long before Versailles had been envisioned. Capital of the Aquitaine region, made a UNESCO World Heritage Site in 2007, Bordeaux is a town full of history.

- **Population:** 239 157.
- **Michelin Map:** 335 H 5
- **Info:** 12 cours du 30-Juillet. ℘05 56 00 66 00. www.bordeaux-tourisme.com.
- **TGV:** Bordeaux St Jean is 3–4hrs from Paris Montparnasse.
- **Flights:** Bordeaux Merignac airport (www.bordeaux.aeroport.fr/en. ℘05 56 34 50 00) is 30min from the city centre; shuttle bus every half hour.
- **Tram:** A 3-line tram network covers the whole of the city (www.infotbc.com)
- **Location:** Bordeaux is on the S bank of the River Gironde, about 48km/29.8mi from the Atlantic, and 216km/157mi N of the Spanish border.
- **Parking:** There are car parks alongside the river.
- **Don't Miss:** The extensive collection of paintings in the Musée des Beaux-Arts. Of course, there are Bordeaux's world-famous wines. Take an excursion to the Bordeaux Vineyards – you won't regret it.
- **Kids:** Workshops for kids at Cap Sciences; films, a sound and light show and fun questionnaire at Planète Bordeaux in Beychac to learn all about wine.

A BIT OF HISTORY

A large settlement even before the Roman conquest, **Burdigala** was always an important trading port, but frequently attacked by sea-going raiders. From 7C, Good King Dagobert took effective control of the town and its region, creating the Duchy of Aquitaine. In 1152, when **Eleanor of Aquitaine** married Henri Plantagenet, Duke of Normandy, Count of Anjou, ruler of Touraine and Maine, the bride's dowry consisted of practically the whole of southwestern France. Two months later her new husband inherited the English Crown, becoming Henry II of England. Bordeaux thus became part of the English kingdom, and so remained for three centuries.

It was the English demand for wine that began the city's tradition of seafaring, and promoted the expansion of the Bordeaux **vineyards**. Even during the Hundred Years' War claret continued to flow north to England. In 1453, Bordeaux and Guyenne (Old English for Aquitaine) were won back for France in the final battle of the Hundred Years' War. The French Crown appointed **Intendants** to rebuild and govern Bordeaux as a well-planned city to replace the tangle of medieval streets. In the course of the 18C they succeeded in transforming Bordeaux, giving it the Classical face it wears today, with grandiose set-pieces of urban design: the quaysides, the Place de la Bourse, the great avenues, the Town Hall (Hôtel de Ville) and the Grand Théâtre.

During the French Revolution, the Bordeaux *députés* formed the group known as the **Girondins**. Accused of conspiring against the Revolution, 22 of them were tried in May 1793 and executed.

In the 18C, goods from the Caribbean added to the huge volume of trade, further stimulating the development of this great port.

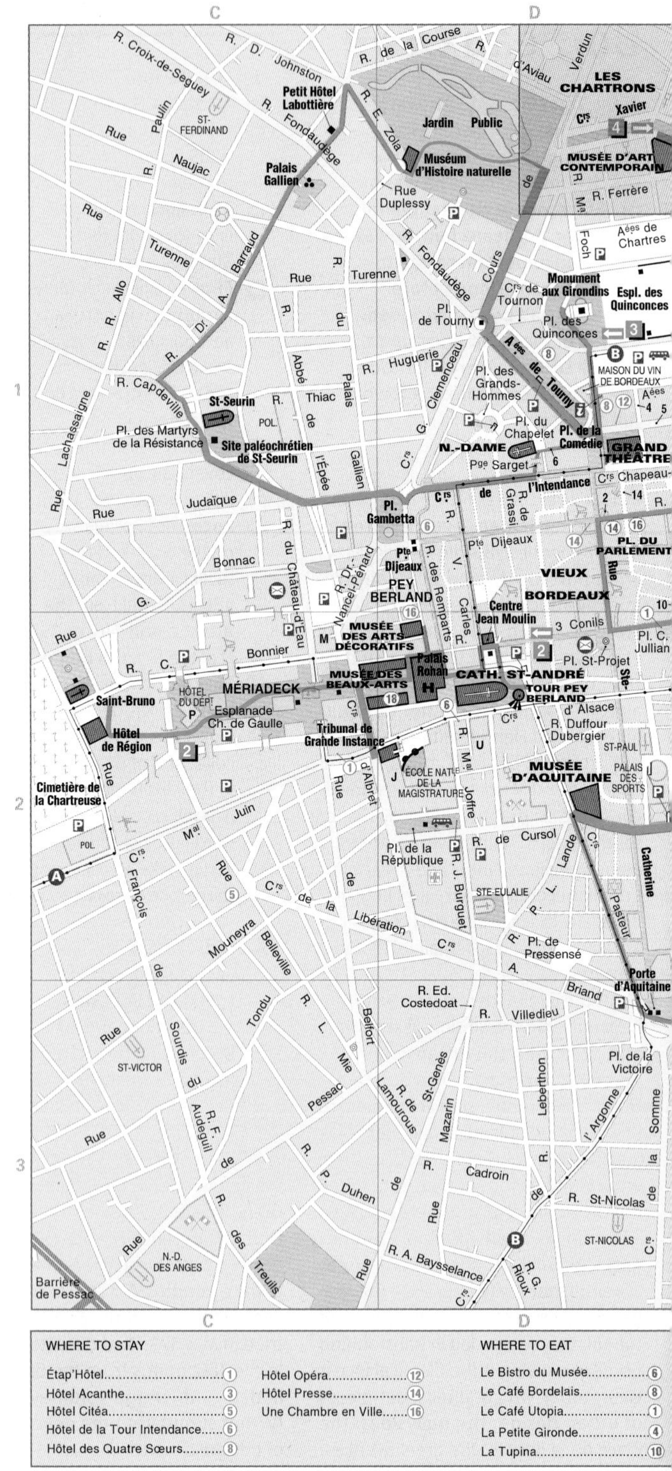
C
D
1
2
3
R. Croix-de-Seguey
R. D. Johnston
R. de la Course
R. d'Aviau
Verdun
LES CHARTRONS
Crs Xavier
4
MUSÉE D'ART CONTEMPORAIN
R. Ferrère
Mal Foch
Aées de Chartres
Petit Hôtel Labottière
R. Fondaudège
R. E. Zola
Jardin Public
Muséum d'Histoire naturelle
ST-FERDINAND
Paulin
Rue Naujac
Palais Gallien
Rue Duplessy
Rue Turenne
R. Dr. A. Barraud
Rue Turenne
R. Fondaudège
Cours de
Monument aux Girondins
Espl. des Quinconces
Crs de Tournon
Pl. de Tourny
Pl. des Quinconces
3
R. R. Allo
R. du Palais Gallien
R. Abbé de l'Épée
R. Huguerie
G. Clemenceau
Aées de Tourny
MAISON DU VIN DE BORDEAUX
Pl. des Grands-Hommes
Pl. du Chapelet
Pl. de la Comédie
GRAND THÉATRE
R. Capdeville
St-Seurin
R. Thiac
POL.
Pl. des Martyrs de la Résistance
Site paléochrétien de St-Seurin
Rue Lachassaigne
N.-DAME
Pge Sarget
Crs de l'Intendance
Crs Chapeau-
Rue Judaïque
Pl. Gambetta
R. de Grassi
Pte Dijeaux
PL. DU PARLEMENT
Bonnac
R. du Château-d'Eau
R. Dr. Nancel-Pénard
Pte Dijeaux
PEY BERLAND
R. des Remparts
V. Carles
VIEUX BORDEAUX
Rue
G.
Centre Jean Moulin
3 Conils
Pl. C. Jullian
MUSÉE DES ARTS DÉCORATIFS
M
Rue Bonnier
R. C.
MÉRIADECK
MUSÉE DES BEAUX-ARTS
Palais Rohan
CATH. ST-ANDRÉ
TOUR PEY BERLAND
Pl. St-Projet
Ste-
HÔTEL DU DÉPt
Esplanade Ch. de Gaulle
Saint-Bruno
Hôtel de Région
2
Tribunal de Grande Instance
Crs d'Alsace
R. Duffour Dubergier
ST-PAUL
Cimetière de la Chartreuse
Rue d'Albret
J
ÉCOLE NATle DE LA MAGISTRATURE
R. Mal Joffre
MUSÉE D'AQUITAINE
PALAIS DES SPORTS
U
POL.
Mal Juin
Crs François
Pl. de la République
R. J. Burguet
R. de Cursol
Lande
Crs Pasteur
Catherine
A
Rue de
Crs de la Libération
STE-EULALIE
Pl. de Pressensé
Mouneyra
Belleville
A. Briand
Porte d'Aquitaine
R. Ed. Costedoat
R. Villedieu
R. L. Mie
Rue Sourdis
Tondu
Belfort
Pl. de la Victoire
ST-VICTOR
Pessac
R. de Lamourous
St-Genès
Mazarin
Leberthon
l'Argonne
Somme
Rue
R. F. Auduguil
R. P. Duhen
R. Cadroin
R. St-Nicolas
Rue
R. des Treuils
ST-NICOLAS
B
R. A. Bayssselance
R. G. Rioux
N.-D. DES ANGES
Barrière de Pessac
WHERE TO STAY
Étap'Hôtel ... 1
Hôtel Acanthe ... 3
Hôtel Citéa ... 5
Hôtel de la Tour Intendance ... 6
Hôtel des Quatre Sœurs ... 8
Hôtel Opéra ... 12
Hôtel Presse ... 14
Une Chambre en Ville ... 16
WHERE TO EAT
Le Bistro du Musée ... 6
Le Café Bordelais ... 8
Le Café Utopia ... 1
La Petite Gironde ... 4
La Tupina ... 10

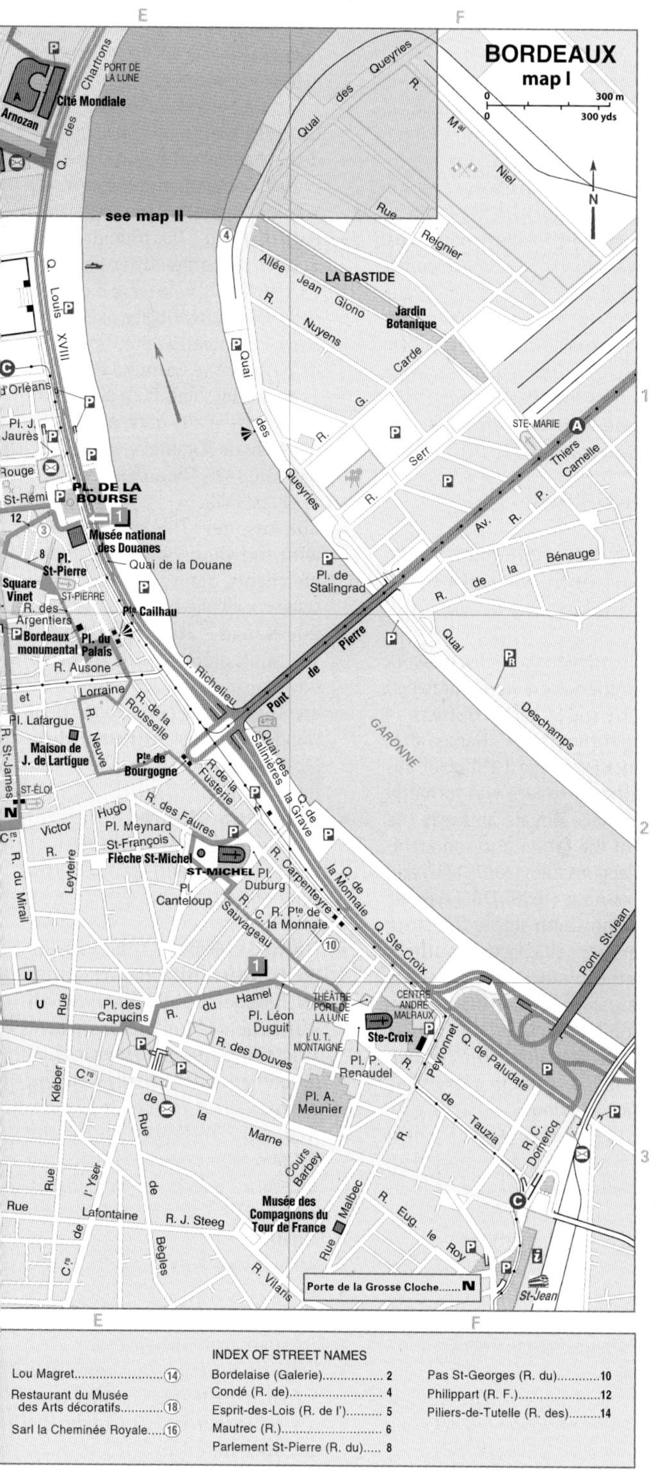

INDEX OF STREET NAMES

Lou Magret........................ (14)
Restaurant du Musée des Arts décoratifs............ (18)
Sarl la Cheminée Royale.... (16)
Bordelaise (Galerie)................. 2
Condé (R. de)........................... 4
Esprit-des-Lois (R. de l')........... 5
Mautrec (R.)............................ 6
Parlement St-Pierre (R. du)..... 8
Pas St-Georges (R. du)............10
Philippart (R. F.).......................12
Piliers-de-Tutelle (R. des).........14

OLD BORDEAUX★★★

Situated between the Chartrons and St-Michel districts, the Old Town, which includes some 5 000 buildings dating from the 18C, has undergone large-scale restoration in an effort to return the city's ancient stonework to its original splendour. The façade of numerous buildings are marked by "mascarons", small carved faces or objects that are often linked to the trades of the bourgeoisie who first owned the houses. The name comes from the Italian word maschera meaning "mask". Often comic or grotesque, there are more than 3 000 examples across the Old Town centre.

WALKING TOUR 1

From la Place de la Bourse to the Quartier St-Michel★★

Bordeaux map I, p514. Allow 1 day.

This stroll leads you through a network of picturesque narrow streets between the St-Pierre and St-Michel districts.

- **Place de la Bourse★★** – Named after the Stock Exchange (La Bourse), this magnificent square was formerly called place Royale and was the work of the father and son architects Jacques Jules (1667–1742) and Jacques-Ange (1698–1782) Gabriel. On the northern side is the Stock Exchange itself. On the southern side is the former Hôtel des Fermes (tax assessors) housing the National Customs Museum.
- **Musée des Douanes** – The Customs Museum is housed in a large hall with fine vaulting.
- **Place du Parlement★** – Parliament Square was once a royal market. This pleasant quadrangle of Louis XV buildings is arranged around a central cobbled courtyard.
- **Place St-Pierre** – Many 18C houses in the St-Pierre district have been restored. On Thursdays the square is livened up by a market of organic produce.
- **Place du Palace** – The square owes its name to the old Palais de l'Ombrière, which was built by the dukes of Guyenne in the 10C, rebuilt in the 13C, used subsequently by the kings of England and finally, under Louis XI, became the seat of the Bordeaux Parliament in 1462. The palace was demolished in 1800 to make way for the present rue du Palais.
- **Porte Cailhau** – This triumphal arch derives its name either from the Cailhau family, who were members of the Bordeaux nobility, or from the *cailloux* (pebbles) washed up around its base by the Garonne and used as ballast by ships. Built on the site of an ancient city gate, east of the old Palais de l'Ombrière, it was completed in 1495. The arch is dedicated to Charles VIII.
- **Rue Ausone** – This street is lined with the shops where the wine merchants, grain and salted meat sellers once plied their trade.
- **Rue Neuve** – Still preserved is a 14C wall, pierced with two windows surrounded with stone tracery. Through the porch to the right stands the city's oldest house, where Montesquieu's wife, Jeanne de Lartigue lived.
- **Basilique St-Michel★** – The construction of St Michael's Basilica began in 1350, and lasted for two centuries, its original design much modified over time.
- **Flèche St Michel** – The people of Bordeaux are justly proud of this late 15C hexagonal Gothic belfry, which stands apart from the basilica. At 114m tall, it is the highest tower in all of southern France, easily dwarfing the cathedral's Pey-Berland Tower.
- **Abbatiale Ste-Croix** – Built in the 12C and 13C and restored during the 19C, this church has a Romanesque **west front★** typical of the Saintonge region.
- **Porte d'Aquitaine** – Triumphal arch.
- **Musée d'Aquitaine★★** – This regional museum traces human occupation of Aquitaine.
- **Porte de la Grosse-Cloche★** – This 15C arched gateway (Great Bell Gate) is another source of local pride. The gateway stands on the site of an

older structure, porte St Éloi (St Eligius' Gateway), which was one of the entrances to the 13C walled town. When it existed, this belfry rang out the news that the grape harvest was to begin.

WALKING TOUR 2

Quartier Pey Berland

Bordeaux map I, p514. Allow half a day.

Cathédrale St-André, with its famous tower, stands in the middle of place Pey Berland, which is flanked by the city's most important museums. On the first Sunday of every month, the town centre is closed to traffic (bikes can be hired on pl. des Quinconces) and admission to museums is free.

- **Cathédrale St-André★** – This cathedral, dedicated to St Andrew, is the most impressive of all the religious buildings in Bordeaux.
- **Tour Pey Berland★** – The tower was built in the 15C on the orders of Archbishop Pey-Berland. 231 steps up a narrow spiral staircase take you to the top from where there is a panoramic **view★★**.
- **Centre Jean Moulin** – This museum, devoted to the Resistance and deportation under the German occupation, presents a panorama of World War II.
- **Palais Rohan** – The City Hall is installed in the former bishop's palace, built in the 18C for Archbishop Ferdinand Maximilian de Meriadek, Prince of Rohan. The building marks the introduction of Neoclassicism to France.
- **Musée des Arts Décoratifs★** – The Lalande mansion, which houses the Museum of Decorative Arts was designed by Laclotte in 1779.
- **Musée des Beaux-Arts★** – The Fine Arts Museum bordering the gardens of City Hall displays a collection of 15–20C paintings.
- **Tribunal de Grande Instance de Bordeaux** – Built in 1998 by architect Richard Rogers, the TGI is found in the heart of the Old Town, a self-contained island for the judiciary that includes the town hall, the former Neoclassical Palais de Justice and the École nationale de la Magistrature. This modern glass, stainless steel and wood structure is found beside some of the oldest vestiges of medieval Bordeaux; the remains of the **fort du Hâ**.
- **Mériadeck District** – Named in honour of Prince Ferdinand Maximilien de Rohan, Archbishop of Bordeaux in the 18C, this ultra-modern complex is the administrative centre of the Aquitaine.
- **Église St-Bruno** – The church, and its Cimetière de la Chartreuse, is worth a detour for its 17C Baroque decoration.

  Following the example of Père-Lachaise, the diversity of mausoleums and chapels creates a dreamy atmosphere.

WALKING TOUR 3

Golden Triangle to Jardin Public

Bordeaux map I, p514. Allow one day (including shopping).

At the centre of this area is the triangle formed by the intersection of cours Clemenceau, cours de l'Intendance and allées de Tourny.

- **Esplanade des Quinconces** – The sheer size (about 126 000sq m) of this rectangular esplanade is very impressive. It was laid out during the Restoration (early 19C) on the site of the old Château Trompette.
- **Grand Théâtre★★** – The recently restored Grand Théâtre, which overlooks the Place de la Comédie, is among the most beautiful in France, and is a potent symbol of the richness of both French architecture and French culture at the time. The building was designed by the architect Victor Louis (1731–1800) and erected between 1773 and 1780 on the site of a Gallo-Roman temple.
- **Église Notre-Dame★** – This church, dedicated to the Virgin, was for-

merly a Dominican chapel. It was built between 1684 and 1707.

- **Cours de l'Intendance** – The main street for high-fashion and luxury goods stores.
- **Place Gambetta** – This square was formerly known as place Dauphine. All the houses were built in the Louis XV style, giving a pleasing architectural unity. An attractive English garden has been laid out at the centre of the square which, during the Revolution, was the site of the scaffold.
- **Basilique St-Seurin** – As with St-André cathedral and the Basilique St-Michel, both of which are also on The Way of St James, the St-Seurin Basilica was declared in 1999 a UNESCO World Heritage Site. Its 11C crypt contains Gallo-Roman capitals and columns, as well as 6C marble sarcophaguses and the 17C tomb of St Fort.
- **Palais Gallien** – All that remains of this Roman amphitheatre which could seat 15 000 spectators are a few rows and arcades overgrown with weeds.
- **Petit Hôtel Labottière** – Laclotte, an architect at the Musée des Arts Décoratifs, designed this Neoclassical private mansion (18C).
- **Jardin Public** – This 18C French-style garden was turned into an English-style park during the reign of Napoléon III.

WALKING TOUR 4

Les Chartrons

Bordeaux map II, p519. Allow half a day.

The Chartrons district extends to the north of Quinconces, between quai des Chartrons and cours de Verdun, Portal and St-Louis. The district was named after the 15C Chartreux convent, and later became the centre of the wine trade. The district was at its height in the 18C, when the rich merchants built numerous sumptuous residences. During the 19C, numerous eschoppes were built – small workers' houses with tall, thin doors and façades that were often sculpted to resemble the wealthier merchant houses. These typical Bordeaux houses are found all over the city.

- **Cours Xavier Arnozan** – This avenue reflects the wealth of the great merchant and wine-growing families of the 1770s, who had their sumptuous town houses built conveniently close to but sufficiently removed from the noisy bustle of the port.
- **Musée d'Art Contemporain★** (CAPC) – The former Lainé **warehouse★★**, built in 1824 for storing goods imported from the French colonies, has been successfully remodelled into a Museum of Contemporary Art.
- **Cité Mondiale** – This glass-fronted commercial centre was designed by local architect Michel Petuaud-Letang, overlooking the quai des Chartrons.
- **Rue Notre-Dame** – This is the backbone of Chartrons: where the wine merchants of the 19C have been replaced by antiquarians in the 21C. Perfect for window shopping, rue Notre-Dame is lined with stone houses and numerous boutiques.
- **Place du Marché des Chartrons** – Architect Charles Burguet built a market hall here in 1869 on the site of the former Convent des Carmes. Today, a cultural centre occupies the space.
- **Église St-Louis-des-Chartrons** – This church marks the heart of the Chartrons district. Inside is the largest organ in Aquitaine. Its two spires are illuminated in blue at night.
- **Musée du Vin et du Négoce à Bordeaux** – This museum is located in three vaulted cellars typical of Chartrons, and tells the history of wine merchants in Bordeaux, and the role of the port.
- **Quai des Chartrons★** – Lined with 18C limestone buildings, the Chartrons quays have been renovated to create cultural spaces, restaurants and boutiques.

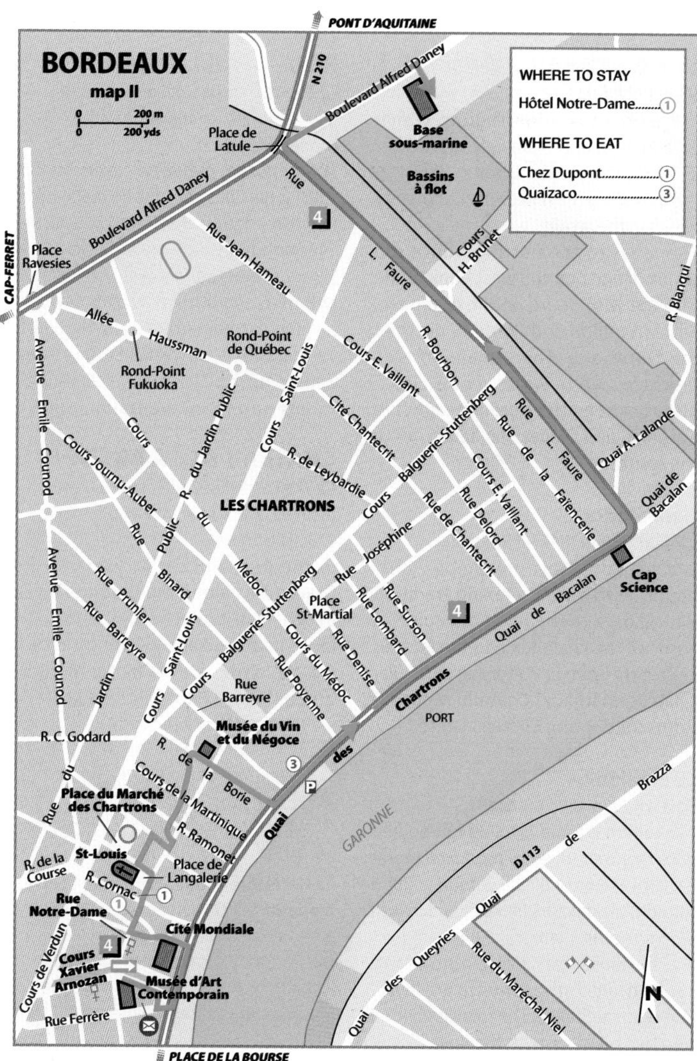

- **Cap Sciences** – The region's biggest science and industry museum offers permanent exhibitions and one-off workshops.
- **Bassins à Flot** – At the far end of the quays from the Old Town, and for years an industrial wasteland, the bassins are undergoing major renovation, with bars, restaurants and an art gallery already opened in Hangar G2.

The **Base sous-marine**, a vast concrete submarine pen from World War II, built between 1941 and 1943 for the 12th flotilla of the German army, is one of the city's most experimental venues, offering exhibitions, music and dance evenings with a distinctly underground feel.

EXCURSIONS

THE BORDEAUX VINEYARDS★

The Bordeaux wine region, which extends over approximately 135 000 ha/333 585 acres in the Gironde *département,* is the largest producer of quality wines in the world.

The areas to the north produce red wines: Médoc on the west bank of the Gironde with Bourg on the east bank, and St-Émilion and Pomerol north of the Dordogne. The remaining area produces white wines: Entre-Deux-Mers between the Dordogne and the Garonne, and Graves and Sauternes to the south.

Haut Médoc

48km/30mi NNW of Bordeaux.

It boasts the most prestigious "châteaux" with a wine-making tradition dating back to the reign of Louis XIV. Some of the châteaux and the famous cellars are open to visitors, in particular Château Margaux, **Château Mouton-Rothschild★** and Château Lafite.

St-Émilion★★

43km/27mi E of Bordeaux.

The region is famous for its full-bodied and fragrant red wines produced under the strict control of the Jurade, a guild founded in the Middle Ages which was reconvened in 1948.

St-Émilion offers both simple and sophisticated attractions to art-lovers and gourmets alike. The town is divided into two hill sites, with the Royal Castle and Deanery (Doyenné) symbolising the age-old rivalry between the civil and religious authorities.

Its sun-baked, pantile-roofed stone houses nestle in an **amphitheatre★★** on the slope of a limestone plateau. Apart from its wines, the town is known for its strange underground church.

Sauternes

50km/31mi SSE of Bordeaux.

The vineyards on the slopes of the lower valley of the Ciron produce renowned sweet white wines, in particular Château d'Yquem.

CHÂTEAU DE ROQUETAILLADE★★

The château is S of Langon on the River Garonne, on the edge of the Landes region.

This imposing medieval castle, built in 1306, is part of a compound made up of two forts dating from the 12C and the 14C within a single walled enclosure. Six enormous round towers, crenellated and pierced with arrow slits, frame a rectangular main structure. In the courtyard stands a powerful square keep and its turret. There are also vaulted rooms and monumental chimneys.

CHÂTEAU DE LA BRÈDE★

The castle lies S of Bordeaux, along the A 62, exit 1.1. Avenue du Château, 33650 La Brède.

In the peaceful countryside of the Graves area along the Garonne River, this **château**, protected by its moat, still keeps its aristocratic 15C appearance. It was the birthplace of **Charles Montesquieu** (1689–1755), Baron de la Brède – a magistrate of Bordeaux.

ADDRESSES

STAY

Hotel ibis budget Bordeaux Centre Mériadeck – 37 cours du Maréchal-Juin. 08 92 68 05 84. www.ibis.com. P. 109 rooms. Chain hotel, but well located for the Old Town.

Hôtel Citéa – 1 bis r. Jean-Renaud, Dandicolle. 05 56 56 18 00. www.adagio-city.com. P. 98 studios and 10 apartments. A new building offering a variety of studios and doubles with an equipped kitchen, or the choice of having breakfast in the main salon.

Hôtel Notre-Dame – 36–38 r. Notre-Dame. 05 56 52 88 24. www.hotelnotredame.free.fr. 22 rooms. An unpretentious little family hotel in an 18C house just the quai des Chartrons.

Hôtel de l'Opéra – 35 r. Esprit de Lois. 05 56 81 41 27. www.hotel-bordeaux-centre.com. Closed 24 Dec–2 Jan. 28 rooms. A modest family hotel near the Grand Théâtre and the allées de Tourny.

⊖⊖ **Chambre d'hôte Une Chambre en Ville** – 35 r. Bouffard. ✆05 56 81 34 53. www.bandb-bx.com. 5 rooms. In the historic Old Town, carefully decorated rooms each with individual theme. Contemporary feel.

⊖⊖ **Hôtel Acanthe** – 12–14 r. St-Rémi. ✆05 56 81 66 58. www.acanthe-hotel-bordeaux.com. Reservations required. 20 rooms. Closed late Dec. A central location and reasonable prices are the strong points of this hotel.

⊖⊖ **Hôtel des Quatre Sœurs** – 6 cours du XXX-Juillet. ✆05 57 81 19 20. www.hotel-bordeaux-4soeurs.com. 34 rooms. Well located and a real institution, celebrated for having housed both musician Richard Wagner and writer John Dos Passos.

⊖⊖ **Hôtel Presse** – 6–8 r. de la Porte Dijeaux. ✆05 56 48 53 88. www.hoteldelapresse.com. 27 rooms. In the pedestrian shopping quarter of the old city, this is a nice little hotel despite the difficult access by car. Modern, functional, cosy rooms.

⊖⊖⊖ **Hôtel de la Tour Intendance** – 14–16 r. de la Vieille-Tour. ✆05 56 44 56 56. www.hotel-tour-intendance.com. P 35 rooms. A successful renovation has restored the traditional Bordeaux façade, and inside the rooms are comfortable, modern and air-conditioned.

EAT

⊖ **Café l'Utopia** – 5 pl. Camille-Jullian. ✆05 56 79 39 25. Open Mon–Fri 12–3pm, 7–11pm, Sat–Sun 12–11.30pm. Former church restored as an art-house cinema with a lively café on the ground floor.

⊖ **La Petite Gironde** – 75 quai des Queyries. ✆05 57 80 33 33. www.lapetitegironde.fr. Closed Sat lunch and Sun. P On the Right Bank of the Garonne, a popular spot with relaxed atmosphere and good traditional menu.

⊖ **Le Bistro du Musée** – 37 pl. Pey Berland. ✆05 56 52 99 69. www.lebistrodumusee.com. Closed Sun and public holidays. This bistro with a pretty green wood entrance makes a promising impression from the start. Thoughtful décor with exposed stone walls, oak parquet, moleskin seats and wine paraphernalia. Southwest cuisine and a fine Bordeaux wine list.

⊖ **Lou Magret** – 62 r. St-Rémi. ✆05 56 44 77 94. Closed evenings (Mon–Thu), Sat lunch and Sun. A pleasant establishment whose speciality is duck.

⊖ **Quaizaco** – 80 quai des Chartrons. ✆05 57 87 67 72. Closed Sat lunch and Sun and 2 wks Aug. Housed behind the façade of 18C warehouses, a contemporary restaurant that also houses art exhibitions

⊖ **Sarl la Cheminée Royale** – 56 r. St-Rémi. ✆05 56 52 00 52. Closed Mon lunch and Sun. Meat is grilled under the enormous chimney in the dining room of this city-centre restaurant.

⊖⊖ **Auberge Inn** – 245 r. de Turenne. ✆05 56 81 97 86. Closed Sat–Sun, 3 wks Aug and 1 wk Dec. Exposed stone walls alternate with muted paint colours in this contemporary-style restaurant, with an attractive terrace.

⊖⊖ **Café Bellini** – 15 allées de Tourny. ✆05 56 81 49 94. On the allées de Tourny, this was formerly called the Brasserie Bordelais, and remains a great place to eat, specialising in tapas-style, chic menus and more gourmet food.

⊖⊖ **Chez Dupont** – 45 r. Notre-Dame. ✆05 56 81 49 59. Closed Sun–Mon. A "cuisine du marché" presented with style in this bistro in the heart of Chartron.

⊖⊖ **Les Restaurants de l'Atrium** – r. du Cardinal.-Richaud. ✆05 56 69 49 00. www.lucienbarriere.com. ♿P. Two restaurants in the casino. First the Atrium, a bistro specialising in seafood and regional food. The restaurant, La Carène, is open evenings only, and serves gourmet food.

⊖⊖ **Restaurant du Musée des Arts décoratifs** – 39 r. Bouffard. ✆05 56 52 60 49. Closed Tue. In the courtyard of this hôtel particulier which houses the Musée des Arts décoratifs, a restaurant-salon de thé offering an elegant place to stop.

⊖⊖⊖ **La Tupina** – 6 r. Porte-de-la-Monnaie. ✆05 56 91 56 37. www.latupina.com. Relaxed atmosphere in this Bordeaux institution. Traditional southwestern food cooked over an open fire.

Arcachon★★

and Le Bassin

A century and a half ago, the site of Arcachon was no more than a pinewood. Today, it is one of the most popular resorts on the French Atlantic.

- **Population:** 10 975.
- **Michelin Map:** 335 D 6-7
- **Info:** Esplanade Georges Pompidou. ℘05 57 52 97 97. www.arcachon.com.
- **TGV:** 4hrs 30mins–5hrs from Paris Montparnasse and 1hr from Bordeaux.
- **Location:** The resort fronts the vast Bassin d'Arcachon inlet, 64km/40mi SW of Bordeaux.

RESORT

Arcachon was born when a couple of speculators, the **Pereire brothers**, laid a railway line to the coast in 1852.

The resort quickly grew and was popular for both winter and summer holidays. It is divided into "seasons" – a winter resort (**ville d'hiver★**), with fine villas among the pines; a summer resort (**ville d'été**), with the seafront and attractive **Boulevard de la Mer★**; and the fashionable autumn and spring districts (**ville d'automne** and **ville de printemps**) with opulent houses near Pereire park.

EXCURSIONS

LE BASSIN★ (BAY)

Bordered by the resorts of Arcachon, Andernos and the wooded dunes of the Cap Ferret peninsula, this vast airy bay, with Bird Island (Île aux Oiseaux) at its centre, extends over an area of 250sq km/96.5sq mi, four-fifths of which is exposed at low tide.

With its great stretches of oyster beds totalling 18sq km/7sq mi in all, Arcachon is one of the main oyster-farming areas. Drive along the waterfront, or take a trip in a pinasse, one of the traditional boats used by the oyster farmers *(many excursions available from Thiers and Eyrac landing stages (Arcachon) and other landing stages around the Bassin. ℘05 57 72 28 28. www.bateliers-arcachon.com)*.

DUNE DU PILAT★★

7.5km/4.5mi S of Arcachon.

This hill of sand, the highest (114m) and longest (2 800m) in Europe, drops on its landward side almost sheer to the pine woodland. Its summit offers a thrilling view along the long, straight sands of the 230km/143mi **Côte d'Argent** (Silver Coast) with its splendid Atlantic rollers. Every year the ocean deposits another 15cu m of sand per m of coastline, continually building up the dune which in 1774 swallowed up the church at **Soulac★**. The **panorama★★** of ocean and forest is lovely at dusk.

ADDRESSES

STAY

Hôtel Le Dauphin – 7 av. Gounod. ℘05 56 83 02 89. www.dauphin-arcachon.com. 50 rooms. Housed in an attractive 19C mansion, this hotel enjoys an excellent location 300m from the sea in one of Arcachon's quiet districts.

EAT

Aux Mille Saveurs – 25 bd Général-Leclerc. ℘05 56 83 40 28. Open daily Jul–Aug; closed Tue evening and Wed rest of year. Dozens of flavour combinations on display here, often subtly spiced.

Cap Pereire – 1 av. du Parc Pereire. ℘05 56 83 24 01. www.cappereire.com. Closed Sun evening, Mon and Jan–mid-Feb. Far from the crowds, with a view of the sea, this attractive colonial-style restaurant is situated next to the tranquil Parc Pereire. The restaurant specialises in fish and seafood.

Biarritz★★★

With its splendid beaches of fine sand and high-quality facilities, golf courses and luxury hotels, this Basque coast resort enjoys an international reputation. Biarritz is Europe's surfing capital and teems with thousands of visitors coming to ride the waves year-round.

- **Population:** 25 306.
- **Michelin Map:** 324 C-D 2
- **Info:** Javalquinto, 64200 Biarritz. ℘05 59 22 37 00. www.biarritz.fr.
- **TGV:** Biarritz is 5hrs 20min direct from Paris Montparnasse.
- **Flights:** Biarritz-Anglet-Bayonne airport (www.biarritz.aeroport.fr. ℘05 59 43 83 83) is just 3km/2mi from the centre of the town, and served by Air France.
- **Location:** 205km/128mi SSW of Bordeaux, and 32km/20mi N of the Spanish border.
- **Don't Miss:** The view of La Perspective, a promenade overlooking Plage des Basques, is one of the highlights of Biarritz.
- **Kids:** Musée de la Mer.

A BIT OF HISTORY

Over a century ago, Biarritz was a place of no particular distinction, its beaches attracting people from nearby Bayonne. Fame came suddenly, with the visits of Empress Eugénie and Napoléon III, followed by many of the illustrious names of the period. Queen Victoria was here in 1889, and after 1906 Biarritz became a favourite of Edward VII.

Now enhanced by modernisation, Biarritz continues to offer pleasures which never pall; its beaches, promenades and gardens to either side of the rocky promontory of the Plateau de l'Atalaye remain as attractive as ever. The orientation of the beaches also produces rollers that attract surfers.

BEACHES

Biarritz owes much of its charm to its hydrangea-lined garden promenades, which follow the contours of the cliffs, over the rocks and along the three main beaches, which have become an international meeting place for surfers and a focal point for local entertainment both day and night.

- **Grande Plage** – Overlooked by the Municipal Casino, the Grande Plage is the largest and most fashionable of Biarritz's beaches. In former times, only the most daring of bathers would swim here, which led to its now forgotten nickname of Plage des Fous ("Madman's Beach"). To the north, it becomes Plage Miramar.
- **Plage du Port-Vieux** – Sheltered by two overhanging cliffs, it is a small family beach and a local favourite.

RESORT

- **Promenades** – Pleasantly shaded and landscaped streets lead from the main beach (*Grande Plage*) to the **Rocher de la Vierge★**. To the south is the **Perspective de la Côte des Basques** and an uninterrupted **view★★** to the mountain peaks of the Basque Country.
- **Musée de la Mer** – A remarkable aquarium set on **Rocher de la Vierge★**, with performing seals at the top floor outdoor pool.
- **Rocher de la Vierge★** – The Virgin's Rock, crowned with a statue of the Virgin Mary, is Biarritz's main landmark. It is surrounded by reefs and joined to the shore by a footbridge, impassable in rough weather with the breaking waves.
- **Villas** – The small fishing port of Biarritz suddenly became extremely fashionable during the second half of the 19C and many sumptuous villas were built in the eclectic style of the period.

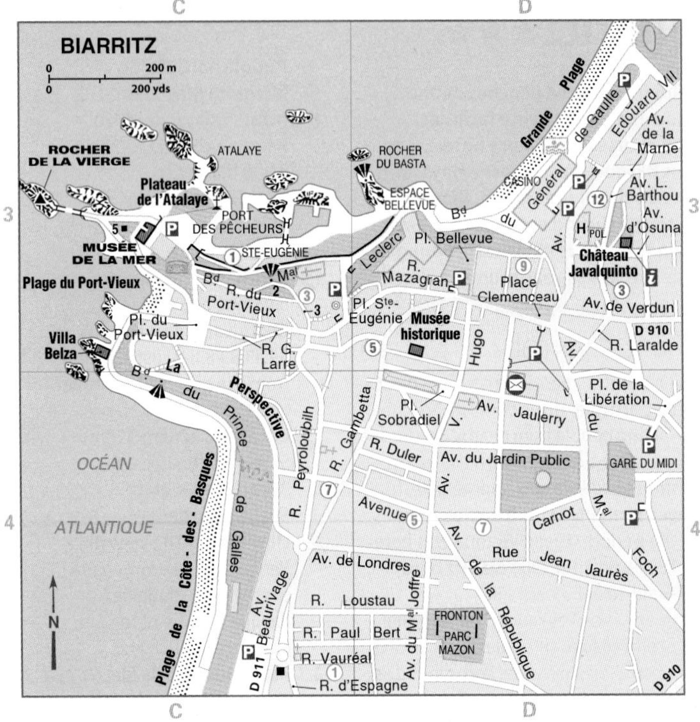

WHERE TO STAY

- Chambre d'hôte Villa Vauréal........ ①
- Hôtel Atalaye........ ③
- Hôtel Gardenia........ ⑤
- Hôtel Maïtagaria........ ⑦
- Le Petit Hôtel........ ⑨

WHERE TO EAT

- Chez Albert........ ①
- Clos Basque........ ③
- Da Vinci........ ⑤
- Il Giardino........ ⑦
- Le Cachaou........ ⑫

STREET NAMES

- Atalaye (Pl.)........ 2
- Goélands (Rue des)........ 3
- Rocher de la Vierge (Espl. du)........ 5

EXCURSIONS

BAYONNE★★

8km/5mi ENE of Biarritz.

Biarritz, Anglet and Bayonne merge to form a single urban area; Bayonne, with its busy quaysides and old streets, is the commercial centre. Its harbour on the estuary of the Adour handles maize, sulphur and chemical products. The picturesque Rue du Pont-Neuf is flanked by arcades and tall houses.

- **Musée Bonnat★★** – This beautiful building houses works by the artist and collector, Léon Bonnat, as well as works by artists and sculptors including Degas and Rubens.
- **Musée Basque★★** – One of the finest regional ethnographic museums in France and probably the best on Basque ethnography. Exhibits cover agriculture, seafaring and *pelota* – a ball game.
- **Cathédrale Sainte-Marie de Bayonne★** – Set in the historic quarter of Bayonne, this Gothic-style building was built in 13–17C. The present cathedral replaced a Romanesque one destroyed by fire in 1258 and again in 1310. Admire the **cloisters★**.

ROUTE IMPÉRIALE DES CIMES★

Bayonne to Hasparren 25km/15.5mi.

This section of Napoléon I's scenic highway was part of an overall project to link Bayonne with **St-Jean-Pied-de-Port★**

for strategic reasons. It follows a sinuous alignment and affords fine **views★** of the Basque coast and countryside.

BIDART★

6km/3.7mi S.

The small resort of Bidart, halfway between Biarritz and St-Jean-de-Luz, is built at the highest point on the Basque coastline, on the edge of a cliff.

From Chapelle Ste-Madeleine (accessible from r. de la Madeleine), the clifftop **view★** looks over the Jaizkibel (a promontory closing off the Fontarabia natural harbour), the Trois Couronnes and La Rhune.

The charming **place centrale** is framed by the church, the pelota (*jai alai*) fronton and the town hall. Local pelota matches and competitions are always watched by enthusiastic crowds. **Rue de la Grande-Plage** and **promenade de la Mer** lead steeply down to the beach.

ADDRESSES

STAY

⊜⊜ **Hôtel Atalaye** – 6 r. des Goëlands, Plateau de l'Atalaye. 05 59 24 06 76. Closed 15 Nov–18 Dec. 25 rooms. This imposing turn-of-the century villa owes its name to the superb Atalaye Plateau overlooking the Atlantic Ocean. Free parking nearby (Oct–mid-Jun).

⊜⊜ **Hôtel Gardenia** – 19 av. Carnot. 05 59 24 10 46. www.hotel-gardenia.com. Closed Dec–Feb. 19 rooms. This central hotel with a pink façade has all the charm of a private home. Its quiet, attractive rooms are regularly redecorated.

⊜⊜⊜ **Chambre d'hôte Villa Vauréal** – 114 r. Vauréal. 06 10 11 64 21. Closed Jan. 5 rooms. Comfortable villa in a large garden full of mature trees, two minutes from the beach.

⊜⊜⊜ **Hôtel Maïtagaria** – 34 av. Carnot. 05 59 24 26 65. www.hotel-maitagaria.com. 15 rooms. A warm, friendly reception in this little hotel near the garden, just 500m from the beach. The rooms, of varying sizes, are bright and functional.

⊜⊜⊜ **Le Petit Hôtel** – 11 r. Gardères. 05 59 24 87 00. www.petithotel-biarritz.com. Closed fortnight in Nov and Feb. 12 rooms. This appealing hotel is ideally located for exploring the town or spending time on the beach. Its soundproofed rooms have been decorated in tones of blue or yellow.

EAT

⊜ **Da Vinci** – 15 r. Gambetta. 05 59 22 50 88. Closed Mon, Jan, Mon–Wed out of season. This restaurant concentrates on Spanish tapas/pintxos-style and regional Basque food.

⊜ **Il Giardino** – 62 r. Gambetta. 05 59 22 16 41. www.ilgiardino-biarritz.com. Open Wed–Sat lunch, Tue and Sun evening. Brightly coloured Italian restaurant. Authentic Italian regional cuisine, with home-cooked feel and generous portions. Well-priced also. Specialities include spinaci ripieni (a kind of home-made spinach ravioli), risotto and spiedini sfiziosi (brochettes of veal cooked with raisins and pine-nuts).

⊜⊜ **Le Cachaou** – 30 av. Édouard-VI. 05 59 22 59 55. This recently opened spot from father-son team serves up traditional southwest food, with a Basque flavour in terms of spices and emphasis on local fish and meats. Well located, close to the Grand Plage, town hall and the casino. Tapas-style food also available, based around fresh seasonal produce.

⊜⊜ **Le Clos Basque** – 12 r. Louis-Barthou. 05 59 24 24 96. Closed Sun evening (Sep–Jun), Mon and a fortnight in Feb and Jun. Excellent local cuisine and a warm, friendly atmosphere mean that there's rarely a spare table in this popular restaurant. Exposed beams and azulejos tiles add an Iberian flavour.

⊜⊜⊜⊜ **Chez Albert** – 51 Bis all Port des Pêcheurs, 64200 Biarritz. 05 59 24 43 84. www.chezalbert.fr. Closed Wed (Sep–Jun) and Jan. Situated close to the church of St Eugénie, this busy fish and seafood restaurant affords fine views over the fishing port.

St-Jean-de-Luz★★

As a smart summer and winter seaside resort, St-Jean-de-Luz only dates back to 1843; however, as a fishing port, the town is ancient. Today only one house survives from before the great fire of 1558, when the place was sacked by the Spanish. The seafront is determinedly modern. Ste-Barbe headland, reached on foot via promenade de la Plage and boulevard Thiers, offers a fine view southwards across the bay to Socoa fort on its rocky promontory. St-Jean-de-Luz, the most Basque of the towns north of the Spanish border, offers all the attractions and amenities of a beach resort together with the picturesque and briny delights of a busy fishing port.

- **Population:** 12 969.
- **Michelin Map:** 342 C 2
- **Info:** Bd. Victor Hugo. ✆05 59 26 03 16. www.saint-jean-de-luz.com.
- **Location:** The town is on the Atlantic seafront just S of Biarritz, close to the Spanish border. The centre is on the right bank of the Nivelle.
- **Don't Miss:** The port area.

A BIT OF HISTORY

The main event to occur in the town was the marriage of Louis XIV of France to the infanta of Spain, Maria-Theresa. The wedding was initially held up by the king's passion for Marie Mancini, but in the end was solemnised here, on 9 June 1660.

PORT★

This is the original St-Jean-de-Luz. As early as the 11C, its sailors were hunting whale off Labrador. By the 15C, their quarry had changed to the abundant cod of the great fishing grounds off Newfoundland. The part of the town known as **La Barre** was where the ship-owners lived; its growth was intimately linked to the fortunes of its fleet. The 16C and 17C brought good times, though the place was burned down by the Spaniards in 1558, then ravaged by high tides in 1749 and 1785.

With whaling a thing of the past, local fishermen nowadays rely on hauls of sardines, anchovies and especially tuna fish for their livelihood.

The port is at the inner end of the only anchorage to break the long straight line of the Atlantic coast between Arcachon and the Bidassoa river. The estuary, nestling between the Socoa and Ste-Barbe headlands, is further protected from westerly gales by massive dykes and the Artha breakwaters. From the quays there are picturesque views across the busy harbour of the Old Town and inland, in the distance, the great pyramid bulk of La Rhune.

The imposing **Maison de l'Infante** seems to be guarding the boats. This elegant building in the Louis XIII style, constructed of brick and stone with Italian-style galleries overlooking the port, belonged to the rich Haraneder family. The Infanta stayed here with her future mother-in-law, Anne of Austria. In the large 17C room, note the immense sculpted and painted fireplace and the beams decorated with paintings from the school of Fontainebleau.

TOWN CENTRE

Modernised now with pedestrian precincts – the town centre has a special charm of its own. The famous "oldest house", its solid dressed-stone construction contrasting with the red-roofed, white-walled Basque buildings nearby, is at 17 rue de la République, near the harbour.

- **Église St-Jean Baptiste★★** – Work on enlarging the church, begun in 1649, had still not been completed when the royal wedding took place here in 1660. It is the finest church in the French Basque country, with a resplendent 17C gilded altarpiece (**retable★**) attributed to Martin de Bidache, a painted wooden ceiling and oak-built galleries on several levels.

EXCURSIONS

CORNICHE BASQUE★★

14km/8.7mi S, then extending S to Hendaye.

The Socoa cliff (**Falaise de Socoa★**), is an unusual example of coastal relief, best seen at low tide.

SARE★

13.5km/8.5mi SE of St-Jean-de-Luz.

This village was described, under the name of Etchezar, by Pierre Loti in his novel Ramuntcho (1897). The high fronton wall of the pelota court, the shaded streets, and the fine church with its galleries, raised chancel and Baroque altarpieces, are all typical of the Basque Country. The upper Sare valley is a pastoral landscape of sheep, dairy cattle, pottock ponies and scattered hamlets.

AINHOA★

25.5km/16mi SE of St-Jean-de-Luz.

Ainhoa, a typical Basque village, was founded in the late 12C by Premonstratensian monks as a staging post on the route to Santiago de Compostela. This brotherhood combined evangelism and work with a contemplative life. The D 20, through the village, is one of the oldest pilgrimage and trade routes to Spain in the Nive-Nivelle region.

ESPELETTE★

22.5km/14mi ESE of St-Jean-de-Luz.

This village dates from medieval times, and remains a sprawling collection of Basque-style red-and-white houses lining narrow, winding streets. Espelette specialises in growing a regional variety of red chilli pepper, but there is also a brisk local trade in a breed of pony called a pottock (a Pottock Fair is held in late January: exhibitions and competitions of pottocks, market with local produce, pelota). The ponies live in herds on the slopes of the mountains along the Spanish border. Once used in the mines because of their docile nature and diminutive stature, these animals are now suited to pony trekking.

CAMBO-LES-BAINS★

35km/22mi E of St-Jean-de-Luz.

Haut Cambo, the upper residential district of this spa, has a number of hotels and villas overlooking the River Nive, whereas Bas Cambo, the lower town, is an old Basque village nestling in a wide curve of the river. At one time Cambo was the navigable limit for barges bringing cargoes inland from Bayonne.

- **Villa Arnaga★★** – The spacious Villa Arnaga was built in the Labourdes Basque style under Rostand's supervision between 1903 and 1906. It stands on a promontory which the writer turned into formal gardens.

LA RHUNE★★

14km/8.7mi SE, then as far as Sare.

Towards the end of the 6C, the Basques were probably pushed northwards by the Visigoths. Those of their number who settled in the plains of Aquitaine intermarried with local people, eventually becoming the Gascons.

Those who remained in the mountains, however, kept their independence and their enigmatic language, thus guaranteeing their very distinct identity.

The mountain called La Rhune ("good grazing" in Basque) is one of the symbols of the Basque country; its **summit** *(accessible by rack-and-pinion railway)* rises to a height of 905m, offering a wonderful **panorama★★★** of the Bay of Biscay, the Landes and the ancient provinces of Labourd, Navarre and Guipuzcoa.

At the foot of the mountain lie the villages of **Ascain★** and **Sare★**, both with many characteristically Basque features. The houses are timber-framed; the white rendering of the walls makes a pleasant contrast to the reddish-brown colour usually applied to the timber.

Dax★

Dax is the most popular spa resort in France, and is reputed for its hot mud treatments. The maceration of silt from the River Adour in water from the hot springs encourages the development of vegetable and mineral algae. The town, built on the edge of the Landes pine forest, is an enjoyable place to visit, with riverside walks and colourful public gardens.

- **Population:** 20 665.
- **Michelin Map:** 335: E-12
- **Info:** 11 cours Foch, Dax. ☎05 58 56 86 86. www.dax-tourisme.com.
- **Location:** 146km/91.5mi SSW of Bordeaux, 65.5km/41mi NE of Biarritz.
- **Parking:** There are car parks near the cathedral and along the banks of the Adour. Some of the streets in the town centre are pedestrianised.
- **Don't Miss:** The Fontaine Chaude and the town's parks and gardens; the duck and goose market (*marché au gras*), held every Saturday morning in the market hall.
- **Timing:** If you enjoy a festival atmosphere, then August is the best time to visit Dax. This is when the town holds its annual *féria*, a week-long festival.
- **Kids:** Musée de l'Aviation Légère de l'Armée de Terre.

A BIT OF HISTORY

A lake village, with houses on stilts, once stood on the site where Dax is built today. However, alluvia from the Adour gradually silted up the lake and the village developed on dry land. The hot springs received favours and prospered after Emperor Augustus brought his daughter Julia here to treat her rheumatism.

After celebration of the marriage between Louis XIV and Maria Teresa in St-Jean-de-Luz, the couple stopped at Dax on their way home to Paris. The townsfolk set up a triumphal arch at the entrance to the town depicting a dolphin emerging from the water, and an inscription in Latin, was a pun on the words dolphin and *dauphin* (identical in French) in the hopes that the couple's stay in Dax would bear fruit.

TOWN CENTRE

- **Fontaine Chaude** – The hot spring at the centre of town is the main attraction in Dax. Its thermal waters have been tapped since Roman times, gush forth at a temperature of 64°C into a huge basin surrounded by arcades. Nearby in place Thiers is the statue of **Borda**, an 18C marine engineer born in Dax.
- **Banks of the Adour** – There are several **riverside walks**. Upstream from the bridge, on the south side, is **Parc Théodore-Denis**, where Gallo-Roman ramparts provide a shady walk under a row of plane trees.

  Downstream is **Jardin de la Potinière**, leading down into the heart of the thermal district, while just beyond is the *Trou des Pauvres* or paupers' hole, once a public bath.
- **Musée de Borda** – The museum contains collections of Gallo-Roman and medieval archaeology (statuettes and 1C bronzes discovered in Dax), 18–20C paintings of the world of bullfighting, and Dutch landscapes.
- **Musée de l'Aviation Légère de l'Armée de Terre (ALAT)** – Take the D 6 southwest towards Peyrehorade, then the D 106 and turn right. The museum houses an historical gallery with collections of documents, memorabilia, uniforms, etc. A hangar contains more than 30 well-preserved aeroplanes and helicopters.

Pau★★

and the Béarn

Overlooking the Gave de Pau torrent, the town has guarded an important route to Spain since Roman times. Since 1450 it has been the capital of the Béarn country, in touch with both the lowlands and the high mountains of this ancient southwestern province of France.

- **Population:** 81 166.
- **Michelin Map:** 342 J 3
- **Info:** Place Royale. ✆05 59 27 27 08. www.pau-pyrenees.com.
- **Location:** Pau lies between Biarritz (121km/76mi to the W) and Toulouse (194km/121mi to the E).
- **Access:** Pau Pyrénées Airport is 10km/6.2mi NW. Train from Bordeaux takes 2hrs 15mins.

A BIT OF HISTORY

The Béarn and its people

The province has an attractively varied landscape of hills, vineyards, orchards and pasture. Houses are large, with steep slate roofs.

Gaston IV Fébus (1331–91), an authoritarian ruler who surrounded himself with men of letters, was the first to fortify Pau. **Jean II d'Albret** acquired the Foix country through his marriage to Catherine de Foix in 1484, but was obliged to abandon southern Navarre to the king of Spain. In 1527, his son Henri II married Marguerite d'Angoulême, the sister of François I: it was she who brought the art of the Renaissance to the castle and, fired with Reformation zeal, made the place one of the intellectual centres of Europe.

Their daughter, **Jeanne d'Albret**, married Antoine de Bourbon, a descendant of Louis IX; this enabled her own son Henri of Navarre (the future Henri IV) to garner the inheritance of the House of Valois on the extinction of the line, thereby "incorporating France into Gascony by way of the Béarn" (Henri IV).

SIGHTS

- **Boulevard des Pyrénées★★** – From this splendid panoramic avenue running along a high ridge between the château and the park, there is a famous **view★★★** over the valley to the Pyrénéan foothills, and, in clear weather, far beyond, to the Pic du Midi de Bigorre and the Pic d'Anie.
- **Château★★** – The castle, built by Gaston Fébus in the 14C on a spur overlooking the river, has lost its military aspect despite the square, brick keep, which still towers over it. Transformed into a Renaissance palace by Marguerite d'Angoulême, the building was completely restored in the 19C in the time of Louis-Philippe and Napoléon III.
- **Musée des Beaux-Arts★** – In the Fine Arts Museum old masters are exhibited next to local artists in tasteful thematic displays of old and contemporary works.

EXCURSIONS

Vallée d'Ossau★★

Invigoratingly beautiful landscape abounds, with mountain peaks reflected in still lakes, and waterfalls cascading down mountain faces. And to complete the picture, turn your eyes skywards to watch birds of prey swooping down on an unaware Pyrénées marmot, or an izard goat nimbly jumping from rock to rock. The magnificent **Col d'Aubisque★★** (1 709m), which separates the Béarn from the Bigorre country, is by far the most spectacular pass in the region.

Vallée d'Aspe★★

One of the three valleys of the Haut-Bárn, the secluded vallée d'Aspe has long been an important thoroughfare through the mountains.

Angoulême★★

Angoulême has a walled historic Upper Town, which rises high above a more industrial modern Lower Town; narrow streets lace through the lofty Upper Town, lined with beautiful old buildings, and the ramparts give immense views. Angoulême is France's "Cartoon Capital", and everywhere you'll see the influence of its celebrated *Festival international de la bande dessinée*, **devoted to the art of the strip cartoon.**

- **Population:** 41 613.
- **Michelin Map:** 324 K-L-M 5-6
- **Info:** 7 bis r. du Chat. ℘05 45 95 16 84. www.angouleme-tourisme.com.
- **TGV:** Angouleme is 2hrs 30mins direct from Paris Montparnasse and 1hr from Bordeaux.
- **Location:** Angoulême is 119km/74.5mi NE of Bordeaux.
- **Kids:** In this cartoon-crazy city, there are brilliant graffiti and *trompe l'œil* everywhere. The tourist office has a map of some of the best, or find their locations online at www.toutenbd.com/murs_peints.

A BIT OF HISTORY

Marguerite d'Angoulême – Marguerite de Valois, François I's sister, also known as Marguerite des Marguerites ("the Pearl of Pearls"), was born in the town in 1492 and spent much of her youth here. She was a woman of great culture and learning – her *Heptameron*, a collection of stories in the style of Boccaccio, won her a permanent place in French literature. She was also famous for her fêtes and parties, and was very influential in Court life. Her name lives on in two kinds of local confectionery: *marguerites* and *duchesses*.

The Two Balzacs – The local lycée (high/secondary school) is named after the author Guez de Balzac (1597–1654), who was born in Angoulême. A rigorous stylist, he was dubbed "the man who restored the French language". The other writer, Honoré de Balzac (1799–1850), the famous French author of La *Comédie Humaine* (The Human Comedy), was adopted by Angoulême and described the town in his famous work *Les Illusions Perdues* (Lost Illusions).

WALKING TOUR

OLD TOWN

Angoulême map, p531.

The district around the cathedral is fairly quiet, but around the Palais de Justice, there are lively bars, restaurants and shops, punctuated by old houses, picturesque streets and small squares. The main highlight is the **Cathedrale St-Pierre★★**. Extensively destroyed by the Calvinists, the cathedral was restored in 1634 and again from 1866 onwards. The early 12C statuary of the west front (**façade★★**) is mostly intact

Next is the **Musée de Angoulême**, housed in the 12C former Bishops' Palace rebuilt in the 15C and 16C. The museum is best known for the quality and wealth of its exhibits from the South Pacific region and Africa.

The **Ancienne Chapelle des Cordeliers** was once a convent church belonging to the Franciscans. **Hôtel St-Simon** has a pretty Renaissance courtyard.

ADDITIONAL SIGHTS

Centre National de la Bande Dessinée et de l'Image – strip-cartoon centre – This seriously wacky cartoon centre houses a museum, temporary exhibitions and a library, all of which are well worth visiting.

Musée du Papier "Le Nil" – The former Bardou-Le-Nil paper mill, which specialised in the production of cigarette papers, operated here on the banks of the River Charente until 1970.

EXCURSIONS

CHÂTEAU DE LA ROCHEFOUCAULD★★

The château and village are in the Charente, NE of Angoulême.
1 r. des Tanneurs. 05 45 63 07 42. www.chateau-la-rochefoucauld.com.

This elegant Renaissance château, reminiscent of the Loire, stands outside a picturesque village of the same name. The property is the seat of a noble family, which gave the name François to all its first-born sons and produced many a distinguished soldier, statesman, artist and churchman. **François VI** (1613–80) established his reputation as the greatest of France's maxim-writers. In his younger days he was a brave soldier but inept plotter; he was imprisoned by Richelieu, fought on the wrong side in the Fronde and was almost blinded by a blast from a harquebus.

With a perception of the world sharpened by an understandable pessimism, he produced the *Maxims* for which he is famous, for example: "Hypocrisy is the tribute vice pays to virtue", and "We are all brave enough to bear other people's misfortunes."

The first fortification here was a wooden structure built by Foucauld, the youngest brother of the Viscount of Limoges, in 980 and named Foucauld's Rock.

During the following century a stone keep with a surrounding wall was constructed and the medieval works were completed by five towers, later raised in height to demonstrate the power of the Rochefoucauld family.

In 1520 François II de la Rochefoucauld and his wife Anne de Polignac transformed the fortress into a sophisticated Renaissance residence, albeit retaining the medieval towers, with a chapel, a terrace and 16C façades. They also added galleries and a staircase based on a design by Leonardo da Vinci that was given to Anne by King François I.

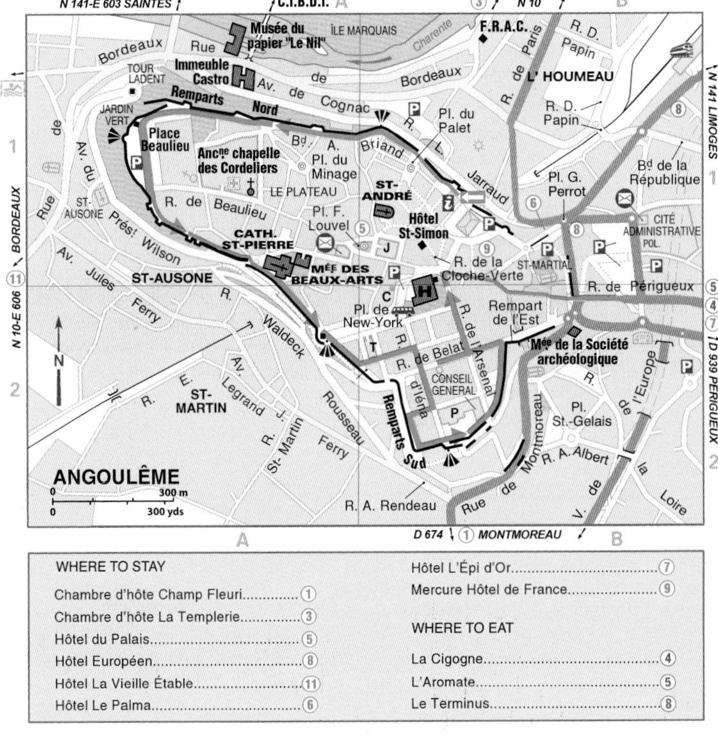

AUBETERRE-SUR-DRONNE★★

48km/30mi S of Angoulême.

Aubeterre is a very old village huddled in a semicircle at the foot of its castle. One of the finest villages in France, it has steep, narrow streets, and stands out against the line of white chalk cliffs that give Aubeterre its name (alba terra in Latin, meaning "white land"). The writer Pierre Véry (1900–60) was born in Bellon, a few miles away from Aubeterre. One of his most famous books was Les Disparus de St-Agil. Aubeterre's **monolithic church★★**, dedicated to St John, is one of a rare type which has been hewn from a single, solid block of rock.

ADDRESSES

STAY

Chambre d'Hôte La Templerie – 440, rue des Lys, Denat, 16430 Champniers (9.5km/6mi N of Angoulême. Take the N 10 towards Poitiers then the D 105 to Balzac). 06 87 13 14 65. www.latemplerie-richon.fr. 5 rooms. You will be lodged in the old utility rooms of this magnificent vineyard farm. Not to worry – every room is very pleasant and colourful.

Chambre d'hôte Champ Fleuri – chemin de l'Hirondelle (2km/1.2mi S of the map). 05 45 68 35 84. www.champ-fleuri.com. 5 rooms. Lovely old house surrounded by a private garden, near to the golf course. Pretty individually decorated rooms, splendid view, terrace and swimming pool: a peaceful haven.

Européen – 1 pl. G-Perot. 05 45 92 06 42. www.europeenhotel.com. Closed 19 Dec–3 Jan. ♿. 31 rooms. Near to the ramparts, family hotel with practical soundproofed rooms.

L'Épi d'Or – 66 bd René-Chabasse. 05 45 95 67 64. www.hotel-epidor.fr. P 33 rooms. Centrally located near to the place Victor-Hugo where there is a lively market.

Hôtel du Palais – 4 pl. Francis-Louvel. 05 45 92 54 11. www.hoteldupalais16.com. 41 rooms. Situated in the centre of the Old Town, housed in a building dating from 1778 that once belonged to the Tiercelettes convent, the rooms are in a beautiful setting. The elegant façade, facing south, looks out over the place Francis-Louvel.

Le Palma – 4 rampe d'Aguesseau. 05 45 95 22 89. Closed Sat noon, Sun and 19 Dec–5 Jan. 9 rooms. Comfortable non-smoking rooms, decorated tastefully with solid wood furniture: natural or painted. The simple restaurant serves daily specials, and a selection of Spanish dishes.

Vieille Etable – Les Plantes, 16440 Roullet-St-Estèphe. 05 45 66 31 75. www.hotel-vieille-etable.com. 29 rooms. Restaurant. Despite lying close to the N 10 road, this restored farmhouse offers quiet accommodation in small chalets dotted around the grounds.

Mercure Hôtel de France – 1 pl. des Halles-Centrales. 05 45 95 47 95. www.mercure.com. 89 rooms Restaurant. The hotel is housed in the birthplace of Guez de Balzac onto which a modern annex has been added. Pleasant modern rooms and pretty garden.

EAT

L'Aromate – 41 bd René-Chabasse. 05 45 92 62 18. Closed Tue, Wed and Sun evenings, Mon, 1–11 May, 25 Jul, 25 Aug and 21 Dec–5 Jan. Convivial atmosphere in this rustic restaurant without frills. Splendid traditional dishes with a touch of innovation.

Le Terminus – 3 pl. de la Gare. 05 45 95 27 13. www.le-terminus.com. Closed Sun. Chic contemporary brasserie, decorated in black and white. The cuisine, also modern, is based on local produce enlivened with the catch of the day from the Atlantic Coast.

La Cigogne – 5 impasse Cabane Bambou. 16800 Soyaux at the town hall. Take r. A-Briand 1.5km/0.9mi. 05 45 95 89 23. www.la-cigogne-angouleme.com. Closed Wed and Sun evenings, Mon, 14–21 Mar, 25 Oct–10 Nov and 22 Dec–3 Jan. P Adjacent to an ancient mushroom farm, the veranda-dining room is modern and bright, complemented by a terrace overlooking the surrounding countryside. The cuisine is a combination of traditional and modern dishes.

Cognac★

For many years Cognac was a river port on the calm waters of the Charente, exporting salt and, from the 11C, wine. In 1570, it was one of the four strongholds conceded to the Protestants under the Treaty of St-Germain. Place Francois I, a busy square with an ornamental fountain, links the old part of Cognac, on the slope above the river Charente, with the sprawling modern town.

- **Population:** 18 557.
- **Michelin Map:** 324 I 5
- **Info:** 16 r. du 14-juillet. ℘05 45 82 10 71. www.tourism-cognac.com.
- **Location:** 43km/27mi W of Angoulême, 123km/77mi NNE of Bordeaux.
- **Don't Miss:** Visit a distillery, although a stroll beside the river is pleasant enough.

A BIT OF HISTORY

Early in the 17C local vintners started to distil wines that travelled badly, in order to help turnover, reduce excise dues and facilitate storage.

The taste for the product spread to Holland, Scandinavia and Britain, whose long association with brandy is reflected in some of the great names of Cognac, Hine, Martell, Hennessy. A century later it was realised that ageing improved the quality of the spirit.

QUARTIER ANCIEN★

The Grande-Rue has a fine half-timbered example dating from the 15C, the Rue Saulnier a number of 16C houses with rusticated stonework and elaborate doorways and windows, while in the Rue de l'Îsle d'Or is the Hôtel de l'Échevinage (House of the Magistrates), distinguished by its corner niches.

Musée d'Art et d'Histoire – This municipal museum is housed in Hôtel Dupuy d'Angeac, in the grounds of the town hall. The displays cover the history and civilisation of the Cognac area from the earliest times to the present.

CELLARS★★

The cellars and storerooms spread out along the riverside quays, near the port and in the suburbs, house the casks in which the slow alchemy between spirit and oak occurs.

Camus – The tour offered by this Cognac trading company, founded in 1863, concentrates on the history of Cognac, its distillation, ageing and blending. Visitors are conducted through the cooper's shop and wine stores before watching the bottling process.

Hennessy – The business was founded in 1765 by a captain of Irish origin serving in Louis XV's Irish Brigade. His descendants still head the company today. A Cooperage Museum **(Musée de la Tonnellerie)** is devoted to the manufacture of brandy casks. The stores of this company are located on both banks of the River Charente. A modern white-stone building, standing on the Right Bank, was designed by Wilmotte. As an introduction to the world of Cognac,

Cognac Production

The production of cognac is the result of a two-stage distillation process, using the special still of the region. The 90 000ha/220 000 acres of vineyards yield a white wine which is light, flowery and quite acid; it takes nine litres of it to make one of brandy. It is then kept in barrels made of porous oak from the Limoges district for at least two and a half years, during which time the brandy absorbs tannin and resins from the wood, and oxygen from the atmosphere, to which it loses 2½ percent of its volume per annum – the "angels' portion", equivalent to 2 million bottles a year!

visitors are first taken across the river by boat and led into the wine stores where the various stages of brandy making are explained with the help of special effects involving sounds and smells.
Rémy Martin – The distillery, founded in 1724, creates its cognac exclusively from the prestigious Grande Champagne and Petite Champagne vintages.
Martell – Founded in 1715, this is the oldest of the famous cognac distilleries. Three rooms of the founder's residence have been restored and convey the working environment of an entrepreneur in the early 18C. Other cognac houses with cellars open to visitors include **Camus**, **Otard** and **Prince Hubert de Polignac**.

ADDITIONAL SIGHTS

Otard★ – The 15C–16C château de Cognac recalls the memory of the Valois family and François I, who was born here. It became the property of the Comte d'Artois (the future Charles X) under Louis XVI and was sequestrated by the Republicans during the Revolution. Since 1795 it has been used as a wine store by the firm Otard, which was originally founded by an old Scottish family. The façade overlooking the Charente has a fine balcony, known as the King's Balcony. Inside the old château, it is possible to visit Helmet Hall, where Richard the Lionheart married his son Philip to Amélie de Cognac. The huge rooms, with their ribbed vaulting are extremely elegant. The tour ends in the wine stores.
Musée des Arts du Cognac★★ – Housed partly in the Hôtel Perrin de Boussac (1567) and partly in a modern building this remarkable museum is entirely dedicated to Cognac and its history.

EXCURSIONS

LA GRANDE CHAMPAGNE CHARENTAISE★

65km/40mi. Allow half a day.

The roads which wind through the Cognac vineyards reveal rural architecture, a string of Romanesque churches, and a host of wine-growers.

- **Ars** – St-Maclou church, late 12C, has a lovely portal with sculptured archivolts. The nave leads to a half-dome apse with a 17C altar.
- **Genté** – The village sits on a hillside, and has splendid views, especially from the church (12C) terrace.
- **Dolmen de St-Fort-sur-le-Né** – Megalithic monument in the middle of the vineyards.
- **Lignières** – A pretty village typical of Grande Champagne with solid stone houses in the centre. There is also a charming river that runs past a 17C château, and a church, with a remarkable sculptured façade.
- **Bouteville** – The village is overlooked by the ruins of its château, rebuilt in the 17C. From the outskirts of its grounds there is a magnificent panorama over the vineyards to Angoulême. Below the village, St-Paul church is all that remains of a 10C Benedictine priory.
- **Segonzac** – The capital of Grande Champagne is home to the Université internationale des eaux-de-vie et boissons spiritueuses.
- **Gensac-la-Pallue** – Before arriving at Gensac, route D 49 skirts the pallue or marshland from which the small town derives its name.

ADDRESSES

STAY

Hôtel François Ier – 3 place François Ier. 05 45 80 80 80. www.hotelfrancoispremier.fr. 21 rooms and 4 suites. A taste of luxury in the centre of Cognac.

EAT

Le Chantilly – 146, avenue Victor Hugo. 05 45 32 43 07. Closed Sat, Sun and public holidays, plus 1st week in Aug. Traditional and regional cuisine, and French specialities.

La Rochelle★★★

This lively port is much frequented by artists and tourists. It owes its origin to the fort built in the 11C during the centuries of English rule.

- **Population:** 75 170.
- **Michelin Map:** 324 D 3
- **Info:** 2 quai Georges Simenon, Le Gabut. 05 46 41 14 68. www.holidays-la-rochelle.co.uk.
- **TGV:** La Rochelle Ville is 3hrs 30mins direct from Paris Montparnasse, and 2hrs 15 mins from Bordeaux St Jean.
- **Location:** La Rochelle is 182km/114mi N of Bordeaux. The town centre lies around the Vieux Port.
- **Timing:** Allow half a day to explore the old port area, but use La Rochelle as a base from which to visit Île de Ré, and the Atlantic coast.
- **Kids:** Aquarium (quai Louis Prunier; www.aquarium-larochelle.com); Musée des Automates (www.musees larochelle.com).

A BIT OF HISTORY

La Rochelle was one of the first places in France where the Reformation took hold. After the St Bartholomew's Day Massacre (1572), La Rochelle became one of the main centres of Protestant resistance.

The religious freedoms secured by the Edict of Nantes in 1598 brought several years of peace. By 1627, however, the town's continued adherence to Protestantism had become intolerable to Richelieu, not least because of its English connection. Richelieu personally directed a siege of La Rochelle that took 15 months to starve the town into submission. 23 000 citizens perished. The 5 000 who survived were spared, though a number of their leaders, including the mayor, Jean Guiton, were banished for a period of several months.

La Rochelle contributed more than its share to the opening up of the world beyond Europe; in the 15C, it was from here that the first colonists embarked for Canada and Jean de Béthencourt sailed to discover the Canary Islands; in the 16C, La Rochelle's fishing fleet operated in the rich fishing grounds off Newfoundland.

Other explorers to set out from here were René-Robert Cavelier, Sieur de La Salle, who sailed down the Mississippi to the Gulf of Mexico in 1681–2, and René Caillié, the first European to get back from Timbuktu alive.

La Rochelle's shipowners profited from international trade, and above all with the West Indies, where they owned vast plantations; they drew wealth, too, from the triangular trade involving selling cloth to Africa, transporting African slaves to the Americas, and bringing American products to Europe.

WALKING TOURS

1 OLD PORT★★

Allow 1hr30min.

The old harbour (the modern harbour has been transferred to La Palice) is located deep inside a narrow bay. You can see the forward harbour, the old harbour, the small dock used by yachts, the outside dock used by trawlers and the reservoir supplied by a canal with water from the River Sèvre.

- **Gabut District** – A picturesque residential and shopping development has been built on the site of an old bastion that was once part of the town's ring of fortifications (demolished in 1858). The façades with their wood cladding recall the fish-lofts and sheds of old-time sailors, while vivid colours and wide windows lend the place a Nordic air.
- **Tour St-Nicolas★** – This slightly leaning tower, 42m high, and dedi-

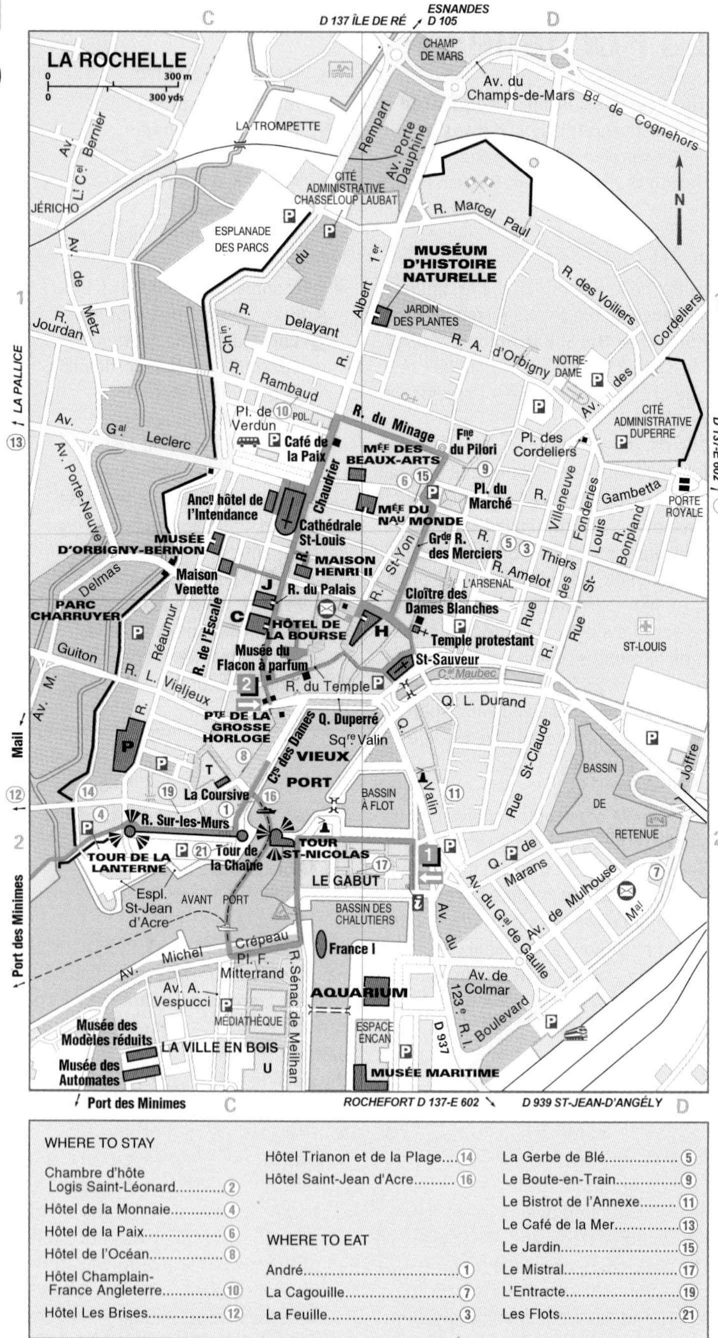

WHERE TO STAY

Chambre d'hôte Logis Saint-Léonard 2
Hôtel de la Monnaie 4
Hôtel de la Paix 6
Hôtel de l'Océan 8
Hôtel Champlain-France Angleterre 10
Hôtel Les Brises 12
Hôtel Trianon et de la Plage 14
Hôtel Saint-Jean d'Acre 16

WHERE TO EAT

André 1
La Cagouille 7
La Feuille 3
La Gerbe de Blé 5
Le Boute-en-Train 9
Le Bistrot de l'Annexe 11
Le Café de la Mer 13
Le Jardin 15
Le Mistral 17
L'Entracte 19
Les Flots 21

cated to the patron saint of sailors, is a fortress in itself.

- **Cours des Dames** – Once the haunt of sardine mongers and fishermen repairing their nets, this esplanade, which is one of the most animated parts of the old port, now features a cinema and terrace restaurants.
- **La Coursive** – Now a theatre, formerly the Ancienne Chapelle des Carmes (chapel).
- **Tour de la Chaîne** – The tower owes its name to a huge and heavy chain that used to be stretched across the harbour mouth between this tower and Tour St-Nicolas at night, closing the port to ships.
- **Rue Sur-les-Murs** – The tower is linked with Tour de la Lanterne by this narrow street which follows the old medieval rampart.
- **Tour de la Lanterne★** – The Lantern Tower is not as old as the other two (it dates from the 15C), and was built with strictly functional concerns in mind, eschewing aesthetic considerations in favour of military imperatives.
- **Parc Charruyer★** – This park, built on the mounds and ditches of the old fortifications, encircles the town.
- **Préfecture** – The préfecture (administrative headquarters of the département) is housed in the former Hôtel Poupet. The Louis XVI style of architecture is typical of local private buildings.
- **Quai Duperré** – The cafés lining this quay offer a view of the waterfront activity.

2 OLD TOWN★★

Allow 1hr30min.

The oldest district of La Rochelle, which was built to a regular plan and protected, until 1913, by Vauban's fine ramparts, exudes an atmosphere part mercantile and part military. The busy, lively shopping centre is based around the town hall, its principal axes Grande-Rue des Merciers and rue du Palais. The streets are still paved with ancient stone slabs, secret passages, arcades and darkened "porches" where passers-by can stroll sheltered from bad weather. Many of the houses are designed on a plan particular to La Rochelle. Almost all of them have two entrances, one on the main street, the other on a lane parallel to it. At ground-floor level, these buildings have one huge room, often converted into a shop, an interior courtyard with a staircase leading to a balconied gallery, and a rear courtyard surrounded by outhouses. On the upper floor is a room looking out on the street, a kitchen overlooking the courtyard, and a "dark room" with no direct light from outside. Half-timbering on the oldest houses is overhung with slates to protect the wood from the rain.

The beaux quartiers, the fashionable areas, are west of rue du Palais. The most stately are rue Réaumur and rue de l'Escale. Here, behind high walls pierced with gateways and sometimes (rue Réaumur) topped with balustrades, the old families live in their 18C mansions.

- **Porte de la Grosse-Horloge★** – This gateway to the town is famous for its oversized clock.
- **Rue du Palais★** – This street links the shopping centre with the residential district.
- **Hôtel de la Bourse★** – The 18C Stock Exchange has been the seat of the local Chamber of Commerce since its founding.
- **Palais de Justice** – The law-courts façade, with its Corinthian columns, was completed in 1789.
- **Rue de l'Escale★** – The picturesque rue de l'Escalea is paved with pebbles that were once used as ballast by ships from Canada.
- **Rue Chaudrier★** – At no. 6 stands an old half-timbered house with slate cladding.
- **Maison Henri II★** – This grand house, built in 1555 for Hugues de Pontard, the Seigneur de Champdeniers, rises at the far end of a garden.
- **Cathédrale Saint-Louis** – The cathedral, sober and severe in aspect, was built in part on the site of a church dedicated to St Bartholomew.

- **Café de la Paix** – This is the sole remaining example in La Rochelle of those flamboyant cafés of the last century, gleaming with gilt and glass, where the local burghers read their newspapers or played billiards.
- **Rue du Minage** – Irregular **arcades★** on each side of the street bring an eccentric element to the street.
- **Grande-Rue des Merciers★** – This shopping street is one of the most characteristic arteries of La Rochelle, bordered by numerous galleries and houses built in the 16C and 17C.
- **Hôtel de Ville★** – The 15–16C town hall was richly decorated, but ravaged by fire in 2013. It is still in ruins.
- **Protestant Church** – This church has a charming façade. The Musée Protestant relates the history of Protestantism, particularly around La Rochelle.
- **Cloître des Dames Blanches** – These cloisters are part of the former Récollets Convent.
- **Église St-Sauveur** – 17–18C church crowned by a lofty 15C bell tower.
- **Musée du Flacon à Parfum** – Charming collection of perfume bottles, powder boxes and labels, from 1920 to the present day.

LA VILLE-EN-BOIS

The "wooden town" lies to the west of the larger tidal basin; it is an area of low wooden houses mainly used in the past as workshops for ships' repairs or chandlers and spare-part shops. Reorganised after a fire, this district has added cultural activities (university, museums) which sit side by side with traditional handicraft centres.

Aquarium★★ – Large, modern aquarium founded by René Coutant with a vast panorama of fauna and flora

EXCURSIONS

ÎLE DE RÉ★

The island, which is also known as White Island and has been linked to the mainland by a bridge since 1988, is a popular, chic and trendy resort. Part of the salt marshes to the north has been set aside as a bird sanctuary.

MARAIS POITEVIN★★

N and NE of La Rochelle.

The vast Poitou marshlands occupy what was once a wide bay, the Golfe du Poitou. It is now a conservation area. Under clear, luminous skies, its meadows are bordered by slender poplar and willow. The boats of the marshlanders glide on a network of waterways.

LES SABLES-D'OLONNE★★

Les Sables-d'Olonne stretches between a small port and an immense beach of fine sand running for more than 3km/2mi at the foot of the Remblai (an embankment-promenade).

Les Sables-d'Olonne is an important seaside resort on the Côte de la Lumière, built on the sands of what was once an offshore bar. Port Olona is the starting point for the round-the-world yacht race held every four years, known as the "Vendée Globe" – a tough challenge for single-handed sailing boats with no ports of call allowed and no help on the way (*www.vendeeglobe.org*).

- **Le Remblai★** – This embankment was built in the 18C to protect the town from the incursions of the sea. Today the fine promenade along its top is bordered by shops, hotels, cafés and luxury apartment blocks with splendid views of the beach and the bay. At the western extremity of Le Remblai is the municipal swimming pool and one of the casinos. Behind the modern blocks, the narrow streets of the old town beckon.
- **La Corniche** – This southerly prolongation of Le Remblai leads to the new residential district of La Rudelière. After 3km/2mi the clifftop route arrives at **Le Puits d'Enfer** (Hell's Well) – a narrow and impressive cleft in the rock, where the sea foams and thrashes.
- **Parc Zoologique** – In this pleasantly laid out "green belt" environment, visitors can observe a variety of wildlife including camels, llamas, kangaroos, monkeys and rare birds.

ROYAN★★

Royan is located on the Atlantic Coast, 35km/22mi SW of Saintes.

The town of Royan, capital of the Côte de Beauté, was rebuilt after the bombardments that flattened it in 1945. Today it has once more found the popularity and prosperity that characterised it at the end of the 19C. Royan is ideally located on a headland at the entrance to the Gironde. At the western end of the seafront is the port. This comprises a dock for trawlers and the sardine boats, a marina for yachts and cruisers, and a tidal basin with the jetty from which the ferry to Pointe de Grave leaves.

Boat trips are organised in summer, especially out to Cordouan lighthouse. **Beaches** of fine sand curve enticingly at the inner end of the town's four bays indenting the coastline. The largest cove is warm and sheltered from the wind. Apart from the natural beauty of the area and a particularly mild climate, Royan also benefits from a seaweed-cure centre and numerous other attractions, hence its popularity.

- **Église Notre-Dame★** – The church (reinforced concrete coated with resin to protect it from wind erosion) was built between 1955 and 1958 to plans by architects Guillaume Gillet and Jean-Albert Hébrard.
- **Les Jardins du Monde★** – On the banks of the marais de Pousseau, in an area which has been drained since the war, this 7.5ha/18.5-acre floral garden is enshrined within a high metallic structure and three large steel sails. The vast semicircular entrance is followed by a large tropical greenhouse which shelters a beautiful **collection of orchids★**.

ZOO DE LA PALMYRE★★★

The zoo is situated in the middle of the Forêt de La Palmyre, 15km/9mi NW of Royan.

This attractive 14ha/33-acre zoo is one of the most visited in France. Every year 250t of fodder, 180t of fruit and vegetables, 70t of straw, 50t of meat,

Marais Poitevin at Abbaye de Maillezais

© Hervé Lenain/hemis.fr

20t of fish, 30t of mixed food and 10t of grain support the animals. The zoo breeds species threatened with extinction (such as elephant and cheetah); the lion cub nursery brings pleasure to young and old alike.

ADDRESSES

STAY

LA ROCHELLE

Chambre d'hôte Logis Saint-Léonard – 6 r. des Chaumes-l'Abbaye, 17139 Dompierre-sur-Mer. 05 46 35 14 65. 5 rooms. This renovated mansion, sitting in beautiful grounds, has rooms in which the décor reflects the travels made by the owners to Polynesia and Africa.

Hôtel de l'Océan – 36 cours des Dames. 05 46 41 31 97. www.hotel-ocean-larochelle.com. Closed 2 wks late Dec–early Jan. 15 rooms. Located at the Vieux Port, this hotel has renovated rooms, bright, comfortable and with air-conditioning. The rooms overlooking the quay are soundproofed, and have a view out to sea.

Hôtel de la Paix – 14 r. Gargoulleau. 05 46 41 33 44. www.hotelalarochelle.com. 19 rooms. Meals. Situated between the old market and the place de Verdun, the Hôtel de la Paix is steeped in history. The guest rooms in this former 18C shipowner's home are spacious and regularly refreshed. Cosy dining room.

Hôtel Les Brises – 1 chemin de la digue Richelieu (off r. Philippe Vincent).

05 46 43 89 37. www.hotellesbrises.eu. 46 rooms. This 1960s hotel is well sited, with ocean views.

Saint-Jean d'Acre – 4 pl. de la Chaîne . 05 46 41 73 33. www.hotel-la-rochelle.com. 60 rooms. Two 18C houses with soundproofed guest rooms, that are little by little being renovated.

Trianon et de la Plage – 6 r. Monnaie. 05 46 41 21 35. www.hoteltrianon.com. Closed 18 Dec–1 Feb. 25 rooms. Meals. This 19C hôtel particulier of standing has been in the same family since 1920. Breakfast room decorated in a winter garden theme. Cosy atmosphere in the restaurant; traditional cuisine.

Best Western Hôtel Champlain – 30 r. Rambaud. 05 46 41 23 99. www.hotelchamplain.com. 36 rooms. On a busy street near the historic district, this old 16C convent has a discreet, pleasant garden. The rooms are decorated with period pieces.

Hôtel de la Monnaie – 3 r. de la Monnaie. 05 46 50 65 65. www.hotelmonnaie.com. 31 rooms. Right behind the Tour de la Lanterne, in this splendid 17C mansion, you'll appreciate the serenity of the rooms between courtyard and garden, as well as the space and modern furnishings.

ROYAN

Belle-Vue – 122 av. de Pontaillac. 05 46 39 06 75. www.bellevue-pontaillac.com. Closed Nov–Mar. 18 rooms. This modernised 1950s villa is situated on a wide avenue. The rooms on the ground floor overlook a small garden.

EAT

LA ROCHELLE

La Feuille – 26 r. Thiers. 05 46 34 31 81. Closed Mon–Thu evening and Sun. Adjacent to the old covered market, this is an appealing restaurant. Range of gourmet salads. Reservation strongly advised.

La Gerbe de Blé – r. Thiers. 05 46 41 05 94. Closed evenings. This very friendly bistro has a limited choice on the menu, but the quality is excellent, especially the snacks.

Le Café de la Mer – Port du Plomb, Lauzières, 17137 Nieul-sur-Mer (take the D 106E1 4km/2.5mi W of Nieul-sur-Mer). 05 46 37 39 37. Closed Oct–Mar. Mouclades (mussels in a spicy cream sauce), oysters and crêpes in the summer, hearty dishes in the winter, all served in generous portions. Little restaurant, with view of Île de Ré bridge.

Le Jardin – 5 bis r. Gargoulleau. 05 46 41 06 42. Closed Sun. ♿. Near to the covered market. Gourmet breakfast, lunchtime giant mixed salads, open sandwiches and home-made desserts.

Le Mistral – 10 pl. des Coureauleurs (in the Le Gabut district). 05 46 41 24 42. Closed Sun–Thu evening (winter). The maritime-style dining room is on the first floor; a terrace overlooks the port.

La Cagouille – bd Joffre. 05 46 27 19 18. ♿ P. The kitchen is open plan, the menu has Charentais specialities. Lovely view of the woodland from the veranda.

L'Entracte – 35 r. St-Jean-du-Pérot. 05 46 52 26 69. www.lentracte.net. ♿. Contemporary bistro decorated with a sense of nostalgia. Modern dishes.

André – 7 r. St Jean. 05 46 41 28 24. www.abcsalles.com. On the old docks, facing the Tour de la Chaîne, this enormous restaurant comprises a dozen bistro-style dining rooms where customers sit elbow to elbow to feast on seafood.

Le Bistrot de l'Annexe – 45 r. St-Nicolas. 05 46 50 67 71. Closed Sun. Creative recipes using local produce.

Le Boute-en-Train – 7 r. des Bonnes-Femmes. 05 46 41 73 74. Closed Sun. Near the markets, this charming restaurant serves a variety of quiches and food fresh from the marketplace.

Les Flots – 1 r. de la Chaîne. 05 46 41 32 51. www.les-flots.com. An 18C tavern at the foot of the Tour de la Chaîne. Seafood dishes prepared with individuality and good wine list.

ROYAN

La Jabotière – 4 espl. de Pontaillac. 05 46 39 91 29. Closed Jan. White-and-blue parasols, a wooden terrace and big bay windows overlooking the Conche de Pontaillac.

Rochefort★★

Rochefort takes pride in an illustrious maritime past. There is still something exotic in the air around the Arsenal, where great expeditions were masterminded.

- **Population:** 25 140.
- **Michelin Map:** 324 E 4
- **Info:** Avenue Sadi-Carnot. ☎05 46 99 08 60. www.rochefort-ocean.com.
- **Location:** Rochefort is 38km/23.5mi SE of La Rochelle.
- **Don't Miss:** The Arsenal district; the Corderie Royale.

A BIT OF HISTORY

In 1665, Colbert chose a site 22km/13.7mi up the River Charente and asked Vauban to extend existing defences. Seven years later, the work was complete, and by 1690 Rochefort rivalled the naval bases of Toulon and Brest. The increasing draught of modern vessels led to the harbour's obsolescence and it closed in 1926.

VISIT

Rochefort's history has left many richly ornamented houses; the former rope-walk (**Corderie Royale★★**), 374m long; the great timber hall built by naval carpenters (now a covered market and conference centre); and the Sun Gateway (*Porte du Soleil*), which formed the entrance to Colbert's **Arsenal**. Admirers of the writer Pierre Loti (1850–1923), a native of Rochefort and lover of the exotic, should pause at the **Maison de Pierre Loti★** (guided tours (45min); €9, now a museum evocative of his travels.

ADDITIONAL SIGHTS

Musée de l'Ancienne Ecole de Médecine Navale★
(25 r. de l'Admiral Meyer).

Musée d'Art et d'Histoire★
(63 av. Charles de Gaulle).

L'Hermione★ – General Lafayette's frigate (restored) (Arsenal maritime, pl. Amiral Dupont. ☎05 46 82 07 07. www.hermione.com).

EXCURSIONS

AULNAY★★

The village of Aulnay sits 58km/36mi inland from Rochefort.

290 av. de l'Église. ☎05 46 33 14 44.

Originally in the province of Poitiers, Aulnay was apportioned to Saintonge when France was divided into *départements* by the Constituent Assembly on 22 December 1789. It is known for its 12C Romanesque **Église St-Pierre★★** on rue Haute de l'Église which stands among the cypresses of its ancient burial ground with its Gothic Hosanna Cross. It was built between 1140 and 1170 at a time when Eleanor of Aquitaine ruled southwestern France as queen first to Louis VII, then to Henry II of England. Its structure, notably its tribune-less triple nave, is essentially in the Romanesque style typical of the Poitou area, while its sculpture is characteristic of Saintonge.

SAINTES★★

Saintes is mid-way between Cognac and Royan, 45km/28mi from Rochefort.

62 cours National. ☎05 46 74 23 82. www.saintes-tourisme.fr.

With its plane trees, white houses and red-tiled roofs, Saintes has a curiously Mediterranean feel. This pleasant regional capital on the River Charente has a rich cultural and historical heritage. Saintes was already a regional capital in Roman times, with a bridge over the Charente aligned on today's r. Victor-Hugo. In the Middle Ages, the town was an important stop on the pilgrims' route to Santiago de Compostela. Two great religious establishments developed on its outskirts: St-Eutrope on the west bank of the river, the **Abbey for Women★** on the east bank.

To the west, on the slopes of the west bank of the river, is an amphitheatre (**arènes★**), one of the oldest (1C AD) in the Roman world.

Poitiers★★

Key events in France's history have occurred in and around this city and the medieval districts in its heart have much of interest to sightseers.

- **Population:** 87 697.
- **Michelin Map:** 322 H-I 5
- **Info:** 45 pl. Charles-de-Gaulle. 05 49 41 21 24. www.ot-poitiers.fr.
- **TGV:** Poitiers is less than 2hrs from Paris Montparnasse, and 2hrs direct from Bordeaux St Jean.
- **Location:** 227km/142mi NE of Bordeaux, 102km/64mi S of Tours. The old town centre sits on a promontory almost surrounded by the rivers Boivre and Clain.
- **Kids:** 12km/7.4mi from Poitiers, the science-themed leisure park Futuroscope is a must.

A BIT OF HISTORY

Poitiers was established in Gallo-Roman times on the promontory overlooking a bend in the River Clain, a site which commanded the "Gate of Poitou", the almost imperceptible rise in the land some 30km/18.6mi south, which divides the Paris Basin from Aquitaine. It was here in 732 that Charles Martel (688–741) won a great victory against invading Arab forces at **Moussais-la-Bataille** on the banks of the Clain, thereby saving Europe from Islamic rule.

Poitiers was under English domination twice: in the 12C and the 14C. On 19 September 1356, a famous episode in the Hundred Years' War took place at **Nouaillé-Maupertuis** on the steep banks of the River Miosson. Jean II le Bon (the Good) was fighting with the French forces, who were defeated. The French king surrendered and was taken to London, where he remained in comfortable exile. The result was the signing four years later of the Treaty of Brétigny under which the French agreed to give Poitiers to the English. In 1372, Bertrand du Guesclin retook the town, presenting it to the king's representative, Duke Jean de Berry, brother of Charles V.

In 1418, the fleeing Charles VII set up his court and parliament here, and four years later he was proclaimed king. In March 1429, in the Gothic Great Hall (**Grande Salle★**) of Poitiers' recently rebuilt Law Courts (**Palais de Justice**), Joan of Arc was subjected to a humiliating ecclesiastical investigation.

In the 16C the city played host to Rabelais, then Calvin and the writers of the Pléiade. In 1569, the place was besieged for seven weeks by a Protestant army under Coligny. In the 18C, under the rule of the centrally appointed governors known as Intendants, Poitiers became a tranquil provincial capital.

WALKING TOUR

1 CITY CENTRE

- **Église Notre-Dame-La-Grande★★** – The name of this former collegiate church stems from Santa Maria Maggiore Church in Rome. The building, with its perfect lines and the aesthetic balance of its architectural features, stands as a supreme example of Romanesque art in France.
- **Palais de Justice** – The Restoration façade of the law courts masks the Great Hall and the original keep of the ancient ducal palace, rare examples of urban civic architecture dating from the Middle Ages. In March 1429 Joan of Arc was subjected to a gruelling interrogation by an ecclesiastical commission, to emerge after three weeks with an enhanced sense of her sacred mission and official recognition that the mission was religiously inspired.
- **Hôtel de l'Échevinage** – This 15C building with its contemporary chapel was once the town hall.
- **Église St-Porchaire** – All that remains today of the original 11C

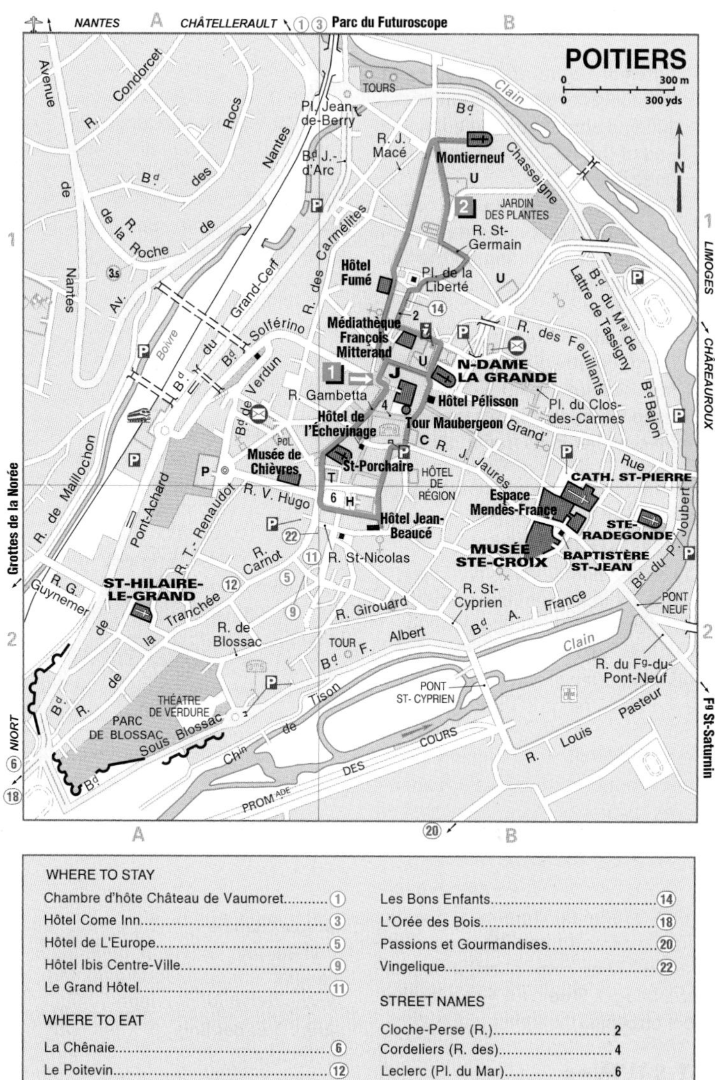

church built on this site is the belfry-porch with its four-sided pyramid roof.

- **Hôtel Jean-Beaucé** – Renaissance.
- **Tour Maubergeon** – This tower dates from the beginning of the 12C. It was converted into apartments for Jean de Berry.
- **Hôtel Pélisson** – The finely decorated façade is a good example of Renaissance architecture.

2 THREE QUARTIERS

Walking through this pleasant but steep district requires a certain amount of energy!

- **Médiathèque** – The multimedia library is one of the most attractive modern buildings in Poitiers.
- **Hôtel Fumé** – Note the Flamboyant dormer windows adorning the restored façade of no 8.

CATHEDRAL QUARTER

- **Cathédrale Saint-Pierre★** – St Peter's was begun at the end of the 12C and almost completed by the end of the 14C. It is striking for its huge size.

  Musée Ste-Croix★★ – Archaeology and painting collections in a modern building on the site of the former Holy Cross abbey (Abbaye Ste-Croix).
- **Église Ste-Radegonde★** – This former collegiate church was founded around AD 552 by Radegund, intended to be the last resting place of her nuns from Holy Cross abbey.

EXCURSIONS

FUTUROSCOPE★★

Northern outskirts of Poitiers. Open year-round, check website for details. €42 (children, 5–16, €34). 05 49 49 11 12. http://en.futuroscope.com.

This vast, science-orientated leisure park offers a range of exciting shows, games and entertainments based on the theme of the screen image. There are restaurants, shops, and "experiences" such as "fly me to the moon" and "the future is wild".

Numerous attractions include **Lac enchanté** and its **Théâtre Alphanumérique. Kinémax, Omnimax, Solido, Showscan** and **Imax 3D** show films using 3D films, hemispherical cinema, etc.). **Images-Studio★★★** shows what goes on behind the scenes.

ST-SAVIN★★

The abbey is on the west bank of the River Gartemps, 42km/26mi E of Poitiers.

The fame of St-Savin rests on its Romanesque **murals★★★**, the finest in the whole of France. They seem to have been painted around 1100 by a single team of artists over a period of only three to four years.

St-Savin lies among the pasturelands of the eastern border of the old province of Poitou, an area of sandy clay soils known as Les Brandes. Its former abbey church still draws visitors in spite of the depredations of the centuries.

ADDRESSES

STAY

€€ **Chambre d'hôte Château de Vaumoret** – r. du Breuil Mingot (10km/6.2mi NE of Poitiers). 05 49 61 32 11. www.chateaudevaumoret.com. 5 rooms. A delightful 17C château with attractive traditionally-furnished guest rooms.

€€ **Come Inn** – 13 r. Albin Haller. 05 49 88 42 42. www.hotelcomeinn.fr. Closed 24 Dec–5 Jan mid-Jul–Aug. P 44 rooms. Meals €. Functional rooms in this hotel situated not far from Aquitaine motorway. Traditional cuisine.

€€ **Hôtel de l'Europe** – 39 r. Carnot. 05 49 88 12 00. www.hotel-europe-poitiers.com. Closed 24 Dec–3 Jan. P 88 rooms. Central location, near to the pedestrianised streets.

€€€ **Hôtel Ibis Centre-ville** – 15 r. du Petit-Bonneveau. 05 49 88 30 42. www.ibis.com. P. 75 rooms. City-centre chain hotel.

€€€ **Le Grand Hôtel** – 28 r. Carnot. 05 49 60 90 60. www.grandhotelpoitiers.fr. 41 rooms. Centrally located hotel with an Art Deco theme.

EAT

€ **Les Bons Enfants** – 11 r. Cloche-Perse. 05 49 41 49 82. Closed Sun evening and Mon. This little restaurant with a green façade specialises in regional cuisine.

€€ **La Chênaie** – Les Hauts de Croutelle La Berlanderie, r. du Lejat. 05 49 57 11 52. www.la-chenaie.com. Old farmhouse serving contemporary dishes.

€€ **L'Orée des Bois** – 13 r. de Naintré, St-Benoît. 05 49 57 11 44. Closed Sat lunch, Sun evening, Mon, and 12–21 August. A restful place serving traditional local fare.

€€ **Passions et Gourmandises** – 6 r. du Square, St-Benoît (4km/2.5mi S of Poitiers via the D 88). 05 49 61 03 99. www.passionsetgourmandises.com. Modern dining room. Lovely terrace.

€€€ **Poitevin** – 76 r. Carnot. 05 49 88 35 04. Closed Sun evening (16 Apr–2 May) and Jul. Accent on traditional regional cuisine.

€€ **Vingelique** – 37 r. Carnot. 05 49 55 07 03. Gastronomic cuisine. Lovely courtyard terrace.

Le Puy du Fou★★★

This huge theme park, based around a real château and its grounds, takes visitors on an adventure through 2 000 years of Vendean history. On summer evenings its château sparkles under the lights of a famous *Son et Lumière*; by day the museum, Écomusée de la Vendée★★, evokes the past of the Vendée region, while various attractions along a trail (Grand Parcours★★) lure visitors into the 12ha/29.6 acres of grounds. Puy du Fou is Latin for "beech hill".

- **Michelin Map:** 316 K 6
- **Info:** 30 r. Georges Clemenceau, BP 25, 85 590 Les Epesses. ☎0820 09 10 10. www.puydufou.com.
- **Location:** 122km/76mi NW of Poitiers, near Cholet.
- **Timing:** There is a hotel and restaurants on the site, ideal for an unhurried visit, including the evening show.

VISIT

Grand Parc★★

☎02 51 64 11 11. Times and admission fees vary; check website for details.

Puy du Fou is a multi-attraction theme park offering ongoing entertainment throughout the day and amazing spectacles in the evening. Even if all you do is follow the paths around lakes and through lovely woodland, visiting the medieval villages and the animal parks, the day will fly by. It is likely that the original **castle**, built in the 15C and 16C, was never completed; it was in any case partly destroyed during the Wars of the Vendée. There remains a fine late Renaissance pavilion at the end of the courtyard, preceded by a peristyle with engaged Ionic columns. This now serves as an entrance. The left wing of the château is built over a long gallery.

Cinéscénie★★★

1hr 45min. Reservations necessary. ☎02 51 64 11 11.

The terrace below the rear façade of the château, together with the ornamental lake below it, makes an agreeable background for the spectacular *"Cinéscénie"* in which "Jacques Maupillier, peasant of the Vendée" directs a company of 700 actors and 50 horsemen in a dazzling show. The history of the Vendée is relived with the help of an impressive array of special effects, fountains, fireworks, laser and other lighting displays.

ADDRESSES

STAY

⊖⊜ **Hôtel de France** – pl. Dr-Pichat, 85290 Mortagne-sur-Sèvre. ☎02 51 65 03 37. Closed Sat–Sun (mid-Oct–mid-May). A 17C coaching inn has guest rooms furnished with period furniture, and two restaurants. The Taverne (classic cuisine), and the Petite Auberge (good daily specials).

⊖⊜⊜ **Chambre d'hôte Le Logis de la Devinière** – 20 r. du Puy-du-Fou, 85590 Les Épesses. ☎02 51 57 30 46. http://logis-la-deviniere.fr. ♿ 5 rooms. Meals⊖⊜⊜. Beautiful 18C house with a pleasant garden. Individually decorated rooms, in a modern or traditional style. Three family rooms. Heated pool, jacuzzi and hammam.

EAT

⊖⊜ **Restaurant L'Auberge** – Domaine du Puy du Fou, 85590 Les Épesses. ☎08 20 09 10 10. www.puydufou.com. Closed Oct–May. At the north end of the Puy du Fou grounds, this auberge serves regional dishes in a convivial setting. Costumed service and an excellent fixed-price "Gourmets" menu.

⊖⊜ **Le Relais de Poste** – Domaine du Puy du Fou. ☎08 20 09 10 10. Closed Oct–mid-Apr. Extended opening hours during Cinéscénie evenings. At the north end of the site, an attractive room opens onto a courtyard where diners can enjoy entertainment as they eat.

Languedoc Roussillon Tarn Gorges

» Region map p548-549
Montpellier p550
Nîmes p558
Gorges du Tarn p562
Carcassonne p564
Narbonne p569
Perpignan p572
Toulouse p577
Albi p584
Lourdes p588

Introduction

Languedoc-Roussillon follows the arc of the coastal plain from the mighty Rhône to the massive barrier of the Pyrénées. Adjoining the Languedoc-Roussillon on its western edge, the Midi-Pyrénées stretches from the mountains of the south to the Massif Central in the north. It is a hugely diverse area, ranging from seaside resorts to mountain villages and rural hamlets, not to mention some large towns and cities in both regions.

Geography – Along the southern edge of the Massif Central stretch the Grands Causses, and to the east, the Cévennes consist of rocky summits, deep, narrow valleys and scrubby *garrigues*. The south is dominated by the Pyrénées mountain range; to the west the Garonne flows through the Midi-Pyrénées, while, to the north, the Lot meanders through the wine region of Cahors.

History – The Languedoc-Roussillon plain was crossed by Hannibal en-route to Rome (214 BCE). By the 2C, the Romans were in control, but eventually the region was ruled by the Counts of Toulouse, until, following the Cathar heresy, French kings took control.

Languedoc nevertheless saw the rise of a Romance language – Langue d'Oc – used by wandering poets (troubadours) entertaining the nobility during the 11C to 13C. Street signs in Occitan appear in many of the region's towns. Its similarity to Catalan, the language of Andorra and an official language of Spain, facilitated a degree of cultural exchange that remains evident today.

Today – The economic diversity of Languedoc-Roussillon and the Midi-Pyrénées ranges from crafting of fine leather goods, to the high-tech aerospace industry around Toulouse. In this part of France, you're never far from vineyards, while much of the Midi-Pyrénées is given over to agriculture and tourism.

With some 15 million visitors a year, tourism is a huge economic player, with summer beach-going on Languedoc's "sunshine coast", cultural tourism, spas and ski resorts.

Highlights

1. The meander of the **Cirque de Navacelles** (p556)
2. Fortified Templar settlement of **La Couvertoirade** (p556)
3. The last Cathar stronghold: **Château de Montségur** (p566)
4. Abbey on an eagle's eyrie: **St-Martin-du-Canigou** (p576)
5. Restored Medieval walled city of **Carcassonne** (p584)

Château de Peyrepertuse © Bertrand Rieger/hemis.fr

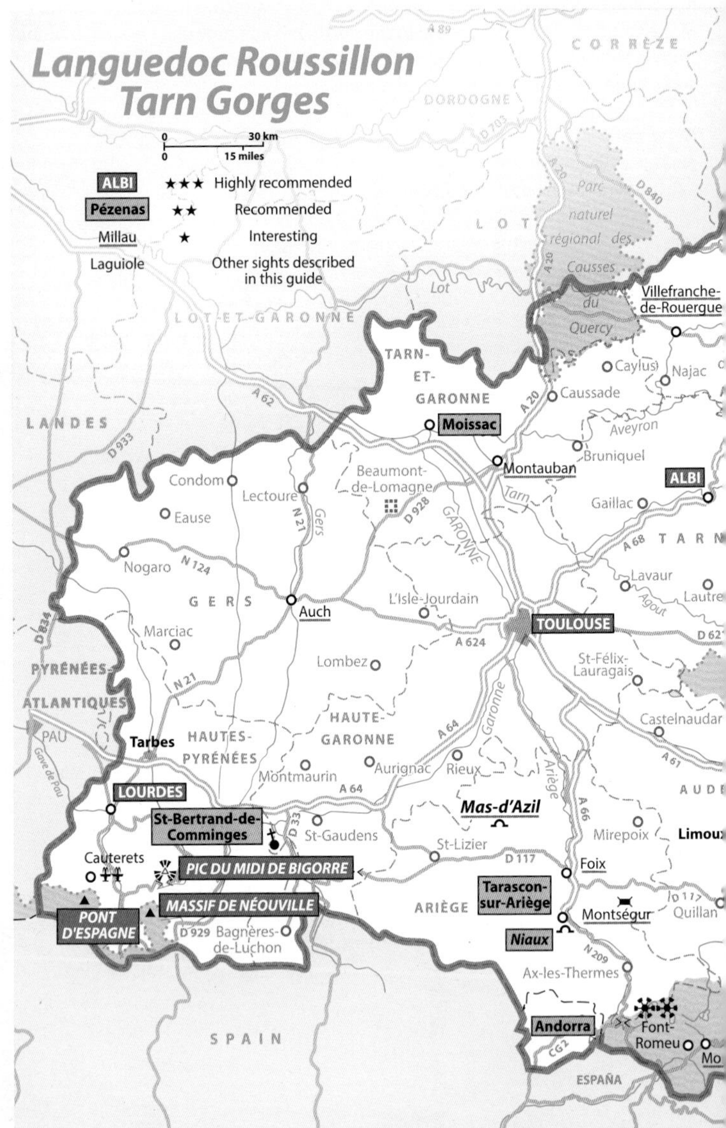
Languedoc Roussillon
Tarn Gorges
0 30 km
0 15 miles
ALBI ★★★ Highly recommended
Pézenas ★★ Recommended
Millau ★ Interesting
Laguiole Other sights described in this guide
CORRÈZE
DORDOGNE
LOT
Parc naturel régional des Causses du Quercy
Villefranche-de-Rouergue
LOT-ET-GARONNE
TARN-ET-GARONNE
Caylus
Najac
Caussade
LANDES
Moissac
Aveyron
Bruniquel
Montauban
Condom
Lectoure
Beaumont-de-Lomagne
ALBI
Eause
Gaillac
Gers
GARONNE
TARN
Nogaro
Lavaur
GERS
Auch
L'Isle-Jourdain
Lautrec
TOULOUSE
Marciac
Lombez
St-Félix-Lauragais
PYRÉNÉES-ATLANTIQUES
Castelnaudary
PAU
Tarbes
HAUTES-PYRÉNÉES
HAUTE-GARONNE
Gave de Pau
Montmaurin
Aurignac
Rieux
Ariège
AUDE
LOURDES
Mas-d'Azil
St-Bertrand-de-Comminges
St-Gaudens
Mirepoix
Limoux
St-Lizier
Cauterets
PIC DU MIDI DE BIGORRE
Foix
Tarascon-sur-Ariège
MASSIF DE NÉOUVILLE
ARIÈGE
Montségur
Quillan
PONT D'ESPAGNE
Bagnères-de-Luchon
Niaux
Ax-les-Thermes
SPAIN
Andorra
Font-Romeu
ESPAÑA

CANTAL
LOIRE
LOZÈRE
Le Malzieu
Langogne
Laguiole
Aubrac
CONQUES
Mende
Rodez
Sévérac-le-Château
GORGES DU TARN
LES CÉVENNES
CHAOS DE MONTPELLIER-LE-VIEUX
AVEN ARMAND
VIADUC DE MILLAU
Millau
MASSIF DE L'AIGOUAL
Caves de Roquefort
CIRQUE DE NAVACELLES
La Couvertoirade
LES DEMOISELLES
St-Sernin-sur-Rance
Sylvanès
St-Guilhem-le-Désert
Lodève
Lacaune
CLAMOUSE
MONTPELLIER
Castres
Lamalou-les-Bains
Olargues
HÉRAULT
LA GRANDE-MOTTE
Aigues-Mortes
Mazamet
St-Pons-de-Thomières
Pézenas
Béziers
Sète
Minerve
CARCASSONNE
LE CAP-D'AGDE
Narbonne
Fontfroide
Gruissan
Les Corbières Cathares
PEYREPERTUSE
Salses
Port-Barcarès
Musée de Tautavel
Perpignan
PYRÉNÉES-ORALES
Canet-Plage
St-Martin-du-Canigou
Serrabone
Côte Vermeille
LE CANIGOU
Argelès-Plage
Banyuls-s-Mer
VALENCE
Parc naturel régional des monts d'Ardèche
ARDÈCHE
RHÔNE
Pont-St-Esprit
Alès
GARD
Bagnols-s-Cèze
Uzès
Pont du Gard
AVIGNON
NIMES
Sommières
Beaucaire
St-Gilles
Parc naturel régional de Camargue
GOLFE DU LION
MEDITERRANEAN SEA
N

Montpellier★★★

As capital of Languedoc-Roussillon, Montpellier is an administrative centre and university city with beautiful historical districts, impressive architecture and superb gardens.

- **Population:** 257 351.
- **Michelin Map:** 339 I-7
- **Info:** 30 allée Jean-de-Lattre-de-Tassigny (espl. Comédie), 34000 Montpellier. ☏04 67 60 60 60. www.ot-montpellier.fr.
- **TGV:** Montpellier St-Roch is 3hrs 30 mins–5hrs 30 mins from Paris Gare de Lyon.
- **Flights:** Montpellier Méditerranée International airport (www.montpellier.aeroport.fr; ☏04 67 20 85 00), is 8km/5mi from the centre of the city.
- **Location:** 170km/106mi west of Marseille.
- **Don't Miss:** Place de la Comédie; a walk in the Old Town; the view from the promenade du Peyrou; the Quartier Antigone; Musée Fabre.
- **Timing:** At least a full day to explore the centre.

A BIT OF HISTORY

Origins – Montpellier had its beginnings with two villages: Montpellieret and Montpellier. In 1204 Montpellier became a Spanish enclave and remained so until 1349 when John III of Majorca sold it to the king of France for 120 000 *écus*. After that, the town developed quickly by trading with the Levant. In the 16C, the Reformation arrived in Montpellier, and Protestants and Catholics in turn became masters of the town. In 1622 royal armies of Louis XIII laid siege to Montpellier's fortifications and Richelieu built a citadel to keep watch over the rebel city.

Modern Montpellier – After the Revolution the town became the simple *préfecture* of the Hérault *département*. When the French returned from North Africa after 1962, it regained its dynamism. The city's dynamism is reflected in the **Corum** conference and concert centre, the **Antigone** district that is linked to old Montpellier by the Triangle and Polygone shopping centres, and the new **Odysseum** leisure district.

WALKING TOUR

HISTORIC MONTPELLIER★★

Montpellier map II, p555. Allow 3hrs.

Between place de la Comédie and the Peyrou Arc de Triomphe are Montpellier's historic districts, last vestiges of the original medieval town. Superb 17C and 18C private mansions, hôtels, line the streets, with their remarkable staircases hidden in inner courtyards.

- **Place de la Comédie** – This lively square links the city's old districts with the new. Place de la Comédie continues north to the Esplanade promenade with plane trees, outdoor cafés and musical bandstands. The **Corum** complex includes the Berlioz opera house. To the east lie the Triangle and the Polygone complex.
- **Hôtel des Trésoriers de France** – This private mansion housing the Musée Languedocien was the Hôtel Jacques-Cœur when the king's treasurer lived here in the 15C. In the 17C it became the Hôtel des Trésoriers de France, occupied by senior magistrates administering the royal estates in Languedoc. Finally it was named "Lunaret" in memory of Henri de Lunaret who bequeathed it to the Société Archéologique de Montpellier. It contains the **Musée Languedocien★**
- **Hôtel de Varennes★** – This mansion houses two museums. The **Musée du Vieux Montpellier** contains local artefacts from the Revolution. The

TRANSPORTATION

TRAMWAY

Transports de l'Agglomération de Montpellier. ℘04 67 07 61 00. www.tam-way.com. A new Montpellier tram allows passengers to go just about anywhere within the city and beyond in minutes. Its four lines (the last two fitted out by Christian Lacroix) enable you to travel around the city in a few minutes (€1.40 single ticket, valid for 1 hr; €10 valid for 10 trips). An end to traffic jams and the hunt for a free parking place! The same it true, of course, of the bus network.

BY BICYCLE

Contact TAM Vélo. ℘04 67 22 87 87. www.montpellier-agglo.com/tam. Cycle hire – Velomagg (€0.50 per hour).

MONTPELLIER CITY CARD

Three options available. 24hrs: from €13.50 (3–12s, €6.75), 48hrs: from €19.80 (3–12s €9.90) and 72hrs: from €25.20 (3–12s €12.60). On sale all year round at the tourist information centre on ℘04 67 60 60 60. This 'Découverte' (discovery) option includes free entry to many sites, discounts for events and leisure facilities as well as a TAM travel card so that you can get about.

Musée **Fougau** preserves 19C arts and traditions.

- **Rue de l'Aiguillerie** – This was the town's street for arts and crafts in the Middle Ages. Some shops still retain their 14–15C vaulted roofs.
- **Hôtel de Cabrières-Sabatier d'Espeyrana** – This grand home (built in 1873) houses a department of the Musée Fabre.
- **Musée Fabre★★** – Founded in 1825 with the generosity of the Montpellier painter François-Xavier Fabre (1766–1837). Greek and European ceramic ware, and paintings from the Spanish, Italian, Dutch and Flemish schools.
- **Hôtel Baudon de Mauny** – elegant Louis XVI façade.
- **Rue du Cannau** – This street is lined with classical town houses.
- **Hôtel de Solas** – 17C townhouse.
- **Hôtel d'Uston** – Early 18C mansion.
- **Place de la Canourgue★** – In the 17C this square was the centre of Montpellier, and numerous hôtels remain around the garden with its Unicorn fountain.
- **Ancien Courrier district** – This is the oldest part of Montpellier; its narrow pedestrian streets are lined with luxury boutiques.
- **Hôtel des Trésoriers de la Bourse★** – An impressive town house by architect Jean Giral.
- **Place St-Ravy** – Retains the Gothic windows of the Palace of the Kings of Majorca.
- **Hôtel St-Côme** – This town house was built in the 18C by Jean-Antoine Giral thanks to the donation of François Gigot de Lapeyronie, surgeon to Louis XV, who bequeathed a part of his fortune to the surgeons of Montpellier for them to build an anatomical theatre similar to the one in Paris.

PROMENADE DU PEYROU★★

The promenade's upper terrace affords a sweeping **view★**. The key feature of the Promenade du Peyrou is the ensemble of the *château d'eau* and St-Clément aqueduct. On Saturday, Promenade des Arceaux becomes a flea market. The late-17C **Arc de Triomphe** depicts the victories of Louis XIV and major events from his reign: the Canal du Midi, revocation of the Edict of Nantes, the capture of Namur in 1692 and the United Provinces of the Netherlands kneeling before Louis XIV.

FACULTÉ DISTRICT

Montpellier map II, p555. Allow 30mins.

- **Faculté de Médecine** – The Montpellier Faculty of Medicine occupies a former Benedictine monastery founded in the 14C by order of Pope

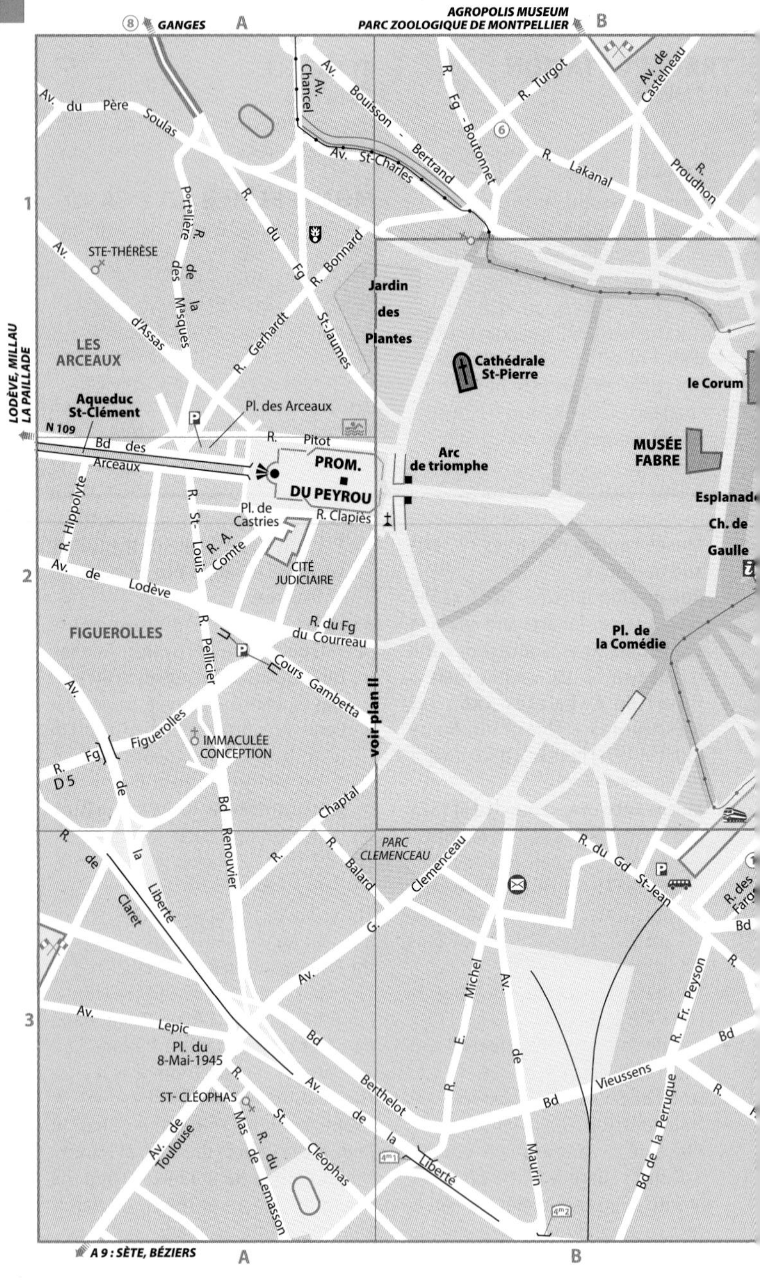

Urban V. It houses two museums. **Musée Atgera** contains drawings bequeathed by Xavier Atger (1758–1833) and works by artists of the French, Italian and Flemish schools; while the **Musée d'Anatomie** contains anatomical collections.

- **Cathédrale St-Pierre** – Towering like a fortress, the cathedral seems more massive with the adjacent

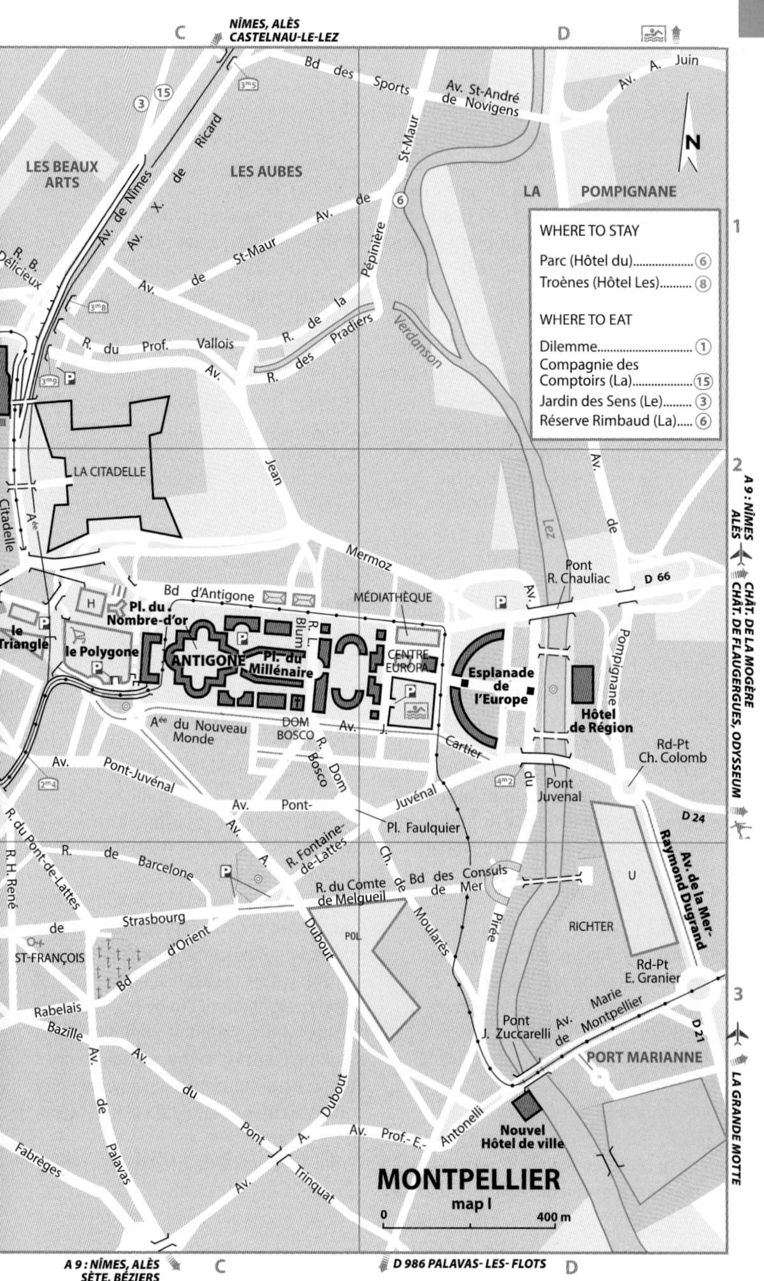

façade of the Faculty of Medicine. It is the only church in Montpellier not completely destroyed during the Wars of Religion. Although built in the Gothic style, the cathedral is reminiscent of the single-nave Romanesque churches along the coast.

- **Jardin des Plantes** – The oldest botanical gardens in France, created in 1593 for the Montpellier Faculty of Botany for the study of medicinal plants, contain various Mediterranean species such as the nettle tree, holm-oak and mock privet (phillyrea). A large ginkgo biloba planted in 1795 is a graft from the first ginkgo plant introduced to France by Antoine Gouan.

ANTIGONE DISTRICT★

Starting from place de la Comédie (east side), walk to the Antigone district via the Polygone shopping centre.
Catalan architect **Ricardo Bofill** designed the bold new Antigone district. This vast Neoclassical housing project combines prefab technology with harmonious design. Behind a profusion of entablatures, pediments, pilasters and columns are low-income housing, public facilities and local shops, arranged around squares and patios. **Place du Nombre-d'Or** continues with the cypress-lined **place du Millénaire**, place de Thessalie then place du Péloponnèse. The vista stretches from the "Échelles de la Ville" past the crescent-shaped buildings of **esplanade de l'Europe**, to the **Hôtel de Région**, converted into a dock for Port Juvénal.

EXCURSIONS

SÈTE

36km/22.5mi SW of Montpellier.
The main strolling and shopping streets are found on the east side of the "island"; beaches to the west.
60, Grand' rue Mario Roustan 34200 Sète. 04 67 74 71 71. www.tourisme-sete.com.

Sète was built on the slopes and at the foot of Mont St-Clair, a limestone outcrop 175m high, on the edge of the Thau lagoon. Once an island, it is linked to the mainland by two narrow sand spits. The new town, east and northeast of Mont St-Clair, runs right up to the sea itself and is divided up by several canals. Sète is the scene of the famous *joutes nautiques*, water-based jousting tournaments, particularly well attended on the day of St-Louis in August.

Vieux port★ – The old harbour, with its picturesque fishing boats and yachts, is the most interesting part of Sète port. **Quai de la Marine** is lined with fish and seafood restaurants, with terraces overlooking the Sète canal. It is the departure point for various **boat trips**.
A little farther down, fishermen and bystanders are summoned by the **"criée électronique"** (electronic auction) when the boats come in around 3.30pm. Sailing is practised at high level near the St-Louis pier. **Promenade de la Corniche** – This busy road, leading to the Plage de la Corniche, situated 2km/1mi from the centre of town, cuts around the foot of Mont St-Clair with its slopes covered by villas. **Plage de la Corniche** – This 12km/7.5mi-long sandy beach stretches across a conservation area.

MASSIF DE L'AIGOUAL★★★

Rising high at the heart of the Cévennes National Park, the Aigoual summit, 37km/23mi S of Florac, is reached on the steep D 118.

The immense forces involved in the formation of the Alps in the Tertiary Era acted on the ancient granitic foundation of this landscape, uplifting it to form a massif which reaches its highest point at **Mont Aigoual★★★**.
Subsequent erosion, all the more vigorous because of high precipitation and the low elevation of the surrounding country, has created a landscape of long straight ridges cut by deep ravines. These well-watered highlands make a striking contrast to the arid landscapes of the neighbouring *causses* where any rainfall is immediately absorbed by the porous limestone.
From 1875 onwards the state undertook a massive programme of forestation; the forest today covers some 140sq km/54sq mi. Tree growth is particularly vigorous on the more exposed western slopes. In the last 20 years conifers have been added to the beeches planted in the 19C. There are sweet chestnuts too, the traditional tree of the Cévennes, growing at altitudes as high as 600–900m.

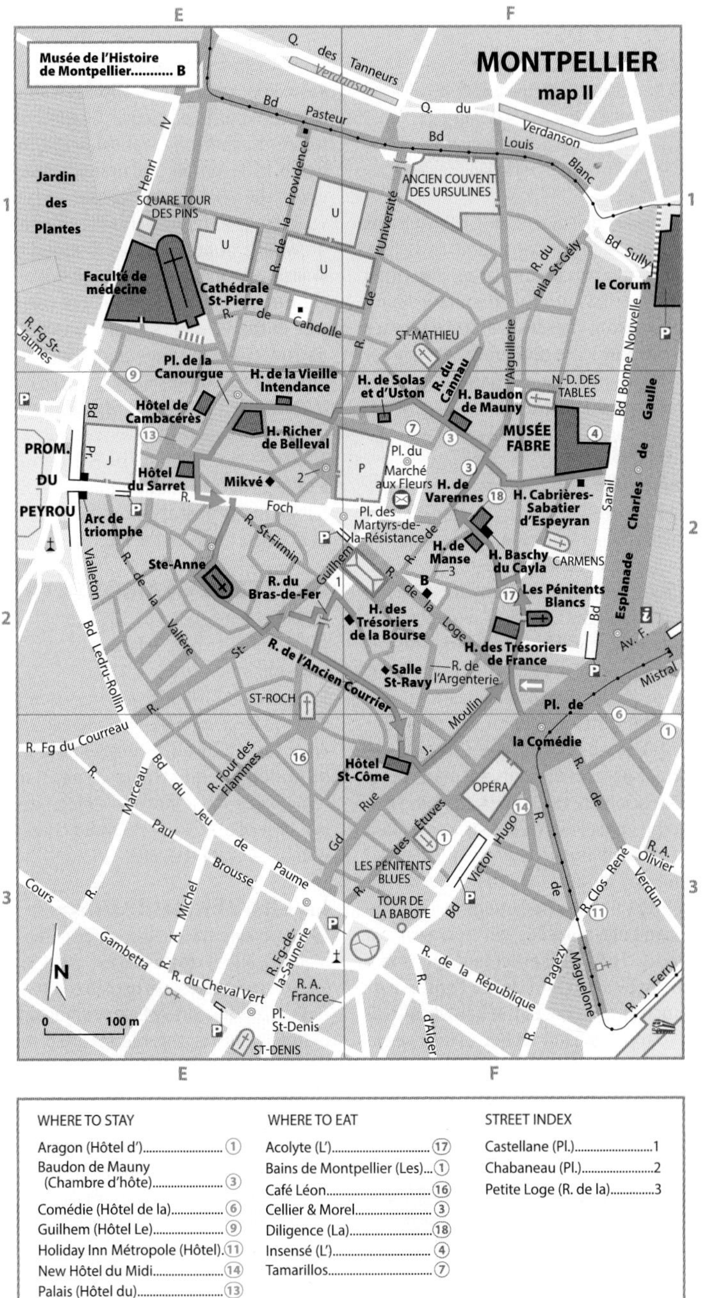

A **panorama★★★** extends over the Causses and the Cévennes from the viewing table at the top of the meteorological station. The clearest days are in winter, when it is sometimes possible to see both Mont Blanc (*see MONT BLANC, p406*) and the Maladeta Massif in the Pyrénées.

GROTTE DES DEMOISELLES★★★

The caves are in the upper Hérault Valley near the town of Ganges. ℘04 67 73 70 02. www.demoiselles.com. €10.50. The temperature in the caves is 14°C.

The cave, discovered in 1770, contains an enthralling underground landscape. Deposition of calcium carbonate within the cave has produced extraordinary forms, from stalactites and stalagmites and translucent draperies, to the great columns and huge organ-case of this underground cathedral.

CIRQUE DE NAVACELLES★★★

The site is reached by turning off the road between **Lodève**★ and Ganges, in the Hérault département.

This spectacular 300m-deep basin, separating the Causses – high plateaux – de Larzac and Blandas marks the former course of the River Vis before it cut through the base of the meander.

On the outer sweep of the meander great screes have been formed; the upper parts of the cliffs are made up of exceptionally thick beds, thinning out at the lower levels where traces remain of old buildings and terraces on the marl and clay deposits. On the valley floor a pretty single-arched bridge leads to the village of Navacelles, which once had a priory. The little settlement clings to a rocky outcrop in order to conserve as much as possible of the belt of cultivable land in the former bed of the river. In contrast to the harsh conditions prevailing on the arid causses, the valley floor has a mild microclimate, which allows figs to be grown.

ST-GUILHEM-LE-DÉSERT★★

The village is in the Hérault gorge, and can be approached via Gignac and Aniane if coming from the E or S, via St-Félix and Montpeyroux if coming from the N or W. ℘04 67 57 70 17. www.saint-guilhem-le-desert.com.

The eponymous Guilhem was born in the mid-8C and renowned for his talent in handling weapons as well as his intelligence and piety. He was brought up with the sons of the Carolingian king, Pepin the Short, and his friendship with one in particular, Charles, the future Charlemagne, was to last until his death. In its remote and dramatic **site**★ where the Val de l'Infernet runs into the valley of the Hérault, this 9C **village**★ grew up around an abbey founded by William of Aquitaine. This timeless place centres on a huge and ancient plane tree in the village centre, from which narrow streets radiate and disappear into inviting corners.

L'Abbaye et le Musée du Cloître★ – Open May–Sep daily except Sun am 10.30am–noon, 1–6pm. This is a Romanesque structure of striking simplicity, famed for its possession of a fragment of the True Cross (*in the south transept*).

GROTTE DE CLAMOUSE★★★

3km/1.8mi S. ℘04 67 57 71 05. www.clamouse.com. Take a sweater; the temperature inside is 17°C.

The caves, a UNESCO World Heritage Site, run beneath the Larzac plateau and were carved by an extensive network of underground streams. There are remarkable stalactites and stalagmites, but best of all are the splendid crystallisations in varied shapes.

LA COUVERTOIRADE★★

The village stands to one side of the highway, which crosses Larzac. ℘05 65 58 55 59. www.lacouvertoirade.com.

High up on the lonely Larzac limestone plateau (*causse*), this old fortified settlement once belonged to the Knights Templar. It has many robustly built houses, typical of the region, with cisterns, outside stairways leading to the main floor, and a vaulted sheep-pen at ground level. Most date from the 17C.

The towers and the sentry-walk of the **ramparts** are particularly interesting. Go through the north gateway and, taking great care, climb the steps at the foot of the Renaissance house, following the watch-path round to the left to the round tower for a view over the town and its main street, rue Droite.

Also see the 14C **fortified church**.

ADDRESSES

STAY

Hotel les Troènes – 17 av. Emile-Bertin-Sans. 04 67 04 07 76. www.hotel-les-troenes.fr. Closed Dec–Feb. 14 rooms. Renovated 1960s hotel, linked to the town centre by the tramway.

Hotel du Parc – 8 r. Achille-Bège. 04 67 41 16 49. www.hotelduparc-montpellier.com. P. Closed Dec–Feb. 19 rooms. A former stately residence, close to the historic centre.

Hôtel de la Comédie – 1 bis r.Baudin. 04 67 58 43 64. www.hotel-montpellier-comedie.com. 10 rooms. Located just off of La Place de la Comédie, this renovated hotel with 19C façade offers modern bedrooms.

Hôtel du Palais – 3 r. du Palais-des-Guilhem. 04 67 60 47 38. www.hotel dupalais-montpellier.fr. 26 rooms. This family hotel near the Peyrou gardens and the Place de la Canourgue has small stylish and well-kept rooms.

Hôtel Le Guilhem – 18 r. Jean-Jacques Rousseau. 04 67 52 90 90. www.leguilhem.com. 36 rooms. Two 16C and 17C houses. Top-floor rooms offer a lovely view of the nearby cathedral.

Hôtel d'Aragon – 10 r. Baudin. 04 67 10 70 00. www.hotel-aragon.fr. 12 rooms. A charming little hotel, completely renovated, with well-kept and pleasantly decorated rooms. Breakfast is served on a sunny veranda.

New Hotel du Midi – 22 bd Victor-Hugo. 04 67 92 69 61. www.new-hotel.com/en. 47 rooms. A stone's throw from the Place de la Comédie, a fine, renovated, hundred-year-old building.

Chambres d'hôte Baudon de Mauny – 1 r. de la Carbonnerie. 04 67 02 21 77. www.baudondemauny.com. 8 rooms. In the heart of old Montpellier, this hotel marries old and new in a stylish and luxurious setting.

EAT

Le Café Léon – 12 r. du Plan-d'Agde. 04 67 60 58 83. Closed Sun. Traditional cuisine in a rustic setting.

Le Dilemme – 12 r. Fargés. 04 67 69 02 13. A well-known place in Montpellier, hidden away behind the station. Unbeatable value for money.

L'Acolyte – 1 r. des Trésoriers-de-France. 04 67 66 03 43. Mon–Sat. 6.30pm–1am. A wine bar with excellent bar snacks and a restaurant (on the first floor) to satisfy bigger appetites.

L'Insensé – Musée Fabre, 39 bd. Bonne-Nouvelle. 04 67 58 97 78. Modern decor and cuisine from the Pourcel brothers, worthy of the famous *Le Jardin des Sens*.

La Compagnie des Comptoirs – 51 av. François-Delmas. 04 99 58 39 29. www.lacompagniedescomptoirs.com. The Pourcel brothers offer a gourmet trip around the Med and Far East.

La Réserve Rimbaud – 820 av. de Saint-Maur. 04 67 72 52 53. Open Tue–Sun, closed Sat lunch, Sun eve, 2 weeks in mid-Aug and first 10 days of Jan. A place of great charm, with an extraordinary terrace overlooking the Lez.

Les Bains de Montpellier – 6 r. Richelieu. 04 67 60 70 87. Les-bains-de-montpellier.com. Reservation recommended. Dine in the shade of the courtyard palm trees or in one of the drawing rooms in these wonderfully restored old 'Parisian baths'.

Cellier Morel – La Maison de la Lozère, 27, r. de l'Aiguillerie. 04 67 66 46 36. www.celliermorel.com. Closed Sun; Mon, Wed, Sat lunch; first 3 weeks Aug. Cuisine inspired by dishes of the Lozère, served in an opulent 13C vaulted room or in a charming 18C courtyard garden.

Tamarillos – 2 pl. du Marché-aux-Fleurs. 04 67 60 06 00. www.tamarillos.biz. Open Tue–Sat, closed Mon and Wed lunch, 1st week Nov and last week Feb. Reservation recommended. Flowers, fruit, colours and desserts to die for, all concocted by a very original chef.

La Diligence – 1 pl. Pétrarque. 04 67 66 12 21. www.la-diligence.com. The vaulted rooms of the fine Hôtel Baudan de Varennes host this restaurant. Whiskey cellar.

Le Jardin des Sens – 11 av. St-Lazare. 04 99 58 38 38. The Pourcel brothers' amphitheatre-like dining room opens onto a Mediterranean garden. Reservation essential.

Nîmes★★★

Nîmes lies between the limestone hills of the Garrigue to the north and the alluvial plain of the Costière du Gard to the south. Its elegant and bustling boulevards are shaded by lotus-trees. The quality of its Roman remains is outstanding.

- **Population:** 142 205.
- **Michelin Map:** 339 L 5
- **Info:** 6 r. Auguste. ℘04 66 58 38 00. www.ot-nimes.fr.
- **TGV:** Nîmes is about 3hrs direct from Paris Gare de Lyon.
- **Flights:** Nîmes-Alès-Camargue-Cévennes Airport (www.aeroport-nimes.fr. ℘04 66 70 49 49) is just 15min from the city centre.
- **Location:** 32km/19.8mi NW of Arles. The main shopping street is Rue de la Madeleine.
- **Parking:** Enter the city along the canal de la Fontaine and boulevard Victor-Hugo, go around the amphitheatre to get to the underground car park beneath the Esplanade.
- **Timing:** Avoid the heat of August. Visitors who object to bull-fighting or crowds are advised to avoid May and September.

A BIT OF HISTORY

Emperor Augustus heaped privileges on Nîmes and allowed the building of fortifications. The town, situated on the Domitian Way, then proceeded to erect splendid buildings: the Maison Carrée along the south side of the forum, an amphitheatre able to hold 24 000 people, a circus, baths fed by an imposing aqueduct, the Pont du Gard. In the 2C the town won favour with Emperors Hadrian and Antoninus Pius (whose wife's family came from Nîmes); it continued to flourish and build and reached the peak of its glory.

In 1873, a Bavarian emigrant to the United States called Lévy-Strauss called his new trousers, made from the blue serge manufactured locally, "Denims", meaning literally "from Nîmes".

WALKING TOURS

1 ROMAN AND MEDIEVAL NÎMES

Nîmes map.

This walk explores the principal monuments and buildings of the Roman city, and the area known as 'Écusson', a maze of narrow alleyways in the medieval quarter. Enjoy the shaded boulevards flanked by beautiful mansions, and, if time allows, stop at a street café for a coffee or refreshing Perrier menthe.

- **Esplanade Charles-de-Gaulle** – This vast square, bordered on one side by the columns of the Palais de Justice and street cafés, opens on the other side onto the avenue Feuchères with its fine aristocratic façades.
- **Arènes★★★** – The magnificent amphitheatre is a splendid illustration of the perfection in design achieved by Roman engineers. This amazing structure was built in the reign of Augustus, 80 years before the corresponding structure at Arles. The scale and concept is hugely impressive demonstrating perfect symmetry. In Roman times the monument could hold 24 000 spectators over 34 rows of terraces divided into four separate areas, and the design allowed an unrestricted view of the whole arena. The stone used comes from quarries at Roquemaillère and Baruthel, near Nîmes. There are certainly bigger Roman amphitheatres, but this is the best preserved of them all.
- **Maison Carrée★★★** – Inspired by the temples of Apollo and Mars Ultor in Rome, the Maison Carrée

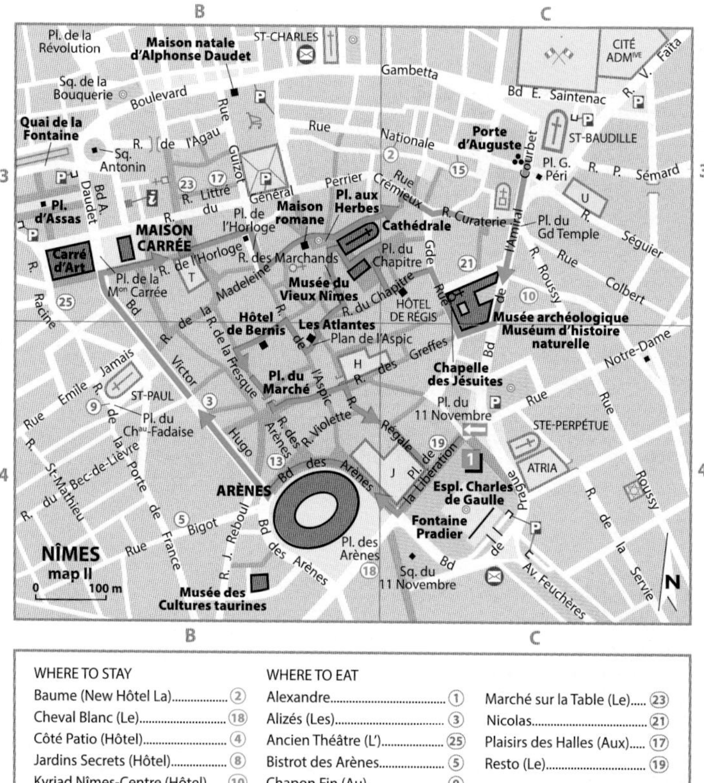

WHERE TO STAY

- Baume (New Hôtel La) 2
- Cheval Blanc (Le) 18
- Côté Patio (Hôtel) 4
- Jardins Secrets (Hôtel) 8
- Kyriad Nîmes-Centre (Hôtel) 10
- Mazade (Chambre d'hôte La) 14
- Orangerie (Hôtel L') 16

WHERE TO EAT

- Alexandre 1
- Alizés (Les) 3
- Ancien Théâtre (L') 25
- Bistrot des Arènes 5
- Chapon Fin (Au) 9
- Lisita (Le) 13
- Magister (Le) 15
- Marché sur la Table (Le) 23
- Nicolas 21
- Plaisirs des Halles (Aux) 17
- Resto (Le) 19

charms visitors with its harmonious proportions. Set in the centre of an elegant paved square separated from the Carré d'Art by the boulevard Victor-Hugo, it is the only completely reserved ancient Roman temple. It is by far the best preserved and purest of all Roman temples, and was built during the time of Augustus (1C BC). The Maison Carrée owes its preservation to its constant use from the 11C; it has served as a consular house, stables, apartments and even as a church. After the French Revolution, it became the headquarters for the first prefecture of the Gard region.

- **Carré d'Art★** – Established in 1993 in a beautiful building designed by Norman Foster, the collection covers contemporary art from 1960 to the present day.
- **Rue de la Madeleine** – The principal business street of the city.
- **Porte d'Auguste** – The Via Domitia arrived here in Nemausus.
- **Musée archéologique★** – Located in the former Jesuit college, the museum exhibits items predating colonisation.
- **Muséum d'histoire naturelle** – Museum of ethnology and natural history.
- **Musée du Vieux Nîmes** – This museum presents a collection of artefacts that evoke the traditional life of Nîmes and its inhabitants.

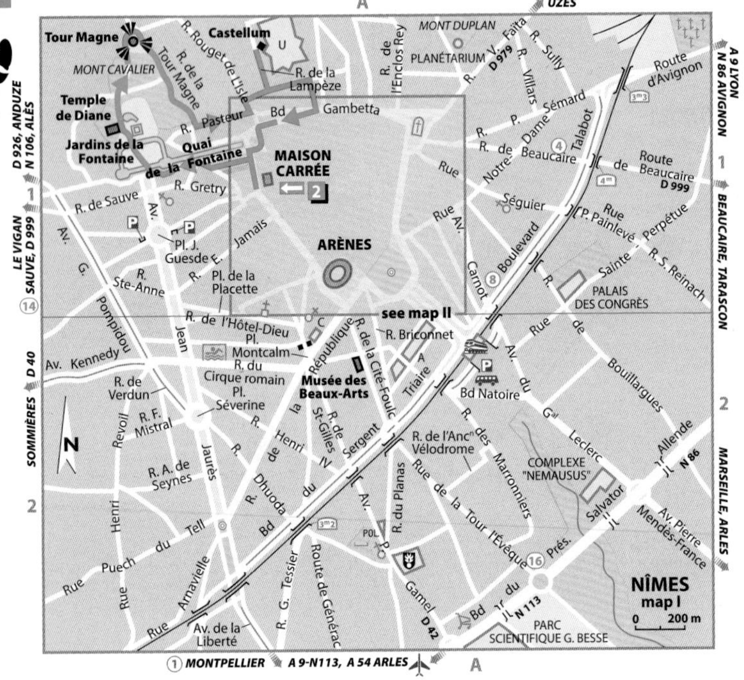

2 RETURN TO THE SOURCE

Nîmes map.

- **Jardins de la Fontaine★★** – In Roman times this was the site of a spring, a theatre, a temple and baths. Today, these shaded gardens exemplify the subtle use of water in the landscapes of Languedoc. The **Tour Magne★**, the Great Tower, is the only remnant of the ancient Augustan fortifications. From a **viewing platform★★** there is a panorama.
- **Castellum** – This circular basin was the culmination of the aqueduct. Rediscovered in 1844, it is one of the few to have survived.

ADDITIONAL SIGHT

- **Musée des Beaux-Arts★** – Refurbished in 1986 around a Roman mosaic discovered in 1883, the museum houses works from the 15C to 19C from the Italian, Dutch and French schools.

EXCURSION
AIGUES-MORTES★★

46.6km/29mi SW of Arles.
Place Saint Louis. 04 66 53 73 00. www.ot-aiguesmortes.fr.

Few places evoke the spirit of the Middle Ages as vividly as Aigues-Mortes, sheltering behind its ramparts in a landscape of marshland, lakes and saltpans. The tourist train offers an overview of the main attractions. Shops, restaurants and hotels lie within the city walls, and a traditional market can be found on Avenue Frédéric-Mistral.

In 1240, Louis IX (St Louis), established Nîmes as a French Mediterranean trade port at a time when Provence was still part of the Holy Roman Empire, Sète did not exist, and Narbonne was silting up. The port launched the failed 7th and 8th Crusades. The silting up of the port and the incorporation of Marseille into the French kingdom in 1481 pushed Aigues-Mortes into decline and the coup de grâce was the founding (17C) and subsequent development of Sète.

ADDRESSES

STAY

Be sure to book well ahead if you intend to stay during the ferias.

Hôtel Côté Patio – 31 r. de Beaucaire. 04 66 67 60 17. www.hotel-cote-patio.com. 17 rooms. Close to old Nîmes and the Arènes.

Le Cheval Blanc – 1 pl. des Arènes. 04 66 76 05 22. 32 rooms. WiFi. Pablo Picasso, Coco Chanel and Jean Cocteau were clients of this legendary hotel, which has found a new lease of life after fifteen years of closure.

Kyriad Nîmes Centre – 10 r. Roussy. 04 66 76 16 20. www.hotel-kyriad-nimes.com. 28 rooms. Close to Écusson, an agreeable hotel in the centre.

L'Orangerie – 755 r. Tour-de-l'Évêque. 04 66 84 50 57. www.orangerie.fr. 37 rooms. Provençal-style rooms; regional cooking.

Hôtel Marquis de la Baume – 21 r. Nationale. 04 66 76 28 42. 34 rooms. Former mansion, delightful hotel.

Jardins Secrets – 3 r. Gaston-Maruejols. 04 66 84 82 64. www.jardins secrets.net. 12 rooms. A rare and secret moment in the heart of the city.

NEARBY

Chambre d'hôte La Mazade – In the village, 30730 St-Mamert-du-Gard. 04 66 81 17 56. www.lamazade.fr. 3 rooms. Colourful and fun, a true family home; al fresco dinner on the terrace.

EAT

Nicolas – 1 r. du Poise. 04 66 67 50 47. www.restaurant-nicolas-nimes.com. Closed Mon, Sat lunchtime and Sun evening. The Martin family have been running this restaurant, with its decor inspired by the course camarguaise, for more than half a century. These fans of Camarguaise bullfighting traditions serve simple but tasty regional recipes from brandade to gardiane de taureau. An institution appreciated by true Nîmois.

Les Alizés – 26 bd Victor-Hugo. 04 66 29 10 10. There's a buzzing atmosphere at this friendly restaurant serving various local specialities and with a pretty tree-shaded street terrace.

Le Chapon Fin – 3 pl. du Château-Fadaise. 04 66 67 34 73. www.chaponfin-restaurant-nimes.com. Closed Sun. Pleasant, air-conditioned restaurant behind the church; local produce.

Bistrot des Arènes – 11 r. Bigot. 04 66 21 40 18. Closed evenings on Mon-Wed. Efficient bistro, close to the amphitheatre.

L'Ancien Théâtre – 4 r. Racine. 04 66 21 30 75 . Closed Sat lunchtime, Sun and 1st 2 weeks in Aug. Arriving straight from Le Grau-du-Roi, fish and seafood are prepared with creativity and sophistication in this restaurant, which lies a little away from the boulevard, behind the Carré d'art.

Le Resto – 6 r. St-Thomas. 04 66 21 80 12. www.leresto-nimes.com. Open Mon–Thu lunchtime and Fri. nice little restaurant working with high-quality produce and situated a stone's throw from the Esplanade.

Aux Plaisirs des Halles – 4 r. Littré. 04 66 36 01 02. www.aux plaisirsdeshalles.com. Closed Sun, Mon. Fine dining room; generous servings, and regional wine list.

Le Marché sur la Table – 10 r. Littré. 04 66 67 22 50. He is a cook from the Cévennes; she is Basque and a sommelier. Together, they have opened this place on the rue Littré, with a lovely dining room opening onto a patio. Here they serve dishes that change depending on availability of produce, and wines by the glass.

Le Magister – 5 r. Nationale. 04 66 76 11 00. Paintings brighten weathered-wooden walls; regional cuisine.

Le Lisita – 2 bd des Arènes. 04 66 67 29 15. www.lelisita.com. Closed Sun, Mon. Opposite the amphitheatre; a beautiful dining room and garden, and arguably the best place in the city centre.

NEARBY

Alexandre – 2 r. Xavier-Tronc (rte de l'aéroport), 30128 Garons (9km/5.5mi SW on the road to Arles, D42). 04 66 70 08 99. www.michelkayser.com. Closed Sun eve and Mon, Tue (Sep–Jun) Sun–Mon (Jul–Aug). Two-starred restaurant under the watchful eye of chef/patron Michel Kayser makes this a favourite place with gourmets and gourmands alike.

Gorges du Tarn★★★

The deep gorges cut by the Tarn through the harsh limestone plateaux to the south of the Massif Central make up one of France's most spectacular natural landscapes. The source of the Tarn lies high (1 575m) in the granitic uplands of Mount Lozère; tumbling torrent-like down the slopes of the Cévennes, the river then enters the most spectacular section of its course at Florac.

- **Michelin Map:** 330 H-J 8-9 and 338 L-N 5
- **Info:** Le Bourg, Le Rozier. ✆05 65 62 60 89. www.officedetourisme-gorgesdutarn.com.
- **Location:** The River Tarn rises on Mont Lozère and runs through the Cévennes before reaching the Causses country, where it has carved its plunging gorge between the limestone plateaux. The road runs at the top of the cliffs. There are small villages, notably Ste-Énimie, along the gorge, but no communities of any great size.
- **Don't Miss:** Pause at the Point Sublime to get the full picture of the Tarn gorge.
- **Timing:** The road along the gorge is narrow, difficult, and in season can be congested. Allow several hours to cover the full distance.

THE AREA

The Tarn River – 381km/237mi long – flows through gorges and canyons, joined by side valleys such as the Jonte and the Dourbie, in Millau.

Escape from the valley bottom is by means of roads that twist and turn up the precipitous slopes to join the roughly planed surface of the Causse Méjean; its porous limestone is deeply fissured and hollowed out to form the caves for which the region is famous.

Most visitors come here when the summer sun is beating down, but the scene is best appreciated in spring and autumn, when the vegetation and local wildlife are flourishing. The spectacle of winter should not be missed, when every feature has its frosty outline.

The hostile landscape here has been humanised by centuries of determined human effort. So, there are villages on the flatter patches of cultivable land that occur on the valley bottom and sides (Ste-Énimie, La Malène, Les Vignes) and the castles of lords and robber-barons on the more easily defended sites overlooking the river. On the plateau above are isolated farms based on the better soils of the little depressions known as dolinas; the drystone walls once made by piling up the boulders collected laboriously from the fields are now supplemented by electric fences, and the thoughtless forest clearance of the 19C is being made good by the planting of Austrian pines. No trace of the underground realm of chasms (**Aven Armand★★★**) and caverns is visible at the surface; those who venture into this unsuspected world are rewarded by the extraordinary spectacle presented by the dissolution of the limestone, and by the strange forms of stalactites and stalagmites.

EXCURSIONS

- **Les Détroits (The Straits)★★** – 36km/22.3mi NE of Gorges du Tarn. This is the narrowest part of the valley, hemmed in by plunging cliffs of coloured limestone and slightly to the east of La Malène.
- **Cirque des Baumes★★★** – 2.4km/1.5mi NW of Les Détroits. Below Les Détroits, the gorge widens, forming a magnificent natural amphitheatre.

- **Le Point Sublime★★★** – Just W of Cirque des Baumes. This splendid viewpoint above the Cirque des Baumes overlooks both the Tarn Canyon and the Tarn Causse.
- **Grotte de l'Aven Armand★★★** – 43km/27mi NE of Millau, Aven Armrand is in the plateau country S of the Gorges du Tarn. The temperature inside is 10°C. One of the wonders of the underground world, this immense cavern is reached down a 200m tunnel in the bleak Causse Méjean.

  Deep within the arid limestone of the Causse Méjean, subterranean waters have created a vast cavern, 60m wide and 120m long, its floor littered with rock fallen from its roof. Four hundred stalagmites, some up to 30m high and christened the "Virgin Forest", make an extraordinary spectacle.
- **Millau★** – 116km/72.5mi N of Montpellier. Millau huddles between two high limestone plateaux, the Causse du Larzac and the Causse Noir, at the meeting-point of the Tarn and the Dourbie.

  The site of a ford in ancient times, it acquired a bridge in the Middle Ages and became a trading centre of some importance. Today it is a lively provincial town, with a southern air, close to a remarkable modern viaduct soaring over the Tarn valley.

  The **Musée de Millau★** is housed in the 18C Hôtel de Pégayrolles. It has a **palaeontology** section and a remarkable collection of Gallo-Roman **earthenware★**.
- **Millau Viaduct/Millau Bridge★★★** – This amazing cable-stayed construction, completed in 2004 and designed by the British architect Norman Foster, spans the 2km/1.2mi-wide Tarn Gorge near Millau. The world's tallest road bridge, it forms part of the A 71-A 75 autoroute from Paris to Béziers.
- **Chaos de Montpellier-le-Vieux★★★** – 18km/11.2mi NE. This extraordinary "ruined city" in fact made entirely of natural rocks, has a bewildering variety of rock formations (the Sphinx, the Elephant, the Gates of Mycaenae).
- **Caves de Roquefort★** – 25km/ 15.5mi SW. The name of the market town of Roquefort, located between Millau and St-Affrique, is synonymous with one of the most famous of French cheeses: the delicious blue-veined Roquefort. In accordance with AOC Roquefort regulations, all production of the cheese must take place underground, in natural caves in which the temperature and humidity are constant. Roquefort cheese is produced exclusively from full-fat, untreated ewe's milk.

ADDRESSES

STAY

Hotel de la Capelle – 7 pl. de la Capelle. ℘05 65 60 14 72. www.hotel-millau-capelle.com. 45 rooms. This hotel has two distinct advantages: reasonable prices and an air of tranquillity.

SHOPPING

Cave des Vignerons des gorges du Tarn – ave Causses 12520 Aguessac. 5km/ 3mi from Millau. ℘05 65 59 84 11. This co-op produces wines with the Vin délémité de qualité supérieure (VDQS) label côtes de Millau (red and rose).

SPORTS AND RECREATION

Walking – The main waymarked footpaths are the GR 62 ("Causse Noir-Lévezou-Rouergue") and several PR, "Causse Noir" (13 itineraries around Millau for rambling and mountain biking), "Millau et les causses majeurs", "St-Affrique-Vallée du Tarn-Pays de Roquefort" (footpaths around St-Affrique, Camarès and Roquefort).

Carcassonne★★★

A visit to fortified Carcassonne, a UNESCO World Heritage Site, is a return to the Middle Ages. On Bastille Day (14 July) a dramatic fireworks display makes the stunning citadel seem to go up in flames. The romantic old town contrasts sharply with the commercial Ville Basse (lower town), a *bastide* town, where Carcassonne shows off its role as the centre of the Aude *département*'s wine-growing industry.

- **Population:** 47 419.
- **Michelin Map:** 344 E-F 3
- **Info:** 28 r. de Verdun. ✆04 68 10 24 30. www.carcassonne-tourisme.com.
- **Location:** The city lies 93km/58mi SE of Toulouse and 59km/37mi W of Narbonne.
- **Parking:** Visitors are not allowed to drive in the Cité.
- **Don't Miss:** The view of the Cité from a distance, especially from *autoroute* A 1, is spectacular.
- **Timing:** Half a day to visit the fortified Cité, and the same for the modern town. Ask at the tourist office about the three guided tours available with the City Pass.

A BIT OF HISTORY

The site of the Cité was first fortified by the Gauls; their entrenched camp served Roman, Visigoth and Frank in turn. In the 9C, Carcassonne became the capital of a county, then of a viscounty subject to the County of Toulouse. In common with the rest of the South of France it enjoyed a long period of prosperity which was brought to an end by the Crusade against the "Albigensians" – Cathars.

On 1 August 1209 the army of crusaders under Simon de Montfort arrived at the walls of Carcassonne and besieged the city. Within a fortnight, the attackers had seized the Viscount, Raymond-Roger Trencavel, and the town capitulated.

WALKING TOUR

LA CITÉ★★★

Carcassonne map, p565. 2hr tour of the ramparts available aboard a tourist train or horse-drawn carriage.

The "Cité" of Carcassonne on the Aude's east bank is the largest fortress in Europe. It consists of a fortified nucleus, the Château Comtal, and a double curtain wall: the outer ramparts, with 14 towers, separated from the inner ramparts (24 towers) by the outer bailey, or lists *(lices)*. A resident population of 139, and school and post office, save Carcassonne from becoming a ghost town.

- **Porte Narbonnaise** – On either side of the gateway to the original fortified town are two massive Narbonne towers, and, between them, a 13C statue of the Virgin Mary. Inside, the 13C rooms restored by Viollet-le-Duc house **temporary exhibitions** of modern art.
- **Rue Cros-Mayrevieille** – This street leads directly to the castle, although you might prefer to get there by wandering along the narrow winding streets of the medieval town, with its many crafts and souvenir shops.
- **Château Comtal** – The castle was originally the palace of the viscounts, built in the 12C by Bernard Aton Trencavel. It became a citadel after Carcassonne was made part of the royal estate in 1226. Since the reign of St Louis IX, it has been defended by a large semicircular barbican and formidable moat.
- **Porte d'Aude** – A fortified path, the Montée d'Aude, weaves from the church of St-Gimer up to this heavily defended gateway. The west and

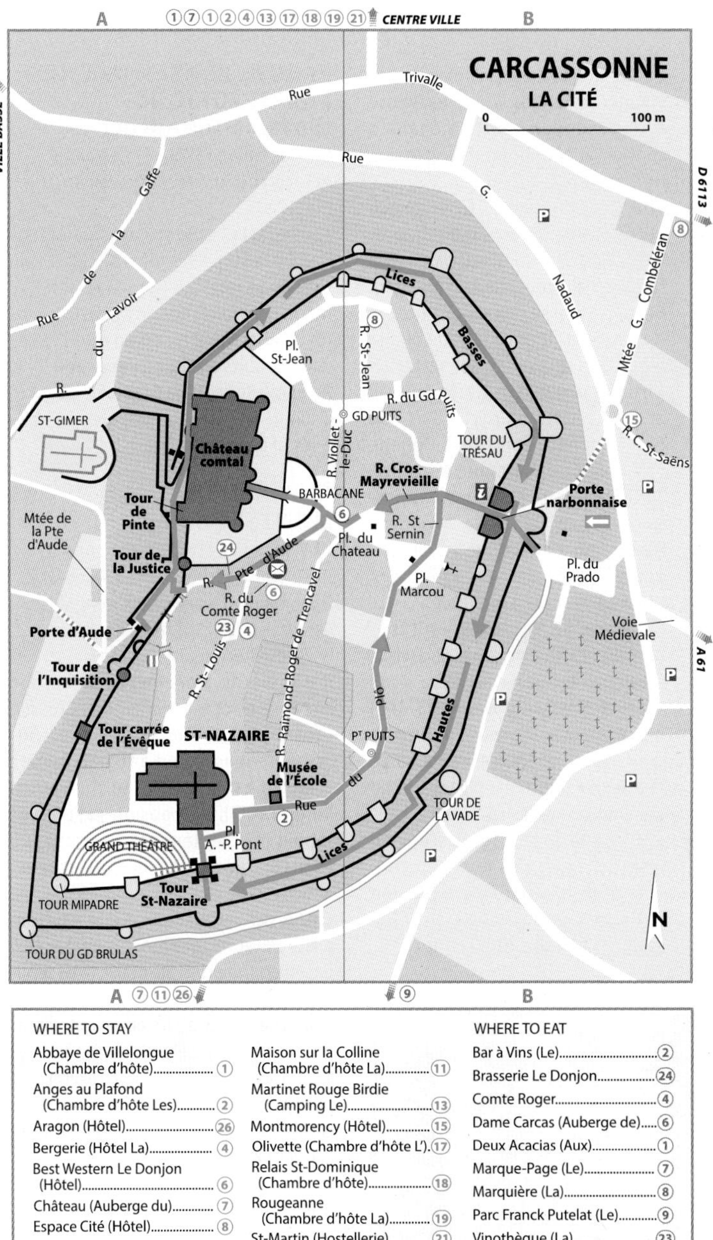

WHERE TO STAY

Abbaye de Villelongue (Chambre d'hôte) 1
Anges au Plafond (Chambre d'hôte Les) 2
Aragon (Hôtel) 26
Bergerie (Hôtel La) 4
Best Western Le Donjon (Hôtel) 6
Château (Auberge du) 7
Espace Cité (Hôtel) 8
Maison sur la Colline (Chambre d'hôte La) 11
Martinet Rouge Birdie (Camping Le) 13
Montmorency (Hôtel) 15
Olivette (Chambre d'hôte L') 17
Relais St-Dominique (Chambre d'hôte) 18
Rougeanne (Chambre d'hôte La) 19
St-Martin (Hostellerie) 21

WHERE TO EAT

Bar à Vins (Le) 2
Brasserie Le Donjon 24
Comte Roger 4
Dame Carcas (Auberge de) 6
Deux Acacias (Aux) 1
Marque-Page (Le) 7
Marquière (La) 8
Parc Franck Putelat (Le) 9
Vinothèque (La) 23

north sections of the outer bailey are called the "lices basses". The **Tour de l'Inquisition** was the seat of the Inquisitor's court, and its central pillar with chains and cell bear witness to the tortures inflicted upon heretics. The Bishop's **Tour carrée de l'Évêque** was much more comfortably appointed.

- The itinerary takes you past the **Tour de la Justice**. The Trencavels, protectors of the Cathars, sought refuge

here with the count of Toulouse during the Albigensian Crusade. This circular tower has windows whose tilting wooden shutters enabled those inside to see (and drop things on) attackers.

- **The "lices hautes"** – The wide gap between the inner and outer ramparts, edged with moats, was used for weapons practice and jousting. Beyond Porte Narbonnaise, note the three-storey Tour de la Vade on the outer curtain wall to the left. This fortified tower kept watch over all of the eastern ramparts. Carry on to the Tour du Grand Brulas, on the corner opposite the Tour Mipadre.
- **Tour St-Nazaire** – This tower's postern was only accessible by ladders. A well and an oven are still in evidence on the first floor. At the top of the tower is a viewing table.
- **Basilique St-Nazaire★** – All that remains of the original church is the Romanesque nave. The basilica's **stained-glass windows★★** (13–14C) are considered the most impressive in the south of France. Remarkable **statues★★** adorn the pillars around the chancel walls.
- **Musée de l'école** – Occupying an old school, this museum consists of documents, materials and furniture evoking education at the beginning of the 20th century.

Château de Montségur

© Bertrand Rieger/hemis.fr

EXCURSIONS

PARC PYRÉNÉEN DE L'ART PRÉHISTORIQUE (Tarascon-sur-Ariège) ★★

104km/65mi SW of Carcassonne. At Lacombe, on the road to Banat via the N 20.

The park, devoted to cave paintings – there are some 12 decorated caves in the Ariège area – comprises a distinctive modern building housing a display area, the Grand Atelier, and an open space with exhibits featuring water and rock. An audio-tour of the Grand Atelier gives a comprehensive account of the discoveries of cave paintings.

CHÂTEAU DE MONTSÉGUR★

77km/48mi SW of Carcassonne, in the foothills of the eastern Pyrénées. Opening times vary; check website for details. €5. 05 61 01 10 27. www.montsegur.org.

It was on this fearsome peak that the last episode of the Albigensian Crusade took place, when its Cathar defenders were massacred and Languedoc eclipsed by the power of the French kingdom. This imposing castle was rebuilt in a pentagonal structure due to the shape of the limestone rock on which it sits.

Catharism – the name is derived from a Greek word meaning "pure" – was based on the principle of the total separation of Good and Evil, of the spiritual from the material. Its adherents comprised ordinary believers and the *"Perfecti"*, the latter living lives of exemplary purity in the light of God. Their austerity contrasted sharply with the venality and laxity of the Catholic clergy.

In the early 13C the local **Cathars** built a castle here to replace an old, since-demolished, fortress. Forty years later, following the ravages of the Albigensian Crusade against the Cathars, the stronghold was occupied by 400 adherents to the faith, from whose ranks was drawn the fierce band which marched on Avignonet to put to the sword the members of the Inquisition meeting there.

This sealed the fate of Montségur; in the absence of Louis IX, who was dealing with disturbances in Saintonge, Blanche of Castille ordered the Crusaders to put the castle to siege. On 2 March 1244, the resistance of the defenders was overcome, but 200 of the faithful refused to retract their beliefs, even after being granted a fortnight in which to reconsider. On 16 March, they were brought down from the mountain to be burnt on a huge pyre.

Musée Historique et Archéologique

Same opening times as the château.
As well as medieval period furniture and objects found in the vicinity of the castle, this museum also has two skeletons and a cast of the cross of Morency.

ADDRESSES

STAY

€€ Hôtel Espace Cité – 132 r. Trivalle. ℘04 68 25 24 24. www.hotelespacecite.fr. Apr. 48 rooms. WiFi. Modern hotel at the foot of the citadel, with bright and functional rooms.

€€ Chambre d'hôte La Maison sur la Colline – Lieu-dit Ste-Croix. ℘04 68 47 57 94. www.lamaisonsurlacolline.com. Closed end Dec–mid Feb. P. 4 rooms. This restored farm has a view of the Cité from its garden. Rooms are spacious and colourful.

€€€ Hôtel Montmorency – 2 r. Camille-St-Saëns. ℘04 68 11 96 70. www.lemontmorency.com. P. 30 rooms. WiFi. Close to La Cité. Very smart rooms, well furnished, but simple.

€€€ Hôtel Aragon – 15 montée Combéléran. ℘04 68 47 16 31. www.hotelaragon.fr. P. 30 rooms. An attractive hotel close to the Porte Narbonnaise. Comfortable rooms and warm welcome.

€€€€ Hôtel Best Western Le Donjon – 2 r. du Comte-Roger. ℘04 68 11 23 00. www.hotel-donjon.fr. 61 rooms. WiFi. This hotel combining old stonework and renovated décor occupies part of a 15C orphanage at the heart of the Cité.

NEARBY

€ Camping Le Martinet Rouge Birdie – 11390 Brousses-et-Villaret. ℘04 68 26 51 98. www.camping-martinet.com. Open Mar–Nov. 63 places. In a fabulous setting in the Montagne Noire.

€€ Chambre d'hôte Le Relais St-Dominique – 11270 Prouille (3km/2mi northeast of Fanjeaux on D 802, D 623, D 4 and D 119). ℘04 68 24 68 17. www.lerelaisdesaintdominique.com. 4 rooms. This rural house, a short way from the medieval village, has a rustic interior which is at once simple and charming. The rooms are comfortable and well-maintained. Breakfast is served on the patio. Beautiful swimming pool and shop selling regional products.

€€ Chambre d'hôte L'Olivette – R. Pierre-Duhem, 11160 Cabrespine. ℘04 68 26 19 25. http://olivette-cabrespine.com. P. 3 rooms. A family home charming in its simplicity, situated not far from the Gouffre de Cabrespine. Three comfortable and well maintained rooms furnished with antiques. The table d'hôte dinner (available by reservation only) is prepared with great enthusiasm and enlivened by local aromatic herbs.

€€ Chambre d'hôte Les Anges au Plafond – R. de la Mairie, 11170 Montolieu. ℘04 68 24 97 19. www.lesangesauplafond.com. 3 rooms. Let your gaze wander upwards and you will understand the name of the establishment, "The Angels on the Ceiling". Above the cafe are three light, bright rooms, each with its own colour scheme down to the painted floorboards. Tea rooms and restaurant open at lunchtime; dinner is available for guests by reservation.

€€ Chambre d'hôte de l'abbaye de Villelongue – À l'abbaye, 11170 St-Martin-le-Vieil. ℘04 68 76 92 58 (after 7.30pm). www.abbaye-de-villelongue.com. 4 rooms. Accommodation at the heart of the abbey, with modern comforts replacing Cistercian austerity. The bedrooms are charming and all open onto the flowery cloister.

€€€ Auberge du Château – Château de Cavanac, 11570 Cavanac. ℘04 68 79 61 04. www.chateau-de-cavanac.fr. P.

29 rooms. Beautiful rooms with view over vineyard; fine restaurant.

Hostellerie St-Martin – 11000 Montredon (4km/2.5mi northeast). 04 68 47 44 41. Closed 12 Nov-19 Mar. 15 rooms. WiFi. This modern building in regional style stands in peaceful grounds. It is surrounded by countryside and has views of the Cité. Pleasant bedrooms.

Hôtel La Bergerie – Allée Pech-Marie, 11600 Aragon. 04 68 26 10 65. www.labergeriearagon.com. Closed three weeks in Feb and two in Oct. 6 rooms. In a lovely village; rooms have views over vineyard. Cuisine and wines of the region.

Chambre d'hôte La Rougeanne – 8 allée du Parc. 11170 Moussoulens, 04 68 24 46 30 or 06 61 94 69 99. www.larougeanne.com. 5 rooms. Enjoy the peace and quiet of this old wine estate house. The rooms (equipped with internet), are lovingly decorated in pastel tones and look onto the tree-filled grounds. Beyond is a view of the Pyrénées. Two rooms on the ground floor, "Verveine " and "Tomette", have mezzanines, making them ideal family accommodation.

EAT

Le Bar à Vins – 6 r. du Plo. 04 68 47 38 38. www.lebaravins.fr. Closed two weeks in Jan or Feb. In the heart of the medieval Cité, this wine bar's shady garden has a view of the St-Nazaire basilica. Tapas and fast food.

La Vinothèque (Comptoir des Vins et Terroirs) – 3 r. du Comte-Roger. 04 68 26 44 76. As its name suggests, this is above all a wine bar where you can taste excellent local vintages, accompanied by toasts, salads and foie gras. Bottles of wine and other regional produce can also be bought here.

Auberge de Dame Carcas – 3 pl. du Château. 04 68 71 23 23. www.damecarcas.com. Closed 24–26 Dec. On the restaurant's logo, Dame Carcas, wife of king Sarrasin, carries a small pig. According to legend, she persuaded Charlemagne to lift his siege of Carcassonne by throwing a fattened suckling pig over the battlements to prove that the inhabitants still had plenty of food. The auberge is renowned for its original dishes.

La Marquière – 13 r. St-Jean. 04 68 71 52 00. Closed Wed and Thu and 10 Jan–10 Feb. Roughcast building near northern ramparts. Serves traditional cuisine.

Brasserie Le Donjon – 4 r. Porte-d'Aude. 04 68 25 95 72. www.brasserie-donjon.fr. Closed Sun evening and Nov–Mar. A master-restaurateur offers the choice of a brasserie menu or a more complete meal combining, among other things, foie gras and an excellent cassoulet.

Au Comte Roger – 14 r. St-Louis. 04 68 11 93 40. www.comteroger.com. Closed 8 Feb–3 Mar, Sun and Mon (except in season) and holidays. A stroll around the Cité can be happily punctuated with a meal at this restaurant on a lively little street that has a modern décor and a shady terrace. The menu is inspired by market availability, and makes excellent use of local produce.

Le Parc Franck Putelat – 80 ch. des Anglais (south of the Cité). 04 68 71 80 80. www.restaurantleparcfranckputelat.fr. Open Tue–Sat. A restaurant of high standing, set in exceptional surroundings, with exquisite décor. Here you can enjoy cuisine that unites tradition with unexpected innovations such as bouillabaisse de foie gras. No gourmet misses this place without good reason. Expect an extended lunch, and don't plan anything for the rest of the day!

NEARBY

Aux Deux Acacias – D 6113, 11150 Villepinte (14km northeast of Fanjeaux by D 4 then D 6113). 04 68 94 24 67. www.les-deux-acacias.fr. 10 rooms. WiFi. The simplicity of the décor in this 15C house is quickly forgotten once you see what is on your plate. You have to realise that the star here is the cassoulet, expertly prepared with fresh ingredients. Warm and convivial. Rooms are air-conditioned.

Le Marque-Page – Pl. de la Liberté, 11170 Montolieu. 04 68 24 76 72. Closed Sun evening, Mon, Wed evening. A pleasant menu (including homemade cassoulet) to enjoy in the shade of the plane trees.

Narbonne★★

Narbonne, which in its time has been the ancient capital of Gallia Narbonensis, the residence of the Visigoth monarchy and an archiepiscopal seat, is now a lively Mediterranean city playing an important role as a wine-producing centre and a road and rail junction.

- **Population:** 51 039.
- **Michelin Map:** 344 I-J 3
- **Info:** 31 r. Jean Jaurès. 04 68 65 15 60. www.mairie-narbonne.fr.
- **Location:** 61km/38mi E of Carcassonne and 96km/60mi SW of Montpelier.
- **Parking:** The centre is pedestrianised. Car parks are on quai Victor-Hugo and beneath cours Mirabeau.
- **Don't Miss:** The Palais des Archevêques.
- **Timing:** Explore early in the morning in summer, before it becomes too hot.

A BIT OF HISTORY

The history of this ancient Mediterranean city is a long one, reaching back many centuries BCE. After the defeat of Hannibal, the Roman Empire chose Narbonne to be the commercial centre of the Celtic province, with an artificial port created by diverting an arm of the River Aude. Finally it was made the capital of Gallia Narbonensis (today's Languedoc and Provence regions) and flourished right up to the end of the Empire and the arrival of the Visigoths, who made it the capital of their kingdom. Trading activity continued (Muslim raiders found the city still worth looting in 793), and medieval shipping made use of the extensive shallow lagoons lining the coast behind the rampart of sand bars. However, in the 14C, the city's large and long-established Jewish community was expelled; the famous port silted up, and the town's prosperity came to an abrupt end. The construction of the Canal du Midi in the 17C, the coming of the railway in the 19C, and the development of tourism on the Languedoc coast in the 20C halted the process of decline.

WALKING TOUR

PALAIS DES ARCHEVÊQUES★

Narbonne map, p571. Allow 2hrs.

The Archbishops' Palace overlooks the lively place de l'Hôtel-de-Ville, in the heart of the city, where a section of the Roman Via Domitia was discovered. It has three square towers: framing the Passage de l'Ancre, the Tour de la Madeleine (the oldest) and Tour St-Martial; farther to the left the Donjon Gilles-Aycelin. Between the last two, Viollet-le-Duc built the present Hôtel de Ville (town hall) in a neo-Gothic style. The Archbishops' Palace is an example of religious, military and civil architecture bearing the imprint of centuries, from the 12C to the 19C Hôtel de Ville.

- **Donjon Gilles-Aycelin★** – This fortified tower stands on the remains of the Gallo-Roman rampart.
- **Palais Neuf** (New Palace) – The New Palace complex surrounds the Cour d'Honneur and comprises the façade over the courtyard of the town hall, the Gilles-Aycelin keep, the St-Martial tower, the synods building and the north and south wings.

  Musée Archéologique★★ – One of the finest collections of **Roman paintings★★** in France.

  Musée d'Art★ – Occupies the old episcopal apartments where Louis XIII stayed during the 1642 siege of Perpignan.

  Salle des Consuls – The room is supported on part of the old Roman fortified city wall.
- **Palais Vieux** (Old Palace) – The two buildings flank the Madeleine tower.

- **Passage de l'Ancre** – This almost fortified street with its impressive walls separates the old and new palaces and leads from place de l'Hôtel-de-Ville to the cloisters.
- **Salle du Pilier** – This 14C room houses the Palais shop.
- **Cathédrale St-Just-et-St-Pasteur★★** – The first stone was laid on 3 April 1272 and by 1332, the radiating chancel had been completed in the same style as the great cathedrals of northern France. The chancel houses numerous works of art. The treasury includes illuminated manuscripts among other items.

WALKING TOUR

OLD NARBONNE

Narbonne map, p571.

- **Place du Forum** – Remnants of a 1C temple on the site of the Antique forum and Capitol.
- **Église St-Sébastien** – This church was built, according to legend, on the site of the saint's birth.
- **La Poudrière** – Situated behind the Jardin des Vicomtes, this 18C powder magazine houses temporary exhibitions.
- **Banks of the Robine** – The Robine canal links together the Sallèles-d'Aude junction canal to Port-la-Nouvelle.
- **Pont des Marchands★** – This picturesque bridge, a pedestrianised street lined with colourful shops overlooking the canal, follows the old Roman road (Via Domitia).

EXCURSIONS

ABBAYE DE FONTFROIDE★★

15km/9.3mi SW.

This former Cistercian abbey nestles in a quiet, restful corner of the countryside. The fine flame-coloured shades of yellow ochre and pink in the Corbières sandstone, which was used to build the abbey enhance the serenity of the sight, particularly at sunset.

RÉSERVE AFRICAINE DE SIGEAN★

18km/11m S of Narbonne and 54km/34m N of Perpignan. After Sigean follow signs. Please observe the safety instructions displayed at the entrance. ♿Open daily, from 9am–4.30pm/6pm depending on season. €31 (children 4–14, €23). 04 68 48 20 20. www.reserveafricainesigean.fr.

This **safari park** owes much of its unique character to the wild landscape of coastal Languedoc, with its *garrigues* dotted with lagoons, and to the fact that for each species large areas have been set aside, which resemble their native environment.

The park can be visited by car or on foot. The car route goes through four areas, reserved for free-ranging animals: African bush, Tibetan bear park, lion park and African savannah. Walking round the safari park, visitors will come across more fauna of various continents.

ADDRESSES

STAY

Hôtel de France – 6 r. Rossini. 04 68 32 09 75. www.hotelnarbonne.com. Closed Jan. 16 rooms. WiFi. Late-19C hotel on a quiet street downtown.

Chambre d'hôte Nuitées Vigneronnes de Beaupré – Rte d'Armissan. 04 68 65 85 57. www.domaine-de-beaupre.fr. 4 rooms. WiFi. Small B&B on a wine estate close to the centre of Narbonne.

Hotel la Résidence – 6 r. du 1er-Mai. 04 68 32 19 41. www.hotelresidence.fr. Closed 20 Jan–15 Feb. 26 rooms. WiFi. A fine hotel in a renovated 19C building.

NEARBY

Château des Fontaines – 2 av. de la Distillerie, 11200 Canet (14km/8.7mi W via the D 6113 in the direction of Lézignan-Corbières, then the D 11 from Villedaigne). 04 68 49 72 48. www.chateau-des-fontaines.com. Open Jun–Sep. 7 rooms. A prestigious 19C house where luxury and serenity reigns.

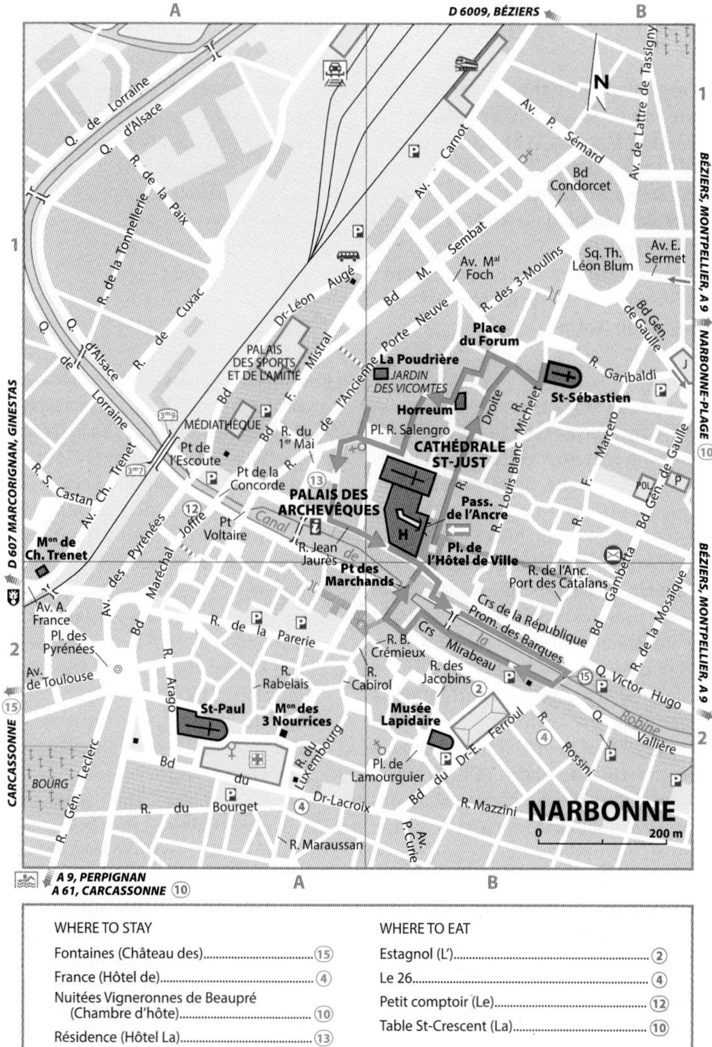

EAT

L'Estagnol – 5 bis Cours Mirabeau. 04 68 65 09 27. www.lestagnol.fr. Closed 16–24 Nov, Sun and Mon eve. Lively brasserie situated near Les Halles, popular with locals. Traditional cuisine.

Le 26 – 8 bd du Dr Lacroix. 04 68 41 46 69. www.restaurantle26.fr. Closed Sun eve and Mon. Slow-cooking fills the restaurant with appetising aromas.

Le Petit Comptoir – 4 bd du Mar.-Joffre. 04 68 42 30 35. www.petitcomptoir.com. Closed 15 days in Jul, Sun–Mon. (May–Sep). Bistro-style restaurant with local specialities.

La Table St Crescent – 68 av. du Gén.Leclerc au Palais du vin. 04 68 41 37 37. www.la-table-saint-crescent.com. Closed Sat lunch, Sun eve and Mon. A former oratory transformed into a temple of wine; inventive cuisine and superb wines.

Perpignan★★

Perpignan, once the capital city of the counts of Roussillon and the kings of Majorca, is an outlying post of Catalan civilisation north of the Pyrénées, and a lively commercial city, with shaded walks lined with pavement cafés. The economy is largely based on tourism, wine and olive oil, and the production of cork, wool and leather.

- **Population:** 117 419.
- **Michelin Map:** 344 I 6
- **Info:** Place François Arago. ℘04 68 66 30 30. www.perpignantourisme.com.
- **Location:** 64km/40mi S of Narbonne.
- **Timing:** Allow a day, or more if you can.

A BIT OF HISTORY

Perpignan prospered in the 13C from growing eastern Mediterranean trade. In 1276, it became capital of Roussillon, part of the Catalan kingdom of Majorca. When the kingdom broke up, Roussillon became part of the principality of Catalonia. From 1463, the French Crown tried in various ways to take possession of Roussillon, but met fierce resistance from the local inhabitants.

The province was briefly given to the monarchs of Spain, who fortified it heavily. Local people rebelled against Spanish rule too, and in 1640 Richelieu offered Roussillon a degree of autonomy if it would become part of France, which it agreed to do, leading to the Siege of Perpignan as the Spanish tried to retain the city. The French victory was ratified by the Treaty of the Pyrénées.

WALKING TOUR

HISTORIC PERPIGNAN

Perpignan map, p574. Allow 2hrs.

- **Le Castillet★** – This monument, an emblem of Perpignan, dominates place de la Victoire. Its two towers are crowned with tall crenellations and machicolations.
- **Promenade des Platanes** – This wide avenue is lined with plane trees and adorned with fountains.
- **La Miranda** – This is a small public park behind the church of St-Jacques. It is given over to the plant life of the *garrigue*.
- **Église St-Jacques** – A vast chapel added in the 18C was reserved for the brotherhood of La Sanch ('of the precious Blood'). From 1416, this penitents' brotherhood performed a solemn procession on Maundy Thursday (now Good Friday), carrying its misteris to the singing of hymns.
- **Cathédrale St-Jean★** – The church was begun in 1324 by Sancho, second king of Majorca, and was consecrated in 1509.
- **Campo Santo** – A vast graveyard and one of the few medieval graveyards remaining in France.
- **Place de la Loge** – This square and the pedestrianised rue de la Loge, paved in pink marble, form the lively centre of town life.
- **Loge de Mera** – This fine Gothic building once housed a commercial tribunal in charge of ruling on claims relating to maritime trade.
- **Hôtel de Ville★** – In the arcaded courtyard is a bronze by Maillol.
- **Palais de la Députation** – During the reign of the kings of Aragón, this 15C palace was the seat of the permanent commission representing the Catalan 'Corts'.
- **Musée des Beaux-Arts Hyacinthe-Rigaud** – Hyacinthe-Rigaud (1659–1743) was a French baroque painter of Catalan origin whose career was largely based in Paris. He is renowned for his portraits of Louis XIV, the royalty and nobility.
- **Place Arago** – Pleasant square adorned with palm trees, magnolias and cafés.

PALAIS DES ROIS DE MAJORQUE★

4 r. des Archers. Open daily: Jun–Sept 10am–6pm; Oct–May 9am–5pm. €4. ✆04 68 34 96 29.

The origin of this Catalan palace lay in the desire of James I of Aragon to make his younger son ruler of the "Kingdom of Majorca", with its mainland seat in Perpignan. When the kings of Majorca came to the throne in 1276, they built their palace on the hill of Puig del Rey.

EXCURSIONS

BEACHES

Colliourse is gorgeous but small and crowded in summer; Racou Plage is less busy, if a bit modernish and not very picturesque. Closer to Perpignan is St Cyprien, go to the northernmost part, which is not crowded.

MUSÉE DE PRÉHISTOIRE DE TAUTAVEL★★

27km/16.7mi NW of Perpignan, 9.4km/5.8mi NE of Estagel.

Open daily: 10am–12.30pm, 2–6pm (Jul–Aug 10am–7pm). €8 (children, 7–14, €4). ✆04 68 29 07 76. www.tautavel.com.

After the discovery in the 1970s of fragments of human skull at Tautavel, this little village gave its name to **"Tautavel man"**, hunters living about 450 000 years ago. Highlights include a reconstruction of the skeleton and a copy of the cave where the bones were found.

LA CÔTE VERMEILLE★★

Between Argelès beach and the Spanish border, small towns and ports huddle in bays along the mountainous coast. The picturesque port **Collioure★★**, below its royal castle, attracted artists of the Fauve School in the early 20C. **Banyuls★** is famous for its sweet wine. In the hills above, the Madeloc Tower enjoys a wide **panorama★★** of the Côte.

FORT DE SALSES★★

20km/12.4mi N of Perpignan.

Rising strangely above the surrounding vine-covered plain north of Perpignan, this huge and intriguing brick fortress, originally 15C, was adapted by Vauban.

LES CORBIÈRES★★

✆04 68 45 69 40. www.corbieres-sauvages.com. Don't miss the chateaux de Peyrepertuse, Quéribus and Puilaurens.

Corbières is best known for its ruined castles and its wine, and for a massif landscape showered with luminous Mediterranean light. The spiny, sweet-smelling *garrigue* covers much of the countryside.

Vines have overgrown the area east of the Orbieu and around **Limoux**, the region producing sparkling white *blanquette*. The **Corbières** has been awarded the *Appellation d'Origine Contrôlée* for its fruity, full-bodied wines (mainly red, some white and rosé) with bouquets evocative of local flora.

MONT-LOUIS★

High in the Pyrénées, east of Font-Romeu and Andorra.

3 r. Lieutenant Pruneta. ✆04 68 04 21 97. http://mont-louis.net.

Mont-Louis occupies a strategic site at the meeting point of three valleys. To the north is the valley of the Aude; its broad upper course is known as the **Capcir**. To the southwest is the Sègre, a tributary of the Ebro, which here flows through the **Cerdagne**, an upland basin; its elevated position diminishes the apparent height of the surrounding peaks, and its high sunshine level led to the construction here in 1949 of the first "solar furnace" **(four solaire)** using parabolic mirrors. Finally, to the west, is the valley of the Têt, which flows out of the Lac des Bouillouses to form the **Conflent**, the major routeway linking the Cerdagne with Perpignan.

The site's importance was confirmed following the **Treaty of the Pyrénées** in 1659, which made the Pyrénées the legal as well as the natural boundary of France. Louis XIV set about giving his newly acquired lands some more solid protection than that afforded by a signature; the great Vauban carried out his survey of Roussillon and the Cerdagne in 1679, and, from 1681 onwards, directed the construction of Mont-Louis.

PERPIGNAN

D 117 FOIX
A 9: NARBONNE
ANDORRE N 116: PRADES
A 9: BARCELONE
A 9: BARCELONE THUIR

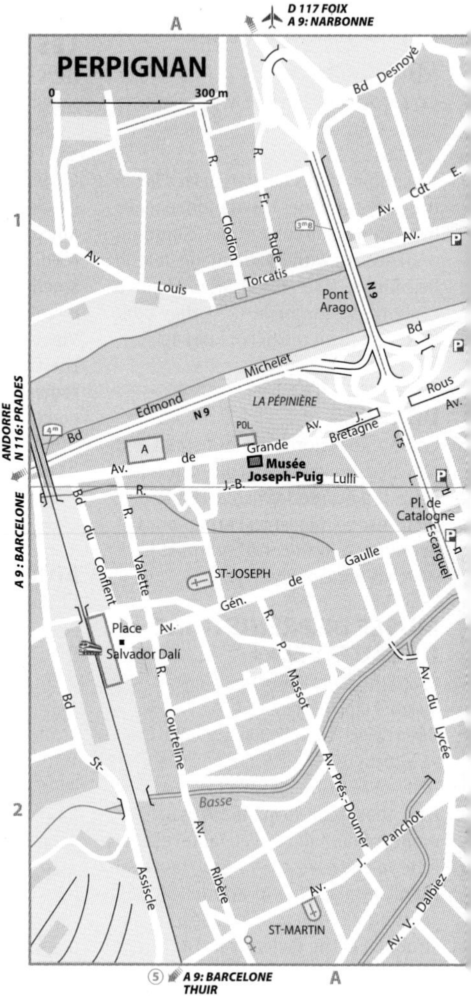

PRINCIPAT D'ANDORRA★★

There are few towns or roads. A single highway crosses the territory through the capital, Andorra La Vella. 0800 680 0694. http://visitandorra.com.

Andorra is an independent state with an area of 468 sq km and more than 1 000 years of history. No mere tax-free shopping haven, this tiny Catalan-speaking nation in the high Pyrénées is also a wild, scenic land of lofty plateaux and precipitous valleys.

Andorra was a possession of Catalan counts and bishops, and from 1278 was shared between the Count of Foix and the Bishop of Urgell ("co-principality"). In 1993 it was given freedom from its feudal status and become an independent state. Despite a remote location, It is prospering with hydroelectric power and all-year-round tourism.

Andorra la Vella is a bustling commercial town. Away from the main road, the town's heart preserves quiet old streets; to the east it merges with Escales.

Port d'Envallra★★ is the highest pass in the Pyrénées (2 409m). It marks the watershed between the Mediterranean and the Atlantic. There is a superb **panorama**.

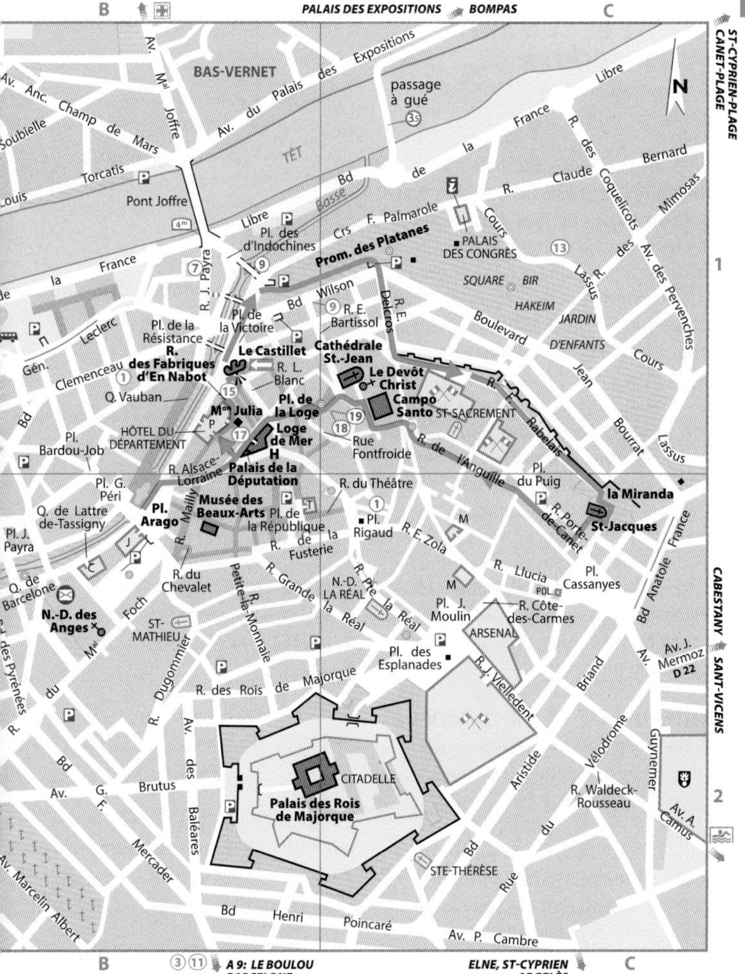

CHÂTEAU DE PEYREPERTUSE★★★

The site is 47km/29mi NW of Perpignan. On D 14, S of Duilhac, look out for the 3.5km/2mi narrow access road to the site.

Open daily, times vary. €6.50 (children 6–15, €3.50). 04 82 53 24 07. www.chateau-peyrepertuse.com.

The dramatic barrier of the Corbières was defended by a number of strongholds of which the ruins of the Château de Peyrepertuse, separated into two distinct castles on their rocky promontory, are the most imposing. The Lower Castle (Château Bas) to the east came under Aragonese rule in 1162. In 1240, it surrendered to the Seneschal of Carcassonne acting in the name of the king. Under the terms of the Treaty of Corbeil in 1258, it became part of the fortified French border facing Spanish Roussillon.

The royal castle raised on the western height is known as St George's Castle. It was built in the course of a single campaign, probably by Philip the Bold. In 1659, the incorporation of Roussillon into France by the Treaty of the Pyrénées stripped Peyrepertuse of its strategic importance.

ABBAYE DE ST-MARTIN-DU-CANIGOU★★

The abbey lies 2.5km/1.5mi S of Vernet-les-Bains.

Guided tours only (1hr): €6. 04 68 05 50 03. http://stmartinducanigou.org.

The abbey of St Martin on Mont Canigou, an eagle's eyrie at 1 055m above sea level, is one of the great sights of the eastern Pyrénées. This Romanesque abbey, built on a rocky pinnacle at 1 094m in around 1001–09, grew up around a monastic community founded here in the 11C.

After falling into disuse at the Revolution, it was restored from 1902–32 and extended from 1952–72. At the beginning of the 20C, all that remained of the **cloisters** were three galleries. As part of the restoration, a south gallery has been rebuilt overlooking the ravine, using the marble capitals from an upper storey which was no longer extant. The abbey is now home to nuns and priests, who lead the silent tours.

PRIEURÉ DE SERRABONE★★

The steep road to Serrabonne is a turning (near Ille-sur-Têt) off the highway Perpignan to Font-Romèu. Boule d'Amont. 04 68 84 09 30.

In a wild and stony setting among austere mountains, this former priory contains superb Romanesque sculpture, its severity relieved by delicate pink marble.

ADDRESSES

STAY

Hôtel de la Loge – 1 r. des Fabriques-d'En-Nabot. 04 68 34 41 02. www.hoteldelaloge.fr. 22 rooms. Beautiful 16C mansion, central location.

Hôtel de France – Quai Sadi-Carnot. 04 68 84 80 35. www.hoteldefrance-perpignan.fr. 24 rooms. WiFi. An historic mansion with small but well sound-proofed rooms. Central location.

Hôtel Alexander – 15 Bd. Clemenceau. 04 68 35 41 41. www.hotel-alexander.fr. 23 rooms. This little downtown hotel has balconied, air-conditioned guestrooms.

Hôtel New Christina – 51 cours Lassus. 04 68 35 12 21. www.hotel-newchristina.com. 25 rooms. A small, modern hotel, near the city centre, with a rooftop pool.

Hôtel Kyriad – 8 bd. Wilson. 0892 23 48 13. www.kyriad.com. 49 rooms. Functional furnishings, integral courtyard with fountain.

NEARBY

Chambre d'hôte du Domaine du Moulin – 66300 Caixas, 6km/4mi S of Fontcouverte (direction Fourques). 04 68 38 87 84. Closed end Nov–Mar. Reservation advised. 3 rooms. In the mountains, a former miller's house, now a B&B with an excellent restaurant.

Chambre d'hôte Domaine du Mas Boluix – Chemin du Pou de les Colobres. 5km/3mi S of Perpignan towards Argelès. 04 68 08 17 70. 5 rooms. Removed from the bustle of Perpignan, this nicely restored 18C mas is a peaceful place in the middle of Cabestany vines.

Le Mas des Arcades – 840 av. d'Espagne 2km/1mi on the D 9. 04 68 85 11 11. www.hotel-mas-des-arcades.fr. 62 rooms. WiFi. Tidy rooms, half with balconies; fine restaurant.

EAT

Le Barathym – 7 r. des Cardeurs. 04 68 50 98 14. This restaurant in a little street near the place de la Loge serves an inspired cuisine and is popular among the people of Perpignan.

Les Antiquaires – Pl. Desprès. 04 68 34 06 58. http://lesantiquairesperpignan.fr.gd. Closed Sun eve and Mon. Family restaurant decorated with antique china. Traditional cuisine.

La Rencontre – 18 r. des Cardeurs. 04 68 34 42 73. www.restaurant-larencontre.fr. Closed lunch Sat–Mon. Menu based on regional and seasonal food.

La Passerelle – 1 cours Palmarole. 04 68 51 30 65. Closed Mon lunch, and Sun. Cosy seafood restaurant.

La Galinette – 23 R. Jean-Payra. 04 68 35 00 90. Contemporary furnishings, beautifully set tables and southern-style dishes.

Toulouse★★★

A vibrant regional capital, attractive with its red-brick architecture, Toulouse is a lively university town with a thriving high-tech industrial sector and, at the same time, plenty of attractions for the visitor to enjoy.

- **Population:** 441 802.
- **Michelin Map:** 343 G 3
- **Info:** Donjon du Capitole. ✆05 40 131 531, or 0892 180 180 (when in France). www.toulouse-visit.com.
- **TGV:** Toulouse Matabiau is 8–9hrs from Paris Austerlitz and 6hrs from Paris Montparnasse.
- **Flights:** Toulouse-Blagnac international airport (www.toulouse.aeroport.fr) is 8km/5mi W of Toulouse, from where the city centre is reached by airport shuttle or by taxi.
- **Location:** Toulouse lies between Bordeaux (243km/152mi to the W) and Narbonne (150km/94mi to the E).
- **Parking:** Cars can be parked free of charge in the "Transit car parks"; you then take the bus or metro into the city. Parking in the city centre can be difficult.
- **Don't Miss:** From the Pont St-Michel, there's a great view of the city, especially when the setting sun picks up the warm red tones of the brickwork.
- **Timing:** If you staying for a few days, buy a Pass Tourisme (€19.50–33.50, 24–72hrs). But, take a guided tour of Toulouse first, to get a better idea of where you want to spend your time; three days will fly by.

A BIT OF HISTORY

Toulouse has long been the focus of diverse influences. It was the capital of the Visigothic kingdom, and enjoyed considerable prosperity between the 9C and 13C under the Raymond dynasty, whose court was one of the most cultured in Europe; their extensive territories were known as the "Langue d'Oc". In the 13C, the whole domain of the Raymonds – most of present-day Languedoc and parts of the Midi-Pyrénées and Provence – embraced **Catharism**. This gave the Capetian kings an opportunity, with the authority of the pope, to launch the **Albigensian Crusade**, which crushed the Raymonds, broke up their territories, and pushed the Capetian frontier southwards into Languedoc.

In 1323, Europe's oldest literary society was founded here to further the cause of the language of southern France (Langue d'Oc). Later, in the 16C, the city flourished again because of a boom in woad, which was widely used for fabric dyeing, yielding a blue-black colour.

As early as 1917, strategic industries like aircraft manufacturing were being set up in southwestern France, as far away as possible from the country's vulnerable eastern border. In the inter-war period, Toulouse became the starting point of France's first scheduled air service. The city has remained the focus of France's aeronautics industry.

BASILIQUE ST-SERNIN★★★

The great church was built to honour the memory of the Gaulish martyr St Sernin (or Saturninus). A first phase of construction lasting from around 1080–1118 was in a mixture of brick and stone, a second phase in brick alone. St-Sernin was one of a number of major Romanesque pilgrimage churches on the route to Compostela. St-Sernin's octagonal bell tower is particularly characteristic of the area, with five levels of twin arches built in brick, the upper two of which are provided with little pediments.

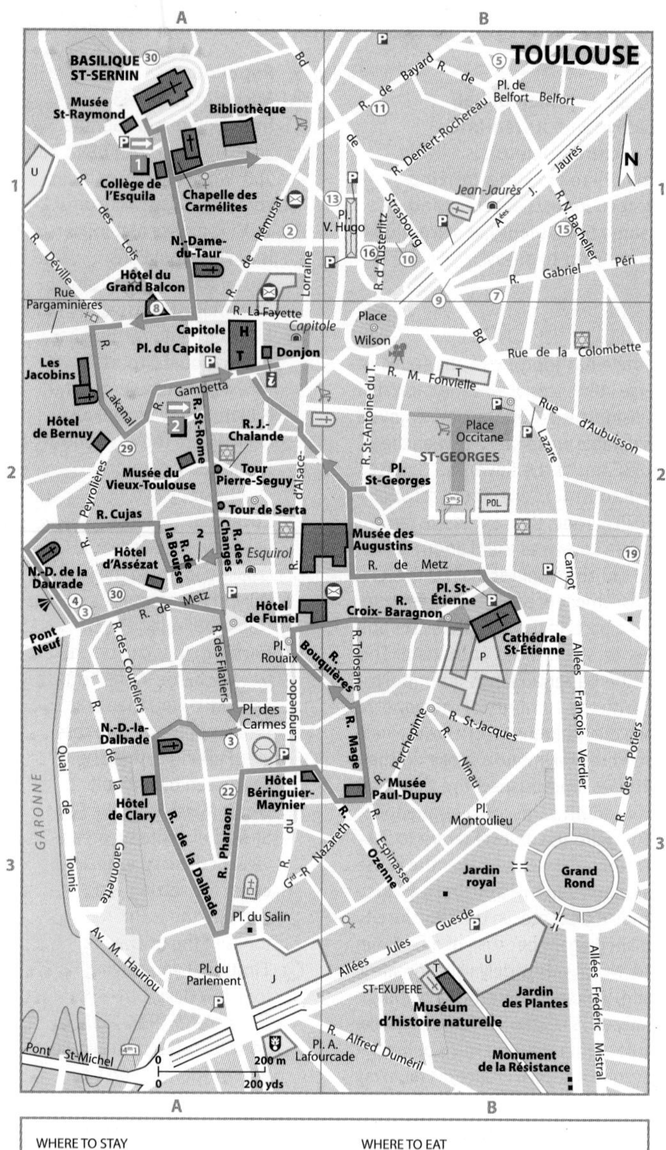

WHERE TO STAY

Albert 1er (Hôtel).......... 2
Beaux-Arts (Hôtel des).......... 3
Boréal (Hôtel).......... 5
Castellane (Hôtel).......... 7
Grand Balcon (Hôtel du).......... 8
Ours Blanc-Centre (Hôtel de l').......... 10
Ours Blanc-Place Victor-Hugo (Hôtel de l').... 13
St-Claire (Hôtel).......... 15

WHERE TO EAT

7 Place St-Sernin.......... 30
"Beaux-Arts" (Brasserie Flo).......... 4
Colombier.......... 11
J'Go.......... 16
Madeleine de Proust (La).......... 19
Mangevins (Le).......... 22
Régalade (La).......... 29
Rôtisserie des Carmes.......... 3

STREET INDEX

Malcousinat (R.).......... 2

PUBLIC TRANSPORT

Toulouse is served by 83 bus routes, two metro lines and a modern tramway. Nine bus routes operate at night on Fri and Sat; the metro runs from 5.15am to midnight from Sun to Thu, and to 00.42am on Fri and Sat. Cars can be parked free of charge in 'transit car parks' at certain metro stations. A **yellow ticket** (€1.60 each) allows you to travel anywhere on the network for 1hr. **Day round-trip** tickets (€3.10), day (€5.50) and season tickets are also available. Other transport options include a tourist road train and **VélôToulouse**, a municipal pick up/drop off bicycle hire scheme. Information: Allô Tisséo; 05 61 41 70 70; www.tisseo.fr.

'PASS TOURISME' CARD

The 'Pass Tourisme' card, available from the tourist information office, gives free or discounted access to several tourist sights, and access to travel freely on the Tisséo network. The card is personal and valid for 1, 2 or 3 days, priced €19.50, €26.50 and €33.50, inclusive of airport shuttle option.

WALKING TOUR

1 OLD TOWN★★★

Toulouse map, p578.

- **Musée St-Raymond★★** – This museum, housed in one of the buildings of the old Collège St-Raymond (13C), rebuilt in 1523 and restored by Viollet-le-Duc, was recently refurbished and now displays its collections of archaeology and antique art.
- **Chapelle des Carmélites** – A fine 18C chapel commemorating the Carmelite order.
- **Bibliothèque d'étude et du patrimoine** – Civic pride and the importance of learning are celebrated in this 1930s library by Montariol.
- **Église Notre-Dame-du-Taur** – This church replaced the sanctuary erected where the martyr saint was buried.
- **Hôtel du Grand Balcon** – In the 1920s this was a pension for pioneers of French aviation working for Aerospatiale.
- **Les Jacobins★★** – St Dominic, alarmed by the spread of the Albigensian heresy, founded the Order of Preachers (Dominican Order) and the first Dominican monastery was founded in Toulouse in 1216.

  Église des Jacobins★★ – The awesome main **body★★** of the church reflects the Dominican Order's prestige, its prosperity and its two aims: serving God and preaching his word.
- **Hôtel de Bernuy** (Lycée Pierre-de-Fermat) – This mansion was built in the early 16C.
- **Place du Capitole** – Along the east side of this vast square, the main meeting point for local residents, stretches the majestic façade of the Capitole building.
- **Capitole★** – This is the city hall of Toulouse, named after the 'capitouls', or consuls, who used to run the city.

WALKING TOUR

2 SOUTH FROM THE PLACE DU CAPITOLE★★★

Toulouse map, p578.

- **Rue St-Rome** – This busy shopping street is part of the old cardo maximus (Roman road through town from north to south).
- **Musée du Vieux Toulouse** – The beautiful Hôtel Dumay was built in red brick embellished with stone at the end of the 16C by Antoine Dumay, chief physician to queen Marguerite de Valois. The museum it now houses brings together collections on the history of Toulouse.

- **Rue des Changes** – The square known as 'Quatre Coins des Changes' is overlooked by the Sarta turret.
- **Rue Malcousinat** – Attractive hôtel and an austere 15C keep.
- **Rue de la Bourse** – No 20, the late-15C Hôtel Delfau, is the house of Pierre Del Fau, who hoped to become a capitoul but who never fulfilled his ambition.
- **Basilique Notre-Dame-de-la-Daurade** – A pagan temple here was first converted into a church in the 5C.
- **Pont Neuf** – Despite the name, this is the city's oldest bridge, completed in 1632.
- **Hotel d'Assézat★★** – This, the finest private mansion in Toulouse, was built in 1555–57 according to the plans of Nicolas Bachelier, the greatest Renaissance architect of Toulouse, for the Capitoul d'Assézat, who had made a fortune from trading in dyer's woad.

  Fondation Bemberg★★ – This impressive collection comprises painting, sculpture and objets d'art from the Renaissance to the 20C.
- **Église Notre-Dame-la-Dalbade** – This church was built in the 16C, on the site of an earlier building.
- **Rue de la Dalbade** – This street is lined with the elegant mansions of former local dignitaries.

Place du Capitole

© Christophe Boisvieux/hemis.fr

- **Rue Pharaon** – Pretty street.
- **Hôtel Béringuier-Maynier** (Hôtel du Vieux-Raisin) – The main building at the back of the courtyard marks the first manifestation of the Italian Renaissance in Toulouse, in the style of the châteaux of the Loire Valley.
- **Rue Ozenne** – At no 9 the Hôtel Dahus and Tournoër turret make a handsome 15C group.
- **Musée Paul-Dupuy★** – This museum, in the Hôtel Pierre-Besson, is devoted to the applied arts from the Middle Ages to the present.
- **Rue Mage** – This is one of the best-preserved streets in Toulouse.
- **Rue Bouquière** – Note the splendid architecture of the Hôtel de Puivert (18C).
- **Hôtel de Fumel** (Palais Consulaire) – This mansion houses the Chamber of Commerce.
- **Place St-Étienne** – In the square stands Toulouse's oldest fountain.
- **Cathédrale St-Étienne★** – Built over several centuries, from the 11–17C.
- **Musée des Augustins★★** – This museum is housed in a former Augustinian monastery designed in the southern French Gothic style (14C and 15C); specifically the chapter-house and the great and small cloisters. Paintings and Romanesque **sculptures★★★**.
- **Galeries Lafayette** – Panoramic view of rooftops and church spires from the terrace on the top floor of this department store.

ADDITIONAL SIGHTS

Muséum d'Histoire Naturelle★★

Open daily except Mon 10am–6pm. Closed 1 Jan, 1 May, 25 Dec. €9. ✆05 67 7384 84. www.museum.toulouse.fr.

The natural history museum has extensive collections, most notably of ornithological, prehistoric and ethnographical exhibits.

Take this opportunity to discover the **Jardin des Plantes**, the **Jardin Royal** and the **Grand Rond**, well-laid-out gardens that make a very pleasant place for a stroll.

EXCURSIONS

CANAL DU MIDI

The Canal runs from Sète on the Languedoc coast to Toulouse, then joins the Canal Lateral to the Garonne and then on to Bordeaux.

It is hard to believe that this calm, beautiful, even elegant waterway, now so popular for leisurely boating holidays, was a daunting engineering achievement enabling the transport of industrial goods directly between the Mediterranean and the Atlantic.

The notion of a canal between the Atlantic and the Mediterranean enabling shipping to avoid the long route via Gibraltar had preoccupied not only the Romans but also François I, Henri IV and Richelieu. The natural obstacles, however, seemed insurmountable.

Then in 1662, Pierre-Paul Riquet (1604–80) succeeded in interesting Colbert in overcoming them. The canal was to prove his ruin; all the work was carried out at his own expense and he died six months before the opening. The completed Canal du Midi is 240km/149mi long and has 103 locks; It proved a huge commercial success – too late for the great man.

Becoming obsolete in the late 19C, the canal provides a perfect illustration of pre-industrial techniques. It passed into state ownership in 1897 and today is used mainly by leisure craft. In 1996 it was named as a World Heritage Site by UNESCO.

AUCH★

Auch lies 76.4km/47.4mi W of Toulouse.

1 r. Dessoles. 05 62 05 22 89. www.auch-tourisme.com.

Auch is an attractive, pleasantly busy local capital in the heart of Gascony. Auch began in ancient times as a fortified Basque settlement beside the River Gers. For 2 000 years it served as a staging post on the old Toulouse–Bordeaux highway; its position avoided the treacherously shifting course of the River Garonne to the north. It owes some fame to the story of *The Three Musketeers* – the real d'Artagnan, Charles de Batz, was from this district.

The **cathedral★★** contains a masterly series of Renaissance **stained-glass windows★★** and some exceptional **choir stalls★★★**.

MONTAUBAN★

The town is 55.3km/34.3mi N of Toulouse (autoroute A 62).

4 r. du Collège. 05 63 63 60 60. www.montauban-tourisme.com.

On the boundary between the hillsides of Bas Quercy and the rich alluvial plains of the Garonne and the Tarn, the old bastide of Montauban, built with a geometric street layout, is an important crossroads and a good point of departure for excursions into the Aveyron gorges. The almost exclusive use of pink brick lends the buildings here a distinctive character, which is also found in most of the towns and villages in Bas Quercy and the Toulouse area.

Place Nationale★ – The square, formerly the Place Royale, dates from the foundation of the town in the 12C. After fire destroyed the wooden roofs or *couverts* above the galleries in 1614 and again in 1649, the arcades were rebuilt in brick in the 17C.

Musée Ingres★ – Devoted to Jean-Auguste-Dominique Ingres' works, the museum is housed in a former bishop's palace.

MOISSAC★★

70km/44mi NW of Toulouse, via A 62.

6 pl. Durand de Bredon. 05 63 04 01 85. www.moissac.fr.

Moissac is situated on a low rise overlooking the fertile flood plain near the meeting point of the Tarn with the Garonne. The place is famous for the white Chasselas dessert grape, which grows here in abundance.

Église St-Pierre★ – The former Benedictine abbey church, founded in the 7C, was consecrated in 1063 and the **cloisters★★** completed 35 years later. It subsequently served as a model for similar work all over Europe.

The church's **south doorway★★★** is a triumph of Romanesque sculpture.

ST-BERTRAND-DE-COMMINGES★★

St-Bertrand lies 112km/70mi SW of Toulouse, S of A 64, junction 17.

This is one of the most picturesque and charming villages in the Pyrénéan foothills, perched on an isolated hill-top, encircled by ancient ramparts and dominated by an imposing cathedral.

A substantial town was founded here in 72 BCE by Pompey. In AD 585 the Burgundians descended on the place and laid it waste. For centuries the site lay abandoned, until in 1073 St Bernard saw its potential for the building of a cathedral and monastery.

Here the rules of the religious reforms of Pope Gregory VII were applied, making the little city the spiritual centre of Comminges, endowing the awkwardly shaped county (sandwiched as it was between the territories belonging to the House of Foix-Béarn and dotted with enclaves) with a religious significance far outweighing its political importance.

GROTTE DU MAS-D'AZIL★

80km/50mi S of Toulouse, in the Ariège hills, 31km/19mi NW of Foix. 05 61 69 97 71. www.grotte-masdazil.com.

This cave is one of the outstanding natural phenomena of southwestern France, as well as a very important prehistoric site. In 1887 Édouard Piette discovered evidence of human habitation during the Azilian period (9 500 BCE). Research continued under Abbé Breuil, Mandement, Boule and Cartailhac.

FOIX★

85km/53mi S of Toulouse.

29 r. Delcassé. 05 61 65 12 12. www.tourisme-foix-varilhes.fr.

In the Middle Ages this hill town was important as the capital of the colourful Counts of Foix. Ruggedly set against a skyline of jagged peaks and three castle towers, it overlooks the Plantaurel hills. Its old narrow streets radiate from Rue de Labistour and Rue des Marchands, starkly contrasting with the 19C administrative area fanning out from the allées de la Villote and the Champ de Mars.

Once part of the Duchy of Aquitaine, the Foix region became a county in the 11C. At the conclusion of the Albigensian Crusade, the Counts, who had favoured the heresy, were obliged to submit to the king of France under the terms of the Treaty of Paris (1229).

Until the late 19C the Ariège River was panned for gold, and many local iron foundries were supplied by the mine at La Rancié until 1931.

From the **Château** rock high above the river there are extensive **views★** over the surrounding region.

ADDRESSES

STAY

Hotel Albert 1er – 8 r. Rivals. 05 61 21 17 91. www.hotel-albert1.com. 47 rooms. Ideally placed from which to explore the city on foot.

Hotel Boréal – 20 r. Caff arelli. 05 61 62 57 21. www.hotel-toulouse-boreal.com. Booking advised. WiFi. 24 rooms. This red-brick hotel is ideally placed between the station and place Wilson; good prices, rooms on three floors.

Hôtel Athénée – 13 bis r. Matabiau. 05 61 63 10 63. www.hotel-toulouse-athenee.com. P. 35 rooms. Just 500m from St Sernin; a lovely relaxing place.

Hôtel de Brienne – 20 bd du Mar.-Leclerc. 05 61 23 60 60. www.hoteldebrienne.com. P. 77 rooms. A place most suitable for business people, but equally appropriate for those on holiday.

Hôtel Castellane – 17 r. Castellane. 05 61 62 18 82. www.castellanehotel.com. P. 53 rooms. This small hotel close to the Capitole is slightly set back from the main thoroughfare. The rooms are housed in three different buildings; some well suited to families.

Hôtel de l'Ours Blanc-Centre – 14 pl. Victor-Hugo. 05 61 21 25 97. www.hotel-oursblanc.com. 44 rooms. Close to the centre of the city; sound-proofed, air-conditioned rooms.

Hôtel de l'Ours Blanc-Place Victor Hugo – 25 pl. Victor-Hugo. 05 61 23 14 55. www.hotel-oursblanc.com. 38 rooms. Opposite the market, but well soundproofed and air-conditioned; simple and very comfortable.

⊖⊖ **Hôtel St-Claire** – 29 pl. Nicolas-Bachelier. ℘05 34 40 58 88. www.stclairehotel.fr. 16 rooms. Five minutes from place Wilson, a small hotel with elegant rooms, inspired by Feng Shui. Discounts at certain periods.

⊖⊖ **Chambre d'hôte Manoir St-Clair** – 20 ch. de Sironis, 31130 Balma. ℘05 61 24 36 98. www.manoirsaintclair.com. 3 rooms. An authentic 17C manor with brick walls circulating a grand park with trees and flowers. The pretty rooms are decorated with inspiration from the region.

⊖⊖⊖ **Hôtel des Beaux-Arts** – 1 pl. du Pont-Neuf. ℘05 34 45 42 42. www.hoteldesbeauxarts.com. 19 rooms. An 18C house refurbished with taste to create cosy and comfortable rooms. Most have a view over the Garonne river and No 42 has its own small terrace.

⊖⊖⊖ **Hôtel Mermoz** – 50 r. Matabiau ℘05 61 63 04 04. www.privilegetoulouse.com/hotel-mermoz. 52 rooms. The inner flower garden of this hotel near the city centre provides a haven of calm. Spacious rooms furnished in 1930s style.

⊖⊖⊖⊖ **Hôtel du Grand Balcon** – 8 r. Romiguières. ℘05 34 25 44 09. www.grandbalconhotel.com. 47 rooms. Very close to the place du Capitole is this legendary hotel which once lodged the pioneer aviators Saint-Exupéry and Mermoz. The rooms and suites are decorated in different styles. The lounges, bars and restaurant all have a touch of elegance about them.

EAT

⊖ **J'Go** – 16 pl. Victor-Hugo. ℘05 61 23 02 03. www.lejgo.com. Closed 1 Jan, 24 and 31 Dec. Both cuisine and decor pay homage to the region. Appreciated by the locals.

⊖ **La Régalade** – 16 r. Gambetta. ℘05 61 23 20 11. Closed 3 wks Aug and weekends. Between the Capitole and the Garonne, a small restaurant behind a red-brick façade. Traditional and regional cuisine.

⊖⊖ **7 Place St-Sernin** – 7 pl. St-Sernin – ℘05 62 30 05 30. www.7placesaintsernin.com. Closed Sat lunch & Sun. The outdoor tables of this well-known restaurant enjoy a view of the Basilica St-Sernin. Exquisite food.

⊖⊖ **Le Bellevue** – 1 av. des Pyrénées, 31120 Lacroix-Falgarde. ℘05 61 76 94 97. www.restaurant-lebellevue.com. Closed Tue, Wed, 15 Oct–15 Nov. This former dance hall was in its prime in the 1940s, but now enjoying a revival of fortunes.

⊖⊖ **Colombier** – 14 r. Bayard. ℘05 61 62 40 05. www.restaurant-lecolombier.com. Closed Mon lunch, Sat lunch & Sun. Reservation recommended. Opened in 1874, this is an essential stopping point for culinary pilgrims in search of authentic cassoulet. Delightful dining room with pink bricks and wall paintings. Friendly and efficient service.

⊖⊖ **La Madeleine de Proust** – 11 r. Riquet. ℘05 61 63 80 88. www.madeleinedeproust.com. Closed Sat lunch, Sun eve and Mon. Childhood memories inspire the original, carefully designed decor of this restaurant featuring yellow walls, waxed tables, antique toys, an old school desk, a time-worn cupboard. The cuisine gives the starring role to vegetables that have fallen from common use.

⊖⊖ **Le Mangevins** – 46 r. Pharaon. ℘05 61 52 79 16. Closed Aug and weekends. In this local tavern where salted foie gras and beef are sold by weight, the bawdy, fun atmosphere is enhanced by ribald songs. There is no menu, but a set meal for hearty appetites.

⊖⊖ **Rôtisserie des Carmes** – 138 r. Polinaires. ℘05 61 53 34 88. Closed Aug, 24–27 Dec, 31 Dec–3Jan, Sat, Sun and public holidays. Next to the market, the chef serves whatever is available that day.

⊖⊖ **La Table des Merville** – 3 pl. Richard. 31320 Castanet-Tolosan. ℘05 62 71 24 25. www.table-des-merville.com. Closed Sun & 24 Dec–4 Jan. The appetising cuisine of this welcoming restaurant reflects the availability of ingredients in the market. Modern art is displayed on the walls.

⊖⊖⊖⊖ **Brasserie Flo 'Beaux Arts'** – 1 quai Daurade. ℘05 61 21 12 12. www.brasserielesbeauxarts.com. Daily. The atmosphere of a 1930s brasserie is recreated here with bistro-style chairs, wall seats, retro lighting, wood panelling and mirrors. The cuisine, in keeping with the decor, features seafood, sauerkraut and a few regional specialities.

Albi★★★

From the bridges spanning the Tarn to the extraordinary cathedral, Albi "the red" is made of brick, which owes its rosy hue to the clays dug from the river's bed.

- **Population:** 48 916.
- **Michelin Map:** 338 D 6, E 7
- **Info:** Palais de la Berbie, pl. Ste-Cécile, Albi. ✆05 63 36 36 00. www.albi-tourisme.fr. The Albi City Pass gives numerous discounts at sites and monuments, shops and attractions. Valid for a year, €12.
- **Location:** Albi is 77km/ 47.8mi NE of Toulouse.
- **Timing:** Allow one day. The town was built around its cathedral, which is best viewed from a distance, preferably the bridge across the Tarn (the Pont du 22-Août), or from one of the streets of Old Albi.
- **Don't miss:** Enjoy a boat trip on the river to appreciate the beauty of the city at its best.

A BIT OF HISTORY

At the start of the 13C, the city was one of the centres of the dualist Cathar doctrine, dubbed the "Albigensian heresy". The subsequent "Albigensian Crusade" of 1209 was directed on the spiritual side by St Dominic and commanded militarily by the fearsome Simon de Montfort; on the ground, armies moved in from north and east to commit the terrible atrocities of Béziers, **Carcassonne★★★**, **Minerve★** and **Lavaur**. The Capetian kings took advantage of the troubles from 1208–1229, to gain a foothold in Languedoc, but Catharism itself was finally stamped out only by the Inquisition and the ghastly funeral pyre at Montségur (*see CHÂTEAU DE MONTSÉGUR, p566*).

CATHÉDRALE STE-CÉCILE★★

5 bd Sybille. ♿Open Nov–Apr Mon–Sat 9am–1pm, 2–6.30pm; May–Oct daily 9.30am–6.15pm (Sun 9.30–10.45am, 2–5.45pm). ✆05 63 43 23 43.

Construction of the cathedral took two centuries, starting in 1282 when work was already well advanced on the neighbouring Berbie Palace and the Dominicans at Toulouse. In the 19C the formidable edifice acquired the three upper storeys of its keep-like bell tower, its machicolations and its inspection gallery.

Inside, the perfect simplicity of the nave with its Southern French Gothic side chapels passes almost unnoticed, such is the exuberance of the Flamboyant decorative scheme. The 1485 **rood screen★★★**, one of the few to have survived, is also one of the most sumptuous. Its white limestone arches, gables, columns and arcading all show extraordinary skill and attention to detail. Old Testament figures are on the outside, those from the New Testament on the side of the choir. The vaults were painted from 1509 to 1512 by Bolognese artists.

The hallucinatory **Last Judgement** is a masterpiece of late 15C mural painting; it was disfigured by the installation in the 17C of the great organ.

PALAIS DE LA BERBIE★

The former Bishops' Palace houses the **Musée Toulouse-Lautrec★★**, devoted to the life and art of Henri de Toulouse-Lautrec (1864–1901). The Collection was bequeathed to Albi by the artist's mother, Comtesse Alphonse de Toulouse-Lautrec, and other family members. Born in Albi at the Hôtel du Bosc, Toulouse-Lautrec was crippled in early life by two accidents. He is revealed here as one of the great painters of everyday life; his vision of the depravity and decadence of late 19C Paris is communicated with restraint and compassion.

WALKING TOUR

OLD ALBI★★

Albi map, p585. Allow 1hr.

- **Hôtel Séré de Rivières** – This 15C–18C mansion belonged to a family of dyer's woad merchants ennobled in the 18C.
- **Maison du vieil Alby** – Restored medieval house, between pretty Croix-Blanche and Puech-Berenguier streets, hosts craft exhibits.
- **Rue Toulouse-Lautrec** – Handsome mansions.
- **Hôtel de Reynès★** – Headquarters of the chamber of commerce.
- **Pharmacie des Pénitents★** – This 16C house features timbering and crisscross-pattern brickwork typical of the Albi region.
- **Collégiale St-Salvi** – St Salvi was a lawyer before becoming Bishop of Albi in the 6C. He brought Christianity to the region and is buried on the site of this church

BERGES DU TARN★★

Follow the Azure circuit starting from the tourist office. The banks of the Tarn offer splendid **views★★** of the town and the old fortifications and a peaceful stroll away from the town's bustle.

EXCURSIONS

CASTRES★

Castres is 40km/25mi S of Albi.
2 pl. de la République. 05 63 62 63 62. www.tourisme-castres.fr.

This industrial town on the **Agout** river has fine 16–17C mansions, a Goya museum, and is a good base for exploring the **Lacaune** and **Montagne Noire** hill country. The Castres area is the French wool carding centre; its wool industry is second only to Roubaix-Tourncoing.

Musée Goya★ – Set up on the second floor of the former episcopal palace (now the Town Hall), this museum specialises in Spanish painting and possesses several outstanding works by Goya.

WHERE TO STAY
- À la Ferme "Naussens" (Chambre d'hôte) ..... ①
- Au Bouquet de Roose (Chambre d'hôte) ..... ②
- Cantepau (Hôtel) ..... ④
- Grand Hôtel d'Orléans ..... ⑦
- Mercure (Hôtel) ..... ⑩

WHERE TO EAT
- Épicurien (L') ..... ②
- Fourchette Adroite (La) ..... ④
- Jardin des Quatre Saisons (Le) ..... ⑤
- Robinson (Le) ..... ⑧
- Table du Sommelier (La) ..... ⑫

STREET INDEX
- Puech-Bérenguier (R.) 3
- Toulouse-Lautrec (R.) 6

- **Hôtel Séré-de-Rivières ..... D**
- **Maison du vieil Alby ..... K**
- **Maison du 15e s. ..... L**
- **Maison natale de T.-Lautrec ..... F**
- **Pharmacie des Pénitents .. R**

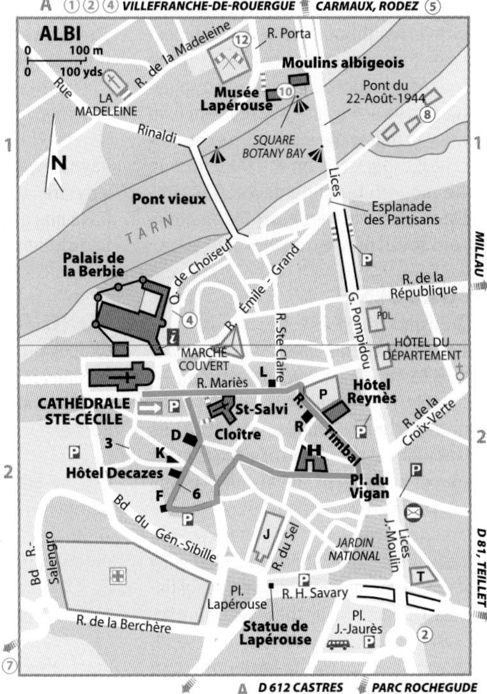

RODEZ★

The town is on a meeting of highways between Languedoc and Auvergne.

10–12 Place de la Cité. 05 65 75 76 77. http://tourisme.grand-rodez.com.

Once the capital of the Rouergue, Rodez is situated on the borders of two very different regions, the dry Causses plateaux and the well-watered Ségale hills. The ancient town stands on a rocky spur high above the meanders of the River Aveyron. Its layout reflects the medieval rivalry of secular and ecclesiastical power: the cathedral and castle districts were both fortified.

Cathédrale Notre-Dame★★ – The 13C red sandstone edifice has a fortress-like west front, once a bastion in the city wall. It has Flamboyant Gothic portals and a magnificent **bell tower★★★**. The interior was completed in the 16C but still in the style of the 13C. Note the 15C former **rood screen★** and the superb 17C carved wooden **organ case★**. The choir **stalls★** are by André Sulpice (15C).

Musée Fenaille★★ – The museum is housed partly in the oldest mansion in Rodez and partly in an adjacent modern building which blends harmoniously with its neighbour. Inside are the most extensive collections concerning the Rouergue region, each section displaying a time scale for easy reference. In order to follow the exhibition's chronological order, start on the third floor in the modern building devoted to prehistory. Note in particular the menhirs from south of Aveyron.

BOZOULS★

20km/12mi NE of Rodez.

pl. de l'Hôtel-de-Ville, 12340 Bozouls. 05 65 48 50 52. www.bozouls.com.

Bozouls is distinguished from afar by its modern church (1964), south of D 20. Its sanctuary in the shape of a ship's prow houses a statue of the Virgin Mary by local sculptor Denys Puech.

Trou de Bozouls★ – The terrace next to the war memorial affords the best view of this 800m canyon, hollowed out of the Causse de Comtal by the River Dourdou. From the town hall, walk round the south side of the "Trou" for the **Ancienne Église Ste-Fauste**. The church's 12C nave, with its raised, semicircular barrel vaulting, was originally roofed with heavy limestone slabs (*lauzes*). Under this enormous weight, the pillars sagged and the roof was replaced by a timber-frame one in the 17C.

VILLEFRANCHE-DE-ROUERGUE★

On the western edge of the Massif Central, the town is at a meeting point of three highways.

05 65 45 13 18. www.villefranche.com.

The ancient bastide of Villefranche, with its rooftops clustered around the foot of the massive tower of its church, lies at the bottom of a green valley surrounded by hills, at the confluence of the Aveyron and the Alzou.

Bastide★ – The old town on the north bank of the River Aveyron has kept many of the typical features of a planned urban foundation of the 13C. Its cobbled streets and narrow alleyways are laid out on a grid pattern with a central square **(Place Notre-Dame★)** with covered walks, dominated by a large metal figure of Christ.

The tall, severe houses are characteristic of the Rouergue area; a number of them have high open balconies with provision for drying grain. The President Raynal House (Maison du Président Raynal) with its 15C façade is particularly striking, and the Maison Dardennes has a fine galleried courtyard. The fortified church **(Église Notre-Dame★)** has splendid ironwork around the font.

CONQUES★★★

100km/63mi NNE of Albi.

This tiny medieval town has a splendid **hillside site★★** best seen from the Rocher du Bancarel (3km/1.8mi south).

Église St-Foy★★

Completely rebuilt between 1045 and 1060, this is one of the oldest Romanesque pilgrimage churches on the route to Santiago de Compostela. Its abbey had a chapel and hospice at Roncesvalles to serve the pilgrims as they made their way across the Pyrénées.

The **tympanum★★★** above the west door with its wealth of sculpture forms a striking contrast to the overall plainness of the west front. It shows how sculpture had evolved away from the static solemnity characteristic of Burgundy and Languedoc, towards the greater freshness and spontaneity evident in the capitals of the churches of the Auvergne. It may be that the weighing of souls, shown below Christ, is an expression of the idea – entirely new at the beginning of the 12C – of the personal nature of the Last Judgement. The **treasury★★★** is among the most important in Europe. Its most precious object is the reliquary statue of St Faith (Ste-Foy). The saint's relics had been brought to Conques at the end of the 9C, when they were venerated by prisoners and by the blind. The statue was put together and added to over a long period; some of its features probably go back as far as the last years of the Roman Empire and consist of reused elements of Roman date (face-mask, intaglio work in precious stones, jewels); the gold and engraved crystal are Merovingian and Carolingian (7–9C). At the close of the 10C the revered statue was renovated here at Conques and adorned with enamels, cabochons and other precious stones. Four more of the treasures are of exceptional significance: the initial "A" given to the abbey, it is said, by Charlemagne (a fragment of the Holy Cross decorated in the 11C with intaglio work and with chased and gilded silver); two portable altars, one, St Faith's, in alabaster and chased silver, the other, Abbot Begon's, from the beginning of the 12C, in porphyry and silver inlaid with niello; and the reliquary of Pope Pascal with filigree work and diadems, also from the early 12C.

CORDES-SUR-CIEL★★★

69m/43mi SW of Conques and 25km/15.5mi NW of Albi.
05 63 56 00 52. http://cordessurciel.eu.
Nestling at the top of the peak, Puech de Mordagne, Cordes has an attractive **site★★** overlooking the Cérou valley. The superb row of **Gothic houses★★** (13–14C) testify to this little town's wealthy. Notice the **Maison du Grand Fauconnier★** and the **Maison du Grand Veneur★**. For more than 50 years, artists and craftsmen have contributed to preserving and restoring local tradition.

ADDRESSES

STAY

Chambre d'hôte à la Ferme "Naussens" – 81150 Castanet. 05 63 55 22 56. 5 rooms. Closed Nov–mid Apr. A convivial farmer's welcome and Mediterranean-accented cuisine.

Chambre d'hôte au Bouquet de Roose – Jussens, 81150 Castelnau-de-Levis (5km/3mi from Albi by D 1). 05 63 45 59 75. 3 rooms. Closed 15 Dec–15 Jan. Peace and quiet within sight of the city centre.

Inter Hotel Albi le Cantepau – 9 r. Cantepau. 05 63 60 75 80. www.hotel-cantepau-albi.com. P. 33 rooms. Wicker furniture and subdued hues lend a colonial feel.

Grand Hôtel d'Orléans – pl. Stalingrad. 05 63 54 16 56. www.hotel-orleans-albi.com. 56 rooms. Simple hotel; swimming pool; traditional dishes.

Hôtel Mercure – 41 bis r. Porta. 05 63 47 66 66. www.mercure.com. P 56 rooms. Modern hotel in an 18C red-brick mill on the banks of the Tarn.

EAT

La Fourchette Adroite – 7 pl. de l' Archevêché. 05 63 49 77 81. Modern decor within ancient walls. Creative cuisine.

L'Épicurien– 42 pl. Jean Jaurès. 05 63 53 10 70. www.restaurantlepicurien.com. Closed Sun and Mon. The address to know in Albi. Comfortable and bright bistro.

Le Jardin des Quatre Saisons – rue de la Pompe. 05 63 60 77 76. www.le-jardin-des-quatre-saisons.com. Closed Sun eve and Mon. A reliable favourite. Good wine selection. Traditional cuisine.

Le Robinson – 142 r. Édouard-Branly. 05 63 46 15 69. Closed Nov–Feb, Mon and Tue. This 1920s dance hall has an exuberant charm. Simple food.

La Table du Sommelier – 20 r. Porta. 05 63 46 20 10. www.latabledusommelier.com. Closed Sun and Mon. Wine-focused bistro; refined cuisine; rustic dining room.

Lourdes★★★

and the Pyrénées

This little market town, sited at the meeting point of mountain and plain, became a pilgrimage place of world renown in the 19C.

- **Population:** 14 743.
- **Michelin Map:** 324 L 4
- **Info:** pl. Peyramale. 05 62 42 77 40. www.lourdes-infotourisme.com.
- **Location:** The town is in the central Pyrénées area, 20km/12.4mi S of the town of Tarbes.
- **Timing:** About an hour will suffice to explore the town centre.

A BIT OF HISTORY

On 11 February 1858, **Bernadette Soubirous** (1844–79), while preparing for her First Communion, is said to have had the first of the 18 visions that led to Lourdes becoming a centre of the cult of Mary, with the grotto and its surroundings attracting pilgrims, and with a special place reserved for the lame and the sick, who come in the hope of a miraculous cure.

The summit of the **Béout** mountain is littered with great erratic blocks that give some idea of the power of the Quaternary glaciers. The **view**★ is an object lesson in physical geography; it extends northwards from the exits of the Lavedan valleys over the morainic terraces through which the Pau torrent winds its sinuous course, to the glacial rock-bar on which the castle is sited, and finally to the great terminal moraine which forces the stream to make an abrupt turn to the west.

VISIT

Château Fort★

The fortress guarding the gateway to the Central Pyrénées, a fine example of medieval military architecture, was

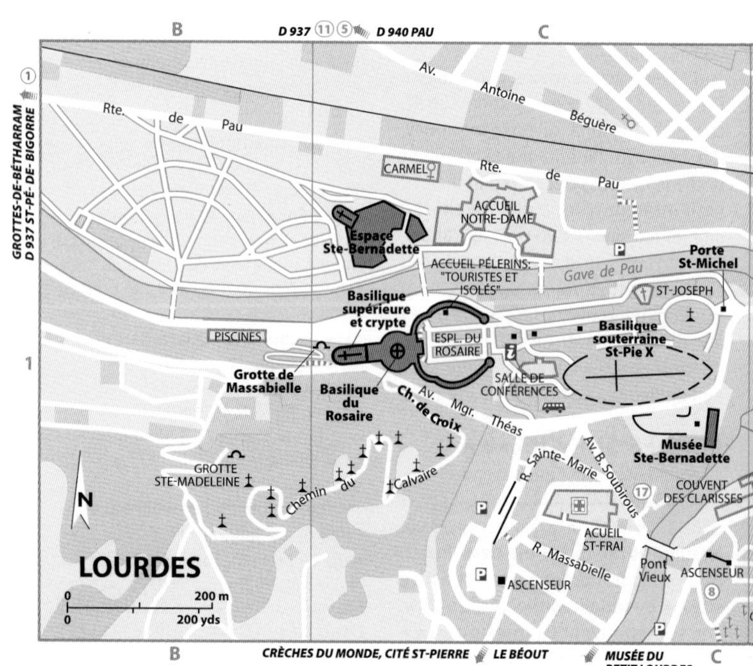

the state prison in the 17C and 18C. The Pointe du Cavalier (Rider's Bluff) panorama covers the valley of the Pau torrent and Pyrenean chain.

The **Pyrenean Folk Museum★** exhibits local costumes, musical instruments, fine ceramics, a Béarnaise kitchen, *surjougs* (harness bells on wooden frames) and displays on palaeontology and prehistory.

Grotto area

The site of the visions is the **Grotto of the Miracles**, where the most moving manifestations of faith take place.

In the summer months the great local, national and international pilgrimages are held here. The degree of spirituality is evident in the scale of the ceremonial and the devotion of the participants.

In neo-Byzantine style, the **Basilica of the Rosary** has two curving approach ramps that have fixed the image of the great building in the popular mind.

The **crypt** is a realm of devotion, contemplation and silence. The **Upper Basilica** is dedicated to the Immaculate Conception and has a vast nave of five bays.

EXCURSIONS

GROTTES DE BÉTHARRAM★★

Saint-Pé-de-Bigorre. 14km/8.7mi W.

This is one of the most popular natural attractions in the Pyrénées area. The caves comprise five separate galleries, one above the other. Notable features include the vast roofs of porous rock of the upper level, a striking column which is still growing and is a typical example of the evolution of stalagmites and stalactites; a collapsed pot-hole 80m deep; and a narrow fissure through which the river flows.

PIC DE PIBESTE★★★

2hr20min climb from Ouzous on D 202.

This peak – alt. 1 349m – provides one of the best viewpoints in the central Pyrénées.

TARBES

19km/12mi NE of Lourdes by N 21.

Tarbes has been the capital of Bigorre since the 9C. Tarbes is also an important trading centre and the traditional home of fairs and markets, as well as the

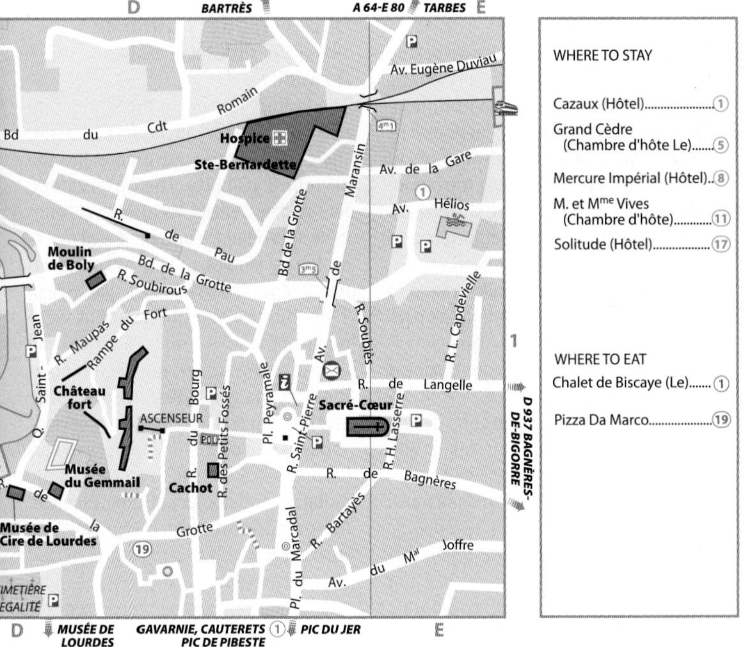

second-largest university centre in the Midi-Pyrénées region after Toulouse.

PIC DU JER★

59 av. Francis-Lagardère; the mountain summit is SE of Lourdes.

A **funicular railway** offers a **panorama** of the Pyrénées rising to 948m.

LE BÉOUT★

Alt. 791m. S of Lourdes. Take the footpath from the Cité-Secours-St-Pierre rescue centre.

The **view** of Lourdes, Pic du Jer, Pic de Montaigu, the Argelès valley, and Bat-Surguère and Castelloubon valleys is splendid. Continue along the ridge to the far end to admire the Pic du Midi de Bigorre, Lac de Lourdes, Pic Long in the Néouvielle massif, the Marboré Cylinder and Monte Perdido.

PARC NATIONAL DES PYRÉNÉES★★★

The park extends for more than 100km/60mi along the French border region from Vallée d'Aspe in the west to Vallée d'Aure in the east. Seven Maisons du Parc and several other seasonal outposts offer maps, brochures and tourist information (*see Useful Addresses, p591*).

The Pyrénées National Park was created in 1967 with the aim of preserving the beauty of the natural environment. The Parc National des Pyrénées and its peripheral area attract thousands of tourists every year. In winter, the mountains are a kingdom where skiers reign – children and adults, beginners and experts alike. In summer, both experienced and occasional walkers take to the mountain trails. Although the park can be toured by car, it can be a convoluted process, and so the countryside is better appreciated on foot.

Geology – The park itself is surrounded by a peripheral area of 206 000ha/795sq mi, including 86 municipalities in the Hautes-Pyrénées and Pyrénées-Atlantiques *départements*. The development programme in this area has concentrated on revitalising the pastoral economy of the mountain villages and improving tourist facilities. The park provides shelter for 4 000 izard, a local species of chamois, particularly in the valleys of Ossau and Cauterets, where they can be easily spotted, as well as more than 200 colonies of marmots. It is now very rare to catch sight of one of the few remaining brown bears, but it is not unusual to see royal eagles or huge bearded vultures in flight in a region still frequented by wood grouse, ptarmigan and Pyrénéan muskrats.

PIC DU MIDI DE BIGORRE★★★

The Pic is a landmark in the Gascon Pyrénées, rising SE of Lourdes.

Subject to change due to weather.

Don't miss the observatory for its **panorama★★★** views of the Pyrénées.

A vertiginous mountain road winds over the Tourmalet Pass (Col du Tourmalet). From the top (2 114m) a rough road leads to Les Laquets; from where there is access to the summit of the Pic du Midi de Bigorre. However, a cable car now operates from La Mongie (0825 20 28 77. www.picdumidi.com. €36 (child, under 12, €23)).

Observatoire et Institut de Physique du Globe du Pic du Midi

The factors favouring the siting here of an observatory include the height, the purity of the atmosphere and the all-round visibility. The observatory, founded by General Nansouty, was originally intended for botanical and meteorological studies, but the astronomical function was soon added. It was here in 1706 that the first observations were made of the solar corona during a total eclipse of the sun. At the beginning of the 20C, the great observatory dome and reflecting telescopes were added. Today, it is used for lunar mapping and research into the solar corona, cosmic radiation and nocturnal luminescence.

At the **summit**, which can only be reached by cable car, a glassed-in gallery and several terraces offer the most impressive panorama in the Pyrénées.

THE PRACTICAL PILGRIM

Tourist train – A small train runs from late Mar–early Nov; departures from place Mgr-Laurence every 20min 9am–noon and 1.30–6.30pm; 8–11pm. ♿ Accessible to persons of impaired mobility. **Pilgrimage** – Before 5am, only the path to the Calvary is open (Les Lacets entrance). At 9am, pilgrims group on the Esplanade du Rosaire to celebrate the Queen of Heaven (Easter to 31 Oct). Then the grotto opens. Thousands of votive candles flicker along the path and in front of the entrance and pilgrims seeking miracle cures immerse themselves in blue marble pools. At 4.30pm, the Holy Eucharist is borne from the Chapelle de l'Adoration to the Esplanade du Rosaire and the blessing of the sick begins.

USEFUL ADDRESSES

Parc National des Pyrénées – 59 rte de Pau, 65000 Tarbes. ✆05 62 44 36 60. www.parc-pyrenees.com.

Maisons du Parc – These visitor centres provide information on the flora and fauna, walking in the mountains, and present exhibits on the Pyrenean bear and the history of mountain exploration.

Maison du Parc (Vallée d'Aure) – 65170 St-Lary-Soulan – ✆05 62 39 40 91

Maison du Parc (Vallée de Luz-Gavarnie) – 65120 Luz-St-Sauveur – ✆05 62 92 38 38

Maison du Parc (Vallée de Luz-Gavarnie) – 65120 Gavarnie – ✆05 62 92 42 48

Maison du Parc (Vallée de Cauterets) – 65110 Cauterets – ✆05 62 92 52 56

Maison du Parc (Vallée d'Azun) – 65400 Arrens-Marsous – ✆05 62 97 43 13

Maison du Parc (Vallée d'Ossau) – 64440 Laruns. ✆05 59 05 41 59

Maison du Parc (Vallée d'Aspe) – 64880 Etsaut. ✆05 59 34 88 30.

Information points in summer: **Réserve Naturelle du Néouvielle** (Vallée d'Aure) and **Pont d'Espagne** (Vallée du Cauterets).

Leisure and Recreation

Activities in the Parc National des Pyrénées – There are more than 350km/210mi of marked footpaths. The GR 10, crosses the park in several places. Hunting, picking flowers, lighting campfires, and dogs are all prohibited. Fishing in streams and lakes is subject to ordinary regulations of the sport.

ADDRESSES

STAY

€ **Hôtel Cazaux** – 2 chemin Rochers. ✆05 62 94 22 65. www.hotel-cazaux-lourdes.federal-hotel.com. Closed Easter–mid Oct. 18 rooms. A small hotel near the market.

€€ **Chambre d'hôte M. and Mme Vives** – 28 rte de Bartrès, 65100 Loubajac , 6km/4mi NW of Lourdes on D 940 towards Pau. ✆05 62 94 44 17. P www.anousta.com. Closed 11 Nov–Feb holiday. 6 rooms. Restaurant €€. A farm with a stunning backdrop of the Pyrenees.

€€ **Le Grand Cèdre** – 6 r. du Barry, 65270 St-Pé-de-Bigorre. P ✆05 62 41 82 04. www.legrandcedre.fr. 5 rooms. This lovely 17C manor has 4 rooms decorated in art deco, Louis XV, Henri II, Louis-Philippe.

€€€ **Hôtel Mercure Impérial** – 3 av. du Paradis. ✆05 62 94 06 30. www.mercure.com. Closed 15 Dec–31 Jan. 93 rooms. This 1935 hotel renovated in its original art deco style, is near the cave.

€€€ **Hôtel Solitude** – 3 passage St-Louis. ✆0562 428 428. www.hotelsolitude.com. Closed 12 Apr–4 Nov. 288 rooms and 5 suites. This imposing hotel on the banks of the Gave de Pau has a small rooftop swimming pool.

EAT

€ **Pizza da Marco** – 47 r. de la Grotte. ✆05 62 94 03 59. Closed Sun and Mon. A pleasant place for crispy pizza and efficient service.

€€ **Le Chalet de Biscaye** – 26 rte du Lac. ✆05 62 94 12 26. Closed 5–21 Jan, Mon eve, and Tue. A family restaurant with a tasty traditional cuisine.

Lac de Gaube

WALKS IN THE PYRÉNÉES

Vallées des Cauterets

Lac de Gaube★★ – 1hr 30min round-trip by GR 10 rambling path, upstream from Pont d'Espagne. The **Gaube chairlift** (open Jul–Aug 9.15am–5.45pm; May–Jun and Sep 9.45am-5.30pm; closed Oct–mid-Dec. €8 round-trip (€7 for Puntas gondola and Gaube chairlift). 05 62 92 52 19) from Plateau de Clots can be taken most of the way, followed by a 20min walk to a bar-café by the lake. At the top of the chairlift, nature information panels describe forest flora and fauna and the izard, a local species of chamois. The austere yet beautiful site provides a view of the Vignemale massif and glaciers. A footpath along the river's west bank looks onto Pique Longue du Vignemale, 3 298m, one of the highest peaks in the Pyrenees.

Vallée du Marcadau★★ – 6.5km/4mi. 6hr round-trip on foot from the Pont d'Espagne parking area. Once a favourite route for crossing into Spain, this path has grass-covered shoulders and meandering mountain streams, alternating with glacial thresholds and twisted mountain pines. The Wallon refuge stands at an altitude of 1 866m, and beyond it is a cirque of pastureland scattered with lakes. Marcadau means market place, which this once was.

Vallée de Lutour★ – 6km/3.6mi. Take the Pont d'Espagne road as far as a series of hairpin bends. Just before the Le Bois thermal establishment, turn sharply left onto the narrow, steep forest road to La Fruitière. The track offers glimpses of the upper Lutour falls, then emerges into peaceful pastureland.

VALLÉE DE GAVARNIE

Cirque de Gavarnie★★★ – 3hr on foot there and back. At the end of the village, take the unsurfaced path then follow the true left bank of the *gave* (mountain stream). Cross an old stone bridge and walk up through the woods, with the river now to your right. The last part of the walk climbs through mixed vegetation to the first rocky folds marking the approach of the Cirque itself. Then the Cirque de Gavarnie comes into view. Gazing at its majesty of sheer walls and tiered snow platforms, Victor Hugo exclaimed: "It is both a mountain and a rampart; it is the most mysterious of structures by the most mysterious of architects; it is Nature's Colosseum – it is Gavarnie!"

Cirque de Gavarnie
© Doug Pearson/age fotostock

Tours on horseback end at the Hôtel du Cirque, but it is possible to continue, on foot (1hr30min there and back), to the Grande Cascade. This impressive waterfall is fed by meltwater from the frozen lake on Monte Perdido on the Spanish side of the frontier. The cascade drops 422m into the void.

Brèche de Roland (Roland's Gap) – 5hr on foot there and back – for experienced and equipped mountain walkers only: beware of the névés Sep–early Jul. Follow the prominent path starting E of Port de Boucharro. The path follows the Haute Route des Pyrénées and fords a waterfall at the foot of the Taillon glacier. From the pass admire the Grande Cascade of the Cirque de Gavarnie. Beyond the Sarradets refuge, the climb to the gap is long and more difficult due to snow and ***névés***. The breach named after the gallant 8C knight Rolland offers a **view** of Monte Perdido and the barren Spanish side.

Massif de Néouvielle★★★

The Massif de Néouvielle is the ideal area for family walks as well as for more demanding treks in the mountains. There are numerous marked itineraries, and appropriate topoguides are on sale in local shops or in the **Maison du Parc** in Saint-Lary-Soulan (05 62 39 40 91); information is available from the **Bureau des Guides** in Saint-Lary-Soulan (05 62 40 02 58 or 05 62 39 41 97).

Col (or hourquette) d'Aubert★★ – 3hr on foot to the pass. From the Lac d'Aubert parking area, follow the marked path that skirts the lake by the NE. Alt. 2 498m. This pass links the depression cradling the Aubert and Aumar lakes with the desolate Escoubous coomb on the slopes towards Barèges. There is a remarkable **view★★** of the tiered lakes at the foot of Pic de Néouvielle.

Massif de Néouvielle viewed from the Lac d'Aumar
© B. Mollaret/Photononstop

Provence

» **Region map p596-597**
Marseille p598
Aix-en-Provence p612
Arles p616
Les Baux-de-Provence p622
Avignon p624
Orange p630

Introduction

The name Provence evokes an image of a magical land in the Midi, or south, of France where the sun always shines and Mediterranean influences are supreme: from the extensive remains of six centuries of Roman occupation to the traditional triumvirate of wheat, vine and olive, alternating with the remnants of the natural forest and the infertile but wonderfully aromatic *garrigues* (arid scrubland). Among the fertile Provençal plains stand the *mas*, shallow-roofed pantiled farmsteads protected from the fierce sun by stone walls with few window openings. Crops and buildings are shielded from the effects of the mistral, the strong regional wind, by serried ranks of cypresses.

Geography – Provence is synonymous with serene landscapes, from sandy beaches to plains of arable land. These plains are flanked by limestone hills running east–west, including the Alpilles, the rugged Luberon range and the Vaucluse plateau with its chasms, gorges and great resurgent spring at Fontaine de Vaucluse.The River Rhône brings down 20 million m^3 of sand, gravel and silt annually, creating the huge delta of the Camargue. Further north the gorges of the Ardèche form one of the most impressive natural sights in France.

History – Provence has been occupied from the earliest times. From the 8C BCE the Celts settled here, but were eventually subdued by the Romans who founded a settlement at Aix in 122 BCE. The collapse of the Roman Empire led to incursions by Visigoths and later by the Franks. Provence was annexed by the Holy Roman Empire in 1032, and the region was incorporated into France in 1486, although the Parliament of Aix remained semi-independent until 1771.

Highlights

1. A walk around the ancient port of **Marseille** (p599)
2. Wetland plain of the Rhône Delta: **La Camargue** (p619)
3. Palace built for the popes in **Avignon**: Palais des Papes (p624)
4. Roman Aqueduct and road bridge: **Le Pont du Gard** (p626)
5. Natural rock arch created by the river: **Pont d'Arc** (p627)

Economy – In recent years Provence has seen much industrial expansion, and increasing tourism has been facilitated by the construction of ***autoroutes*** and high-speed train lines. The climate is conducive to the production of wine, olive oil, fruit and vegetables.

Le Pont du Gard

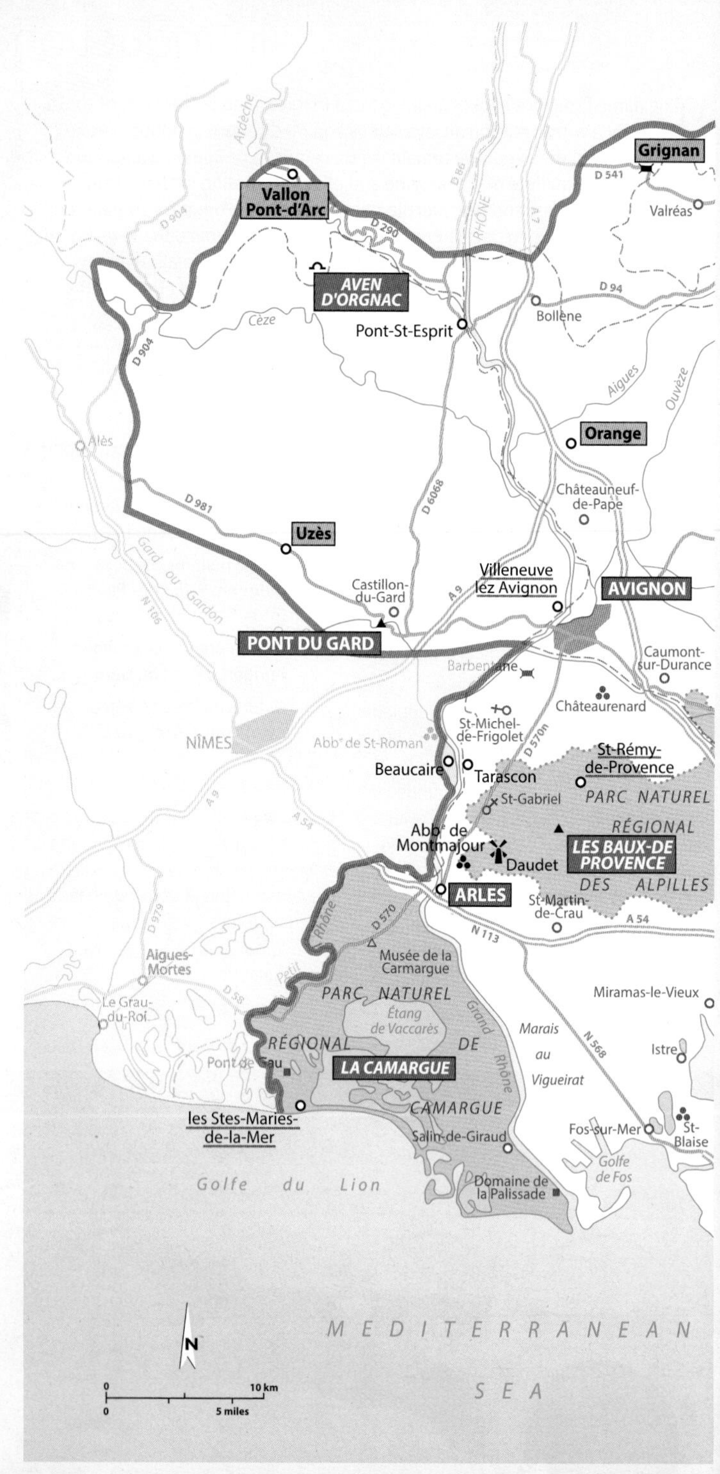

Grignan
Vallon Pont-d'Arc
AVEN D'ORGNAC
Valréas
Bollène
Pont-St-Esprit
Orange
Châteauneuf-de-Pape
Uzès
Castillon-du-Gard
Villeneuve lez Avignon
AVIGNON
PONT DU GARD
Barbentane
Caumont-sur-Durance
Châteaurenard
St-Michel-de-Frigolet
NÎMES
Abbe de St-Roman
St-Rémy-de-Provence
Beaucaire
Tarascon
St-Gabriel
PARC NATUREL RÉGIONAL DES ALPILLES
Abbe de Montmajour
LES BAUX-DE PROVENCE
Daudet
ARLES
St-Martin-de-Crau
Aigues-Mortes
Musée de la Carmargue
Miramas-le-Vieux
Le Grau-du-Roi
PARC NATUREL RÉGIONAL DE CAMARGUE
Étang de Vaccarès
Marais au Vigueirat
Istre
Pont de Gau
LA CAMARGUE
les Stes-Maries-de-la-Mer
Salin-de-Giraud
Fos-sur-Mer
St-Blaise
Golfe de Fos
Golfe du Lion
Domaine de la Palissade
MEDITERRANEAN SEA
N
0 10 km
0 5 miles

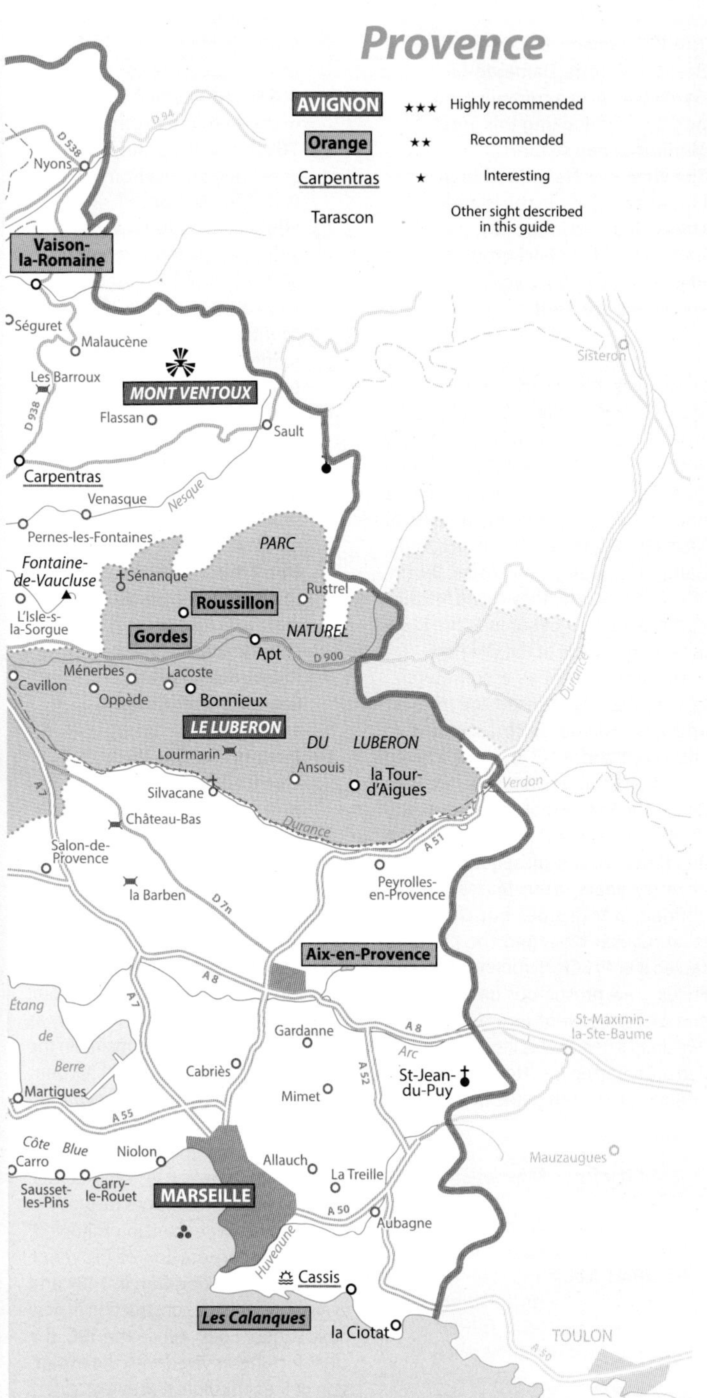
Provence
AVIGNON
★★★ Highly recommended
Orange
★★ Recommended
Carpentras
★ Interesting
Tarascon
Other sight described in this guide
Nyons
D 538
D 94
Vaison-la-Romaine
Séguret
Malaucène
Les Barroux
MONT VENTOUX
D 938
Flassan
Sault
Sisteron
Carpentras
Venasque
Nesque
Pernes-les-Fontaines
PARC
Fontaine-de-Vaucluse
Sénanque
Rustrel
Roussillon
L'Isle-s-la-Sorgue
Gordes
NATUREL
Apt
D 900
Durance
Cavillon
Ménerbes
Lacoste
Oppède
Bonnieux
LE LUBERON
DU LUBERON
Lourmarin
Ansouis
la Tour-d'Aigues
Verdon
A 7
Silvacane
Château-Bas
Durance
A 51
Salon-de-Provence
Peyrolles-en-Provence
la Barben
D 7n
Aix-en-Provence
A 8
Étang de Berre
A 7
Gardanne
A 8
St-Maximin-la-Ste-Baume
Arc
Cabriès
A 52
St-Jean-du-Puy
Martigues
Mimet
A 55
Côte Blue
Niolon
Carro
Allauch
La Treille
Mauzaugues
Sausset-les-Pins
Carry-le-Rouet
MARSEILLE
A 50
Aubagne
Huveaune
Cassis
Les Calanques
la Ciotat
TOULON
A 50

Marseille★★★

The 19C Romano-Byzantine Basilica of Notre-Dame-de-la-Garde stands in a commanding position overlooking this great Mediterranean seaport. The view★★★ from the church is immense, taking in the islands standing guard in the bay, the harbour, and the background of limestone hills as well as the sprawling city itself.

- **Population:** 850 726.
- **Michelin Map:** 340 H 6
- **Info:** 11 La Canabière. 0826 500 500 (€0.15/min). www.marseille-tourisme.com.
- **TGV:** Marseille St Char is 3hrs 15mins direct from Paris Gare de Lyon.
- **Flights:** Marseille Provence airport (www.mp.aeroport.fr. 04 42 14 14 14) is used by 29 airlines, linking 27 countries. Shuttle service to the city centre (25 min) operates every 15 minutes.
- **Location:** On the Mediterranean coast, 32km/20mi S of Aix-en-Provence.
- **Parking:** There are several underground car parks around town.
- **Don't miss:** Bouillabaisse: this is arguably the best place in France to enjoy this popular and filling dish.
- **Kids:** Hook up to the Count of Monte Cristo at Château d'If.
- **Timing:** From the Vieux Port, it takes about 2hr to walk along the Canebière. Afterwards, allow 1hr for the old Le Panier district.

A BIT OF HISTORY

Marseille began life as a trading post set up by Greeks from Asia Minor around 600 BCE. Its inhabitants soon established other commercial bases both in the interior and on the coast, at Nice, Antibes, the Lérins Islands, Agde, Glanum (St-Rémy) and Arles. By the 3C–2C BCE the city they called Massilia covered an area of some 50ha/123.5 acres to the north of the Old Port.

A cultural as well as a commercial centre, the city aroused the interest and envy of the Celto-Ligurians of Entremont, and in 123 BC Massilia found it prudent to conclude an alliance with Rome. The Senate took the opportunity to begin its programme of expansion into Provence and subsequently Gaul. Seventy years later, Marseille was obliged to take sides but chose the loser. Caesar besieged the city and sacked it in 49 BCE. Narbonne, Arles and Fréjus grew prosperous on the spoils, and Marseille went into decline, yet remained a free city. Its life as a port carried on, based on the "Horn" (corne), the original basin sited to the northeast of today's Old Port, which itself came more and more into use as an outer harbour. Nevertheless, the decline of the city as a whole made it difficult to maintain the installations, and the original harbour gradually silted up, finally becoming completely blocked in the 11C.

The Crusades, together with the growth of the rivalry between Pisa and Genoa, led to a revival of the city's fortunes in the 12C. Further expansion followed, with the incorporation of Provence into the French kingdom in 1481 and even more with the construction of new quays under Louis XIII. In the 19C, the city's fortunes revived with the expansion of French colonial activity.

City Pass Marseille

This is an all-inclusive pass giving free access to **museums, public transport, a boat trip** to the Château d'If and even the little tourist train. €24/1 day–€39 for 3 days. Enquire at the tourist office.

GETTING AROUND TOWN

METRO–THE RTM – This is the most convenient mode of transport; the two lines operate from 5am–1am. ✆04 91 36 58 11. www.rtm.fr. **Tickets** are valid for a single trip (€1.50), 1 day (carte journée: €5.20 or for several journeys. In addition, there are no fewer than 80 bus and 2 tramway lines. Bus timetables and network maps are available at ticket offices. ✆04 91 91 92 10. www.rtm.fr.

FERRY BOAT – Trips from one side of the Vieux Port to the other (saving you about 800 paces!): place aux Huiles to the town hall. Journeys daily 9am–7pm. No charge.

WALKING TOURS

Marseille map II, p602.

1 OLD PORT★★

The Phocaeans landed in this creek in 600 BCE. It was here that, until the 19C, all Marseille's maritime life was concentrated. The quays were constructed under Louis XII and Louis XIII. In the 19C, the depth of two fathoms was found to be insufficient for steamships of large tonnage and new docks were built.

- **Hôtel de Ville** – A town hall has existed on this site since the 13C. The present building is Provençal Baroque, middle-17C.
- **Musée des Docks Romains★** – During reconstruction work in 1947 the remains of some commercial Roman warehouses used for storing dolia (large earthenware jars) were uncovered, dating from the 1C to the 3C. The museum contains objects found on the site, which date from the Greek period to the Middle Ages.
- **Hôtel de Cabre** – Built in 1535, this is one of the oldest houses in the city, in Gothic style.
- **Le Panier★** – Built on the Moulins hill on the site of ancient Massalia, the Panier district is all that remains of old Marseille since the Liberation. This charming and highly picturesque quarter of Marseille can be seen as a melting pot where Naples, Catalonia and the Mediterranean coast mingle with the French West Indies, Vietnam and the Comoro Islands to produce scenes which delight the senses: washing hangs from windows, the air is full of the scents of basil and ratatouille, and bursts of Marseille French, with its inimitable turns of phrase, can be heard everywhere. In recent years, trendy restaurants, art galleries and boutiques have begun to open in Le Panier, giving it a dynamic new edge.
- **Centre de la Vieille Charité★★** – This well-restored former hospice is a fine architectural unit built from 1671 to 1749, based on the plans of Pierre and Jean Puget.

  The rich and varied collection, bringing together some 900 artefacts from the Near East, Greece, Etruria and Rome, makes this one of the few provincial museums able to offer an almost complete picture of ancient Mediterranean civilisations. The building houses the Musée d'Archéologie Méditerranéenne, the museum of African, Oceanic and native American art (MAAOA), a poetry centre and a variety of exhibitions. At the time of printing, it houses the Musée des Beaux-Arts collection.
- **Cathédrale de la Major** – A huge and sumptuous construction started in 1852 in Roman-Byzantine style. It was originally built at the instigation of the future Napoléon III, who wished to reconcile the Church and the people of Marseille in one fell swoop.
- **Ancienne Cathédrale de la Major★** – A fine example of mid-11C Romanesque architecture.
- **Belvédère St-Laurent** – A fine **view★**.
- **Fort Saint-Jean-MuCEM** – This national museum is dedicated to the cultures of Europe and the Mediter-

WHERE TO STAY

Chambre d'hôte Villa Marie-Jeanne 7

Chambre d'hôte Villa Monticelli 10

Hôtel Ibis Euroméditerranée 19

Hôtel Le Corbusier 25

Hôtel Le Richelieu 28

Hôtel Pullman Palm Beach 30

WHERE TO EAT

Chez Fonfon 1

Cyprien 10

L'Épuisette 13

L'Hippocampe 20

Le Petit Nice 36

Les Akolytes 38

Les Grandes Tables 41

Péron 45

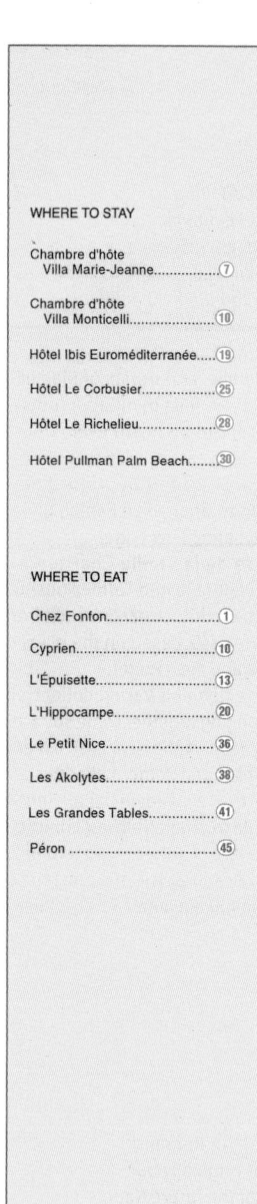

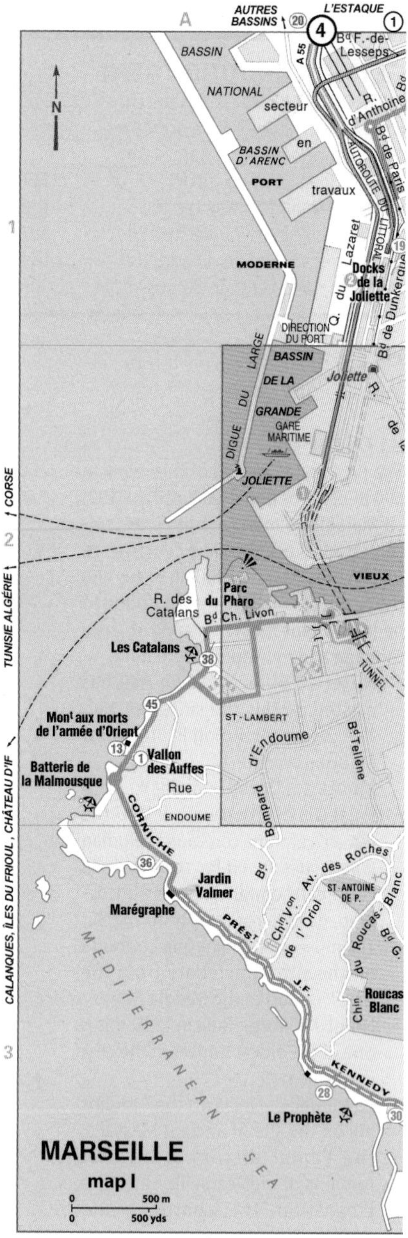

ranean, bringing together the collections of the Musée des Arts et Traditions Populaires and of the European section of the Musée de l'Homme.

- **Place de Lenche** – This lively square whose façades are embellished with wrought-iron balconies is located on the presumed site of the agora of the Greek town.

2 RIVE NEUVE

- **Quai de Rive-Neuve** – It was only relatively recently that the shallows that inconvenienced this part of the

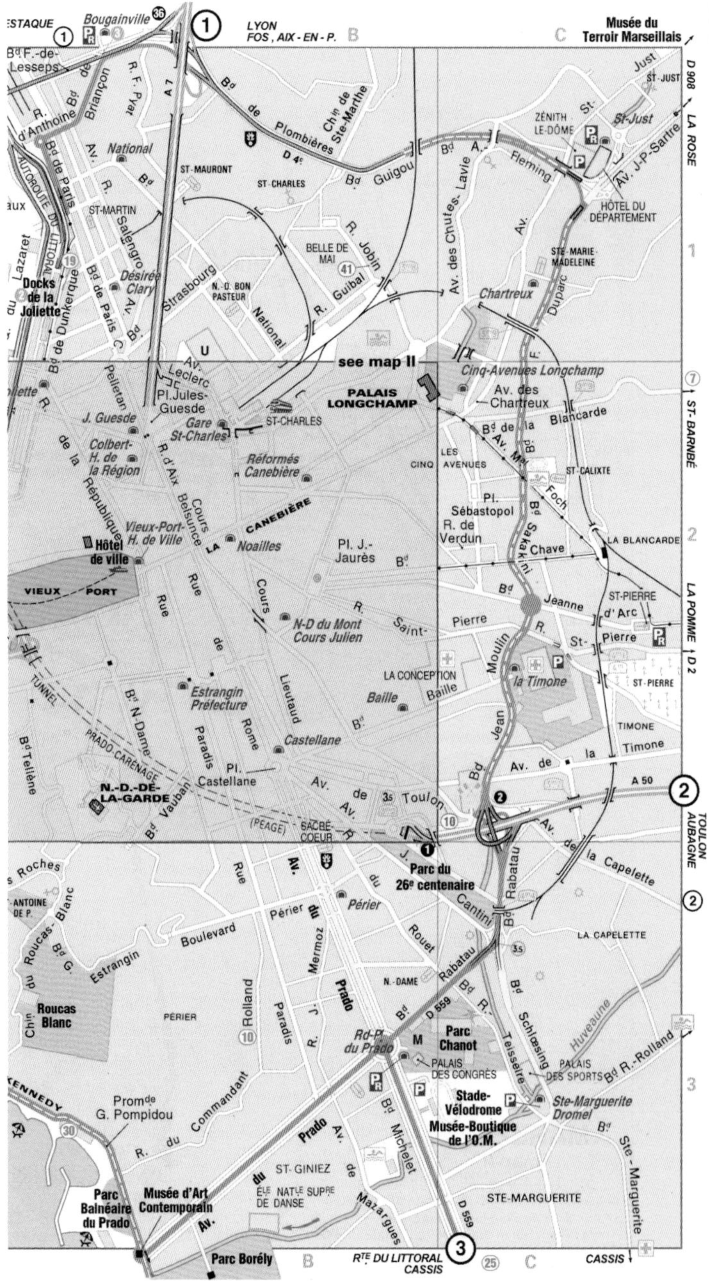

port were dredged and the quayside improved. Surrounded by beautiful buildings in Neoclassical style, the quai de Rive-Neuve is livelier now than its opposite bank.

- **Quartier des Arcenaulx** – In the Italian-style cours Honoré-d'Estienne-d'Orves are several cafés and restaurants, as well as the remains of the Arsenal's buildings, at no 23 and no 25.
- **Carré Thiars** – This network of streets around the pleasant 18C square of the same name devel-

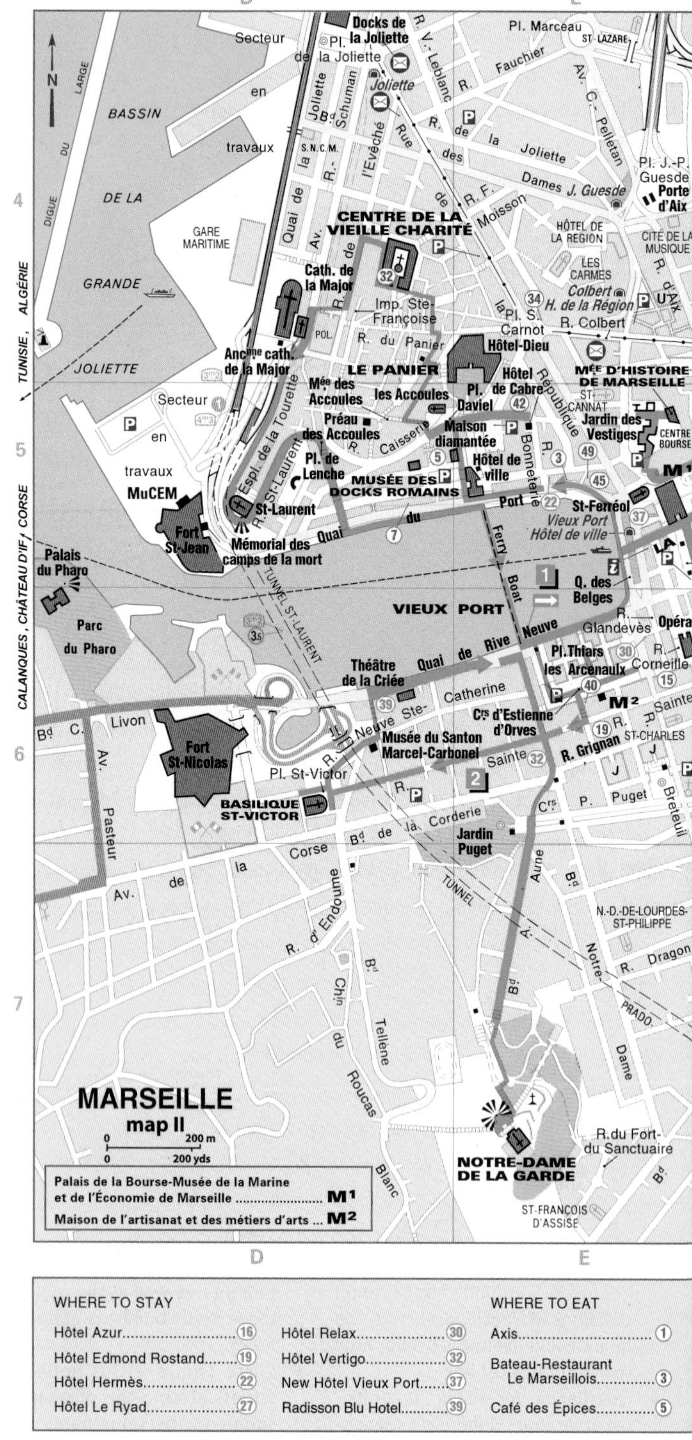

WHERE TO STAY			
Hôtel Azur	16	Hôtel Relax	30
Hôtel Edmond Rostand	19	Hôtel Vertigo	32
Hôtel Hermès	22	New Hôtel Vieux Port	37
Hôtel Le Ryad	27	Radisson Blu Hotel	39

WHERE TO EAT	
Axis	1
Bateau-Restaurant Le Marseillois	3
Café des Épices	5

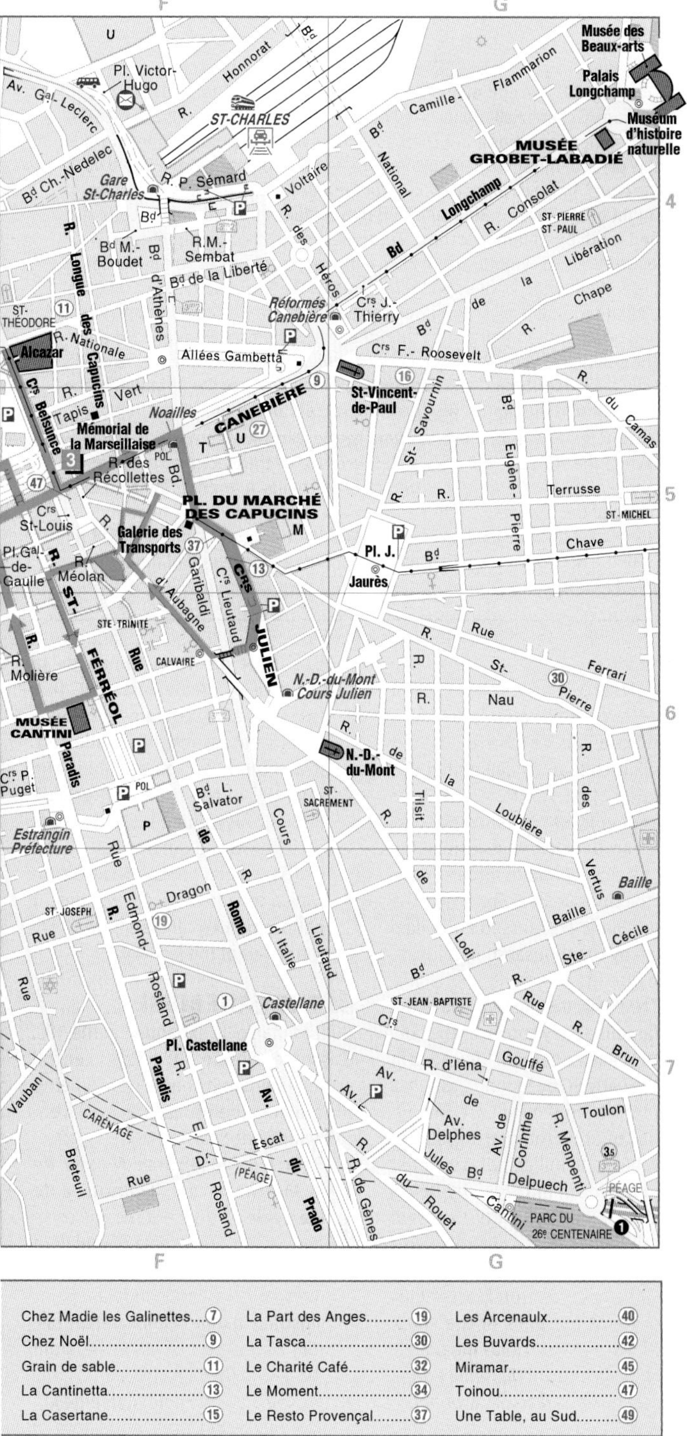

Chez Madie les Galinettes....(7)	La Part des Anges.........(19)	Les Arcenaulx...............(40)
Chez Noël.........................(9)	La Tasca.......................(30)	Les Buvards...................(42)
Grain de sable..................(11)	Le Charité Café.............(32)	Miramar.........................(45)
La Cantinetta....................(13)	Le Moment.....................(34)	Toinou...........................(47)
La Casertane.....................(15)	Le Resto Provençal........(37)	Une Table, au Sud.........(49)

La Marseillaise

On 20 April 1792, Revolutionary France declared war against Austria. In Strasbourg, General Kellerman asked Claude Joseph Rouget de l'Isle, a captain in the engineering corps and a composer-songwriter in his spare time, to write a "new piece of music to mark the departure of the volunteers"; the *Chant de guerre pour l'Armée du Rhin (War Song for the Rhine Army)* was written during the night of 25–26 April. Soon adopted by a battalion from Rhône-et-Loire and carried south by commercial travellers, the Chant reached Montpellier on 17 June. On 20 June, a young patriot from Montpellier on assignment in Marseille, François Mineur, sang it at a banquet offered by the Marseille Jacobin club, located at r. Thubaneau. Enthusiasm was such that the words of the song were passed on to 500 national guards from Marseille, who had been called to arms for the defence of Paris. Renamed *Chant de guerre aux armées des Frontières (War song for the Border Armies)*, the anthem was sung at each of the 28 stages of the journey towards the capital, with growing success and virtuosity.

On 30 July, the impassioned verses sung by the warm southern voices, ringing out across the St-Antoine district, was referred to by the electrified crowd as the *Chant des Marseillais* (Song of the people of Marseille). A few days later, on the storming of the Tuileries, the new anthem was given its definitive name. *La Marseillaise* became the French national anthem on 26 Messidor an III (14 July 1795) of the Republican calendar, and again, after a long period of obscurity, on 14 July 1879.

oped on the site of the old naval yard. Now it is a lively area full of restaurants, bars and nightclubs.

- **Basilique Saint-Victor★** – It is in this church that Marseille's famous religious festival, the Fête de la Chandeleur, has been celebrated on 2 February every year since the Middle Ages. Candles, green in colour to symbolise the virginity of the Virgin Mary, are blessed and taken home by the thousands of pilgrims who attend.

  The basilica is the last relic of the famous abbey known as the "key to Marseille harbour", founded in the early 5C by St John Cassian, a monk from the Far East, in honour of St Victor, patron saint of sailors and millers, who suffered martyrdom in the 3C by being slowly ground between two millstones. Make sure you visit the **crypt★★**.
- **Musée du Santon Marcel-Carbonel** – At the back of the shop, this small museum holds the private collection of one of Marseille's great santon makers, Marcel Carbonel.
- **Basilique de Notre-Dame de la Garde★★** – Now restored, this famous basilica gleams resplendently in the bright Marseille sun. It was built by Espérandieu in the mid-19C in the then fashionable Romano-Byzantine style. It stands on a limestone outcrop (alt 162m) on the site of a 13C chapel also dedicated to Our Lady. A magnificent **panorama★★★** can be enjoyed from the parvis of the basilica.

3 THE CANEBIÈRE

Built as Marseille expanded in the 17C, this wide avenue – the city's central artery – derives its name from a hemp rope factory (hemp: canèbe in Provençal) which once existed here.

- **Palais de la Bourse-Musée de la Marine et de l'Économie de Marseille** – This maritime and commercial museum displays models of sailboats and steamships; paintings, watercolours, engravings and plans illustrate marine history and the history of the port of Marseille, from the 17C to the present.
- **Musée d'Histoire de Marseille★** – This museum traces the history of

Marseille in its Provençal context from prehistoric to Gallo-Roman times through archaeological finds, documents and models.

- **Cours Julien** – Until 1972 this was the Marseille wholesale market for fruit and vegetables. It has now been renovated and here you will find specialist restaurants, antique shops, fashion boutiques, galleries and so on. The clubs and cafés come to life as night falls.
- **Place du marché des Capucins**, opposite Noailles metro station, is a hub for local stall holders or partisanes. The air rings with their loud cries, urging passers-by to purchase their lemons and beans. In the narrow **rue Longue-des-Capucins** the atmosphere is part souk, part flea market. With a fascinating mix of traders, from African countries especially, selling their foodstuffs here, the air is full of different scents: spices mingled with freshly baked flatbreads, coffee, dates, pitted or marinated olives, anchovies, herbs and dried fruit.
- **Rue des Halles-Charles-Delacroix** (a former fish market, now demolished), lined with grocery stores and shops selling exotic wares, leads to **rue Vacon**, where Provençal fabrics are displayed, as well as to "**Saint-Fé**", the rue St-Ferréol, which is the main pedestrian-only shopping street of the city.
- **Musée Cantini★** – This museum specialises in 20C art after World War II until 1960, with particular attention to Fauvist, early Cubist, Expressionist and Abstract art.

LONGCHAMP DISTRICT

Musée Grobet-Labadié★ – The bourgeois interior of this town house has been preserved.

Palais Longchamp – This remarkable building with its monumental fountains was constructed by the Nîmes architect Henri Espérandieu from 1862 to 1869, to celebrate the completion of the Durance to Marseille canal. There is a **Musée des Beaux-Arts** in the left wing and a **Musée d'Histoire Naturelle★** in the right wing.

LA CORNICHE★★

You can drive up the Corniche but it is almost impossible to find a parking place. The 83 bus goes from the Vieux Port as far as the Prado beach, and from there the 19 bus goes on to the Pointe-Rouge beach.

Parc du Pharo – This park is situated on a promontory above the entrance to the Vieux Port. Enjoy the view from the terrace near the Pharo palace (www.palaisdupharo.marseille.fr), built for Napoléon III.

Corniche Président-J.-F.-Kennedy★★ – This Corniche runs for nearly 5km/3mi – almost entirely along the seafront. Be sure to have a look at the elegant villas built by wealthy families at the end of the 19C.

Vallon des Auffes – This tiny fishing port, crowded with traditional boats and ringed with small fishermen's cottages, seems worlds away from city life.

Jardin Valmer – The most elegant public garden in the city.Crowned by the Villa Valmer, a sumptuous neo-Renaissance-style bastide built in 1865 by a wealthy industrialist (*a guided tour can be arranged through the tourist office*), the park offers dramatic views of the Mediterranean from the hills of Marseilleveyre in the south to the pointe de Carry in the north. In the heat of the summer you will especially appreciate the dense shade.

Promenade de la Plage – The corniche's southern extension, running alongside the plages Gaston-Defferre. The Pointe Rouge is an important sailing centre.

Château et Parc Borély – Built between 1767 and 1778 by the Borély, a family of wealthy merchants, the château houses the town's Museum of Decorative Arts. The park, with its network of paths, extends to the east

Musée de la Faïence★ – In the Château Pastré, this museum is devoted to the art of ceramics, from the early Neolithic era up to the present day.

EXCURSIONS

ÎLES DU FRIOUL

Sea crossing: leaves from quai des Belges, Vieux Port. €10.50 return to If or Frioul, and €15.60 to both. ✆04 96 11 03 50. www.frioul-if-express.com.

Château d'If★★ – Alexandre Dumas (1802–70), the popular 19C French author of *The Three Musketeers*, gave this castle literary fame by imprisoning three of his heroes here: the Man in the Iron Mask, the Count of Monte Cristo and Abbé Faria. Built rapidly from 1524 to 1528, Château d'If was an outpost destined to protect the port of Marseille. After falling into disuse, it became a state prison where Huguenots and various political prisoners were held; their cells can be visited.

MASSIF DES CALANQUES★★

No access either on foot or by car to the *calanques* between 1 July and the second Sunday in September, or on days when the mistral is blowing fiercely. Even when access to the calanques is permitted, restrictions may apply in bad weather conditions, particularly on weekends. Some paths are very dangerous for children.

The Massif des Calanques, with Mont Puget (565m) its highest peak, stretches almost 20km/12.4mi between Marseille and Cassis. With its solid limestone, dazzling whiteness, and weather-worn pinnacles, it has long attracted nature lovers for its wild beauty. However, its unique character and exceptional charm stem above all from its deep and narrow indentations, the famous *calanques*, which have been chiselled out along its coastline, creating a majestic union of sea, sky and rocks. There are no direct approach roads by car to the *calanques* with the exception of the less attractive coves of Goudes, Callelongue and Port-Miou.

The only way to reach the others is on foot. Footpaths are often steep and rocky: it is advisable to get yourself the IGN map *Les Calanques de Marseille à Cassis (www.ign.fr)*. Make sure you are equipped with walking boots; carry water with you as there is none available.

Calanque d'En-Vau

Leave Marseille by the promenade de la Plage.

Goudes

An old fishing village, nestled amid grandiose rocky scenery. There is no beach, but there are a number of small local restaurants frequented by the local Marseillais.Lunch in the sun here is a delight.

Continue as far as Callelongue where the tarmac road ends.

Callelongue

(45min). From there you can get to the calanque of Marseilleveyre and its little pebble beach.

This tiny cove has several *cabanons* (cabins) and provides shelter for a small flotilla of boats.

Sormiou★

(45min) Leave Marseille on either ave de Hambourg or chemin de Sormiou. Park in the car park at the entrance to the tarmac road blocked off to vehicles. Walk down to the calanque.

Considered by the local Marseillais population to be the best of all the *calanques*, there are numerous *cabanons*, a small port, a beach, and several fish restaurants. Sormiou is separated from Morgiou by the **Cap Morgiou**, a viewpoint affording magnificent views of both *calanques* and the eastern side of the massif.

Morgiou★★

(2hr) From Marseille take the same route initially as for Sormiou; turn left and follow the "calanque Morgiou" signs (you will pass the famous prison, Les Baumettes). Park near the "sens interdit" (no entry) sign; continue on foot along the paved road.

A wild setting with tiny creeks for swimming, crystal-clear water, *cabanons* clustered at the far end of the valley, restaurant, small port. Not to be missed!

Sugiton★★

(1hr30min) From Marseille take bd Michelet as far as Luminy; park in the car park near the École d'Art et d'Architecture and continue on foot along the forest track.

A small *calanque* with turquoise water, it is well sheltered by its surrounding high cliffs. It is popular with naturists.

En-Vau★★

(2hr 30min) Access via Col de la Gardiole (Route Gaston-Rebuffat beginning opposite the Carpiagne military camp); leave your car in the Gardiole car park.

(2hr) Or, from Cassis, walk past Port-Miou and Port-Pin calanques.

The best known of all the *calanques* with its white cliffs, emerald water and stony beach. It is encircled by a forest of rock pinnacles overlooked by the "Doigt de Dieu" (Finger of God).

Port-Pin★

Access via Col de la Gardiole (same directions as En-Vau – 3hr) or Cassis (skirting Port-Miou calanque).

A spacious *calanque* with a sandy beach surrounded by pine trees.

Cassis

25km/15.5mi E of Marseille. Quai des Moulins, Cassis. 08 92 25 98 92. www.cassis.fr. Your best bet is to get the bus from Marseille (40min).

Cassis, a bustling fishing port, lies in an attractive **setting★** at the end of a bay between the Puget heights and Cap Canaille. It is a popular summer resort with three beaches. Boat trips to the *calanques* are a popular excursion.

DRIVING TOUR

Corniche des Crêtes★★

From Cassis to La Ciotat 19km/12mi.

The stretch of coast road between Cassis and La Ciotat skirts the crests of the Canaille, a limestone range that rises from the sea in white cliffs, some of the tallest in France.

Leave Cassis in an easterly direction, on the road to Toulon (D 559), and during the ascent take a signposted road to the right. At Pas de la Colle, turn left.

Mont de la Saoupe

The **panorama★★** from the television mast at the top includes Cassis, the **Île de Riou** and Chaîne St-Cyr to the west, the Chaîne de l'Étoile and Massif de la Ste-Baume to the north, La Ciotat and Cap de Sicié to the southeast.

Return to Pas de la Colle and continue uphill.

Cap Canaille★★★

From the guard rail on the cape there is an outstanding **view★★★** of the cliff face, Massif de Puget and the *calanques* and Massif de Marseilleveyre.

Beyond Grande Tête, turn right towards the coastguard station.

From the **Coastguard station (semaphore)** the **view★★★** embraces La Ciotat, Cap Sicié and Cap Canaille (telescope).

Return to the crest road; bear right for La Ciotat.

The descent into town passes quarries, pinewoods, and the "pont naturel", a natural limestone arch.

ADDRESSES

STAY

€ **Hotel Vertigo** – 2 r. des Petites-Maries. Ⓜ Gare-St-Charles. ☎ 04 91 91 07 11. www.hotelvertigo.fr. 18 rooms. Situated in the historic Belsunce neighbourhood, this simple place offers various types of accommodation from hostel-style sharing to twin or double rooms. Nicely renovated.

€ **Hôtel Relax** – 4 r. Corneille. Ⓜ Vieux Port. ☎ 04 91 33 15 87. www.hotelrelax.fr. 21 rooms. Situated near Marseille's shopping area and a 2-minute walk from Vieux Port, the location is ideal. Rooms are small but well kept and air-conditioned.

€ **Hotel Marseille Richelieu** – 52 Corniche du Président Kennedy. ☎ 04 91 35 78 78. www.hotel-marseille-richelieu.com. P. 19 rooms and 2 suites. Charming hotel on the Corniche near the Catalans beach. Seven types of rooms and prices with or without views (and bathrooms!).

€ **Hôtel Azur** – 24 cour Franklin Roosevelt. Ⓜ Réformés. ☎ 04 91 42 74 38. www.azur-hotel.fr. 18 rooms. Restaurant €€. Very near the Canabière, this hotel is in typical Provençal style. Rooms are spread across four floors; some open on to the garden, where you can have breakfast.

€€ **Hôtel Hermès** – 25 r. Bonneterie. Ⓜ Vieux Port. ☎ 04 96 11 63 63. www.hotelmarseille.com/hermes. 29 rooms. Unpretentious, centrally located hotel with small, well-kept rooms; those on the fifth floor have a terrace overlooking the quayside. Panoramic rooftop sundeck.

€€ **Hôtel Edmond Rostand** – 31 r. du Dragon. Ⓜ Castellane. ☎ 04 91 37 74 95. www.hoteledmondrostand.com. 15 rooms. Simple contemporary rooms in a quiet neighbourhood.

€€ **Hôtel Ibis Euroméditerranée** – 25 bd de Dunkerque. ☎ 04 91 99 25 20. www.ibis.com. 192 rooms. Straightforward rooms, but air-conditioned and comfortable. A good base to explore the area between Joliette docks and rue de la République.

€€ **Chambre d'hôte Villa Marie - Jeanne** – 4 r. Chicot. Ⓜ Cinq Avenue Long Champs. ☎ 04 91 85 51 31. 3 rooms. A 19C building in a residential quarter of the city. Traditional, Provençal touches, old-fashioned furniture with modern amenities.

€€ **Hôtel Le Ryad** – 16 r. Sénac de Meilhan. Ⓜ Vieux Port. ☎ 04 91 47 74 54. www.leryad.fr. P. 9 rooms. Restaurant €€€. Step off the Canebière and into Morocco! Cosy and elegant, with a tea room and Moroccan restaurant.

€€€ **Chambre d'hôte Villa Monticelli** – 96 r. du Cdt-Rolland. Ⓜ Rond-Point-du-Prado. ☎ 04 91 22 15 20. www.villamonticelli.com. 5 rooms. This Art Deco villa in the Prado area has small but tastefully decorated rooms. A stroll from the beach.

€€€ **Hôtel Le Corbusier** – 280 bd Michelet. ☎ 04 91 16 78 00. www.hotellecorbusier.com. 21 rooms. P. Closed 1 week in Jan. Restaurant €€€. Architects and designers love this unique hotel in Le Corbusier's innovative 1940s apartment block, La Cité Radieuse. Rooms all have original features and accessories and there's a 360-degree view from the roof. The excellent restaurant, Le Ventre de l'Architecte, has similar period décor.

€€€€ **New Hôtel Vieux Port** – 3 bis r. Reine-Elisabeth. Ⓜ Vieux Port. ☎ 04 91 99 23 23. www.new-hotel.com. 42 rooms. Well located just a few steps from the Vieux Port, this hotel, recently refurbished, has rooms decorated with exotic themes: Pondicherry, Rising Sun, Arabian Nights, Vera Cruz or Tropical Africa.

€€€€ **Hôtel Pullman Palm Beach** – 200 corniche J.-F.-Kennedy. ☎ 04 91 16 19 00. www.pullmanhotels.com. 160 rooms. Restaurant €€€€. Facing the Île du Château d'If, this stylish contemporary hotel has a nautical feel. Extremely comfortable, well-equipped rooms all with sea view. The very modern restaurant gives the sunny flavours of the south a new twist.

€€€€ **RadissonBlu Hotel** – 38 quai de Rive Neuve. Ⓜ Vieux Port. ☎ 04 88 92 19 50. www.radissonblu.com. 189 rooms. Restaurant €€€. Right by Vieux Port, this smart, designerish hotel, between Fort St-Nicolas and Théâtre de la Criée, is furnished beautifully and provides the latest high-tech gadgets. Immaculate, bright rooms, some with harbour views.

EAT

Les Buvards – 34 Grand'Rue. Vieux Port. 04 91 90 69 98. Closed Sun lunch. Unpretentious bistro with simple food and an interesting selection of wines to drink in or take away.

Le Charité Café – 2 r. de la Charité. Colbert. 04 91 91 08 41. Open 9am–5pm, closed Mon. A pleasant brasserie right beside the Vieille Charité. Salads, plats du jour, afternoon tea etc.

Les Grandes Tables de la Friche – 41 r. Jobin (Friche de la Belle de Mai). 04 95 04 95 85. Open lunch Mon–Fri; dinner Thu–Sat, closed Sun. Bar open Fri–Sat from 5pm. Out from the centre, this is a key address for Marseille's trendy, artistic types. It is part of the Friche de la Belle de Mai, an artists' colony housed in an old tobacco factory, hence the post-industrial-chic feel of the restaurant's vast dining room with its raw concrete and stainless steel. This café-"neo-brasserie" serves retro-style comfort food.

La Part des Anges – 33 r. Sainte. Vieux Port. 04 91 33 55 70. www.lapartdesanges.com. This cosy, old-fashioned wine bar has an excellent selection of wines by the glass or bottle to enjoy on the spot or take away. It also serves simple food. Lively in the evening.

Le Resto Provençal – 64 cours Julien. Cours-Julien. 04 91 48 85 12. Closed Sun, Mon, Thu eve. A cosy place with Provençal specialities including sea bream soup and fig tart.

Toinou – 3 cours St-Louis. Noailles. 0 811 45 45 45. www.toinou.com. Closed Sun afternoons. This famous Marseille fishmonger has been here nearly 50 years. Right by the stall in cours St-Louis, the restaurant allows you to sit down and enjoy some shellfish or a fine seafood platter, washed down with a little glass of chilled white wine. Home deliveries.

Les Akolytes – 41 r. Papety. Bus 83, 54. 04 91 59 17 10. Closed Sat lunch and Sun. Opened by three young people, this trendy spot focuses on "gastronomic tapas". The fashionable modern interior matches the clientele, especially in the evening. Fantastic sea views are a bonus, and after dinner you can enjoy a walk on the plage des Catalans, just opposite.

Axis – 8 r. Sainte-Victoire. Castellane. 04 91 57 14 70. www.restaurant-axis.com. Closed Sat lunch, Sun, Mon eve. The seasonal, contemporary-style cuisine makes this establishment worth a detour. Modern décor, with views of the chefs in action. Charming welcome.

Le Café des Épices – 4 r. Lacydon. Vieux Port. 04 91 91 22 69. Closed Sat eve, Sun and Mon. Reservations advised. This tiny, trendy restaurant seats just 20, but the esplanade terrace and its olive grove in the background are delightful, as is the creative cuisine.

La Cantinetta – 24 cours Julien. N.-D.-du-Mont. 04 91 48 10 48. Closed Sun, Mon. This young Italian restaurant is making a reputation for itself for its surprisingly spot-on food that uses all fresh ingredients, and for its bistro décor and pleasant garden. Excellent value for money. Booking strongly advised.

La Casertane – 71 r. Francis-Davso. Vieux-Port. 04 91 54 98 51. Closed Mon–Sat dinner and Sun. A stone's throw from the Vieux Port, this restaurant and delicatessen delights its regulars with antipasti and copious pasta dishes at very reasonable prices. Do keep a bit of room for the excellent traditional tiramisu. You can shop for goodies before you leave.

Chez Madie Les Galinettes – 138 quai du Port. Vieux Port. 04 91 90 40 87. Closed Sat lunch in Jul, Sun. Near the museums of Old Marseille, this Provençal restaurant with terrace sits on the Vieux Port. Traditional dishes.

Chez Noël – 174 la Canebière. Réformés-Canebière. 04 91 42 17 22. Closed Mon, Aug. Some say that these are the best pizzas in Marseille. The atmosphere is great. A small family business that is going strong.

Cyprien – 56 av. de Toulon. La Castellane. 04 91 25 50 00. Closed 23 Jul–4 Sep, 24 Dec–5 Jan, Mon eve, Sat lunch, Sun, public holidays. This restaurant near the place Castellane offers classic, tasty cuisine and a décor to match. Interior adorned with floral touches and paintings.

⊖⊖ **L'Hippocampe –** 151 plage de l'Estaque (L'Estaque). Bus 35. ✆04 91 03 83 78 . Closed Sun dinner, Mon. From outside this restaurant doesn't look that great, but the dining room overlooking the Vieux Port and the terrace right beside the water make it worthwhile. Salads, beef kebabs and Provençal specialities. A singer, too, on Friday and Saturday evenings and on Sunday at midday.

⊖⊖ **La Tasca** – 102 r. Ferrari. Ⓜ N.-D.-du-Mont. ✆04 91 42 26 02. www.latasca.fr. Closed Sun, Mon. Opposite the Poste à Galène theatre, La Tasca is the place to go for a tapas evening. Tucked away, a large garden is open year-round. Good Spanish tapas, with traditional plates of jamon Serrano y manchego (Serrano dry-cured ham and cheese), tortillas y patatas bravas (Spanish omelette with potatoes) and some 65 other varieties of tapas.

⊖⊖⊖ **Les Arcenaulx** – 25 cours d'Estienne-d'Orves. Ⓜ Vieux Port. ✆04 91 59 80 30. www.les-arcenaulx.com. Closed Sun. Dine surrounded by the books that cover the walls of this restaurant: it's combined with a bookshop and publishers, located in the original warehouses of the 17C Arsenal des Galères.

⊖⊖⊖ **Chez Fonfon** – 140 r. du Vallon-des-Auffes. ✆04 91 52 14 38. www.chez-fonfon.com. Closed 2–23 Jan, Mon lunch, Sun. The dining room of this renowned restaurant is a landmark in the tiny harbour of the Vallon des Auffes.

⊖⊖⊖ **Le Moment** – 5 pl. Sadi Carnot. Ⓜ Vieux-Port. ✆04 91 52 47 49. www.le moment-marseille.com. Closed Sun and Mon eve. Run by talented chef Christian Ernst, this ultra-modern restaurant near the Vieux Port also offers top-notch takeaway food and cookery classes. Exciting cooking in refined surroundings.

⊖⊖⊖⊖ **l'Épuisette** – 156 r. du Vallon des Auffes. ✆04 91 52 17 82. Closed 5 Aug–5 Sep, Sun–Mon. Perched on rocks beside the sea in the picturesque Vallon des Auffes, this restaurant has long been a Marseille favourite, especially for fish. Wonderful seascapes and attentive staff.

⊖⊖⊖⊖ **Miramar** – 12 quai du Port. Ⓜ Vieux Port. ✆04 91 91 10 40. www.bouillabaisse.com. Closed Sun and Mon. This 1960s-style restaurant on the Vieux Port is famous for its bouillabaisse and other fish specialities. High prices do not deter faithful customers! After eating bouillabaisse don't expect to do much other than relax.

⊖⊖⊖⊖ **Péron –** 56 corniche J.-F.-Kennedy. ✆04 91 52 15 22. www.restaurant-peron.com. Closed 1 week Mar, 1 week Nov. In a great location on the Corniche, this well-known restaurant, decorated in the style of a transatlantic steamer, has giddy views out to the îles du Frioul. Mediterranean cooking in a modern vein.

⊖⊖⊖⊖ **Une Table, au Sud** – 2 quai du Port. Ⓜ Vieux Port. ✆04 91 90 63 53. www.unetableausud.com. Closed Aug, 3–11 Jan, Sun–Mon. This colourful restaurant delights both the eye and the taste buds, thanks to inventive cuisine with delicious southern accents. No terrace, so book a window table for a view over the Vieux Port.

⊖⊖⊖⊖ **Le Petit Nice** – Anse de Maldormé, corniche J.-F.-Kennedy. ✆04 91 59 25 92. www.passedat.fr. Closed 1–20 Jan, Feb school holidays, Whitsun holidays. Chef Gérald Passédat's refined and inventive cooking (of fish and seafood especially), combined with magical sea views, a soigné atmosphere and well-trained staff, has made this restaurant a top address.

NIGHTLIFE

Bar de la Marine – 15 quai Rive-Neuve. Vieux Port. ✆04 91 54 95 42. The setting for Marcel Pagnol's **Marius et Fanny** trilogy; you're likely to find the beautiful people having a drink here these days.

Café Parisien – 1 pl. Sadi-Carnot. Colbert. ✆04 91 90 05 77. Closed Sun. At weekends this attractive Baroque-style café hosts musical events based on the themes presented in the monthly art exhibitions.

TOURS

Guided Tours – By reservation at the tourist office. Guided tours (of varying duration) take place on various themes, in several languages, most days.

City Tour Marseille (bus) – Leaves from 9, La Canebière, near the Palais de la Bourse and tourist office. ✆04 86 09 50 34. Two audioguided circuits (8 languages) that take you around all the major sights: one last 2 hrs (€16), the other 3 hrs (€20). Tickets available online or at the tourist office.

Tourist train – Leaves from quai du Port. €8 (children 3–11, €4). 04 91 25 24 69. www.petit-train-marseille.com. There are three itineraries: (1) Notre-Dame de la Garde going past the Basilica of St-Victor, and Le Panier; (2) the old town (Vieux Marseille); (3) Le Frioul, which is actually a boat trip.

EVENTS

Programmes are listed in local newspapers, and the tourist office also distributes a small monthly magazine, In Situ.

Festival de Marseille – Jun–Jul. 04 91 99 02 50. www.festivaldemarseille.com. Theatre, music and dance festival takes place in atmospheric venues in the city.

Fiesta des Suds – 12 rue Urbain V, 13002 Marseille. 04 91 99 00 00. www.dock-des-suds.org. In late October, this world music festival brings 50 000 spectators to Marseille and vibrates with the music and traditions of the Mediterranean.

Folklore – International Folklore Festival at Château-Gombert takes place in early July (www.roudelet-felibren.com).

Pétanque World Championships – A very popular event frequented by celebrities who, after a few throws, let the champions take over. First week in July.

SHOPPING

BOOKS

Librairie-galerie-restaurant des Arcenaulx – 25 cours d'Estienne d'Orves. Vieux-Port. 04 91 59 80 40. www.les-arcenaulx.com. Specialises in books on Marseille, Provence and food; old and rare books. Quality gifts; restaurant.

CLOTHES

The main shopping street is rue St-Ferréol, which has many individual and chain boutiques plus Galeries Lafayette. Adventurous dressers might like to visit Marseille's well-known designer, **Madame Zaza** (73 cours Julien. Notre Dame du Mont. 04 91 48 05 57), for daring outfits.

MARKETS

Fish market every morning on quai des Belges. **Food** markets are open Mon–Sat mornings in cours Pierre Puget, place Jean-Jaurès (la Plaine), place du Marché-des-Capucins and avenue du Prado. Boulevard La Canebière has a **flower** market every Tuesday and Saturday morning; this market is also on avenue du Prado Friday morning.

OLIVE OIL

Lei Moulins – 6 bd Tellène. Estrangin Préfecture. 04 91 59 49 78. Closed Sun, Mon. Cave-like shop in the St-Victor quarter. You'll find an interesting selection of olive oil from the Med and also a selection of jams made on the premises.

SANTONS

Santons Marcel Carbonel – 47–49 r. Neuve-Ste-Catherine. Vieux Port. Open 10am–12.30pm, 2–6.30pm: Jan–Nov Tue–Sat; Dec Mon–Sat. 04 91 13 61 36. www.santonsmarcelcarbonel.com. Visit the workshop where the famous ***santons*** are made. Take a browse through the museum before hitting the shop to buy some of the traditional clay figurines .

SOAP

La Compagnie de Provence – 18 r. Francis Davso. Vieux Port. Mon–Thu 9am–1pm, 2–6pm, Fri 9am–1pm. 04 95 06 92 44. www.compagniedeprovence.com. Marseille soap and natural products make this shop smell wonderful.

Savonnerie Marseillaise de la Licorne – 34 cours Julien. Notre Dame du Mont. 04 96 12 00 91. www.savon-de-marseille-licorne.com. Mon–Fri 8am–5pm, Sat 10am–6pm. Visit the workshop, free, at 11am, 3pm and 4pm. The only artisan-made soap in the centre of town.

BOAT TRIPS

From Marseille – ICARD Maritime, quai des Belges. 04 91 33 36 79. www.visite-des-calanques.com. Boat trips to Cassis along the coast.

From Cassis – Les Bateliers de Cassis. 06 86 55 86 70. www.calanques-cassis.com. Departure from the port of Cassis visiting Port-Miou, Port-Pin and En-Vau, without landing.

From La Ciotat – Les Amis des Calanques, 34, rue Grand Madier, Le Ciotat. 06 09 35 25 68. www.visite-calanques.fr.

See also the Petit Train trips to Le Frioul. www.petit-train-marseille.com (p608).

Aix-en-Provence★★★

The old capital of Provence has kept much of its 17C and 18C character: elegant mansions, charming squares, avenues and lovely fountains. It is a lively city whose large student population is in evidence on the café terraces. The new part of town is expanding and attracting more residents; it has established itself as a city of arts, a thermal spa and an important centre for industry and tourism.

- **Population:** 141 438.
- **Michelin Map:** 340 H-I 4
- **Info:** Les Allées Provençales 300 avenue Giuseppe Verdi. ℘04 42 161 161. www.aixenprovencetourism.com.
- **Location:** 32km/20mi N of Marseille and 35km/22mi SE of Salon-de-Provence.
- **Don't Miss:** Vieil Aix, the charming medieval heart of the city.
- **Timing:** The first thing to do in Aix is walk along the majestic Cours Mirabeau under its handsome plane trees, pause for a drink at one of the many cafés and then stroll through Vieil Aix. Allow at least a half day. But, for an overview of the city, join a guided tour (the tourist office has details).

A BIT OF HISTORY

Aix is the legacy of King René (1409–80). The Roman city Aquae Sextiae had long before destroyed by the Lombards (574) and by Saracens; its deserted buildings served as a quarry for building materials for a six centuries. Then in the 12C its fortunes were restored by the Counts of Provence.

The most illustrious of the line was René, Duke of Anjou, Lorraine and Bar, King of Naples, Count of Provence and Piedmont, and ally of Charles VII against the English and Burgundians. This enlightened monarch supported literature and the arts and completed Aix cathedral. Towards the end of his life he made Charles of Maine his heir; Charles however was to die childless, enabling Louis XI to incorporate Provence into France (1486). Harsh times intervened; invasion by Imperial troops, feuding, and religious conflict.

While the Aix Parliament was putting up a strong resistance to Richelieu's policies, an administrative class grew and prospered. Intellectual life continued to flourish and the roll-call of great men who were born or who lived in Aix is a long one, including the 17C astronomer Fabri de Peiresc, and, of course, Paul Cézanne (1839–1906), one of the founders of modern painting. The room devoted to him in the Musée Granet houses among other paintings his *Still Life with Sugar-bowl, Nude at the Mirror* and the monumental *Bathers.* footsteps of CÉZANNE

- **Atelier Paul Cézanne** ★ (Cézanne's Studio) – In 1897, Cézanne had a traditional Provençal-style house built, surrounded by a garden with plants growing right up to the windows. The studio, called the Lauves, has been left as it was at the time of his death in 1906.
- **Le jas de Bouffan**★ – This fine 18C bastide on the edge of Aix later provided the painter with memories of his youth and his family. Aged 20, he used the downstairs salon as a studio and painted the four seasons on the walls.
- **Carrières de Bibémus**★ (Bibémus quarries) – Cézanne came to these quarries to paint, producing 11 oil paintings and 16 watercolours.
- **Café-brasserie Les Deux Garçons** – It was in this famous brasserie that Cézanne and his friend Émile Zola came to round off the day after classes at the collège Bourbon.

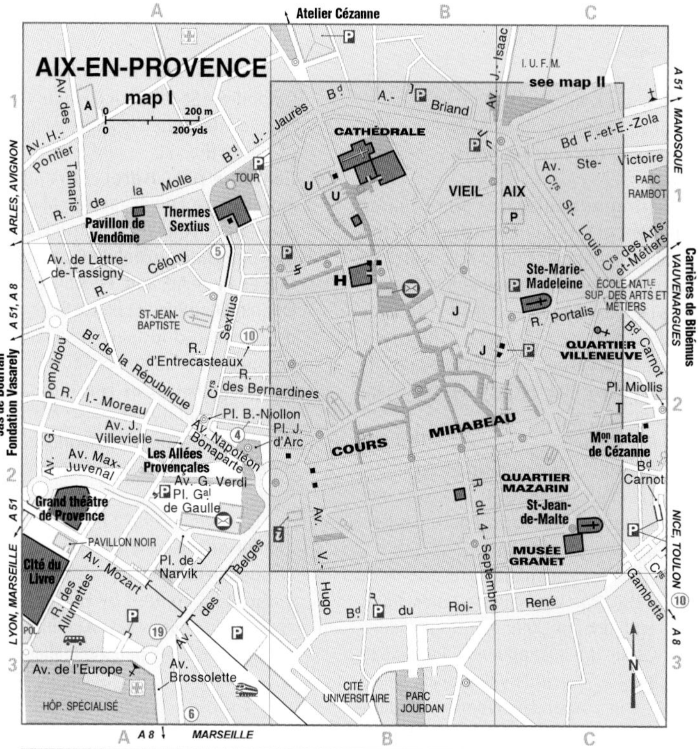

AIX-EN-PROVENCE
map I

0 — 200 m
0 — 200 yds

Atelier Cézanne — see map II — CATHÉDRALE — VIEIL AIX — Thermes Sextius — Pavillon de Vendôme — Ste-Marie-Madeleine — ÉCOLE NAT.LE SUP. DES ARTS ET MÉTIERS — QUARTIER VILLENEUVE — COURS MIRABEAU — Les Allées Provençales — Grand théâtre de Provence — Cité du Livre — PAVILLON NOIR — QUARTIER MAZARIN — St-Jean-de-Malte — MUSÉE GRANET — Mon natale de Cézanne — PARC RAMBOT — CITÉ UNIVERSITAIRE — PARC JOURDAN — HÔP. SPÉCIALISÉ — ST-JEAN-BAPTISTE — I. U. F. M.

A 51 MANOSQUE — Carrières de Bibémus VAUVENARGUES — NICE, TOULON — A 8 — A 8 MARSEILLE — LYON, MARSEILLE A 51 — Jas de Bouffan Fondation Vasarely — A 51, A 8 — ARLES, AVIGNON

WHERE TO STAY		WHERE TO EAT			
Hôtel du Globe	5	Chez Charlotte	4	L'Auberge Provençale	10
Hôtel Le Manoir	10	Les 2 Frères	6	Yamato	19

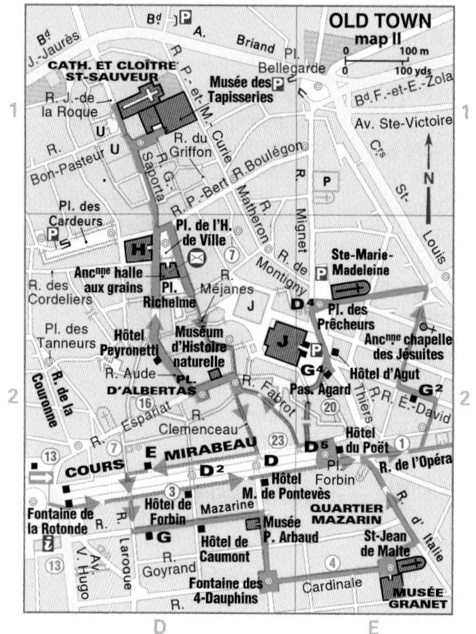

WHERE TO STAY

- Hôtel Cardinal ... 4
- Hôtel des Augustins ... 7
- Hôtel St-Christophe ... 13

WHERE TO EAT

- Basilic et Citronnelle ... 1
- Côté Cour ... 3
- Chez Féraud ... 7
- La Cigale ... 13
- Le Formal ... 16
- Pierre Reboul ... 20
- Pizza Capri ... 23

Fontaine mousse	D
Fontaine des Neufs Canons	D2
Fontaine des Prêcheurs	D4
Fontaine du Roi René	D5
Hôtel d'Arbaud-Jouques	E
Hôtel de Marignane	G
Hôtel de Panisse-Passis	G2
Hôtel de Roquesante	G4
Hôtel de Ville	H

WALKING TOUR

OLD AIX★★

Aix Old Town map, p613. Allow half a day, including 1hr30min for Quartier Mazarin.

The ring of boulevards and squares that encircles the old town marks the line of the ancient ramparts. North of cours Mirabeau, the town's focal point, lies Old Aix, tucked between the cathedral and place d'Albertas. The many pedestrian streets criss-crossing this area make it the perfect setting for an exploratory stroll.

- **Fontaine de la Rotonde** – This is a fountain on a monumental scale. Erected in 1860, it marked the entrance to the town. Photographed by everybody and depicted on countless postcards, this fountain is the town's most important symbol and most popular meeting place.
- **Cours Mirabeau★★** – This wide avenue, shaded by fine plane trees, is the hub of Aix, where a verdant tunnel of foliage protects against the hot Provençal sun.
- **Rue de l'Opéra** – There are a number of houses of interest on this street, including Cézanne's birthplace at No. 28.
- The route continues past **Hôtel de Panisse-Passis, Église Ste-Marie-Madeleine, Fontaine des Prêcheurs** and the **Muséum d'histoire naturelle.**
- **Place d'Albertas★** – This square is arranged very much in the style of Parisian squares and has lovely mansions all around it. Concerts are held here every summer.
- The route continues past **Hôtel d'Albertas, Hôtel Peyronetti** and **Hôtel d'Arbaud** to **Place Richelme**; every morning there is a fresh fruit and vegetable market.
- **Place de l'Hôtel de Ville★** – The northwest corner of this attractive square is overlooked by the clock tower and town hall.
- Continue past the **Ancienne Halle aux Grains**, to the **Musée des Tapisseries★**, housed in the 17C former archbishop's palace and the Romanesque **Cloître St-Sauveur★**. **Cathédrale St-Sauveur★** is a curious building decorated in all styles from the 5C to the 17C
- Continue past **Hôtel d'Arbaud-Jouques** to the **Quartier Mazarin★**. Here you will find the **Hôtel de Marignane, Hôtel de Caumont, Musée Paul-Arbaud, Fontaine des Quatre-Dauphins★, Église St-Jean-de-Malte** and **Musée Granet★★**. The museum's fine collection of paintings includes the legacies of the Aix painter François Marius Granet (1775–1849) and works from the great 16–19C European schools.

ADDITIONAL SIGHT

- **Fondation Vasarely★★** – On the Jas de Bouffan hill west of Aix stands the foundation created by Hungarian artist Victor Vasarely (1906–97), an early practitioner of op art.

ADDRESSES

STAY

Hôtel Cardinal – 24 r. Cardinale. 04 42 38 32 30. www.hotel-cardinal-aix.com. 29 rooms. In an 18C building, in the quiet Mazarin quarter, this hotel has old-fashioned elegance and today's comfort. Its location is perfect for exploring the town on foot.

Hôtel des Augustins – 3 r. de la Masse. 04 42 27 28 59. www.hotel-augustins.com. 28 rooms. Stone vaulting and stained glass are reminders of the origins of this hotel, a stone's throw from cours Mirabeau, which was originally a 15C convent. The rooms, of which two have terraces with rooftop views, are decorated in a modern style.

Hôtel du Globe – 74 cours Sextius. 04 42 26 03 58. www.hoteldu globe.com. Closed 15 Dec–mid-Jan. 46 rooms. Rooms are bright, well kept and soundproofed but not luxurious. Good value. Sunny roof-terrace.

Hôtel St-Christophe – 2 av. Victor-Hugo. 04 42 26 01 24. www.hotel-saintchristophe.com. 67 rooms. Restaurant. This hotel is right in the centre of the city, near cours

Mirabeau, and rooms are decorated in either 1930s or Provençal style. The lively Brasserie Léopold, decorated in the Art Deco style, offers regional cuisine and typical brasserie dishes. Pavement terrace in fine weather.

Domaine de la Brillane – 195 rte de Couteron. Leave Aix on N 296 (direction Sisteron), exit 12 (Aix-Les Plataners), then on towards Couteron (signposted). 04 42 54 21 44. www.labrillane.com. 5 rooms. A British banker turned wine producer has made one floor of his fine domaine at the foot of Sainte-Victoire into a comfortable B&B.

Le Mas d'Entremont – 315 rte Nationale 7, 13090 Aix-en-Provence. 04 42 17 42 42. www.masdentremont.com. Open mid-Mar–mid-Oct. 20 rooms. In the hills above Aix, this fine *bastide* nestles in a park with pool, fountains and antique columns. Spacious rooms with individual touches.

EAT

Basilic et Citronelle – 3 r. de l'Opéra. 04 42 27 58 77. Open noon–2pm. Closed Sun. A small, brightly coloured restaurant offering fresh, home-cooked food. The menu changes every day, as do the vegetarian plates, tarts and pastries. Eat in or take away. Booking recommended.

Pizza Capri – 1 r. Fabrot. 04 42 38 55 43. Open 6am–1.30pm (Fri–Sat 3.30pm). www.pizza-capri.fr. Very good pizzeria, also serving panini. Good value for money.

La Grignote – 22 r. Mignet, 13120 Gardanne. 04 42 58 30 25. Closed Mon–Thu eve, Sat lunch, Sun. Close to the cours Forbin, this restaurant focuses on traditional cooking. Air-conditioned dining room and shady terrace.

L'Auberge Provençale – 13590 Meyreuil (near Le Canet-de-Meyreuil). 04 42 58 68 54. www.auberge-provencale.fr. Closed Tue–Wed (Jul–Aug). . This pretty roadside inn has agreeable dining rooms with a southern feel. Traditional cooking, generous and carefully executed, plus a good list of local wines.

Chez Charlotte – 32 r. des Bernardines. 04 42 26 77 56. Closed Aug, Sun–Mon. Nostalgia sets the tone here; the main dining room's décor is dedicated to the cinema. Focusing on traditional and seasonal cuisine.

Le Formal – 32 r. Espariat. 04 42 27 08 31. Closed Sat lunch, Sun–Mon. A restaurant occupying 15C vaulted cellars adorned with a collection of contemporary paintings. Inventive, well-presented cuisine.

Le Grand Puech – 8 r. St-Sébastien, 13105 Mimet. 04 42 58 91 06. Closed Sun eve and Mon. In the heart of the old village of Mimet this restaurant serves Florentine specialities. Good selection of pastas. One of the dining rooms has a breathtaking view of the Pilon du Roi.

La Table de Muriel– 42 r. Jean-Jaurès, 13120 Gardanne. 04 42 58 14 60. www.latabledemuriel.fr. Closed Mon–Wed eve, Sun, Aug. Behind a fairly anonymous façade lies a restaurant which pays homage to Provence and the Mediterranean. Local specialities are tinged with Armenian flavours.

Les 2 Frères – 4 av. de la Reine-Astrid. 04 42 27 90 32. www.les2freres.com. As the name suggests, this restaurant is run by two brothers: the older one prepares the fashionable, modern food, while his sibling works front of house.

Côté Cour – 19 cours Mirabeau. 04 42 93 12 51. Closed 25–26 Dec, Mon lunch, Sun. This is a retreat with a luminous, verdant patio-veranda. All the flavours of Provence and Italy are at your fingertips.

La Cigale – 48 r. Espariat. 04 42 26 20 62. Closed Sun. In addition to pizzas, classic dishes are on offer. Graceful décor and a terrace in good weather.

Chez Féraud – 8 r. du Puits-Juif. 04 42 63 07 27. Closed Aug, Sun–Mon. Tucked away in a lane in the Old Quarter, an appealing place with typical local cuisine (pistou, daube) and grills.

Yamato – 21 av. des Belges. 04 42 38 00 20. Closed Mon, Tue lunch. Guests are made to feel very welcome by Mme Yuriko in this small Japanese restaurant, decorated in traditional style.

Pierre Reboul – 11 Petite-Rue-St-Jean. 04 42 20 58 26. www.restaurant-pierre-reboul.com. Closed Sun–Mon. In the heart of the old town, this elegant contemporary restaurant specialises in delicious and innovative cuisine, with a strong focus on top-quality ingredients.

Arles★★★

Arles is one of the most important centres of Provençal culture, proud of its past and famed for an exceptional Roman and medieval heritage, yet vibrantly modern and forward-looking. Van Gogh produced many of his greatest works here; what he loved was not the culture or history, but the brilliance of the light. The town continues to play a role in artistic life, hosting a renowned annual summer photography festival, Les Rencontres d'Arles.

- **Population:** 52 661.
- **Michelin Map:** 340 C 3
- **Info:** 43 bd de Craponne. ✆04 90 18 41 20. www.arlestourisme.com.
- **Location:** Arles stands on the edge of the Camargue wetlands and the Rhône delta, 80km/50mi W of Aix-en-Provence and 45km/28mi S of Avignon.
- **Parking:** Park under the plane trees of bd Georges-Clemenceau.
- **Don't Miss:** Roman arena; the café on the Place de Forum as painted in September 1888 by Van Gogh.
- **Timing:** Visitor passes are available at the tourist office or at any of the monuments and museums (except Museon Arlaten). The tourist office has information on walking tours. Expect to spend a couple of days if you want to see everything.

A BIT OF HISTORY

The ancient Celtic-Ligurian town was colonised by the Greeks of Marseille as early as the 6C BCE and was already a thriving town when the Romans conquered the region. They built a canal linking it to the sea so that it could be supplied directly from Rome.

Growing into a prosperous port town, and well placed on the major Roman highways, it became an administrative and political capital of Roman Gaul, with many magnificent buildings.

WALKING TOUR

PUBLIC BUILDINGS

Arles map, p617.

- **Roman Theatre★★** (Théâtre Antique) – Built during Augustus' reign c. 27–25 BCE, this theatre was gradually dismantled. As early as the 5C, it was used as a quarry for the construction of churches. In the 9C it was transformed into a redoubt before disappearing completely under houses and gardens. From 1827 to 1855 it was excavated. The theatre measured 102m in diameter and had a seating capacity of 12 000. It was backed up by a 27-arched portico made up of three levels of arcades, of which only one bay remains. Although little of the original stage survived intact, restoration work carried out in 2010 means that shows can now be staged here using modern equipment.
- **Amphitheatre★★** (Arènes) – This amphitheatre probably dates from the end of the 1C. Transformed into a fortress during the early Middle Ages, it constituted a system of defence. Later on, the arena was transformed into a town of 200 houses and two chapels, built with materials taken from the building itself, which was mutilated but saved from complete destruction. The excavation and restoration began in 1825.
- **Fondation Vincent van Gogh** – Permanent collection of works of art assembled in homage to Van Gogh

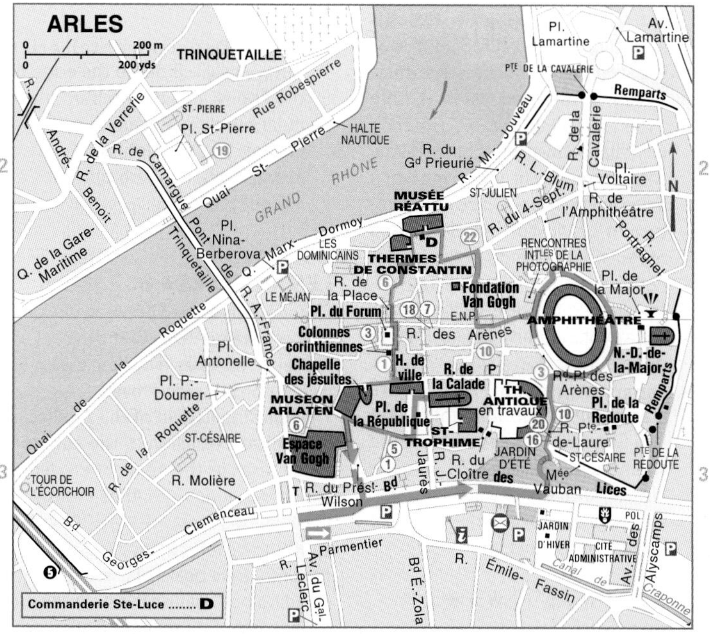

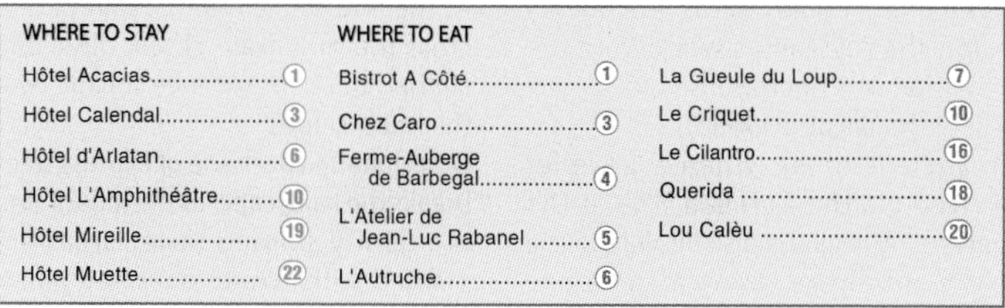

WHERE TO STAY		WHERE TO EAT			
Hôtel Acacias	1	Bistrot A Côté	1	La Gueule du Loup	7
Hôtel Calendal	3	Chez Caro	3	Le Criquet	10
Hôtel d'Arlatan	6	Ferme-Auberge de Barbegal	4	Le Cilantro	16
Hôtel L'Amphithéâtre	10	L'Atelier de Jean-Luc Rabanel	5	Querida	18
Hôtel Mireille	19	L'Autruche	6	Lou Calèu	20
Hôtel Muette	22				

- **Musée Réattu★** – The museum takes its name from the painter Jacques Réattu (1760–1833), who lived here and whose work is exhibited in the museum's galleries. There are also works from the 16C–18C Italian, French, Dutch and Provençal Schools, as well as a collection of modern and contemporary art.
- **Thermes de Constantin★** – The baths of Arles are the largest (98 x 45m) remaining in Provence. They date from Constantine's era (4C).
- **Place du Forum** – The actual place du Forum is not on the site of the ancient forum, which lay more to the south.
- **Hôtel de Ville** – When he rebuilt it in 1675 following the plans of Hardouin-Mansart, the Arles architect Peytret retained the clock tower (16C) inspired by the mausoleum on the Plateau des Antiques.
- **Cryptoportiques★** – This double gallery underground, in the form of a horseshoe, dates from the end of the 1C BCE.
- **Église St-Trophime★** – This church, dedicated to St Trophimus, possibly the first bishop of Arles in the early 3C, was built on a site first occupied by an ancient temple, then, in the Carolingian era, by a church. Its construction began around 1100.
- **Cloître St-Trophime★★** – These cloisters, the most famous in Provence for the elegance of their carved decoration, may have been carved with the help of the craftsmen of St-Gilles.

- **Museon Arlaten★** – This fascinating Provençal Museum was created by the writer Frédéric Mistral in 1896 and installed, from 1906 to 1909, in the 16C Hôtel de Castellane-Laval, bought by Mistral with the money he was given when awarded the Nobel Prize for Literature in 1904. Worried by the loss of Provençal identity in the face of national centralisation policies, Mistral wanted to preserve the details of Provençal daily life for future generations.
- **Espace Van Gogh** – This centre was originally a hospital where Van Gogh was treated in 1889. The site now houses the Médiathèque d'Arles, with the city archives, several bookstores, and the school of literary translators.

LES ALYSCAMPS★★★

Allow 30 mins.

From Roman times to the late Middle Ages, the Alyscamps was one of the most famous necropolises (cemeteries) of the Western world.

In ancient times, when a traveller arrived via the Aurelian Way at the gates of Arles, he made his way to the city's entrance passing along a line of inscribed tombs and mausoleums. And yet the Alyscamps' great expansion occurred during the Christianisation of the necropolis around the tomb of St Genesius, a Roman civil servant, beheaded in 250 for having refused to write down an imperial edict persecuting the Christians. Miracles began to happen on this site, and the faithful asked to be buried here. Added to all this was the legend of St Trophimus, who was buried here.

The transfer of St Trophimus' relics to the cathedral in 1152 reduced the prestige of this cemetery. During the Renaissance, the necropolis was desecrated. City councillors took to offering their guests carved sarcophagi as presents, and monks in charge took funerary stones to build churches and convents and to enclose monastery grounds.

ADDITIONAL SIGHT

- **Musée Départemental Arles Antique★★** – Built on the edge of the Rhône, this daring blue triangular building, designed by Henri Ciriani, houses behind its vivid enamel walls a superb collection of ancient art.

EXCURSION

LES ALPILLES★★

The area is divided between the Alpilles des Baux in the W and the Alpilles d'Eygalières in the E; in the middle is St-Rémy-de-Provence.

The limestone chain of the Alpilles, a geological extension of the Luberon range, rises in the heart of Provence between Avignon and Arles. From afar, these jagged crests rising 300–400m appear to be lofty mountains.

The arid, white peaks of these summits standing out against the blue sky are reminiscent of some Greek landscapes. At the mouths of the dry valleys that cross the mountain chain, olive and almond trees spread their foliage over the lower slopes.

Occasionally a dark line of cypress trees breaks the landscape. In the mountains, the gently sloping lower areas are planted with *Kermes* oaks and pines, but often the rock is bare and peppered with a few scraggy bushes covered by *maquis* or poor pasture suitable only for sheep.

Due to the high risk of fire, access to the forested areas of the Alpilles is forbidden from July to mid-September.

DRIVING TOURS

LES BAUX ALPILLES★★

Round trip starting from St-Rémy-de-Provence. 40km/25mi. Allow 4hr.

St-Rémy-de-Provence★

See ST-RÉMY-DE-PROVENCE p623.

Leave St-Rémy-de-Provence going SW on chemin de la Combette; turn right into Vieux Chemin d'Arles. After

3.8km/2.3mi, turn left at a T-junction onto D 27 (signposted: Les Baux).

Les Baux Panorama (Table d'Orientation)★★★

Just before reaching the top of the hill, on your left, you will see a road tracing the ledge where you can stop and gaze at the magnificent **panorama★★★** of Les Baux (*see Les BAUX-DE-PROVENCE, p622*).

Return to D 27; bear left on it.

The road winds through Val d'Enfer *see Les BAUX-DE-PROVENCE, p622.*

Les Baux-de-Provence★★★

See Les BAUX-DE-PROVENCE, p622.

Continue along D 27, then take a right before Maussane-les-Alpilles to connect to Paradou on D 17.

La Petite Provence du Paradou

75 ave de la Vallée des Baux, Le Paradou (towards Fontvieille (D 17) on the right). Open daily Jan–Mar and Oct–Nov 10am–12.30pm, 2–6pm; Apr–May and Dec 10am–12.30pm, 2–6.30pm; Jun–Sept 10am–7pm. €8.50 (children 6–11, €5). 04 90 54 35 75. www.lapetiteprovenceduparadou.com.

In a décor redolent of rural Provence, *santons* are produced here by *santon*-makers from **Aubagne**. They are dressed in the local costumes and some are even mobile.

They are arranged into evocative scenes of Provence past, with trades (fisherman, miller, shepherd), festivals, daily life (drinking holes, games of cards), and the like.

Return to the village, taking D 78 to the right through an olive grove.

Aqueducs de Barbegal

5min round-trip on foot: follow the signposts for 'Aqueduc Romain'.

Note the impressive ruins, on the left in particular, of a pair of Gallo-Roman aqueducts. The aqueduct branching off to the west supplied Arles with water from Eygalières. The other one cut through the rock and served a 4C hydraulic flour mill on the slope's south side, the ruins of which provide a rare example of Gallo-Roman mechanical engineering.

Go right on D 33.

Fontvieille

Avenue des Moulins. 04 90 54 67 49. www.fontvieille-provence.com.

For centuries, the main industry in this small town, where Alphonse Daudet is remembered for his *Lettres de mon Moulin* (1869), has been the quarrying of Arles limestone.

Moulin de Daudet (Daudet's Mill)

Between Arles and Les Baux-de-Provence, the admirers of Alphonse Daudet's works can make a literary pilgrimage to his mill, the inspiration for his famous *Lettres de mon Moulin (Letters from my Mill)*, a charming and whimsical series of letters and tales from Provence. A lovely avenue of pines leads from Fontvieille to the mill.

Alphonse Daudet, the son of a silk manufacturer, was born in Nîmes on 13 May 1840 (d. 1897). An outstanding author of tales of Provençal life and member of the Académie Goncourt, he was also a contemporary of such important 19C literary figures as Zola and Mistral. The **view★** from the mill is an inspiration, embracing the Alpilles, **Beaucaire★** and **Tarascon★** castles, the vast Rhône valley, and the **abbaye de Montmajour**.

Take D 32 to return to St-Rémy-de-Provence.

La Camargue★★

The main town in the Camargue is Les Saintes-Maries-de-la-Mer on the coast. Try to catch sight of the three creatures that symbolise the Camargue – white horses, black bulls and pink flamingos.

The Rhône delta forms an immense wetland plain. Product of the interaction of the Rhône, the Mediterranean and the winds, this remarkable area has a culture and history all its own, as well as distinctive flora and fauna. It is divided into three distinct regions: a cultivated region north of the delta, salt marshes west of the Petit Rhône, and the watery nature reserve to the south.

Parc Naturel Régional de Camargue

Beware mosquitoes during summer (http://vigilance-moustiques.com).

The nature park includes the communes of Arles and Stes-Maries-de-la-Mer. Together with the nature reserve, **Réserve Nationale de Camargue**, it aims to protect the fragile ecosystem of the region with its exceptional variety of flora and fauna – there are some 400 bird species. The traditional image of the Camargue is associated with the **herds** (*manades*) and the **horsemen** (*gardians*). Many horse owners hire out their mounts for organised rides among the animals.

The *manade* designates livestock and all that relates to the upkeep of the herd: herdsmen, pastureland, horses, etc. The *gardian*, an experienced rider, is the symbol of the *manade* with his large felt hat and long three-pronged stick; he watches over the herd, cares for the sick animals and selects the bulls for the bullfights.

Les Stes-Maries-de-la-Mer

At the heart of the Camargue is situated Les Stes-Maries-de-la-Mer, clustered around its fortified church. The town, which is now at some distance from the coastline of medieval times, is protected by dikes to counter the encroachment of the sea.

A large, colourful **Gypsy Pilgrimage★★** in honour of Sarah, whom they consider as their patron, takes place 24–25 May, attracting thousands of gypsies.

Musée Camarguais at Pont de Rousty

Located in Park Information Centre, Parc naturel régional de Camargue, Mas du Pont de Rousty, 13200 Arles. ♿ Open Apr–Sept daily 9am–12.30pm, 1–6pm; Oct–Mar Wed–Mon 10am–12.30pm, 1–5pm. Closed 1 Jan, 1 May, 25 Dec. €5. ☎04 90 97 10 82. www.parc-camargue.fr.

Occupying a former sheep farm deep in the Camargue, the museum traces the history of human activity in the delta. Much of the exhibition is devoted to life in a *mas* or traditional farmhouse during the 19C, but also features the economic activities of the present time: wine production, rice growing, sea salt.

ADDRESSES

STAY

€€ Hôtel de l' Amphithéâtre – 5 r. Diderot. ☎04 90 96 10 30. www.hotelamphitheatre.fr. 33 rooms. Inside this fine 17C building are cosy, renovated rooms; those in the adjoining mansion are larger and more elegant. Pretty breakfast room.

€€ Hôtel de la Muette – 15 r. des Suisses. ☎04 90 96 15 39. www.hotel-muette.com. Closed Feb. 18 rooms. The lovely 12C façade of this small hotel overlooks a little square. Exposed stonework, old beams and the colours of the south in the bedrooms. The breakfast room has interesting bullfighting photos on its walls.

€€ Hôtel des Acacias – 2 r. de la Cavalerie. ☎04 90 96 37 88. www.hotel-acacias.com. Closed late Oct–end Mar. 33 rooms. This refurbished hotel near the porte de la Cavalerie has a Camarguaise ambiance downstairs and Provençal décor in its bright rooms.

€€€ Hôtel d'Arlatan – 26 r. du Sauvage. ☎04 90 93 56 66. www.hotel-arlatan.fr. Closed late Nov–early Apr. 41 rooms. The past lives on in this gracious 15C mansion thanks to an exhibition of archaeological remains.

€€€ Hôtel Calendal – 5 r. Porte-de-Laure. ☎04 90 96 11 89. www.lecalendal.com. 38 rooms. Delightful bedrooms have views of the Théâtre Antique, the Arènes or a lovely garden. In the salon de thé, Provençal salads are just right for a summer lunch.

€€€ Hôtel Mireille – 2 pl. St-Pierre. ☎04 90 93 70 74. www.hotel-mireille.com. Closed early Jan–end Feb. 34 rooms.

Restaurant ⊖⊜⊜. Out from the centre on the right bank of the Rhône, this hotel has charming Provençal-style rooms. Good service, high-quality breakfasts and a shop selling fine local produce add to its appeal, as do an attractive terrace and pool.

EAT

⊖ **Querida** – 37 r. des Arènes. ℘04 90 98 37 81. Open Thu–Mon noon–3pm, 7–11pm. Just a few steps away from the Arènes, this wine bar has a Spanish feel, thanks in part to the Spanish wines and tapas that it serves.

⊖ **L'Autruche** – 5 r. Dulau. ℘04 90 49 73 63. Closed Sun, Mon. A friendly couple run this attractive little restaurant. Elegant décor, southern cuisine.

⊖⊜ **Chez Caro** – 21 pl. du Forum. ℘04 90 97 94 38. www.chezcaro.fr. Closed Tue, Wed. At this small, unpretentious bistro, the menu changes every other day. It features beautifully presented dishes made from fresh ingredients and cooked by creative, expert hands.

⊖⊜ **Le Criquet** – 21 r. Porte-de-Laure. ℘04 90 96 80 51. Closed Mon, early Jan–mid-Feb. With its beams and stone walls, the dining room of this small restaurant near the Arènes is more appealing than the terrace. The young chef's specialities include *bourride*.

⊖⊜ **La Gueule du Loup** – 39 r. des Arènes. ℘04 90 96 96 69. Closed Sun and Mon lunch, Oct–Mar weekends, Apr–Sep. In the historic centre, it's easy to spot this restaurant by the greenery on the outside. On the first floor, the air-conditioned dining room is pleasantly cool. Provençal cuisine with a focus on fish and Camargue beef. Attentive service.

⊖⊜ **Lou Calèu** – 27 r. Porte-de-Laure. ℘04 90 49 71 77. Closed early Jan–mid-Feb, Sun, Mon. This traditional, popular Arles restaurant is famous for little purple artichokes *à la barigoule*, shrimp tail *mille-feuilles* and all sorts of other delights. Excellent wine list.

⊖⊜⊜ **Bistrot à Côté** – 19 r. des Carmes. ℘04 90 47 61 13. www.bistro-acote.com. Next door to the Atelier of prominent Arles chef Jean-Luc Rabanel (see below), this affordable eatery has a relaxed, rather Spanish atmosphere and quality produce.

⊖⊜⊜ **Le Cilantro** – 31 Porte de Laure. ℘04 90 18 25 05. www.restaurantcilantro.com. Closed Mon (except Mon eve Jul–Aug), Sat lunch, Sun, early Nov and late Feb–early Mar. Behind the Théâtre Antique, this is a place to enjoy confident, modern cuisine from a talented chef, either in a smart, contemporary interior or on the terrace.

⊖⊜⊜ **Ferme-Auberge de Barbegal** – D 33, 13280 Raphèle-les-Arles. ℘04 90 54 63 69. www.barbegal.fr. Reserve at least 48 hrs in advance. ♿ 🅿 ⊄. 5 rooms. The owners of this magnificently restored 300-year-old farm raise sheep and poultry, and grow vegetables and olives.

⊖⊜⊜⊜ **L'Atelier de Jean-Luc Rabanel** – 7 r. des Carmes. ℘04 90 91 07 69. www.rabanel.com. Closed Mon, Tue. Regarded as a true artist in the kitchen, well-known chef Jean-Luc Rabanel serves up innovative, elegant food based on organic local produce.

SHOPPING

Markets – Browse traditional markets every Wed in bd Émile-Combes and every Sat in bd des Lices and boulevard Clemenceau. **Antique market** first Wed of the month in bd des Lices.

Les Étoffes de Romane – 10 bd des Lices. ℘04 90 93 53 70. Choose from wonderful **Provençal fabrics**.

Olive Oil – Best quality Provençal olive oil is found (together with other olive specialities) at **Fad'ola** (46 r. des Arènes; ℘04 90 49 70 73).

EVENTS

Festival Les Suds – mid-Jul. www.suds-arles.com. World music festival.

Fête des Gardians – 1 May. ℘04 90 18 41 20. Mass is held in Provençal dialect, with the blessing of horses, typical Camargue games, local folk music and dances.

Les Rencontres d'Arles – 10 rond-point-des Arènes. ℘04 90 96 76 06. www.rencontres-arles.com. This photography festival is a feast of exhibitions, talks and activities in locations throughout the town, including the Roman Theatre.

Les Baux-de-Provence★★★

With its ruined castle and deserted houses capping an arid rocky spur plunging abruptly to steep ravines on either side, the old village of Baux has the most spectacular of sites. Baux has also given its name to bauxite, a mineral first discovered here in 1822 that led to the development of aluminium.

- **Population:** 436.
- **Michelin Map:** 340 D 3
- **Info:** Maison du Roy, r. Porte-Mage. ☏04 90 54 34 39. www.lesbauxdeprovence.com.
- **Location:** 30km/18.6mi S of Avignon and 9.5km/6mi SW of St-Rémy-de-Provence, in the Chaîne des Alpilles.
- **Parking:** Park the car in one of the car parks at the foot of the escarpment, before the road up to the village (where cars are not allowed). In high season the car parks can be full, so you may need to park by the roadside some way down from the village.
- **Timing:** A walk through the streets of Les Baux is a magical experience. Take 1hr to see the village and the same for the château.

A BIT OF HISTORY

The lords of Baux were renowned in the Middle Ages, described by Mistral as "warriors all – vassals never". They traced their ancestry back to the Magi king Balthazar and boldly placed the Star of Bethlehem on their coat of arms.

VILLAGE

The original entrance into the village is guarded by a gate (Porte Eyguières). Go through the fortified gateway and simply wander the old streets.

The **Place St-Vincent★**, pleasantly shaded by elms and lotus-trees, has a terrace giving views of the small Fontaine valley and Val d'Enfer. The 17C former Town Hall (Hôtel de Ville) has rooms with ribbed vaulting.

The church (Église St-Vincent) dates from the 12C; dressed in their long capes, the shepherds from the Alpilles hills come here for their **Christmas festival★★**, celebrated at Midnight Mass. The **Rue du Trencat★** was carved into the solid rock which has been pitted and eroded by wind and rain.

Château des Baux

Opening times vary, but generally 10am–5pm, later in summer. €8–€10 according to season. ☏04 90 54 55 56. www.chateau-baux-provence.com.

By the 11C the lords of Baux, "that race of eagles", were among the most powerful rulers in the south of France.

Their turbulent ways, together with their support for the Reformation, were a great irritant to Louis XIII who in 1632 ordered the castle and ramparts to be dismantled; this was the town's death-blow.

From the remains of the 13C keep a fine **panorama★★** unfolds over the Alpilles with the windmills of Fontvieille to the west. One of them is Daudet's Mill (Moulin de Daudet).

It was here that **Alphonse Daudet**, the Nîmes-born author very popular in France (and available in English translation), is supposed to have written his delightful *Letters from My Mill*, creating the characters of the Woman of Arles (*L'Arlésienne*), Monsieur Seguin's goat, the Pope's grumpy mule and Dom Balaguère the gourmand.

Musée Yves-Brayer★

pl. François-de-Hénain. Closed Jan–Feb. €5. ☏04 90 54 36 99. www.yvesbrayer.com.

The museum houses works by Yves Brayer (1907–90), a figurative painter deeply attached to Les Baux (he is buried in the village cemetery).

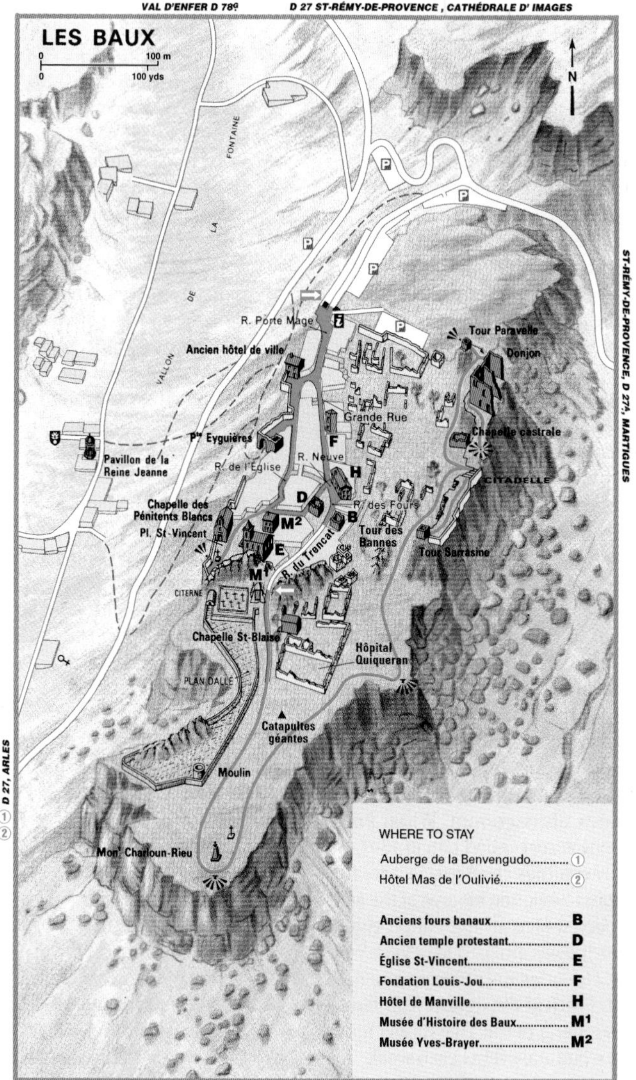

EXCURSIONS

St-Rémy-de-Provence★

The little town is just north of Les-Baux-de-Provence.

pl. Jean-Jaurès. 04 90 92 05 22. www.saintremy-de-provence.com.

Just to the north of the jagged peaks of the Alpilles, St-Rémy encapsulates the character of inland Provence; plane trees shade its boulevards from the intense light and there are charming old alleyways.

Les Antiques★★

1km/0.6mi S of the town.

These fascinating remains mark the site of the prosperous Roman city of Glanum. The **mausoleum★★** of the 1C BCE is the best preserved of its kind in the Roman world; it was erected in memory of the Emperor Augustus' grandsons Gaius and Lucius, whose early death deprived them of their Imperial inheritance. The **triumphal arch★**, is one of the oldest sin the south of the country.

Avignon★★★

Protected by a ring of imposing ramparts, the historic core of Avignon is a lively centre of art and culture. For 68 years it was the residence first of seven French popes, then of three others once Pope Gregory XI had returned to Rome in 1377; the Papal Legates remained until the city was united with France in 1791.

- **Population:** 89 683.
- **Michelin Map:** 32 B-C 10
- **Info:** 41 cours Jean-Jaurès. ✆04 32 74 32 74. www.avignon-tourisme.com.
- **Location:** Avignon is located 37km/23mi N of Arles.
- **TGV:** Avignon TGV station is a little over 2hrs 30min direct from Paris Gare de Lyon, and 6hrs 30min direct from London.
- **Flights:** Airport Avignon Caumont (www.avignon.aeroport.fr. ✆04 90 81 51 51) is 8km/5mi from Avignon and handles internal and UK flights.
- **Parking:** There are paying and free car parks outside the ramparts – don't try to park in the centre.
- **Don't Miss:** The Palais des Papes, and the Pont St-Bénézet. The Rocher des Doms gives an excellent view of the surrounding countryside.
- **Timing:** With so much to do in Avignon, allow a couple of days for a visit including half a day for the old town and an hour for the Palais des Papes. Expect crowds during the festival in July.
- **Kids:** There's an old-fashioned carousel in Place de l'Horloge. A fun way to see the sights is via "Le Petit Train d'Avignon": every 20 mins from Place du Palais des Papes – 40min, daily. €7 (under 9, €4).

A BIT OF HISTORY

Very little remains of the Roman settlement of Avenio which fell into ruin after the Barbarian invasions of the 5C. At the beginning of the 14C the popes felt the need to escape from the turbulent political life of Rome. Avignon formed part of the papal territories, and occupied a central position in the Europe of the time. The case for moving there was put by Philippe le Bel (the Fair), possibly with a view to involving the papacy in his own political manœuvrings. In 1309 Pope Clement V took the plunge, and Avignon became for most of a century the capital of Western Christendom. When Pope Clement VI succeeded him in 1342, he greatly enlarged the Papal Palace, and brought to Avignon his love of the arts. Avignon remains an influential cultural centre. It owes much to Jean Vilar, who in 1947 founded the prestigious annual event, **Festival d'Avignon**. This led to a blossoming of the arts: it now hosts various cultural events each week.

SIGHTS

Palais des Papes★★★

Open daily Mar 9am–6.30pm; Apr–Jun and Sept–Oct 9am–7pm; Jul 9am–8pm; Aug 9am–8.30pm; Nov–Feb 9.30am–5.45pm. €11 (Combined ticket with Pont St-Bénézet €13.50). ✆04 90 27 50 50. www.palais-despapes.com.

The huge feudal structure, fortress as well as palace, conveys an overwhelming impression of defensive strength with its high bare walls, its massive corbelled crenellations and stalwart buttresses. Inside, a maze of galleries, chambers, chapels and passages contains almost no furnishings. While the popes were in residence the palace was extremely luxuriously equipped.

Pont St-Bénézet★★

Stepping out into the swirling Rhône, and coming to an abrupt end in midstream, this beautiful bridge was first built in 1177, according to legend, by a shepherd-boy called Bénézet.

Until the Bridge Brotherhood (Frères Pontifes) built **Pont-St-Esprit** more than a century later this was the only stone bridge over the Rhône. It helped the economic development of Avignon long before becoming a useful link with Villeneuve when the Cardinals built their villas there. Eighteen arches were destroyed by the floodwaters in the 17C.

Petit Palais

pl. du Palais des Papes.

This was formerly Cardinal Arnaud de Via's residence (*livrée*) before being bought by the pope in 1335 to house the bishopric. The building deteriorated during the different sieges imposed upon the Palais des Papes, and had to be repaired and transformed in the late 15C, especially by Cardinal della Rovere, who subsequently became Pope Julius II.

Rocher des Doms★★

There is a well laid-out garden planted with different species on this bluff. From the terraces you will encounter superb **views★★** of the Rhône and Pont St-Bénézet, Villeneuve-lez-Avignon with Tour Phillipe-le-Bel and Fort St-André, the Dentelles de Montmirail, Mont Ventoux, Vaucluse plateau, the Luberon hills and the Alpilles.

Musée Calvet★

This celebrated museum is named after its creator, the physician Esprit Calvet. Highlights include a range of sculptures, a collection of silverware and faïence, and French, Italian and Flemish painting from the 16C to the 19C.

Musée Lapidaire★

Located in the former chapel of the 17C Jesuit College, this building has a unique nave and is flanked by side galleries where you will find displays of sculpture and stone carvings that together represent the different civilisations that left their mark on the region.

EXCURSIONS

UZÈS★★

38km/24mi W of Avignon.

This, the first duchy of France, is set amid a landscape of garrigue and austere charm that dazzles whatever the season. With its shaded boulevards, medieval streets and russet-faced mansions, built mainly in the 17C–18C, when the production of cloth, serge and silk made the city wealthy, Uzès exudes a quiet but radiant beauty.

VILLENEUVE-LÈS-AVIGNON★

2km/1.2mi W, on the west bank of the river.

At the point where St Bénézet's bridge originally touched French territory Philippe le Bel built a small fort (only a tower remains).

Half a century later, feeling hemmed in at Avignon, the Cardinals crossed the river and built themselves 15 fine houses (*livrées*) here. At the same time, Jean le Bon (John the Good) erected the St-André fortress on the hill which was already crowned by an abbey. Protected by its walls and with a splendid twin-towered gatehouse, this vast building complex offers (from its Romanesque Chapel of Notre-Dame de Belvézet) one of the finest views over the Rhône Valley. In the foreground is the gateway, Porte St-André, and beyond, on the far bank, the Palace of the Popes.

In 1352 the General of the Carthusian Order had been elected pope but humbly refused the throne. Pope Innocent VI, elected in his stead, founded a charterhouse, **La Chartreuse★** (open daily Apr–Sep 9.30am–6.30pm; Oct–Mar 10am–5pm; closed 1 Jan, 1 May, 1, 11 Nov, 25 Dec. ☎04 90 15 24 24) to commemorate the gesture. It soon became the greatest charterhouse in France. It has a monumental 17C gateway, small cloisters and graveyard cloisters, the latter fringed by the cells of the Fathers.

LE PONT DU GARD★★★

Pont du Gard site, rte du Pont du Gard 04 66 37 50 99. www.pontdugard.fr. Both banks of the river have a large car park, open 7am–1am (€18 per vehicle, giving access to the site).

This superb aqueduct and road bridge was built between AD 40 and 60. It formed part of a water-supply system with a total length of 49km/30mi, stretching from its source near Uzès via a whole series of cuttings, trenches, bridges and tunnels to supply the Roman city of Nîmes with fresh water. The three great rows of arches of the aqueduct rise 49m above the valley of the Gardon: imagine the effect such a structure must have had on the imagination of the local Gauls, impressing with the power and prestige of Roman achievement.

A slight curve in the upstream direction increases its ability to withstand seasonal high waters, while the independent construction of the arches lends a certain flexibility to the whole. Careful calculation of the dimensions of the huge blocks of stone meant that they could be put in place without the use of mortar. The channel on the topmost level was faced with stone in order to maintain water quality and alongside it ran the carriageway of a Roman road. The Pont du Gard fulfilled its function until the 9C, when lack of maintenance and blocking by deposits of lime finally put it out of use.

LE LUBERON★★★

La Maison du Parc, 60 pl. Jean Jaurès, Apt. 04 90 04 42 00. www.parcduluberon.fr.

Midway between the Alps and the Mediterranean lies the mountainous Luberon range. This region is full of charm: striking solitary woods and rocky countryside plus picturesque hilltop villages and dry-stone huts. The diversity of the vegetation is a delight to nature lovers: oak forests, Atlas cedar (planted in 1862) on the heights of the Petit Luberon, beech, Scots pine, moors of broom and boxwood, *garrigues*, an extraordinary variety of aromatic plants (herbs of Provence) clinging here and there to the rocky slopes.

The Luberon has been inhabited by humans since prehistoric times. Villages appeared during the Middle Ages, clinging to the rock face near a waterhole.

FONTAINE DE VAUCLUSE

The village of Fontaine de Vaucluse is at the end of a 7km/4.3mi-long country road from the town of L'Isle sur la Sorgue. chemin de la Fontaine. 04 90 20 32 22. The fountain is much more impressive in spring than in autumn.

This impressive resurgent spring was famous enough to figure in Strabo's *Geography* 2 000 years ago.

The humanist poet Petrarch retired here in 1337 to write his "Sonnets to Laura" inspired by the beautiful Laura de Noves with whom Petrarch had fallen in love whilst living in Avignon.

Gushing forth at the foot of a cliff among trees in an enclosed valley, this is one of the most spectacular phenomena of its kind. Fed by rain falling on the Vaucluse hills, the water penetrates the limestone uplands and collects in a vast cavern from which it is forced out under pressure. In late winter, the flow can amount to 100cu m per second. At such times the waters foam and spray against the rocks, a magnificent natural spectacle.

GORDES★

The village is in scenic back-country 40km/25mi E.

Le Château. 04 90 72 02 75. www.gordes-village.com.

The **site★** is outstanding, the charming village rising in tiers up rocky slopes.

The imposing Renaissance **château** stands dramatically on the village's highest point, facing Old Gordes.

Today it houses the **Musée Pol Mara**, displaying the work of this Flemish artist who lives in the village.

VILLAGE DES BORIES★

3.5km/2mi SW.

Curious dry-stone structures of this kind exist from Iceland to the Middle East. In Vaucluse they were built between the 14C and the 19C. The village consists of

Parc Naturel Régional du Luberon

Founded in 1977, the park incorporates 60 communes covering 185 145ha/457 503 acres including the *départements* of Vaucluse and Alpes-de-Haute-Provence (that is, from Manosque to Cavaillon and the Coulon – or Calavon – valley to the Durance). Its goal is to preserve the natural balance of the region with the aim of improving the living conditions of villagers, the promotion of agricultural activity through irrigation, mechanisation and the reorganisation of the holdings. The main developments in the tourist industry are the opening of tourist information offices and museums at **Apt**, Buoux and **La Tour-d'Aigues**, and the creation of nature trails through the cedar forest at **Bonnieux★**, the ochre cliffs of Roussillon, the Viens *bories* and the cultivation terraces at Goult, as well as thematic tourist routes such as the "Route de Vaudois". It also produces attractive publications.

a number of dwellings as well as structures for threshing, baking, oil pressing, and housing animals.

GORGES DE L'ARDÈCHE★★★

The Ardèche gorge runs most of the way from Vallon Pont d'Arc to St Martin-d'Ardèche.

Vallon-Pont d'Arc. 04 75 88 04 01.

The Ardèche rises in hills to the north of the Col de la Chavade and flows 119km/74mi before joining the Rhône. It is notorious for spring floods and sudden spates which can increase its flow by as much as 3 000 percent, causing immense damage. Vertical cliffs, dramatic meanders and rapids, alternating with calm stretches, are a lesson in the geography of river formation. Prehistoric people settled here very early, and dolmens and cave-dwellings in the area date from the Bronze Age.

Aven de Marzal★

North bank.

At the bottom of this deep swallowhole the Gallery of Diamonds glitters with calcite crystals. A museum presents a display of equipment used by the great explorers of these caverns. Nearby, the popular **Prehistoric Zoo** features reproductions of prehistoric animals.

Gorges: From Vallon Pont d'Arc to Pont-St-Esprit

47km/29.2mi.

The meanders of the river mark the course it originally followed on the ancient surface of the plateau before cutting down through the rocks as they were uplifted during the Alpine-building period. Great sweeps of vertical cliffs with dramatic meanders cut deep into the rock and rapids alternating with calm stretches of water combine to form a very impressive natural site.

Pont-d'Arc★★

Spanning the width of the river, the arch of this gigantic natural bridge is 34m high and 59m wide. It is a recent phenomenon, caused by the action of the river, helped by the presence of fissures in the limestone, which eroded the base of a meander.

Haute Corniche (Scenic route)★★★

The road links a number of splendid viewpoints. From the Serre de Tourre can be seen the Pas du Mousse meander, where the river has still to cut through the wooded isthmus; the view from the Morsanne Needles (Aiguilles de Morsanne) gives a good idea of the structure of the plateau as it dips down to the south. Limestone ridges can be viewed from Gournier, while the rock spires of the Rocher de la Cathédrale lend this natural monument the appearance of a ruined cathedral.

Aven d'Orgnac★★★

Guided tours (1hr): Feb–Mar 10.30am, 11.30am, 2.25pm, 3.30pm, 4.45pm; Apr–Jun and Sept every 30mins 10am–noon,

2–5.30pm; Jul–Aug regularly throughout the day; Oct–mid-Nov every 40 mins. €12.50 (includes museum). 04 75 38 65 10. www.orgnac.com.

This extraordinary chasm, Aven d'Orgnac, lies among the woods covering the Ardèche plateau. It was first explored by Robert de Joly (1887–1968) on 19 August 1935. Joly was an electrical engineer, fascinated by cars and planes but above all by speleology.

Of the four caverns at Orgnac, only **Orgnac I** has so far been opened up to the public. Orgnac III is known to have been inhabited 300 000 years ago; the **museum** has displays on the cultures which flourished in the region before the Bronze Age.

ADDRESSES

STAY

La Ferme – 110 chemin des Bois, Île de la Barthelasse, 5km/3mi N. 04 90 27 15 47. 20 rooms. Closed Mon lunch, Wed lunch. Country-style dining room with beams, fireplace and old stone can be found at this haven of peace.

Bagatelle – 25 allées Antoine Pinay, Île de la Barthelasse. 04 90 86 30 39. www.campingbagatelle.com. 10 rooms for 2–4 people at the hotel, 230 placements at the campsite. Large campground with a separate hotel. Great setting near Pont St-Bénezet.

Hôtel Boquier – 6 r. du Portail Boquier. 04 90 82 34 43. www.hotel-boquier.com. 12 rooms. Each room is individually and tastefully decorated.

Hôtel Bristol – 44 cours J.-Jaurès. 04 90 16 48 48. www.bristol-hotel-avignon.com. 11 rooms. Closed 15 Dec –14 Jan. Situated on the main avenue of the walled city. Spacious and sensibly functional rooms.

Chambre d'hôte Villa Agapè – 13 r. Agricol. 04 90 85 21 92. 3 rooms. Closed 1–15 May, Jul, Feb. It's easy to forget the town-centre location of this attractive villa, with its verdant terrace and swimming pool.

Le Colbert – 7 r. Agricol Perdiguier. 04 90 86 20 20. www.avignon-hotel-colbert.com. Closed Nov–Feb. 15 rooms. Simplicity and family home atmosphere in this discreet hotel. Bedrooms are decorated with Provençal colours, antiques and billboards. No lift.

Hôtel de Blauvac – 11 r. de la Bancasse. 04 90 86 34 11. www.hotel-blauvac.com. 16 rooms. The former home of the Marquis de Tonduly, Lord of Blauvac, in the 17C, is one of the best value-for-money hotels in town.

Mignon – 12 r. Joseph Vernet. 04 90 82 17 30. www.hotel-mignon.com. 16 rooms. A small hotel in the heart of Avignon's historic centre. All rooms are soundproofed.

La Banasterie – 11 r. de la Banasterie. 06 87 72 96 36. www.labanasterie.com. 5 rooms. A Virgin with Child adorns the listed façade of this 16C edifice. A cosy, romantic interior.

Hôtel Cloître St-Louis – 20 r. Portail Boquier. 04 90 27 55 55. www.cloitre-saint-louis.com. 77 rooms. Restaurant. Situated in 16C cloisters, part of this hotel was designed by Jean Nouvel.

Hôtel Palais des Papes – 1 r. Gérard Philipe. 04 90 86 04 13. www.hotel-avignon.com. 27 rooms. Beautiful rooms and beautiful views at this luxurious, reasonably priced hotel in the old centre.

Maison d'hôte Lumani – 37 r. du Rempart St-Lazare. 04 90 82 94 11. www.maison-lumani.com.5 rooms. Artists are particularly welcome in this fine 19C manor house.

EAT

Ginette et Marcel – 25 pl. des Corps Saints. 04 90 85 58 70. More a bisto/caféteria than a restaurant, you can grab a decent sandwich or salad here.

Entrée des Artistes – 1 pl. des Carmes. 04 90 82 46 90. Closed Sat–Sun. The dining room is decorated in the style of a Parisian bistro, with old posters and movie memorabilia.

L'Ami Voyage... en compagnie – 5 r. Prevot. 04 90 82 41 51. French cuisine is served at this cute place set in an old library. An air of elegance reigns here.

Le Jardin de la Tour – 9 r. de la Tour. 04 90 85 66 50. http://restaurant-lejardindelatour.com. Closed Sun–Mon.

Situated near the ramparts, this restaurant has a lovely garden. Provençal cuisine.

⊜⊜ **L'Isle Sonnante** – 7 r. Racine. ℘04 90 82 56 01. Closed lunch in Aug, Sun, Mon. This restaurant near the town hall is proud of its Rabelaisian name. Interior combines rustic style with warm tones.

⊜⊜ **Piedoie** – 26 r. 3-Faucons. ℘04 90 85 17 32. Closed last week Aug, last week Nov, Feb school holidays, Mon off season, Wed. Beams, parquet flooring and white walls hung with contemporary paintings for the décor and creative cuisine based on market produce. A family atmosphere.

⊜⊜⊜ **Restaurant Christian Étienne** – 10 r. Mons. ℘04 90 86 16 50. www.christian-etienne.fr. A long-established Michelin restaurant in the centre of Avignon, not far from the Palais des Papes.

⊜⊜⊜ **Le Grand Café** – La Manutention, r. des Escaliers Ste Anne. ℘04 90 86 86 77. Closed Sun and Mon. Backing onto the buttresses of the Palais des Papes, these old barracks have become an essential part of local life.

⊜⊜⊜ **Le Moutardier du Pape** – 15 pl. du Palais-des-Papes. ℘04 90 85 34 76. Closed Wed from Oct–Mar. This 18C building, listed in France's National Heritage, makes an exceptional setting for a simple, fresh meal.

⊜⊜⊜⊜ **L'Essentiel** – 2 r. Petite-Fusterie. ℘04 90 85 87 12. www.restaurantlessentiel.com. Closed Sun. Generous cuisine.

⊜⊜⊜⊜ **La Mirande** – 4 pl. Amirande. ℘04 90 14 20 20. www.la-mirande.fr. Closed Tue–Wed. An 18C Provençal décor, antiques, ornaments and a profusion of refined detail set the scene here.

NIGHTLIFE

La Cave Breysse – 41 r. des Teinturiers. ℘04 32 74 25 86. Closed Sun. A very popular wine bar, this is a nice place to enjoy a well-priced glass of wine or an apéritif, and to take in the night.

Café In et Off – pl. du Palais-des-Papes. ℘04 90 85 48 95. Closed mid-Nov–late Feb. Don't miss the only café that enjoys views of the Palais des Papes.

Cloître des Arts – 83 r. Joseph-Vernet. ℘04 90 85 99 04. Open Mon–Sat 7am–1.30am (during the festival 7am–3am). Closed the first fortnight of Jan. 60+ varieties of beer from all over the world.

SHOWTIME

Le Rouge Gorge – 10 bis, r. Peyrolerie. ℘04 90 14 02 54. Closed Sun, Jul–Aug. The only cabaret in Avignon, the Rouge Gorge, modestly sheltered by the Palais des Papes, unveils the sensual charms of its show every Friday and Saturday.

SHOPPING

Markets – **Les Halles Centrales**, pl. Pie, traditional covered market Tue–Sun. **Flower market** Sat in pl. des Carmes. **Fair** Sat and Sun, rempart St-Michel. **Flea market** Sun in pl. des Carmes.

Honey – **La Boutique de la Miellerie**, 189 r. de la Source, St-Saturnin-lès-Avignon. ℘04 90 22 47 52. www.miellerie.fr. Honey, pollen, and royal jelly-based products.

LEISURE ACTIVITIES

Avignon by boat – CroisiEurope. ℘08 26 10 12 34. www.croisieurope.com. Audioguide tours from 1hr30 to 4hr of Avignon and along the Rhône.

Coach excursion – **Provence Vision (Cars Lieutaud)** – 36 bd St-Roch. ℘04 90 86 36 75. www.cars-lieutaud.fr. Offers half- and full-day excursions from Avignon to the Camargue, Pont du Gard, Fontaine-de-Vaucluse, the Alpilles, a lavender tour and a wine tour.

Trips on the Rhône – "Grands Bateaux de Provence" (℘04 90 85 62 25. www.avignon-et-provence.com/mireio) organises several full-day round-trip boat outings from Avignon along the Rhône.

EVENTS

Festival d'Avignon – Every July. It promotes France's cultural life through theatre, dance, lectures, exhibitions and concerts in and around Avignon. Information: ℘04 90 27 66 50. Reservations ℘04 90 14 14 14. www.festival-avignon.com.

Booking "Festival Off" – ℘04 90 85 13 08. www.avignonleoff.com. The programme for Avignon's Fringe Festival is available mid-June.

Hivernales d'Avignon – This contemporary dance festival takes place during two weeks in July. ℘04 90 82 33 12. www.hivernales-avignon.com.

Animo Nature – Early Oct at Parc des Expositions d'Avignon. ℘04 90 84 02 04. www.animo-nature.com. The largest animal show in France.

Orange★★

Gateway to the Midi, Orange is famous for its remarkable Roman remains, including the triumphal arch and the Roman Theatre, as well as for its prestigious international music festival, Chorégies d'Orange.

- **Population:** 29 135.
- **Michelin Map:** 332 B 9
- **Info:** 5 cours Aristide Briand. ✆04 90 34 70 88. www.otorange.fr.
- **Location:** Orange, on the River Meyne, close to the Rhône, is at the meeting of *autoroutes* and other highways, 32km/20mi N of Avignon.
- **Don't miss:** The stunning Théâtre Antique, and, if you have time, go to Vaison-la-Romaine for the Tuesday market.

A BIT OF HISTORY

Orange flourished in the days of the Pax Romana as an important staging post on the great highway between Arles and Lyon. In the 16C, it came into the possession of William the Silent, ruler of the German principality of Nassau, then Stadtholder of the United Provinces. He took the title of Prince of Orange and founded the Orange-Nassau line. Orange is still proud of its association with the royal house of the Netherlands, whose preferred title is Prince (or Princess) of Orange. In 1678 under the Treaty of Nijmegen, the town became French territory.

ROMAN MONUMENTS

- **Théâtre Antique★★★** – Dating from the reign of Roman **Emperor Augustus**, this theatre is the best-preserved structure of its type in the whole of the Roman world. The stage wall measures 103m x 36m; Louis XIV called it "the finest wall in all the kingdom". Its outer face is of striking simplicity, interrupted only by the mounts for the poles supporting the awnings shading the audience from the sun. On the auditorium side, the wall has lost its marble facing and mosaic decoration, its columns and its statues.

  The great statue of Augustus has been replaced in its central niche; together with some remaining hammer-finished granite blocks, it gives some idea of how the theatre must have appeared originally.
- **Arc de Triomphe★★** – A UNESCO World Heritage Site, Orange's Arc de Triomphe was built between the years AD 21 and 26 as a tribute to Emperor Augustus. It is a remarkable piece of architecture covered with beautiful sculptures. On its north and east sides are reliefs depicting the exploits of the Second Legion in Gaul (weapons both of Gauls and of Amazons), the triumph of Rome (captured Gauls in chains) and Roman domination of the seas following the naval battle of Actium (anchors, oars, warships).

WALKING TOURS

OLD ORANGE

Orange map, p631.

The streets of the old town centre are very animated and pleasant to stroll along. Turn right into rue Fuséerie and after place du Cloître, left into rue de Renoyer. Note the statue of the troubadour-prince Raimbaut d'Orange while crossing place de la République and heading towards the cathedral, the ancienne Cathédrale Notre-Dame de Nazareth.

- There are plenty of lively cafés and restaurants with pavement terraces in place Georges-Clemenceau, where you can admire the Hôtel de Ville with its 17C belfry. From place de la République, rue Stassart leads

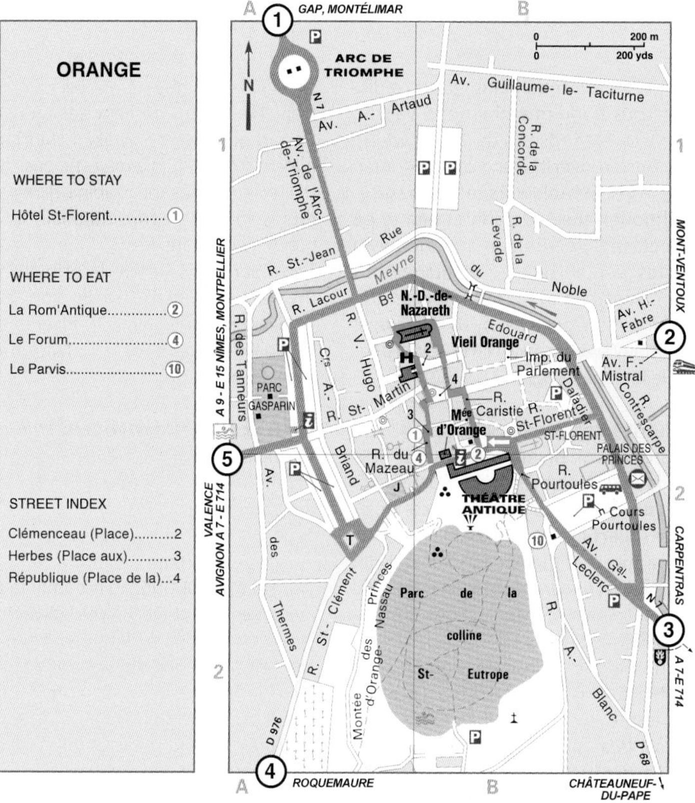

to a little square shaded with plane trees, place aux Herbes, which you cross to return to the theatre via rue du Mazeau.

- **Colline St-Eutrope** (St Eutrope Hill) – The main avenue crosses the moat of the former castle of the Princes of Orange; the excavations (left of square Reine-Juliana) have uncovered important ruins. At the far north end of the park, near a statue to the Virgin, there is a viewing table offering a beautiful viewa of the Roman Theatre in the foreground, the city of Orange with its tiled roofs, and the Rhône plain enclosed by mountains including majestic Mont Ventoux.

EXCURSIONS

VAISON-LA-ROMAINE★★

The town is on the N slopes of the Dentelles de Montmirail hills, some 30km/18.6mi E of the Rhône Valley and the town of Orange. pl. du Chanoine Sautel. ℘04 90 36 02 11. www.vaison-la-romaine.com.

This charming old market town near Mont Ventoux has outstanding and extensive ruins of the original Gallo-Roman town, as well as a Romanesque cathedral and cloisters.

Founded 60 years before Caesar's conquest of Gaul, Vaison was the capital of a Celtic tribe, the Vocontii. Under Roman rule it became the seat of great landed proprietors, a flourishing city possibly as large as Arles or Fréjus, one of the centres of Transalpine Gaul and subsequently of Narbonensis. It fell into ruin at the time of the barbarian invasions, and was covered in debris. In the Middle Ages the town grew again, but around the castle of the Counts of Toulouse on the other side of the river. In the 17C and 18C, new dwellings were built on the right bank, on top of the Roman site. Its ruins were discovered in the 19C, and began to be excavated in the early 20C.

In 1992, torrential rains caused a disastrous flood in and around Vaison. The Ouvèze rose to the point where it flowed over the top of the Roman bridge, which was undamaged, although the 16C parapet had to be replaced. The Roman and medieval sites were virtually undamaged but a campsite and modern houses and commercial premises by the river were entirely swept away. Thirty-seven people lost their lives.

Ruines Romaines★★

The layout of modern Vaison has allowed two parts of the Roman city to be excavated. The La Villasse quarter **(quartier de la Villasse)** lies to the southwest of the Avenue Général-de-Gaulle on either side of a paved central street; there are shops, houses and a basilica.

The Dolphin House (Maison du Dauphin) dating from 30 BCE is particularly interesting, as is the House of the Silver Bust (Maison du Buste-d'argent). The **quartier de Puymin** lies to the east of the avenue. Here there is the House of the Messii (Maison des Messii) with its atrium, peristyle and baths, as well as the Roman Theatre.

The latter structure (*approached via a tunnel*) dates from the time of the Emperor Augustus; the pits containing the machinery and curtain have been well preserved and the tiers of seating were reconstructed in 1932.

Musée Archéologique Théo-Desplans★

♿Open daily Nov–Feb 10am–noon, 2–5pm; Mar and Oct 10am–12.30pm, 2–5.30pm; Apr–May 9.30am–6pm; Jun–Sep 9.30am–6.30pm.
€8 (including Roman Ruins).
✆04 90 36 50 05.

This fascinating archaeological museum displays the finds excavated at Vaison. Different aspects of Gallo-Roman civilisation are presented thematically: religion, living quarters, pottery, glassware, arms, tools, ornaments, toiletries and imperial coins. The statues are remarkable. They are all in white marble; in chronological order: Claudius (dating from 43) wearing a heavy oak crown; Domitian in armour; naked Hadrian (dating from 121) in a majestic pose in the Hellenistic manner; Sabina, his wife, represented more conventionally as a great lady in state dress.

Two other pieces are worthy of interest: the 2C marble head of Apollo crowned with laurel leaves, and a 3C silver bust of a patrician and mosaics from the Peacock Villa.

CHÂTEAU DE GRIGNAN★★

Grignan is SE of Montélimar, E of the Rhône.
12 place du Jeu de Ballon.
✆04 75 46 56 75. www.tourisme-paysdegrignan.com.

The old town of Grignan is dominated by its medieval château, which owes its fame to the delightful letters written in the 17C, over a twenty-year period, by Mme de **Sévigné** to her daughter Mme de Grignan. The letters were to create a new literary genre; they are full of keen observation, wit and spontaneity.

The medieval castle was remodelled in the 16C. In 1669, the Count of Grignan married the daughter of Mme de Sévigné, who became a frequent visitor.

The Renaissance south front of the château was restored early in the 20C following a fire. With its superimposed columns, moulded pilasters, mullioned windows and shell-decorated niches, it marks the arrival of the Renaissance in Provence.

The original courtyard is flanked by a Gothic pavilion and opens out onto the terrace with a **view**★★ over the Tricastin area and Mont Ventoux. Inside are evocative furnishings **(mobilier**★**)** of many periods and Aubusson tapestries.

MONT VENTOUX★★★

The massif is served by a scenic route 67km/41.6mi long between Vaison and Carpentras. The road was used for motor racing until 1973, and the ascent is a major challenge in those years when it features as part of the Tour de France. The mountain's upper section is blocked by snow mid-Nov–mid-March.

Mount Ventoux enjoys an isolated position far from any rival summit, making it a commanding presence in northwestern Provence, visible over vast distances especially when topped in winter with a sparkling coat of snow.

Summit★★★

1 909m.

The top of the mountain consists of a vast field of white shingle from which protrude numerous masts and instruments, radar equipment, a TV transmitter and a weather station.

Mont Ventoux, the Windy Mountain, is so named because of the mistral which blasts it with a force unequalled elsewhere. On average, the temperature here is 11°C lower than in the valley. The flora even includes polar vegetation. In the early morning and late afternoon, as well as in autumn, the vast **panorama★★★** extends from the Écrins Massif to the northeast to the Cévennes and the shore of the Mediterranean.

Below the resort of Chalet-Reynard on the descent southward are fine stands of Aleppo and Austrian black pine and Atlantic cedar, as well as beeches and oaks. Finally, beyond St-Estève, vines and fruit trees make an appearance.

ADDRESSES

STAY

Hôtel Le St-Florent – 4 r. du Mazeau. 04 90 34 18 53. www.hotel-orange-saint florent.com. 15 rooms. Closed Dec–Feb. A stone's throw from the Roman Theatre, this is an attractive little hotel with individually decorated rooms and paintings by the owner.

Chambre d'hôte Le Clos des Grenadiers – 400 rte des Plaines, 84350 Courthézon. 04 90 70 29 76. www.closdes grenadiers.fr. 2 rooms. Representing the seventh generation at Châteauneuf-du-Pape estate Mourre du Tendre, Florence Paumel has two very well-appointed rooms for guests in her lovely home. Each has a private terrace and a luxurious bathroom, and breakfasts are delicious. A fine garden with pool and views to Mont Ventoux, plus Châteauneuf wine estates on the doorstep.

La Bastide des Princes – chemin de Bigonnet, 84860 Caderousse. 04 90 51 04 59. www.bastide-princes.com. Restaurant (table d'hote). In quiet countryside near Orange, well-known local chef Pierre Paumel and his wife have created attractively traditional rooms in this old bastide. Its greatest feature, however, is the chef's cooking.

EAT

Le Pistou – 15 r. Joseph-Ducos, 84230 Châteauneuf-du-Pape. 04 90 83 71 75. Closed Sun eve and Mon. A cosy, unpretentious little bistro whose menu focuses on traditional Provençal dishes.

Auberge Le Tourne au Verre – Rte de Ste-Cécile, 84290 Cairanne. 04 90 30 72 18. www.letourneauverre.com. Closed Sun and Wed. A wine bar in the heart of a wine village. Impressive selection of Côtes du Rhone wines.

Restaurant La Rom'Antique – Rue Madeleine Roch, 5 pl. Silvain. 04 90 51 67 06. ♿. Closed 3 weeks in Jan, 2 weeks in Oct, Sat lunch, Sun eve, Mon. Sit on the terrace if possible so that you can take in views of the Roman Theatre.

Le Forum – 3 r. de Mazeau. 04 90 34 01 09. www.restaurantleforum.com. Closed 20 Aug–3 Sep, 23 Feb–5 Mar, Sun and Tue. Small restaurant hidden in a tiny, narrow street near the Roman theatre. Elegant Provençal-style décor.

Le Parvis – 55 cours Pourtoules. 04 90 34 82 00. Closed 8 Nov–1 Dec, 10 Jan–1 Feb, Sun–Mon. Polished parquet flooring and contemporary paintings create an elegant atmosphere in this restaurant. Contemporary cuisine with a Provençal note.

French Riviera and Corsica

» Region map p636–637
Nice p638
Monaco p646
Menton p652
Cannes p654
St-Tropez p660
Toulon p663
Corsica p665

Introduction

The Riviera's abundant sunshine, exotic vegetation and dramatic combination of sea and mountains have made it a fashionable place of pleasure since its "discovery" in the 19C. The coast is densely built up, the resorts linked by triple corniche roads. Further north are the Maritime Alps, dissected by the upper valleys of the Var, Tinée, Vésubie and Roya. To the west of Nice the coast flattens out, forming wide bays with fine beaches, before again rising beyond Cannes to higher ground.

Geography – The bustle of the coast is in contrast to the quieter charm of the interior, with its olive groves, spectacular gorges and hill villages. There is no defined boundary for the Riviera, but it is widely accepted as extending from the border with Italy, west to St-Tropez. Between Nice and Menton, the Pre-Alps plunge into the sea while the limestone plâteaux of the Provence tableland are separated from the sea by two massifs, Estérel and Maures. Its coastline has great promontories extending into the sea defining wide bays like that of the Gulf of St-Tropez. The Toulon coast is characterised by vertical cliffs, and a number of attractive beaches; to the north rise the limestone heights of the Provençal ranges.

History – Although preceded by the Ligurians and Greeks, the Romans had established themselves in the region by the 1C AD and evidence of their presence can be seen today at Fréjus and Cimiez (Nice). In the Middle Ages, Provence changed hands several times and was not a part of France until the late 15C. Nice remained part of Savoy and not restored to France until 1860.

Highlights

1. The fascinating old quarter of **Nice** (p639)
2. Exciting drives and fine views: **Corniches de la Riviera** (p643)
3. The capital of the city of Monaco: **Le Rocher** (p646)
4. Ancient village in natural amphitheatre: **Saorge** (p652)
5. Tour of the Old Town of **Ajaccio** on Corsica (p666)

Economy – The Riviera, also known as the Côte d'Azur, is dominated by tourism, which began in the 19C. This most important industry is why Nice, the largest city in the region, has France's second-busiest airport. After tourism, the best-known industry on the Riviera is perfume, but there is also a burgeoning industry, producing olives and olive oil; that is also a major contributor to the economy.

Roquebrune-Cap-Martin, Corniches de la Riviera

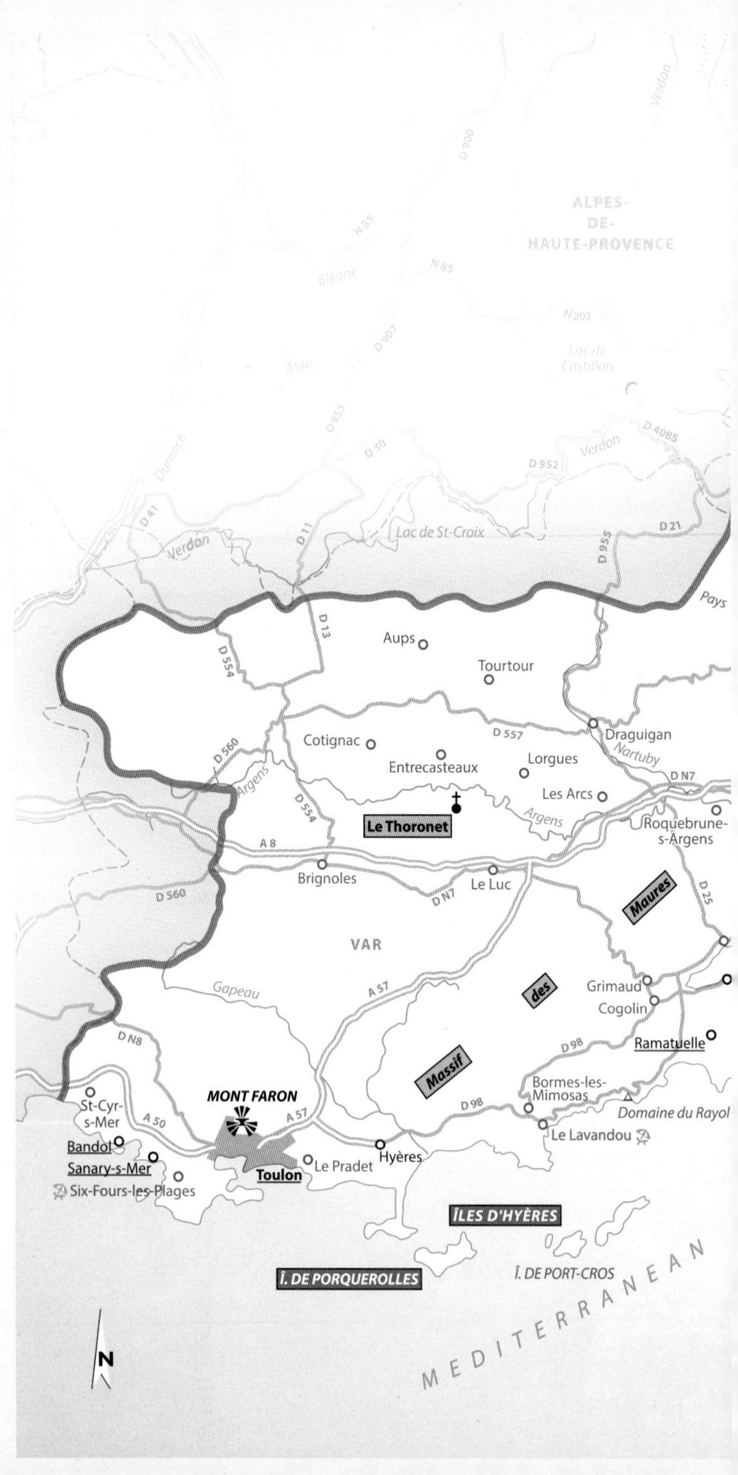

ALPES-DE-HAUTE-PROVENCE
Verdon
D 900
N 85
Bléone
N 202
Lac de Castillon
D 907
Asse
D 953
D 30
Durance
D 952
Verdon
D 4085
D 41
D 11
Lac de St-Croix
D 21
Verdon
D 955
Pays
D 13
Aups
Tourtour
D 554
Draguigan
D 557
Cotignac
Entrecasteaux
Lorgues
Nartuby
D 560
Argens
D N7
Les Arcs
D 554
Le Thoronet
Argens
Roquebrune-s-Argens
A 8
Brignoles
Le Luc
D N7
Maures
D 25
D 560
VAR
des
Grimaud
Gapeau
A 57
Cogolin
D N8
D 98
Ramatuelle
Massif
MONT FARON
Bormes-les-Mimosas
St-Cyr-s-Mer
A 50
A 57
D 98
Domaine du Rayol
Bandol
Le Lavandou
Sanary-s-Mer
Toulon
Le Pradet
Hyères
Six-Fours-les-Plages
ÎLES D'HYÈRES
Î. DE PORQUEROLLES
Î. DE PORT-CROS
MEDITERRANEAN
N

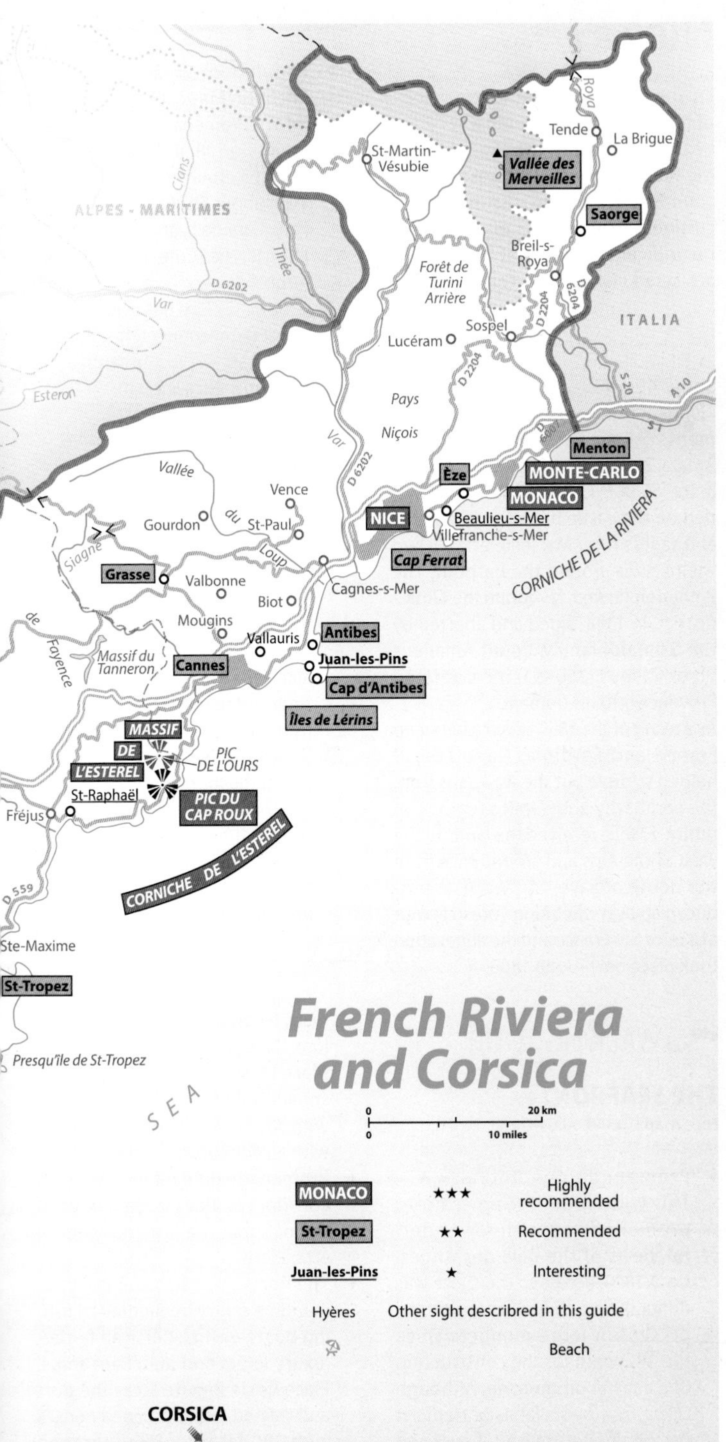
ALPES - MARITIMES
ITALIA
St-Martin-Vésubie
Vallée des Merveilles
Tende
La Brigue
Roya
Saorge
Breil-s-Roya
Forêt de Turini Arrière
Sospel
Lucéram
Pays Niçois
Menton
MONTE-CARLO
MONACO
Èze
NICE
Beaulieu-s-Mer
Villefranche-s-Mer
Cap Ferrat
CORNICHE DE LA RIVIERA
Vence
St-Paul
Gourdon
Vallée du Loup
Grasse
Valbonne
Biot
Cagnes-s-Mer
Mougins
Vallauris
Antibes
Juan-les-Pins
Cap d'Antibes
Cannes
Massif du Tanneron
Îles de Lérins
MASSIF DE L'ESTEREL
PIC DE L'OURS
PIC DU CAP ROUX
St-Raphaël
Fréjus
CORNICHE DE L'ESTEREL
Ste-Maxime
St-Tropez
Presqu'île de St-Tropez
SEA
Cians
Tinée
Var
Esteron
Siagne
de Fayence
D 6202
D 2204
D 6204
D 559
S 20
A 10
French Riviera and Corsica
0 20 km
0 10 miles
MONACO ★★★ Highly recommended
St-Tropez ★★ Recommended
Juan-les-Pins ★ Interesting
Hyères Other sight described in this guide
Beach
CORSICA

Nice★★★

Enclosed by an amphitheatre of hills, extending around a beautiful blue bay, the capital of the Riviera has artistic treasures, countless attractions, distinctive cuisine, a wonderful climate and a magnificent setting that has long attracted visitors year round.

- **Population:** 343 304.
- **Michelin Map:** 341 E 5
- **Info:** 5 Promenade des Anglais. ℘08 92 70 74 07. www.nicetourisme.com.
- **TGV:** about 6h–6h30 from Paris Gare de Lyon.
- **Flights:** Nice Côte d'Azur Airport (www.nice-aeroport.fr. ℘0820 423 333) has over 100 direct flight connections. Bus shuttle service to city centre.
- **Location:** Nice is 27km/17mi W along the coast from the border with Italy.
- **Parking:** Try one of the many underground car parks. The Nice City Passport app for smartphones allows you to locate empty parking places and pay for them instantly (www.parkings-semiacs.com).
- **Don't Miss:** A stroll along the Promenade des Anglais; the panorama from the château hill.
- **Timing:** At least a full day: spend the morning on the seafront and in Vieux Nice; reserve the afternoon for Cimiez, and, if you have time, choose an art museum according to your taste.

A BIT OF HISTORY

Some 400 000 years ago, bands of elephant hunters made their encampments on the fossil beach at Terra Amata, 26m above the present sealevel. In the 6C BCE, Celto-Ligurians first settled on the castle hill; later merchants and sailors from Marseille established themselves around the harbour. The Romans followed, favouring the Cimiez district. In 1388, aided and abetted by the **Grimaldi** family, Count Amadeus VII of Savoy (1360–91) incorporated Provence into his domain.

As a result of the 1859 alliance between France and Sardinia, Napoléon III helped to drive out the Austrians from the Lombardy and Veneto regions; in return, France received the lands to the west of the Alps and around Nice from the House of Savoy. A plebiscite produced an overwhelming vote in favour of a return to France and the annexation took place on 14 June 1860.

WALKING TOUR

THE SEAFRONT★★

Nice map I, p640. Allow 2hrs.

- **Promenade des Anglais★★** – This wide south-facing seafront promenade provides wonderful views of the Baie des Anges. Until 1820, access to the shore was difficult, so rich English residents, present in large numbers since the 18C, paid for the construction of a coastal promenade. Although taken over by six lanes of traffic, it has retained its mythical aura and many legendary buildings still overlook the sea.
- **Place Masséna** – This harmonious square built in Turin style is lined with restored, red ochre buildings with arcades at street level. .
- **Promenade du Paillon** – A "green corridor" to the marble cubes of the national theatre and modern art gallery.
- **The Port** – Nice harbour is a busy maritime centre frequented by fishing boats, yachts, Corsican ferries, luxury liners and merchant ships. Place Île de Beauté faces the port and is lined with porticoed houses with 19C façades. Stroll through

PRACTICAL INFORMATION

Sightseeing and Tours

Admission to Nice's municipal museums and galleries is free.

Guided tours – 5 Promenade des Anglais. ℘04 92 00 41 90. Closed Jan. Tours of the Old Town (2hr 30min). €12, bookable at the tourist office.

French Riviera Pass – A 1-, 2- or 3-day sightseeing pass with free entry to many sights, tours and shopping and dining advantages (€26, €38 and €56. Available at the tourist office or online at www.frenchrivierapass.com.

Petits Trains Touristiques – ♿Tours (50min) departing every 30min: Oct–Mar 10am–5pm; Apr–Sept 10am–7pm. €8 (children 4–12, €4). ℘06 08 55 08 30; www.trains touristiquesdenice.com. Departures from the Promendade des Anglais. Tours of the Old Town, port and château.

Nice l'Open Tour – Departs from avenue des Phocéens (Maison du Département): every 30 min 10am–6pm: Apr–Oct, hourly Nov–Mar. €22 (children 4–11, €8). ℘04 92 29 17 00. Double-decker, open-top bus tours with commentary in English *(90min)*. Hop-on, hop-off the 14 different stops from the Promenade des Anglais, Cimiez and the Port.

Trans Côte d'Azur – Operates Apr–Oct Tue–Sun 11am and 3pm. ℘04 92 00 42 30; www.trans-cote-azur.com. €17.50. Guided tours (1hr) of the coast of Nice, Bay of Villefranche and Baie des Anges. ***Reservations essential.***

Public transport

Bus/Tram – The Ligne d'Azur network (℘08 1006 1006; www.lignedazur.com) includes buses for the city of Nice and its suburbs, and a new tram line in central Nice. Individual tickets, 10-journey cards and unlimited travel passes (1- and 7-day) available. The TAM coach network (various departure points across the city. ℘0800 06 01 06; www.rca.tm.fr) has services to towns such as Antibes, Cannes and Grasse.

TER Train – SNCF Gare, Avenue Thiers. ℘0 891 70 30 00. www.ter-sncf.com/paca. Local train services to Draguignan, Fréjus, St-Raphaël, Cannes, Grasse, Antibes, Menton, Vintimille (Vintimiglia in Italy), Monaco. The Nice-Cuneo line crosses the Bévéra and Roya valleys.

Rental Bikes and Cars – Nice has set up dozens of self-service **bicycle rental** docking stations **(vélos bleues)** across the city. Guidelines and rates (per hour, day, week or month) are available at www.velobleu.org (℘04 93 72 06 06). A similar scheme for electric cars, **Auto Bleue**, was launched in 2011 with a slightly more complicated registration process. For details visit www.auto-bleu.org (℘0977 406 406).

the flea markets at quai Lunel, then return along quai Rauba Capeu, which connects Promenade des Anglais.

WALKING TOUR

OLD NICE★

Nice map II, p643. Allow 2hrs.

The core of the city, huddling at the foot of the castle hill, has a lively, utterly Mediterranean character.

- **Cours Saley★** – Lined with shops and restaurants, this elegant Baroque square is home to a famous flower and vegetable market (antiques on Monday). Matisse lived here 1921–1938 at the Caïs de Pierla Palace.
- **Chapelle de la Miséricorde★** – This Niçois Baroque chapel belongs to the Black Penitents.
- **Chapelle de l'Annonciation** – Built in the 13C and remodelled in the 17C, this chapel, known locally as the Chapelle Ste-Rita, has a typically

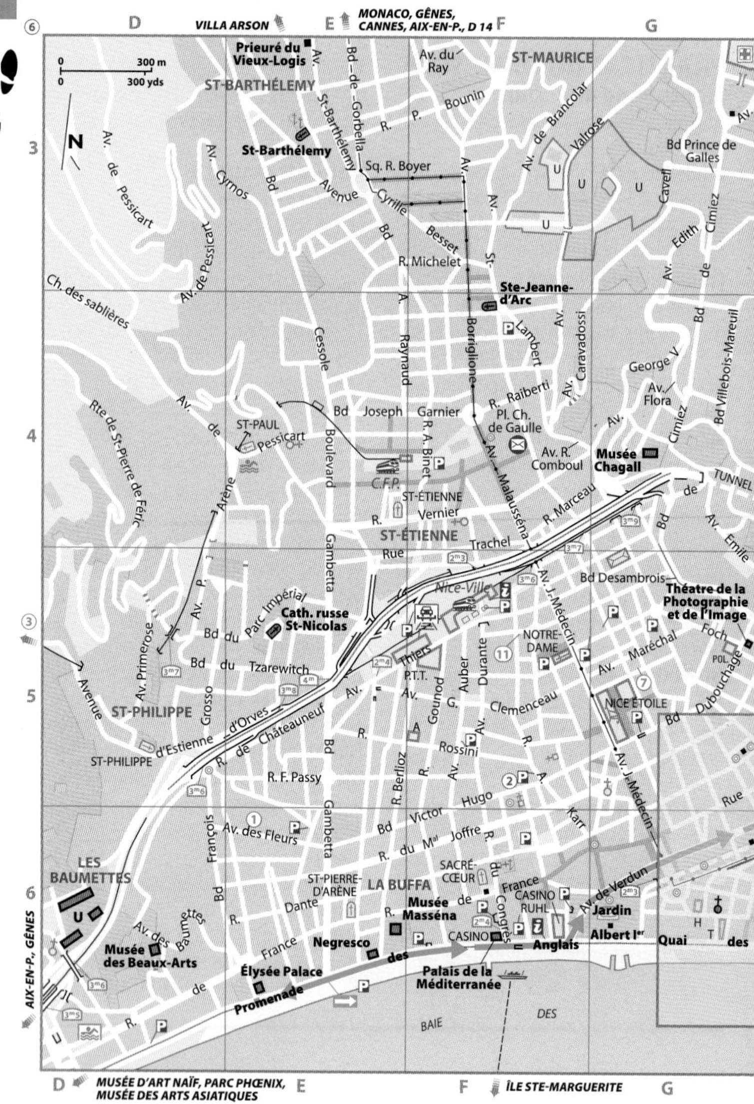

stern Nice Baroque exterior and a lavish Baroque **interior★**.

- **Église St-Jacques or Gésu★** – Built as a chapel in the 17C (the façade dates from 1825), this church is typical of the Counter Reformation style.
- **Cathédrale Ste-Réparate** – The cathedral (1650) is topped by an 18C bell tower and a magnificent dome of 14 000 glazed tiles. The **interior★** is a riot of Baroque plasterwork and marble.
- **Palais Lascaris, Musée de la Musique** – This Genoese-style palace, influenced by local tradition, was built in 1648 by J.B. Lascaris, a descendant of the counts of Ventimiglia. On the ground floor a pharmacy from Besançon (1738) has been reconstructed.

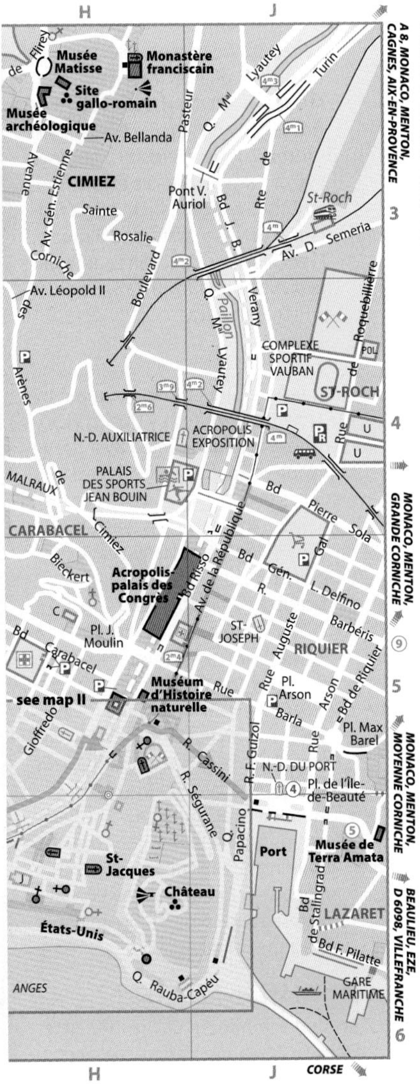

NICE
map I

WHERE TO STAY

Armenonville (Hôtel)	1
Castel Enchanté (Chambre d'hôte)	3
Clair H.	5
Normandie (Hôtel de)	11
Star (Hôtel)	7
Villa la Lézardière (Chambre d'hôte)	9

WHERE TO EAT

Chez Cicion	6
le Local	4
Stéphane Viano	2

- **Place St-François** – This square, home to the morning fish market, is overlooked by a fine 18C building, the former labour exchange, behind which is the St-François clock tower, once part of the Franciscan monastery transferred to Cimiez.
- **Place Garibaldi** – One of the most attractive squares in Nice, place Garibaldi was laid out in the 18C in typical Piedmont style and is lined with Sardinian-red and yellow ochre arcaded buildings. It marks the northern limit of the Old Town and the beginning of the new, and was the start of the royal route to Turin in the 1700s.
- **Église St-Martin-St-Augustin** – This is the oldest parish in Nice, dating back to 1510. Garibaldi was baptised here and Martin Luther once performed a mass here.

- **Château Hill** – This 302m high hill, arranged as a garden walk, was where Nice's fortress stood until it was destroyed in 1706 on the orders of Louis XIV.
- **Tour Bellanda** – Despite its appearance, this imposing circular bastion is a 19C reconstruction of one of the towers of the citadel destroyed in 1706.

ART

- **Musée des Beaux-Arts Jules-Chéret★★** – This 1878 residence, built in the style of a 17C Genoese Renaissance palace for the Russian princess Kotschoubey, houses a rich collection of works sent to Nice by Napoléon III in 1860, along with a number of donations.
- **Musée Matisse★★** – Built on the site of a cabin (cabanoun) surrounded by the ancient remains of Cimiez, this 17C Genoese villa with a pebble-dash façade and trompe-l'oeil decoration extended by balustraded terraces was once owned by the Consul of Nice. After it fell into ruin, the city of Nice bought it in 1950. Since its redevelopment in 1993, it has housed the Musée Matisse. This collection includes over 30 paintings and provides an overview of Henri Matisse's career (1869–1954).
- **Musée Marc-Chagall★★** – This museum, built in 1972, houses the most important permanent collection of the painter's works, including all 17 canvasses which make up the "Biblical Message".
- **Musée d'Art Moderne et d'Art Contemporain★★** – Designed by Yves Bayard and Henri Vidal, the Museum of Modern and Contemporary Art is made up of four square towers with roof-top terraces linked by glass passageways. The collections present works by the Nice School and the French and American avant-garde art movements from the 1960s to the present day.
- **Musée des Arts Asiatiques★★** – Delicately poised on the lake in Phœnix Park, this white marble construction (1998) by the Japanese architect Kenzo Tange presents sacred and traditional objects from Asia.
- **Musée d'Art Naïf Jakovsky★** – Housed in an elegant château, the Anatole Jakovsky Bequest comprises 600 canvasses by naïve artists from around the world, including Croatian artists Generalic and Rabuzin, French artists Bauchant and Vieillard, and works from Italy, Belgium and the Americas.

CIMIEZ

Long before Cimiez was occupied by the French and visited by Queen Victoria (who is commemorated by a statue at the top of Boulevard de Cimiez), this was the site of the Roman city Cemelenum. In 2C there were at least 20 000 Romans living here. Many vestiges of their city remain.

- **Site archéologique gallo-romain★** – The Cimiez district originated in the Roman settlement whose growth soon eclipsed that of the older town laid out around the harbour. The archaeological site consists of medium-size amphitheatres and the area around the baths.
- **Monastère de Cimiez★** – The Franciscans, who in the 16C took over the buildings of a former Benedictine monastery founded in the 9C, have restored and considerably enlarged the abbey church.

RUSSIAN HERITAGE

Around the middle of the 19C, after Empress Alexandra Fedorovna, widow of Tsar Nicolas I, settled in Nice, many wealthy Russian aristocrats chose the city as their winter residence. These "eccentrics", as the locals called them, recreated the atmosphere of their native land on the Riviera.

- **Cathédrale Orthodoxe Russe St-Nicolas★** – With its six gilded onion domes and its ochre brick façade, the Russian Orthodox cathedral is the largest Russian religious building outside Russia.

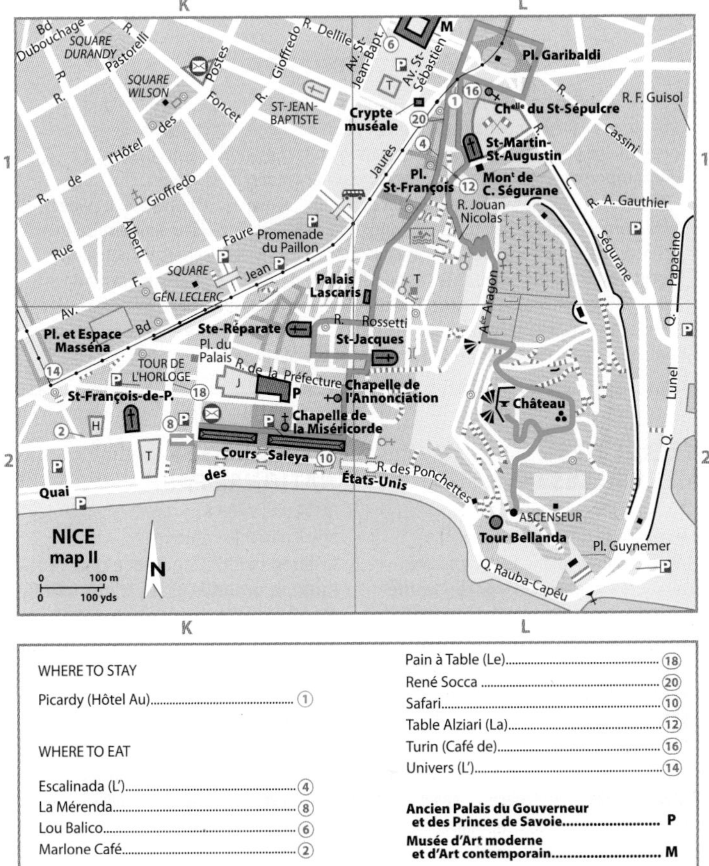

ADDITIONAL SIGHTS

- **Musée Masséna★** – Recently reopened after a major renovation, this museum explores the history of Nice from the 19C to the 1930s.
- **Acropolis-Palais des Congrès★** – This enormous convention centre resembles a majestic vessel anchored to five robust vaults spanning the River Paillon. Designed by a group of local architects it features works by contemporary artists.

EXCURSIONS

CORNICHES DE LA RIVIERA★★★

Circular tour of 41km/25.4mi.

The Lower Corniche road skirts the foot of Mont Boron, giving fine views over Villefranche-sur-Mer and its bay.

The highly indented coastline is the result of the recent folding and subsequent drowning of the limestone Pre-Alps.

Both **Cap Ferrat★★** and the nearby headland, Pointe St-Hospice, offer splendid views of the Riviera with its corniche roads; the village of Èze-Bord-de-Mer, the fashionable resort of **Beaulieu★**, Cap d'Ail can all be identified, and rising out of the sea in the distance is Cap Martin. Clinging like an eagle's nest to its inaccessible rock spike, **Èze★★** seems the very archetype of a hill village. It was inhabited by the Ligurians and by the Phoenicians, then fortified against raiders from the sea. In 1706 both the village and its castle were demolished on the orders of Louis XIV, but it was rebuilt after 1760.

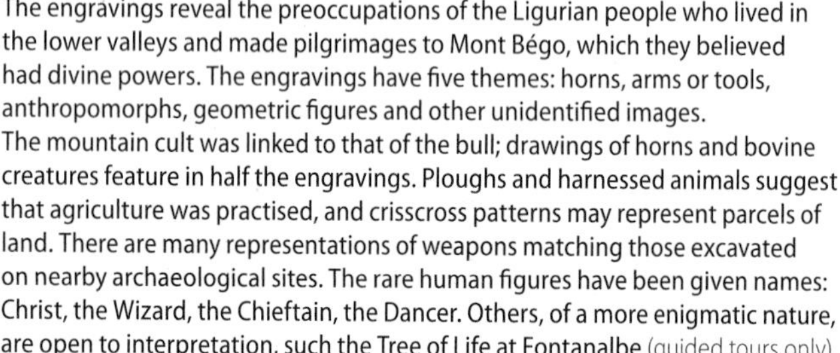

Magic Mountain

The engravings reveal the preoccupations of the Ligurian people who lived in the lower valleys and made pilgrimages to Mont Bégo, which they believed had divine powers. The engravings have five themes: horns, arms or tools, anthropomorphs, geometric figures and other unidentified images.

The mountain cult was linked to that of the bull; drawings of horns and bovine creatures feature in half the engravings. Ploughs and harnessed animals suggest that agriculture was practised, and crisscross patterns may represent parcels of land. There are many representations of weapons matching those excavated on nearby archaeological sites. The rare human figures have been given names: Christ, the Wizard, the Chieftain, the Dancer. Others, of a more enigmatic nature, are open to interpretation, such the Tree of Life at Fontanalbe (guided tours only).

VALLÉE DES MERVEILLES★★

78km/49mi NE from Nice.

The whole of the site known as the vallée des Merveilles consists of seven distinct regions around Mont Bégo: the vallée des Merveilles itself, which is the largest; the vallée de Fontanalbe, which is narrower; the Valmasque, Valaurette, Lac Sainte-Marie, Col du Sabion and Lac Vei del Bouc.

At the foot of **Mont Bégo** lies a region of glacial lakes, valleys and rocky cirques formed during the Quaternary Era, cut off by the scarce roads and harsh mountain climate. In this dramatic landscape is the Vallée des Merveilles, famous for the thousands of prehistoric rock engravings found there.

The Engravings – The name Bégo is derived from an Indo-European root which means the sacred mountain (*Be*) inhabited by the bull-god (*Go*).

The region of Mont Bégo is an **open-air museum** comprising over 40 000 engravings. Cut into the rock face worn smooth by glacial erosion 15 000 years ago, the linear engravings date from the Gallo-Roman period through the Middle Ages to the present. The most interesting ones to the archaeologists date back to the early Bronze Age.

MERCANTOUR NATIONAL PARK

04 93 16 78 88. www.parc-mercantour.eu.

Created in 1979, and once part of the hunting grounds of the kings of Italy, Mercantour is now twinned with the Parco Naturale delle Alpi Marittime across the border in Italy. These two parks work together to protect their natural and cultural heritage. More than 800 000 visitors reach the park each year to enjoy its 600km/275mi of footpaths, more than 2 000 species of plants, and 58 species of mammal.

ADDRESSES

STAY

⊖ **Au Picardy Hôtel** – 10 blvd. Jean-Jaurès. 04 93 85 75 51. 11 rooms. Between the train station and Old Town, this friendly, family-run hotel has basic rooms: small, yet soundproofed.

⊖ **Clair Hotel** – 23 blvd. Carnot, Impasse Terra Amata. 04 93 89 69 89. 10 rooms. This converted schoolhouse near the archaeological museum has rooms all on one floor (in the old classrooms) and a Mediterranean garden terrace, where breakfast is served in summer. Quiet neighbourhood.

⊖⊖ **Hôtel Armenonville** – 20 ave. des Fleurs. 04 93 96 86 00. www.hotel-armenonville.com. 12 rooms. P. At the end of a passage in the old Russian district of Nice, this retro hotel built in

1900 has charming rooms decorated with antiques. WiFi, garden, air-conditioning and free parking.

⊖⊖ **Hôtel de Normandie** – 18 rue Paganini. ℘04 93 88 48 83. www.hotel-normandie.com. 44 rooms. Practical location near the train station with a typical Niçoise decor. Rooms are simple, yet well-equipped; free WiFi and a hot meal distributor in the lobby.

⊖⊖ **Star Hôtel** – 14 rue Biscarra. ℘04 93 85 19 03. www.hotel-star.com. 24 rooms. Small hotel close to the Nice Étoile shopping centre, offering simple accommodation with air-conditioning and free Internet access.

⊖⊖⊖ **Chambre d'hôte Castel Enchanté** – 61 route St-Pierre-de-Féric. ℘04 93 97 02 08. www.castel-enchante.com. ⊭. 4 rooms. Closed mid-Nov–mid-Mar. A beautiful 19C villa on the hills above Nice, with a huge terrace surrounded by orchards. Rooms are lovingly decorated.

⊖⊖⊖ **Chambre d'hôte Villa la Lézardière** – 87 blvd. de l'Observatoire. ℘04 93 56 22 86. 5 rooms. P. Perched on the Grande Corniche, this Provençal-style villa has great **views** over the Alps. Personalised bedrooms, some with kitchenettes. Also a large pool and enclosed garden.

EAT

***Salade niçoise, socca, pan bagnat, poutine, tourte aux blettes, beignets de fleurs de courgettes**...* to experience the best in local cuisine, look for the restaurants displaying the "Cuisine Nissarde" label. Get a guide to these restaurants from the tourist office.

⊖ **Lou Balico** – 22 ave. St-Jean-Baptiste. ℘04 93 85 93 71. www.loubalico.com. Three generations of the same family have been serving classic Niçois dishes in this cosy dining room, adorned with a piano and guest book with signatures from around the world.

⊖ **Marlone Café** – 4 rue de l'Opéra. ℘04 93 85 96 15. www.marlonecafe.com. Closed Mon. A gourmet refuge just off Place Masséna, with traditional meals and a comfortable, thoughtfully decorated dining room.

⊖ **Le Pain à Table** – 3 rue St-François-de-Paul (cours Saleya). ℘04 93 62 94 32. Sit at one of the communal wooden tables and order fresh breads with spreads, salads, open sandwiches and brunch on the weekend.

⊖ **Réné Socca** – 2 rue Miralhéti. ℘04 93 92 05 73. ⊭. Closed Mon. The most popular "Nissart" restaurant in town. Follow the line, order your food and sit at one of the long tables with your meal. Don't miss the ***socca***, cooked fresh in the wood-fired oven, or the *pissaladière*.

⊖ **Restaurant Safari** – 1 cours Saleya. ℘04 93 80 18 44. http://restaurantsafari.fr. A trendy address overlooking the market at Cours Saleya, this restaurant has a beautiful terrace and local specialities, including seafood.

⊖ **La Table d'Alziari** – 4 rue François-Zannin. ℘04 93 80 34 03. Closed mid-Jan, early Jun, early Oct, mid-Dec, Sun–Mon. Unpretentious family restaurant in a small alley of the old town. Typical dishes from Nice and the Provence area.

⊖⊖ **L'Escalinada** – 22 rue Pairolière. ℘04 93 62 11 71. www.escalinada.fr. ⊭. Closed mid-Nov–mid-Dec. Nestled in the old quarter, this charming restaurant offers attractively presented regional cuisine in a spruce dining room with rustic overtones. Friendly service.

⊖⊖ **Grand Café de Turin** – 5 pl. Garibaldi. ℘04 93 62 29 52. This brasserie, which is over 200 years old, has become an institution in Nice. It serves seafood dishes à la carte at reasonable prices throughout the day. Pleasant, welcoming setting, although a bit noisy on the terrace.

⊖⊖ **Le Local** – 4 rue Rusca. ℘04 93 14 08 29. Minimalist decor for this deli-restaurant specialising in Neopolitan and Sicilian dishes.

⊖⊖⊖ **La Mérenda** – 4 r. Raoul Bosio F. ℘04 93 14 08 29. ⊭. Uncomfortable stools, no telephone and credit cards are not accepted. Despite all of this, crowds flock to La Mérenda every day to sample its authentic Niçoise cuisine!

⊖⊖⊖⊖ **L'Univers-Christian Plumail** – 54 blvd. J. Jaurès. ℘04 93 62 32 22. www.christian-plumail.com. Closed Sat and Mon, Sun. Decorated with modern paintings and sculptures, this prestigious Niçois restaurant serves regional cuisine with a twist. Very reasonable set menus.

Monaco★★★

The Principality of Monaco, world-famous haunt of the super-rich, is a sovereign state. Inhabited since prehistoric times and later a Greek settlement (5C BCE) and a Roman port, its history really began when the Grimaldi family bought it from the Republic of Genoa in 1308. Prince Rainier III ruled the principality from 1949–2005 with the assistance of a National Council. His only son Prince Albert then took power, but because he has no children, it seems certain that the line of succession will pass to Rainier's daughter, Princess Caroline. Four districts make up the town: Monaco-Ville, the historic seat of the Principality; Monte-Carlo, the district surrounding the casino; La Condamine, around Port Hercule and Fontvielle, the new industrial area built on land reclaimed from the sea.

- **Population:** 37 418.
- **Michelin Map:** 341 F 5
- **Info:** 2a bd des Moulins. ℘00 377 92 16 61 66. www.visitmonaco.com.
- **TGV:** 6–8hrs from Paris. Gare de Lyon.
- **Location:** The territory includes the Old Town or Monaco Ville on the Rock (Rocher de Monaco); the new town of Monte-Carlo and the port area at La Condamine linking the two.
- **Parking:** Park in the underground garage (parking des Pêcheurs creusé) of Le Rocher, and take the lift up to the Old Town on the Rock.
- **Don't Miss:** The Musée Océanographique or the Palais Princier.
- **Timing:** Allow 3hr in Old Monaco before visiting Monte-Carlo, where you can try your luck in the casino. November is very busy.
- **Kids:** Musée Océanographique; Collection des Voitures Anciennes; Musée National des Automates et Poupées d'Autrefois à Monaco.

WALKING TOUR

THE ROCK★★

Monaco Monte Carlo map, p648. 3hr.

Crowned by the old town of Monaco-Ville and its ramparts, the Rocher de Monaco juts 800m out to sea over the bay. Resembling a studio set, its neat little 18C houses with their salmon-pink façades are squeezed along quaint alleyways. This is the medieval heart of the Principality, home to some of its most popular sights.

- **Musée Océanographique★★** – The Oceanographic Museum and Research Institute overlooks the Mediterranean from an impressive cliff (85m). Founded in 1910 by marine research enthusiast Prince Albert I to house his scientific collections, it has one of the most impressive **aquariums★★** in Europe.
- **Jardins St-Martin★** – The shaded pathways of this Mediterranean garden have delightful sea views.
- **Cathédrale** – Houses a series of royal family tombs.
- **Chapelle de la Miséricorde** – This chapel's classic pink and white Baroque façade was built between 1639 and 1646 by the Black Penitents brotherhood.
- **Place du Palais★** – Don't miss the Changing of the Guard.
- **Palais Princier★** – The palatial home of the Grimaldi family was built in the 17C on the site of the original 13C Genoese fortress.

PRACTICAL INFORMATION

Telephone

To telephone Monaco from France, dial 00 followed by 377 (code for Monaco) and then the 8-digit telephone number.

Currency and Postage

Monaco uses euros just like France, but it has an independent postal system. All letters mailed from within the Principality must have Monégasque stamps.

Public lifts

Large-capacity lifts are available to make it easier to move around certain neighbourhoods. The main roads and sites served are: pl. Ste-Dévote to blvd. de Belgique (the longest route), plages du Larvotto (and Musée national) to pl. des Moulins, ave. Hector-Otto to blvd. de Belgique, auditorium Rainier-III (blvd. Louis-II) to the casino terraces, the Pêcheurs car park to the Musée océanographique, ave. de Grande-Bretagne to ave. des Citronniers, Centre Commercial de Fontvieille to pl. d'Armes, port de Monaco to ave. de la Costa.

TOURS AND PUBLIC TRANSPORT

BUS: C.A.M. – ✆00 377 97 70 22 22. www.cam.mc. Service every 10min from 7.30am–8.30pm. Tickets €2 each or €5.50 for day pass. Six regular bus lines loop around the Principality. Maps available at the tourist office.

TAXI: Two main **taxi** stands are located near the casino and at the train station. ✆00 377 93 50 56 28 or 00 377 93 15 01 01.

TOURIST BUS: Le Grand Tour – Twelve stops around the Principality, including the Palais Princier and the Casino. ✆00 377 97 70 26 36. http://monacolegrandtour.com. €21. This small hop-on, hop-off tourist bus makes 1hr round trip journeys around the Principality.

BATEAU BUS – Quai des Etats-Unis. ✆00 377 92 16 15 15; www.riviera-navigation.com. Bateau Bus is a solar/electric powered boat conducting sea tours of Monaco and the surrounding towns. They even offer night time tours during the summer and fireworks season and go hunting for whales on their sea safari tours! Tickets can be bought online and on the boat itself.

HELICOPTER: Héli Air Monaco – Héliport de Monaco, Fontvieille. ✆00 377 92 05 00 50; www.heliairmonaco.com. Regular daily service between Monaco and the Aéroport de Nice-Côte d'Azur. Also 10min sightseeing tours of Monaco, and daily flights between Monaco and Fréjus.

SPORT: For tennis fans, the **Monte Carlo Country Club** has 23 courts (✆04 93 41 30 15; www.mccc.mc). Golfers will enjoy the prestigious **Monte Carlo Golf Club**, which boasts an 18-hole course at an altitude of 810m (✆04 92 41 50 70).

LA CONDAMINE

In the Middle Ages this term applied to land owned by a lord and cultivated exclusively for him at the foot of a village or castle. Nowadays La Condamine is the commercial district and port stretching between the Rock and Monte-Carlo.

- **Port Hercule** – Prince Albert I commissioned this harbour, with its promenade and luxury yachts.
- **Église Ste-Dévote** – Ste-Dévote was martyred in Corsica in the 3C when, legend has it, a dove guided her boat to these shores.

MONTE-CARLO★★★

Europe's gambling capital was launched by François Blanc, director of the casino in Bad Homburg in Germany. The place's success has led to high-density building, but Monte-Carlo retains its attractiveness with its luxurious casino, its sumptuous villas, de luxe shops and pretty gardens. There is a fine view from the Casino's **terrace★★**.

MONACO MONTE-CARLO

0 200 m
0 200 yds

WHERE TO STAY

France (Hôtel de) ④
Miramar (Hôtel) ⑦
Novotel ①

WHERE TO EAT

Bistroquet (Le) ①
Castelroc ④
Loga ⑦
Maison du Caviar (La) ⑩
Maison du Caviar-Pétrossian (La) ⑯
Paris (Café de) ⑬
Polpetta ⑱
Zebra Square ⑰

INDEX OF STREET NAMES

Basse (R.) 3
Castro (R. Col.-de) 7
Comte-Félix-Gastaldi (R.) 10
Princesse-Marie-de-Lorraine (R.) 15

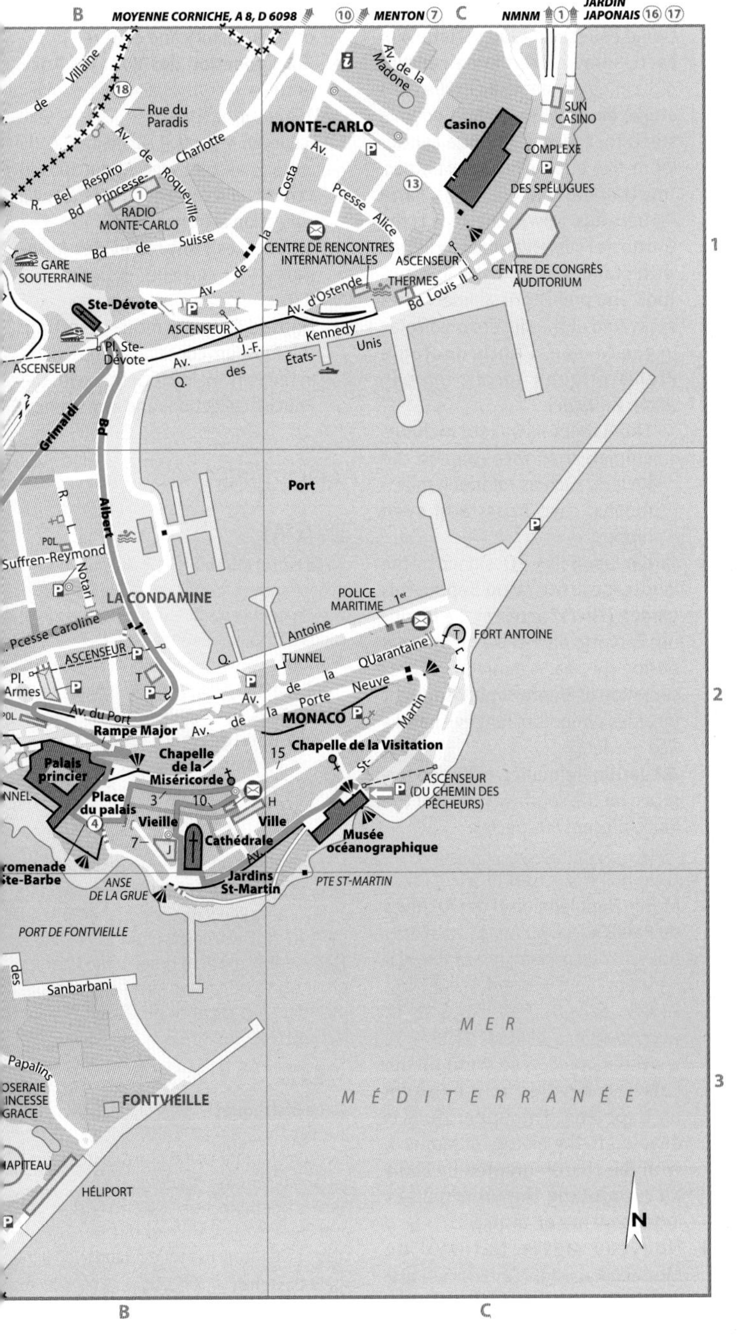
MOYENNE CORNICHE, A 8, D 6098
MENTON
NMNM
JARDIN JAPONAIS
MONTE-CARLO
Casino
SUN CASINO
COMPLEXE DES SPÉLUGUES
Rue du Paradis
RADIO MONTE-CARLO
CENTRE DE RENCONTRES INTERNATIONALES
ASCENSEUR
THERMES
CENTRE DE CONGRÈS AUDITORIUM
GARE SOUTERRAINE
Ste-Dévote
Pl. Ste-Dévote
Port
LA CONDAMINE
POLICE MARITIME
FORT ANTOINE
TUNNEL
MONACO
Rampe Major
Chapelle de la Miséricorde
Chapelle de la Visitation
Palais princier
Place du palais
Vieille
Ville
Cathédrale
Musée océanographique
ASCENSEUR (DU CHEMIN DES PÊCHEURS)
Jardins St-Martin
ANSE DE LA GRUE
PTE ST-MARTIN
PORT DE FONTVIEILLE
FONTVIEILLE
HÉLIPORT
MER MÉDITERRANÉE
N

GARDENS

- **Jardin Exotique★★** – This exceptional collection (900 varieties) of cacti, some more than a century old, clings dramatically to the cliffs above Monaco, cascading down a steep rock face with huge candelabra-like euphorbia, giant aloes, "mother-in-law cushions" and Barbary figs. Down 279 steps is the **Grotte de l'Observatoire★**, adorned with stalactites and stalagmites. Tools and prehistoric animal bones excavated at the site are on display in the **Musée d'Anthropologie Préhistorique★** (*access through Jardin Exotique*).

  The Rainier III Gallery includes animals that once roamed the Riviera, such as reindeer, mammoths, cave bears and even hippos.
- **Jardin Japonais★** – Designed by the landscape artist Yasuo Beppu, this garden (7ha/17 acres) in the luxurious Larvotto district is a green oasis beside the sea. A miniature representation of Shintoist philosophy, it includes symbols of longevity and a Zen garden.
- **Jardin Animalier** – The zoo terraces, on the southwest face of the Rock, present 50 species.

ADDITIONAL SIGHTS

- **Musée Napoléonien et des Archives du Palais★** – pl. du Palais. Open daily Apr–Oct 10am–6pm; rest of the year 10.30am–5pm. Closed 1 Jan, Nov, 25 Dec. €4. 00 377 93 25 18 31; www.palais.mc. 00 377 93 25 18 31. www.palais.mc. One wing of the Palace is devoted to a museum on Napoléon. The upper floor is devoted to the history of Monaco, with the charter granted by Louis XII recognising the Principality's independence on display.
- **Nouveau Musée National de Monaco★** – bd du Jardin Exotique. Open daily 8am–6pm (Jun–Sept 11am–7pm). Closed 1 Jan, 1 May, Grand Prix weekend, 19 Nov and 25 Dec. €6 (under 26 free). www.nmnm.mc. This museum in the charming Villa Paloma hosts temporary exhibitions on local history and culture.
- **Collection des Voitures Anciennes★** – Fontvieille. Open daily 10am–6pm. Closed 25 Dec. €6.50 (children 8-14, €3). 00 377 92 05 28 56. www.palais.mc. About 100 old vehicles and carriages from the royal collection are on display.
- **Musée des Timbres et des Monnaies** – Fontvieille. Open daily 9.30am–5pm; Jul–Sept until 6pm. €3. Housed in a very modern setting, this museum contains stamps made in the Principality together with the Princes' collections and rare stamps.

ADDRESSES

STAY

Hôtel Miramar – 126 ave. du 3-Septembre, Cap d'Ail. 04 93 78 06 60. www.monte-carlo.mc/hotel-miramar-capdail. 25 rooms. Closed Feb. P
A good-value, family-run hotel in the neighbouring village of Cap d'Ail. Rooms have WiFi; some face the sea.

Hôtel de France – 6 rue de la Turbie. Near the train station. 00 377 93 30 24 64. www.monte-carlo.mc/france. 26 rooms. Charming, soundproofed rooms decorated in Provençal hues. Modern breakfast lounge.

Novotel Monte Carlo – 16 blvd. de la Princesse Charlotte. 00 377 99 99 83 00. www.novotel.com. 218 rooms. P. A stylish, modern hotel in the heart of Monaco with all the latest amenities, including heated pool, fitness centre, bar and restaurant.

EAT

Le Bistroquet – Galerie Charles III, ave. des Spéluges. 00 377 93 50 65 03. Lively restaurant and bar with a heated terrace facing the casino gardens. Serves a combination of bistro fare and French classics; wines by the glass. Live music Fri–Sat evenings.

Castelroc – pl. du Palais. 00 377 93 30 36 68. Closed mid-Dec–mid-Jan, Sat. The terrace under the trees with a **view** of the palace makes a lovely setting for a meal of Mediterranean specialities.

La Maison du Caviar – 1 ave. St-Charles. 00 377 93 30 80 06. Closed Sat lunch, Sun. This prestigious house has been serving choice caviar to Monaco's residents for the past 50 years. In an unusual setting made up of bottle racks and wooden panelling, you can also purchase salmon and foie gras.

Polpetta – 2 r. Paradis. 00 377 93 50 67 84. Closed early–late Jun, first half Nov, Sat lunch and Mar. This small Italian restaurant offers three different settings: the veranda close to the road; the rustic dining room; and a more intimate cosy space to the rear. Don't miss the family specialities.

Café de Paris – pl. du Casino. 00 377 98 06 76 23. An elegant and chic brasserie with terraces overlooking the casino square and the sea. Seafood and traditional French dishes, as well as light salads and sandwiches.

Loga – 25 blvd. des Moulins. 00 377 93 30 87 72. Closed Sun. A friendly family-run establishment popular with the locals, serving traditional regional cuisine and daily specials on the slate board.

Petrossian – 11 ave. Princesse Grace. 00 377 97 77 00 24. www.petrossian.fr. Closed Sun–Mon. The romantic dining room of this caviar house is decorated in luminous shades of white and mother-of-pearl. Specialities focus on fresh seafood to complement the caviar, as well as gourmet foie gras and rare vodkas.

Zébra Square – 10 ave. Princesse-Grace, 98000 Monaco. 00 377 99 99 25 50. www.zebrasquare.com. Same trendy feel, zebra theme and modern cuisine as its big Parisian sister, with a terrace overlooking the sea.

NIGHTLIFE

Casino de Monte-Carlo – pl. du Casino. 00 377 92 16 20 00. www.casino-montecarlo.com. Europe's leading casino. The gambling salons and lavish dining hall Le Train Bleu, decorated in the style of the Orient-Express, are truly impressive.

La Terrasse (Bar du Vistamar) – square Beaumarchais. 00 377 92 16 40 00. www.montecarloresort.com. This famous bar has been patronised by many celebrities, such as Onassis and Maria Callas.

Le Jimmy'z – quai Princesse-Grace. 00 377 92 16 22 77. http://fr.jimmyzmontecarlo.com. It would be unthinkable to leave Monte-Carlo without having paid a visit to Jimmy'z club. Formal evening wear.

SHOPPING

All the famous fashion brands have boutiques in Monte-Carlo. Shops specialising in traditional goods are to be found in the narrow streets of the Rock (Le Rocher) opposite the palace.Hunt out Boutique du Rocher on ave. de la Madonne for traditional Monégasque handicrafts, made in the on-site workshops.

If exclusive brands such as Dior and Chanel on ave. des Beaux Art are beyond your reach, head for the Fontevielle shopping centre, where you'll find dozens of ready-to-wear chain stores, a hypermarket and fast-food outlets. Most of the Principality's high-street stores (music, books, electronic equipment, furniture and cosmetics) are situated in Monte-Carlo along ave. Saint-Charles (which is where you'll also find the Marché de Monte-Carlo, selling fresh fruit and vegetables) and further south around ave. des Spélugues. For traditional open-air markets, hop over to the port d'Hercule in the Espace Commercial de la Condamine, where you'll also find a host of specialist delicatessens.

CALENDAR

Monte-Carlo Rally – Held every year since 1911 at the end of January.

Feast of Ste-Dévote – Monaco's Patron Saint feast, 27 January.

Sciaratù Carnival – Monégasque festival during the week of Mardi Gras.

Spring Arts Festival – Art, music, theatre and dance festival, in April.

International Tennis Masters Series – Held every April.

Monaco Grand Prix – Every May in the streets of the Principality on a winding circuit (2mi/3 145km).

Monte-Carlo Golf Open – Held in the hills of Mont Agel every June.

National Day of Monaco – Picturesque procession around the Rocher, plus a range of other cultural events and shows: 19 November.

Menton★★

Between mountain and Mediterranean, Menton stretches out agreeably on its sunny site★★ on the lower slopes of a picturesque natural amphitheatre of mountains. The town is known for its citrus groves and dazzling annual Lemon Festival. On the cliffs around are the remains of fortifications and human settlement going back to Neolithic times. The town was bought by the Grimaldi family of Monaco in the 14C, then incorporated into the French kingdom.

- **Population:** 28 858.
- **Michelin Map:** 341 F 5
- **Info:** 8 ave Boyer. ✆04 92 41 76 76. www.menton.fr.
- **TGV:** Just under 7hrs from Paris Gare de Lyon.
- **Location:** The last town on the Riviera before the Italian border, 29km/18mi E of Nice.

WALKING TOUR

OLD TOWN★★

Menton map, p653. Allow 1hr.

- **Rue St-Michel** – This pedestrian street linking the old and new towns is bordered by boutiques and orange trees.
- **Rue Longue** – Formerly the main street of Menton and formerly part of the Via Julia Augusta.
- **Parvis St-Michel★★** – At the top of the steps is a charming mosaiced square in the Italian style.
- **Façade of the Chapelle de la Conception★** – The façade of this chapel of the White Penitents has statues of the theological virtues.
- **Basilique St-Michel-Archange** – This is the largest and finest Baroque church in the region.
- **Cimetière du Vieux-Château** – This international cemetery recalls Menton's rich residents from around the world.

ADDITIONAL SIGHTS

- **Promenade du Soleil★★** – The wide promenade follows the shore beneath the old town.
- **Musée des Beaux-Arts (Palais Carnolès)★** – This former summer residence of the princes of Monaco houses collections of religious and contemporary art.
- **Musée Jean-Cocteau** – This 17C bastion was converted into a museum by Cocteau, the "Prince of the Poets", in 1957.
- **Serre de la Madone★** – The gardens feature rare plants from around the world.

EXCURSIONS

ROQUEBRUNE-CAP MARTIN★★

2km/1.2mi SW.

Roquebrune is a most picturesque hilltop village (**village perché★★**), where the tourist can stroll through the small streets towards the **keep★** From the top, wonderful **panorama★★** of the sea, Cap Martin, the Principality of Monaco and the Mont Agel.

SAORGE★★

The village is high in the back country of the Riviera, close to the Italian border.

The **gorges★★** of the Upper **Roya** form a spectacular **setting★★** for the village clinging to the steep, south-facing slopes which rise abruptly from the river far below. Saorge was originally a Ligurian settlement and then later a Roman colony. In the Middle Ages the town was said to be impregnable, but it has yielded twice since: in 1794 to the French and again in April 1945.

Saorge is dominated by the belfries of its churches and monasteries, overlooking terraces and balconies, old houses with open-fronted drying lofts and roofs tiled with heavy stone slabs. A maze of stepped and tunnelled streets completes this highly picturesque townscape.

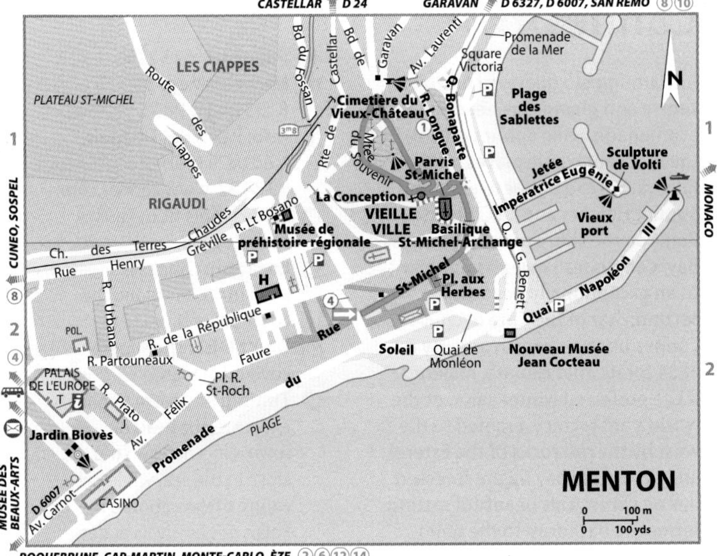

WHERE TO STAY

Aiglon (Hôtel L')	2
Chambord (Hôtel)	4
Londres (Hôtel de)	6
Napoléon (Hôtel)	8
Paris Rome (Hôtel)	10
Prince de Galles (Hôtel)	12
Princess et Richmond (Hôtel)	14

WHERE TO EAT

A Braijade Méridiounale	1
Cantinella (La)	4
Pierrot-Pierette (Auberge)	8

ADDRESSES

STAY

€ Hôtel de Londres – 15 ave. Carnot. ☎04 93 35 74 62. www.hotel-de-londres.com. 27 rooms. Restaurant €€€. Near the coast. Soundproofed rooms.

€€ Hôtel Paris Rome – 79 ave. porte de France. ☎04 93 35 73 45. www.paris-rome.com. 22 rooms. Restaurant €. Rustic Provençal hotel and restaurant.

€€ Hôtel L'Aiglon – 7 ave. Madone. ☎04 93 57 55 55. www.hotelaiglon.net. 29 rooms. P. Restaurant€€. Beautiful villa with terrace and pool.

€€ Hôtel Chambord – 6 ave. Boyer. ☎04 93 35 94 19. www.hotel-chambord.com. 40 rooms. P. Modern, hotel near the Palais de l'Europe and casino.

€€ Hôtel Prince de Galles – 4 ave. General de Gaulle. ☎04 93 28 21 21. www.princedegalles.com. 64 rooms. P Restaurant€€. Modern comforts and sea views. The Petit Prince restaurant has a large garden terrace.

€€ Hôtel Princess et Richmond – 617 promenade du Soleil. ☎04 93 35 80 20. www.princess-richmond.com. 46 rooms. P. Restaurant€. Seaside hotel, pebble beach, solarium and Jacuzzi.

€€€ Hôtel Napoléon – 29 porte de France. ☎04 93 35 89 50. www.napoleon-menton.com. 43 rooms. P. Restaurant €€. Elegant, contemporary hotel right on the beach.

EAT

€€ Auberge Pierrot-Pierrette – pl. de l'Église, Monti. ☎04 93 35 79 76. Provençal food in a tranquil hamlet perched on the hills above Menton.

€€ A Braijade Méridiounale – 66 rue Longue. ☎04 93 35 65 65. www.abraijade.fr. Homely restaurant hidden in an alley of the old quarter. Provençal dishes and grilled meats at very reasonable rates.

€€ La Cantinella – 8 rue Trenca. ☎04 93 41 34 20. The Sicilian owner delights in sharing his Mediterranean-influenced cuisine in a friendly, laid-back atmosphere.

Cannes★★★

A charming old quarter, chic town centre and glamorous beachside promenade make Cannes one of the most enjoyable places on the Riviera. Spread out between the Suquet Heights and La Croisette Point on the shore of La Napoule Bay, Cannes also owes its popularity to an exceptionally beautiful setting. Star of the Côte d'Azur, Cannes became known as early as 1834 for its mild climate, making it the preferred winter salon of the world's aristocracy. Framed to the west by the red rocks of the Esterel and across the bay by the forested Îles de Lérins, this beautiful setting forms the backdrop to the palm-lined beaches of La Croisette and the world-famous Cannes Film Festival.

- **Population:** 73 234.
- **Michelin Map:** 341 B-D 5 and D P-Q 5
- **Info:** Palais des Festivals, 1 bd de la Croisette. ✆04 92 99 84 22. www.cannes.com.
- **TGV:** 5–6hrs from Paris Gare de Lyon.
- **Location:** Cannes is situated 34.4km/21.3mi along the coast SW of Nice.
- **Don't Miss:** The superb covered market.
- **Timing:** As a town Cannes is extensive; the heart of town is in a narrow strip close to the sea, while the centre of the action is the Palais des Festivals et des Congrès. One day may be sufficient, but there are many temptations to stay longer.

A BIT OF HISTORY

In 1834, the former Lord Chancellor of England, Lord Henry Brougham, was on his way to Italy when he was prevented from entering the County of Nice, then part of Italy, due to a cholera epidemic. Forced to wait, he made an overnight stop at a fishing village called Cannes. Enchanted by the place, he built a villa here and returned to it every winter, establishing a trend among the English aristocracy and stimulating Cannes' first period of growth, ultimately leading to its establishment as a holiday resort.

WALKING TOURS

1 SEAFRONT★

Cannes map II, p656. Allow 2hrs.

- **Boulevard de la Croisette★** – Locals and visitors congregate along this wide, attractive seafront road, with delightful gardens along its centre. To one side extends the splendid sandy beach and broad promenade, while the landward side of

TOURS AND TRANSPORTATION

Bus – Gare routière, pl. de l'Hôtel-de-Ville. ✆0800 06 01 06. www.rca.tm.fr. TAM buses operate between Cannes and Nice, with direct airport service.

Train Station – SNCF Gare de Cannes. ✆0 892 35 35 35. www.ter-sncf.com/paca. This train station is served by SNCF trains, the TGV and the local TER trains (service between Mandelieu-La-Napoule and Vintimille).

Trans Côte d'Azur – 3 quai des Îles. ✆06 19 20 49 74/04 92 98 71 30; www.trans-cote-azur.com. Reservations essential. Regular service to Île Ste-Marguerite from Cannes (*Jun–Sept. €32.50 return, children 4–10, €20*), plus tours to l'Île de Porquerolles, Monaco, St-Tropez, etc..

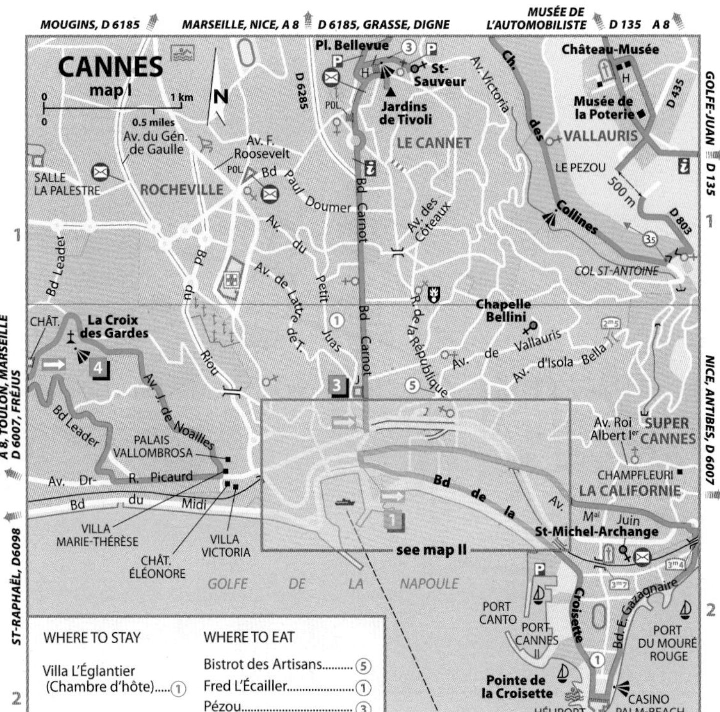

the boulevard is lined with the dignified and impeccably maintained façades of four luxury "palace" hotels and exclusive boutiques. At the eastern end of La Croisette is a marina, busy with yachts and pleasure craft, and at its western end another, overlooked by the Festival and Conference Centre (Palais des Festivals et des Congrès) where the Cannes International Film Festival is held every May – the town's most spectacular and prestigious event.

- **Pointe de la Croisette★** – This point offers splendid views of Cannes, the Îles de Lérins and the Esterel. Modern tourist developments include artificial beaches and the Palm Beach Casino complex. Beyond Palm Beach is a splendid **view★** of Golfe-Juan and Cap d'Antibes.
- **Quartier de la Californie** – East of the town lie several residences that marked its history: on avenue du Roi-Albert-Ier, the villa Kazbeck was the scene of sumptuous parties given by the Russian Grand Duke Mikhail Mikhaïlovitch; the villa Champfleuri remains famous for its gardens. The Mystery of the Yellow Room (1930) by Marcel L'Herbier was shot in the château Scott, a Flamboyant neo-Gothic pile.

2 OLD CANNES AND THE PORT

Cannes map II, p656. Allow 1.5hrs.

- **The Harbour** – Between the Palais des Festivals and Le Suquet lies the Old Port, teeming with fishing boats, luxury yachts, shops and restaurants. The embarkation point for trips to the Îles de Lérins lies to the southwest.
- **Allées de la Liberté** – Beneath the plane trees, overlooking the port, is a large square featuring a statue of Lord Brougham, where an early

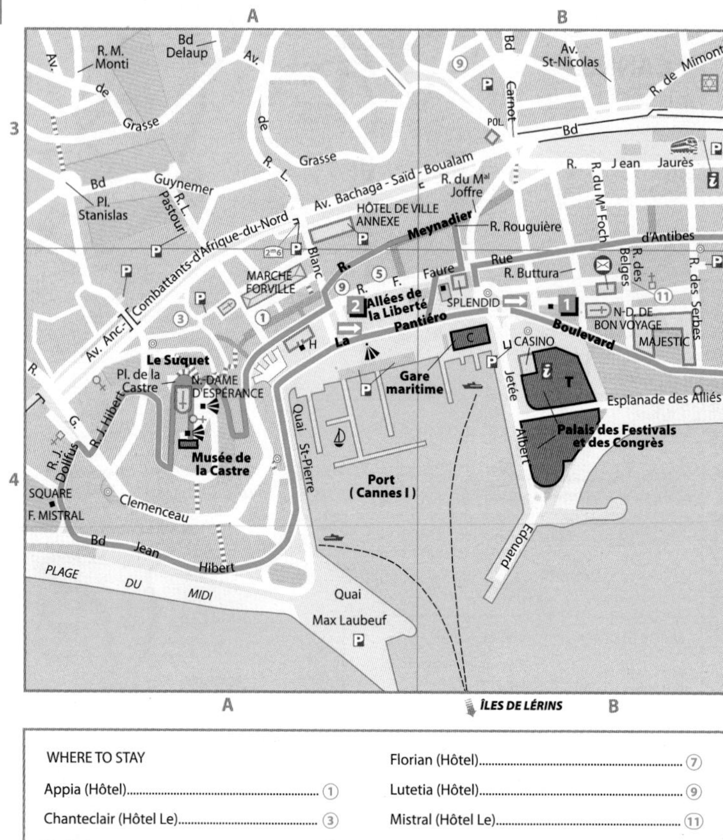

WHERE TO STAY

Appia (Hôtel)	1
Chanteclair (Hôtel Le)	3
Festival	5
Florian (Hôtel)	7
Lutetia (Hôtel)	9
Mistral (Hôtel Le)	11

morning flower market gives way to afternoon pétanque matches.

- **Rue Meynadier** – Formerly the main street linking the new town to Le Suquet, rue Meynadier is bordered by specialist shops.
- **Le Suquet** – The old town is built on the site of the former Canoïs castrum or "citadel" on the slopes of Mont Chevalier. Rue Perrissol leads to Place de la Castre, surrounded by a wall and dominated by Notre-Dame-d'Espérance.
- **Musée de la Castre★★** – This 11C castle, built by the Lérins monks to guard the harbour, houses substantial archaeological and ethnographic collections.

3 LE CANNET

Cannes map I, p655.

Sheltered from the wind by a circle of wooded hills, Le Cannet, at an altitude of 110m, offers breathtaking views. The artist Pierre Bonnard (1867–1947) spent the last years of his life painting views of Le Cannet from the Villa Le Bosquet (avenue Victoria).

- **Le Vieux Cannet** – The old town is reached by rue St-Sauveur, lined with 18C houses and pleasant shady squares. Place Bellevue offers a superb view of Cannes and the Îles de Lérins. The old Calvys Tower (12C) still stands nearby, as well as the taller Danys Tower (14C). The Jardins de Tivoli can be reached from

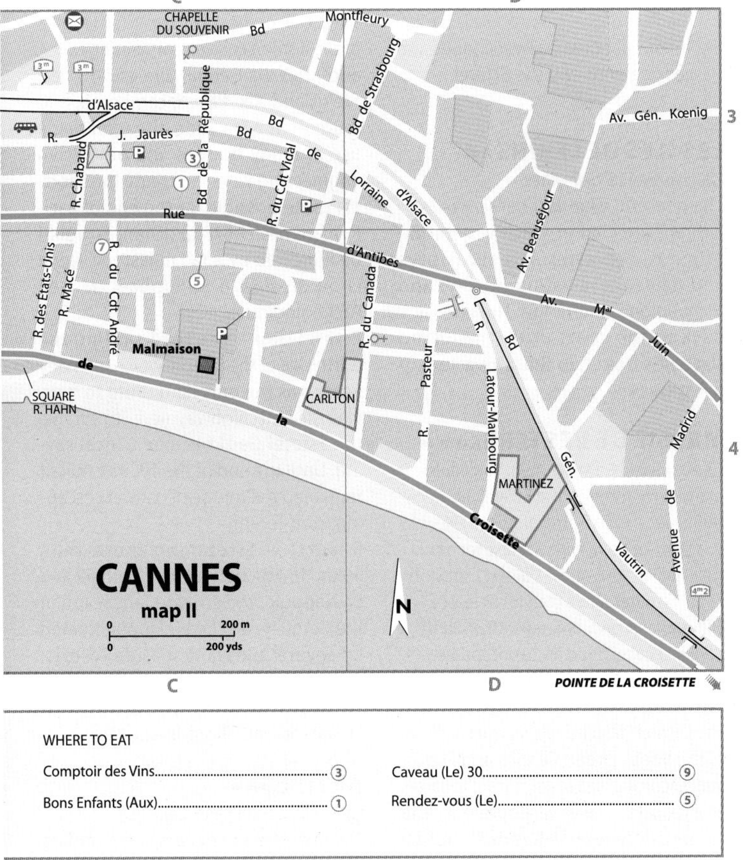

the Hôtel de Ville via the pedestrian rue Cavasse, passing luxurious villas.

- **Chemin des Collines★** – This road along the flanks of the hills above Cannes offers fine views over La Napoule bay and the Îles de Lérins.
- **Vallauris** – Pablo Picasso chose to spend his final years in this small village on a gently sloping hill, where he indulged his passion for ceramics and revived the village's ancient pottery-making traditions.

4 LA CROIX DES GARDES★

Cannes map I, p655.

To the west of Cannes, this hill offers a wonderful panorama over the bay, both day and night. Begin your tour at the early 20C château de la Croix des Gardes, which has an interesting Florentine façade. Continue towards Lord Brougham's villa (Château Eleonore) and its neighbour, the villa Marie-Thérèse, at no 2 av. J.-de-Noailles. Once the residence of the dowager baroness de Rothschild and now home to the town's media library, it is set in pleasant parkland. The palais Vallombrosa and its park and the villa Victoria, once belonging to Victorian property developer and botany enthusiast Sir Thomas Robinson Woolfield, continue this prestigious promenade.

- Take the footpath to the top of the hill (alt 164m) and a strategically-placed 12m-high cross, which gave the area its name in the 16C. From the foot of the cross there is a marvellous panoramaa over Cannes, the Îles de Lérins and the Esterel.

EXCURSIONS

LES ÎLES DE LÉRINS★★

3km/2mi SE of Cannes.

The peaceful **islands** (*boat service from Cannes*) are clad in a rich vegetation of pines, cypresses and eucalyptus and have a fascinating historic and archaeological heritage. The fine view back to the coast of the mainland stretches from **Cap Roux★★★** to **Cap d'Antibes★★**.

MASSIF DE L'ESTEREL★★★

40km/24.8mi W by N 98. You could easily drive through the Esterel along N98 coastal road from Cannes to Fréjus in less than an hour, with a pause for a short walk at Dramont or the Point d'Esquillon. For the longer walks plan for at least a half day, and be prepared with enough drinking water, food and appropriate footwear. It is advisable to remove all valuables from your car when walking.

The Esterel stretches along the coastline of the Var between Cannes and Fréjus, and encompasses several small villages and resorts such as **St-Raphaël★**. The Esterel between St-Raphaël and La Napoule is an area of breathtaking natural beauty. One of the loveliest parts of Provence, it was opened to large-scale tourism by the Touring Club's creation in 1903 of the scenic road known as the Corniche d'Or (Golden Scenic Route). The fiery red of the rocks forms a strong contrast with the deep blue of the sea, while the bustling life along the coast contrasts with the seclusion of the inland roads.

The Massif – The massif's jagged relief of volcanic rock (red porphyry) worn by erosion dips vertically into the deep blue sea between La Napoule and St-Raphaël. The rugged coastline is fringed with rocks, islets and reefs. From **Mont Vinaigre★★★**, its highest peak (alt 618m), a vast panorama unfolds.

Via Aurelia – The Esterel was bordered to the north by the Via Aurelia (Aurelian Way), one of the most important routes of the Roman Empire, connecting Rome and Arles via Genoa, Cimiez, Antibes, Fréjus and Aix. Paved, cambered, and more than 2.5m wide, the road made use of many bridges and other civil engineering works to create the shortest route possible. At the end of each Roman mile (1 478m) distances would be indicated by a tall milestone – one is on display in St-Raphaël (Musée Archéologique).

Esterel Gap – The road skirting the north side of the Esterel, which for many years was the only land route to Italy, was rife with highwaymen; "to survive the Esterel Gap" became a local saying. Until the end of the 19C the massif remained the refuge of convicts escaping from Toulon.

Resorts – Stretching more than 30km/18.6mi between St-Raphaël and La Napoule, the striking landscape of the Corniche de l'Esterel is punctuated by several pleasant seaside resorts, including **Boulouris**, **Agay**, **Anthéor**, **Le Trayas**, **Miramar**, **La Galere**, **Port-la-Galère**, and **Théoule-sur-Mer**.

ANTIBES★★

11.5km/7mi ENE of Cannes.

The first settlement here was a trading post founded by Greek merchants from Marseille in the 4C BCE. Reconstructed in the 16C, the **Château Grimaldi** dates from the 12C, when it was built on the site of a Roman encampment to protect the coast from the incursions of Barbary pirates. Inside, the **Musée Picasso★** (Picasso Museum, 4 r. des Cordiers; 04 92 90 54 20) has a superb selection of the master's works, including ceramics, drawings, prints and tapestries (*The Lobster, Two Nudes and a Mirror*), as well as paintings (*Still Life with Watermelon*). The town was purchased from the Grimaldi family by Henri IV because of its strategic position in relation to the Kingdom of Savoy. It was fortified first by François I, then by Vauban. To the west of the **Cap d'Antibes★★** stretches the fine sandy beach of Golfe-Juan.

GRASSE★★

19km/12mi NNW of Cannes.

Prettily located on the slopes of the Grasse Pre-Alps, the Old Town (**Vieille Ville★**) has picturesque streets lined with tall Provençal houses. Grasse's most famous son is **Jean-Honoré Fragonard** (1732–1806), a painter known for witty depictions of the frivolities of 18C court life. The Salle Fragonarda in the Villa-Musée Fragonard has two of the artist's self-portraits as well as his *Landscape with Washerwomen* and *Three Graces.*

For the past three centuries, Grasse has been the world's most important centre of the perfume industry, with perfume manufacturers open to the public and two museums, the **Musée international de la Parfumerie** (*2 bd du Jeu de Ballon; www.museesdegrasse.com*) and the **Musée d'Art et d'Histoire de Provence** (*2 r. Mirabeau*).

To the north of the **Pas de la Faye** with its **view★★** over mountains and Mediterranean, the road enters Haute Provence through the Seranon valley.

ADDRESSES

STAY

Le Chanteclair – 12 rue Forville. 04 93 39 68 88. Closed mid-Nov–late Jan. 15 rooms. Selection of rooms of differing comfort. Breakfast is served in a pleasant inner courtyard.

Hôtel Lutetia – 6 rue Michel-Ange. 04 93 39 35 74. www.hotel-lutetia-cannes.com. 8 rooms. A simple and comfortable hotel on a quiet side street, with air-conditioning and Provençal decor, close to the train station.

Hôtel Florian – 8 rue du Cdt André. 04 93 39 24 82. www.hotel-leflorian.com. 20 rooms. A family-run hotel between the train station and the Palais des Festivals, on a semi-pedestrian street in the old town.

Hôtel National – 9 rue du Maréchal-Joffre. 04 93 39 91 92. 17 rooms. Located near the Palais des Festivals and the sea. Small, but clean and well maintained en-suite rooms.

Hôtel Appia – 6 rue Marceau. 04 93 06 59 59. www.appia-hotel.com. Closed mid-Nov–late Dec. 31 rooms. Practicality takes precedence over comfort in this downtown hotel with well-kept, small rooms.

Chambre d'hôte Villa L'Églantier – 14 rue Campestra. 04 93 68 22 43. www.maison-eglantier.com. 3 rooms. Impressive white villa dating from 1920, surrounded by palm trees and other exotic species.

Hôtel Festival – 3 rue Molière. 04 97 06 64 40. www.hotel-festival.com. 14 rooms. Recently renovated family-run hotel within walking distance of the Croisette and the rue d'Antibes shopping area. Jacuzzi and sauna available for guests.

Hôtel Le Mistral – 13 rue des Belges. 04 93 39 91 46. www.mistral-hotel.com. Closed mid-Nov–late Dec. 10 rooms. A new boutique hotel with modern decor, just behind the Palais des Festivals.

EAT

Aux Bons Enfants – 80 rue Meynadier. No phone. Closed Aug, Sat eve off-season, Sun. An old-fashioned cantina near the Forville market serving ratatouille, grilled anchovies, aïoli, stuffed sardines, etc. Family-friendly.

Le Caveau 30 – 45 rue F.-Faure. 04 93 39 06 33. www.lecaveau30.com. Large restaurant comprising two dining rooms decorated in the style of a 1930s brasserie. The terrace overlooks a shaded square. Fish and seafood.

Le Comptoir des Vins – 13 blvd. de la République. 04 93 68 13 26. Closed Tue eves, Sat lunch, Sun–Mon. This handsomely stocked wine boutique leads to a colourful dining area, where light snacks are served with wine.

Le Rendez-Vous – 35 rue F.-Faure. 04 93 68 55 10. A chic bistro with an Art Deco-style ceiling, serving fish, seafood and Mediterranean dishes.

Fred L'Écailler – 7 pl. de l'Étang. 04 93 43 15 85. www.fredlecailler.com. A large neon sign marks the entrance to this rustic restaurant. Fine selection of freshly-caught fish and seafood.

Bistrot des Artisans – 67 blvd. de la République. 04 93 68 33 88. Generous portions of lovingly prepared Mediterranean food.

St-Tropez★★

After half a century of fame, the little town of St-Trop' (as the locals call it) is still in fashion, thanks to an exquisitely picturesque harbour, a stunning location, and a constant stream of artists, journalists and photographers.

- **Population:** 4 532.
- **Michelin Map:** 340 O 6
- **Info:** quai Jean-Jaurès. ✆0892 68 48 28. www.ot-saint-tropez.com.
- **Location:** 86km/54mi from Cannes, via the congested road that encircles the peninsula. The easiest route is the short passenger ferry from Port Grimaud across the bay.
- **Timing:** A day should be more than enough to explore.

VISIT

Celebrities can sometimes be spotted in St-Tropez and the atmosphere is created by an impressive array of luxury charter yachts moored in the picturesque harbour, which teems with life.

The old fishing village, which was discovered by writer **Guy de Maupassant** and his friend painter **Paul Signac**, and went on to attract Matisse and major post-Impressionist artists as well as the writer **Colette**, remains a fashionable resort frequented by writers and artists and more recently by celebrities from the entertainment world.

Two *Bravades*, or "acts of defiance", take place each year in May. The first is a religious procession in honour of St-Tropez, while the second commemorates an event of local history from 1637.

THE PORT★★

Lined with luxury yachts, the bustling centre of life in cosmopolitan St-Tropez is a star-spotter's paradise. The old pink and yellow houses of the waterfront and neighbouring streets have been converted into cafés and pastry shops, cabarets and restaurants, luxury boutiques, galleries and antique shops.

THE BEACHES

The 10km/6mi of beaches around St-Tropez are truly heavenly, with their fine sand and charming rocky coves. The nearest is Bouillabaisse Beach (perfect for windsailing when the mistral is blowing). To the east of the town lies **Graniers Beach** (access from rue Cavaillon). Further east round the headland stretches **Les Salins Beach** (ave. Foch).

But by far the most appealing and the most fashionable are the **Pampelonne Beaches**, well sheltered from the mistral winds. Reached by a **coastal path** that skirts the entire peninsula, Cannebiers Bay affords glimpses of the superb villas of the rich and famous.

WALKING TOUR

SEAFRONT★

St-Tropez map, p661.

- **Môle Jean-Réveille** – Attractive **panorama★** from the jetty.
- **La Ponche Quarter** – Tucked between the port and the citadel, this is the oldest and most charming district of St-Tropez.
- **Citadelle★** – The citadel stands on a hillock at the east end of town. The hexagonal keep with three round towers was built in the 16C. The ramparts command a fine **panorama★**.
- **Notre-Dame-de-l'Assomption** – Built in the Italian Baroque style in the early 19C, this church has a finely carved woodwork interior.
- **Place aux Herbes** – Small morning market. Charming backdrop.
- **Rue Laugier, rue Gambett** – Lively shopping streets.
- **Place des Lices** – Popular square with cafés, market and leafy trees.

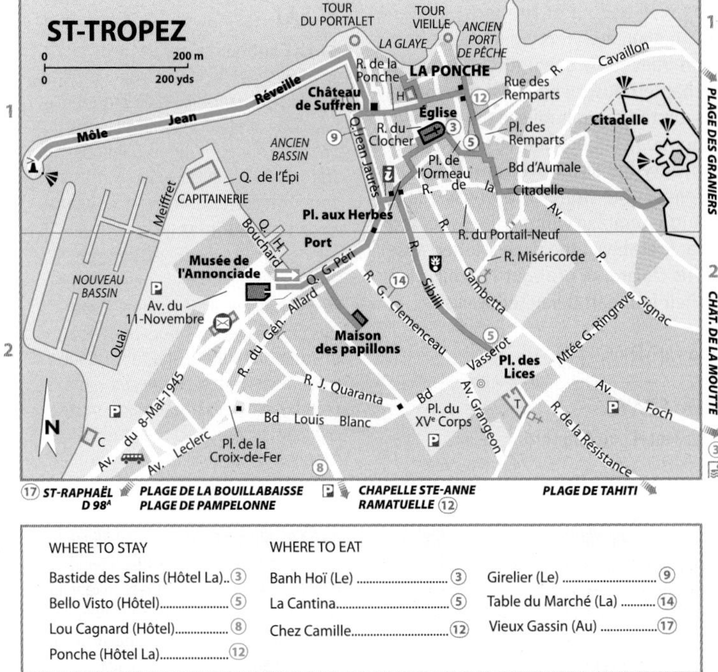

ADDITIONAL SIGHT

Musée de l'Annonciade★★

pl. Georges Grammont. Open daily except Tue 10am–1pm, 2–6pm. Closed Nov, 1 Jan, 1 May, Ascension Day, 25 Dec. €6. ☏04 94 17 84 10.

The museum, in an old house delightfully positioned on a bend in the quayside, has an impressive permanent collection, including post-Impressionist pictures of St-Tropez and also some remarkable temporary exhibitions.

EXCURSIONS

ST-TROPEZ PENINSULA★★

St-Tropez is located on the north coast of the peninsula. Its east coast is fringed with popular sandy beaches, notably the famous **Plage de Pampelonne**. The south coast has some scenic rocky headlands. The interior is hilly and rustic, with small vineyards, pine copses and two charming old villages commanding wide views, **Ramatuelle★** and smaller **Gassin**. A **footpath** extends around the coast of the whole peninsula.

MASSIF DES MAURES★★★

The long, low parallel ranges of the massif unfold from Fréjus to Hyères. Its fine forests of pine, cork oak and chestnut trees have often been devastated by fire. Chapels, monasteries and small villages are dotted in the hinterland, while the coast is fringed by coves, bays and small beach resorts.

Abbaye du Thoronet★★

The abbey can be reached from autoroute A 8, junction 13.

♿Open daily: Apr–Sep 10am–6.30pm, Sun 10am–noon, 2–6.30pm; Oct–Mar Mon–Sat 10am–1pm, 2–5pm, Sun 10am–noon, 2–5pm. Closed 1 Jan, 1 May, 1 and 11 Nov, 25 Dec. €7.50. ☏04 94 60 43 90/98. http://thoronet.monuments-nationaux.fr.

Of the "Three Cistercian Sisters of Provence" (the others are Silvacane and Sénanque), Le Thoronet is the earliest; it was founded in 1136, when St Bernard was still alive. It is one of the most characteristic of Cistercian abbeys, as well as one of the most austere. The plain architecture of the abbey is unrelieved by decoration, save in the chapterhouse, where just two roughly sculpted capitals relieve the prevailing rigour. The abbey **church★** has a simple beauty. Built from 1160 onwards, it has remarkable stonework which was cut and assembled without the use of mortar (notably in the oven-vaulted apse). The **cloisters★** of about 1175 have kept their four barrel-vaulted walks.

ADDRESSES

STAY

Hôtel Lou Cagnard – ave. Paul-Roussel. 04 94 97 04 24. www.hotel-lou-cagnard.com. Closed Nov–Dec. P 19 rooms. Enjoy breakfast seated in the shade of a mulberry tree in the tiny garden of this Provençal house, just off Place des Lices. At night you'll be lulled to sleep by the chirping of cicadas. Very reasonable prices.

Bello Visto – pl. deï Barri, Gassin. 04 94 56 17 30 or 04 94 56 47 33. 9 rooms. Restaurant. A small family-run hotel and restaurant posted on Place des Remparts (*barri*), at the top of Gassin. The majority of the rooms, such as the terrace, profit from **views** over the Massif des Maures and the gulf of St-Tropez. Dining room with fireplace and Provençal cuisine.

Bastide des Salins – 2.5mi/4km southeast of St-Tropez. 04 94 97 24 57. www.bastidedessalins.com. P 13 rooms. You will be greeted like friends of the family at this old Provençal house surrounded by extensive leafy grounds. Barely 5min from Place des Lices and yet totally isolated, this hotel offers large rooms decorated in the Provençal spirit, appointed with great simplicity.

Hôtel Ponche – pl. Révelin. 04 94 97 02 53. www.laponche.com. Closed Nov– Mar. P. 18 rooms. Restaurant. The rooms of this cosy hotel occupy four village houses formerly belonging to fishermen; the blue one was a favourite of Romy Schneider's. Warm, bright hues and considerate service make the Hôtel Ponche an absolute must.

EAT

La Cantina – 16 rue des Remparts. 04 94 97 40 96. Closed Nov–Mar. After sipping your tequila, savour generous helpings of Mexican cuisine in this typical setting featuring religious statues and painted wood furnishings. Youngish clientele, relaxed ambience.

La Table du Marché – 38 rue Georges-Clémenceau. 04 94 97 85 20. www.christophe-leroy.com. A temple of gastronomy located near Place des Lices, open all hours of the day. In addition to the restaurant offering traditional French cuisine, La Table du Marché also sells homemade pastries: croissants, cakes and the legendary "gendarme de St-Tropez" – mouth-watering chocolate mousse filled with vanilla crême brûlée.

Au Vieux Gassin – pl. deï Barri, Gassin. 04 94 56 14 26. Closed mid-Oct–mid-Mar. A ravishing little hilltop village serves as the backdrop for this popular restaurant. A terrace with **panoramic views** is partially enclosed and heated in cooler weather, taking over a large section of the charming place deï Barri. The regional menu has a few "exotic" specialities.

Le Banh Hoï – 12 r. Petit St-Jean. 04 94 97 36 29. Closed 12 Oct–3 Apr. Low lighting, black lacquer walls and Asian artworks decorate this restaurant specialising in Thai and Vietnamese cuisine.

Chez Camille – quai de Bonne Terrasse. 04 98 12 68 98. Closed early Oct–early Apr. A family-run restaurant on the waterfront serving bouillabaisse (spicy fish stew) and grilled fish since 1913. Ask about the boat shuttle service.

Le Girelier – quai Jean-Jaurès. 04 94 97 03 87. www.legirelier.fr. Closed Nov–mid-Mar. A harbourside fishermen's hut converted into a stylish, contemporary dining room with simply-cooked shellfish platters and bouillabaisse.

Toulon★★

Backed by high hills whose summits are crowned by forts, Toulon is France's second most important naval base, set in one of the Mediterranean's most beautiful harbours. The Old Town of Toulon is located on the Old Port, or Vieille Darse, bounded to the east by Cours Lafayette, to the west by Rue Anatole-France and to the north by Rue Landrin. The greater Toulon area includes the towns surrounding the harbours (Grande Rade and Petite Rade) as well as the Bay of Lazaret formed by the peninsula of the Presqu'île de St-Mandrier. The Old Town is accessible to pedestrians only.

- **Population:** 164 532.
- **Michelin Map:** 340 K 7
- **Info:** 12 pl Louis Blanc. ✆04 94 18 53 00. www.toulontourisme.com.
- **TGV:** 4–4hrs 30mins from Paris Gare de Lyon.
- **Flights:** The Aéroport International Toulon-Hyères is just 20 minutes from the centre of Toulon. Taxis and shuttle/buses.
- **Location:** The city is 64km/39.7mi E of Marseille.
- **Parking:** Park on the Place d'Armes, Place de la Liberté/Palais Liberté, and at the Centre Mayol.
- **Don't Miss:** A boat trip around the immense natural harbour (*rade*) is especially enjoyable (✆04 94 93 07 56). Also don't miss the winding streets of the Old Town and Old Port around the Arsenal and Quai Cronstadt.

SIGHTS

La Rade★★

Construction of Toulon's Old Port (Darse Vieille) began under Henri IV. Richelieu appreciated the strategic advantages of the roadstead and ordered the building of the first naval installations. In the reign of Louis XIV, the base was extended and the New Port (Darse Neuve) laid out by Vauban. In the 19C, the Mourillon extension and the Castigneau basin were built, completing the naval base which had become the home port of the Mediterranean Fleet.

Port★

To the west of the Quai Cronstedt (landing-stage for boat trips) is the **Navy Museum** (Musée de la Marine). Once the entrance to the old Arsenal, its doorway is a Louis XV masterpiece; it is flanked by sculptures of Mars and Bellona and has marble columns with Doric capitals framing tableaux of maritime motifs. The balcony of the former **Town Hall** is supported by two splendidly muscular **Atlantes★**, the work of Pierre Puget.

Mont Faron★★★

This distinctive yet small massif rising behind the town is the easternmost of the limestone ranges that were raised up in Provence on the fringe of the great earth movements associated with the formation of the Alps. A telepherique travels over pine-clad slopes to the summit, an exciting experience, with thrilling views of Toulon, the inner and outer anchorages, the St-Mandrier and Cap Sicié peninsulas and **Bandol★** (bd Amiral Vence. €7. ✆04 94 92 68 25).

Musée-mémorial du Débarquement en Provence★

Open daily except Mon: 10am–noon, 2–4.30pm. €4. ✆04 94 88 08 09.

From the tower, Tour Beaumont, there are fine views inland as well as a magnificent seaward **panorama★★★** over the Hyères Islands, the Toulon roadstead and the whole of the coast between **Sanary★** and **Bandol★**. The diorama explains the course of the landings, which took place on the night of 14–15 August 1944.

EXCURSIONS

HYÈRES★

The palm trees and mild climate of this resort are a good indication of what has attracted winter visitors to Hyères (aka Hyères-les-Palmiers) for more than a century. Its magnificent villas and Belle Époque palace hotels reveal the faded glory of the town once populated by wealthy aristocrats. Excavations on the coast reveal that Greeks from Marseille set up a trading station called **Olbia**, which was succeeded by a Roman town **Pomponiana**, and then a convent called **St-Pierre-d'Almanarre** during the Middle Ages, when the inhabitants moved further up the hill. The town became a well-known resort in the 19C. In the 20C, tourism led to the development of the beaches, although Hyères is a lively town all year.

Beaches

The long sandy beach of **L'Almanarre** is near the ancient site of the Greek town of Olbia and used by many surfing schools. The Route du Sel (accessible only in summer) leads along the peninsula, passing a vast salt marsh and then the Étang des Pesquiers, home to many aquatic birds. The old port of Hyères, **Ayguade-le-Ceinturon**, is where St Louis disembarked on his return from the Seventh Crusade.

Jardins Olbius-Riquier

Open daily 7.30am–5pm. No charge.

Extensive gardens with a rich variety of tropical plants, palms and cacti. In the **greenhouse** more fragile species can be seen together with a few rare animals.

Villa de Noailles

Open Jul–Sept daily except Tue and public holidays 2–7pm (Fri 4–10pm); Oct–Jun daily except Mon, Tue and public holidays 1–6pm (Fri 3–8pm). No charge. ✆04 94 08 01 98. www.villanoailles-hyeres.com.

In 1923 the Noailles commissioned ths winter villa from the Belgian architect Mallet-Stevens. With its covered swimming pool and 60 or so rooms, it was one of the first modern homes on the Riviera, and became a favourite rendez-vous for avant-garde artists of the 1920s. The city restored the villa in 1986, and temporary exhibitions are held on the first floor.

ÎLES D'HYÈRES★★★

No matter which island you visit, be sure to take plenty of drinking water. TLV-TVM has a year-round direct ferry service to all three islands from La Tour fondue, Gare Maritime (✆04 94 58 21 81. www.tlv-tvm.com). Vedettes Ile d'Or has boat tours to the three islands, Porquerolles, Port-Cros, Le Levant as well as along the coast (✆04 94 71 01 02. www.vedettesilesdor.fr).

These popular Côte d'Azur islands off the Hyères harbour are just a short sea crossing from the coast, and offer many beautiful scenic walking trails, sandy beaches and rocky inland hills. These islands are also known as the **Îles d'Or** due to the fact that in certain lights their mica shale rocks cast golden reflections.

Île de Porquerolles★★★

Porquerolles was called Protè (First) by the Greek settlers who came to live along its shores. The best way to discover the island is by bicycle (hired in the village). The north coast has sandy beaches bordered by pine trees, heather and scented myrtle; the south coast is steep and rugged with one or two inlets that are easily accessible.

Île-de Port-Cros★★★

Port-Cros Island is hillier, more rugged, and higher above the sea than its neighbours, and its lush vegetation is unrivalled on the coast. A few fishermen's cottages, a bunch of shops and a small church adorn the area around the bay, which is commanded by Fort du Moulin (aka the "Château"). Port-Cros, together with Île de Bagaud and neighbouring islets is designated a **Parc National**.

Île du Levant

The island consists of a rocky spine rimmed by vertical cliffs. Ninety percent of the island is occupied by the Marine Nationale (*access is forbidden*). Much of the rest is private nudist beaches.

Corsica★★★

***Kallisté*, the name given to Corsica by the ancient Greeks, means "most beautiful", and even today the French refer to it as *L'Île de Beauté*. This mountainous island lies some 170km/105.6mi off the coast of mainland France. With its intense light, its superbly varied and dramatic coast and its wild and rugged interior, it is a place of distinct natural identity, enhanced by the succession of peoples who have been attracted here to settle or to rule; these have included megalith builders and mysterious Torreans, Greeks and Romans, Pisans and Genoese, French and British, though the somewhat absurd interlude of the Anglo-Corsican Viceroyalty of 1794–96 seems to have left little trace.**

- **Population:** 322 120.
- **Michelin Map:**
- **Info:** Federation Régionale des Offices de Tourisme et Syndicats d'Iniative de Corse, Quartier Citadelle, 20250 Corte. ✆04 95 37 18 07. www.frotsi-corse.com.
- **Location:** Accessible by air (4 airports on the island) and by sea from Nice and Toulon (www.visit-corsica.com).

GEOGRAPHY

The gulfs of Corsica's west coast are of extraordinary beauty, the jagged headlands and precipitous cliffs rising from the Golfe de Porto being especially memorable. The Cap Corse promontory prolongs the island's backbone of schistic rocks 40km/25mi northwards into the sea.

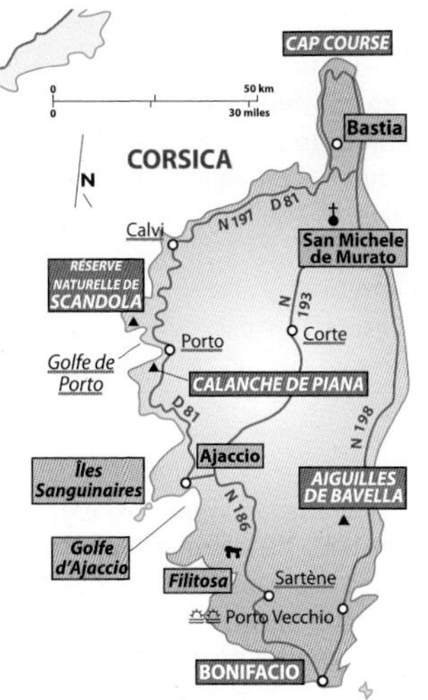

The coastal plains of Bastia and Aléria to the east constitute the only substantial areas of flat land. The interior is penetrated by a network of narrow and winding roads as well as by a remarkable 1m-gauge railway. Here are villages of tall granite houses overlooking deep gorges, as well as forests of oak, Corsican pine and sweet chestnut. Above the tree line rise the high bare summits, all the more imposing because of their proximity to the sea.

History – Remarkably Corsica has been part of France only since the late 19C, and before that it had a succession of occupiers including Greeks, Romans, Byzantines, Saracens (who gave the island its symbol, the Moor's Head) and finally the Genoese. During the War of Independence in the 19C the nationalist movement, led by the Corsican hero Pasquale Paoli, had some success, but despite the support of the British during the rather absurd Anglo-Corsican Viceroyalty of 1794–96, the island was absorbed into France in 1796. Corsica's most famous son is Napoléon.

ECONOMY

Corsica is an unspoilt Mediterranean island, and this, allied with beautiful mountains, a magnificent coastline and an agreeable climate, attracts the many tourists who are the mainstay of the economy. The island also produces honey, chestnuts, cheese, wine and sausages. The nationalist movement remains active.

AJACCIO★★

Ajaccio is on the W coast of Corsica, 82.4km/51mi SW of Corte along the N 193. Place Foch is the heart of town. The tourist office has information on guided tours. 3 bd du Roi-Jérôme, 20181 Ajaccio (Aiacciu). 04 95 51 53 03. www.ajaccio-tourisme.com.

Ajaccio occupies a natural amphitheatre looking out over its splendid bay. The town was founded in 1492 by the Office of St George which governed Corsica on behalf of the Republic of Genoa. Native Corsicans were forbidden residence there until 1553, when, in the course of the first French intervention in the island, it was taken by the legendary military adventurer Sampierro Corso (1498–1567), born in the village of Bastelica, 25km/15.5mi to the northeast.

A BIT OF HISTORY

It was here, at 1am on 13 September 1943, that the first Free French forces to land on the territory of France disembarked from the submarine *Casabianca*, under Commander L'Herminier.

Ajaccio's historic importance is due above all to its being the birthplace of **Napoléon Bonaparte**. The town continues to revere the memory of its "glorious child prodigy". Born on 15 August 1769, the son of Charles-Marie Bonaparte and Letizia Romolino, he entered the military school at Brienne (*Aube*) at the age of 10. At 27 he married Josephine Tascher de la Pagerie, widow of General Beauharnais, before directing the Italian campaign (Battle of Arcole) and, two years later, the expedition to Egypt. In 1804, taking the title of Napoléon I, he crowned himself Emperor of the French.

On 26 August the following year he launched the *Grande Armée* (Grand Army) against Austria from the encampment at Boulogne whence he had threatened England with invasion. By 1807, at the age of 38, he dominated Europe. It was then, however, that coalitions originally formed to resist the French Revolution were turned against the Empire. England was deeply involved in them all, in the colonies and on the high seas as well as in Europe. Though bloated and prematurely aged, Napoléon rose to the challenge, never more formidable than from 1809 on, the years of struggle against the Fifth and Sixth Coalitions. But France and her Emperor were out of touch with a changed Europe. There was now a strong desire for national independence among the peoples of Europe.

The Napoleonic Age was brought to a close on 18 June 1815 by the Battle of Waterloo. On 15 July Bonaparte sailed to exile on St Helena, where he died on 5 May 1821.

SIGHTS

Old Town★

It is the heart of Ajaccio's old town that holds the most interest. Here, a network of ancient streets spreads north and south from place Foch, which itself opens out to the seafront close by the port and marina. Place de Gaulle is essentially the town centre, and from here the main highway, cours Napoléon, extends parallel to the sea in a northeasterly direction.

Salon Napoléonien★

Hôtel de Ville, Place Foch. Open mid Jun–mid-Sep Mon–Fri 9–11.45am, 2–5.45pm; mid-Sep–mid-Jun Mon-Fri 9–11.45am, 2–4.45pm. Closed Mon morning. €2.50. 04 95 51 52 62. www.napoleon.org.

Situated in the Hôtel de Ville, this early 19C Restoration-style room displays paintings and sculptures relating to the Imperial era in addition to coins and medals also from the period.

Maison Bonaparte★

r. St-Charles Open daily: Apr–Sep 10.30am–12.30pm, 1.15–6pm; Oct–Mar 10am–noon, 2–4.45pm. €7. 04 95 21 43 89. http://musees-nationaux-malmaison.fr.

A typical house of the Genoese quarter, the Bonaparte family moved here from Italy in 1743. Napoléon is supposed to have been born on a couch in the antechamber on the first floor.

The family enjoyed a reasonable standard of living. In May 1793, the Bonapartes, loyal to Republican ideas, were forced by the followers of Pascal Paoli to abandon the house, which was sacked and the adjoining family properties laid waste. On her return to Ajaccio in 1798, Napoléon's mother put the house back in order with the help of her half-brother, Abbot Fesch (a future cardinal). The work was financed in part by a grant from the Directory, in part by sums sent to his brother Joseph by Napoléon (now in Egypt), enabling him to acquire the upper storeys and the adjoining house. On his return from Egypt on 29 September 1799, Bonaparte stopped off at Ajaccio to see the family home. He is supposed to have slept in the alcove on the second floor. After six days he slipped away via a trap-door, never to see his birthplace again. A diverse collection of memorabilia is displayed.

Palais Fesch: musée des Beaux-Arts★★★

50–52 r. Cardinal Fesch. Open: Oct–Apr Mon, Wed, Sat 10am–5pm, Thu–Fri noon–5pm (Sun, 3rd weekend of month, noon–5pm); May–Sep Mon, Wed, Sat 10.30am–6pm, Thu, Sun noon–6pm, Fri noon–6pm. €8. ✆04 95 26 26 26. www.musee-fesch.com.

The building was constructed for Cardinal Fesch, uncle of Napoléon I, in order to establish an Institute of Arts and Sciences. Born in Ajaccio in 1763, the cardinal died in Rome in 1839, and bequeathed to his home town more than 1 000 works of art. The museum is the most important in France after the Louvre as regards Italian painting.

Place Maréchal-Foch

This fine square, the focus of Ajaccio's outdoor social life, is shaded by palm trees; its upper part is dominated by a marble statue by Laboureur of Napoléon as First Consul.

EXCURSIONS

Aiguilles de Bavella★★★

The Aiguilles rise above the Col de Bavella, the mountain pass on D268, which runs from Sartène in SW Corsica to Solenzara on the southeast coast. The nearest community is Zonza.

There is no tourist office nearby, but the Mairie (town hall, ✆04 95 78 66 87) in Zonza can assist with information. For more on this region of Corsica, see www.alta-rocca.com.

The Bavella Pass is the starting point for many walks and trails for all levels of ability, and is on the long-distance path **GR20** (see p668). It is one of the most dramatic locations in Corsica. From the Bavella Pass, Col de Bavella, there is an awesome view of the jagged Bavella or Asinao Peaks in a spectacular, stark setting; the changing light plays on the sheer rock walls rising above the pine trees at the base.

Forêt de Bavella★★

The dense forest growing at an altitude of 500m–1 300m has been damaged repeatedly by fire and has been extensively replanted with maritime and laricio pines, cedars and fir trees. A hunting preserve shelters herds of wild sheep which can be glimpsed perched high up on the sheer rocks. Just before the pass are low buildings formerly used as sheep-pens, and an inn, **Auberge du Col**, the starting-point for walks around the pass to the Trou de la Bombe and La Pianona.

Col de Bavella★★★

The mountain ridge crowning the island is indented by the Bavella Pass marked by a cross and the statue of **Notre-Dame-des-Neiges**.

The setting and the panorama over the summits are spectacular. To the west the Bavella Peaks rise above the forest of twisted pine trees, while to the east the rock wall of Calanca Murata and the jagged ridge of red rock of Punta Tafonata di Paliri stand out against the backdrop of the Tyrrhenian Sea.

Golfe de Porto★★★

The Gulf is the large bay on the shores of which the town of Porto stands, in western Corsica. Qtr. de la Marine, ✆04 95 26 10 55. www.porto-tourisme.com.

The Bay of Porto is one of the most splendid destinations on the coast,

Walking in Corsica

The scope for walking in Corsica is great, but it covers a vast range of terrain including rough, stony mountainsides, exposed airy ridges, rock slabs, earth-based paths through woodland and pastureland, sandy beaches and numerous river crossings, the latter generally achieved by fording. Most paths have clear waymarking, although numbering of them is rare. Waymarking uses the conventional system of painted stripes on rocks common to anyone who has walked elsewhere in France.

The GR20, the so-called high-level route, is a tough and unremitting trail that heads high into the mountains and stays there for days. The landscape through which it passes is awesome, passing from Calenzana in the north to Conca in the south, a distance of around 190km/118mi.

Two excellent guides are Walking in Corsica, by Gillian Price, and GR20 – Corsica by Paddy Dillon, both available from www.cicerone.co.uk.

owing to its sheer size, range of colours and varied natural sights. Imposing cliffs of red granite contrast with the deep-blue waters. The area is part of a nature park, Parc naturel régional de Corse, listed as a World Heritage Site.

Calanches de Piana★★★

Boat trips (1hr30min) leaving from Porto. Easter–Oct: departure 2pm, 4pm, 6pm. www.otpiana.com.

The deep creeks (*calanches*) dominating the Bay of Porto are remarkable; the chaotic landscape is shaped by erosion of the granite, jagged rocks and spherical cavities known as "taffoni", and integral feature of the picturesque landscape of Corsica.

A road (D 81) runs through the calanche for 2km/1.2mi affording splendid viewpoints over the rock piles and the sea. Starting from the terrace of the **Chalet des Roches bleues**, several walks lasting about one hour allow visitors to admire at close range the distinctive form of some of the rocks: the Turtle, the Bishop, a human head and a castle.

Réserve Naturelle de Scandola★★★

The Presqu'île de Scandola rises between the Punta Rossa to the south and the Punta Nera to the north.

The majestic massif is of volcanic origin and features numerous taffoni.

BONIFACIO★★★

At the southern tip of the island: 122km/76mi S of Ajaccio. ℹ 2 r. Fred Scamaroni. ✆04 95 73 11 88. www.bonifacio.fr.

Projecting into the sea on Corsica's southern tip, the old town occupies the top of a high wedge of rock with exceptional views, while the harbour and new town at the foot of the cliff is the busy centre of commerce and activity.

A BIT OF HISTORY

Greek and Roman remains have been found at Bonifacio but the town's history really begins when Bonifacio, Marquis of Tuscany, gave it his name in AD 828. Its strategic position controlling the Western Mediterranean was appreciated by the Genoese, who took it in 1187.

The town was besieged many times, most notably in 1420 by King Alfonso V of Aragon. Legend has it that his soldiers cut the famous stairway of 187 steps into the cliff-face in the course of a single night.

VISIT

Site★★★

Bonifacio is magnificently sited on a long, narrow promontory protecting its "fjord" in the far south of Corsica and it is reached from the rest of the island across a vast, arid plain. The town is divided in two, the **"Marine"★**, the port quarter offering a safe anchorage for warships, fishing boats and pleasure craft, and the **Upper Town★★** overlooking the sea from 60m-high cliffs. Its old houses, many of them four or five storeys, are joined by buttress-like rainwater channels feeding the town's cisterns.

The great loggia of the Church of Ste-Marie-Majeure is built over a huge cistern with a capacity of 650m^3; under Genoese rule this is where the affairs of the town were deliberated upon by four elders, who were elected for three months at a time.

Twice a week the *podesta*, the mayor, who lived opposite, would mete out justice from here.

Parc Marin International des Bouches de Bonifacio★★

The Nature Reserve of Bonifacio was founded at the initiative of the Ministry of Environment and Territorial Collectivity of Corsica, to preserve and enhance the natural heritage of this strait. This reserve is home to marine and coastal environments and exceptional landscapes: the Lavezzi islands, Cerbicales, Bruzzi Moines, and the cliffs of Bonifacio.

Coastline

With 70km/44mi of coastline, Bonifacio has sandy beaches, coves, islands, archipelagos, fishing ports and marinas. Worthy of a visit are the Bay of **Rondinara★★★**, regarded by many as the **most beautiful beach in France**, Fazzio, Sant'Amanza, and the wild beaches of Tonnara and Petit Sperone.

EXCURSIONS

Grotte du Sdragonato★

45min by boat.

The dragon's cave is dimly lit by a shaft in the shape of Corsica in reverse. 12km/7.4mi away across the sometimes choppy waters of the Bonifacio Straits (Bouches de Bonifacio) is Sardinia. The trip gives good views of the high limestone cliffs of the promontory and of the King of Aragon's steps.

Filitosa★★

The site, overlooking the Taravo valley, is located in the commune of Sollacaro, 17km/10.5mi N of Propriano, in southern Corsica. Place St Marcel. 95 37 18 07. www.frotsi-corse.com.

This fascinating site was discovered in 1946; the beginnings of Corsican history are all visible here, from the Neolithic to the Megalithic and the Torreen, and finally to the Roman.

Site archéologique★★

Apr–mid-Oct: 9am–7pm. Preferably in the middle of the day: good light to study the sculptures and engravings. Sound recordings in 4 languages. 04 95 74 00 91.

By the path leading to the prehistoric site stands the superb menhir known as **Filitosa V**, bearing, in front, a long sword and an oblique dagger, and, behind, anatomical or clothing details. A stone wall built by the Megalithic people encloses the site. Within it, four striking groups of monuments testify to the domination exercised by the Torreens: the **East Monument** which they filled in; the remains of **huts** (*cabanes*) which they re-used, the circular **Central Monument**, and the fragments of menhir-statues. The latter had been made by the Megalithic people; the Torreens cut them up and re-used them, face downwards, in the construction of the Central Monument, doubtless to signal their supremacy. Some of them, however, have been placed upright again, and Filitosa IX and XIII frame the way into the Central Monument.

The **West Monument** is Torreen, and is built on Megalithic foundations.

The five menhir-statues near an age-old olive tree on the far slope of the valley mark the end of the Megalithic period in this area.

Sartène★

The town is 51km/31.7mi NW of Bonifacio. Place de la Libération. 04 95 77 74 01.

The writer Prosper Mérimée thought Sartène, 305m above the Bay of Valinco, the "most Corsican of Corsican towns".

Vieille ville (Old Town)★★

Go through the arch of the town hall (Hôtel de ville) and take the street opposite (Rue des Frères-Bartoli). The narrow stone-flagged alleyways, some stepped or vaulted, are lined by tall granite-built houses with a fortress-like air. The **Quartier de Santa Ann★★★** has this kind of characteristic townscape.

Place de la Libération – The shady square is the focus of local life. It is overlooked by the **Église Ste-Marie**, built in granite. To the left of the main entrance are the chains and the heavy cross of oak borne by Catenacciu, the anonymous red-robed penitential figure at the centre of the nocturnal procession on Good Friday. This **procession du Catenacciu★★** is probably the island's most ancient ceremony.

BASTIA★★

Bastia lies on the northeaastern coast of the island, 57.5km/92mi NE of Ajaccio.

Place St-Nicolas. 04 95 54 20 40. www.bastia-tourisme.com.

The overriding impression of Bastia, the island's most successful commercial town, is one of aged distress and charm. Thankfully, the town's industry lies to the south, among the lowlands. Bastia has two ports which co-exist amicably and between them portray the old and the new aspects of this time-worn place.

SIGHTS

Old Town (Terra Vecchia)★

The old quarter, the Terra Vecchia, consists of a tightly packed mishmash of streets, Flamboyant Baroque churches and lofty tenements, displaying crumbling ochre walls against a scented backdrop of maquis-covered hills.

Bastia dates from Roman times, when a camp was established at Biguglia to the south, close by a freshwater lagoon. Little remains of this former colony, but the site is worth a day-trip for the well-preserved pair of Pisan churches at Marana, rising from the southern fringes of Poretta airport. Bastia began to thrive under the Genoese, when wine was exported to the Italian mainland from Porto Cardo, as the old port was originally called. Despite the fact that in 1811 Napoléon made Ajaccio the capital of the island, initiating a competitiveness between the two towns that is evident to this day, Bastia soon developed the stronger trading position with mainland France. The Nouveau Port, created in 1862 to the north of the town to cope with the increasing traffic with France and Italy, became the mainstay of the local economy, exporting chiefly agricultural products from Cap Corse, Balagne and the eastern plain.

Citadel and ramparts★

Constructed in the 15–17C by the Genoese, the citadel of Bastia is almost a town in its own right, known as Terra Nova, which you enter through the Louis XVI gate, which gives onto the place du Donjon. Entrenched behind the citadel walls, the villagers lived peaceably for nearly three centuries, and styled the centre on the grid plan of Roman cities.

Today, the houses seem to be stacked above one another, presenting a colourful picture to the port. The narrow streets have great allure, beckoning like an impatient child, leading into a maze of alleyways that confuse and amuse in equal measure.

EXCURSIONS

Cap Corse★★★

Cap Corse can be reached from either the east or the west coast. The city of Bastia stands at the base of the "finger" on the east coast.

Base Nautique, Port de Plaisance Macinaggio. 04 95 35 40 34. www.macinaggiorogliano-capcorse.fr.

Make time to visit the superb covered market, near the Old Port, daily except Monday.

Cap Corse is the finger of mountain range that prolongs the island's ridge of rock 40km/24.8mi into the sea.

A Seafaring People – In contrast to the rest of the Corsican population, local inhabitants responded to the call of the sea and took up trade and travel to distant lands. In the 19C they set up the first trading-posts in North Africa. A large number emigrated to South America; many became prosperous and built great houses in colonial or Renaissance style in their native village. These styles have influenced the architecture of the region. This northernmost part of Corsica is in fact its sunniest and is ideal for walking and cycling. The east side of the Cap has small villages like Erbalunga nestling in coves, while on the west side the villages of Nonza and Canari are on higher ground.

San Michele de Murato★★

22km/13.6mi SW via N193 and D62.

The church and village of Murato are just north of the village of Murato in the Bevinco valley, this 13C Romanesque church is Pisan in style, of uneven stripes of beautiful green serpentine and white limestone blocks.

Corte★

67km/41mi SW via N193. 04 95 46 26 70. www.corte-tourisme.com.

Corte owes its fame to its **site★** among gorges and ravines, as well as to two great men, Gaffori and Paoli, who were instrumental in making it one of the strongholds of Corsican patriotism.

Jean-Pierre Gaffori (1704–53) was born here. He was a member of the Triumvirate "Protectors of the Nation", who took up arms against Genoa. In 1746, supported by his indomitable wife Faustine, he succeeded in wresting the town from the Genoese. In 1750 they returned, taking the citadel but failing to overcome the town's defences; Gaffori's house still bears the scars of the Genoese guns. In June 1751, Gaffori was made "General of the Nation" and granted executive power. But two years later he was killed in an ambush.

After this an appeal was made for **Pascal Paoli** (1725–1807), then in exile in Italy, to return to his native land. He was proclaimed "General of the Nation" in his turn. By 1764, the island was united under his leadership, with only the Genoese coastal forts holding out against him. For 14 years he made Corte his capital, drew up a constitution, founded a university, minted money, reformed the system of justice, encouraged industry and stimulated agricultural production. Having failed to put down the Corsicans' long struggle for independence (1729–69), the Republic of Genoa requested the intervention of France. A mission of conciliation arrived, headed by the future French Governor, Marbeuf. Paoli unwisely prevaricated and was bypassed by events; on 15 May 1768, by the Treaty of Versailles, Genoa provisionally gave up its rights over the island to France. Paoli proclaimed a mass uprising, but was defeated at **Ponte Nuovo** on 8 May 1769.

Paoli went into exile, spent mostly in England, where he was lionised by the court of George III. Amnestied at the outbreak of the French Revolution, he met with a triumphal reception in Paris before returning to Corsica.

Later, after his denunciation as a counter-revolutionary, he sought aid from the English. Nelson's victories over the French at St-Florent, Bastia and Calvi did not, however, fulfil Paoli's hopes of independence under the English Crown, but led to the short-lived Anglo-Corsican kingdom and renewed exile in London for Paoli. He died there in 1807.

Ville Haute★

Dominated by the **citadel★** perched high up on its rock, old Corte, with its cobbled, stepped streets and tall houses, still has the air of the island capital it once was.

In the Place Paoli stands the statue of the great man, in bronze. Further up is the Place Gaffori, where, behind the monument to the General of the Nation, is his house. A ramp opposite the National Palace (Palais National) leads to a **viewpoint★**.

INDEX

A

Abbaye Bénédictine de Cluny........ 381
Abbaye de Fontenay................. 373
Abbaye de Fontfroide 570
Abbaye de Jumièges 217
Abbaye de Noirlac................... 488
Abbaye de St-Benoît-sur-Loire 311
Abbaye de St-Martin-du-Canigou 576
Abbaye du Bec 216
Abbaye du Thoronet 661
Abbot Suger 125
Abers, Les.......................... 261
Aber Wrac'h......................... 262
Academicism 106
Académie française.................. 76
Accessibility.......................... 47
Accommodation 52
Activities for Kids..................... 33
Adam brothers 101
Ader, Clément........................ 81
Affair of the Régale 77
Agay................................ 658
Agincourt.............................74
Aigues-Mortes 560
Aiguille des Grands-Montets......... 410
Aiguille du Midi 409, 410
Aiguilles de Bavella.................. 667
Aiguilles de Port-Coton.............. 272
Ainhoa.............................. 527
Airbus 83
Airports.............................. 44
Aix-en-Provence 612
Aix-les-Bains........................ 402
Ajaccio.............................. 666
Alabaster Coast 223
Albi................................. 584
Albigensian Crusade.................. 73
Alençon 240
Algerian crisis 82
Alignements de Kerlescan 270
Alignements de Kermario............ 270
Alignements du Ménec.............. 270
Alignements Mégalithiques
de Lagatjar....................... 262
Allegrain, GC........................ 103
L'Almanarre 664
Alpilles, Les 618
Alps, The............................ 396
Alsace Lorraine Champagne 312
Alsace wine tours 32
Alyscamps, Les...................... 618
Amboise............................ 300
Amboise Conspiracy.................. 75
American War of Independence....... 78
Amiens 185
Amphion-les-Bains.................. 406
Ancenis............................. 277
Ancienne Abbaye St-Vaast 183
Ancien Régime........................ 78
Andelys, Les 216
Andlau.............................. 346
Andorra............................. 574
Ange-Jacques....................... 126
Angers...................... 23, 284
Cathédrale St-Maurice................. 285
Château 284
Collégiale St-Martin 285
Doutre, La 288
Église St-Serge 286
Galerie David-d'Angers................ 285
Hôtel du Croissant.................... 285
Hôtel Pincé 285
Jardin des Plantes 287
Jardin du Mail......................... 287
Maison d'Adam 285
Monastery buildings 285
Musée des Beaux-Arts................. 285
Musée Jean-Lurçat et de la Tapisserie
contemporaine 288
Musée Turpin de Crissé 286
Muséum des Sciences Naturelles........ 286
Old Town 285
Parc de Balzac......................... 287
Parc de la Maine....................... 287
Parc de l'Arboretum 287
Parc St-Nicolas 287
Place du Ralliement 285
Quai, Le.............................. 288
St-Laud district........................ 286
Tour St-Aubin 285
Walking tour.......................... 285
Ango, Jean.......................... 77
Angoulême 530
Annecy 399
Ancien Palais Épiscopal................ 401
Avenue d'Albigny 399
Cathédrale St-Pierre................... 401
Eat 404
Église Notre-Dame-de-Liesse.......... 401
Église St-François-de-Sales 400
Église St-Maurice...................... 400
Jardins de l'Europe 399
Musée-Château d'Annecy 400
Palais de l'Île.......................... 400
Palais de l'Île.......................... 400
Parc de l'Impérial...................... 399
Place Notre-Dame..................... 401
Pont des Amours...................... 399

Pont sur le Thiou 400
Rue Ste-Claire 401
Stay 403
Anne of Austria 76, 126
Anthéor 658
Antibes 658
Antiques, Les 623
Antiques shopping 35
Aqueducs de Barbegal 619
Aquitaine 15
Arago 128
Arcachon 522
Arc-et-Senans 392
Archipel du Frioul 27
Architecture 84
Art and architecture, 19C 105
Art and architecture, 20C 108
Arènes, Nîmes 558
Argentière 409
Arles 616
Arman 109
Arras 183
Arromanches-les-Bains 231
Ars 534
Art and Culture 84
Art Nouveau 107
Atelier Paul Cézanne 612
Atlantic Coast 15, 510
ATMs 56
Aubeterre-sur-Dronne 532
Auch 581
Aulnay 541
Auray Port St Goustan 270
Autun 379
Auvergne Rhône Valley 14, 426
Auvers-Sur-Oise 173
Auxerre 383
Avant-garde art and architecture 108
Aven de Marzal 627
Aven d'Orgnac 627
l'Aventure Michelin 470
Avignon 624

B

Bagnoles-de-l'Orne 241
Baie de Lampaul 262
Baie du Stiff 262
Balcon du Haut Planet 207
Balcons de la Mescla 423
Baltard, V 106
Balzac 129
Banks 56
Banne d'Ordanche 472
Barcelonnette 415
Barfleur 236
Bar-le-Duc 356
Barneville-Carteret 236
Baron Haussmann 106, 129
Baroque Gothic art and architecture 93
Barraques-en-Vercors, Les 421
Bartholomé 108
Basilique Ste-Marie-Madeleine 387
Bassin du Bourg d'Oisans 420
Bassin, Le 522
Bastia 670
Bastille 78, 125, 126
Battlefields of Verdun 321
Battle of Austerlitz 79
Battle of Bouvines 74
Battle of Denain 77
Battle of Hastings 233
Battle of Leipzig 79
Battle of Marignano 74
Battle of Poitiers 74
Battle of Sedan 80
Battle of Ulm 79
Battle of Waterloo 79
Baule, La 278
Baule-les-Pins, La 278
Baume-aux-Pigeons 424
Baux Alpilles, Les 618
Baux-de-Provence, Les 622
Bayeux 232
Bayeux Tapestry 232
Bayle 128
Bayonne 524
Béarn, The 529
Beaufort 412
Beaufortain 412
Beaugency 306
Beaulieu 643
Beaulieu-sur-Dordogne 504
Beaune 377
Bastion des Filles 378
Bastion Notre-Dame 378
Collégiale Notre-Dame 378
Hôtel de la Rochepot 378
Hôtel-Dieu 377
Musée du Vin de Bourgogne 378
Place de la Halle 378
Ramparts 378
Rempart des Dames 378
Rempart Madeleine 378
Walking tour 377
Beauvais 181
Bed and breakfast 52
Bélanger 103
Belle Époque 80

Belle-Île. 26, 243, 272
Bellevue 410
Belvédère de Rancoumas 425
Belvédère du Point Sublime. 424
Béout, Le 590
Bérarde, La. 420
Bergerac. 499
Berges du Tarn 585
Berlioz. 129
Bernard, Émile 107
Bernard, J. 108
Berry 14, 482
Bertholet 128
Besançon 389
Cathédrale Saint-Jean 391
Chapelle Notre-Dame-du-Refuge. 391
Citadelle. 389
Collégiale Sainte-Madeleine. 391
Grande-Rue. 390
Hôpital Saint-Jacques 391
Hôtel Bonvalot. 391
Hôtel de Champagney. 391
Hôtel de Ville 390
Maison espagnole. 391
Musée des Beaux-Arts et d'Archéologie . 389
Musée du Temps 391
Old Town 389, 391
Palais de Justice. 391
Palais Granvelle 391
Place de la Révolution 389
Porte Rivotte. 391
Préfecture 391
Rue Mégevand. 391
Tour de la Pelote 391
Vestiges Romains 391
Walking tour. 389
Besbre. 478
Beuil. 415
Beynac-et-Cazenac 498, 501
Biarritz. 523
Bidart. 525
Bizet. 130
Black Prince, The 74
Blais, Jean-Charles. 109
Blanchard, remi 109
Blériot-Plage 200
Blois. 304
Blum, Léon. 82
Boisrond, François. 109
Bollée, Amédée 290
Bollène-Vésubie, La 416
Bolline, La. 416
Boltanski. 109
Bonaparte, Napoléon. 666
Bonifacio 668
Bonnard 107
Bordeaux 15, 22, 23, 513
Abbatiale Ste-Croix 516
Basilique St-Michel. 516
Basilique St-Seurin 518
Bassins à Flot. 519
Cap Sciences. 519
Cathédrale St-André. 517
Centre Jean Moulin. 517
Chartrons, Les. 518
Cité Mondiale. 518
Cours de l'Intendance 518
Cours Xavier Arnozan 518
Église Notre-Dame 517
Église St-Bruno. 517
Église St-Louis-des-Chartrons. 518
Esplanade des Quinconces 517
Flèche St Michel. 516
Golden Triangle 517
Grand Théâtre 517
History 513
Jardin Public 517, 518
Mériadeck District. 517
Musée d'Aquitaine 516
Musée d'Art Contemporain 518
Musée des Arts Décoratifs 517
Musée des Beaux-Arts. 517
Musée des Douanes. 516
Musée du Vin et du Négoce à Bordeaux . 518
Palais Gallien. 518
Palais Rohan 517
Petit Hôtel Labottière 518
Place de la Bourse. 516
Place du Marché des Chartrons 518
Place du Palace 516
Place du Parlement. 516
Place Gambetta 518
Place St-Pierre 516
Porte Cailhau 516
Porte d'Aquitaine 516
Porte de la Grosse-Cloche 516
Quai des Chartrons. 518
Quartier Pey Berland 517
Quartier St-Michel. 516
Rue Ausone 516
Rue Neuve 516
Rue Notre-Dame 518
Tour Pey Berland 517
Tribunal de Grande Instance
de Bordeaux 517
Bordeaux Vineyards 520
Bordeaux wine tours 32
Bouchardon. 102

Boucher 101
Boudin.......................... 126, 412
Bouguereau......................... 106
Bouillé.............................. 127
Boulogne-sur-Mer................... 201
Boulouris 658
Bourbons, The 75, 125
Bourdelle 108, 131
Bourg-en-Bresse 447
Bourgeois, Louise 109
Bourges.........................485
Cathédrale St-Étienne 485
Digue de l'Yèvre 488
Eat 490
Église Notre-Dame 487
Église St-Bonnet 488
Église St-Pierre-le-Guillard.............. 487
Grange aux Dîmes....................... 487
Hôtel Cujas 487
Hôtel des Échevins 487
Hôtel Lallemant......................... 488
Jacques Cœur's "Birthplace" 487
Jardin des Prés-Fichaux................. 488
Jardins de l'Archevêché................. 487
Maison de Pelvoysin.................... 487
Marais, Les............................. 488
Musée des Meilleurs Ouvriers de France. 488
Musée du Berry 487
Musée Estève 487
Old Town 487
Palais Jacques Cœur.................... 487
Place des Quatre-Piliers 487
Place Étienne-Dolet 487
Place Gordaine......................... 488
Promenade des Remparts 487
Rue Bourbonnoux....................... 488
Rue Coursalon 488
Rue des Linières........................ 487
Rue Joyeuse 488
Rue Mirebeau.......................... 487
Stay 489
Bourg-St-Maurice 412
Bouteville........................... 534
Bozouls............................. 586
Brancusi 131
Branly 130
Brantôme........................... 495
Braque.............................. 108
Braque, Georges 223
Breakdown (vehicle)................. 49
Breath test kits....................... 50
Brèche de Roland 593
Brest................................ 261
Brévent, Le.......................... 410
Briançon............................ 422
Briare............................... 385
Brignogan-Plages 261
Brioude............................. 460
Brochon 374
Brongniart...................... 103, 128
Brosse, Salomon de.................. 125
Brun, Charles le 100
Burgundy Jura 364
Burgundy Jura wine tours............ 32
Burgundy's vineyards................ 376
Buses to France 45
Business hours 54

C

Cabanel............................. 106
Caen.............................224
Abbaye-aux-Dames 225
Abbaye-aux-Hommes.................... 225
Château Ducal 225
Cour des Imprimeurs 224
Église St-Pierre......................... 224
Église St-Sauveur....................... 224
Hôtel d'Escoville 224
Mémorial, Le........................... 225
Musée de la Poste et des Techniques de Communication.................. 224
Musée de Normandie 225
Musée des Beaux-Arts.................. 225
Place de la République 224
Place Malherbe 224
Place St-Martin......................... 225
Place St-Sauveur 225
Rue du Vaugueux 225
Rue Froide 224
Rue St-Pierre........................... 224
Walking Tour........................... 224
Cahors.............................. 506
Cairn de Gavrinis 270
Calais............................... 196
Calanches de Piana.................. 668
Callelongue......................... 606
Calle, Sophie 109
Calvados....................... 228, 230
Calvaire de Plougastel-Daoulas 261
Calvin................................ 75
Camaret-sur-Mer.................... 262
Camargue, La 619
Cambo-les-Bains.................... 527
Camisard revolt 77
Camping.............................. 53
Camus.............................. 533
Canal Cruising........................ 29
Canal du Midi 581

Cancale 256
Cannes........................654
Allées de la Liberté 655
Boulevard de la Croisette 654
Cannet, Le 656
Chemin des Collines.................... 657
Croix des Gardes, La.................... 657
Eat 659
History 654
Musée de la Castre 656
Old Cannes 655
Pointe de la Croisette................... 655
Port 655
Quartier de la Californie 655
Rue Meynadier.......................... 656
Seafront 654
Stay 659
Suquet, Le 656
Vallauris 657
Walking tours.......................... 654
Canoeing 28
Cap Blanc-Nez....................... 200
Cap Canaille......................... 607
Cap Corse........................... 670
Cap d'Antibes 658
Cap de la Chèvre 262
Cap de la Hague...................... 236
Cap d'Erquy.......................... 256
Capet, Hugh 73
Capetians, The 73, 125
Cap Ferrat........................... 643
Cap Fréhel 256
Cap Gris-Nez......................... 200
Cap Martin........................... 652
Cap Roux 658
Cap Sizun 264
Carcassonne 564
Carnac.............................. 270
Carnot, Sadi......................... 128
Carolingians, The..................... 73
Carpeaux 106, 130
Carrefour du Grand Baliveau 207
Car rental 49
Cartellier............................ 106
Cartier, Jacques 77
Cascade du Hérisson 395
Cascade du Ray-Pic.................. 462
Casse Déserte....................... 414
Cassis............................... 607
Castellane 423
Castres 585
Cathars 74
Cathédrale de Beauvais.............. 181
Cathédrale Saint-Cyr-et-Ste-Julitte ... 380
Catherine de' Medici 75
Catholic League...................... 75
Causse de Gramat 503
Caves de Roquefort.................. 563
Celts................................. 71
Cénac............................... 501
Cerceau, Du......................... 125
César 109
Cézanne 107, 108, 612
Chablais 411
Chablis 386
Chagall 131
Chaise-Dieu, La 460
Chalgrin 128
Châlons-en-Champagne............. 356
Chalon-sur-Saône 380
Chambéry 402
Chambolle-Musigny................. 374
Chamonix-Mont-Blanc............... 408
Champagne......................... 312
Champagne-Ardenne wine tours...... 32
Champaigne, Philippe de 99
Champs-Élysées..................... 149
Channel Tunnel 83
Chaos de Montpellier-le-Vieux....... 563
Chaos de Trescaïre.................. 424
Chapelle de Ronchamp 393
Chardin.........................101, 126
Charlemagne 73
Charles IX............................ 75
Charles the Bald..................... 293
Charles the Simple 73
Charles V............................ 125
Charles VI 74
Charles VIII.......................... 125
Charles X.........................79, 128
Chartres 203
Château d'Alleuze 475
Château d'Amboise.................. 300
Château d'Ancy-le-Franc............ 386
Château d'Angers 284
Château d'Auvers.................... 174
Château d'Azay-le-Rideau 302
Château de Blérancourt............. 180
Château de Blois 304
Château de Bonaguil 505
Château de Breteuil 164
Château de Brissac 288
Château de Carrouges 241
Château de Castelnau-Bretenoux 505
Château de Castelnaud 501
Château de Chambéry............... 402
Château de Chambord............... 306
Château de Chantilly 176

Château de Chaumont-sur-Loire 300
Château de Chenonceau 300
Château de Cheverny 306
Château de Chinon 296
Château de Combourg 249
Château de Compiègne 178
Château de Cormatin 381
Château de Courances 172
Château de Dampierre 165
Château de Dinan 255
Château de Fontainebleau 170
Château de Fougères 249
Château de Gevrey-Chambertin 374
Château de Grignan 632
Château de Hautefort 495
Château de Josselin 271
Château de La Brède 520
Château de Langeais 296
Château de La Palice 478
Château de La Rochefoucauld 531
Château de Loches 301
Château de Meillant 488
Château de Milandes 501
Château de Montal 505
Château de Montfort 501
Château de Montségur 566
Château de Murol 472
Château de Peyrepertuse 575
Château de Pierrefonds 180
Château de Pirou 236
Château de Polignac 460
Château de Rambouillet 205
Château de Roquetaillade 520
Château de Saumur 293
Château de Savigny-lès-Beaune 378
Château des Ducs de Wurtemberg ... 344
Château de Serrant 288
Château de St-Germain-en-Laye 173
Château de St-Malo 251
Château de Sully-sur-Loire 311
Château de Suscinio 270
Château de Thoiry 174
Château de Tournoël 477
Château de Tours 298
Château de Valençay 307
Château de Vaux-le-Vicomte 169
Château de Vendôme 307
Château de Versailles 161
Château de Villandry 302
Château de Vitré 249
Château d'If 606
Château du Haut-Kœnigsbourg 341
Châteaudun 311
Château d'Ussé 301
Château Gaillard 217
Château Mouton-Rothschild 520
Châtillon-sur-Seine 373
Chaudet 106
Cheese 36, 67
Chémoulin 278
Chénier, André 127
Chenôve 373
Cherbourg 236
Children 33
Chinon 296
Chirac, Jacques 83
Cime de Caron 418
Cingle de Montfort 501
Ciotat, La 607
Circuit de la Sarthe 291
Cirque de Baume 395
Cirque de Gavarnie 592
Cirque de Navacelles 556
Cirque des Baumes 562
Cities of France 23
Clairière de l'Armistice 179
Classicism - art and architecture 99
Clemenceau 131
Clément, Jacques 125
Clermont-Ferrand 23, 464
Basilique Notre-Dame-du-Port 468
Carrefour des Taules 468
Cathédrale Notre-Dame-de-l'Assomption 468
Église Notre-Dame-de-Prospérité 469
Église St-Pierre-les-Minimes 465
Fontaine d'Amboise 465
Fontaine du Lion 470
Halle aux Toiles 469
History 464
Hôtel de Fontenilhes 470
Hôtel de Fontfreyde 470
Hôtel de la Faye des Forges 468
Hôtel de la Porte 468
Hôtel de Lignat 470
Hôtel d'Étienne Pradal 469
Hôtel Doyac 468
Hôtel du Bailliage 468
Hôtel Gaschier 470
Hôtel Mallet-de-Vandègre 470
Hôtel Regin 468
Maison d'Adam et d'Eve 469
Maison de l'Ange 470
Maison de l'Apothicaire 469
Maison de l'Élephant 469
Marché St-Pierre 465
Musée d'Art Roger-Quilliot 469
Old Clermont 465

- Old Montferrand . . . 468
- Place de Jaude . . . 465
- Place de la Rodade . . . 468
- Place de la Victoire . . . 468
- Rue des Chaussetiers . . . 468
- Rue des Cordeliers . . . 468
- Rue des Gras . . . 465
- Rue des Petits-Gras . . . 468
- Rue du Port . . . 468
- Rue Pascal . . . 468
- Walking tour . . . 465

Climate . . . 43, 113
Clos-Lucé . . . 300
Clovis . . . 71, 125
Cluny . . . 381
Clusaz, La . . . 412
Cluse de Pontarlier . . . 393
Cluses . . . 411
Coaches to France . . . 45
Cocteau . . . 131
Code Napoléon . . . 78, 128
Cognac . . . 533
Cognac (brandy) shopping . . . 36
Colbert . . . 77
Col d'Aubert . . . 593
Col d'Aubisque . . . 529
Col d'Aussois . . . 418
Col de Balme . . . 410
Col de Bavella . . . 667
Col de Couilloie . . . 415
Col de la Cayolle . . . 415
Col de la Croix des Frêtes . . . 418
Col de la Schlucht . . . 349
Col de la Vanoise . . . 418
Col de Rousset . . . 421
Col des Saisies . . . 412
Col de St-Martin . . . 416
Col de Tourne . . . 418
Col de Turini . . . 416
Col de Valberg . . . 415
Col de Vars . . . 415
Col d'Iseran . . . 413
Col d'Izoard . . . 414
Col du Bonhomme . . . 349
Col du Galibier . . . 413
Col du Lautaret . . . 413
Col du Palet . . . 418
Coligny . . . 75
Collection Schlumpf . . . 347
Collonges-la-Rouge . . . 504
Colmar . . . 340
Colmiane, La . . . 416
Colonne de la Grande Armée . . . 202
Combas, Robert . . . 109
Combe du Queyras . . . 414
Combe Laval . . . 421
Combourg . . . 249
Commune, The . . . 127, 130
Compiègne . . . 178
Concarneau . . . 266
Condamine, Charles de la . . . 126
Condé . . . 75
Condé-sur-Noireau . . . 228
Congress of Vienna . . . 79
Conques . . . 586
Conquet, Le . . . 262
Consulates . . . 55
Consulate, The . . . 128
Continental Blockade . . . 79
Convention, The . . . 78, 127
Corbières, Les . . . 573
Corbusier, Le . . . 131
Cordes-sur-Ciel . . . 587
Cormet de Roselend . . . 412
Corniche Basque . . . 527
Corniche des Crêtes . . . 607
Corniches de la Riviera . . . 643
Corniche Sublime, La . . . 423
Cornouaille, La . . . 264
Corot . . . 107, 128
Corsica . . . 16, 77, 634, 665
Côte d'Albâtre . . . 223
Côte d'Amour . . . 278
Côte d'Azur . . . 16
Côte de Beaune . . . 376
Côte de Grâce . . . 221
Côte d'Émeraude . . . 256
Côte de Nacre . . . 230
Côte de Nuits . . . 376
Côte De Nuits . . . 373
Côte Sauvage, Belle-Île . . . 272
Côte Sauvage, Île d'Ouessant . . . 262
Côte Sauvage, La Baule . . . 278
Côte Vermeille, La . . . 573
Cottages . . . 52
Cotte, Robert de . . . 126
Coulée de Serrant . . . 289
Couloir de Samson . . . 423
Couloir Samson . . . 424
County of Nice . . . 80
Courbet . . . 106
Courchevel . . . 417
Courchevel 1550 . . . 417
Courchevel 1850 . . . 417
Courtonne . . . 101
Coustou . . . 101
Coutances . . . 235
Couvertoirade, La . . . 556

Coypel, Antoine 101
Coysevox, Antoine 100
Creac'h 262
Credit cards 56
Cressent 102
Cresson 102
Croisica, Le 278
Croisic, Le 278
Crozon Peninsula 262
Cru bourgeois 69
Cubism 108
Cuisine 67
Culoz 448
Culture 84
Curie, Marie 131
Currency 56
Currency exchange 56
Customs Regulations 46
Cutlery shopping 36
Cuvier 128
Cycling 28

D

Dagobert I 71
Daguerre 128
d'Alambert 126
Daudet's Mill 619
Daumesnil 128
Daumier 106, 129
Dauphiné, The 74
David 127
David, JL 104
Dax 528
D-day landings 230
Deauville 227
Degas 107, 130
Delacroix 106, 128
Delamair 101
Delanois, Louis 104
Denis 107
Derain, A 108
Descartes 76
Desmalter 106
Desportes 101
Desserts 67
De Stijl 108
Détroits, Les 562
Dezeuze, Daniel 109
Diderot 126
Dien Bien Phu 82
Dieppe 223
Dietrich, Frédéric de 330
Dijon 368
Chartreuse de Champmol 372
Eat 375
Église Notre-Dame 371
Église Saint-Philibert 372
Église St-Michel 372
History 368
Hôtel de Vogüé 372
Hôtel Fyot-de-Mimeure 372
Jardin des Sciences 372
Municipal Library 372
Musée Amora 373
Musée Archéologique 372
Musée de la Vie bourguignonne 373
Musée des Beaux-Arts 370
Musée Magnin 372
Muséum de la ville de Dijon 372
Palace of the Dukes and States of Burgundy ... 369
Palais de Justice 372
Palais des Ducs 370
Place de la Libération 371
Place des Ducs-de-Bourgogne 372
Place François-Rude 371
Quartier Notre-Dame 371
Rue des Forges 371
Rue Vauban 372
Rue Verrerie 372
Square Darcy 372
Stay 375
St-Bénigne's Cathedral 372
Walking tour 370
Dinan 254
Dinan Castle 262
Dinard 256
Directory, The 78, 128
Disneyland Resort Paris 166
Dives 233
Documents (driving) 49
Documents (international travel) 46
Dole 395
Dolmen de St-Fort-sur-le-Né 534
Dombes, La 446
Domme 498, 501
Dorat, Le 492
Dordogne Berry Limousin 14, 482
Dordogne in the Périgord 501
Dreux 218
Dreyfus Affair 81
Driving in France 48
Driving licence 49
Driving to France 45
Dubois 106
Dubois, René 104
Dubuffet 109
Duchamp 109

Du Guesclin........74, 246
Duke Henri of Guise........75
Duke of Orléans........77
Duke of Sully........76
Dumas........129
Dumas, Alexandre........129
Dune du Pilat........522
Dunkerque........198
Duplessis-Mornay........293
Dupuytren........128

E

Early Middle Ages - art and architecture........85
Eclecticism........106
Ecomusée d'Alsace........348
Economy........66
Écrins, Les........420
Edict of Nantes........75
Edict of Nantes, revocation........77
Edward III of England........74
Edward the Confessor........233
Eguisheim........346
EHIC cards........47
Eiffel, Gustave........130, 146
Eiffel Tower........81
Eleanor of Aquitaine........73, 233
Electricity........54
Embassies........55
Embrun........415
Emergencies........55
Emperor of the French........79
Empire........126
Empire, The........128
Enclos Paroissial de Guimiliau........260
Enclos Paroissial de St-Thégonnec........260
Enlightenment........78
Enlightenment, The........126
Ensemble Mégalithique de Locmariaquer........270
Entente Cordiale........81
Entrées........67
En-Vau........607
Espace Rambouillet........207
Espelette........527
Esterel Gap........658
Étang de la Porte Baudet........207
Étangs de Hollande........207
Étangs de St-Bonnet........481
Étienne Marcel........125
Étretat........222
Étroit des Cavaliers........424
Euro........56, 83
European Community........83
Eurostar........45
Eurotunnel........45
Éventail........395
Events........38
Évian-les-Bains........405
Évreux........217
Eyrignac gardens........501
Eyzies-de-Tayac, Les........498
Èze........643

F

Faience shopping........36
Falaise........228
Falaise d'Amont........222
Falaise d'Aval........222
Falaise des Cavaliers........423
Falconet, EM........103
Family-friendly holidays........33
Family, the........66
Faucigny........411
Fauvism........108
February Revolution........79
Fécamp........222
Ferries to France........44
Ferry, Jules........81
Festival of the Supreme Being........127
Festivals........38
Fêtes des Gayants........193
Field of the Cloth of Gold........74
Fifth Republic........82, 83
Figeac........508
Filitosa........669
Films........111
Finistère........263
First Empire........78
Fishing........28
Fixin........374
Flamboyant Gothic art and architecture........89
Flégère, La........410
Flights to France........44
Flights to Paris........123
Foix........582
Foliot........102
Fontaine........105, 128
Fontainebleau........170
Fontaine de Vaucluse........626
Fontevraud l'Abbaye........295
Fontvieille........619
Food glossary........68
Forain........130
Forêt de Bavella........667
Forêt de Rambouillet........206
Forêt de Tronçais........480

Fôret de Turini ... 416
Fort de Latte ... 256
Fort de Salses ... 573
Fort La Latte ... 256
Fort National, St-Malo ... 254
Fort Tournoux ... 415
Fosse, Charles de la ... 101
Foucault, Léon ... 129
Fougères ... 249
Four Ordinances of St-Cloud ... 79
Fourth Republic ... 82
Fragonard ... 101
France Today ... 64
François I ... 74
François II ... 74
Franco-Prussian War ... 80
Free French ... 82
Frémiet ... 106
French Alps ... 396
French Art and Culture ... 84
French cuisine ... 67
French East India Company ... 77
French History ... 70
French Revolution ... 126
French Revolution, The ... 78
French Riviera ... 16, 634
French Rocaille art and architecture .. 101
French Wine ... 69
Fronde ... 126
Futaie Colbert ... 481
Futuroscope ... 544

G

Gabriel ... 126
Gaffori, Jean-Pierre ... 671
Galere, La ... 658
Gallé ... 107
Gallo-Roman art and architecture ... 85
Galois, Evariste ... 129
Garnier ... 106
Garouste, Gérard ... 109
Gasoline ... 50
Gassin ... 661
Gauguin ... 107
General de Gaulle ... 82
Gensac-la-Pallue ... 534
Genté ... 534
Geography ... 112
Geology ... 113
Geometric abstract art ... 109
Gerbier de Jonc ... 462
Géricault ... 128
Germigny-des-Prés ... 311
Gevrey-Chambertin ... 374
Girardon, François ... 100
Girault ... 131
Girodet-Trioson, AL ... 105
Gîtes ... 52
Glacier de Rhême-Golette ... 418
Gleizes, A ... 109
Gobelins ... 100
Gold Beach ... 231
Golf ... 28
Golfe de Porto ... 667
Golfe du Morbihan ... 268, 270
Gordes ... 626
Gorges de Daluis ... 415
Gorges de la Bourne ... 421
Gorges de l'Ardèche ... 627
Gorges du Cians ... 415
Gorges du Piaon ... 416
Gorges du Pont du Diable ... 411
Gorges du Tarn ... 15, 562
Gothic art and architecture ... 89
Goudes ... 606
Gouffre de Padirac ... 503
Gour de Tazenat ... 478
Government ... 66
Grand Aquarium, St-Malo ... 254
Grand Ballon ... 349
Grand Canyon du Verdon ... 423
Grand Colombier ... 448
Grand cru ... 69
Grande Champagne Charentaise ... 534
Grand Saut ... 395
Grands Goulets ... 421
Grand Taureau ... 393
Grasse ... 659
Grave, La ... 414
Great Outdoors, The ... 28
Great Schism, The ... 74
Greeks in France ... 71
Grenoble ... 419
Gros ... 128
Gros, AJ ... 105
Grotte de Clamouse ... 556
Grotte de Lascaux ... 499
Grotte de l'Aven Armand ... 563
Grotte des Demoiselles ... 556
Grotte du Mas-d'Azil ... 582
Grotte du Pech-Merle ... 508
Grotte du Sdragonato ... 669
Grottes de Bétharram ... 589
Guebwiller ... 346
Guérande ... 278
Guérande Peninsula ... 278
Guillaume ... 106
Guillaumes ... 415

Guillestre . . . 414
Guimard . . . 107
Guimiliau . . . 260
Guise . . . 75

H

Haras de Jardy . . . 164
Hardouin-Mansart, Jules. . . . 100
Harold Godwinson . . . 233
Haussmann . . . 106, 129
Hautecombe . . . 402
Haut Médoc. . . . 520
Havas, Charles. . . . 129
Havre, Le. . . . 220
Health . . . 47
Hennebont . . . 267
Hennessy . . . 533
Henri II. . . . 74
Henri III . . . 75, 125
Henri IV . . . 75, 76, 125, 293
Henri of Navarre. . . . 75
Henry VIII of England . . . 74
Herbin . . . 109
Highway code. . . . 49
History. . . . 70
Hittorff . . . 106
Hohneck. . . . 349
Hollande, François. . . . 83
Honfleur . . . 221
Hostels . . . 53
Hôtel de la Ronade . . . 475
Hotels . . . 52
Houches, Les. . . . 410
Houdon, JA . . . 103
Hugo, Victor . . . 129
Huguenots. . . . 75
Humbert II . . . 74
Hundred Days. . . . 79
Hundred Years' War . . . 74
Hunspach. . . . 337
Hyères . . . 664

I

Île aux Moines. . . . 270
Île Beaulieu . . . 277
Île d'Aix . . . 27
Île d'Arz. . . . 270
Île de Batz. . . . 26, 278
Île de Bendor. . . . 27
Île de Bréhat . . . 26, 258
Île de Groix. . . . 26, 267
Île de Keller . . . 262
Île de Molène . . . 26
Île de Noirmoutier. . . . 27
Île de Porquerolles . . . 664
Île-de Port-Cros . . . 664
Île de Ré . . . 27, 538
Île de Riou . . . 607
Île de Sein. . . . 26, 266
Île d'Hoedic. . . . 26
Île d'Houat. . . . 26
Île d'Oléron . . . 27
Île d'Ouessant. . . . 26, 262
Île du Levant . . . 664
Île d'Yeu . . . 27
Îles Chausey. . . . 26, 256
Îles de Glénan . . . 26
Îles de Lérins . . . 27, 658
Îles des Calanques. . . . 27
Îles d'Hyères . . . 27, 664
Îles d'Or. . . . 664
Îles du Frioul . . . 606
Îles du Golfe de Morbihan . . . 26, 270
Îles du Levant . . . 27
Îles du Ponant. . . . 26
Îles Lavezzia . . . 27
Îles Sanguinaires . . . 27
Illumination. . . . 93
Îlot de Cadoran. . . . 262
Impressionists . . . 107
Ingres . . . 106
Inspiration . . . 22
Insurance (car) . . . 49
Internet. . . . 55
Inter-war years . . . 81
Introducing France . . . 60
Islands of France . . . 26
Issoire . . . 471

J

Jardins de Kerdalo. . . . 259
Jardins de la Fontaine, Nîmes . . . 560
Jardins de Marquessac. . . . 501
Jardins de Marqueyssac. . . . 501
Jaurès, Jean . . . 131
Joan of Arc. . . . 74, 125
John the Fearless of Burgundy . . . 74
Joubert . . . 102
Julien, P. . . . 103
July Monarchy, The . . . 79
July Revolution. . . . 79
Juno Beach . . . 231
Jussieu. . . . 126

K

Kallisté. . . . 665
Kaysersberg. . . . 341
Kerlescan . . . 270

Kermario............................ 270
Kernascléden 267
Kids 33
King John the Good 74
Klein, Yves 109

L

Lac de Chaillexon.................... 392
Lac de Gaube 592
Lac de la Plagne..................... 418
Lac de la Sassière.................... 418
Lac de St-Point 393
Lac d'Issarlès........................ 462
Lac du Bouchet...................... 460
Lac du Bourget...................... 402
Lac du Grattaleu 418
lacier de Bionnassay................ 410
Lac Léman 411
Laënnec 128
Lafayette 78
Lagatjar............................. 262
Lake Geneva 411
Lalande............................. 77
Lamartine........................... 129
Lampaul 262
Lanceolate Gothic art and architecture 91
Landscapes 113
Languedoc Roussillon Tarn Gorges . 15, 546
Languedoc-Roussillon wine tours 32
Lannion............................. 259
Laon................................ 182
Lardin 126
Largillière........................... 101
Larmor-Plage 267
Laurens, Henri 109
Laval 240
Lavaudieu 460
Ledoux, Claude-Nicolas.............. 103
Lefuel, H 106
Léger............................... 131
Léger, F 109
Légué 258
Lemercier........................... 126
Lens 22, 184
Lens and the Bassin Minier
- Musée Louvre-Lens 184

Léon plateau........................ 262
Lessay 236
Lights (vehicles)..................... 50
Lignières............................ 534
Lille 190
- Citadelle, La.......................... 191
- Douai............................... 193
- Eat 194
- Entertainment 195
- Euralille............................... 192
- Hospice Comtesse..................... 193
- Musée d'Art Moderne 192
- Musée des Beaux-Arts................. 191
- Old Lille.............................. 190
- Place Louise-de-Bettignies 191
- Porte de Paris 191
- Quartier St-Sauveur 191
- Rue de la Monnaie 191
- Shopping 195
- Stay 194
- Vieille Bourse 190

Limoges 491
Limoges Enamel 491
Limousin.........................14, 482
Lisieux.............................. 221
Littré, Émile......................... 130
Loches.............................. 301
Locmariaquer 270
Locronan 264
Loire Valley wine tours............... 32
Lons-le-Saunier 395
Lorient..........................77, 267
Lorraine 77, 312
Louis IX 74
Louis Philippe I...................... 79
Louis VII 73
Louis XIII........................76, 125
Louis XIV.................... 76, 126, 161
Louis XV 77, 126
Louis XVI........................78, 126
Louis XVIII 79, 128
Lourdes............................ 588
Louvre, The 135
Luberon, Le 626
Lyon 23, 432
- Amphithéâtre des Trois Gaules.......... 443
- Ancienne Chapelle de la Vierge 438
- Ancienne Église St-Pierre 440
- Aquarium............................. 446
- Basilique Notre-Dame.................. 438
- Basilique St-Martin-d'Ainay............. 442
- Carnot 442
- Centre d'Histoire de la Résistance et de la Déportation 446
- Cité Internationale 443
- Condition Publique des Soies........... 443
- Cordeliers, Les 442
- Cour des Voraces...................... 443
- Crédit Lyonnais Tower................. 446
- Croix-Rousse, La 442
- Eat 449
- Église St-Bonaventure.................. 442

Festival of Lights.......................436
Fourvière Hill..........................438
Gerland District........................446
Grande-Côte............................443
Halle Tony-Garnier......................446
History................................432
Hôtel-Dieu..............................442
Jardin Archéologique..................438
Jardin Botanique.......................444
Jardin des Plantes......................443
Jardin du Rosaire.......................438
Jardin Zoologique.......................445
Left Bank..............................443
Maison des Canuts......................443
Manécanterie..........................437
Montée des Chazeaux...................438
Montée du Gourguillon..................438
Montée Nicolas-de-Lange...............439
Montées, The..........................438
Musée Africain.........................446
Musée d'Art Contemporain.............443
Musée de Fourvière....................438
Musée de Gallo-Romains de
Lyon-Fourvière......................439
Musée de l'Imprimerie..................440
Musée des Beaux-Arts..................440
Musée des Moulages...................446
Musée des Tissus & Musée des Arts
Décoratifs...........................442
Musée Gadagne.........................438
Musée Historique de Lyon..............438
Musée International de la Marionnette..438
Musée Lumière.........................446
Opéra de Lyon.........................440
Palais St-Pierre........................440
Parc Archéologique de Fourvière.......440
Parc de la Tête d'Or....................444
Parc des Hauteurs......................439
Part-Dieu district.......................446
Place Bellecour.........................442
Place Chardonnet.......................443
Place de la Trinité.....................438
Place des Jacobins.....................442
Place des Tapis........................443
Place des Terraux......................440
Place des Terreaux.....................440
Place du Change.......................438
Place du Gouvernement................438
Place Louis-Pradel.....................442
Place Neuve-St-Jean....................438
Place Rouville..........................443
Place Sathonay.........................443
Place St-Jean...........................437
Plateau, Le............................443
Practical Information...................433
Presqu'île, La..........................440
Primatiale St-Jean......................437
Quai de la Pêcherie.....................440
Quai St-Vincent........................440
Quartier de Saint-Nizier: Église St-Nizie..440
Quartier des Canuts....................443
Quartier des Célestins..................442
Quartier St-Jean........................437
Quaysides.............................445
Rue de la République...................440
Rue des Tables-Claudiennes............443
Rue des Trois-Maries...................438
Rue du Bœuf..........................438
Rue Grenette..........................442
Rue Juiverie...........................438
Rue Lainerie..........................438
Rue Mercière...........................442
Rues de Bouchons.....................440
Rue St-Georges........................438
Rue St-Jean...........................438
Saint-Nizier............................440
Serres.................................444
Shopping..............................433
Stay...................................448
St-Georges District.....................438
Lyrical abstract......................109

M

Maginot Line.......................... 81
Magritte............................109
Mail................................55
Maillol.............................108
Maison Carrée.......................558
Majorelle...........................107
Manet.........................107, 129
Mannerist - art and architecture....... 96
Mansart.............................126
Mans, Le............................289
Marais Poitevin......................538
Marguerite d'Angoulême.............530
Marmoutier..........................337
Marquet, A..........................108
Marsannay-la-Côte..................374
Marsat.............................477
Marseillaise, La......................604
Marseille.................... 23, 598
Ancienne Cathédrale de la Major........599
Basilique de Notre-Dame de la Garde...604
Basilique Saint-Victor...................604
Belvédère St-Laurent...................599
Canebière.............................604
Carré Thiars...........................601
Cathédrale de la Major.................599

Centre de la Vieille Charité.............. 599
Château et Parc Borély 605
Corniche, La 605
Corniche Président-J.-F.-Kennedy 605
Cours Julien............................ 605
Fort Saint-Jean-MuCEM 599
History 598
Hôtel de Cabre......................... 599
Hôtel de Ville 599
Jardin Valmer 605
Longchamp District 605
Musée Cantini.......................... 605
Musée de la Faïence.................... 605
Musée des Beaux-Arts.................. 605
Musée des Docks Romains............... 599
Musée d'Histoire de Marseille........... 604
Musée d'Histoire Naturelle 605
Musée du Santon Marcel-Carbonel 604
Musée Grobet-Labadié................. 605
Palais de la Bourse-Musée de la Marine et de l'Économie de Marseille 604
Palais Longchamp...................... 605
Panier, Le 599
Parc du Pharo 605
Place de Lenche........................ 600
Place du marché des Capucins 605
Promenade de la Plage 605
Quai de Rive-Neuve 600
Quartier des Arcenaulx 601
Rive Neuve............................. 600
Rue des Halles-Charles-Delacroix 605
Stay 608
Vallon des Auffes....................... 605
Walking tours.......................... 599
Marshal Ney........................... 79
Marshal Pétain 82, 130
Martel, Charles 72
Martell............................... 534
Massif de l'Aigoual 554
Massif de l'Authion, Le................ 416
Massif de la Vanoise 418
Massif de l'Esterel 658
Massif de Néouvielle 593
Massif des Aravis 412
Massif des Calanques................ 606
Massif des Maures................... 661
Massif Du Ézenc..................... 460
Massif du Vercors.................... 421
Masson 109
Mathieu 109
Matisse 108
Maurienne........................... 413
Maximilien de Béthune 76
Mazarin.............................. 76
Media 55
Medieval art and architecture.......... 85
Megalithic culture.................... 71
Ménec............................... 270
Menton.............................. 652
Mer de Glace, Chamonix 409
Mérimée............................. 130
Merovingian - art and architecture 85
Merovingians, The.................... 71
Merovius............................. 72
Mescla............................... 424
Messager, annette.................... 109
Métezeau 125
Métro, The 123
Metz............................316
Arsenal 318
Cathédrale St-Étienne 318
Centre Pompidou-Metz 319
Chapelle des Templiers................. 318
Eat 320
Église St-Eucaire 318
Église St-Martin-aux-Champs........... 318
Église St-Maximin 318
Église St-Pierre-aux-Nonnains 318
History 316
Jardin des Régates 318
Moyen Pont........................... 318
Musées de la Cour d'Or 319
Notre-Dame-de-l'Assomption 318
Old Town 317
Palais de Justice....................... 318
Place d'Armes......................... 317
Place de la République 318
Place du Général-de-Gaulle............ 318
Place St-Louis......................... 318
Porte des Allemands 318
Stay 319
Walking Tour.......................... 317
Metzinger, J.......................... 109
Meuse Ardennaise, La 357
Migeon 102
Military architecture.................. 94
Millau............................... 563
Millau Viaduct....................... 563
Millet 106
Miramar 658
Mitterrand, François.................. 83
Modane 413
Modigliani 131
Moissac............................. 581
Monaco........................ 646
Cathédrale............................ 646
Chapelle de la Miséricorde............. 646
Collection des Voitures Anciennes 650

Condamine, La . . . 647
Église Ste-Dévote . . . 647
Jardin Animalier . . . 650
Jardin Exotique . . . 650
Jardin Japonais . . . 650
Jardins St-Martin . . . 646
Monte-Carlo . . . 647
Musée d'Anthropologie Préhistorique . . . 650
Musée des Timbres et des Monnaies . . . 650
Musée Napoléonien et des Archives du Palais . . . 650
Musée Océanographique . . . 646
Nouveau Musée National de Monaco . . . 650
Palais Princier . . . 646
Place du Palais . . . 646
Port Hercule . . . 647
Practical Information . . . 647
Stay . . . 650
Walking tour . . . 646
Monet . . . 107, 130
Money . . . 56
Montagne de Beaune . . . 379
Montagne de Locronan . . . 265
Montauban . . . 581
Montbard . . . 373
Mont de la Saoupe . . . 607
Monte-Carlo . . . 647
Mont Faron . . . 663
Montgolfier brothers . . . 77
Monthermé . . . 357
Mont-Louis . . . 573
Mont Mézenc . . . 462
Montmorency . . . 75
Montpellier . . . 24, 550
Ancien Courrier district . . . 551
Antigone District . . . 554
Cathédrale St-Pierre . . . 552
Eat . . . 557
Faculté District . . . 551
History . . . 550
Hôtel Baudon de Mauny . . . 551
Hôtel de Cabrières-Sabatier . . . 551
Hôtel de Solas . . . 551
Hôtel des Trésoriers de France . . . 550
Hôtel des Trésoriers de la Bourse . . . 551
Hôtel de Varennes . . . 550
Hôtel d'Uston . . . 551
Hôtel St-Côme . . . 551
Jardin des Plantes . . . 553
Musée du Vieux Montpellier . . . 550
Musée Fabre . . . 551
Musée Fougau . . . 551
Place de la Canourgue . . . 551
Place de la Comédie . . . 550
Place St-Ravy . . . 551
Promenade du Peyrou . . . 551
Rue de l'Aiguillerie . . . 551
Rue du Cannau . . . 551
Stay . . . 557
Mont Saint Odile . . . 345
Monts Dore, Les . . . 472
Montss du Cantal . . . 474
Mont-St-Michel . . . 22, 238
Mont Ventoux . . . 632
Mont Vinaigre . . . 658
Morgat . . . 262
Morgiou . . . 607
Moriond-Courchevel 1650 . . . 417
Morlaix . . . 264
Morocco . . . 82
Morzine . . . 411
Motor boating . . . 28
Moulin de Daudet . . . 619
Moulinet . . . 416
Moulins . . . 476, 480
Mourre de Chanier . . . 425
Moustiers-Ste-Marie . . . 423
Mozac . . . 477
Mulhouse . . . 347
Muscadet . . . 277
Musée Bargoin . . . 470
Musée de l'Automobile, Mulhouse . . . 347
Musée de Préhistoire de Tautavel . . . 573
Musée Ingres . . . 581
Musée Louvre-Lens . . . 184
Musée Marc-Chagall . . . 642
Musée Matisse . . . 642
Musée Picasso . . . 658
Musée Unterlinden . . . 340
Musset, Alfred de . . . 129

N

Nabis . . . 107
Nain, Le . . . 99
Nancy . . . 323
Arc de Triomphe . . . 325
Basilique St-Epvre . . . 326
Cathédrale . . . 326
Eat . . . 328
Église des Cordeliers . . . 327
Église Notre-Dame-de-Bon-Secours . . . 327
Église St-Sébastien . . . 326
History . . . 323
Hôtel de ville . . . 324
Jardin botanique du Montet . . . 327
Maison des Adam . . . 326
Musée-aquarium de Nancy . . . 326
Musée de l'École de Nancy . . . 326

Musée des Beaux-Arts 326
Musée Lorrain 326
New Town 326
Old Town 326
Palais ducal 326
Palais du Gouverneur 326
Pépinière, La 326
Place d'Alliance 326
Place de la Carrière 325
Place Stanislas 323
Porte de la Craffe 326
Practical information 323
Stay 327
Nantes 24, 273
Ancienne Île Feydeau 277
Cathédrale St-Pierre-et-St-Paul 276
Château des Ducs de Bretagne 276
Eat 279
Église Notre-Dame-de-Bon-Port 277
History 273
Île Beaulieu 277
Lieu Unique, Le 276
Lycée Clemenceau 276
Musée Archéologique 277
Musée de l'Imprimerie 277
Musée des Beaux Arts 276
Musée Dobrée 277
Muséum d'Histoire Naturelle 277
Old Nantes 277
Place Maréchal-Foch 276
Plateau Ste-Croix 276
Porte St-Pierre 276
Psalette, La 276
Quai de la Fosse 277
Quartier Graslin 277
Stay 279
Walking Tour 276
Napoléon 78
Napoléon Bonaparte 128
Napoléonic Wars 78
Napoléon III 80, 129
Narbonne 569
National Assembly 78, 126
National calls 57
Natoire 101
Nattier 101
Nature 112
Nausicaä 201
Nazis 82
Neoclassical art and architecture 103
Neolithic art and architecture 85
Nevers 380
New Realism 109
Nez de Jobourg 236
Nice 24, 638
Acropolis-Palais des Congrès 643
Cathédrale Orthodoxe Russe St-Nicolas . 642
Cathédrale Ste-Réparate 640
Chapelle de la Miséricorde 639
Chapelle de l'Annonciation 639
Château Hill 642
Cimiez 642
Cours Saley 639
Eat 645
Église St-Jacques or Gésu 640
Église St-Martin-St-Augustin 641
History 638
Monastère de Cimiez 642
Musée d'Art Moderne et d'Art Contemporain 642
Musée d'Art Naïf Jakovsky 642
Musée de la Musique 640
Musée des Arts Asiatiques 642
Musée des Beaux-Arts Jules-Chéret 642
Musée Marc-Chagall 642
Musée Masséna 643
Musée Matisse 642
Old Nice 639
Palais Lascaris 640
Place Garibaldi 641
Place Masséna 638
Place St-François 641
Port 638
Practical information 639
Promenade des Anglais 638
Promenade du Paillon 638
Seafront 638
Stay 644
Tour Bellanda 642
Walking tour 638
Nid d'Aigle 410
Nîmes 558
Nominoé 73, 268
Norman Conquest, The 233
Normandy 208
Normandy Landing Beaches 230
Normandy landings 82
Northern France 158
Notre-Dame Cathédral 132
Nôtre, Le 100, 126
Nouveau Réalisme 109
Nuits-St-Georges 374

O

Obernai 337, 345
Océanopolis 261
Odo 125
L'Oisans 420

Olbia ... 664
Omaha Beach ... 231
Opening hours ... 54
Operation Overlord ... 82, 230
Oradour-sur-Glane ... 492
Orange ... 630
Oratoire du Chazelet ... 413
Orcival ... 471
Ordinance of Villers-Cotterêts ... 75
Orléans ... 309
Orne ... 228
Otard ... 534

P

Pagès ... 109
Paimpol ... 258
Painting ... 84
Palaeolithic art and architecture ... 85
Palais des Papes ... 624
Palais des Rois de Majorque ... 573
Palais, Le (Belle-Île) ... 272
Panhard ... 130
Paramé ... 256
Parc Astérix ... 175
Parc du Marquenterre ... 187
Parc Européen du Volcanisme Vulcania ... 470
Parc floral de la Source ... 310
Parc Marin International des Bouches de Bonifacio ... 669
Parc National des Pyrénées ... 590
Parc Naturel Régional de Camargue .. 620
Parc Pyrénéen de l'Art Préhistorique . 566
Paris ... 24, 116
- Addresses ... 154
- Arc de Triomphe ... 150
- Arc de Triomphe du Carrousel ... 134
- Arrondissements 1-4 ... 132
- Arrondissements 5-7 ... 142
- Arrondissements 8-10 & 17 ... 148
- Arrondissements 11-15 ... 151
- Arrondissements 18-20 ... 152
- Avenue des Champs-Élysées ... 149
- Bastille ... 151
- Bercy ... 151
- Canal Saint-Martin ... 149
- Catacombes, Les ... 151
- Centre Georges-Pompidou ... 138
- Cité des Sciences et de l'Industrie ... 152
- Conciergerie ... 133
- Eat ... 155
- École Militaire ... 147
- Église de Saint-Sulpice ... 144
- Église de St-Germain-des-Prés ... 144
- Église du Dôme ... 146
- Église Notre-Dame-du-Val-de-Grâce ... 151
- Église St-Eustache ... 140
- Église St-Séverin ... 142
- Eiffel Tower ... 147
- Entertainment ... 156
- Exhibitions ... 157
- Fairs ... 157
- Faubourg Saint-Germain ... 144
- Galerie Carrousel du Louvre ... 134
- Géode, La ... 152
- Getting Around ... 123
- Getting There ... 123
- Grand Palais ... 149
- Grands Boulevards ... 148
- History ... 125
- Hôtel de Ville ... 134
- Invalides, Les ... 145
- Jardin des Tuileries ... 148
- Jardin du Carrousel ... 148
- Luxembourg Palace ... 142
- Madeleine ... 148
- Marais, Le ... 141
- Marché aux Puces de Saint-Ouen ... 152
- Métro ... 123
- Montmartre ... 152
- Montparnasse ... 151
- Musée de l'Orangerie ... 148
- Musée des Arts et Métiers ... 140
- Musée d l'Armée ... 146
- Musée d'Orsay ... 145
- Musée du louvre ... 135
- Musée du Quai Branly ... 147
- Musée national d'Art moderne ... 139
- Musée National du Moyen Âge ... 144
- Notre-Dame Cathédral ... 132
- Opéra National de Paris ... 150
- Palais Bourbon ... 145
- Palais de Chaillot ... 147
- Palais de Justice ... 133
- Palais de la Découverte ... 149
- Palais de l'Élysée ... 150
- Palais du Louvre ... 135
- Palais Garnier ... 150
- Palais-Royal ... 150
- Panthéon ... 143
- Paris docks ... 142
- Parks ... 153
- Père-Lachaise Cemetery ... 153
- Place de la Concorde ... 148
- Planning your trip ... 122
- Quai Austerlitz ... 142
- Quartier de St-Germain-des-Prés ... 144
- Quartier Latin ... 142

Sainte-Chapelle........................ 133
Seine................................. 123
Shopping............................. 157
Sport................................. 157
St-Germain-des-Prés.................. 144
Tour Montparnasse.................... 151
Vélib.................................. 123
Vélodrome d'Hiver..................... 131
Villette, La........................... 152
Voie Triomphale, La................... 148
Paris Commune....................... 81
Paris docks........................... 22
Parking regulations................... 50
Pas-de-Peyrol....................... 475
Passports........................... 46
Pasteur............................. 130
Pau................................ 529
Pays d'Auge......................... 221
Peace of Westphalia.................. 77
Pedestrian priority................... 50
Peisey-Nancroix..................... 418
Penchâteau.......................... 278
Peninsular War....................... 79
Penn-ar-Ru-Meur..................... 262
People.............................. 65
Pepin I.............................. 73
Percier......................105, 128
Périgord........................... 501
Périgueux.......................... 494
Pérouges........................... 446
Perpignan.......................... 572
Perret brothers..................... 108
Perros-Guirec....................... 259
Peyron, JFP........................ 104
Philip IV............................74
Philippe Auguste............ 73, 125, 293
Philippe d'Orléans.................. 126
Philippe, Louis..................... 129
Philippe VI of Valois.................74
Picabia............................ 109
Picasso............................ 108
Pic de Colmiane.................... 416
Pic de Pibeste...................... 589
Pic du Jer.......................... 590
Pic du Midi de Bigorre............... 590
Pierre, BM......................... 104
Pigalle, JB......................... 104
Pinel............................... 128
Pirot............................... 481
Pissarro.....................107, 130
Places to Stay and Eat................ 52
Plage de Pampelonne................ 661
Plages du débarquemet.............. 230
Plan de l'Aiguille................... 410
Planète Sauvage.................... 278
Planning Your Trip.................... 20
Plantagenets..........................74
Plougastel-Daoulas.................. 261
Ploumanach........................ 259
Pointe de Chémoulin................ 278
Pointe de Dinan..................... 262
Pointe de Penchâteau............... 278
Pointe de Penhir.................... 262
Pointe des Espagnols................ 262
Pointe des Poulains.................. 272
Pointe du Chardonnet............... 418
Pointe du Grouin.................... 256
Pointe du Raz.................. 264, 266
Pointe du Van...................... 266
Pointe St-Mathieu.................. 261
Point Sublime...................424, 563
Poitiers............................ 542
Poitou-Charentes.....................15
Pompidou, Georges.................. 83
Pomponiana........................ 664
Pontarlier.......................... 393
Pont-Aven......................... 266
Pont-Aven School................... 107
Pont-d'Arc......................... 627
Pont de Normandie.................. 221
Pont de Tusset...................... 425
Pont du Gard, Le.................... 626
Pont-en-Royans..................... 421
Pony trekking....................... 29
Pope Pius VII........................ 79
Popular Front....................... 82
Population.......................... 65
Porcelain shopping.................. 36
Pornichet.......................... 278
Port-Coton......................... 272
Port-Donnant....................... 272
Port-Goulphar...................... 272
Port-la-Galère...................... 658
Port-Louis.......................... 267
Port-Navalo........................ 270
Port-Pin............................ 607
Post................................ 55
Pottery shopping.................... 37
Pouliguen, Le....................... 278
Pourville-sur-Mer................... 223
Poussin............................. 99
Practical A-Z........................ 54
Practical Info........................ 43
Pralognan.......................... 418
Praz 1300, Le....................... 417
Pre-Classicism - art and architecture... 98
Prehistoric Art....................... 85
Presqu'île de Crozon................ 262

Presqu'île de Guérande.............. 278
Presqu'île de Penmarch.............. 264
Presqu'île de Quiberon 26, 270
Presqu'ile du Cotentin, La............ 235
Prieuré de Serrabone................ 576
Principat d'Andorra.................. 574
Provence..........................16, 594
Provence wine tours.................. 32
Provins 168, 363
Public holidays....................... 56
Puget, Pierre......................... 100
Putanges 228
Puvis de Chavannes 130
Puy de Dôme, Le 471
Puy de Sancy, Le 472
Puy du Fou, Le 545
Puy-en-Velay
- Cathédrale Notre-Dame............... 458
- Old quarter 459
- Rocher Corneille 459
- St-Michel-d'Aiguilhe 459

Puy-en-Velay, Le 458
Puy Mary, Le 475
Pyrénées, The...................588, 592

Q

Queyras............................ 414
Quimper............................ 263

R

Ramatuelle 661
Rambouillet......................... 205
Ramplas 416
Raspail............................. 129
Ravel, Maurice 131
Refuge de Prariond.................. 418
Reims...................24, 82, 350
- Basilique St-Rémi 354
- Basses et Hautes Promenades 351
- Cathédrale Notre-Dame................ 351
- Cryptoportique gallo-romain........... 351
- Eat 355
- Église St-Jacques 351
- History 350
- Hôtel des Comtes de Champagne....... 351
- Hôtel de ville.......................... 351
- Hôtel Saint-Jean-Baptiste de la Salle 351
- Palais du Tau.......................... 354
- Place Drouet-d'Erlon 351
- Place Royale 351
- Porte du Chapitre 351
- Porte Mars............................ 351
- Rue de Mars........................... 351
- Stay 354

Religion.............................. 66
Rémy Martin 534
Renaissance - art and architecture..... 96
Renault 131
Rennes 246
- Cathédrale St-Pierre................... 247
- Champs Libres 248
- Église St-Germain 248
- Getting around 246
- History 246
- Hôtel de Ville 248
- Musée des Beaux-Arts.................. 249
- Old Town 247
- Palais du Parlement de Bretagne........ 248
- Palais St-Georges 248
- Place de l'Hôtel-de-Ville 248
- Place des Lices 248
- Place Ste-Anne......................... 248
- Portes Mordelaises..................... 248
- Rue du Champ-Jacquet................. 248
- Rue du Pont-aux-Foulons............... 248
- Rue St-Georges 248
- Rue St-Michel.......................... 248
- Walking Tour........................... 247

Renoir 107, 130
Republic, The 78
Réserve Africaine de Sigean.......... 570
Réserve naturelle de la Grande Sassière 418
Réserve Naturelle de Scandola....... 668
Réserve naturelle de Tuéda 418
Resistance, The...................... 82
Restany, Pierre 109
Restaurants.......................... 52
Restoration, The.................79, 128
Restout 101
Retable d'Issenheim................. 340
Retreat, The.......................... 79
Revocation of the Edict of Nantes 293
Revolution 126
Revolution of 1848 79
Revolution, The 78
Rhineland occupation 81
Rhône Valley....................14, 426
Rhône valley wine tours 32
Rhune, La 527
Richard II.............................74
Richelieu.........................76, 126
Riding 29
Rigaud.............................. 101
Rights of Man 78, 127
Riom 477
Riopelle............................. 109
Riquewihr........................... 344

River cruising ... 29
Robert Pothier ... 126
Robespierre ... 127
Rocaille ... 101
Rocamadour ... 503
Roc au Chien, Le ... 241
Roche aux Moines ... 289
Rochefort ... 541
Rochelle, La ... 535
Café de la Paix ... 538
Cathédrale Saint-Louis ... 537
Cloître des Dames Blanches ... 538
Cours des Dames ... 537
Coursive, La ... 537
Eat ... 540
Église St-Sauveur ... 538
Gabut District ... 535
Grande-Rue des Merciers ... 538
History ... 535
Hôtel de la Bourse ... 537
Hôtel de Ville ... 538
Maison Henri II ... 537
Musée du Flacon à Parfum ... 538
Old Town ... 537
Palais de Justice ... 537
Parc Charruyer ... 537
Porte de la Grosse-Horloge ... 537
Préfecture ... 537
Quai Duperré ... 537
Rue Chaudrier ... 537
Rue de l'Escale ... 537
Rue du Minage ... 538
Rue du Palais ... 537
Rue Sur-les-Murs ... 537
Stay ... 539
Tour de la Chaîne ... 537
Tour de la Lanterne ... 537
Tour St-Nicolas ... 535
Ville-en-Bois ... 538
Rocher de Bellevarde ... 418
Rochers d'Angennes ... 207
Rock climbing ... 29
Rococo ... 101
Rocroi ... 76, 357
Rodez ... 586
Rodin ... 107
Roland's Gap ... 593
Rollo ... 73
Romanesque art and architecture ... 86
Romans ... 71
Roquebrune-Cap Martin ... 652
Roque-Gageac, La ... 501
Roscoff ... 260
Rouault, Georges ... 131
Roubion ... 415
Rouen ... 212
Abbatiale Saint-Ouen ... 213
Aître St-Maclou ... 213
Archevêché ... 213
Cathédrale Notre-Dame ... 212
Église Saint-Godard ... 213
Église Ste-Jeanne-d'Arc ... 216
Église St-Maclou ... 213
Jardin des Plantes ... 216
Musée de la Céramique ... 213
Musée des Beaux-Arts ... 213
Musée Jeanne-d'Arc ... 216
Musée Le Secq des Tournelles ... 213
Musée national de l'Éducation ... 213
Nightlife ... 219
Old Rouen ... 213
Palais de Justice ... 213
Place de la Cathédrale ... 213
Place du Vieux-Marché ... 213
Rue Damiette ... 213
Rue du Gros-Horloge ... 216
Rue Eau-de-Robec ... 213
Rue Martainville ... 213
Rue Saint-Romain ... 213
Shopping ... 219
Showtime ... 219
Stay ... 218
Walking Tour ... 213
Rouffach ... 346
Roure ... 416
Roussillon ... 15, 546
Route des Crêtes ... 349, 423
Route des Grandes Alpes ... 411
Route des Vins ... 344
Route Impériale des Cimes ... 524
Route planning ... 51
Royal Academy of Painting and Sculpture ... 99
Royan ... 539
Royat ... 470

S

Sables-d'Olonne, Les ... 538
Sailing ... 29
Saintes ... 541
Saint-Véran ... 414
Saisies Pass ... 412
Salers ... 475
Salian Franks ... 72
Salisbury ... 74
Saloup ... 481
Sancerre ... 488
San Michele de Murato ... 671

Sans-culottes 127
Santos-Dumont 131
Saorge 652
Sare 527
Sarkozy, Nicolas 83
Sarlat-la-Canéda 496
Sarrazin, Jacques 99
Sartène 669
Saulire, La 417
Saumur 293
Saut de la Forge 395
Saut du Doubs 391
Sauternes 520
Sauzon 272
Saverne 337
Savoy 80
School holidays 56
Scuba-diving 30
Sculpture 84
Seasons 43
Second Empire 80, 129
Second Republic 80, 129
Section d'Or 109
Segonzac 534
Seine River 123
Sélestat 341
Sené 102
Senlis 177
Sens 385
Sentier de Découverte des Lézards ... 424
Sentier Martel 423
September Massacres 127
Séries de l'Ouest 481
Serres 444
Serres, Olivier de 76
Sérusier, Paul 107
Sète 554
Seulecq 130
Seurat 130
Seurat, G. 107
Shopping 34
Signac 107
Silk shopping 37
Sisteron 425
Site de Montfort 501
Skiing 30
Slodtz 101
Smoking 57
SNCF 47
Snowsports 30
Solignac 492
Sormiou 606
Sospel 416
Soufflot 126
Souillac 504
Soulages 109
Soups 67
Source de la Loue 393
Soutine 131
Souvigny 477
Spas 33
Speed limits 50
Sport 66
Stael, Nicolas de 109
Stained glass 93
St Bartholomew's Day Massacre 125
St-Bertrand-de-Comminges 582
St-Brieuc 258
Ste-Anne-la-Palud 265
Ste-Marguerite-sur-Mer 223
St-Émilion 520
Stendhal 129
Stes-Maries-de-la-Mer, Les 620
St-Étienne 456
St-Flour 475
St-Georges-sur-Loire 289
St-Germain-en-Laye 173
St-Guilhem-le-Désert 556
Stiff 262
St-Jean-de-Luz 526
St Ké 258
St-Lô 235
St Louis 74
St-Loup-de-Naud 363
St-Lunaire 256
St-Malo 251
St-Martin-d'Entraunes 415
St-Martin-Vésubie 416
St-Nazaire 278
St-Nectaire 472
St-Omer 199
St-Pierre-d'Almanarre 664
St-Pol-de-Léon 260
St-Quay-Portrieux 258
St-Raphaël 658
Strasbourg 24, 330
Barrage Vauban 334
Cathédrale Notre-Dame 331
Cour du Corbeau 334
Eat 338
Église St-Pierre-le-Jeune 335
Église St-Pierre-le-Vieux 334
Église St-Thomas 334
History 330
La Petite France 334
Musée Alsacien 336
Musée Archéologique 336
Musée d'Art Moderne et Contemporain . 336

Musée de l'Œuvre Notre-Dame 336
Musée des Arts Décoratifs 336
Musée des Beaux-Arts 336
Old Town 334
Palais de l'Europe 337
Palais de Rohan 336
Palais des Droits de l'Homme 337
Place Broglie 335
Place de la Cathédrale 334
Place du Château 334
Place du Marché-aux-Cochons-de-Lait .. 334
Place Gutenberg 334
Place Kléber 335
Pont du Corbeau 334
Ponts Couverts 334
Port Autonome 337
Practical information 335
Quai St-Nicolas 334
Rue du Bain-aux-Plantes 334
Rue du Dôme 335
Stay 338
Walking tours 334
Strasbourg Oaths 330
Stravinsky 131
Street life 65
St-Rémy-de-Provence 623
St-Sauveur-sur-Tinée 416
St-Savin 544
St-Thégonnec 260
St-Tropez 660
St-Tropez Peninsula 661
Sue, Eugène 129
Sueur, Eustache le 99
Sugiton 607
Suisse Normande, La 228
Sun King 76, 161
Support-Surface 109
Surrealism 109
Sword Beach 231

T

Talleyrand 79, 127
Talleyrand-Périgord,
Charles-Maurice de 308
Talus de Guègues 424
Tapisserie de la Reine Mathilde 232
Tarascon-sur-Ariège 566
Tarbes 589
Tarentaise 413
Tarn Gorges 15, 546, 562
Tautavel 573
Telephones 57
Temperature 42
Terroir 69
Terror, The 127
Tertre Aubé 258
TGV 48, 83
Thann 349
Théoule-sur-Mer 658
Thermidorian Convention 127
Third Republic 80
Thonon-les-Bains 411
Thury-Harcourt 228
Tignes 418
Tignes Dam 413
Time 57
Tinée, La 415
Tipping 57
Tolls 52
Topography 113
Toul 329
Toulon 663
Toulouse 24, 577
Basilique Notre-Dame-de-la-Daurade ... 580
Basilique St-Sernin 577
Bibliothèque d'étude et du patrimoine .. 579
Capitole 579
Cathédrale St-Étienne 580
Chapelle des Carmélites 579
Église des Jacobins 579
Église Notre-Dame-du-Taur 579
Église Notre-Dame-la-Dalbade 580
Galeries Lafayette 580
Hôtel Béringuier-Maynier 580
Hotel d'Assézat 580
Hôtel de Bernuy 579
Hôtel de Fumel 580
Hôtel du Grand Balcon 579
Jacobins, Les 579
Musée des Augustins 580
Musée du Vieux Toulouse 579
Musée Paul-Dupuy 580
Musée St-Raymond 579
Muséum d'Histoire Naturelle 580
Place du Capitole 579
Place St-Étienne 580
Pont Neuf 580
Rue Bouquière 580
Rue de la Bourse 580
Rue de la Dalbade 580
Rue des Changes 580
Rue Mage 580
Rue Malcousinat 580
Rue Ozenne 580
Rue Pharaon 580
Rue St-Rome 579
Walking tour 579
Toulouse-Blagnac 22

Toulouse-Lautrec 130
Toulouse school...................... 99
Touquet, Le......................... 202
Tour, Georges de la................... 99
Tourist Offices........................ 58
Tournier, Nicolas 99
Tour, Quentin de la 101
Tours.............................. 298
Trade unions......................... 81
Trafalgar............................ 79
Trains in France....................... 47
Trains to France 45
Trains to Paris 123
Transitional Gothic - art and
architecture 89
Trayas, Le 658
Treaty of Brétigny 74
Treaty of Frankfurt 81
Treaty of Le Cateau-Cambrésis 75
Treaty of Nijmegen 77
Treaty of Picquigny....................74
Treaty of St-Clair-sur-Epte............ 73
Treaty of Troyes 74
Treaty of Verdun 73
Treaty of Versailles 78, 81
Trébeurden 258
Trégastel........................... 258
Tréguier 259
Trinité-sur-Mer, La.................. 270
Trois Vallées........................ 417
Troyes 358
Basilique St-Urbain.................... 359
Cathédrale St-Pierre et St-Paul......... 359
Eat 362
Église Ste-Madeleine.................. 359
Église St-Pantaléon.................... 359
Maison de l'Outil et de la
Pensée ouvrière..................... 358
Musée d'Art Moderne 359
Musée de Vauluisant 359
Musée St-Loup........................ 359
Pharmacie Musée 359
Stay 359
Tunisia.............................. 82
Turckheim 346
TVA............................. 37, 59

U

UNESCO World Heritage Sites 31
Utah Beach 231
Uzès............................... 625

V

Vaison-la-Romaine 631
Vaïsse, CM 106
Val André, Le........................ 256
Val d'Isère........................... 413
Vallée d'Aspe........................ 529
Vallée de Gavarnie................... 592
Vallée de la Var...................... 415
Vallée de Lutour..................... 592
Vallée de Ponturin................... 418
Vallée des Chapieux 412
Vallée des Merveilles 644
Vallée d'Ossau 529
Vallée du Gouët...................... 258
Vallée du Marcadau 592
Vallée du Vénéon..................... 420
Vallées des Cauterets................ 592
Vallon de la Madone de Fenestre..... 416
Vallon du Boréon.................... 416
Valognes............................ 236
Valois, The 74
Valois, The House of 125
Van Gogh 107
Vannes 268
Varangeville-sur-Mer 223
Vassieux-en-Vercors................. 421
Vauban 77, 192, 425
Vau, Louis le......................... 100
VDQS............................... 69
Vehicle registration................... 49
Vélib' 123
Vendée, The......................... 78
Vendôme 307
Verberckt 101
Vercors Regional Natural Park........ 421
Verdun 81, 321
Stay 321
Versailles 161
Versailles Classicism -
art and architecture 100
Vesunna 495
Veules-les-Roses 223
Vézelay 387
Via Aurelia 658
Viaduc de Garabit 475
Viallet, Claude....................... 109
Vichy 82, 476
Vichy Springs 479
Vieil-Armand........................ 349
Vien, JM 104
Vienne.............................. 452

Vierge Island 262
Village des Bories 626
Villefranche-de-Rouergue 586
Villeneuve d'Entraunes 415
Villeneuve-lès-Avignon 625
Villers-le-Lac 392
Vimy Canadian Memorial 184
Vincennes Porcelain Factory 102
Vin de pays 69
Vin de table 69
Viollet-le-Duc 106
Vionèse, La 415
Virieu-le-Petit 448
Visas 46
Visigoths 72
Viticulture 69
Vitré 249
Vlaminck, M de 108
Vosne-Romanée 374
Vougeot 374
Vuillard 107

W

Walking 30
War of the Breton Succession ... 249, 259, 266
War of the Spanish Succession 77
Wars of Religion 75
Watteau 101
Weather 44
What's Hot 22
What to Buy 34
When to Go 43
Where to Shop 34
Whites and Blues 78
William, Duke of Normandy 73, 233
Wimereux 200
Wine 69
Wine tasting 69
Wine tours 32
Winterhalter 106
Winter sports 30
Wissant 200
World Fair 80
World War I 81
World War II 82
Wright, Wilbur 290

Y

Yvoire 406

Z

Zadkine 131
Zoo de la Palmyre 539

STAY

Aix-en-Provence 614
Albi 587
Amiens 188
Angoulême 532
Annecy 403
Arcachon 522
Arles 620
Arras 184
Auxerre 387
Avignon 628
Barneville-Carteret 237
Bayeux 234
Beaune 382
Belle-Île 272
Besançon 394
Biarritz 525
Blois 308
Bordeaux 520
Bourges 489
Caen 229
Cahors 509
Cannes 659
Carcassonne 567
Cherbourg-Octeville 237
Clermont-Ferrand 473
Cognac 534
Colmar 342
Compiègne 181
Courchevel 418
Dijon 375
Évian-les-Bains 407
Fontainebleau 172
Gorges du Tarn 563
Grenoble 421
Lille 194
Limoges 493
Lourdes 591
Lyon 448
Mans, Le 291
Marseille 608
Menton 653
Metz 319
Monaco 650
Montpellier 557
Monts du Cantal 475
Mont-St-Michel 239
Moulins 481
Nancy 327
Nantes 279
Narbonne 570
Nice 644
Nîmes 561
Orange 633
Paris 154
Périgueux 495
Perpignan 576
Poitiers 544
Puy du Fou, Le 545
Puy-en-Velay 462
Quimper 266
Reims 354
Rennes 250
Riquewihr 346
Rochelle, La 539
Rouen 218
Route des Grandes Alpes 416
Sarlat-la-Canéda 502
Saumur 297
St-Brieuc 259
St-Étienne 457
St-Lô 237
St-Malo 257
Strasbourg 338
St-Tropez 662
St-Vaast-la-Hougue 237
Toul 329
Toulouse 582
Troyes 359
Valognes 237
Vannes 271
Versailles 165
Vichy 478
Vienne 453

EAT

Aix-en-Provence 615
Albi 587
Amiens 189
Angoulême 532
Annecy 404
Arcachon 522
Arles 621
Arras 184
Auxerre 388
Avignon 628
Barneville-Carteret 237
Bayeux 234
Beaune 382
Belle-Île 272
Biarritz 525
Blois 308
Bordeaux 521
Bourges 490
Caen 229
Cahors 509
Cannes 659
Carcassonne 568
Cherbourg-Octeville 237
Clermont-Ferrand 473
Cognac 534
Colmar 343
Compiègne 181
Coutances 237
Dijon 375
Évian-les-Bains 407
Fontainebleau 172
Lille 194
Limoges 493
Lourdes 591
Lyon 449
Menton 653
Metz 320
Montpellier 557
Moulins 481
Nancy 328
Nantes 279
Narbonne 571
Nice 645
Nîmes 561
Orange 633
Paris 155
Périgueux 495
Perpignan 576
Poitiers 544
Puy du Fou, Le 545
Puy-en-Velay 463
Quimper 266
Reims 355
Rennes 250
Riquewihr 346
Rochelle, La 540
Sarlat-la-Canéda 502
Saumur 297
St-Étienne 457
St-Germain-en-Laye 174
St-Lô 237
St-Malo 257
Strasbourg 338
St-Tropez 662
St-Vaast-la-Hougue 237
Toul 329
Toulouse 583
Tours 303
Troyes 362
Valognes 237
Vannes 271
Verdun 322
Versailles 165
Vichy 478
Vienne 453

Thematic Maps

Principal Sights Map... Inside front cover
Paris Métro and
Arrondissements ... Inside back cover
The Growth of France 72

Maps and Plans

Paris
Region map.....................118-119
Central Paris 120-121
Arrondissements of Paris 124

Northern France
Region map........................ 160
Château de Versailles: The Park.......163
Fontainebleau: Château 171
Chartres: Cathédral Notre-Dame 204
Rambouillet: Château............... 205

Normandy
Region map.....................210-211
Rouen 214-215
Caen...........................226-227
Mont-St-Michel 239

Brittany
Region map.....................244-245
Rennes 247
St-Malo 252-253, 254
Quimper.......................263, 265
Vannes 269
Nantes......................... 274-275

Châteaux of the Loire
Region map.................... 282-283
Angers.........................286-287
Saumur............................ 294
Blois.............................. 305

Alsace Lorraine Champagne
Region map................... 314-315
Metz...............................317
Verdun 322
Nancy 324, 325
Strasbourg.................332-333, 334
Colmar.........................342, 343
Riquewihr.......................... 345
Reims.......................... 352-353
Troyes 360-361

Burgundy Jura
Region map.....................366-367
Dijon 369, 370-371
Beaune 379
Auxerre........................... 384
Besançon 390, 392

French Alps
Region map....................... 398
Annecy 400, 401
Évian-les-Bains.................... 406

Auvergne Rhône Valley
Region map.................... 430-431
Lyon...........................434-435
Vieux-Lyon-Fourvière 439
Lyon, La Presqu'ile................. 441
Lyon, La Croix-Rousse 444-445
Vienne.........................454-455
Le Puy-en-Velay.................... 461
Old Clermont 465
Clermont-Ferrand..............466-467
Old Montferrand 469

Dordogne Berry Limousin
Region map........................ 484
Bourges 486
Vieux Sarlat....................... 497
Cahors............................. 507

Atlantic Coast
Region map.........................512
Bordeaux 514-515, 519
Biarritz............................ 524
Angoulême..........................531
La Rochelle 536
Poitiers 543

Languedoc Roussillon Tarn Gorges
Region map....................548-549
Montpellier 552-553, 555
Nîmes 559, 560
Carcassonne 565
Narbonne.......................... 571
Perpignan 574-575
Toulouse.......................... 578
Albi............................... 585
Lourdes........................588-589

Provence
Region map....................596-597
Marseille.............600-601, 602-603
Aix-en-Provence 613
Arles...............................617
Les Baux-de-Provence.............. 623
Orange 631

French Riviera and Corsica
Region map....................636-637
Nice 640-641, 643
Monaco.........................648-649
Menton............................ 653
Cannes 655, 656-657
St-Tropez 661
Corsica 665

★★★ **Highly recommended**

★★ **Recommended**

★ **Interesting**

Tourism

Sightseeing route with departure point indicated	AZ B Map co-ordinates locating sights
Ecclesiastical building	Tourist information
Synagogue – Mosque	Historic house, castle – Ruins
Building (with main entrance)	Dam – Factory or power station
Statue, small building	Fort – Cave
Wayside cross	Prehistoric site
Fountain	Viewing table – View
Fortified walls – Tower – Gate	Miscellaneous sight

Recreation

Racecourse	Waymarked footpath
Skating rink	Outdoor leisure park/centre
Outdoor, indoor swimming pool	Theme/Amusement park
Marina, moorings	Wildlife/Safari park, zoo
Mountain refuge hut	Gardens, park, arboretum
Overhead cable-car	Aviary, bird sanctuary
Tourist or steam railway	

Additional symbols

Motorway (unclassified)	Post office – Telephone centre
Junction: complete, limited	Covered market
Pedestrian street	Barracks
Unsuitable for traffic, street subject to restrictions	Swing bridge
Steps – Footpath	Quarry – Mine
Railway – Coach station	Ferry (river and lake crossings)
Funicular – Rack-railway	Ferry services: Passengers and cars
Tram – Metro, underground	Foot passengers only
Bert (R.)... Main shopping street	③ Access route number common to MICHELIN maps and town plans

Abbreviations and special symbols

A	Agricultural office (Chambre d'agriculture)	P	Local authority offices (Préfecture, sous-préfecture)
C	Chamber of commerce (Chambre de commerce)	POL.	Police station (Police)
			Police station (Gendarmerie)
H	Town hall (Hôtel de ville)	T	Theatre (Théâtre)
J	Law courts (Palais de justice)	U	University (Université)
M	Museum (Musée)		Hotel
			Park and Ride

Some town plans are extracts from plans used in the Green Guides to the regions of France.

Useful Words and Phrases

SIGHTS

	Translation
Abbey	Abbaye
Belfry	Beffroi
Bridge	Pont
Castle	Château
Cemetery	Cimetière
Chapel	Chapelle
Church	Église
Cloisters	Cloître
Convent	Couvent
Courtyard	Cour
Fountain	Fontaine
Garden	Jardin
Gateway	Porte
Hall	Halle
House	Maison
Lock (Canal)	Écluse
Market	Marché
Monastery	Monastère
Museum	Musée
Park	Parc
Port/harbour	Port
Quay	Quai
Ramparts	Remparts

"Fourchette" and "Couteau" ©Andrew Johnson/iStockphoto.com

Square	Place
Street	Rue
Statue	Statue
Tower	Tour
Town Hall	Mairie
Windmill	Moulin

NATURAL SITES

	Translation
Abyss	Abîme
Swallow-hole	Aven
Dam	Barrage
Viewpoint	Belvédère
Waterfall	Cascade
Pass	Col
Ledge	Corniche
Coast, Hillside	Côte
Forest	Forêt
Cave	Grotte
Lake	Lac
Beach	Plage
River	Rivière
Stream	Ruisseau
Beacon	Signal
Spring	Source
Valley	Vallée

ON THE ROAD

	Translation
Car Park	Parking
Driving Licence	Permis de conduire
East	Est
Garage (For Repairs)	Garage
Left	Gauche
Motorway/Highway	Autoroute
North	Nord
Parking Meter	Horodateur
Petrol/Gas	Essence
Petrol/Gas Station	Station essence
Right	Droite
South	Sud
Toll	Péage
Traffic Lights	Feu tricolore
Tyre	Pneu
West	Ouest
Wheel Clamp	Sabot
Pedestrian crossing	Passage clouté

TIME

	Translation
Today	Aujourd'hui
Tomorrow	Demain
Yesterday	Hier
Winter	Hiver
Spring	Printemps
Summer	Été
Autumn/Fall	Automne
Week	Semaine
Monday	Lundi
Tuesday	Mardi
Wednesday	Mercredi
Thursday	Jeudi
Friday	Vendredi
Saturday	Samedi
Sunday	Dimanche

NUMBERS

	Translation
0	zéro
1	un
2	deux
3	trois
4	quatre
5	cinq
6	six
7	sept
8	huit

9	neuf
10	dix
11	onze
12	douze
13	treize
14	quatorze
15	quinze
16	seize
17	dix-sept
18	dix-huit
19	dix-neuf
20	vingt
30	trente
40	quarante
50	cinquante
60	soixante
70	soixante-dix
80	quatre-vingt
90	quatre-vingt-dix
100	cent
1000	mille

SHOPPING

	Translation
Bank	Banque
Baker's	Boulangerie
Big	Grand
Butcher's	Boucherie
Chemist's	Pharmacie
Closed	Fermé
Cough mixture	Sirop pour la toux
Cough sweets	Cachets pour la gorge
Entrance	Entrée
Exit	Sortie
Fishmonger's	Poissonnerie
Grocer's	Épicerie
Newsagent, Bookshop	Librairie
Open	Ouvert
Post Office	Poste
Push	Pousser
Pull	Tirer
Shop	Magasin
Small	Petit
Stamps	Timbres

FOOD AND DRINK

	Translation
Beef	Bœuf
Beer	Bière
Butter	Beurre
Bread	Pain
Breakfast	Petit-déjeuner
Cheese	Fromage
Dessert	Dessert
Dinner	Dîner
Fish	Poisson
Fork	Fourchette
Fruit	Fruits
Glass	Verre
Chicken	Poulet
Ice cream	Glace
Ice cubes	Glaçons
Ham	Jambon
Knife	Couteau
Lamb	Agneau
Lunch	Déjeuner
Lettuce salad	Salade
Meat	Viande
Mineral water	Eau minérale
Mixed salad	Salade composée
Orange juice	Jus d'orange
Plate	Assiette
Pork	Porc
Restaurant	Restaurant
Salt	Sel
Spoon	Cuillère
Sugar	Sucre
Vegetables	Légumes
Water	De L'eau
White/Red Wine	Vin blanc/rouge
Yoghurt	Yaourt

TRAVEL

	Translation
Travel	Voyager
Airport	Aéroport
Credit card	Carte de crédit
Customs	Douane
Passport	Passeport
Platform	Voie
Railway station	Gare
Shuttle	Navette
Suitcase	Valise
Train Ticket	Billet de train
Plane Ticket	Billet d'avion
Wallet	Portefeuille

CLOTHING

	Translation
Coat	Manteau
Jumper	Pull
Raincoat	Imperméable
Shirt	Chemise
Shoes	Chaussures
Socks	Chaussettes
Stockings	Bas
Suit	Costume
Tights	Collants
Trousers	Pantalon

COMMON WORDS

	Translation
Goodbye	Au revoir
Hello/Good Morning	Bonjour
How	Comment
Excuse Me	Excusez-moi
Thank You	Merci
Yes/No	Oui/Non
I Am Sorry	Pardon
Why	Pourquoi
When	Quand
Please	S'il vous plaît

USEFUL PHRASES

Do you speak English? Parlez-vous anglais?

I don't understand Je ne comprends pas

Talk slowly Parlez lentement

Where is...?. Où est...?

When does the ... leave? À quelle heure part...?

When does the ... arrive? À quelle heure arrive...?

When does the museum open? À quelle heure ouvre le musée?

What does it cost? Combien cela coûte?

Where can I buy a newspaper in English? Où puis-j'acheter un journal en anglais?

Where is the nearest petrol/gas station? Où se trouve la station essence la plus proche?

Where are the toilets? Où sont les toilettes?

Do you accept credit cards? Acceptez-vous les cartes de crédit?

USEFUL TO KNOW

On national and departmental roads, there are often roundabouts (traffic circles) just outside the towns, which serve to slow traffic down.
At a French roundabout **(rond point)**, you are likely to see signs pointing to **Centre Ville** (city centre) or to other towns (the French use towns as directional indicators, rather than cardinal points). You are also likely to see a sign for **Toutes Directions** (all directions – this is often the bypass road to avoid going through the town) or **Autres Directions** (other directions – in other words, any place that isn't indicated on one of the other signs on the roundabout!).

YOU ALREADY KNOW THE GREEN GUIDE, NOW FIND OUT ABOUT THE MICHELIN GROUP

The Michelin Adventure

It all started with rubber balls! This was the product made by a small company based in Clermont-Ferrand that André and Edouard Michelin inherited, back in 1880. The brothers quickly saw the potential for a new means of transport and their first success was the invention of detachable pneumatic tires for bicycles. However, the automobile was to provide the greatest scope for their creative talents. Throughout the 20th century, Michelin never ceased developing and creating ever more reliable and high-performance tires, not only for vehicles ranging from trucks to F1 but also for underground transit systems and airplanes.

From early on, Michelin provided its customers with tools and services to facilitate mobility and make traveling a more pleasurable and more frequent experience. As early as 1900, the Michelin Guide supplied motorists with a host of useful information related to vehicle maintenance, accommodation and restaurants, and was to become a benchmark for good food. At the same time, the Travel Information Bureau offered travelers personalised tips and itineraries.

The publication of the first collection of roadmaps, in 1910, was an instant hit! In 1926, the first regional guide to France was published, devoted to the principal sites of Brittany, and before long each region of France had its own Green Guide. The collection was later extended to more far-flung destinations, including New York in 1968 and Taiwan in 2011.

In the 21st century, with the growth of digital technology, the challenge for Michelin maps and guides is to continue to develop alongside the company's tire activities. Now, as before, Michelin is committed to improving the mobility of travelers.

MICHELIN TODAY

WORLD NUMBER ONE TIRE MANUFACTURER

- 70 production sites in 18 countries
- 111,000 employees from all cultures and on every continent
- 6,000 people employed in research and development

Moving for a world

Moving forward means developing tires with better road grip and shorter braking distances, whatever the state of the road.

CORRECT TIRE PRESSURE

RIGHT PRESSURE

- Safety
- Longevity
- Optimum fuel consumption

-0,5 bar

- Durability reduced by 20% (- 8,000 km)

- Risk of blowouts
- Increased fuel consumption
- Longer braking distances on wet surfaces

forward together
where mobility is safer

It also involves helping motorists take care of their safety and their tires. To do so, Michelin organises "Fill Up With Air" campaigns all over the world to remind us that correct tire pressure is vital.

WEAR

DETECTING TIRE WEAR

The legal minimum depth of tire tread is 1.6mm. Tire manufacturers equip their tires with tread wear indicators, which are small blocks of rubber moulded into the base of the main grooves at a depth of 1.6mm.

Tires are the only point of contact between the vehicle and road.

The photo below shows the actual contact zone.

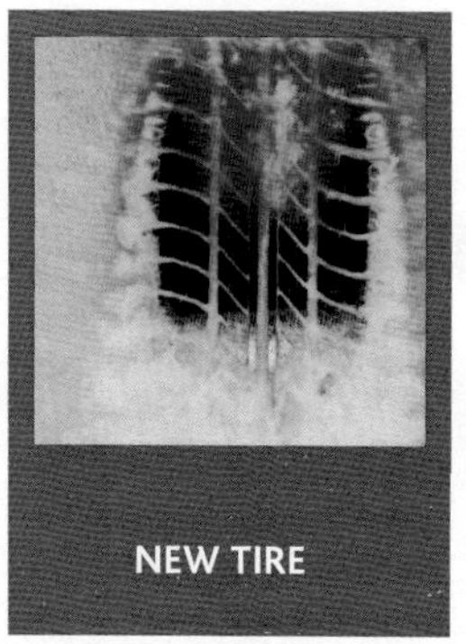

NEW TIRE

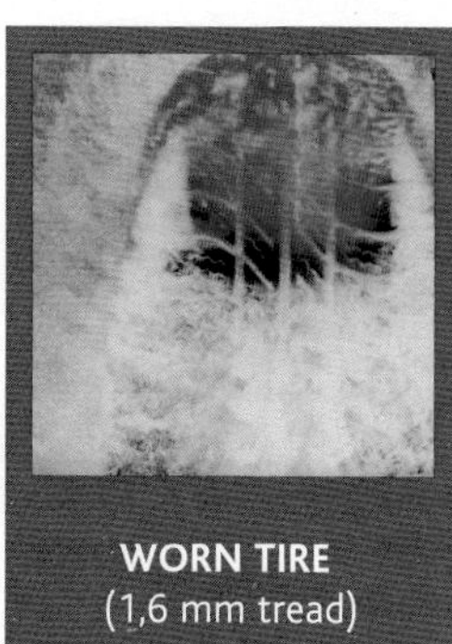

WORN TIRE
(1,6 mm tread)

If the tread depth is less than 1.6mm, tires are considered to be worn and dangerous on wet surfaces.

Moving forward means sustainable mobility

INNOVATION AND THE ENVIRONMENT

By 2050, Michelin aims to cut the quantity of raw materials used in its tire manufacturing process by half and to have developed renewable energy in its facilities. The design of MICHELIN tires has already saved billions of litres of fuel and, by extension, billions of tons of CO2.

Similarly, Michelin prints its maps and guides on paper produced from sustainably managed forests and is diversifying its publishing media by offering digital solutions to make traveling easier, more fuel efficient and more enjoyable!

The group's whole-hearted commitment to eco-design on a daily basis is demonstrated by ISO 14001 certification.

Like you, Michelin is committed to preserving our planet.

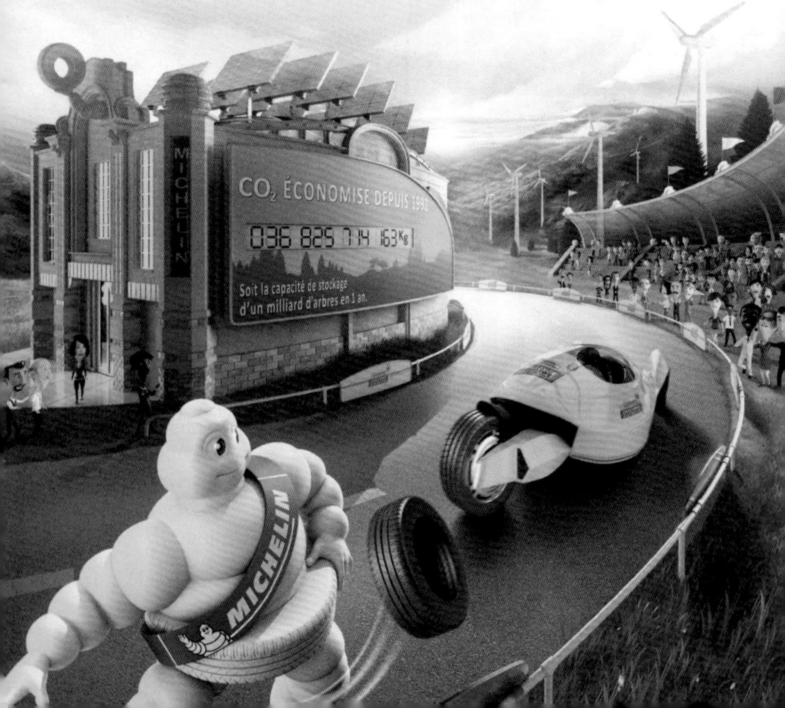

Chat with Bibendum

Go to
www.michelin.com/corporate/en
Find out more about
Michelin's history and the
latest news.

QUIZ

Michelin develops tires for all types of vehicles.
See if you can match the right tire with the right vehicle…

Solution : A-6 / B-4 / C-2 / D-1 / E-3 / F-7 / G-5

THE GREEN GUIDE **FRANCE**

Editorial Director	Cynthia Clayton Ochterbeck
Principal Writer	Terry Marsh
Production Manager	Natasha George
Cartography	John Dear
Picture Editor	Yoshimi Kanazawa
Interior Design	Natasha George, Jonathan P. Gilbert
Cover Design	Chris Bell, Christelle Le Déan
Layout	Natasha George, Jonathan P. Gilbert
Cover Layout	Michelin Travel Partner, Natasha George

Contact Us

Michelin Travel and Lifestyle North America
One Parkway South
Greenville, SC 29615
USA
travel.lifestyle@us.michelin.com

Michelin Travel Partner
Hannay House
39 Clarendon Road
Watford, Herts WD17 1JA
UK
℘01923 205240
travelpubsales@uk.michelin.com
www.ViaMichelin.com

Special Sales

For information regarding bulk sales, customized editions and premium sales, please contact us at:
travel.lifestyle@us.michelin.com

Michelin Travel Partner

Société par actions simplifiées au capital de 11 288 880 EUR
27 cours de l'Ile Seguin - 92100 Boulogne Billancourt (France)
R.C.S. Nanterre 433 677 721

ISBN 978-2-067206-63-2
Printed: September 2015
Printed and bound in Belgium : GEERS Offset, Gent